PRINCIPLES OF MEDICAL LAW

PRINCIPLES OF
MEDICAL
LAW

Edited by

IAN KENNEDY

Professor of Health Law, Ethics and Public Policy,
School of Public Policy, University College London

ANDREW GRUBB

Professor of Medical Law, Cardiff Law School, Cardiff University

OXFORD UNIVERSITY PRESS
1998

Oxford University Press, Great Clarendon Street, Oxford OX2 6DP
www.oup.co.uk

Oxford New York
Athens Auckland Bangkok Bogota Bombay Buenos Aires
Calcutta Cape Town Dar es Salaam Delhi Florence Hong Kong Istanbul
Karachi Kuala Lumpur Madras Madrid Melbourne Mexico City
Nairobi Paris Singapore Taipei Tokyo Toronto Warsaw
and associated companies in
Berlin Ibadan

Oxford is a registered trade mark of Oxford University Press

Published in the United States
by Oxford University Press Inc., New York

British Library Cataloguing in Publication Data
Data available

Library of Congress Cataloging in Publication Data
Principles of medical law/edited by Ian Kennedy, Andrew Grubb.
p.   cm.
Includes bibliographical references.
1. Medical laws and legislation—Great Britain. 2. Medical care—Law and
legislation—Great Britain. I. Kennedy, Ian, 1941–   . II. Grubb, Andrew.
KD3395.P75   1998
344.41'041-dc21   98–29926

main work ISBN 0–19–826861–0
main work with First Supplement ISBN 0–19–825808–9

1 3 5 7 9 10 8 6 4 2

Typeset by J&L Composition Ltd, Filey, North Yorkshire
Printed in Great Britain
on acid-free paper by
Bookcraft Ltd, Midsomer Norton, Somerset

EDITORS

Ian Kennedy
Professor of Health Law, Ethics and Public Policy,
School of Public Policy, University College London

Andrew Grubb
Professor of Medical Law, Cardiff Law School, Cardiff University

CONTRIBUTORS

Christopher Newdick
Reader in Health Law, University of Reading

Diana Kloss
Senior Lecturer in Law, University of Manchester

James Munby QC
Barrister, 1, New Square, Lincoln's Inn, London

Michael A Jones
Hill Dickinson Professor of Law, University of Liverpool

Kristina Stern
Barrister, 39, Essex Street, London

Michael Freeman
Professor of English Law, University College London

Adrian Whitfield QC
Barrister, 3, Serjeants' Inn, London

Harvey Teff
Professor of Law, University of Durham

Bernard Dickens
Professor of Law, University of Toronto

Alexander McCall Smith
Professor of Medical Law, University of Edinburgh

PREFACE

Medical Law has come a long way since its early days. It was once dominated by medical negligence actions and disciplinary cases arising out of the failure to adhere to the GMC's standards on the 'three A's': adultery, alcohol and advertising. The last decade or so has seen judicial and legislative intervention into the health care setting in an unprecedented way.

It is well known that there has been a rise (some would say a surge) in medical negligence litigation. But, the area of real judicial intervention has been in the so-called treatment decisions cases, such as *Re B* (1988); *Re F* (1990); *Bland* (1993); *Re MB* (1997). Here the courts have risen to the challenge to fashion the common law (both its substance and process) not only to resolve particular disputes but to meet the legitimate needs of patients, doctors and institutions for a clear statement of the law governing a particular aspect of medical practice. These are times of genuine excitement for medical lawyers as the law has yet to fulfil its potential.

However, there has been and is more to medical law than this. Public law has become a major mechanism for judicial regulation within the NHS. The political ambition to restructure the NHS manifested in the National Health Service and Community Care Act 1990 has increased the potential for judicial control through the mechanism of judicial review. The creation of the 'internal market' which is being retained in form, if not in substance, by the current Government and the reforms of primary care provision in the National Health Service (Primary Care) Act 1997 impress a framework upon the NHS which makes decision-making more visible and, therefore, a more likely judicial target. The growth in primary and secondary legislation and their sibling of doubtful parentage, quasi-legislation and the 'Executive Letter' has been phenomenal. The last of these has, without a doubt, become *the* method of 'command and control' from the top (whether from the UK Health Departments or the NHS Executive) since the 1990 reforms. Also guidance and guidelines from such bodies as the Royal Medical Colleges and elsewhere have created a transparent form of regulation, ostensibly extra-legal but ultimately providing a template for legal control when breached.

This volume, *Principles*, is what it purports to be. It is not a book about the practice and process of litigation. It seeks to expound the principles of law that govern medical practice and which form the corpus of medical law. We use the latter term to encompass 'health care services' in general although, often, it is the doctor (or institution) – patient relationship that throws up the difficult legal problems. *Principles* is intended to provide the courts, legal practitioners, academic lawyers and others with as comprehensive and, it is hoped, as authoritative an account as possible of the developing law in England and Wales. Necessarily in this fast moving area of law, developments outstrip publishing schedules. This edition itself has a brief supplement to make it as up-to-date as possible. Further supplements will seek to chart developments between editions.

The preparation of *Principles* for publication has been a long one. During those years much has changed and perceptions of what medical law is all about have evolved: expanded may be the most appropriate term. The next edition will include a chapter on the civil commitment and treatment of those suffering from mental disorder. We are already aware that this omission needs to be rectified. More pervasive, in terms of forthcoming editions, will be the effect of the Human Rights Act 1998 and its impact on medical law. Little of medical law is likely to be left untouched by the incorporation of the European Convention on Human Rights.

In preparing this edition we would, of course, like to thank the contributing authors for their hard work, persistence and good humour throughout. Those at Oxford University Press, past and present, who conceived the project and saw it through to birth also deserve recognition, probably through a long service medal. Our gratitude goes out to them. We hope that the wait was worth it.

The law in the main text is stated at 31 December 1997, although some later developments have been incorporated where possible.

Ian Kennedy
Andrew Grubb
1 June 1998

OUTLINE TABLE OF CONTENTS

IV SPECIFIC ISSUES

TABLE OF CONTENTS

I THE HEALTH CARE SYSTEM

1 THE ORGANISATION OF HEALTH CARE

2 THE HEALTH CARE PROFESSIONS

III MEDICAL NEGLIGENCE

5 DUTIES IN CONTRACT AND TORT

6 BREACH OF DUTY

17 DEATH

TABLE OF CASES

l

TABLE OF STATUTES

TABLE OF STATUTORY INSTRUMENTS

TABLE OF LEGISLATION FROM OTHER JURISDICTIONS

TABLE OF TREATIES AND CONVENTIONS

1

THE HEALTH CARE SYSTEM

1

THE ORGANISATION OF HEALTH CARE

This chapter on the organisation of health care considers (A) the system of fund- **1.01**
ing the National Health Service (NHS) and (B) the regulation of the Service.

A. Funding the National Health Service

How is funding allocated to health service bodies? The following examines **1.02**
(1) the components of the National Health Service, (2) the funding of
purchasers of health care, and (3) the funding of providers of health care.[1]

---

[1] See generally Newdick, C, *Who Should We Treat?—Law, Patients and Resources in the NHS*
(Oxford University Press, 1995) ch 2 and Montgomery, J, *Health Care Law* (Oxford University
Press, 1997) ch 4.

1. Components of the National Health Service

1.03 The NHS is organised in accordance with the National Health Service Act 1977, the National Health Service and Community Care Act 1990, and the National Health Service (Primary Care) Act 1997. Organisational structure in the Service evolves continuously. For the present, the salient components of the NHS are as follows.[2] Under the 1977 Act, the Secretary of State is given wide enabling powers to fulfil his, or her, statutory obligations, supported by a team of ministerial colleagues to whom specific responsibilities may be delegated. The Secretary of State determines matters of policy and priorities, and approves the allocation of resources to meet those objectives. The task of the Department of Health is to support the Secretary of State in carrying out these responsibilities, including advising on the development of policy, taking forward legislation, liaising with other government departments, collecting data and monitoring health, and regulating the safety of medicinal products.

1.04 Strategic and managerial responsibility within the NHS lies with the National Health Service Executive (NHSE) which is concerned to ensure that resources are used appropriately, effectively and efficiently. Matters of this nature may also require it to advise on policy matters. Although the NHSE is a non-statutory body, its chief executive is directly accountable to the Secretary of State.[3] The NHSE may issue directions and guidance to other bodies within the NHS by means of health service circulars (HSCs) (which were previously known as executive letters (ELs), health service guidance (HSGs) and finance directorate letters (FDLs)). An important link between ministers and the NHSE is available through the NHS Policy Board, another non-statutory body chaired by the Secretary of State.

1.05 Operational matters at local level are the responsibility of bodies which are loosely referred to by the National Health Service and Community Care Act 1990 as 'acquirers' (or 'purchasers') and 'providers' of health care. Until 1999, the purchasers are health authorities,[4] general practitioner (GP) fund-holders and (in future) total purchasing pilots, under the National Health Service (Primary Care) Act 1997. After that time, primary legislation is proposed in the White Paper *The New NHS—Modern, Dependable*,[5] which will distance

---

[2] See *Managing the New NHS—Functions and Responsibilities in the New NHS* (NHSE, 1994) and *The Purpose, Organisation, Management and Funding of the National Health Service* (Department of Health, 1997).   [3] ibid.
[4] And special health authorities, with responsibility, for example, for purchasing supplies for the NHS, the training of doctors in medical schools and special, high security hospitals.
[5] Cm 3807 (1997).

health authorities from direct involvement in purchasing by giving them a greater strategic policy-making role.[6] In their place, 'Primary Care Groups' will undertake responsibility for agreeing and paying for 'service contracts' with NHS hospitals, within the framework agreed with health authorities. Primary care groups will be led by health professionals and represent around 100,000 patients each. At the same time, the practice of GP fund-holding will cease.[7] By contrast, the *provision* of health care takes place in NHS community and hospital trusts whose income is derived from entering 'NHS Contracts' with purchasers and others (for example private sources) to provide services for patients.[8] In addition, primary care is also provided by ordinary (non-fund-holding) GPs whose expenditure is the responsibility of health authorities.

2. Funding Purchasers of Health Care

Subject to the primary legislation proposed in 1999, health authorities, GP **1.06** fund-holders and total purchasing pilots may commission, or purchase, health care from hospitals on behalf of patients.

(i) *Health Authorities*

The National Health Service Act 1977 imposes on the Secretary of State a **1.07** duty to pay to each health authority sums which are attributable to (a) the payment of remuneration of those who provide services under the 1977 Act and (b) the reimbursement of expenses of persons providing services thereto.[9] It is also the duty of the Secretary of State:

> to pay in respect of each financial year to each Health Authority sums not exceeding the amount allotted for that year by the Secretary of State to the Health Authority towards meeting the expenditure of the Health Authority which . . . is attributable to the performance by the Health Authority of their functions in that year . . .[10]

Correspondingly, it is the duty of each health authority, to perform its **1.08** functions in a manner which does not exceed the amounts allotted to it

---

[6] ibid, ch 4.   [7] ibid, ch 5.
[8] The Labour government proposes to preserve the principle which separates purchasers from providers, but reduce the perceived short-term and adversarial nature of the current system. See *The New NHS—Modern, Dependable* (n 5 above), ch 5.
[9] S 97(1) and (2), National Health Service Act 1977, as substituted by ss 2(1) and 8, Sch 1, para 47, Health Authorities Act 1995.
[10] S 97(3), National Health Service Act 1977, as substituted by ss 2(1) and 8, Sch 1, para 47, Health Authorities Act 1995.

either under the 1977 Act, or otherwise (for example by means of bequests)[11] and to pay to GP fund-holding practices an 'allotted sum' representing the fund for which they have accepted responsibility.[12] The small minority of hospitals remaining within health authority control continue to receive their funding from that source.

1.09 The distribution of NHS resources to Health Authorities is calculated on the basis of a weighted capitation formula[13] which assesses health needs according to: (i) the projected size of the population concerned, (ii) the numbers of elderly people in the population, (iii) the health needs of the population, distinguishing between general, acute and psychiatric care and morbidity and mortality ratios, and (iv) an allowance to allow for local market forces with respect to the cost of labour and the higher costs of the Thames' Regions.

1.10 It is difficult to conceive of circumstances in which the formula for allocating funds could be successfully challenged, say, by a health authority which considered it had received inadequate funding. An analogous issue arose concerning expenditure guidance issued by the Secretary of State for the Environment to local authorities, which was challenged for being *Wednesbury* unreasonable, ie so unreasonable that no reasonable person addressing himself to the issue in question could have come to such a decision. Lord Scarman dealt with the claim as follows:

> We are in the field of public financial administration and we are being asked to review the exercise by the Secretary of State of an administrative discretion which inevitably requires political judgment on his part . . . I cannot accept that it is constitutionally appropriate, save in very exceptional circumstances, for the courts to intervene on the ground of 'unreasonableness' to quash guidance framed by the Secretary of State and by necessary implication approved by the House of Commons, the guidance being concerned with the limits of public expenditure by local authorities and the incidence of the tax burden as between taxpayers and ratepayers . . . these are matters of political judgment for him and for the House of Commons. They are not matters for the judges . . . I refuse in this case to examine the detail of the guidance or its consequences.[14]

1.11 On the other hand, different considerations arise if funds, once allocated, are misapplied. The 1977 Act provides that the Secretary of State may issue

---

[11] S 97A, National Health Service Act 1977, as substituted by ss 2(1) and 8, Sch 1, para 48, Health Authorities Act 1995.

[12] See 1990 Act, s 15(1) as amended by s 2(1), Sch 1, para 74, Health Authorities Act 1995.

[13] See *Hospital and Community Health Services Resource Allocation: Weighted Capitation Formula* (NHS Executive, 1994).

[14] *R v Secretary of State for the Environment, ex p Nottinghamshire County Council* [1986] AC 240, 247. And see the consideration of the case in *R v Secretary of State for the Environment, ex p Hammersmith and Fulham London Borough Council* [1991] 1 AC 521.

directions to health authorities and special health authorities with respect to the ways in which their allocations shall be applied, and 'it is the duty of the Health Authority or Special Health Authority to comply with the directions.'[15] Such directions as to the allocation of monies have to be clear and precise but

> they do not have to be given in any particular form. It must be made clear that funds have to be used in a particular manner. There is no magic form of words that is required and I do not think that the use of the word 'direct' is necessary in order to constitute a 'direction'.[16]

Thus, funds paid to a health authority for specific purposes such as reimbursing GPs for the costs of employing suitable staff at their practices, the cost rent scheme, and premises improvement grants could not be diverted to other uses, notwithstanding that those uses were intended to promote 'general medical services' which were otherwise the health authority's responsibility.[17] **1.12**

(ii) *GP Fund-holders and the Allotted Sum*

The perceived benefit of allocating funds directly to fund-holding practices is **1.13** that individual GPs or practices may thereby exercise greater control over the ways in which resources are used. The new Labour government 'has signalled its intention to explore with all interested parties, the development of new models of primary care led commissioning, based on the principles of fairness and meeting local needs'[18] and, subject to Parliamentary approval, proposes to end fund-holding in 1999. For the present, however, the regulations governing fund-holding remain intact.

Practices may apply for fund-holding status to the Health Authority which **1.14** shall recommend to the Secretary of State whether the application should be granted.[19] The conditions for recognition are, *inter alia*, that there are at least 5,000 patients on the lists of the members of the practice, that the application is made by all the members of the partnership, and that the practice is capable

---

[15] S 97(6) and (7), National Health Service Act 1977, as substituted by s 6, Health Services Act 1980 and amended by ss 2(1), 8 and Sch 1, para 47, Health Authorities Act 1995.
[16] *R v Secretary of State for Health, ex p Manchester LMC* 25 BMLR 77, 89, *per* Collins J.
[17] ibid. [18] *Changing the Internal Market* (NHSE, EL(97)33), annex A.
[19] See reg 3, National Health Service (Fund-holding Practices) Regulations 1996, SI 1996/706.

of managing an allotted sum effectively and efficiently.[20] Fund-holding gives GPs a much more explicit role in the management of NHS resources.

1.15 Successful applicants shall be paid an 'allotted sum' which shall be 'determined in such manner and by reference to such factors as the Secretary of State may direct' and shall be awarded annually by the Health Authority.[21] The uses to which the fund may be put are closely restricted.[22] Fund-holders remain bound by their Terms of Service to the Health Authority and thus, except in limited circumstances, may not use the sum as a means of remunerating themselves.[23] Since fund-holding GPs are already bound by their Terms of Service with the Health Authority to provide 'general medical services' to patients,[24] the regulations provide that the allotted sum shall be applied so as to secure the purchase of goods and services, 'other than general medical services'.[25]

1.16 Thus, the sum shall be used to provide additional goods and services within the practice which have been approved by the Secretary of State.[26] Such goods and services may be supplied by the doctors themselves or by consultants, or employees.[27] The sum shall be applied

> so as to secure the purchase of such goods and services . . . as are necessary for the proper treatment of individuals on the lists of patients of the members of the

---

[20] ibid, Sch 1. The regulations also permit more limited 'community fund-holding' available to practices with 3,000–5,000 patients (see reg 5), and 'GP commissioning groups', introduced by the National Health Service (Fund-holding Practices) Amendment Regulations 1997, SI 1997/747. The Audit Commission considers that some fund-holders do not manage their funds well, and comments that the NHS Executive has provided no detailed definition of efficiency. See *What the Doctor Ordered—A Study of GP Fundholders in England and Wales* (Audit Commission, 1996) paras 69–75.

[21] National Health Service and Community Care Act 1990, s 15(1) as amended by s 2(1), Sch 1, para 74, Health Authorities Act 1995.

[22] See National Health Service and Community Care Act 1990, s 15(6) and (7), and reg 20(2), National Health Service (Fund-holding Practices) Regulations, 1996, SI 1996/706.

[23] See the National Health Service (General Medical Services) Regulations 1992, SI 1992/635, para 38. A doctor 'shall not, otherwise than by virtue of these Regulations, demand or accept a fee or other remuneration for any treatment . . . whether under these terms of service or not, which he gives to a person for whose treatment he is responsible under paragraph 4' (which describes 'a doctor's patients').

[24] The obligation arises under the GPs' Terms of Service. Thus, the costs incurred in prescribing drugs, medicines and listed appliances may be recovered by the Health Authority from the allotted sum, see the National Health Service and Community Care Act 1990, s 15(7)(a). The Terms of Service are discussed below.   [25] See ibid, reg 20(1).

[26] See ibid, reg 20(2). The list is published in a letter from the NHS Executive and adjusted from time to time.

[27] The allotted sum may be used to pay the salaries of those who provide additional services to patients, as well as in connection with the management or administration of the practice. See SI 1996/706 (*supra*), reg 23. For the range of additional services provided, see *What the Doctor Ordered—A Study of GP Fundholders in England and Wales* (Audit Commission, 1996) para 38.

practice and are appropriate in all the circumstances having regard, in particular, to the needs of all those individuals.[28]

The circumstances in which fund-holders may purchase goods are restricted. **1.17**
Thus, the allotted sum shall not, without the consent of the health authority, be used to purchase goods or services from a patient of a doctor of the practice, nor from a provider with which a member of the practice is 'connected'.[29] The specific approval of the health authority is required before a doctor who is a member of the practice may derive additional income by providing goods and services to patients of the practice. Such consent shall only be given provided that the practitioner possesses suitable competence and experience, that suitable premises and facilities are available, that the payment is reasonable, represents value for money and is made 'directly to the medical practitioner who provides the services or to the partnership of which he is a member and not to any third party.'[30]

(a) Savings from the 'Allotted Sum'

Many fund-holders have been able to achieve savings from their allotted **1.18**
sums.[31] Savings may be ploughed back into the practice. Thus, in respect of any financial year, after the practice accounts have been audited by the Audit Commission a fund-holding practice has four years in which to accumulate savings.[32] Such monies may continue to be spent on the provision of additional medical goods or services to its patients, the payment of approved salaries, or remuneration. In addition, savings may be applied for, *inter alia*:

(a) the purchase of material or equipment which
  (i)   can be used for the treatment of patients of the members of the practice, or
  (ii) enhances the comfort or convenience of patients of the members of the practice, or
  (iii) enables the practice to be managed more effectively and efficiently; or
(b) the purchase of material or equipment relating to health education; or

---

[28] ibid, reg 20(2). The precise arrangements under which fund-holders are regulated differs from region to region. [29] ibid, reg 20(7), (8) and (11).
[30] ibid, reg 24 and *GP fund-holding practices: the provision of secondary care* (HSG(93)14, NHSME, 1993).
[31] In 1992–93, fund-holders made savings of £28.3 million from the sums allotted to them. See *General Practitioner Fundholding in England* (HC 51, Session 1994–95, National Audit Office), para 4.11 and *GP Fundholding: Use of Savings* (HSG(95)46).
[32] Reg 25(2), National Health Service (Fund-holding Practices) Regulations 1996, SI 1996/706.

(c) in relation to any premises from which the members of the practice carry on their practice:

   (i) improvements to the premises, including alterations to or decoration of the premises and the purchase of furniture and furnishing, and

   (ii) building an extension provided that no acquisition of land is involved.[33]

1.19 Any such application of savings must have the consent of the Health Authority which must be satisfied that the expenditure would '(a) be for the benefit of the patients of the members of the practice; and (b) represent value for money.'[34] Presumably a practice will be permitted to effect essential repairs to its premises by using its savings. But would it be allowed to purchase practice (*sic*, company) cars for the partners? Ought patients on waiting lists to be dealt with before money is spent on interior redecoration, if needs be, by paying for treatment under an additional NHS contract? Arguably, the obligations imposed by the GPs' Terms of Service to render 'all necessary and appropriate personal medical services of the type usually provided by general practitioners'[35] require that, as a general rule, patients should come first. In any event, the Secretary of State may recover any parts of the sum which have been misapplied by any one or more of the members of a fund-holding practice[36] by an action in civil debt against them, jointly, or severally.[37]

1.20 Many practices have used savings to improve their own practice premises under sub-paragraph (c), above.[38] Clearly, any increase in the capital value of premises accrues to the benefit of partners when they leave the practice. Misgivings have been expressed about the propriety of such a financial benefit, and the Audit Commission has suggested that the NHSE should 'seek agreement from practices which spend savings on premises that assets funded from the scheme are held in trust and cannot add to GPs' personal

---

[33] ibid, reg 25(2).

[34] ibid, reg 25(3). Appeal against a refusal of consent is available to the Secretary of State, see reg 25(5).

[35] See the National Health Service (General Medical Services) Regulations 1992, SI 1992/635, Sch 2, para 12(1), discussed below. Note also that 'action taken . . . in connection with any allotted sum paid to members of the practice' is now amenable to investigation by the Health Service Ombudsman. See s 3(1B), Health Service Commissioners Act 1993, as amended by s 2(2), Health Service Commissioners (Amendment) Act 1996.

[36] National Health Service (Fund-holding Practices) Regulations 1996, SI 1996/706, reg 26.

[37] ibid, reg 25(8). Once a practitioner leaves a fund-holding practice, savings which remain in the fund-holder's account should be returned to the Health Authority on a pro rata basis, see reg 10(5).

[38] See *General Practitioner Fundholding in England* (HC 51, Session 1994–95, National Audit Office), para 4.11.

wealth when they leave the practice.'[39] For the present, however, so long as the improvements have the approval of the health authority, the consequential gain to the partners appears to be lawful.

(b) Exceeding the 'Allotted Sum'

What if a fund-holding practice is unable to remain within the sum allotted **1.21** to it? Good reasons may well exist to explain such an overspend. Additional patients may have been accepted onto the doctor's list, or there may have been an increased demand for prolonged care amongst a group of patients, or the original allotment may simply have been wrong. The Department of Health must hold funds in reserve to deal with this possibility.[40]

When overspending cannot be justified the money may be deducted from **1.22** future allocations, or the status of fund-holder may be withdrawn from the practice, either with effect from the start of the next financial year, or immediately.[41] In this case the rights and liabilities of the fund-holding practice shall transfer to the Health Authority.[42] This may pose a dilemma for the practice. A fund-holding practice which has spent its money imprudently at the start of the financial year cannot attempt to retrieve the situation by failing to purchase the care required by its patients. Fund-holders are obliged to account to the health authority for their use of the fund on a monthly basis[43] and scrutiny of the accounts might identify why the problem has arisen. They also remain bound by their Terms of Service to provide care for their patients. It would not be proper for a practice to attempt to remedy its own errors and shortcomings by failing to provide patients with the standard of care they are entitled to expect. Arguably, were a doctor to do so, he would breach his Terms of Service with the Health Authority.[44]

---

[39] *What the Doctor Ordered—a Study of GP Fundholders in England and Wales* (Audit Commission, 1996), 78. Also, hospitals frequently fail to invoice fund-holders for services provided to patients. NHS contracts permit practices to withhold payment after a period of six weeks. See ibid, para 103. Why should such a windfall benefit, caused by managerial inefficiency elsewhere, credit the fund-holder's account? In *Changing the Internal Market* (NHSE, EL(97)33), annex B, the NHSE states that 'GP fundholders should return any "windfall" savings, and should hold other savings against the possibility of a future overspend.'

[40] The amount allotted to a practice may be made by 'payments on account of the allotted sum at such times and in such manner as the Secretary of State may direct'. See the National Health Service and Community Care Act 1990, s 15(3)(a).

[41] Part III, National Health Service (Fund-holding Practices) Regulations 1996 (SI 1996/706). Such a procedure is uncommon, but see 'GP surgery first to be stripped of fundholding', *The Independent*, 10 Mar 1993.   [42] ibid, reg 12(7).   [43] ibid, reg 19(1).

[44] The Terms of Service are discussed below. For discussion of the position of the fund-holder who deliberately refused to fund a particular category of treatment, see Newdick, C, *Who Should We Treat?—Law, Patients and Resources in the NHS* (Oxford University Press, 1995), 178 and 219.

(iii) *Total Purchasing Pilots*

1.23 Since the creation of the NHS in 1946, primary care within the NHS has been provided (a) only by general practitioners, (b) only by means of their Terms of Service with health authorities which, alone, have a 'duty . . . to provide personal medical services for all persons in the locality . . . ',[45] and (c) the relationship between doctor and health authority has only been one of principal and independent contractor, and not employer and employee.[46] Now, Part I of the National Health Service (Primary Care) Act 1997 deregulates these arrangements by enabling the Secretary of State to agree to 'pilot schemes', namely 'one or more agreements made by an authority . . . under which personal medical services are provided (otherwise than by the authority).'[47] The purpose of the Act is to encourage experimentation as to differing methods of delivering health care. The scheme must be reviewed within three years of their creation with a view to their being either adopted as permanent arrangements, or re-incorporated into the traditional framework. The Act has considerable implications for the manner in which health care is provided within the NHS.

1.24 Diversity in the provision of health care is encouraged by the categories from whom applications may be considered. An agreement to enter into a pilot scheme may be made by a health authority[48] with any one or more of the following: (a) an NHS Trust, (b) a suitably experienced medical practitioner, (c) an NHS employee, or a pilot scheme employee, (d) a qualifying body, or (e) an individual who is providing personal medical services under that or another pilot. 'A qualifying body' means a company which is limited by shares all of which are beneficially and legally owned by persons falling within (a), (b), (c), or (e).[49] Thus, instead of primary care being the sole responsibility of health authorities, pilot schemes permit the creation of limited companies of doctors, nurses and other NHS employees as well as nurse partnerships which engage doctors as salaried employees. Arrangements of this kind will be subject to undertakings agreed between the pilot scheme and health authority, and the approval of the Secretary of State.[50] Although the GP's Terms of Service

---

[45] S 29(1), National Health Service Act 1977. The Terms of Service are discussed below.
[46] See s 29(4), National Health Service Act 1977.
[47] Ss 1(1)(a) and 5. See Coulter, A and Mays, N, 'Deregulating Primary Care', (1997) 314 *British Medical Journal* 510. GPs providing services under pilot schemes, independent of the 'general medical services' regulations may be referred to as 'Part I practitioners', see s 14(3), 1997 Act.
[48] See the National Health Service (Proposals for Pilot Schemes) and (Miscellaneous Amendments) Regulations 1997, SI 1997/2289. [49] See s 2(2) and (3).
[50] See ss 4 and 5, National Health Service (Primary Care) Act 1997.

will not apply to these agreements,[51] s 1(8) of the 1997 Act requires that the quality of the services provided by each pilot shall be 'of a kind that may be provided by a general practitioner. . . under the 1977 Act'.[52] In this way patients within pilot schemes should not suffer any reduction in standards of care, indeed the intention of the Act is to discover ways of improving services to patients.

A number of brief observations can be made about the 1997 Act. First, it may **1.25** blur the distinction between primary and secondary care. GPs may be engaged, or employed by NHS hospitals, or community trusts; or they may agree to be funded to provide a full range of both primary and secondary care in consortium with a hospital. In this way responsibility for the entire range of health services is contained within one organisation. Secondly, it undermines the operation of the internal market for health which seeks to separate purchasers and providers of health care in order to encourage bargaining as a way of driving up standards. By contrast, the 1997 Act enables doctors to join health authorities, or NHS trusts, and become responsible both for purchasing and providing care. This signals much greater commitment to the benefits to be gained from co-operation, rather than competition in health care. Thirdly, it permits private interests to become directly involved with the provision of care within the NHS. Paragraphs (b) and (d) include the possibility of private practitioners and companies becoming 'health service bodies' within the National Health Service and Community Care Act 1990,[53] with the right to enter NHS contracts with other health service bodies[54] and receive funding for doing so.

Lastly, as we have seen, it permits GPs to work as employees. Many newly **1.26** qualified doctors do not wish to join a practice as partners and prefer the flexibility offered by employment which enables them to move practices from time to time. Equally, practices in some areas of the country find it more difficult to recruit new partners to their practices and welcome the advantages of employment. The possibility of joining a pilot scheme as an employee clearly has its advantages. At the same time, it may increase the sense of a 'third party' in the surgery. Will the doctor's commitment to promoting his patients' best interests be devalued if he also carries commitments to his employer? What comes first, the patient's need for costly treatment, or the bonus that will be achieved if the doctor

---

[51] See s 9, National Health Service (Primary Care) Act 1997 and s 13, National Health Service Act 1977. The GP's Terms of Service are considered at paras 1.127–1.172 below.
[52] The framework within which such agreements should be made are discussed in *Personal Medical Services Pilots Under the NHS (Primary Care) Act 1997—A Comprehensive Guide* (NHS Executive, 1997) and closely resembles the major provisions of the GP's Terms of Service. This guidance will be enforced under directions to be issued by the Secretary of State.
[53] Within the meaning of s 4, National Health Service and Community Care Act 1990, discussed below. See the National Health Service (Pilot Schemes—Health Service Bodies) Regulations 1997, SI 1997/2929.   [54] S 16, 1997 Act.

is able to keep his spending within agreed limits? Traditionally, this has been a matter of concern more in America than the UK.[55]

1.27 In December 1997, 94 pilot schemes were approved, which commence operation in April 1998. They focus on three main areas of patient need, namely: attracting doctors to those parts of the country where recruitment of GPs is difficult; improving co-operation between GPs and community nurses so as to create a more integrated service for patients; and focusing care on specific patient groups such as children, the elderly, the mentally ill, ethnic minorities, and the homeless in parts of the country which experience high levels of illness.[56]

3. Funding Providers of Health Care

1.28 The providers of health care are, in the main, hospitals. The following section considers (1) managed competition amongst hospitals, (2) NHS Trust Hospitals, (3) NHS 'contracts' (4) raising revenue from patients and (5) the private finance initiative.

(i) *Managed Competition among Hospitals*

1.29 Before 1990, the system of funding the National Health Service was thought to encourage inefficiency. Financial resources were allocated to Regions according to the perceived 'needs' of a resident population (by reference to its rates of mortality and morbidity) without regard to the efficiency of the hospitals responsible for their treatment. This became known as the 'efficiency trap'. When there is no relationship between the amount of money allocated to a district and the numbers of patients it is able to treat, the more efficient hospital appears to suffer a penalty. By treating more patients it spends its allocation more quickly and exhausts its funds before the end of the financial year. One commentator, who influenced the shape of the health service reforms, said of the NHS in 1985 that:

> the system contains no serious incentives to guide the NHS in the direction of better quality care and service at reduced cost . . .
> In fact, the structure of the NHS contains perverse incentives. For example, a District that develops an excellent service in some specialty that attracts more referrals is likely to get more work without getting more resources to do it. A

---

[55] See Richards, T, 'HMOs: America Today, Britain Tomorrow', 298 *British Medical Journal* 292, 460, and 539 (1986) and Rodwin, M, 'Consumer Protection and Managed Care: The Need for Organised Consumers', (1996) 15 *Health Affairs* 110.
[56] See *New Pilots Will Improve Quality in Primary Care Services*, NHS Executive Press Release 97/416.

District that does a poor job will 'export' patients and have less work, but not correspondingly less resources, for its reward . . . ; management and consultants in a District risk weakening the case for a new hospital wing they have been campaigning for by solving their waiting list problem by referring patients to other districts with excess capacity . . .[57]

The 'internal market' for health was proposed to encourage providers of health   **1.30**
care to compete with one another for quality and price and, thus, to reward the most efficient.[58] The market is 'internal' in the sense that its buyers and sellers are confined to those identified in health service legislation; and the level of funding in the system is limited by the Secretary of State (and the Treasury). In principle, purchasers may favour those hospitals which provide best care and value for money by entering NHS 'contracts' with them. The most efficient hospitals ought to receive the highest level of funding from purchasers of health care. This may be referred to as contract funding.

However, the logic of this principle began to be questioned soon after the   **1.31**
internal market commenced operation for a number of reasons. First, the incentive to attract more patients may have enabled some hospitals to do more work than others. It has not, however, entirely resolved the problem of the efficiency trap. Most hospital revenue will arise from large-scale 'block' contracts from health authorities, in which lump sum payments are agreed for categories of work over a period of time. But those hospitals which are able to deal with patients most quickly and efficiently will still face the prospect of exhausting their revenue before the end of the financial year by virtue of the fact that the money available to purchasers within the NHS remains limited.

Secondly, the application of pure market principles to the provision of health   **1.32**
care may not always be practicable, or desirable. Effective markets require consumers to have good information to distinguish between good value and poor, and to enable them to exert pressure on sellers to improve quality, or to lower prices. But patients and doctors may not have the information necessary to enable them to act in this way. Until very recently, it was true to say that 'such is the design of hospital information systems that no real distinction is made between patients who leave hospital alive and those who die there',[59] so that it was extremely difficult to know which hospitals achieved the highest

---

[57] Enthoven, A, *Reflections on the Management of the National Health Service—An American looks at incentives to efficiency in health services management in the UK* (Nuffield Provincial Hospitals Trust, 1985), 13–15.

[58] Although it rejects the application of pure market principles to health care, the Labour Party has given qualified support to 'a system of rewards for those units which demonstrate high quality and increased productivity'. See *Health 2000* (The Labour Party, 1994), para 6.5.

[59] Kind, P, *Hospital Deaths—The Missing Link: Measuring Outcome in Hospital Activity Data* (Office of Health Economics, 1988), 1.

standards. Now, the NHS Executive has committed itself to improving information about hospital activity and performance tables were introduced in 1994 which compare waiting times and (in Scotland) clinical outcomes for certain clinical procedures. But measurements of waiting times, although easy to quantify, are not necessarily a good indication of the quality of care provided. Even the more sensitive clinical outcome indicators used in Scotland, which reveal differences in success rates between clinical procedures and in different hospitals, have to be used with great caution. The Clinical Outcomes Working Group emphasise that

> no conclusions can or should be drawn from the comparisons in this report about the quality or the efficacy of the treatment provided . . . or for patients admitted to different hospitals. Despite the standardisation for age and sex, and in many cases for deprivation and commorbidity as well, it is still just as likely that the observed differences in outcome are due to differences in patients, or in diagnostic criteria, as they are due to differences in treatment.[60]

1.33 Also, the devolution of power to the market will not necessarily be desirable since it may not promote national strategy established by the Department of Health. Before 1990, the system of distributing resources allowed national policy to be imposed on health authorities and hospitals. With the creation of GP fund-holders and NHS Trusts, however, decision-making power has been devolved away from the centre. This may have advantages for doctors and patients, but it is not clear how the policy objectives of the Secretary of State, or the overall stability of hospitals, are promoted by such a system.

1.34 Take the case of fund-holding GPs. Some have combined to form consortia. A consortium of five or six practices may represent a considerable number of patients, but with no corresponding obligations with respect to policy laid down centrally. No contracts manager in a hospital can afford to lose the custom of doctors with a potential buying power of, perhaps, 50,000 patients. Inevitably, these local pressures may tend to distort policy established by the Department of Health. For example, as an incentive to attract fund-holding revenue, some hospitals offered a fast-track to fund-holders' patients which gave preferential access based on the status of the GP rather than the clinical merits of the case. This led to charges of 'two-tierism' in the NHS and new guidelines have forbidden the practice by insisting on the use of common hospital waiting lists for both urgent and non-urgent patients.[61]

1.35 Considerations of this nature explain the commitment of the Labour

---

[60] *Clinical Outcome Indicators* (Clinical Outcomes Working Group, Scottish Office, 1995), 4.
[61] See *Access to Secondary Care Services* (EL(97)42). From April 1998, 'hospitals cannot offer preferential appointments for the patients of fund-holders . . . ' (para 6).

Government to modify the operation of the internal market[62] and the bipartisan support for the National Health Service (Primary Care) Act 1997 (discussed above) which modifies some features of the old 'internal market' for health care by encouraging co-operation between the component parts of the system.

(ii) *NHS Trust Hospitals*

Section 5(1) of the National Health Service and Community Care Act 1990 **1.36** provides that the Secretary of State may by order establish bodies, to be known as NHS Trusts:

(a) to assume responsibility, in accordance with this Act, for the ownership and management of hospitals or other establishments or facilities which were previously managed or provided by Health Authorities or Special Health Authorities, or

(b) to provide and manage hospitals or other establishments or facilities.

The order shall be made by statutory instrument and may be amended or **1.37** revoked.[63] The NHS Trust shall carry out 'effectively, efficiently and economically the functions for the time being conferred on it by [such] an order'[64] so that its annual revenue is sufficient to meet its outgoings.[65] NHS Trust Hospitals are funded from the revenue generated by contracting with NHS purchasers and others. Before acquiring trust status, the health authority is obliged to consult the Community Health Councils of the relevant area and other persons or bodies as they consider appropriate.[66] The nature and function of NHS Trust hospitals is set down in the regulations by which they have been created which generally provide as follows:

(1) The trust is established for the purposes specified in section 5(1)(a) of the [1990] Act.

(2) The trust's functions (which include the functions which the Secretary of State considers appropriate in relation to the provision of services by the trust for one or more health authorities) shall be—

(a) to own and manage hospital accommodation and services provided at [name and address];

---

[62] And see *Changing the Internal Market* (NHSE, EL(97)33).

[63] The requirements of such an order are specified in the National Health Service and Community Care Act 1990, sch 2, Part I, as amended by s 2(1), Sch 1, para 69(a), Health Authorities Act 1995. [64] Sch 2, para 6(1), 1990 Act.

[65] See 1990 Act, s 10. See also the restrictions imposed on the powers to borrow money in sched 7B of the 1990 Act.

[66] S 5(2), National Health Service and Community Care Act 1990 and the National Health Service Trusts (Consultation on Establishment and Dissolution) Regulations 1996, SI 1996/653.

(b) to manage community health services provided from [name and address].[67]

1.38 NHS Trusts may have better access to information and be able to promote themselves more effectively than hospitals managed by the Health Authority. The additional freedom conferred is that, subject to specific financial provisions,[68]

> . . . an NHS Trust shall have power to do anything which appears to it to be necessary or expedient for the purposes of or in connection with the discharge of its functions, including in particular power—
>
> (a) to acquire and dispose of land or other property;
> (b) to enter into such contracts as seem to the trust to be appropriate;
> (c) to accept gifts of money, land or other property, including money, land or other property to be held on trust, either in general or for any specific purposes of the NHS trust or for all or any purposes relating to the health service; and
> (d) to employ staff on such terms as the trust think fit.[69]

(iii) NHS 'Contracts'

1.39 What are 'NHS contracts' and to what extent do they resemble contracts at common law? The following considers (i) the parties to NHS contracts, (ii) the contracts and (iii) resolving disputes concerning NHS contracts.

(a) The Parties

1.40 The system of contract funding requires hospitals to engage in a competitive process in order to secure revenue by selling goods and services to purchasers of health care. This is achieved by entering 'NHS contracts':

> . . . the phrase 'NHS contract' means an agreement under which one health service body ('the acquirer') arranges for the provision to it by another health service body ('the provider') of goods and services which it reasonably requires for the purposes of its functions.[70]

And 'health service body' means any of the following, namely—

(a) a health authority;
(b) a health board;
(c) the Common Services Agency for the Scottish Health Service;
(d) . . . ;

---

[67] This example is taken from the Harrow and Hillingdon Healthcare National Health Service Trust (Establishment) Order 1994, SI 1994/848.
[68] Detailed in the National Health Service and Community Care Act 1990, Sch 3.
[69] ibid, Sch 2, para 16(1).   [70] S 4(1), 1990 Act.

(e) an NHS Trust;

(f) a recognised fund-holding practice;

(g) the Dental Practice Board or the Scottish Dental Practice Board;

(h) the Public Health Laboratory Service Board; and

(i) the Secretary of State.[71]

In addition an NHS Trust may also provide services under arrangements made with a 'qualifying body' under section 2(2)(d) of the National Health Service (Primary Care) Act 1997.[72]

NHS contracts are intended to enable the parties to agree matters of quality, **1.41** quantity, and cost. In one sense they introduce pressures common to ordinary business contracts between commercial parties. Parties may need to consider compromises between competing objectives. Perhaps the quantity of a particular service ought to be reduced to expand facilities elsewhere; or prices ought to be reduced to attract more custom. Similarly, there is the need to balance administrative and transaction costs (the costs of providing and monitoring the service) with the money devoted to the services themselves. But the matter 'should not be approached as a legalistic or adversarial exercise but as an opportunity to discuss and agree how improvements to patient care can be secured and over what time'.[73]

Clearly, NHS contracts will force the parties to be explicit about the services **1.42** they wish to provide and, by implication, those they do not. In this respect, they make more visible than ever before the judgments that have been made between patients when demand for health care exceeds the resources made available. For the present, the evidence suggests that there has been little change in the patterns of priorities identified by health authorities, though a process of evolution may be under way.[74]

(b) The Contracts

Most commissioning of health care takes place between hospitals (as providers, **1.43** or sellers), and health authorities and GP fund-holders (as purchasers). Health authorities still retain the major responsibility for purchasing. In 1994–95, providers derived 86 per cent of their income from health authorities and 6 per cent from GP fund-holders.[75] On average, hospitals appear to work with

---

[71] S 4(2), 1990 Act. Para (d) referred to FHSAs, and is deleted by s 2(1), Sch 1, para 68, Health Authorities Act 1995.

[72] See nn 50 and 51 above and Sch 2, para 65(2) of the 1997 Act, amending s 5(6) of the National Health Service and Community Care Act 1990.

[73] *Contracts for Health Services: Operating Contracts* (EL(90)MB/24, NHSME, 1990), 1.

[74] Redmayne, S, *Small Steps, Big Goals—Purchasing Policies in the NHS* (Centre for the Analysis of Social Policy, University of Bath, 1996). [75] See para 1.05 above.

around thirty generic contracts with health authorities. Parties to NHS contracts may undertake such obligations as they see fit, but (subject to the legislative changes proposed for 1999 in which primary care groups will be responsible for entering 'service agreements' with NHS trusts[76]) three models of contract have been suggested as the suitable means of commencing the process, ie 'block contracts', 'cost and volume contracts' and 'cost per case contracts'.

1.44 Block contracts are agreements in which hospital units undertake to provide an unlimited number of facilities, or a maximum number, expressed, for example in terms of beds, over a specified period of time. Under these arrangements health authorities may commit resources to a hospital provider irrespective of the actual usage of the facilities and, in so doing, will have difficulty being precise with respect to quality. In its most simple form, the block contract ought to decline and be replaced by more sophisticated agreements in which standards of performance are monitored more accurately and terms may be adjusted according to agreed maxima and minima.[77]

1.45 Cost and volume contracts offer the opportunity for the parties to agree a particular service, or range of services, for a specific price. Its emphasis is on output in the sense that the parties agree to a specific requirements for an exact price.

> The various advantages to both contracting parties—the opportunity for [Health Authorities] to link payment with activity; and for units to match funding to workload and deploy their resources more flexibly—suggest that cost and volume contracts are likely to be widely used as negotiating skills improve and more detailed information becomes available.[78]

1.46 Arrangements of this nature may enable quality to be monitored, by reference to, for example, waiting times, admission and discharge procedures, the facilities provided to patients, out-patients clinics, correspondence with referring doctors and the provision of performance data to health authorities.[79] As has been noted above, however, for the moment, data which compares the quality of clinical care and outcomes is largely unavailable.[80]

1.47 Cost per case contracts, or individually agreed contracts may be used most

---

[76] See Appleby, J, *Developing Contracting: A National Survey of District Health Authorities, boards and NHS Trusts* (NAHAT, 1995), 8. Non-NHS and private work made up the majority of the remainder.
[77] See Appleby, J, Smith, P, *et al*, 'Monitoring Managed Competition', in Robinson, R, and Le Grand, J (eds), *Evaluating the NHS Reforms* (King's Fund Institute, 1994), ch 2.
[78] *Contracts for Health Services: Operating Contracts* (EL(90)MB/24, NHSME, 1990), para 3.38.
[79] See *The Patient's Charter: Hospital and Ambulance Services—Comparative Performance Guide 1993–94* (NHS Executive, 1994). [80] See para 1.32 above.

frequently by fund-holding GPs. Because they inevitably carry larger transaction costs they will be less commonly used by health authorities. In addition purchasers may be reluctant to enter cost per case contracts based on a day per day basis for fear of losing control over their resources. The alternative is to use the contract as a means of negotiating entire episodes of care, with the emphasis on the provider to assess the average cost of each episode, allowing for occasional complications, or to refine cost and volume contracts after specified threshold targets have been achieved.

(c) Disputes

Parties to NHS contracts will be keen to ensure that the terms of their agreements are adhered to. Health authorities and GP fund-holders will monitor the performance of the hospitals to which patients have been sent with a view to encouraging improvements in standards, or a change of hospital, if performance is unsatisfactory. And hospitals themselves may make 'tertiary referrals' of patients who need specialist treatment to other hospitals with particular expertise. They too will want to safeguard quality. Each will want to know that it has received the goods and services paid for in the right quantity, quality, and at the right time. In cases of dispute what action may be taken where an amicable settlement between the parties is impossible? **1.48**

The 1990 Act removes the possibility of disputes over NHS contracts from proceeding to the courts on grounds of breach of contract. It provides: **1.49**

> Whether or not an arrangement which constitutes an NHS contract would, apart from this subsection, be a contract in law, it shall not be regarded for any purposes as giving rise to contractual rights and liabilities, but if any dispute arises with respect to such an arrangement, either party may refer the matter to the Secretary of State for determination.[81]

An adjudication may:

> contain such directions (including directions as to payment) as the Secretary of State or, as the case may be, the person appointed under subsection (5) . . . considers appropriate to resolve the matter in dispute; and it shall be the duty of the parties to the NHS contract in question to comply with any such directions.[82]

The adjudicator also has authority to vary the terms of an NHS contract, or bring it to an end.[83] In addition to these rules which assume the existence of an NHS contract, a procedure is available to negotiators who consider that: **1.50**

---

[81] National Health Service and Community Care Act 1990, s 4(3). The matter may be determined either by the Secretary of State, or by his appointee. See s 4(5), 1990 Act.
[82] See s 4(7), 1990 Act.   [83] See s 4(8), 1990 Act.

(a) the terms proposed by another health service body are unfair by reason that the other party is seeking to take advantage of its position as the only, or the only practicable, provider of the goods and services concerned or by reason of any other unequal bargaining position as between the prospective parties to the proposed arrangement, or

(b) that for any other reason arising out of the relative bargaining position of the prospective parties any of the terms of the proposed arrangement cannot be agreed . . .[84]

1.51 The procedure by which such disputes should be resolved is set down in regulations,[85] but no substantive guidelines have been suggested as a means of settlement. The explanatory notes state, rather ambiguously, that the adjudicator's decisions:

> will not constitute precedents for the determination of other disputes, but they will be useful learning tools for all parties in reaching a shared understanding of the ways contracts might develop.[86]

1.52 Generally, statutes do not exclude the right to natural justice and judicial review would be available to parties who consider they have been dealt with unfairly by an informal adjudicatory body. Both parties must be heard in order for the adjudicator to have a balanced view of the dispute;[87] and the adjudication must be fair, in the sense that it must be truly independent of the parties.[88] Given that one of the parties to an NHS contract may be the Secretary of State, particular care will be required by the courts to ensure independence. There is a 'presumption . . . that the outcome will give effect to the agreement which was originally reached, rather than a new agreement which the parties should have reached'.[89] Some measure of consistency ought to exist between adjudications. If similar cases were to be treated inconsistently, the matter could be amenable to judicial review.[90] In this way a common stock of responses to NHS contractual disputes might accumulate for the benefit of the parties.

1.53 Some have suggested that, though the courts are excluded from intervening in

---

[84] See s 4(4), 1990 Act.

[85] See the National Health Service Contracts (Dispute Resolution) Regulations 1996, SI 1996/623.

[86] See *NHS Contracts: Arrangements for Resolving Disputes*, HO 302/6 and EL(91)11 (NHSME, 1991).

[87] *Ridge v Baldwin* [1964] AC 40, *Schmidt v Secretary of State for Home Affairs* [1969] 2 Ch 149.

[88] *R v Kent Police Authority, ex p Gooden* [1971] 2 QB 662, *Metropolitan Properties Co (FGC) Ltd v Lannon and Others* [1969] 1 QB 577.

[89] *NHS Contracts: Arrangements for Resolving Disputes*, HO 302/4 (NHSME, 1991).

[90] See *Metropolitan Properties Ltd v Lannon* [1969] 1 QB 577, which concerned consistency between levels of rent established by rent assessment committees.

the substantive matters relating to NHS *contracts*, there remains the possibility of a party pursuing a remedy in the law of Restitution.[91] The action does not require the existence of a contract but it is capable of achieving similar objectives, ie the payment of money for the value of goods or services which the other party has received and from which he has taken benefit. Common law dislikes a party being unjustly enriched at the expense of another. Even when the absence of a contract is because legislation has precluded its existence, courts have sympathised with the plaintiff and provided a remedy in restitution.[92]

Could such an approach be adopted with respect to NHS contracts? As a general rule, the courts interpret narrowly statutes which erode common law rights. Arguably, therefore, assuming NHS contracts to be contracts at common law,[93] the exclusion from litigation of 'contractual rights' ought not to exclude other remedies available to the parties.[94] On the other hand, the policy of the Act is to exclude the courts from resolving disputes between parties to NHS contracts. It would be strange if, on identical disputes, one alone was to be admitted by reason simply of the plea of restitution, rather than breach of contract, in the statement of claim. Such a ploy would undermine the intention of the Act and, incidentally, exclude those whose complaints were based on executory contracts (i e those to be performed in the future) and who had yet to confer benefit on the other party. This seems arbitrary. Thus, the courts will be reluctant to enable the intention of the Act to be bypassed in this way and will allow the internal system to operate 'provided they are satisfied that such claims can be enforced in another way; and provided they retain the ultimate power to review statutory arbitration decisions which are irrational, or beyond the powers of the arbitrator'.[95]

1.54

---

[91] Jacob, J, 'Lawyers go to Hospital', [1991] Public Law 255, 274.
[92] See the Australian case of *Pavey & Mathews v Paul* [1986] 162 CLR 221. See also *Delgman v Guaranty Trust Co of Canada* [1954] 3 DLR 785.
[93] Arguably, NHS contracts are not contracts at common law, in which a fundamental requirement is the freedom of the parties to enter the contract and negotiate terms. Complete freedom does not exist in relation to NHS contracts because the parties are obliged to enter agreements in order to fulfil their statutory responsibilities. See *Pfizer v Minister of Health* [1965] AC 512.
[94] See *Metropolitan Film Studios Ltd v Twickenham Film Studios Ltd* [1962] 1 WLR 1315, 1323, and *Allen v Thorn Electrical Industries Ltd* [1968] 1 QB 487.
[95] See Barker, K, 'NHS Contracts, Restitution and the Internal Market', (1993) 56 Modern Law Review 832, 840.

(iv) *Raising Revenue from Patients*

1.55 Revenue may be raised from (i) private patients and (ii) NHS patients.

(a) Private Care in NHS Hospitals

1.56 As a general rule the services provided to patients in the NHS 'shall be free of charge except in so far as the making and receiving of charges is expressly provided for by or under any enactment . . . '.[96] However, private, fee-paying care may be provided in NHS hospitals. Thus, '[i]n order to make income available for improving the health service',[97] to such extent as it may determine,

> a Health Authority or Special Health Authority may make available at a hospital or hospitals for which they have responsibility accommodation and services for patients who give undertakings (or for whom undertakings are given) to pay, in respect of the accommodation and services made available, such charges as the Authority may determine . . . on any basis that the Authority considers to be the appropriate commercial basis . . .[98]

1.57 Similarly, under arrangements made with medical or dental practitioners, a health authority may allow accommodation and services to be made available for the treatment of private patients of the practitioner.[99] Single beds may be used for private, fee-paying patients in a way that is indistinguishable from normal NHS facilities, or whole wards or wings may be dedicated to private use. Beds, wards, or units utilised in this way are a source of revenue for hospitals and the Secretary of State has power to direct that activities of this nature are undertaken.[100] For the moment, the numbers of complete units dedicated to private care is relatively small. At the beginning of 1995, there were believed to be 72 dedicated NHS pay bed units in NHS hospitals with a

---

[96] S 1(2), 1977 Act. See also ss 25, 63, 65, 77–83 and Sch 12 for circumstances in which fees may be charged.

[97] Agreements may also be entered into with respect to goods, land, and other services. See Health and Medicines Act 1988, s 7(1) and (2).

[98] See s 65(1) 1977 Act, as amended by the Health and Medicines Act 1988, s 7(10), the National Health Service and Community Care Act 1990, s 25(2), and the Health Authorities Act 1995, s 2(1), Sch 1, para 38(a). Agreements may also be entered into with respect to goods, land, and other services 'in order to make income available for improving the health service . . .' See Health and Medicines Act 1988, s 7(2).

[99] S 65(2) 1977 Act, as amended by the Health and Medicines Act 1988, s 7(2) and the National Health Service and Community Care Act 1990, s 25(5).

[100] See the Health and Medicines Act 1988, s 7(3).

total of 1,367 beds.[101] The units are generally managed by the hospitals themselves, although they may have private staffing arrangements. Total income from this source amounted to £185 million in the year 1993–94.[102] In the past, private hospital care has tended to concentrate on acute (curable) conditions, rather than chronic (long-term) ones.

The power of a health authority to use its resources for private care is restricted so that: **1.58**

> it shall permit facilities to be used in this way only if and to the extent that the Authority is satisfied that to do so
> (a) will not to a significant extent interfere with the performance by the Authority of any function conferred on the Authority under [the 1977] Act to provide accommodation or services of any kind; and
> (b) will not to a significant extent operate to the disadvantage of persons seeking or afforded admission or access to accommodation or services at health service hospitals (whether as resident or non-resident patients) otherwise than under this section.[103]

The power to offer treatment privately is also available to NHS Trust hospitals.   **1.59**
Thus, 'an NHS trust may make accommodation or services or both available for patients who give undertakings (or for whom undertakings are given) to pay, in respect of the accommodation or services (or both) such charges as the trust may determine.'[104] The specific restrictions on this freedom which apply to hospitals directly managed by health authorities do not apply to NHS Trust hospitals[105] which, it will be recalled, make up the vast majority of all NHS hospitals. Given their obligation to 'ensure that revenue is not less than sufficient, taking one financial year with another, to meet outgoings properly chargeable to revenue account',[106] there may be an incentive for them to use fee-paying patients as a means of balancing their books.[107] Conceivably,

---

[101] *Are Pay-Beds Profitable?* (National Economic Research Associates, 1995), 6. See generally *Laing's Review of Private Health Care* (Laing and Buisson, 1995). Previously, s 75 of the National Health Service Act 1977 required a register of private use to be kept. The provision was repealed by the Health Services Act 1980. No other central record of private use of NHS facilities appears to have been kept.   [102] *Are Pay-Beds Profitable?* (n 101 above), 8.
[103] S 65(1) 1977 Act, as substituted by the Health and Medicines Act 1988 s 7, and amended by the National Health Service and Community Care Act 1990, s 25(2) and the Health Authorities Act 1995, s 2(1), Sch 1, para 38(a). If the powers are exercised by the Secretary of State, the same restrictions apply, see the Health and Medicines Act 1988, s 7(8)(a).
[104] Sch 2, para 6(14), National Health Service and Community Care Act 1990.
[105] See s 65(4), 1977 Act, added by the National Health Service and Community Care Act 1990, s 66(1), Sch 9, para 18(4).
[106] See National Health Service and Community Care Act 1990, s 10.
[107] Spending by NHS Trust hospitals on private health care rose by 265% between 1991–92 and 1992–93, ie from around £12 million to £44 million. The comparable increase by district health authorities was 17%, from around £160 million to £187 million. See 'NHS Trust Spending on Private Care up by 265% in a Year', *News Release* (The Labour Party, 22 Dec 1993).

commercial incentives could induce an NHS Trust to allocate its resources to fee-paying patients in a way that interfered with the duty imposed on the Secretary of State to provide a 'comprehensive health service' and this may create concern. On the other hand, NHS trust hospitals remain committed to honouring their responsibilities under NHS contracts and they could not use income from private patients in a way that compromised those obligations. The Secretary of State retains power to issue directions to health authorities in respect of the freedom to use facilities for private patients[108] and those powers have been extended to NHS Trusts. Thus,

> [a]n NHS Trust shall comply with any directions given to it by the Secretary of State with respect to . . . compliance with guidance or directions given (by circular or otherwise) to health authorities, or particular descriptions of health authorities . . .[109]

This enables the Secretary of State to interfere with improper commercial strategies adopted by NHS trust hospitals, if circumstances so require.

(b) Revenue from NHS Patients

1.60 By section 7(2) of the Health and Medicines Act 1988, the Secretary of State may authorise certain accommodation to be made available for patients:

> and recover such charges as he may determine in respect of such accommodation and calculate them on any basis that he considers to be the appropriate commercial basis.[110]

1.61 Section 7(8) restricts the exercise of the discretion so that the power shall be exercised only to the extent that he is satisfied that anything he proposes to do

> (a) will not to a significant extent interfere with the performance by him of any duty imposed on him by the National Health Service Act 1977 . . . ; and
> (b) will not to a significant extent operate to the disadvantage of persons seeking or afforded admission or access to accommodation or services vested in the Secretary of State for the purposes of his functions under [the Act] . . .

1.62 In this way, income may be generated from NHS patients who choose, for example, to be treated in a private room or a small ward which are not otherwise needed by any patient on medical grounds. Income from the use of

---

[108] See s 65(3), National Health Service Act 1977, substituted by s 25(5), National Health Service and Community Care Act 1990, and s 2(1), Sch 1, para 38(d), Health Authorities Act 1995.

[109] National Health Service and Community Care Act 1990, Sch 2, para 6(2)(e). But see also the National Health Service Act 1977, s 72 in relation to private, non-resident patients, with respect to whom permission to treat must be sought from the Secretary of State and is subject to restrictions.

[110] S 63(1), 1977 Act, as amended by the Health and Medicines Act 1988, s 7(9).

NHS beds for paying patients has increased steadily, from around £78 million in 1988–89, to £157 million in 1992–93.[111]

Similar powers are available to NHS trust hospitals which, '[f]or the purpose of making additional income available in order better to perform [their] functions, . . . shall have the powers specified in section 7(2) of the Health and Medicines Act 1988'.[112]   **1.63**

(v) *The Private Finance Initiative*

The Private Finance Initiative intends to encourage private investment in the NHS by expanding hospital facilities in ways that could not be achieved from public sources alone. The power of NHS trusts 'to enter into such contracts as seem to the trust to be appropriate' already exists under the National Health Service and Community Care Act 1990,[113] but following a Court of Appeal decision in which a development agreement between a bank and local authority was held to be ultra vires the powers of the authority and, therefore, unenforceable,[114] an Act was passed to provide further reassurance to financiers. Under the National Health Service (Private Finance) Act 1997,[115] the powers of a National Health Service trust expressly include the power to enter into externally financed development agreements (EFDAs). An agreement is an EFDA if it is so certified by the Secretary of State and such a certificate may be issued if   **1.64**

(a) in his opinion the purpose or main purpose of the agreement is the provision of facilities in connection with the discharge by the trust of any of its functions; and

(b) a person proposes to make a loan to, or provide any form of finance for, another party in connection with the agreement.[116]

The words 'another party' excludes reference to the trust itself[117] so that any such scheme would usually involve a private loan to (say) a consortium which would propose to finance the development of 'facilities' for an NHS trust. This could serve to shield the trust from exposure to the same degree of risk as that undertaken by the consortium. The word 'facilities' includes (a) works,   **1.65**

---

[111] A full break-down of statistics by year and by region is supplied by the Secretary of State in a Parliamentary written answer at *Hansard*, HC col 532 (31 January 1994). This form of business activity may work against private hospitals.

[112] Sch 2, para 6(15), National Health Service and Community Care Act 1990.

[113] Sch 2, para 16(1)(b), 1990 Act.

[114] See *Crédit Suisse v Allerdale BC* [1996] 4 All ER 129.

[115] Similar assurance to those who have obtained rights from trusts which cease to exist is available from the National Health Service (Residual Liabilities) Act 1996.

[116] S 1.   [117] S 1(5).

buildings, plant, equipment or other property; and (b) services.[118] A sensitive matter of policy concerns the 'services' which may be included and whether, and, if so, to what extent, they should include clinical services. The Labour government has committed itself to excluding all clinical services from certification under the Act and to formulate a list by which clinical, and non-clinical will be distinguished.[119] Exactly where such a boundary should be drawn will inevitably provoke disagreement.

1.66 The basis on which the Secretary of State will exercise his discretion to issue an EFDA certificate is to be explained in guidelines which may include such factors as improved clinical quality of services, improved strategic fit, better use of resources, and better access to services.[120] Precise quantification of the advantages and disadvantages of a privately financed scheme will be difficult and the scope of the discretion in this respect is likely to be very broad.

B. Regulating Health Care[121]

1.67 What controls exist within the NHS to regulate doctors, health authorities and hospitals? The following examines (1) the status of Directions and Guidelines, (2) internal regulation of standards, (3) the provision of hospital care and (4) the provision of primary care by GPs.

1. The Status of Directions and Guidelines

1.68 Internal regulation of the health service is most commonly achieved by means of health service circulars (previously known as executive letters (ELs), health service guidelines (HSGs)), and various other statements of policy from the NHS Executive and the Department of Health. What is their legal status? There are a number of considerations. First, internal regulations must remain within the statutory and common law framework which surrounds the NHS. Any contradiction between the two must be resolved in favour of the statute. In reviewing this matter, the court must

> begin by examining the nature of the statutory power which the administrative authority . . . has purported to exercise and asking, in the light of that

---

[118] ibid.

[119] Given the open-ended manner in which the words 'facilities' in sub-s (3)(a) and 'services' in sub-s (5) are expressed in the Act, would such a self-imposed restriction on the Secretary of State's powers be an unreasonable fetter on his discretion?

[120] See discussion in *Hansard*, HC, vol 297, cols 139–142 (14 July 1997).

[121] See generally Newdick, C, *Who Should We Treat?—Law, Patients and Resources in the NHS* (Oxford University Press, 1995).

examination, what were, and were not, relevant considerations for the authority to take into account in deciding to exercise its power.[122]

Provided the regulations are lawful in this sense, one must ask whether they have **1.69** the status of 'directions', or mere 'guidance'. By section 13 of the National Health Service Act 1977, the Secretary of State may direct a health authority

> to exercise on his behalf such of his functions relating to the health service as are specified in the directions, and it shall be the duty of the health authority to comply with the directions.[123]

And 'it shall be the duty of a Health Authority or Special Health Authority to **1.70** whom directions are given . . . to comply with the directions.'[124] The distinction between directions and guidance was considered in *R v North Derbyshire HA, ex p Fisher*[125] with respect to *New Drugs for Multiple Sclerosis* (EL (95)97) which included the following statements:

> 7. Key aims . . . are to: target the drug appropriately at patients who are most likely to benefit from treatment . . . 9. Purchasing authorities and providers are asked . . . to develop and implement a prescribing approach for Beta Interferon through hospitals . . . 10 . . . providers are asked to give sympathetic consideration to such GP referrals, taking into account local priorities.[126]

Dyson J considered the distinction as follows. He said: **1.71**

> The difference between a policy which provides mere guidance and one in which the health authority is obliged to implement is crucial. Policy which is in the form of guidance can be expressed in strong terms and yet fall short of amounting to direction. There is no reference in the circular to the word 'directions' and read as a whole there is no indication that the circular is intended to trigger the statutory duty of compliance to be found in section 13 of the 1977 Act. The circular includes words such as 'asks', 'suggested', 'taking into account', it does not include the word 'shall' or any of the other badges of mandatory requirement.
> . . . If the circular provided no more than guidance, albeit in strong terms, then the only duty placed upon the health authority was to take it into account in the discharge of their functions. That would be susceptible to challenge only on *Wednesbury* principles if they failed to consider the circular, or they misconstrued or misapplied it whether deliberately or negligently.[127]

On this analysis, the directions that must, and the guidance that may be **1.72** followed, serve to regulate NHS bodies with respect to, for example, issues of

---

[122] *Per* Lord Bridge in *Gillick v West Norfolk and Wisbech AHA* [1985] 3 All ER 402, 426. The question may be far from straightforward, as the disagreement between the Court of Appeal and House of Lords in *Gillick* demonstrates.
[123] S 13, National Health Service Act 1977 as amended by the National Health Service and Community Care Act 1990, s 66(2) and sch 10. [124] ibid, s 17(2).
[125] [1997] 8 Med LR 327. See also *R v Secretary of State for Health, ex p Manchester LMC* 25 BMLR 77, 89, *per* Collins J. [126] ibid, 330.
[127] ibid, 331.

management, or the achievement of targets.[128] But they will not necessarily confer rights on individual patients. By contrast, if such measures create a legitimate expectation that certain rights will be conferred, they may succeed in doing so. Rights arising in this way have been explained as follows:

> If a public body has made a representation to a specific individual or group of individuals that a particular policy will be followed, or that they will be informed before such a change of policy takes place, then the individual will be entitled to insist that the policy is pursued in relation to the instant case, provided the implementation of the policy does not conflict with the authority's statutory duty.[129]

1.73 Most commonly, such rights will be in the nature of promises that certain procedures will be followed before decisions are reached. Thus, a recent case has conferred the right of residents of a nursing home to be consulted about proposals to close the residence and accommodate them elsewhere. They had been 'enjoying some benefit or advantage of which the county council now propose[d] to deprive them.'[130] Their legitimate expectation that they would be able to stay was sufficient to confer a right to have their views heard before a decision on the matter was taken. This approach applies equally to the status of, for example, some of the assurances given in the *Patient's Charter*.[131]

1.74 Given the improved reliability of the clinical evidence of the medicines, techniques, and procedures which tend to be most effective (and those which do not), together with the variations of practice between doctors which cannot be explained simply by the different mix of patients for whom they are responsible, one would expect health service managers to make increasing use of measures of this nature to influence clinical practice.[132] Inevitably, such action will provoke dispute between the professions as to the legitimate areas of responsibility of clinicians and managers.

---

[128] See targets for the reduction of specific areas of mortality and morbidity established by *The Health of the Nation* (Department of Health, 1992).

[129] See Craig, P, *Administrative Law* (Sweet & Maxwell, 3rd edn, 1994) 395 and *Council for Civil Service Unions v Minister for the Civil Service* [1985] 1 AC 374, 408 *per* Lord Diplock.

[130] See *R v Devon County Council, ex p Barker* [1995] 1 All ER 73, 91 *per* Simon Brown LJ.

[131] See *The Patient's Charter and You* (Department of Health, 1996), *Services for Children and Younger People* (Department of Health, 1996), and *Mental Health Services* (Department of Health, 1997).

[132] *Variations in Health: What can the Department of Health and the NHS Do?* (Department of Health, 1995).

2. Internal Regulation of Standards

Although specific guidance and directions are referred to throughout this **1.75** chapter, special consideration is given to regulations designed to improve standards of management in the NHS.

Following concern about the mismanagement of funds within the NHS,[133] **1.76** guidance has been issued which is intended to enhance the quality of corporate governance in the NHS. The principles of corporate governance comprise

> [1] **Accountability**—meaning that everything done by those who work in the NHS must be able to stand the test of parliamentary scrutiny, public judgements on propriety and professional codes of conduct. [2] **Probity**—meaning that there should be an absolute standard of honesty in dealing with the assets of the NHS: integrity should be the hallmark of all personal conduct in decisions affecting patients, staff and suppliers, and in the use of information acquired in the course of the NHS duties. [3] **Openness**—meaning that there should be sufficient transparency about the NHS activities to promote confidence between the NHS authority or trust and its staff, its patients and the public.[134]

The following considers these principles in relation to (1) health authorities **1.77** and NHS trusts and (2) primary care medicine.

(i) *Health Authorities and NHS Trusts*

Three detailed codes now govern standards in the NHS; namely a *Code of* **1.78** *Conduct*, a *Code of Accountability*,[135] and a *Code of Practice on Openness in the NHS*.[136] It is not proposed to consider each in detail. The broad principles behind the codes, however, can be summarised as follows. With respect to conduct, those who work in the NHS 'have a responsibility to respond to staff, patients and suppliers impartially, to achieve value for money from the public funds with

---

[133] See, eg *West Midlands RHA: Regional Managed Services Organisation*, (HC 485, 1993, Report of the Public Accounts Committee). And see generally, *Standards of Public Life* (Cm 2850, 1995, The 'Nolan' Report).
[134] *Public Enterprise Governance in the NHS* (NHSE, 1994), 9 and *Code of Conduct for NHS Boards* (Department of Health, 1994), 2. See generally, Longley, D, *Public Law and Health Service Accountability* (Open University Press, 1993). For the additional regulation provided by other statutory bodies such as the Audit Commission see Newdick, C, *Who Should We Treat?—Law Patients and Resources in the NHS* (Oxford University Press, 1995) ch 6 and Montgomery, J, *Health Care Law* (Oxford University Press, 1997) ch 3.
[135] Both contained in *Code of Conduct. Code of Accountability* (Department of Health, 1994).
[136] NHS Executive, 1995. And see generally, Belcher, A, 'Codes of Conduct and Accountability for NHS Boards', [1995] Public Law 288.

which they are entrusted and to demonstrate high ethical standards of personal conduct.'[137] Greater emphasis should be placed on openness and public responsibility. Thus, there should be a willingness to be open with the public, patients and staff as the need for change emerges. Major changes should always be consulted upon before decisions are reached and information supporting those decisions should be made available and positive responses should be given to reasonable requests for information.[138] Chairmen and board members should act impartially and shall never use their public position to further their private interests. Every potential for a conflict of interest of this nature should be declared and recorded in the board minutes, and entered onto a publicly available register.[139]

1.79 All board members of NHS authorities and trusts must subscribe to the *Code of Accountability* on appointment, and firm, prompt and fair disciplinary action must be taken against any executive director who acts in breach of the code.[140] The chief executive of the NHS Executive is accountable to Parliament through the Public Accounts Committee. NHS boards must co-operate fully with the NHS Executive and the Audit Commission when required to account for their use of public funds, the delivery of patient care, or compliance with statutes, directions, guidance and the policies of the Secretary of State.[141] NHS boards have six key objectives for which they are held accountable by the NHS Executive, and about which it must publish an annual report to the NHS Executive, the Audit Commission, and the local community; namely

> [1] to set the strategic direction of the organisation within the overall policies and priorities of the Government and the NHS, define its annual and longer term objectives and agree plans to achieve them; [2] to oversee the delivery of planned results by monitoring performance against objectives and ensuring corrective action is taken when necessary; [3] to ensure effective financial stewardship through value for money, financial control and financial planning and strategy; [4] to ensure that high standards of corporate governance and personal behaviour are maintained in the conduct of the business of the whole organisation, [5] to appoint, appraise and remunerate senior executives, and [6] to ensure that there is effective dialogue between the organisation and the local community on its plans and performance and that these are responsive to the community's needs.[142]

1.80 The basis of the *Code of Practice on Openness* 'is that the NHS should respond positively to requests for information' except in certain circumstances.[143]

---

[137] *Code of Conduct* (n 128 above), 2.   [138] ibid, 3.   [139] ibid, 4.
[140] ibid, 6.   [141] ibid, 7.
[142] ibid, 8. For an overview of the plans adopted by a cross-section of health authorities, see Redmayne, S, *Small Steps, Big Goals—Purchasing Policies in the NHS* (Centre for the Analysis of Social Policy, University of Bath, 1996).
[143] *Code of Practice on Openness in the NHS* (n 129 above), 2, 5 and 6. See also *Guidance on Implementation of Code of Practice on Openness in the NHS* (NHSE, 1995). The codes do not affect the statutory duties of disclosure discussed elsewhere.

People must have access to information about the services provided in the NHS, their cost, and the extent to which targets have been achieved. They must also have access to information about, and the opportunity to influence, proposals to change NHS services. In addition, they are entitled to know of reasons for decisions which affect their own care and, generally, know what information is available and how to obtain it.[144] On the other hand, information about third parties and confidential information should not normally be disclosed. Nor should NHS authorities and trusts be expected to entertain unreasonable requests for information, or those which would require disproportionate resources to answer, or matters relating to internal discussion where disclosure would hinder frank discussion. Information concerning matters of management are protected if disclosure would prejudice the administration of justice, as is information relating to personnel management or commercial activities (other than internal NHS contracts).[145]

(ii) *Primary Care Medicine*

Increasing responsibility is being devolved to GPs both to manage and allocate health care resources. For fund-holding GPs, this matter is dealt with in *An Accountability Framework for GP Fundholding*,[146] which requires fund-holding practices to submit an annual plan to the health authority which describes how the practice intends to use its funds and the contribution the plan will make to national and local targets. The plan should notify the health authority of major shifts in purchasing intentions to assist a coordinated approach to planning, and performance should be monitored by regular review meetings.[147] Similar candour is expected toward patients, who should have access to practice plans from the practice itself, the health authority, and community health council, so that patients may be involved in service planning.[148] Complaints procedures must be available within the practice,[149] and financial accounts must be submitted annually to the Audit Commission[150] and be made available to the public.

1.81

---

[144] ibid, 3 and 11.   [145] ibid, 6. This list is not exhaustive.   [146] NHSE, 1995.

[147] ibid, para 5.

[148] ibid, para 6. No mechanism for such patient involvement is suggested.

[149] ibid, para 6, also required by the National Health Service (General Medical Services) Amendment Regulations 1996, SI 1996/702, amending the 1992 regulations. See generally, Montgomery, J, *Health Care Law* (Oxford University Press, 1997), ch 5

[150] ibid, para 7, also required by s 20, National Health Service and Community Care Act 1990.

1.82 One would expect equally extensive principles to apply to total purchasing pilots,[151] which may accumulate still larger influence over decisions on resource allocation. The criteria on which pilots will be approved and assessed, and the nature of the targets they will be expected to achieve have yet to be published. Clearly, many of these requirements will carry the force of directions, rather than guidance, which the relevant health service bodies will be obliged to adopt under section 13 of the 1977 Act.[152] At the same time, one should not overestimate the significance of the rhetoric on openness and the involvement of the public in this area. There appears to be no significant appetite for decisions of this nature to be influenced to any large extent by the public. Indeed, such a policy would introduce the risk of periodic alterations of strategy which would make long-term planning impossible. Thus, it is only at the margins that change is possible in the short term, assuming always that those responsible for decision-making in this area consider it desirable and consistent with targets established nationally.[153]

3. The Provision of Hospital Care

1.83 The Secretary of State's obligations are based on the principle that he should promote 'a comprehensive health service'. This section considers (1) the meaning of these words, (2) the provision of care in hospital, and (3) the contracting out of services to private providers.

(i) *A 'Comprehensive Health Service'*

1.84 The National Health Service Act 1977 imposes on the Secretary of State a:

> duty to continue the promotion . . . of a comprehensive health service designed to secure improvement (a) in the physical and mental health of the people of those countries, and (b) in the prevention, diagnosis and treatment of illness, and for that purpose to provide or secure the effective provision of services in accordance with this Act.[154]

The Secretary of State's duty is amplified in section 3(1), as follows:

> It is the Secretary of State's duty to provide . . . to such extent as he considers necessary to meet all reasonable requirements—
> (a) hospital accommodation;

---

[151] Established under the National Health Service (Primary Care) Act 1997, see above.
[152] See paras 1.68–1.74 above.
[153] See Redmayne, S, *Small Steps, Big Goals—Purchasing Policies in the NHS* (Centre for the Analysis of Social Policy, University of Bath, 1996), 7.
[154] S 1. See Montgomery, J, *Health Services Law* (Oxford University Press, 1997), ch 3.

(b) other accommodation for the purpose of any service provided under this Act;

(c) medical, dental, nursing and ambulance services;

(d) such other facilities for the care of expectant mothers and nursing mothers and young children as he considers are appropriate as part of the health service;

(e) such facilities for the prevention of illness, the care of persons suffering from illness and the after-care of persons who have suffered from illness as he considers are appropriate as part of the health service;

(f) such other services as are required for the diagnosis and treatment of illness.[155]

The Act also sets out a number of 'specified health service functions'[156] which health authorities shall provide on behalf of the Secretary of State, including the provision by every health authority of accident and emergency, and ambulance services for all persons present in their area.[157]

Section 3(1) was first considered in *R v Secretary of State for Social Services, ex p Hincks*,[158] in which plans for a new orthopaedic unit in Birmingham, approved by the Secretary of State in 1971, were postponed by him in 1973 and 'virtually abandoned'[159] soon thereafter. Although there was an acknowledged need for the service, it did not command sufficient priority in the overall scheme of health service finances. The applicants alleged that the Secretary of State had failed in his duty to provide a comprehensive health service in their area. Since he had approved the plans to build the unit and acknowledged the need for the facility, section 3(1) obliged him to set aside the funds to fulfil his duty. No limitation was expressed in the statute to restrict the duty, so 'if the Secretary of State needs money to do it, then he must see that Parliament gives it to him. Alternatively if Parliament does not give it to him, then a provision should be put in the statute to excuse him from his duty.'[160] **1.85**

The Court of Appeal decided, however, that section 3(1) cannot impose an absolute duty to provide services, irrespective of economic decisions taken at national level. The provision has to be read subject to the implied qualification that the Secretary of State's duty was 'to meet all reasonable requirements such as can be provided within the resources available',[161] which 'must be determined in the light of current Government economic policy'.[162] In addition, given the fact that there were twelve hospitals competing for **1.86**

---

[155] S 3(1), 1977 Act. See also Sch 8, concerning mothers and young children; prevention and after care; and home help.

[156] See ss 17 and 18, 1977 Act. The phrase is used to describe the functions listed in the National Health Service (Functions of Health Authorities and Administrative Arrangements) Regulations 1996, SI 1996/708, sch 1. [157] ibid, reg 3(1).

[158] (1992) 1 BMLR 93 (decided in 1980). [159] ibid, at 95, *per* Lord Denning MR.

[160] ibid, *per* Lord Denning MR summarising the 'attractive argument' of Mr Blom-Cooper, counsel for the applicants. [161] ibid.

[162] ibid, 97 *per* Bridge LJ.

resources in this particular area, Lord Denning endorsed the opinion of the judge at first instance that 'I doubt very much whether under s 3(1) it is permissible to put the spotlight, as it were, upon one particular department of one hospital and to say that conditions there are unsatisfactory.'[163]

1.87 Much the same has been said of those awaiting treatment in hospital.[164] In *R v Secretary of State, ex p Walker*,[165] the Health Authority was satisfied that a premature baby required an operation to repair his heart. However, it was unable to staff all the intensive care units in its neonatal ward and the operation was cancelled. The plaintiff alleged that her baby had been denied the surgical care the hospital acknowledged he needed. Rejecting the application for an order that the operation be performed, Macpherson J said:

> I say at once that I find it quite impossible to say there is in the decision made by the health authority, or by the surgeons who act on their behalf, any illegality, nor any procedural defect, nor any such unreasonableness. The fact that the decision in unfortunate, disturbing and in human terms distressing, simply cannot lead to a conclusion that the court should interfere in a case of this kind . . . . It seems to me that this case is not truly an attack upon the actual decision made . . . I detect a general criticism of the decisions as to staffing and financing of the National Health Service and of those who provide its funds and facilities. It has been said before, and I say again, that this court can no more investigate that on the facts of this case than it could do so in any other case where the balance of available money and its distribution and use are concerned . . . they are questions to be raised, answered and dealt with outside this court.[166]

1.88 Dismissing the appeal, the Master of the Rolls, Sir John Donaldson, said:

> It is not for this court, or indeed any court, to substitute its own judgment for the judgment of those who are responsible for the allocation of resources. This court could only intervene where it was satisfied that there was a prima facie case, not only of failing to allocate resources in the way in which others would think that resources should be allocated, but of a failure to allocate resources to an extent which was *Wednesbury* . . . unreasonable.[167]

1.89 Note that in *Walker*, Macpherson J 'stressed that at present the evidence establishes that there is no danger to the baby' and that, were an emergency

---

[163] ibid.

[164] Action should normally be taken against the hospital or health authority in question, and not the Secretary of State. See s 8(1), National Health Service and Community Care Act 1990 and sch 5, para 15(1), National Health Service Act 1977 respectively. However, in *Re HIV Haemophiliac Litigation* (CA, 1990, unreported) Ralph Gibson LJ said 'if . . . it could be shown that the Secretary of State was independently in breach of the relevant duty, the wording of paragraph [15(1)] does not provide any protection.'

[165] (1992) 3 BMLR 32 (decided in 1987).   [166] ibid, 34.   [167] ibid, 35.

to arise, the operation would have been performed.[168] What is the position when facilities are not made available to patients whose health will be damaged, or whose lives will be at risk, as a result? The matter was considered in *R v Central Birmingham Health Authority, ex p Collier*,[169] which concerned a four-year old boy suffering from a hole in the heart. In September 1987 his consultant said that 'he desperately needed open heart surgery' and placed the boy at the top of the waiting list, expecting that intensive care facilities would be made available by the hospital within a month. By January 1988 the operation had been arranged, but then cancelled, on three occasions and had still not been carried out. The reason was that no intensive care bed was available. The Court of Appeal was invited to order that, given that the boy would probably die unless the operation were performed, the operation should be carried out. It said, however, that:

> even assuming that [the evidence] does establish that there is immediate danger to health . . . the legal principles to be applied do not differ from the case of *Re Walker*. This court is in no position to judge the allocation of resources by this particular health authority . . . there is no suggestion here that the hospital authority has behaved in a way which is deserving of condemnation or criticism. What is suggested is that somehow more resources should be made available to enable the hospital authorities to ensure that the treatment is immediately given.

1.90 To what extent should these decisions be taken to mean that section 3 does not create rights to health service resources and that it should be considered only as a target, or an aspiration without legal effect?

(a) Wednesbury Unreasonableness

1.91 Decisions to allocate facilities between deserving patients are extremely difficult and judges have no particular expertise in doing so. In theory, however, they have reserved the right to review the decisions of managers and administrators if they are *Wednesbury* unreasonable.[170] Lord Diplock has described the power of review as follows:

> It applies to a decision which is so outrageous in its defiance of logic or of accepted moral standards that no sensible person who had applied his mind to the question to be decided could have arrived at it. Whether a decision falls within this category is a question that judges by their training and experience

---

[168] ibid, 34.
[169] Unreported, 1988, reproduced in part in Kennedy, I, and Grubb, A, *Medical Law—Text with Materials* (Butterworths, 1994, 2nd edn), 428.
[170] Following the case of *Associated Provincial Picture Houses Ltd v Wednesbury Corporation* [1948] 1 KB 223.

1: The Organisation of Health Care

should be well equipped to answer, or else there would be something badly wrong with our system.[171]

1.92 The function of the court is not to substitute its own judgment for that under review and it may uphold the decision even if, had the matter been within its own power, it would have decided otherwise.[172] Its function is limited to considering whether the decision-maker was unreasonable and, particularly in matters concerning the allocation of scarce resources, it will be most reluctant to do so.[173] In practice, however, outside the medical context, it has been observed that this distinction is extremely blurred and the courts have intervened even when there are arguments to support both sides to the dispute, so that neither party can be described as wholly unreasonable, simply because they feel strongly inclined to do so.[174]

1.93 There has been less inclination to do so, however, with respect to health service resources. Thus, in *Collier*, the Court said: 'This is not the forum in which a court can properly express opinions upon the way in which national resources are allocated or distributed.'[175] Understandably, the courts must be extremely careful before becoming involved in telling hospital managers which cases should take priority over others. During litigation on behalf of an individual patient, who will speak for the large numbers of patients who are not party to the dispute but who may be affected by its outcome, and for those particular patients whose operations will have to be cancelled if someone else is treated first? This point was made subsequently in the Court of Appeal, by Balcombe LJ, who said:

> I would stress the absolute undesirability of the court making an order which may have the effect of compelling a doctor or health authority to make available scarce resources (both human and material) to a particular child, without knowing whether or not there are other patients to whom those resources might more advantageously be devoted.[176]

---

[171] In *Council of Civil Service Unions v Minister for the Civil Service* [1985] AC 374, 410.
[172] See eg *R v Secretary of State for the Environment, ex p Knowsley Metropolitan BC* (1991) *The Independent* 11 June.
[173] See *Rowling v Takaro Properties Ltd* [1988] AC 473, 501, *per* Lord Keith.
[174] See the discussion by Jowell, J and Lester, A, 'Beyond *Wednesbury*: Substantive Principles of Administrative Law', [1987] PL 368. See also *West Glamorgan County Council v Rafferty* [1987] 1 WLR 457, in which the Court of Appeal held a local authority unreasonable for seeking a possession order against gypsies occupying its land. Nevertheless, Ralph Gibson said of the dispute (at 477) that 'there are admissible factors on both sides of the question'.
[175] n 169 above.
[176] *Re J* [1992] 4 All ER 614, 625. But compare Lord Mustill in *Airedale NHS Trust v Bland* [1993] 1 All ER 821, 879, who said: ' . . . it is not legitimate for a judge in reaching a view as to what is for the benefit of the one individual whose life is in issue to take into account the wider practical issues as to allocation of limited financial resources . . . '

Nevertheless, the case of *Collier* concerned a child, as everyone agreed, in   **1.94**
need of common, if not routine, life-saving cardiac surgery who had been
placed at the top of the waiting list by his responsible doctor, yet the hospital
was unable to make facilities available. Bear in mind that this was a paediatric, rather than a neonatal, case with correspondingly smaller implications
for resources. On what system of priorities could a responsible health authority have repeatedly elevated other demands on its resources to a level of
importance greater than that of saving the life of such a patient? Were nursing
staff attending to other patients in greater need of care? Could the operation
not have been performed in another hospital? Was it impossible to borrow
nursing staff from elsewhere? Had managerial priorities taken priority over
clinical ones? Astonishingly, no one seemed to know exactly why intensive
care facilities could not be made available to this patient. Counsel for the boy
accepted that he simply did not know why the surgery had been cancelled; as
he said, 'it may be good reason or bad reason.' And, in the absence of an
explanation, Ralph Gibson LJ commented, somewhat wistfully:

> No doubt the health authority would welcome the opportunity to deal with
> such matters so that they could explain what they are doing and what their
> problems are.

A similar response was given in *R v Sheffield HA ex p Seale*,[177] although the   **1.95**
case had considerably less strength than that of *Ex p Collier*. The plaintiff was
refused in vitro fertilisation treatment because she was thirty seven. The upper
age limit set for such procedures by Sheffield HA was thirty five. She alleged
that the policy was illegal for being contrary to section 3 of the National
Health Service Act 1977, and that it was irrational. As to the allegation of
illegality, Auld J said:[178]

> it is not arguable . . . that [the HA] is bound, simply because it has undertaken
> to provide such a service, to provide it on demand to any individual patient for
> whom it may work, regardless of financial and other constraints upon the
> authority. In my view it is clear that if the Secretary of State has not limited
> or given directions as to the way in which such a service, once undertaken,
> should be provided, the authority providing it is entitled to form a view as to
> those circumstances and when they justify provision and when they do not.

Further, the the age limit was held not to be irrational or absurd for failing to   **1.96**
take account of the clinical circumstances of each individual case. His Lordship said:[179]

> a clinical decision on a case by case basis is clearly desirable and, in cases of
> critical illness, a necessary approach. However, it is reasonable, or at least not

---

[177] (1995) 25 BMLR 1.   [178] ibid, 3.   [179] ibid.

> *Wednesbury* unreasonable . . . of an authority to look at the matter in the context of the financial resources available to it and the many other services for which it is responsible. I cannot say that it is absurd for this authority . . . to take [35] as an appropriate criterion when balancing the need for such provision against its ability to provide it . . .

1.97 Note, however, that although the application was refused on its merits, the case distinguishes between critical and other illnesses. If critical illness necessitates an individual clinical decision, it is not clear how *Wednesbury* can apply,[180] or at least, it may have a much narrower application. Arguably, *ex p Seale* suggests that cases with clinical merits as strong as those in *Collier* deserve (as a minimum) an explanation of the reasons why treatment has been refused. In such a case, perhaps Lord Denning's reasoning, expressed in a different context, could be employed: namely that some cases give rise to a presumption in favour of an explanation so that 'a Minister should give reasons, and if he gives none the court may infer that he had no good reasons . . . in particular in cases which affect life, liberty and property.'[181] Has there been any subsequent indication of willingness on the part of the courts to take a less passive role in cases of this nature?

(b) The Role of the Courts: A Broader View?

1.98 Three cases have suggested the possibility of a more critical attitude toward health authority decisions to restrict access to care. *R v Cambridge DHA, ex p B*[182] concerned a ten year-old girl suffering from leukaemia who had been in the care of the Health Authority since 1990. By 1995 her prognosis was very poor. Without treatment, her doctors expected she would die within a matter of months. The Health Authority refused to provide her with remedial (as opposed to palliative) treatment that might have prolonged her life. One of the factors it had in mind was based on the availability of resources, since the treatment could cost up to £75,000. The child's father sought a declaration to the effect that treatment ought to be provided.

1.99 The Court of Appeal heard detailed evidence of the grounds on which the decision to refuse treatment had been based. Thus: (i) the doctors responsible for treatment considered it to be 'experimental', (ii) its prospects of success were very small, i e between 10 and 20 per cent for the first stage of treatment

---

[180] In *Joyce v Wandsworth HA* [1996] 7 Med LR 1, 20, Hobhouse LJ doubted the use of the 'Wednesbury unreasonableness' test to describe unacceptable medical conduct (as suggested by Dillon LJ in *Bolitho v City of Hackney HA* 13 BMLR 111. 132). He said, correctly, that this concept from administrative law did not assist an understanding of medical negligence.

[181] *Secretary of State for Employment v ASLEF* [1972] 2 QB 455, 493.

[182] [1995] 2 All ER 129.

and, *if* that were to be successful, between 10 and 20 per cent for the second stage of treatment; ie between 1 and 4 per cent overall, (iii) it would have debilitating side-effects which, given her prospects, were not in her best interests, and (iv) given her prospects, the total cost of the two stages of procedures could not be justified. In these circumstances, the unanimous clinical view of the doctors was that the procedure should not be carried out and they advised the Health Authority accordingly. The Health Authority accepted their opinions, confirming at the same time that the decision had been taken in the light of 'all the clinical and other relevant matters . . . and not on financial grounds.'[183] Having heard in detail the precise medical evidence on which the decision to withhold care was based, the Master of the Rolls, Sir Thomas Bingham, found it 'impossible to fault that process of thinking . . . '[184]

On one view of the case, the result is indistinguishable from that of *Collier* **1.100** and confirms the exteme reluctance of the courts to be drawn into arbitration over matters of this nature. Indeed, as the Master of the Rolls observed:

> Difficult and agonizing judgments have to be made as to how a limited budget is best allocated to the maximum advantage of the maximum number of patients. That is not a judgment the court can make. In my judgment, it is not something that a health authority . . . can be fairly criticised for not advancing before the court.[185]

On the other hand, the case offers a striking contrast to *Collier* by its will- **1.101** ingness to hear the evidence on which the decision was based and the primacy given to the *clinical* evidence which was used to support the decision. Certainly, it is asking too much for the courts to become familiar with the principles (if there are any) which seek to ensure that maximum numbers of patients receive maximum benefits, ie the 'macro' policies of resource alloca- tion. To this extent, the observation of the Master of the Rolls must be correct. Matters concerning the general distribution of funds between differ- ent hospitals, categories of patients or treatments, medical research, new equipment, staffing, and so on, are largely unjusticiable and His Lordship's observation serves to confirm the decision in *Hincks*.

In the light of *Collier*, however, one is concerned to ask whether the courts are **1.102** competent to hear evidence why a *particular* patient has been refused care, i.e the 'micro' issue. *Ex p B* demonstrates that it is entirely possible for health authorities to present the evidence on which individual decisions have been based. For the court to review the reasons for such a decision does not require

---

[183] ibid, 133. A refusal to refer the patient on financial grounds would have breached the NHS Executive's own guidelines. See below text accompanying para 1.165 below.
[184] ibid, 138.   [185] ibid, 133.

it to substitute its own. Such a requirement is necessary to enable the court to be sure that decisions have been taken in the light of relevant considerations, and have excluded irrelevant ones. Naturally, given the limitations of its expertise in the area, a fairly low threshold of satisfaction will tend to be required. Indeed, few such cases will have realistic prospects of success. But the very fact that such clinical evidence may be required would focus minds on ensuring that these unenviable decisions are reasonable and defensible, and satisfy patients, and the public, that the question has been properly addressed. It was the failure to do so in *Collier* which makes that case so unsatisfactory. Some support for the proposition that decisions concerning resource allocation cannot be the exclusive domain of health service managers is available from Lord Donaldson MR who has said that when there is agreement amongst doctors as to the treatment that ought to be provided, it would be unreasonable for managers to decide otherwise and so upset clinicians' assessment of priorities. He said:

> Health authorities are supported by medical and administrative staff. In the context of medical decisions, it would be perverse for it to act otherwise than in accordance with the advice of its medical staff when the advice was unanimous . . . .[186]

1.103 *Ex p B* does not expressly require that clinical evidence of this nature should be presented to the court, though the decision itself appears to rely upon it.[187] By contrast, in *R v North Derbyshire HA, ex p Fisher*,[188] the court was so dissatisfied with the Health Authority's explanations for failing to provide treatment that it overturned the decision. The applicant suffered from the relapsing form of multiple sclerosis (MS). Beta Interferon was a newly licensed medicine which had undergone clinical trials suggesting that it could delay the onset of the symptoms of the disease and enable sufferers to remain active.

1.104 The NHS Executive issued guidelines by means of an executive letter to health authorities and NHS trust hospitals recommending that the drug be made available to this category of patient, although no additional funds were made available to assist their doing so. However, the respondents did not favour use of Beta-Interferon for two reasons. First, they felt that the product had not been sufficiently tested. Also, the clinical evidence suggested that the drug would only postpone the onset of the debilitating symptoms of the disease for a relatively short period of time. The authority appears to have considered that, given its commitments to other patients, the costs of achieving such a modest benefit did not justify its purchase. Accordingly, the

---

[186] *Re J (a minor)* [1992] 4 All ER 614, 619.
[187] Arguably, however, the *Codes of Accountability* and *Openness*, discussed above, require disclosure to the patient of information of this nature, or confer a legitimate expectation that it will be disclosed. See paras 1.78–80 above. [188] [1997] 8 Med LR 327.

applicant was denied access to the drug and correspondence was entered into in which the respondents presented a number of reasons for their refusal.

Originally, it said that it would only purchase Beta-Interferon for MS patients   **1.105**
who were participating in a national clinical trial. But this was during a time when no trial had been undertaken and, indeed, even after the Prime Minister had confirmed that no such trial would take place. Of this reason, Dyson J said:

> the policy was plainly not in accordance with the circular . . . One of the [circular's] key aims was said to be to 'target the drug appropriately at patients who were most likely to benefit from treatment.' In other words . . . how most effectively Beta-Interferon could be introduced into the NHS as a drug to be prescribed to treat patients. [Yet] the primary aim of the [clinical] trial is not to prescribe drugs in order to treat patients, but to test their efficacy. I do not consider that the respondent's policy could at any time have been described as a reasonable way of giving effect to the circular.[189]

Once the 'within-a-trial only' policy became unsustainable, the authority's   **1.106**
chief executive said that:

> they could not support, in cost effective terms, the use of the drug Beta Interferon for relapsing multiple sclerosis patients and also they could not identify any new money to give priority to the use of this drug. This was based on the unanimous views of their professional advisors. However, they also made it clear that they could not restrict clinicians . . . prescribing this drug where appropriate based on individual patient need and within existing contracts.[190]

Dyson J, however, criticised this explanation. He said: **1.107**

> Of course, they could not stop clinicians writing prescriptions but the respondents knew that, at any rate within the Trust hospitals, those prescriptions would not be dispensed and treatment would not be given unless additional funds were made available.[191]

Then the authority argued that its refusal to fund the drug was based on   **1.108**
considerations of fairness. Any such funding, it said, would have to be on the basis of a 'first come, first served' basis. But that created the risk that deserving patients who presented for treatment later in the year, perhaps with more treatable symptoms, would find that the funds set aside had been exhausted and therefore be denied treatment. Of this, the judge said

> I regard this as an irrational reason. If correct it would be a reason for refusing to make any expensive treatment available in almost all circumstances. When

---

[189] (1997) 8 Med L Rev 327.   [190] ibid, 334.
[191] ibid, 335. This view may be considered harsh on the health authority. Like health authorities, NHS trust hospitals ought to hold monies in reserve in order to meet unplanned demands arising during the year. Was it correct that no treatment could have been given by the hospital and paid for from such reserves? On this point there was no evidence.

deciding whether to prescribe treatment to a patient a clinician has to have regard to many factors including the resources available for that treatment and the needs of and likely benefit to that patient as compared with other patients who are likely to be suitable . . . It is absurd to suppose that before any patient is prescribed any expensive treatment a survey must be made of all patients who are, or might be, in need of the same treatment in the area. I do not accept that this was a rational justification for not releasing additional funds. Indeed, I have considerable doubts as to whether it was a true reason.[192]

1.109 Alternatively, the health authority argued, contradicting the statement of the chief executive (above) that 'they could not identify any new money to give priority to the use of this drug', that it had set £50,000 aside for the purpose of funding Beta-Interferon but that toward the end of the year, that sum no longer existed 'because it had not been ring fenced'. Contrast the response of Dyson J with the uncritical acceptance by the Court of Appeal of the assertions presented to it in *ex p Collier*. He said:

I am bound to express surprise [that] this important aspect of the dispute should have been dealt with in this unsatisfactory way. No explanation has been given as to why, if [the statement as to the availability of funds] was in error, the true position has not been explained in a further affidavit. I am not willing to accept what I have been told on instructions.[193]

1.110 In all the circumstances, Dyson J held that the health authority had behaved unreasonably by misinterpreting, or failing to take proper account of the NHS Executive's guidance. The lawfulness of the health authority's policy had to be judged:

in accordance with *Wednesbury* principles against the background of national policy which was set out fully and firmly in the guidance to be found in the circular. The respondents had to have regard to that national policy, they were not obliged to follow the policy [since it amounted to guidance, rather than directions] but if they decided to depart from it, they had to give clear reasons for doing so . . . This is not a case in which a health authority departed from a national policy because there were special factors which it considered exceptionally justified departure. The respondent failed to implement any aspect of national policy principally because they disagreed with it altogether.[194]

1.111 Thus, he issued a declaration that the policy adopted by the respondents in relation to the executive letter was unlawful; certiorari, quashing the decision to make funds available to the applicant; and mandamus, requiring the respondent to reformulate and implement a policy taking full and proper account of national policy as stated in the executive letter. Of course, there was no order that treatment be provided to the applicant. On the contrary, Dyson J expected that 'the applicant's case will be reconsidered and that,

---

[192] ibid, 337.   [193] ibid, 336.   [194] ibid, 336.

subject to clinical judgment and *availability of resources*, he will receive treatment' (emphasis added).

The case demonstrates that the intractable problems of allocating scarce health service resources are not the unique responsibility of health service managers. The reasons given for their decisions must be candid, consistent, and cogent. It would be wrong, however, to think that the case provides patients with greater access to expensive medicines. Indeed, had the refusal to treat been based on a proper consideration of the relevant factors, including the executive letter, the most recent clinical trials, the policies adopted by other health authorities, and the competing demands on the authority's resources, the application might have failed. The costs of prescribing a relatively small number of new drugs designed to delay the symptoms of chronic illnesses such as Alzheimer's disease and motor neurone disease, would be capable of absorbing a disproportionate quantity of the NHS drugs budget and, thereby, in the absence of increased funding, deprive other, equally deserving patients of, perhaps, more effective medicines. The case does not affect the need to make choices.

Lastly, the most notable example of a dispute in which the patient has succeeded in gaining access to health service resources was referred to the Health Service Ombudsman. Leeds Health Authority adopted a policy whereby it made no provision for the continuing care of patients with chronic neurological conditions. The chief executive said that the Authority: **1.113**

> could not meet every health need. Present policy was for shorter inpatient stays with continuing care being provided in the community. The Authority did not provide for any long stay medical beds in hospital or have any contractual arrangements for such beds in private nursing homes.[195]

Thus, the Health Authority devoted its resources to providing acute hospital care. Conditions of chronic illness which had stabilized and were no longer amenable to improvement were discharged into the community. This policy was applied to a patient who had suffered a severe stroke. The doctors' clinical decision was that no further benefit could be achieved in the acute unit. Nevertheless, the patient needed continuing nursing care. He had suffered severe neurological damage, a heart attack, had a renal tumour and was being given nursing care in a private nursing home. This policy had financial consequences. Health care is provided free without direct charges to patients. Community care is chargeable.[196] In this case, the cost to the family was **1.114**

---

[195] *Failure to Provide Long term NHS Care for a Brain-damaged Patient* (Health Service Commissioner, HC 197, Session 1993–94), para 18.
[196] S 44, National Health Service and Community Care Act 1990.

£6,000 per year. In a most significant decision, the Ombudsman, Mr William Reid QC, said:

> the contract for neurological services makes no reference to continuing institutional care. The patient was a highly dependent patient in hospital . . . ; and yet, when he no longer needed care in an acute ward but manifestly still needed what the National Health Service is there to provide, they regarded themselves as having no scope for continuing to discharge their responsibilities to him because their policy was to make no provision for continuing care . . . . In my opinion the failure to make available long-term care within the NHS for this patient was unreasonable and constitutes a failure in the service provided by the Health Authority.[197]

1.115 The complaint was upheld and the Health Authority agreed to make a payment to the complainant to cover her out-of-pocket expenses incurred by way of fees for the private nursing home and to pay for the future cost of the patient's care. The result of the case was the introduction of new NHS guidelines which confirm that 'the NHS is responsible for arranging and funding a range of services to meet the needs of people who require continuing physical or mental health care.'[198] Speaking of the guidelines, the Secretary of State for Health said 'Health Authorities who follow the new guidelines should not find themselves in a position of being rebuked by the Ombudsman.'[199]

(ii) *NHS Hospitals*

1.116 A small minority of hospitals remain within the direct control of health authorities, which are accountable to the Secretary of State via the NHS Executive. By contrast, NHS trust hospitals have been created with greater independence of action. As the Department of Health put it: 'Trusts have the power to make their own decisions—right or wrong!—without being subject to bureaucratic procedures, processes or pressure from higher tiers of management.'[200] Thus 'an NHS trust shall have power to do anything which appears to it to be necessary or expedient for the purposes of or in connection with

---

[197] ibid, para 22. Subsequently, the Chief Executive of the NHS, Mr Alan Langlands told the House of Commons Health Committee: 'if a similar case were to crop up . . . tomorrow then the expectation would be that there should be a continuing commitment from the NHS. So, in other words, we accept that the Ombudsman was right in his judgment.' (*Priority Setting in the NHS: Purchasing* HC 134–II, Session 1994–95), para 849.

[198] See *NHS Responsibilities for Meeting Continuing Health Care Needs* (HSG,(95)8; LAC (95)5, DoH, 1995), para 10 and generally. See also Newdick, C, 'Patients, or Residents? Long-term Care in the Welfare State', (1996) 4 Med L Rev 144.

[199] *Priority Setting in the NHS: Purchasing, vol II* (Health Committee, HC 134–II, Session 1994–95), para 853. See also *White v Chief Adjudication Officer* 17 BMLR 68 (1994) for an analogous case.   [200] *NHS Trusts: A Working Guide* (HMSO, 1990), 2.

the discharge of its functions . . .[201] 'Trusts are accountable to the Secretary of State in four ways:

[1] for each accounting year an NHS Trust shall prepare and send to the Secretary of State an annual report in such form as may be determined by the Secretary of State;[202]

[2] an NHS Trust shall furnish to the Secretary of State such reports, returns and other information, including information as to its forward planning as, and in such form as, he may require;[203]

[3] at such time or times as may be prescribed, an NHS Trust shall hold a public meeting at which its audited accounts and annual report and any report on the accounts made pursuant to subsection (3) of section 15 of the Local Government Finance Act 1982 shall be presented,[204] and

[4] in such circumstances and at such time or times as may be prescribed, an NHS Trust shall hold a public meeting at which such documents as may be prescribed may be presented.[205]

'An NHS Trust shall not be regarded as the servant or agent of the Crown',[206] **1.117** so it cannot be said that, as agents of the Secretary of State, its duty is identical to that imposed by section 3 of the National Health Service Act 1977 to provide 'a comprehensive health service'. However, each trust is created by regulation and may be pursued in its own name[207] for failing in the duty imposed upon it to 'manage hospital accommodation and services'.[208] Also, residual power is vested in the Secretary of State to control a range of activities undertaken by NHS Trusts. Thus, an NHS Trust 'shall comply' with any directions given to it by the Secretary of State with respect, *inter alia*, to:

> prohibiting or restricting the disposal of, or any interest in, any asset . . . in respect of which the Secretary of State considers that the interests of the National Health Service require that the asset should not be disposed of; [and] compliance with guidance or directions given (by circular or otherwise) to health authorities, or particular descriptions of health authorities.[209]

Note also the obligation that every health authority 'shall exercise the specified **1.118**

---

[201] Sch 2, para 16(1), National Health Service and Community Care Act 1990.
[202] 1990 Act, Sch 2, para 7(1).   [203] ibid, para 8.   [204] ibid, para 7(2).
[205] ibid, para 7(3).
[206] National Health Service and Community Care Act 1990, Sch 2, para 18.
[207] See s 8(1), 1990 Act and the Regulations by which it is created.
[208] See, by analogy, *Bromley LBC v Greater London Council* [1982] 1 AC 768.
[209] Sch 2, para 6(2)(d) and (e) of the 1990 Act. Note, however, that the Secretary of State's supervisory powers over health authorities in respect of income generation do not extend to NHS Trust hospitals. See s 65(4) of the 1977 Act, added by the National Health Service and Community Care Act 1990, Sch 9, para 18(4).

health service functions on behalf of the Secretary of State . . .' (which are listed in regulations[210]), for the benefit of patients. These regulations empower the Secretary of State to issue directions with respect to the provision of services to patients and it shall be the duty of the health authority to whom they have been directed to comply with them.[211] Alternatively, the Secretary of State may order an enquiry into an alleged failure of a health service body (including an NHS Trust) to carry out its functions under the 1977 Act or 1990 Act and, after such an enquiry, may by order declare the body to be in default.[212] In such a case, the members of the body shall vacate their office and the order shall provide for new members to act in their place. In circumstances of emergency, when it is necessary to ensure provision of a service under the 1977 Act or 1990 Act, he may direct that a function conferred on any body, or person, under the 1977 Act is performed, either exclusively or concurrently, by another body or person and it shall be the duty of such a body or person to comply with directions.[213]

1.119 There are, therefore, powers enabling the Secretary of State to intervene in suitable circumstances. However, so long as health authorities or primary care groups remain the major commissioners of health care, NHS Trusts will effectively be obliged to offer a cross-section of services to NHS purchasers in order to generate the funding required to fulfil their financial obligations. In practice, therefore, the need for directions ought not to arise.

(iii) *Contracting Out Services to Private Suppliers*

1.120 NHS services may be provided by private hospitals and suppliers, as follows:

> The Secretary of State may, where he considers it appropriate, arrange with any person or body (including a voluntary organisation) for that person or body to provide, or assist in providing, any service under [the 1977] Act.[214]

Facilities, including goods, materials, plant, apparatus and premises may be made available for this purpose on such terms as may be agreed, including the making of payments by, or to, the Secretary of State.[215] In future, the traditional split between public and private providers will be more difficult to recognise. NHS patients may receive treatment in private hospitals, and staff engaged by private health companies may provide NHS care. The

---

[210] See the National Health Service (Functions of Health Authorities and Administrative Arrangements) Regulations 1996, SI 1996/708.
[211] See National Health Service Act 1977, ss 12 and 13, and Sch 5, Part III as amended.
[212] See s 85, 1977 Act, as amended by the Health Services Act 1980, ss 1, 2 and Sch 1, para 65 and the National Health Service and Community Care Act 1990, s 66, sch 9, para 18(7).
[213] See s 86, 1977 Act as amended by s 66(1) and Sch 9, para 18(8) of the 1990 Act.
[214] See National Health Service Act 1977, s 23(1).   [215] See s 23(2) and (3), 1977 Act.

Conservative government encouraged the use of private providers because external competition was thought to enhance quality by increasing the range of options available to patients and their GPs, as well as enabling different institutions to learn from one another.[216] It remains to be seen what view the Labour government will take on this matter.

Private hospitals are not 'health service bodies',[217] and cannot, therefore, enter into NHS contracts. Nevertheless, they make a significant contribution to the work of the NHS. Nearly a tenth of the UK's health care provision is supplied by the independent sector.[218] In the past, its main contribution has been in the field of nursing homes for elderly people and care for those in hospices. Arrangements made with private hospitals have often been short term, in the sense that they have been designed to relieve occasional pressure on NHS institutions. In 1986, however, the Government introduced the Waiting List Initiative under which sums of money were made available annually to ease pressures caused by long lists,[219] and there has also been an increase in private acute care, a development which has been actively encouraged by the government.[220]

1.121

One of the reasons for encouraging this collaboration is 'because it relieves pressure on the NHS'.[221] On the other hand, were the private sector to undergo significant expansion, a government might reconsider the funding needed by NHS hospitals. Presumably, an NHS hospital which found itself unable to compete with a service provided by a private facility would find it difficult to sustain funding. Purchasers would send their patients to the less expensive private alternative and the revenue within the NHS unit would decline. In this sense, although private services may reduce pressure on the NHS in the short term, the longer term implications ought to be recognised. The logic of this development is that a significant quantity of NHS care could be purchased from private providers whose hospital services have tended to

1.122

---

[216] See *Working for Patients* (Cm 555, 1989), ch 9.   [217] Under s 4, 1990 Act.

[218] *NHS Made Easy* (NHSME, 1992), para 35.

[219] See *The NHS and Independent Hospitals* (National Audit Office, HC 106, 1989).

[220] In 1988, some 17% of all elective surgery was carried out by the independent sector at a cost of around £50 million to the NHS. See *The NHS and Independent Hospitals* (National Audit Office, HC 106, 1989), paras 2(3) and 2(8).

[221] *Working for Patients* (Cm 555, 1989), para 9.4.

exclude those with chronic illnesses[222] and over whom the Department of Health, and the *Patient's Charter*, have no power.[223]

1.123 What is the position of those who are injured by the negligence of a private contractor? Say a caterer provides contaminated food, or a private radiography service provides inaccurate reports so that a crucial diagnosis is missed, or it ceases trading as soon as a writ is served upon it? There are two ways in which this question may be considered, under statute and in common law. Under statute, services may be contracted out either by means of the Deregulation and Contracting-Out Act 1994, or within the National Health Service Act 1977 or the National Health Service and Community Care Act 1990. Contracting out under the 1994 Act requires specific procedures by which the Minister issues an order identifying the contracted-out service.[224]

In these circumstances, anything done or omitted to be done by the private contractor in connection with the contracted-out service 'shall be treated for all purposes as done or omitted to be done . . . in the case of a function of a Minister or office-holder, by or in relation to the Minister or office-holder in his capacity as such'.[225]

Thus, liability for a failure of services contracted-out under the 1994 Act rests with the public authority, which may pursue its own remedies against the private contractor responsible for the fault.[226]

1.124 .Certainly, NHS services may be contracted-out under the 1994 Act, in which case the question of liability when things go wrong will not be in doubt. However, it seems unlikely that NHS services will be contracted-out in this way because provision for doing so already exists under the 1977 Act (with respect to health authorities)[227] and the 1990 Act (with respect to NHS Trusts).[228] Significantly, the policy of retaining public authority liability for the acts and omissions of private contractors underlying the 1994 Act plays no part in the 1977 and 1990 Acts. Thus, there appears to be 'Contracting-Out' (under the 1994 Act) and 'contracting-out'. Neither the 1977 Act, nor

---

[222] There has been 'no consideration of the problem of the relationship between a private sector concentrating on the potentially lucrative and easier elective surgery and a public sector which has to deal with priority care services and the elderly.' See *Resourcing the National Health Service: The Government's Plans for the Future of the National Health Service* (Social Services Committee, HC 214–III, Session 1988–1989), para 2.38.

[223] The private sector depends heavily on doctors who have been trained at the expense of the NHS. If it were to undergo significant expansion, it might be required to contribute to the costs of medical training. See *The NHS and Independent Hospitals* (National Audit Office, HC 106, 1989), para 2.47.   [224] See s 72(2) of the 1994 Act.

[225] See s 72(2) of the 1994 Act.   [226] See s 72(3) of the 1994 Act.

[227] See s 23(1) of the 1977 Act.   [228] See Sch 2, para 16 to the 1990 Act.

the 1990 Act resolve the question of the proper location of responsibility for the acts and omissions of private contractors. Though the distinction is unattractive, contracting-out within the statutes which govern the NHS appears to be subject to regulation by the common law.

In general, the common law of vicarious liability applies as between employer **1.125** and employee, but not as to those who engage independent contractors to perform work on their behalf. However, some duties have been described as 'non-delegable', in which case responsibility for the performance of an independent contractor will remain with the principal and cannot be delegated away. The nature and extent of these non-delegable duties is yet to receive thorough judicial analysis and it is unclear whether such a rule would apply to services contracted-out within the NHS[229] The question is considered elsewhere in this volume and will not be elaborated upon here.

The issue of contracting-out NHS services to private suppliers arises parti- **1.126** cularly, though not exclusively, in connection with the National Health Service (Private Finance) Act 1997, under which NHS building projects may be financed from the private sector. To what extent should NHS hospital services be provided privately? Under the previous Conservative administration, no restrictions were proposed as to the nature of the services that could be contracted-out, in the interests of the perceived benefits of competition. Although Labour supported the 1997 Act with respect to some services, it intends to exclude contracting-out from 'clinical' services. The distinction between a 'clinical' and 'non-clinical' service is to some extent arbitrary (consider, for example, non-touching services such as pathology and radiology) and the matter will be resolved by a specific list of such services (which is expected during the Summer of 1998). Some may prefer this policy of retaining a core of services within the fabric of the NHS. Inevitably, if a broad range of services were absorbed by the private sector in the long-term, the prospect would arise of the NHS becoming a funding institution only, and not primarily concerned with the provision of health care. Such a fundamental transformation of the character of the NHS deserves to be debated as an issue in its own right.

---

[229] See *Cassidy v Minister of Health* [1951] 1 All ER 574 (although the point was not addressed specifically) and *McDermid v Nash Dredging Ltd* [1987] 2 All ER 878. Australian and Canadian authorities lean against imposing liability in these circumstances, see *Ellis v Wallsend District Hospital* [1990] 2 Med LR 103 and *Yepremian v Scarborough General Hospital* (1980) 110 DLR (3d) 513. See also Kennedy, I, and Grubb, A, *Medical Law, Text with Materials*, 2nd edn, (Butterworths, 1994) 404–11 and Newdick, C, *Who Should We Treat?—Law, Patients and Resources in the NHS* (Oxford University Press, 1995) 101–6.

4. The Provision of Primary Care by GPs

1.127 Except for those who have agreed to provide their services under the National Health Service (Primary Care) Act 1997,[230] GPs are regulated by their 'Terms of Service' with health authorities. The following examines (1) the relationship between GP and health authority and (2) the duties owed to 'a doctor's patients'.

(i) *The Relationship between GP and Health Authority*

1.128 A specific duty has been imposed on health authorities by the National Health Service Act 1977 to provide general medical services. Thus:

> (1) It is the duty of every Health Authority, in accordance with regulations, to arrange as respects their area with medical practitioners to provide personal medical services for all persons in the area who wish to take advantage of the arrangements;
>
> (2) . . . the arrangements will be such that all persons availing themselves of those services will receive adequate personal care and attendance, and the regulations shall include provision—
>
> (a) for the preparation and publication of lists of medical practitioners who undertake to provide general medical services;
>
> (b) for conferring a right on any person to choose, in accordance with the prescribed procedure, the medical practitioner by whom he is to be attended, subject to the consent of the practitioner and to any prescribed limit on the number of patients to be accepted by any practitioner;
>
> (c) for the distribution among medical practitioners whose names are on the list of any persons who have indicated a wish to obtain general medical services but who have not made any choice of general practitioner or have been refused by the practitioner chosen . . . .[231]

1.129 The 'personal medical services' which it is the duty of health authorities to provide must include:

> (a) all necessary and appropriate personal medical services of the type usually provided by general medical practitioners;
>
> (b) child health services;
>
> (c) contraceptive services, that is to say—
>
> (i) the giving of advice to women on contraception,
>
> (ii) the medical examination of women seeking such advice,

---

[230] See paras 1.23–1.27 above.

[231] S 29, 1977 Act, as amended by the National Health Service and Community Care Act 1990, s 2(1).

    (iii) the contraceptive treatment of such women, and
    (iv) the supply to such women of contraceptive substances and appliances;
(d) maternity medical services; and
(e) minor surgery services.[232]

The imprecision of paragraph (a) has given rise to difficulties between the **1.130** British Medical Association (BMA) and health authorities. The source of the problem is the increasing numbers of patients who have been discharged from hospitals and nursing homes into the community and the associated increase in workload which falls to GPs. Accordingly, the BMA have recommended a distinction between 'core services', for which GPs should continue to be responsible, and non-core services, for which additional remuneration should be paid.[233] What are 'services of the type usually provided by general practitioners', and is the matter within the *Bolam* discretion of the medical profession, or the *Wednesbury* discretion of health service managers? Given the expansion of responsibility of primary care doctors, the matter ought to be resolved by regulations, rather than litigation.

GPs may apply to be included on a health authority's Medical List[234] in order **1.131** to provide general medical services to patients under an agreement known as the Terms of Service.[235] The Medical List contains, *inter alia*, the names of the doctors who have agreed to provide general medical services, the nature of the services they have agreed to provide, their practice address and the times during which they will be available to see patients. In addition, each health authority must prepare and keep up to date a list of the patients for whom doctors on the Medical List are responsible.[236] Doctors may withdraw their names from the Medical List,[237] and will have their names removed if they have died, ceased to be doctors, or had their names struck off, or suspended from, the Medical Register by the General Medical Council.[238]

As a general rule, doctors make their services available as independent **1.132**

[232] See the National Health Service (General Medical Services) Regulations 1992, SI 1992/635, reg 3.
[233] See *Defining Core Services in General Practice—Reclaiming Professional Control* (British Medical Association, 1996).
[234] National Health Service (General Medical Services) Regulations 1992, SI 1992/635, regs 4–7. Doctors whose application to join the list is refused may appeal to the Secretary of State, see ibid, reg 17.
[235] Contained in the National Health Service (General Medical Services) Regulations 1992, SI 1992/635, Sch 2.　　　　　　　[236] ibid, reg 19.
[237] ibid, reg 6. Unless it is impracticable to do so, the doctor shall give the authority three months notice of his intention to leave the Medical List and the authority shall make the necessary adjustment to it, see ibid reg 6(2) and (3).
[238] ibid, reg 7. The power of the General Medical Council to remove doctors from the Medical Register is contained in ss 36 and 38 of the Medical Act 1983. Reg 7 permits the doctor to appeal against such a removal to the Secretary of State.

contractors, not employees.[239] Their remuneration is provided by the health authority and they may not receive fees from their patients.[240] Nevertheless, the use of the law of contract to describe the relationship between GP and health authority has been doubted. The matter was considered in a dispute concerning the remuneration due to a GP from his Family Practitioner Committee (FPC) (the authority formerly responsible for these functions). The preliminary question arose whether the dispute should be dealt with as if it were a matter of private law between private bodies, or as one of public law involving individuals and government departments. Lord Bridge dealt with the question as follows:

> I do not think the issue in the appeal turns on whether the doctor provides services pursuant to a contract with the family practitioner committee. I doubt if he does and am content to assume that there is no contract. Nevertheless, the terms which govern the obligations of the doctor on the one hand, as to the services he is to provide, and of the family practitioner committee on the other hand, as to the payments which it is required to make to the doctor, are all prescribed in the relevant legislation and it seems to me that the statutory terms are just as effective as they would be if they were contractual to confer upon the doctor an enforceable right in private law to receive the remuneration to which the terms entitle him.[241]

1.133 The question has also arisen in a case in which a doctor was unavailable to patients during a time in which he had agreed to be on duty. On the recommendation of the FPC, the Secretary of State exercised his discretion to withhold £2,000 from the doctor's remuneration.[242] The doctor appealed on the ground that, since the nature of the relationship between him and the FPC was analogous to contract, the powers of the Secretary of State should be confined to a right to recover a proper sum of compensation for the loss caused by the breach. He should not, however, be entitled to impose a penalty on the GP far in excess of the damage actually suffered. Having examined the Terms of Service and the provisions regulating the power to discipline GPs, Potts J said:

> the terms of the relevant statutes and regulations are such as to indicate unequivocally that the power to withhold money extends beyond, and is different from, any power to recover money as compensation for the lost value

---

[239] See s 29(4), 1977 Act. Significantly, under s 2 of the National Health Service (Primary Care) Act 1997, GPs may be employed by NHS trusts, other GPs on the medical list, or other GPs providing services under a pilot scheme. It remains to be seen whether the dual obligations owed to patient and employer will affect the traditional view of the doctor–patient relationship.   [240] ibid, Sch 2, para 38.

[241] *Roy v Kensington and Chelsea FPC* [1992] 1 All ER 705 at 709.

[242] See generally the powers provided in the National Health Service (Service Committees and Tribunal) Regulations 1992, SI 1992/664, as amended by SI 1994/634.

of services not performed. It forms part of a clear disciplinary scheme to ensure control of the service . . .[243]

Thus, he refused to interfere with the sanction. This suggests that the relationship between doctors and health authorities has to be considered in its regulatory context and that the law of contract cannot be used as a framework for analysis.

1.134

(ii) *Duties owed to a Doctor's Patients*

'A doctor's patients' are those recorded by the health authority as being on the doctor's list, or those whom the doctor has accepted onto his list, whether or not it has received notification that he has done so; but it also includes a number of other categories, in which there is no agreement between doctor and patient.[244] The duties owed by a doctor to his patients are described in paragraph 12 of the Terms of Service as follows:

1.135

(1) A doctor shall render to his patients all necessary and appropriate personal medical services of the type usually provided by general practitioners.
(2) The services which a doctor is required by paragraph (1) to render shall include the following:[245]
   (a) giving advice, where appropriate, to a patient in connection with the patient's general health, and in particular about the significance of diet, exercise, the use of tobacco, the consumption of alcohol and the misuse of drugs;
   (b) offering to patients consultations and, where appropriate, physical examinations for the purpose of identifying, or reducing the risk of disease or injury;
   (c) offering to patients, where appropriate, vaccination or immunisation against measles, mumps, rubella, pertussis, poliomyelitis, diphtheria and tetanus;
   (d) arranging for the referral of patients, as appropriate, for the provision of any other services under this Act; and

---

[243] *R v Secretary of Health, ex p Hickey* 10 BMLR 126, 137 (1993).
[244] See reg 4(1)(a) and (b) of the National Health Service (General Medical Services) Regulations 1992, SI 1992/635.
[245] Also note the special requirement that 'a doctor shall' invite newly registered patients (para 14) and patients aged 75 years and over (para 16) to participate in a consultation, either at the practice premises, or elsewhere. Patients not seen within 3 years should be provided with a consultation if they request it (para 15, as amended by SI 1993/540). This 'preventive', rather than curative function, is described in great detail in the regulations. For example, for newly registered patients and those not seen within 3 years, the doctor is obliged to record in the patient's medical notes details of previous illnesses, immunisations, allergies, diseases, and medication, offer a physical examination, record the findings and offer appropriate advice.

(e) giving advice, as appropriate, to enable patients to avail themselves of services provided by a local social services authority.[246]

1.136 The following discusses a number of specific duties arising under the Terms of Service.

(a) Duty to Prescribe

1.137 Paragraph 43 of the Terms of Service requires that:

> a doctor shall order any drugs or appliances which are needed for the treatment of any patient to whom he is providing treatment under these terms of service by issuing to that patient a prescription form.[247]

1.138 GP spending on pharmaceuticals is now subject to regulation by indicative amounts,[248] or 'target budgets'.[249] The scheme, which does not apply to GP fund-holders,[250] requires health authorities to impose a notional amount on GP drug spending. The corresponding duty of GPs is contained in section 18 of the National Health Service and Community Care Act 1990:[251]

> The members of a practice shall seek to secure that, except with the consent of the relevant health authority or for good cause, the orders for drugs, medicines and listed appliances given by them . . . in any financial year does not exceed the indicative amount notified for the practice . . .

1.139 The object of the scheme is not to inhibit clinical discretion. In proper circumstances, GPs will be entitled to exceed the amount indicated by the health authority. One of the salient principles underlying the scheme is that of the 'patient's entitlement to receive all the medicines they [sic] require'.[252] An influx of new patients to the list, or unexpectedly expensive requirements

---

[246] National Health Service (General Medical Services) Regulations 1992, SI 1992/635, Sch 2. para 12.

[247] ibid, sch 2, para 43. But the doctor 'shall provide' medicines which are immediately needed by a patient. See the National Health Service (Pharmaceutical Services) Regulations 1992, SI 1992/662, reg 19(a). These obligations are subject to para 44 of the General Medical Regulations which concerns the Limited List of drugs which may not be prescribed under the Terms of Service. Note also that new, or experimental treatments, with which the GP could not be expected to be familiar, should normally remain the responsibility of the hospital consultant (see para 12(1)), eg *New Drugs for Multiple Sclerosis* (EL(95)97, NHSE, 1995).

[248] See s 18, National Health Service and Community Care Act 1990 and National Health Service (Indicative Amounts) Regulations 1991, SI 1991/556.

[249] The phrase is informally introduced in *Prescribing Expenditure: guidance on allocations and budget setting 1994/95* (EL(94)2, NHSME, 1994), which discusses the principles on which the amounts shall be assessed.

[250] See the National Health Service and Community Care Act 1990, s 18(2). Fund-holders are responsible for their own budgets.

[251] As amended by s 2(1), Sch 1, para 77, Health Authorities Act 1995.

[252] *Prescribing Expenditure: guidance on allocations and budget setting 1994/95* (EL(94)2, NHSME, 1994), para 2.

from particular patients would justify exceeding the recommended amount.[253] However, the ultimate sanction against overspending is for a deduction to be made from a GP's remuneration when:

> the cost of any drug or appliance ordered by a doctor on a prescription form in relation to any patient is, by reason of the character of the drug or appliance in question or the quantity in which it was so ordered, in excess of that which was reasonably necessary for the proper treatment of that patient . . .[254]

One would expect discussions between the GP concerned and the health **1.140** authority to avoid the need for invoking this procedure, so that it will be used very rarely. In serious cases, however, the amount of money to be deducted from a doctor's remuneration should relate to the costs incurred by the excessive prescribing.[255] What counts as 'excessive'? Guidance from the NHS Executive suggests that:

> there are several types of prescribing which may give rise to a perception on the [health authority's] part that there may have been excessive prescribing [e.g.] . . . where it appears that far too much of a drug is prescribed for the condition under treatment . . . ; where two drugs with the same apparent mode of action are prescribed when beneficial synergy is not expected . . . ; where too many drugs appear to have been prescribed for a single condition. This may be where treatment is begun or drugs are added without deletion of previous treatment . . . ; [or] where additional drugs are routinely prescribed prophylactically to meet infrequent side effects.[256]

This suggests that the scheme is designed to cut out waste. It is not intended **1.141** to inhibit the GP's reasonable clinical discretion. Doctors obviously have widely differing opinions about what is reasonable and excusable and ought to remain the ultimate arbiters in matters of clinical discretion which should be insulated from interference by the Health Authority. This view apears to have the support of the Department of Health which has said '[t]he Government fully recognises that effective patient care may sometimes require the prescribing of relatively costly drugs. It remains committed to ensuring that

---

[253] See the selection of ministerial statements gathered by J Jacob in his annotations to s 18 of the 1990 Act in *Current Law Statutes Annotated, 1990*, vol 2.

[254] See the National Health Service (Service Committees and Tribunal) Regulations 1992, SI 1992/644, reg 15(1) and paras 15 and 16. Appeal against such a decision, either as to the decision to make a deduction, or the amount, is available to the Secretary of State. See para 15(19)–(31).

[255] ibid, para 13. The principle is flexible. Such a sum may be reduced in cases concerning very expensive drugs, or increased in cases of very inexpensive drugs or persistent excessive prescribing. See para 14.

[256] *Excessive prescribing by GPs: referral to a Professional Committee* (EL(92)90, NHSME, 1992), annex B, para 8.

patients get the drugs that their doctors judge appropriate to their clinical needs.'[257]

1.142 What, then, is the effect of the requirement in paragraph 43 that the doctor 'shall' prescribe the medicines which are 'needed'? Does it mean that it would be unreasonable for a health authority to inhibit GPs from prescribing according to the clinical requirements of each case, even when it is doing its reasonable best to manage scarce resources? An anlogous point arose under the Chronically Sick and Disabled Persons Act 1970 in which the word 'need' fell to be interpreted as imposing either an absolute obligation on the public authority to respond to the individual as his needs required, or alternatively a relative duty dependent on the resources made available to it. Under s 2(1), where, in the case of any disabled person, a local authority is satisfied:

> that it is necessary in order to meet the needs of that person for that authority to make arrangements for [services specifed in paras. (a)–(h)] . . . then . . . it shall be the duty of that authority to make those arrangements

1.143 The issue arose in *R v Gloucestershire CC, ex p Barry*.[258] The applicant had been assessed as needing certain services under the 1970 Act. The question arose whether those services could be withdrawn in the light of financial constraints. A majority of the Court of Appeal held that the word 'need', in its context, imposed an absolute duty. In the Court of Appeal, Sir John Balcombe said, with reference to section 2(1) that 'the point of reference in assessing those needs can only be the requirements of the individual concerned: it cannot extend to a consideration of the resources available to the local authority.' He continued:

> 'Need' as a noun is a common Englsh word. The Shorter Oxford English Dictionary (3rd ed.) gives as definition 6 of 'need': 'A condition marked by the lack or want of some necessary thing, or requiring some extraneous aid or addition'. Simply as a matter of the ordinary use of language, I do not see how the resources available to a local authority can be relevant to the determination of the needs of a particular person.[259]

1.144 On this delicate point, however, a bare majority of the House of Lords considered that local authority resources were relevant to the assessment of an individual's needs. Lord Clyde considered, notwithstanding the wording of the section that it was unlikely that Parliament could have intended that the relevant service might be provided regardless of the costs involved.[260] And Lord Nicholls said that '[a] person's needs for a particular type or level of

[257] *Priority Setting in the NHS: The NHS Drug Budget. Government Response to the Second Report from the Health Committee Session 1993–94* (Cm 2686, 1994) at 11.
[258] [1997] 1 All ER 1. [259] *R v Gloucestershire CC, ex p Barry* [1996] 4 All ER 421, 440.
[260] N 244, above, 17.

service cannot be decided in a vacuum from which all considerations of cost have been expelled.'[261] On the other hand, he also considered the argument that:

> if a local authority may properly take its resources into account in the way I have described, the s 2(1) duty would in effect be limited to making arrangements to the extent only that the authority should decide to allocate money for this purpose. The duty, it was said, would collapse into a power. I do not agree. A local authority must carry out its functions under s 2(1) in a responsible fashion. In the event of a local authority acting with *Wednesbury* unreasonbleness . . . a disabled person would have a remedy.[262]

Were a similar approach to be adopted to the difficulties faced by health authorities, doctors could not be said to have a right under paragraph 43 to prescribe simply according to their responsible clinical discretion. And although a remedy would be available to patients under the *Wednesbury* principle to challenge a health authority's decision to restrict the availability of medicines, the remedy is limited to requiring the authority to reconsider its decision and is not a guarantee of access to care.[263]   **1.145**

Once a doctor has given the patient a prescription, those who are obliged to pay prescription charges do so at a flat rate, notwithstanding that many medicines purchased privately cost less than the prescription charge.[264] Since prescription only medicines may not be obtained without a prescription form, may a doctor give an NHS patient a private prescription in order to enable the patient to make the saving by buying it privately? The Terms of Service provide that the GP shall issue to the patient 'a prescription form',[265] namely 'a form provided by a health authority . . .'[266] In the normal course of a consultation within the framework of the NHS, therefore, the doctor is obliged to give the patient a form which will attract the standard prescription charge.[267]   **1.146**

---

[261] ibid, 11.   [262] ibid, 12.   [263] See paras 1.91–1.112 above.

[264] A minister for health, Mr Mawhinney, explained that the additional charge was levied by way of 'a contribution to the NHS'. Only around 20% of NHS prescriptions are paid for. The remainder are exempt from charges. See *Priority Setting in the NHS: The NHS Drugs Budget* (HC 80–vii, Session 1993–94), para 878. Many drugs, of course, cost vastly more than the standard prescription charge.

[265] National Health Service (General Medical Services) Regulations 1992, SI 1992/635, Sch 2, para 43.   [266] ibid, Sch 2, para 1 (interpretation paragraph).

[267] A different view appears to be taken in *General Practitioner Terms of Service: Private Prescriptions* (FHSL (94)26, NHSE, 1994).

(b) Duty to Visit

1.147 Medical services will normally be rendered by a doctor 'at his practice premises.'[268] However, when 'in the doctor's reasonable opinion it would be inappropriate for the patient to attend the practice', it may be necessary for the doctor to visit the patient at the patient's home, or elsewhere within the doctor's practice area.[269] Doctors must be available to their patients twenty four hours a day. The Terms of Service require that:

> a doctor is responsible for ensuring the provision for his patients of the services referred to in paragraph 12 throughout each day during which his name is included in the [Health Authority's] medical list.[270]

1.148 Not surprisingly, the obligation to undertake calls throughout the night is unpopular, largely because of the numbers of patients who are perceived to abuse the service. In one survey, GPs said that fewer than half of their out-of-hours visits concerned genuine emergencies.[271] The difficulty, of course, is to know what should count as 'abuse'. Patients are not encouraged to make their own diagnoses of illness and, particularly with children, will naturally be inclined to be safe than sorry when something unexpected occurs. Clearly, it would be undesirable if a policy designed to attack outright abuse had the additional effect of deterring those for whom care is needed. Specific regulations now provide for the provision of services to patients outside normal hours. Thus, if in the doctor's reasonable opinion a consultation is needed before the next time at which the patient could be seen during normal hours, he may render the relevant services at any of the places discussed above (including the practice premises). In addition, greater freedom has been given to doctors to use primary care centres outside normal hours. Thus, the services may be rendered:

> at such other place as the [Health Authority] has agreed . . . , and he has informed the patient, . . . is a place where he will treat patients outside normal hours.[272]

---

[268] National Health Service (General Medical Services) Regulations 1992, SI 1992/635, Sch 2, para 13(a), as amended by National Health Service (General Medical Services) Amendment Regulations 1995, SI 1995/80, reg 3.

[269] National Health Service (General Medical Services) Regulations 1992, SI 1992/635, Sch 2, para 13(b), as amended by National Health Service (General Medical Services) Amendment Regulations 1995, SI 1995/80, reg 3(2)(b).

[270] National Health Service (General Medical Services) Regulations 1992, SI 1992/635, Sch 2, para 18(1). On the duty to visit, see *Sa'd v Robinson* [1989] 1 Med L 41 and *Morrison v Forsyth* 23 BMLR 11 (1995).

[271] See Johnson, P, 'Doctor come now, my tortoise has gone', *The Doctor* 17 Feb 1994, 32.

[272] National Health Service (General Medical Services) Regulations 1992, SI 1992/635, Sch 2, para 13, as amended by National Health Service (General Medical Services) Amendment Regulations 1995, SI 1995/80, reg 3(4)(b).

Use of such centres requires the formal approval of the Health Authority, **1.149** which must be satisfied that the premises 'are likely to be reasonably convenient to the doctor's patients' and correspond with the general needs of the locality.[273] In this way, practices may co-operate with one another on a rota basis which spreads the load of their out-of-hours obligations. (Doctors may agree to deputise for other doctors by undertaking responsibility for their patients.[274]) An invitation to patients to leave their homes and attend a health centre during the night may have the benefit of reducing needless out-of-hours visits, but it should not be used as a blanket response to all such calls. The threat of a negligence action requires that patients who ought reasonably to have the benefit of a home visit do indeed receive one.

(c) Emergency Cases

Duties are also owed to patients who are not on the doctor's list. The Terms of **1.150** Service require doctors to provide care at the site of an emergency in certain circumstances. Paragraph 4(1)(h) provides that a doctor's patients include:

> persons to whom he may be requested to give treatment which is immediately required owing to an accident or other emergency at any place in his practice area provided that . . . he is available to provide such treatment . . . [and] provided there is no doctor who, at the time of the request, is under an obligation otherwise than under this head to give treatment to that person, or there is such a doctor but, after being requested to attend, he is unable to attend and give treatment immediately required . . .

The obligation is restricted to 'treatment which is immediately required' in **1.151** the doctor's own practice area, or in the area of the health authority in which he is included, provided no other doctor is obliged, or available, to provide care. The logic of the geographical restriction may be that visitors to an area will always be able to find medical help in emergency circumstances by contacting a local doctor. Equally, a doctor should not be expected to be on duty throughout the country wherever he happens to be.

---

[273] National Health Service (General Medical Services) Regulations 1992, SI 1992/635, Sch 2, para 29A, added by National Health Service (General Medical Services) Amendment Regulations 1995, SI 1995/80, reg 3(5).

[274] National Health Service (General Medical Services) Regulations 1992, SI 1992/635, Sch 2, para 25, as amended by National Health Service (General Medical Services) Amendment Regulations 1995, SI 1995/80, reg 3(3). The use of deputies is discussed below.

(d) Patients Treated by a Deputy

1.152 As a general rule 'a doctor shall give treatment personally.'[275] It would not be reasonable, however, to expect doctors to be personally responsible for their patients every hour of every day. For this reason, doctors have long made use of deputies, or deputising services, under which another doctor takes responsibility for a doctor's patients for a limited period of time. This approach has been reflected in the Terms of Service, which provide that the doctor:

> . . . shall be under no obligation to give treatment personally to a patient provided that reasonable steps are taken to ensure continuity of the patient's treatment, and in these circumstances treatment may be given—
> (a) by another doctor acting as a deputy, whether or not he is a partner or assistant of the patient's doctor; or
> (b) in the case of treatment which it is clinically reasonable in the circumstances to delegate to someone other than a doctor, by a person whom the doctor has authorised and who he is satisfied is competent to carry out such treatment.[276]

1.153 What if something goes wrong during the time that the patient is being treated by, or awaiting treatment by, a doctor acting as a deputy? The Terms of Service distinguish between deputies whose names are on the medical list of a health authority and those that are not. The patient's own doctor bears direct responsibility for the acts and omissions of deputies whose names are not on a medical list.[277] He is not responsible, however, for deputies who are already on a medical list. Thus, under paragraph 21(2):

> Where a doctor whose name is included in the medical list is acting as deputy to another doctor whose name is also included in the list, the deputy is responsible for—
> (a) his own acts and omissions in relation to the obligations under these terms of service of the doctor for whom he acts as deputy; and
> (b) the acts and omissions of any person employed by him or acting on his behalf.

1.154 This distinction may often be sufficient to insulate a doctor from a complaint

---

[275] National Health Service (General Medical Services) Regulations 1992, SI 1992/635, Sch 2 para 19(1).

[276] National Health Service (General Medical Services) Regulations 1992, SI 1992/635, Sch 2, para 19(2). Note the special requirements that doctors who use 'organisations providing deputy doctors' are satisfied that the deputy is qualified. See the National Health Service (General Medical Services) Amendment Regulations 1997, SI 1997/730, reg 3. The scheme extends to arrangements made by, or with, GPs practising outside the 1992 regulations by virtue of the National Health Service (Primary Care) Act 1997; see s 15.

[277] National Health Service (General Medical Services) Regulations 1992, SI 1992/635, Sch 2, para 20(1), as amended by SI 1994/633.

by the health authority but it does not affect the position at common law. In negligence a doctor may be liable whether or not the deputy is on the medical list if he has failed to take reasonable care of his patient. The obvious danger in using deputies, particularly from outside the practice, is that the deputy will probably not know the history of the patients he is expected to treat and will be more likely to miss signs or symptoms that would have been recognised by the patient's doctor. Also, deputising services may not appreciate the urgency with which a patient requires a visit through ignorance of the patient's particular condition. In principle, therefore, '[a]ny deputising arrangements should make provision for prompt and proper communication between the deputy and the doctor who has primary responsibility for the patients' care.'[278] There are obvious dangers in using deputies and reasonable care should be taken to minimise them.

In one circumstance, however, this analysis may need to be modified. Amendments to the Terms of Service have introduced the concept of 'out of hours arrangements.'[279] Formal arrangements may be agreed between a GP and the health authority whereby a doctor may 'transfer his obligations under these terms of service during part or all of the out of hours period' to a 'transferee doctor', namely a doctor who is on the medical list who 'has undertaken to carry out the obligations of another doctor under these terms of service'.[280] The transfer may cover some, or all of his patients and be agreed during such times as the doctors, and the health authority, agree. Health authority approval of such an arrangement is required, which shall be given if it is satisfied: **1.155**

(a) having regard, in particular, to the interests of the doctor's patients, that the arrangement is reasonable;
(b) . . . that the arrangement is practicable and will work satisfactorily;
(c) that it will be clear to the doctor's patients how to seek personal medical services during the out of hours period; and
(d) that if the arrangement does come to an end, the doctor has in place proper arrangements for the immediate resumption of his responsibilities.[281]

This approval of the arrangements may provide prima facie evidence that the arrangement is reasonable for providing proper care to the doctor's patients. In this case, during the relevant period, all the doctor's duties to the relevant patients, including those in negligence, are transferred to the transferee **1.156**

---

[278] *Professional Conduct and Discipline: Fitness to Practise* (General Medical Council, 1993), para 41.
[279] Sch 2, para 18A, National Health Service (General Medical Services) Regulations 1992, SI 1992/635, added by reg 5(5), National Health Service (General Medical Services) Amendment Regulations 1996, SI 1996/702. [280] ibid, para 18A(1) and (2).
[281] ibid, para 18A(9).

doctor. In other words, during the active period of the arrangement, the patient is no longer one of the 'doctor's patients' under paragraph 4 of the terms of service. Instead, the patient is transferred to the list of the transferee doctor, who is entirely responsible for his care.[282] On the other hand, there may be circumstances in which the doctor knows, or ought to know that the arrangement has broken down. In this case a common law duty would arise on his part to provide alternative cover for his patients.[283]

(e) Violent Patients and 'Assignees'

1.157 Under the principle that primary care under the NHS should be available 'for all persons in the locality who wish to take advantage of the arrangements',[284] GPs' Terms of Service permit the health authority to 'assign' unpopular patients to GPs with or without agreement. Thus, where a patient who is not on a doctor's list is refused acceptance by a doctor for inclusion on his list, he may apply to the authority in writing for assignment to a doctor. The application shall be considered by the authority,

> which shall assign the patient to such doctor in its medical list as it thinks fit, having regard to—
> (a) the respective distances between the person's residence and the practice premises . . . ;
> (b) whether within the previous six months the person has been removed from the list of any doctor in that part of the locality at the request of that doctor; and
> (c) such other circumstances, including those concerning the doctors in that part of the locality and their practices, as the [Health Authority] think relevant.[285]

1.158 Such patients are included in the description of 'a doctor's patients' in the Terms of Service, to whom a GP is bound to make services available,[286] and so the doctor has a corresponding obligation to accept health authority 'assignees'.

1.159 Obviously, there will be occasions when the duty to accept unpopular patients causes anxiety. In particular, in areas where the number of medical practices is

---

[282] As they are now deemed to be, see ibid, sch 2, para 4(1)(m); added by reg 5(3)(b), National Health Service (General Medical Services) Amendment Regulations 1996, SI 1996/702.

[283] This prima facie focus of liability on the deputy, unless additional circumstances prevail, is also contained in the new disciplinary procedures introduced by the National Health Service (Service Committees and Tribunal) Amendment Regulations 1996, SI 1996/703 reg 4(6). [284] See s 29, 1977 Act.

[285] National Health Service (General Medical Services) Regulations 1992, SI 1992/635, reg 21(2).

[286] National Health Service (General Medical Services) Regulations 1992, SI 1992/635, Sch 2, para 4(1)(d): ' . . . a doctor's patients are . . . persons who have been assigned to him under regulation 21 . . . '

small, doctors may find that a patient seems to be assigned to them with great regularity and that they share a patient with one other practice on a 'three months on, three months off' basis. A doctor to whom a patient has been assigned may make representations to the health authority against the assignment and require it to hear his case against it.[287] Within seven days of the representation the health authority must reconsider the decision in order to confirm or revise it,[288] pending which the doctor remains responsible for the patient.[289] No person who participated in making the initial assignment shall participate in the review.[290]

What is the nature of the obligation to accept assignees in relation to patients who threaten, or use violence, toward a doctor, or his staff?[291] The problem was considered sufficiently serious to merit an amendment to the Terms of Service between doctors and health authorities. Now, where a person on the doctor's list has committed an act of violence against the doctor or has behaved in such a way that the doctor has feared for his safety, and the doctor has reported the matter to the police, 'the doctor may notify the [Health Authority] that he wishes to have that person removed from his list with immediate effect.'[292] In these circumstances, although the patient will cease to be on the doctor's list from the time the doctor has notified the Authority (by telephone, or fax, provided the message is confirmed subsequently in writing[293]), the doctor may still not be able to terminate his obligations immediately because the patient remains one of the 'doctor's patients'.[294] Consequently, the doctor must continue to give the person any 'immediately necessary treatment until the expiry of 14 days beginning with the date . . . when he requested the immediate removal of that person from his list, or until that person has been accepted by or assigned to another doctor, whichever occurs first.'[295]

1.160

---

[287] National Health Service (General Medical Services) Regulations 1992, SI 1992/635, Sch 2, para 21(5).   [288] ibid, para 21(6) and (9).
[289] ibid, para 21(10).   [290] ibid, para 21(8).
[291] See Schnieden, V, 'How doctors can deal with violence in their workplace', *BMA News Review*, Feb 1994, 11 and Chadwick, J, 'Fighting against the threat of brutality', *The Doctor*, 27 Jan 1994, 40.
[292] See the National Health Service (General Medical Services) Regulations 1992, SI 1992/635, para 9A(1), as inserted by the National Health Service (General Medical Services) Amendment Regulations 1994, SI 1994/633, para 8(4).
[293] National Health Service (General Medical Services) Amendment Regulations 1994, SI 1994/633, Sch 2, para 6.
[294] See para 4(1)(c) of the Terms of Service which specifically includes those to whom treatment must be given for 14 days.
[295] ibid, the amendment is made to para 4(4) of the 1992 Regulations by para 8(2) of the 1994 Regulations. Under the new Regulations, before an assignment is made, the authority is obliged to consider the circumstances in which a patient has been removed from another doctor's list. See para 21(11) of the 1992 Regulations, as amended by para 7 of the 1994 Regulations.

1.161 Notice that the treatment required is restricted to that which is 'immediately necessary', rather than that which is routine. Perhaps this more limited obligation could be fulfilled by referring the patient directly to the accident and emergency unit of a hospital, or by making home visits dependent on attendance by the police.[296] No doctor is obliged to put him or herself at unreasonable risk by virtue of the Authority's decision. In such a case, the doctor might be able to exclude such a patient from the practice premises by means of an injunction and insist that any future consultations take place in the presence of a policeman, or at a police station. Ultimately, however, if reasonable safety cannot be assured, it is suggested that the doctor would be entitled to refuse to accept the Authority's assignment.

(f) Duty to Refer

1.162 In the past, the recommendation of the British Medical Association has been that 'general practitioners should always acquiesce in any reasonable request by a patient for a second opinion'[297] with the presumption that the choice of consultant was a matter for the referring doctor to decide. What freedom do GPs retain in the choice of consultant?

1.163 The idea of NHS contracts in the National Health Service and Community Care Act 1990 requires health authorities to make agreements with hospitals with respect to the services required by its residents. In doing so, they will seek to make provision for those most often in need of care and the most common conditions of illness. 'Block contracts' lead to economies of scale that make for the most efficient provision of health care.

1.164 This system will only work effectively, therefore, if GPs are prepared to adhere to the arrangements made by the Health Authority, by referring their patients to hospitals with whom sizeable contractual arrangements have been established. If GPs refuse to do so and refer their patients to hospitals extra-contractually, the cost of these one-off referrals will adversely affect the management of the annual budget. This degree of flexibility has almost certainly been restricted under the block contract system. If this is the case, what is the position of the GP who considers that his patient reasonably requires the services of a consultant on an extra-contractual basis? Could the authority simply refuse to hold reserve funds for this purpose, or to pay for any extra-contractual referrals (ECRs)?

1.165 NHS guidance suggests that the grounds on which an ECR could be refused

---

[296] See *Violence Against GPs: Time for Resolute Action* (British Medical Association, 1994).
[297] *Rights and Responsibilities of Doctors*, (British Medical Association, 1988), 85.

are limited. Purchasers should respect the clinical judgment of GPs and other clinicians who decide on individual referrals so that it will be rare for a clinician's choice of consultant to be judged to be unwarranted. In particular 'it is not acceptable for a purchaser to refuse authorization solely on the grounds of the proposed cost of the treatment in relation to the contracted services.'[298] The only grounds on which refusal may be acceptable are as follows:

(a) the patient is not the purchaser's responsibility, i e the patient is not a district resident or the patient is, for the treatment planned, a responsibility of a GP fund-holder;

(b) where prior authorization for the ECR was not sought where it was medically reasonable to expect the provider to have done so;[299]

(c) the referral is not justified on clinical grounds. In making such judgments the [Health Authority] would be expected to ensure that it takes appropriate clinical advice. This would include instances where such clinical advice has led to the development and agreement of clear referral protocols and the threshold has not been met;

(d) an alternative referral would be equally efficacious for the patient, taking account of the patient's wishes.[300]

This will reassure those with conditions which are so uncommon that their health authority has not arranged a block contract with a hospital, and those whose conditions become so serious that they have to be dealt with in specialist units as tertiary referrals. **1.166**

Some money, therefore, must be allocated by health authorities to cover the costs incurred by extra-contractual referrals.[301] Health authorities have a good idea of previous referral patterns and are obliged to make reasonable provision based on their past experience. **1.167**

(g) Freedom to Enter and Leave the Doctor–Patient Relationship

In principle, the parties are entirely free to enter, or leave, the doctor–patient relationship. The procedure for doing so is simple and neither is obliged to tolerate the other against his or her wishes. The mechanism for applying to a doctor to be accepted onto his or her list is straightforward: **1.168**

An application to a doctor for inclusion in his list for the provision of general

---

[298] *Guidance on Extra Contractual Referrals* (NHSME, 1993), para 51.

[299] 'GPs should be encouraged to discuss any referrals outside contracts with a named contact point in the [HA] before referral . . . though purchasers should not insist on such discussions prior to the referral.' ibid, para 4.   [300] ibid, paras 49–52.

[301] For the system of payment for extra contractual referrals, see 'Tariffs for Extra Contractual Referrals' FDL(91)34 (NHSME) and 'Information to Support Invoicing for Extra Contractual Referrals' FDL(91)37 (NHSME).

medical services shall be made by delivering to the doctor a medical card or a form of application signed (in either case) by the applicant or a person authorised on his behalf.[302]

1.169 Doctors, however, are in private practice. They are not employees of a health authority and are free to decide for themselves whether or not to accept an applicant on to their list. Thus, a doctor may agree to accept a person on his list if the person is eligible to be accepted by him,[303] but is not obliged to do so. Equally, patients are not tied to any particular GP once they have joined a GP's practice. They, too, are free to leave their current practitioner and apply to join another in the usual way. Thus:

> A person who is on a doctor's list of patients may apply to any other doctor providing general medical services for acceptance on that other doctor's list of patients.[304]

1.170 Alternatively, the doctor may wish to sever his or her relationship with the patient and is free to do so, subject only to giving the health authority an opportunity to offer the patient another practice. Thus:

> A doctor may have any person removed from his list and shall notify the [health authority] in writing that he wishes to have a person removed from his list and . . . the removal shall take effect (a) on the date on which the person is accepted by or assigned to another doctor; or (b) on the eighth day after the FSA receives the notice, whichever is the sooner.[305]

1.171 Patients, therefore, retain absolute freedom to leave the list of a medical practitioner. Although the Terms of Service appear to permit the same freedom to doctors, the General Medical Council has expressed its view that doctors may not do so for illegitimate reasons. Thus doctors are advised that they may not remove patients from their lists for economic reasons, for example, their need for expensive drug therapy, or a patient's refusal to participate in screening or immunisation programmes. The Council expressed itself on the matter as follows:

> . . . family doctors, as the professionals involved, have special responsibilities for making the relationship work. In particular, it is unacceptable to abuse the right to refuse to accept patients by applying criteria of access to the practice list which discriminate against groups on grounds of their age, sex, sexual orienta-

---

[302] National Health Service (General Medical Services) Regulations 1992, SI 1992/635, reg 20(1). For applications on behalf of others, see reg 20(2).

[303] National Health Service (General Medical Services) Regulations 1992, SI 1992/635, Sch 2, para 6.

[304] National Health Service (General Medical Services) Regulations 1992, SI 1992/635, Sch 2, para 22(3). See also reg 23(1).

[305] National Health Service (General Medical Services) Regulations 1992, SI 1992/635, Sch 2, para 9(1).

tion, race, colour, religious belief, perceived economic worth or the amount of work they are likely to generate by virtue of their clinical condition.[306]

These standards of conduct, required by a professional body, do not necessarily represent a good statement of law, although breach may expose the individual to the disciplinary procedure of the General Medical Council. Though it appears unprofessional for doctors to be able to pick and choose between patients for reasons of this nature, in the absence of obligations imposed by the Terms of Service to the contrary, it is probable that GPs are not obliged as a matter of law to accept patients onto their lists and, subject to anti-discrimination laws, may strike them off for good reasons or bad. The sole disincentive for doing so is the Professional Standards Committee of the Council itself. The Health Authority, on the other hand, may be in a different position. Its obligation to provide general medical services 'for all persons in the area who wish to take advantage of the arrangements'[307] suggests that it ought not to tolerate GPs who frustrate that objective by refusing to accept certain categories of patient. Evidence that such a practice was affecting patients' access to GPs could give rise to an action in judicial review against the Health Authority. **1.172**

---

[306] See *Removal of Patients from GP Lists* (GMSC, 1994). Increasing numbers of GPs are refusing certain patients to their lists, eg 'troublemakers', those with mental illness and elderly patients with chronic conditions. See *Association of Community Health Councils for England and Wales: Annual Report 1993–94*, 4.

[307] S 29, National Health Service Act 1977, as amended by s 2(1), Sch 1, para 18(a), Health Service Act 1995.

2

THE HEALTH CARE PROFESSIONS

A. Regulation and the Health Care Professions

2.01 Self-regulation is often seen as the hallmark of professional status. Parliament delegates to the profession itself the responsibility to control the education, accreditation and discipline of its members.[1] The key to self-regulation is found in the maintenance of the professional register. Aspiring professionals must gain admission to the register and maintain the requisite standard of conduct and competence to remain on it. Erasure from the register deprives the professional of virtually all career prospects. Nurses struck off the register by the United Kingdom Central Council (UKCC) will thereafter be unable to work in the nursing field other than as unqualified care assistants. Self-regulation has two functions which occasionally conflict. First, the profession

---

[1] Moran, M, and Wood, B, *States, Regulation and the Medical Profession* (Open University Press, 1993); McVeigh, S, and Wheeler, S, (eds) *Law, Health and Medical Regulation* (Dartmouth, 1992).

protects the public against charlatans and inadequate practitioners. Secondly, the profession preserves its own valuable monopoly of professional services.

Many professionals, like most solicitors and barristers, practise as self- **2.02** employed practitioners, answerable only to the professional bodies and the courts. Their clients for the most part have a choice. An incompetent solicitor will find it difficult to make a good living. Health professionals, however, are in the main employed in the National Health Service (NHS). Their patients have far less choice of who is to care for them, and an incompetent doctor, unlike an incompetent solicitor, can kill or seriously maim his patient.

Consideration of the health care professions must thus address three main **2.03** questions:

(1) How do the health care professions regulate themselves, and how effectively does that professional regulation protect the public?
(2) How do NHS authorities control those professionals whom they employ or with whom they have a contract for services?
(3) What special procedures for the investigation of patients' complaints and for ensuring the quality of health care services have been established in the NHS?

1. The Medical Profession

The organisation of the medical profession in the United Kingdom has a long **2.04** history.[2] The Royal College of Physicians received its charter in 1518 and the College of Surgeons (later the Royal College) separated from the Company of Barbers in 1745. The Society of Apothecaries represented the ancestors of the general practitioners of today. However, the first comprehensive move to regulate medical education and qualifications was the Medical Act 1858 which created the General Medical Council. Under this and successive legislation (most recently the Medical Act 1983) the State delegated to the medical profession itself the regulation of medical education and the control of medical practitioners.

This pattern has been followed in relation to other health care professions. **2.05** The Dentists Act 1984, the Pharmacy Act 1954, the Pharmacists (Fitness to Practice) Act 1997, the Nurses Midwives and Health Visitors Act 1997, the

---

[2] Stacey, M, *Regulating British Medicine: The General Medical Council* (John Wiley, 1992); Stacey, M, 'The General Medical Council and Professional Accountability' (1989) 4 *Public Policy and Administration*, 12–27.

Professions Supplementary to Medicine Act 1960 (chiropodists, dietitians, medical laboratory technicians, occupational therapists, physiotherapists, radiographers, remedial gymnasts and orthoptists), the Opticians Act 1989, the Hearing Aid Council Act 1968 (suppliers of hearing aids) have recently been joined by legislation regulating osteopaths and chiropractors (Osteopaths Act 1993 and Chiropractors Act 1994).[3]

2. What is a Doctor?

2.06   A common error is to suppose that the law prevents the practice of medicine or any of the other health professions by unqualified persons. What the legislation seeks to achieve is to enable the general public to identify those who have qualifications and skills recognised by responsible members of their peer group, and who are therefore likely to provide a competent and reliable service. The Medical Act 1983, section 49,[4] provides that it is a criminal offence for any person wilfully and falsely to pretend to be or to take and use the name or title of physician, doctor of medicine, licentiate in medicine or surgery, bachelor of medicine, surgeon, general practitioner or apothecary, or any name, title, addition or description implying that he is recognised by law as a physician or surgeon or licentiate in medicine or surgery or a practitioner in medicine or an apothecary. This pattern is followed in legislation relating to other professions, including those until recently regarded as somewhat outside the mainstream of conventional medicine. Section 32 of the Osteopaths Act 1993, for example, makes it a crime for any person expressly or by implication to describe himself as an osteopath, osteopathic practitioner, osteopathic physician, osteopathist, osteotherapist, or any kind of osteopath unless he is registered.

2.07   In addition, any person who dishonestly obtains money, property or services by deception (eg that he has medical qualifications) may be convicted of an offence under section 15 Theft Act 1968. This would extend to the obtaining of paid employment and to representations of all kinds, as for example that a job applicant has experience or has achieved high marks in examinations.

2.08   Where a patient has consented to treatment in the belief, induced by a bogus person, that he possessed recognised qualifications, this will constitute both the crimes and the torts of assault and battery. No person is entitled to recover any charge for any medical advice or attendance, or for the performance of

---

[3] Stone, J, and Matthews, J, *Complementary Medicine and the Law* (Oxford University Press 1996).
[4] *Younghusband v Luftig* [1949] 2 KB 354; *Wilson v Inyang* [1951] 2 KB 799; *R v Sheppard* [1981] AC 394.

any operation, or for any medicine that he has both prescribed and supplied, unless he proves that he was fully registered at the time the services were rendered.[5] However, a person who is not registered under the Medical Act may recover payment for treatment which does not amount to performing a function regarded as the prerogative of those who are medically qualified, for example, manipulation by an osteopath. A person other than a registered midwife or a registered medical practitioner may not attend a woman in childbirth, on pain of conviction of a criminal offence.[6] The only exceptions are where there is sudden or urgent necessity (many fathers and ambulance personnel are covered by this provision), or where the helper is in training with a view to becoming a doctor or midwife.

3. Registration and Qualifications

The pattern of all the legislation which regulates the various professions is to establish a central Council with power to create and maintain a register of qualified practitioners. In the case of doctors, this is the General Medical Council, in the case of nurses the United Kingdom Central Council of Nursing, Midwifery and Health Visiting, and in the case of dentists the General Dental Council.   **2.09**

The Medical Register consists of four lists: the principal list, the overseas list, the visiting overseas doctors list and the visiting European practitioners list.[7] There is also a register of doctors with limited registration. A copy of the printed register, which is published annually by the Registrar, is evidence that the persons included are fully registered, and the absence of a person's name from the register is evidence that that person is not registered.[8]   **2.10**

---

[5] Medical Act 1983, s 46(1); by s 47 Medical Act 1983, unregistered practitioners are banned from holding an appointment as physician, surgeon or other medical officer in the naval, military or air service, in any hospital or other place for the reception of persons suffering from a mental disorder or in any other hospital not supported wholly by voluntary contributions, in any prison or any other public establishment, body or institution. Only fully registered medical practitioners may be entered on the list of practitioners undertaking to provide general medical services in the NHS: National Health Service (General Medical Services) Regulations 1992, SI 1992/635. Only registered medical practitioners can sign birth, still-birth and death certificates: Medical Act 1983, s 48; *Halls v Trotter* (1921) 38 TLR 30 DC. It is an offence to provide HIV testing services unless the person providing them is a registered medical practitioner, or acting under the direction of or at the request of a registered medical practitioner: HIV Testing Kits and Services Regulations 1992, SI 1992/460. In any area in which the Venereal Disease Act 1917 is in force, no person other than a duly qualified medical practitioner may, for reward, treat any person for venereal disease. There are also statutory provisions which prohibit certain advertisements: Cancer Act 1939, s 4(1)(a); Medicines (Advertising) Regulations 1994, SI 1994/1932.

[6] Nurses, Midwives and Health Visitors Act 1997, s 16.   [7] Medical Act 1983, s 2.

[8] Medical Act 1983, s 34.

2.11 Applicants for registration who are qualified to the satisfaction of the Registrar must be issued with a certificate of registration. Any person who holds one or more primary UK qualifications, has passed a qualifying examination and has complied with the regulations laid down by the General Medical Council as to a period of experience is entitled to registration on payment of the appropriate fee.[9]

2.12 The primary qualifications which entitle an applicant to be entered in the Medical Register are specified in legislation.[10] Certain universities, and the Royal Colleges and the Society of Apothecaries, are entitled to hold qualifying examinations with the approval and under the direction of the education committee of the General Medical Council. In addition, a person must satisfy requirements as to experience in employment in a resident medical capacity in one or more approved hospitals or approved institutions, and obtain a certificate to that effect from his examining body, before being entitled to full registration.

2.13 Provisional registration may be sought by those who, having completed the necessary examinations, are undertaking a period of employment in order to obtain the experience necessary for full registration. A person who is provisionally registered is deemed to be registered as a fully registered medical practitioner only so far as it is necessary to enable him to be engaged in employment in a resident medical capacity in one or more hospitals or institutions.[11]

2.14 The fundamental principle that nationals of member states of the European Union should be free to practise their profession in all other member states has necessitated the mutual recognition of qualifications. In the medical field, two key Directives of 1975[12] provided that each member state should recognise qualifications obtained in other member states, and also laid down minimum standards which those qualifications must reach, for example, that there must be suitable clinical experience in a hospital under appropriate supervision. At the same time two committees were established by the European Council of Ministers: the Advisory Committee on Medical Training and the Committee of Senior Officials in Public Health. In 1993[13] a further

---

[9] Medical Act 1983, s 3.
[10] Medical Act 1983; Medical Qualifications (Amendment) Act 1991.
[11] Medical Act 1983, s 15.
[12] 75/362/EEC; 75/363/EEC; Medical Qualifications (EEC Recognition) Order 1977, SI 1977/287; European Primary Medical Qualifications Regulations 1996, SI 1996/1591; Dental Qualifications (Recognition) Regulations 1996, SI 1996/1496; European Nursing and Midwifery Qualifications Designation Order 1996, SI 1996/3102.
[13] 93/16/EEC; Vocational Training for General Medical Practice (European Requirements) Regulations 1994, SI 1994/3130, amending NHS Vocational Training Regulations 1979, SI 1979/1644, and similar regulations for Scotland and Northern Ireland.

Council Directive consolidated the Directives of 1975 and subsequent amendments, including a requirement that those entering general practice should have a minimum of two years' specific vocational training. From 1 January 1994 the provisions on training and mutual recognition for doctors have also applied in certain EFTA countries (Austria, Norway, Sweden, Finland and Iceland) which, together with the European Union member states and Liechtenstein, constitute the European Economic Area. Austria, Sweden and Finland became members of the European Union on 1 January 1995.

2.15 A national of a member state of the European Union who is lawfully established in medical practice in a state other than the UK may lawfully render medical services here as a visitor if he makes a written declaration showing the services he intends to provide and produces a certificate showing that he holds recognised medical qualifications in another member state. He may not, other than in an emergency, render medical services except in accordance with his declaration.[14] If such a person wishes to practise here permanently, he must apply for full registration in the principal list. Although European Directives do not in general permit states to impose a test of linguistic competence on doctors from other European states, doctors seeking employment in the National Health Service may be required by the prospective employer to prove that they can communicate effectively in English.

2.16 Doctors whose qualifications have been obtained outside the European Union are not in such a strong position. Responsibility for establishing the sufficiency of the education received by this group rests with the overseas committee of the GMC. A distinction must be made between recognised foreign qualifications, where the foreign medical school has been recognised by the GMC, and acceptable foreign qualifications which are accepted by the GMC as a sufficient guarantee of the possession of the knowledge and skill required to practise under the supervision of a person who is registered as a fully registered medical practitioner. Many overseas doctors are given only limited registration for a period of up to five years.[15] Limited registration is obtained by satisfying the Registrar that the applicant has been offered employment in the UK or the Isle of Man, that he holds an acceptable overseas qualification, that he has the necessary knowledge of English, that he is of good character, and that he has the knowledge, skill, and experience required. From 1 January 1996 the GMC has accepted the World Health Organisation's list of primary medical qualifications as acceptable for limited registration. Overseas doctors who undertake postgraduate training in the hospital service and who intend to leave the UK on completion of training are able to enter without a work

---

[14] Medical Act 1983, s 18.   [15] Medical Act 1983, s 22.

permit under the Immigration Rules for up to four years.[16] Extension of this period for up to two years may exceptionally be permitted by the Home Office. An alternative to the need to pass the English and clinical tests set by the Professional and Linguistic Assessment Board (PLAB) is that the doctor should be sponsored by a consultant or senior doctor in the NHS who undertakes to supervise and provide training.

2.17 The GMC Annual Report of 1995 concluded that, in future, assessment of all doctors applying for limited registration will be based on objective evidence, either the PLAB tests or, for example, a postgraduate qualification. It is possible for an overseas doctor with only limited registration to apply for full registration. The Review Board for Overseas Qualified Practitioners has power to review decisions of the GMC relating to overseas practitioners under section 29 Medical Act 1983. It was held in *Khan v General Medical Council*[17] that the existence of this right of appeal excluded a right to complain to an industrial tribunal about racial discrimination under the Race Relations Act 1976. The Court of Appeal again considered the powers of the GMC with respect to overseas practitioners in *R v General Medical Council, ex p Virik*.[18] Dr Virik, who had qualified in Malaysia and India, had obtained limited registration under the Medical Act 1983, s 22, for five years. His application for full registration was refused, and his appeal to the review board was unsuccessful. The GMC's guidance for doctors with limited registration recommended that applicants for full registration should have experience as a registrar or senior house officer and an additional qualification. The same requirements were not specified for holders of UK or European Union qualifications, or those with a recognised overseas qualification. It was held that there was no legal duty to apply a comparative test with UK/ European Union doctors. The GMC had a wide discretion, with which the court would only interfere if the decision was manifestly unreasonable.[19] The GMC proposed in 1995 that overseas practitioners should first be granted a training registration which would be similar to limited registration in that they would be required to work under the supervision of a fully qualified medical practitioner.[20]

2.18 Where experience is lacking, an overseas practitioner who has a recognised

---

[16] (1994) HC 395, paras 70, 71; Thompson, J, 'Admission in the academic and medical fields' (1993) *Immigration and Nationality Law and Practice 124.*

[17] [1994] IRLR 646 CA; cf *GMC v Goba* [1988] ICR 885 EAT; *Rovenska v General Medical Council* [1997] IRLR 367 CA.   [18] [1996] ICR 433.

[19] The GMC (Review Board for Overseas Qualified Practitioners Rules) Order 1979, SI 1979/29, requires that written reasons must be given for their decisions.

[20] *GMC News Review,* Oct 1995.

qualification and good English may be granted provisional registration.[21] A further possibility is temporary full registration for those who intend to visit the UK for up to a year in order to provide medical services of a specialist nature.[22] They must possess recognised or acceptable qualifications and special knowledge and skill in a particular branch or branches of medicine. However, the Immigration Rules prohibit such a person with the immigration status of visitor from undertaking paid employment in the UK,[23] that is, the doctor would need a work permit.

As a result of the publication of the NHS Executive booklet: *Ethnic Minority* **2.19** *Staff in the NHS: A Programme of Action* (1993), there has been a review by the Working Group on Specialist Medical Education of the employment and training of overseas doctors entering specialist training. It has recommended that all overseas doctors coming for training, without exception, pass a standard test of English competence before applying to the GMC for registration, and also demonstrate clinical competence to a level comparable with UK doctors.[24]

The Medical (Professional Performance) Act 1995, section 2, permits the **2.20** GMC to make regulations, subject to approval by the Secretary of State, authorising the Registrar to erase from the register of medical practitioners the name of any person who applies for his name to be erased from the register.

4. The General Medical Council

This is a body corporate which consists of fifty four elected members, elected **2.21** by medical practitioners, twenty five appointed members, chosen by certain universities and other bodies, and not more than twenty five members nominated by the Queen. Only nominated members may be, and a majority of the nominated members must be, lay persons without medical qualifications.[25] Under the Medical Act the Council has power to provide advice for members of the medical profession on standards of professional conduct and medical ethics.[26]

The Council, through its Education Committee, controls medical education.[27] **2.22** The appointed members still dominate the education committee. The

---

[21] Medical Act 1983, s 21.   [22] Medical Act 1983, s 27.
[23] (1994) HC 395, para 41.
[24] Supplementary Report by the Working Group commissioned to consider the Implications for Overseas Doctors arising from the Calman Report on Specialist Medical Training, March 1995, NHS Executive.
[25] Medical Act 1983, s 1 and Part 1 of Sch 1; GMC General Medical Council (Constitution) Order 1979, SI 1979/112, as amended.   [26] Medical Act 1983, s 35.
[27] Medical Act 1983, s 5.

committee must determine the prescribed knowledge and skill required to qualify as a doctor, ensure that instruction given in the universities is sufficient to equip students with that knowledge and skill, determine the standard of proficiency to be expected from candidates in examinations and prescribe patterns of experience in employment in a residential medical capacity in approved hospitals and institutions in order to qualify for full registration. Visitors to medical schools and approved hospitals and institutions, and examination inspectors, may be appointed.

2.23 Before 1978 the GMC had no role in postgraduate medical education, but this was placed under the aegis of the education committee by the Medical Act of that year. However, the content and day-to-day supervision of postgraduate medical education and assessment is left to the universities and the Royal Colleges. Postgraduate education is divided into two stages: basic specialist training for two or three years after full registration and higher specialist training for a further three to five years. Without official accreditation as a specialist, a doctor is highly unlikely to obtain a post as a consultant in the NHS or to be recognised by the private health insurers. However, there is no legal barrier to any doctor with basic medical qualifications setting himself up as a specialist in any field.

2.24 In other states of the European Union specialisation is more common, is undertaken earlier in the doctor's career and is recognised by legal qualifications. Membership of the European Union necessitated the recognition of these qualifications in the Certificate of Specialist Training; however, accreditation by the Royal Colleges maintained its supremacy until it was challenged as being discriminatory by the European Commission, on the ground that it created a two-tier system of UK accredited specialists and those from other member states with the Certificate of Specialist Training whose qualification was regarded as inferior in the UK.[28] In January 1991 the GMC began to add the letter T to the medical register against the names of those who were accredited or accorded equivalent status by being appointed a consultant. It did not include the letter T against the names of doctors whose only specialist qualifications were awarded in other member states. The Council maintained an unpublished list of those who had received the Certificate of Specialist Training, but, as inclusion on this list was not regarded as prima facie

---

[28] *R v Joint Committee on Higher Medical Training, The Specialist Advisory Committee on Rheumatology, ex p Goldstein* [1992] 3 Med LR 278; *R v Secretary of State for Health, ex p Goldstein* [1993] 4 Med LR 336; *Knoors v Secretary of State for Economic Affairs (Netherlands)* [1979] 2 CMLR 357.

evidence of sufficient training to qualify for a consultant post, an entry in the list had little value.

The Chief Medical Officer, Dr Calman, recommended in his report *Hospital* **2.25**
Doctors: Training for the Future (1993) that each specialty should publish a curriculum and its advice on how that could be provided through a planned, structured training programme, that there should be a new unified training grade to deliver higher specialist training, that progress through the grade and the award of a Certificate of Completion of Specialist Training (CCST) should be based on an assessment of competence and that consultant numbers should be increased well above previous targets. In future, mutual recognition will be afforded to certificates awarded in other member states of the European Union on the same basis as specialist qualifications obtained here. The Government accepted the recommendations in the report, and on 12 January 1996 implementing legislation came into force.[29]

Two competent authorities are appointed for the UK in relation to specialist **2.26**
medical qualifications: the GMC and a new body called the Specialist Training Authority of the medical Royal Colleges (STA). The STA issues CCSTs to doctors with the required qualifications and training. The GMC has established and published a register of specialists, including not only those who have been awarded a CCST, but also European doctors with specialist qualifications awarded elsewhere in the EEA whose qualifications are entitled to automatic recognition. From 1 January 1997 it is a condition of appointment as a consultant in the NHS in a specialty other than general practice that the doctor be included in the specialist register. Doctors who are already consultants should apply for inclusion before 1 January 1998. The STA has power to hear appeals against its decisions, and to remove and suspend doctors from the specialist register.

Control of fitness to practise is in the hands of committees of the Council. The **2.27**
Medical (Professional Performance) Act 1995 has added two new committees to those already established. The Professional Conduct Committee, the Health Committee and the Preliminary Proceedings Committee are charged with the task of establishing whether a medical practitioner has been guilty of serious professional misconduct, or whether his fitness to practise is seriously impaired by reason of his physical or mental condition.[30] The Assessment Referral Committee and the Committee on Professional Performance were created by the 1995 Act. Their task is to deal with allegations that the standard of professional performance of a doctor has been seriously deficient.

[29] European Specialist Medical Qualifications Order 1995, SI 1995/3208.
[30] Medical Act 1983, ss 36, 37, 42.

5. The United Kingdom Central Council of Nursing, Midwifery and Health Visiting

2.28 This was established by the Nurses, Midwives and Health Visitors Act 1979, which was consolidated, with subsequent amendments, in the Nurses, Midwives and Health Visitors Act 1997. It consists of such number of members, not greater than sixty, and a multiple of three, as approved by the Secretary of State.[31] Two-thirds of the members of the Council are elected and the remaining one-third appointed by the Secretary of State from among persons who are either registered nurses, midwives or health visitors or medical practitioners, or have such qualifications and experience in education or other fields as, in the opinion of the Secretary of State, will be of value to the Council in the performance of its functions. The Secretary of State shall have especially in mind the need to secure a geographical balance, so that each part of the United Kingdom is represented, and the need to ensure that qualifications and experience in the teaching of the relevant disciplines are adequately represented.

2.29 The Council must maintain a register of those qualified in the relevant professions, must determine the training to be undertaken in order to entitle an applicant to be admitted to the register, and also adjudicate on fitness to practise. The Acts establish a national board for each of England, Wales, Scotland and Northern Ireland. The members of the boards are all appointed by the Secretary of State.[32] The principal function of the national boards is to validate and supervise courses of training and examinations, in accordance with standards laid down by the Council.

2.30 The professional register is divided into fifteen parts. These include first and second level general nurses, first and second level mental illness and mental handicap nurses, paediatric nurses, midwives and health visitors. A person seeking admission to a part of the register must have undergone the training and passed the examinations required by the rules of the Council, must be a person of good character and must pay a fee. Registration is subject to renewal every three years, on payment of a fee.[33]

2.31 The Council is under a duty to make rules regulating the practice of midwives[34] and these rules may, in particular, determine the circumstances in

---

[31] Nurses, Midwives and Health Visitors Act 1997, s 1.
[32] Nurses, Midwives and Health Visitors Act 1997, s 5.
[33] *R v UKCC, ex p Bailey* [1991] 2 Med LR 145, CA.
[34] Nurses, Midwives and Health Visitors Rules 1983, SI 1983/873.

which, and the procedure by means of which, midwives may be suspended from practice, require midwives to give notice of intention to practise to the local supervising authority, the health authority, and require registered midwives to attend courses of instruction in accordance with the rules. The midwifery committee of the UKCC deals with proposals to make, amend or revoke such rules, which must be approved by the Secretary of State in order to come into force.

A national of any member state of the European Union who applies for **2.32** registration in the United Kingdom and has professional qualifications designated by statutory instrument as equivalent to UK qualifications must be registered in the relevant part of the register on payment of a fee as long as he satisfies the Council that he is of good character.[35] A visiting European Union national who is lawfully practising in another member state as a nurse responsible for general care, or as a midwife, and who holds the appropriate qualifications, may practise in the UK on a temporary basis on making a written declaration to the Council of his intention to practise in the UK and on the production of documents establishing his qualifications in the other state. Registration in a country outside the European Union may be recognised as permitting an individual to be registered in the UK, following individual evaluation of the knowledge and competence of that individual, including proficiency in English.[36]

Fitness to practise is under the control of the Council, which has established a **2.33** Professional Conduct Committee and a Health Committee. The function of these committees is to determine whether a person on the register has been guilty of professional misconduct, ie 'conduct unworthy of a nurse, midwife or health visitor', (compare the wording with 'serious professional misconduct' in the Medical Act), or whether his fitness to practise has been seriously impaired by reason of his physical or mental condition.[37]

6. General Dental Council

The profession of dentistry is governed by the Dentists Act 1984. The General **2.34** Dental Council maintains a register of qualified persons and has the power through its Professional Conduct Committee to order the suspension for up to twelve months, or erasure from the register, of dentists found guilty of criminal offences or of serious professional misconduct. The Health Committee of the

---

[35] European Nursing and Midwifery Qualifications Designation Order 1996, SI 1996/ 3102.   [36] Nurses, Midwives and Health Visitors Act 1997, s 8.
[37] Nurses, Midwives and Health Visitors (Professional Conduct) Rules 1993, SI 1993/893; Pyne, R, 'The Professional Dimension' in Tingle, J and Cribb, A (eds) *Nursing Law and Practice* (Blackwell Science, 1995).

Council has power to suspend the registration of a registered dentist whose fitness to practise is judged to be seriously impaired by reason of his physical or mental condition and to impose conditions upon his registration. Powers in relation to the dental profession, as with the medical profession, are conferred on the Privy Council, including a right of appeal against a decision of the Professional Conduct Committee.

B. Disciplinary Procedures

1. The Nature of Professional Disciplinary Proceedings

2.35 The professional bodies see their primary responsibility as the protection of the public and the maintenance of professional and ethical standards. As it is difficult to encompass all the professions in a work such as this, the major emphasis will be placed on the doctors, but much of what follows applies *mutatis mutandis* to all the health professions.[38]

2.36 A function of great importance is the giving of advice on ethical standards. A practitioner who observes the rules laid down by his professional body is unlikely to become involved in disciplinary proceedings. The General Medical Council publishes a series of booklets: 'Good Medical Practice', 'Confidentiality', 'Advertising' and 'Serious communicable diseases' under the general heading of 'Duties of a Doctor'. The United Kingdom Central Council for Nursing, Midwifery and Health Visiting has produced the *Code of Professional Conduct for the Nurse, Midwife and Health Visitor*. Further documents elaborate some parts of the Code, for example *The Scope of Professional Practice*. The General Dental Council issues *Professional Conduct and Fitness to Practise*. None of these publications has direct legal effect, yet they are obviously extremely influential. All of them are regularly updated.

2.37 The powers of the General Medical Council to discipline registered practitioners are set out in section 36, Medical Act 1983 and in the Medical (Professional Performance) Act 1995. Where a fully registered person is found by the Professional Conduct Committee to have been convicted in the British Isles of a criminal offence, whether while so registered or not, or is judged by the Professional Conduct Committee to have been guilty of serious profes-

---

[38] Rosenthal, MM, *The Incompetent Doctor* (Open University Press, 1995); Stacey, M, *Regulating British Medicine* (n 2 above, 1992); Robinson, J, *A Patient Voice at the GMC: a Lay Member's View of the GMC*, Report 1, Health Rights (1992); Smith, RG, *Medical Discipline: The Professional Conduct Jurisdiction of the General Medical Council 1858–1990* (Oxford University Press, 1994). 'Medical Discipline in Cross-Cultural Perspective: the US, Britain and Sweden' in Dingwall, R and Fenn, P (eds) *Quality and Regulation in Health Care* (Routledge, 1992).

sional misconduct, whether while so registered or not, the Committee may, if they think fit, either direct that his name be erased from the register, or that his registration shall be suspended for up to twelve months, or that his registration shall be conditional on his compliance for up to three years with such requirements as the Committee thinks fit to impose for the protection of members of the public or in his interests.[39]

The purpose of giving a disciplinary committee powers over a professional **2.38** who has been convicted of a crime is to protect the public and maintain the good name of the profession. The maxim that noone should be punished twice for the same offence does not apply to disciplinary proceedings.[40] A serious failure to achieve the standards expected by the profession is enough: it is not necessary to prove dishonesty or moral turpitude.[41]

It is obvious that the Professional Conduct Committee (PCC) is a powerful body. **2.39** Its membership is elected annually by the Council and consists in all of thirty two members, eighteen doctors and six lay members. Eleven members, including two lay members, sit on each case. The proceedings before the Committee are very formal: witnesses may be subpoenaed and give evidence on oath. It is usual for doctors who appear before the Committee to be legally represented. The Committee is advised by a Legal Assessor who must be a barrister, advocate or solicitor of not less than ten years' standing. There is a heavy burden of proof: the case must be proved beyond a reasonable doubt.[42] Proceedings are held in public.

Not all complaints against doctors could or should reach the PCC. There **2.40** must be a preliminary stage at which unmeritorious allegations can be excluded. The procedure is that relevant matters are brought to the notice of the Council either by a public body, such as the police, a health authority, or by a patient, doctor or member of the public. Complaints from individuals must be supported by sworn affidavits. A complaint against an NHS doctor which relates to poor practice rather than personal misconduct will be referred back to the complainant with the advice that he must first exhaust the NHS complaints procedures. The case will only be taken up by the

---

[39] Medical Act 1983, s 36; General Medical Council Preliminary Proceedings Committee and Professional Conduct Committee (Procedure) Rules 1988, SI 1988/2255; General Medical Council Professional Conduct Committee (EC Practitioners) (Procedure) Rules 1989, SI 1989/1837; GMC Health Committee (Procedure) Rules 1987, SI 1987/2174. Periods of suspension may be renewed for up to 12 months at a time, and of conditional registration for up to three years at a time.

[40] *R v Statutory Committee of the Pharmaceutical Society of GB, ex p Pharmaceutical Society of GB* [1981] 2 All ER 805, DC; *Zidermann v General Dental Council* [1976] 2 All ER 334.

[41] *Doughty v General Dental Council* [1988] AC 164, PC; *McEniff v General Dental Council* [1980] 1 All ER 461, PC.

[42] *Bhandari v Advocates Committee* [1956] 1 WLR 1442, PC.

Council if the NHS system finds against him. Initially, the matter is referred to the President who sends the matter to a medical member of the Council who acts as a preliminary screener. A decision not to proceed is taken only after consultation with a lay member. Where it is decided to proceed, the matter is referred to the Preliminary Proceedings Committee consisting of eleven members elected annually and also advised by a Legal Assessor. This Committee takes into account the written submissions of the accused doctor. Many cases of relatively minor offences, eg a conviction for shoplifting, are dealt with by sending the doctor a warning letter. Only serious cases are sent on to the Professional Conduct Committee for a full hearing.

2.41 Where the evidence discloses a possible impairment of the doctor's fitness to practise arising from a physical or mental condition, the Committee may refer the case to the Health Committee rather than the Professional Conduct Committee. This jurisdiction is to be found in section 37(1) of the Medical Act 1983. The proceedings of the Health Committee are conducted entirely in private. The Committee arranges an independent medical examination by a senior specialist. It is common for this Committee to adjourn its proceedings to allow for the doctor to receive treatment. Cases of doctors addicted to drugs or alcohol are now referred to this procedure. In *R v General Medical Council, ex p Phillips*[43] it was held that the Health Committee is entitled to seek an undertaking that the practitioner abstains from alcohol while continuing to practise, and to suspend him for breach of that undertaking.

2.42 The UKCC has a similar regulatory structure. The Nurses, Midwives and Health Visitors Act 1992 instituted some important changes. The Preliminary Proceedings Committee and the Professional Conduct Committee now have power to issue a formal caution. This will frequently be used by the Preliminary Proceedings Committee where it has been notified of a practitioner's conviction in a criminal court, but it is unnecessary for the matter to go to a full hearing. The Preliminary Proceedings Committee may also convene a hearing as a matter of urgency and order the immediate intermediate suspension of the practitioner's registration pending further disciplinary proceedings.

2.43 The UKCC places great emphasis on the accountability of nurses, midwives and health visitors for their own practice. As independent professionals they must not shelter behind the doctor. However, it is often difficult in practice for a nurse to oppose the decisions of a doctor. Only where the nurse

---

[43] [1996] 7 Med LR 31, CA. In *Finegan v GMC* [1987] 1 WLR 121, PC, it was held that a prohibition on prescribing controlled drugs or prescription only medicines was justified even though it precluded the practitioner from continuing in general practice. Subsequent periods of suspension should be used only for the purpose of monitoring the practitioner, not merely to punish him: *Taylor v GMC* [1990] 2 AC 539, PC.

considers that the doctor is 'manifestly' wrong should she be prepared to disobey instructions.[44]

2. Appeals

The doctor, but not the complainant, has the right of appeal against any decision of the PCC to the Judicial Committee of the Privy Council. The appeal includes a detailed re-examination of the evidence. However, the Privy Council is unlikely to interfere with the PCC's ruling on the scope of serious professional misconduct, confining itself to an examination of the procedure and the law applied by the PCC.[45] Decisions of the Professional Conduct Committee of the General Dental Council may also be appealed to the Privy Council, but the Privy Council has no jurisdiction with respect to the nursing profession. **2.44**

Appeal lies from any decision of the United Kingdom Central Council for Nursing, Midwifery and Health Visiting to withdraw any person from the register or alter any entry in respect of him to the High Court in England and Northern Ireland or the Court of Session in Scotland. It must be made within three months of notice of the decision of the Council. The order of the court is final. Again, it is unlikely that the court will interfere with professional judgment on what constitutes professional misconduct. Errors of procedure are far more likely to lead to a successful appeal.[46] **2.45**

In addition, an application may be made to the High Court for judicial review of the decision of a disciplinary committee. This may arise where there is an allegation of a mistake of law, or a failure to follow a fair procedure, or where there is a submission that irrelevant considerations were taken into account, or that the decision was so unreasonable that no reasonable committee could have made it. **2.46**

Where a person's name has been erased from the register, the Professional Conduct Committee of either the General Medical Council or the General Dental Council may direct that the name be restored to the register, but no application may be made within ten months of erasure, or within ten months of a previous application. The Professional Conduct Committee of the UKCC also has the power to restore a practitioner's name to the register. **2.47**

---

[44] UKCC Exercising Accountability (1989).
[45] *Libman v GMC* [1972] AC 217; *Hossack v GDC* (1997) *The Times*, 22 Apr.
[46] *Hefferon v UKCC* (1988) 10 BMLR 1; *Slater v UKCC* (1987) *The Times*, 10 June, DC; Pyne, RH, *Professional Discipline in Nursing, Midwifery and Health Visiting* (Blackwell Science, 1992).

3. Serious Professional Misconduct

2.48 The definition of serious professional misconduct (SPM) (or unworthy conduct in the case of the nursing profession) is for the profession to determine. This is, after all, a system of peer review. The phrase originates in the Medical Act 1969. Before that, the legislation referred to 'infamous conduct in a professional respect'. One important question is whether relevant conduct is confined to conduct in the practice of the profession, or whether 'extra-mural' conduct may also justify disciplinary action. In *Marten v Royal College of Veterinary Surgeons*,[47] the Divisional Court refused to interfere with the findings of the Disciplinary Committee of the Royal College of Veterinary Surgeons to the effect that cruelty to animals on a veterinary surgeon's own farm was relevant to the surgeon's fitness to practise on other people's livestock. In *Dennis v UKCC*[48] a nurse's name was removed from the register on the ground that she had committed a number of road traffic offences. It was held that the Professional Conduct Committee should have informed the nurse's representative of his error in conducting her defence solely on the basis that the criminal offences were not connected with being a nurse.

2.49 The medical profession was in the past adamant that errors of clinical judgment should not give rise to disciplinary proceedings. It is, however, often difficult to draw a line between cases where a doctor is 'ordinarily incompetent' and those where he fails in his professional duty to such an extent as to give rise to accusations of SPM. Paragraph 38 of the GMC 'Blue Book' (1993) stated that: 'The Council is concerned with errors in diagnosis and treatment, and with the kind of matters which give rise to action in the civil courts for negligence, only when the doctor's conduct in the case has involved such a disregard of professional responsibility to patients or such a neglect of professional duties as to raise a question of serious professional misconduct'.

2.50 In 1995 a gynaecologist whose surgical blunders in performing keyhole surgery caused serious injury to women patients was struck off the register. The Privy Council examined whether seriously negligent medical treatment could amount to serious professional misconduct in *McCandless v GMC*.[49] Lord Hoffman stated that it was clear that since the enactment of 'serious professional misconduct' as a disciplinary offence, the higher expectations of the public, the range of sanctions now available, and decisions since 1960 all

---

[47] [1966] 1 QB 1, DC.   [48] [1993] 4 Med LR 252, DC.
[49] [1996] 7 Med LR 379 PC; *Doughty v General Dental Council* [1988] AC 164 PC.

pointed to the conclusion that a doctor who, like Dr McCandless, had been held to have fallen deplorably short of the standard which patients were entitled to expect from their general practitioners was guilty of serious professional misconduct.

In 1995 the GMC substantially rewrote its advice on ethical practice.[50] More **2.51** emphasis has been placed on the patient's right to be consulted and involved in his treatment plan. Doctors are required to treat every patient politely and considerately, respect patients' dignity and privacy, listen to patients and respect their views and give patients information in a way they can understand. It is stressed that doctors must be able to work constructively within multi-disciplinary teams and to respect the skills and contributions of colleagues. Doctors are encouraged to provide factual information about their professional qualifications and services, but must not advertise so aggressively as to put patients under pressure.[51]

The decisions of the Professional Conduct Committee will necessarily always **2.52** reflect medical opinion. Certain offences, illegal abortion is one, a sexual relationship with a patient another, almost invariably lead to striking off the register. In 1992, Dr Nigel Cox remained on the register despite having been convicted of the attempted murder of a patient dying in intolerable pain to whom he administered an injection of a lethal drug with no pain-relieving properties.[52] Though the case was referred to the General Medical Council, the only penalty was an admonition. The doctor's employing authority imposed on him a period of supervised practice as a condition of allowing him back to work in his NHS post.

Serious cases of medical incompetence which were held not to constitute **2.53** SPM gave rise to public disquiet about the laxity of the GMC. One *cause célèbre* was that of Alfie Winn, the mascot of West Ham United Football Club. His general practitioner, Dr Archer, rudely refused to examine the seriously ill child in his home and failed to arrange appropriate specialist treatment. The child died later of meningitis. The following year Dr Archer again appeared before the PCC on another serious charge. This time he was found guilty of SPM and referred to the Health Committee.[53] Alfie's MP,

---

[50] 'Good Medical Practice'.
[51] *Colman v GMC* [1990] 1 Med LR 241 CA (a case about the advice given by the GMC in 1988 to practitioners about advertising. The advice was revised following a reference to the Monopolies and Mergers Commission which found that a complete ban on advertising was contrary to the public interest). Reference should now be made to the GMC booklet: 'Advertising' (1995). [52] *R v Cox* (1992) 12 BMLR 38.
[53] Robinson, J, *A Patient Voice at the GMC* (n 38 above). See now 'GMC Performance Procedures' (November 1995).

Nigel Spearing, proposed the creation of a second tier of disciplinary offence: unacceptable medical conduct. His 1983 Private Member's Bill failed, but led to the setting up of a GMC Working Party which reported in 1984. A second GMC Working Party reported in 1989, and in 1992 it published its recommendations in a Consultation Paper, *Proposals for New Performance Procedures*, which were adopted by the Council. These proposals are enacted in the Medical (Professional Performance) Act 1995, which came into force in 1997. Its provisions will enable the GMC to investigate cases where a doctor's standard of professional performance is alleged to be seriously deficient. The newly established Committee on Professional Performance may impose conditions on his registration for up to three years or suspend his registration for up to twelve months. The period of suspension may be renewed for further periods of twelve months and there is a power to direct indefinite suspension. The period of conditional registration may be renewed for further periods of three years.

2.54   The procedure is that a complaint about standards of professional performance will first be received by a medical member of the Council appointed as a preliminary screener who may decide to refer the matter for assessment if he concludes that there is evidence of possible serious deficiency of performance. It may be necessary for the screener to be either an expert in the same specialty or to have advice from such a person. If the medical screener decides to take no further action, a non-medical screener will be consulted. Sometimes the screener may conclude that poor performance has been the result of ill-health and cross-refer the complaint to the preliminary screener of health cases. The screener should ask whether action is being taken by another body, for example an NHS trust or a Royal College. There will be a discretion to decide whether to postpone GMC action pending the completion of such procedures.

2.55   Assessments will be carried out by Assessment Panels which have power to order the production of medical records. If necessary, a search warrant may be obtained from a magistrate. If the doctor refuses to undergo assessment the case will be referred to the Assessment Referral Committee, with power to order an assessment. The Assessment Panels will be composed of a least two doctors drawn from a panel of specialists and one lay member. The assessment is likely to include a review of the doctor's clinical record-keeping, an extended interview with the doctor, and inquiries of third parties with direct knowledge of the doctor's performance. The main purpose of the exercise will be to make recommendations for counselling, remedial action, usually further training, or limitations on practice, where these are thought to be necessary. In serious cases a doctor might be recommended to retire. Only a doctor who fails to co-operate or fails to improve will face further proceedings before the Committee on Professional Performance which may then hold a further hearing and impose sanctions as it thinks fit. It will have no power to strike a doctor off the register, but it may impose indefinite suspension of his registration. The Committee will comprise eighteen Council members, including four lay members, who will sit in panels of eight members.

As an alternative to undergoing assessment, a doctor might decide voluntarily 2.56 to remove his name from the register. If he were subsequently to apply for restoration, he would first have to complete a satisfactory performance assessment.

4. The Disciplinary Powers of the Employer

Employers are unable to deprive an employee of his professional qualifica- 2.57 tions, but they can dismiss him, or discipline him in some other way within the contract of employment.[54] A doctor who is sacked for gross misconduct or incompetence will find it difficult to obtain another post, and may find that his case has been referred to the GMC by his employer. Employees who have worked continuously for the employer for two years or more at the date of dismissal may complain to an employment tribunal that they have been unfairly dismissed under the Employment Rights Act 1996. Misconduct and incapability (including ill-health) are potentially fair reasons for dismissal, but the employer must also follow a fair procedure. For example, dismissal for misconduct will probably be held to be unfair unless the employer has made a proper investigation and allowed the employee to speak in his own defence.[55] The tribunals do not have power to force the employer to reinstate the unfairly dismissed employee, and there is an upper limit on the compensation which may be awarded. Further, the legislation does not protect the self-employed. In exceptional cases an employee dismissed by his employer in breach of contract of employment may obtain an injunction from the High Court effectively reinstating him, if only for a temporary period while an appeal against dismissal can be heard.[56]

Most health professionals, including consultants, are employed by NHS 2.58 trusts, though there is a growing private sector, and there is a minority who work for health authorities. A much more substantial number are self-employed doctors, dentists, pharmacists and opticians providing primary care. Until recently they were independent contractors of the Family Health

---

[54] du Feu, V and Warnock, O, *Employment Law in the NHS* (Cavendish Publishing Ltd, 1995).　　　　　　　　　[55] *BHS v Burchell* [1980] 1 CR303n, EAT.
[56] *Irani v Southampton and South West Hampshire HA* [1985] IRLR 203.

Services Authorities (formerly known as Family Practitioner Committees), responsible to the Regional Health Authorities. These authorities were obliged by statute[57] to arrange for the provision in their area of personal medical services. In Scotland and Northern Ireland this function is performed by Health Boards. The National Health Service (General Medical Services) Regulations 1992[58] incorporate the terms of service under which the general practitioners provide general medical services. In April 1996 the Regional Health Authorities, the District Health Authorities and the Family Health Services Authorities were abolished, and replaced by Health Authorities (often known as Health Commissions) and Special Health Authorities.[59]

2.59   The relationship between the health authority and the general medical practitioner was explored in *Roy v Kensington and Chelsea FPC*.[60] A doctor was refused the full rate of the basic practice allowance by the Family Practitioner Committee on the ground that he was not devoting a substantial amount of time to his NHS practice. The House of Lords ruled that the doctor had a bundle of private rights against the committee including the right to be paid for work done, and that these rights could be pursued through an action commenced by writ. It was not necessary to use the judicial review procedure. Both Lord Bridge and Lord Lowry said obiter that general medical practitioners did not in strict law have contracts with the family practitioner committees. In consequence, the Sex Discrimination and Race Relations Acts do not apply to appointments of general practitioners.[61]

2.60   Health professionals employed directly by health authorities and NHS trusts are employed under a contract of service, giving them the status of employees. In *R v East Berkshire Health Authority, ex p Walsh*,[62] a senior nursing officer was employed by the health authority under a contract which, with the approval of the Secretary of State under powers given him by the National Health Service Act 1977, incorporated terms and conditions jointly agreed for the health service through collective bargaining. When he was dismissed, he sought to challenge the dismissal through judicial review under Order 53 Rules of the

---

[57] National Health Service Act 1977; National Health Service and Community Care Act 1990.
   [58] SI 1992/63; NHS (General Dental Services) Regulations 1992, SI 1992/661; NHS (Pharmaceutical Services) Regulations 1992, SI 1992/662.   [59] Health Authorities Act 1995.
   [60] [1992] 1 AC 624; Fredman, S and Morris, G, 'The Costs of Exclusivity, Public and Private Re-Examined' (1994) Public Law 69.
   [61] *Wadi v Cornwall and Isles of Scilly Family Practitioner Committee* [1985] ICR 492 EAT; *Ealing, Hammersmith and Hounslow FHSA v Shukla* [1993] ICR 710 EAT. Judicial review may be granted of the Secretary of State's decision to uphold the rejection of a doctor's application to the medical practices committee to be appointed as a general practitioner in that committee's area: *R v Secretary of State for Health, ex p Gandhi* (1991) *The Times*, 23 Jan, CA.
   [62] [1985] QB 152.

Supreme Court, arguing that termination of his employment by a public body was a public law issue. The Court of Appeal rejected this argument. Breach of contract is a matter of private law, even when the employment is in the public sector with some measure of public control. Mr Walsh was directed to the industrial tribunal where he might complain that his dismissal was unfair. Health service employees have the right to complain to employment tribunals on the same basis as employees in the private sector. Since the National Health Service and Community Care Act 1990 came into force, terms and conditions of employment of those employed by NHS trusts are open to individual negotiation without interference by the Secretary of State.

Health professionals employed in the private sector are, of course, not **2.61** affected by circulars and regulations relating to the National Health Service. Private hospitals which employ staff directly may set up their own disciplinary and complaints procedures in order to be able to satisfy an employment tribunal that they treat employees fairly. However, many doctors and nurses who work in private medicine are self-employed and are therefore outside the employment protection legislation.

How will the employer discover misconduct or incompetence? Very often **2.62** through a complaint by a patient who has suffered at the hands of the practitioner. Fellow employees are usually reluctant to 'blow the whistle' on their colleagues. In general practice the partners of the problem individual may cover up for him, especially if he is undergoing a personal crisis. The professional bodies have in recent times begun to stress that there may be an ethical duty to expose incompetence or wrongdoing by colleagues for the protection of patients. The UKCC Code of Conduct, clauses 11 and 12, states that a nurse, midwife, or health visitor must report to an appropriate person or authority any circumstances in the environment of care which could jeopardise standards of practice, and any circumstances in which safe and appropriate care for patients and clients cannot be provided. The GMC in its guidance on AIDS and HIV infection[63] advises doctors that it is their ethical duty to disclose to the employer the HIV status of an infected health professional who refuses to modify practice so as to prevent the spread of infection. The GMC advises doctors that it is their duty to inform the appropriate person or body where a colleague's professional conduct or fitness to practise may be called in question.[64] And in 1995 a Working Party chaired by the Chief Medical Officer recommended that doctors in the health service should be placed under a contractual duty to report on colleagues who constitute a danger to patients.

---

[63] 1988, amended 1993 and 1997.   [64] 'Good Medical Practice' (GMC, 1995).

2.63 The Department of Health circular HC (82) 13 advises health authorities to set up a panel of senior medical and dental staff to take appropriate action on any report of physical or mental incapacity of a doctor or dentist, including addiction. A sub-committee of the panel will investigate the allegations in confidence, reporting to the Medical Director if they find cause for concern. This is familiarly known as the 'Three Wise Men' procedure. It was held to be a breach of contract to suspend a doctor until he agreed to undergo a psychiatric examination after the Three Wise Men had declared him sane.[65]

5. NHS Disciplinary Procedures

2.64 Though the relationship between the NHS trust and the employee is one of contract, the terms of the agreement are affected by collective agreements and Government circulars.[66] Where the employee is disciplined for personal conduct, that is 'performance or behaviour of practitioners due to factors other than those associated with the exercise of medical or dental skills', the matter was until recently governed by section 40 of the NHS 'Blue Book' (the General Whitley Council Conditions of Service) which applies to all employees from porters to senior medical and nursing staff. Personal misconduct includes dishonesty and the use of violence. Section 40 was replaced in March 1995 by section 42. There is, in fact, little guidance on the details of the disciplinary procedures in either section 40 or section 42. Most NHS trusts have drafted their own rules with reference to the ACAS Code of Practice on Disciplinary Practice and Procedures in Employment (1977). There should be a right of appeal from the decision of the manager to dismiss, but section 42 is less specific than section 40 about the detailed procedure for the conduct of the appeal.

2.65 Discipline for professional conduct or competence of hospital doctors was reviewed and updated by circular HC(90)9.[67] Professional misconduct is defined as 'performance or behaviour of a practitioner arising from the exercise of medical or dental skills', for example rudeness to patients. Professional competence relates to 'the adequacy of performance of practitioners related to the exercise of their medical or dental skills and professional judgment', for example negligent diagnosis or treatment. It is not clear whether the circular is binding on trusts, or for guidance only. It is, of course, neither statute nor statutory instrument. When Dr Marietta Higgs, a consultant

[65] *Bliss v SE Thames Regional Health Authority* [1987] ICR 700.
[66] Raymond, B, 'The Employment Rights of the NHS Hospital Doctor', in Dyer, C, (ed) *Doctors, Patients and the Law*, (Blackwell Scientific Publications, 1992).
[67] du Feu and Warnock (n 54 above), 118.

paediatrician, was disciplined by the Northern Regional Health Authority after she had been criticised by the Butler-Sloss report on alleged child abuse in Cleveland in 1987, Lord Donaldson MR said in argument in the Court of Appeal[68] that health authorities are bound to follow procedures laid down by the Minister (the case was eventually settled out of court), though Hutchison J had held at first instance that the procedures for investigating professional incompetence had not been incorporated into the contract.[69] The argument presumably would be that there is an implied term in the contracts of employment of health service doctors that their employer will give regard to the circular.

HC(90)9 advises the setting up of a professional review panel which normally **2.66** consists of the chairman of the Medical Staff Committee and two consultants. A fourth member is co-opted from the specialty of the defendant in the case. Referral may be made by any person and must be in writing. An informal meeting will be held; if the panel considers that there is substance in the allegation a second meeting will be arranged within the next six months. If there is no improvement, the case will be referred to the Medical Director who may decide to institute one of the disciplinary procedures.

The circular envisages two kinds of procedure: the intermediate procedure for **2.67** less serious cases and the inquiry procedure for major allegations of incompetence. The Medical Director initiates the intermediate procedure by asking the Joint Consultants' Committee to nominate assessors, and by informing the doctor of the allegations which are to be investigated. The assessors, who will be consultants from a different employing body, one from the same specialty as the accused, will take evidence in private and in the absence of the accused and then produce a report with findings of fact, findings of fault, if applicable, and recommendations as to how any mistakes might have been avoided. The Medical Director will then decide what action to take. An appeal against his decision will lie to an appeals committee similar to that appointed to deal with cases of personal misconduct.

Where serious allegations have been made, it is common for the trust **2.68** authority to suspend the doctor pending the setting up of a full inquiry. The decisions whether there is a prima facie case to answer and whether to suspend are in the hands of the trust chairman. Suspension on full pay in the past continued for lengthy periods, since the law permits the employer to remove the employee from his job as long as he continues to pay him.[70] Some

---

68 Raymond, B (n 66 above), 198.
69 *Higgs v Northern Regional Health Authority* [1989] 1 Med LR 1.
70 *Lyndon v Yorkshire Regional Health Authority* (1991) 10 BMLR 49, CA.

consultants have been suspended for many years, most notoriously Dr Bridget O'Connell, who was suspended for twelve years without any disciplinary inquiry being held before agreeing to early retirement. The 1990 circular attempts to avoid this by laying down prescribed time limits. The majority of cases should be completed within thirty two weeks.

2.69 A full inquiry should not be held if the facts are undisputed or have been established by an official inquiry or in criminal proceedings. The panel normally sits in private and follows a formal disciplinary procedure. The accused is entitled to be present, to be represented by a lawyer, and to hear and cross-examine all the witnesses against him. The panel, which consists of a legally qualified chairman and two doctors, or one doctor and a lay person in the event of an allegation of misconduct, reports on its findings of fact and its views as to whether the practitioner was at fault. It may also be asked to make recommendations about disciplinary action, but the employing body takes the decision whether or not to dismiss. In the event of a dismissal, there is the right of appeal to the Secretary of State, but this does not apply in cases of summary dismissal.[71] The procedure is laid down in paragraph 190 of the Hospital Medical and Dental Whitley Council Agreement (HC(90)(9) Annex C). The right of appeal is confined to consultants who have been dismissed for professional misconduct or incompetence. Only those who are SHMO, SHDO, Associate Specialists, Transferred Child Psychiatrists and Hospital Practitioners are included. The consultant must serve notice of appeal to the Secretary of State within four months of receiving notice of dismissal, unless it was not reasonably practicable to do so. The appeal panel is appointed by the Secretary of State and chaired by the Chief Medical Officer or his deputy. Both parties are entitled to full legal representation. The committee may uphold the dismissal, withdraw it, or direct a compromise solution agreed by the parties, for example allowing the consultant to continue under supervision.

2.70 Health professionals employed within NHS trusts are employees of the trusts, which are independent legal entities. Employees who were transferred to trusts from health authorities have the same rights against the trust as they had against the health authority which previously employed them, and this would include NHS disciplinary procedures. The National Health Service and Community Care Act 1990 makes specific provision for those who are employed to work solely at, or for the purposes of, a hospital or other establishment or facility which is to become the responsibility of the trust.[72]

---

[71] *R v Secretary of State for Health and Trent Regional Health Authority, ex p Guirgis* [1989] 1 Med LR 91.
[72] National Health Service and Community Care Act 1990, s 6.

An employee whose contract includes a mobility clause obliging him to work in a number of different hospitals, not all of which are transferred to the trust, will fall outside this,[73] and will not be able to establish continuity of employment under the statute between the old and new jobs. However, the Transfer of Undertakings (Protection of Employment) Regulations 1981[74] apply whenever there is a transfer of an undertaking in whole or in part to another employer, and provide that employees of the undertaking are automatically transferred with the undertaking and are entitled to the same terms and conditions of employment. The transfer of paediatric and neo-natal services from Grantham to Nottingham in the wake of the conviction of Beverly Allitt, a nurse at the Grantham Hospital, of the murder and attempted murder of several child patients was held to fall within the regulations.[75]

Employees of trusts may agree to vary the terms of their contracts after transfer, and new employees can be offered different terms and conditions from those previously established for NHS employees (including disciplinary and grievance procedures). The trust has power to employ staff on such terms as the trust thinks fit.[76] Thus, the Board of Directors of a trust may establish new disciplinary rules and procedures with the agreement of its staff, avoiding the cumbersome procedures set out in collective agreements and circulars. Where trades unions were recognised prior to the setting up of the trust, they must be consulted about changes in terms and conditions of employment.[77] Trusts are not to be regarded as servants or agents of the Crown and do not enjoy Crown privilege or immunity, so that the legal status of trust employees is for the most part comparable to that of employees in the private sector.[78]   **2.71**

Until recently discipline of general practitioners has to a large extent been regulated by the complaints procedure. The power of the health authority was limited to trying to ensure that the practitioner complied with the terms of   **2.72**

---

[73] *Northern General Hospital NHS Trust v Gale* [1993] ICR 638.   [74] SI 1981/1994.
[75] *Porter and Nanayakkara v Queen's Medical Centre, Nottingham University Hospital Trust* [1993] IRLR 486, EAT.
[76] National Health Service and Community Care Act 1990, Sch 2, para 16(1)(d); the Transfer of Undertakings (Protection of Employment) Regulations 1981 protect transferred employees from the imposition of different terms and conditions of employment by the transferee employer, unless for an economic, technical or organisational reason entailing changes in the workforce, *Porter and Nanayakkara v Queen's Medical Centre, Nottingham University Hospital Trust* [1993] IRLR 486; *Burke v Royal Liverpool Hospital NHS Trust* [1997] ICR 730, EAT.
[77] In the event that a trade union was not recognised elected worker representatives must be consulted, Transfer of Undertakings (Protection of Employment) Regulations 1981, SI 1981/1994 as amended by the Collective Redundancies and Transfer of Undertakings (Protection of Employment) (Amendment) Regulations 1995, SI 1995/2587.
[78] National Health Service and Community Care Act 1990, Sch 2, para 18.

his contract. Legislation to separate the handling of complaints from disciplinary action came into force in April 1996.[79] The new disciplinary procedures may only be initiated by the health authority whose list includes the practitioner's name. To this extent, the patient has lost the right to bring disciplinary procedures against the practitioner, and must be content with the complaints procedures. Health authorities should set up reference committees to make decisions whether to refer. Personnel involved with the complaints procedure should play no part in reference committees. If the health authority decides that the matter should be investigated by a discipline committee, it must refer it to the discipline committee of another health authority. Referral must be made within strict time limits, and there is no discretion to allow a case to be brought out of time. Where there has been an independent review under the complaints procedure, referral must be made within twenty eight days of receiving the report, or within thirteen weeks of the relevant act or omission by the practitioner in other cases, except where the matter concerns misconduct on the part of a dentist. In the latter case, the referral must be within six months of the completion of the relevant course of treatment, where the allegation concerns the treatment of a patient, or in other cases, within thirteen weeks of the date the matter came to the notice of the Dental Practice Board, if they have reported it, or within thirteen weeks of the matter coming to the attention of the health authority, where a report has been received from some other source.

2.73 'Disciplinary proceedings should not be used to punish genuine mistakes or conscientiously taken decisions which might, with the benefit of hindsight, have been different'.[80] It is, of course, open to the health authority where a serious breach of discipline has been discovered to refer the matter to the NHS Tribunal, the professional body, or the police. Such a referral normally halts the complaints procedure.

2.74 Documents used in the investigation of a patient complaint by an Independent Review Panel cannot be used by the health authority before the discipline committee. The health authority will have to obtain fresh statements. Discipline committees must have a legally qualified chairman, and lay members and professional members. Proceedings are in private. Legal representation is not permitted. The discipline committee reports to the health authority which decides whether to adopt its recommendations. The committee can recommend recovery of an amount from the practitioner's

---

[79] National Health Service (Service Committees and Tribunal) Amendment Regulations 1995, SI 1995/3091.
[80] 'FHS Disciplinary Procedures: A Guide for Health Authorities', NHS Executive, August 1996.

remuneration, as well as a warning. Only the practitioner may appeal to the Family Health Services Appeal Authority.

In a serious case the authority can refer the practitioner to the relevant profes- **2.75** sional body or recommend to the National Health Service Tribunal that he be removed from the list of practitioners in his area. The National Health Service (Amendment) Act 1995 has extended the powers of the Tribunal to permit it to order that the defaulting practitioner be disqualified from being engaged in the provision of any professional services listed in Part II of the National Health Service Act 1977. The NHS Tribunal can also make orders for interim suspension of NHS practitioners, if it considers it necessary to protect patients. The Chairman is appointed by the Lord Chancellor, and parties may be legally represented. Similar Tribunals have been constituted for Scotland and Northern Ireland. Appeal lies from the Tribunal to the High Court on points of law. The health authority has power, in consultation with the Local Medical Committee, to take over the running of a practice where the practitioner has been suspended, or is unable to manage it efficiently or attend to patients.[81]

C. Complaints and Inquiries

National Health Service complaints procedures were comprehensively **2.76** reviewed by a Committee chaired by Professor Alan Wilson which reported in May 1994.[82] This reflected the philosophy behind the introduction of an internal market by the National Health Service and Community Care Act 1990, with an increased emphasis on the rights of the consumer. Both the Citizen's and the Patient's Charters require effective complaints handling as a key aspect of high quality public services. The Patient's Charter (which does not have the force of law) provides that patients have the right to have any complaints about NHS services—whoever provides them—investigated, and to receive a prompt written reply from the chief executive or general manager. From 1 April 1992, health authorities and NHS authorities have had to publish details regularly of both the number of complaints and how long it has taken to deal with them.

---

[81] National Health Service Act 1977, s. 7(a); NHS (General Medical Services) Regulations 1992, SI 1992/635, reg 25(6); National Health Service (General Medical Services) Amendment (No 2) Regulations 1995, SI 1995/3093.

[82] 'Being heard', (Department of Health, 1994); Hanna, J, 'Internal Resolution of NHS Complaints' (1995) Med L Rev 177; Mulcahy and Lloyd-Bostock, S, 'Complaining—What's the Use?' in Dingwall, R and Fenn, P, *Quality and Regulation in Health Care: International Perspectives* (Routledge, 1992).

2.77 Procedures to implement the recommendations in the Wilson Report came into effect on 1 April 1996.[83] Two separate systems of complaints had evolved, one for the primary care sector and one for hospital services. This was partly for historical reasons and partly because of the different employment status of general practitioners and hospital staff. The new procedures extend to hospital, primary care and community services, as well as to complaints against purchasing authorities and private sector providers of services to NHS patients.

2.78 Most complainants are not skilled in advocacy, but the Community Health Councils can advise and in some cases provide a representative to assist the patient. Also, some NHS trusts have set up their own patient advocacy/patient friend schemes to encourage and support patients in pursuing complaints.

Primary Care

2.79 General practitioners have been encouraged to set up practice-based complaints procedures as a first step in dealing with patients' complaints. The patient who is still dissatisfied may complain to the health authority. Until 1996, the system for dealing with complaints against doctors, dentists and pharmacists was through Service Committees which had power to rule that the practitioner had breached his contract with the Family Health Services Authority, and to impose financial penalties.

2.80 New procedures separating complaints from discipline were brought into effect in April 1996. Local Resolution of complaints will be dealt with by practice-based procedures, while Independent Review panels may be appointed for complaints which remain unresolved.

Hospital Procedures

2.81 The Hospital Complaints Procedures Act 1985 did not, as its name implies, initiate comprehensive procedures, but merely placed a legal responsibility on health authorities to introduce such procedures and advertise their availability.[84] NHS trusts were placed under similar obligations by the Secretary of State acting under powers conferred by the National Health Service and Community Care Act 1990.[85]

---

[83] National Health Service (Functions of Health Authorities) (Complaints) Regulations 1996, SI 1996/669.

[84] Directions were given for implementation of the Act in HC(88)37.

[85] Sch 9, para 29.

As a result of the recommendations of the Wilson Committee, new complaints procedures following the same pattern for general practitioner services, hospital services, and community health services were introduced in April 1996. There are separate procedures for dealing with complaints about serious untoward incidents involving harm to a patient, disciplinary proceedings, physical abuse of patients, possible criminal offences and the conduct of the designated complaints officer himself. **2.82**

1. NHS Complaints Procedures

The Wilson Committee recommended that the procedures for the providers of primary and secondary care should follow the same pattern.[86] Another important change has been to separate complaints procedures from disciplinary action, although a complaint, once investigated, may lead to such action by the employer or by the professional regulatory body. Where purchasers of health care refer patients to providers in the private sector they should specify complaints requirements in their contracts. Where a trust has purchased a service, the NHS Independent Review procedure will apply. **2.83**

The Committee identified two distinct stages: Local Resolution and Independent Review. There should be a three-fold initial response to complaints: an immediate first-line response within forty eight hours of the complaint, investigation and/or conciliation, and action by an officer of the health authority for primary care services or by the Chief Executive for trusts. There should be well-publicised access for complainants to a named person such as a complaints manager. Complaints must normally be made within six months of the event, with a discretion to extend the time limit. Special attention should be paid to the needs of vulnerable groups for support and representation in making complaints. Oral and written complaints should receive the same consideration and sensitive treatment. Where the complainant remains dissatisfied or the matter is complex, there should be an investigation and the offer of conciliation. Once investigation or conciliation has taken place, a written response should be sent by a senior person to the complainant. At this stage, where the complaint relates to primary services, it will be dealt with within the relevant practice. **2.84**

Further procedures are designed to deal with complaints which are not adequately dealt with under internal procedures. The patient may feel that his complaint has not been properly investigated, or has been brushed aside. **2.85**

---

[86] Miscellaneous directions to health authorities for dealing with complaints were issued by the National Health Service Executive on 20 March 1996.

If complaints cannot be resolved by service providers, complainants have the option of asking for a further review which may include the establishment of a panel to reconsider the complaint. (The complaints procedure should cease if the complainant explicitly indicates an intention to take legal action). Such panels have a lay chair and a majority of members who are totally independent from the provider of the service. Co-operation with the new complaints procedure is now one of the NHS terms of service for primary care practitioners.[87] Independent clinical assessors will provide advice in appropriate cases. There is a time limit of one year after the event being complained about for a complaint to be made, with the discretion to waive this in appropriate cases. Community health councils continue to carry out their role in supporting claimants. Where preliminary screening by a convenor, who will be either a non-executive director of a trust or a non-executive member of a health authority, decides that a panel hearing is inappropriate, the complainant will still be able to put the case directly to the Health Service Commissioner (Ombudsman), whose jurisdiction has been extended to complaints against family health service practitioners. The Ombudsman is likely to interfere only where the convenor has failed to give reasons for the refusal, or has failed to follow a fair procedure. He cannot change the decision, but he can recommend that it be reconsidered. Where an Independent Review Panel has been convened, the Ombudsman has the power to investigate a complaint again if the procedure has been at fault, or the panel has not given a full report.

2.86   This is a new and fairer NHS complaints procedure. It has necessitated legislative changes in the existing structure of the committees which review complaints against general medical practitioners, dentists and pharmacists.[88] It has also extended mandatory procedures to complaints against purchasing authorities and services purchased for NHS patients from the private sector. The right in the Patient's Charter to receive a full and prompt written reply from the Chief Executive to any formal complaint against a trust has been retained.

2.87   Most complaints relate to the conduct of health service providers, but a minority concern the activities of purchasing authorities. However, it would be inappropriate for the complaints procedures to challenge purchasing policy as such. Only where there appears to have been specific harm or injustice caused to an individual as a result of a decision by a purchaser

---

[87] For doctors, see NHS (General Medical Services) Regulations 1992, SI 1992/635, Sch 2, as amended. The terms of service of other primary care practitioners have been similarly amended.
[88] NHS (Service Committees and Tribunal) Amendment Regulations 1996, SI 1996/703.

will it be appropriate as, for example, where a patient has been denied treatment without the health authority or GP fundholder taking proper clinical advice and engaging in proper consultation.

2. The Health Service Commissioner

The Ombudsman, as he is most often known, is empowered to receive and **2.88** investigate complaints against NHS authorities. His office is now regulated by the Health Service Commissioners Act 1993. An Act to expand his jurisdiction to cover general medical and dental practitioners and pharmacists came into force on 1 April 1996.[89] The Act also removes the greatest restriction on his powers up to now, that is his inability to investigate complaints about clinical judgment. Over the years, several committees recommended that he be given this power, most recently the Select Committee on the Parliamentary Commissioner for Administration 1993–94, *First Report: the Powers, Work and Jurisdiction of the Ombudsman* and the Review Committee on NHS Complaints Procedures (Wilson Committee) 1994.

The Commissioner can investigate avoidable delay in providing care, not **2.89** following proper procedures, rudeness or discourtesy, not explaining decisions, and failing to answer complaints fully and promptly. He can also inquire into an NHS authority's failure to provide information on request in accordance with the 1995 Code of Practice on Openness in the NHS. The Commissioner has the duty to protect patients rather than employees: he cannot look into personnel matters, like appointments or removals, pay, discipline and superannuation.

Complainants must first take up their complaint with the authority involved. **2.90** They must either be the person directly involved or someone acting on his behalf. Family members may complain on behalf of deceased or incompetent complainants. The Ombudsman cannot investigate complaints until the new NHS complaints procedure has been invoked and exhausted, other than in exceptional circumstances. The complaint must be made no later than one year from the date when the person complaining became aware of the events complained of, other than in exceptional circumstances. The investigating officer carries out his investigation in private and has the same power as a court of law to compel the disclosure of documentary and other evidence. The Ombudsman has recruited medical and nursing advisers and engages independent professional advisers to assist him with allegations relating to clinical judgment. A sample of investigations is published by HMSO every six

---

[89] Health Service Commissioners (Amendment) Act 1996.

months. There is no appeal against the findings of the Ombudsman who has no power to award damages or any other legal remedy but may make recommendations as to redress and changes in procedures.

2.91 There is a potential conflict between an investigation by the Ombudsman and legal proceedings. The Commissioner may not pursue a complaint where the complainant is likely to have a remedy through the courts unless he is satisfied that it is not reasonable to expect him to take legal proceedings, for example because the measure of damages would be very small. In addition, he may not conduct an investigation in respect of action which has been, or is, the subject of an inquiry under section 84 of the National Health Service Act 1977 or section 76 of the National Health Service (Scotland) Act 1978. These Acts empower the Secretary of State for Health to set up an inquiry into any matter arising under the National Health Service Acts.

(i) Health Authority Inquiries

2.92 The disciplinary procedure will be activated where one or more individuals can be identified as being guilty of misconduct or incompetence. In some cases blame cannot be apportioned until there is a full investigation of what has occurred. The health authority may decide to deal with such cases, particularly if they have attracted media attention, by setting up an independent inquiry with a legally qualified chairman.[90] One difficulty is that no person can be compelled to attend the inquiry or to give evidence to it, so that it may be difficult to ascertain the facts.

3. Private Medicine

2.93 Neither National Health Services procedures nor the Health Service Commissioner can have any influence on doctors and hospitals employed by paying patients. Only market forces, the professional bodies, and the courts regulate private medicine. Many private hospitals have set up voluntary complaints procedures.

4. Inquiries by the Secretary of State

2.94 The Secretary of State for Health has power to set up an inquiry into any case in connection with any matter arising under the National Health Service Act where he deems it advisable to do so, and such bodies have similar powers to

---

[90] HM (66) 15.

courts of law, in that they can compel witnesses to give evidence and order the production of documents.[91] It is power which is rarely exercised.

D. Medical Audit

Until very recently health service managers had little idea of the real costs of **2.95** medical and surgical treatments or whether they were good value for money, since research on their success or otherwise did not exist. With the introduction of an internal market in the National Health Service and Community Care Act 1990, dividing the purchaser health authorities with taxpayer's money to spend from the provider NHS trusts, it became vital to be able to assess the cost and quality of medical care. Medical audit was described in Working Paper 6, which expanded the principles laid down in the Government's White Paper, *Working for Patients*, as 'the systematic, critical analysis of the quality of medical care, including the procedures used for diagnosis and treatment, the use of resources, and the resulting outcome and quality of life for the patient'.[92] In the following year the Standing Medical Advisory Committee gave the following definition: 'A frank discussion between doctors, on a regular basis and without fear of criticism, of the quality of care provided as judged against agreed standards but in a context which allows evolutionary change in such standards'.[93] Working Paper 6 set out the aim of medical audit as 'to provide the necessary reassurance to doctors, patients and managers that the best possible quality of service is being achieved within the resources available'. The process of audit involves examining the cost of resources, like buildings and staff, the kinds of medical and surgical treatment being undertaken and the outcome of those treatments. Outcome is not merely to be measured in terms of extra years of life. The quality of that life is also important: relative mobility, freedom from pain, and relief of symptoms. Health economists have coined the term 'quality adjusted life years' (QALYS). The possible range of audit activity encompasses both random reviews of individual cases, to try to find out what went wrong, and also evaluations of specific areas of practice, such as the use of diagnostic facilities.

The medical profession, with some reservations, has welcomed audit[94], espe- **2.96**

---

[91] National Health Service Act 1977, s 84; National Health Service (Scotland) Act 1978, s 76.

[92] See further, Paton, A, 'NHS Review Working Papers—Medical Audit' *Brit J Hosp Med*, (1989) 41(4) 383; Jost, T S, 'Assessing the quality of medical practice' (Kings Fund, 1990).

[93] 'The Quality of Medical Care' (HMSO, 1990).

[94] Smith, H E, 'Medical audit: the differing perspectives of managers and clinicians' *JR Coll Physicians* (1992) 26, 177–80.

cially as part of the process of medical education, both for junior doctors and as part of a continuing education programme.[95] Money was made available by the Department of Health to introduce a national framework for audit. The duty to ensure that regular, systematic medical audit took place throughout the health service was imposed on the health authorities who place contracts for health care with the NHS trusts.[96] The purchasers will not pay for services unless the providers can demonstrate value for money. In the field of general practice, new contracts were introduced in 1990 setting out in far greater detail than ever before the services which a general practitioner must offer his patients.[97] For example, targets for vaccination and cervical smear tests must be met, or the doctor will lose part of his remuneration. Thus, the doctor will have to keep detailed records of many of his activities in order to claim payment. Wider projects evaluating the success of practitioners and treatments in primary care are undertaken by the Medical Audit Advisory Group, appointed by the health authority. All doctors must take part.

2.97 The results of medical audit in respect of individual patients must remain confidential. The need for professionals other than those caring for the patients to consider medical records in the course of audit or investigation is probably justified in law by the implied consent of the patient, but confidential information should be disseminated on a strictly 'need to know' basis.[98] Reports to managers should be anonymised. The General Medical Council gives the following guidance. 'Patients' consent to disclosure of information for teaching and audit must be obtained unless the data have been effectively anonymised'.[99]

2.98 In addition, if doctors are to co-operate they must not feel threatened by the process of audit. The Royal College of Physicians has stressed that audit must be regarded as an educational activity with the object of improving patient care.[100] A doctor who is criticised by name in an audit report might be able to sue either for defamation (libel or slander) or, if the facts are true, for breach of confidence. Truth is a complete defence to an action in defamation.[101] It is also a defence to defamation that the communication is covered by qualified

---

[95] Standing Committee on Postgraduate Medical Education (1989) 'Medical Audit: the educational implications'.

[96] Medical Audit in the Hospital and Community services HC (91) 2; Medical Audit in the Family Practitioner Services HC (FP) (90) 8.

[97] National Health Service (General Medical Services) Regulations 1992, SI 1992/635, Sch 2; Chisholm, J (ed), *Making Sense of the New Contract*, (Radcliffe Medical Press, 1990).

[98] The Protection and Use of Patient Information (Department of Health, 1996).

[99] Guidance for doctors on Confidentiality (1995), para 17.

[100] Royal College of Physicians (1989) 'Medical audit: a first report. What, why and how?'

[101] *McPherson v Daniels* (1829) 10 B and C 263.

privilege, that is that there is a legal, moral or social duty to publish potentially defamatory allegations to another.[102] Thus, if a doctor considers that the practice of a colleague gives cause for concern and should be reported to the Medical Director, he will not be liable for defamation unless he is motivated by malice[103], a desire to harm the other, rather than a proper concern for the patients. He must prove an honest belief in the truth of his statement. He should make the report only to senior management or in the course of audit. Privilege is lost if information is disseminated too widely, for example to the media.[104]

The GMC guidance on Good Medical Practice, para 18, states:　　　　　　**2.99**

> You must protect patients when you believe that a colleague's conduct, performance or health is a threat to them. Before taking action, you should do your best to find out the facts. Then, if necessary, you must tell someone from the employing authority or from a regulatory body. Your comments about colleagues must be honest . . . . The safety of patients must come first at all times.

The action for breach of confidence lies against anyone who reveals to a third　**2.100** party information which he knows was given in confidence either to him or to some other person.[105] It is, however, a defence to show that it was necessary in the public interest to make disclosure.[106] The detection and investigation of sub-standard medical practice by the proper authorities must be in the public interest. The General Medical Council has stated that there will be no direct connection between medical audit and the new procedure to investigate professional performance under the Medical (Professional Performance) Act 1995. The Council can only instigate action on receipt of a complaint. However, the health authority or trust may exceptionally make a reference to the GMC where the matter is regarded as so serious that the doctor's registration should be reviewed.

More general investigations may be undertaken by the Audit Commission,　**2.101** which examines both the accounts of NHS bodies, and the efficiency of the services provided.[107] Areas which have undergone scrutiny are mental health services (1994), hospital medical records (1995) and accident and emergency services (1996). The Clinical Standards Advisory Group investigates the standards and delivery of clinical care. It has reported on the provision of

---

[102] *Toogood v Spyring* (1834) 1 CM and R 181; *Adam v Ward* [1917] AC 309.
[103] *Horrocks v Lowe* [1975] AC 135.　　　[104] *Oddy v Lord Paulet* (1865) 4 F and F 1009.
[105] *A-G v Guardian Newspaper* [1987] 1 WLR 1248, HL.
[106] *X v Y* [1988] 2 All ER 415; *W v Egdell* [1990] Ch 359, CA.
[107] Code of Audit Practice for Local Authorities and the NHS in England and Wales (1990).

care for diabetics, maternity services and services for those with schizophrenia.[108] The Health Advisory Service advises on standards of organisation and delivery of patient care services, but will not investigate individual complaints or matters of clinical judgment. It reports directly to the Secretary of State for Health. Topics dealt with have included suicide and the homeless mentally ill.

---

[108] See assessment by Longley, D, *Public Law and Health Service Accountability* (Open University Press, 1993) 113; Director of the Health Advisory Service, Annual Report 1994–95 (HMSO, 1996).

II

CONSENT TO TREATMENT

3

CONSENT TO TREATMENT:
THE COMPETENT PATIENT

A. Consent and Battery

1. Introduction

The law relating to consent is of central importance in medical law. The **3.01** legality of a medical treatment or procedure[1] will largely turn upon whether the patient has given a valid consent to it.[2] Treatment without consent may

---

[1] Medical *treatment* involves a procedure carried out by, or on behalf of, a medical or health care practitioner for a therapeutic purpose. By contrast, a medical *procedure* includes interventions where the therapeutic intention may be absent, for example, the taking of blood to test for the benefit of others, organ or tissue donation and non-therapeutic research.

[2] But see below, paras 3.28–3.33.

amount to the tort of battery[3] or the crime of assault.[4] Consent, or more accurately the need for it, is the legal reflection of the ethical principle of respect for autonomy. In this particular context, this notion might be better expressed as respect for a person's bodily integrity stemming from a right of self-determination.[5] It is a 'fundamental principle, now long established, that every person's body is inviolate.'[6]

3.02 The law may be stated simply as follows: any intentional touching of a person is unlawful and amounts to the tort of battery unless it is justified by consent or other lawful authority. In medical law this means that a doctor may only carry out a medical treatment or procedure which involves contact with a patient[7] if there exists a valid consent by the patient (or another person authorised by law to consent on his behalf) or if the touching is permitted notwithstanding the absence of consent.[8] The legal position in England is often stated adopting the famous words of Cardozo J in *Schloendorff v Society of New York Hospital*:[9]

> Every human being of adult years and sound mind has a right to determine what shall be done with his own body; and a surgeon who performs an operation without his patient's consent commits an assault, for which he is liable in damages.

3.03 English courts have unreservedly accepted that a patient's bodily integrity in inviolable such that any physically invasive medical treatment or procedure, however trivial, is unlawful unless authorised by consent or other lawful authority.[10] In *Re F*, Lord Goff stated that:

---

[3] Battery is the intentional application of physical contact to the person without consent or other lawful justification: see *Faulkner v Talbot* [1981] 3 All ER 468 (DC) *per* Lane LCJ at 471 and *Collins v Wilcock* [1984] 3 All ER 374 (DC) *per* Goff LJ at 379. For a discussion of the elements of the tort, see Trindade, F, 'Intentional Torts: Some Thoughts on Assault and Battery' (1982) 2 OJLS 211.

[4] The crime of 'common assault' includes an assault *strico sensu* (ie, where the victim merely apprehends a 'touching') and a 'battery' where the 'touching' actually occurs: *DPP v Little* [1992] 1 All ER 299.

[5] *Malette v Shulman* (1990) 67 DLR (4th) 321 (Ont CA), *per* Robins JA at 327–8. See also *Airedale NHS Trust v Bland* [1993] AC 789; [1993] 1 All ER 821 (HL), *per* Lord Goff at 866.

[6] *Re F (Mental Patient: Sterilisation)* [1990] 2 AC 1; [1989] 2 All ER 545 (HL), *per* Lord Goff at 563. See also, *Re T (Adult: Refusal of Treatment)* [1993] Fam 95; [1992] 4 All ER 649 (CA).

[7] It would have no relevance, therefore, where the medical 'intervention' did not involve a touching even where there has been no consent; for example, causing a patient to take a drug where the patient is unaware that he is part of a research project. Contrast the US case of *Mink v University of Chicago* (1978) 460 F Supp 713 (battery action allowed to continue on these facts) which would not be followed, on this point, in England.

[8] For treatment without consent involving an incompetent patient or a child see Ch 4 below.

[9] (1914) 211 NY 125 at 126. Cited with approval in *Re F* (n 6 above), *per* Lord Goff at 564 and in *Airedale NHS Trust v Bland* (n 5 above) *per* Lord Goff at 866.

[10] eg, *Re F* (n 6 above) *Re T* (n 6 above); *Re MB* [1997] 8 Med LR 217 (CA).

It is well established that, as a general rule, the performance of a medical operation on a person without his or her consent is unlawful . . .[11]

Consequently, the medieval tort of battery—developed to deal with fist and sword fights—is the defining legal framework for determining whether a medical treatment or procedure is lawful. At one time, it was suggested that trespass to the person (here, battery) was irrelevant in the case of medical treatment because a battery could only be committed if the defendant acted with 'hostility'.[12] If this were so, rarely, if ever, would the medical treatment be caught by battery even if there was no consent because the doctor's motives would usually be *bona fide*, acting as he would be, in the best interests of the patient. This view has now been conclusively rejected by the House of Lords in *Re F.*[13] It is, as we have seen, the issues of consent or other lawful authority (if any) which are determinative of the legality of the treatment or procedure.

It is important to notice the extent of the relevance of consent. First, a valid consent licenses what would otherwise be unlawful. However, to be a valid consent, the law requires **3.04**

(1) that it be given by a competent person;
(2) that the person must be adequately informed about the 'nature' of what he is agreeing to; and
(3) that the person should be acting voluntarily and not under the undue influence of another.

Each of these requirements—competence,[14] information,[15] and voluntariness[16]—will be considered separately in this chapter. In particular, it should be noticed that the first requirement means that adults of sound mind may consent to medical treatment, as may children who are sufficiently mature, but those persons who suffer from mental disorder or disability or are immature such that they are not capable of understanding what is involved in the treatment or procedure, may not give a valid consent in law.[17]

Secondly, in such instances the law will look to another source of justification **3.05** for the treatment which may, in the case of children, be the consent of a 'proxy' such as parents or a lawful justification based upon 'necessity' to make, what would otherwise be an unauthorised touching, lawful.[18]

---

[11] N 6 above at 562. See also at 563 and *per* Lord Brandon at 550–1.

[12] *Wilson v Pringle* [1987] QB 237, *per* Croom Johnson LJ at 253. For a critisism see Kennedy, I and Grubb, A, *Medical Law* (1st edn, 1989), 172–3.

[13] N 6 above, *per* Lord Goff at 563–4. No other member of the House of Lords commented on this issue. [14] See below, 3.63–3.85.

[15] See below, 3.86–3.100. [16] See below, 3.143–3.147.

[17] See below, 3.63–3.64 (competence and adults) and Ch 4 (children).

[18] See Ch 4.

3.06 Thirdly, consent is a 'necessary' but it is not a 'sufficient' condition for a patient to be treated. A patient cannot compel a doctor or NHS Trust to provide treatment that is determined by the doctor's clinical judgment not to be in the patient's 'best interests' or which cannot be provided because of limited resources. The courts will not force a doctor or NHS Trust to treat a patient in a manner contrary to their wishes.[19] There are three reasons for this. As a matter of policy, the court will not make an order compelling a doctor to treat a patient in a manner contrary to his clinical judgment and professional duty. Also, it would be impracticable and uncertain for the court to enforce a mandatory order in this context. Finally, the courts are most reluctant to enter into investigations about the proper allocation of resources within the health service. The court will, as a consequence, simply decline to adjudicate in disputes between patients, doctors and health service institutions arising out of the denial of treatment where, in fact, the issue is one of lack of resources or the allocation of scarce resources to other patients or other forms of treatment.[20] Where the court disagrees with the views of the responsible doctor, the solution lies in finding another doctor who will act on the court's direction, rather than to coerce the patient's existing doctor.

3.07 Fourthly, in England, the courts have concluded that the burden of proving lack of consent is upon the patient. The defendant does not have to prove he consented.[21] In other words, intentional touching is not *prima facie* unlawful unless it is proved to be justified.[22] In Canada and Australia the rule is otherwise: the defendant bears the burden of proving consent.[23] In the Australian High Court, McHugh J rationalised this view as follows:

> The contrary view is inconsistent with a person's right of bodily integrity. Other persons do not have the right to interfere with an individual's body unless he or she proves lack of consent to the interference.[24]

Given the importance the law places on the inviolability of the person and the protection of bodily integrity of the individual, it is suggested

---

[19] *Re J (A Minor) (Wardship: Medical Treatment)* [1993] Fam 15; [1992] 4 All ER 614 (CA) and *Re R (A Minor) (Wardship: Medical Treatment)* [1992] Fam 11; [1991] 4 All ER 177 (CA), *per* Lord Donaldson MR at 187.

[20] *Re J* (n 19 above), *per* Lord Donaldson MR at 623, *per* Balcombe LJ at 625 and *per* Legatt LJ at 626.

[21] *Freeman v Home Office (No 2)* [1984] QB 524, *per* McCowan J at 524. The Court of Appeal did not specifically refer to the point.

[22] However, judges frequently refer to consent being a 'defence': see eg, *Collins v Wilcock* [1984] 3 All ER 374, *per* Goff LJ at 378.

[23] Picard, E and Robertson, G, *Legal Liability of Doctors and Hospitals in Canada* (3rd edn, 1996), 55.

[24] *Secretary, Department of Health and Community Services v JWB* (1992) 66 ALJR 300, 337.

that the Commonwealth view is the better one and should be adopted in England.[25]

2. Refusal of Consent

(i) *The General Principle*

Consent and refusal of consent to treatment are, as expressions of the patient's **3.08** right to self-determination, opposite sides of the same coin. Where consent to treatment is legally necessary, a refusal by a competent patient acts as a veto to the prohibited treatment.[26] For the doctor to act in the face of such a refusal would be unlawful amounting to a battery.[27] The refusal may be total: 'I don't want any treatment'; or it may be partial: 'I don't want a blood transfusion'. In either case, the refusal is legally effective to prevent the prohibited treatment even if the patient may, or will certainly, die.[28] In *Re T,* Lord Donaldson MR stated:[29]

> An adult patient who . . . suffers from no mental incapacity has an absolute right to choose whether to consent to medical treatment, to refuse it or to choose one rather than another of the treatments being offered . . . This right of choice is not limited to decisions which others might regard as sensible. It exists notwithstanding that the reasons for making the choice are rational, irrational, unknown or even non-existent.

In the same case Butler-Sloss LJ said:[30]

> A man or woman of full age and sound understanding may choose to reject medical advice and medical or surgical treatment either partially or in its entirety. A decision to refuse medical treatment by a patient capable of making the decision does not have to be sensible, rational or well-considered.

Staughton LJ also stated:[31]

> An adult whose mental capacity is unimpaired has the right to decide for herself whether she will or will not receive medical or surgical treatment, even in

---

[25] Notice the confusing approach in the criminal case of *R v Brown* [1994] 1 AC 212; [1993] 2 All ER 75 (HL), *per* Lord Jauncey at 92, Lord Slynn at 119 and Lord Mustill at 103. It may be, however, that criminal cases are unhelpful in determining upon whom the onus of proof would be in a civil context given the very limited situations where in the former a defendant bears the onus of proof.

[26] *Sidaway v Bethlem Royal Hospital* [1985] AC 871; [1985] 1 All ER 643, *per* Lord Scarman at 649.

[27] eg, *Re T* (n 6 above), *per* Lord Donaldson MR at 653. See also *Re MB,* (n 10 above) *per* Butler-Sloss LJ at 221.

[28] *Airedale NHS Trust v Bland* (n 5 above) *per* Lord Goff at 866 citing *Nancy B v Hôtel-Dieu de Québec* (1992) 86 DLR (4th) 385 (competent adult patient on ventilator entitled to refuse further intervention). See also *per* Lord Keith at 860 and *per* Lord Mustill at 889.

[29] N 6 above at 652–3.   [30] ibid, 664.   [31] ibid, 668.

circumstances where she is likely or even certain to die in the absence of treatment.

Consequently, providing the patient is competent, she may refuse any treatment including a life-saving operation such as a blood transfusion,[32] anaesthesia and surgery necessary to prevent harm to her and her unborn child,[33] and even artificial feeding.[34]

3.09 A refusal of medical treatment may be made contemporaneously or in anticipation of becoming incapacitated in the form[35] of an advance directive or, as it is sometimes known, a 'living will'.[36] The legal conditions for a valid advance directive are clear.[37] It must have been made by a patient who was competent and understood what the treatment-refusal decision entailed and it must have been intended to apply in the circumstances that subsequently arise (ie the patient's current medical condition and the procedure that is required). If the 'advance directive' is 'clearly established',[38] then it is as legally binding upon a doctor as would be a contemporaneous refusal.[39]

(ii) *The Exceptions*

3.10 There are a number of exceptions to the competent patient's right to refuse any or all medical treatments.

(a) Children

3.11 In the case of children, a parent (or other with parental authority) or the court may override the patient's refusal if that is in her best interests. In principle, this applies to competent, as well as incompetent, children although in the case of competent children it is arguable that the ability to do so is more

---

[32] eg, *Re T* (n 6 above) (held to be acting under the undue influence of her mother on facts). [33] eg, *Re MB*, (n 10 above) (held incompetent on facts).
[34] *Secretary of State for the Home Department v Robb* [1995] 1 All ER 677 and Kennedy (1995) 3 Med L Rev 189 (Commentary).
[35] The advance directive may be oral or in writing. One advantage, however, of the latter is that it is more likely to reduce evidential difficulties.
[36] For a discussion see Ch 4, paras 4.105–4.114.
[37] *Re T* (n 6 above), and See Grubb (1993) 1 Med L Rev 84 (Commentary).
[38] If there is doubt about the patient's capacity or the directive's applicability, then it seems that a doctor may act as if the patient were incompetent in his best interests, particularly if this will preserve his life: see *Re T* (n 6 above) *per* Lord Donaldson MR at 661.
[39] *Re T* (n 6 above); *Airedale NHS Trust v Bland* (n 5 above) *per* Lord Keith at 860, *per* Lord Goff at 866, *per* Lord Mustill at 892.

limited requiring a situation where serious harm or death will ensue if the child's refusal is respected.[40]

(b) Part IV of the Mental Health Act 1983[41]

There are statutory exceptions to the 'right of refusal' of a competent patient,   **3.12**
in particular, in Part IV of the Mental Health Act 1983 where the treatment is
for the 'mental disorder' of a detained patient.[42] In particular section 63
provides that:

> The consent of a patient shall not be required for any medical treatment given
> to him for a mental disorder from which he is suffering, not being treatment
> falling within sections 57[43] or 58[44] above, if the treatment is given by or under
> the direction of the responsible medical officer.

It is clear, therefore, that section 63 provides in practice a broad exception to   **3.13**
the common law rule that medical treatment may only be given to a competent adult patient with consent. Section 63 licenses what would otherwise be
trespassory touchings. It is, however, limited to patients 'detained' under the
1983 Act;[45] applies only to treatment 'for the mental disorder' (and not for
other physical ailments or conditions); and the treatment must be given 'by or
under the direction' of the RMO.

A series of cases, culminating in the authoritative decision of the Court of   **3.14**
Appeal in *B v Croydon HA*[46] has extended the scope of section 63 of the 1983
Act beyond the paradigm of medical treatment falling within it, namely that
which directly cures or alleviates the effects of the *mental disorder itself.* The

---

[40] See, *Re W (A Minor) (Medical Treatment: Court's Jurisdiction)* [1993] Fam 64; [1992] 4
All ER 627 (CA) and *Re R (A Minor) (Wardship: Medical Treatment)*[1991] 4 All ER 177 (CA).
See Ch 4.

[41] For a full discussion of Part IV see Hoggett, B, *Mental Health Law* (4th edn, 1996), ch 6;
Gostin, L, *Mental Health Services—Law and Practice* (1986), ch 20; and Jones, R, *Mental
Health Act Manual* (5th edn, 1996), 215–38.

[42] See, especially, ss 63, 58 and 62 (urgent treatment).

[43] Section 57 applies to psychosurgery and the surgical implantation of hormones to reduce
male sex drive where both consent *and* a second medical opinion are required for treatment: s
57(1)(a) and the Mental Health (Hospital, Guardianship and Consent to Treatment) Regulations 1983 (as amended), SI 1983/893, reg 16(1).

[44] Section 58 applies to ECT and medication given for more than three months where
consent *or* a second medical opinion is required: s 58(1)(b) and the Mental Health (Hospital,
Guardianship and Consent to Treatment) Regulations 1983, ibid, reg 16(2).

[45] Although it does not apply to all: see s 56(1). Part IV of the 1983 Act does not apply to a
patient 'subject to after-care under supervision' pursuant to ss 25A–I introduced by the Mental
Health (Patients in the Community) Act 1995.

[46] [1995] 1 All ER 683 (CA) and Grubb (1995) 3 Med L Rev 192 (Commentary). See also,
Riverside Mental Health NHS Trust v Fox [1994] 1 FLR 614 (Stuart-White J and CA) and Grubb
(1994) 2 Med L Rev 96 (Commentary); *Re KB (Adult) (Mental Patient: Medical Treatment)*
(1994) 19 BMLR 144 (Ewbank J) and Grubb (1994) 2 Med L Rev 208 (Commentary).

Court of Appeal accepted that section 63 applied not only to the treatment of the 'mental disorder' itself but also to its symptoms, such as a refusal to eat. The Court of Appeal noted that the 'emergency' provisions in section 62 of the 1983 Act clearly contemplates the treatment of symptoms as well as the condition itself as falling within Part IV of the 1983 Act. Also, section 145(1) of the 1983 Act defined 'medical treatment' very widely indeed and so as to include 'a range of acts ancillary to the core treatment'.[47] As a result, the courts have included medical treatments which 'treat' the *symptoms of the mental disorder*, for example, force-feeding an anorectic patient who refused food,[48] force-feeding a patient with borderline personality disorder whose compulsion to self-harm led her to refuse food[49] and force-feeding a suicidal depressive who refused food and water.[50]

3.15 In each of the cases, the condition that was to be treated (the need for food and/or water) was directly related to the patient's mental disorder.[51] It was a manifestation of the mental disorder itself and thus should not be distinguished from it. The mental disorder caused the need for treatment in each of the cases. In one case, however, the court went further. In *Tameside and Glossop NHS Trust v CH*,[52] the patient was a paranoid schizophrenic detained under the 1983 Act. She was found to be pregnant. By the thirty-first week of pregnancy, there was evidence of intra-uterine growth retardation, and her obstetrician was of the opinion that an induced labour might become necessary to safeguard the life of the foetus. However, as a long term sufferer of schizophrenia, she was prone to delusions, and had resisted some of the attempts to monitor her pregnancy in the belief that her obstetrician and psychiatrist were intent on harming the baby. Her doctors applied to the court for a declaration that it would be lawful to carry out obstertric intervention, including a Caesarian section. The patient's consultant psychiatrist gave evidence first, giving the opinion that stillbirth (the alternative to the procedures) would lead to a profound deterioration in the patient's mental health; and secondly, that the pregnancy had interrupted the patient's treatment with strong anti-psychotic medication because of the dangers to her foetus. Wall J concluded on the basis of this evidence that the treatment of the patient's pregnancy fell within section 63. He said:

---

[47] *B v Croydon HA* (n 46 above), *per* Hoffman LJ at 687–8. See also *per* Neill LJ at 689–90.
[48] *Riverside Mental Health NHS Trust v Fox*, (n 46 above), and *Re KB (Adult) (Mental Patient: Medical Treatment)* (n 46 above).   [49] *B v Croydon HA* (n 46 above)
[50] *Re VS (Adult: Mental Disorder)* (1995) 3 Med L Rev 292 (Douglas Brown J).
[51] Contrast *Re C (Adult: Refusal of Medical Treatment)* [1994] 1 All ER 819 (Thorpe J) and Grubb (1994) 2 Med L Rev 93 (Commentary) where the mentally disordered patient's physical condition (gangrene) was 'entirely unconnected with the mental disorder', *per* Hoffman LJ in *B v Croydon HA* (n 46 above), 688.
[52] [1996] 1 FLR 762 and Grubb (1996) 4 Med L Rev 194 (Commentary).

[I]t is not . . . I think stretching language unduly to say that achievement of a successful outcome to her pregnancy is a necessary part of the overall treatment of her mental disorder.

Nevertheless, the decision must be questionable especially on the latter basis that the termination of the woman's pregnancy was treatment 'for [her] mental disorder' because she was unable to receive the appropriate medication until then.[53]

Consequently, there are a number of situations which could arise where a   **3.16** detained patient is in need of medical treatment (broadly defined in section 145 of the 1983 Act to include 'nursing' and also 'care, habilation and rehabilitation under medical supervision'):

(i) where the treatment is given to treat directly the mental disorder, for example, psychotropic medication (within s 63);

(ii) where the treatment is for a physical condition which is causing or contributing to the mental disorder, for example, a brain tumour producing or contributing to psychological effect (within s 63);

(iii) where the treatment is given to alleviate the symptoms or consequences of (and which are related to) the mental disorder, for example, force-feeding where the patient's mental disorder leads to a refusal of food and/or water or stomach pumping following an attempted suicide (within s 63[54]);

(iv) where the treatment is for a condition (usually physical) which is unrelated to the mental disorder, for example, an appendectomy (not within s 63). The mental disorder is only relevant to the patient's competence to make the decision to refuse the treatment.[55]

(c) Necessity and Unknown Competence

Interventions (including medical treatment) may be justified at common law to   **3.17** the extent that it is reasonable to do so in the circumstances, and providing what is done is reasonable, where the competence of the individual is unknown. The common law justification of 'necessity' would come to the aid of the doctor. It would not be illegal, for example, to temporarily restrain a 'jumper' in order to ensure their intentions and competence. Likewise, an apparent suicide victim may be treated to save her life unless it is absolutely clear that the patient was both attempting to kill herself and was competent at the time to make that decision.[56]

---

[53] See Grubb, (1996) 4 Med L Rev 193, 194–8 (Commentary).
[54] After *B v Croydon HA* (n 46 above).
[55] *Re C (Adult: Refusal of Medical Treatment)* (n 51 above).
[56] For an explanation which would extend further, see Skegg, P D G *Law, Ethics, and Medicine* (1984), 110–16. The more recent recognition of a competent patient's right to refuse all treatment has, probably, superseded Professor Skegg's suggested explanation. But note the reference by Butler-Sloss LJ in *Re T* to 'preventing suicide' (n 6 above) at 665.

Even if it subsequently transpired that she was competent and wished to kill herself, the intervention would still be legal.[57] Faced with a patient in a casualty department who has taken a drugs overdose, a doctor would be entitled to entertain these doubts and so act 'out of necessity' to save her life, albeit on a temporary basis.

(d) Public Policy

3.18 Finally, the common law may justify interventions against a competent patient's wishes in wholly exceptional circumstances on the grounds of public policy.[58] Consequently, a patient could not refuse measures designed to maintain basic hygiene and pain relief.[59] The explanation for this is two-fold: the patient may not require his carers, in effect, to abandon him and also the interests of third parties—such as nurses and others affected by the consequences of the patient's decision to 'turn his back to the wall'—outweigh his interests in this singular situation.[60]

3. Withdrawal of Consent

3.19 The law's recognition and protection of the inviolability of the patient's bodily integrity includes the right to withdraw consent after it is given. A withdrawal of consent is indistinguishable, in principle, from an initial refusal of consent. To continue treatment after a patient has validly withdrawn his consent will be unlawful as a battery. There is no relevant English case. However, the issue was considered by the Canadian Supreme Court in *Ciarlariello v Schacter*[61] and there is no doubt that the decision reflects English law.[62]

3.20 The plaintiff was diagnosed with a suspected aneurism. She underwent a diagnostic cerebral angiogram. During the procedure she experienced discomfort and hyperventilation and she asked the doctor to stop which he did. When she had calmed down, the plaintiff told the doctor to continue the procedure. She suffered a rare reaction to the dye which was injected during the course of the procedure. The plaintiff sued the doctor, *inter alia*, for battery alleging that she had withdrawn her consent during the procedure and

---

[57] Of course, if the patient was known to be suffering from a mental disorder which rendered her incompetent, there would be no legal difficulty in treating her under the common law or, if detained, under section 63 of the Mental Health Act 1983 (latter applying even if she is competent): see para 3.14 above and *Re VS (Adult: Mental Disorder)* (1995) 3 Med L Rev 292.   [58] See Kennedy, I and Grubb, A, *Medical Law* (2nd edn, 1994), 1277.
[59] Notice the Law Commission's proposals in relation to anticipated refusals of treatment: Law Commission Report No 251, *Mental Incapacity*, 1995, para 5.34 and Draft Bill, cl 9(7)(a) and (8).   [60] See Grubb, (1993) 1 Med L Rev 84, 85 (Commentary).
[61] (1993) 100 DLR (4th) 609 (SCC) and Kennedy, (1994) 2 Med L Rev 117 (Commentary).   [62] Kennedy, ibid, 118.

its continuation amounted to a battery. The Supreme Court dismissed her action for battery. The court accepted that a patient had a right to withdraw her consent during a procedure. Cory J stated:[63]

> An individual's right to determine what medical procedures will be accepted must include the right to stop a procedure. It is not beyond the realm of possibility that the patient is better able to gauge the level of pain or discomfort that can be accepted or that the patient's premonitions of tragedy or mortality may have a basis in reality. In any event, the patient's right to bodily integrity provides the basis for the withdrawal of a consent to a medical procedure even while it is underway. Thus, if it is found that the consent is effectively withdrawn during the course of the procedure then it must be terminated.

The Court noted that a consent could only validly be withdrawn if the patient was, in law, capable of doing so. A patient's capacity to withdraw consent, just as his capacity to consent, might be affected by the circumstances. Cory J stated that:[64] **3.21**

> If sedatives or other medication were administered to the patient, then it must be determined if the patient was so sedated or so affected by the medication that consent to the procedure could not effectively have been withdrawn. The question whether a patient is capable of withdrawing consent will depend on the circumstances of each case. Expert medical evidence will undoubtedly be relevant, but will not necessarily be determinative of the issue.

Also, the court must decide whether the patient had, in fact, withdrawn his consent. Cory J said: **3.22**

> The words used by a patient may be ambiguous. Even if they are apparently clear, the circumstances under which they were spoken may render them ambiguous. On some occasions, the doctors conducting the process may reasonably take the words spoken by the patient to be an expression of pain rather than a withdrawal of consent.[65]

Cory J referred to two Canadian cases where contrasting views were taken on the evidence before the courts. In *Mitchell v McDonald*,[66] the plaintiff during a cortisone injection into a chest muscle cried out 'For God's sake stop'. Cory J regarded as 'reasonable' the trial judge's view in that case that the plaintiff's exclamation was a 'cry of pain' equivalent to 'My God, stop hurting me', rather than an attempt to withdraw consent.[67] By contrast, in *Nightingale v Kaplovitch*[68] the patient was undergoing a sigmoidoscopic examination which had become extremely painful and screamed 'Stop, I can't take this any more'. **3.23**

---

[63] *Ciarlariello v Schacter* (n 61 above), 619. [64] ibid, 619–20.
[65] ibid, 618. [66] (1987) 80 AR 16 (Alta QB).
[67] n 61 above, 618 *per* Cory J. [68] [1989] OJ No 585 (QL) (HC).

The doctor continued and was held liable in battery as this amounted to a valid withdrawal of consent by the patient.

3.24   In the *Ciarlariello* case it was recognised that the patient's right meant that it was incumbent upon a doctor, where there was any question that the patient was attempting to withdraw his consent, to enquire whether this was the case, and not blithely continue.[69] Although the Court did not spell out the implications of not doing so, they are obvious. Continuation in the face of what is subsequently interpreted as a withdrawal of consent will be a battery.

3.25   The Canadian Supreme Court acknowledged that the 'right' to withdraw consent was not absolute where the effect of terminating: 'would be either life threatening or pose immediate and serious problems to the health of the patient'.[70] In this situation, presumably, the Court took the view that as a matter of public policy the 'refusal' is not valid because of the doctor's overriding duty of care to the patient which would be breached if such serious harm occurred. However, nowhere in the judgment is the basis of this limitation on the 'right' spelt out. Clearly, it must be limited to allowing continued intervention to secure the patient from the immediate peril, and not necessarily completion of the procedure, when the patient's 'right' will again take precedence. In practical terms, of course, the 'right' to withdraw during a procedure cannot apply to major surgical operations performed under general anaesthetic and is limited to more minor surgery or diagnostic procedures (as in *Ciarlariello* itself) performed, at worst, under a local anaesthetic, and it may be, therefore, that the limitation will not usually apply.

3.26   On the facts, the Court held that the plaintiff had validly withdrawn her consent but this had been complied with by the doctors. The only issue remaining for the court was whether the procedure had been lawfully recommenced. For the court this meant, first, whether there had been a valid consent, and secondly, whether the patient had been sufficiently informed for the purposes of negligence. Cory J concluded both questions in the defendants' favour:[71]

> . . . the patient may still consent to the renewal or continuation of the process. That consent must also be informed. Although it may not be necessary that the doctors review with the patient all the risks involved in the procedure, the patient must be advised of any material change in the risks which has arisen and would be involved in continuing the process. In addition, the patient must be informed of any material change in the circumstances which could alter his or her assessment of the costs or benefits of continuing the procedure. Here, there had been no material change in the circumstances and a valid consent was given to the continuation of the process.

---

[69] n 61 above, *per* Cory J at 618.   [70] ibid, *per* Cory J at 619.   [71] ibid, 624.

In England, the law would similarly require that the patient should give a   **3.27**
valid consent to continuation and also would impose a duty to provide
information relevant to that decision. The content of that duty would be a
matter for the law of negligence and an application of the *Sidaway* decision.[72]
While medical evidence of actual (or potential) practices would be highly
influential, it would not be determinative.

4. Limits to Consent

(i) *The General Approach*

Thus far it has been stated that the presence of a patient's consent[73] determines   **3.28**
the legality of a medical treatment or intervention. In the context of a *tort* action
in battery, the patient's consent (or that of an appropriate proxy) is a sufficient
condition for legality. The public policy considerations which apply in criminal
law to limit the extent of harm that a person may legitimately consent to have
little impact on the civil law, concerned as it is with compensation for, rather
than prohibition of, harm.[74] However, a medical intervention may also amount
to the crime of assault or an aggravated form of it under sections 47, 20 and 18
of the Offences Against the Person Act 1861. In England, a person may not
consent to anything which is intended to, or which does, cause more than actual
bodily harm.[75] Of course, many surgical interventions cause serious injury even
though the doctor's intention is to benefit the patient—unlike the usual violent
offender charged under the 1861 Act. English law could take the view that
'medical treatment' is wholly outside the violence offences of the 1861 Act
because the effects of surgery do not amount to 'injury' or 'harm' when viewed
in their totality or in the light of the doctor's intention.[76] The law does not,
however, adopt that approach.[77] Instead, it assumes the doctor's actions do
prima facie fall within the criminal prohibition but then creates a specific
exemption from the law's refusal to accept consent as a defence to anything
which amounts to more than actual bodily harm.[78] In *Attorney-General's*

---

[72] See below, 3.101–3.138.
[73] Or that of a proxy acting in the patient's 'best interests'.
[74] See Skegg (n 56 above), 39.
[75] *R v Brown* [1994] 1 AC 212; [1993] 2 All ER 75 (HL).
[76] See Skegg (n 56 above), 30–2.   [77] *R v Brown* (n 75 above).
[78] The exception should extend to any qualified *health care practitioner*, for example, a
dentist or nurse who is acting within their area of competence (ie providing they have the
appropriate qualification, clinical competence, and professional regulation). Examples arise
under the Medicinal Products: Prescription By Nurses etc Act 1992 and the Medicines
(Products Other than Veterinary Drugs) (Prescription Only) Order 1983, SI 1983/1212 as
amended), Art 9(2) and Sch 3, Part III creating an exception to s 58(2)(b) of the Medicines Act
1968.

Reference (No 6 of 1980),[79] Lord Lane CJ stated that 'reasonable surgical interference' fell outside the criminal law.[80] Subsequently in *Airedale NHS Trust v Bland*, Lord Mustill stated the 'medical exception' as follows:

> . . . proper medical treatment stand[s] completely outside the criminal law. The reason why the consent of the patient is so important is not that it furnishes a defence in itself, but because it is usually essential to the propriety of medical treatment. Thus, if consent is absent, and is not dispensed with in special circumstances by operation of law, the acts of the doctor lose their immunity.[81]

3.29 In *R v Brown*,[82] the House of Lords accepted the existence of the 'medical exception' and Lord Mustill remarked that 'proper medical treatment . . . is in a category of its own'.[83] Thus, there is no doubt that the consent of a patient to 'proper medical treatment' is valid notwithstanding that the procedure will cause injury which the patient could not otherwise lawfully consent to.

(ii) *Therapeutic Procedures*

3.30 The scope of the 'medical exception' remains unclear.[84] In large part this is because a wholly satisfactory account of the basis of the 'medical exception' is elusive, although it must lie in public policy. It is suggested that, in general, the legitimising criterion for an invasion of bodily integrity must be the doctor's 'therapeutic purpose' or his 'intention to benefit' the patient.[85] The criterion is that the procedure is *intended* to be therapeutic/beneficial to the patient, not whether it *did* actually benefit the patient. The crucial question, in determining whether an intervention falls within the medical exception, must be the doctor's *purpose* given the patient's decision to consent to the procedure reflecting his judgment about its therapeutic or beneficial character.

3.31 Obviously, within this context, the reference to 'benefit' solely relates to a benefit to the patient's *life or physical or mental health*.[86] Consequently, a patient could not consent to serious injury, for example the amputation of a leg, in order to enhance her financial interests.[87] A contrasting case which though superficially similar, falls clearly on the other side of the line, would

---

[79] [1981] QB 715; [1981] 2 All ER 1057 (CA). [80] ibid, 1059.
[81] [1993] 1 All ER 821, 889. [82] [1993] 2 All ER 75. [83] ibid, 110.
[84] See Skegg (n 56 above), ch 2 and Williams, G, *Textbook of Criminal Law* (2nd edn, 1983), 589–91. [85] See Kennedy and Grubb (n 58 above), 245–51.
[86] See the Prohibition of Female Circumcision Act 1985, s 2(1)(a) drawing the line between legitimate and criminal activity at an operation which is 'necessary for the *physical or mental health* of the person on whom it is performed . . .'.
[87] See the guarded comment of Neill LJ in *Re F (Mental Patient: Sterilisation)* [1990] 2 AC 1, 29.

be where the patient wishes desperately to be rid of his leg, the presence of which he says is causing him severe distress. If the surgeon performs the amputation, honestly intending to benefit the patient's mental health, while many might disagree with that decision, it is not for the criminal law to second guess the patient's own determination of their health interests.

Providing the therapeutic purpose exists, a patient may consent to serious **3.32** injury, for example, gender re-assignment surgery.[88] A patient's consent to a procedure will also be valid even if it exposes him to the risk of death providing the procedure, on balance, is in his best medical interests, for example, heart transplant surgery.[89] Of course, if the patient dies as a result of the surgeon's gross negligence, he might be guilty of manslaughter regardless of the validity of the patient's consent.[90]

(iii) *Other Procedures*

This account does not, however, deal with all procedures which appear to fall **3.33** within the medical exception. A number of procedures, though not necessarily intended for the medical benefit of the individual, are widely regarded as socially acceptable and ones to which the individual may consent: research,[91] donation of organs and tissue,[92] contraceptive sterilisation,[93] abortion,[94] and cosmetic surgery. No doubt the courts would accept—and already do accept—an individual's consent to such procedures. There would, of course, be limits: the courts would not allow a person to donate his heart if, as it usually would, this would lead to his death.[95] There is no 'golden thread' or commonality which would explain this collection of procedures other than that they are currently socially acceptable and thus, as a matter of public

---

[88] *Corbett v Corbett (Otherwise Ashley)* [1971] P 83.

[89] *R v Hyam* [1975] AC 55 (HL) at 74 and 77–8 *per* Lord Hailsham.

[90] *R v Adomako* [1995] AC 171; [1994] 3 All ER 79 (HL) and Grubb (1994) 2 Med L Rev 362 (Commentary).

[91] The propriety of non-therapeutic research in prescribed circumstances is recognised in the European Convention on Human Rights and Biomedicine (1996), Arts 16 and 5, and *Local Research Ethics Committees* (DoH, 1991, HSG(91)5), paras 3.7–3.10.

[92] The Human Organ Transplants Act 1989, s 2, and the Human Organ Transplants (Unrelated Persons) Regulations 1989, SI 1989/2480.

[93] Originally the National Health Service (Family Planning) Act 1967; now National Health Service Act 1977, s 5(1)(b). Contrast the comments of Denning LJ in *Bravery v Bravery* [1954] 1 WLR 1169 at 1180–1 which no longer can be taken seriously as representing public policy: *Cataford v Moreau* (1978) 114 DLR (3d) 585.   [94] Abortion Act 1967.

[95] Contrast the procedure known as a 'domino transplant' where a person in need of a lung transplant for medical reasons receives both lungs and a new heart, making his heart available for donation.

policy, they are, or would be, recognised by the judges as lawful. Without statutory guidance,[96] the courts can do no better than to deal with each procedure, as and when it comes before them, and apply their sense of what are the proper limits of public policy.[97]

B. The Nature of Consent

1. Forms of Consent

3.34 Consent is a state of mind personal to the patient whereby he agrees to the violation of his bodily integrity.[98] Not every agreement to undergo treatment is, in law, a valid consent because it may be based upon inadequate information to make a meaningful decision whether to undergo the procedure[99] or it may be the product of circumstances, or others' desires, which render the decision involuntary or one which is not really the patient's because of undue influence.[100]

3.35 A patient's consent need not be given in writing. The common law does not impose such a requirement, although in analogous circumstances statutory provisions may do so.[101] However, "consent" are routinely used in hospitals when a patient undergoes a surgical intervention.[102] They do not, as is sometimes assumed within the medical profession, in themselves constitute a patient's consent. Their function, in law, is purely evidentiary. In stating that the patient has agreed to a particular procedure which has been explained to him and which he has understood, the "consent" will not be worth the paper it is written on if these recitations are not, in fact, true. It is the patient's *actual state of mind* which is crucial. Consent expressed 'in form only' is no consent at all.[103] An identical approach is called for in respect of forms which purport to

---

[96] The Law Commission has provisionally proposed a statutory base, including a statutory list of 'borderline' procedures, for the exception: see *Consent and the Criminal Law*, Consultation Paper No 139 (1995), Part VIII.

[97] Jurisdictions with Criminal Codes often seek to deal with the 'medical exception' albeit in general terms: see, ss 61 and 61A, Crimes Act 1961 (NZ); ss 45 and 216, Criminal Code (Can); ss 282 and 288 Criminal Code (Qld). For a discussion of the latter, see O'Regan, R S, 'Surgery and Criminal Responsibility under the Queensland Criminal Code' (1990) 14 Crim LJ 73.

[98] *Sidaway v Bethlem Royal Hospital Governors* [1985] 1 All ER 643, 658 *per* Lord Diplock.

[99] See below, paras 3.86–3.100.   [100] See below, paras 3.86–3.100.

[101] Human Fertilisation and Embryology Act 1990, Sch 3. Discussed below, Ch 10.

[102] Model consent forms are recommended by the Department of Health in England: see *A Guide To Consent for Examination or Treatment* (DoH, 1990, HC (90)22 as amended by HSG (92)32), Appendix A.   [103] *Chatterton v Gerson* [1981] 1 All ER 257, 265 *per* Bristow J.

record a patient's refusal of treatment, for example, of a blood transfusion. Speaking of such forms in *Re T,* Lord Donaldson MR stated:[104]

> They will be wholly ineffective . . . if the patient is incapable of understanding them, they are not explained to him and there is no good evidence (apart from the patient's signature) that he had that understanding and fully appreciated the significance of signing it.

(i) *Express Consent*

(a) Actual Consent

A patient's consent may be express or implied. Express consent is often treated **3.36** as synonymous with *expressed* consent, that is where the patient demonstrates orally or in writing that he agrees to the treatment or procedure. While this will often be the case, it is sometimes misleading to regard it in these terms. More accurately, the issue is whether the patient has given *actual* consent to the treatment or procedure whether or not this is demonstrated orally or in writing. Consent is, as was seen earlier, a state of mind of the patient. A valid legal consent is given even where the patient does not demonstrate his agreement providing that the state of his mind was, in fact, that he agreed. In other words, an unexpressed *actual* consent is, in law, a valid consent. Of course, there may be evidential difficulties in establishing the patient's actual consent if it is not *expressed* but this does not detract from the analysis of what consent, in law, really is.

(b) Implied and Inferred Consent

Any other form of consent—such as *implied* consent—is strictly speaking not **3.37** a 'consent' given by the patient at all.[105] So, where the patient conducts himself such that it is reasonable to *imply* that he consented to the treatment or procedure, the law merely prohibits the patient because of his conduct from denying that he consented even though, in fact, he did not.[106] This is not to say that consent cannot be *inferred* from the patient's conduct and behaviour: it can be, but it should be distinguished from *implied* consent.[107] The latter is a legal device whereby the legality of a treatment or procedure is recognised even though the patient does not, in fact, consent. A patient who allows a doctor to carry out a procedure in full knowledge of what is to be done will have given *actual* consent to the procedure. His consent is not

[104] [1992] 4 All ER 649, 663.   [105] See below, para 3.40.
[106] *Sidaway v Bethlem Royal Hospital Governors* [1985] 1 All ER 643, 658 *per* Lord Diplock.
[107] Kennedy, I and Grubb, A, *Medical Law* (2nd edn, Butterworths, 1994), 101–4.

implied but rather *inferred*. Evidentially, the fact that the patient did not express his consent is not conclusive. Rather, faced with these facts, what other inference is it proper for the court to make other than that the patient was actually consenting.

(ii) *Implied Consent*

3.38 The outward appearance and conduct of the patient may lead to the conclusion that the patient has consented to the treatment or procedure. In these circumstances, it is said that the patient's consent is *implied* and the doctor has a defence to an action in battery. The classic illustration is found in the US case of *O'Brien v Cunard SS Co.*[108] The plaintiff was vaccinated against smallpox by a surgeon on board a boat bound for Boston. She joined a line of passengers whom the surgeon was examining and vaccinating if necessary. When the surgeon told her she should be vaccinated she held out her arm and he did so. She sued claiming battery on the basis that she had not consented to the vaccination. The Supreme Judicial Court of Massachusetts dismissed her action. The court held that her consent should be implied from the circumstances and her conduct. Knowlton J said:[109]

> If the plaintiff's behavior was such as to indicate consent on her part, [the surgeon] was justified in his act, *whatever her unexpressed feelings may have been.* In determining whether she consented, he could be guided only by her overt acts and the manifestations of her feelings.

3.39 Properly understood, *O'Brien* is almost certainly a case of *inferred* consent. It might be thought that the plaintiff's conduct irresistibly led to the inference that she actually had consented to the vaccination. What else was she doing in the line, having spoken to the surgeon, holding her arm out. However, as the emphasised words from Knowlton J's judgment show, the court seems not to have inferred that she actually consented. Rather, he conceded that she did not but nevertheless debarred her from relying upon that because of the circumstances and her behaviour: her consent was *implied*.[110] On the facts, no doubt the court was influenced by the fact that notices had been posted around the ship in various languages that day to indicate the need for vaccination; the plaintiff had stood in line and seen what was happening to other passengers and she had not offered any objection to the surgeon when he went to vaccinate her.

---

[108] (1891) 28 NE 266 (Mass Sup Jud Ct).   [109] ibid, 266 (emphasis added).
[110] See also *Allan v New Mount Sinai Hospital* (1980) 109 DLR (3d) 634, 641 *per* Linden J.

Thus, it is suggested that implied consent is not a species of consent at all. To **3.40** describe the situation in the *O'Brien* case as one of consent would be fictional. Rather, implied consent is more properly understood as a species of estoppel.[111] Where the patient so conducts himself in the circumstances that it is reasonable to conclude that he has consented to a treatment or procedure, the patient will not subsequently be permitted to rely on the fact that he did not actually consent. The doctor will have a defence to what would otherwise be an unlawful touching based upon the patient's implied consent.

Whether a patient will be taken to have impliedly consented to a particular **3.41** treatment or procedure will be a question of fact in every case. Where a *reasonable* person looking on to the situation would conclude that the patient had agreed to the intervention, even if the patient has not, the doctor will have a defence based upon implied consent.[112] It would be dangerous for a doctor to conclude that a patient's silence alone constituted agreement. The issue is one of reasonable deduction based upon all the circumstances, in particular, taking account of the patient's conduct and anything known about the patient.

Implied consent is frequently relied upon by doctors as a justification for **3.42** carrying out treatments or interventions upon patients. The extent to which consent may be implied is, often, controversial.[113] Given that implied consent, though no consent at all, nevertheless licenses an interference with the patient's right of self-determination, the circumstances necessary to impute it require a clear (perhaps unequivocal) indication that the patient appeared to be giving his consent.[114] Some situations, however, should not be analysed as ones where the patient has impliedly consented: two, in particular, are important. Traditionally, it has been argued that treatment of an unconscious or otherwise incompetent patient may be justified on the basis of implied consent.[115] As regards the former, it has been said that the patient would agree to an intervention which was in their 'best interests' if they were able and so their consent to the intervention may be implied.[116] Clearly, the implication or inference of consent is inappropriate where the patient is unable to consent due to incompetence. It is particularly artificial in the case of patients whose

---

[111] *Sidaway v Bethlem Royal Hospital Governors* [1985] 1 All ER 643, 658 *per* Lord Diplock.

[112] See e g *Canadian AIDS Society v Ontario* (1995) 25 OR (3d) 388 ('reasonable blood donor test' used).

[113] e g, in the context of HIV testing, see Grubb, A and Pearl, D, *Blood Testing, AIDS and DNA Profiling—Law and Policy* (Jordans, 1991), 11–13.

[114] *Schweiser v Central Hospital* (1974) 53 DLR (3d) 494, 508 *per* Thompson J.

[115] e g Skegg, P D G, 'A Justification for Medical Procedures Performed Without Consent' (1974) 90 LQR 512. Professor Skegg's more recent views rest more strongly on the doctrine of necessity: see his *Law, Ethics and Medicine* (n 56 above) ch 5.

[116] See e g *Mohr v Williams* (1905) 104 NW 12 (Minn Sup Ct).

mental disability is permanent to justify, for example, sterilisation of mentally disabled women.[117] The more appropriate legal justification in these cases is the principle of necessity as recognised by the House of Lords in *Re F* and not implied consent.[118]

3.43 Implied consent is also often utilised by doctors to justify treatment or interventions which are considered to be routine by the medical profession. For example, diagnostic tests are regularly performed during maternity care without the explicit consent of the patient. Other examples[119] might include procedures carried out by students as part of their training.[120] To what extent does the law accept that a patient has impliedly consented to interventions of this kind when, *a fortiori*, the patient has not given actual consent? The answer will depend upon the circumstances.

3.44 It will only be proper to imply consent if the reasonable onlooker would conclude, albeit wrongly, that the patient had agreed to the intervention. As a basic minimum, this should require that the patient be given notice of the possibility of the 'extra' intervention and be given an opportunity to 'opt out' which is not taken. Hence, where information sheets or prominent notices in doctors' surgeries or clinics indicate what may occur, a reasonable onlooker might well conclude that a patient had tacitly agreed if he remains silent and does not exercise his right to 'opt out'.[121] The implication is not, of course, dependent upon the patient having *read* the information sheet or notice providing reasonable steps were taken to bring the information to the patient's attention and the information was presented in a reasonable manner (ie visible and intelligible to the average reader). Merely being in a teaching hospital would not, on this basis, be sufficient to give rise to an implication that students may engage in touchings for their own benefit. That fact would have to be brought to the patient's attention or reasonable steps be taken to do so.

3.45 Importantly, consent should not be implied unless the patient has had an opportunity (if the notice etc is read) to opt out of the 'extra' intervention.[122] Otherwise, it would not, it is suggested, be reasonable to imply the patient's

---

[117] See *Re F (Mental Patient: Sterilisation)* [1989] 2 All ER 545, 563 *per* Lord Goff.
[118] See below Ch 4.
[119] An analogous situation is the use of medical records for research, especially epidemiological research.
[120] This should not, however, be done without the explicit (ie actual/expressed) consent of the patient: *Medical Students in Hospitals* (1991, HC (91)18). See also, *The Patient's Charter & You* (DoH, 1995), 6.
[121] Analogous situations may be the use of confidential information (*The Protection and Use of Patient Information* (DoH, HSG(96)18) and the use of tissue for research, training and teaching removed without explicit consent (*Human Tissue: Ethical and Legal Issues* (Nuffield Council on Bioethics, 1995)).   [122] Contrast *Human Tissue*, ibid, at para 13.12.

agreement merely as the result of his silence. Also, it may only be proper to imply the patient's agreement or accord with procedures which involve minor interventions and are not controversial in nature. In other situations, the importance the law places upon the inviolability of the patient's bodily integrity strongly point to the law requiring explicit consent. Hence, it would not be proper to imply that a woman in a teaching hospital (even with her knowledge) impliedly consented to intrusive gynaecological investigations by students for the purposes of teaching. Equally, it would be wrong to imply that a patient by agreeing to the taking of blood agrees to it being tested for HIV infection or genetic conditions. The implications of the results of such tests for the patient (and others) is such that the law would only countenance explicit consent as justifying the taking from a competent adult.

2. Scope of Consent

The law of consent requires that the patient authorise the procedure which is carried out. A procedure may be unauthorised for a number of reasons and, subject to what is said below, in such circumstances the doctor will commit a battery. As one Canadian judge put it: **3.46**

> It is the patient, not the doctor, who decides *whether* the surgery will be performed, *where* it will be done, *when* it will be done and *by whom* it will be done.[123]

However, it is important to determine what has, or has not, been authorised by the patient. The following situations illustrate the divide between authorised and unauthorised procedures.

(i) *Absence of Real Consent*

A patient may agree to a medical procedure but without understanding the basic 'nature and purpose' of what it involves. It is clear that in this situation a patient's agreement is not a valid consent to the medical touching and a battery action will lie.[124] **3.47**

---

[123] *Allan v New Mount Sinai Hospital* (1980) 109 DLR (3d) 634, 642 *per* Linden J (emphasis added).
[124] *Chatterton v Gerson* [1981] QB 432, 443 *per* Bristow J; approved in *Sidaway v Governors of Bethlem Royal Hospital* [1985] AC 871 (HL) and see below, paras 3.86–3.100.

(ii) *In Face of a Valid Refusal*

3.48 As was seen above,[125] a valid refusal of treatment by a competent adult patient acts as a veto to any intervention covered by the refusal. The refusal may relate to all medical interventions or limit the range of interventions which the doctor may perform by, for example, instructing a doctor not to inject an anaesthetic into a particular arm[126] or not to perform a sterilisation.[127] In these circumstances, it will not be a defence that the doctor considered the procedure to be medically desirable.[128] The doctor's duty to act in the best medical interests of the patient is limited by the patient's right to refuse.[129]

(iii) *Conditional Consent/Refusal*

3.49 A patient may conditionally consent to treatment and thereafter the treatment is carried out even though the condition is not satisfied. In such an instance, the procedure will be unauthorised in the prevailing circumstances and a battery will be committed. For example, the patient agrees to a blood transfusion providing the blood is provided by a relative[130] or only if the procedure is performed by a particular doctor.[131] In both cases, when the doctor carried out the surgery he carried out a procedure which, in the circumstances, was unauthorised. Looking at it another way, until the condition upon which consent is dependent is satisfied, the patient, in fact, *refused* consent to the procedure. While, in principle, a patient in England could bring a battery action where a different doctor than was anticipated operated,[132] in practice it is unlikely to arise. This is because within an NHS hospital there is no expectation that a particular procedure will be carried out by a particular doctor. This is made plain in the standard consent form used for surgical procedures.[133]

---

[125] See above, paras 3.08–3.09.
[126] *Allan v New Mount Sinai Hospital* (1980) 109 DLR (3d) 634 (Ont HCt).
[127] *Cull v Royal Surrey County Hospital* [1932] 1 BMJ 1195.
[128] *Mulloy v Hop Sang* [1935] 1 WWR. 714 (Alta CA) (prohibited amputation which was necessary amounted to a battery).
[129] See *Airedale NHS Trust v Bland* [1993] 1 All ER 821, 866 *per* Lord Goff and *Mohr v Williams* (n 116 above). [130] *Ashcraft v King* (1991) 278 Cal Rptr 900.
[131] *Perna v Perozzi* (1983) 457 A 2d 431.
[132] *Michael v Molesworth* [1950] 2 BMJ 171.
[133] See *A Guide to Consent for Examination or Treatment* (DoH, HC(90)22, Appendix A(1)).

(iv) *'Further' or 'Additional' Procedures*

What is the legal position when the patient consents to procedure 'X' and the   **3.50**
doctor carries out procedure 'Y' (instead of, or in addition to, 'X')? This
could arise, for example, where the doctor discovers condition 'Y' during
surgery for condition 'X'. In principle, a patient would have a claim in battery
for the performance of the unauthorised procedure.[134] However, it may be
that what on the face of it seems an unauthorised[135] procedure was, in fact,
authorised or otherwise justified.

(a) Principle of Necessity[136]

Taking the last possibility first, the unauthorised procedure may be justified   **3.51**
in law if it is *necessary* in the sense that the patient's medical condition is such
that it would be unreasonable (and not merely inconvenient) to delay the
procedure until the patient regains consciousness and can decide for himself.[137] The distinction is highlighted by the Canadian cases of *Marshall v
Curry*[138] and *Murray v McMurchy.*[139]

In *Marshall v Curry*, the doctor discovered a grossly diseased testicle during a   **3.52**
hernia operation being performed on the patient. He removed it, as part of
the hernia operation, but also because he considered it to be gangrenous and a
threat to the patient's life and health. The patient's battery action was dismissed on the basis that a doctor may act without consent 'in order to save the
life or preserve the health of the patient'.[140] However, as *Murray v McMurchy*
shows, the scope of this apparently broad statement is more limited than
providing a justification for exceeding a patient's consent whenever it is considered in his 'best interests' to do so. In the *Murray* case, the patient underwent a
Caesarian section during the course of which she was sterilised because the
doctor considered that the condition of her uterus—she had fibroid tumours—
would make future pregnancies hazardous for her. The court upheld her battery

---

[134] eg *Mohr v Williams* (1905) 104 NW 12 (Sup Ct Minn) (no consent to operation on left
ear during operation on right ear); *Murray v McMurchy* [1949] 2 DLR 442 (BC Sup Ct);
Hamilton v Birmingham RHA [1969] 2 BMJ 456 (no consent to sterilisation during caesarian
section); and *Devi v West Midlands RHA* (1981) (CA Transcript 491) (no consent to sterilisation
performed during operation to repair ruptured uterus).
[135] See eg *Abbass v Kenney* (1995) 31 BMLR 157 (Gage J).
[136] More fully discussed below Ch 4.
[137] See *Re F* (n 6 above), 37 *per* Butler-Sloss LJ (CA) and at 76–7 *per* Lord Goff (HL). See
also Skegg, *Law, Ethics and Medicine* (n 56 above), 102–4:
[138] [1933] 3 DLR 260 (Sup Ct NS).   [139] [1949] 2 DLR 442 (Sup Ct BC).
[140] N 138 above, *per* Chisholm CJ at 265.

action. There was no evidence of any immediate danger to her life; it was merely convenient to carry out the sterilisation whilst she was unconscious.[141]

3.53 There is no directly relevant English case concerned with the temporarily incapacitated. However, in *Re F* the matter was touched upon both in the House of Lords and the Court of Appeal. Lord Goff, in his speech, stated that the doctor 'should do no more than is reasonably required, in the best interests of the patient, before he recovers consciousness'.[142] While he was prepared to identify the correct legal question he declined to go further and discuss *Marshall* and *Murray*.[143] In the Court of Appeal, having referred to the Canadian cases, Butler-Sloss LJ concluded that where the patient was temporarily incapacitated a procedure which was 'necessary for the preservation of life or for the preservation of health' could be lawfully performed.[144] Neill LJ spoke in terms which mirror the essence of the Canadian cases:

> The treatment which can be . . . given . . . is, within broad limits, confined to such treatment as is necessary to meet the emergency and as such needs to be carried out at once and before the patient is likely to be in a position to make a decision for himself.[145]

3.54 Consequently, English law limits the application of the 'necessity' principle in situations where the patient is temporarily incompetent to permit procedures which it would have been unreasonable to delay because of the imminent danger to the life or health of the patient.

(b) Within the 'Broad Nature' of the Consent Given

3.55 It is important to determine precisely what the patient has agreed to prior to the procedure. It may be that looking at all the circumstances surrounding the patient giving consent that the apparently unauthorised procedure was agreed to even it is not included on the consent form.[146] Two cases illustrate how the patient's agreement may be interpreted as broad enough to encompass the 'additional' procedure. In *Davis v Barking, Havering and Brentwood HA*[147] the plaintiff underwent an operation for the removal of a cyst. She signed a consent form in which it was stated that she consented to the 'administration of general, local or other anaesthetics'. She was told that a general anaesthetic would be used. During the procedure, in addition to this, a caudal block was given. After the operation the plaintiff temporarily lost movement over her

---

[141] See also *Parmley v Parmley* [1945] 4 DLR 81 (patient undergoing limited tooth extraction and dentist removed all the patient's teeth because he discovered advanced tooth decay and gum disease—held a battery). [142] [1990] 2 AC 1, 77.
[143] ibid. [144] ibid, 37. [145] ibid, 30.
[146] See *O'Bonsawin v Paradis* (1993) 15 CCLT (2d) 188.
[147] [1993] 4 Med LR 85; Grubb, (1993) 1 Med L Rev 389 (Commentary).

legs and control of her bladder, but was left with some minor problems. She sued in battery and negligence alleging, in respect of battery, that the anaesthetist had administered the caudal block without her consent and which had caused her injury. McCullough J dismissed her action in battery. He concluded that it would be wrong to sectionalise what the plaintiff had consented to. There were not two separate operations which had been performed for which consent to each would have been necessary. The correct question was 'Have the defendants shown that the plaintiff consented to a procedure the nature and effect of which had in broad terms been explained to her?'[148] The judge held that the plaintiff had understood in 'broad terms' the nature of what was to be done to her, namely that she would receive an anaesthetic. The judge did not rely upon the broadly drafted terms of the consent form.[149] Instead, his conclusion was that, viewed 'in the round' the caudal block was 'part and parcel' of the anaesthetic she had (with knowledge) agreed to.[150]

A case adopting a similar approach is the Canadian decision of *Brushnett v* **3.56** *Cowan*.[151] The plaintiff agreed to undergo a muscle biopsy and signed a consent form stating that she agreed to such 'further or alternative measures as may be found to be necessary during the course of the operation'. During the operation, the defendant carried out a bone biopsy as well as the muscle biopsy. The plaintiff subsequently fell and damaged her leg at the site of the bone biopsy. She sued the defendant, *inter alia*, in battery arguing she had not consented to the bone biopsy. The Newfoundland Court of Appeal dismissed her action in battery. The court held that in order to determine what the patient had consented to, it was necessary to look at all the circumstances leading up to the signing of the consent form and not at that alone. On the facts, the plaintiff had agreed not merely to a muscle biopsy, but to an investigatory procedure for the persistent problem in her right thigh which was 'the overriding general purpose and intent' of the patient consulting the doctor.[152] The court concluded, in effect, that what the plaintiff had agreed to was, in 'broad terms', an investigatory procedure which included both a muscle and a bone biopsy. Thus, the procedure complained of fell, as in *Davis*, within the scope of what the patient had understood she had given consent for. In addition, the court referred to the broadly worded consent form covering 'further and alternate measures' to support its conclusion.[153]

---

[148] ibid, 91.
[149] See below, paras 3.57–3.61 and *Pridham v Nash* (1986) 33 DLR (4th) 304.
[150] For a criticism of the case, see Grubb, (1993) 1 Med L Rev 389 (Commentary).
[151] (1990) 69 DLR (4th) 743; [1991] 2 Med LR 271 (Newfd CA).   [152] ibid, 275.
[153] ibid.

This, however, is a different and altogether more difficult basis for finding that the patient consented to what was done.

(c) Consent Forms[154]

3.57 Standard surgical consent forms in England have long contained clauses which indicate, variously expressed, that the patient agrees to 'such further or alternative operative measures or treatment as may be found necessary during the course of the operation or the treatment'.[155] There can be no doubt that these clauses were included on behalf of doctors to license and provide a legal basis for 'further' or 'additional' procedures carried out for the benefit of the patient during an operation. The current model consent form recommended by the Department of Health is somewhat different in its construction although the substance remains much the same.[156] It does not state that the patient 'agrees' to these procedures but rather that 'I understand' that such a procedure will 'only be carried out if it is necessary and in my best interests and can be justified for medical reasons'.[157] What is the legal effect of this kind of clause?

3.58 On the face of it, the clause cannot in itself evidence (let alone amount to) express consent. For that, the patient must understand the 'nature and purpose' of the additional or further procedure and have agreed to it.[158] By definition, reliance is placed upon this clause when the patient has not understood even in broad terms the nature of the additional procedure. At best, these clauses could only give rise to the argument that the patient had waived his right to the basic information—a claim which is highly problematic legally—or that by signing the consent form containing the clause he is taken thereby to have impliedly consented to the additional or further procedure. The latter arises, as we have seen already, where the patient has conducted himself such that it is reasonable to imply that he agreed and, importantly, understood what would or might happen. A prerequisite of

---

[154] For the 'evidentiary' effect of consent forms, see above, para 3.35.

[155] See eg, the previous DoH standardised consent form agreed with the medical protection organisations: HSC (IS)197 (October 1975). The form is discussed in Farndale, WAJ and Larman, E C, *Legal Liability for Claims arising from Hospital Treatment* (2nd edn, 1976), 19–29.

[156] *A Guide To Consent for Examination or Treatment* (DoH, 1990, HC (90)22 as amended by HSG (92)32), Appendix A(1).

[157] In full it states: 'I understand that any procedure in addition to the investigation or treatment described on this form will only be carried out if it is necessary and in my best interests and can be justified for medical reasons.' For a discussion of the form, see Brazier, M, 'Revised Consent Forms in the NHS' (1991) 7 Professional Negligence 148.

[158] eg *Abbass v Kenney* (1995) 31 BMLR 157: on facts held patient consented to operation carried out and no reliance placed upon the clause in consent form stating she consented to 'further or alternative operative measures as may be found to be necessary'.

implied consent is that the patient has actual or constructive notice of the information which he is thereafter estopped from denying. Obviously, this cannot be applied in the context of vaguely drafted clauses in consent forms.[159] Notwithstanding the logic of these arguments, the case law seems to give these clauses some credence. It was referred to as supporting the court's decision in *Brushnet v Cowan*.[160] More importantly, however, it was the basis for the decision in *Pridham v Nash*.[161]

The plaintiff underwent a laparoscopic abdominal examination to determine **3.59** the cause of pelvic pain. The plaintiff had agreed to this and had signed a consent form which stated, *inter alia*, that she consented to 'additional or alternative procedures as may be necessary or medically advisable during the course of the procedure'. During the procedure, the doctor discovered adhesions between her pelvis and abdominal wall. The doctor divided the adhesions using a forceps. Later, the plaintiff developed complications including peritonitis caused by the procedure. The plaintiff sued in battery and negligence claiming that she had only consented to the investigation and that she not consented to the procedure to release the adhesions. Holland J disagreed. He concluded that the additional procedure was simple and minor and fell within the words of the consent form. The plaintiff had, therefore, expressly consented to it.

Holland J's reasoning is, for the reasons given earlier, open to doubt. Unless **3.60** the curative procedure fell within the 'broad terms' of the investigative procedure (as in *Davis* and *Brushnett*), it is difficult to see how the plaintiff *expressly* consented to something she had not contemplated let alone understood its 'nature and purpose'.

How far should the reasoning of Holland J be taken? Would it permit *any* **3.61** additional procedure for the benefit of the patient? If it did, there would be no need in practice to rely upon the principle of necessity (or its limitations) in this context providing that a standard consent form had been signed. It is difficult to imagine that the courts would be prepared to allow doctors a *carte blanche* based upon the vague terms of the usual clause to act without— whatever they say—the express consent of the patient. In fact, Holland J himself restricted the impact of the clause in *Pridham* limiting it to minor, and excluding major, surgery. He said:[162]

---

[159] For the same reasons it is not conclusive that the form states that 'I have told the doctor . . . about any additional procedures I would *not* wish to be carried out straightaway without my having the opportunity to consider them first.' (emphasis in original). Unless the patient has been advised about the possible further procedures he will not have adequate information for his silence in respect of the particular procedure to amount to an 'implied consent'.   [160] (1990) 69 DLR (4th) 743; [1991] 2 Med LR 271 (Newfd CA).
[161] (1986) 33 DLR (4th) 304.   [162] ibid, 308.

If the laparoscopic examination, an investigative procedure, had revealed a major problem requiring surgery then, in my view, the surgeon would not be entitled to rely on the original consent and the general words of the consent . . . to carry out the major surgery. The surgeon would have been required to consult further with the patient and obtain a further consent to the major operation.

C. Elements of Consent

3.62 For a consent to treatment, or a refusal of treatment, to be legally valid it must be

(1) made by a person with *capacity*;
(2) *real*, ie based upon adequate information; and
(3) *voluntary* and not made under the undue influence of another.

1. Capacity

(i) *General Approach*

3.63 Legal capacity or competence to consent to treatment is not based upon a person's status or age.[163] Consequently, being a child or suffering from a mental disability or disorder does not mean, in law, that a person is necessarily incompetent. There is a rebuttable presumption that an adult is competent to consent (or refuse) treatment.[164] Equally, in relation to children[165] who have attained the age of sixteen there is a similar presumption created by section 8 of the Family Reform Act 1969 in relation to 'medical, surgical or dental treatment' including diagnostic and ancillary procedures.[166] However, the presumption is otherwise in respect of younger children (ie those below sixteen) where it must be established following the decision of the House of Lords in *Gillick v Wisbech and Norfolk AHA*[167] that the particular child has the capacity to consent to the particular treatment contemplated.[168]

3.64 Capacity is a question of fact in every case and requires that the patient is able to understand what is involved in the decision to be taken.[169] In children the issue will frequently be a developmental one, namely whether the patient has

---

[163] *Gillick v West Norfolk and Wisbech AHA* [1986] AC 112; [1985] 3 All ER 402 (HL); *Johnston v Wellesley Hospital* (1970) 17 DLR (3d) 139, 144–5 *per* Addy J. See also Skegg, P D G *Law, Ethics and Medicine* (n 56 above), at 49–56 (children) and 56–7 (adults).
[164] *Re T (Adult: Refusal of Medical Treatment)* [1992] 4 All ER 649, 661 *per* Lord Donaldson MR.   [165] ie those who have not reached the age of 18.
[166] See below, Ch 4.   [167] N 163 above.   [168] See below, Ch 4.
[169] *Gillick v West Norfolk and Wisbech AHA* [1985] 3 All ER 402.

acquired sufficient maturity and intelligence to understand what is involved.[170] In adults, the issue may be the same but usually it will not be. The law will not question the degree of intelligence or education of an adult.[171] In most instances the issue will be whether the patient's mental disability or disorder is such that he has *lost* the capacity to consent (or refuse) treatment or has never acquired it. A patient may have the capacity to make some but not all treatment decisions.[172] For example, a young child may be sufficiently mature to be able to understand what is involved in a minor form of treatment, such as bandaging a wound, but not a major one, such as a heart by-pass operation. Equally, a patient may be incompetent to understand any decision, for example, where the patient is unconscious or suffers from a severe mental disability. While developmental capacity of a child will be attained once and forever,[173] a competent child or adult's capacity may be lost (or absent) temporarily, for example, through an accident rendering the patient unconscious. It may also be permanently absent, for example, where the patient is born mentally disabled.

(a) Mistake as to Capacity

A doctor who mistakenly believes that a patient has capacity to consent to (or **3.65** refuse) medical treatment does not necessarily act unlawfully.[174] For example, in the Scottish legislation dealing with the competence of a child under sixteen to consent to medical treatments or procedures, Parliament has merely required that 'in the opinion of the doctor' the patient has capacity.[175] In England, a doctor's conduct cannot be based upon a legally valid consent (or refusal). If the doctor treats the patient, who is subsequently found to have been incompetent, he may be justified in treating the patient under the principle of necessity in his 'best interests'.[176] By contrast, a doctor who respects the patient's refusal in such circumstances will only be liable to the extent that he was negligent in not treating the patient, and injury to the patient resulted.

(b) Mistake as to Incapacity

More problematic is the doctor who acts notwithstanding a competent **3.66** patient's refusal, believing it to be invalid. At common law, there would

---

[170] ibid. See below, Ch 4, paras 4.54 ff.
[171] *Re T* (n 164 above), 661 *per* Lord Donaldson MR.
[172] *Gillick* (n 169 above), *per* Lord Fraser at 409 and *per* Lord Scarman at 422 and 423–4 (children); *Re T* (n 164 above), *per* Lord Donaldson MR at 661–2 (adults).
[173] See *Re R (A Minor) (Wardship: Medical Treatment)* [1992] Fam 11; [1991] 4 All ER 177 (CA) and *Re W (A Minor) (Medical Treatment)* [1993] Fam 64; [1992] 4 All ER 627 (CA).
[174] See Kennedy and Grubb, *Medical Law* (n 58 above), 241–2.
[175] *Re F* (n 117 above). See below Ch 4.
[176] *Re T* (n 164 above), *per* Staughton LJ at 670.

appear to be no defence since the patient's refusal is valid and the doctor commits a battery.[177] It is likely that in England the judges would fashion a defence of mistake, probably reasonable mistake, if called upon to do so.[178]

3.67 A number of important points arise from this general account of the nature of capacity/incapacity in law to make a decision about medical treatment.

(c) Ability to Understand Versus Actual Understanding

3.68 Capacity to consent is a question of the person's *ability* to understand that which the law requires the patient to understand.[179] The law looks to the person's innate facility or aptitude to understand what is involved in giving consent to (or refusing) the treatment.[180] Of course, it is relevant whether a patient does *actually* understand what is involved and in two ways. It will be necessary if the patient's consent is to be *real*, and thus, valid.[181] An uncomprehending 'consent' (or 'refusal') is no consent at all but it does not mean necessarily. or otherwise, that the patient is incompetent. The patient may have the *ability* to understand but not, perhaps because of the incomplete or inadequate explanation offered by the doctor, *actually* understand the information. The patient is not thereby rendered incompetent and unable to decide for himself. Rather, the law imposes an obligation upon the doctor to disclose the information in a reasonably comprehensible way or the consent will be invalid and the touching arising out of the treatment (of the competent patient) will be unlawful. Also, the patient's actual understanding will, of course, assist the doctor and, ultimately, the court in some cases to determine whether the patient is able to understand what is involved. In other words, the patient's actual understanding will be a useful 'yardstick' by which to assess the patient's capacity. But, for the reasons just given, it is no more than that and it is not conclusive.

(d) Ability to Understand What?

3.69 If legal capacity requires the patient to be able to understand what is involved in the proposed procedure, the question arises as to precisely what that entails. Does it require the patient to be able to understand only that information which, if understood, will make the patient's consent real and

---

[177] Age of Legal Capacity (Scotland) Act 1991, s 2(4).

[178] *Re MB (Medical Treatment)* (1997) 38 BMLR 175 (CA) at 188 *per* Butler-Sloss LJ: 'The only situation in which it is lawful for the doctors to intervene is if it is *believed* that the patient lacks the capacity to decide' (emphasis added).

[179] See discussion in Kennedy and Grubb, *Medical Law* (n 58 above), 120–2.

[180] eg, Mental Health Act 1983, ss 57 and 58; Age of Legal Capacity (Scotland) Act 1991, s 2(4).

[181] See below paras 3.86–3.100.

the doctor's touching not a battery? In other words, the patient must be able to understand the 'broad nature and purpose' of the procedure. This would have a certain legal symmetry about it and would be consistent with the current view of the Court of Appeal that consent in medical law simply has the function of licensing that which would otherwise be a battery.[182] At the other extreme, the law could require the patient to have an ability to understand all information which the law requires the patient to have in mind when consenting whether in order to avoid a battery claim or because of the doctor's obligation in negligence to provide information. This would, therefore, encompass much more than the 'broad nature and purpose' of the procedure and include some risks etc. There is a logical basis for this approach since it would be curious if the law required disclosure of information which the patient was simply unable to comprehend. However, as is often the case, the law takes a middle course. The patient must be able to understand more than the 'broad nature and purpose' of the procedure. He must also be able to understand the likely (or possible) effects or consequences of undergoing (or not) the procedure in question.[183] In one case, the court stated that the patient should have the ability to understand the 'nature, purpose and effects' of the procedure which was the amputation of part of a leg.[184] More recently, the Court of Appeal in *Re MB* spoke of the patient having capacity if she was able to understand 'the information which is material to the decision, especially as to the likely consequences of having or not having the treatment in question'.[185]

In children cases, there is some suggestion in the case law that the patient **3.70** must have a much greater ability to understand than has been suggested above.[186] In the *Gillick* case, for example, the child had to understand the 'moral and family questions' associated with her decision to engage in sexual intercourse and to seek contraceptive treatment secretly without involving her parents.[187] To require this of a child is indeed to expect a lot: more, quite frankly, than could, or indeed would, be expected of an adult patient. It is better to understand the remarks in *Gillick*, at worst, as restricted to the particular context of contraception and the court's desire to move slowly

---

[182] See *Re R* (n 173 above), *Re W* (n 40 above), and *Re T* (n 164 above).

[183] See formulation in Age of Capacity (Scotland) Act 1991, s 2(4) and Law Commission, Report 251, *Mental Incapacity* (1995), 'reasonably foreseeable consequences of deciding one way or another or of failing to make a decision.' (cl 2(2)(a) of Draft Bill).

[184] *Re C (Adult: Refusal of Medical Treatment)* [1994] 1 All ER 819 *per* Thorpe J at 824.

[185] N 178 above, at 187 *per* Butler-Sloss LJ.

[186] For a discussion of the capacity of children to consent (or refuse) medical treatment, see below Ch 4.   [187] N 169 above, especially *per* Lord Scarman at 424.

forward in emancipating children or, at best, as simply wrong, going beyond anything that the law could reasonably expect of anyone.[188]

(ii) *Determining a Patient's Capacity*

(a) The *Re C* Three-Stage Test

3.71 While it is clear that a patient's capacity to consent to (or refuse) treatment is concerned with his *ability to understand* what is involved, how does the law approach a determination of whether the patient has that ability? The courts have developed a three-stage test to assess a patient's capacity or ability to understand. In *Re C (Adult: Refusal of Medical Treatment)*[189] Thorpe J stated that the patient must be able to (i) *comprehend and retain* the relevant information; (ii) *believe* it; and (iii) *weigh* it in the balance so as to *arrive at a choice*. Subsequent courts have applied the so-called '*Re C* three-stage test'. Indeed, it has been applied not only in adult cases, but also in child cases where the issue of the child's capacity is not a developmental one of maturity but is raised by the child's mental disability.[190] In *Re MB* the Court of Appeal authoritatively approved the test.[191] Speaking for the Court of Appeal, Butler-Sloss LJ stated:[192]

> A person lacks capacity if some impairment or disturbance of mental functioning renders the person unable to make a decision whether to consent to or refuse treatment: That inability to make a decision will occur when
> (a) the patient is unable to comprehend and retain the information which is material to the decision, especially as to the likely consequences of having or not having the treatment in question.
> (b) the patient is unable to use the information and weigh it in the balance as part of the process of arriving at the decision. If . . . a compulsive disorder or phobia from which the patient suffers stifles belief in the information presented to her, then the decision may not be a true one.

3.72 The *Re C* test requires that the patient have the ability to 'comprehend' the relevant information in making the decision. It does not require the patient to make a 'mature' or 'wise' decision. Nor does it require the patient to achieve

---

[188] See *C v Wren* (1987) 35 DLR (4th) 419 (Alta CA) and *Ney v Attorney-General of Canada* (1993) 102 DLR (4th) 136 (BC Sup Ct).

[189] [1994] 1 All ER 819, 824; and Grubb, (1992) 2 Med L Rev 92 (Commentary).

[190] See *Re C (Detention: Medical Treatment)* [1997] 2 FLR 180; and Grubb, (1997) 5 Med L Rev 227 (Commentary). See also *Re B (A Minor) (Treatment and Secure Accommodation)* [1997] 1 FCR 618; and Grubb, (1997) 5 Med L Rev 233 (Commentary).

[191] [1997] 2 FLR 426, 433: 'the test to be applied where the issue arose as to capacity . . .' *per* Butler-Sloss LJ.   [192] ibid, 437.

the unattainable such as fully appreciating the consequences of his decision (such as the impact of his death upon his family and others).[193]

In addition to requiring the patient to be able to 'believe' and 'weigh' the information, the test requires that the patient be able to 'retain' it. In some exceptional circumstances, the patient's mental disability may preclude the patient from retaining the information long enough to make a decision, for instance, in some cases of degenerative brain disease such as Alzheimer's Disease or where the patient has suffered a specific brain injury that destroys short-term memory capacity. Clearly if a patient cannot retain the relevant information long enough (or at all) in order to make a choice, the patient should not be competent in law to make that (or indeed, any) decision. **3.73**

(b) Applying the *Re C* Test

A patient's capacity to decide may be called into question for a number of reasons: through mental disability or disorder, an inability to communicate a decision or because of external factors such as fatigue, pain, or sedation. In general, where a patient is suffering from a mental disorder or disability, a doctor's assessment of a patient's capacity should be confirmed by a psychiatrist. Of course, this may not be necessary in the case of children where the issue is one of 'maturity',[194] or in an obvious case, for example, where the patient is unconscious. In cases of doubt about the competence of a patient, a ruling from the court should be obtained[195] either by way of declaratory proceedings (in the case of adults), or under the Children Act 1989 or the court's inherent jurisdiction (in the case of children). A judgment about the application of the *Re C* test should, except in the most exceptional circumstances of urgency, preferably be supported by such evidence where a court is asked to determine a patient's capacity to consent to (or refuse) treatment.[196] **3.74**

In applying the *Re C* test, the courts have repeatedly stated that the patient's capacity must be 'commensurate with the gravity of the decision . . . .The more serious the decision, the greater the capacity required.'[197] Precisely what this means is not clear, but in practice the courts give most careful scrutiny to **3.75**

---

[193] See Gunn, M, (1994) 2 Med L Rev 8, 18–20. For two decisions involving children wrongly requiring this level of 'appreciation', see *Re E (A Minor)* (1990) 9 BMLR 1 and *Re S (A Minor) (Consent to Medical Treatment)* [1994] 2 FLR 1065. For a criticism, see Grubb, (1995) 3 Med L Rev 84, 85–6 (Commentary).

[194] Perhaps the evidence of other experts, such as developmental psychologists, would be helpful in such cases.   [195] See *Re MB* (n 191 above), 445 *per* Butler-Sloss LJ.

[196] ibid.

[197] See *Re T* (n 164 above), 661–2 *per* Lord Donaldson and *Re MB* (n 191 above), 437 *per* Butler-Sloss LJ.

decisions which may (or will) have deleterious consequences for the patient, such as a decision to refuse treatment, in particular life-sustaining treatment. A useful division of the possible situations that could arise, though not comprehensive, is as follows: (i) a patient's beliefs or value system; (ii) misperception of reality; (iii) compulsive or driven behaviour; (iv) external factors; and (v) inability to communicate a decision.

Beliefs and Value Systems

3.76 In applying the *Re C* test, the courts are not concerned with the reasonableness of the patient's decision or his reasoning process.[198] Nor is the law concerned with the rationality of the patient's decision or its basis unless that leads the court to conclude that the patient is suffering from a mental disability which deprives him of the ability to 'comprehend', 'retain', 'believe' or 'weight' the information.[199] In *Re T (Adult: Refusal of Treatment)*, Lord Donaldson MR stated that a competent adult patient had a right to consent to, or refuse, medical treatment based upon reasons which were 'rational, irrational, unknown or even non-existent'.[200] Consequently, religious beliefs which lead patients to refuse some or all medical treatment do not affect a patient's capacity, however irrational the belief may seem.[201] A Jehovah's Witness who refuses a blood transfusion or a Christian Scientist who refuses all medical intervention is not, by reason of the irrationality or otherwise of their beliefs, incompetent to make decisions about their medical treatment. Providing they are able to understand what is involved—'comprehending', 'believing', and 'weighing' the information—their refusals will be legally binding upon the doctors.[202] There are two explanations of the law's position here. First, the law defers to religiously based decisions made by adults, though not those made on behalf of children,[203] as a matter of social tolerance. Providing the person understands what is entailed in their decision, there is no reason for the law to deprive the individual of decision-making power. It would be an act of unjustified state interference to override decisions made on religious grounds. Secondly, and perhaps of more general importance for medical law, such decisions do not stem from any mental disability or mental malfunctioning on the part of the patient. Apart from situations

---

[198] *Re T* (n 164 above), 664 *per* Butler-Sloss LJ: 'a decision . . . does not have to be sensible, rational or well considered.' See also *Smith v Auckland Hospital Board* [1965] NZLR 191 (NZCA), 219 *per* Gresson J.

[199] *Re MB* (n 191 above). See also *Sidaway v Bethlem Royal Hospital Governors* [1985] 1 All ER 643 *per* Templeman at 666.

[200] N 164 above, 653. See also *Re MB* (n 191 above), *per* Butler-Sloss LJ at 432 and 436–7.

[201] *Re W* (n 173 above), 637 *per* Lord Donaldson MR.   [202] *Re T* (n 164 above).

[203] See eg, *Re S (A Minor) (Medical Treatment)* [1993] 1 FLR 376; *Re E (A Minor)* (1990) 9 BMLR 1; *Re R (A Minor)* [1993] 2 FLR 5. See below, Ch 4, paras 4.96–4.98.

where the patient is unable to communicate his decision, a necessary condition for depriving an individual of decision-making power, and justifying state intervention in his 'best interests', is that the patient is suffering from a mental malfunctioning having a pathological or psychological etiology. It is the impairment or disturbance in the patient's mental ability to understand which potentially renders him, in law, incompetent.[204]

Misperception of Reality

In order for a patient to have capacity to decide, he must be able to understand **3.77** the material information to making the decision. As part of this, a patient must be able to understand what is wrong with him and which requires treatment, and he must be able to understand the consequences to him of undergoing or declining the treatment. However, an irrational belief, whether long-held or of contemporary origin, which affects or influences a patient's judgment about medical treatment will not lead to a finding of incompetence unless it results in an inference that the patient is suffering from a mental disability. In *Re MB* the Court of Appeal acknowledged that it would not be proper to find a patient incompetent merely because his decision was 'irrational', meaning one 'so outrageous in its defiance of logic or of accepted moral standards' that 'no sensible person who had applied his mind to the question to be decided could have arrived at it'.[205] The Court of Appeal accepted, however, that if the patient's irrational decision was based upon a misperception of reality stemming from a mental disorder, then the patient might lack the ability to 'comprehend' or 'believe' the information under the *Re C* test.[206]

The general approach can be illustrated by the following examples taken from **3.78** the case law. A patient who denies that she is ill or diseased and in need of treatment is incompetent if that belief derives from a mental disability because she will not be able to 'comprehend' or 'believe' the information relevant to making a decision.[207] Hence a patient who, due to a mental disability, denies that she has a gangrenous foot in need of amputation is incompetent to make a decision. A patient suffering from anorexia nervosa who is unable, because of her mental disorder, to understand her failing physical condition lacks the capacity to refuse food and nutrition.[208] Likewise a patient suffering from paranoid schizophrenia, who denies during a lucid moment that there is anything wrong with her and that she needs treatment to

---

[204] See Law Commission proposals, *Mental Incapacity* (Report 251, 1995), paras 3.8–3.12 and Draft Bill cl 2(1)(a) and (2).
[205] N 191 above 437 *per* Butler-Sloss LJ.   [206] ibid.
[207] See eg, *State of Tennessee v Northern* (1978) 563 SW 2d 197 (Tenn CA).
[208] *Re W* (n 173 above).

prevent a deterioration in her mental health, is incompetent because she is unable by reason of her mental illness to 'comprehend' or 'believe' the information about her illness and its prognosis.[209]

3.79 However, it is essential to a finding of incompetence that the patient's 'disbelief' derives from a mental disability. Not every patient who disbelieves their doctor's advice fails the second stage of the *Re C* test and is incompetent: indeed most will not be incompetent. An important distinction has to be drawn between outright disbelief due to mental disorder where the patient is 'impervious to reason, divorced from reality, or incapable of adjustment after reflection' and 'the tendency which most people have when undergoing medical treatment to self assess and then puzzle over the divergence between medical and self-assessment'.[210] Merely to take a different view of the world from a doctor may result in a patient 'disbelieving' him but it does not render the patient incompetent and thus unable to decide, as a matter of law, for themselves.[211] Even a skewed, and indefensible view of the world, does not have this effect *unless* it has its genesis in what might be termed, mental 'malfunctioning'.[212] Hence, a patient's irrational fear of surgery[213] or a particular medical procedure[214] are not sufficient in themselves to make the patient incompetent in law to make a decision about their treatment. Only if the 'fear' acts on the patient's mind so as to 'paralyse the will and thus destroy the capacity to make a decision' will a finding of incompetence be justified.[215]

Compulsive or Driven Behaviour

3.80 Certain mental disorders result in a patient being deprived of the ability to make a real or true choice. Examples of these are compulsive eating disorders such as anorexia nervosa and compulsive phobias or personality disorders. A patient who is forced or compelled to reach a particular decision, usually to refuse the treatment, is not in law competent to make that decision. The patient is, under the *Re C* test, unable to 'weigh' the information and 'make a choice'. Consequently, a refusal of treatment by a patient suffering from anorexia nervosa,[216] from a borderline personality disorder resulting in

---

[209] *Re R* (n 173 above).
[210] *B v Croydon HA* (1994) 22 BMLR 13 *per* Thorpe J at 20.
[211] *Re C (Adult: Refusal of Medical Treatment)* [1994] 1 All ER 819.
[212] See e g, *Tameside and Glossop Acute Services Trust v CH* [1996] 1 FLR 762 where the patient had a deluded belief that her doctors were maliciously trying to hurt her and her unborn child. See Grubb, (1996) 4 Med L Rev 193 (Commentary).
[213] See e g, *Re Maida Yetter* (1973) 96 D & C 2d 619 (Comm Pleas Pa) and *Lane v Candura* (1978) 376 NE 2d 1232 (Mass App Ct).
[214] See e g, *Re MB* (n 191 above), 437 *per* Butler-Sloss LJ.
[215] ibid, 437 *per* Butler-Sloss LJ.   [216] *Re W* (n 173 above).

self-harm,[217] or a 'needle phobia' compelling the patient to panic and refuse the procedure,[218] will not be valid in law because the patient will be incapable of 'weighing' the information relevant to the decision.

In addition, the patient's mental disorder may cause the patient to 'skew' the **3.81** information given to her such that she distorts the relevant factors in her own mind. Hence, a patient whose mental illness leads her to minimise past events and selectively ignore or distort information given about her condition will be 'unable to weigh treatment information, balancing risks and needs', and hence not competent to make a decision about the treatment for her mental disorder.[219]

However, caution must be exercised in applying the third stage of the *Re C* **3.82** test. It is potentially an open invitation to make a finding of incompetence because the doctor (or court) finds the patient's decision difficult to understand. This is not what the courts intend. That a patient must have the ability to 'weigh' information does not mean that every incongruous decision is an incompetent one. The court is not entitled simply to re-weigh the factors relevant to the patient's decision and, because it would come to a different decision treat the patient as incompetent. It is the patient's ability to weigh, rather than the actual weight given to particular factors, which is at the core of the third stage of the *Re C* test. A patient may have the ability to weigh the information but for reasons particular to him, reach a decision that the doctor (or court) would not. That is the patient's choice and the decision may be based upon the patient's own perception of the world or values providing it is not the product of distorted or deluded perceptions stemming from mental malfunctioning, in particular the very mental disorder for which treatment is needed.[220] To do otherwise, would be to introduce a test of unreasonableness or irrationality which the courts have rejected.

External Factors

A patient's ability to understand may be temporarily affected by external **3.83** factors such as confusion, shock, fatigue, pain, or medication.[221] Such factors may render a patient incapable of making a decision because the patient is

---

[217] *B v Croydon HA* [1995] Fam 133; [1995] 1 All ER 683 (CA). See Grubb, (1995) 3 Med L Rev 191 (Commentary).

[218] See *Re MB* (n 191 above), and *Re L (Patient: Non-Consensual Treatment)* [1997] 2 FLR 837.

[219] eg, *Re C (Detention: Medical Treatment)* [1997] 2 FLR 180. See also, *Re MB* (n 191 above), 437 *per* Butler-Sloss LJ.

[220] See *B v Croydon HA* (1994) 22 BMLR 13, 20 *per* Thorpe J, and see also *Re MB* (n 191 above), *per* Butler-Sloss LJ at 436–7.

[221] *Re T* (n 164 above), 661 *per* Lord Donaldson MR.

unable to 'weigh' the information and make a choice.[222] However, the court will require a demonstrable effect of the patient's ability to reason and decide before such a finding will be permissible. It is not sufficient that the patient's capacity is merely reduced. The patient's capacity must be 'completely erode[d] . . . to such a degree that the ability to decide is absent.'[223] In *Re MB* Butler-Sloss LJ illustrated how the patient's panic and fear could make them incompetent:[224]

> Another . . . influence may be panic induced by fear. Again careful scrutiny of the evidence is necessary because fear of an operation may be a rational reason for refusal to undergo it. Fear may also, however, paralyse the will and thus destroy the capacity to make a decision.

3.84   The importance of the limited scope of this basis for a finding of incompetence is illustrated by two cases involving obstetric treatment. In one case,[225] a patient in the late stages of labour was held to be incompetent because, in the words of Johnson J, '[s]he was called upon to make the decision at a time of acute emotional stress and physical pain in the ordinary course of labour made even more difficult for her because of her own particular mental history.'[226] The patient denied she was pregnant. Even though the psychiatric evidence was that she was not suffering from a mental disorder within the Mental Health Act 1983, she had a history of psychiatric treatment and it is difficult to believe that her denial of the obvious was based upon a difference of opinion or values rather than having a psychiatric etiology. Johnson J was not, therefore, relying upon the patient's circumstances in reaching his decision that she was incompetent. However, in another case decided on the same day,[227] the same judge did make such a finding where the patient had no psychiatric history. Despite the consultant obstetrician's view that she was competent to decide, Johnson J held:[228]

> The patient was in the throes of labour with all that involved in terms of pain and emotional stress. I concluded that a patient who could, in those circumstances, speak in terms which seemed to accept the inevitability of her own death, was not a patient who was able properly to weigh-up the considerations that arose so as to make any valid decision, about anything of even the most trivial kind, surely less one which involved her life.

In *Re MB*, the Court of Appeal rightly doubted this finding.[229]

---

[222] An alternative way of determining such cases would be to say that the patient was acting involuntarily or under undue influence: *Beausoleil v Soeur de la Charité de la Providence* (1964) 53 DLR (2d) 65 (patient sedated). See discussion below paras 3.143–3.147.
[223] *Re MB* (n 191 above), 437 *per* Butler-Sloss LJ.   [224] ibid.
[225] *Norfolk and Norwich Healthcare (NHS) Trust v W* [1997] 1 FCR 269.
[226] ibid, 272.   [227] *Rochdale Healthcare (NHS) Trust v C* [1997] 1 FCR 274.
[228] ibid, 275.   [229] N 191 above.

Inability to Communicate

The patient's incapacity may arise because he is unable to communicate a **3.85** decision to the doctor. Here, there is no necessity for the incapacity to arise from a 'mental malfunctioning'. It may result from a purely physical disability impairing the patient's facility to communicate. It will usually arise in practice where the patient is unconscious. The incapacity may be temporary, as where the patient has been injured in an accident, or permanent, for example, where the patient is in a persistent vegetative state. The inability to communicate may arise otherwise, for example, in rare cases where the patient is 'locked in' or the patient is somehow physically disabled from communication. Providing all reasonable steps have been taken to communicate their decision, the law regards patients in this residual category of case as incompetent to make a treatment decision.

2. Information

(i) *Battery*

In order to give a valid legal consent (or refusal) to treatment, a patient must **3.86** understand adequately what is involved in the procedure (or in refusing it). It is sometimes said that the patient's consent must be 'informed'. This is an unfortunate phrase and one prone to mislead.[230] It is an expression used by courts in other countries, particularly in America, to describe the scope of a doctor's duty in the tort of negligence to disclose information.[231] It is better avoided in any discussion in the context of battery or, indeed, in negligence in England. In battery, it is more helpful to say that the patient's consent must be 'real'.

On the face of it, if the patient's consent is not 'real' then the doctor commits **3.87** battery by touching the patient. However, where the patient does not understand the 'nature' of the procedure, a doctor who mistakenly (and reasonably) believes that he does *may* have a defence in that the patient may be estopped from denying he possessed the information if he has lead the doctor 'reasonably to assume the relevant information was known to him'.[232]

---

[230] *Rogers v Whitaker* (1992) 109 ALR 625, 633 (H Ct Aust): *Reibl v Hughes* (1980) 114 DLR (3d) 1, 11.   [231] Most famously in *Canterbury v Spence* (1972) 464 F 2d 772 (DC Cir).
[232] See *Sidaway v Bethlem Royal Hospital Governors* [1985] 1 All ER 643 *per* Lord Diplock at 658. See discussion above, paras 3.65–3.66 (mistake as to capacity). On the related, but distinct point, of whether a patient has to understand information for the purposes of negligence see Kennedy and Grubb, *Medical Law* (n 58 above), 243–5, and *Ciarlariello v Schacter* (1993) 100 DLR (4th) 609, 622–3 *per* Cory J (positive duty to ensure patient understands).

(a) 'Nature'

3.88　When will a patient's consent be 'real'? The patient must understand in broad terms the 'nature' of the procedure he is agreeing to.[233] Providing the patient does, and he is competent and acting voluntarily, his consent will be 'real' and legally valid. No action in battery will lie. It is another question whether he may have a claim in negligence for non-disclosure of other information and this will be discussed later.[234] It is sometimes erroneously, but understandably, thought that a doctor has a duty to disclose that information relevant to the 'nature' of the procedure in order for the patient's consent to be real.[235] In fact, this is not the case since battery and consent are not concerned with the doctor's duty to disclose but rather with the actual knowledge and understanding of the patient. A patient's consent will be real if he understands the 'nature' of a procedure regardless from where he acquired the information. It need not have been from his doctor or other health carer. Of course, by the very nature of things, usually the information will come from the doctor (or other health carers such as a nurse) because that will be the only source of information for the patient. By contrast, in the tort of negligence the law is concerned with the doctor's duty to volunteer information or answer questions posed by the patient.[236]

3.89　What is meant by the 'nature' of a procedure? The *Oxford English Dictionary*[237] defines, *inter alia*, 'nature' as

> [t]he essential qualities or properties of a thing; the inherent and inseparable combination of properties essentially pertaining to anything and giving it its fundamental character.

In relation to what constitutes the 'nature' of a medical procedure, no general answer can be given other than to say that it is a relatively narrow notion encompassing by *description* the character of the act(s) to be done by the doctor and, *qualitatively*, the intended effect(s) of the procedure and its purpose. There is no doubt that 'nature' includes an understanding of the purpose or intended effect of the procedure. Indeed, although initially refer-

---

[233] *Chatterton v Gerson* [1981] QB 432, 443 *per* Bristow J; *Sidaway v Governors of Bethlem Royal Hospital* [1984] 1 All ER 1018 (CA), 1026 *per* Sir John Donaldson MR at 1029 *per* Dunn LJ; *Rogers v Whitaker* (1992) 109 ALR 624 (H Ct Aust), 633.
[234] See below paras 3.101–3.138.
[235] In *Abbass v Kenney* (1995) 31 BMLR 157, Gage J (at 163) stated that 'a doctor has a duty to explain what he intends to do and the implications of what he is going to do'. However, the plaintiff case was pleaded soley in *negligence* even though the essence of her claim was that she had not consented to the operation.　[236] See below.
[237] OUP, 1971.

ring only to the 'nature' of the procedure, for clarity it is now commonplace for judges to talk of the 'nature and purpose' of the procedure.[238]

The information needs to state in 'broad terms' what is to be done to the **3.90** patient and why.[239] However, this information need not descend into minute, or indeed any, real detail. In practice, judges have considerable leeway in determining what information is relevant to the 'nature and purpose' of a procedure and what is co-lateral to that and, therefore, immaterial to the reality of the patient's consent. For example, it may be enough that the patient knows that a diagnostic procedure of a certain type is to be undertaken, such as a biopsy, and what that involves in terms of contact with the patient and incision. Even if the doctor had been speaking in terms of a particular kind of biopsy such as a muscle biopsy, knowledge of this will be sufficient to amount to a real consent to a bone biopsy carried out at the same time.[240]

The courts' reluctance to read more into the 'nature and purpose' requirement **3.91** is linked to their unwillingness to expand the tort of battery in medical cases. Instead, they wish to leave claims by patients who have not been informed of relevant information to their decision to consent to the tort of negligence. The judges have 'deplor[ed] reliance' upon battery in medical cases.[241] They have done so for a number of reasons. First, battery is an intentional tort usually involving hostile action by an aggressor. Medical cases rarely, if ever, fit this perception of battery particularly when the issue is non-disclosure of information by the doctor. Secondly, to face a civil claim for battery carries a stigma with it for the doctor given the association that could occur in the public's mind with the crime of assault. Thirdly, a battery action affords the patient certain advantages over a claim in negligence; for example, proving negligence and establishing causation may be difficult in a negligence action.[242] In a battery claim, expert evidence of professional practice—and the *Bolam*[243] test—will not avail a doctor as a defence to an allegation of wrongful non-disclosure. Also, establishing what injury flowed from the procedure which was not consented to will, as a matter of causation, usually

---

[238] eg *Sidaway v Bethlem Royal Hospital Governors* [1985] 1 All ER 643, 647 *per* Lord Scarman. [239] *Chatterton v Gerson* (n 233 above).
[240] See *Brushnett v Cowan* [1991] 2 Med LR 271 and the discussion above, paras 3.58–3.61.
[241] *Hills v Potter* [1983] 3 All ER 716, 728 *per* Hirst J; *Chatterton v Gerson* (n 233 above), 265 *per* Bristow J; *Sidaway v Bethlem Royal Hospital Governors* (n 232 above), 650 *per* Lord Scarman; *Abbass v Kenney* (1995) 31 BMLR 157, 163–4 *per* Gage J.
[242] See Robertson, G, 'Informed Consent to Medical Treatment' (1981) 97 LQR 102, 123–4.
[243] *Bolam v Friern HMC* [1957] 1 WLR 582 as interpreted by the House of Lords in *Bolitho v City & Hackney HA* [1997] 4 All ER 771.

be obvious in a battery action whereas establishing in a negligence action what the patient would have done if he had known the information which was not disclosed, may create evidential (and legal) difficulties.[244]

Risks and Alternatives

3.92 The most obvious limitation imposed by the judges upon the information relevant to the 'nature' and 'purpose' of a procedure relates to non-disclosure of risks inherent in, and alternatives to, the procedure. Such information is not considered to affect the reality of the patient's consent. In *Chatterton v Gerson*[245] the plaintiff was treated for chronic pain around the area of an operation scar following a hernia operation. The patient was given an injection of phenol to relieve the pain. Subsequently, this led to her leg becoming numb and thereby impairing her mobility. Although the doctor had described the procedure to the patient he had not informed her of the risk of numbness. She sued in battery and negligence. The court dismissed both actions. As regards her claim in battery, Bristow J held that she had given a 'real' consent even though she had not known the risk of the side-effect. He said:

> I think that justice requires that in order to vitiate the reality of consent there must be a greater failure of communication between the doctor and patient than that involved in a breach of duty if the claim is based on negligence . . . .In my judgment, once the patient is informed in *broad terms of the nature of the procedure* which is intended, and gives her consent, that consent is real, and the cause of action on which to base a claim for failure to go into risks and implications is negligence, not trespass.[246]

3.93 Later cases in England have affirmed this approach, in particular, both the Court of Appeal and House of Lords in *Sidaway v Bethlem Royal Hospital Governors*.[247] In *Sidaway*, the plaintiff underwent an operation upon her neck to relieve pain. Although she was told about the danger of disturbing a nerve root and the consequences of that, she was not told of the risk of damage to her spinal cord and the catastrophic consequences if, which it did, this happened. She sued unsuccessfully in the tort of negligence.[248] It was not argued that her claim could lie in battery.[249] In the Court of Appeal, the judges observed that the plaintiff had consented to the 'nature of the act'[250] (that is, the procedure carried out or 'the nature of what [was] to be done'),[251] hence

---

[244] See below paras 3.139–3.142.   [245] [1981] 1 All ER 257.
[246] ibid, 265 (emphasis added).
[247] [1984] 1 All ER 1018 (CA) and [1985] AC 871 (HL).
[248] See below, paras 3.113–3.122.
[249] This is clear from the transcript of the trial judgment of Skinner J delivered on 19 Feb 1982 (1977 S 8348).   [250] N 247 above, *per* Dunn LJ at 1029.
[251] ibid, *per* Sir John Donaldson MR at 1026; see also *per* Browne-Wilkinson LJ at 1032.

her consent was 'real' for the purposes of battery. Dunn LJ expressly approved *Chatterton v Gerson*.[252] On appeal to the House of Lords, the contrary was simply not suggested and it was accepted that the plaintiff had given a valid consent.[253] Subsequently, in *Freeman v Home Office (No 2)*,[254] Sir John Donaldson MR stated:

> If there was real consent to the treatment, it matters not whether the doctor was in breach of his duty to give the patient the appropriate information before the consent was given. Real consent provides a complete defence to a claim in the tort of trespass to the person . . . .[S]ubject to the patient having been informed in broad terms of the nature of the treatment, consent in fact amounts to consent in law.

Thus, the law in England is clear and, though arguments can be made that the tort of battery could be extended,[255] there seems no prospect that the courts will do so.

Other common law jurisdictions have taken the same view. The Canadian **3.94** Supreme Court in *Reibl v Hughes*[256] and the Australian High Court in *Rogers v Whittaker*[257] have adopted the same demarcation line between battery and negligence.[258]

What is Being Done

The notion of the 'nature' and 'purpose' of a procedure is not limited to a **3.95** factual description of the essence of what is being done. In addition to information which describes the act of the doctor, it also includes an account of the intrinsic quality of what is being done and, of course, why it is being done. Hence, in other contexts for a woman to agree to the act of sexual intercourse (the 'act') is not, in law, for her to consent to it if she is wrongly led to believe that it is a medical treatment or voice training (the 'intrinsic quality').[259] She has not consented to sexual intercourse even though she fully understood the 'act' because the intrinsic quality of what she thought was being done was different. Thus, in the medical context a patient who agrees

---

[252] N 245 above, 1029.   [253] [1985] 1 All ER 643 at 647 *per* Lord Scarman.
[254] [1984] 1 All ER 1036, 1044.
[255] See Somerville, M, 'Structuring the Issues in Informed Consent' (1981) 26 McGill LJ 740; and Keng Feng, T, 'Failure of Medical Advice: Trespass or Negligence?' (1987) 7 LS 149.
[256] (1980) 114 DLR (3d) 1, especially *per* Laskin CJ at 10.
[257] (1992) 109 ALR 625, especially *per* Mason CJ, Brennan, Dawson, Toohey and McHugh JJ at 632–3.
[258] For a curious Australian decision where the court held it to be trespass when a patient underwent 'reduction mammoplasty' without being told of all the breast incisions which would be made, that there would be stitching, that there would be some loss of sensation, and that there would be some permanent scarring, see *D v S* (1981) LS (SA) JS 405.
[259] *R v Flattery* (1877) 2 QBD 410 and *R v Williams* [1923] 1 KB 340.

to a procedure believing it to be for his benefit (therapeutic) whilst, in fact, it is not because the doctor is conducting non-therapeutic research upon him, has not given a valid consent.[260] Similarly, a doctor who carries out an unnecessary intimate examination of a woman wholly for his own sexual gratification would commit a battery.[261] Where a procedure is carried out as part of a teaching exercise in a hospital without the patient's knowledge, the patient's agreement to the 'act' will not amount to a consent in law since she will be unaware of the 'intrinsic quality' of the touching.

3.96 The only reported English case in which a health care professional has been held liable for battery where, on the face of it, the patient agreed to what was done is *Appleton v Garrett*.[262] The plaintiffs underwent at the hands of the defendant unnecessary dental work. The defendant carried out extensive restorative treatment on teeth which were healthy for financial gain. Dyson J held that the defendant had committed a battery on his patients. In respect of those teeth that were healthy, the judge concluded that the patients' consents were not 'real'. The basis for his decision is not clear but seems, in some part, to be based upon the defendant's fraud and 'bad faith'.[263] However, it is most certainly correct. The patients did not consent even if they were aware of the nature of the 'act' performed by the defendant. They were not aware of its 'intrinsic quality', namely that it was of no benefit to them, in fact rather the contrary was the case. Agreeing to treatment on unhealthy teeth is to agree to a fundamentally different act to that which was carried out.[264]

3.97 How far the courts will go in atomising the 'quality' of a touching by a doctor will, ultimately, be a matter of policy and which will give rise to differences of judicial opinion. In one case,[265] a majority of the Canadian Supreme Court held that a patient had given a valid consent to an intimate examination by a doctor in circumstances where he had done so in the presence of a friend, whom he had told the patient was a medical intern. The judges considered that the patient was aware of the 'nature and quality of the act to be done'. Spence J, however, dissented stating that the patient 'only gave [her] consent to such a serious invasion of her privacy on the basis that [the friend] was a

---

[260] *Halushka v University of Saskatchewan* (1965) 52 WWR 608.
[261] Contrast *R v Mobilio* [1991] 1 VR 339 where it was held that a patient had given a valid consent to unnecessary transvaginal ultrasound examinations by a technician because she knew 'the nature and character of the act which was done' (at 352). In England, the courts should not follow this decision since the non-therapeutic character of the procedure changed the 'nature' and 'purpose' of what was done.
[262] [1997] 8 Med LR 75 and Kennedy, (1996) 4 Med L Rev 311 (Commentary).
[263] On these see below, para 3.100.
[264] On this basis an English court would not follow *R v Mobilio* [1991] 1 VR 339 (n 261 above). [265] *R v Bolduc and Bird* (1967) 63 DLR (2d) 82.

doctor intending to commence practice and who desired practical experience in such matters . . .'[266] At one level the disagreement can be seen as a semantic one but, in truth, it is over the proper scope of battery and the policy of the law. A somewhat similar disagreement could arise in respect of a consent given by a person to the taking of a blood sample which is subsequently used for genetic testing or to determine the individual's HIV status. If the patient is only told about what is descriptively to be done (that is, the taking of blood and the method (the 'act') and that it will be used to 'run some tests'), will the person's consent be valid if they are unaware of the precise purpose that the blood will be put to? Is the person aware of the 'intrinsic quality' of what is being done? On one view, he is because he knows that it will be used for his benefit (the tests). On another view, however, it could be said that the significance of genetic and HIV testing for the person (and indeed others close to him) is such that without knowledge of that, the quality of the act is different.[267] Ultimately, however, the issue is a question of policy but given the potential for stigmatisation, discrimination, and personal anxiety to the person, it is suggested that the law should require explicit agreement in these situations.

Who is Carrying Out the Procedure

In some situations who is carrying out the procedure may affect the 'nature' and **3.98** 'purpose' of what is being done. It is well recognised elsewhere in the law, for example the criminal law, that the identity of the actor may vitiate an individual's consent. Hence, in the law of rape the identity of the man with whom the woman is having sexual intercourse will be relevant.[268] The 'quality' of what is agreed to when a woman consents to sexual intercourse with a man who is impersonating her husband is affected by her misunderstanding. Even though she understands the nature of the 'act' (sexual intercourse), it is of a different 'quality' (adulterous) from that which she believes it to be (marital).[269] Likewise a patient who consents to be touched by a doctor will not, in law, have given a valid consent when she is touched by that person if he turns out to be impersonating a doctor even if what is actually done is exactly what she expected.[270] The descriptive nature of the 'act' remains the same but its 'intrinsic quality' changes.

---

[266] ibid, 87.

[267] For different views on this, and other analogous situations, of HIV testing, see Grubb, A and Pearl, D, *Blood Testing, AIDS and DNA Profiling* (Jordans, 1990), ch 1 and Keown, J, (1989) 52 MLR 790.

[268] *R v Linekar* [1995] 3 All ER 69 and *R v Elbekkay* [1995] Crim LR 163.

[269] In fact, the criminal law goes further than this and regards any mistake as to identity as vitiating consent: see ibid. Quaere whether the 'quality' of the act changes in these cases?

[270] *R v Maurantonio* (1967) 65 DLR (2d) 674. See also *De May v Roberts* (1881) 9 NW 146.

3.99 However, the identity of the person carrying out the procedure will not always change the 'nature' or 'quality' of what has been agreed to by the patient. For example, a patient who agrees to a therapeutic procedure which, unbeknownst to him, is carried out by a student or trainee, will have given a valid consent since the 'quality' of the act will not change.[271] It would be different if the agreement was to a therapeutic procedure but the student carried out an unnecessary procedure *simply* in order to learn how to do it or to gain experience. Then, the 'purpose' of the procedure would be radically changed and the patient's consent would not be valid.[272] A change in doctor would not, at least in England,[273] affect the consent given. Even if the patient expected a particular doctor to carry out the procedure, the consent form is likely to indicate that this is a misplaced expectation.[274] In any event, the nature and purpose of what is being done will not change. The only legal relevance of the change in doctor might be that the patient's consent was conditional on that doctor carrying out the procedure: if he did not then there was no consent by the patient at all.[275]

(b) Fraud and Misrepresentation

3.100 Does fraud or a misrepresentation by the doctor as to information about the procedure to be performed affect the validity of the patient's consent? In Canada, the Supreme Court has held that fraud or misrepresentation (even a negligent one) will unravel what would otherwise be a valid consent.[276] It would seem that in Canada there will not be a valid consent in these circumstances even though it is 'real', in other words, even though the patient understands the 'nature' and 'purpose' of the procedure. Fraud or misrepresentation as to co-lateral matters will suffice.[277] In England, the position is otherwise. Notwithstanding one or two broader statements at first instance,[278] the only issue in England is whether the patient has understood the 'nature' and 'purpose' of the procedure. A misunderstanding of that may, of course, arise through fraud or misrepresentation, but it may arise simply through mistake by the patient. If fraud or misrepresentation has occurred, that may provide good evidence that the patient's consent was not 'real'. But, it is the non-consent to

---

[271] Good practice is, however, that explicit consent be obtained: see *Medical Students in Hospitals* (DoH, 1991, HC(91)18).   [272] See above, para 3.95.
[273] But see *Perna v Pirozzi* (1983) 457 A 2d 431.   [274] See above, para 3.49.
[275] ibid.
[276] *Reibl v Hughes* (1980) 114 DLR (3d) 1, 11 *per* Laskin CJ.
[277] But contrast *Lokay v Kilgour* (1984) 31 CCLT 177 (misrepresentation must go to 'the very nature of the procedure'). See discussion in Picard, E and Robertson, G, *Legal Liability of Doctors and Hospitals in Canada* (3rd edn, 1996), 57–60.
[278] *Chatterton v Gerson* (n 245 above), 265 *per* Bristow J and *Appleton v Garrett* (n 262 above), 77 *per* Dyson J.

the procedure rather than the fraud which makes an apparent consent not a real one.[279] Fraud or misrepresentation as to a co-lateral matter, such as an inherent risk in the procedure or an alternative procedure, will not, however, affect the patient's consent. In *Sidaway*,[280] Sir John Donaldson MR stated that:

> [i]t is only if the consent is obtained by fraud or by misrepresentation of the nature of what is to be done that it can be said that an apparent consent is not a true consent.

Of course, the patient may have an action in deceit or negligent misrepresentation in such circumstances but he will not have a claim in battery. In England there is no so-called 'fraud exception' to the 'nature' and 'purpose' rule.[281]

(ii) *Negligence*

(a) Introduction

When a doctor or other health care professional has no consent at all to touch   **3.101**
someone, it has been seen that an action in battery will lie at the suit of the person touched unless some justifying or excusing circumstance exists.[282] It has also been seen, however, that English law is reluctant to see the law of battery invoked in the context of medical care.[283] Thus, provided that the person touched knows 'in broad terms'[284] the general nature and purpose of the touching, this will be regarded as sufficient to constitute a valid consent, so as to defeat a claim in battery.

But this is not the end of the story. Any purported consent must also meet the   **3.102**
requirements of the tort of negligence. This immediately needs explanation. Negligence is concerned not with the presence or absence of consent, but with the defendant's failure to comply with a legally imposed duty of care. Thus, if the tort of negligence is to have a role, two matters must be established: that a *duty* exists and the *content* of that duty, (the *quantum* of care demanded). Clearly, a duty exists to take care not to harm the patient through careless acts. But what is being considered here are not the doctor's acts. Instead, the concern is with what the doctor must do *prior to* acting, so as to ensure that

---

[279] See, in the context of rape, *R v Linekar* [1995] 3 All ER 69, 73 *per* Morland J.

[280] [1984] 1 All ER 1018, 1026. See also Dunn LJ at 1029.

[281] Notice, however, the remark of Sir John Donaldson MR in *Freeman v Home Office (No 2)* [1984] 1 All ER 1036 at 1044 apparently recognising a wider 'fraud exception'. *Freeman* was decided 2 weeks after *Sidaway* in the Court of Appeal and it is most unlikely that the Master of the Rolls intended to recant on his clear statement in *Sidaway*.

[282] See above, para 3.01 *et seq.*   [283] See above, para 3.91.

[284] *per* Bristow J in *Chatterton v Gerson* (n 103 above), and see *Hills v Potter* (n 241 above). See further, Kennedy and Grubb, *Medical Law* (n 58 above), 151 *et seq.*

proper consent has been given for those acts. In particular, the concern is with the knowledge or information which the patient is entitled to be given, (assuming the patient to be competent), before any purported consent is valid. It is important to recognise that, where any complaint arises, what the patient is complaining of is not that a particular procedure was carried out without proper care and skill, (it may have been performed with the utmost skill), but rather, that it was carried out without proper permission.

3.103 Expressed in this way, it is immediately apparent that if the patient is entitled to be informed, the doctor is under a duty to provide the information. To so assert, however, is to place on the doctor a duty of affirmative action. It is trite law that English law regards such a duty as exceptional. While it is one thing to expect people to refrain from careless behaviour, English law, with its aversion to the 'officious intermeddler',[285] will not ordinarily impose a duty to do something on behalf of another. The first step, therefore, is to examine the legal basis for the doctor's duty to inform a patient, so as to obtain valid consent to treatment.

(b) A Duty to Inform

3.104 One well-established ground on which a duty to inform could be based would be to find that, as between the doctor and the patient, there exists a 'special relationship', giving rise to a duty to act. The traditional example is the parent–child and, by extension, the teacher–child relationship. In effect, therefore, the duty is derived from the status of the parties. The common law has not, however, regarded the doctor–patient relationship as falling into the category of special relationship. Its legal origins lay in the law of contract and thus in an assumption that the parties were at arm's length. The notion of vulnerability which underpins the law's recognition of a special relationship, while clearly a central feature of modern medicine, did not colour the earlier development of the law. Thus, a duty to inform cannot be derived from the existence of a special relationship.

3.105 An alternative ground on which English law could base an affirmative duty to inform can be derived from the law of equity. If the relationship between the doctor and patient were fiduciary in nature, a duty to inform could be readily recognised, as an incidence of the more general duty to seek to maximise the interests of the beneficiary. This was the approach adopted by certain courts in the US.[286] Since these courts had previously categorised the doctor–patient relationship as fiduciary, they had little difficulty in carving out and devel-

---

[285] See eg the discussion in Birks, P, *Introduction to the Law of Restitution* (Oxford University Press, 1989), 102–3.
[286] See eg *Canterbury v Spence* (n 231 above), and *Cobbs v Grant* (1972) 502 P 2d 1.

oping a duty to inform. English law, however, has never regarded the doctor–patient relationship as fiduciary. Indeed, when asked to do so, the House of Lords expressly refused.[287] Furthermore, despite some academic support for the idea,[288] it is unlikely that there will be a change of mind. Thus, any duty to inform cannot be based on a fiduciary relationship.

So, where does the duty come from? Curiously, when the English courts very belatedly got round to examining whether a doctor is under a duty to inform a patient, the legal-technical difficulties involved in actually finding some juristic basis for a duty of affirmative action were largely ignored. Instead, the general duty of care owed by a doctor to a patient was interpreted as extending not only to acts but also omissions, in this case the failure properly to inform.[289] As ever, the law of torts displayed the English law's preference for pragmatism over principle. From an analytical point of view, what this appears to mean is that once a doctor's assistance has been sought and the doctor has undertaken to offer treatment, (that is, a doctor–patient relationship has come into existence), this undertaking includes a duty to act affirmatively on the patient's behalf. This, in turn, translates into a duty to inform so as to obtain from a patient a valid consent. **3.106**

As regards the existence of the duty, the remaining point to notice is the point at which the duty arises and for how long it continues. Clearly, it arises whenever the doctor proposes a therapeutic intervention. Valid consent must be obtained prior to embarking on therapy, whether it involves touching the patient or prescribing medicines or other such treatment. Moreover, it is a continuing duty. This means that whenever the doctor engages in any new or additional therapeutic intervention, not covered by the previous consent, there arises a fresh duty to obtain consent and, thus, to inform before proceeding. This is rather easier to stipulate than apply, as cases in the US demonstrate.[290] The general law may well be that where the doctor intends to embark on a course of conduct which is sufficiently different from that previously agreed to and as regards which the appropriate legal standard would demand that the patient be informed, a new duty to inform arises. **3.107**

---

[287] In *Sidaway v Board of Governors of the Bethlem Royal Hospital* (n 26 above), 650–1.

[288] See eg, Bartlett, 'Doctors as Fiduciaries' [1997] 5 Med L Rev 193.

[289] See eg, the speech of Lord Scarman in *Sidaway* (n 26 above), 652, '[i]f it be recognised that a doctor's duty of care extends not only to the health and well being of his patient but also to a proper respect for his patient's rights, the duty to warn [and, generally, to inform] can be seen to be a part of the doctor's duty of care'.

[290] See Commentary, [1995] 3 Med L Rev 209 (I K), on the cases of *Rizzo v Schiller* (1994) 445 SE 2d 153 and *Sinclair by Sinclair v Block* (1993) 663 A 2d 1137, both of which involved the question whether a separate and further consent was called for before resort to forceps during childbirth, given the specific and new risks associated therewith.

This analysis is somewhat delphic because it will be clear that the separation between the existence of a duty and its content breaks down in this situation. If the duty to inform is part of the duty of care, then, depending on who determines the extent of that duty, a new duty will arise when the extent of that duty is exceeded. Whether it is exceeded depends, therefore, on who determines its extent.

(c) Content of the Duty

3.108 The first question to ask is what sort of information could a duty to disclose be concerned with? Obviously, the range includes information about the proposed procedure, risks which arise from it, their likelihood and the consequences if they eventuate, other therapeutic options which exist, including the option not to receive any treatment at all, and the implications of these options.

3.109 The next question, of course, is what, from this range, is the doctor under a duty to pass on to the patient? Analytically, this translates into the question, what is the criterion by reference to which the duty is determined in law. Beginning from the first principles, there at least *three options*. The *first* is that the doctor should be under a duty to pass on all that information which the patient being treated wishes to know. This is a subjective test. The underlying philosophy is rights-based. The patient has a right to know as a necessary feature of the overarching right to self-determination. Even as stated, however, this criterion is not free from difficulty. Should it be expressed as what the patient wishes to know or what the patient would wish to know, (if only he knew)? The former is hard enough to satisfy. The latter verges on the impossible.

3.110 A *second* option is that the doctor should pass on that information which any reasonable patient would wish to know before giving consent. The weakness of this approach is clear. It is a compromise. It purports to take account of the patient's right to be informed but does so at the cost of converting the actual patient into a hypothetical reasonable patient. To that extent, the particular circumstances of the patient are in danger of being ignored. At some point, indeed, the purported subjectivity of the test could evaporate into an objective examination of reasonableness.

3.111 A *third* option is that the doctor's duty should be to inform the patient of that which doctors as a profession think it appropriate for the patient to know. Clearly, this test has no element of subjectivity. It reflects a philosophy of paternalism, according to which the doctor is the better judge of what should inform the medical transaction. Not surprisingly, this option has not been free from criticism in an age in which paternalism has fewer defenders.[291] Quite apart from any ethical attack, the option is vulnerable to at least two further criticisms. First, it assumes that information relevant to making a decision about treatment is a matter of technical medical expertise, properly within the purview of medical expertise. Clearly, diagnosis, treatment and prognosis are uniquely matters of medical expertise. How to respond to these; whether to go ahead and accept (ie consent to) treatment, seems to be of a different order. If anything, it would appear to be uniquely within the competence of the patient (the first option set out earlier). Certainly, it would appear hard to describe it as within the *unique* competence of doctors. This is not to say that doctors should have no role in setting the boundaries of the process of gaining consent. If patients expect them to be sensitive in how they communicate what may sometimes be difficult news, doctors are entitled to make judgements as to how to proceed. But this concerns the 'how' of imparting information, which is undoubtedly a matter of medical expertise. It does not relate to 'whether' to inform, which is what is of concern here. It is hard to see how this is a matter for doctors alone. The second criticism which can be raised is that, if the content of the doctor's duty is to pass on that information which other doctors would, it assumes a degree of professional agreement which is unlikely to be demonstrable in practice. Doctors clearly and quite properly may disagree on diagnosis or treatment. There is, however, some structure of learning about these which all (or virtually all) accept and to which all refer, even though they may derive divergent views from it. There is no such body of learning concerning what information a patient should be told which all doctors accept and draw upon. Thus, the idea of a professional standard of disclosure may proceed from a completely false premiss.

Whatever the weaknesses of this third option, it represents the current **3.112** position in English law. The starting point for an examination of the doctor's duty of care must, of course, be *Bolam v Friern Barnet Hospital Management Committee*.[292] As has been suggested, this case established that the criterion against which a doctor's conduct falls to be judged is by whether it complies with the views of a responsible body of medical opinion.[293] Put another way, to prove breach of duty a patient would have to show that no responsible doctor would have done what was done. The shortcomings of this approach are well known and set out elsewhere.[294] Equally, a slow reappraisal of *Bolam*

---

[291] See eg Brazier, M, *Medicine, Patients and the Law*, 2nd edn (Penguin, 1992), 78 *et seq.*
[292] N 243 above. For a critical appraisal of *Bolam*, see Kennedy and Grubb (n 58 above), 440 *et seq.*
[293] 'A doctor is not guilty of negligence if he has acted in accordance with a practice accepted as proper by a responsible body of medical men skilled in that particular art', ibid, *per* McNair J.
[294] See eg, Kennedy and Grubb (n 58 above), 440 *et seq.*

by the higher courts has been taking place.[295] Thus, there are two matters of importance here. The first is to notice the effect which *Bolam* had on the duty to inform, culminating in the leading case in the House of Lords, *Sidaway v Governors of Bethlem Hospital*.[296] The second is to enquire what any reappraisal of *Bolam* may mean for the law as currently set out in *Sidaway*.

(d) *Sidaway*[297]

3.113 Mrs Sidaway brought an action against the Hospital complaining that she had not been warned, when she consented to surgery on her neck to relieve pain, that it carried a small but acknowledged risk of causing damage to the spinal column and nerve roots. Her surgeon had died before the trial, thus making it impossible to establish what precisely passed between him and Mrs Sidaway. For this reason alone, Mrs Sidaway's case was lost. But the courts, right up to and including the House of Lords, opted to take the opportunity to set out the law on the duty to inform.

3.114 It may seem remarkable that English law had to wait until 1985 for an authoritative statement of the law. Indeed, prior to the *Sidaway* case, there had been only two first instance decisions (other than *Bolam*, which, *inter alia*, was concerned with the doctor's duty to inform) which had clearly addressed the question and both were in the early 1980s.[298] The explanation is complex but, at bottom, reflects the emerging clash between the traditional reluctance to challenge the long-established acquiescence and a preparedness to hold professionals to account.[299]

Lord Diplock

3.115 There are three distinct strands in the speeches delivered by their Lordships in *Sidaway*.[300] The first is that of Lord Diplock. To him, the duty to inform was not a separate duty but part of the overarching duty of care owed by the doctor to the patient. The doctor's 'normal duty of care . . .. has

---

[295] *Bolitho v City* and *Hackney HA* (n 243 above) represents the current (and less than satisfactory) state of reappraisal.   [296] N 26 above.

[297] ibid. For a detailed analysis of the case, see Kennedy, *Treat Me Right* (Oxford, 1992), ch 9. See also, Brazier (n 291 above); Mason and McCall Smith, *Law and Medical Ethics*, 4th edn (Butterworths, 1994), 237 *et seq*; and Kennedy and Grubb (n 58 above), 173 *et seq*.

[298] *Chatterton v Gerson* (n 103 above) and *Hills v Potter* (n 214 above), decided in 1981 and 1984.

[299] See further, Kennedy (n 297 above).

[300] For a different interpretation, see Jones, *Medical Negligence*, 2nd edn (Sweet and Maxwell, 1996), 337 *et seq*. Jones' view, when originally advanced in his first edition in 1991, required what was at the time a heroic reading of *Bolam*, not previously endorsed by the courts. The House of Lords' decision in *Bolitho* (n 243 above) suggests that while the courts may not have realised it, Jones was right all the time.

hitherto been treated as a single comprehensive duty covering all the ways in which a doctor is called upon to exercise his skill and judgement . . .'.[301] Lord Diplock stated that 'this general duty is not subject to dissection into a number of component parts to which different criteria of what satisfy the duty of care apply, such as diagnosis, treatment, advice (including warning of any risks of something going wrong however skillfully the treatment advised is carried out)'.[302] The content of this duty was set out in *Bolam*. Thus, *Bolam* applied. The doctor's duty in obtaining a patient's consent is to provide the patient with that information which a responsible body of doctors would judge to be appropriate. If, therefore, doctors in their wisdom choose to withhold certain information, out of a concern, as they see it, for the patient's interests, it is not for the courts to gainsay them. The extent and limits of the doctor's duty to disclose are, therefore, *per* Lord Diplock, for doctors to determine, through expert evidence of contemporary professional practice. The third of the options set out in paragraph 3.111 above prevails.

Lord Bridge

The second strand is that developed by Lord Bridge and, with some variation, **3.116** Lord Templeman. Lord Bridge, with whose speech Lord Keith concurred, also relied on *Bolam*. But, he then appeared to add a gloss which suggests that the content of the duty to inform may, for him, be more than just *Bolam* simpliciter. For, in his speech, Lord Bridge insisted that the doctor's duty must '*primarily* be a matter of clinical judgement', and thus to be derived from *Bolam*.[303] Undoubtedly, the reason for his adding this rider was his anxiety not to be seen to be handing over the content of the duty entirely to the medical profession. In this regard, he can be seen to be echoing the similarly cryptic assertion of Sir John Donaldson MR in the Court of Appeal, when he held that, 'the duty is fulfilled if the doctor acts in accordance with a practice rightly accepted as proper by a body of skilled and experienced medical men'.[304] The difficulty, however, lies in understanding what, if anything, Lord Bridge's gloss amounts to. He did provide some guidance. He intimated that where the circumstances were such as to give rise to a 'substantial risk of grave adverse consequences',[305] the doctor could well be under

---

[301] *Sidaway*, (n 26 above), 657.
[302] ibid.
[303] Sidaway, (n 226 above), 663 (emphasis added). Lord Bridge had previously spent some time analysing North American jurisprudence, particularly the cases of *Canterbury v Spence* (n 31 above), and *Reibl v Hughes* (n 23 above). While he 'appreciate[d] the force of [the] reasoning', he chose not to follow it, for reasons which are less than wholly persuasive, see Kennedy (n 297 above).
[304] *Sidaway* [1984] 1 All ER 1018, 1028 (emphasis added) (Court of Appeal).
[305] *Sidaway v Bethlem Royal Hospital Governors* (n 26 above)

a duty to inform the patient, whatever the prevailing medical view. The example Lord Bridge chose to illustrate this proposition were the circumstances which arose in the Canadian Supreme Court case of *Reibl* v *Hughes*.[306] In that case, there was a 10 per cent risk of a stroke following surgery. 'In such a case', Lord Bridge averred, 'in the absence of some cogent clinical reason why the patient should not be informed, a doctor, recognising and respecting his patient's right of decision, could hardly fail to appreciate the necessity for an appropriate warning'.[307]

3.117 It is clear that, by his gloss on *Bolam*, Lord Bridge was seeking to articulate the view that doctors ordinarily were entitled to set the legal standard of disclosure, but at some point, where the patient might be expected to want a say in things, the doctor could not merely rely on what fellow professionals did but must take account of what the patient may wish to know, indeed the patient's right to know. Lord Bridge's approach may, therefore, be categorised as a combination of old-fashioned paternalism and, at some ill-defined point, modern consumerism based on patients' rights. Quite apart from the unattractiveness of the former and the difficulty in operating the latter, a further weakness lies in knowing when the latter is supposed to displace *Bolam*. The words 'substantial risk of grave adverse consequences' are particularly unhelpful, not least because the question of who determines 'substantial' or 'grave' is the same question as who sets the content of the duty. Furthermore, it is unhelpful to offer by way of guidance an approach based on percentages. Not only does this purport to reduce what is a matter of values to a mathematical calculation, but it also invites medical experts to shift the argument from whether the profession would have informed the patient, to the probability, in percentage terms, of an occurrence and its comparative gravity. Furthermore, it confuses the likelihood of something happening with its gravity,[308] if it does. It is trite to observe that a 1 per cent risk of catastrophic injury may be less attractive than a 20 per cent risk of minor inconvenience. Thus, while Lord Bridge's endorsement of *Bolam* was not wholesale, it is not easy to determine what he seeks to add to it. It is not entirely clear that he has adopted the second of the options set out in paragraph 3.110 above, although not wholly endorsing the third. It may not come as a surprise, therefore, that Lord Bridge's speech, though much pored over by commentators, has not been taken up by later courts.

---

[306] N 230 above.   [307] *Sidaway* (n 26 above), 663.
[308] See further, Kennedy (n 297 above).

Lord Templeman

Turning to the speech of Lord Templeman, it too equivocates between an **3.118** acceptance of *Bolam* and a hint of something more. The difficulty lies in identifying precisely what it is that Lord Templeman adds to *Bolam*. The key appears to lie in the distinction he draws between 'general' dangers (or risks), and 'special' dangers.[309] As regards the former, 'a simple and general explanation . . . should have been sufficient to alert [the patient]'.[310] At least, therefore, there is some duty to inform, albeit vestigial. As regards the latter dangers (or risks), the doctor is under a duty to inform the patient. There is, for Lord Templeman, 'no doubt that a doctor ought to draw the attention of a patient to a danger which may be special in kind or magnitude or special to the patient'.[311] Two objections can immediately be made to Lord Templeman's differentiation of these categories of danger or risk. The first is that it may be wrong as a matter both of fact and policy to assume that all patients are aware of, and, therefore, the doctor has no duty to warn of, 'general' risks, such as the risks arising from anaesthesia.[312] Secondly, the terms 'general' and 'special', are not terms of art and it is fair to say that Lord Templeman's attempt to differentiate them is not wholly clear. Indeed, he ultimately falls back on the flawed idea of percentages, endorsed by Lord Bridge. Moreover, it must be self-evident that what might be 'general' to one patient may be 'special' to another, depending on their different circumstances. Thus, the central issue remains unsolved, namely who it is who defines and operates these criteria, the medical profession or the court. In summary, therefore, if Lord Templeman does regard the doctor's duty as being more than *Bolam*, (and it is certainly arguable that he does), his speech, when read as a whole, is at best equivocal and certainly does not offer a clear guide.

Lord Scarman

Lord Scarman took a different track from the rest of the court. To him the **3.119** argument was ultimately one of rights.[313] In analysing the issue in this way, Lord Scarman distanced himself from the other Law Lords. To that extent, although all of their Lordships concurred in dismissing Mrs Sidaway's appeal, Lord Scarman's speech is often referred to as if he were in dissent. For Lord Scarman, a patient has a right to know[314] what treatment entails so as to be

---

[309] *Sidaway* (n 26 above), 664–5.
[310] ibid, 664.   [311] ibid, 665.   [312] Compare Lord Scarman's view, ibid, 654.
[313] '[T]he doctor's duty arises from his patient's rights', ibid, 654.
[314] Indeed, Lord Scarman termed it a 'basic human right', ibid, 649, terminology which acquires added significance as English law moves gradually to an acceptance of rights-based arguments and the incorporation of the European Convention on Human Rights into English law.

able to make a reasoned choice and, thus, give a valid consent. This right, he held, finds its expression in English law in the doctor's duty to inform the patient. Unlike Lord Diplock, Lord Scarman was prepared to see that the duty to provide information is of a different order from the duty to take care in treatment. It is not, for Lord Scarman, a matter to be decided solely on the basis of evidence as to prevailing medical practice. This is not to say that Lord Scarman regarded such evidence as irrelevant.[315] It is, of course, relevant, but, beginning from a premiss of patients' rights, it cannot be determinative.

3.120 Lord Scarman chose as his guide the case law which had evolved in both the US and Canada in the previous two decades, particularly *Canterbury v Spence*[316] and *Reibl v Hughes*[317] respectively. Although not prepared analytically to adopt the rights based approach reflected in the North American doctrine of 'informed consent', preferring the common law's duty approach, he was clearly persuaded of the underlying correctness of these cases. But, if Lord Scarman recognised a duty to inform a patient, how did he respond to the oft-repeated sore that this would put every doctor under a legal obligation to pass on to the patient in, at most, a couple of conversations, what it had taken the doctor years of Medical School and experience to acquire? Though such rhetoric may go down well at School reunions, it is, of course, an example of reductio ad absurdum. What the law can properly expect of doctors, on Lord Scarman's approach, is that they provide the patient with sufficient, or adequate, information to make a considered decision. It could not require, nor has it ever been suggested, that the doctor pass on to the patient everything there is to know about a condition or its treatment.

3.121 How is this general idea of the doctor's duty translated by Lord Scarman into more detailed law? He first settles on the concept of 'materiality' found in the North American cases. The doctor is under a duty to inform the patient of that information which is 'material' to making a decision.[318] This, in turn, causes Lord Scarman to have to identify what 'material' means. At this point, it is clear that Lord Scarman must choose whether to prefer the first or the second of the options set out in paragraphs 3.109 and 3.110 above, (he obviously rejects the third). Information could be material, and thus the doctor would be under a duty to disclose it to the patient, if it were something which the particular patient would wish to know, or, if it were that which a reasonable patient, in the particular patient's circumstances, would

---

[315] ibid, 654.
[316] N 231 above.   [317] N 230 above.
[318] *Sidaway* (n 26 above), 655.

wish to know. The analytical difficulties associated with adopting the former meaning were referred to in paragraph 3.109. It is also important to notice a pragmatic difficulty. A court hearing a claim in negligence based on a doctor's alleged breach of the duty to inform could be met with evidence from the patient that, had a particular fact been disclosed, he would never have agreed to the procedure which was carried out. If believed, the patient would prevail. However, this may be to cast too onerous a burden on doctors. The law would, in effect, allow them to be judged against the 20/20 vision of hindsight.[319]

It is not entirely surprising, therefore, that Lord Scarman chose to define 'material' by reference to the reasonable patient, following and endorsing the reasoning in *Reibl* and *Canterbury*. '[T]he duty [to warn] is confined to material risk. The test of materiality is whether in the circumstances of the particular case the court is satisfied that a reasonable person in the patient's position would be likely to attach significance to the risk'.[320] The duty to disclose, therefore, was made subject to the traditional constraint of the tort of negligence—that reasonableness should be a central feature. Lord Scarman then went on to add a further constraint to the duty. To meet the frequent objection, (evidence for which is not easily obtained) that it would be better not to inform a patient of certain matters, Lord Scarman added to his analysis a further element: what is called in North America the 'therapeutic privilege'. By this, a doctor is absolved from the duty to inform if, by complying with it the patient would suffer more harm than good. A commonly cited example is the patient who needs an operation but has an abiding fear of anaesthesia, such that, if advised of the risks involved, he might refuse the operation. In such a case, it is argued that the doctor should have a discretion not to inform that patient, out of a concern for the wider interests of the patient. Expressed in this way, the potential drawbacks of the doctrine are immediately apparent. It marks a reversion to the paternalism of *Bolam*, which, if not carefully controlled, could have the effect of reintroducing the professional standard of whether to inform through the back door. Nonetheless, Lord Scarman recognised the validity, in principle, of the doctrine and with suitable words of warning[321] made it part of his overall design for the duty to inform.

3.122

---

[319] See Lord Scarman's remarks: 'Ideally, the court should ask itself whether in the particular circumstances the risk was such that this particular patient would think it significant if he was told it existed. I would think that, as a matter of ethics, this is the test of the doctor's duty. The law, however, operates not in Utopia but in the world as it is: and such an enquiry would prove in practice to be frustrated by the subjectivity of its aim and purpose', ibid, 654.
[320] ibid. It is important to note that, although Lord Scarman referred only to risks, he accepted that the duty to inform extends also to information about alternatives: ' . . . the options of alternative treatment', as he put it, ibid, 645.
[321] '[I]t is a defence available to the doctor which, if he invokes it, he must prove', ibid, 654.

Breach of Duty

3.123 A final question which should be asked relates to breach of duty. What must the doctor do so as to comply with the duty to inform? Must the doctor make sure that the patient *has understood* what he has been told or need the doctor only *take reasonable steps* to ensure that this is so? Clearly, the former is a particularly onerous duty and, some might argue, impossible to achieve. The doctor may inform, using the best possible techniques of communication, until the cows come home but the patient may still not understand. The view has prevailed, therefore, that English law only requires the doctor to behave reasonably. The issue arose in *Smith v Tunbridge Wells HA*.[322] In that case, Moreland J took what, on its face, seems a rather surprising view. He stated '. . . the doctor, when warning of the risks, must take reasonable care to ensure that his explanation of the risks is intelligible to his patient'. So far, so good. The doctor must behave reasonably and 'ensure' (strong word) that the explanation is 'intelligible' (weaker word). Intelligible only means that someone is capable of understanding, not, critically, that he does so. But then Moreland J goes on to say that: '[t]he doctor should use language [which] . . . will be understood by the patient'. This, with respect, cannot be right, if it means that the doctor must make the patient understand. It would cast too great a burden on the doctor, as well as threaten to bring into disrepute the very notion of the duty to inform, (which, in any event. is not without its detractors).[323]

Summary

3.124 At the end of this review of the three strands in the *Sidaway* case, it may be helpful to draw them together to identify what the case on its face decided. The House of Lords held that the doctor's duty to inform is part of the duty to exercise reasonable care and skill. The content of the duty is governed, wholly or in very large part, by the *Bolam* principle: a doctor must pass on to the patient that information which, according to medical evidence, is thought appropriate by a responsible body of medical opinion. The speeches of Lords Bridge and Templeman add a somewhat indistinct caveat to *Bolam*, in somewhat ill-defined circumstances, suggesting some limit to the operation of *Bolam* in the context of the duty to inform. The North American doctrine of 'informed consent', (always something of a misnomer), is not part of English law. The 'reasonable patient' test, adopted by *Reibl* and espoused by Lord Scarman, is equally not part of English law. As a consequence, the

---

[322] [1994] 5 Med LR 334.
[323] See further, Commentary on *Smith*, 3 Med L Rev 198, 201, (AG).

doctrine of the therapeutic privilege, only necessary, if at all, if there were a prima facie right to know, is not part of English law.

(e) *Gold v Haringey HA*[324]

It is trite law that cases become authority for those propositions which courts later identify as the ones which they intend to follow. After *Sidaway*, there was genuine disagreement as to its precise significance. It was recognised that a later court could not follow Lord Scarman, since he was in a minority of one. What was important was whether the doctrine emerging from *Sidaway* was seen as being '*Bolam* simpliciter' or '*Bolam* plus', and if the latter, what the 'plus' element might be. It was not a long wait. Within two years, in *Gold*, the Court of Appeal, in the person of Lloyd LJ (with whom Watkins and Stephen Brown LJJ agreed), came down firmly on the side of *Bolam* simpliciter. In referring to *Sidaway*, Lloyd LJ chose to rely exclusively on the speech of Lord Diplock. The apparent agonising of Lords Bridge and Templeman did not appear to move him. Thus, the doctor's duty to inform was to be measured not by what the patient, or a reasonable patient, would wish to know so as to make an informed choice, but by what a responsible body of medical opinion would regard as proper to tell him.[325]   **3.125**

The fact that the first law relating to what, in ethical terms, is seen to be a critical aspect of the doctor–patient relationship did not emerge until the early to mid-1980s was remarkable enough. Even more remarkable, perhaps, is the fact that in two years the courts had travelled backwards to *Bolam*, while other jurisdictions scrambled to consign the medical paternalism and lack of concern for patients' rights, which *Bolam* can be said to represent, to the archives. Any attempt to explain the courts' preference for *Bolam* cannot, of course, overlook the traditional tenderness which, despite all claims to the contrary, the law has shown to the medical profession. Nor can it overlook the aversion to the possibility of an increase in malpractice litigation which the courts routinely display. Beyond these and a natural conservatism, it is hard to find an explanation for so significant a dissonance between prevailing ethical analysis and public opinion on one hand and the judicial response on the other.   **3.126**

---

[324] [1988] QB 481.

[325] The view taken in *Gold* has subsequently been followed in a number of cases, e g, *Palmer v Eadie* (18 May 1987, unreported (Court of Appeal)); *Blyth v Bloomsbury HA* [1993] 4 Med LR 151 (Court of Appeal); *Moyes v Lothian Health Board* [1990] 1 Med LR 463 (Court of Session, Outer House); and see *Powell v Boldaz* (1 July, 1997 (Court of Appeal)). See further, Kennedy and Grubb (n 258 above), 187.

(f) Beyond Giving Information: Answering Questions Truthfully

3.127   It is possible, of course, to draw some distinction between an affirmative duty to volunteer information and a duty to respond to questions. The latter seems that much more recognisable as a legal duty, since it assumes an existing relationship between doctor and patient. On reflection, however, both derive from an undertaking of responsibility and, thus, are both aspects of the general duty to exercise due care and skill. To say that there is a duty to respond is not, however, to indicate the content of the duty. Remarkably, in this day and age, it remains an issue whether the duty is to answer truthfully, or to give that answer which a responsible body of the medical profession would regard as appropriate, even if it is only part of the truth or no truth at all. This distinction can only exist, of course, if there is a view within the medical profession that truth is not always the appropriate option.

3.128   That such a view used to exist emerged in the well-known case of *Hatcher v Black*.[326] Moreover, in that case, Lord Denning went so far as to endorse it, remarking that, while not telling the truth to a patient might be ethically wrong, it was not necessarily a breach of the doctor's duty of care in law, if it conformed with professional practice. '[The doctor] told a lie, but he did it because he thought that in the circumstances it was justifiable . . . [T]he law does not condemn the doctor when he only does that which many a wise and good doctor would do.'[327] That was in 1954. By the time *Sidaway* reached the House of Lords, it may be thought that attitudes had changed. The speech of Lord Bridge, with which the Lords Diplock and Templeman agreed on this point, suggested that they had. Lord Bridge stated unequivocally that, '[w]hen questioned specifically by a patient . . . about risks involved in a particular treatment proposed, the doctor's duty must, in my opinion, be to answer truthfully and as fully as the questioner requires'.[328] Thus, it seemed, at least that part of the duty to inform which involved answering questions was not to be governed by *Bolam*. But this was to reckon without the Court of Appeal. In *Blyth v Bloomsbury HA*,[329] the Court of Appeal decided that a doctor is not under a duty to respond truthfully when asked question. Rather, the duty is as laid down in *Bolam*.[330]

[326] *The Times*, 2 July 1954.   [327] ibid.
[328] *Sidaway* (n 26 above) and see further, Kennedy and Grubb (n 258 above), 203 *et seq*.
[329] N 325 above.
[330] See eg, the observation of Kerr LJ that 'the *Bolam* test is all-pervasive in this context', *Gold* (n 324 above).

(g) Post-Treatment Disclosures

There is one final element of the duty to inform which warrants mention. It **3.129** relates not to volunteering information before treatment, nor to answering questions, but to volunteering information *after* treatment, specifically where something has gone wrong and an explanation is called for. It might be thought that if *Bolam* governs the first two of these duties, there is not much likelihood of a different standard applying to the third, if, indeed, it is a duty at all. Sir John Donaldson MR appeared to take a different view on two separate occasions. In *Lee v South West Thames RHA*[331] and again in *Naylor v Preston AHA*,[332] he suggested, albeit in what amounted to judicial asides, that there may well be what he termed a 'duty of candour' or 'duty of candid disclosure', as being 'but one aspect of the duty of general care'.[333] By this, he meant that a doctor who knows or, perhaps has reason to suspect, that something has gone wrong in the treatment of a patient owes a duty to inform the patient. This is a far-reaching observation. It may be ethically appealing, but in the context of the trench warfare of medical negligence, it would not be regarded by those who advise doctors as a duty but rather an act of folly. In the event, although his comments have attracted the attention of commentators, they have not been endorsed by the courts. One reason may be that, quite apart from being obiter, Sir John Donaldson MR relied on the speeches of *Sidaway* regarding the duty to answer questions truthfully which, as has been seen, were subsequently disavowed by the Court of Appeal. That said, however, Stuart-Smith LJ, writing for the Court of Appeal in *Powell v Boldaz*,[334] appears not to have entirely closed the door on Sir John Donaldson MR's newly fashioned duty. He held that it could not avail the plaintiff, but seemed to avoid disavowing it completely.[335]

(h) *Sidaway*: The Future

As has been seen, *Sidaway* and the other cases on the duty to inform, derive their **3.130** sustenance from *Bolam*. If the link between *Bolam* and *Sidaway*, or the very authority of *Bolam* itself, were to be undermined, the duty to inform could well undergo a significant transformation. It is important to assess the likelihood of this happening, not least so as to be able to plot the law's future course.

Perhaps, the first point to notice is the current state of common law else- **3.131** where. In the US, despite the assumption that the doctrine of informed

---

[331] [1985] 2 All ER 385. [332] [1987] 1 WLR 958.
[333] See further, the discussion in Kennedy and Grubb (n 58 above), 230 *et seq.*
[334] N 325 above. [335] ibid, Transcript, p 18.

consent as expressed in, for example, *Canterbury v Spence*,[336] is all pervasive, the truth is that the majority of States still adhere to the professional practice standard.[337] Thus, the pro- and anti-*Bolam* argument is as alive in the US as in the UK. In Canada, as has been seen, the argument is long over. The Supreme Court in *Reibl*[338] came down firmly in favour of the 'reasonable patient' test. Indeed, in subsequent decisions, the Court has flirted with the extent to which the doctor–patient relationship should properly be categorised as fiduciary.[339] Such a categorisation would, of course, fix the doctor with significantly increased duties. Whatever the fate of this line of reasoning, it is clear, therefore, that there is unlikely to be any going back in Canada as regards the doctor's duty to inform. If anything, the duty is set to make somewhat greater demands of the doctor, in an attempt to ensure that the inevitable imbalance in power between patient and doctor is both recognised and alleviated by law.

3.132 Perhaps the most interesting common law development has been in Australia. In *Rogers v Whitaker*,[340] the Australian High Court delivered a blistering criticism of *Sidaway* and the approach it represented. While accepting the analytical starting point in *Sidaway*, that there was a 'single, comprehensive duty' of care which covered diagnosis, treatment, and the provision of information so as to secure consent, the High Court made it clear that the content of the duty varies depending on which activity the doctor is engaged in. Even as regards diagnosis and treatment, the Court was reluctant to endorse the *Bolam* approach, holding only that medical evidence 'will have an influential, often decisive, role to play'. As regards the duty to inform, the Court was in no doubt. Whether a patient has received sufficient information to allow him to make a reasoned choice whether or not to consent to treatment 'is not a question the answer to which depends on medical standards or practices'. The content of this aspect of the doctor's duty was that 'a doctor has a duty to warn a patient of a material risk inherent in the proposed treatment; a risk is material if, in the circumstances of the particular case, a reasonable person in the patient's position, if warned of the risk, would be likely to attach significance to it, or if the medical practitioner is or should reasonably be

---

[336] N 231 above.
[337] See Rosenblatt, Law, and Rosenbaum, *Law and the American Health Care System* (Foundation Press, 1997), 901. [338] N 230 above.
[339] See eg, *McInerney v McDonald* (1992) 93 DLR (4th) 415 and *Norberg v Wynrib* (1992) 92 DLR (4th) 449, and the discussion in Kennedy, 'The Fiduciary Relationship and its Application to Doctors and Patients', in Birks (ed), *Wrongs and Remedies in the Twenty-First Century* (Oxford, 1996).
[340] (1992) 67 ALJR 47. References are to the judgment of the majority, Mason CJ, Brennan, Dawson, Toohey and McHugh JJ. Gaudron J agreed with the majority but wrote a separate judgment.

aware that the particular patient, if warned of the risk, would be likely to attach significance to it. This duty is subject to the therapeutic privilege.' (It may be added parenthetically that, of course, the case concerned risks but the duty is not limited merely to warnings about risks. It extends to information concerning any alternatives which may exist for the patient).

The Australian High Court, therefore, has followed the analysis favoured by the Canadian Supreme Court and by Lord Scarman in *Sidaway*. It has done so by recognising that while doctors must be listened to when questions are raised as to the exercise of their technical expertise, it is patients, or at least the notional reasonable patient, who should decide what they ought to be told before treatment may begin. Thus, the High Court broke the link between *Bolam* and the duty to inform. Perhaps even more significantly, the High Court also cast doubt on the continued validity of the *Bolam* principle itself. 'In Australia . . . [e]ven in the sphere of diagnosis and treatment . . . the *Bolam* principle has not always been applied.' The significance of the Court's judgment here lies in the fact that this potentially opens a second front against the prevailing English law approach. It is clear, (and always has been), that the duty to inform can be uncoupled from *Bolam*. This is something the English courts have so far chosen not to do. But, secondly, and independently, *Bolam*'s standing can be cast into doubt. If *Bolam* were to be undermined in English law, *Sidaway*, which is entirely a creature of *Bolam*, would appear ripe for re-evaluation by the courts. Any such re-evaluation would, arguably, involve a movement towards the reasonable patient standard, as articulated in Lord Scarman's speech in *Sidaway*.

3.133

The decision of the Court of Appeal in *Bolitho v City and Hackney HA*[341] may have marked the beginning of the undermining of *Bolam*. (The later decision of the House of Lords will be examined below, but there is value first in noticing the tentative steps taken by the lower court). *Bolitho* was not concerned with the duty to inform but with the quantum of care to be expected of a doctor in caring for a patient, that is to say, it was a straightforward *Bolam* case. The Court of Appeal in *Bolitho* sent a signal that the *Bolam* principle was increasingly regarded as anachronistic. (Subsequently, in a number of cases, the courts have begun to redefine the relative roles of the medical profession and the courts in determining the content of the duty

3.134

---

[341] (1992) 13 BMLR 1111 and see Commentary (1993) 1 Med. L Rev. 241 (AG). See also, for a similar re-thinking of their *Bolam*-like approach, the decision of the Irish Supreme Court in *Dunne v National Maternity Hospital* [1988] IR 91.

owed to the patient.[342] Lord Scarman's assertion in *Sidaway* (when referring to diagnosis and treatment), that 'the law imposes the duty of care; but the standard of care is a matter of medical judgement', may come to be seen as the high water mark of the law's acquiescence to professional practice). In *Bolitho*, the Court of Appeal took the first steps away from *Bolam*. Both Dillon and Farquharson LJJ, albeit in obiter dicta and in their different ways sought to reaffirm the classic legal proposition that (*pace* Lord Scarman in *Sidaway* and *Maynard*), the content of the duty of care is for the courts. The Court of Appeal was mindful, of course, that in technical medical matters it must lean heavily on evidence of professional practice. But, nonetheless, it was held that the last word lay with the courts. Of course, the big question then becomes; under what circumstances will the court impose its view of the doctor's duty, even in the face of contrary medical evidence.[343]

3.135 Dillon LJ took the view that it was only when medical evidence met the public law threshold of being *Wednesbury*[344] unreasonable that the court should supplant it. Farquharson LJ set the threshold somewhat lower. He was of the view that medical evidence should be subjected to 'a hard look' before being accepted, to decide whether it put 'the patient unnecessarily at risk'.[345] Thus began what Grubb has termed 'the new *Bolam*'.[346] As has been said, a series of cases has emerged, all of which have doubted the perceived underlying rationale of *Bolam* as expressed by Lord Scarman: that the court has no role. Moreover, as time has gone on and the courts have gained in confidence, so they have moved away from the extremely restrictive criterion of *Wednesbury* unreasonableness towards a more general preparedness to subject the evidence of professional practice to judicial scrutiny. *Joyce v*

---

[342] See, in particular, *Gascoigne v Ian Sheridan and Co (a firm)* [1994] 5 Med. LR 437, (High Court); *Smith v Tunbridge Wells HA* (n 322 above), (High Court), and Commentary thereon, 3 Med L Rev 198 (AG); *Bowers v Harrow HA* [1995] 6 Med LR 16, (High Court), *De Freitas v O'Brien* [1995] 6 Med LR 108 (Court of Appeal), and see Commentary thereon, 3 Med L Rev 195 (IK); *McAllister v Lewisham and North Southwark HA* [1994] 5 Med LR 343, (High Court), and Commentary thereon, 3 Med L Rev 201 (AG); and *Joyce v Merton, Sutton and Wandsworth HA* [1996] 7 Med LR 1 (Court of Appeal), and Commentary thereon, 4 Med L Rev 86 (AG).

[343] For a fascinating discussion of precisely the same issue, see the decision of the Canadian Supreme Court in *ter Neuzen v Korn* (1995) 127 DLR (4th) 577, and Commentary thereon, 5 Med L Rev 130 (IK). Sopinka J drew a distinction between matters of technical complexity, as regards which evidence of professional practice would be conclusive, and matters of common sense calling for obvious and reasonable precautions, as regards which the court was entitled to form its own view, regardless of expert medical evidence. '[E]xperts remain witnesses', he reminded the Court. While the distinction which he draws is not entirely satisfactory, the importance of the restatement that the duty of care is always for the court cannot be overstated.

[344] *Associated Provincial Picture Houses v Wednesbury Corporation* [1948] 1 KB 223.

[345] *Bolitho* (n 341 above), 119.   [346] Commentary on *Joyce* (n 342 above).

Merton, Sutton and Wandsworth HA[347] may serve as an example. The Court of Appeal followed Farquharson LJ's lead in *Bolitho* and subjected the medical evidence to 'a hard look'. In doing so, however, Hobhouse LJ made it clear that the criterion for review proposed by Dillon LJ in *Bolitho*, that of *Wednesbury* unreasonableness, was far too limited. It was specifically rejected. Then, Roch LJ went on to make it clear that the purpose of exposing the evidence to this 'hard look' was because otherwise it 'leaves . . . the decision of negligence or no negligence in the hands of the doctors, whereas that question must at the end of the day be one for the courts'.[348] As Grubb concludes, 'new *Bolam*' is the law unless the House of Lords says otherwise'.[349]

The House of Lords *did not* say otherwise when *Bolitho* came before them.[350] **3.136** Lord Browne-Wilkinson, speaking for the House, went back to the words of McNair J and fastened specifically on the words 'responsible' in the expression 'responsible body of medical men' and 'reasonable' in the expression 'reasonable body of opinion'. To these he added Lord Scarman's reference to 'a 'respectable' body of professional opinion' in *Maynard*. These words, ignored by the courts hitherto, separately and taken together, Lord Browne-Wilkinson reasoned, 'all show that the court has to be satisfied that the exponents of the body of opinion relied on can demonstrate that such opinion has a logical basis'. '[I]f, in a rare case,' he went on, 'it can be demonstrated that the professional opinion is not capable of withstanding logical analysis, the judge is entitled to hold that the body of opinion is not reasonable or respectable'. Later courts will have to make sense of Lord Browne-Wilkinson's rather odd use of the word 'logical', but the message is clear. The defences of *Bolam* have been breached. The court's role as the final arbiter of the quantum of care has been reasserted. Admittedly, no sooner had Lord Browne-Wilkinson let in the anti-*Bolam* marauders than he emphasised that 'it will very seldom be right for a judge to reach the conclusion that views genuinely held by a competent medical expert are unreasonable'. But this can be put down to the caution inherent in taking any new step.

The relevance of this move away from *Bolam* simpliciter is clear. With the **3.137** loosening of the courts' commitment to *Bolam*, it can only be a matter of time (and not much time) before *Sidaway* is also consigned to history. It was never necessary anyway to derive the rule in *Sidaway* from *Bolam*. With *Bolam* itself being refashioned, *Sidaway* (apart from Lord Scarman's speech), becomes even less sustainable. Moreover, it is most significant that in his speech in *Bolitho* refashioning *Bolam*, Lord Browne-Wilkinson made no

---

[347] N 342 above.   [348] ibid, 13–14.   [349] Commentary (n 342 above).
[350] N 243 above.

reference at all to the duty to inform. In discussing those cases which cast doubt on the traditional *Bolam* approach, he specifically referred to them as 'cases of diagnosis and treatment' and went on, 'I am not here considering questions of disclosure of risk'. This can, of course, be interpreted in two ways. First, Lord Browne-Wilkinson could be taken to mean that the duty to disclose was unaffected by the developments in *Bolitho* and still remained firmly in the grip of *Bolam*. Alternatively, he could be saying that the duty to disclose was a separate issue, to which *Bolam* and *Bolitho* were not relevant. Only this second interpretation has any plausibility.

3.138 It follows that the effect of *Bolitho* is to enable, indeed require, the courts to cast aside *Sidaway*, based as it is on a flawed interpretation of *Bolam*, and adopt the view that the content of the duty to inform is a matter for the court to determine, guided by but not ruled by the approach(es) to informing patients adopted by the medical profession. It must be obvious to all that English law cannot much longer resist the adoption of the following principles. A doctor has a duty to inform a patient, prior to any medical procedure, of any material facts relating to risks and alternatives. Material facts are those which a reasonable person in the patient's position would regard it as significant to know.[351] In exceptional circumstances, where the doctor could prove that passing on such information would deleteriously affect the patient's health or well-being, the doctor would, to that extent, be justified in invoking the 'therapeutic privilege'[352] and not informing the patient.

(i) Causation

3.139 A patient who complains of a doctor's breach of the duty to inform must, as in any action in negligence, show, as *a matter of fact*,[353] that the damage complained of was caused by the defendant doctor. The damage referred to here, of course, is not that the procedure or operation was badly carried out. Indeed, it may have been performed with consummate skill. It is that it was done without proper consent. It is this damage which the patient must show the doctor caused. The patient must, in other words, show that if he had been properly informed, he would not have consented. Expressed in this way, it will be immediately obvious that the crucial question becomes; what test of

---

[351] On the concept of the 'reasonable patient', see eg, Victorian, New South Wales and Australian Law Reform Commissions, *Informed Decisions about Medical Procedures* (1989).

[352] See further, Kennedy and Grubb (n 58 above), 211–14.

[353] Only issues of factual causation are raised here since no special problems of remoteness appear to arise in this context; see Kennedy and Grubb (n 58 above), 229 and *Moyes v Lothian Health Board* (n 325 above). On factual causation, see further, Kennedy and Grubb (n 58 above), 216–29.

proof must the patient satisfy? If the test is subjective, it may merely become a matter of ex post facto assertion. If, by contrast, it is entirely objective, reflecting what a 'reasonable patient' would have done, it may be difficult for the patient to succeed. This is because, except for a procedure which was truly elective, such that the patient really could take it or leave it, it will be hard to persuade a court that a reasonable patient would have refused treatment which has been carried out with due care and skill and which proved beneficial.

The issue of which test of factual causation should be employed has only commanded the attention of the English courts on three occasions. This is not, perhaps, surprising given that English law required the patient to surmount the initial barrier of *Bolam/Sidaway*. In *Chatterton v Gerson*[354] however, the issue attracted the observations of Bristow J. He commented that, '[w]hen the claim is based on negligence the plaintiff must prove not only the breach of duty to inform but had the duty not been broken she [the patient] would not have chosen to have the operation'. On its face, this appears to adopt a subjective approach. But, on the facts, the judge rejected what the patient claimed that she would have decided, in favour of a reasonable inference of what someone 'desperate for pain relief' (as she admittedly was) would choose. The net effect of Bristow' J's approach, therefore, appears to be a *hybrid* test of causation. The starting point is subjective: what the particular patient would have chosen to do, if informed. The patient's expressed view, then, undergoes an objective appraisal as to whether it is reasonably believable. In other words, the particular patient is expected to behave as, and will be judged as if he were, a reasonable patient (unless the contrary can be explicitly proved).

3.140

This hybrid approach of Bristow J has found favour in two other first instance decisions. In *Smith v Barking, Havering and Brentwood HA*,[355] Hutchison J adopted a 'subjective' test but employed an 'objective' yardstick by which to test the plaintiff's subjective evidence. Moreland J did the same in *Smith v Turnbridge Wells HA*.[356] Notwithstanding this apparent agreement, these first instance decisions may well find themselves tested on appeal to put beyond doubt the proper test of causation. Thus, it may be helpful to notice the contrasting approaches adopted in Canada and Australia respectively. In Canada, the Supreme Court in *Reibl*[357] opted for the objective approach. Laskin CJC expressed the fear that a subjective test would 'result inevitably in liability', once a breach of duty was established. For this reason, he held that

3.141

[354] N 103 above.   [355] [1994] 5 Med LR 285.
[356] [1994] 5 Med LR 334, and see Commentary, 3 Med L Rev 198 (AG), discussing both *Smith* cases.   [357] N 230 above.

'the objective standard is the preferable one on the issue of causation'.[358] Subsequently, by contrast, the New South Wales Court of Appeal in *Ellis v Wallsend District Hospital*[359] took a different tack. Both Samuels JA and Kirby P delivered powerful judgments endorsing the subjective approach and rejecting the reasoning in *Reibl*. Kirby P puts the test clearly as being 'whether, in particular circumstances . . . the particular patient . . . if told, would not have accepted the treatment'.

3.142 Both of these positions may be thought to go too far for the pragmatic English common law. The effect of the Canadian approach is to give with one hand and take away with the other. The duty to inform is established and then a test of causation adopted which will effectively frustrate most claims based on a breach of the duty. The Australian approach may be thought to give too much ground to the value of hindsight. It is likely, therefore, that if there is any development of the duty to inform in English law, the test of causation will reflect the hybrid approach in paragraph 3.140 rather than either of the alternative polar positions.

3. Voluntariness

(i) *Introduction*

3.143 Before any consent is valid in law, there is a third requirement which must be satisfied, in addition to the need to show that the person consenting is competent to do so and is properly informed. The consent must be given voluntarily and freely. In the context of medical care, this requirement may appear to be easily satisfied, since compulsion, force and deception are not features of the medical armamentarium.[360]

3.144 It would be wrong, however, to forget that there are certain situations in which coercion may at least hover nearby, such as when medical care may be given in prisons or certain mental hospitals. Further, when voluntariness is defined in such a way as to take account of the more or less subtle pressures to

---

[358] On the effect of this ruling on litigation, see Robertson, 'Informed Consent 10 Years Later: The impact of *Reibl v Hughes*' (1991) Canadian Bar Review 423, (where the objective test was employed, 56% of patients failed to satisfy the test and so failed in their actions, despite proving breach of the duty to inform). See also, Dugdale, 'Diverse Reports: Canadian Professional Negligence Cases' (1984) 2 Professional Negligence 108, particularly the discussion of *White v Turner* (1981) 120 DLR (3d) 269. [359] (1989) 17 NSWLR 553.

[360] With the exception of the very rare case in which the treatment of a mentally disturbed person may warrant some degree of coercion, limited in law to that which is reasonable in the circumstances.

which patients may be exposed, there may be a role for the law in drawing a line between the permissible and the impermissible.

In drawing any line, it is helpful to notice that there are two contexts in which a claim of lack of voluntariness could arise, the first rather more obvious than the second. In the first, the patient may claim that he was treated after a consent which was, in fact, improperly gained. In the second, it may be alleged that the patient's refusal of consent was the consequence of improper pressure, thereby seeking to justify treatment despite the apparent refusal. It is something of a *canard*, (and, therefore, like all *canards*, true in part), that it is only when he disagrees that it cannot safely be relied upon. The law, of course, should seek to be even-handed and have no truck with such presumptions.[361]

3.145

(ii) *The Current Law*

In *Freeman v Home Office (No 2)*,[362] an argument of some importance was advanced on behalf of the plaintiff, a prisoner serving a life sentence, who had received medical treatment which, he claimed was administered against his will. It was not merely argued that, on the facts, Freeman had not consented voluntarily. A much more challenging argument was advanced. Not only had Freeman not consented, but there are certain contexts, not least that of being a prisoner where the doctor was also a prison officer, in which consent could never, by virtue of this context, be voluntary. Plausible as the argument may be, it was roundly rejected by the Court of Appeal. Whether someone had consented voluntarily or not was simply a matter of fact in each case. If the patient were confined, or if his liberty were otherwise limited, this should merely put the court on notice to be vigilant in examining the facts. For Stephen Brown LJ the 'matter is one of fact'. He referred with approval to the trial judge's view that, '. . . a court must be alive to the risk that what may appear, on the face of it, to be real consent is not in fact so'.[363] Thus, whatever the circumstances, the issue of voluntariness is an issue of fact.

3.146

The leading English case is *Re T (adult: refusal of medical treatment)*.[364] In that case, the Court of Appeal recognised that, for the most part, as has been said, claims of lack of voluntariness do not involve brute force or duress. Instead, the pressure may be more insidious. To respond to this, the Court prayed in

3.147

---

[361] Nor should it have any truck with cases such as *Latter v Bradell* (1881) 50 LJQB 448, (in which a servant was required to submit to a medical examination but failed in her action against the doctor) which can safely be consigned to the archives.
[362] [1984] 1 All ER 1036.   [363] ibid.   [364] N 6 above

aid a well recognised and understood doctrine in English law, that of 'undue influence'. Potentially, the Court, while still insisting that everything turned on the facts, thereby widened the scope of the various factors, the influences or circumstances which could render a patient's consent invalid. This is because 'undue influence' is clearly a more insidious and subtle process than overt pressure and, therefore, calls for a closer examination of the facts to determine what, if anything, may lie beneath those facts. As it happens, the case was concerned with a young woman's *refusal* of consent and whether it was voluntary, in view of the influence exercised over her by her mother. As has been said, a court may be more eager to see lack of voluntariness when the patient is 'defying' rather than agreeing to medical advice. That said, however, the case stands as clear authority that involuntariness can be proved by evidence of undue influence as well as the more obvious examples of circumstances which might overbear the will of the patient.

4

CONSENT TO TREATMENT: CHILDREN AND THE INCOMPETENT PATIENT

It is a fundamental principle that a doctor who gives medical treatment or **4.01** performs surgery[1] without the consent of his patient is prima facie guilty of

---

[1] In this Chapter 'treatment' is used as a generic term covering all forms of examination, assessment, diagnosis, treatment, or care, and all procedures, whether surgical, medical, psychiatric, dental, or nursing, which involve any physical touching or penetration of the patient's body, however trivial. 'Doctor' is similarly used as a generic term covering everyone involved in providing 'treatment'.

both a tort and a crime. The adult who is sui juris is recognised as having the fundamental human and personal right to control his own body, the right to self-determination or right of autonomy, the right to decide for oneself to the exclusion of others. Two classes of patient lack the capacity to give a valid consent and are therefore unable to exercise their right to self-determination: children,[2] who by reason of non-age lack the *legal* capacity to give consent, or whose refusal of consent can be overridden by others; and those adults[3] who are incompetent,[4] that is to say who by reason of mental disability, lack the *mental* capacity to give a valid consent to treatment, or who by reason of mental or physical disability are permanently unable to communicate. In addition there are children who, by reason of mental disability, lack both the *legal* and the *mental* capacity to give consent. The unborn child or foetus (in legal terminology the child *en ventre sa mère*) occupies a special position which requires to be separately considered.

A. Sources of the Law

1. Parens Patriae

Children

4.02   In relation to children the Crown retains a prerogative power as parens patriae exercisable by the judges of the High Court. This power, often though not necessarily exercised by means of wardship, is of considerable importance in relation to the resolution of difficult or disputed questions about the treatment of children.[5]

Incompetent Adults

4.03   In relation to incompetent adults the Crown's prerogative power as parens patriae was abrogated in 1960 upon the coming into force of the Mental

---

[2]   The terminology is capable of confusing, for 'child' has very different meanings in the law of succession, in the law of persons and in colloquial usage. In this Chapter it is used in the same sense as in the Children Act 1989, s 105(1), that is, as meaning a person who is under the age of 18. In this sense 'child' is the modern equivalent of the older expressions 'minor' and 'infant'. Both 'child' and 'infant' are also used colloquially, even by judges, to refer to younger, and in the case of 'infant' very young, children.

[3]   In this Chapter 'adult' is used to mean a person who has attained the age of 18.

[4]   In this Chapter 'incompetent', whether on its own or in the phrase 'adult incompetent', is used to refer to a person who, irrespective of whatever other capacity he may or may not have for other purposes, lacks, by reason of mental disability, the mental capacity to give a valid consent to treatment or who, by reason of mental or physical disability, is permanently unable to communicate.   [5] See further paras 4.39–4.44 below.

Health Act 1959.[6] Despite subsequent expressions of judicial regret it has not been reinstated.

The Court of Protection

The Court of Protection has no jurisdiction (whether in relation to a child or an adult incompetent) in respect of treatment or other issues relating to bodily welfare. Its jurisdiction is limited by the Mental Health Act 1983, sections 93(2) and 95(1)(d), to the management of the patient's 'affairs', and that expression is confined to business matters, legal transactions, and other dealings of a similar kind.[7]   **4.04**

2. Statute

Certain miscellaneous and socially controversial procedures are now specifi-   **4.05**
cally regulated by statute, for example, tattooing,[8] the taking of blood samples,[9] certain forms of treatment for mental disorder,[10] female circumcision,[11] and organ transplants.[12]

There are two provisions of general application which are directly relevant to   **4.06**
the treatment of children or incompetents.

Children

Section 8 of the Family Law Reform Act 1969 provides: **4.07**

(1) The consent of a minor who has attained the age of sixteen years to any surgical, medical or dental treatment which, in the absence of consent, would constitute a trespass to his person, shall be as effective as it would be if he were of full age; and where a minor has by virtue of this section given an effective consent to any treatment it shall not be necessary to obtain any consent for it from his parent or guardian.

---

[6] *In re F (Mental Patient: Sterilisation)* [1990] 2 AC 1, 51, 54, 57–58, 70, 71, 83. See also *T v T* [1988] Fam 52, *Re C (Mental Patient: Contact)* [1993] 1 FLR 940, *Airedale NHS Trust v Bland* [1993] AC 789.
[7] *In re F (Mental Patient: Sterilisation)* [1990] 2 AC 1, 51, 58–60, 70–71, 83.
[8] The Tattooing of Minors Act 1969.
[9] The Family Law Reform Act 1969, s 21(1) (competent adults), s 21(2) (minors who have attained the age of 16), s 21(3) (minors under the age of 16), s 21(4) (persons suffering from mental disorder within the meaning of the Mental Health Act 1983).
[10] As defined in the Mental Health Act 1983, s 1(2). For the treatments in question see the Mental Health Act 1983, s 57(1)(a) (surgical operations for destroying brain tissue or the functioning of brain tissue), s 57(1)(b) (surgical implantation of hormones for the purpose of reducing male sexual drive), s 58(1)(a) (electro-convulsive therapy), s 58(1)(b) (administration of medicine—as to which see *B v Croydon Health Authority* [1995] Fam 133, 137–138). See also the Mental Health Act 1983, ss 56, 59–62, 64.
[11] The Prohibition of Female Circumcision Act 1985.
[12] The Human Organ Transplants Act 1989.

(2) In this section 'surgical, medical or dental treatment' includes any procedure undertaken for the purposes of diagnosis, and this section applies to any procedure (including, in particular, the administration of an anaesthetic) which is ancillary to any treatment as it applies to that treatment.

(3) Nothing in this section shall be construed as making ineffective any consent which would have been effective if this section had not been enacted.

Section 8 does not extend to the donation of organs, or of blood or other bodily substances, nor even to the taking of a blood sample (for which separate provision is made in section 21(2)), for none of these procedures constitutes either treatment or diagnosis.[13]

Persons Suffering from Mental Disorder

4.08 Section 63 of the Mental Health Act 1983 (which applies by virtue of section 56 of the Act only to patients liable to be detained under the Act) provides:

The consent of a patient shall not be required for any medical treatment given to him for the mental disorder[14] from which he is suffering, not being treatment falling within section 57 or 58 above[15] if the treatment is given by or under the direction of the responsible medical officer.

Section 145(1) of the Act provides that

'medical treatment' includes nursing, and also includes care, habilitation and rehabilitation under medical supervision

'Medical treatment' in section 63 means treatment which, taken as a whole, is calculated to alleviate or prevent a deterioration of the mental disorder from which the patient is suffering, and includes a range of acts ancillary to the core treatment, including those which prevent the patient from harming himself or which alleviate the symptoms of the disorder.[16]

[R]elieving symptoms is just as much a part of treatment as relieving the underlying cause.[17]

'Medical treatment' in section 63 thus includes forcible feeding for the treatment of anorexia nervosa[18] or other psychiatric illnesses[19] and inducing

---

[13] *In re W (A Minor) (Medical Treatment: Court's Jurisdiction)* [1993] Fam 64, 78, 83, 92, 94.
[14] As defined in the Mental Health Act 1983, s 1(2).
[15] For which see para 4.05 above.
[16] *B v Croydon Health Authority* [1995] Fam 133, 138–140, affirming [1995] 1 FCR 332.
[17] *Re KB (Adult) (Mental Patient: Medical Treatment)* (1994) 19 BMLR 144, 146 *per* Ewbank J approved *B v Croydon Health Authority* [1995] Fam 133, 139, 141.
[18] *Riverside Mental Health NHS Trust v Fox* [1994] 1 FLR 614; *Re KB (Adult) (Mental Patient: Medical Treatment)* (1994) 19 BMLR 144; *B v Croydon Health Authority* [1995] Fam 133, affirming [1995] 1 FCR 332.
[19] *Re VS (Adult: Mental Disorder)* (1995) Aug 17 (Douglas Brown J), [1995] Med L Rev 292. Contrast *Secretary of State for the Home Department v Robb* [1995] Fam 127 (forcefeeding of competent adult prisoner).

labour and performing a caesarian section on a pregnant paranoid schizo-phrenic where effective treatment of the schizophrenia required that the patient give birth to a live baby and resume medication necessarily inter-rupted by her pregnancy,[20] including, if necessary, restraint and the use of reasonable force.[21]

3. Common Law

Save to the limited extent to which particular matters are regulated by statute, **4.09** or, in the case of children, by the Crown's prerogative power as parens patriae, the treatment of children and incompetent adults, and related issues of consent, are regulated by the general principles of the common law.

B. Consent

1. Children

The Need for Consent

The law normally requires a valid consent before any treatment can lawfully **4.10** be given to a child. In certain circumstances the law recognises as valid the child's own consent.[22] In those cases where the child is unable to give a valid consent,[23] and in cases where the child is able to give a valid consent but refuses to do so,[24] the law recognises as valid a proxy or substitute consent given on behalf of the child either by a parent (or someone having parental responsibility) or by the court. In cases of emergency a doctor can provide treatment notwithstanding the absence of parental or judicial consent.[25]

The Purpose of Consent

The giving of consent to medical treatment has two main functions. **4.11**

> There seems to be some confusion in the minds of some as to the purpose of seeking consent from a patient (whether adult or child) or from someone with authority to give that consent on behalf of the patient. It has two purposes, the one clinical and the other legal. The clinical purpose stems from the fact that in many instances the co-operation of the patient and the patient's faith or at least

---

[20] *Tameside and Glossop Acute Services Trust v CH* [1996] 1 FLR 762, 771–774. Contrast *In re C (Adult: Refusal of Treatment)* [1994] 1 WLR 290 (schizophrenic held entitled to refuse consent to amputation of gangrenous leg) where the gangrene was 'entirely unconnected' with the mental disorder: *B v Croydon Health Authority* [1995] Fam 133, 139.

[21] *Tameside and Glossop Acute Services Trust v CH* [1996] 1 FLR 762, 771, 774.

[22] See paras 4.62, 4.66 below.   [23] See para 4.53 below.

[24] See paras 4.63, 4.65, 4.67, 4.68 below.   [25] See para 4.18 below.

confidence in the efficacy of the treatment is a major factor contributing to the treatment's success. Failure to obtain such consent will not only deprive the patient and the medical staff of this advantage, but will usually make it much more difficult to administer the treatment. I appreciate that this purpose may not be served if consent is given on behalf of, rather than by, the patient. However, in the case of young children knowledge of the fact that the parent has consented may help. The legal purpose is quite different. It is to provide those concerned in the treatment with a defence to a criminal charge of assault or battery or a civil claim for damages for trespass to the person. It does not, however, provide them with any defence to a claim that they negligently advised a particular treatment or negligently carried it out.[26]

4.12 In the case of a child the right of self-determination plays no part and the clinical purpose of consent is thus limited. Plainly, except as a legal fiction, a proxy or substitute consent is quite inconsistent with a right of *self*-determination. Moreover, even in those cases where a child is treated as having the capacity in law to *give* a valid consent to treatment, he is not treated as having the capacity effectively to *refuse* consent to treatment, since such a refusal can always be overridden by the giving of consent either by the child's parent (or someone having parental responsibility) or by the court.[27] The law thus denies even the competent child any right of autonomy, in the sense of the right to decide for oneself to the exclusion of others. Hence the main purpose of consent in the case of a child is to provide the doctor with a defence to a charge of assault or a claim in trespass.

4.13 As with an adult patient, so with a child, the right to consent is merely a power to consent, not a power to compel. In the case of a child neither the parent nor the child can compel an unwilling doctor or health authority to provide treatment, whether that refusal is based on the doctor's clinical or ethical judgment or on a lack of resources. In such a case the patient's only remedy is to find another doctor, if he can, who is prepared to give the desired treatment.

4.14 Nor is the child any better off by seeking to invoke the assistance of the court. The court, even if it is exercising its inherent parens patriae jurisdiction, will never make an order requiring a particular doctor or health authority to treat a child in a manner contary to their wishes.[28] There are two reasons for this. The first is because, as a matter of policy, the court will never make an order compelling a doctor to treat a patient in a manner contrary to his clinical

---

[26] *In re W (A Minor) (Medical Treatment: Court's Jurisdiction)* [1993] Fam 64, 76 *per* Lord Donaldson of Lymington MR.   [27] See further paras 4.63, 4.65, 4.67, 4.68 below.
[28] *In re J (A Minor) (Wardship: Medical Treatment)* [1991] Fam 33, 41, 48; *In re R (A Minor) (Wardship: Consent to Treatment)* [1992] Fam 11, 22, 26; *In re J (A Minor) (Child in Care: Medical Treatment)* [1993] Fam 15, 27, 29, 31. See further para 4.100 below.

judgment and professional duty.[29] Where the court disagrees with the views of the attending physician the solution is to find another doctor who shares the court's view, not to coerce the existing doctor. Secondly, because, again as a matter of policy, the court declines to become involved in questions relating to the resource implications of proposed treatment, and refuses to adjudicate in disputes between patients, doctors, and health authorities arising out of the denial of treatment because of a lack of resources or the allocation of scarce resources to other patients or other forms of treatment.[30]

The Effect of Consent

In the case of a child it would seem that the effect of a consent will be the same as the effect of a consent given by an adult who is sui juris in those cases where the consent is given either by the child himself (assuming, that is, that the child in question has the capacity to give a valid consent at all) or by the court on his behalf. **4.15**

The effect of a proxy or substitute consent given on behalf of a child by a parent (or by someone having parental responsibility) is more limited, for such a consent will not necessarily provide the doctor with an absolute defence. The right of the parent to give a valid proxy or substitute consent is subject to a variety of limitations,[31] and a doctor cannot rely upon a 'consent' which he knows, or ought to know, ought not to have been given by the parent. **4.16**

> [B]ecause parents are given authority to act for the benefit of the child, their authority is limited to those acts which advance or protect the welfare of the child. This criterion is a matter which must be determined objectively and not by reference to the good faith opinions of the parent. A parent has no authority, therefore, to consent to medical treatment unless it can be seen objectively that the treatment is for the welfare of the child. If a parent purports to give consent to treatment which is not for the welfare of the child, the consent is of no effect. A person who acts on such 'consent' is guilty of assaulting the child if the treatment involves any physical interference with the child[32]

---

[29] *In re J (A Minor) (Child in Care: Medical Treatment)* [1993] Fam 15, 26–27, 29–31.
[30] *R v Secretary of State for Social Services, West Midlands Regional Health Authority and Birmingham Area Health Authority (Teaching), ex p Hinck* (1980) 1 BMLR 93 (patients on waiting list for orthopaedic surgery); *R v Central Birmingham Health Authority, ex p Walker* (1987) 3 BMLR 32 (premature baby requiring heart surgery); *R v Central Birmingham Health Authority, ex p Collier* [1988] CAT 88/1 (4–year old child in immediate danger to health requiring heart surgery); *In re J (A Minor) (Wardship: Medical Treatment)* [1991] Fam 33, 41; *In re J (A Minor) (Child in Care: Medical Treatment)* [1993] Fam 15, 28, 30–31; *R v Cambridge Health Authority, ex p B* [1995] 1 WLR 898, reversing [1995] 1 FLR 1055 (experimental treatment of 10–year old child suffering from leukaemia). [31] See further paras 4.71–4.80 below.
[32] *Secretary, Department of Health and Community Services v JWB and SMB* (1992) 175 CLR 218, 316 *per* McHugh J. To the same effect *In re F (Mental Patient: Sterilisation)* [1990] 2 AC 1, 20 *per* Lord Donaldson of Lymington MR (child would 'undoubtedly have . . . a very substantial claim for damages').

The Role of the Doctor

4.17   In practical terms parental decision-making in relation to the medical treatment of children is subject to control by the doctor. In the final analysis much, if not most, of the ultimate process of decision-making is necessarily borne by the doctor. The doctor is not bound to do what the parent wants, and even if he has the parent's consent he is not necessarily protected from legal proceedings.

4.18   On the other hand, the doctor who wishes to treat a child is not necessarily fettered by the absence, or even the refusal, of parental consent. Except in an emergency,[33] or where parents have abandoned their parental responsibilities without the child yet having been taken into the care of a local authority or someone else in loco parentis,[34] a doctor should always discuss with the child's parents the treatment he proposes and obtain their consent.[35] If a consent which he believes is necessary is not forthcoming he can invoke the assistance of the court. But in a case of emergency, when there is no time to obtain a decision from the court, a doctor can proceed notwithstanding the absence of parental or judicial consent and, if the parents are acting unreasonably or contrary to the best interests of the child, even despite a parental refusal of consent.[36]

The Role of Parental Consent

4.19   It will be seen, therefore, that consent plays a very much more limited role in the case of the patient who is a child than in the case of a patient who is sui juris. Parental consent is only one factor, and except in the case of routine treatment rarely a determining factor, in the treatment of a child. Not even the approval of the court is determinative.

> The doctors owe the child a duty to care for it in accordance with good medical practice recognised as appropriate by a competent body of professional opinion: . . . This duty is, however, subject to the qualification that, if time permits, they must obtain the consent of the parents before undertaking serious invasive treatment. The parents owe the child a duty to give or to withhold consent in the best interests of the child and without regard to their own interests. The court when exercising the parens patriae jurisdiction takes over the rights and duties of the parents, although this is not to say that the parents will be excluded

---

[33] *Gillick v West Norfolk and Wisbech Area Health Authority* [1986] AC 112, 181–182, 194, 200.
[34] ibid, 165, 170, 182, 194.
[35] ibid, 169, 173–174, 189; *In re J (A Minor) (Wardship: Medical Treatment)* [1991] Fam 33, 41; *Re R (A Minor) (Blood Transfusion)* [1993] 2 FLR 757, 760.
[36] *Gillick v West Norfolk and Wisbech Area Health Authority* [1986] AC 112, 200; *In re J (A Minor) (Wardship: Medical Treatment)* [1991] Fam 33, 41; *In re R (A Minor) (Wardship: Consent to Treatment)* [1992] Fam 11, 26.

from the decision-making process. . . . No one can dictate the treatment to be given to the child—neither court, parents nor doctors. There are checks and balances. The doctors can recommend treatment A in preference to treatment B. They can also refuse to adopt treatment C on the grounds that it is medically contra-indicated or for some other reason is a treatment which they could not conscientiously administer. The court or parents for their part can refuse consent to treatment A or B or both, but cannot insist upon treatment C. The inevitable and desirable result is that choice of treatment is in some measure a joint decision of the doctors and the court or parents. This co-operation is reinforced by another consideration. Doctors nowadays recognise that their function is not a limited technical one of repairing or servicing a body. They are treating people in a real life context. This at once enhances the contribution which the court or parents can make towards reaching the best possible decision in all the circumstances. Finally mention should be made of one problem to the solution of which neither court nor parents can make any contribution. In an imperfect world resources will always be limited and on occasion agonising choices will have to be made in allocating those resources to particular patients. It is outwith the scope of this judgment to give any guidance as to the circumstances which should determine such an allocation. . . . neither the court in wardship proceedings, nor, I think, a local authority having care and control of the baby is able to require the [health] authority to follow a particular course of treatment. What the court can do is to withhold consent to treatment of which it disapproves and it can express its approval of other treatment proposed by the authority and its doctors.[37]

No doctor can be required to treat a child, whether by the court in the exercise of its wardship jurisdiction, by the parents, by the child or anyone else. The decision whether to treat is dependent upon an exercise of his own professional judgment, subject only to the threshold requirement that, save in exceptional cases usually of emergency, he has the consent of someone who has authority to give that consent. In forming that judgment the views and wishes of the child are a factor whose importance increases with the increase in the child's intelligence and understanding.[38]

2. The Incompetent Adult

The Role of Consent

Except as specifically provided by statute,[39] consent plays no part in the **4.20** treatment of the adult incompetent, because the patient himself is, by definition, unable to give a valid consent to treatment and the common law does not recognise anyone else as having the legal capacity to give or refuse consent on his behalf. A spouse or relative does not have any power either to consent

---

[37] *In re J (A Minor) (Wardship: Medical Treatment)* [1991] Fam 33, 41, 48 *per* Lord Donaldson of Lymington MR.
[38] *In re R (A Minor) (Wardship: Consent to Treatment)* [1992] Fam 11, 26 *per* Lord Donaldson of Lymington MR.
[39] eg, the Mental Health Act 1983, s 63 (treatment of mental disorder), the Family Law Reform Act 1969, s 21(4) (taking of blood samples).

or to refuse consent to medical treatment on behalf of an incompetent adult.[40] Nor does the court, for neither the Court of Protection nor the High Court has any parens patriae or other jurisdiction over the person, as opposed to the property, of an adult incompetent.[41]

The Role of the Court

4.21 However, the High Court, in exercise of its inherent jurisdiction and/or its statutory jurisdiction under RSC Order 15 Rule 16, can grant declaratory relief to determine questions relating to the lawfulness or unlawfulness of the proposed treatment or care, including the proposed medical treatment or care, of an incompetent adult.[42]

Necessity

4.22 In the case of an adult who is incompetent or permanently unable to communicate,[43] the principle of necessity renders lawful, despite the absence of consent, such treatment which in the absence of consent would otherwise be tortious,[44] as a reasonable doctor would in all the circumstances give, acting in the best interests of the patient.[45]

C. The Unborn Child

4.23 As has been said

> From the earliest times the posthumous child has caused a certain embarrassment to the logic of the law, which is naturally disposed to insist that at any given moment of time a child must either be born or not born, living or not living. This literal realism was felt to bear hardly on the interests of posthumous children and was surmounted in the Civil Law by the invention of the fiction

---

[40] *In re T (Adult: Refusal of Treatment)* [1993] Fam 95, 103. See also *T v T* [1988] Fam 52; *In re F (Mental Patient: Sterilisation)* [1990] 2 AC 1; *Re C (Mental Patient: Contact)* [1993] 1 FLR 940.
[41] *T v T* [1988] Fam 52; *In re F (Mental Patient: Sterilisation)* [1990] 2 AC 1; *Re C (Mental Patient: Contact)* [1993] 1 FLR 940.
[42] *In re F (Mental Patient: Sterilisation)* [1990] 2 AC 1; *Airedale NHS Trust v Bland* [1993] AC 789.
[43] The doctrine of necessity also applies if the patient is competent, 'in cases of emergency where the patient is unconscious, and where it is necessary to operate before consent can be obtained': '*Schloendorff v Society of New York Hospital* (1914) 105 NE 92, 93 *per* Cardozo J. Necessity applies in such a case if (i) it is impossible to communicate with the patient (e g, because the patient is unconscious or under anaesthetic) and (ii) urgent action is imperative in the best interests of the patient but consent cannot be obtained until it is too late and (iii) the doctor or surgeon does no more than is reasonably required in the best interests of the patient in the interim before the patient recovers the ability to communicate: *In re F (Mental Patient: Sterilisation)* [1990] 2 AC 1, 71–77.
[44] *In re F (Mental Patient: Sterilisation)* [1990] 2 AC 1, 73–76.   [45] ibid, 51, 56, 75.

that in all matters affecting its interests the unborn child in utero should be deemed to be already born.[46]

Perhaps not surprisingly, the law is both unclear and confused. Thus it has been said that the law treats the foetus as being 'an integral part of the mother' until it has a separate existence of its own, so much so that an injury to the foetus is treated as being an injury to a part of the mother in the same way as would be an injury to her arm or leg.[47] That view, however, has since been rejected by the House of Lords in favour of the view that the foetus, although dependent upon the mother for its survival until birth, is, from the moment of conception, an organism separate and distinct from the mother.[48]

> There was, of course, an intimate bond between the foetus and the mother, created by the total dependence of the foetus on the protective physical environment furnished by the mother, and on the supply by the mother through the physical linkage between them of the nutriments, oxygen and other substances essential to foetal life and developmeFnt. The emotional bond between the mother and her unborn child was also of a very special kind. But the relationship was one of bond, not of identity. The mother and the foetus were two distinct organisms living symbiotically, not a single organism with two aspects. The mother's leg was part of the mother, the foetus was not. . . . [T]he foetus does not (for the purposes of the law of homicide and violent crime) have any relevant type of personality but is an organism sui generis lacking at this stage the entire range of characteristics both of the mother to which it is physically linked and of the complete human being which it will later become.[49]

Be that as it may, the criminal law has long protected the unborn child and the civil law recognises that an unborn child can have an independent and legally enforceable right separate and distinct from any right of its mother.[50]

1. The Status of the Unborn Child

Both at common law[51] and by statute[52] the criminal law protects the unborn child. **4.24**

---

[46] *Elliot v Lord Joicey* [1935] AC 209, 238 *per* Lord Macmillan.
[47] *Attorney-General's Reference (No 3 of 1994)* [1996] QB 581, 591, 593, 598 *per* Lord Taylor of Gosforth CJ.
[48] *Attorney-General's Reference (No 3 of 1994)* [1997] 3 WLR 421, 429, 440.
[49] ibid, 428–429 *per* Lord Mustill.
[50] *Schofield v Orrell Colliery Company Ltd* [1909] 1 KB 178, 181; *Watt v Rama* [1972] VR 353, 376.
[51] *R v Senior* (1832) 1 Mood 346; *R v West* (1848) 2 Car & K 784; *Attorney-General's Reference (No 3 of 1994)* [1997] 3 WLR 421.
[52] Offences against the Person Act 1861, ss 58, 59, Infant Life (Preservation) Act 1929, s 1 (as to which see *C v S* [1988] QB 135; *In re F (In Utero)* [1988] Fam 122), Road Traffic Act 1972, s 1 (as to which see *McCluskey v HM Advocate* [1989] RTR 182; *Attorney-General's Reference (No 3 of 1994)* [1996] QB 581, 597–598, [1997] 3 WLR 421, 442). The criminal law is of course

4.25   The position of the unborn child in civil law is much less clear.[53] There are in reported cases broad and unqualified statements to the effect that, until it is born, a foetus has no status, that it does not exist as a legal person and has no independent legal personality, that it lacks the status to have any legal right or to be the subject of any legal duty, and that it cannot have a right of action and cannot be a party to an action.

> [I]n England and Wales the foetus has no right of action, no right at all until birth . . . [It is] undefined in law and without status.[54]

> The human being does not exist as a legal person until after birth. The foetus enjoys no independent legal personality . . . An unborn child lacks the status to be the subject of a legal duty.[55]

> It . . . is established beyond doubt for the criminal law, as for the civil law . . . that the child en ventre sa mere does not have a distinct human personality, whose extinguishment gives rise to any penalties or liabilities at common law.[56]

Two judgments, of Sir George Baker P[57] and of Heilbron J[58] at first instance, have been particularly influential:

> The foetus cannot, in English law, in my view, have a right of its own at least until it is born and has a separate existence from its mother. That permeates the whole of the civil law of this country (I except the criminal law, which is now irrelevant) . . . For a long time there was great controversy whether after birth a child could have a right of action in respect of pre-natal injury . . . but it was universally accepted . . . that in order to have a right the foetus must be born and be a child . . . [T]here can be no doubt, in my view, that in England and Wales the foetus has no right of action, no right at all, until birth. The succession cases have been mentioned. There is no difference. From conception the child may have succession rights by what has been called a 'fictional construction' but the child must be subsequently born alive: see per Lord Russell of Killowen in *Elliot v Lord Joicey* [1935] AC 209, 233[59]

---

greatly modified by the Abortion Act 1967 (as amended by the Human Fertilisation and Embryology Act 1990).

[53] For a recent partial survey see *Burton v Islington Health Authority* [1993] QB 204, 226–227. For the position in Scotland see *Kelly v Kelly* [1997] 2 FLR 828.

[54] *B v Islington Heath Authority* [1991] 1 QB 638, 644, 647 *per* Potts J, on appeal [1993] QB 204.

[55] *De Martell v Merton and Sutton Health Authority* [1993] QB 204, 213, 218 *per* Phillips J, on appeal [1993] QB 204, 223.

[56] *Attorney-General's Reference (No 3 of 1994)* [1997] 3 WLR 421, 434 *per* Lord Mustill. To similar effect see also Lord Mustill at 429 ('foetus does not . . . have any relevant type of personality', 'foetus does not have the attributes which make it a "person"'), 435–436 (foetus 'not a person').   [57] *Paton v British Pregnancy Advisory Service Trustees* [1979] QB 276.

[58] *C v S* [1988] QB 135.

[59] *Paton v British Pregnancy Advisory Service Trustees* [1979] QB 276, 279 *per* Sir George Baker P, followed *C v S* [1988] QB 135, 140 (Heilbron J), approved *In re F (In Utero)* [1988] Fam 122, 138 (May LJ), see also at 140–141 (Balcombe LJ), applied *B v Islington Health Authority* [1991] 1 QB 638, 644 (Potts J).

The authorities, it seems to me, show that a child, after it has been born, and only then, in certain circumstances, based on he or she having a legal right, may be a party to an action brought with regard to such matters as the right to take, on a will or intestacy, or for damages for injuries suffered before birth. In other words, the claim crystallises upon the birth, at which date, but not before, the child attains the status of a legal persona, and thereupon can then exercise that legal right. . . . In my judgment, there is no basis for the claim that the foetus can be a party, whether or not there is any foundation for the contention with regard to the alleged threatened crime.[60]

There seems little doubt that these statements, at least in their general and unqualified form, are wrong. English law adopts, though only for the purpose of enabling the unborn child to take a benefit which, if born, it would be entitled to,[61] the fiction of the civil law that **4.26**

> Qui in utero est, perinde ac si in rebus humanis esset, custoditur, quoties de commodis ipsius partus quaeritur: quanquam alii, antequam nascatur, nequaquam prosit . . . Qui in utero sunt in toto paene jure civili intelliguntur in rerum natura esse.

> [A child in the womb is protected just as if it had been born whenever the question concerns benefits which depend on its existing: but another person cannot be advantaged before the child is actually born . . . Children in the womb are regarded as having been born for almost all the purposes of the civil law.][62]

The principle is applicable not merely to real and personal property but also to claims by unborn children under Lord Campbell's Act[63] and the Workmen's Compensation Acts[64] and even, it seems, to actions in negligence for pre-natal injuries.[65]

---

[60] *C v S* [1988] QB 135, 140–141 *per* Heilbron J, approved *In re F (In Utero)* [1988] Fam 122, 138 (May LJ), see also at 140–141 (Balcombe LJ).

[61] *Burnet v Mann* (1748) 1 Ves Sen 156; *Doe d Clarke v Clarke* (1795) 2 H Bl 399, 401; *Blasson v Blasson* (1864) 2 De G J & S 665, 670; *Villar v Gilbey* [1907] AC 139, 145–146, 149, 151–152 *Williams v The Ocean Coal Company Limited* [1907] 2 KB 422, 429; *Schofield v Orrell Colliery Company Ltd* [1909] 1 KB 178, 181–183 *Elliot v Lord Joicey* [1935] AC 209, 215, 222, 226, 231, 233–234, 238–240, 241; *Burton v Islington Health Authority* [1993] QB 204, 226–227, 230.

[62] *Blasson v Blasson* (1864) 2 De G J & S 665, 670; *Elliot v Lord Joicey* [1935] AC 209, 238; *Burton v Islington Health Authority* [1993] QB 204, 226.

[63] *The George and Richard* (1871) LR 3 A & E 466, 480–482; *Manns v Carlon* [1940] VR 280 (as to which see *Watt v Rama* [1972] VR 353, 358, 375–376).

[64] *Williams v The Ocean Coal Company Limited* [1907] 2 KB 422, 429, 432; *Schofield v Orrell Colliery Company Ltd* [1909] 1 KB 178 (as to which see *Watt v Rama* [1972] VR 353, 358, 376).

[65] *Montreal Tramways v Leveille* [1933] 4 DLR 337, 346; *Watt v Rama* [1972] VR 353, 376–377; *Burton v Islington Health Authority* [1993] QB 204, 227. For a contrary view see *B v Islington Health Authority* [1991] 1 QB 638, 649.

The Unborn Child as Litigant

4.27 So also, a child en ventre sa mère can be a party to an action, an action for damages or for an injunction can be brought on its behalf, and an injunction can be granted in its favour.[66]

> It is certain that a child en ventre sa mère is protected by law, and may even be party to an action.[67]

> The principal reason I go upon in the question is, that the plaintiff was en ventre sa mère at the time of her brother's death, and consequently a person in rerum natura, so that both by the rules of the common and civil law, she was, to all intents and purposes, a child, as much as if born in the father's life-time. . . . First, As to the common law, there is the trite case of an infant en ventre sa mère being vouched in common recovery; a mother also may justify the detaining of charters on behalf of it; a devise to him is good, by the opinion of Treby and Powell, in Scatterwood and Edge, 1 Salk 229, a bill may be brought in his behalf, and this court will grant an injunction in his favour to stay waste, 2 Vern 710, Musgrave versus Parry et al. . . . Secondly, As to the civil law, nothing is more clear, than that this law considered a child in the mother's womb absolutely born, to all intents and purposes, for the child's benefit.[68]

> The next objection is, that, supposing, he meant a child en ventre sa mère, and had expressly said so, yet the limitation is void. Such a child has been considered as a non-entity. Let us see, what this non-entity can do. He may be vouched in a recovery, though it is for the purpose of making him answer over in value. He may be an executor. He may take under the Statute of Distributions. (22 & 23 Ch II c 10.) He may take by devise. He may be entitled under a charge for raising portions. He may have an injunction; and he may have a guardian. Some other cases put this beyond all doubt. . . . Why should not children en ventre sa mère be considered generally as in existence? They are entitled to all the privileges of other persons.[69]

---

[66] Lutterel's case temp Lord Bridgman LC cited *Hale v Hale* (1692) Pre Ch 50 (action on behalf of child en ventre sa mère to stay waste: injunction granted); *Musgrave v Parry* (1715) 2 Vern 710, 711; *Wallis v Hodson* (1740) 2 Atk 114, 117; *Thellusson v Woodford* (1799) 4 Ves 227, 322; *The George and Richard* (1871) LR 3 A & E 466, 468, 473, 474, 480, 481–482 (child en ventre sa mère held entitled to bring claim under Lord Campbell's Act; assessment of damages adjourned until birth of child); *Villar v Gilbey* [1907] AC 139, 144; *Manns v Carlon* [1940] VR 280, 284 (child en ventre sa mère held to have right of action under Victorian equivalent of Lord Campbell's Act; trial of action stayed until birth of child); *Watt v Rama* [1972] VR 353, 358, 375–376.

[67] *Villar v Gilbey* [1907] AC 139, 144 *per* Lord Loreburn LC.

[68] *Wallis v Hodson* (1740) 2 Atk 114, 117–118 *per* Lord Hardwicke LC (as to which see *Thellusson v Woodford* (1799) 4 Ves 227, 322, (1805) 11 Ves 112, 139; *Villar v Gilbey* [1907] AC 139, 141, 142, 149; *Montreal Tramways v Leveille* [1933] 4 DLR 337, 343; *Watt v Rama* [1972] VR 353, 375; *Burton v Islington Health Authority* [1993] QB 204, 229–230).

[69] *Thellusson v Woodford* (1799) 4 Ves 227, 321–322, 323 *per* Buller J, on appeal (1805) 11 Ves 112 (as to which see *Montreal Tramways v Leveille* [1933] 4 DLR 337, 340).

2. Medical Treatment and the Unborn Child

(i) *General Principles*

Consent

There can be no doubt that, as a general principle, the only consent which is **4.28** either required or relevant for the medical treatment of either the foetus or its mother is that of the pregnant woman. The giving or refusing of consent by the child's father is legally irrelevant, whether or not he is married to the child's mother. Subject only to the provisions of the criminal law, the consent of a pregnant woman makes any treatment either of her or of the foetus lawful, irrespective of any adverse effects which the foetus may suffer, and whether or not the child's father has consented. Conversely, the refusal of consent by the mother is normally decisive, whatever the adverse implications for the foetus. This reflects the biological fact that, until birth, the foetus lives in a symbiotic relationship with, and is totally dependent for its survival upon, the pregnant woman,[70] the very limited rights of the father, whether or not he is married to the child's mother,[71] and the public policy which recognises the extreme undesirability of creating conflict between the mother and her unborn child and the insuperable difficulties of attempting to manage the lifestyle or control the actions of an uncooperative mother.[72]

In the same way the law, as a general principle, treats the interests of the **4.29** foetus as being so bound up with the interests of its mother that the mother's best interests are treated as being likewise those of the foetus and vice versa.

Wardship and the Unborn Child

Consistently with this principle, it has been held that the court cannot **4.30** exercise its inherent parens patriae jurisdiction in relation to an unborn child or over the mother of an unborn child, nor can it make such a child a ward of court.[73]

Abortion

Similarly, although the reasoning in the cases may be criticised insofar as they **4.31** proceed on the footing of the alleged inability of the unborn child to have legal rights or be a party to litigation, there is no doubt that neither the

---

[70] *Attorney-General's Reference (No 3 of 1994)* [1997] 3 WLR 421, 428–429, 440.
[71] *Paton v British Pregnancy Advisory Service Trustees* [1979] QB 276, 279–281, 282.
[72] *In re F (In Utero)* [1988] Fam 122, 131–132, 138, 143, 144–145.   [73] ibid.

unborn child,[74] nor its father,[75] nor the husband of its mother,[76] can obtain an injunction to restrain the performance of a lawful abortion to which the mother has consented.[77]

(ii) *Possible Exceptions*

4.32 Whether, and if so in what circumstances, the law will have regard to the independent medical interests of the unborn child, or allow legal intervention by or on its behalf for the purpose of protecting its bodily interests, are questions the answers to which are both uncertain and controversial. There would appear to be no absolute bar as a matter of principle. The law recognises the foetus as an entity capable of having rights, separate and distinct from the rights of its mother, and capable of suing to vindicate those rights. There is no reason in principle why any distinction should be drawn for this purpose between property interests and bodily welfare.

> I can find no logical reason for rejecting the notion that the common law would protect a child en ventre sa mère against careless acts causing him or her injury. As its property, real or personal, is protected, so should its physical substance be similarly protected.[78]

Moreover, the law does not eschew the application of restraint and the use of reasonable force for the purpose of compelling a pregnant child[79] or an incompetent pregnant adult woman[80] to submit to a caesarian section.

4.33 Thus it might be thought that a child en ventre sa mere could sue for an injunction to restrain violent assaults upon its mother of a kind likely to put it in peril even if the mother, for some reason, was not willing herself to bring proceedings against the assailant. On the other hand it has been held that the

---

[74] *Paton v British Pregnancy Advisory Service Trustees* [1979] QB 276, 279, *Dehler v Ottawa Civic Hospital* (1979) 101 DLR (3d) 686, 694–700, appeal dismissed (1980) 117 DLR (3d) 512, *Medhurst v Medhurst* (1984) 9 DLR (4th) 252, 255–257.
[75] *Paton v British Pregnancy Advisory Service Trustees* [1979] QB 276, 279–280; *C v S* [1988] QB 135, 140, 141, 148.
[76] *Paton v British Pregnancy Advisory Service Trustees* [1979] QB 276, 280, 281, 282; *Medhurst v Medhurst* (1984) 9 DLR (4th) 252, 257–259; *C v S* [1988] QB 135, 140, 141.
[77] *Paton v British Pregnancy Advisory Service Trustees* [1979] QB 276, 280–281, 282. The position is the same in Scotland: *Kelly v Kelly* [1997] 2 FLR 828.
[78] *Watt v Rama* [1972] VR 353, 376 *per* Gillard J.
[79] *A Metropolitan Borough Council v AB* [1997] 1 FLR 767.
[80] *Tameside and Glossop Acute Services Trust v CH* [1996] 1 FLR 762; *Norfolk and Norwich Healthcare (NHS) Trust v W* [1996] 2 FLR 613; *Rochdale Healthcare (NHS) Trust v C* [1997] 1 FCR 274; *Re L (Patient: Non-consensual Treatment)* [1997] 2 FLR 837; *Re MB (Medical Treatment)* [1997] 2 FLR 426.

unborn child[81] cannot obtain an injunction to restrain the performance of an unlawful (and thus necessarily criminal) abortion.[82] Other cases are more difficult. Where the mother if competent is refusing or if incompetent is unable to consent to treatment which is in her unborn child's interests, to what extent are the unborn child's interests to be taken into account, and can proceedings be taken by or on behalf of the unborn child for the purpose of authorising or compelling its mother to undergo treatment—for example, if the child requires minor but life-saving treatment in the womb, or if the child's welfare dictates a caesarian section, or if the question is whether a pregnant woman who is in an irreversible coma should be kept artificially alive for the sole purpose of enabling her viable foetus to be born?

The Unborn Child and the Incompetent Mother

Such problems are likely to be less acute where the mother is herself incompetent or a child and where there is, accordingly, no question of overriding the decision of a competent patient who is sui juris. In such cases the court will be astute to find that a procedure which is medically in the interests of the child, even if not of its mother, is nevertheless in the mother's best emotional and psychological interests, so that it can authorise (in the case of a child) or declare lawful (in the case of an adult incompetent) the necessary treatment.[83] But even in this situation the only interests that can properly be taken into account are the interests of the mother, not those of the foetus.[84]   **4.34**

> In our judgment the court does not have the jurisdiction to take the interests of the foetus into account in a case such as the present appeal [a case involving an incompetent adult mother] and the judicial exercise of balancing those interests does not arise. . . . The foetus up to the moment of birth does not have any separate interests capable of being taken into account when a court has to consider an application for a declaration in respect of a caesarian section operation.[85]

---

[81] Whether the father of an unborn child, or the husband of its mother, can obtain an injunction to restrain the performance of an unlawful (and thus necessarily criminal) abortion is uncertain: *Paton v British Pregnancy Advisory Service Trustees* [1979] QB 276, 282 (leaving the question undecided); *Medhurst v Medhurst* (1984) 9 DLR (4th) 252, 259–261 (holding that he could); *C v S* [1988] QB 135, 149, 153 (leaving the question undecided).

[82] *Dehler v Ottawa Civic Hospital* (1979) 101 DLR (3d) 686, appeal dismissed (1980) 117 DLR (3d) 512; *C v S* [1988] QB 135, 140–141.

[83] Consider the analyses in *Tameside and Glossop Acute Services Trust v CH* [1996] 1 FLR 762; *In re Y (Mental Patient: Bone Marrow Donation)* [1997] Fam 110; *Norfolk and Norwich Healthcare (NHS) Trust v W* [1996] 2 FLR 613; *Rochdale Healthcare (NHS) Trust v C* [1997] 1 FCR 274; *A Metropolitan Borough Council v AB* [1997] 1 FLR 767; *Re L (Patient: Non-consensual Treatment)* [1997] 2 FLR 837; *Re MB (Medical Treatment)* [1997] 2 FLR 426.

[84] *Norfolk and Norwich Healthcare (NHS) Trust v W* [1996] 2 FLR 613, 616; *Re MB (Medical Treatment)* [1997] 2 FLR 426, 440.   [85] *Re MB* (n 84 above), 440, 444.

Thus, this approach will not resolve the problem presented by the mother in an irreversible coma who may, in truth, have no interests at all.[86]

The Unborn Child and the Competent Mother

4.35 The difficulties are particularly acute where a competent mother is refusing treatment in circumstances gravely prejudicial to the life or welfare of her unborn child. The law, however, is clear: the doctor and the court are powerless to act.[87]

> A competent woman who has the capacity to decide may, for religious reasons, other reasons, for rational or irrational reasons or for no reason at all, choose not to have medical intervention, even though the consequence may be the death or serious handicap of the child she bears, or her own death. In that event the courts do not have the jurisdiction to declare medical intervention lawful and the question of her own best interests objectively considered, does not arise. . . . If therefore the competent mother refuses to have the medical intervention, the doctors may not lawfully do more than attempt to persuade her. If that persuasion is unsuccessful, there are no further steps towards medical intervention to be taken. . . . The only situation in which it is lawful for the doctors to intervene is if it is believed that the adult patient lacks the capacity to decide. . . . The law is, in our judgment, clear that a competent woman who has the capacity to decide may, for religious reasons, other reasons, or for no reasons at all, choose not to have medical intervention, even though . . . the consequence may be the death or serious handicap of the child she bears or her own death. . . . The court does not have the jurisdiction to declare that such medical intervention is lawful to protect the interests of the unborn child even at the point of birth.[88]

D. Children

1. Who Can Consent

(i) *Common Law*

Parents and the State

4.36 The common law imposes responsibility for the care, nurture and protection of children on parents, as their guardians by the law of nature, and on the Crown as parens patriae. The powers of the child's parents are limited by law. The prerogative powers of the Crown as parens patriae are theoretically

---

[86] Compare *Airedale NHS Trust v Bland* [1993] AC 789 and see further para 4.214 below.
[87] *Re MB* (n 84 above), 436, 438, 440, 441, 444 overruling the extremely controversial decision in *In re S (Adult: Refusal of Treatment)* [1993] Fam 123.
[88] *Re MB (n 84 above)*, 436–438, 444 *per* Butler-Sloss LJ.

without limit, though in practice they are exercised only within recognised limits.[89] The Crown normally chooses not to exercise its parens patriae powers in relation to children, being content most of the time to leave responsibility for the care, nurture and protection of a child to its parents.

> The best person to bring up a child is the natural parent. It matters not whether the parent is wise or foolish, rich or poor, educated or illiterate, provided the child's moral and physical health are not endangered. Public authorities cannot improve on nature. Public authorities exercise a supervisory role and interfere to rescue a child when the parental tie is broken by abuse or separation. In terms of the English rule the court decides whether and to what extent the welfare of the child requires that the child shall be protected against harm caused by the parent.[90]

> Parenthood, in most civilised societies, is generally conceived of as conferring upon parents the exclusive privilege of ordering, within the family, the upbringing of children of tender age, with all that that entails. That is a privilege which, if interfered with without authority, would be protected by the courts, but it is a privilege circumscribed by many limitations imposed both by the general law and, where the circumstances demand, by the courts or by the authorities upon whom the legislature has imposed the duty of supervising the welfare of children and young persons.[91] When the jurisdiction of the court is invoked for the protection of the child the parental privileges do not terminate. They do, however, become immediately subservient to the paramount consideration which the court has always in mind, that is to say, the welfare of the child.[92]

> The first [submission] was that the court should never override the decision of a devoted and responsible parent such as this mother was found to be. I would for my part accept without reservation that the decision of a devoted and responsible parent should be treated with respect. It should certainly not be disregarded or lightly set aside. But the role of the court is to exercise an independent and objective judgment. If that judgment is in accord with that of the devoted and responsible parent, well and good. If it is not, then it is the duty of the court, after giving due weight to the view of the devoted and responsible parent, to give effect to its own judgment. That is what it is there for. Its judgment may

---

[89] See further para 4.39 below.

[90] *In re KD (A Minor) (Ward: Termination of Access)* [1988] AC 806, 812 *per* Lord Templeman. Consistently with this approach, the common law gives the child no cause of action against a parent for bad parenting, as opposed to parenting which exposes the child to physical dangers: see the discussion in *Surtees v Kingston-upon-Thames Borough Council* [1991] 2 FLR 559 of *McCallion v Dodd* [1966] NZLR 710, *Hahn v Conley* (1971) 126 CLR 276.

[91] See now the Children Act 1989, s 31(2), as explained by the House of Lords in *In re M (A Minor) (Care Orders: Threshold Conditions)* [1994] 2 AC 424; *In re H (Minors) (Sexual Abuse: Standard of Proof)* [1996] AC 563.

[92] *In re KD (A Minor) (Ward: Termination of Access)* [1988] AC 806, 825 *per* Lord Oliver of Aylmerton.

of course be wrong. So may that of the parent. But once the jurisdiction of the court is invoked its clear duty is to reach and express the best judgment it can,[93]

In making that decision the court will always act cautiously, 'acting in opposition to the parent only when judicially satisfied that the welfare of the child requires that the parental rights should be suspended or superseded'.[94]

(a) Parental Power

4.37 At common law responsibility for the care, nurture and protection of a child (including responsibility for the medical treatment of a child) is an aspect of the parental right of custody, the 'bundle of rights' or 'bundle of powers' which enable a parent to exercise physical control over the person of the child, control over the education, religion and marriage of the child and control over the administration of the child's property.[95] Custody in all its aspects necessarily comes to an end with the child's majority at the age of eighteen, but that part of custodial power which enables a parent to exercise physical control over the person of the child (which is that aspect of custody which is most relevant in the context of treatment) ceases when the child reaches 'the years of discretion'.[96] Thus, custody

> is a dwindling right which the courts will hesitate to enforce against the wishes of the child, and the more so the older he is. It starts with a right of control and ends with little more than advice.[97]

> It is, in my view, contrary to the ordinary experience of mankind, at least in Western Europe in the present century, to say that a child or a young person remains in fact under the complete control of his parents until he attains the definite age of majority, now 18 in the United Kingdom, and that on attaining that age he suddenly acquires independence. In practice most wise parents relax their control gradually as the child develops and encourage him or her to become increasingly independent. Moreover, the degree of parental control actually exercised over a particular child does in practice vary considerably according to his understanding

---

[93] *In re Z (A Minor) (Identification: Restrictions on Publication)* [1997] Fam 1, 32–33 *per* Sir Thomas Bingham MR, adopted in *In re T (A Minor) (Wardship: Medical Treatment)* [1997] 1 WLR 242, 250 *per* Butler-Sloss LJ, 255 *per* Roch LJ.
[94] *In re Z (n 93 above)*, 31 *per* Ward LJ (quoting *In re O'Hara* [1902] 2 IR 232, 240 *per* FitzGibbon LJ, approved in *J v C* [1970] AC 668, 715). The test is, of course, easier to state than to apply: compare the facts and the contrasting decisions in *J v C* [1970] AC 668 and *Re M (Child's Upbringing)* [1996] 2 FLR 441 (further proceedings *Re M (Application for Stay of Order)* [1996] 3 FCR 185 and *Re M (Petition to European Commission of Human Rights)* [1996] 3 FCR 377) and consider the, it might be thought surprising, decision in *In re T (A Minor) (Wardship: Medical Treatment)* [1997] 1 WLR 242. See further paras 4.72, 4.75–4.76, 4.162–4.163 below.
[95] *In re Z (A Minor) (Identification: Restrictions on Publication)* [1997] Fam 1, 25–26.
[96] *Hewer v Bryant* [1970] 1 QB 357, 372–373 (a classic description and analysis of custody by Sachs LJ approved in *Gillick v West Norfolk and Wisbech Area Health Authority* [1986] AC 112, 184).
[97] *Hewer v Bryant* [1970] 1 QB 357, 369 *per* Lord Denning MR approved in *Gillick v West Norfolk and Wisbech Area Health Authority* [1986] AC 112, 172, 186.

and intelligence and it would, in my opinion, be unrealistic for the courts not to recognise these facts. Social customs change, and the law ought to, and does in fact, have regard to such changes when they are of major importance.[98]

Custody of a legitimate child is vested in both its parents; in the case of an illegitimate child custody is vested in the mother alone. Rights of custody vested in both parents can be exercised by either and thus either parent can consent to a child's medical treatment.[99]   **4.38**

(b) The Crown as Parens Patriae

Nature and Extent of the Jurisdiction.[100]

The Crown as parens patriae is empowered and obliged 'to protect the person and property of . . . those unable to look after themselves, including infants'.[101] The Sovereign, as parens patriae, has a duty to protect those of his subjects who are unable to protect themselves, particularly children who are the generations of the future.[102] The powers of the Crown as parens patriae, and of the court when exercising the parental power of the Crown as part of its inherent jurisdiction, are theoretically without limit, are more extensive than the custodial powers of a parent, and extend beyond anything that either the child, the child's parents, or even an adult sui juris, could authorise or require, but in practice the court declines to exercise a limitless jurisdiction,   **4.39**

---

[98] *Gillick v West Norfolk and Wisbech Area Health Authority* [1986] AC 112, 171 *per* Lord Fraser of Tullybelton.

[99] *In re L (An Infant)* [1968] P 119, 132, 135, 136, 155, 160, 172. Because of the potential difficulties that arise where parents do not follow the same cultural tradition the BMA has strongly recommended that the written consent of both parents should be obtained for circumcision: 'Circumcision of Male Infants: Guidance for Doctors' (Sept 1996). The General Medical Council has ruled that a doctor must obtain the permission of both parents whenever possible, but in all cases obtain valid consent in writing from a person with parental responsibility: 'Guidance for Doctors who are asked to Circumcise Male Children' (Sept 1997).

[100] See generally *In re Z (A Minor) (Identification: Restrictions on Publication)* [1997] Fam 1. For illuminating discussions of the Crown as parens patriae, viewed from the perspectives of Canada, Australia, pre-partition Ireland and Scotland respectively, see *Re Eve* (1986) 31 DLR (4th) 1, 13–22 *per* La Forest J; *Secretary, Department of Health and Community Services v JWB and SMB* (1992) 175 CLR 218, 258–260 *per* Mason CJ, Dawson, Toohey and Gaudron JJ, 279–285 *per* Brennan J, 301–302 *per* Deane J; *In the matter of a Ward of Court (withholding medical treatment) (No 2)*[1996] 2 IR 79, 102–107 *per* Hamilton CJ, 139–40 *per* Blayney J; *Law Hospital NHS Trust v Lord Advocate* [1996] 2 FLR 407, 418–423 *per* Lord Hope of Craighead LP, 427–431 *per* Lord Cullen, 434–436 *per* Lord Clyde.

[101] *In re D (A Minor) (Wardship: Sterilisation)* [1976] Fam 185, 192.

[102] *In re X (A Minor) (Wardship: Jurisdiction)* [1975] Fam 47, 51–52; *In re C (A Minor) (Wardship: Medical Treatment) (No 2)* [1990] Fam 39, 46; *In re J (A Minor) (Wardship: Medical Treatment)* [1991] Fam 33, 50; *In re R (A Minor) (Wardship: Consent to Treatment)* [1992] Fam 11, 25.

even when what is in question is the protection as opposed to the custody of the child.[103]

4.40 The powers of the Crown as parens patriae are exercised by the judges of the High Court, prior to 1971 by the Judges of the Chancery Division, since then by the Judges of the Family Division, as part of their inherent jurisdiction as the successors of the judges of the High Court of Chancery.

Wardship

4.41 The inherent parens patriae jurisdiction is often, though not necessarily, exercised by means of wardship. Wardship is merely machinery by which the court exercises parens patriae powers in relation to children: the court can exercise its parens patriae jurisdiction whether or not the child is a ward of court.[104] The substantive powers of the court are the same whether it is exercising the inherent jurisdiction or the wardship jurisdiction, for the court, when exercising the wardship jurisdiction, is in truth exercising the inherent jurisdiction, albeit in a particular manner. The only practical difference between wardship and an exercise of the inherent jurisdiction not involving wardship is that in the former case, but not in the latter, the child acquires the *status* of a ward of court.[105]

4.42 The court cannot exercise its inherent parens patriae jurisdiction in relation to an unborn child or over the mother of an unborn child, nor can it make such a child a ward of court.[106]

4.43 The court cannot exercise its inherent parens patriae jurisdiction in relation to a child who has died, nor can it make such a child a ward of court: it can, however, grant declaratory relief in relation to such a child.[107]

---

[103] *Thomasset v Thomasset* [1894] P 295, 299; *Hewer v Bryant* [1970] 1 QB 357, 372; *In re X (A Minor) (Wardship: Jurisdiction)* [1975] Fam 47, 58, 61; *In re X (A Minor) (Wardship: Injunction)* [1984] 1 WLR 1422; *In re C (A Minor) (Wardship: Medical Treatment) (No 2)* [1990] Fam 39, 46; *In re R (A Minor) (Wardship: Criminal Proceedings)* [1991] Fam 56, 63–64, 66; *Re C (A Minor) (Wardship: Jurisdiction)* [1991] 2 FLR 168, 178–179, 184; *In re R (A Minor) (Wardship: Consent to Treatment)* [1992] Fam 11, 25, 28; *Secretary, Department of Health and Community Services v JWB and SMB* (1992) 175 CLR 218, 259, 302; *In re J (A Minor) (Child in Care: Medical Treatment)* [1993] Fam 15, 29; *In re W (A Minor) (Medical Treatment: Court's Jurisdiction)* [1993] Fam 64, 81, 85, 91; *In re Z (A Minor) (Identification: Restrictions on Publication)* [1997] Fam 1, 14–18, 23.
[104] *In re N (Infants)* [1967] Ch 512, 530–531; *In re L (An Infant)* [1968] P 119, 156–157; *In re C (A Minor) (Wardship: Medical Treatment) (No 2)* [1990] Fam 39, 46; *In re M and N (Minors) (Wardship: Publication of Information)* [1990] Fam 211, 223; *In re W (A Minor) (Medical Treatment: Court's Jurisdiction)* [1993] Fam 64, 73, 85; *In re Z (A Minor) (Identification: Restrictions on Publication)* [1997] Fam 1, 13–14.
[105] *In re W (A Minor) (Medical Treatment: Court's Jurisdiction)* [1993] Fam 64, 73.
[106] *In re F (In Utero)* [1988] Fam 122.
[107] *Re A* [1992] 3 Med L Rev 303 (child brain-stem dead: jurisdiction to make declaration that child dead and accordingly lawful to disconnect ventilator).

No 'important' or 'major' step in the life of a ward of court can be taken without **4.44** the prior consent of the court.[108] What precisely counts as an 'important' or 'major' step has never been defined, but the principle plainly extends to the more significant forms of medical treatment, for example, a sterilisation,[109] an abortion,[110] and even a psychiatric examination undertaken for forensic purposes.[111] No doubt it extends to other procedures. Moreover, a child who is a ward of court can neither marry nor leave the jurisdiction without the consent of the court. These matters apart, the status of wardship confers neither disadvantage nor privilege: a child who is a ward of court should be treated medically in exactly the same way as one who is not (though the doctor will be looking to the court rather than to the parent for any necessary consent), and the fact that a child either is or is not a ward of court is totally irrelevant when it comes to choosing how to allocate scarce medical resources.[112]

(ii) *The Children Act 1989*

The effect of the Children Act 1989 is to alter the law in detail but without **4.45** affecting its substance to any significant extent.

(a) Parental Power

Parental Responsibility

The common law concept of custody has been replaced by the statutory **4.46** concept of parental responsibility, defined in section 3(1) as meaning 'all the rights, duties, powers, responsibilities and authority which by law a parent has in relation to the child and his property'. Parental responsibility thus defined plainly includes power to consent to medical treatment.[113] The Act recognises (section 2(5)) that more than one person may have parental responsibility for the same child at the same time and provides (section 2(7)) that where more

---

[108] *In re S (Infants)* [1967] 1 WLR 396, 407; *In re D (A Minor) (Wardship: Sterilisation)* [1976] Fam 185, 196; *Re G-U (A Minor) (Wardship)* [1984] FLR 811; *In re C (A Minor) (Wardship: Medical Treatment)* [1990] Fam 26, 32, 38; *In re J (A Minor) (Wardship: Medical Treatment)* [1991] Fam 33, 49; *In re R (A Minor) (Wardship: Consent to Treatment)* [1992] Fam 11, 25; *In re W (A Minor) (Medical Treatment: Court's Jurisdiction)* [1993] Fam 64, 73.

[109] *In re D (A Minor) (Wardship: Sterilisation)* [1976] Fam 185, 196.

[110] *Re G-U (A Minor) (Wardship)* [1984] FLR 811.

[111] *In re S (Infants)* [1967] 1 WLR 396, 407.

[112] *In re J (A Minor) (Wardship: Medical Treatment)* [1991] Fam 33, 41, 42; *In re R (A Minor) (Wardship: Criminal Proceedings)* [1991] Fam 56, 65–66.

[113] *In re Z (A Minor) (Identification: Restrictions on Publication)* [1997] Fam 1, 25–26.

than one person has parental responsibility each may act alone and without the other.[114]

4.47 The Act provides that the following have parental responsibility: the child's father and mother, where they were married to each other at the time of his birth (section 2(1)); the child's mother, but not the father, where they were not so married (section 2(2)), unless the father acquires parental responsibility either by order of the court under section 4(1)(a) or pursuant to a 'parental responsibility agreement' with the mother under section 4(1)(b); a person appointed as the child's guardian (section 5(6)); a person in whose favour the court makes a residence order with respect to the child (section 12(2)); the local authority designated in a care order made with respect to the child (section 33(3)(b));[115] the local authority or other authorised person who has obtained an emergency protection order with respect to the child (section 44(4)(c)).[116]

Carers

4.48 A person who does not have parental responsibility for a particular child but has care of the child—for example, a relative, a child-minder, a school-teacher, or even a doctor, if for instance the child is an in-patient in a hospital—may do what is reasonable in all the circumstances of the case for the purpose of safeguarding or promoting the child's welfare (section 3(5)). In an appropriate case such a person can consent to medical treatment on behalf of the child, though it will presumably only be reasonable to act without first obtaining the consent of the child's parents or whoever else has parental responsibility in an emergency or if the treatment is trivial.

(b) Parens Patriae

4.49 Section 100(2) of the Act follows the common law in distinguishing between 'the High Court's inherent jurisdiction with respect to children' (that is, the exercise by the High Court of the parens patriae jurisdiction) and 'wardship'. Section 100(2)(c), following the common law, recognises that the High Court can exercise its inherent parens patriae jurisdiction without making the child a ward of court.

4.50 In addition to exercising its parens patriae powers either under the inherent jurisdiction or in wardship the court can in some cases exercise comparable

---

[114] See n 99 above.
[115] For an example of consent by a local authority to the treatment of a child in care (voluntary admission to a mental hospital), see *R v Kirklees Metropolitan Borough Council, ex p C* [1992] 2 FLR 117, [1993] 2 FLR 187.
[116] *Re O (A Minor) (Medical Treatment)* [1993] 2 FLR 149, 151.

powers under section 8, by making either a prohibited steps order or a specific issue order.

2. The Three Stages of Childhood

Upon attaining the age of eighteen a child who is not mentally incompetent **4.51** becomes sui juris and absolutely entitled to decide whether or not to consent to treatment. Prior to that the normal developing child will have passed through three successive stages of development recognised by the law.

(i) *The Child of Tender Years*

Manifestly a young child who has not yet reached 'the years of discretion' **4.52** lacks the capacity to consent to medical treatment, because he lacks the intellectual ability to understand what is involved and the maturity to form a balanced judgment.

Who Can Consent

In the case of a child of tender years consent to medical treatment can **4.53** lawfully be given by the court, by any person with parental responsibility, and, to the extent that it is reasonable in all the circumstances for the purpose of safeguarding or promoting the child's welfare, by any person who, although he does not have parental responsibility, has care of the child.[117]

(ii) *The 'Gillick competent' Child*

(a) The Test of Competence

If and when the child achieves a sufficient understanding and intelligence to **4.54** enable him to understand fully what is proposed he is treated as having the capacity to give a valid consent to medical treatment.[118] The conventional shorthand is to refer to such a child as having 'Gillick capacity' or as being 'Gillick competent'.

---

[117] See paras 4.37, 4.39, 4.46, 4.47, 4.48 above.
[118] *Gillick v West Norfolk and Wisbech Area Health Authority* [1986] AC 112, 169, 186, 188–189, 195, 201.

The Test of 'Gillick Competence'

4..55 The key to 'Gillick competence' is the child's understanding and intelligence.[119] 'Gillick competence' in relation to a particular child is a question of fact for the judge (or jury).[120]

4.56 In determining whether or not a particular child is 'Gillick competent' in relation to a particular proposed treatment what is being looked for is the capacity to reach a mature and balanced judgment, 'the attainment by a child of an age of sufficient discretion to enable him or her to exercise a wise choice in his or her own interests'.[121] The factors to be taken into account are: the child's understanding and intelligence, his chronological, mental and emotional age, intellectual development and maturity, his capacity to make up his own mind, and his ability to understand fully, and to appraise, the medical advice being given, the nature, consequences and implications of the advised treatment, the potential risks to health and the emotional impact of either accepting or rejecting the advised treatment, and any moral and family questions involved.[122]

> I would hold that as a matter of law the parental right to determine whether or not their minor child below the age of 16 will have medical treatment terminates if and when the child achieves a sufficient understanding and intelligence to enable him or her to understand fully what is proposed. It will be a question of fact whether a child seeking advice has sufficient understanding of what is involved to give a consent valid in law. . . . When applying these conclusions to contraceptive advice and treatment it has to be borne in mind that there is much that has to be understood by a girl under the age of 16 if she is to have legal capacity to consent to such treatment. It is not enough that she should understand the nature of the advice which is being given: she must also have a sufficient maturity to understand what is involved. There are moral and family questions, especially her relationship with her parents; long term problems associated with the emotional impact of pregnancy and its termination; and there are the risks to health of sexual intercourse at her age, risks which contraception may diminish but cannot eliminate. It follows that a doctor will have to satisfy himself that she is able to appraise these factors before he can safely proceed upon the basis that she has at law capacity to consent to contraceptive treatment[123]

Youth and the potential for development may make it difficult, or indeed

---

[119] ibid, 171, 186, 189, 201; *In re W (A Minor) (Medical Treatment: Court's Jurisdiction)* [1993] Fam 64, 81.
[120] *Gillick v West Norfolk and Wisbech Area Health Authority* [1986] AC 112, 172, 189.
[121] ibid, 188 *per* Lord Scarman.
[122] ibid, 174, 189, 190, 201; *In re R (A Minor) (Wardship: Consent to Treatment)* [1992] Fam 11, 26.
[123] *Gillick v West Norfolk and Wisbech Area Health Authority* [1986] AC 112, 188–189 *per* Lord Scarman.

impossible, to make the relevant findings of fact to the necessary standard of proof. It must also be borne in mind that, even with an adult, there may be considerable barriers, conscious and unconscious, intellectual and emotional, to a full understanding of the implications of accepting or refusing the advised treatment.

Gillick competence reflects the staged development of a normal child and the **4.57** progressive transition of the adolescent from childhood to adulthood. The capacity to understand reflects and is conditioned by the gradual acquisition of maturity and the capacity to consent will vary with the gravity of the treatment proposed. A child who has Gillick capacity to consent to dental treatment, the mending of a broken arm, a tonsillectomy or even an appendectomy, may lack the capacity to consent to more serious treatment.[124]

> [T]he extent of the legal capacity of a young person to make decisions for herself or himself is not susceptible of precise abstract definition. Pending the attainment of full adulthood, legal capacity varies according to the gravity of the particular matter and the maturity and understanding of the particular young person.[125]

Mental disability

Mental disability is not of itself incompatible with a child having 'Gillick **4.58** capacity', at least for some purposes.

> The age at which intellectually disabled children can consent will be higher than for children within the normal range of abilities. However, terms such as 'mental disability', 'intellectual handicap' or 'retardation' lack precision. There is no essential cause of disability; those who come within these categories form a heterogeneous group. And since most intellectually disabled people are borderline to mildly disabled, there is no reason to assume that all disabled children are incapable of giving consent to treatment. In the case of children with intellectual disabilities, the situation is further complicated by the need for future, as well as present, assessment. . . . It may also be said, in this context, that not only are there widely varying kinds and consequences of intellectual disability but such handicaps, possibly more so than other forms of disability, are often surrounded by misconceptions on the part of others in society, misconceptions often involving an underestimation of a person's ability. . . . [I]t is important to stress that it cannot be presumed that an intellectually disabled child is, by virtue of his or her disability, incapable of giving consent to treatment. The capacity of a child to give informed consent to medical treatment depends on the rate of development of each individual.[126]

---

[124] ibid, 169, 201; *In re R (A Minor) (Wardship: Consent to Treatment)* [1992] Fam 11, 25, 31; *In re W (A Minor) (Medical Treatment: Court's Jurisdiction)* [1993] Fam 64, 81.
[125] *Secretary, Department of Health and Community Services v JWB and SMB* (1992) 175 CLR 218, 293 *per* Deane J.
[126] ibid, 238–239 *per* Mason CJ, Dawson, Toohey and Gaudron JJ.

Fluctuating Capacity

4.59 Gillick competence is a developmental concept and will not be lost or acquired on a day to day or week to week basis. Mental disability must be taken into account particularly where it is fluctuating in its effect[127] or (as with anorexia nervosa) has as one of its features that it is capable of destroying the ability to make an informed choice and creates a wish not to be cured and a compulsion to refuse treatment or accept only ineffective treatment.[128]

> But there is no suggestion that the extent of this competence can fluctuate upon a day to day or week to week basis. What is really being looked at is an assessment of mental and emotional age, as contrasted with chronological age, but even this test needs to be modified in the case of fluctuating mental disability to take account of that misfortune. It should be added that in any event what is involved is not merely an ability to understand the nature of the proposed treatment . . . but a full understanding and appreciation of the consequences both of the treatment in terms of intended and possible side effects and, equally important, the anticipated consequences of a failure to treat. On the evidence in the present case . . . even if she was capable on a good day of a sufficient degree of understanding to meet the Gillick criteria, her mental disability, to the cure or amelioration of which the proposed treatment was directed, was such that on other days she was not only 'Gillick incompetent', but actually sectionable. No child in that situation can be regarded as 'Gillick competent'.[129]

The Standard of Proof

4.60 The standard of proof must be the more rigorous the more serious the implications for the child of either giving or refusing consent. Where life or serious injury to health is at stake, and the child's decision appears to be unreasonable, the doctor (or the court) can be astute to find a lack of capacity to consent.

> I find that A is a boy of sufficient intelligence to be able to take decisions about his own well-being, but I also find that there is a range of decisions of which some are outside his ability fully to grasp their implications. Impressed though I was by his obvious intelligence, by his calm discussion of the implications, by his assertion even that he would refuse well knowing that he may die as a result, in my judgment A does not have a full understanding of the whole implication of what the refusal of that treatment involves. . . . I am quite satisfied that A does not have any sufficient comprehension of the pain he has yet to suffer, of the fear that he will be undergoing, of the distress not only occasioned by that fear but also—and importantly—the distress he will inevitably suffer as he, a loving son, helplessly watches his parents' and his family's distress. They are a

---

[127] *In re R (A Minor) (Wardship: Consent to Treatment)* [1992] Fam 11, 26, 31–32.
[128] *In re W (A Minor) (Medical Treatment: Court's Jurisdiction)* [1993] Fam 64, 81, 83.
[129] *In re R (A Minor) (Wardship: Consent to Treatment)* [1992] Fam 11, 25–26 *per* Lord Donaldson of Lymington MR.

close family, and they are a brave family, but I find that he has no realisation of the full implications which lie before him as to the process of dying. He may have some concept of the fact that he will die, but as to the manner of his death and to the extent of his and his family's suffering I find that he has not the ability to turn his mind to it nor the will to do so. Who can blame him for that? If, therefore, this case depended upon my finding of whether or not A is of sufficient understanding and intelligence and maturity to give full and informed consent, I find that he is not.[130]

The doctor (or the court) must be astute to the possibility that conscious or sub-conscious influence is being exerted on a child either by his parents or, where religious beliefs are involved, by religious advisers.[131]   **4.61**

(b) Who Can Consent

The child's consent

A 'Gillick competent' child's consent to treatment is as valid and effective as the consent of an adult who is sui juris.   **4.62**

Parental Consent

A parent can lawfully consent to the treatment of a 'Gillick competent' child who is refusing to consent.[132] A parent cannot overrule a 'Gillick competent' child's consent to treatment,[133] but can, in effect, overrule a 'Gillick competent' child's refusal to consent to treatment: the parent and the child have concurrent powers to consent and where more than one person has a power of consent, only a failure to, or refusal of, consent by all creates a veto.[134]   **4.63**

The law is clear and settled (short of the House of Lords) but the cases in which the law was thus established by the Court of Appeal are controversial and have been heavily criticised by academic writers on a number of grounds.[135] First, it is said that the law as laid down by the Court of Appeal   **4.64**

---

[130] *Re E (A Minor) (Wardship: Medical Treatment)* [1993] 1 FLR 386, 391 *per* Ward J (15–year old Jehovah's Witness refusing blood transfusion necessary to save his life). Similarly, *Re S (A Minor) (Consent to Medical Treatment)* [1994] 2 FLR 1065.
[131] *Re S (A Minor) (Consent to Medical Treatment)* [1994] 2 FLR 1065 ($15\frac{1}{2}$ –year old Jehovah's Witness refusing blood transfusion necessary to save her life).
[132] *In re R (A Minor) (Wardship: Consent to Treatment)* [1992] Fam 11, 23–25, 26; *In re W (A Minor) (Medical Treatment: Court's Jurisdiction)* [1993] Fam 64, 84, 86, 87; *Re K, W and H (Minors) (Medical Treatment)* [1993] 1 FLR 854, 859.
[133] *In re R (A Minor) (Wardship: Consent to Treatment)* [1992] Fam 11, 23, 26; *In re W (A Minor) (Medical Treatment: Court's Jurisdiction)* [1993] Fam 64, 83.
[134] *In re R (A Minor) (Wardship: Consent to Treatment)* [1992] Fam 11, 22, 26.
[135] See, for example, Bainham, 'The Judge and the Competent Minor' (1992) 108 LQR 194, 198–9; Thornton, 'Multiple Keyholders' [1992] CLJ 34; Dyer (ed), *Doctors, Patients and the Law* (1992), 58–61 (Kennedy), 75–7 (Gostin), 156–7 (Dodds-Smith) Brazier, *Medicine, Patients and the Law* (ed; 2), 345–6.

conflicts with Lord Scarman's analysis in *Gillick* when he described what he called the parents' 'right to determine whether or not their minor child . . . will have medical treatment' as terminating when the child becomes 'Gillick competent'. The words 'whether or not' certainly suggest[136] that, in Lord Scarman's opinion, the parent's consent is not effective where a 'Gillick competent' child has refused consent. Lord Scarman clearly viewed the policy of the common law as dictating that, once a child of whatever age has the capacity to give an informed and valid consent, that terminates the parent's right to veto the child's views *one way or the other*. Nothing in Lord Scarman's speech in *Gillick* supports the view that the parent's right to consent and the child's right to consent are ever co-existent or co-terminous. Secondly, it is said to be illogical to accept that a parent cannot veto the competent child's consent to treatment while asserting that the parent can overrule the child's refusal of treatment. Such a view is wholly destructive of the child's right to self-determination and capable of producing some extremely odd results: it is not easy to see what social purpose or principle of public policy is served by treating the parent, for example, as powerless to veto an abortion which the child wants but the parent objects to, while treating the parent as competent to authorise an abortion which the child does not want but the parent does. The Court of Appeal sought to meet this objection by dismissing the example as 'hair-raising' but inconceivable in real life.[137] But this does not meet the argument of principle and logic. Moreover, and perhaps more to the point, it is difficult to see what purpose is achieved by conferring on parents a power which in practice cannot be exercised. Thirdly, it is said that the distinction drawn between 'consent' and 'determination' is fallacious and unworkable. The Court of Appeal sought to avoid the difficulties created by Lord Scarman's concept of 'determination' by accepting that there is no parental right to determine, in the sense of a right to nullify or veto the 'Gillick competent' child's consent, and asserting only a 'concurrent' parental right to 'consent'. But the truth is (so it is said) that in a case where the child has refused to consent, and the parent then supplies his own concurrent consent, the parent is 'determining' the matter—so the suggested distinction between 'determination' and 'consent' falls apart. Fourthly, it is said to run counter to the philosophy of the Children Act 1989, which, in the context of certain forms of medical and psychiatric examination, assessment and treatment, recognises and gives effect to the child's right to self-determination and treats his objection as conclusive whenever he has 'sufficient understanding to make an

---

[136] As Staughton LJ recognised in *In re R (A Minor) (Wardship: Consent to Treatment)* [1992] Fam 11, 27–28.
[137] *In re W (A Minor) (Medical Treatment: Court's Jurisdiction)* [1993] Fam 64, 79, 89–90.

informed decision' (sections 38(6), 43(8), 44(7), Schedule 3, paras 4(4)(a), 5(5)(a)).

The court

The court is not bound by the wishes or decision of a 'Gillick competent' child.[138] Thus the court, if only it chooses to exercise its inherent powers,[139] can always outflank what might appear to be the perfectly clear legislative policy laid down in the Children Act 1989 and can do the very things which the Act has said that it shall not do. It is not easy to reconcile this view of the law with the principle that prerogative power yields to inconsistent statutory provisions.[140]

4.65

(iii) *The 16 or 17-year old Child*

Section 8 of the Family Law Reform Act 1969 provides:

4.66

(1) The consent of a minor who has attained the age of sixteen years to any surgical, medical or dental treatment which, in the absence of consent, would constitute a trespass to his person, shall be as effective as it would be if he were of full age; and where a minor has by virtue of this section given an effective consent to any treatment it shall not be necessary to obtain any consent for it from his parent or guardian.

(2) In this section 'surgical, medical or dental treatment' includes any procedure undertaken for the purposes of diagnosis, and this section applies to any procedure (including, in particular, the administration of an anaesthetic) which is ancillary to any treatment as it applies to that treatment.

(3) Nothing in this section shall be construed as making ineffective any consent which would have been effective if this section had not been enacted.

Section 8 does not extend to the donation of organs, or of blood or other bodily substances, nor even to the taking of a blood sample (for which

---

[138] *In re R (A Minor) (Wardship: Consent to Treatment)* [1992] Fam 11, 25, 26, 28, 31, 32; *In re W (A Minor) (Medical Treatment: Court's Jurisdiction)* [1993] Fam 64, 81, 84, 88, 93; *South Glamorgan County Council v W and B* [1993] 1 FLR 574, 584. The previous cases bearing on the point were: *B(BR) v B(J)* [1968] P 466; *Re P (A Minor)* [1986] 1 FLR 272, *Re G-U (A Minor) (Wardship)* [1984] FLR 811; *Re E (A Minor) (Wardship: Medical Treatment)* [1993] 1 FLR 386; *Re B (Wardship: Abortion)* [1991] 2 FLR 426.

[139] As in *South Glamorgan County Council v W and B* [1993] 1 FLR 574 (order under inherent jurisdiction for psychiatric examination and assessment of 'Gillick competent' child who had validly refused consent under section 38(6)). See also *In re W (A Minor) (Medical Treatment: Court's Jurisdiction)* [1993] Fam 64, 82.

[140] *AG v De Keyser's Royal Hotel Ltd* [1920] AC 508; cf also *Richards v Richards* [1984] AC 174.

separate provision is made in section 21(2)), for none of these procedures constitutes either treatment or diagnosis.[141]

Parental Consent

4.67 As in the case of a 'Gillick competent' child, and for the same reasons, a parent cannot overrule a sixteen or seventeen–year old child's consent to treatment but can, in effect, overrule such a child's refusal to consent to treatment.[142] This view of the law has, again, been the subject of severe academic criticism, as involving an inappropriately narrow construction of the langauge of section 8, which had previously been considered as conferring 'complete autonomy' on the sixteen or seventeen–year old child.

The Court

4.68 Notwithstanding section 8 of the 1969 Act, the court in the exercise of its inherent parens patriae jurisdiction is not bound by the wishes of a sixteen or seventeen–year old child.[143]

(iv) *The Mentally Incompetent Child*

The Mentally Incompetent Child Under the Age of 16.

4.69 A mentally incompetent child may, because of its mental disability, never acquire 'Gillick competence'. Alternatively, it may have 'Gillick competence' for some limited purposes but lack the capacity to give a valid consent to a particular form of medical treatment. In such a case the power to decide whether or not the child should be treated will remain in the parents or the court.

The Mentally-Incompetent 16 or 17-year old Child

4.70 All that section 8(1) of the Family Law Reform Act 1969 does is to deem the sixteen–year old child to have the same *legal* capacity as he would if he were eighteen ('consent . . . shall be as effective as . . . if he were of full age'). The bare fact of age apart, section 8(1) does not deem the child to have any *mental* capacity which in fact he lacks. Thus in the case of a mentally incompetent sixteen–year old the power to decide will, notwith-standing section 8, remain in the parents or the court until the child

---

[141] *In re W (A Minor) (Medical Treatment: Court's Jurisdiction)* [1993] Fam 64, 78, 83, 92, 94.
[142] *In re R (A Minor) (Wardship: Consent to Treatment)* [1992] Fam 11, 24, 26; *In re W (A Minor) (Medical Treatment: Court's Jurisdiction)* [1993] Fam 64, 74–79, 83–84, 86–87.
[143] *In re R (A Minor) (Wardship: Consent to Treatment)* [1992] Fam 11; *In re W (A Minor) (Medical Treatment: Court's Jurisdiction)* [1993] Fam 64, 81, 83–84, 91–92.

attains the age of eighteen.[144] Consistently with section 8(1) the mental competence of a sixteen or seventten–year old child is judged by reference not to 'Gillick capacity' but to the test applicable in the case of an adult, that is, the test in *In re C (Adult: Refusal of Treatment)* [1994] 1 WLR 290.[145]

3. The Ambit of Parental Consent

Limitations on the Parental Power to Consent

Even where the law recognises the capacity of a parent to give a proxy or substitute consent on behalf of a child, the parental right to decide is not absolute. The parental power to give a valid consent is subject to five limitations. In the first place no parent can consent to any procedure which is unlawful. Secondly, where the child is a ward of court parental power is limited by the principle that it is necessary to obtain the prior consent of the court before any 'important' or 'major' step is taken in the life of the child.[146] Thirdly, any parental giving or refusal of consent must be in the best interests of the child. Fourthly, there are certain procedures, not unlawful in themselves, but which are nonetheless considered to be of such a nature as to require the prior sanction of the court. Fifthly, there are limits to the consent which a parent can give in the case of a child old enough to understand what is involved.

4.71

Control by the Court

Consistently with the principle that the parental right to decide is not absolute, the court is not bound by and can override a parent's decision;[147] the court can overrule parental consent to treatment which is not in the best interests of the child[148] and overrule parental refusal to consent to treatment which is in the best interests of the child.[149] However, the court always acts

4.72

---

[144] *In re R (A Minor) (Wardship: Consent to Treatment)* [1992] Fam 11, 24.

[145] *A Metropolitan Borough Council v AB* [1997] 1 FLR 767, 773; *Re C (Detention: Medical Treatment)* [1997] 2 FLR 180, 195. See further paras 4.111–4.113 below.

[146] See para 4.44 above.

[147] *Gillick v West Norfolk and Wisbech Area Health Authority* [1986] AC 112, 184, 200; *In re C (A Minor) (Wardship: Medical Treatment) (No 2)* [1990] Fam 39, 46; *In re J (A Minor) (Wardship: Medical Treatment)* [1991] Fam 33, 52; *In re R (A Minor) (Wardship: Consent to Treatment)* [1992] Fam 11, 25; *In re W (A Minor) (Medical Treatment: Court's Jurisdiction)* [1993] Fam 64, 93; *In re Z (A Minor) (Identification: Restrictions on Publication)* [1997] Fam 1, 30–31.

[148] *In re D (A Minor) (Wardship: Sterilisation)* [1976] Fam 185 (sterilisation restrained despite parent's consent: as Heilbron J said, 194, 'in wardship proceedings parents' rights can be superseded').

[149] *In re B (A Minor) (Wardship: Medical Treatment)* [1981] 1 WLR 1421 (order directing life-saving operation on 10-day old mongol child notwithstanding parents' bona fide decision to let nature take its course); *Re P (A Minor)* [1986] 1 FLR 272 (order directing abortion

cautiously and will act in opposition to the parent only when judicially satisfied that the parental rights should be suspended or superseded.[150] The question is not whether the parent is acting reasonably but what is in the best interests of the child.[151] But the law recognises that there is a 'margin of appreciation' within which parental decision-making is unlikely to be superseded by the court:

> The law's insistence that the welfare of a child shall be paramount is easily stated and universally applauded, but the present case[152] illustrates, poignantly and dramatically, the difficulties that are encountered when trying to put it into practice. . . . It is not an occasion—even in an age preoccupied with 'rights'—to talk of the rights of a child, or the rights of a parent, or the rights of the court. The cases . . . are uncompromising in their assertion that the sole yard-stick must be the need to give effect to the demands of paramountcy for the welfare of the child. They establish that there are bound to be occasions when such paramountcy will compel the court, acting as a judicial parent, to substitute the judge's own views as to the claims of child welfare over those of natural parents—even in a case where the latter are supported by qualities of devotion, commitment, love and reason. . . . All these cases depend on their own facts and render generalisations—tempting though they may be to the legal or social analyst—wholly out of place. It can only be said safely that there is a scale, at one end of which lies the clear case where parental opposition to medical intervention is prompted by scruple or dogma of a kind which is patently irreconcilable with principles of child health and welfare widely accepted by the generality of mankind; and that at the other end lie highly problematic cases where there is genuine scope for a difference of view between parent and judge. In both situations it is the duty of the judge to allow the court's own opinion to prevail in the perceived paramount interests of the child concerned, but in cases at the latter end of the scale, there must be a likelihood (though never of course a certainty) that the greater the scope for genuine debate between one view and another the stronger will be the inclination of the court to be influenced by a reflection that in the last analysis the best interests of every child include an

---

on 15–year old girl notwithstanding parents' bona fide objections on religious and other grounds); *Re E (A Minor) (Wardship: Medical Treatment)* [1993] 1 FLR 386 (order directing blood transfusion for 15–year old leukaemic Jehovah's Witness notwithstanding parents' religious objections); *Re B (Wardship: Abortion)* [1991] 2 FLR 426 (order directing abortion on 12–year old girl notwithstanding parent's bona fide objections); *Re S (A Minor) (Medical Treatment)* [1993] 1 FLR 376 (order directing blood transfusion for 4–year old leukaemic child of Jehovah's Witnesses); *Re O (A Minor) (Medical Treatment)* [1993] 2 FLR 149 (order directing blood transfusion for 2–month old child with respiratory problems of Jehovah's Witnesses); *Re R (A Minor) (Blood Transfusion)* [1993] 2 FLR 757 (order directing blood transfusion for 10–month old leukaemic child of Jehovah's Witnesses).

[150] *In re Z (A Minor) (Identification: Restrictions on Publication)* [1997] Fam 1, 31. See further para 4.36 above, paras 4.75–4.76, 4.162–4.163 below.

[151] *In re T (A Minor) (Wardship: Medical Treatment)* [1997] 1 WLR 242, 250–251, 253–256. See further paras 4.75–4.76, 4.90, 4.137 below.

[152] For the facts of which see below and para 4.201 below.

expectation that difficult decisions affecting the length and quality of its life will be taken for it by the parent to whom its care has been entrusted by nature.[153]

Moreover, even in the case of potentially life-saving treatment, the court may be more willing to overrule parental refusal to consent where the child's life-threatening condition can be cured by a simple 'one-off' operation[154] than where the child requires complicated surgery and the total commitment to the treatment, and many years of special care, by a parent upon whom the child's welfare depends but who has conscientiously come to the conclusion that such treatment, with all that it may entail for the child in terms of risks, discomfort and distress, a lifetime of drugs, and the possibility of further invasive surgery, would not be in the child's best interests[155]

Control by the Doctor

As has already been seen, parental decision-making is in practical terms   **4.73**
subject to considerable control by the doctor.[156]

(i) *Unlawful Procedures*

Some forms of interference with the body are unlawful, in the sense that even   **4.74**
a competent adult cannot give a consent which the law recognises as lawful and effective.[157] The general rule, however, is that 'reasonable surgical interference' is lawful as being in the public interest.[158] Nonetheless, from time to time it has been suggested that certain surgical procedures are unlawful. Thus it has been said that female circumcision for non-therapeutic purposes is unlawful at common law[159] (it has now been made illegal by statute[160]). On the other hand, there is no doubt that male circumcision, for whatever reason it is performed, is not as such unlawful,[161] nor is a 'sex-change' or 'gender

---

[153] *In re T (A Minor) (Wardship: Medical Treatment)* [1997] 1 WLR 242, 253–254 *per* Waite LJ.

[154] As in *In re B (A Minor) (Wardship: Medical Treatment)* [1981] 1 WLR 1421. See *In re T (A Minor) (Wardship: Medical Treatment)* [1997] 1 WLR 242, 252 *per* Butler-Sloss LJ.

[155] As in *In re T (A Minor) (Wardship: Medical Treatment)* [1997] 1 WLR 242 (child suffering from life-threatening liver defect requiring liver transplant). See the critical discussion by Professor Grubb in [1996] Med L Rev 315.

[156] See paras 4.17–4.18 above.

[157] *Attorney-General's Reference (No 6 of 1980)* [1981] QB 715; *R v Brown* [1994] AC 212.

[158] *Attorney-General's Reference (No 6 of 1980)* [1981] QB 715, 719.

[159] Lord Hailsham of St Marylebone LC (1983) 441 HL Deb cols 676–7, 694–5; Mackay, 'Is Female Circumcision Unlawful?' [1983] Crim LR 717; Hayter, 'Female Circumcision—Is there a legal solution?' [1984] JSWL 323.

[160] Prohibition of Female Circumcision Act 1985.

[161] *R v Brown* [1994] AC 212, 231 and see The National Health Service (General Medical Services) Regulations 1992, SI 1992/635, Sch 2, para 38(i) (which permits a doctor to

reassignment' operation whether from male to 'female' (involving castration and removal of the penis)[162] or from female to 'male',[163] nor is a sterilisation, for whatever reason it is performed.[164]

(ii) *Best Interests*

4.75 Parental rights exist not for the benefit of the parent or anyone else but for the benefit of the child.[165] The parental power to give a substituted consent to medical treatment for a child must be exercised in the best interests of the child, objectively assessed on a judgment of what is best for the welfare of the particular child.[166]

> Parental rights clearly do exist, and they do not wholly disappear until the age of majority. Parental rights relate to both the persons and the property of the child—custody, care, and control of the person and guardianship of the property of the child. But the common law has never treated such rights as sovereign or beyond review and control. Nor has our law ever treated the child as other than a person with capacities and rights recognised by law. The principle of the law . . . is that parental rights are derived from parental duty and exist only so long as they are needed for the protection of the person and property of the child. . . . [P]arental right must be exercised in accordance with the welfare principle and can be challenged, even overridden, if it be not. . . . [P]arental right endures only so long as it is needed for the protection of the child.[167]

charge a fee for 'circumcising a patient for whom such an operation is requested on religious grounds and is not needed on any medical ground'.). See also *Hickey v Croydon Area Health Authority* (1985) *The Times* Mar 6 (claim for damages for negligence in circumcising adult who sought operation to 'improve his sex life': Michael Davies J justified the legality of the operation by reference to Gen xvii: vv 10–14).

[162] *Corbett v Corbett* [1971] P 83, 99. See also *R v Tan* [1983] QB 1053.
[163] *In re A* (1993) 16 Fam LR 715 (Family Court of Australia).
[164] Denning LJ's dicta in *Bravery v Bravery* [1954] 1 WLR 1169, 1180–1181, if they were ever good law (Evershed MR and Hodson LJ expressed the contrary view, 1175–1176), are now universally regarded as no longer representing the law: *In re B (A Minor) (Wardship: Sterilisation)* [1988] AC 199; *In re F (Mental Patient: Sterilisation)* [1990] 2 AC 1; *Secretary, Department of Health and Community Services v JWB and SMB* (1992) 175 CLR 218, 234.
[165] For the suggestion that the parental role is fiduciary, and that a parent with a conflicting interest to that of the child is therefore disqualified from giving consent, see *Secretary, Department of Health and Community Services v JWB and SMB* (1992) 175 CLR 218, 317.
[166] *Gillick v West Norfolk and Wisbech Area Health Authority* [1986] AC 112, 170, 173, 183–185, 200; *Secretary, Department of Health and Community Services v JWB and SMB* (1992) 175 CLR 218, 240, 278, 295, 316.
[167] *Gillick v West Norfolk and Wisbech Area Health Authority* [1986] AC 112, 183–185 *per* Lord Scarman.

Community Standards and Parental Views

In determining what is in the best interests of their children, parents are **4.76** entitled to follow their own moral and social views within the limits set by the general standards of society.

> [O]ne can identify two broad common law propositions relating to the authority of parents to authorise surgery in the case of . . . a child who is, as a matter of fact, completely unable to make a reasoned decision for herself or himself about the desirability of the particular treatment. The first of those propositions is that parental authority exists to authorise such surgery for the purpose, and only for the purpose, of advancing the welfare of the child. It does not extend to authorising surgery because of a perception that it is in the interests of those responsible for the care of the child or in the interests of society in general (eg, for eugenic reasons). That which constitutes the welfare of a child in a particular case falls to be determined by reference to general community standards, but making due allowance for the entitlement of parents, within the limits of what is permissible in accordance with those standards, to entertain divergent views about the moral and secular objectives to be pursued for their children. The second broad proposition is that, at least in relation to a serious matter such as a major medical procedure, parental authority can be validly exercised only after due inquiry about, and adequate consideration of, what truly represents the welfare of the child in all the circumstances of the case.[168]

This approach is reflected in the cases[169] and is mirrored both by commentators[170] who acknowledge that, in bringing up their children, parents have to address the basic moral issue of what sort of child they wish to raise and have a wide range of discretion to pursue goals which society as a whole may find undesirable, but which it will tolerate, and by those commentators[171] who justify infant male circumcision (in contrast to female circumcision) on the basis of immemorial usage and social or religious toleration.[172]

Procedures not Contrary to the Child's Interests

Some commentators have suggested that a parent can lawfully give consent to **4.77** any procedure to which a 'reasonable parent' would consent and which, even

---

[168] *Secretary, Department of Health and Community Services v JWB and SMB* (1992) 175 CLR 218, 295 *per* Deane J.

[169] See *In re T (A Minor) (Wardship: Medical Treatment)* [1997] 1 WLR 242, esp, 254 *per* Waite LJ quoted at para 4.72 above.

[170] McCall Smith, 'Is Anything Left of Parental Rights?' in Sutherland and McCall Smith (eds), *Family Rights: Family Law and Medical Advance* (1990), 4; Bainham, 'Non-Intervention and Judicial Paternalism' in Birks (ed), *The Frontiers of Liability, Volume 1* (1994), 173.

[171] Glanville Williams, 'Consent and Public Policy' [1962] Crim LR 74, 154, 157, Glanville Williams, *Textbook of Criminal Law* (2nd edn), 575, 586; Mackay, 'Is Female Circumcision Unlawful?' [1983] Crim LR 717, 719; Hayter, 'Female Circumcision—Is there a legal solution?' [1984] JSWL 323, 326.   [172] See further paras 4.162–4.163 below.

if not positively beneficial to the child, is neither cruel, nor excessive nor clearly against the child's interests. It is on this basis that some commentators justify routine neonatal male circumcision on the footing that the attendant risks are not so great as to be 'contrary to the child's interest'.[173] Such a principle is said to be supported by the decision of the House of Lords that a child can be blood-tested for forensic purposes even if it cannot be shown that a blood-test will be in its best interests.[174]

> It is a legal wrong to use constraint to an adult beyond what is authorised by statute or ancient common law powers connected with crime and the like. But it is not and could not be a legal wrong for a parent or person authorised by him to use constraint to his young child provided it is not cruel or excessive. There are differences of opinion as to the age beyond which it is unwise to use constraint, but that cannot apply to infants or young children. So it seems to me to be impossible to deny that a parent can lawfully require that his young child should submit to a blood test. . . . [S]urely a reasonable parent would have some regard to the general public interest and would not refuse a blood test unless he thought that would clearly be against the interests of the child.[175]

This perhaps reflects a suggested wider principle of the child's civic duty:

> Children, whether wards of court or not, are citizens owing duties to society as a whole (including other children), which are appropriate to their years and understanding. Those duties are defined both by the common law and by statute.[176]

This view of the ambit of parental power, at least if it is to be relied upon as a rule of wide-ranging application, is difficult to reconcile either with basic principle or with more recent cases. It is best treated as confined to procedures which involve no more than 'minimal' or 'negligible' risk and discomfort, e g, the taking of nasal or throat swabs and urine or blood samples (including the taking of a blood sample by venepuncture).

---

[173] Skegg, *Law, Ethics, and Medicine* (2nd edn), 66; Poulter, *English Law and Ethnic Minority Customs*, para 6.28. This is very questionable given the nature of the attendant risks: see further paras 4.148, 4.150 below.

[174] *S v McC, W v W* [1972] AC 24 discussed in *In re Z (A Minor) (Identification: Restrictions on Publication)* [1997] Fam 1, 20, 28–29. See also the Family Law Reform Act 1969, s 21(3); *In re F (A Minor) (Blood Tests: Parental Rights)* [1993] Fam 314; *Re L (A Minor) (Blood Tests)* [1996] 2 FCR 649; *In re H (A Minor) (Blood Tests: Parental Rights)* [1997] Fam 89; *Re R (a Minor) (Blood Test: Constraint)* [1998] 1 FCR 41.

[175] *S v McC, W v W* [1972] AC 24, 43–44 *per* Lord Reid. See also, 48, 51 *per* Lord MacDermott (blood test will not be ordered if it 'would prejudicially affect the health of the infant'), 58–59 *per* Lord Hodson ('protection may be needed for health reasons').

[176] *In re R (A Minor) (Wardship: Criminal Proceedings)* [1991] Fam 56, 65 *per* Lord Donaldson of Lymington MR.

(iii) *Procedures Requiring the Sanction of the Court*

Concern, in particular at the prospect of parents consenting to the non- **4.78** therapeutic sterilisation of mentally-handicapped children,[177] has led the courts in a number of jurisdictions to consider whether there are not certain procedures, not unlawful in themselves, but which are nonetheless of such a nature that the prior sanction of the court ought, either as a matter of law or at the very least as a matter of good practice, always to be obtained. Thus at first it was suggested[178] that a court exercising the inherent parens patriae jurisdiction is the only author-ity empowered to authorise such a drastic step as sterilisation. And the High Court of Australia has since held that, as a matter of law, a parent lacks the capacity to give a valid consent to the non-therapeutic sterilisation of a child.[179] In England, however, it would now seem that, unless the child is already a ward of court, the prior sanction of the court is never required as a matter of law,[180] though 'as a matter of good practice' it should always be obtained[181] in those cases falling within what has been described as a 'special category'.[182] A similar approach has been adopted in relation to adult incompetents.[183]

Precisely which cases are to be treated as falling within the special category has **4.79** deliberately been left undefined, to be considered on a case-by-case basis.[184] Initially, it was suggested that the special category would or might include

---

[177] There is no doubt that in this country *In re D (A Minor) (Wardship: Sterilisation)* [1976] Fam 185 (in which a highly qualified medical practitioner supported by a caring mother, who were proposing to sterilise a mentally handicapped 11–year old girl, were held by Heilbron J not to be acting in her best interests, although no one had challenged their skill, bona fides, or quality of care) had a powerful effect in influencing the development of this branch of the law: see *In re F (Mental Patient: Sterilisation)* [1990] 2 AC 1, 20, 41, 69 ('stark warning of the danger'), 79 ('vivid illustration').

[178] *In re B (A Minor) (Wardship: Sterilisation)* [1987] 2 All ER 206, 210, [1988] AC 199, 206.

[179] *Secretary, Department of Health and Community Services v JWB and SMB* (1992) 175 CLR 218.

[180] But cf *Re E (A Minor) (Medical Treatment)* [1991] 2 FLR 585, 587 which can be read as suggesting that it is because the parents of a mentally retarded child are in a position to give a valid consent to a therapeutic sterilisation that 'accordingly' the consent of the court is not required—from which it might be deduced that the consent of the court is required in those cases in which the parents are not in a position to give a valid consent.

[181] In some cases the court, once it has been able to investigate the matter fully, may be willing to devolve the final decision to the attending doctor subject to suitable safeguards: *Re R (Adult: Medical Treatment)* [1996] 2 FLR 99, 104, 106–110. See further para 4.129 below.

[182] *In re F (Mental Patient: Sterilisation)* [1990] 2 AC 1, 19–20, 33, 42, 51, 56–57, 78–80, 83. See also *Airedale NHS Trust v Bland* [1993] AC 789, 805–806, 815–816, 859, 873–874.

[183] See further para 4.123 below.

[184] *In re F (Mental Patient: Sterilisation)* [1990] 2 AC 1, 57.

sterilisation, abortion, organ donation, and the disconnection of life-support machines.[185] Subsequent decisions indicate that the special category of cases which require the prior sanction of the court includes a non-therapeutic sterilisation,[186] the donation of regenerative tissues (bone marrow),[187] the withdrawal of food from a patient in the permanent (formerly called persistent) vegetative state,[188] cases where the capacity of a pregnant woman to consent to or refuse a caesarian section is in issue,[189] and any case in which the application of restraint or use of force on a non-compliant patient is envisaged,[190] but that it does not include a brain scan,[191] psychiatric treatment,[192] an abortion,[193] or a therapeutic sterilisation.[194] It is clear that the donation of a non-regenerative organ (e g, a kidney) falls within the special category,[195] so also, it is suggested, would a 'sex-change' or 'gender reassignment' operation.[196] Whether, and if so to what extent and in which circumstances, the withholding of life-saving treatment generally falls within the special category is unclear.[197]

(iv) *The Older Child*

4.80 There are two further limitations upon the parent's power to consent to treatment in the case of an older child. In the first place, the commentators

---

[185] ibid, 19, 33, 40, 42.   [186] ibid.

[187] *In re Y (Mental Patient: Bone Marrow Donation)* [1997] Fam 110, 116: quaere in relation to donations of blood or other regenerative bodily fluids.

[188] This was said to be for 'the protection of patients, the protection of doctors, the reassurance of patients' families and the reassurance of the public': *Airedale NHS Trust v Bland* [1993] AC 789, 815 *per* Sir Thomas Bingham MR, approved, 859 *per* Lord Keith of Kinkel, 874 *per* Lord Goff of Chieveley. See further para 4.118 below.

[189] *Re MB (Medical Treatment)* [1997] 2 FLR 426.

[190] *Re VS (Adult: Mental Disorder)* (1995) Aug 17 (Douglas Brown J), [1995] Med L Rev 292; *Tameside and Glossop Acute Services Trust v CH* [1996] 1 FLR 762, 774.

[191] *Re H (Mental Patient: Diagnosis)* [1993] 1 FLR 28 (a case involving an adult incompetent).   [192] *Re K, W and H (Minors) (Medical Treatment)* [1993] 1 FLR 854.

[193] *Re SG (Adult Mental Patient: Abortion)* [1991] 2 FLR 329 (adult incompetent).

[194] *Re E (A Minor) (Medical Treatment)* [1991] 2 FLR 585 (consent of court not necessary for therapeutic hysterectomy to relieve serious menorrhagia of severely mentally handicapped 17–year old girl: parents able to give valid consent, as sterilisation would not be the purpose, although the inevitable and incidental result, of the operation). Similarly in the case of a mentally incompetent adult: *Re GF (Medical Treatment)* [1992] 1 FLR 293 (declaration of court not needed regarding legality of hysterectomy to relieve excessively heavy periods which would have the incidental effect of sterilising a mentally handicapped woman of 29 if two medical practitioners are satisfied that the operation is necessary for therapeutic purposes and in the best interests of the patient and that there is no practicable less intrusive means of treating the condition).

[195] *In re F (Mental Patient: Sterilisation)* [1990] 2 AC 1, 19, 33, 40; *In re W (A Minor) (Medical Treatment: Court's Jurisdiction)* [1993] Fam 64, 79, 94.

[196] So held by the Family Court of Australia: *In re A* (1993) 16 Fam LR 715.

[197] Compare *In re J (A Minor) (Wardship: Medical Treatment)* [1991] Fam 33, 51; *Re C (A Baby)* [1996] 2 FLR 43, 45; *Re R (Adult: Medical Treatment)* [1996] 2 FLR 99.

suggest, and it would seem correct in principle (for it corresponds with the principle adopted by the court in the exercise of its jurisdiction[198]), that parental consent will not be sufficient in the case of a non-therapeutic procedure if the child is old enough to understand what is involved and is either left uninformed or actually withholds his or her consent.[199] This principle would apply, for example, to a blood-test[200] or the ritual circumcision of an older boy. Secondly, and even in the case of therapeutic procedures, the jurisdiction of the court should always be invoked where parents are prepared to consent, but a child capable of understanding what is involved, is refusing to consent to some major form of treatment.[201]

4. The Court

(i) *When the Court is Involved*

The court may be involved in matters relating to the medical treatment of a **4.81**
child for a variety of different reasons: if the child is already a ward of
court, because the law requires prior judicial consent before any 'important'
or 'major' step in the ward's life is taken;[202] if there are disputes between
parents and doctor, or between parents and child or between the parents
themselves, so that the court can decide what the best interests of the child
require; or in cases falling within the 'special category', so that the court can
decide whether or not to give the prior sanction which good practice
requires[203]

The Need to Involve the Court

It is necessary to involve the court only if the child is already a ward of court **4.82**
or if the case falls within the 'special category'. In cases not falling within the
'special category' there is no need to involve the court unless the child is
already a ward of court.

Involving the Court Unnecessarily

Where there is no disagreement between the child's parents and the doctor, **4.83**
and the proposed treatment is not one which, either because of its nature or
because the child is a ward of court, requires the prior sanction of the court,
the court will treat the parents' consent as sufficient authority and protection

---

[198] See further paras 4.95, 4.170, 4.181 below.
[199] Glanville Williams, *Textbook of Criminal Law* (2nd edn), 576, Poulter, *English Law and Ethnic Minority Customs*, para 6.28.   [200] *S v McC, W v W* [1972] AC 24, 45.
[201] *In re W (A Minor) (Medical Treatment: Court's Jurisdiction)* [1993] Fam 64, 79, 90, 94.
[202] See para 4.44 above.   [203] See paras 4.78–4.79 above.

for the doctor and refuse to grant relief.[204] The court may decline to act even though there is a dispute between a 'Gillick competent' child, who is refusing to consent, and its parents, so long as the parents have given the doctor their consent to the proposed treatment.[205]

(ii) *The Jurisdiction of the Court*

4.84 The court may be involved in the exercise of its inherent parens patriae jurisdiction, the wardship jurisdiction, or its statutory jurisdiction under the Children Act 1989.[206] In relation to the medical treatment of children the substantive powers of the court are the same, and are exercised in accordance with precisely the same principles, whichever jurisdiction is being exercised.[207]

Invoking the Jurisdiction of the Court

4.85 If the child is already a ward of court application is made by summons in the wardship.[208] If the child is not a ward, and there are no other relevant proceedings pending, the court's assistance can be invoked, unless the applicant is a local authority, either under the inherent jurisdiction[209] or by an ad hoc wardship (that is, by making a child a ward of court for the purpose of resolving a question relating to the child's medical treatment)[210] or by an

---

[204] *Re SG (Adult Mental Patient: Abortion)* [1991] 2 FLR 329 (abortion—a case involving an adult incompetent); *Re E (A Minor) (Medical Treatment)* [1991] 2 FLR 585 (therapeutic sterilisation); *Re GF (Medical Treatment)* [1992] 1 FLR 293 (therapeutic sterilisation—adult incompetent); *Re H (Mental Patient: Diagnosis)* [1993] 1 FLR 28 (brain scan—adult incompetent).

[205] *Re K, W and H (Minors) (Medical Treatment)* [1993] 1 FLR 854 (psychiatric treatment).

[206] See paras 4.41, 4.49, 4.50 above.

[207] *Re K, W and H (Minors) (Medical Treatment)* [1993] 1 FLR 854, 859.

[208] As in *In re C (A Minor) (Wardship: Medical Treatment)* [1990] Fam 26; *In re J (A Minor) (Wardship: Medical Treatment)* [1991] Fam 33.

[209] As in *In re J (A Minor) (Child in Care: Medical Treatment)* [1993] Fam 15; *In re W (A Minor) (Medical Treatment: Court's Jurisdiction)* [1993] Fam 64; *South Glamorgan County Council v W and B* [1993] 1 FLR 574; *Re O (A Minor) (Medical Treatment)* [1993] 2 FLR 149; *A Metropolitan Borough Council v AB* [1997] 1 FLR 767; and (arguably incorrectly in the light of *Re R (A Minor) (Blood Transfusion)* [1993] 2 FLR 757) in *Re S (A Minor) (Medical Treatment)* [1993] 1 FLR 376; *Re S (A Minor) (Consent to Medical Treatment)* [1994] 2 FLR 1065; *In re T (A Minor) (Wardship: Medical Treatment)* [1997] 1 WLR 242; *Re C (Detention: Medical Treatment)* [1997] 2 FLR 180.

[210] As in *In re D (A Minor) (Wardship: Sterilisation)* [1976] Fam 185 (sterilisation); *In re B (A Minor) (Wardship: Medical Treatment)* [1981] 1 WLR 1421 (life saving surgery); *Re P (A Minor)* [1986] 1 FLR 272 (abortion), *In re B (A Minor) (Wardship: Sterilisation)* [1988] AC 199 (sterilisation); *Re P (A Minor) (Wardship: Sterilisation)* [1989] 1 FLR 182 (sterilisation); *Re E (A Minor) (Wardship: Medical Treatment)* [1993] 1 FLR 386 (blood transfusion); *Re E (A Minor) (Medical Treatment)* [1991] 2 FLR 585 (sterilisation); *Re B (Wardship: Abortion)* [1991]

application for either a prohibited steps order or a specific issue order under the Children Act 1989, section 8.[211] Different views have been expressed as to whether, other things being equal, the preferred course is to invoke the inherent jurisdiction or section 8.[212]

Applications by Local Authorities

Applications by a local authority are governed by the Children Act 1989, section 100(2)(c) (which prevents a child who is in care from being made a ward of court), section 100(3) (which requires a local authority to obtain the leave of the court before invoking the court's inherent jurisdiction), and section 100(4) (which provides that such leave can be granted only if (*inter alia*) the result which the local authority wishes to achieve cannot be achieved through the making of (*inter alia*) a prohibited steps order or a specific issue order under section 8). In the case of a child in care a local authority is precluded by section 9(1)[213] from obtaining either a prohibited steps order or a specific issue order. The combined effect of the statutory provisions thus appears to be that an application by a local authority in relation to a child in care must be made under the inherent jurisdiction[214] but an application by a local authority in relation to a child who is not in care must be made by way of an application for a section 8 order.[215]

4.86

---

2 FLR 426 (abortion); *In re R (A Minor) (Wardship: Consent to Treatment)* [1992] Fam 11 (psychiatric treatment with anti-psychotic drugs).

[211] As in *Re K, W and H (Minors) (Medical Treatment)* [1993] 1 FLR 854; *Re HG (Specific Issue Order: Sterilisation)* [1993] 1 FLR 587; *Re R (A Minor) (Blood Transfusion)* [1993] 2 FLR 757.

[212] *Re O (A Minor) (Medical Treatment)* [1993] 2 FLR 149, 155 (inherent jurisdiction preferable); *Re R (A Minor) (Blood Transfusion)* [1993] 2 FLR 757, 760 (section 8 preferable). The Official Solicitor's view is that the procedural and administrative difficulties attaching to applications under s 8 are such that the preferred course is to apply within the inherent jurisdiction: Practice Note (Official Solicitor: Sterilisation) [1996] 2 FLR 111, para 2.

[213] cf also ss 9(2), 9(5), 91(1), 91(2) and 100(2).

[214] *South Glamorgan County Council v W and B* [1993] 1 FLR 574 (explaining, 583–584 that the Children Act, s 100(2)(d), is no bar to exercising the inherent jurisdiction); *Re O (A Minor) (Medical Treatment)* [1993] 2 FLR 149.

[215] *Re R (A Minor) (Blood Transfusion)* [1993] 2 FLR 757; *Re J (Specific Issue Order: Leave to Apply)* [1995] 1 FLR 669, 673. The point seems to have been overlooked in *Re S (A Minor) (Medical Treatment)* [1993] 1 FLR 376; *Re S (A Minor) (Consent to Medical Treatment)* [1994] 2 FLR 1065; *In re T (A Minor) (Wardship: Medical Treatment)* [1997] 1 WLR 242; and *Re C (Detention: Medical Treatment)* [1997] 2 FLR 180 (but see at 190) where local authorities were given leave under s 100(3) to invoke the inherent jurisdiction even though the child was not in care.

Hearing by High Court Judge

4.87 Whichever form of procedure is invoked the proceedings should be commenced in the High Court, not in the Family Proceedings Court or the County Court, and should be heard by a High Court Judge.[216]

(iii) *The Official Solicitor*

4.88 As part of his wide-ranging duties and responsibilities[217] the Official Solicitor is involved, either ex officio or as next friend or guardian ad litem or by instructing an amicus curiae, in virtually all cases relating to the treatment of adult incompetents and in most cases of any significance relating to the treatment of children. Members of his legal staff are prepared to discuss such cases before proceedings have been issued. The Official Solicitor issues Practice Notes (which are revised from time to time) detailing the procedure and the nature of his role in cases involving sterilisation[218] and patients in a vegetative state.[219]

4.89 Generally, the Official Solicitor should be invited to act in all cases of any complexity.[220]

(iv) *Exercise of the Jurisdiction*

(a) General Principles

4.90 The sole and paramount criterion[221] for the exercise by the court of its jurisdiction, whether it be the inherent parens patriae jurisdiction, the

---

[216] *Re HG (Specific Issue Order: Sterilisation)* [1993] 1 FLR 587, 596; *Re O (A Minor) (Medical Treatment)* [1993] 2 FLR 149, 155; *Re R (A Minor) (Blood Transfusion)* [1993] 2 FLR 757, 760. See also *Re HIV Tests* [1994] 2 FLR 116.
[217] As to which see the Supreme Court Act 1981, s 90, the Supreme Court Practice, 1997, Vol 2, paras 5303–5304, the Lord Chancellor's Directions under the Supreme Court Act 1981, s 90(3)(b), Practice Direction (Mental Health: Appeal) [1989] 1 WLR 133, Lord Chancellor's Direction (Duties and Functions of Official Solicitor under the Children Act 1989) [1991] 2 FLR 471 and, in particular, Practice Note (The Official Solicitor: Appointment in Family Proceedings) [1995] 2 FLR 479 (replacing earlier Practice Note reported, [1993] 2 FLR 641).
[218] Practice Note (Official Solicitor: Sterilisation) [1996] 2 FLR 111 (replacing earlier Practice Notes reported, [1989] 2 FLR 447, [1990] 2 FLR 530 and [1993] 3 All ER 222).
[219] Practice Note (Official Solicitor: Persistent Vegetative State) [1996] 2 FLR 375 (replacing earlier Practice Note reported, [1994] 2 All ER 413).
[220] *Re B (Wardship: Abortion)* [1991] 2 FLR 426, 428; *Re HG (Specific Issue Order: Sterilisation)* [1993] 1 FLR 587, 597. See also Practice Note (The Official Solicitor: Appointment in Family Proceedings) [1995] 2 FLR 479 (replacing previous Practice Note reported [1993] 2 FLR 641).
[221] *In re B (A Minor) (Wardship: Sterilisation)* [1988] AC 199, 212.

wardship jurisdiction, or its statutory jurisdiction under the Children Act 1989, is the welfare of the child. This was the rule adopted by the High Court of Chancery and is now given statutory force by the Children Act 1989, section 1(1)(a).[222]

> The welfare of this child is the paramount consideration and the court must act in her best interests.[223]

> The first and paramount consideration is the well being, welfare, or interests (each expression occasionally used, but each, for this purpose synonymous) of the human being concerned, that is the ward himself or herself.[224]

Welfare

The courts have traditionally been reluctant to articulate the principles and values to be applied in operating the best interests test,[225] but it is clear that welfare for this purpose must be taken in the widest sense[226] and that it includes the child's ethical, moral, spiritual and religious welfare.[227]   **4.91**

> The dominant matter for the consideration of the Court is the welfare of the child. But the welfare of a child is not to be measured by money only, nor by physical comfort only. The word welfare must be taken in its widest sense. The moral and religious welfare of the child must be considered as well as its physical well-being. Nor can the ties of affection be disregarded.[228]

An Objective Standard[229]

In deciding questions of welfare, the court, acting as 'the judicial reasonable parent', acts by reference to the objective standard of the ordinary reasonable and responsible mother and father,[230] but having regard to the subjective needs of the particular child.[231] Thus in deciding whether to authorise or direct medical treatment the court adopts that course which, objectively considered, is in the particular child's best interests.[232]   **4.92**

---

[222] *In re Z (A Minor) (Identification: Restrictions on Publication)* [1997] Fam 1, 28–29.
[223] *In re D (A Minor) (Wardship: Sterilisation)* [1976] Fam 185, 194 *per* Heilbron J.
[224] *In re B (A Minor) (Wardship: Sterilisation)* [1988] AC 199, 202 *per* Lord Hailsham of St Marylebone LC.   [225] See further paras 4.138–4.139 below.
[226] See further paras 4.145–4.167 below.
[227] *In re K (Minors) (Children: Care and Control)* [1977] Fam 179, 187, 191. See further para 4.152 below.   [228] *Re McGrath* [1893] 1 Ch 143, 148 *per* Lindley LJ.
[229] See further para 4.143 below.
[230] *J v C* [1970] AC 668, 723; *In re D (A Minor) (Wardship: Sterilisation)* [1976] Fam 185, 194; *Re E (A Minor) (Wardship: Medical Treatment)* [1993] 1 FLR 386, 392–393; *In re J (A Minor) (Wardship: Medical Treatment)* [1991] Fam 33, 50; *In re R (A Minor) (Wardship: Consent to Treatment)* [1992] Fam 11, 25; *Re O (A Minor) (Medical Treatment)* [1993] 2 FLR 149, 153.
[231] *Re E (A Minor) (Wardship: Medical Treatment)* [1993] 1 FLR 386, 392.
[232] *In re B (A Minor) (Wardship: Sterilisation)* [1988] AC 199, 210.

Prevention of Harm

4.93 'It has always been the principle of this court, not to risk the incurring of damage to children which it cannot repair, but rather to prevent the damage being done'.[233] Moreover, the court is justified in interfering not only where there is a 'likelihood' of damage to the child but even if there is no more than 'an apprehension or suspicion of it'.[234]

(b) The Child's Wishes

4.94 In relation to medical treatment generally, the court is bound (whether or not the case strictly falls within the Children Act 1989, section 1(4))[235] to have regard to the ascertainable wishes and feelings of the child, considered in the light of his age and understanding.[236] However the court is not bound by the wishes even of a 'Gillick competent' child, or a child who has attained the age of sixteen, though it will not lightly override the child's decision, particularly if the child's decision is sensible or the treatment is invasive.[237]

> This is not, however, to say that the wishes of 16– and 17–year-olds are to be treated as no different from those of 14– and 15–year-olds. Far from it. Adolescence is a period of progressive transition from childhood to adulthood and as experience of life is acquired and intelligence and understanding grow, so will the scope of decision-making which should be left to the minor, for it is only by making decisions and experiencing the consequences that decision-making skills will be acquired. As I put it in the course of the argument, and as I sincerely believe, 'good parenting involves giving minors as much rope as they can handle without an unacceptable risk that they will hang themselves'. As Lord Hailsham of St Marylebone LC put it in *Re B* [1988] AC 199, 202, the 'first and paramount consideration [of the court] is the well being, welfare or interests [of the minor]' and I regard it as self-evident that this involves giving them the maximum degree of decision-making which is prudent. Prudence does not involve avoiding all risk, but it does involve avoiding risks which, if they eventuate, may have irreparable consequences or which are disproportionate to the benefits which could accrue from taking them.[238]

---

[233] *Wellesley v Duke of Beaufort* (1827) 2 Russ 1, 18 *per* Lord Eldon LC (cited in *In re X (A Minor) (Wardship: Jurisdiction)* [1975] Fam 47, 51; *In re D (A Minor) (Wardship: Sterilisation)* [1976] Fam 185, 194).

[234] *In re X (A Minor) (Wardship: Jurisdiction)* [1975] Fam 47, 51 quoting *Chambers on Infants* [ed 1842], 20.

[235] *In re W (A Minor) (Medical Treatment: Court's Jurisdiction)* [1993] Fam 64, 93.

[236] *B(BR) v B(J)* [1968] P 466, 473, 481; *Re P (A Minor)* [1986] 1 FLR 272, 276–279; *Re E (A Minor) (Wardship: Medical Treatment)* [1993] 1 FLR 386, 393; *Re B (Wardship: Abortion)* [1991] 2 FLR 426, 428–429. cf the Children Act 1989, s 1(3)(a).

[237] *In re W (A Minor) (Medical Treatment: Court's Jurisdiction)* [1993] Fam 64, 81–82, 84, 88, 93.   [238] ibid, 81–82 *per* Lord Donaldson of Lymington MR.

Thus in practice the court is unlikely to overrule the competent child's decision in the ordinary run of relatively routine surgical, medical or dental treatment, though even then it has the power to do so.[239] Moreover, where the views of a competent child conflict with those of its parents, the court is likely to adopt the views of the child rather than the parents.[240] On the other hand there will be cases where, having given proper weight to the child's views, it is nonetheless appropriate for the court to overrule either a 'Gillick competent' or even a sixteen or seventeen–year old child's decision, for example where that is necessary in order either to save the child's life or to prevent really serious and irreparable harm to the child, for as a general principle the protection of the child's welfare implies at least the protection of the child's life and it is generally the duty of the court to preserve life and ensure so far as it can that children survive to attain the age of eighteen.[241] The court has not hesitated, for example, to override the refusal of teenagers to consent to a life-saving blood transfusion[242] or other essential treatment,[243] and, one imagines, would readily overrule a promiscuous teenager's frivolous decision to be sterilised. Likewise, the court would probably be very slow indeed to allow even a willing and 'Gillick competent' teenager to donate an organ.

Non-Therapeutic Procedures

Where the procedure in question is non-therapeutic, and the child is old **4.95** enough to understand, the court should not subject it to the operation against its will, certainly unless to do so is 'clearly' in the child's interests.[244]

---

[239] ibid, 94.

[240] As in *Re P (A Minor)* [1986] 1 FLR 272 (where a pregnant 15–year old girl of strong personality and mature views, and able to understand the implications, wanted an abortion but was opposed by her Seventh Day Adventist parents on bona fide religious and other grounds: the court treated the child's welfare, but not her views and wishes, as paramount and, although giving weight to her parents' feelings and taking into account their deeply and sincerely held religious objections, directed the abortion) and *Re B (Wardship: Abortion)* [1991] 2 FLR 426 (where a pregnant 12–year old girl's wish to have an abortion was opposed by her mother: the court directed an abortion). See also *In re W (A Minor) (Medical Treatment: Court's Jurisdiction)* [1993] Fam 64, 90, 94.

[241] *In re B (A Minor) (Wardship: Medical Treatment)* [1981] 1 WLR 1421, 1424–1425; *In re W (A Minor) (Medical Treatment: Court's Jurisdiction)* [1993] Fam 64, 88, 94.

[242] *Re E (A Minor) (Wardship: Medical Treatment)* [1993] 1 FLR 386; *Re S (A Minor) (Consent to Medical Treatment)* [1994] 2 FLR 1065.

[243] *In re R (A Minor) (Wardship: Consent to Treatment)* [1992] Fam 11; *In re W (A Minor) (Medical Treatment: Court's Jurisdiction)* [1993] Fam 64; *A Metropolitan Borough Council v AB* [1997] 1 FLR 767; *Re C (Detention: Medical Treatment)* [1997] 2 FLR 180.

[244] *In re L (An Infant)* [1968] P 119, 140; *B(BR) v B(J)* [1968] P 466, 469, 473–474, 481; *S v McC, W v W* [1972] AC 24, 45. See also *In re D (A Minor) (Wardship: Sterilisation)* [1976] Fam 185, para 4.80 above and paras 4.170, 4.181 below.

(c) The Court's Approach to Religious Issues

Religion[245]

4.96 The court recognises no religious distinctions and passes no judgment on religious beliefs unless they are 'immoral or socially obnoxious' or 'pernicious'.[246] Indeed the court pays every respect and gives great weight to the family's religious principles.[247]

4.97 But, although the parents' views and wishes as to the child's religious upbringing are of great importance, and will be seriously regarded by the court, they will be given effect to by the court only so far as and in such manner as is in accordance with the best interests of the child's welfare. In matters of religion, as in all other aspects of a child's upbringing, the interests of the child are the paramount consideration.[248]

> Parents may be free to become martyrs themselves. But it does not follow that they are free, in identical circumstances, to make martyrs of their children before they have reached the age of full and legal discretion when they can make the choices for themselves.[249]

4.98 Where a child is old enough to be able to express sensible views on the subject of religion, even if not old enough to take a mature decision, the court will pay great regard to (though it cannot be bound by) the child's wishes, and will be slow to dictate the child's religious upbringing.[250] But, just as the court

---

[245] See further paras 4.162–4.163 below.

[246] *Stourton v Stourton (1857)* 8 DeGM&G 760, 771; *Re T (Minors) (Custody: Religious Upbringing)* (1981) 2 FLR 239, 244–245; *Re B and G (Minors) (Custody)* [1985] FLR 134, 157; *Re R (A Minor) (Residence: Religion)* [1993] 2 FLR 163, 171.

[247] *Re P (A Minor)* [1986] 1 FLR 272, 281; *Re E (A Minor) (Wardship: Medical Treatment)* [1993] 1 FLR 386, 394; *Re O (A Minor) (Medical Treatment)* [1993] 2 FLR 149, 153.

[248] *Stourton v Stourton (1857)* 8 DeGMG 760, 771; *Re McGrath* [1893] 1 Ch 143, 148, 149; *In re W, W v M* [1907] 2 Ch 557, 566–567; *Ward v Laverty* [1925] AC 101, 108; *Re Aster* [1955] 1 WLR 465, 468; *In re E (An Infant)* [1964] 1 WLR 51, 57–58; *J v C* [1970] AC 668, 713, 715; *Re P (A Minor)* [1986] 1 FLR 272, 281; *Re E (A Minor) (Wardship: Medical Treatment)* [1993] 1 FLR 386, 391–394; *Re S (A Minor) (Medical Treatment)* [1993] 1 FLR 376, 380; *Re S (A Minor) (Consent to Medical Treatment)* [1994] 2 FLR 1065. See para 4.72 above.

[249] *Prince v Massachusetts* (1944) 321 US 158, 170 *per* Rutledge J (cited in *Re E (A Minor) (Wardship: Medical Treatment)* [1993] 1 FLR 386, 394, where the passage, due to an error by counsel, is wrongly attributed to Holmes J).

[250] *Stourton v Stourton (1857)* 8 DeGMG 760 (where the LJJ themselves interviewed a nine-year old boy); *Re E (A Minor) (Wardship: Medical Treatment)* [1993] 1 FLR 386, 393, 394 (where the judge interviewed a 15–year old boy); *Re S (Minors) (Access: Religious Upbringing)* [1992] 2 FLR 313, 321; *Re R (A Minor) (Residence: Religion)* [1993] 2 FLR 163, 173–174, 175, 179–180.

will not allow a parent to make a martyr of his child, so the court will be very slow to allow a child to martyr himself.[251]

(d) The Court and the Doctor

The court will naturally pay great respect to, and will not lightly disregard, the **4.99** opinion of the doctor treating or proposing to treat the child. However, in the final analysis it is for the court, and not for doctors, however eminent, to reach a decision as to what is in the best interests of the particular child.[252] And where there is a diversity or conflict of medical opinion the court is necessarily obliged to choose which view to adopt. In the case of a child, therefore, the 'Bolam' test plays little part:[253] its only function is to identify the opinion of a particular doctor either as being one which can reasonably be held by a competent practitioner (and is therefore deserving of proper consideration by the court) or as being one which fails to meet that criterion (and is therefore not deserving of consideration by the court).

The court, depending on the circumstances, can either make an order for- **4.100** bidding something to be done to the child (for example, an order restraining a proposed sterilisation)[254] or make an order 'authorising' or 'authorising and directing' something to be done to the child (for example, an order authorising and directing surgery).[255] But the court will never make a compulsive order requiring a particular doctor or health authority to treat a child in a manner contrary to their wishes.[256] It follows that, even when the court 'authorises and directs' treatment, what it is really doing is to authorise the proposed treatment and to indicate that such authorisation is to be effective notwithstanding the absence or refusal of parental consent.[257] To avoid confusion or misunderstanding the court should avoid the 'authorise and direct' form of order and simply make an order 'authorising' the relevant treatment.[258]

---

[251] *Re E (A Minor) (Wardship: Medical Treatment)* [1993] 1 FLR 386, 394; *In re W (A Minor) (Medical Treatment: Court's Jurisdiction)* [1993] Fam 64, 88; *Re S (A Minor) (Consent to Medical Treatment)* [1994] 2 FLR 1065.

[252] cf *In re F (Mental Patient: Sterilisation)* [1990] 2 AC 1, 80; *Frenchay Healthcare National Health Service Trust v S* [1994] 1 WLR 601, 609–610.

[253] Contrast where the patient is an adult incompetent: *In re F (Mental Patient: Sterilisation)* [1990] 2 AC 1; *Airedale NHS Trust v Bland* [1993] AC 789. See further paras 4.135–4.136 below.

[254] *In re D (A Minor) (Wardship: Sterilisation)* [1976] Fam 185.

[255] *In re B (A Minor) (Wardship: Medical Treatment)* [1981] 1 WLR 1421, 1424–1425.

[256] See para 4.14 above.

[257] cf *Secretary, Department of Health and Community Services v JWB and SMB* (1992) 175 CLR 218, 259, 267–268.

[258] *In re J (A Minor) (Wardship: Medical Treatment)* [1991] Fam 33, 48; *In re J (A Minor) (Child in Care: Medical Treatment)* [1993] Fam 15, 29, 31; *In re W (A Minor) (Medical Treatment: Court's Jurisdiction)* [1993] Fam 64, 81.

E. Incompetent Adults

1. General Principles

The Role of Consent

4.101 Except as specifically provided by statute,[259] consent plays no part in the treatment of the adult incompetent, because the patient himself is, by definition, unable to give a valid consent to treatment and the common law does not recognise anyone else as having the legal capacity to give or refuse consent on his behalf. A spouse or relative does not have any power either to consent or to refuse consent to medical treatment on behalf of an incompetent adult.[260] Nor does the court, for neither the Court of Protection nor the High Court has any parens patriae or other jurisdiction over the person, as opposed to the property, of an adult incompetent.[261]

The Role of the Court

4.102 However, the High Court, in exercise of its inherent jurisdiction and/or its statutory jurisdiction under RSC Order 15 Rule 16, can grant declaratory relief to determine questions relating to the lawfulness or unlawfulness of the proposed treatment or care (including the proposed medical treatment or care) of an incompetent adult.[262]

Necessity

4.103 In the case of an adult who is incompetent or permanently unable to communicate,[263] the principle of necessity renders lawful, despite the absence of consent, such treatment which in the absence of consent would otherwise be tortious[264] as a reasonable doctor would in all the circumstances give, acting in the best interests of the patient.[265] But this principle is qualified by the rule that a doctor is *never* entitled to give treatment, even in cases of emergency or to an unconscious or incompetent patient, which is contrary to the known, competent, wishes of the patient.

---

[259] eg the Mental Health Act 1983, s 63 (treatment of mental disorder), the Family Law Reform Act 1969, s 21(4) (taking of blood samples).

[260] *In re T (Adult: Refusal of Treatment)* [1993] Fam 95, 103. See also *T v T* [1988] Fam 52; *In re F (Mental Patient: Sterilisation)* [1990] 2 AC 1; *Re C (Mental Patient: Contact)* [1993] 1 FLR 940.

[261] *T v T* [1988] Fam 52; *In re F (Mental Patient: Sterilisation)* [1990] 2 AC 1; *Re C (Mental Patient: Contact)* [1993] 1 FLR 940.

[262] *In re F (Mental Patient: Sterilisation)* [1990] 2 AC 1; *Airedale NHS Trust v Bland* [1993] AC 789.

[263] *In re F (Mental Patient: Sterilisation)* [1990] 2 AC 1, 71–77.   [264] ibid, 73–76.

[265] ibid, 51, 56, 75.

[T]he basic requirements, applicable in these cases of necessity, [are] that, to fall within the principle, not only (1) must there be a necessity to act when it is not practicable to communicate with the assisted person, but also (2) the action taken must be such as a reasonable person would in all the circumstances take, acting in the best interests of the assisted person. On this statement of principle, I wish to observe that officious intervention cannot be justified by the principle of necessity. So intervention cannot be justified when another more appropriate person is available and willing to act; nor can it be justified when it is contrary to the known wishes of the assisted person, to the extent that he is capable of rationally forming such a wish.[266]

Best Interests

What is meant by a patient's best interests is dealt with below.[267] **4.104**

2. Advance Directives and the Incompetent Adult

A competent adult patient has an absolute right (the right of self-determina- **4.105**
tion) to refuse consent to any medical treatment or invasive procedure, whether the reasons are rational, irrational, unknown or non-existent, and even if the result of refusal is the certainty of death. Consistently with this, a competent patient's anticipatory refusal of consent (a so-called 'advance directive' or 'living will') is binding and effective notwithstanding that the patient has subsequently become and remains incompetent.[268]

(i) *Proving an Advance Directive*

Burden and Standard of Proof

The burden of proof is on those who seek to establish an advance directive **4.106**
refusing life-saving treatment or life-sustaining artificial feeding. If there is doubt 'that doubt falls to be resolved in favour of the preservation of life'.[269] The evidence must be scrutinised with 'especial care'. The advance directive must be 'clearly established' and not speculative, and must be expressed 'in clear terms'.[270]

---

[266] ibid, 75–76 *per* Lord Goff of Chieveley.   [267] See paras 4.137–4.167 below.
[268] *In re T (Adult: Refusal of Treatment)* [1993] Fam 95, 102, 115, 116, 120–121; *Airedale NHS Trust v Bland* [1993] AC 789, 808–809, 816–817, 828, 857, 864, 891–892, 894; *In re C (Adult: Refusal of Treatment)* [1994] 1 WLR 290, 294–295, 295–296. The British Medical Association has published guidance on advance directives: 'Advance Statements about Medical Treatment: Code of Practice with explanatory notes' (Apr 1995), 'BMA Views on Advance Statements' (Nov 1992, revised May 1995).
[269] *In re T (Adult: Refusal of Treatment)* [1993] Fam 95, 112 *per* Lord Donaldson of Lymington MR.
[270] *In re T (Adult: Refusal of Treatment)* [1993] Fam 95, 103, 112; *Airedale NHS Trust v*

Formal Validity

4.107 There are no formal requirements for a valid advance directive. An advance directive need not be in, or evidenced by, writing,[271] and may be proved by a single witness deposing to a conversation with the patient on a single occasion; there is no requirement of corroboration. However the court will plainly scrutinise with great care the evidence of any witness whose interests conflict with those of the patient,[272] and it may well be easier to establish the existence of an oral advance directive if more than one witness is able to depose to more than one conversation with the patient.

Matters to be Proved

4.108 There are five matters which have to be proved in order to establish an advance directive binding and effective in relation to an adult incompetent:

(1) That at the date of the advance directive the patient was of sound mind, i e, competent.[273]

(2) That the patient knew in broad terms the nature and effect of the procedure to which he was giving or refusing consent.[274]

(3) That the patient's decision was (i) voluntary and unequivocal, (ii) 'real' and not 'expressed in form only' and (iii) free of vitiating influences (e g, coercion or undue influence, the withholding of relevant information, misinformation or mistake).[275]

(4) That the patient's decision was made with reference to and was intended to cover the particular (and perhaps changed or unforeseen) circumstances which have in fact subsequently occurred.[276]

(5) That the patient's expressed views represented a 'firm and settled com-

---

Bland [1993] AC 789, 864. English law thus corresponds to the 'specific-subjective-intent rule' applied in the United States of America by the courts of New York and Missouri, which requires 'clear and convincing, inherently reliable evidence': *Re O'Connor* (1988) 531 NE 2d 607, 608, 611–612, 613–614; *Cruzan v Harmon* (1988) 760 SW 2d 408, 414–415, 424–426, appeal dismissed (1990) 497 US 261.

[271] cf *In re T (Adult: Refusal of Treatment)* [1993] Fam 95, 102.
[272] *Airedale NHS Trust v Bland* [1993] AC 789, 817.
[273] See paras 4.110–4.113 below.
[274] *Chatterton v Gerson* [1981] QB 432, 442, 442–443; *In re T (Adult: Refusal of Treatment)* [1993] Fam 95, 115. But note that English law does not recognise the doctrines of 'informed consent' or 'informed refusal of consent' in the sense in which those terms are used in North America: *Sidaway v Board of Governors of the Bethlem Royal Hospital and the Maudsley Hospital* [1985] AC 871. cf *Malette v Shulman* (1987) 47 DLR (4th) 18, 47–48, (1990) 67 DLR (4th) 321, 336. Nor is it any part of a doctor's duty to dissuade a patient from a decision made on a non-medical (often religious or quasi-religious) basis.
[275] *Chatterton v Gerson* [1981] QB 432, 443; *In re T (Adult: Refusal of Treatment)* [1993] Fam 95, 113–114, 115, 116, 117, 119–120, 121.
[276] *In re T (Adult: Refusal of Treatment)* [1993] Fam 95, 103, 114, 116, 117, 120, 121–122.

mitment' rather than 'informally expressed reactions to other people's medical condition and treatment' or 'an offhand remark about not wanting to live under certain circumstances made by a person when young and in the peak of health'.[277]

The question for the court is well summarised as follows:

> [T]he 'clear and convincing' evidence standard requires proof sufficient to persuade the trier of fact that the patient held a firm and settled commitment to the termination of life supports under the circumstances like those presented.[278]

(ii) *Capacity to Make an Advance Directive*

The fact that someone is a 'patient' within the meaning of the Mental Health **4.109** Act 1983, section 94(2), or RSC Order 80 Rule 1, as being 'incapable, by reason of mental disorder, of managing and administering his property and affairs', does not of itself render him incapable of giving a legally effective consent or entering into a legally effective transaction. Subject to the principle that a person who is a 'patient' actually subject to the jurisdiction of the Court of Protection cannot lawfully enter into any transaction which 'raises a conflict with the court's control of his affairs'[279] (and that principle cannot apply in relation to the patient's medical treatment[280]) the question whether a 'patient' can lawfully give his consent depends solely upon whether or not he has capacity to do so at common law.

Burden of Proof

An adult is presumed to have capacity.[281] The burden of proof is therefore on **4.110** those who seek to rebut the presumption and who assert a lack of capacity.

---

[277] *Re Conroy* (1985) 486 A 2d 1209, 1230, 1232; *Re Jobes* (1987) 529 A 2d 434, 443; *Cruzan v Harmon* (1988) 760 SW 2d 408, 424.

[278] *Re O'Connor* (1988) 531 NE 2d 607, 613 *per* Wachtler CJ.

[279] *In re Walker (A Lunatic so Found)* [1905] 1 Ch 160, 172, 179; *In re Marshall* [1920] 1 Ch 284; *In re W(EEM)* [1971] Ch 123, 143; *In re Beaney* [1978] 1 WLR 770, 772. Thus a patient subject to the Court of Protection, unless of course he lacks testamentary capacity, can make a will (because a will, taking effect only on death, does not interfere with the court's control of his affairs) but cannot without the consent of the court make a valid inter vivos disposition of his property.

[280] Because the jurisdiction of the Court of Protection, being confined to his 'affairs', does not extend to questions affecting the patient's person or body: *In re F (Mental Patient: Sterilisation)* [1990] 2 AC 1, 59. See further para 4.04 above.

[281] *R v Sullivan* [1984] AC 156, 170, 171 (approving *M'Naghten's Case* (1843) 10 Cl & F 200, 210); *In re T (Adult: Refusal of Treatment)* [1993] Fam 95, 112, 115; *In re C (Adult: Refusal of Treatment)* [1994] 1 WLR 290, 295; *Cambridgeshire County Council v R (An Adult)* [1995] 1 FLR 50, 54; *Re MB (Medical Treatment)* [1997] 2 FLR 426, 436.

The Test of Capacity

4.111 Whatever the context in which the question arises, the test of capacity at common law is essentially one of the person's 'understanding' of the 'nature' 'character' and 'effect' of the act or transaction in question.[282] The test of capacity is in essence the same in relation to medical treatment: the question is whether the patient is 'competent to appreciate the issues involved'[283] so as to be able to exercise a 'right of choice',[284] and whether he sufficiently 'understand[s] the nature, purpose and effects of the treatment'.[285]

4.112 The degree of capacity required varies with the circumstances of the particular treatment; it must be commensurate with the gravity of the decision,[286] for 'the more serious the decision, the greater the capacity required'.[287] A high degree of capacity is required to refuse life-saving treatment.[288]

4.113 There are three aspects to be considered in any analysis of the patient's capacity.[289]

(1) The patient's ability (whether or not actually exercised) to function rationally. This involves three questions:[290] (i) Can the patient take in, comprehend and retain treatment information? (ii) Does he believe that information? (iii) Can he weigh the information in the balance so as to arrive at a choice? It is not necessary for the patient to understand everything about a complicated decision, so long as he can understand the essentials if explained to him in broad terms and simple language.[291]

(2) The extent to which the patient's normal capacity may have been tem-

---

[282] *Boughton v Knight* (1873) LR 3 P & D 64, 71–75; *Cambridgeshire County Council v R (An Adult)* [1995] 1 FLR 50, 53.
[283] *In re F (Mental Patient: Sterilisation)* [1990] 2 AC 1, 12 *per* Lord Donaldson of Lymington MR. [284] ibid, 31, 34 *per* Neill and Butler-Sloss LJJ.
[285] *In re C (Adult: Refusal of Treatment)* [1994] 1 WLR 290, 295 *per* Thorpe J.
[286] *Re MB (Medical Treatment)* [1997] 2 FLR 426, 437.
[287] *In re T (Adult: Refusal of Treatment)* [1993] Fam 95, 113, 116 *per* Lord Donaldson of Lymington MR.
[288] cf *Re E (A Minor) (Wardship: Medical Treatment)* [1993] 1 FLR 386, 391.
[289] See generally *In re T (Adult: Refusal of Treatment)* [1993] Fam 95; *In re C (Adult: Refusal of Treatment)* [1994] 1 WLR 290; *Re MB (Medical Treatment)* [1997] 2 FLR 426, 433–437.
[290] *In re C (Adult: Refusal of Treatment)* [1994] 1 WLR 290, 292, 295, followed in *Cambridgeshire County Council v R (An Adult)* [1995] 1 FLR 50, 53–54; *Tameside and Glossop Acute Services Trust v CH* [1996] 1 FLR 762, 766, 769; *Norfolk and Norwich Healthcare (NHS) Trust v W* [1996] 2 FLR 613; *Rochdale Healthcare (NHS) Trust v C* [1997] 1 FCR 274; *Re L (Patient: Non-consensual Treatment)* [1997] 2 FLR 837 and, in relation to 16 and 17–year old children, in *A Metropolitan Borough Council v AB* [1997] 1 FLR 767; *Re C (Detention: Medical Treatment)* [1997] 2 FLR 180, and approved by the Court of Appeal in *Re MB (Medical Treatment)* [1997] 2 FLR 426, 433, 437. See further para 4.70 above.
[291] *Cambridgeshire County Council v R (An Adult)* [1995] 1 FLR 50, 54.

porarily reduced by the effects, for example, of injury, illness, drugs, confusion, shock, pain, anxiety, depression, fatigue or panic induced by fear.[292]

(3) The extent to which the patient had the capacity to make not merely a present but also an anticipatory decision, that is, the capacity to weigh the consequences of future hypothetical circumstances.[293]

(iii) *Effect of Valid Advance Directive*

If a competent adult has expressed an unequivocal decision to refuse **4.114** treatment, it is not for the doctor or the court to speculate as to the strength of the patient's personal or religious convictions or as to his reasons for refusing consent. Nor is it for the doctor or the court to speculate as to what the patient's decision might have been if he had been alive to the current crisis, or if he had been more fully informed, or if he had had more forcibly brought home to him all the implications of his refusal. If it is not possible to say what the patient's decision would have been if he had been given more information, his expressed decision, if he was competent to make it, is decisive, even if it was not made in contemplation of life threatening circumstances.[294]

3. The Court's Declaratory Jurisdiction

The Role of the Court

As has been seen,[295] the court has no jurisdiction either to consent or to refuse **4.115** consent to the medical treatment of an incompetent adult. Its only jurisdictions are (1) to award damages and/or grant an injunction (including, in appropriate cases, a quia timet injunction) in respect of anything tortious[296] and (2) to make a declaration either under the inherent jurisdiction or pursuant to RSC Order 15 rule 16.[297] In practice most applications to the court are for declarations.

---

[292] *In re T (Adult: Refusal of Treatment)* [1993] Fam 95, 111, 113, 115, 118, 122; *Re MB (Medical Treatment)* [1997] 2 FLR 426, 437.

[293] *In re C (Adult: Refusal of Treatment)* [1994] 1 WLR 290, 295.

[294] *Malette v Shulman* (1987) 47 DLR (4th) 18, 42–44, 47–48, (1990) 67 DLR (4th) 321, 331–333, 335–338.

[295] See paras 4.20, 4.101 above.

[296] For an example see *In re C (Adult: Refusal of Treatment)* [1994] 1 WLR 290.

[297] See paras 4.21, 4.102 above.

(i) *The Basis of the Declaratory Jurisdiction*

4.116 The jurisdiction is based upon the physical presence of the incompetent adult within the jurisdiction, irrespective of his nationality or domicile. Jurisdiction is not displaced by the appointment of a guardian by a foreign court of competent jurisdiction. Although the English court is not bound to accede to the wishes of such a guardian it will place weight upon considerations of comity and the guardian's views.[298]

(ii) *The Scope of the Declaratory Jurisdiction*

The Effect of a Declaration

4.117 It is axiomatic that a declaration is, as its name indicates, merely declaratory in its effect. A declaration changes nothing; it cannot make lawful that which, absent a declaration, would be unlawful. Conversely, that which is declared lawful by declaration is equally lawful absent a declaration.[299] There is therefore never any legal necessity to obtain a declaration before proceeding either to treat or to stop the treatment of an incompetent adult (though the courts have indicated that, in certain circumstances, good practice requires that a declaration should be sought).[300]

The Purpose of Obtaining Declaratory Relief

4.118 The purpose of proceedings for a declaration is thus primarily one of protection of the patient and doctors and reassurance, both of the patient's family and the public, that what is proposed to be done (or not, as the case may be) is lawful.[301]

4.119 It is also axiomatic that a declaration can be granted only in relation to legal (or equitable) rights and obligations and not in relation to questions, however pressing, which are merely moral, ethical, or social.[302] The efficacy of the

---

[298] *In re S (Hospital patient: Foreign Curator)* [1996] Fam 23, 30, 31, 32.

[299] *Airedale NHS Trust v Bland* [1993] AC 789, esp 888–890 *per* Lord Mustill.

[300] See paras 4.78–4.79 above, para 4.123 below.

[301] *Airedale NHS Trust v Bland* [1993] AC 789, 805, 815, 859, 874, 875. See further para 4.79 above.

[302] *Malone v Metropolitan Police Commissioner* [1979] Ch 344, 353 (court can make binding declarations only as to legal and equitable rights, and not as to moral, social or political matters). For a neat illustration of the point compare *Re C (Mental Patient: Contact)* [1993] 1 FLR 940 (jurisdiction to grant declaration that adult incompetent had right of access to non-custodial parent) and *Cambridgeshire County Council v R (An Adult)* [1995] 1 FLR 50 (no jurisdiction to grant declaration that adult incompetent had 'right' of non-access from non-custodial parent) as explained in *In re S (Hospital Patient: Court's Jurisdiction)* [1995]

declaration as a means of determining questions of medical treatment which often involve very complex moral and ethical issues derives from two principles of substantive law that underpin the entire jurisdiction: first, the principle that any touching or other interference with the integrity of the human body is, prima facie, unlawful, being both a tort and a crime;[303] secondly, the principle that a doctor (or layman) who, whether or not under any obligation to do so, assumes the responsibility of caring for or looking after a helpless individual, thereby assumes the legal duty to provide, whether himself or by calling for the assistance of others, for that individual's needs, and will be liable if he wrongfully abandons the person he is caring for.[304]

The efficacy of the declaration is further enhanced by the willingness of the **4.120** courts (at least in this context) to grant declaratory relief not merely in relation to future questions for example, in declaring whether or not it will be lawful to administer or withhold treatment in the future, but even in relation to purely contingent questions,[305] for example, in declaring whether or not, in the event of a patient's family assuming the domiciliary care of a patient currently being cared for in hospital, it will be lawful for the family to administer or withhold treatment in the future.[306]

Scope of the Declaratory Jurisdiction: Treatment

It follows that the declaratory jurisdiction is available whether the question **4.121** relates to medical treatment in the narrow sense, to professional nursing care (for example in a hospital or nursing home), or to care in the widest sense of the word (for example the domiciliary feeding and care by relatives of a bedridden patient). The declaratory jurisdiction extends to the lawfulness or unlawfulness of all aspects of an incompetent adult's 'treatment' and 'care'. Treatment and care are not confined to medical treatment, but include whatever is 'necessary to preserve . . . life, health or well-being' or 'carried

---

Fam 26, 32, appeal dismissed [1996] Fam 1, further proceedings *In re S (Hospital patient: Foreign Curator)* [1996] Fam 23. See also *Re V (Declaration against Parents)* [1995] 2 FLR 1003.

[303] *In re F (Mental Patient: Sterilisation)* [1990] 2 AC 1.

[304] Thus the breach of that duty, if it leads to the death of the patient, renders the carer, depending upon his mens rea, liable to prosecution for manslaughter or murder: *R v Gibbins* (1918) 13 Cr App R 134; *R v Stone* [1977] QB 354; *In re F (Mental Patient: Sterilisation)* [1990] 2 AC 1, 55–56, 77; *Airedale NHS Trust v Bland* [1993] AC 789, 858, 866, 881, 893; *Swindon and Marlborough NHS Trust v S* (1994) *Guardian* Dec 10, [1995] Med L Rev 84. See further paras 4.193–4.196 below.

[305] *Re R (Adult: Medical Treatment)* [1996] 2 FLR 99. See further para 4.129 below.

[306] *Re C (Mental Patient: Contact)* [1993] 1 FLR 940; *Swindon and Marlborough NHS Trust v S* (1994) *Guardian* Dec 10, [1995] Med L Rev 84; *In re S (Hospital Patient: Court's Jurisdiction)* [1995] Fam 26, appeal dismissed [1996] Fam 1, subsequent substantive proceedings *In re S (Hospital patient: Foreign Curator)* [1996] Fam 23.

out in order either to save . . . lives, or to ensure improvement or prevent deterioration in . . . physical or mental health'.[307] In addition to appropriate medical, dental and surgical treatment, treatment includes, in the case of someone who is permanently or semi-permanently incapable, care, as part of daily life, of a basic, simple or humdrum nature, such as dressing, undressing, feeding, looking after, and putting to bed, and including the actions of the relative, friend or neighbour who comes in to look after the patient.[308] Treatment and care extend to 'action . . . such as a reasonable person would in all the circumstances take, acting in the best interests of the assisted person'[309] and thus to everything that conduces to the welfare and happiness of the patient, including companionship and the patient's domestic and social environment.[310]

Scope of the Declaratory Jurisdiction: Future Questions

4.122   Likewise, the declaratory jurisdiction is available whether the question relates to the proposed administration of treatment (for example the performance of a sterilisation[311]), or to the proposed withholding or termination of treatment (for example the discontinuance of artificial hydration or nutrition).[312]

(iii)   *The Need to Involve the Court*

4.123   Although there is never any legal necessity to obtain a declaration before proceeding either to treat or to stop the treatment of an incompetent adult,[313] the courts have indicated that, as in the case of a child, so in the case of an adult incompetent, 'as a matter of good practice', a declaration should always be obtained in those cases falling within what has been described as a 'special category'. This topic has already been dealt with in relation to children;[314] the same principles apply in relation to incompetent adults. Where the court is involved unnecessarily, it may decline to act.[315]

---

[307]   *In re F (Mental Patient: Sterilisation)* [1990] 2 AC 1, 52 *per* Lord Bridge of Harwich, 55 *per* Lord Brandon of Oakbrook.   [308]   ibid, 72, 76 *per* Lord Goff of Chieveley.
[309]   ibid, 75 *per* Lord Goff of Chieveley.
[310]   *Re C (Mental Patient: Contact)* [1993] 1 FLR 940.
[311]   As in *In re F (Mental Patient: Sterilisation)* [1990] 2 AC 1, esp, 81–82.
[312]   As in *Airedale NHS Trust v Bland* [1993] AC 789, esp 862–863, 880–881, 888–890 (stressing how intolerable it would be if a carer could not obtain authoritative judicial guidance in advance as to the legality of proposed action or inaction). See further para 4.129 below.
[313]   See para 4.117 above.   [314]   See paras 4.78–4.79 above.
[315]   See further para 4.83 above.

(iv) *Locus Standi*

Three categories of individual have locus standi to apply for a declaration:[316] **4.124**

(1) The patient (acting by some suitable individual as his next friend): his own legal rights are, of course, in issue.

(2) Any actual or prospective carer, whether professionally qualified or not: the carer's own (albeit prospective) legal rights and liabilities are in issue and the prospective carer needs to know, for example, if he will be acting lawfully or unlawfully (tortiously and criminally) if he arranges for the patient to be accommodated at a place of the carer's choosing, undertakes the task of caring for the patient, and adopts a particular regime for the medical or other treatment and care of the patient.[317]

(3) Anybody whose past or present relationship with the patient, whether formal or informal (for example as parent, spouse, sibling, mistress,[318] or friend), gives him a genuine and legitimate interest in obtaining a decision, in contrast to being a stranger or an officious busybody.[319]

A spouse or relative does not, qua spouse or relative, have any status either to   **4.125**
consent or to refuse consent to medical treatment[320] and therefore cannot, qua spouse or relative, have locus to seek a declaration. Nor, if the question is whether or not a patient under the care of doctors can lawfully be treated by those doctors, can a spouse or relative have locus qua carer. In such circumstances, a spouse or relative can, and normally will, have locus only as a person with a genuine and legitimate interest in the patient.

Likewise in the case of a local authority.   **4.126**

Thus the declaratory jurisdiction has been successfully invoked in cases involv-   **4.127**
ing the medical treatment of incompetent or competent but unconscious

---

[316] *In re S (Hospital Patient: Court's Jurisdiction)* [1995] Fam 26, appeal dismissed [1996] Fam 1, further proceedings *In re S (Hospital patient: Foreign Curator)* [1996] Fam 23.

[317] See, for example, *In re S (Hospital Patient: Court's Jurisdiction)* [1995] Fam 26, 35, appeal dismissed [1996] Fam 1, further proceedings *In re S (Hospital patient: Foreign Curator)* [1996] Fam 23.

[318] For an example see *In re S (Hospital Patient: Court's Jurisdiction)* [1995] Fam 26 (where the relevant factors were listed by Hale J, 35), appeal dismissed [1996] Fam 1. For the subsequent substantive proceedings see *In re S (Hospital patient: Foreign Curator)* [1996] Fam 23.

[319] *In re S (Hospital Patient: Court's Jurisdiction)* [1996] Fam 1, 18, 19, dismissing appeal from [1995] Fam 26. For the earlier cases see, in particular, *Royal College of Nursing of the United Kingdom v Department of Health and Social Security* [1981] AC 800; *Gillick v West Norfolk and Wisbech Area Health Authority* [1986] AC 112; *In re F (Mental Patient: Sterilisation)* [1990] 2 AC 1, 81–82; *Airedale NHS Trust v Bland* [1993] AC 789, 862.

[320] See paras 4.20, 4.101 above.

adults by the patient (acting by a next friend)[321] by a doctor or health authority,[322] by a relative (applying qua relative),[323] by a local authority,[324] by a mistress,[325] and by the prospective donee from an adult incompetent of bone marrow.[326]

(v) Form of Declaratory Relief

Interim or Final?

4.128 Cases in which the court's declaratory jurisdiction is invoked often arise at very short notice and as a matter of extreme urgency; many require to be resolved within a day or two, and some within a matter of a few hours or even minutes. But the court cannot grant an interim declaration (there being no such thing known to the law), only a final declaration.[327] In practice, this theoretical difficulty presents no real problem. In the first place, the court is willing to grant a final declaration following an inter partes hearing arranged, if the circumstances warrant, at extremely short notice and, if need be, out of normal court hours.[328] Moreover, the court can grant an ex parte final

---

[321] *In re F (Mental Patient: Sterilisation)* [1990] 2 AC 1; *Re SG (Adult Mental Patient: Abortion)* [1991] 2 FLR 329; *Re W (Mental patient) (Sterilisation)* [1993] 1 FLR 381.
[322] *Re H (Mental Patient: Diagnosis)* [1993] 1 FLR 28; *Airedale NHS Trust v Bland* [1993] AC 789; *Riverside Mental Health NHS Trust v Fox* [1994] 1 FLR 614; *Frenchay Healthcare National Health Service Trust v S* [1994] 1 WLR 601; *Re KB (Adult) (Mental Patient: Medical Treatment)* (1994) 19 BMLR 144; *Re G (Persistent Vegetative State)* [1995] 2 FCR 46; *Swindon and Marlborough NHS Trust v S* (1994) *Guardian* Dec 10, [1995] Med L Rev 84; *Re C (Adult Patient: Restriction of Publicity after Death)* [1996] 2 FLR 251; *Tameside and Glossop Acute Services Trust v CH* [1996] 1 FLR 762; *Re R (Adult: Medical Treatment)* [1996] 2 FLR 99; *Norfolk and Norwich Healthcare (NHS) Trust v W* [1996] 2 FLR 613; *Rochdale Healthcare (NHS) Trust v C* [1997] 1 FCR 274; *Re L (Patient: Non-Consensual Treatment)* [1997] 2 FLR 837; *Re D* (1997) 38 BMLR 1; *Re MB (Medical Treatment)* [1997] 2 FLR 426; *Re H (adult: incompetent)* (1997) 38 BMLR 11; *Re D* (1997) Nov 26 (Sir Stephen Brown P).
[323] *Re GF (Medical Treatment)* [1992] 1 FLR 293 (mother—proposed sterilisation); *In re T (Adult: Refusal of Treatment)* [1993] Fam 95 (father—blood transfusion after caesarian). See also *Re C (Mental Patient: Contact)* [1993] 1 FLR 940 (mother—contact with adult incompetent).
[324] *Re NK* (1990) Feb 28 (Ewbank J), (1990) Apr 4 (Scott Baker J); *Re LC (Medical Treatment: Sterilisation)* [1997] 2 FLR 258 (proposed sterilisation). See also *Cambridgeshire County Council v R (An Adult)* [1995] 1 FLR 50.
[325] *In re S (Hospital Patient: Court's Jurisdiction)* [1995] Fam 26, appeal dismissed [1996] Fam 1. For the subsequent substantive proceedings see *In re S (Hospital patient: Foreign Curator)* [1996] Fam 23.
[326] *In re Y (Mental Patient: Bone Marrow Donation)* [1997] Fam 110.
[327] *Riverside Mental Health NHS Trust v Fox* [1994] 1 FLR 614.
[328] *In re Y (Mental Patient: Bone Marrow Donation)* [1997] Fam 110, 116. Thus in *Swindon and Marlborough NHS Trust v S* (1994) *Guardian* Dec 10, [1995] Med L Rev 84 an inter partes hearing with medical evidence on both sides was arranged late on a Friday afternoon and took place, after the patient had been examined by the Official Solicitor's doctor on Saturday morning, on Saturday afternoon.

declaration, and will do so in cases of extreme emergency.[329] Even if the only substantive relief sought is a declaration, the court can grant an interlocutory injunction to 'hold the ring' pending trial.[330] Furthermore, the practice of the court, even when making a final declaration, is to confine the declaration to the state of affairs as it exists at the date of the hearing and to grant liberty to all parties to apply for further declaratory relief in the event of any material change in circumstances.[331]

Prospective Relief

In an appropriate case the court can make a prospective declaration to cover the happening of a future event, and declare that steps taken on the happening of that event will, subject to specified conditions and safeguards, be lawful. Thus in one case[332] a declaration was granted in the following terms, the court in effect devolving the future decision to the attending doctor subject to the twin safeguards of a second medical opinion and parental consent: **4.129**

> Ordered and declared that notwithstanding (a) that the patient is unable to give a valid consent thereto and (b) if such be the case that no further order of the court shall have been obtained in the meantime it shall be lawful as being in the patient's best interests for the Trust and/or the responsible medical practitioners having the responsibility at the time for the patient's treatment and care . . . to withhold the administration of antibiotics in the event of the patient developing a potentially life-threatening infection which would otherwise call for the administration of antibiotics but only if immediately prior to withholding the same (a) the Trust is so advised both by the general medical practitioner and by

---

[329] *In re S (Adult: Refusal of Treatment)* [1993] Fam 123; *Riverside Mental Health NHS Trust v Fox* [1994] 1 FLR 614, 616, 622. The judge faced with an apparently urgent case where it has proved impossible to arrange an inter partes hearing at short notice (as was possible in *Swindon and Marlborough NHS Trust v S* (1994) *Guardian* Dec 10, [1995] Med L Rev 84) may be placed in very great difficulty in deciding whether to proceed ex parte (as in *In re S (Adult: Refusal of Treatment)* [1993] Fam 123) or trying to proceed ex parte 'on notice' (as in *Frenchay Healthcare National Health Service Trust v S* [1994] 1 WLR 601); plainly it is imperative, if at all possible, to proceed inter partes or, at the very least ex parte 'on notice': see *Riverside Mental Health NHS Trust v Fox* [1994] 1 FLR 614, 617, 621–622; *Frenchay Healthcare National Health Service Trust v S* [1994] 1 WLR 601, 606, 607, 609–610; *Re MB (Medical Treatment)* [1997] 2 FLR 426, 445.

[330] *In re S (Hospital Patient: Court's Jurisdiction)* [1995] Fam 26, 35–36, appeal on another point dismissed [1996] Fam 1.

[331] See, for example, the declarations granted in *In re F (Mental Patient: Sterilisation)* [1990] 2 AC 1; *Airedale NHS Trust v Bland* [1993] AC 789, and the precedents in Practice Note (Official Solicitor: Sterilisation) [1996] 2 FLR 111; Practice Note (Official Solicitor: Persistent Vegetative State) [1996] 2 FLR 375.

[332] *Re R (Adult: Medical Treatment)* [1996] 2 FLR 99, 104, 106, 109, 110, justified by Sir Stephen Brown P for the reasons set out, 106–107, 108–109. See also *Re D* (1997) Nov 26 (Sir Stephen Brown P) where the declaration was in terms that it was lawful not to treat 'in circumstances in which in the opinion of the medical practitioners responsible for such treatment it is not reasonably practicable so to do'.

the consultant psychiatrist having the responsibility at the time for the patient's treatment and care and (b) one or other or both of the [patient's] parents first give their consent thereto.

Precedents

4.130   The forms of declaration granted in a variety of cases can be found in the reports.[333] Precedents for use in cases relating to sterilisation[334] and the withdrawal of artificial nutrition and hydration from patients in a permanent (formerly called persistent) vegetative state[335] are set out in the Official Solicitor's Practice Notes and can readily be adapted for use in other cases.

(vi)   *Injunctions in Support of Declaratory Relief*

4.131   Where proceedings are brought to restrain a threatened tort involving an interference with the patient's body, the court can grant an injunction, including, in an appropriate case, a quia timet injunction.[336] Even if the only substantive relief sought is a declaration, the court can grant an interlocutory injunction to 'hold the ring' pending trial.[337]

(vii)   *Procedure*

4.132   Proceedings should be commenced in the High Court.[338] Details of the procedure to be adopted in applications to the court in relation to pregnant women have been laid down by the Court of Appeal.[339] Details of the procedure to be adopted in applications to the court in relation to sterilisation[340] and the withdrawal of artificial nutrition and hydration from patients in a permanent (formerly called persistent) vegetative state[341] are set out in the Official Solicitor's Practice Notes. These reflect views expressed by the

---

[333] See, for example, *In re F (Mental Patient: Sterilisation)* [1990] 2 AC 1; *Airedale NHS Trust v Bland* [1993] AC 789; *Tameside and Glossop Acute Services Trust v CH* [1996] 1 FLR 762; *Re R (Adult: Medical Treatment)* [1996] 2 FLR 99; *In re Y (Mental Patient: Bone Marrow Donation)* [1997] Fam 110.

[334] Practice Note (Official Solicitor: Sterilisation) [1996] 2 FLR 111.

[335] Practice Note (Official Solicitor: Persistent Vegetative State) [1996] 2 FLR 375.

[336] *Egan v Egan* [1975] Ch 218. For an example see *In re C (Adult: Refusal of Treatment)* [1994] 1 WLR 290.

[337] *In re S (Hospital Patient: Court's Jurisdiction)* [1995] Fam 26, 35–36, appeal on another point dismissed [1996] Fam 1.   [338] See para 4.87 above.

[339] *Re MB (Medical Treatment)* [1997] 2 FLR 426, 439, 445.

[340] Practice Note (Official Solicitor: Sterilisation) [1996] 2 FLR 111.

[341] Practice Note (Official Solicitor: Persistent Vegetative State) [1996] 2 FLR 375.

House of Lords in the leading cases[342] and, mutatis mutandis, can be taken as applying in other applications for declaratory relief.[343]

4. Best Interests and the 'Bolam' Test

The 'Bolam' test[344]

Prima facie, and as a starting point, the answer to the question, Is the course **4.133** proposed to be adopted one which is in the best interests of the patient? is given by the answer to the question, 'Is the proposed action in accordance with an accepted body of medical opinion?': in other words, by applying the 'Bolam' test.[345]

The 'Bolam' test governs the legality of action taken without reference to the **4.134** court.

But, once the matter is put before the court, the 'Bolam' test alone does not **4.135** supply the definitive answer to the question, 'Is the proposed action in the best interests of the patient?' That is always, in the final analysis, a matter for judicial decision; the court has to reach its own judgment, on the evidence before it, as to the incompetent's best interests. It is not enough, it is submitted,[346] for the court merely to determine whether the judgment formed, for example, by the patient's doctor, is within the limits reasonably open to him, and lawful as falling within the bounds of reasonable professional judgment.

The Function of the Court

The function of the court, and the manner in which it approaches the question **4.136** of what is in the incompetent's best interests can be summarised as follows:

(1) The overriding consideration is always the patient's best interests.[347]
    More than one alternative may satisfy the 'Bolam' test, but the court is

---

[342] *In re F (Mental Patient: Sterilisation)* [1990] 2 AC 1; *Airedale NHS Trust v Bland* [1993] AC 789.

[343] For the role and involvement of the Official Solicitor see paras 4.88–4.89 above. Further aspects of the procedure in sterilisation cases were considered in *Practice Note (Mental Patient: Sterilisation)*; *J v C* [1990] 1 WLR 1248. On the question of whether the court should sit in public, and attendant questions of protecting the patient's anonymity, see *Re G (Adult Patient: Publicity)* [1995] 2 FLR 528; *Re C (Adult Patient: Restriction of Publicity after Death)* [1996] 2 FLR 251; *Re R (Adult: Medical Treatment)* [1996] 2 FLR 99, 110; *In re Y (Mental Patient: Bone Marrow Donation)* [1997] Fam 110, 116.

[344] See *Bolam v Friern Hospital Management Committee* [1957] 1 WLR 582.

[345] *In re F (Mental Patient: Sterilisation)* [1990] 2 AC 1, 52, 68, 78; *Airedale NHS Trust v Bland* [1993] AC 789, 870, 883, and cf, 874, 884, 898.

[346] Notwithstanding what was said by Lord Browne-Wilkinson in *Airedale NHS Trust v Bland* [1993] AC 789, 884. Contrast the views of Lord Goff of Chieveley in *In re F (Mental Patient: Sterilisation)* [1990] 2 AC 1, 77, 80, 83 and in *Airedale NHS Trust v Bland* [1993] AC 789, 874–875 and of Lord Mustill in the latter case, 898–899.

[347] *In re F (Mental Patient: Sterilisation)* [1990] 2 AC 1, 55, 56, 64, 69, 70, 75, 77, 78, 79, 83.

concerned to identify what is in the incompetent's best interests. Best must mean best. Therefore if differing opinions are put forward as to what is in the incompetent's best interests the court must select that course which it believes to be in the incompetent's best interests.[348] Two diametrically opposed courses of action cannot both be in the best interests of the patient.[349]

(2) When the court considers the best interests of an incompetent patient it has to consider more than purely medical factors.[350] In many cases it has to consider ethical, social and moral questions in relation to which a doctor has no special qualifications and as to which a judge is as well qualified to express an opinion as a doctor.[351]

(3) The court is not bound by, although it will obviously pay great respect to, the evidence of the medical experts.[352]

(4) The court's function when considering an adult incompetent patient is, in practical terms, the same as that of a court exercising the parens patriae jurisdiction in relation to a child.[353]

> The jurisdiction is not strictly speaking the exercise of a parens patriae jurisdiction but is similar to it . . . it is clear that the result of the decision in *Re F* was that a case of this nature did give to the court a jurisdiction which has been referred to as patrimonial and not strictly 'parens patriae' but similar in all practical respects to it.[354]

---

[348] It is respectfully submitted that Hale J was wrong in suggesting the contrary in *In re S (Hospital Patient: Court's Jurisdiction)* [1995] Fam 26, 32, appeal on another point dismissed [1996] Fam 1. Contrast the same judge's approach in the subsequent substantive proceedings: *In re S (Hospital patient: Foreign Curator)* [1996] Fam 23, 32–33.

[349] For these reasons, it is submitted, Ewbank J in *Re NK (No 1)* (1990) Feb 28 and Scott Baker J in *Re NK (No 2)* (1990) Apr 4 were wrong in holding that two alternative courses of treatment could both be in an incompetent's best interests. In that case there was a difference of medical opinion, one doctor taking the view that a hysterectomy was needed, the other that alternatives (laparotomy and other procedures) should be explored. On a preliminary issue Ewbank J held that the court could entertain the application for a declaration. The final order made by Scott Baker J was in the following terms: '1 It is declared that the operation of hysterectomy proposed to be performed on [NK] being in the existing circumstances in her best interests can lawfully be performed on her despite her inability to consent to it, and 2 It is declared that laparotomy as a diagnostic procedure followed by such appropriate medical treatment as may be necessary proposed to be performed on [NK] being in the existing circumstances in her best interests can lawfully be performed on her despite her inability to consent to it'.

[350] *In re F (Mental Patient: Sterilisation)* [1990] 2 AC 1, 72, 76; *In re S (Hospital Patient: Court's Jurisdiction)* [1995] Fam 26, 31–32, appeal dismissed [1996] Fam 1.

[351] *Airedale NHS Trust v Bland* [1993] AC 789, 877, 878, 887, 890, 898.

[352] *In re F (Mental Patient: Sterilisation)* [1990] 2 AC 1, 80.

[353] ibid, 18, 77, 83. Consider also Hale J's approach to the evaluation of best interests in a case which had turned into a 'battle' between two 'very polarised positions' which the judge had to choose between: *In re S (Hospital patient: Foreign Curator)* [1996] Fam 23, 25–26, 32–33.

[354] *Re G (Adult Patient: Publicity)* [1995] 2 FLR 528, 530 *per* Sir Stephen Brown P (with the

(5) In the final analysis the court has the ultimate power and duty[355] to review the doctors' decision and, in the light of all the facts and having heard and appraised the witnesses, to come to its own conclusion as to what is in the best interests of the incompetent.[356]

F. Best Interests

As has been seen, the defining criterion for the legality of any invasive **4.137** procedure proposed to be performed on an incompetent adult is the patient's best interests.[357] Best interests is also the criterion by which, normally,[358] the propriety of performing an invasive procedure on a child is determined, whether the decision is that of the court[359] or of a parent.[360]

What exactly is meant by a patient's best interests is neither self-evident nor **4.138** altogether clear. The problem is well illustrated by the uncertainties which have long surrounded, and to an extent still surround, the ambit of the parental power, in furthering the best interests of the child, to consent or refuse consent[361] to medical treatment.[362] Earlier controversies concerned such questions as the blood-testing of children for forensic rather than therapeutic purposes and female circumcision. More recent controversy has focussed on the non-therapeutic sterilisation of children and incompetent adults. Difficulties and obscurities currently surround such issues as the withholding of life-saving treatment from children (particularly neonates) and incompetent adults and the donation by children and incompetent adults of regenerative tissue or bodily fluids and, more particularly, non-regenerative organs.

---

consequence that a court exercising the declaratory jurisdiction in relation to an incompetent adult has power to sit in private under the first exception to the rule in *Scott v Scott* [1913] AC 417).

[355] Even in the context of an action for negligence, and applying the 'Bolam' test, the court has the ultimate right and duty to determine the propriety of the doctor's actions: *Sidaway v Board of Governors of the Bethlem Royal Hospital and the Maudsley Hospital* [1985] AC 871, 900, 903; *Edward Wong Finance Co Ltd v Johnson Stokes & Master* [1984] AC 296 (solicitor); *Bolitho v City and Hackney Health Authority* [1997] 3 WLR 1151.

[356] *In re F (Mental Patient: Sterilisation)* [1990] 2 AC 1, 79; *Airedale NHS Trust v Bland* [1993] AC 789, 875; *Frenchay Healthcare National Health Service Trust v S* [1994] 1 WLR 601, 609, 610.

[357] See paras 4.22, 4.102, 4.104 above.   [358] But see para 4.77 above.

[359] See para 4.90 above.   [360] See paras 4.75–4.76 above.

[361] For a recent vivid example see the, it might be thought surprising, decision in *In re T (A Minor) (Wardship: Medical Treatment)* [1997] 1 WLR 242.

[362] The most recent comprehensive, if inconclusive, judicial consideration of the basis and scope of the common law power of a parent to consent to medical treatment is in *Secretary, Department of Health and Community Services v JWB and SMB* (1992) 175 CLR 218, esp, 239–240, 278–279, 291–301, 312–317.

4.139 There are two reasons for this uncertainty. First, the question has been given surprisingly little consideration by the courts.[363] Secondly, and notwithstanding strong criticism, the courts have traditionally failed,[364] and even on occasions refused,[365] to articulate any principles or values to be applied in operating the best interests test.

> The 'best interests' approach focusses attention on the child whose interests are in question. . . . But, that said, the best interests approach does no more than identify the person whose interests are in question: it does not assist in identifying the factors which are relevant to the best interests of the child. The summary rejection by the House of Lords of the criterion offered by *Re Eve* left their Lordships without any guidelines by which to decide *Re B* or, at least, any guidelines that could be articulated for general application. That is because the best interests approach offers no hierarchy of values which might guide the exercise of a discretionary power . . ., much less any general legal principle which might direct the difficult decisions to be made in this area by parents, guardians, the medical profession and the courts. . . . [B]y transforming a 'complex moral and social question' into a question of fact, the best interests approach leaves the court in the hands of 'experts' who assemble a dossier of fact and opinion on matters which they deem relevant 'without reference to any check-list of legal requirements'.[366]

> To say that a medical or surgical procedure is in the best interests of a child, however, is merely to record a result. Before the best interests of the child can be determined, some principle, rule or standard must be applied to the facts and circumstances of the case.[367]

---

[363] *Secretary, Department of Health and Community Services v JWB and SMB* (1992) 175 CLR 218, 312.

[364] *In re B (A Minor) (Wardship: Sterilisation)* [1988] AC 199 is a well-known and much criticised example of such failure.

[365] As in *In re J (A Minor) (Wardship: Medical Treatment)* [1991] Fam 33, 52 *per* Balcombe LJ: 'I would deprecate any attempt by this court to lay down such an all-embracing test . . . I do not know of any demand by the judges who have to deal with these cases at first instance for this court to assist them by laying down any test beyond that which is already the law: that the interests of the ward are the first and paramount consideration, subject to the gloss on that test . . . that in determining where those interests lie the court adopts the standpoint of the reasonable and responsible parent who has his or her child's best interests at heart'. See also *In re T (A Minor) (Wardship: Medical Treatment)* [1997] 1 WLR 242, 254 *per* Waite LJ: 'All these cases depend on their own facts and render generalisations—tempting though they may be to the legal or social analyst—wholly out of place'.

[366] *Secretary, Department of Health and Community Services v JWB and SMB* (1992) 175 CLR 218, 270, 272–273 *per* Brennan J.   [367] ibid, 320 *per* McHugh J.

1. Best Interests and Substituted Judgment

The propriety of an invasive medical procedure proposed to be performed on a child or an incompetent adult is judged by reference to the patient's best interests, not by the application of a substituted judgment. The test of best interests is objective, assessed with respect to the particular patient and from the point of view of a person suffering his handicaps.

4.140

(i) *Best Interests or Substituted Judgment?*

(a) The Patient's Property and Affairs

So far as concerns questions relating to the patient's property and affairs, the court applies,[368] and has always applied, a substituted judgment test.[369] The principle is an old one.[370]

4.141

(b) The Patient's Physical and Bodily Welfare

Some jurisdictions in the United States of America have extended the substituted judgment test[371] to questions relating to the patient's body.[372] However, English law, in common with a number of other jurisdictions in the United States of America which also apply a best

4.142

---

[368] Where a true substituted judgment is impossible because the patient has always lacked capacity, the court 'must assume that she would have been a normal decent person, acting in accordance with contemporary standards of morality': *Re C (A Patient)* [1991] 3 All ER 866, 870 *per* Hoffmann J.

[369] *In re D(J)* [1982] Ch 237, 244 *per* Megarry VC ('court must seek to [do that] which the actual patient, acting reasonably, would have [done] if notionally restored to full mental capacity, memory and foresight').

[370] *Ex p Whitbread* (1816) 2 Mer 99, 102 ('looking at what it is likely the Lunatic himself would do, if he were in a capacity to act'); *Re Blair* (1836) 1 My & Cr 300; *Re Earl of Carysfort* (1840) Cr & Ph 76, 77 ('one which the lunatic, if he should ever recover, would approve'); *Re Croft* (1863) 32 LJ(Ch) 481; *In re Frost (A Person of Unsound Mind)* (1870) LR 5 Ch App 699; *In re Evans (A Person of Unsound Mind)* (1882) 21 ChD 297; *In re Darling (A Person of Unsound Mind)* (1888) 39 ChD 208, 211, 212 ('what the lunatic would have done himself if of sound mind'), 213 ('what it is likely the lunatic himself would do if sane'); *In re Alice Pauline Freeman (A Person of Unsound Mind Not so Found)* [1927] 1 Ch 479; *In re DML* [1965] Ch 1133; *In re L(WJG)* [1966] Ch 135; *In re TB* [1967] Ch 247.

[371] Explicitly by adopting the English *property* cases and, in particular, *ex p Whitbread* (1816) 2 Mer 99.

[372] *Strunk v Strunk* (1969) 445 SW 2d 145, 147–148 (Ky); *Hart v Brown* (1972) 289 A 2d 386, 387 (Conn); *Re Quinlan* (1976) 355 A 2d 647, 663, 664, 666 (NJ); *Superintendent of Belchertown State School v Saikewicz* (1977) 370 NE 2d 417, 431 (Mass); *Re Doe* (1992) 583 NE 2d 1263, 1267, 1273 (Mass).

interests test,[373] has rejected the substituted judgment test so far as concerns questions relating to the patient's physical and bodily welfare in favour of a best interests test.[374] The reason for the divergence in English law between the objective test applied in cases affecting the person of the incompetent and the substituted judgment test applied in cases relating to his property has never been explained or explored.

(ii) *Objective or Subjective?*

4.143   The test of best interests is objective.[375] One does not, therefore, attempt to find a speculative answer to the question, 'What would this patient have chosen if he had the capacity to make a choice?'[376] But although the test is objective one is necessarily concerned with the question, 'What is in the best interests of *this* particular patient?' One therefore looks at the case not from the point of view of an ordinary or normal fit person but from the assumed point of view of a person suffering the handicaps of the particular patient.[377] In this sense the standard is subjective.[378]

(iii) *Best Interests and the Patient's Wishes*

4.144   Regard must be had to the ascertainable wishes and feelings of the patient, considered in the light of his age and understanding.[379] Even if the patient lacks the capacity to decide for himself, and has never made an effective advance directive, the personality of the particular patient and the expressed views, wishes and feelings of the patient, whether past or present, are relevant and must be taken into account as a very material factor in ascertaining his best interests.[380]

---

[373]   *Re Richardson (1973)* 284 So 2d 185, 187 (La); *Lausier v Pescinski* (1975) 226 NW 2d 180, 181–182, 184 (Wis); *Little v Little* (1979) 576 SW 2d 493, 497–498 (Tex); *Curran v Bosze* (1990) 566 NE 2d 1319, 1326, 1331 (Ill).
[374]   *Airedale NHS Trust v Bland* [1993] AC 789, 871–872, 894–895.
[375]   See further para 4.92 above.
[376]   *In re T (Adult: Refusal of Treatment)* [1993] Fam 95, 103.
[377]   *In re J (A Minor) (Wardship: Medical Treatment)* [1991] Fam 33, 44, 46–47, 55.
[378]   *Re E (A Minor) (Wardship: Medical Treatment)* [1993] 1 FLR 386, 392.
[379]   See further, particularly in relation to children, paras 4.94, 4.95, 4.98 above.
[380]   *In re W (A Minor) (Medical Treatment: Court's Jurisdiction)* [1993] Fam 64, 88; *In re T (Adult: Refusal of Treatment)* [1993] Fam 95, 103; *Airedale NHS Trust v Bland* [1993] AC 789, 872.

2. Applicability of the Best Interests Test

The best interests test governs all aspects of a child's 'upbringing'[381] and all **4.145** aspects of an incompetent adult's 'treatment' and 'care'. 'Treatment' and 'care' are not confined to medical treatment.

Treatment and care include whatever is 'necessary to preserve . . . life, health **4.146** or well-being' or 'carried out in order either to save . . . lives, or to ensure improvement or prevent deterioration in . . . physical or mental health'.[382] In addition to appropriate medical, dental and surgical treatment, treatment includes, in the case of someone who is permanently or semi-permanently incapable, care, as part of daily life, of a basic, simple or humdrum nature, such as dressing, undressing, feeding, looking after, and putting to bed, and including the actions of the relative, friend or neighbour who comes in to look after the patient.[383]

Treatment and care extend to 'action . . . such as a reasonable person would in **4.147** all the circumstances take, acting in the best interests of the assisted person'[384] and thus to everything that conduces to the welfare and happiness of the patient, including companionship and the patient's domestic and social environment.[385]

3. Best Interests and Medical Interests

Best interests or best medical interests? **4.148**

An invasive medical procedure can be in a patient's best interests even though

(a) it is not therapeutically required;[386]

(b) it is not, of itself, of any medical benefit at all to the patient;

(c) it is attended with some medical risks or disadvantages;[387] and

---

[381] cf the Children Act 1989, s 1(1)(a); *In re Z (A Minor) (Identification: Restrictions on Publication)* [1997] Fam 1, 28–29.

[382] *In re F (Mental Patient: Sterilisation)* [1990] 2 AC 1, 52 *per* Lord Bridge of Harwich, 55 *per* Lord Brandon of Oakbrook.   [383] ibid, 72, 76 *per* Lord Goff of Chieveley.

[384] ibid, 75 *per* Lord Goff of Chieveley.

[385] *Re C (Mental Patient: Contact)* [1993] 1 FLR 940.

[386] *In re B (A Minor) (Wardship: Sterilisation)* [1988] AC 199 (non-therapeutic sterilisation of minor for contraceptive purposes); *In re F (Mental Patient: Sterilisation)* [1990] 2 AC 1 (non-therapeutic sterilisation of incompetent adult for contraceptive purposes).

[387] Thus ritual or other non-therapeutic circumcision of minor male children (eg, the routine non-therapeutic circumcision of neonates for reasons which are social or conventional rather than religious) is permissible even though the preponderance of current medical opinion, at least in the United Kingdom, is that circumcision is normally of no medical benefit and devoid of rational justification, and notwithstanding that circumcision is not without risks and that the procedure can lead to complications, serious injury, and even death: see Skegg,

(d) the primary purpose of the procedure is to further the interests of a third party.[388]

Factors other than the narrowly therapeutic or medical can therefore properly be taken into account in assessing whether or not an invasive medical procedure is in the patient's best interests.[389]

Best interests are not limited to best medical interests.[390]

Countervailing Advantages

4.149 Such a procedure may nonetheless be in the patient's best interests if (i) it is not seriously detrimental to the patient[391] and (ii) it is compensated by sufficient countervailing benefits or advantages to the patient, in other words if, having regard to all relevant factors, the balance of benefit and detriment overall is such that it is in the patient's best interests to subject him to the procedure.

4.150 Thus a non-therapeutic sterilisation may be justified as being for the benefit of a child or incompetent adult patient's psychological health and well-being.[392] Likewise the donation of bone-marrow to a sibling may be justified as serving the emotional and psychological welfare of an incompetent adult.[393] So also a blood test for purely forensic purposes may be in a child's best interests if the potential personal or financial benefits to the child of ascertaining his paternity outweigh any possible medical disadvantages,[394] and notwithstanding that its primary purpose is to further the interests of another, for example, the blood-testing of a child in order to resolve an issue of adultery in a divorce suit.[395] So also the ritual circumcision of male

---

Law, Ethics, and Medicine (edn 2), 66; Poulter, *English Law and Ethnic Minority Customs*, para 6.26; *Gray v LaFleche* [1950] 1 DLR 337; *Iqbal v Irfan* [1994] CLY 1642; *R v Alam* (1994) *Independent* July 9, Nov 15.

[388] So the blood-testing of a child in order to resolve an issue of adultery in a divorce suit: *B(BR) v B(J)* [1968] P 466. Or the donation of bone-marrow in order to save a sibling's life: *In re Y (Mental Patient: Bone Marrow Donation)* [1997] Fam 110.

[389] See *In re T (A Minor) (Wardship: Medical Treatment)* [1997] 1 WLR 242.

[390] *Re MB (Medical Treatment)* [1997] 2 FLR 426, 439.

[391] cf *S v McC, W v W* [1972] AC 24, 44 *per* Lord Reid (referring to blood-testing): 'unless . . . clearly . . . against the interests of the child'.

[392] *In re B (A Minor) (Wardship: Sterilisation)* [1988] AC 199; *In re F (Mental Patient: Sterilisation)* [1990] 2 AC 1.

[393] *In re Y (Mental Patient: Bone Marrow Donation)* [1997] Fam 110.

[394] *In re L (An Infant)* [1968] P 119, 141, 158, 160, 161; *B(BR) v B(J)* [1968] P 466, 473, 477; *S v McC (orse S) and M (DS intervener)* [1970] 1 WLR 672, 675–676, 679, 681–682. These cases were decided before *S v McC, W v W* [1972] AC 24, and thus at a time when it was generally held that a child could be blood-tested for forensic purposes only if it was in the child's best interests that it should be. Orders were refused, as not being in the child's best interests, in *M(DK) v M(SV) and G (M intervening)* [1969] 1 WLR 843; *B v B and E* [1969] 1 WLR 1800; *W v W* [1970] 1 WLR 682.   [395] *B(BR) v B(J)* [1968] P 466.

children, on the basis that, on balance, the perceived religious advantages out-weigh both the absence of medical benefit and the risk of occasionally serious complications.[396] So also a 'sex-change' or 'gender reassignment' operation.[397]

There are other applications of the same principle: Payment away of trust monies to a third party may be for the 'benefit' of a beneficiary if it enables him thereby to discharge what he recognises to be his moral obligation to the third party.[398] Public exploitation in the media of a child's medical problems may be in the best interests of the child if it enables her father, by sale of the story to a newspaper, to raise money needed to pay for the child's further possibly life-saving medical treatment.[399]

4.151

4. Factors in the Best Interests Equation

(i) *Personal Factors*

In assessing an individual's best interests, relevant factors may, in an appropriate case, include: his psychological health, well-being, amenity and quality of life;[400] his ethical, moral, spiritual and religious welfare;[401] his relationship with his parents or other carers;[402] his financial interests;[403] ties of affection;[404] and moral obligations, whether or not they are yet the object of public or social pressure, but only if he himself recognises and feels the moral obligation.[405]

4.152

---

[396] *R v Brown* [1994] AC 212, 231, *Secretary, Department of Health and Community Services v JWB and SMB* (1992) 175 CLR 218, 297 *per* Deane J (parents 'plainly' able to consent to 'male circumcision for perceived hygienic—or even religious—reasons'); Kennedy & Grubb, *Medical Law: Text with Materials*, (edn 2 1994), 270 ('Regard may, of course, be paid to a religious view . . . when the effect on the child is not significant (eg male circumcision)'). It is not altogether easy to accept these rationalisations given the possible seriousness of the attendant risks and the fact that (at least until recently) routine non-therapeutic circumcision of neonates was widespread for reasons which were social or conventional, rather than religious.

[397] So held by the Family Court of Australia: *In re A* (1993) 16 Fam LR 715.

[398] *In re Clore's Settlement Trusts* [1966] 1 WLR 955.

[399] *R v Cambridge District Health Authority, ex p B (No 2)* [1996] 1 FLR 375. Contrast *In re Z (A Minor) (Identification: Restrictions on Publication)* [1997] Fam 1 (not in best interests of child of prominent public figure to appear in television documentary showing her receiving treatment).

[400] *In re B (A Minor) (Wardship: Sterilisation)* [1988] AC 199, 202–203, 206, 208–210; *In re F (Mental Patient: Sterilisation)* [1990] 2 AC 1, 52, 76 ('life, health or well-being'), 55 (steps taken to 'ensure improvement or prevent deterioration in . . . physical or mental health').

[401] *In re K (Minors) (Children: Care and Control)* [1977] Fam 179, 187, 191.

[402] *In re T (A Minor) (Wardship: Medical Treatment)* [1997] 1 WLR 242.

[403] *R v Cambridge District Health Authority, ex p B (No 2)* [1996] 1 FLR 375.

[404] *Re McGrath* [1893] 1 Ch 143, 148 *per* Lindley LJ quoted para. 4.91 above.

[405] *In re Clore's Settlement Trusts* [1966] 1 WLR 955, 959–960; *In re CL* [1969] 1 Ch 587, 599–600.

(ii) *Third Party Interests*

4.153   The best interests in question are those of the child or adult incompetent patient, not those of a third party or of society. Benefits accruing to the third party are material only insofar as they further the interests of the patient.

Third Parties

4.154   The interests of a third party can legitimately be taken into account in assessing all the relevant facts, choices and other circumstances which have to be taken into account in determining whether or not what is proposed is in the best interests of the patient.[406] But an invasive medical procedure which is not, of itself, of any medical benefit to the patient cannot be justified as being in his best interests merely because it confers a benefit (even a very substantial benefit indeed) on a third party; what has to be shown is some countervailing benefit or advantage *to the patient himself.*

4.155   There is no legal (as opposed to moral, ethical or civic) obligation to provide medical assistance to another[407] or to subject oneself to a medical procedure[408] for the benefit of another.[409] This is merely the application in the medical context of the general principle that, in the absence of special relationship or assumption of responsibility, the law imposes no obligation to go to the assistance of someone in peril, however immediate and mortal the peril to the person in danger and however trivial or even non-existent the possible risk to the rescuer.[410]

4.156   Thus an invasive medical procedure cannot be justified merely because it will lighten the burden on those who care for the patient.[411] So also the giving or

---

[406]   *In re Z (A Minor) (Identification: Restrictions on Publication)* [1997] Fam 1, 28.

[407]   *In re F (Mental Patient: Sterilisation)* [1990] 2 AC 1, 77; *Capital & Counties PLC v Hampshire County Council* [1997] QB 1004, 1035.

[408]   This is so even in the case of a mother with a viable foetus: see further paras 4.34–4.35 above.

[409]   *In re T (Adult: Refusal of Treatment)* [1993] Fam 95, 99, 102 and, in the United States of America, *McFall v Shrimp* (1978) 10 Pa D&C 3d 90 (see Kennedy and Grubb, *Medical Law: Text with Materials*, 2nd edn (1994), 1097–1101); *Re AC* (1990) 573 A 2d 1235, 1243–1244, *Re Baby Boy Doe* (1994) 632 NE 2d 326, 333–334.

[410]   *Donoghue v Stevenson* [1932] AC 562, 580; *Home Office v Dorset Yacht Co Ltd* [1970] AC 1004, 1027, 1034, 1042, 1060; *The Ogopogo* [1969] 1 LlR 374, 378, [1970] 1 LlR 257, 261, 265, further appeal [1971] 2 LlR 410.

[411]   *In re B (A Minor) (Wardship: Sterilisation)* [1988] AC 199, 204, 212; *Secretary, Department of Health and Community Services v JWB and SMB* (1992) 175 CLR 218, 295–296, 297, 300–301. On the other hand, the easing of that burden may indirectly further the interests of the patient: ibid, 300–301. See further *In re T (A Minor) (Wardship: Medical Treatment)* [1997] 1 WLR 242. The welfare of even an insentient patient may be

withholding of medical treatment is not to be determined by reference to the medical[412] or financial[413] implications of the decision for other members of the patient's family. On the other hand the court can be astute to find that a procedure which is in the medical interests of a third party, though not necessarily of the patient, is nevertheless in the patient's best interests inasmuch as it furthers the patient's emotional and psychological welfare.[414]

Conflicting Interests of Child Siblings

Where both the patient and the third party are children (for example, where what is in question is a transplant between minor siblings) it is still the interests of the patient (donor), and not of the third party (donee), which are paramount, for it is the patient (donor) whose interests are directly involved.[415]   **4.157**

(iii) Public Interests

In the same way, the general public interest and the moral and civic obligations of the patient can legitimately be taken into account in determining whether or not what is proposed is in the best interests of the patient.[416] But it is still necessary to show some benefit or advantage *to the patient* from what is proposed.[417]   **4.158**

---

adversely affected if his carers are subjected to pressure or put under emotional or other stress, e g, as a result of massive media intrusion: *In re C (A Minor) (Wardship: Medical Treatment) (No 2)* [1990] Fam 39, 47–48, 51–52, 54–55.

[412] *In re Y (Mental Patient: Bone Marrow Donation)* [1997] Fam 110 (whether adult incompetent should donate bone-marrow to be determined by reference to the best interests of the donor and not of the donee, notwithstanding that the donee would die if the operation did not take place).

[413] *Airedale NHS Trust v Bland* [1993] AC 789, 879–880 (not proper to alter the time of death of patient in permanent vegetative state in order to manipulate third party property rights). See further para 4.195 below.

[414] See the analyses in *Tameside and Glossop Acute Services Trust v CH* [1996] 1 FLR 762 (caesarian section); *In re Y (Mental Patient: Bone Marrow Donation)* [1997] Fam 110 (bone-marrow donation); *Norfolk and Norwich Healthcare (NHS) Trust v W* [1996] 2 FLR 613; *Rochdale Healthcare (NHS) Trust v C* [1997] 1 FCR 274; *A Metropolitan Borough Council v AB* [1997] 1 FLR 767; *Re L (Patient: Non-Consensual Treatment)* [1997] 2 FLR 837; *Re MB (Medical Treatment)* [1997] 2 FLR 258 (caesarian section) but note the qualification in para 4.34 above.

[415] *Birmingham City Council v H (A Minor)* [1994] 2 AC 212; *F v Leeds City Council* [1994] 2 FLR 60; *Re F (Contact: Child in Care)* [1995] 1 FLR 510; *Re T and E (Proceedings: Conflicting Interests)* [1995] 1 FLR 581.

[416] *S v McC, W v W* [1972] AC 24, 44; *In re R (A Minor) (Wardship: Criminal Proceedings)* [1991] Fam 56, 65; *In re Z (A Minor) (Identification: Restrictions on Publication)* [1997] Fam 1, 28.

[417] Note the emphatic rejection in English law of the doctrine that the public interests of the state can ever prevail over the competent patient's right of self-determination: *In re T (Adult: Refusal of Treatment)* [1993] Fam 95, 102; *Secretary of State for the Home Department v Robb* [1995] Fam 127.

4.159   The performance of a moral, social or civic obligation can be of benefit to the patient, and his moral, social or civic obligations are therefore relevant, only if the patient is able to recognise, and in fact himself recognises and wishes to give effect to, the obligation.[418]

4.160   Thus the sterilisation of a child or mentally incompetent adult cannot be justified for eugenic purposes[419] or with a view to population control. So also the public interest in publicising a unique and specialised form of treatment with a view to bringing strength and encouragement to other patients and encouraging the use of the treatment in the United Kingdom did not justify the child of a prominent public figure appearing in a television documentary showing her receiving the treatment, bearing in mind the adverse effects upon her of the publicity which the broadcast would generate.[420]

5. The Best Interests Balancing Exercise

4.161   The relevant inquiry is thus whether the procedure is, overall, in the best (though not necessarily in the best medical) interests of the child or adult incompetent patient. The balancing exercise may arise in two different ways. A procedure which is medically indicated may be resisted on grounds of religious or other beliefs or principles. On the other hand, an attempt may be made to justify some procedure which is not medically indicated, serves no therapeutic purpose, and may even be attended with some medical risk or disadvantage, on the basis of some non-medical benefit sufficient (so it is said) to justify a procedure which, if harmless, serves no medical purpose or which (it is said) outweighs any medical risk or disadvantage there may be.

---

[418] *In re Clore's Settlement Trusts* [1966] 1 WLR 955 and see paras. 4.151–4.152 above. This reveals an important practical difference between the best interests test and a substituted judgment test. The discharge on behalf of an incompetent adult of moral or social obligations (e g, financial obligations to family or former employees) may be justified by reference to a substituted judgment test whether or not the incompetent is in fact able to recognise, and wishes to give effect to, the obligation: see the authorities referred to in para 4.141 above. The discharge of such an obligation will not, however, satisfy the best interests test unless the incompetent is in fact able to recognise, and in fact wishes to give effect to, the obligation.

[419] *In re B (A Minor) (Wardship: Sterilisation)* [1988] AC 199, 202, 204, 207, 212; *Re M (A Minor) (Wardship: Sterilisation)* [1988] 2 FLR 497; *Secretary, Department of Health and Community Services v JWB and SMB* (1992) 175 CLR 218, 295.

[420] *In re Z (A Minor) (Identification: Restrictions on Publication)* [1997] Fam 1, 10, 11, 12, 30–31, 32, 33.

(i) *The Balancing Exercise and Community Standards*

Community Standards[421]

Best interests have to be assessed by reference to general community stan- **4.162**
dards, making due allowance for the entitlement of people, within the limits
of what is permissible in accordance with those standards, to entertain
divergent views about the moral and secular objectives they wish to pursue.[422]
Within limits the law will tolerate things which society as a whole may find
undesirable. Thus the court passes no judgment on religious beliefs or on the
tenets doctrines or rules of any particular section of society so long as they are
'legally and socially acceptable' and not 'immoral or socially obnoxious' or
'pernicious'.[423]

It follows that an invasive medical procedure which is not of itself of any **4.163**
medical benefit to the patient can never be in the best interests of the patient
if, judged by albeit flexible and tolerant general community standards, it is
'cruel or excessive'[424] or involves 'mutilation'.[425] Nor will a religious, cultural
or social justification be accepted which, judged by the same standards, is
'immoral or socially obnoxious'[426] or 'pernicious'.[427]

(ii) *Application of the Balancing Exercise*

(a) Procedures which are Medically Indicated

It follows that there are limits to the extent to which countervailing interests **4.164**
will be permitted to stand in the way of performing a procedure which is
medically indicated, especially if the patient's condition is life-threatening or

---

[421] See further paras 4.76, 4.96 above. For a valuable survey of the legal problems presented
by a variety of ethnic minority customs see Poulter, *English Law and Ethnic Minority Custom*,
esp, paras 6.15–6.33, 10.03, 10.24–10.26.
[422] *Secretary, Department of Health and Community Services v JWB and SMB* (1992) 175
CLR 218, 295, 297, 300, 301. And see *In re T (A Minor) (Wardship: Medical Treatment)*
[1997] 1 WLR 242, esp, 254 *per* Waite LJ quoted para 4.72 above.
[423] *Re T (Minors) (Custody: Religious Upbringing)* (1981) 2 FLR 239, 244–245; *Re B and G
(Minors) (Custody)* [1985] FLR 134, 157; *Re R (A Minor) (Residence: Religion)* [1993] 2 FLR
163, 171.
[424] *S v McC, W v W* [1972] AC 24, 43 *per* Lord Reid.
[425] *Secretary, Department of Health and Community Services v JWB and SMB* (1990) 14
FamLR 427, 448 *per* Nicholson CJ, on appeal (1992) 175 CLR 218.
[426] *Re T (Minors) (Custody: Religious Upbringing)* (1981) 2 FLR 239, 244 *per* Scarman LJ.
[427] *Re B and G (Minors) (Custody)* [1985] FLR 134, 157 *per* Latey J (referring to
scientology).

likely to cause serious harm.[428] Thus the court will readily order a life-saving blood transfusion for a child notwithstanding the sincere and strong religious convictions of the child and his parents.[429] So also the court will refuse to allow the religious objections of a pregnant child's parents to stand in the way of her abortion.[430]

(b) Procedures which are not Medically Indicated

4.165 In the same way there are limits to the extent to which countervailing interests, whether religious, social or financial, will suffice to justify an invasive medical procedure which either has no medical benefit or is attended by possible medical disadvantages.

4.166 It is suggested that an invasive medical procedure which is not, of itself, of any medical benefit at all to a child or adult incompetent patient will be in the best interests of the patient, if but only if:

(a) the procedure is not seriously detrimental to the patient;

(b) judged by flexible and tolerant general community standards, the procedure is not cruel or excessive, does not involve mutilation, and would not be considered immoral, socially obnoxious or pernicious;

(c) it is compensated by countervailing benefits or advantages to the patient which are (i) real or substantial, as opposed to fanciful, insubstantial, hypothetical, speculative, nebulous or illusory and (ii) significant and not de minimis;

(d) those countervailing benefits and advantages clearly (if not necessarily by any very great margin) outweigh both the absence of any medical benefit and any possible medical risks or other disadvantages of the procedure;

so that

(e) having regard to all relevant factors, the balance of benefit and detriment overall is such that it is in the patient's best interests to subject him to the procedure.

4.167 Thus, as has already been seen,[431] a non-therapeutic sterilisation, male circumcision for ritual or other non-therapeutic reasons, a blood-test for forensic purposes, the donation of regenerative tissue (for example, bone-marrow), or a 'sex-change' or 'gender reassignment' operation may all be justified as being, overall, in the patient's best interests. So also ear piercing

---

[428] But see *In re T (A Minor) (Wardship: Medical Treatment)* [1997] 1 WLR 242 considered in para 4.72 above, para 4.201 below.   [429] See paras 4.94, 4.97, 4.98 above.   [430] See para 4.94 above.   [431] See paras 4.76, 4.148, 4.150 above.

and cosmetic surgery.[432] On the other hand female circumcision for religious, cultural or social reasons is not justifiable at common law.[433] Nor is ritual incision of the face.[434] Amputation of a child's hand as a punishment for theft cannot be justified on religious grounds.[435] Nor can amputation of a child's limb so as to exploit it for the purpose of gain, for example, by cutting off its foot so that it can earn a living begging.[436] Likewise the common law would surely not permit the removal from a child or incompetent adult of a non-regenerative organ (for example, a kidney) for the purpose of sale.[437]

G. Particular Cases

Reported cases cover a wide range of different forms of care and treatment. **4.168**
Thus, in addition to cases dealing with the blood-testing of children[438] and

---

[432] *Secretary, Department of Health and Community Services v JWB and SMB* (1992) 175 CLR 218, 297 *per* Deane J (parents 'plainly' able to consent to 'plastic surgery to correct serious disfigurement for purely cosmetic purposes' even though 'not "therapeutic" within the accepted meaning of that word'). To the same effect *Re a Teenager* (1988) 94 FLR 181, 212 *per* Cook J ('cosmetic surgery to a child with malformed features'); *Re Jane* (1988) 94 FLR 1, 31, but see *Secretary, Department of Health and Community Services v JWB and SMB* (1990) 14 FamLR 427, 448 *per* Nicholson CJ ('there may well be some limitations upon the power to consent to cosmetic surgery on a child, depending upon its purpose').

[433] *Secretary, Department of Health and Community Services v JWB and SMB* (1990) 14 FamLR 427, 448, (1992) 175 CLR 218, 242–243, 252.

[434] *R v Adesanya* (1974) *The Times* July 16, 17.

[435] *Secretary, Department of Health and Community Services v JWB and SMB* (1992) 175 CLR 218, 297.

[436] *Secretary, Department of Health and Community Services v JWB and SMB* (1990) 14 FamLR 427, 448 ('mutilation'), (1992) 175 CLR 218, 240.

[437] Thus, the common law rule. A number of socially controversial invasive procedures are regulated by statute. The Tattooing of Minors Act 1969 makes it a criminal offence to tattoo a minor 'except when the tattoo is performed for medical reasons'. The Prohibition of Female Circumcision Act 1985 makes female circumcision in all its forms a criminal offence unless it is either 'necessary for the physical or mental health of the person on whom it is performed' or 'performed for purposes connected with . . . labour or birth'. S 2 of the Act draws an interesting distinction between mental health and customary or ritual belief by providing that 'In determining . . . whether an operation is necessary for the mental health of a person, no account shall be taken of the effect on that person of any belief on the part of that or any other person that the operation is required as a matter of custom or ritual'. The Human Organ Transplants Act 1989 makes it a criminal offence to make or receive payment for the supply of an organ (as defined in s 7(2), that is any part of a human body . . . which, if wholly removed, cannot be replicated by the body) or to transplant an organ otherwise than between genetically related persons unless authorised by the Unrelated Life Transplant Regulatory Authority in accordance with the Human Organ Transplants (Unrelated Persons) Regulations 1989.

[438] *S v McC, W v W* [1972] AC 24; *In re F (A Minor) (Blood Tests: Parental Rights)* [1993] Fam 314; *Re L (A Minor) (Blood Tests)* [1996] 2 FCR 649; *In re H (A Minor) (Blood Tests: Parental Rights)* [1997] Fam 89; *Re R (a minor) (blood test: constraint)* [1998] 1 FCR 41.

with the general care of the handicapped child or adult,[439] there are reported cases dealing with: the therapeutic[440] and non-therapeutic sterilisation[441] of children and incompetent adults; the abortion[442] of children[443] and incompetent adults;[444] complications during the labour of children[445] and incompetent adult women;[446] the psychiatric assessment and treatment of children[447] and incompetent adults;[448] the forcefeeding of children[449] and incompetent adults[450] for the treatment of anorexia nervosa or other psychiatric illnesses; the administration of blood transfusions to child[451] and incompetent adult[452] Jehovah's Witnesses; the donation of bone-marrow by an

---

[439] *Re C (Mental Patient: Contact)* [1993] 1 FLR 940; *Cambridgeshire County Council v R (An Adult)* [1995] 1 FLR 50; *In re S (Hospital Patient: Court's Jurisdiction)* [1995] Fam 26, appeal dismissed [1996] Fam 1, subsequent substantive proceedings *In re S (Hospital patient: Foreign Curator)* [1996] Fam 23; *Re V (Declaration against Parents)* [1995] 2 FLR 1003.

[440] *Re E (A Minor) (Medical Treatment)* [1991] 2 FLR 585; *Re GF (Medical Treatment)* [1992] 1 FLR 293.

[441] *In re D (A Minor) (Wardship: Sterilisation)* [1976] Fam 185; *In re B (A Minor) (Wardship: Sterilisation)* [1988] AC 199; *T v T* [1988] Fam 52; *Re M (A Minor) (Wardship: Sterilisation)* [1988] 2 FLR 497; *Re P (A Minor) (Wardship: Sterilisation)* [1989] 1 FLR 182; *In re F (Mental Patient: Sterilisation)* [1990] 2 AC 1; *Re NK* (1990) Feb 28 (Ewbank J), (1990) Apr 4 (Scott Baker J); *Re W (Mental patient) (Sterilisation)* [1993] 1 FLR 381; *Re HG (Specific Issue Order: Sterilisation)* [1993] 1 FLR 587; *Re LC (Medical Treatment: Sterilisation)* [1997] 2 FLR 258.

[442] See paras 4.28, 4.31, 4.33 above for cases dealing with the interests of the foetus and its father.

[443] *Re P (A Minor)* [1986] 1 FLR 272; *Re B (Wardship: Abortion)* [1991] 2 FLR 426.

[444] *Re SG (Adult Mental Patient: Abortion)* [1991] 2 FLR 329.

[445] *A Metropolitan Borough Council v AB* [1997] 1 FLR 767.

[446] *In re T (Adult: Refusal of Treatment)* [1993] Fam 95; *Tameside and Glossop Acute Services Trust v CH* [1996] 1 FLR 762; *Norfolk and Norwich Healthcare (NHS) Trust v W* [1996] 2 FLR 613; *Rochdale Healthcare (NHS) Trust v C* [1997] 1 FCR 274; *Re L (Patient: Non-Consensual Treatment)* [1997] 2 FLR 837; *Re MB (Medical Treatment)* [1997] 2 FLR 426. For the procedure to be adopted in such cases see *Re MB*, ibid, 439, 445. For the proper approach to the issue of capacity in such cases see *Re MB*, ibid, 436–437. For the position where the mother is a competent adult see para 4.35 above.

[447] *In re R (A Minor) (Wardship: Consent to Treatment)* [1992] Fam 11; *Re K, W and H (Minors) (Medical Treatment)* [1993] 1 FLR 854; *South Glamorgan County Council v W and B* [1993] 1 FLR 574; *R v Kirklees Metropolitan Borough Council, ex p C* [1992] 2 FLR 117, [1993] 2 FLR 187; *A Metropolitan Borough Council v AB* [1997] 1 FLR 767.

[448] *Re H (Mental Patient: Diagnosis)* [1993] 1 FLR 28.

[449] *In re W (A Minor) (Medical Treatment: Court's Jurisdiction)* [1993] Fam 64; *Re C (Detention: Medical Treatment)* [1997] 2 FLR 180.

[450] *Riverside Mental Health NHS Trust v Fox* [1994] 1 FLR 614; *Re KB (Adult) (Mental Patient: Medical Treatment)* (1994) 19 BMLR 144; *B v Croydon Health Authority* [1995] Fam 133, affirming [1995] 1 FCR 332; *Re VS (Adult: Mental Disorder)* (1995) Aug 17 (Douglas Brown J), [1995] Med L Rev 292. For a case involving the forcefeeding of a competent adult prisoner see *Secretary of State for the Home Department v Robb* [1995] Fam 127.

[451] *Re E (A Minor) (Wardship: Medical Treatment)* [1993] 1 FLR 386; *Re S (A Minor) (Medical Treatment)* [1993] 1 FLR 376; *Re O (A Minor) (Medical Treatment)* [1993] 2 FLR 149; *Re R (A Minor) (Blood Transfusion)* [1993] 2 FLR 757; *Re S (A Minor) (Consent to Medical Treatment)* [1994] 2 FLR 1065.   [452] *In re T (Adult: Refusal of Treatment)* [1993] Fam 95.

incompetent adult;[453] the withholding of life-saving treatment (surgery,[454] a liver transplant,[455] haemodialysis (kidney dialysis[445a]), artificial ventilation,[456] cardio-pulmonary resuscitation,[457] and antibiotics[458]) from a child,[459] the handicapped[460] or the dying,[461] and the withdrawal of artificial nutrition and hydration from patients in a permanent (formerly called persistent) vegetative state[462] or in a vegetative, but not (on one view) strictly speaking a permanent vegetative, state.[463] There are also reported cases dealing with the circumstances in which detention for the purposes of treatment[464] or the application of restraint or the use of force[465] is permis-

---

[453] *In re Y (Mental Patient: Bone Marrow Donation)* [1997] Fam 110.

[454] *In re B (A Minor) (Wardship: Medical Treatment)* [1981] 1 WLR 1421.

[455] *In re T (A Minor) (Wardship: Medical Treatment)* [1997] 1 WLR 242.

[455a] *Re D* (1997) Nov 26 (Sir Stephen Brown P).

[456] *In re J (A Minor) (Wardship: Medical Treatment)* [1991] Fam 33; *In re J (A Minor) (Child in Care: Medical Treatment)* [1993] Fam 15; *Re C (A Baby)* [1996] 2 FLR 43; *Re C (a minor) (medical treatment)* [1998] 1 FCR 1.

[457] *Re R (Adult: Medical Treatment)* [1996] 2 FLR 99. The BMA has published guidance on cardio-pulmonary resuscitation: 'Decisions relating to Cardiopulmonary Resuscitation: A Statement from the BMA and RCN in association with the Resuscitation Council (UK)' (Mar 1993).   [458] *Re R (Adult: Medical Treatment)* [1996] 2 FLR 99.

[459] *In re T (A Minor) (Wardship: Medical Treatment)* [1997] 1 WLR 242. The Royal College of Paediatrics and Child Health has published guidance: 'Withholding or Withdrawing Life Saving Treatment in Children: A Framework for Practice' (Sept 1997).

[460] *In re B (A Minor) (Wardship: Medical Treatment)* [1981] 1 WLR 1421, reversing (1982) 3 FLR 117; *R v Arthur* (1981) 12 BMLR 1; *In re J (A Minor) (Wardship: Medical Treatment)* [1991] Fam 33; *In re J (A Minor) (Child in Care: Medical Treatment)* [1993] Fam 15; *Re C (A Baby)* [1996] 2 FLR 43; *Re R (Adult: Medical Treatment)* [1996] 2 FLR 99; *Re D* (1997) Nov 26 (Sir Stephen Brown P).

[461] *R v Bodkin Adams* (1957) Apr 8–9 (Devlin J), [1957] Crim LR 365; *In re C (A Minor) (Wardship: Medical Treatment)* [1990] Fam 26; *R v Cox* (1992) 12 BMLR 38; *Re C (a minor) (medical treatment)* [1998] 1 FCR 1. The BMA has published guidance: 'End of Life Decisions: Views of the BMA' (Sept 1996).

[462] *Airedale NHS Trust v Bland* [1993] AC 789; *Frenchay Healthcare National Health Service Trust v S* [1994] 1 WLR 601; *Re G (Persistent Vegetative State)* [1995] 2 FCR 46; *Swindon and Marlborough NHS Trust v S* (1994) *Guardian* Dec 10, [1995] Med L Rev 84; *Re C (Adult Patient: Restriction of Publicity after Death)* [1996] 2 FLR 251. The BMA has published guidance on PVS: 'BMA guidelines on treatment decisions for patients in persistent vegetative state' (revised June 1996).

[463] *Re D* (1997) 38 BMLR 1; *Re H (adult: incompetent)* (1997) 38 BMLR 11. See further paras 4.211, 4.215 below.

[464] *In re R (A Minor) (Wardship: Consent to Treatment)* [1992] Fam 11; *In re W (A Minor) (Medical Treatment: Court's Jurisdiction)* [1993] Fam 64; *South Glamorgan County Council v W and B* [1993] 1 FLR 574; *Re C (Detention: Medical Treatment)* [1997] 2 FLR 180. For the inter-relationship between the court's inherent power to order the detention of a child for the purposes of treatment and its limited power to make a secure accommodation order under the Children Act 1989, s 25, see *In re CB (A Minor) (Wardship: Local Authority)* [1981] 1 WLR 379, 387; *Re SW (A Minor) (Wardship: Jurisdiction)* [1986] 1 FLR 24; *South Glamorgan County Council v W and B* [1993] 1 FLR 574; *A Metropolitan Borough Council v AB* [1997] 1 FLR 767; *Re C (Detention: Medical Treatment)* [1997] 2 FLR 180. For the power of a parent, or a local authority having parental responsibility, to authorise the admission of a child to a secure

sible in relation to a non-compliant child[466] or incompetent adult[467] patient either under the Mental Health Act 1983, section 63,[468] or at common law.[469] Other procedures are considered mainly in the academic literature: male

unit or as a voluntary patient under the Mental Health Act 1983 see *Re K, W and H (Minors) (Medical Treatment)* [1993] 1 FLR 854 (parent—secure unit); *R v Kirklees Metropolitan Borough Council, ex p C* [1992] 2 FLR 117, [1993] 2 FLR 187 (local authority—voluntary patient), and, for the explanation of the underlying principle, *R v Rahman* (1985) 81 Cr App R 349, 353, 354; *R v Deputy Governor of Parkhurst Prison, ex p Hague* [1992] 1 AC 58, 162; *In re M (A Minor) (Secure Accommodation Order)* [1995] Fam 108, 117. For the older cases dealing with the common law power to restrain and detain, where appropriate for the purposes of treatment, a lunatic who is a danger either to himself or to others, see *Brookshaw v Hopkins* (1772) Lofft 240; *Anderdon v Burrows* (1830) 4 Car & P 210; *In re Shuttleworth* (1846) 9 QB 651; *In re Greenwood* (1855) 24 LJQB 148; *Fletcher v Fletcher* (1859) 1 El & El 420; *Scott v Wakem* (1862) 3 F & F 328; *Symm v Fraser* (1863) 3 F & F 859; *Townley v Rushforth* (1964) 62 LGR 95; *B v Forsey* [1988] SC(HL) 28, 38–39, 44–45, 52, 56, 59–60, 63, 68.

[465] *Riverside Mental Health NHS Trust v Fox* [1994] 1 FLR 614; *Re KB (Adult) (Mental Patient: Medical Treatment)* (1994) 19 BMLR 144; *Re S (A Minor) (Consent to Medical Treatment)* [1994] 2 FLR 1065; *B v Croydon Health Authority* [1995] Fam 133; *Re VS (Adult: Mental Disorder)* (1995) Aug 17 (Douglas Brown J), [1995] Med L Rev 292; *Tameside and Glossop Acute Services Trust v CH* [1996] 1 FLR 762; *Norfolk and Norwich Healthcare (NHS) Trust v W* [1996] 2 FLR 613; *Rochdale Healthcare (NHS) Trust v C* [1997] 1 FCR 274; *A Metropolitan Borough Council v AB* [1997] 1 FLR 767; *Re L (Patient: Non-Consensual Treatment)* [1997] 2 FLR 837; *Re C (Detention: Medical Treatment)* [1997] 2 FLR 180; *Re MB (Medical Treatment)* [1997] 2 FLR 426, 439; *Re R (A Minor) (Blood Test: Constraint)* [1988] 1 FCR 41; *Re D* (1997) Nov 26 (Sir Stephen Brown P).

[466] *In re R (A Minor) (Wardship: Consent to Treatment)* [1992] Fam 11; *In re W (A Minor) (Medical Treatment: Court's Jurisdiction)* [1993] Fam 64; *South Glamorgan County Council v W and B* [1993] 1 FLR 574; *Re S (A Minor) (Consent to Medical Treatment)* [1994] 2 FLR 1065; *A Metropolitan Borough Council v AB* [1997] 1 FLR 767; *Re C (Detention: Medical Treatment)* [1997] 2 FLR 180; *Re R (A Minor) (Blood Test: Constraint)* [1988] 1 FCR 41.

[467] *Riverside Mental Health NHS Trust v Fox* [1994] 1 FLR 614; *Re KB (Adult) (Mental Patient: Medical Treatment)* (1994) 19 BMLR 144; *B v Croydon Health Authority* [1995] Fam 133; *Re VS (Adult: Mental Disorder)* (1995) Aug 17 (Douglas Brown J), [1995] Med L Rev 292, *Tameside and Glossop Acute Services Trust v CH* [1996] 1 FLR 762; *Norfolk and Norwich Healthcare (NHS) Trust v W* [1996] 2 FLR 613; *Rochdale Healthcare (NHS) Trust v C* [1997] 1 FCR 274; *Re L (Patient: Non-Consensual Treatment)* [1997] 2 FLR 837; *Re MB (Medical Treatment)* [1997] 2 FLR 426, 439; *Re D* (1997) Nov 26 (Sir Stephen Brown P).

[468] *Riverside Mental Health NHS Trust v Fox* [1994] 1 FLR 614; *Re KB (Adult) (Mental Patient: Medical Treatment)* (1994) 19 BMLR 144; *B v Croydon Health Authority* [1995] Fam 133; *Re VS (Adult: Mental Disorder)* (1995) Aug 17 (Douglas Brown J), [1995] Med L Rev 292; *Tameside and Glossop Acute Services Trust v CH* [1996] 1 FLR 762.

[469] *In re R (A Minor) (Wardship: Consent to Treatment)* [1992] Fam 11; *In re W (A Minor) (Medical Treatment: Court's Jurisdiction)* [1993] Fam 64; *South Glamorgan County Council v W and B* [1993] 1 FLR 574; *Re S (A Minor) (Consent to Medical Treatment)* [1994] 2 FLR 1065; *Norfolk and Norwich Healthcare (NHS) Trust v W* [1996] 2 FLR 613; *Rochdale Healthcare (NHS) Trust v C* [1997] 1 FCR 274; *A Metropolitan Borough Council v AB* [1997] 1 FLR 767; *Re L (Patient: Non-Consensual Treatment)* [1997] 2 FLR 837; *Re C (Detention: Medical Treatment)* [1997] 2 FLR 180; *Re MB (Medical Treatment)* [1997] 2 FLR 426, 439; *Re R (A Minor) (Blood Test: Constraint)* [1998] 1 FCR 41. For the court's approach in deciding whether or not to adopt coercive measures, and the safeguards to be applied, see *Re C (Detention: Medical Treatment)* [1997] 2 FLR 180, 196–199 (and see the form of the order at 199–201); *Re MB (Medical Treatment* [1997] 2 FLR 426, 445. For the problem presented

circumcision;[470] female circumcision;[471] 'sex-change' or 'gender reassignment' operations;[472] ear piercing and cosmetic surgery;[473] ritual incision of the face;[474] and tattooing.[475]

Six topics require more detailed consideration: sterilisation; abortion; the treatment of the mentally disordered; blood-testing; organ and tissue donation; and issues of life and death. **4.169**

1. Sterilisation

Therapeutic and Non-Therapeutic Sterilisation

The House of Lords has dismissed the suggested distinction between thera- **4.170** peutic and non-therapeutic sterilisations as being 'meaningless', 'irrelevant', 'not helpful', and giving rise to 'arid semantic debate'.[476] The distinction[477] is, nonetheless, of importance for at least two reasons. In the first place, whereas the prior sanction of the court is not required for a therapeutic sterilisation[478] (unless, that is, the patient is a child who happens to be a ward of court already[479]), it is required for any non-therapeutic sterilisation of a child or adult incompetent.[480] Secondly, although there may be circumstances[481] in

---

by the incompetent patient who is unwilling to submit to treatment see *Re D* (1997) Nov 26 (Sir Stephen Brown P) (49–year old chronic but fluctuating psychotic suffering from chronic renal failure at near-end stage and high blood pressure requiring haemodialysis for four hours three or four times each week to keep him alive but unable because of his mental condition to understand the need for treatment and strongly objecting to procedure: held lawful in the last resort 'not to impose haemodialysis upon him in circumstances in which in the opinion of the medical practitioners responsible for such treatment it is not reasonably practicable so to do', the judge accepting that in the circumstances dialysis, which requires the co-operation of the patient, could only be performed under general anaesthetic which was neither practicable nor desirable in a patient suffering D's disabilities).

[470] See paras 4.74, 4.76, 4.77, 4.80, 4.148, 4.150, 4.167 above. The BMA has published guidance: 'Circumcision of Male Infants: Guidance for Doctors' (Sept 1996). So too has the GMC: 'Guidance for Doctors who are asked to Circumcise Male Children' (Sept 1997).

[471] See paras 4.05, 4.74, 4.76, 4.138, 4.167 above. The BMA has published guidance: 'Guidance for Doctors Approached by Victims of Female Genital Mutilation' (Jan 1996).

[472] See paras 4.74, 4.79, 4.150, 4.167 above.   [473] See para 4.167 above.

[474] See para 4.167 above.   [475] See paras 4.05, 4.167 above.

[476] *In re B (A Minor) (Wardship: Sterilisation)* [1988] AC 199, 204, 205, 211.

[477] For the most recent and comprehensive judicial consideration of the distinction between therapeutic and non-therapeutic sterilisation see *Secretary, Department of Health and Community Services v JWB and SMB* (1992) 175 CLR 218, esp, 243, 250, 253, 269, 274, 296–297, 306. See also *Re E (A Minor) (Medical Treatment)* [1991] 2 FLR 585, 587 where Sir Stephen Brown P referred to the 'clear distinction' between therapeutic and non-therapeutic sterilisations.

[478] *Re E (A Minor) (Medical Treatment)* [1991] 2 FLR 585; *Re GF (Medical Treatment)* [1992] 1 FLR 293.   [479] *In re D (A Minor) (Wardship: Sterilisation)* [1976] Fam 185, 196.

[480] *In re F (Mental Patient: Sterilisation)* [1990] 2 AC 1.

[481] By analogy with *In re R (A Minor) (Wardship: Consent to Treatment)* [1992] Fam 11; *In re W (A Minor) (Medical Treatment: Court's Jurisdiction)* [1993] Fam 64.

which the court would authorise the therapeutic sterilisation of a child who either has, or may in later years have, the capacity to make her own choice (for example if the removal of a cancerous womb was necessary to save the life of a 'Gillick competent' girl who was refusing her consent to a hysterectomy), the court will not subject such a child to a non-therapeutic sterilisation.[482]

Form of Procedure

4.171 Details of the procedure to be adopted in applications to the court are set out in the Official Solicitor's Practice Note.[483]

Therapeutic Sterilisations

4.172 In cases where it is appropriate to invoke the court's assistance at all, it will readily authorise, in the case of a child,[484] or declare lawful, in the case of an adult incompetent,[485] an operation (for example, a hysterectomy) required for genuine therapeutic reasons, even if such an operation will inevitably result in the sterilisation of the patient.

Non-Therapeutic Sterilisations

4.173 The court will never sanction a sterilisation for eugenic purposes.[486] In the case of a non-therapeutic sterilisation for contraceptive purposes the court adopts a rigorous approach; the kind of considerations which the court is likely to have in mind are set out in paragraphs 8 and 10 of the Official Solicitor's Practice Note.[487] The court will not sanction the non-therapeutic sterilisation of a girl[488] who has, or may in later years have, the capacity to

---

[482] *In re D (A Minor) (Wardship: Sterilisation)* [1976] Fam 185, and see further paras 4.80, 4.95 above.

[483] Practice Note (Official Solicitor: Sterilisation) [1996] 2 FLR 111, issued June 1996 following the decision in *Re G (Adult Patient: Publicity)* [1995] 2 FLR 528, and replacing with modifications the earlier Practice Notes: Practice Note (Official Solicitor: Sterilisation) [1989] 2 FLR 447 (issued Sept 1989, following the decision in *In re F (Mental Patient: Sterilisation)* [1990] 2 AC 1), Practice Note (Official Solicitor: Sterilisation) [1990] 2 FLR 530 (issued Sept 1990, following the decision in *Practice Note (Mental Patient: Sterilisation), J v C* [1990] 1 WLR 1248), Practice Note (Official Solicitor: Sterilisation) [1993] 3 All ER 222, [1993] 2 FLR 222 (issued May 1993, following the decision in *Re HG (Specific Issue Order: Sterilisation)* [1993] 1 FLR 587). See further para 4.132 above.

[484] *Re E (A Minor) (Medical Treatment)* [1991] 2 FLR 585.

[485] *Re GF (Medical Treatment)* [1992] 1 FLR 293.

[486] *In re B (A Minor) (Wardship: Sterilisation)* [1988] AC 199, 202, 204, 207, 212; *Re M (A Minor) (Wardship: Sterilisation)* [1988] 2 FLR 497.

[487] Practice Note (Official Solicitor: Sterilisation) [1996] 2 FLR 111.

[488] It is a matter for comment, and a revealing insight into societal attitudes to gender, sexuality and contraception, that all the known cases of sterilisation relate to girls: the question of male sterilisation seems never to arise.

make her own choice whether or not to be sterilised.[489] Where the child is severely mentally handicapped, will never have the capacity to decide about sterilisation for herself and is likely to be exposed to the risk of a pregnancy which she would not understand and the consequences of which would be harmful to her, and other contraceptive methods are inappropriate, the court may come to the view that a sterilisation so as to prevent future pregnancy is necessary in her own best interests.[490] So in the case of an incompetent adult.[491]

2. Abortion

Abortion is not a procedure which of its nature requires the sanction of the court,[492] unless the patient is a child who is already a ward of court.[493]   **4.174**

In cases where it is appropriate to invoke the court's assistance at all, it will authorise or declare lawful (as the case may be) an abortion if satisfied that the requirements of the Abortion Act 1967, as amended by the Human Fertilisation and Embryology Act 1990, are met and that an abortion is in the best interests of the pregnant child[494] or adult incompetent.[495]   **4.175**

As has already been seen,[496] neither the unborn child, nor its father, nor the husband of its mother, can obtain an injunction to restrain the performance of a lawful abortion to which the mother has consented. It make no difference that the mother is either a child or an adult incompetent; it is quite clear[497] that the only questions which arise in such a case are, first, whether the   **4.176**

---

[489] *In re D (A Minor) (Wardship: Sterilisation)* [1976] Fam 185 (11–year old girl suffering from Sotos syndrome, of dull normal intelligence, whose future prospects were unpredictable, but with sufficient capacity to marry and likely to be able to make her own choice in later years).

[490] *In re B (A Minor) (Wardship: Sterilisation)* [1988] AC 199 (17–year old girl with mental age of 5 or 6); *Re M (A Minor) (Wardship: Sterilisation)* [1988] 2 FLR 497 (17–year old girl suffering from Fragile X Syndrome with an emotional and psychological age of 5 or 6); *Re P (A Minor) (Wardship: Sterilisation)* [1989] 1 FLR 182 (17–year old girl with mental age of 6); *Re HG (Specific Issue Order: Sterilisation)* [1993] 1 FLR 587 (17–year old severely epileptic girl with mental age of an infant).

[491] *T v T* [1988] Fam 52; *In re F (Mental Patient: Sterilisation)* [1990] 2 AC 1; *Re W (Mental patient) (Sterilisation)* [1993] 1 FLR 381. In *Re LC (Medical Treatment: Sterilisation)* [1997] 2 FLR 258 the court refused to make an order.

[492] *Re SG (Adult Mental Patient: Abortion)* [1991] 2 FLR 329.

[493] *Re G-U (A Minor) (Wardship)* [1984] FLR 811.

[494] *Re P (A Minor)* [1986] 1 FLR 272; *Re B (Wardship: Abortion)* [1991] 2 FLR 426.

[495] *Re SG (Adult Mental Patient: Abortion)* [1991] 2 FLR 329.

[496] See paras 4.28, 4.31 above.

[497] *Re P (A Minor)* [1986] 1 FLR 272; *Re SG (Adult Mental Patient: Abortion)* [1991] 2 FLR 329; *Re B (Wardship: Abortion)* [1991] 2 FLR 426.

requirements of the Abortion Act 1967 are met and, secondly, whether an abortion is in the best interests of the mother.

3. Treatment of the Mentally Disordered

4.177 Save to the limited extent to which particular matters are regulated by statute, or, in the case of children, by the Crown's prerogative power as parens patriae, the treatment of the mentally disordered, whether for their mental disorder or otherwise, is regulated by the general principles of the common law.

Statutory Exceptions

4.178 There are three statutory exceptions. All are confined to persons suffering from mental disorder as that expression is defined in the Mental Health Act 1983, section 1(2). Two relate to specific procedures: the taking of blood samples,[498] and certain forms of treatment for mental disorder.[499]

General Provision

4.179 There is one provision of general application. Section 63 of the Mental Health Act 1983 (which applies by virtue of section 56 of the Act only to patients liable to be detained under the Act) provides:

> The consent of a patient shall not be required for any medical treatment given to him for the mental disorder from which he is suffering, not being treatment falling within section 57 or 58 above,[500] if the treatment is given by or under the direction of the responsible medical officer.

Section 145(1) of the Act provides that:

> 'medical treatment' includes nursing, and also includes care, habilation and rehabilitation under medical supervision . . .

'Medical treatment' in section 63 means treatment which, taken as a whole, is calculated to alleviate or prevent a deterioration of the mental disorder from which the patient is suffering, and includes a range of acts ancillary to the core treatment, including those which prevent the patient from harming himself or which alleviate the symptoms of the disorder.[501]

---

[498] The Family Law Reform Act 1969, s 21(4) (persons suffering from mental disorder).
[499] For the treatments in question see the Mental Health Act 1983, s 57(1)(a) (surgical operations for destroying brain tissue or the functioning of brain tissue), s 57(1)(b) (surgical implantation of hormones for the purpose of reducing male sexual drive), s 58(1)(a) (electro-convulsive therapy), s 58(1)(b) (administration of medicine—as to which see *B v Croydon Health Authority* [1995] Fam 133, 137–138). See also the Mental Health Act 1983, ss 56, 59–62, 64.   [500] See para 4.178 above.
[501] *B v Croydon Health Authority* [1995] Fam 133, 138–139, 140, affirming [1995] 1 FCR 332.

[R]elieving symptoms is just as much a part of treatment as relieving the underlying cause.[502]

'Medical treatment' in section 63 thus includes forcible feeding for the treatment of anorexia nervosa[503] or other psychiatric illnesses[504] and inducing labour and performing a caesarian section on a pregnant paranoid schizophrenic where effective treatment of the schizophrenia required that the patient give birth to a live baby and resume medication necessarily interrupted by her pregnancy,[505] including, if necessary, restraint and the use of reasonable force.[506]

4. Blood-Testing

Consent to Blood-Testing

Consent to the taking of blood samples is now regulated by statute.[507] In addition the court can authorise the taking of a blood sample from a child,[508] though not from a competent adult.[509]   **4.180**

Blood-Testing of Children

The court can authorise the taking of a blood sample from a child even if it cannot be shown that a blood-test will be in its best interests, unless it is satisfied that it would be against the child's interests.[510] In the case of an older   **4.181**

---

[502] *Re KB (Adult) (Mental Patient: Medical Treatment)* (1994) 19 BMLR 144, 146 *per* Ewbank J approved *B v Croydon Health Authority* [1995] Fam 133, 139, 141.
[503] *Riverside Mental Health NHS Trust v Fox* [1994] 1 FLR 614; *Re KB (Adult) (Mental Patient: Medical Treatment)* (1994) 19 BMLR 144; *B v Croydon Health Authority* [1995] Fam 133, affirming [1995] 1 FCR 332.
[504] *Re VS (Adult: Mental Disorder)* (1995) Aug 17 (Douglas Brown J), [1995] Med L Rev 292. Contrast *Secretary of State for the Home Department v Robb* [1995] Fam 127 (forcefeeding of competent adult prisoner).
[505] *Tameside and Glossop Acute Services Trust v CH* [1996] 1 FLR 762, 771–774. Contrast *In re C (Adult: Refusal of Treatment)* [1994] 1 WLR 290 (schizophrenic held entitled to refuse consent to amputation of gangrenous leg) where the gangrene was 'entirely unconnected' with the mental disorder: *B v Croydon Health Authority* [1995] Fam 133, 139.
[506] *Tameside and Glossop Acute Services Trust v CH* [1996] 1 FLR 762, 771, 774. For the common law power to use restraint and reasonable force see para 4.168 above.
[507] The Family Law Reform Act 1969, s 21(1) (competent adults), s 21(2) (minors who have attained the age of 16), s 21(3) (minors under the age of 16), s 21(4) (persons suffering from mental disorder within the meaning of the Mental Health Act 1983). S 8 of the Act does not apply to the taking of a blood sample: *In re W (A Minor) (Medical Treatment: Court's Jurisdiction)* [1993] Fam 64, 92.
[508] On the question whether, in the case of a child under the age of 16, it should do so without the consent referred to in the Family Law Reform Act 1969, s 21(3), see *S v McC, W v W* [1972] AC 24, 44; *In re F (A Minor) (Blood Tests: Parental Rights)* [1993] Fam 314, 318; *In re H (A Minor) (Blood Tests: Parental Rights)* [1997] Fam 89, 100–101; *Re R (a minor) (blood test: constraint)* [1998] 1 FCR 41.   [509] *S v McC, W v W* [1972] AC 24, 43.
[510] *S v McC, W v W* [1972] AC 24; *In re F (A Minor) (Blood Tests: Parental Rights)* [1993] Fam 314, 318; *Re L (A Minor) (Blood Tests)* [1996] 2 FCR 649, 653; *In re H (A Minor) (Blood Tests: Parental Rights)* [1997] Fam 89, 103–104. For the approach adopted by the court see

child, however, the court will not order a blood-test against the child's will unless it would 'clearly' be in the child's interests.[511] Similar principles would appear to apply to the giving of consent[512] by the parent or other person having the care and control of the child.[513]

5. Organ and Tissue Donation

4.182 The donation of organs, tissues or body fluids[514] is not illegal, in the sense of being, as such, either prohibited by law or criminal. Transplants of organs (that is, as defined in section 7(2), 'any part of a human body . . . which, if wholly removed, cannot be replicated by the body') are regulated by the Human Organ Transplants Act 1989.[515]

Non-Regenerative Organs and Regenerative Tissue or Body Fluids

4.183 There is (quite apart from the fact that the distinction is drawn for the purposes of the criminal law by the Human Organ Transplants Act 1989) an important distinction between the donation of a non-regenerative organ (for example, a kidney) and the donation of regenerative tissue or body fluids (for example, bone marrow or blood). The donation of regenerative tissue or body fluids by a child or incompetent adult (for example, bone marrow) can, in appropriate circumstances, satisfy the best interests test. Whether the donation of a non-regenerative organ by a child or incompetent adult can ever satisfy the best interests test, and would therefore ever be sanctioned by the court, is an unresolved and very difficult question, which must be open to considerable doubt.[516]

In re H (A Minor) (Blood Tests: Parental Rights) [1997] Fam 89, 104–108; *Re R (a minor) (blood test: constraint)* [1988] 1 FCR 41. For the approach adopted by the court in relation to testing for HIV see *Re O (Minors) (Medical Examination)* [1993] 1 FLR 860; *Re HIV Tests* [1994] 2 FLR 116.

[511] *In re L (An Infant)* [1968] P 119, 140; *B(BR) v B(J)* [1968] P 466, 469, 473–474, 481; *S v McC, W v W* [1972] AC 24, 45.

[512] Under the Family Law Reform Act 1969, s 21(3). Query whether, in the light of ss 21(1), 21(2) and 21(3), a parent can give a valid consent in the case of a child who has attained the age of 16.   [513] *S v McC, W v W* [1972] AC 24, 44, 45.

[514] Useful general discussions are to be found in Kennedy and Grubb, *Medical Law: Text with Materials* (2nd edn, 1994), 1081–1087; Mason and McCall Smith, *Law and Medical Ethics* (4th edn, 1994), 291–300; Brazier, *Medicine, Patients and the Law* (2nd edn, 1992), 395–402; Dyer (ed), *Doctors, Patients and the Law* (1992), 120–126; Meyers, *The Human Body and the Law* (2nd edn, 1990), 198–203, 206–208; Skegg, *Law, Ethics, and Medicine* (1990), 60–68. The GMC has published guidance: 'Guidance for Doctors on Transplantation of Organs from Live Donors' (Nov 1992).

[515] The Act makes it a criminal offence to make or receive payment for the supply of an organ or to transplant an organ otherwise than between genetically related persons unless authorised by the Unrelated Life Transplant Regulatory Authority in accordance with the Human Organ Transplants (Unrelated Persons) Regulations 1989.

[516] Consider, for example, the views expressed by Kennedy and Grubb (n 514 above), 1086–1087; Mason and McCall Smith (n 514 above), 295–296; Brazier (n 514 above), 398

Donation by Children

The extent to which a child or its parent can validly consent to the donation **4.184** of organs, tissues or body fluids is obscure. Section 8 of the Family Law Reform Act 1969 does not extend to the donation of organs, or of blood or other bodily substances, for none of these procedures constitutes either treatment or diagnosis.[517] Whatever may be the position in strict legal theory, it has been said to be 'inconceivable' that any doctor should proceed with an organ transplant in the case of a child donor without the consent of both the child and its parents.[518]

Need to Involve the Court

The prior sanction of the court is required for the donation of regenerative **4.185** tissue (bone marrow) by a child or incompetent adult.[519] Assuming that the court would ever be prepared to sanction such procedure, the prior sanction of the court will also be required for the donation of a non-regenerative organ (for example, a kidney) by a child or incompetent adult.[520]

Best Interests

Consistently with principle, the determining criterion is the best interests of **4.186** the donor. The interests of the potential recipient, however compelling, are relevant only insofar as they further the interests of the donor.[521]

> The test to be applied in a case such as this is to ask whether the evidence shows that it is in the best interests of the [donor] for such procedures to take place. The fact that such a process would obviously benefit the [potential recipient] is not relevant unless, as a result of the [donor] helping the [recipient] in that way, the best interests of the [donor] are served. The approach is as set out in *In re F (Mental Patient: Sterilisation)* [1990] 2 AC 1 . . . The lawfulness of the action depends upon whether the treatment is in the best interests of the patient . . . This case is different from the case of *In re*

(children), 399 (incompetent adults); Dyer (ed) (n 514 above), 124; Meyers (n 514 above), 203, 208; Skegg (n 514 above), 61–62, 68. See also the recommendations of the Law Commission in: Consultation Paper No 129, Mentally Incapacitated Adults and Decision-Making, Medical Treatment and Research, 1993, para 6.9; Report Law Com No 231, Mental Incapacity, 1995, para 6.5. See further para 4.192 below.

[517] *In re W (A Minor) (Medical Treatment: Court's Jurisdiction)* [1993] Fam 64, 78, 83, 92, 94.
[518] ibid, 78–79 *per* Lord Donaldson of Lymington MR.
[519] *In re Y (Mental Patient: Bone Marrow Donation)* [1997] Fam 110, 116. Query in relation to donations of blood or other regenerative bodily fluids.
[520] *In re F (Mental Patient: Sterilisation)* [1990] 2 AC 1, 19, 33, 40; *In re W (A Minor) (Medical Treatment: Court's Jurisdiction)* [1993] Fam 64, 79, 94.
[521] See paras. 4.153–4.157 above. Thus it would seem that it cannot be lawful to take tissue from a donor who is in an irreversible coma or who is unconscious and dying: compare the problem of the pregnant woman in a coma considered in para 4.34 above.

F (Mental Patient: Sterilisation) because it involves the concept of donation of bone marrow by a donor who is incapable of giving consent where a significant benefit will flow to another person. There was no other person in *In re F* who would have benefitted directly as a result of the declaration sought, the benefits of sterilisation attaching solely to the mentally incapacitated subject of the application. Nonetheless, I am satisfied that the root question remains the same, namely, whether the procedures here envisaged will benefit the [donor] and accordingly benefits which may flow to the [potential recipient] are relevant only insofar as they have a positive effect upon the best interests of the [donor].[522]

4.187 Decisions in the United States of America[523] are important because of the reliance placed in the only English case which has yet been decided[524] upon the reasoning in a recent decision of the Supreme Court of Illinois.[525]

4.188 The American authorities identify, with varying degrees of enthusiasm or scepticism, five factors potentially relevant to the question of whether or not the donation of an organ or tissue is in the best interests of a child or adult incompetent donor:[526]

(1) If the potential recipient dies as a result of the transplant not taking place:

    (a) The adverse emotional or psychological effect on the donor (where the recipient is a sibling with whom the donor has a strong identification, or upon whom the donor is emotionally or psychologically dependent), whether that adverse effect is caused by (i) the mere fact of the sibling's death or (ii) the fact that the relationship no longer continues.

    (b) The loss of a prospective carer for the donor after the donor's parents are dead.

    (c) Feelings of guilt on the part of the donor.

---

[522] *In re Y (Mental Patient: Bone Marrow Donation)* [1997] Fam 110, 113 *per* Connell J.

[523] *Strunk v Strunk* (1969) 445 SW 2d 145 (Court of Appeals of Kentucky, donation of kidney by adult incompetent authorised); *Hart v Brown* (1972) 289 A 2d 386 (Superior Court of Connecticut, donation of kidney by child authorised); *Re Richardson* (1973) 284 So 2d 185 (Court of Appeal of Louisiana, donation of kidney by child refused); *Lausier v Pescinski* (1975) 226 NW 2d 180 (Supreme Court of Wisconsin, donation of kidney by adult incompetent refused); *Little v Little* (1979) 576 SW 2d 493 (Court of Civil Appeals of Texas, donation of kidney by child authorised); *Curran v Bosze* (1990) 566 NE 2d 1319 (Supreme Court of Illinois, donation of bone marrow by children refused).

[524] *In re Y (Mental Patient: Bone Marrow Donation)* [1997] Fam 110, 113–114.

[525] *Curran v Bosze* (1990) 566 NE 2d 1319, containing full discussions, 1322–1326 of whether the relevant test was best interests or substituted judgment (holding, 1331 that the test was best interests), 1326–1332 of the previous American case-law and, 1332–1345 of a substantial body of evidence directed to the risks and benefits to the donor of a bone marrow transplant.

[526] These may usefully be compared with the factors referred to in para 4.152 above identified in English cases.

(2) If the transplant does take place

    (d) The increased happiness and gratification of, and psychological benefit to, the donor from having been able to save another person's life.

    (e) The fact that the donor is better off in a family that is happy (because the recipient is alive) than in a family that is distressed (because the potential recipient has died).

The approach adopted in the American cases accords, broadly speaking, with English law, though, consistently with principle[527] (and, indeed, to an extent recognised in the American cases), factors (a)(i), (c) and (d) cannot be relevant unless the donor has sufficient cognitive and social awareness to be able to understand the abstract concept of death, understands that he is in a position to ameliorate the recipient's condition and in fact wishes to do so.

The critical task is to evaluate the emotional, psychological and social effects **4.189** on the donor of what is proposed[528] In the typical case,[529] the benefits to the donor which have to be shown if the best interests test is to be satisfied will be found, if at all, in the pre-existing family relationships between the donor, the potential recipient and other members of their family; the critical factor will be proof that there will be emotional, psychological or social benefits to the donor in maintaining an existing, close family relationship which will be interrupted or lost if the donation does not take place.[530]

The Balancing Exercise

Those benefits then have to be balanced against the possible disadvantages[531] **4.190** to the donor. The best interests balancing exercise has to be performed by considering (a) if the transplant takes place, (i) the psychological and other benefits to the donor, including any enhancement of his relationships with the potential recipient and other members of his family, balanced against (ii) the medical risks and other possible disadvantages of the procedure; and (b) if the transplant does not take place, (i) the psychological and other detriments to

---

[527] See paras 4.151, 4.152, 4.159 above.

[528] *In re Y (Mental Patient: Bone Marrow Donation)* [1997] Fam 110, 116.

[529] As in ibid, where, on the evidence, factor (b) was not material, where the patient's low level of cognitive and social awareness, and lack of ability to understand both her own plight and that of the potential recipient, meant that factors (a)(i), (c) and (d) could not be relevant and where, for the same reason, there could not be any question of the patient benefitting from the performance by her of any perceived moral, social or civic obligation.

[530] ibid, 114–116, adopting, 113–114 the approach of Calvo J in *Curran v Bosze* (1990) 566 NE 2d 1319, 1331, 1343–1344, 1345.

[531] For example as in *In re Y (Mental Patient: Bone Marrow Donation)* [1997] Fam 110, 115–116.

the donor, including any damage to or loss of his relationships with the potential recipient and other members of his family, balanced against (ii) the avoidance of the medical risks and other possible disadvantages of the procedure.

> I must look therefore at the situation of the [donor] and ask whether the proposals placed before the court would benefit her and, if yes, whether those benefits outweigh any possible detriment to her.[532]

Bone Marrow Transplants

4.191 Applying these principles the court has declared lawful the donation of bone marrow by an adult incompetent.[533]

Other Procedures

4.192 Whether the court would ever be willing to authorise (in the case of a child) or to declare lawful (in the case of an adult incompetent) any procedure more serious than a donation of bone marrow must be open to considerable doubt.[534]

> I should perhaps emphasise that this is a rather unusual case and that the family of the [potential recipient] and the [donor] are a particularly close family. It is doubtful that this case would act as a useful precedent in cases where the surgery involved is more intrusive than in this case, where the evidence shows that the bone marrow harvested is speedily regenerated and that a healthy individual can donate as much as two pints with no long term consequences at all. Thus, the bone marrow donated by the [donor] will cause her no loss and she will suffer no real long term risk[535]

6. Life and Death

(i) *General Principles*

The Duty to Care

4.193 A doctor (or layman) who has assumed the responsibility of caring for a helpless patient thereby becomes subject to a duty to care for him. The breach of that duty, if it leads to the death of the patient, renders the carer, depending upon his mens rea, liable to prosecution for manslaughter or murder.[536] The critical inquiry is, therefore, as to the duration and extent

---

[532] *In re Y (Mental Patient: Bone Marrow Donation)* [1997] Fam 110, 114 *per* Connell J.
[533] ibid.   [534] See para 4.183 above.
[535] *In re Y (Mental Patient: Bone Marrow Donation)* [1997] Fam 110, 116 *per* Connell J.
[536] *R v Gibbins* (1918) 13 Cr App R 134; *R v Stone* [1977] QB 354; *In re F (Mental Patient: Sterilisation)* [1990] 2 AC 1, 55–56, 77; *Airedale NHS Trust v Bland* [1993] AC 789, 858, 866, 881, 893; *Swindon and Marlborough NHS Trust v S* (1994) *Guardian* Dec 10, [1995] Med L Rev 84.

of the duty, because that determines whether or not there has been a breach of duty.

The duty to care does not oblige a doctor or other carer to pursue invasive treatment or artificial feeding with a view to prolonging life at all costs and regardless of the circumstances.[537]   **4.194**

The crucial question

In determining the duration and extent of the duty, the question which has to be asked is not, 'Is it in the best interests of the patient that he should die?' The question which has to be asked is, 'Is it in the best interests of the patient that treatment (feeding) which has the effect of artificially prolonging his life should be continued?' If the answer to that question is that the patient's best interests no longer require that it should be, then the withdrawal of the treatment will be lawful; indeed, the continuation of the treatment will be unlawful.[538] This is so even though it may not be possible to say that it is in the patient's best interests that the treatment should be ended.[539]   **4.195**

> [I]t cannot be too strongly emphasised that the court never sanctions steps to terminate life. That would be unlawful. There is no question of approving, even in the case of the most horrendous disability, a course aimed at terminating life or accelerating death. The court is concerned only with the circumstances in which steps should not be taken to prolong life. . . . [T]he court in these cases has to decide, not whether to end life, but whether to prolong it by treatment without which death would ensue from natural causes. . . . I repeat, because of its importance, the debate here is not about terminating life but solely whether to withhold treatment designed to prevent death from natural causes.[540]

It is crucial for the understanding of this question that the question itself should be correctly formulated. The question is not whether the doctor should take a

---

[537] *In re J (A Minor) (Wardship: Medical Treatment)* [1991] Fam 33, 52, 54, 55; *Airedale NHS Trust v Bland* [1993] AC 789, 864, 865, 867. The BMA has published guidance on various relevant topics: 'End of Life Decisions: Views of the BMA' (Sept 1996); 'Decisions relating to Cardiopulmonary Resuscitation: A statement from the BMA and RCN in association with the Resuscitation Council (UK)' (Mar 1993); 'BMA guidelines on treatment decisions for patients in persistent vegetative state' (revised June 1996). So also the Royal College of Paediatrics and Child Health: 'Withholding or Withdrawing Life Saving Treatment in Children: A Framework for Practice' (Sept 1997).

[538] *Airedale NHS Trust v Bland* [1993] AC 789, 883–884, 885, 897, 898. It follows that, if the *patient's* best interests no longer require that his life be artificially prolonged, he cannot lawfully be kept alive with a view to benefitting third parties, e g for the purpose of enabling his organs or tissues to be harvested (whether before or after his death) or for the purpose of obtaining a financial or fiscal benefit: see further paras 4.156, 4.186 above. If the patient is pregnant with a viable foetus: see paras 4.33–4.34 above.

[539] *Airedale NHS Trust v Bland* [1993] AC 789, 857–858, 868, 873, 883–885, 896–898.

[540] *In re J (A Minor) (Wardship: Medical Treatment)* [1991] Fam 33, 53, 54 *per* Taylor LJ. To the same effect *Re R (Adult: Medical Treatment)* [1996] 2 FLR 99, 107 *per* Sir Stephen Brown P.

course which will kill his patient, or even take a course which has the effect of accelerating his death. The question is whether the doctor should or should not continue to provide his patient with medical treatment or care which, if continued, will prolong his patient's life. The question is sometimes put in striking or emotional terms, which can be misleading. For example, in the case of a life support system, it is sometimes asked: should a doctor be entitled to switch it off, or to pull the plug? And then it is asked: can it be in the best interests of the patient that a doctor should be able to switch the life support system off, when this will inevitably result in the patient's death? Such an approach has rightly been criticised as misleading . . . This is because the question is not whether it is in the best interests of the patient that he should die. The question is whether it is in the best interests of the patient that his life should be prolonged by the continuance of this form of medical treatment or care. The correct formulation of the question is of particular importance in a case such as the present, where the patient is totally unconscious and where there is no hope whatsoever of any amelioration of his condition. In circumstances such as these, it may be difficult to say that it is in his best interests that the treatment should be ended. But if the question is asked, as in my opinion it should be, whether it is in his best interests that treatment which has the effect of artificially prolonging his life should be continued, that question can sensibly be answered to the effect that his best interests no longer require that it should be.[541]

The Presumption in Favour of Life

4.196 But although the question is, 'Is it in the best interests of the patient that treatment should be continued?' (and not, 'Is it in the best interests of the patient that treatment be discontinued?'), there is a very strong presumption in favour of taking all steps which will prolong life; in the great majority of cases, save in exceptional circumstances or where the patient is dying, the best interests of the patient will require such steps to be taken.[542] The burden of proof is accordingly on those who assert that life-saving treatment or life-sustaining artificial feeding should be discontinued.

(ii) *The Dying Patient*

Life-Prolonging Treatment

4.197 In the case of life-prolonging treatment—that is treatment the purpose of which is merely to prolong the life of a terminally ill patient who cannot be expected to recover from a condition which is incurable—the court will

---

[541] *Airedale NHS Trust v Bland* [1993] AC 789, 868 *per* Lord Goff of Chieveley.
[542] *In re J (A Minor) (Wardship: Medical Treatment)* [1991] Fam 33, 46, 51, 53; *Airedale NHS Trust v Bland* [1993] AC 789, 867.

authorise or declare lawful (as the case may be) such treatment as is appropriate to the patient's condition.

In such a case the goal should be to ease suffering and, where appropriate, to 'ease the passing' rather than to achieve a short prolongation of life.[543]   **4.198**

> If the first purpose of medicine, the restoration of health, can no longer be achieved . . . a doctor . . . is entitled to do all that is proper and necessary to relieve pain and suffering, even if the measures he takes may incidentally shorten life[544]

Withdrawal of Treatment

Consistently with this approach there may be circumstances in which it is   **4.199**
appropriate to withdraw life-prolonging treatment from a dying patient,[545] but a doctor is never justified in taking active steps in order to kill his patient by the introduction of an external agency (for example, the administration of a fatal drug) with the intention of bringing about the patient's death: 'mercy killing' by active means is murder.[546]

Indirect Consequences

Also consistent with this approach is the recognition[547] by English law of the   **4.200**
theological doctrine of double effect:

> 'Thou shalt not kill' is an absolute commandment in this context. But, to quote the well known phrase of Arthur Hugh Clough in 'The Latest Decalogue,' in this context it is permissible to add 'but need'st not strive officiously to keep alive'. The decision on life and death must and does remain in other hands. What doctors and the court have to decide is whether, in the best interests of the child patient, a particular decision as to medical treatment should be taken which *as a side effect* will render death more or less likely. This is not a matter of semantics. It is fundamental. At the other end of the age spectrum, the use of drugs to reduce pain will often be fully justified, notwithstanding that this will hasten the moment of death. What can never be justified is the use of drugs or surgical procedures with the primary purpose of doing so.[548]

---

[543] *In re C (A Minor) (Wardship: Medical Treatment)* [1990] Fam 26, 32, 33, 37, 38; *Re C (A Minor) (Medical Treatment)* [1988] 1 FCR 1. The BMA has published guidance: 'End of Life Decisions: Views of the BMA' (Sept 1996).
[544] *R v Bodkin Adams* (1957) Apr 8–9 (Devlin J), [1957] Crim LR 365.
[545] cf *Airedale NHS Trust v Bland* [1993] AC 789.
[546] *R v Bodkin Adams* (1957) Apr 8–9 (Devlin J), [1957] Crim LR 365; *R v Cox* (1992) 12 BMLR 38; *Airedale NHS Trust v Bland* [1993] AC 789, 831, 865–866, 892.
[547] By Devlin J in *R v Bodkin Adams* (1957) Apr 8–9, [1957] Crim LR 365.
[548] *In re J (A Minor) (Wardship: Medical Treatment)* [1991] Fam 33, 46 *per* Lord Donaldson of Lymington MR. The distinction was central to the issue for the jury in *R v Cox* (1992) 12 BMLR 38. For a case turning on double effect which attracted much publicity, though it never proceeded to judgement, see *Lindsell v Holmes* (1997) *Guardian*, Oct 29.

(iii) *The Normal Patient*

4.201   In the case of life-saving treatment—that is treatment the purpose of which is to enable the patient to recover from a life-threatening condition which is potentially curable—there is usually no difficulty in arriving at the appropriate decision. For reasons which are obvious the court will normally[549] authorise or declare lawful (as the case may be) such treatment in the case of a child or incompetent adult, irrespective of the views of either the child, the child's parents or the patient's relatives, for generally the duty of the court is to preserve life. Thus where it is necessary to preserve the patient's life the court, notwithstanding religious or other objections, will authorise or declare lawful (as the case may be) the administration of blood transfusions to child[550] and incompetent adult[551] Jehovah's Witnesses, the force-feeding of children[552] and incompetent adults[553] for the treatment of anorexia nervosa or other psychiatric illnesses, and the administration, if need be by force, of surgical procedures necessary to preserve the life of a child[554] or an incompetent woman[555] suffering complications during labour.

---

[549] But not always. Thus 'on the most unusual facts' the court in *In re T (A Minor) (Wardship: Medical Treatment)* [1997] 1 WLR 242 refused to overrule the parents' refusal to consent to a liver transplant on a 17–month old boy suffering from biliary atresia, a life-threatening liver defect, notwithstanding unanimous medical opinion that without a transplant the child would not live beyond the age of 2 to $2^1/_2$ whilst the prospects of a successful operation leading to many years of normal life were good. This decision might be thought surprising: see the critical discussion by Professor Grubb in [1996] Med L Rev 315 and see further para 4.72 above.

[550] *Re E (A Minor) (Wardship: Medical Treatment)* [1993] 1 FLR 386; *Re S (A Minor) (Medical Treatment)* [1993] 1 FLR 376; *Re O (A Minor) (Medical Treatment)* [1993] 2 FLR 149; *Re R (A Minor) (Blood Transfusion)* [1993] 2 FLR 757; *Re S (A Minor) (Consent to Medical Treatment)* [1994] 2 FLR 1065.

[551] *In re T (Adult: Refusal of Treatment)* [1993] Fam 95.

[552] *In re W (A Minor) (Medical Treatment: Court's Jurisdiction)* [1993] Fam 64; *Re C (Detention: Medical Treatment)* [1997] 2 FLR 180.

[553] *Riverside Mental Health NHS Trust v Fox* [1994] 1 FLR 614; *Re KB (Adult) (Mental Patient: Medical Treatment)* (1994) 19 BMLR 144; *B v Croydon Health Authority* [1995] Fam 133, affirming [1995] 1 FCR 332; *Re VS (Adult: Mental Disorder)* (1995) Aug 17 (Douglas Brown J), [1995] Med L Rev 292.

[554] *A Metropolitan Borough Council v AB* [1997] 1 FLR 767. See further paras 4.94, 4.168 above.

[555] *In re T (Adult: Refusal of Treatment)* [1993] Fam 95; *Tameside and Glossop Acute Services Trust v CH* [1996] 1 FLR 762; *Norfolk and Norwich Healthcare (NHS) Trust v W* [1996] 2 FLR 613; *Rochdale Healthcare (NHS) Trust v C* [1997] 1 FCR 274; *Re L (Patient: Non-Consensual Treatment)* [1997] 2 FLR 837; *Re MB (Medical Treatment)* [1997] 2 FLR 426.

(iv) *The Handicapped Patient*

The court does not adopt any different approach merely because a patient is **4.202**
physically or mentally handicapped. The fact that the patient is handicapped
cannot of course be ignored, for the question is never what treatment would
be appropriate for a non-handicapped patient but always, what is the treatment appropriate for this patient given his condition?[556] Nonetheless,

> where . . . the child is severely handicapped although not intolerably so and
> treatment for a discrete condition can enable life to continue for an appreciable
> period, albeit subject to that severe handicap, the treatment should be given.[557]

Thus, in the leading case,[558] parents had refused consent to surgery on their
ten–day old mongol baby to relieve an intestinal blockage, taking the bona
fide view that 'God or nature has given the child a way out'. Without surgery
the baby would have died; the surgery, if carried out, would enable the baby
to live the same life as any other mongol child. The Court of Appeal
recognised that the child would have a short life expectancy and would be
very severely mentally and physically handicapped and thus not able to have
anything like a normal existence,[559] but directed surgery.

> If the operation takes place and is successful then the child may live the normal
> span of a mongoloid child with the handicaps and defects and life of a mongol
> child, and it is not for this court to say that life of that description ought to be
> extinguished.[560]

> The child should be put into the same position as any other mongol child and
> must be given the chance to live an existence.[561]

The principle has subsequently been explained as being that

> It [is] not for the court to decide that the child should not have the chance of the
> normal life span of a mongoloid child with the handicaps, defects and life of
> such a child.[562]

[556] *In re C (A Minor) (Wardship: Medical Treatment)* [1990] Fam 26, 32.
[557] *In re J (A Minor) (Wardship: Medical Treatment)* [1991] Fam 33, 54 *per* Taylor LJ.
[558] *In re B (A Minor) (Wardship: Medical Treatment)* [1981] 1 WLR 1421, reversing
(1982) 3 FLR 117, subsequently considered and explained in *In re C (A Minor) (Wardship: Medical Treatment)* [1990] Fam 26; *In re J (A Minor) (Wardship: Medical Treatment)*
[1991] Fam 33.
[559] *In re B (A Minor) (Wardship: Medical Treatment)* [1981] 1 WLR 1421, 1423.
[560] *In re B (A Minor) (Wardship: Medical Treatment)* [1981] 1 WLR 1421, 1424 *per*
Templeman LJ.   [561] ibid, 1424 *per* Dunn LJ.
[562] *In re C (A Minor) (Wardship: Medical Treatment)* [1990] Fam 26, 35 *per* Lord Donaldson of Lymington MR. In the light of the decisions in *In re B (A Minor) (Wardship: Medical
Treatment)* [1981] 1 WLR 1421; *In re C (A Minor) (Wardship: Medical Treatment)* [1990]

(v) *The Gravely Handicapped Patient*

4.203 On the other hand there are cases in which the degree of handicap is so great that it is not in the best interests of the patient to give or to continue (as the case may be) treatment which if given will artificially prolong life. The law recognises three situations where that is so.[563]

Intolerability

4.204 The first is where the nature of the patient's condition and the nature of the proposed treatment are such that, taking everything into account, the patient's life, even if he survives, will be 'intolerable',[564] as it has been put, so intolerable, so full of pain and suffering and so awful,[565] that life-saving treatment would not be appropriate. It is on this footing that the withholding or withdrawal of treatment can be justified in the case of gravely handicapped but sentient patients.[566]

Futility

4.205 The second is where the disability is such that the treatment would be 'futile', 'useless' or 'pointless'. In such a case it is the futility of the treatment which justifies its withholding or withdrawal. It is on this footing that the with-drawal of artificial nutrition and hydration is justified in the case of patients in a permanent (formerly called persistent) vegetative state.[567] Treatment can properly be categorised as futile if it cannot cure or palliate the disease or illness from which the patient is suffering and thus serves no therapeutic purpose of any kind.

Impracticability

4.206 The third is where it is simply impracticable to administer the proposed treatment, for example, where it is impracticable to give the treatment against

---

Fam 26 and *In re J (A Minor) (Wardship: Medical Treatment)* [1991] Fam 33 it is doubtful whether any useful principles can be extracted from *R v Arthur* (1981) 12 BMLR 1.

[563] cf *Airedale NHS Trust v Bland* [1993] AC 789, 868–869.

[564] *In re J (A Minor) (Wardship: Medical Treatment)* [1991] Fam 33, 54, 55 *per* Taylor LJ; *Re R (Adult: Medical Treatment)* [1996] 2 FLR 99, 107, 108, 110 *per* Sir Stephen Brown P.

[565] *In re B (A Minor) (Wardship: Medical Treatment)* [1981] 1 WLR 1421, 1424. But note that these words are not to be taken as providing a quasi-statutory yardstick: *In re J (A Minor) (Wardship: Medical Treatment)* [1991] Fam 33, 46.

[566] As in *In re J (A Minor) (Wardship: Medical Treatment)* [1991] Fam 33; *In re J (A Minor) (Child in Care: Medical Treatment)* [1993] Fam 15; *Re C (A Baby)* [1996] 2 FLR 43; *Re R (Adult: Medical Treatment)* [1996] 2 FLR 99.

[567] *Airedale NHS Trust v Bland* [1993] AC 789, 869, 870, 884.

the wishes of a patient who, though incompetent, strongly objects to and is not prepared to submit to the relevant procedure.[567a]

(a) The Gravely Handicapped but Sentient Patient

Thus in the leading case mechanical ventilation was held not to be necessary **4.207** in the case of a 'gravely damaged' five–month old baby who was suffering from an 'appalling catalogue of disabilities'.[568]

> [T]here is a balancing exercise to be performed in assessing the course to be adopted in the best interests of the child. . . . This brings me face to face with the problem of formulating the critical equation. In truth it cannot be done with mathematical or any precision. There is without doubt a very strong presumption in favour of a course of action which will prolong life, but . . . it is not irrebuttable. . . . [A]ccount has to be taken of the pain and suffering and quality of life which the child will experience if life is prolonged. Account has also to be taken of the pain and suffering involved in the proposed treatment itself. . . . But in the end there will be cases in which the answer must be that it is not in the interests of the child to subject it to treatment which will cause increased suffering and produce no commensurate benefit, giving the fullest possible weight to the child's, and mankind's, desire to survive.[569]

> There is only the one test: that the interests of the ward are paramount. Of course the court will approach those interests with a strong predilection in favour of the preservation of life, because of the sanctity of human life. But there neither is, nor should there be, any absolute rule that, save where the ward is already terminally ill, that is dying, neither the court nor any responsible parent can approve the withholding of life-saving treatment on the basis of the quality of the ward's life. . . . [I]t could in certain circumstances be inimical to the interests of the ward that there should be such a requirement: to preserve life at all costs, whatever the quality of the life to be preserved, and however distressing to the ward may be the nature of the treatment necessary to preserve life, may not be in the interests of the ward.[570]

> [T]he court's high respect for the sanctity of human life imposes a strong presumption in favour of taking all steps capable of preserving it, save in

---

[567a] *Re D* (1997) Nov 26 (Sir Stephen Brown P) (49-year old chronic but fluctuating psychotic suffering from chronic renal failure at near-end stage and high blood pressure requiring haemodialysis for four hours three or four times each week to keep him alive but unable because of his mental condition to understand the need for treatment and strongly objecting to procedure: held lawful in the last resort 'not to impose haemodialysis upon him in circumstances in which in the opinion of the medical practitioners responsible for such treatment it is not reasonably practicable so to do', the judge accepting that in the circumstances dialysis, which requires the co-operation of the patient, could only be performed under general anaesthetic which was neither practicable nor desirable in a patient suffering D's diasabilities).

[568] *In re J (A Minor) (Wardship: Medical Treatment)* [1991] Fam 33, 49, 56.

[569] ibid, 46–47 *per* Lord Donaldson of Lymington MR.

[570] ibid, 51–52 *per* Balcombe LJ.

exceptional circumstances. . . . Despite the court's inability to compare a life afflicted by the most severe disability with death, the unknown, . . . there must be extreme cases in which the court is entitled to say: 'The life which this treatment would prolong would be so cruel as to be intolerable'. . . . Once the absolute test is rejected, the proper criteria must be a matter of degree. At what point in the scale of disability and suffering ought the court to hold that the best interests of the child do not require further endurance to be imposed by positive treatment to prolong its life? Clearly, to justify withholding treatment, the circumstances would have to be extreme. . . . I consider the correct approach is for the court to judge the quality of life the child would have to endure if given the treatment and decide whether in all the circumstances such a life would be so afflicted as to be intolerable to that child. I say 'to that child' because the test should not be whether the life would be tolerable to the decider. The test must be whether the child in question, if capable of exercising sound judgment, would consider the life tolerable.[571]

4.208 In the particular circumstances of that case the reasons for arriving at the decision that life-saving treatment should not necessarily be given were that

mechanical ventilation is itself an invasive procedure which, together with its essential accompaniments . . . would cause the child distress. Furthermore the procedures involve taking active measures which carry their own hazards, not only to life but in terms of causing even greater brain damage. This had to be balanced against what could possibly be achieved by the adoption of such active treatment. The chances of preserving the child's life might be improved, although even this was not certain and account had to be taken of the extremely poor quality of life at present enjoyed by the child, the fact that he had already been ventilated for exceptionally long periods, the unfavourable prognosis with or without ventilation and a recognition that if the question of reventilation ever arose, his situation would have deteriorated still further.[572]

4.209 There are other reported examples of the application of these principles.[573]

Life-Saving Treatment and the Quality of Life

4.210 As can be seen, the Court of Appeal[574] has accepted that the quality of life is

---

[571] ibid, 53, 55 *per* Taylor LJ.

[572] ibid, 47–48 *per* Lord Donaldson of Lymington MR.

[573] In relation to gravely handicapped children see *In re J (A Minor) (Child in Care: Medical Treatment)* [1993] Fam 15 (artificial ventilation); *Re C (A Baby)* [1996] 2 FLR 43 (artificial ventilation). For a case where the decision went the other way, see *Re Superintendent of Family & Child Service and Dawson* (1983) 145 DLR (3d) 610, esp 611, 615, 616, 620–621; *Re SD* [1983] 3 WWR 597 considered in *In re C (A Minor) (Wardship: Medical Treatment)* [1990] Fam 26; *In re J (A Minor) (Wardship: Medical Treatment)* [1991] Fam 33. For a case involving a gravely handicapped adult see *Re R (Adult: Medical Treatment)* [1996] 2 FLR 99 (cardio-pulmonary resuscitation and antibiotics).

[574] In *In re J (A Minor) (Wardship: Medical Treatment)* [1991] Fam 33. For comments by the House of Lords on this case see *Airedale NHS Trust v Bland* [1993] AC 789, 858,

something that can be taken into account in deciding whether or not a gravely handicapped but sentient patient should receive life-saving treatment. But this does not mean that, in the case of a sentient patient, the withholding or withdrawal of life-saving treatment or artificial feeding can ever be justified solely by reference to an assessment of the quality of the patient's life, let alone because of physical or mental handicap, however grave. Withdrawal is justified only in extreme circumstances and if the court is satisfied to a high degree of probability that the patient's quality of life (and any prospects of improvement) are demonstrably so very poor as not to be commensurate with the extreme pain, suffering, or distress (physical or mental) being experienced as a result of the patient's condition (including any pain, suffering, and distress resulting from, and any hazards involved in, the treatment itself). In other words, the determining factor is not the patient's quality of life as such but pain, suffering or distress, whether physical or mental, so extreme that the artificial prolongation of the patient's agony cannot be justified.[575]

(b) The Patient in a Permanent (Formerly Called Persistent) Vegetative State

The essence of the permanent vegetative state (PVS)[576] is that the patient is **4.211** alive, is not dying (and, if properly treated may live for many years), but is totally insensate, and therefore can feel neither pain nor distress, has no cognitive functions, requires artificial nutrition and hydration to remain alive, and has no hope of either recovery or improvement.

868–869, 872, esp Lord Goff of Chieveley's reservation, 869, and see also, 885, 899. For subsequent comments by the Court of Appeal see *Frenchay Healthcare National Health Service Trust v S* [1994] 1 WLR 601, 607, 610.

[575] *In re J (A Minor) (Wardship: Medical Treatment)* [1991] Fam 33, 46, 47–48, 55, 56; *Airedale NHS Trust v Bland* [1993] AC 789, 858, 868.

[576] PVS was fully described in *Airedale NHS Trust v Bland* [1993] AC 789, 795–796, 797–798, 806–807, 860–861. At that time PVS was called the persistent vegetative state. It has since been renamed the permanent vegetative state, so as better to emphasise the fundamental essence of the condition. As currently understood, PVS is defined, albeit slightly differently, in the 'International Working Party Report on the Vegetative State' (The Royal Hospital for Neuro-Disability, London, Feb 1996) and in 'The permanent vegetative state', a Review by a working group convened by the Royal College of Physicians, endorsed by the Conference of Medical Royal Colleges and their Faculties in the United Kingdom (Royal College of Physicians of London, Ap (1996). A patient may be within the criteria identified by the International Working Party whilst not meeting the more stringent criteria identified by the Royal College: *Re D* (1997) 38 BMLR 1; *Re H (adult incompetent)* (1997) 38 BMLR 11. See further para 4.215 below. The BMA has published guidance on PVS: 'BMA guidelines on treatment decisions for patients in persistent vegetative state' (revised June 1996).

Need to Involve the Court

4.212 Withdrawal of artificial nutrition and hydration from a patient in a permanent vegetative state requires the prior sanction of the court.[577]

4.213 Details of the procedure to be adopted in applications to the court are set out in the Official Solicitor's Practice Note.[578]

Withdrawal of Treatment

4.214 Where a patient is diagnosed as being in a permanent vegetative state the court will authorise or declare lawful (as the case may be) the withdrawal of artificial nutrition and hydration.[579] This is essentially on the ground that artificial nutrition and hydration is medical treatment[580] and that in the case of a patient in a permanent vegetative state such treatment is futile: the patient has no further interest in being kept alive, his interest in life being in truth null.[581] The function of the court is to verify the diagnosis of the patient as being in a permanent vegetative state. The views of the patient's relatives or of others close to the patient will be taken into account by the court but cannot act as a veto.[582]

Related Conditions

4.215 Given the categorisation by the courts of artificial nutrition and hydration as medical treatment, it is suggested that there can be no arbitrary reason for distinguishing in this context between those patients who are in a permanent vegetative state and those who are not: the matter must, in

---

[577] *Airedale NHS Trust v Bland* [1993] AC 789, 805, 815, 824, 833, 859, 873, 875.

[578] Practice Note (Official Solicitor: Persistent Vegetative State) [1996] 2 FLR 375, issued July 1996 following the decisions in *Re G (Adult Patient: Publicity)* [1995] 2 FLR 528; *Re G (Persistent Vegetative State)* [1995] 2 FCR 46; *In re S (Hospital Patient: Court's Jurisdiction)* [1996] Fam 1; *Re C (Adult Patient: Restriction of Publicity after Death)* [1996] 2 FLR 251 and the issue of Practice Note (Official Solicitor: Sterilisation) [1996] 2 FLR 111, and replacing with modifications the earlier Practice Note: Practice Note (Official Solicitor: Persistent Vegetative State) [1994] 2 All ER 413, [1994] 1 FLR 654 (issued Mar 1994, following the decisions in *Airedale NHS Trust v Bland* [1993] AC 789; *Frenchay Healthcare National Health Service Trust v S* [1994] 1 WLR 601). See further para 4.132 above.

[579] *Airedale NHS Trust v Bland* [1993] AC 789; *Frenchay Healthcare National Health Service Trust v S* [1994] 1 WLR 601; *Re G (Persistent Vegetative State)* [1995] 2 FCR 46; *Swindon and Marlborough NHS Trust v S* (1994) *Guardian* Dec 10, [1995] Med L Rev 84; *Re C (Adult Patient: Restriction of Publicity after Death)* [1996] 2 FLR 251.

[580] *Airedale NHS Trust v Bland* [1993] AC 789.

[581] ibid, 858, 859, 868, 869, 884, 885, 897, 899.

[582] ibid, 871; *Re G (Persistent Vegetative State)* [1995] 2 FCR 46, 51.

each case, be resolved by applying the two criteria of intolerability[583] or futility. This accords with the view adopted by those courts, not only in this country[584] but also in New Zealand,[585] Eire,[586] and Jersey,[587] which have authorised the withdrawal of artificial nutrition and hydration from incompetent patients who, although not in a permanent vegetative state, lack all awareness. The question of the withdrawal of artificial nutrition and hydration from a patient whose condition falls significantly short of the permanent vegetative state (for example, because there is some, albeit slight, chance of improvement or the patient has what has been described as 'very slight sensate awareness'[588] or the 'glimmerings of awareness'[589]) has been expressly left open for future decision by the House of Lords,[590] the Court of Appeal,[591] and the President of the Family Division.[592] The courts will probably be very slow indeed to take this further step. As the President of the Family Division has said:

> No declaration to permit or to sanction the taking of so extreme a step could possibly be granted where there was any real possibility of meaningful life continuing to exist.[593]

---

[583] Consider, for example, the patient 'suffering the mental torture of Guillain-Barre syndrome, rational but trapped and mute in an unresponsive body': *Airedale NHS Trust v Bland* [1993] AC 789, 897 *per* Lord Mustill. For Guillain-Barre syndrome see *Nancy B v Hotel-Dieu de Quebec* (1992) 86 DLR (4th) 385; *Auckland Area Health Board v AG* [1993] 1 NZLR 235.

[584] *Re D* (1997) 38 BMLR 1 (adult in a vegetative state, 'totally unaware of herself or of her surroundings' and of 'anything which is going on about her', but whose condition did not in all respects meet the Royal College's criteria for PVS); *Re H (adult: incompetent)* (1997) 38 BMLR 11 (insentient adult in vegetative state, unable to communicate at all or to appreciate anything taking place around her, whose condition met the International Working Party's criteria but not the Royal College's criteria for PVS).

[585] *Auckland Area Health Board v AG* [1993] 1 NZLR 235 (Guillain-Barre syndrome).

[586] *In the Matter of a Ward of Court (withholding medical treatment) (No 2)* [1996] 2 IR 79 (adult in condition 'nearly, but not quite,' a permanent vegetative state).

[587] *In the Matter of an Infant* [1995] JLR 296, sv *Re Representation Attorney General* [1995] Med L Rev 316 (child in a non-cognitive but not permanent vegetative state).

[588] *Airedale NHS Trust v Bland* [1993] AC 789, 885 *per* Lord Browne-Wilkinson.

[589] ibid, 898 *per* Lord Mustill.   [590] ibid, 869, 879, 885, 899.

[591] *Frenchay Healthcare National Health Service Trust v S* [1994] 1 WLR 601, 607, 610.

[592] *Re R (Adult: Medical Treatment)* [1996] 2 FLR 99, 105 (adult in low-awareness state).

[593] *Re D* (1997) 38 BMLR 1, 10 *per* Sir Stephen Brown P.

III

MEDICAL NEGLIGENCE

5

DUTIES IN CONTRACT AND TORT

A. Introduction

Most litigation against doctors concerns actions for medical negligence or, as it **5.01** is sometimes called in 'transatlantic' language, medical malpractice. It is the principal action by which patients seek compensation for injuries caused within the National Health Service (NHS). The only other action which features to any extent is battery.[1] Actions in battery are however rare, not least because they require the patient to prove the doctor acted without the patient's consent, which is not usually the case. Claims for damages generally arise out of treatment or care to which the patient has consented, but which went wrong or did not produce the desired or expected outcome. The essence of the patient's claim is that the doctor was negligent in that he breached his duty to exercise reasonable care and skill in diagnosing, advising or treating the patient.

The frequency and volume of medical negligence actions has increased con- **5.02** siderably in recent years.[2] Prior to the 1980s these actions were relatively rare

---

[1] See above, Ch 3.
[2] For a discussion of the problems of the present system and suggestions for reform see Kennedy, I and Grubb, A, *Medical Law: Text with Materials*, 2nd edn (Butterworths, 1994) ch 6.

in England; reported cases were few and far between. Since that time a significant upsurge in litigation has occurred and led some to argue that claims for medical negligence are now out of control, just as in the United States of America, and that litigation has reached 'crisis proportions'.[3] This trend, it is said, can only have bad consequences for patients because of the transaction and direct costs it imposes upon the limited NHS budget. It is also said that the fear of being sued has, or will, encourage doctors to respond in a defensive and undesirable way and lead them to practise 'defensive medicine' whereby their behaviour towards a patient is modified solely to reduce the risk of legal action.[4] Although it is clear that both the number of claims and their costs are rising,[5] there is no hard evidence of the latter practice. In fact, the introduction of 'risk management' systems—defensive practices of a sort—both in clinical and other services provided within the NHS is more likely to contribute to a higher level of care to patients and others. Awareness of risk and a concern to reduce it will, inevitably, reduce accidents and hence take away the basis for some litigation. It will not, however, contribute to a reduction of claims in some situations, for instance, where a doctor's clinical judgment is at the core of the action. Clinical judgment is notoriously difficult to challenge in court either at the level of showing it was a *mis*judgment or, if it was, that it was a negligent one.[6] However, the development of protocols and, particularly, practice guidelines may have implications by going some way to standardise medical responses and inform doctors (and others) on the available options to treat a particular patient.[7]

5.03 It is also clear that the NHS has taken negligence litigation altogether more seriously in recent years prompted in part by the volume and cost of litigation but also because of the continuing squeeze upon NHS resources and the discipline of the cost-saving regime of the 'internal market'. The introduction of 'NHS Indemnity' in 1990[8] and the subsequent 'Clinical Negligence Scheme for Trusts' administered by the National Health Service Litigation

---

[3] The litigation boom (actual or perceived) and its implications is discussed in Jones, M, *Medical Negligence* (2nd edn, 1996), ch 1 and Kennedy, I, 'Confidentiality, Competence and Malpractice' in Byrne, P (ed), *Medicine in Contemporary Society* (1987), 40, 51–61.

[4] For a discussion of the issue of 'defensive medicine' see Jones, M, *Medical Negligence*, ibid, 5–7 and 139–44.

[5] See the figures discussed in Jones, M, ibid, 3–5. Some of the studies are discussed in Montgomery, J, *Health Care Law* (1997), 203–9. The characterisation of the situation as one of 'crisis' has been questioned: see Ham, C, Dingwall, R, Fenn, P and Harris, D, *Medical Negligence: Compensation and Accountability* (1988).   [6] See below, Ch 6.

[7] On which, see Deighan, M, and Hitch, S (eds), *Clinical Effectiveness from Guidelines to Cost-Effective Practice* (1995, Health Service Management Unit) and Hurwitz, B, 'Clinical Guidelines and the Law: Advice, Guidance or Regulation?' (1995) 1 *Journal of Evaluation in Clinical Practice 49*, and see below, Ch 8, para 8.18.

[8] Circular HC (89)34; now updated as HSG (96)48.

Authority[9] introduced on 1 March 1996,[10] represent attempts at more
centralised control to effect a rationalisation of negligence litigation within
the NHS.[11] It is also likely that, if introduced, 'conditional fee' agreements
and the removal of legal aid for medical negligence actions would 'dampen'
the volume of litigation considerably.

Medical negligence is, in reality, no more than an application of the tort of **5.04**
negligence to professionals such as doctors, nurses and others involved in the
provision of health care services. Hence, the law of negligence is applicable (with
some peculiar adaptions) to the medical context and medical negligence is a
specific form of negligence liability in the professional context.[12] The general
principles of liability in negligence are well-known and can be found elsewhere.[13]

There are, however, particular factual and legal problems thrown up in the **5.05**
medical context which necessitates a separate account from the general principles of negligence (and professional) liability. A patient may have an action
for breach of contract, in the tort of negligence[14] or for misrepresentation.[15]

B. Breach of Contract

1. Treatment under the National Health Service

(i) *No Contractual Relationship*

Historically,[16] the legal obligations of a doctor were derived from his status **5.06**
and 'common calling', that is, to exercise the skill and diligence expected of

---

[9] The National Health Service Litigation Authority (Establishment and Constitution)
Order 1995, SI 1995/2800; The National Health Service Litigation Authority Regulations
1995, SI 1995/2801.
[10] Pursuant to the National Health Service and Community Care Act 1990, s 21. See the
National Health Service (Clinical Negligence Scheme) Regulations 1996, SI 1996/251, as
amended by SI 1997/527. [11] Discussed below, paras 8.17–8.18.
[12] On which, see Jackson, R and Powell, J, *Professional Negligence* (4th edn, 1997); Dugdale, A and Stanton, K, *Professional Negligence* (3rd edn, 1995).
[13] eg, *Clerk & Lindsell on Torts* (17th edn, M Brazier (ed), 1995); Buckley, R, *The Modern
Law of Negligence* (3rd edn, 1996).
[14] Other actions may include false imprisonment (where the patient is unlawfully
restrained) or battery (where the touching is without consent or lawful justification). These
torts are discussed in the context of consent and the competent (Ch 3 above) and the
incompetent patient (Ch 4 above).
[15] Under the common law principle in *Hedley Byrne & Co Ltd v Heller & Partners Ltd*
[1964] AC 465 or, under the Misrepresentation Act 1967, where the patient has been induced
to enter into a contract for the provision of the medical services.
[16] See Teff, H, *Reasonable Care* (1995), 159–60 and 173–80 and references contained
therein, and Picard, E and Robertson, G, *Legal Liability of Hospitals and Doctors in Canada*
(3rd edn, 1996), 1–3.

his calling.[17] Whilst delictual in nature, it was recognised that an action in assumpsit and later contract lay against a doctor who treated a patient for payment.[18] Until the NHS was created in 1948, treatment was either provided privately or on a charitable basis. However, even in the latter instance, when the patient provided no tangible consideration, the courts held that the patient's submission to treatment was sufficient consideration for a contract.[19] Within the NHS today it is generally accepted that there is no contractual relationship between a doctor (whether general practitioner or hospital doctor) and the patient.[20] Equally, there is no contractual relationship between the patient and the hospital, such as the NHS Trust, where the patient is cared for. Any claim for damages based upon a breach of duty lies only in tort and, in particular, in an action for negligence.[21]

(ii) *A Contrary Argument*

5.07 The basis for the orthodoxy is two-fold. First, medical services within the NHS are provided to the patient pursuant to a statutory obligation. Such compulsion to provide a service is considered to be inconsistent with a contractual arrangement.[22] Secondly, the patient fails to provide the consideration in return for the doctor (or other's) promise to treat which is necessary if a contract is to exist. This position is not, however, beyond challenge. The statutory context, for example within which a GP functions, is not necessarily inconsistent with a contractual arrangement.[23] Also, it could be argued, for example, that in the case of a GP consideration may indirectly be provided by the patient since his inclusion upon the doctor's medical list will result in remuneration being paid by the Health Authority to the doctor. Also, in the

---

[17] The first report case against a doctor is *The Surgeon's Case* (or *Morton's Case*) (1374) 48 Edw 11.
[18] *Everard v Hopkins* (1615) 80 ER 1164 and *Slater v Baker and Stapleton* (1767) 95 ER 860.
[19] *Coggs v Bernard* (1703) 92 ER 107.
[20] Relying on *Pfizer Corp v Ministry of Health* [1965] AC 512 (HL): medicines supplied under prescription not a 'sale' even if some payment is made. See Kennedy and Grubb, *Medical Law* (n 2 above), 52–3. See also Teff, *Reasonable Care* (n 16 above), 161–2 note 138 and Pearson Commission, *Civil Liability and Compensation for Personal Injury* (Cmnd 7054, 1978) para 1313.
[21] However, a duty may also arise under a contract between a doctor or health institution by virtue of a contractual arrangement if the treatment is provided outside the NHS and the requirements for a legally binding contract are satisfied: namely, (1) there is an intention to create legal relations; (2) the parties have contractual capacity; (3) the terms are certain or ascertainable; and (4) there is consideration. On contractual actions in the medical context, see below. [22] *Pfizer Corp v Ministry of Health* (n 20 above).
[23] See *Roy v Kensington & Chelsea FPC* [1992] 1 All ER 705 (HL).

case of an NHS Trust, it could be argued again that the patient indirectly provides remuneration in cases where his treatment will generate distinct future (and not past) consideration from the NHS provider whether GP fund-holder or Health Authority. Treatment under an 'extra-contractual' referral most closely fits this description.

In the Canadian decision of *Pittman Estate v Bain*,[24] an Ontario court went **5.08** even further and held that a contractual relationship existed between the patient and a hospital on the basis that the hospital received funding from the Government funded health insurance scheme. The patient indirectly contributed to this through taxes and health premiums. Further, the hospital obtained a benefit, both financial and in reputation, when patients choose to receive treatment.

However attractive in principle the arguments may appear, there are two **5.09** factors which tell against them. And, as we shall see, there is in truth no real reason for an English court to divine a contract between the parties. First, the structure of health care provision within the 'internal market' of the NHS is antithetical to contractual arrangements; for example, the National Health Service and Community Care Act 1990 specifically states that agreements between 'purchasers' and 'providers' are not legally enforceable contracts.[25] While the 1990 Act does not deal with agreements with patients, the ethos of regulation of the NHS is *ex pactum*. Secondly, the statutory and regulatory context in which health services are provided may lead a court to infer that the parties had no intention to create legal relations in the form of a contract. In any event, the argument in *Pittman Estate* is most unlikely to be followed by an English court. It stretches the factual boundaries of what amounts to consideration almost to breaking point: the consideration is probably too remote.

A contractual claim will not, in most cases, affect the content of the legal **5.10** rights and obligations of the parties. Even if the courts did determine that a contractual relationship existed, the scope of the duty owed to the patient is unlikely to be any different from that in the tort of negligence.[26] In the end, however, in England a contractual basis for the legal obligations of a doctor or hospital is restricted to treatment which is provided privately. It is important to notice that private treatment is not exclusively provided outside NHS

---

[24] (1994) 112 DLR (4th) 257 (Ont Gen Div); further reasons, (1994) 112 DLR (4th) 482, (1994) 112 DLR (4th) 494, and (1994) 35 CPC (3d) 67.   [25] S 4(3).

[26] Subject to the express terms, the law will imply a duty to exercise reasonable care and skill identical to that imposed in the tort of negligence: *Thake v Maurice* [1986] QB 644 (CA); *Eyre v Measday* [1986] 1 All ER 488 (CA); Supply of Goods and Services Act 1982, s 13. See below, Ch 5, paras 5.19–5.20.

facilities. To the extent that it is provided within the NHS in, for example, 'pay beds' then a contractual basis for the parties legal obligations will apply.[27]

2. Private Treatment

(i) *Express Terms*

5.11 When treatment or other health care is provided privately, a contractual relationship will arise between the doctor and the patient, and usually the clinic or institution and patient. The nature, scope, and terms of these contracts will depend upon the circumstances. Although there are a variety of ways in which contractual relationships may exist for private health care, commonly the patient will make separate arrangements with the doctor (for the treatment and aftercare) and with the clinic for the provision of facilities (such as the operating theatre) and staff (such as nurses). This will be the usual arrangement where the patient consults a doctor privately who then arranges for the patient to be treated at a clinic with which he (the doctor) has an agreement to admit patients. In other situations the arrangement may be directly with the clinic for the provision of the 'services' sought including the doctors who will carry out the procedure. There may, then, be no separate contractual arrangement with the doctor. Examples of this occur in cases of infertility treatment where the patient seeks treatment at an IVF clinic where particular doctors work.

5.12 The terms of these contracts will primarily be a matter for agreement between the parties and then subsequently included expressly in the written contract, if one exists. Terms as to payment, the provision of facilities and staff will be common depending upon the circumstances. The consent form, if any, signed by the patient will form part of the contract.[28] The contract may also specify who is to be the treating doctor and, in such circumstances, it will be a breach of contract if another doctor treats the patient.[29] The obligations of the parties will, therefore, be a matter of construing the terms in the contract in each case, subject to the constraints of public policy.[30]

5.13 One question which has arisen is whether a doctor contractually guarantees the outcome of the treatment. Hence a patient might be able to claim when the treatment does not effect a cure or produce the intended result. An action would certainly be sustainable if the doctor failed to carry out the procedure

---

[27] Discussed in relation to 'vicarious liability' and 'primary duty', below, Ch 8, paras 8.07 *et seq.*

[28] eg, *Thake v Maurice* (n 26 above) and *Eyre v Measday* (n 26 above).

[29] See *Morris v Winsbury-White* [1937] 4 All ER 494.

[30] eg, restricting liability: *Tunkl v Regents of the University of California* (1963) 383 P 2d 441 (Cal Sup Ct) and Unfair Contract Terms Act 1977, s 2(1).

at all, through oversight or whatever.[31] The possibility of a contractual warranty action is important because no such duty arises in negligence: the only obligation of the doctor is to act reasonably. There is no doubt that a doctor may enter into a contractual guarantee. However, in order to do so, he must use explicit and unequivocal words such as 'I guarantee you will be cured', 'I will guarantee to make the hand a 100 per cent perfect hand'[32] or 'I assure you will never have children again—you will be infertile'. Absent words of this nature forming part of the contract, the courts will not usually construe contractual terms as amounting to a guarantee of success.

The American case of *Guilmet v Campbell*[33] illustrates the lengths to which a **5.14** doctor must go before he warrants an outcome for a patient. The doctor treated the plaintiff for a bleeding ulcer. Prior to the operation the doctor told the patient:

> Once you have an operation it takes care of all your troubles. You can eat as you want to, you can drink as you want to, you can go as you please . . . . there is nothing to it at all—it's a very simple operation. You'll be out of work three to four weeks at most. There is no danger at all in this operation. After the operation you can throw away your pill box.[34]

Unfortunately, the plaintiff suffered serious physical after-effects. The Michigan Supreme Court upheld a jury verdict in the plaintiff's favour that the defendant had contractually guaranteed to cure his peptic ulcer. The court emphasised that it was not saying that a doctor necessarily contracted to produce a cure in these circumstances[35] but rather that there was sufficient evidence for the jury to conclude:

> that the doctor made a specific, clear and express promise to cure or effect a specific result which was in the reasonable contemplation of [the doctors] and the plaintiff which was relied upon by the plaintiff.[36]

The leading English decision concerned with a guarantee of cure or an effect **5.15** is *Thake v Maurice*.[37] The plaintiffs, a married couple consulted the defendant, a surgeon, privately in order for the husband to undergo a vasectomy as they did not wish to have any more children. The defendant explained the procedure to the plaintiffs and he pointed out that although it was possible to restore the husband's fertility he could not guarantee it, and that the plaintiffs

---

[31] See eg, *Zehr v Haughen* (1994) 871 P 2d 1006 (Ore Sup Ct): action for breach of contract held to be sustainable where doctor had failed to carry out at all the sterilisation operation he had contracted to undertake.
[32] *Hawkins v McGhee* (1929) 146 A 641 (NH).
[33] (1971) 188 NW 2d 601 (Mich Sup Ct). For the US cases, see *Annotation*, 99 ALR 3d 303.
[34] ibid, 606.   [35] ibid, *per* Kavanagh J.   [36] ibid, 607 *per* Kavanagh J.
[37] [1986] QB 644; [1986] 1 All ER 479 (CA). See Grubb, A, [1986] CLJ 197.

should regard the operation as permanent. The plaintiffs signed a consent form which stated, *inter alia*, 'I have been told that the object of the operation is to render me sterile and incapable of parenthood. I understand that the effect of the operation is irreversible.' The operation was carried out and appeared successful. However, almost three years later, the wife discovered that she was pregnant. The operation had naturally reversed itself by a process known as late recanalisation and the husband's fertility had been restored. Subsequently, a child was born and the plaintiffs sued the defendant in negligence and for breach of contract.[38] The plaintiffs claimed that they had not been warned of the risk of reversal and that this was negligent. Further they claimed a breach of contract in that the defendant had guaranteed the success of the operation namely, the husband's infertility. Peter Pain J held the defendant had not, in fact, warned the plaintiffs of the small risk of reversal. He was liable in negligence for this. Also, Peter Pain J held that the defendant was liable in contract as he had given a contractual warranty of success. The Court of Appeal unanimously upheld the judge on the negligence ground but, by a majority,[39] reversed him on the contract claim.

5.16   Emphasising the inexact nature of medical science and unpredictability of medical treatment, Nourse and Neill LJJ held that a doctor would only be held to have guaranteed the success of an operation if he expressly said so in clear and unequivocal terms.[40] Neither the circumstances of the case, nor the use of the word 'irreversible' could lead the court to reach the conclusion that the defendant had guaranteed the husband's sterility.[41] The defendant had only contracted to exercise reasonable care and skill, which he breached by failing to warn the plaintiffs of the risk of reversal as was his normal practice. Nourse LJ said:[42]

> . . . a professional man is not usually regarded as warranting that he will achieve the desired result. Indeed, it seems that that would not fit well with the universal warranty of reasonable care and skill, which tends to affirm the inexactness of the science which is professed. I do not intend to go beyond the case of the doctor. Of all sciences medicine is one of the least exact. In my view a doctor cannot be objectively regarded as guaranteeing the success of any operation or treatment unless he says as much in clear and unequivocal terms.

Neill LJ agreed, adding that while both the plaintiffs and the defendant expected that sterility would result, that[43]

---

[38] For a discussion of the 'failed sterilisation' cases: see below, Ch 12.
[39] Nourse and Neill LJ. Kerr LJ dissenting.
[40] N 37 above, at 511–2 and 510 respectively.
[41] Likewise, therefore, it cannot amount to a misrepresentation so as to found a claim for negligent misrepresentation on the basis of *Hedley Byrne*: see *Gold v Haringay HA* [1988] QB 481; [1987] 2 All ER 888 (CA) at 895–6 *per* Lloyd LJ. See also *Worster v City & Hackney HA, The Times*, 22 June 1987.   [42] N 37 above, 512.   [43] ibid, 510.

does not mean, however, that a reasonable person would have understood the defendant to be giving a binding promise that the operation would achieve its purpose or that the defendant was going further than to give an assurance that he expected and believed that it would have the desired result.

In the *Thake* case all the judges accepted that in some circumstances a **5.17** guarantee of success might be understood from the words used by a doctor.[44] Nourse LJ postulated that a reasonable person might do this where 'the general experience of mankind' was that a particular outcome would, as a matter of fact, result from a procedure. He instanced a surgical procedure to amputate a limb.[45] Nourse LJ contrasted this situation with one 'where an operation is of modern origin, its effects untried over several generations'.[46] There, a reasonable person, even faced with apparently clear and straightforward assurances would not believe that a guarantee of success was being given. In reality, virtually every medical treatment and procedure will fall into the latter, rather than the former, category. As a result, there is little mileage in couching a claim in contract. It will be a wholly exceptional set of facts where the plaintiff will be able to persuade a court that the doctor was guaranteeing an outcome.

An example of such a case arose in Canada in respect of cosmetic surgery. In **5.18** *LaFleur v Cornelis*[47] the defendant, a cosmetic surgeon performed a procedure to reduce the size of the plaintiff's nose. He failed to inform her that there was a 10 per cent risk of scarring. She was, in fact, scarred. Barry J held the defendant liable in negligence and for breach of contract. He distinguished between 'an ordinary physician' and a cosmetic surgeon.[48] The defendant had told the plaintiff what she needed done, had drawn a diagram of what he would do and how she would look and had said: 'no problem. You will be very happy.'[49] Barry J concluded that this, in the light of his failure to warn of the risk of scarring, amounted to a warranty of success. While other courts have similarly regarded cosmetic surgeons, it is not at all clear that English law would follow them. The uncertainties of such surgery are surely no less, usually, than any other. Not every client can be made to look perfect! Absent an undertaking to make the plaintiff 'stunningly beautiful', 'handsome beyond words', or 'drop-dead gorgeous', even in this context it is suggested that all the surgeon undertakes (as viewed through the eyes of Nourse LJ's perceptive reasonable person) is to exercise reasonable care and skill.

---

[44] See also, ibid, *per* Kerr LJ at 505.
[45] ibid, 511. Kerr LJ, dissenting, considered the instant case as involving 'something in the nature of an amputation', ibid, 505.   [46] ibid.
[47] (1979) 28 NBR (2d) 569 (QB).   [48] ibid, 577.   [49] ibid.

(ii) *Implied Terms*

5.19 More important in practical terms are the terms *implied* in the contract between doctor (or hospital) and patient. The law implies terms in respect of services or goods provided to patients. Many of these obligations are statutory and cannot be excluded: such as those implied by the Supply of Goods and Services Act 1982 in relation to 'fitness for purpose' and 'satisfactory quality' where goods alone are supplied or together with services, for example, a prosthesis, vaccine, or medicinal product.[50] Further, the law will imply an obligation to respect a patient's confidences which, of course, would otherwise arise by virtue of an equitable obligation alone.[51]

5.20 In the context of medical negligence, the important term that the law implies into the contract is, in the case of doctors, to exercise reasonable care and skill when diagnosing, advising and treating[52] and, in the case of hospitals, for example, in the provision of staff and facilities.[53] These are the very same obligations implied generally in the contracts of other professions and are indistinguishable from the duty of care in the tort of negligence.[54] Hence, in two cases[55] where the patients underwent a sterilisation operation, the Court of Appeal held that the contract between the doctor and patient had implied into it a duty to exercise reasonable care and skill in carrying out the operation. In *Eyre v Measday*,[56] the Court of Appeal concluded that a warranty of success would not be implied where the doctor had stated that the procedure would be 'irreversible'. No 'intelligent lay bystander' would reasonably infer that the defendant was guaranteeing sterility.[57]

C. Negligence: Duty of Care

5.21 Actions for breach of contract will be the exception in the medical context. Where a patient is injured allegedly as a result of a doctor's negligence by far

---

[50] See below, Ch 14.

[51] eg, *W v Egdell* [1990] Ch 359 (CA). For a discussion of 'confidentiality', see below, Ch 9.

[52] *Greaves & Co (Contractors) Ltd v Baynham Meikle & Partners* [1975] 3 All ER 99, 103–4 *per* Lord Denning MR.

[53] There appears to be no English case. For a Canadian case in which a hospital was held to have impliedly contracted to exercise reasonable care in providing a safe system of work, see *Osburn v Mohindra* (1980) 29 NBR (2d) 340 (QB). The obligations would be identical to those imposed in the tort of negligence, on which, see below, Ch 8.

[54] Thus little, if anything, turns upon whether the patient pleads the 'negligence' in tort or contract. Indeed, the patient may sue in both tort and contract: see eg, *Thake v Maurice* (n 37 above).

[55] *Thake v Maurice* [1986] 1 All ER 497; *Eyre v Measday* [1986] 1 All ER 488.

[56] ibid.   [57] ibid, 495 *per* Slade LJ.

the most common basis for a claim will be in the tort of negligence. The plaintiff (patient) must establish:

(1) that a duty of care was owed to him by the defendant (health professional or hospital[58]);

(2) that the defendant was in breach of that duty by not exercising reasonable care and skill;[59] and

(3) that the breach of duty caused damage, namely the injuries suffered by the patient.[60]

Beyond these—which constitute the legal elements of a claim for medical negligence—there may arise issues concerned with defences to the action,[61] for example, limitation and also calculations of the quantum of damages.[62]

When will a doctor or other health professional owe a duty of care to another?[63] Usually, this question will not give rise to any difficulty in a medical negligence case. It will be obvious, and accepted, that a duty was owed to the plaintiff who is the doctor's patient. The real issues in the case will revolve around, for example, breach and causation. There will, however, be problems where the doctor–patient relationship has not been forged fully or at all, for example, where the doctor is employed by another such as an insurance company or a prospective employer to examine the plaintiff or is a third party who suffers injury as a result of the doctor's negligence (for example, a total stranger injured by the patient or a relative of the patient). Also, legal problems arise where the injury suffered by the patient (or other) is not personal injury arising out of the treatment but rather financial loss or psychiatric harm. **5.22**

1. To Patients

It may seem blindingly obvious that a doctor owes a duty of care to his patients.[64] It is a duty to exercise reasonable care and skill in diagnosing, advising and treating the patient.[65] The duty is the same regardless of the **5.23**

---

[58] Discussed in Chapter 8. [59] Discussed in Chapter 6.
[60] Discussed in Chapter 7. [61] Discussed in Chapter 7.
[62] For quantum of damages in general, see *McGregor on Damages* (ed H McGregor, 16th edn, 1997); and in respect of medical negligence claims, Jones, M, *Medical Negligence* (n 3 above), ch 9.
[63] See also Kennedy and Grubb, *Medical Law* (n 2 above), 67–9 and 73–80. For 'institutional liability' see below, Ch 8.
[64] For a discussion of who are a general practitioner's patients, see above, Ch 1.
[65] *Sidaway v Bethlem Royal Hospital Governors* [1985] AC 871; [1985] 1 All 643, 657 *per* Lord Diplock, describing it as a 'single comprehensive duty covering all the ways in which a doctor is called on to exercise his skill and judgment in the improvement of the physical or mental condition of the patient'.

experience of the doctor, being instead, as a matter of public policy, tailored to the task that he undertakes and the specialty he professes.[66] Consequently, inexperience is not a defence to a medical negligence action.[67] An action in negligence lies for a breach of this duty which causes injury. The basis for this duty is an 'undertaking' of care of the person as a patient.[68] An undertaking of care may be expressly made by the doctor or implied by the law arising out of the circumstances. As long ago as 1957 Nathan[69] put it as follows:

> The medical man's duty of care arises . . . quite independently of any contract with his patient. It is based simply upon the fact that the medical man *undertakes the care and treatment of the patient.*

Later Nathan stated that the doctor's duty arises because he has 'assumed responsibility for the care, treatment or examination of the patient'.[70] The language of 'undertaking' and 'assumption of responsibility' reflects the modern approach of the courts when imposing positive duties of care, particularly upon professionals.[71] In general the duty will stem from the doctor's voluntary agreement to 'care for' or 'treat' the person.[72] This will, in turn, lead the law to characterise the doctor's conduct as amounting to 'an assumption' of responsibility to the person. It is important to notice that for a duty to exist, there need be no reciprocation of agreement by the patient. A doctor will equally owe a duty of care to an incompetent adult, for example, an unconscious patient in an Accident and Emergency (A & E) department, or young child brought to his surgery who is too young to consent and whom he examines.[73]

5.24 *The same analysis applies to other health care professionals, such as nurses, who come into contact with a patient: the crucial issue being whether that* professional has assumed responsibility by undertaking the 'care' of the person.[74]

---

[66] *Maynard v West Midlands RHA* [1984] 1 WLR 634 (HL), 638 *per* Lord Scarman.
[67] *Wilsher v Essex AHA* [1987] QB 730 (CA); the point was not raised in the House of Lords. For a discussion, see below, Ch 6.
[68] *Jones v Manchester Corp* [1952] QB 852, 867 *per* Denning LJ (referring to the liability of the hospital). See also *Cassidy v Ministry of Health* [1951] 2 KB 343, 360 *per* Denning LJ. On the latter, see below, Ch 8. See also, *R v Bateman* (1925) 94 LJKB 791, 794 per Hewart LCJ.
[69] Nathan, H, *Medical Negligence* (1957), 8 (emphasis added).   [70] ibid, 10.
[71] See eg, *White v Jones* [1995] 2 AC 207 (HL); *Henderson v Merrett Syndicates Ltd* [1995] 2 AC 145 (HL); *Capital and Counties plc v Hampshire CC* [1997] 2 All ER 865 (CA), especially *per* Stuart-Smith LJ at 883 *et seq*; *Kirkham v Chief Constable of Greater Manchester Police* [1990] 2 QB 283 (CA).
[72] See *Capital and Counties plc v Hampshire CC* (n 71 above), 883 and 884 *per* Stuart-Smith LJ.
[73] *Re F (Mental Patient: Sterilisation)* [1990] 2 AC 1 (HL), 56 *per* Lord Brandon and at 77 *per* Lord Goff.
[74] See *Barnett v Chelsea and Kensington HMC* [1969] 1 QB 428: nurse in casualty department owed duty to plaintiff when he presented himself complaining of illness. Of course, she was not in breach of her duty because she contacted the duty doctor: See also *Junor v McNicol,*

(i) *General Practitioners*

(a) **In General**

As we saw earlier,[75] a general practitioner's patients are determined by his **5.25** Terms of Service contained in Schedule 2 of the National Health Service (General Medical Services) Regulations 1992.[76] The Regulations set out a procedure whereby an individual may request, and a doctor may accept him, onto his 'list' of patients.[77] Hence, a GP's patients include individuals recorded by the Health Authority as being on his 'list' and those accepted by the doctor on his 'list' even if the HA has not been notified.[78] In addition, in some circumstances an individual may be a GP's patient under the Regulations even where he has not been accepted by the doctor or, even, where he has been removed from the doctor's 'list'.[79] The Regulations set out a range of duties imposed upon the doctor, including, providing 'personal medical services', relating to visits, prescribing etc.[80]

Undoubtedly, the obligations imposed by the 1992 Regulations will guide the **5.26** courts in determining the scope and content of the doctor's duty at common law, though they will not be determinative or exclusive. They will, for example, be crucial in reaching a view on whether a GP was negligent. However, it does not follow that just because the Regulations impose a duty on a GP, that a duty of care will arise at common law. The 1992 Regulations set out the situations whereby the formal relationship of doctor–patient is created. It would be artificial to state that a GP owes all the patients, for example, on his 'list' a duty of care at all times. Apart from the initial meeting, the GP may never see or hear from the patient subsequently. A GP, in general, only owes his 'formal' patient a duty of care *at common law* when he has knowledge (actual or constructive) of the circumstances which trigger his obligations under the 1992 Regulations. Thus, without a direct or indirect request for 'care' from the patient, the GP does not owe a duty of care.[81] It will be different where

---

The Times, 11 Feb 1959 (HL) (house surgeon not negligent acting on instructions of consultant); *Wilsher v Essex AHA* [1987] QB 730 (CA) (house officer not negligent as sought opinion of registrar).

[75] The 1992 Regulations are considered in detail above, Ch 1.
[76] SI 1992/635, as amended.   [77] ibid, Sch 2, paras 5 and 6.
[78] ibid, para 4(1)(a) and (b) respectively.
[79] ibid, para 4(1)(c), (d) and (e) respectively.
[80] ibid, paras 12 and 13 (general); para 14 (newly registered patients); para 15 (patients not seen for 3 years); para 16 (patients aged 75 and over).
[81] An alternative analysis would be that the duty always exists and the doctor's knowledge (actual or constructive) is relevant only to the issue of breach of duty. Perhaps it makes no difference in practice which analysis is correct. However, it is suggested that the better one is

the obligation under the 1992 Regulations is a continuing one or one that imposes a responsibility upon the GP to seek out the patient. An example of this arises in relation to patients aged 75 or over who should be offered an annual consultation.[82] A GP who fails to do this could be liable in negligence if it is shown that his failure was negligent and caused injury (or death) to the patient. It is irrelevant that the patient did not request a consultation.

5.27 Also, the Regulations are not determinative of when a duty of care ceases to a particular patient. The Regulations set out the circumstances in which a doctor may terminate the relationship to his patient, in general[83] or because the patient is violent.[84] Merely by complying with this procedure does not necessarily terminate the doctor's duty of care *at common law*. First, the Regulations themselves contemplate a continuing obligation to provide treatment which is 'immediately necessary' when requested by a patient who is not yet on another doctor's 'list'.[85] Secondly, the GP continues to owe his (former) patient a duty at common law until such time as it is reasonable for that treatment to be taken over by another doctor. The common law will not allow a GP to 'abandon' his (former) patient. A duty of care continues until such time as it is reasonable for it to cease although, of course, the content of that duty may be different in the circumstances, for example, where the patient behaves violently towards the doctor.[86]

(b) Deputies and Others

5.28 Sometimes a GP's patients will be treated by another doctor, for example, a locum whilst the GP is away on holidays. More frequently, the workload of GPs is such that they often use deputies to cover for them at night. The Terms of Service allow for this practice where it is reasonable to do so.[87] Will a GP be liable for the acts (or omissions) of a deputy? Under the Terms of Service, a GP is not accountable for a deputy who is on the Medical List of a Health Authority (whether that of the GP or another): the deputy alone is responsible.[88] By

---

that postulated in the text. See eg, analogous situations in relation to a landowner's duty to his neighbours for the state of his premises: *Goldman v Hargrave* [1967] 1 AC 645 (PC) and *Smith v Littlewoods Organisation* [1987] AC 241 (HL), 272–3 *per* Lord Goff.

[82] SI 1992/635 (as amended), Sch 2, para 16.
[83] SI 1992/635 (as amended), Sch 2, para 9.
[84] ibid, para 9A, inserted by The National Health Service (General Medical Services) Amendment Regulations 1994, SI 1994/633, reg 8(4).
[85] N 82 above, para 4(4) as substituted by SI 1994/633, reg 8(2). The obligation is to do so for 14 days or until the person finds another GP.
[86] That an obligation to continue to provide 'immediately necessary treatment' exists is made explicit: ibid, para 4(4)(c) as inserted by SI 1994/633, reg 8(2).
[87] The National Health Service (General Medical Services) Regulations 1992, SI 1992/635 (as amended), Sch 2, paras 18–25.   [88] ibid, combined effect of para 20(1) and (2).

contrast, a GP remains responsible for a GP who is not on a Health Authority's Medical List.[89] Of course, the Terms of Service are only explicitly concerned with the GP's obligations *vis à vis* his Health Authority. What is the extent of the GP's duty of care at common law? Is he liable for the acts and omissions of his deputy? The position is not free from doubt.[90] If the deputy were his employee, then the GP would be liable on the basis of vicarious liability.[91] However, this is doubtful as the deputy is likely to be an independent contractor.[92] To the extent that the GP has already 'undertaken' the care of the patient—that is, gone beyond the formal relationship under the Regulations—then the GP will be liable for the deputy's conduct to the extent that he (the GP) is personally in breach of his duty of care. Hence, if the GP was at fault in selecting a competent deputy or in providing the deputy with adequate information about the patient, the GP could be liable in negligence.[93] However, providing there was no fault of this kind, the GP could not be liable for the negligence of the deputy unless, as a matter of law, the GP is under a non-delegable duty to ensure that care is taken of his patient. It is rare for the common law to impose such a duty which does not look to the personal fault of the defendant but of another and, rather like the devise of vicarious liability, nevertheless places responsibility on the defendant for the fault of another.[94] While this has never been decided in England, it is arguable that the GP's duty is non-delegable. The statutory context in which care is provided under the NHS by general practitioners is that patients look to the personal care of that individual. Everyone who is registered with a GP is registered with a particular doctor. The deputy will not be associated with the patient's GP or his practice. While delegation to another doctor within a partnership or practice is reasonable and leaves the patient with some assurance of continuity of care, delegation to outsiders lacks this quality. The law would go some way to redress this imbalance by recognising the non-delegability of the GP's duty of care in such cases.

A somewhat similar set of arguments arise where the GP delegates to another, but not a deputy, the performance of a procedure within his surgery or practice. For example, a nurse carries out an examination or administers an injection on the doctor's behalf. In these circumstances, the GP will be vicariously liable for the negligence of the practice nurse (or whoever) who is his employee.[95] In any event, as the arguments in the preceding paragraph show, the GP may be in breach of *his* duty of care if he is personally at fault, for example, by unreasonably delegating a task to a nurse or other. Equally, it was argued that the law might impose upon a GP a non-delegable duty which would entail liability for the negligent acts and omissions of others acting on his behalf, such as nurses.

5.29

---

[89] ibid.   [90] See also below, para 8.12.   [91] See ibid.   [92] See ibid.
[93] ibid.   [94] See discussion below, paras 8.21 *et seq.*   [95] See below, para 8.12.

(c) In Emergencies

5.30   Unlike continental legal systems, English law is chary of imposing positive duties upon individuals.[96] As a consequence, doctors are generally not required to act as 'good Samaritans', going to the aid of others who appear to require medical assistance even in emergency situations.[97] There is no legal duty on a doctor to answer the call 'Is there a doctor in the house?'.[98] Doctors who come upon an accident may legally 'pass on the other side', though their conduct if it came to the attention of the General Medical Council might lead to disciplinary action.[99] English law, as ever, looks for an 'undertaking' of care or an express or implied assumption of responsibility by the doctor. Uniquely, in the case of GPs, the Terms of Service may create a doctor–patient relationship (in the formal sense) between a GP and the victim of an accident.[100] The Regulations contemplate *two* situations.

5.31   First, a GP who is requested to give treatment which is 'immediately required' to a person involved in an accident or other emergency in his practice area, must do so. There are further conditions, such as the GP must be 'available to provide such treatment', but providing these are satisfied failure to provide the treatment will put him in breach of his Terms of Service and liable to disciplinary action by the Health Authority. Secondly, where the accident or other emergency, though not in his practice area, is in the locality of his Health Authority, he must provide treatment which is 'immediately required' if requested *and he agrees* to do so. The obligation only arises if the victim does not have a GP to provide the treatment or, if he does, he has been requested to provide it but is 'unable to attend'. Consequently, before the obligation in this latter situation comes into existence, the GP must, in effect, be the only (or only reasonably) available GP and, of course, he must *agree* to provide the treatment.

5.32   The Terms of Service are not conclusive of the existence or scope of a duty of care at common law. Clearly, the second situation involves an 'undertaking' or 'assumption of responsibility' by the doctor and would, on this basis alone, be

---

[96] See eg, *Smith v Littlewoods Organisation* [1987] AC 241, 271 *per* Lord Goff. See generally, Markesinis, B, 'Negligence, Nuisance and Affirmative Duties of Action' (1989) 105 LQR 104.

[97] See *Capital and Counties plc v Hampshire CC* [1997] 2 All ER 865 (CA), 883 *per* Stuart-Smith LJ.   [98] *Re F (Mental Patient: Sterilisation)* [1990] 2 AC 1, 77–8 *per* Lord Goff.

[99] As 'serious professional misconduct' under the Medical Act 1983, s 35. See GMC, *Duties of A Doctor (Good Medical Practice)* (1995), para 4: 'In an emergency, you must offer anyone at risk the treatment you could reasonably be expected to provide.'

[100] The National Health Service (General Medical Services) Regulations 1992, SI 1992/ 635 (as amended), Sch 2, para 4(1)(h).

sufficient for the doctor to owe a duty of care to the victim. However, the common law may go further and reflect the fact that a GP at a site of an accident or emergency within his practice area has *impliedly* assumed a responsibility towards the victim because of his Terms of Service. By contrast, it is unlikely that a GP owes such a duty if he were elsewhere in the country and happened upon an accident: to impose a duty of care here would be to make the doctor a 'good Samaritan' quite contrary to the general approach of English law.

A recent decision in Australia raises the possibility that the common law in England might contemplate a duty arising where a doctor is requested in a professional context to provide advice or treatment. In *Lowns v Woods*,[101] the plaintiff was an eleven-year-old boy with a history of epileptic seizures. Whilst on holiday, one morning his mother returned from a walk to find him undergoing a seizure. She sent another of her sons to get an ambulance and her daughter to get a doctor. About five minutes later she arrived at the defendant's surgery. Although it was disputed, the trial judge[102] (Badgery-Parker J) found that the daughter explained the situation and asked the defendant to come but he refused telling her to bring the plaintiff to him. By the time she returned to her mother, the ambulance had arrived and the plaintiff was taken to hospital. Unfortunately, the plaintiff suffered profound brain damage and was quadriplegic as a result of the uncontrolled seizure. It was claimed, *inter alia*, by the plaintiff that the defendant was under a duty of care, which included an obligation to attend him, and if he had the defendant would have administered Valium which would have controlled the seizure and prevented his injuries.

5.33

By a majority,[103] the New South Wales Court of Appeal upheld the trial judge's ruling that the defendant owed the plaintiff a duty of care. The essence of the court's ruling is stated by Cole JA:[104]

5.34

> Dr Lowns accepted that injury ('damage') to a fitting child was foreseeable if he, once requested, did not attend to treat the child. There was obvious physical proximity, for Joanna [the daughter] had come on foot. There also existed an adequate 'circumstantial proximity' in the sense that Dr Lowns was a medical practitioner to whom a direct request for assistance was made in circumstances where, on the evidence presented, there was no reasonable impediment or circumstance diminishing his capacity or indicating significant or material inconvenience or difficulty in him responding to the request, in circumstances where he knew . . . that serious harm could occur to [the plaintiff] if he did not respond to the request and provide treatment.

---

[101] (1996) Feb 5 (unreported) (NSW CA).
[102] (1995) 36 NSWLR 344 (NSW Sup Ct).
[103] Kirby P and Cole JA; Mahoney JA dissenting.   [104] N 101 above.

5.35 Cole JA also relied on the terms of section 27(2) of the Medical Practitioners Act 1938 which imposed a professional obligation (enforceable through disciplinary proceedings) upon a doctor to attend when requested to do so a person in need of urgent medical attention. While the wording of section 27(2) differs from a GP's Terms of Service, reliance upon it by the court is significant and there is no reason to doubt that an English court would look to the Terms of Service for guidance. However, the decision is a limited one. The doctor had been requested to provide treatment and had refused. It was accepted (even by him) that in these circumstances he ought to do so and it was not inconvenient or otherwise unreasonable for him to attend. Whether the case can be seen as going much further is not clear.[105] Certainly, Cole JA approved the view of Badgery-Parker J that, in general, a doctor had no duty to rescue another.[106] The trial judge had, nevertheless, been influenced by an argument that a doctor 'in a professional context' should respond to requests for urgent help.[107] The defendant was at his surgery when asked for help. The Court of Appeal did not deal with this point but nothing in the judgment of Cole JA (or of Kirby P) rejected Badgery-Parker J's approach. At least, then, it could be argued that a doctor who is requested to provide help or, even if not, but finds himself 'in a professional context', may have to volunteer help or be liable in negligence. Driving past an accident on the way to the shops with your family is one thing; momentarily stopping at an accident in a car marked 'doctor on call' before driving on, is quite another. English law may well impose a duty of care in the latter situation regardless of the precise requirements of the GP's Terms of Service.

5.36 A related, though distinct, point concerns the scope of the GP's duty if he does render help. Properly understood, this must be a matter of what a 'reasonable doctor' would do (or not do) in the circumstances. It is not a question of whether a duty of care exists but rather a question of whether there has been a breach of duty and, therefore, ultimately a matter for determination in each case. No a priori generally applicable statement of the doctor's obligations can be made. In the particular circumstances, a reasonable doctor might only provide temporary relief, such as stemming the flow of blood. In other circumstances, he might have to go further and

---

[105] In particular, it would not, it is suggested, be extended to other doctors who happened upon an accident notwithstanding the wording of the GMC's advice, cited above (n 101). It has been suggested that in Canada the law might go further: see Picard, E and Robertson, G, *Legal Liability of Doctors and Hospitals in Canada* (n 16 above), 9–10.

[106] N 101 above, referring to (1995) 36 NSWLR 344, 354.

[107] N 102 above, 357–8. Citing English academic authority, inter alia, Jones, M, *Medical Negligence* (1991), para 2.21 (now 2nd edn, at para 2–026) and Kennedy and Grubb, *Medical Law* (2nd edn, 1994), 79.

provide more treatment for the victim. In one recent case, however, the Court of Appeal has in an obiter statement suggested that the doctor's 'only duty as a matter of law is not to make the victim's condition worse'.[108] There is no basis for stating this as matter of law and there is no English authority for so limiting the content of the doctor's duty.[109] A doctor who allows a road accident victim to die by failing to deal with his injuries does not make the victim's condition 'worse'—assuming he would have died without immediate treatment. Yet, there can be no doubt that medical evidence will in many circumstances suggest that the doctor could reasonably have done something to *improve*, or *prevent a deterioration in*, the victim's condition. Such a doctor is in breach of his duty to act reasonably in preventing foreseeable injury to the victim and should be liable in negligence.[110]

(ii) *Hospital Doctors*

Hospital doctors working within an NHS Trust and, to the extent that they still do so, in Health Authority managed units are in a different position to GPs. The 1992 Regulations do not apply to them. Their employment structure is different and there is normally an employment relationship. A patient who is admitted to a hospital under the care of a particular consultant will be owed a duty of care by that consultant.[111] He will have 'undertaken' the care of that patient. Equally all those in the consultant's 'team', or 'firm' as it is often known, will owe a duty to the patient as soon as they individually 'undertake' the patient's care. When this happens will depend upon the circumstances but would not necessarily require a 'laying on of hands'. The consultant will, at all times, remain legally responsible for the patient's care.

5.37

---

[108] *Capital and Counties plc v Hampshire CC* [1997] 2 All ER 865 (CA) *per* Stuart-Smith LJ at 883.

[109] Reference was made to the Canadian decision of the *Ogopogo* [1970] 1 Lloyd's Rep 257 (Ont CA); [1971] 2 Lloyd's Rep 410 (Can Sup Ct). This case did not involve a rescue by a professional but rather, the private owner of a boat whose guest fell overboard. The decision of the Ontario Court of Appeal (the point being left open in the Supreme Court) may be seen as being concerned with the standard of care expected of a rescuer, in effect, not requiring more than not to make the situation worse. Whilst it is obviously correct that less may be expected in an emergency, perhaps even of professionals, it is not at all clear why professional rescuers such as firemen, police, or doctors are given the benefit of the lower duty.

[110] In America, most state legislatures have sought to exclude physician liability (or limit it to cases of 'gross negligence') in emergency situations through so-called 'Good Samaritan' statutes: see Furrow, B, Greaney, T, Johnson, S, Jost, T and Schwartz, R, *Health Law* (1995), Vol 1, 387–90 and *Annotation*, 68 ALR 4th 294. For Canada see Picard, E and Robertson, G, *Legal Liability of Doctors and Hospitals in Canada* (n 16 above), 178–80.

[111] *Capital and Counties plc v Hampshire CC* [1997] 2 All ER 865 (CA) *per* Stuart-Smith LJ at 883.

He cannot delegate it to another but given the 'team' nature of hospital care in the modern age, it may well be reasonable for him to leave the patient, at any one time, in the immediate care of a team member whether doctor or other health care professional. He cannot be liable for their acts of negligence as there is no employment relationship giving rise to vicarious liability.[112] Of course, he may be in breach of his own duty if he has entrusted the care to an inappropriate 'team' member who, for instance, lacks experience or competence. Equally, he may be in breach of his duty if he unreasonable fails to provide any, or adequate, instructions to his 'team' or supervision of its more junior members.[113] These issues are, however, related to breach of his duty rather than to its existence.

5.38   More problematic is the question of the point at which a hospital doctor comes under a duty of care, if at all, prior to a patient's admission.[114] Could a patient who collapses in the A & E department of a hospital claim in negligence against the doctor on duty? The answer depends upon whether an express or implied undertaking of care has been given by the doctor. The only relevant English authority is *Barnett v Chelsea and Kensington HMC*.[115] The deceased, along with two workmates, drank some tea and began vomiting. They went to the casualty department of the defendant's hospital. The deceased lay down and looked ill. One of the other men told the nurse on duty what had happened. She telephoned the doctor on duty who, being unwell himself, did not see the deceased but told the nurse to send them home and call their own doctors. Some hours later, the deceased died from arsenic poisoning. Nield J dismissed the action on the basis that even if the doctor had seen them, that would have made no difference because an effective antidote could not have been administered in time. Thus, any negligence had not caused the death. However, on the issue of whether the doctor and nurse owed the deceased a duty of care, Nield J concluded that they did because there was a 'close and direct relationship' between them.[116] Of course, in *Barnett* there is no doubt that both the nurse and doctor assumed a responsibility to the deceased by helping and advising him. The latter, but not the former, was patently negligent in not seeing, examining and admitting the deceased to hospital. Thus, on its facts the case is unexceptional.

---

[112] See below, para 8.05, n 45 (nurses).   [113] eg, *Wilsher* (n 74 above).
[114] For a discussion of the hospital's duty, see below, Ch 8.
[115] [1969] 1 QB 428; [1968] 1 All ER 1068.
[116] [1969] 1 QB 428; [1968] 1 All ER 1072. The judgment is not entirely clear and he may have been concerned primarily with the hospital's duty to the deceased. Later he speaks of 'a close and direct relationship between the hospital' and the deceased (ibid). See below, para 8.14.

What the *Barnett* case does not determine is whether the doctor will be under   **5.39**
a duty of care if he simply refuses to have anything to do with the deceased.
There will, in these circumstances, be no express assumption of responsibility
of the care of the individual. However, as was suggested earlier a GP 'in a
professional context' *impliedly* undertakes the care of emergency patients: a
fortiori a doctor in an open A & E department. The *Barnett* case does not go
this far but in principle the duty exists because of the holding out by the
doctor that he is there to deal with emergency cases that present themselves.[117]

(iii) *Liability for Financial Loss*

Generally speaking an action in negligence against a doctor will be for   **5.40**
personal injury or death caused during a medical procedure or it may arise
from the illness or disease for which the patient sought advice or treatment.
However, a doctor may also cause his patient financial loss. Whether a doctor
owes a duty of care in respect of this type of loss will depend upon an
application of the complex case law relating to recovery for negligently
inflicted economic loss.[118] Where a doctor advises a patient in circumstances
where he knows (or ought to know) that the patient will rely upon it, and the
patient thereby suffers economic loss, then under the principle in *Hedley
Byrne v Heller & Co*[119] the doctor will owe a duty of care.

If the doctor is consulted by a patient for a particular purpose which the   **5.41**
doctor is aware of, then it is likely that, on the basis of *Hedley Byrne*, a duty of
care to exercise reasonable care and skill in preparing the report will be owed
by the doctor to the patient. However, where the doctor is unaware that the
patient intends to rely upon his advice or, more likely, the patient relies upon
it for an unrelated and unexpected purpose, then a duty of care will probably
not exist.[120] The point is illustrated by *Stevens v Bermondsey and Southwark
Group HMC*.[121] The plaintiff was advised by a casualty officer at a hospital,
following an accident, that there was nothing wrong with him. In fact, the

---

[117] In *Egedebo v Windermere District Hospital Assn* (1993) 78 BCLR (2d) 63 (BC CA), a
doctor who happened to be in a hospital emergency department, but not 'on call', owed a duty
of care to a patient whom he knew required attention but whom he left for the 'on call' doctor
who was, at that time, busy.
[118] See *Clerk & Lindsell on Torts* (n 13 above), paras 7.54–7.95. The recent decisions of the
House of Lords are discussed in McBride, N and Hughes, A, '*Hedley Byrne* in the House of
Lords: an Interpretation' (1995) 15 LS 376.   [119] [1964] AC 465 (HL).
[120] See for the general issue, albeit in a different context, *Caparo Industries plc v Dickman*
[1990] 2 AC 605 (HL).   [121] (1963) 107 SJ 478.

plaintiff had suffered an injury and subsequently developed spondylosis of the spine. However, relying on what he had been told, the plaintiff had already settled his claim against the local authority which was liable for the accident for a small sum of money. He sued the hospital arguing that the doctor's negligent diagnosis had caused him to suffer economic loss since had he been properly advised he would only have settled his claim for more. Paull J held that the defendant was not liable. The hospital doctor had no duty in respect of the plaintiff's financial affairs, only his physical condition. The answer would, as the judge acknowledged, have been different if the doctor had been consulted with a view to providing advice about litigation. The case remains good law even in the light of developments since *Hedley Byrne*. The doctor did not know, nor in the circumstances of an A & E department should he have known, that the patient would rely upon his advice in settling his claim. It would have been different if he had known.[122] The doctor had assumed a responsibility to him but only in respect of caring for him *qua* doctor and not as providing the professional services of an expert witness.[123]

5.42 However, a doctor may not only owe a duty of care not to cause his patients financial loss on the basis of a narrow application of the *Hedley Byrne* case. A broader basis of liability was accepted by the House of Lords in *Henderson v Merritt Syndicates Ltd*[124] and *White v Jones*[125] whereby a duty of care may exist where the defendant assumes a responsibility to the plaintiff.[126] The assumption may be express—arising from an undertaking by the defendant—or implied by the law—arising from the conduct of the defendant and surrounding circumstances. Hence, an employer has been held to owe a duty to an ex-employee when he carelessly produced a reference for the employee's new employer thereby causing the employee to lose the job and suffer financial loss.[127] Likewise, a doctor who was employed by the plaintiff's potential employer to examine him prior to confirming his job owed a duty of care to the plaintiff not carelessly to produce a report resulting in the plaintiff losing the job and suffering financial loss.[128] The plaintiff in this case was not

---

[122] On which, see *McGrath v Keily and Powell* [1965] IR 497 (Ir H Ct).

[123] However, if the medical expert's report is prepared as a witness in a trial (*Evans v London Hospital Medical College* [1981] 1 WLR 184) or at a pre-trial stage so intimately connected with the conduct of the case that it affects the way a case is to be conducted (*Landall v Dennis Faulkner & Alsop* [1994] 5 Med LR 268), then 'witness immunity' applies and no action can arise. [124] [1995] 2 AC 145 (HL). [125] [1995] 2 AC 207 (HL).

[126] For a criticism of 'assumption of responsibility' as a basis of liability, see Barker, K, 'Unreliable Assumptions in the Modern Law of Negligence' (1993) 109 LQR 461.

[127] *Spring v Guardian Assurance plc* [1995] 2 AC 296 (HL). Although only Lord Goff relied upon the 'touchstone' of 'assumption of responsibility' to decide the case, the subsequent decisions of the House of Lords in *Henderson v Merit* and *White v Jones* have adopted the approach of Lord Goff.

[128] *Baker v Kaye* [1997] IRLR 219 (Robert Owen QC) (doctor not liable on facts because he was not careless).

in a conventional doctor–patient relationship with the doctor and, as will be seen, the issue of what duty is owed in such situations is not clear in England.[129] However, if a doctor assumes a responsibility to an examinee in such a case, a fortiori in the case of a patient when he produces a report at the patient's request or otherwise for a particular purpose. *Baker v Kaye* illustrates that a duty of care may arise for negligent advice given by a doctor to a patient who consults him for the purpose of a 'medical reference' which the doctor knows (or ought to know) will be relied upon by the patient or a third party to whom it is to be supplied.

(iv) *For Psychiatric Injury*[130]

A patient who suffers emotional distress, grief, or anguish arising out of injuries resulting from medical negligence will, in the usual way, be able to recover general damages to reflect this in addition to the other non-pecuniary and pecuniary damages recoverable for his personal injuries.[131] A patient who does not suffer any personal injury may not, however, recover damages for mere distress or mental anguish.[132] An action could only be brought if psychiatric injury is caused, that is, there is a recognised psychiatric illness.[133] The complex and limiting rules in *McLoughlin*[134] and *Alcock*[135] which are applied to 'secondary victims' who suffer psychiatric injury, do not apply. The doctor owes the patient a duty of care not to cause personal injury which, for this purpose, includes psychiatric injury. The pre-existing duty owed to the patient, as the 'primary victim', will suffice to base an action for psychiatric injuries even where no other injury is suffered.[136] The duty would also extend to allow a claim for psychiatric injury caused by the *fear* of being injured by a doctor, for example, on discovering that a doctor who had treated the patient was infected with HIV.[137] Providing there was a foreseeable risk of injury

5.43

---

[129] See below, paras 5.88–5.104.

[130] See the comprehensive study, Mullany, N and Handford, P, *Tort Liability for Psychiatric Damage* (1993).

[131] eg, *Kralj v McGrath* [1986] 1 All ER 54 (contract and negligence actions).

[132] eg, *Reilly v Merseyside RHA* [1995] 6 Med LR 246 (CA).

[133] cf *Grieve v Salford HA* [1991] 2 Med LR 295; *Bagley v North Hertfordshire HA* (1986) 136 NLJ 1014.   [134] *McLoughlin v O'Brien* [1983] AC 410; [1982] 2 All ER 298 (HL).

[135] *Alcock v Chief Constable of South Yorkshire Police* [1992] 1 AC 310; [1991] 4 All ER 907 (HL).

[136] *Alcock*, ibid, 923–4 *per* Lord Oliver; *Page v Smith* [1996] AC 155 (HL); *Frost v Chief Constable of the South Yorkshire Police* [1997] 1 All ER 540 (CA).

[137] For a discussion of the 'AIDS phobia' cases in an instructive US case, see *Faya and Rossi v Almaraz* (1993) 620 A 2d 327 (My CA).

to the patient,[138] the psychiatric injury claim would fall within the approach of the House of Lords in *Page v Smith*.[139]

5.44 An illustration of the 'primary victim' approach can be found in the case of *Tredgett and Tredgett v Bexley HA*.[140] The plaintiffs, who were married, suffered psychiatric illness as a result of the defendants' negligence during the birth of their child who subsequently died. Judge White awarded both plaintiffs damages for their psychiatric illnesses. He relied on the participants' category identified by Lord Oliver in *Alcock* which obviously covered the mother but also, he held, the father.[141]

5.45 Another situation in which a doctor might cause psychiatric injury to a patient is where he gives false information or communicates accurate information carelessly to the patient after treatment. If a doctor did so deliberately, intending to cause harm to the patient, there would be liability under the rule in *Wilkinson v Downton*.[142] This, of course, will be rare. In principle, however, a duty of care exists between a doctor and patient which would encompass negligent post-operative advice whether in its content or in its method of communication.

5.46 In *AB v Tameside and Glossop HA*,[143] the parties conceded that the defendant[144] owed a duty of care when negligently communicating accurate information to obstetric patients (present and former) about their possible exposure to a health worker infected with HIV. While noting that no previous case seemed to deal with this point, the Court of Appeal accepted the concession and were content to state that 'we do not have to decide this point, or to consider whether such a duty exists, or the parameters of that duty, where there is no pre-existing relationship of care.'[145] By embarking upon communication with the patient, the doctor assumes a duty of care in respect of what he is undertaking whether it be diagnosis, pre-treatment advice, treatment or *post-treatment* advice.[146] Providing it is reasonably fore-

---

[138] It may also be necessary for the patient to show a 'shocking' event (cf *Walker v Northumberland CC* [1995] 1 All ER 737) but this could lie in the manner in which the risk of infection was discovered: *Sion v Hampstead HA* [1994] 5 Med LR 170 (CA) *per* Peter Gibson LJ at 176.   [139] N 136 above.
[140] [1994] 5 Med LR 178. Grubb, (1995) 3 Med L Rev 213, 215–6 (Commentary).
[141] *Alcock* (n 135 above), 923–4 *per* Lord Oliver.
[142] [1897] 2 QB 57. See also *Powell v Boldaz* (1997) 39 BMLR 35 (CA).
[143] [1997] 8 Med LR 91 (CA). See Kennedy (1997) 5 Med L Rev 338 (Commentary).
[144] The case concerned the duty of the hospital but there is no difference, in principle, if the advice is given by a doctor.   [145] N 143 above, 93 *per* Brooke LJ.
[146] There may be a duty to volunteer information about medical mistakes: *Lee v South Thames RHA* [1985] 2 All ER 385 (CA), 389 *per* Sir John Donaldson MR; *Naylor v Preston AHA* [1987] 2 All ER 353 (CA), 360 *per* Sir John Donaldson MR; *Stamos v Davies* (1986) 21 DLR (4th) 507 (Ont H Ct); *Gerber v Pines* (1934) 79 SJ 13; *Daniels v Heskin* [1954] IR 73 (Ir Sup Ct). For a discussion see Robertson, G, 'Fraudulent Concealment and the Duty to Disclose Medical Mistakes' (1987) 25 Alta LR 215.

seeable that this negligent advice could cause psychiatric injury, as it may well be depending upon the nature of the advice, then a duty of care will exist. Hence, at least in the case of existing, and even former, patients the concession was surely properly made.[147]

2. To Third Parties

Although a doctor owes a duty of care to his patients, it is unclear whether a **5.47** doctor will ever owe a duty of care to third parties who are not his patients.[148] In one recent decision, speaking on behalf of the Court of Appeal, Stuart-Smith LJ went so far as to say that a doctor only owed a duty of care to his patients and never anyone else, including in that case the parents of the deceased patient.[149] The statement of the Court of Appeal should, perhaps, be understood as merely asserting the limited proposition that a doctor only owes a duty *qua* doctor *to treat* his patients. This is not, of course, the same as saying he does not owe a duty of care, the content of which might include warning or advising others but not requiring him to act as their doctor. In certain circumstances, a doctor may owe a duty of care to someone who is not his patient. It is helpful to consider three situations: (1) the dangerous patient; (2) financial loss; and (3) psychiatric injury.

(i) *Dangerous Patients*

As a result of his treatment and responsibility for the care of a patient, a **5.48** doctor may know (or reasonably ought to know) that his patient is a danger to others. A number of examples can be contemplated:

(1) a doctor who knows that his patient suffers from an infectious disease which he is likely to transmit to others through sexual contact or otherwise;[150]

(2) a psychiatrist whose mentally ill patient threatens to injure or kill another person and does so;[151]

(3) a general practitioner who has an epileptic patient who drives and injures or kills someone during an attack;[152]

---

[147] The legal basis of the duty will be negligence if injury is suffered as a result of non-disclosure. If no such injury is caused the duty must rest elsewhere, for example, as an aspect of the parties fiduciary relationship: *Gerula v Flores* (1995) 126 DLR (4th) 506 (Ont CA). See generally, Grubb, A, 'The Doctor as Fiduciary' (1994) 47 CLP 311 especially at 335–8.
[148] See generally, Giesen, D, *International Medical Malpractice Law* (1988), 157–61.
[149] *Powell v Boldaz* (1997), 39 BMLR 35, 45 (CA).
[150] eg, *Pittman Estate v Bain* (1994) 112 DLR (4th) 257 (Ont Gen Div).
[151] eg, *Tarasoff v Regents of the University of California* (1976) 551 P 2d 334 (Cal Sup Ct).
[152] eg, *Toms v Foster* (1994) Ont CA LEXIS 346.

(4) a male patient who is wrongly advised that a vasectomy operation has been successful and need not take any contraceptive precautions with the result that his sexual partner becomes pregnant.[153]

Does a doctor owe a duty to any of these 'injured' third parties?

(a) Some Overseas Authority

Infectious Diseases

5.49 In the context of transmission of infectious or contagious diseases by a patient to a third party, US courts have held doctors liable for (i) failing to diagnose the disease; (ii) failing to inform the third party (or others) of the danger; (iii) negligently advising the third party that there is no danger; and (iv) failing to prevent the spread of the disease.[154] Usually, however, the courts have restricted the group of potential victims who are owed a duty by the doctor to, for example, close family[155] or sexual partners.[156]

5.50 A number of recent cases have concerned the transmission of HIV by a patient to another. In *DiMarco v Lynch Homes-Chester County*[157] a blood technician accidentally infected herself with hepatitis through a sharps' injury. Her doctors told her that if she remained symptom free for six weeks, it would mean that she had not been infected. She was not advised to refrain from sexual intercourse although she did for eight weeks. She remained symptom free and, thereafter, she resumed sexual relations with her boyfriend (the plaintiff) who became infected. The plaintiff sued the doctors arguing that they should have advised the patient to refrain from sexual relations for six months otherwise she could infect her sexual partner. The Pennsylvania Supreme Court (by a majority of 4–3) held that the doctors owed the plaintiff a duty of care. The Court was greatly influenced by public health policy concerns to prevent the spread of communicable diseases and to further that policy by placing responsibility, in these circumstances, on the only person who was aware of the danger—the doctor. One passage in the majority judgment of Larsen J is particularly important:[158]

> When a physician treats a patient who has been exposed to or who has contracted a communicable and/or contagious disease, it is imperative that the

---

[153] eg, *Goodwill v BPAS* [1996] 2 All ER 161 (CA).
[154] See *Annotation*, 3 ALR 5th 370.
[155] eg, *Bradshaw v Daniels* (1993) 854 SW 2d 865 (Tenn Sup Ct) ('Rocky Mountain Fever' transmitted by ticks). See Kennedy, (1994) 2 Med L Rev 237 (Commentary).
[156] eg, *Gammell v United States* (1984) 727 F 2d 950 (10th Circ). See Grubb, A and Pearl, D, *Blood Testing, AIDS and DNA Profiling: Law and Policy* (1990), 49–52.
[157] (1990) 525 Pa 558 (Pa Sup Ct).   [158] ibid, 562–2.

physician give his or her patient the proper advice about preventing the spread of the disease. Communicable diseases are so named because they are readily spread from person to person. Physicians are the first line of defense against the spread of communicable diseases, because physicians know what measures must be taken to prevent the infection of others. The patient must be advised to take certain sanitary measures, or to remain quarantined for a period of time, or to practice sexual abstinence or what is commonly referred to as 'safe sex'.

Such precautions are not taken to protect the health of the patient, whose well-being has already been compromised, rather such precautions are taken to safeguard the health of others. Thus, the duty of a physician in such circumstances extends to those 'within the foreseeable orbit of risk of harm' . . . If a third person is in that class of persons whose health is likely to be threatened by the patient, and if erroneous advice is given to that patient to the ultimate detriment of the third person, the third person has a cause of action against the physician, because the physician should recognize that the services rendered to the patient are necessary for the protection of the third person.

The majority emphasised the breadth of their decision. The duty was not owed only to married partners:[159] to so limit it would be 'exalting an unheeded morality over reality'.[160] Also, while it might be thought that in *DiMarco* the plaintiff was both known and identifiable to the defendants, in fact this played no part in the majority's reasoning.[161] The duty was also not so limited: it was owed to 'anyone who is physically intimate with the patient'.[162]

Unlike the situation where a patient suffers from a contagious or infectious disease,[163] in an HIV case a duty of care would not be owed to the patient's 'extended family' since they would not be at risk of infection.[164] It may, however, extend to future as well as current sexual partners who are subsequently put at risk of infection. In *Reisner v Regents of California*,[165] the California Court of Appeal adopted and applied this reasoning and rejected the argument that to impose a duty on the defendants would not prevent future harm. The patient received a transfusion of blood and blood products infected with HIV antibodies. Her doctor, on discovering this the following day, decided not to tell her or her family. Some years later, she commenced a sexual relationship with the plaintiff and, unknowingly, infected him with the HIV virus. Shortly before her death, the patient was told she had AIDS and

5.51

---

[159] See also *Pittman Estate v Bain* (1994) 112 DLR (4th) 257 (Ont Gen Div); additional reasons, (1994) 112 DLR (4th) 482, (1994) 112 DLR (4th) 494 and (1994) 35 CPC (3d) 767 (duty owed to wife of HIV positive patient).
[160] N 157 above, 564 *per* Larson J.   [161] See ibid, 565 *per* Flaherty J (dissenting).
[162] ibid, 563 *per* Larson J.
[163] eg, *Gammell v United States* (1984) 727 F 2d 950 (10th Circ).
[164] See *Lemon v Stewart* (1996) 682 A 2d 1177 (Ms Ct Spec App).
[165] (1995) 37 Cal Rptr 2d 518.

immediately communicated this fact to the plaintiff, who subsequently learned of his own sero-positive status. In his action in negligence, the California Court of Appeal held that the doctor's duty of care extended to the plaintiff. Although not readily identifiable, the plaintiff, as a sexual partner of the patient, was a foreseeable victim even though the injury he complained of occurred some years after the negligent act. The defendant's duty was to warn the patient or her parents, who were likely to have warned the plaintiff of the risks and thereby have avoided the risk of transmission by abstaining from sexual contact or practising 'safe sex'. Vogel J said:[166]

> Civil liability for a negligent failure to warn under the circumstances of this case may not hasten the day when AIDS can be cured or prevented but it may, in the meantime, protect one or more persons from unnecessary exposure to this deadly virus.

Psychiatric Patients

5.52 Likewise in cases of dangerous psychiatric patients, some US courts have recognised that a psychiatrist owes a duty of care to potential victims of a dangerous patient.[167] Most famously, the California Supreme Court held such a duty existed in *Tarasoff v Regents of University of California*.[168] The Supreme Court held that a psychotherapist owed a duty of care to his patient's victim whom he knew was the patient's intended target. Tobriner J stated:[169]

> Although . . . under the common law, as a general rule, one person owed no duty to control the conduct of another, nor to warn those endangered by such conduct, the courts have carved out an exception to this rule in cases in which the defendant stands in some special relationship to either the person whose conduct needs to be controlled or in a relationship to the foreseeable victim of that conduct.

5.53 The Court balanced the public interest in maintaining the confidentiality of the defendant's client against the public interest in protecting others from assaults and concluded that the defendant had a legal duty to take reasonable steps to avert the danger by warning the victim, the police or others who might appraise her of the danger. Tobriner J said:[170]

> In this risk-infested society we can hardly tolerate the further exposure to danger that would result from a concealed knowledge of the therapist that his patient was lethal.

5.54 In *Tarasoff*, it was important that the victim was known and identified to the defendant by his patient. In other US jurisdictions courts have interpreted

---

[166] ibid, 522.   [167] *Annotation*, 83 ALR 3d 1201.
[168] (1976) 551 P 2d 334 (Cal Sup Ct).   [169] ibid, 343.   [170] ibid, 347.

Tarasoff in different ways. Some have interpreted it widely so as to impose a duty to warn whenever it is foreseeable that a person may be endangered.[171] On the whole, however, courts have taken a more limited view, requiring not only that the victim be foreseeable, but also that the particular victim be identifiable.[172] Some jurisdictions have rejected the duty altogether.[173]

Dangerous Drivers

A patient may be a danger to others because of his medical condition, for **5.55** example, if he were to drive a car or other vehicle. In a number of US[174] and Canadian cases, courts have held doctors liable to passengers and other road users who have been injured when a patient lost control of a car or other vehicle when he was unfit to drive[175] and suffered, for example, an epileptic fit,[176] a diabetic attack,[177] or drowsiness brought on by medication prescribed by the doctor. Liability has been imposed in three sorts of situations: where the doctor (1) created the 'dangerous' condition, for example, by prescribing drugs;[178] (2) was aware of the patient's physical condition;[179] and (3) affirmatively advised the patient that it was safe to drive.[180] The duty of care is owed to the third party but the negligence consists of failing to warn *the patient* of his dangerous condition.[181] Where it has been suggested that the doctor should control the patient by stopping him driving, the courts have been reluctant to impose this onerous (and legally impossible) obligation.[182] The duty is generally held to be owed to all foreseeable road users even though the injured person's precise identity is not known.[183] However, recently, some courts have adopted a more restrictive approach derived, by

---

[171] eg, *Bardoni v Kim* (1986) 390 NW 2d 218 (Mich CA) (foreseeable individual); *Lipari v Sears, Roebuck & Co* (1980) 497 F Supp 185 (DC) (foreseeable class).
[172] See eg, *Thomson v County of Alameda* (1980) 614 P 2d 728 (Cal Sup Ct).
[173] eg, *Cole v Taylor* (1981) 301 NW 2d 766 (Iowa Sup Ct).
[174] Discussed, *Annotation*, 43 ALR 4th 153.
[175] *Joy v Eastern Main Medical Center* (1987) 529 A 2d 1364 (Me Sup Ct) (failure to warn not to drive wearing an eye-patch); *Toms v Foster* 1994 Ont CA Lexis 346 (driver suffering from cervical spondylosis).
[176] eg, *Spillane v Wasserman* (1992) 13 CCLT 267 (Ont H Ct).
[177] eg, *Myers v Quesenberry* (1983) 193 Cal Rptr 733 (Cal CA).
[178] eg, *Gooden v Tips* (1983) 651 SW 2d 364 (Tex CA); *Kaiser v Suburban Transportation System* (1965) 398 P 2d 14 (Wash Sup Ct); *Schuster v Altenberg* (1988) 424 NW 2d 159 (Wis Sup Ct).
[179] eg, *Myers v Quesenberry* (n 177 above); *Freese v Lemmon* (1973) 210 NW 2d 576 (Iowa Sup Ct), subsequently, following trial, held no negligence: (1978) 267 NW 2d 680.
[180] eg, *Freese v Lemmon*, ibid.   [181] See *Myers v Quesenberry* (n 177 above), 733.
[182] eg, *Purdy v Estate of Shaw* (1987) 514 NYS 2d 407 (NY App Div) (no duty on health facility to restrain licensed driver).
[183] See *Myers v Quesenberry* (n 177 above), 733. See also *Duvall v Goldin* (1984) 362 NW 2d 275 (Mich CA); *Freese v Lemmon* (1973) 210 NW 2d 576 (Iowa Sup Ct); *Gooden v Tips* (1983) 651 SW 2d 364 (Tex CA).

analogy, from the 'dangerous psychiatric patient' cases such as *Tarasoff*. Consequently, courts have refused to impose a duty of care unless the third party is 'known and identifiable'[184] or where there is a 'special relationship' between the doctor and the patient whereby the doctor has control over the patient.[185] In context, the latter approach virtually eliminates claims against doctors by injured passengers or other road users.

Genetic Conditions

5.56 Analogous to the situations of the infectious or dangerous psychiatric patient are those where the patient is not strictly speaking 'dangerous' but because of information gained during the course of the doctor–patient relationship the doctor knows that harm may come to the other. An illustration of this occurs where the doctor discovers genetic information about his patient which has relevance to the genetic health of members of the patient's family. The increasing potential for determining a patient's genetic 'make-up' will, undoubtedly, increase the incidence of such cases in the future. In two American decisions, courts have held that a doctor owed a duty of care to the children of a patient whom he discovered had a serious inheritable genetic condition. In *Pate v Threlkel*,[186] the defendant treated his patient for thyroid cancer which was genetically inheritable. Three years later, the patient's adult daughter discovered that she suffered from the same condition which was, by this time, incurable. She claimed that if her father had been told, she would have been tested and taken preventative steps which would, more likely than not, have resulted in a cure. The Florida Supreme Court held that a doctor could owe a duty of care to someone who was not his patient. The court concluded that a doctor owed a duty only to 'known' and 'identifiable' individuals who were at risk.[187] Thus, he owed the patient's daughter a duty to warn the patient of the danger of his children inheriting the condition. Further, the court held that the doctor's duty was to warn the patient and not to breach the confidentiality of the patient by directly warning the child. Wells J stated:[188]

---

[184] See *Werner v Varner, Stafford & Seaman* (1995) 659 So 2d 1308 (Fla CA) (duty not owed to public at large); applying *Pate v Threlkel* (1995) 661 So 2d 278 (Fla Sup Ct) (duty to children of patient in respect of the patient's inheritable genetic condition), and see below, para 5.56.

[185] See *Caldwell v Hassan* (1996) 925 P 2d 422 (Kan Sup Ct) (failure to warn patient who suffered from daytime sleep disorder not to drive). The court left open whether liability might exist if the doctor 'created a risk of harm' to the plaintiff (at 431) but, on the facts, there was no evidence that the medication prescribed by the doctor 'caused or worsened [the patient's] daytime drowsiness problem' (ibid). [186] (1995) 661 So 2d 278 (Fla Sup Ct).

[187] Relying on an 'infectious disease' case: *Hofmann v Blackmon* (1970) 241 So 2d 752 (Fla CA). [188] N 186 above, 282.

. . . the patient ordinarily can be expected to pass on the warning. To require the physician to seek out and warn various members of the patient's family would often be difficult or impractical and would place too heavy a burden upon the physician. Thus, we emphasis that in any circumstances in which the physician has a duty to warn of a genetically transferable disease, that duty will be satisfied by warning the patient.

The reasoning of the Florida Supreme Court is, however, of limited importance in England. First, the court applied a test for determining a duty of care based, in essence, upon 'foreseeability of risk'.[189] English law would require more to establish a duty of care in this context applying the three-stage test in the *Caparo* case. Secondly, the court relied heavily upon the expert evidence that it was a doctor's professional obligation to warn of the dangers of inheriting the condition.[190] While this may be some evidence supporting the imposition of a legal duty of care, English law would not necessarily adopt the professional standard.[191] **5.57**

In the second American case, *Safer v Pack*,[192] a New Jersey appellate court also imposed a duty of care in the context of genetic disease. The defendant treated his patient for a genetically related form of colon cancer from which the patient eventually died. At the time the plaintiff was aged ten, and twenty-six years later she was diagnosed as suffering from the same condition. The plaintiff alleged that the defendant knew of the inheritable nature of the condition and should have warned those at risk so that they might take early preventative measures. The New Jersey court held that the doctor did owe a duty of care to the plaintiff. Relying on cases concerned with the transmission of infectious disease and physical threats by dangerous patients,[193] the court held that the duty was owed to all 'members of the immediate family of the patient who may be adversely affected'.[194] Kesten J stated[195] that '[t]he individual or group at risk is easily identified, and substantial future harm may be averted or minimized by a timely and effective warning'. The court accepted that the limited duty to warn of an avertible risk those defined by familial connection was 'sufficiently narrow to serve the interests of justice'.[196] **5.58**

As for the content of the duty, the court concluded that the duty 'require[d] that reasonable steps be taken to assure that the information reaches those likely to be affected or is made available for their benefit'.[197] This, the court **5.59**

[189] ibid, 280.   [190] ibid, 281 and 282.
[191] But contrast *Baker v Kaye* [1997] IRLR 219.
[192] (1996) 677 A 2d 1188 (Super Ct App Div).
[193] *McIntosh v Milano* (1979) 403 A 2d 500; *Tarasoff v Regents of University of California* (1976) 551 P 2d 334.
[194] N 192 above, 1192 citing *Schroeder v Perkel* (1981) 87 NJ 53, 65.
[195] ibid, 1192.   [196] ibid, 1192 *per* Kestin J.

contemplated, might be satisfied by warning the patient in a case like *Safer* where the third party was a young child when the genetic condition was discovered. However, unlike the court in *Pate v Threlkel*, the New Jersey court refused to rule out the possibility that the duty might entail an obligation to warn the family member *directly*. Kestin J said:[198]

> It may be necessary, at some stage, to resolve a conflict between the physician's broader duty to warn and his fidelity to an expressed preference of the patient that nothing be said to family members about the details of the disease.

(b) English Law

5.60 English law has never directly addressed the question of a doctor's liability in any of these four situations. The analytical structure of English law is, however, clear: it is the 'three-stage' test propounded by the House of Lords in *Caparo Industries plc v Dickman*.[199] For the doctor to owe the third party a duty of care there must be *'foreseeability'*, *'proximity'* of relationship and the imposition of a duty must be *'fair, just, and reasonable'*.[200] In this context 'foreseeability' of injury is unlikely to be a problem, the real 'battle ground' will be 'proximity' and the policy issues under the third limb. It is probably unduly narrow to see these requirements as wholly distinct and hermetically sealed from each other because particular factors may well influence a court in reaching a view on both requirements. The law will develop incrementally by analogy to existing situations of recognised liability. There are a number of formidable difficulties in the way of a plaintiff establishing such a claim.

Omissions and Third Parties

5.61 First, the third party's claim will often be that the doctor *failed* to protect him by, for example, warning him or another of the danger. English law is generally reluctant to impose a duty of care where the defendant is alleged to have failed to act (ie, for an omission).[201] Secondly, the plaintiff may be relying on the doctor's failure to prevent an intermediary voluntarily and intentionally injuring the third party.[202] Generally, this person alone is viewed as responsible for the plaintiff's injuries.[203] A duty may exist, however, if the defendant could (and should) have controlled that intermediary who was the direct cause of the plaintiff's harm.[204] This is unlikely unless, for

---

[197] ibid, 1192 *per* Kestin J.   [198] ibid, 1192.
[199] [1990] 2 AC 605; [1990] 1 All ER 568 (HL).
[200] See especially, ibid, *per* Lord Bridge at 574 and *per* Lord Oliver at 585.
[201] See *Smith v Littlewoods Organisation Ltd* [1987] 1 AC 241.
[202] As in the 'dangerous patient' or 'driver' cases or 'infectious disease' cases. Not, however, in the 'genetic' transmission cases.   [203] *Smith* (n 201 above).
[204] *Home Office v Dorset Yacht* [1970] AC 1004; [1970] 2 All ER 294 (HL).

example, the patient is a psychiatric patient who has been detained under the Mental Health Act 1983 and is prematurely released, or should have been but the doctor fails to instigate the procedure for detention under the Act. Another illustration could arise in the area of infectious diseases, but only where the provisions of the Public Health (Control of Diseases) Act 1984 allow for detention. In one case, a hospital[205] was held liable where it released a dangerous patient who assaulted and injured the plaintiff, having broken into her home.[206] However, the authority of this case is somewhat limited: it was a summing up to a jury and the judge assumed a duty of care arose and was more concerned with the issue of breach. Liability may be restricted to injuries caused to others themselves within the control of the defendant[207] or where, once escaped, the 'dangerous patient' injures those in a close vicinity during his escape.[208] It may, therefore, not be followed in the future.[209]

Increased Risk of Injury

Thirdly, the courts are unwilling to shoulder a doctor with the burden of liability where he has not made the plaintiff's position worse and they may well insist that he has *increased the risk* of the intermediary harming the plaintiff.[210] Hence, a doctor who, for example, creates a risk of 'injury' by infecting a patient with HIV[211] could be liable whilst one who merely failed to avert the risk by warning of the danger will not.[212] Consequently, for this reason a failure to advise a third party of their genetic condition will probably not give rise to an action. Ultimately, of course, this is an unsatisfactory distinction. Being the agent of the risk creation is only one indicium of culpability—it increases the moral turpitude of the individual—but there are others. Furthermore, it will inevitably lead to fine distinctions being drawn in cases as to which particular category any given set of facts falls into,[213] but

5.62

---

[205] The duty is probably that of the institution rather than any particular doctor.
[206] *Holgate v Lancashire Mental Hospitals Board* [1937] 4 All ER 19.
[207] See *Ellis v Home Office* [1953] 2 QB 135 (CA) (injury caused by one prisoner to another). The same reasoning would apply if the injured party was a visitor or, indeed, himself injured: see eg, *Hay v Grampian Health Board* [1995] 6 Med LR 128 and Grubb, A, (1995) 3 Med L Rev 299 (Commentary).
[208] As in *Dorset Yacht* itself (n 204 above). Contrast, *Marti v Smith and Home Office* (1981) 131 NLJ 1028.
[209] In *Home Office v Dorset Yacht* (n 204 above), Lord Diplock reserved his opinion on its correctness (at 328) explaining it as a case involving a person not responsible for his actions; Lord Reid appears to have considered it correct as a matter of private law (but doubted the public law issue raised, at 301–2); Lord Morris considered it correct (at 309).
[210] eg *Hill v Chief Constable of West Yorkshire* [1989] AC 53, explaining *Dorset Yacht*.
[211] *Reisner v Regents of the University of California* (1995) 37 Cal Rptr 2d 518 (Cal CA).
[212] *Goodwill v BPAS* [1996] 2 All ER 161 (CA), discussed below, paras 5.65–5.67.
[213] Hence, a doctor who prescribes a medication to a patient 'creates' a risk to other road users whilst a doctor who only fails to diagnose or inform a patient of an existing condition does not: see its acceptance in *Calwell v Hassan* (1996) 925 P 2d 422 (Kan Sup Ct). The satisfactory nature of this distinction is questionable.

it seems to appeal to the English judiciary as encapsulating a necessary condition for culpability.

Identifiable Victims

5.63 Fourthly, liability would not be based upon foreseeability of injury to another alone; certainly if all that is foreseeable is injury to others in general. Even if all the other requirements for liability were in place, English law would seek to limit the range of liability by closely circumscribing the breadth of liability through other control mechanisms.[214] At the very least, foreseeability of harm to a particular person or perhaps a small identifiable group would be essential.[215]

Policy and Confidentiality

5.64 Finally, the courts will investigate the policy arguments that might tell against imposing liability upon the defendant, such as the burdens it would create, the inconveniences that would be generated, and any deleterious effects such a duty might have upon the medical profession. In particular, the courts will be reluctant to impose a duty upon a doctor which requires him to disclose information in breach of confidence. This may not be crucial where the duty only contemplates disclosure to the patient rather than to the third party (or another). Hence, in the *Reisner* case, no breach of confidence was contemplated.[216] The doctor only has a duty to tell his patient in order for her to act responsibly by desisting from risky behaviour or warning her partners of the risk they might be running. Where a breach of confidence is contemplated (even one which could be justified), however, the better position is to *allow* disclosure (a discretion) where there are exceptional circumstances of danger (or harm) to others, but not to *require* it (a duty).[217] In other words, the law should only provide a justification for a breach of confidence. This is consistent with the ethical guidance issued by the General Medical Council[218] and the Department of Health[219] and, in the genetics context, by other bodies.[220]

---

[214] *Dorset Yacht* (n 204 above); *Hill* (n 210 above) and *Caparo* (n 199 above).

[215] See eg, *Osman v Ferguson* [1993] 4 All ER 344 (CA) where it was accepted by two judges in the Court of Appeal that there was proximity between the police and a specific individual who was known to them to be at risk: see McCowan LJ at 350; Simon Brown LJ agreed; Beldam LJ at 354 expressing no view.

[216] See also *Pate v Threlkel* (n 186 above). This would also be the case in the 'dangerous driver' cases where the duty is to advise the driver/patient himself.

[217] See Grubb, A and Pearl, D, *Blood Testing, AIDS and DNA Profiling* (n 156 above), 48–55.

[218] *Duties of Doctors: Confidentiality* (para 18) and their specific guidance in relation to HIV (contrast, *HIV and AIDS* (para 19)).

[219] *The Protection and Use of Patient Information* (1996) para 5.6.

[220] Nuffield Council on Bioethics, *Genetic Screening* (1993), ch 5.

Goodwill v BPAS

One English case which does concern the liability of a doctor to a third party **5.65**
is *Goodwill v BPAS*.[221] The defendant performed a vasectomy on his patient
and subsequently advised him that the operation had been successful and that
he need not take further contraceptive measures. Three years later the patient
met the plaintiff. He told her about the vasectomy and after she had consulted her own doctor, who confirmed there was almost no chance of her
becoming pregnant, they started a sexual relationship. The plaintiff became
pregnant and, following the birth of a healthy child, she sued the defendant in
negligence for the costs arising out of the birth. The defendant's action in
negligence was struck out because the Court of Appeal held that he did not
owe the plaintiff a duty of care.

Interestingly, the court did not reach its conclusion by deciding in limine that a **5.66**
doctor could not owe a duty to the patient's future sexual partner. Instead, the
court applied the approach adopted in negligent advice cases where the defendant's advice is passed on to a third party/plaintiff. The court held that there was
no special relationship between the doctor and plaintiff since he did not know
(nor could he have known) that his advice would be passed onto the plaintiff and
relied upon by her. Thus, the doctor had not voluntarily assumed a responsibility
to her. The court distinguished the earlier case of *Thake v Maurice*[222] where the
plaintiff was present when the advice was given to both her and her husband.

As argued, *Goodwill* is a difficult decision to accept. Curiously, it was argued **5.67**
on the basis that the plaintiff had suffered economic loss. She had not, since
the earlier decision of the Court of Appeal in *Walkin v South Manchester
HA*[223] clearly establishes that the plaintiff had suffered 'personal injury'.
Walkin was not referred to by the court in *Goodwill* and it was binding
upon the judges. This might have made a difference to the reasoning of the
court (and thus the outcome) because the court relied almost exclusively on
the case law concerned with the liability of auditors for economic loss caused
to third parties as a result of negligent advice.[224] It is not entirely clear why
the particular description of 'proximity' in these cases has anything to do with
failed sterilisations. The context is so different and the demands of policy are
not, manifestly, the same. There is no reason to generalise from the

---

[221] [1996] 2 All ER 161 (CA).   [222] [1986] QB 644 (CA), discussed below, Ch 12.
[223] [1995] 4 All ER 132 (CA), and see Grubb, A, (1996) 4 Med L Rev 94 (Commentary).
[224] eg, *Caparo*, (n 199 above), and *James McNaughton Papers Group Ltd v Hicks Anderson
& Co (A Firm)* [1991] 1 All ER 134 (CA).

contraceptive advice context of *Goodwill* to all the situations of injury to third parties considered here.[225]

5.68 Thus, in conclusion, there are considerable difficulties in establishing the necessary ingredients of 'proximity' and 'public policy' for a duty of care to be accepted by an English court where a doctor's patient causes physical injury to a third party.[226] It is likely that a court would require a third party to establish as relevant: that the doctor had 'control' over the patient; that the doctor 'increased the risk of harm' to the patient; that the patient was 'identifiable to a high degree of specificity'; and that no (unjustified?) breach of confidence was contemplated. Even then, it may be that the court would invoke public policy to exclude liability.

(ii) *For Financial Loss*

5.69 A doctor who is requested by his patient to provide a medical report to a third party, for example, an insurance company or potential employer, may owe a duty of care to that third party to do so carefully so that the third party does not incur economic loss.[227] Following *Hedley Byrne v Heller* a doctor, knowing whom the recipient of the report is to be, the purpose for which it will be used, and that the third party will (or is likely to) rely upon it, undertakes (or assumes) a responsibility to the third party sufficient to impose a legal duty to exercise reasonable care and skill in preparing the report.[228]

5.70 In the unlikely event that the doctor provides a medical report on the patient without knowing what use it will be put to, or if the report is put to an unexpected use or one which could not reasonably be anticipated by the doctor, it may well be that the all important 'assumption of responsibility' is absent. It will not, however, be necessary for the doctor to know the precise identity of the third party providing he knows the nature of the third party's use, for example, that it is an insurance company.

---

[225] For further discussion of *Goodwill* (n 221 above), see Grubb, A,(1997) 5 Med L Rev 250, 255–6.

[226] See also discussion in Jones, *Medical Negligence* (n 3 above), 73–9.

[227] See eg, *Wharton Transport Corp v Bridges* (1980) 606 SW 2d 521 (Tenn Sup Ct) (failure by doctor to report to employer the disabilities of an employee resulting in claim by injured person against employer for negligence of employee). See also *North American Co for Life & Health Insurance v Berger* (1981) 648 F 2d 305 (5th Cir) (insurance company had action against doctor for negligent medical assessment of employee entitlement under insurance coverage).

[228] This should follow from the reasoning in *Spring v Guardian Assurance plc* [1995] 2 AC 296; [1994] 3 All ER 129 (HL), but notice the reservation by Lord Goff at 147.

The same reasoning would apply if the doctor had no pre-existing relation- **5.71** ship with the 'patient' but was specifically engaged directly by the third party to provide the medical report. Here, there would undoubtedly be an undertaking or assumption of responsibility to the third party who requested the report. And, of course, there would almost certainly be a contract between the doctor and third party which would include an implied term which could be the basis for a contractual negligence claim unconstrained by requirements for recovering economic loss in the tort of negligence.[229]

(iii) *For Psychiatric Injury*

The circumstances in which damages may be recovered for negligently caused **5.72** nervous shock (psychiatric injury) are confusing and, often, uncertain.[230] A distinction has to be drawn between 'participants' or 'primary victims' and others who are merely 'secondary victims' of the defendant's negligence.[231] As regards the latter, the House of Lords in the two cases of *McLoughlin v O'Brien*[232] and *Alcock v Chief Constable of South Yorkshire*[233] imposed arbitrary limits upon claims for psychiatric injury not for any logical reason but rather to reflect 'the court's perception of what is the reasonable area for the imposition of liability'.[234] The courts have explicitly accepted that they are making policy choices about the scope of liability. In particular, the law requires

(i)   a close relationship between the victim and the plaintiff (either presumed, eg, parent and child or established in fact, eg, brother and sister) such that psychiatric injury is foreseeable to the plaintiff;

(ii) propinquity in time and space between the victim's 'accident' and the plaintiff's discovery of the victim's injury (ie at the scene or its 'immediate aftermath');

(iii) that the plaintiff discover that injury by sight and sound; and

(iv) that as a result the plaintiff suffers psychiatric illness through an affront to her senses.

By contrast, as regards those who are 'participants' or 'primary victims' of the defendant's negligence, *Page v Smith*[235] has made it clear that the *McLoughlin/Alcock* rules do not apply. It suffices that a duty of care arises

---

[229] *Spring* (n 228 above).
[230] For a comprehensive study, see Mullany, N, and Handford, P, *Tort Liability for Psychiatric Damage* (1993). [231] See also discussion, above, paras 5.45–5.46.
[232] [1983] AC 410; [1982] 2 All ER 298 (HL).
[233] [1992] 1 AC 310; [1991] 4 All ER 907 (HL). [234] ibid, *per* Lord Oliver at 926.
[235] [1996] AC 155 (HL).

because it is reasonably foreseeable that the plaintiff will suffer personal injury whether or not it is also foreseeable that he will suffer psychiatric injury, and the 'proximity' requirements identified in *McLoughlin/Alcock* need not be satisfied.

5.73 These, perhaps deceptively, simple rules apply in medical negligence cases where the issue is whether a third party, usually a relative of the patient, may recover for the psychiatric injury caused by the doctor's negligence directed towards the patient. Claims for psychiatric injury arising out of negligent medical treatment have not until recently troubled the courts in England.[236] Three reported decisions: *Tredgett and Tredgett v Bexley HA*[237]; *Sion v Hampstead HA*[238] and *Taylor v Somerset HA*[239] illustrate the application of the general rules in the context of medical negligence.

(a) Participant/Primary Victim Cases

5.74 We are not, of course, here concerned with the claim by a patient for psychiatric injury arising out of her treatment.[240] Rather, the issue is whether a relative, usually a close relative such as a spouse, partner or parent, may claim for their psychiatric injury triggered by the negligent care of their relative. It seems that, in some instances, the courts will regard the relative as so involved in the events of medical negligence that the relative will not be seen as a 'secondary victim' but will be regarded as a 'participant' or 'primary victim'. In *Tredgett and Tredgett v Bexley HA*,[241] the plaintiffs, who were married, suffered psychiatric illness as a result of the defendants' negligence during the birth of their child who died forty-eight hours later. The course of the birth was horrendous in circumstances described as amounting to 'chaos' and 'pandemonium'. Mr Tredgett who was present throughout and witnessed what was taking place, was shaken and stunned by what he saw. After the birth both plaintiffs witnessed the child in intensive care prior to its life-support being switched off. Judge White awarded both plaintiffs damages. He held that they had each suffered a recognised psychiatric illness—pathological grief reaction. This had been caused by 'shock' resulting from their involvement in the birth process and subsequent events. Judge White held that it would be unrealistic to isolate the birth from the continuing events leading up to the child's death forty-eight hours later. He applied the 'participant' category identified in *Alcock* which obviously covered the mother but also, he held, the father. As regards the latter, he relied upon 'the degree of involvement in and the immediacy of the parents to the birth of the child'.[242] Hence,

---

[236] cf USA, see *Annotation*, 77 ALR 3d 436.   [237] [1994] 5 Med LR 178.
[238] [1994] 5 Med LR 170.   [239] (1993) 16 BMLR 63.
[240] See above, paras 5.43–5.46.   [241] N 237 above.   [242] ibid, 184.

in obstetric cases where a father is present and (as will often be the case) is actively encouraging and supporting his partner, a claim for psychiatric illness caused by negligence in the birth could be brought.

This will not be the only situation in which a relative will be considered a **5.75** 'participant'; there will be others. It will be a matter of fact determined by the closeness and immediacy of involvement of the relative. At the very least, however, the relative will have to be present at the time of the negligence: merely witnessing the effect of the negligence on the patient will not do. In *Tredgett*, of course, the father was actually involved in his wife's care and it may well be that something of this sort will be necessary for the more restrictive *McLoughlin/Alcock* rules not to apply. It is important to note, however, that relatives who merely conduct a vigil at the bedside of the injured patient or are otherwise present at the hospital where the medical negligence occurs will not be considered 'participants'. Rather, their actions for psychiatric injury must fall within the 'secondary victim' rules of *McLoughlin/Alcock* and, as will be seen shortly, are unlikely to succeed.

(b) Witnessing a Traumatic Event

Damages for psychiatric illness will be recoverable if the plaintiff witnessed a **5.76** traumatising event that compromised the medical negligence: providing always that the other *McLoughlin/Alcock* rules are satisfied, for example, that the plaintiff has a sufficiently close relationship with the 'primary' victim of the medical negligence. Arguably, in *Tredgett* the husband's claim would still have succeeded even if he had only witnessed what the judge described as the 'chaos' and 'pandemonium' at the time of the birth. Thus, seeing a loved one suffer, if sufficiently traumatic, at the hands of a doctor may do. The decision of the Court of Appeal in *Sion v Hampstead HA*[243] illustrates the application of the 'secondary victim' rules.

The plaintiff's son was injured in a motor-cycle accident and was admitted to **5.77** hospital. The plaintiff stayed at his son's bedside for fourteen days watching him deteriorate in health, suffer a heart attack, fall into a coma, and eventually die. The plaintiff claimed that the hospital had been negligent in that they had failed to diagnose bleeding from his son's left kidney as a result of which he had fallen into a coma. The plaintiff alleged that he had suffered psychiatric illness as a result of what he had seen whilst at the hospital. The Court of Appeal stuck out his action. The plaintiff's psychiatric illness had not been caused by 'shock' as required under the *McLoughlin/Alcock* rules.

---

[243] N 238 above. See Grubb, A, (1994) 2 Med L Rev 365 (Commentary).

There was no evidence that it had arisen from a 'sudden appreciation by sight or sound of a horrifying event'. Instead, the court held that the plaintiff's condition had arisen from a continuing exposure to the events beginning with his first arriving at the hospital and concluding with the appreciation at the inquest that there had been negligence by the hospital.

5.78 *Sion* is an important case even though the plaintiff was unsuccessful because it is clear from the judgments, particularly that of Peter Gibson LJ, that a nervous shock claim could arise out of medical negligence.[244] Apart from the necessary relationship to the patient, as *Sion* makes clear, it is crucial if a claim for psychiatric illness is to have any chance of success that what the plaintiff sees 'shocks' her. Relatives who suffer recognised psychiatric illness subsequent to the death or illness of their loved one, such as pathological grief disorder (PGD), will be able to recover providing the 'traumatising' or 'shocking' event was, at least, a contributory cause of the their psychiatric illness.[245] Likewise, if the subsequent events aggravate or prolong 'shock'-induced psychiatric illness then damages may be recovered even if this is characterised as pathological grief disorder.[246] It will be otherwise, however, where the PGD is wholly caused by subsequent events which do not fall within the *McLoughlin/Alcock* rules.[247] Much will therefore turn on the expert evidence of what caused the plaintiff's psychiatric illness and will require a degree of sophistication.

5.79 However, the need for a 'shocking' event must not be misunderstood. In *Sion*, it was argued that the defendant's conduct must be 'shocking' in the sense of a sudden and violent incident. The Court of Appeal disagreed. Peter Gibson LJ made this clear, doubting the statement of Auld J in *Taylor v Somerset HA*[248] to the contrary. He said:[249]

> I see no reason in logic why a breach of duty causing an incident involving no violence or suddenness, such as where the wrong medicine is negligently given to a hospital patient, could not lead to a claim for damages for nervous shock, for example where the negligence has fatal results and a visiting close relative, *wholly unprepared for what has occurred*, finds the body and thereby sustains a sudden and unexpected shock to the nervous system.

5.80 The crucial factor is the unexpected nature of what the plaintiff *witnesses* through sight or sound rather than the character of the event in itself.

---

[244] N 238 above, especially at 176.
[245] *Vernon v Bosley (No 1)* [1997] 1 All ER 577 (CA). [246] ibid.
[247] See *Calascione v Dixon* (1993) 19 BMLR 97 (CA) (claim for PGD not allowed) as explained by the majority of the Court of Appeal in *Vernon v Bosley (No 1)* ibid, *per* Evans LJ at 600 and *per* Thorpe LJ at 609–10. [248] (1993) 16 BMLR 63.
[249] N 238 above, 176 (emphasis added).

Though, of course, merely to be *told* the unexpected is quite illogically not enough.[250] In *Sion*, the plaintiff's psychiatric illness arose from the gradual realisation that his son would not survive. Hence, his death was not surprising but expected.

What is not covered by the 'secondary victim' rules is, as *Sion* itself shows, a **5.81** situation where the relative's psychiatric illness arises from a vigil at the bedside and the gradual realisation of the victim's fate.[251] *A fortiori* a claim would not arise if the plaintiff's illness arose from the long-term care of the victim of medical negligence at home.[252]

(c) Witnessing the Immediate Aftermath

In addition to situations where the plaintiff witnesses the event, the **5.82** *McLoughlin/Alcock* rules contemplate recovery for psychiatric injury as a result of witnessing the 'immediate aftermath'. In *McLoughlin* itself, the House of Lords accepted a claim where the plaintiff visited the hospital some two hours after the car accident and saw her family in the state they had been brought in. By contrast, in *Alcock* the House of Lords rejected a claim where relatives had visited a mortuary and saw their dead family members eight or nine hours after their death. The distinction between these two factual applications of the 'immediate aftermath' requirement cannot simply be one of time. One important difference is that in *McLoughlin* the victims were in much the same condition as they were immediately following the accident. In *Alcock*, however, the victims had been cleaned up. A further difference is that in *McLoughlin*, the plaintiff arrived at the hospital not knowing what to expect. In *Alcock*, the plaintiffs knew their relatives were dead and had come to identify them. Applying the 'suddenness' or 'unexpected' requirement of *Sion*,[253] identifying a body will rarely give rise to an *unexpected* shock, unless perhaps in cases where the body is badly mutilated or has not been cleaned up. In *Calascione v Dixon*,[254] the plaintiff recovered damages for psychiatric injury (post-traumatic stress disorder, 'PTSD') as a result of seeing her dead son's body in a hospital following a road accident. His body was described as 'barely recognisable'.

Consequently, there will be little scope for applying the 'immediate after- **5.83** math' requirement in medical negligence cases. A plaintiff who arrives at the

---

[250] See *Ravenscroft v Rederiaktiebolaget Transatlantic* [1992] 2 All ER 470 (CA).
[251] See also *Anderson v Smith* (1990) 101 FLR 34 (15 months vigil) and *Beecham v Hughes* (1988) 52 DLR (4th) 625 (BCCA): gradual realisation that wife severely injured.
[252] *Alcock* (n 238 above), *per* Lord Ackner at 917; *Andrewartha v Andrewartha* (1987) 44 SASR 1 (South Aust Sup Ct). [253] N 238 above. See para 5.79.
[254] N 247 above.

hospital after the patient has died or been injured will only possibly have a claim if the condition of the plaintiff creates an unexpected (and immediate) reaction in the plaintiff. Identifying a dead body is very unlikely to qualify. In *Taylor v Somerset HA*[255] the plaintiff's husband suffered a heart attack. He was taken to hospital and died. The plaintiff was informed that he was ill and had been taken to hospital. She was told after a short time that her husband had died. Not believing what she was told and in shock, she asked to see the body and identified him in the hospital mortuary. The sight of his body caused her shock and distress. She sued the defendant alleging that she had suffered psychiatric injury as a result of the death of her husband which the defendant had negligently caused by failing to diagnose and treat his serious heart condition. Auld J rejected her claim. He held that she could not claim for any psychiatric injury arising from being told that her husband was dead. Further, her visit to the mortuary did not fall within the 'immediate aftermath' requirement. She had gone there to identify her husband and apart from the 'obvious shock to her of the sight of his dead body, it bore no marks or signs to her of the sort that would have conjured up for her the circumstances of his fatal attack'.[256] The absence of the latter was crucial and distinguished the case from *McLoughlin*.

(d) Delivering 'Bad News'[257]

5.84 A final situation which should be considered is where a person is negligently told bad news about a relative and, as a consequence, suffers a shock which causes psychiatric injury.[258] The negligence may lie in the way the information is communicated or in its accuracy. It is clear that an action will not lie against the primary defendant where an intermediary acts as a conduit to tell the plaintiff of injuries that have been inflicted upon the plaintiff's relative.[259] Unlike that situation, however, we are concerned with the liability of the *intermediary* himself. Can a doctor[260] be liable for negligently[261] breaking 'bad news' to the relatives? In principle there is no reason why he should not.[262] The three elements required for a duty of care—'foreseeability', 'proximity', and the 'fair, just, and reasonable' requirement—seem satisfied. It is readily foreseeable that carelessness might produce an adverse psychiatric

---

[255] (1993) 16 BMLR 63.   [256] ibid.

[257] See Mullany, N and Handford, P, *Tort Liability for Psychiatric Injury* (n 230 above), at 183–91.

[258] See above, para 5.46 for the related issue of liability to the patient.

[259] See above, para 5.80.   [260] Or other, such as a counsellor.

[261] See *Wilkinson v Downton* [1897] 2 QB 57 for malicious communication.

[262] *Jinks v Cardwell* (1987) 39 CCLT 168 (Ont H Ct) (doctor held liable for psychiatric injury caused to a wife when he told her, falsely, that her husband had committed suicide).

reaction. There is a 'close and direct' relationship between the doctor and relative sufficient to create a proximate relationship. Finally, it is not obvious what policy reasons mitigate against imposing liability in this particular context. It should not matter whether the negligence lies in the falsity of the communication or in the method or nature of a (true) communication. As regards the latter situation, there is certainly some analogy with the duty of a doctor to exercise reasonable care when informing his patients post-operatively.[263] However, the contrary has been suggested at least where the information is true.[264]

The decision of the Court of Appeal in *Powell v Boldaz*[265] appears to limit the **5.85** scope of a doctor's liability in these circumstances. The plaintiffs, a married couple, brought an action claiming damages for psychiatric injury arising out of the death of their son. He suffered from a rare condition known as 'Addison's Disease'. It was accepted that there had been negligence in failing to diagnose and treat his condition and that had he been treated in time he would have survived. Sometime after their son's death, the plaintiffs were told the reason for his death and were shown his medical records. No complaint was made about this. However, they alleged that seven months later they discovered that their son's medical notes had been tampered with by the defendants. They alleged that their general practitioners had conspired to 'cover-up' the cause of their son's death and that their realisation of this caused them each to suffer post-traumatic stress disorder. The judge struck out their actions. The Court of Appeal dismissed the appeal on the basis that no duty of care was owed by the defendants in respect of the post-death allegations. The Court of Appeal held that a duty of care would only arise if the defendants had been called upon or undertook to treat the plaintiffs as patients. While the defendants were the plaintiffs' GPs, the court held that at the relevant time they had not been counselling or treating the plaintiffs. Stuart-Smith LJ said:[265a]

> I do not think that a doctor who has been treating a patient who has died, who tells relatives what has happened, thereby undertakes the doctor–patient relationship towards the relatives. It is a situation that calls for sensitivity, tact and discretion. But the mere fact that the communicator is a doctor, does not, without more, mean that he undertakes the doctor–patient relationship.

---

[263] See *AB v Tameside & Glossop Health Authority* [1997] 8 Med LR 91 (CA), and above, para 5.46.

[264] *Mount Isa Mines v Pusey* (1970) 125 CLR 383 (Aust H Ct), *per* Windeyer J at 407. But note *Guay v Sun Publishing Co* [1953] 4 DLR 577 (Can Sup Ct) (no liability for false story published in newspaper). [265] (1997) 39 BMLR 35.

[265a] ibid, 45.

Later, he stated that the case law did not establish

> some kind of free-standing duty of candour, irrespective of whether the doctor–patient relationship exists in a healing or treating context, breach of which sounds in damages, such damages involving personal injury. This would involve a startling expansion of the law of tort.[265b]

5.86 Three observations on this decision are worth making. First, the plaintiffs only alleged that their discovery of the 'conspiracy' caused them psychiatric injury and not the communication by the GPs to them of false, inaccurate or insensitively communicated information. Arguably, the plaintiffs' claim would have been stronger if this had been the case. Secondly, the almost mesmeric effect on the Court of Appeal of the label 'doctor–patient relationship' has to be questioned. It is not a necessary condition for a doctor to owe another a duty of care.[266] It is as if the court thought that the plaintiffs were alleging that the defendants had negligently failed to treat them. If they had, the existence of the relationship would have been important, though even then not conclusive, to the action. But this was in fact irrelevant in the case because it was not what they alleged. The real question was whether the defendants owed a duty not to harm the plaintiffs, rather than one not to diagnose or treat them negligently. Thirdly, the Court of Appeal's denial of a duty of care in circumstances such as these was not quite categorical. The court accepted that if the doctor realised that the news he had broken had shocked the recipient such as to call for treatment, he might be liable for not carrying on and treating the individual. Stuart-Smith LJ stated that it would be 'a question of fact and degree in each case whether the doctor–patient relationship came into existence by the doctor undertaking to treat and heal the person as a patient.'[266a]

5.87 It is suggested that the reasoning of the Court of Appeal is so open to question that it is extremely unlikely to survive scrutiny in a future case where a doctor negligently *advises* a relative of a patient's death or injuries and thereby causes psychiatric injury.

3. Doctors Engaged by Others

5.88 In a number of situations a doctor may be requested and engaged by a third party to examine and provide a report on an individual's health. For example, a doctor may be engaged to provide a medical report by an insurance company prior to writing a policy or by a prospective employer to ensure the individual's fitness for the job.[267] In addition, a police surgeon may be called upon to

---

[265b] ibid, 46.   [266] See below, paras 5.88 *et seq.*   [266a] N 265 above, 45.
[267] Other examples might include the preparation of a report for the purposes of litigation or for assessing the individual's entitlement under an insurance policy or a statutory benefits scheme.

examine the person at a police station prior to detention, or a doctor may be requested by a local social services authority to determine whether there is evidence of child abuse, or requested to provide a statutory opinion necessary for the detention of the person under the Mental Health Act 1983. What, if any, duty does the doctor owe the individual examined who is not, in conventional terms, his patient? Is the doctor's duty limited to not harming the individual during the examination or does it go further and require the doctor, for example, to appraise the person of anything relevant to his health discovered during the examination? The answer in England is not clear, not least because of the paucity of authority on the issue although it has been suggested that English law only accepts the limited duty.[268] Courts in other jurisdictions, particularly in America. have however addressed this question.

(i) *Overseas Authorities*

In other jurisdictions, particularly America, courts have reached different conclusions.[269] Some courts have dismissed claims brought against doctors engaged by (prospective) employers or insurance companies for failure to diagnose a medical condition or, having done so, to inform or advise the person of it.[270] The absence of a doctor–patient relationship is seen as crucial; without it courts have allowed actions only where the person has been injured during the examination.[271] However, some courts have taken a slightly wider view of liability imposing a duty of care where the doctor undertakes to advise the person of his condition and misrepresents or conceals the results[272] and the advice is relied upon to his detriment.[273] Liability in the last two situations, though extending beyond cases where injury is caused by the doctor, can be premised upon rules of liability for negligent misrepresentation and assumption of responsibility to the individual and should, it is suggested, be followed in England.[274]
5.89

However, increasingly American courts are extending liability to cases involving a pure failure to warn or advise a patient about a known (or knowable)
5.90

---

[268] *X v Bedfordshire CC* [1995] 2 AC 633; [1995] 3 All ER 353.
[269] Many of the cases are helpfully collected in the judgment of the Supreme Court of Montana in *Webb v TD* (1997) 95 P 2d 1008. See also, *Annotation*, 10 ALR 3d 1071.
[270] e g, *Beaman v Helton* (1990) 573 So 2d 776 (Miss Sup Ct) (no liability for failing to advise examinee that x-ray disclosed cancer).
[271] *Beadling v Sirotta* (1964) 197 A 2d 857 (NJ Sup Ct).
[272] *Hoover v Williamson* (1964) 203 A 2d 861 (Md CA).
[273] *Heller v Community Hospital* (1993) 603 NYS 2d 548.
[274] *Baker v Kaye*, (n 128 above) is an example of a duty of care based upon assumption of responsibility.

health condition discovered during the examination. In *Green v Walker*[275] an employee was required to undergo annual health checks. The doctor carried out the tests, found all the results to be normal and classified the employee as 'employable without restriction'. One year later, the employee was diagnosed with lung cancer. He sued the doctor in negligence alleging that his failure to diagnose the cancer was careless; the failure to disclose these findings and the consequent delay in treatment had reduced his chances of survival. The employee subsequently died. The 5th Circuit Court of Appeals held that the defendant owed the employee a duty of care notwithstanding the examination occurred ostensibly for the benefit of the employer. The duty required the doctor to carry out the tests and diagnosis carefully and to advise the employee of any findings that 'pose an imminent danger to [his] physical or mental well-being'. Subsequent decisions have approved the court's decision.[276] There is a strong argument for finding that a doctor impliedly assumes a responsibility to the individual by examining the patient and refraining from disclosing the results or taking other appropriate action to appraise the individual of the need for further investigation. An individual is as likely to rely upon the silence of the doctor as upon a positive misrepresentation of his good health.[277] One American court persuasively put it as follows:[278]

> When a doctor conducts a physical examination, the examinee generally assumes that 'no news is good news' and relies on the assumption that any serious condition will be revealed.

5.91 Similar decisions to *Green v Walker* have been reached in Australia[279] and Canada[280] where the doctor was engaged by a third party.

(ii) *English Law*

5.92 The leading English decision relevant to the issue of whether a doctor engaged by a third party owes a duty to the examinee is the House of Lords in *X v Bedfordshire CC*.[281] The complex legal and facts issues raised by this

---

[275] (1990) F 2d 291 (5th Cir).
[276] See *Daly v United States* (1991) 946 F 2d 1467 (9th Cir); *Cleghorn v Hess* (1993) 853 P 2d 1260 (Nev Sup Ct); *Baer v Regents of University of California* (1994) 884 P 2d 841 (NM CA); *Webb v TD* (1997) 951 P 2d 1008 (Mont Sup Ct).
[277] See, *Webb v TD*, ibid, *per* Trieweiler J, (Leaphart and Gray JJ dubitante).
[278] *Betesh v United States* (1974) 400 F Supp 238 (DC Dist Ct), *per* Bryant J at 246 (liability for failing to advise examinee during military pre-induction physical examination of abnormality on x-ray indicating cancer). [279] *Thomsen v Davison* [1975] Qd R 93.
[280] *Parslow v Masters* [1993] 6 WWR 273 (action to obtain medical report).
[281] [1995] 2 AC 633; [1995] 3 All ER 353.

case can be found elsewhere.[282] The important issue here, however, is whether a psychiatrist who interviews and examines a child for suspected sexual abuse at the behest of the local social services can be liable to the child for psychiatric injury caused when it is unnecessarily taken into care. The House of Lords held that the psychiatrist did not owe the child a duty of care in such circumstances. Beyond the duty not to injure the child during the examination, the psychiatrist's duty was owed solely to the local authority: there was no proximity between the child and doctor.[283] Lord Browne-Wilkinson stated that the psychiatrist did not

> by accepting the instructions of the local authority, assume any general professional duty of care to the plaintiff children. The professionals were employed or retained to advise the local authority in relation to the well-being of the plaintiffs but not to advise or treat the plaintiffs.[284]

Lord Browne-Wilkinson drew an analogy with the situation where a doctor is retained by an insurance company to examine an applicant for life insurance. He said:[285]

5.93

> The doctor does not, by examining the applicant, come under any general duty of medical care to the applicant. He is under a duty not to damage the applicant in the course of the examination: but beyond that his duties are owed to the insurance company and not to the applicant.

No authority is given for this analysis of the relationship in the insurance context; indeed there could not be, since it does not appear that the issue has ever directly arisen in England. It was, however, crucial to the view taken by at least four of the judges in the House of Lords.[286] A similar analogy was drawn by a majority of the Court of Appeal.[287] Staughton LJ asserted (and it was no more) that the psychiatrist was in precisely the same position as a doctor who examined a person for insurance purposes or takes a blood sample from a suspected drunk driver at a police station. The doctor owed the person a duty not to cause harm during the examination but 'the general duty to perform the task allocated with reasonable skill and care' was owed to the insurance company or police authority only.[288] By contrast Sir Thomas Bingham MR dissented on the issue of the psychiatrist's duty. He concluded that a duty of care was owed to the child because it was for the child alone that the psychiatrist was 'being invited to exercise her professional skill and judgment'.[289]

5.94

---

[282] See Cane, P, 'Suing Public Authorities in Tort' (1996) 112 LQR 13 and Oliphant, K, 'Tort' (1996) 49 CLP 29, 31–44.

[283] Lord Nolan dissented on this point (n 281), at 400.

[284] ibid, 384.   [285] ibid, 383.

[286] Lord Nolan disagreed that an analogy could be drawn between the relationship of the insurance doctor and an examinee and the psychiatrist in *X* (ibid, 400).

[287] [1994] 2 WLR 554.   [288] ibid, 582. See also Peter Gibson LJ at 591.

[289] ibid, 570.

(a) Return to General Principle

5.95 There is no doubt that the doctor owes the person a duty of care in negligence not to cause injury in the course of the examination.[290] Consequently, the doctor who carelessly carries out a medical procedure during the examination, such as taking a blood sample and puncturing an artery, and injures the person will be liable in negligence. This is not the problematic case. The question is whether the doctor owes the patient a broader duty of care than that. To the extent that a doctor already has a relationship with the person (for example, he is that individual's GP), his pre-existing duty of care would extend to all reasonably foreseeable harm.[291]

5.96 There is only one English case which has directly addressed the issue of a doctor's duty to a person when the doctor is engaged by a third party.[292] In *Baker v Kaye*[293] the plaintiff was a television sales executive. He was offered a job with a company subject to a satisfactory medical report from the company's doctor. On the strength of this offer, the plaintiff resigned his existing job. The defendant, a GP in private practice, was employed by the company to carry out a medical examination on the plaintiff. The results of blood tests taken during the examination suggested to the defendant that the plaintiff had an alcohol problem; consuming excessive amounts of alcohol made him unsuitable for the demanding job with the company. Consequently, the defendant told the company that he could not recommend the plaintiff for the job. The company, as a result, withdrew their offer of employment to the plaintiff. The plaintiff sued alleging that the defendant had negligently interpreted the test results and, as a result, he had suffered economic loss, namely his lost salary.

5.97 Robert Owen QC (sitting as a Deputy High Court Judge) held that a duty

---

[290] See eg, *Leonard v Knott* [1980] 1 WWR 813 (BC CA) (liability for patient who died during annual check-up from an allergic reaction during a procedure). See also *Greenberg v Perkins* (1993) 845 P 2d 530 (Colo Sup Ct) (liability for injury caused to person undergoing tests during medical examination for purposes of litigation).

[291] The fragmentation of a GP's duty proposed in *Powell v Boldaz* (n 265 above), para 5.85 is unsupportable.

[292] In *R v Croydon HA* [1998] Lloyd's Rep Med 44 (CA) it was admitted that the duty of a radiologist engaged by an employer to carry out a chest x-ray included a duty to ensure that she was fit for work and would be protected from personal injury whilst in employment by reason of an existing health condition.

[293] [1997] IRLR 219 (Robert Owen QC). For factually similar cases in the US see *Olson v Western Airlines Inc* (1983) 191 Cal Rptr 502 (liability); *Armstrong v Morgan* (1976) 545 SW 2d 45 (Tex CA) (liability). Contrast *Rand v Miller* (1991) 408 SE 2d 655 (W Va Sup Ct App) (no liability); *Felton v Schaeffer* (1991) 279 Cal Rptr 713 (Cal CA) (no liability); *Keene v Wiggins* (1977) 138 Cal Rptr 3 (Cal CA) (no liability).

of care was owed to the plaintiff by the defendant. There had, obviously, been no reliance by the plaintiff upon the defendant's advice. It was the company in making its decision to withdraw their offer of employment who had relied upon the defendant. Nevertheless, applying the three-stage test in *Caparo*,[294] the judge held that a duty of care existed. First, he held that economic loss to the plaintiff was foreseeable. Secondly, he concluded that there was a proximate relationship between the parties: (1) the defendant knew the plaintiff's employment depended upon his medical advice to the company; (2) the plaintiff entrusted himself and information to the defendant; and (3) the defendant regarded himself as under a duty to advise the plaintiff of anything untoward about his health which he might discover during the examination. Finally, the judge could see no policy reason why it was not 'just, fair and reasonable' to impose a duty of care upon the defendant. In the end, however, he held that the defendant was not liable because he had not been negligent.

The decision in *Baker v Kaye* is, however, arguably only of limited impor- **5.98** tance. It concerned an (allegedly) negligent report produced by a doctor in the knowledge that it would be relied upon and if false was likely to cause loss to the plaintiff. Thus, liability fell squarely within the case law of the House of Lords beginning with *Hedley Byrne* and, in particular, the employee reference case of *Spring v Guardian Assurance*.[295] Nevertheless, in principle, applying the well-known *Caparo* test, there is no difficulty in holding a doctor liable for *all* the immediate consequences of a failure to exercise reasonable care and skill in the course of the examination. Consequently, he could be liable for failing (carelessly) to diagnose a medical condition which could have been treated or its symptoms alleviated if it had been diagnosed earlier. Injury to the person would be foreseeable and there would be a proximate relationship based upon an implied assumption of responsibility by the doctor. The expectation of both examinee and doctor will usually be that the doctor will perform his professional obligations to the person which would include alerting the person to anything untoward. In one American case the court succinctly stated:[296]

> In placing oneself in the hands of a person held out to the world as skilled in a
> medical profession, albeit at the request of one's employer, one justifiably has

---

[294] *Caparo Industries plc v Dickman* [1990] 2 AC 605 (HL).
[295] [1995] 2 AC 296. Notwithstanding the doubts of the judge, the two cases are very close indeed.
[296] *Webb v TD* (1997) 95 P 2d 1008 (Mont Sup Ct) *per* Trieweiler J (liability for failing to diagnose back condition resulting in injury at work).

the reasonable expectation that the expert will warn of any incidental dangers of which he is cognizant due to his peculiar knowledge of his specialization.

5.99   Obviously, in this situation the doctor would only be required to exercise *reasonable* care. The doctor's duty would not necessarily, perhaps rarely, be to treat the patient. Rather, it would be sufficient for him to discharge his legal duty if he alerted the patient to the danger and advised him to see his own doctor. Likewise, subject to arguments of public policy, a psychiatrist could, in principle, be liable to a child for the consequences of misdiagnosing child abuse or to a detained patient for negligently signing the necessary recommendation under the 1983 Act.

(b) Specific Situations

Insurance and Employment Examinations

5.100   In the private, commercial context of insurance and employment the statutory framework which inhibited the application of a common law duty of care in *X v Bedfordshire CC* is absent. It is clear from the judgments in *Bedfordshire* that the courts were heavily influenced by the statutory framework within which the psychiatrist was functioning. All the actions against the local authority in the child abuse case were dismissed for this very reason. It was not 'just, fair, and reasonable' to impose a duty of care. It would have been remarkable if the psychiatrist (and vicariously the health authority) had been the only proper defendant in the case given that it concerned alleged negligence in social services rather than health service functions. It is worth noting that Lord Browne-Wilkinson relied upon public policy as an additional ground for denying the action against the psychiatrist and it was the only basis upon which Lord Nolan agreed with the other Law Lords.[297] It is suggested that two factors may mitigate against imposing the relevant duty to the individual: the statutory framework, and the potential for a conflict between the duty owed to the third party and the person. Certainly the former was present in the *Bedfordshire* case; although arguably not the latter as Sir Thomas Bingham made clear in the Court of Appeal.[298] Nevertheless, the former was sufficient to expunge the duty (based upon implied undertaking) which would otherwise have existed.

5.101   Further, there is really no conflict that would arise between the duty owed to the insurance company or employer and the duty which would be owed to the examinee. If there were, then a duty of care should not be imposed.[299] The

---

[297] N 281 above, at 384 and 400 respectively.   [298] N 287 above, 571–2.
[299] A possible example is where a doctor is requested by an insurance company to consider a person's entitlement under an *existing* policy providing, for example, disability or health

doctor's duty in relation to both would be to exercise reasonable care in carrying out the examination and in interpreting the results. What is reasonable for the doctor *vis à vis* the insurance company is reasonable *vis à vis* the person examined. The doctor's obligations will be tailored to the tasks he undertakes for the third party and what he could (and should) discover and conclude thereafter. A duty to advise the person on the basis of the examination and assessment of his health is entirely consistent with his legal obligations to the third party.

Police Surgeons

The same rationale applies to the police surgeon examining a detained suspect at a police station, with this proviso: the nature of the examination by a police surgeon may be much more limited than for doctors in the other contexts, for example, if the surgeon is merely engaged to take a blood sample. The person's general health condition does not arise. However, if the doctor is engaged to determine the person's fitness to be detained in a police cell overnight, why should not the doctor owe the person a duty to carry out the examination carefully. If a careless mistake is made which leads to the person suffering harm whilst detained, the doctor should, in principle, be liable to the detained person.

5.102

Psychiatric Recommendation Leading to Detention

What is the position of a psychiatrist who negligently recommends that a person be detained under the Mental Health Act 1983? Usually two doctors must recommend detention,[300] at least, one of which will not have a previous relationship with the 'patient'.[301] There is considerable authority to support the view that a doctor owes the (ultimately) detained patient a duty to exercise reasonable care in certifying the patient.[302] The only remaining

5.103

---

coverage. Here, the interests of the company and the individual are, arguably, different. The latter is concerned to minimise exposure (down-playing medical condition) while the individual is concerned to discover the full extent of their condition: see eg, *Keene v Wiggins* (1977) 138 Cal Rptr 3 (Cal CA), *per* Cologne J at 7. The divergence or conflict of interest does not occur when the policy is only in contemplation.

[300] Under ss 2(3) (assessment), 3(3) (treatment) and 7(3) (guardianship); only one in an emergency (s 4(3)). See discussion in Hoggett, B, *Mental Health Law* (4th edn, 1996), 66–71.

[301] Section 12(2). One doctor must be 'approved': s 12(2).

[302] See *Harnett v Fisher* [1927] AC 573 (HL); *Hall v Semple* (1862) 3 F & F 337 (Crompton J) and *De Freville v Dill* [1927] All ER Rep 205 (McCardie J) and cases cited therein. More recently, *Winch v Jones* [1986] QB 296 (CA) and *James v London Borough of Havering* (1992) 15 BMLR 1 (CA). See Hoggett, *Mental Health Law* (n 300 above), 248 and Gostin, L, *Mental Health Services—Law and Practice* (1986), para 21.04.1. The position of the approved social worker, who initiates the admission process, is no different in all probability and does not raise the kind of policy questions associated with negligence actions

issues being proof of breach, causation, and damage.[303] In *X v Bedfordshire CC*, Lord Browne-Wilkinson[304] doubted the authority of one of the earlier 'negligent certification' cases.[305] However, liability falls within the principles already discussed and thus, on balance, a social worker or doctor providing a medical recommendation could be liable in negligence. As Lord Denning put it in his famous dissenting judgment in *Candler v Crane Christmas & Co*,[306] the doctor is liable 'because [he] knows that his certificate is required for the very purpose of deciding whether the man should be detained or not'. In modern terminology, there is an assumption of responsibility by the doctors and social worker.

5.104 Nevertheless, it may be that on public policy grounds the courts may not recognise a duty of care owed to detained patients in respect of *the decision to admit* them under the 1983 Act.[307] The statutory (and discretionary) nature of this action, the potential 'chilling' effect of liability in negligence coupled with the spirit of non-liability of hospital managers and others for false imprisonment contained in section 6(3) of the Mental Health Act 1983, could lead a court to decide that no duty is owed. Indeed, the court might accept the argument that the hospital managers are immune because of the quasi-judicial nature of their function.[308]

---

arising out of the performance of statutory functions exemplified by *X v Bedfordshire CC* (nn 281, 287 above), and see *Buxton v Jayne* [1960] 1 WLR 783 (CA) and *James v London Borough of Havering*, above.

[303] On which see *Everett v Griffiths* [1920] 3 KB 163 (CA) *per* Atkin LJ at 219 (Scrutton LJ disagreed at 196–7); [1921] 1 AC 631 (HL) *per* Viscount Finlay at 666–7 and *De Freville v Dill* (n 302 above), *per* McCardie J at 212–3 (certification is a cause).

[304] N 281 above, 384.

[305] *Everett v Griffiths* [1920] 3 KB 163 (CA) and [1921] 1 AC 631 (HL). The House of Lords held the certifying doctor not liable because he had exercised reasonable care. The Law Lords did not resolve the different views expressed in the Court of Appeal on the duty issue. Bankes LJ had concluded that a duty to exercise reasonable care but not skill existed (at 183–4). Scrutton LJ held that no duty of care was owed (at 195–6) and Atkin LJ held that a duty to exercise reasonable care existed (at 218). In the House of Lords, Viscount Haldane thought it probable a duty to exercise reasonable care existed (at 657). Viscounts Finlay and Cave and Lords Moulton and Atkinson assumed the duty existed (at 669, 680–1, 697, and 681 respectively). [306] [1951] 1 All ER 426, 435.

[307] cf, liability for negligence once the patient is detained: Jones, M, *Medical Negligence* (2nd edn, 1996), paras 4.096–4.109.

[308] See *X v A, B and C and the Mental Health Act Commission* (1991) 9 BMLR 91 (Morland J): Mental Health Act Commission and appointees not liable for negligent certification that treatment fell within s 57. But contrast the liability of 'second opinion doctor' under ss 57 and 58, *per* Morland J at 99.

6

BREACH OF DUTY

A. Reasonableness

1. The Reasonable Man

The basic test for negligence is whether the defendant's conduct was reason- **6.01**
able in all the circumstances of the case. Reasonable conduct is not negligent;
unreasonable conduct is culpable. In *Blyth v Birmingham Waterworks Co*[1]
Alderson B said that:

> Negligence is the omission to do something which a reasonable man, guided
> upon those considerations which ordinarily regulate the conduct of human

---

[1] (1856) 11 Exch 781, 784.

affairs, would do, or doing something which a prudent and reasonable man would not do.

This is an objective standard which does not take account of the subjective attributes of the particular defendant.[2] It is sometimes said that the standard required is that of the reasonable man, the ordinary man, the average man, or the man on the Clapham omnibus.[3] Despite references to the average man, the standard of care is not necessarily determined by the average conduct of people in general if that conduct is routinely careless. Nor is there any concept of an 'average' standard of care by which a defendant might argue that he has provided an adequate service on average and should not be held liable for the occasions when his performance fell below the norm. No matter how competent the defendant's conduct was on average, he will be responsible for damage caused by even a single lapse below the standard of reasonable care.[4]

2. The Reasonable Doctor

6.02 An individual who professes a special skill is judged, not by the standard of the man on the Clapham omnibus, but by the standards of his peers. For the 'reasonable man' is substituted the 'reasonable professional', be it doctor, lawyer, accountant, architect, etc.[5] The classic statement of the test of professional negligence is the direction to the jury of McNair J in *Bolam v Friern Hospital Management Committee*.[6] Now widely known as the '*Bolam* test', this statement of the law has been approved by the House of Lords on no fewer than four occasions as the touchstone of liability for medical negligence.[7] McNair J said:

But where you get a situation which involves the use of some special skill or

---

[2] *Glasgow Corporation v Muir* [1943] AC 448, 457.

[3] *Hall v Brooklands Auto Racing Club* [1933] 1 KB 205, 217.

[4] *Wilsher v Essex Area Health Authority* [1986] 3 All ER 801, 810, *per* Mustill LJ. The English courts have not accepted a distinction between 'ordinary' negligence and 'gross' negligence. In *Wilson v Brett* (1843) 11 M & W 113 Rolfe B said that there was no difference: 'it was the same thing with the addition of a vituperative epithet'.

[5] 'The public profession of an art is a representation and undertaking to all the world that the professor possesses the requisite ability and skill. An express promise or express representation in the particular case is not necessary'; *per* Willes J in *Harmer v Cornelius* (1858) 5 CB. (NS) 236, 246.

[6] [1957] 2 All ER 118. See more generally, Powers and Harris, *Medical Negligence* (Butterworths, 2nd edn, 1994); and Jones, *Medical Negligence*, (Sweet & Maxwell, 2nd edn, 1996).

[7] *Whitehouse v Jordan* [1981] 1 All ER 267; *Maynard v West Midlands Regional Health Authority* [1984] 1 WLR 634; *Sidaway v Bethlem Royal Hospital Governors* [1985] 1 All ER 643; *Bolitho v City and Hackney Health Authority* [1997] 4 All ER 771. See also *Chin Keow v Government of Malaysia* [1967] 1 WLR 813, PC. The *Bolam* test is not restricted to doctors, but is of general application to any profession or calling which requires special skill, knowledge or experience: *Gold v Haringey Health Authority* [1987] 2 All ER 888, 894, CA.

competence, then the test whether there has been negligence or not is not the test of the man on the Clapham omnibus, because he has not got this special skill. The test is the standard of the ordinary skilled man exercising and professing to have that special skill. A man need not possess the highest expert skill at the risk of being found negligent . . . it is sufficient if he exercises the ordinary skill of an ordinary competent man exercising that particular art.[8]

His Lordship agreed that counsel's statement that 'negligence means failure to act in accordance with the standards of reasonably competent medical men at the time' was an accurate statement of the law, provided that it was remembered that there may be one or more perfectly proper standards:A doctor is not guilty of negligence if he has acted in accordance with a practice accepted as proper by a responsible body of medical men skilled in that particular art . . . Putting it the other way round, a doctor is not negligent, if he is acting in accordance with such a practice, merely because there is a body of opinion that takes a contrary view.[9]

6.03

In *Hunter v Hanley* Lord President Clyde dealt with the question of different professional practices in these terms:

> In the realm of diagnosis and treatment there is ample scope for genuine difference of opinion and one man clearly is not negligent merely because his conclusion differs from that of other professional men, nor because he has displayed less skill or knowledge than others would have shown. The true test for establishing negligence in diagnosis or treatment on the part of a doctor is whether he has been proved to be guilty of such failure as no doctor of ordinary skill would be guilty of if acting with ordinary care.[10]

There is a distinction, however, between a test of negligence based on the standards of the *ordinary* skilled professional and one based on the *reasonably* competent professional. The former places emphasis on the standards which are in fact adopted by the profession, whereas the latter makes it clear that negligence is concerned with departures from what *ought* to have been done in the circumstances, which is measured by reference to the hypothetical 'reasonable doctor'.[11] Of course, what the profession does in a given situation will be an important indicator of what ought to have been done, but it should not necessarily be determinative. In the final analysis it is for the court to

---

[8] [1957] 2 All ER 118, 121.

[9] ibid, 122. Similar formulations of the standard of care required of the medical profession can be found in other Commonwealth jurisdictions: *Crits v Sylvester* (1956) 1 DLR (2d) 502, 508; aff'd (1956) 5 DLR (2d) 601 (SCC). This standard also allows for differences of view within the medical profession: see *Lapointe v Hôpital Le Gardeur* (1992) 90 DLR (4th) 7, 15 (SCC); *F v R* (1982) 33 SASR 189, 190, *per* King CJ.

[10] 1955 SC 200, 204–5. This statement of the law has also been approved by the House of Lords: *Maynard* (n 7 above), 638; *Sidaway* (n 7 above), 660, *per* Lord Bridge. See also *Dunne v National Maternity Hospital* [1989] IR 91, 109 (Supreme Court of Ireland).

[11] See Montrose (1958) 21 MLR 259.

determine what the reasonable doctor would have done, not the profession, drawing upon the evidence presented. The *Bolam* test fails to make this distinction between the ordinary skilled doctor and the reasonably competent doctor. The distinction is potentially significant when the question arises whether compliance with common professional practice can be negligent.

3. Reasonable Care

6.04 Reasonable care can only be measured by reference to the defendant's conduct in the circumstances. It is meaningless to say that the standard required is reasonable care, without knowing the particular situation with which the defendant was confronted. For example, a defendant faced with an emergency and who has to act on the spur of the moment will not be judged too critically simply because with hindsight a different course of action might have avoided the harm.[12] This clearly applies to medical practitioners.[13] None the less, the test remains reasonable care in all the circumstances. If the error is one which a reasonably competent doctor could have made in the circumstances the defendant was not negligent, but if a reasonably competent doctor would not have made that error, the defendant will be liable, notwithstanding the fact that it occurred in the course of an emergency.[14]

6.05 The obligation is to exercise *reasonable* care, and therefore doctors do not guarantee a favourable outcome to their efforts. The medical practitioner is not an insurer and cannot be blamed every time something goes wrong. Indeed, it is widely acknowledged that in medicine, in particular, things can go wrong in the treatment of a patient even with the very best available care.[15] The practitioner is not judged by the standards of the most experienced, most skilful, or most highly qualified member of the profession, but by reference to the standards of the ordinarily competent practitioner in that particular field.[16] Nor is the doctor to be judged by the standards of the least

---

[12] *Parkinson v Liverpool Corporation* [1950] 1 All ER 367; *Ng Chun Pui v Lee Chuen Tat* [1988] RTR 298, 302 (both non-medical cases).

[13] In *Wilsher v Essex Area Health Authority* [1986] 3 All ER 801, 812 Mustill LJ said that an emergency may overburden the available resources, and, if an individual is forced by circumstances to do too many things at once, the fact that he does one of them incorrectly should not lightly be taken as negligence.

[14] Where an emergency is foreseeable the hospital authority may be negligent if there is an inadequate system for dealing with the known risks that the emergency is likely to create: *Bull v Devon Area Health Authority* (1989), [1993] 4 Med LR 117, CA; *Meyer v Gordon* (1981) 17 CCLT 1 (BCSC).

[15] *Hancke v Hooper* (1835) 7 C & P 81, 84, *per* Tindal CJ; *Mahon v Osborne* [1939] 2 KB 14, 31, *per* Scott LJ; *Daniels v Heskin* [1954] IR 73, 84.

[16] *Lanphier v Phipos* (1838) 8 C & P 475, 479, *per* Tindal CJ; *R v Bateman* (1925) 94 LJKB 791, 794, *per* Lord Hewart CJ. See also *Greaves & Co (Contractors) Ltd v Baynham Meikle and Partners* [1975] 3 All ER 99 at 103–4, *per* Lord Denning MR.

qualified or least experienced. It is not a defence that he acted in good faith, to the best of his ability, if he has failed to reach the objective standard of the ordinarily competent and careful doctor. Nor is it a defence to say that a doctor has committed an 'error of professional judgment' or a 'mere' error of judgment, since this gives no indication as to whether there has been negligence. Some such errors may be consistent with the due exercise of professional skill, but other acts or omissions in the course of exercising 'clinical judgment' may be so glaringly below proper standards as to make a finding of negligence inevitable.[17] If the error of judgment is one that would not have been made by a reasonably competent professional person professing to have the standard and type of skill that the defendant held himself out as having, and acting with ordinary care, then it is negligent. If, on the other hand, it is an error that a person, acting with ordinary care, might have made, then it is not negligent.[18]

Within the broad term 'reasonable care' it is possible to identify some general principles which the courts have used in the decision-making process about what constitutes negligence. They are, however, no more than guidelines, and competing principles can point to different outcomes. Medical evidence is invariably a vital element in an action for medical negligence, but the importance attached to expert opinion should not obscure the underlying basis for a finding that the defendant has been negligent. This is that, in the light of the expert evidence, the defendant has taken an unjustified risk, for example, or has failed to keep up to date, or has undertaken a task beyond his competence, or conversely that the risk was justified by the potential benefit to the patient, or the harm was unforeseeable, and so on. In other words, expert opinion about the defendant's conduct (whether favourable or unfavourable) should itself be measured against the general principles applied to the question of breach of duty. This point has been emphasised by the House of Lords in *Bolitho v City and Hackney Health Authority*[19] where Lord Browne-Wilkinson made it clear that the court has to weigh expert evidence in a form of risk–benefit analysis: **6.06**

> the court has to be satisfied that the exponents of the body of opinion relied upon can demonstrate that such opinion has a logical basis. In particular in cases involving, as they so often do, the weighing of risks against benefits, the judge before accepting a body of opinion as being responsible, reasonable or respectable, will need to be satisfied that, in forming their views, the experts have directed their minds to the question of comparative risks and benefits and have reached a defensible conclusion on the matter.

---

[17] *Whitehouse* (n 7 above), 276 *per* Lord Edmund-Davies.
[18] ibid, 281, *per* Lord Fraser. See also *per* Lord Diplock in *Saif Ali v Sydney Mitchell & Co* [1980] AC 198, 220   [19] [1997] 4 All ER 771, 778.

B. The Standard of Care Required

1. Common Professional Practice

6.07 As a general rule, the fact that a defendant acted in accordance with the common practice of others in a similar situation is strong evidence that he has not been negligent.[20] Following a common practice is only *evidence*, however, it is not conclusive, since the court may find that the practice is itself negligent.[21] There could be many reasons, such as convenience, cost, or habit, why a particular practice is commonly followed, which have nothing to do with exercising reasonable care to avoid harming others.[22] There is no reason in theory why the general approach taken by the courts to compliance with accepted practice should not also apply to actions for medical negligence and it is frequently an issue in such cases.

6.08 In *Vancouver General Hospital v McDaniel*,[23] Lord Alness said that a defendant charged with negligence can 'clear his feet' if he shows that he has acted in accordance with general and approved practice, and there are numerous cases in which actions for medical negligence have been dismissed on the basis that the doctor conformed to an accepted practice of the profession.[24] Where there is more than one common practice, as the *Bolam* test contemplates, compliance with one of the practices will normally excuse the defendant. In *Maynard v West Midlands Regional Health Authority*,[25] Lord Scarman said that:

> It is not enough to show that there is a body of competent professional opinion which considers that theirs was a wrong decision, if there also exists a body of professional opinion, equally competent, which supports the decision as reasonable in the circumstances . . . Differences of opinion and practice exist, and will always exist, in the medical as in other professions. There is seldom any one answer exclusive of all others to problems of professional judgment. A court

---

[20] *Morton v William Dixon Ltd* 1909 SC 807, 809; *Morris v West Hartlepool Steam Navigation Co Ltd* [1956] AC 552, 579.

[21] See e g *Lloyds Bank Ltd v EB Savory & Co* [1933] AC 201; *Cavanagh v Ulster Weaving Co Ltd* [1960] AC 145; *General Cleaning Contractors v Christmas* [1953] AC 180, 193, *per* Lord Reid; *Roberge v Bolduc* (1991) 78 DLR (4th) 666, 710 (SCC).

[22] As Lord Tomlin commented in *Bank of Montreal v Dominion Gresham Guarantee and Casualty Co* [1930] AC 659, 666: 'Neglect of duty does not cease by repetition to be neglect of duty'; *Carpenters' Co v British Mutual Banking Co Ltd* [1937] 3 All ER 811, 820, *per* Slesser LJ.

[23] (1934) 152 LT 56, 57–8; *Marshall v Lindsey County Council* [1935] 1 KB 516, 540, *per* Maugham LJ.

[24] *Vancouver General Hospital v McDaniel* (1934) 152 LT 56; *Whiteford v Hunter* [1950] WN 553; *Bolam* (n 8 above); *Gold* (n 7 above). [25] [1984] 1 WLR 634.

may prefer one body of opinion to the other: but that is no basis for a conclusion of negligence.[26]

It is ostensibly for the court to decide whether, on the evidence before it, the **6.09** body of opinion which approved of the defendant's conduct could be said to be responsible. However, there are some judicial statements which suggest that the practice of the medical profession is determinative of the issue, and that it is not open to the court to condemn as negligent a commonly adopted practice. In *Maynard's* case Lord Scarman suggested that the 'seal of approval' of a distinguished body of professional opinion, held in good faith, would acquit the defendant of negligence.[27] His Lordship appeared to equate a *competent* (or 'responsible') body of professional opinion with 'distinguished' or 'respectable' in fact. This tends to conflate accepted practice with the absence of negligence, and, indeed, a 'responsible body of opinion' with the views of distinguished or respectable expert witnesses. This approach is even more apparent in Lord Scarman's speech in *Sidaway v Bethlem Royal Hospital Governors* where he said:

> The *Bolam* principle may be formulated as a rule that a doctor is not negligent if he acts in accordance with a practice accepted at the time as proper by a responsible body of medical opinion even though other doctors adopt a different practice. *In short, the law imposes the duty of care; but the standard of care is a matter of medical judgment.*[28]

As Lord Scarman himself recognised 'the implications of this view of the law are disturbing. It leaves the determination of a legal duty to the judgment of doctors'. On the other hand, this interpretation of the *Bolam* test was not accepted by Lord Bridge in *Sidaway* who said:

> . . . the issue whether non-disclosure in a particular case should be condemned as a breach of the doctor's duty of care is an issue to be decided primarily on the basis of expert medical evidence, applying the *Bolam* test . . . Of course, if there is a conflict of evidence whether a responsible body of medical opinion approves of non-disclosure in a particular case, the judge will have to resolve that conflict. But, even in a case where, as here, no expert witness in the relevant medical field condemns the non-disclosure as being in conflict with accepted and responsible

---

[26] ibid, 638; *Ratty v Haringey Health Authority* [1994] 5 Med LR 413, 416, CA; *Dunne* (n 10 above); *Kaban v Sett* [1994] 1 WWR 476, 479–80 (Man QB). On the other hand, where there has been no considered clinical judgment, but rather 'a catalogue of errors', the approach in *Maynard* to competing bodies of professional opinion will not be relevant: *Le Page v Kingston and Richmond Health Authority* [1997] 8 Med LR 229, 240.

[27] [1984] 1 WLR 639.

[28] [1985] 1 All ER 643, 649 (emphasis added); cf Sir John Donaldson MR in the Court of Appeal, [1984] 1 All ER 1018, 1028: 'The definition of the duty of care is a matter for the law and the courts. They cannot stand idly by if the profession, by an excess of paternalism, denies its patients a real choice. In a word, the law will not permit the medical profession to play God.'

medical practice, I am of opinion that the judge might in certain circumstances come to the conclusion that disclosure of a particular risk was so obviously necessary to an informed choice on the part of the patient that no reasonably prudent medical man would fail to make it.[29]

In other words, the court may condemn even a universally followed practice concerning risk disclosure as negligent on the basis that the hypothetical reasonable doctor would not have adopted it. There is no reason to confine this approach to risk disclosure since the majority of their Lordships in *Sidaway* said that the *Bolam* test applied to all aspects of the doctor's duty of care: diagnosis, advice, and treatment.[30]

6.10 Outside the context of medical negligence actions, the courts have had no difficulty with the notion that commonly adopted practices may themselves be negligent. This has been most apparent in cases of employers' liability,[31] but it is also evident in some cases involving professional liability.[32] There is no basis for applying a different rule about the effect of complying with common practice to the medical profession from that which is applied to all other professions, particularly since the Court of Appeal has emphasised that the *Bolam* test applies to all professions equally.[33] In other common-law jurisdictions the courts have been careful to ensure that, ultimately, decisions as to what constitutes negligence remain for the court to determine. In *Anderson v Chasney*,[34] Coyne JA commented that if general practice was a conclusive defence:

> a group of operators by adopting some practice could legislate themselves out of liability for negligence to the public by adopting or continuing what was an

---

[29] ibid, 662–3. See also Sir John Donaldson MR in *Sidaway* (n 28 above), 1028: '. . . in an appropriate case, a judge would be entitled to reject a unanimous medical view if he were satisfied that it was manifestly wrong and that the doctors must have been misdirecting themselves as to their duty in law.' Thus, a practice must be 'rightly' accepted as proper by the profession. His Lordship drew a specific analogy with the cases in which the courts had held the common practice of employers to be negligent. See further the comment of Farquharson LJ in *Bolitho v City and Hackney Health Authority* [1993] 4 Med LR 381, 386.

[30] See, however, *Gordon v Wilson* [1992] 3 Med LR 401, 426 (Court of Session) where Lord Penrose appeared to suggest that Lord Bridge's comments were confined to the disclosure of information to patients, and that 'nothing in the speech of Lord Bridge was intended to qualify the *Bolam* test'. With respect, though this last observation is accurate, it is clear that the *Bolam* test applies to all aspects of a doctor's duty of care to a patient.

[31] As eg in *Cavanagh* (n 21 above); *Morris* (n 20 above); *Stokes v Guest, Keen & Nettlefold (Bolts & Nuts) Ltd* [1968] 1 WLR 1776, 1783.

[32] *Lloyds Bank Ltd v Savory & Co.* [1933] AC 201, 203; *Edward Wong Finance Co Ltd v Johnson, Stokes and Masters* [1984] AC 296; *Re The Herald of Free Enterprise: Appeal by Captain Lewry* (1987) *Independent*, 18 Dec, Div Ct; *Roberge* (n 21 above).

[33] *Gold* (n 7 above), 894, *per* Lloyd LJ; *Whitehouse* (n 7 above), 276 *per* Lord Edmund-Davies.

[34] [1949] 4 DLR 71, 85 (Man CA); aff'd [1950] 4 DLR 223 (SCC). See also *Hajgato v London Health Association* (1982) 36 OR (2d) 669, 693, *per* Callaghan J.

obviously negligent practice, even though a simple precaution, plainly capable of obviating danger which sometimes might result in death, was well known.

Thus, expert evidence from doctors as to a general or approved practice could not be accepted as conclusive on the issue of negligence, especially where the conduct in question did not involve a matter of technical skill and experience.[35] In *F v R*[36] King CJ acknowledged that professions may adopt unreasonable practices. Practices may develop in professions, not because they serve the interests of clients, but because they protect the interests or convenience of members of the profession. The court has an obligation to scrutinize professional practices to ensure that they accord with the standard of reasonableness imposed by the law. The ultimate question was not whether the defendant's conduct was in accord with the practices of the profession or some part of it, but whether it conformed to the standard of reasonable care demanded by the law. That was a question for the court and the duty of deciding it could not be delegated to any profession or group in the community.[37]

There are, moreover, some English cases in which, on the facts, compliance **6.11** with common practice has been said to have been negligent. In *Clarke v Adams*[38] the plaintiff was being treated for a fibrositic condition of the heel and he was warned by the physiotherapist to say if he felt anything more than a 'comfortable warmth'. He suffered a burning injury resulting in the leg being amputated below the knee. Slade J held the defendant liable for giving an inadequate warning to enable the plaintiff to be safe, although it was the

---

[35] See also *Crits* (n 9 above); *Reynard v Carr* (1983) 30 CCLT 42, 68 (BCSC), *per* Bouck J; *Winrob v Street* (1959) 28 WWR 118, 122 (BCSC); *Hajgato* (n 34 above), 693; *Goode v Nash* (1979) 21 SASR 419, 422 (SC of S Aus); *O'Donovan v Cork County Council* [1967] IR 173, 193, *per* Walsh J; *Albrighton v Royal Prince Alfred Hospital* [1980] 2 NSWLR 542, 562–3, *per* Reynolds JA (NSWCA); *Roberge* (n 21 above), 710 *per* L'Heureux-Dubé J.

[36] (1982) 33 SASR 189, 194 (SC of S Aus), approved by Zelling J in *Battersby v Tottman* (1985) 37 SASR 524, 537; and Lockhart, Sheppard and Pincus JJ in *E v Australian Red Cross Society* (1991) 105 ALR 53, 68, 82–3, 87 (Aus Fed CA).

[37] This view was approved by the High Court of Australia in *Rogers v Whitaker* (1992) 109 ALR 625; [1993] 4 Med LR 79, where it was accepted that, while evidence of acceptable medical practice might be regarded as a useful guide, it was for the court to determine whether the defendant's conduct conformed to the standard of reasonable care demanded by the law; Trindade (1993) 109 LQR 352; McDonald and Swanton (1993) 67 ALJ 145; Malcolm (1994) 2 Tort L Rev 81. See also *Dunne* (n 10 above).

[38] (1950) 94 SJ 599; see also *Jones v Manchester Corpn* [1952] 2 All ER 125, 129, *per* Singleton LJ citing Oliver J, the trial judge. Some commentators consider *Clarke v Adams* to be of questionable authority on the basis that it predates *Bolam* (n 8 above); see Montgomery (1989) 16 J of Law and Soc 319, 323; Dugdale and Stanton, *Professional Negligence* (1989), 2nd edn, para 15.23, n 5. The *Bolam* test, however, was not new, it simply encapsulated earlier statements of the law. This, at least, was Lord Diplock's interpretation in *Sidaway* (n 28 above), 657.

very warning that the defendant had been taught to give. In *Hucks v Cole* Sachs LJ said that:

> When the evidence shows that a lacuna in professional practice exists by which risks of grave danger are knowingly taken, then, however small the risks, the courts must anxiously examine that lacuna—particularly if the risks can be easily and inexpensively avoided. If the court finds, on an analysis of the reasons given for not taking those precautions that, in the light of current professional knowledge, there is no proper basis for the lacuna, and that it is definitely not reasonable that those risks should have been taken, its function is to state that fact and where necessary to state that it constitutes negligence. In such a case the practice will no doubt thereafter be altered to the benefit of patients.[39]

His Lordship added that the fact that other practitioners would have done the same thing as the defendant was a weighty factor to be put in the scales on his behalf, but it was not conclusive. The court had to be vigilant to see whether the reasons given for putting a patient at risk were valid in the light of any well-known advance in medical knowledge, or whether they stemmed from a residual adherence to out of date ideas.[40]

6.12 In *Bolitho v City and Hackney Health Authority*[41] a two-year-old boy suffered brain damage as a result of cardiac arrest caused by an obstruction of the bronchial air passages. The plaintiff was in hospital at the time for the treatment of croup. The defendants admitted that there had been negligence, in that a doctor who had been summoned for assistance on more than one occasion had failed to attend. It was also common ground that had the plaintiff been seen by a doctor and intubated, clearing the obstruction, the brain damage could have been avoided. There were two schools of thought, however, as to whether in the circumstances it was appropriate to intubate.

---

[39] (1968), [1993] 4 Med LR 393, 397. See also the comments of Thomas J in *Wiszniewski v Central Manchester Health Authority* [1996] 7 Med LR 248, 261, that where analysis of the expert evidence 'shows that a decision made by a doctor and supported by experts cannot be justified as one that a responsible medical practitioner would have taken, then a judge should not preclude himself from reaching that conclusion simply because clinical judgment is involved'.

[40] In *Bolitho v City and Hackney Health Authority* [1993] 4 Med LR 381, 392 Dillon LJ suggested that the court could only adopt the approach of Sachs LJ and reject medical opinion on the ground that the reasons of one group of doctors does not really stand up to analysis if the court, fully conscious of its own lack of medical and clinical experience, was none the less clearly satisfied that the views of that group of doctors were *Wednesbury* unreasonable, i e views such as no reasonable body of doctors could have held. In *Joyce v Wandsworth Health Authority* [1996] 7 Med LR 1, 20, however, Hobhouse LJ took a different view: 'In my judgment (*pace* Dillon LJ [1993] 4 Med LR at 392), it does not assist to introduce concepts from administrative law such as the *Wednesbury* test; such tests are directed to very different problems and their use, even by analogy, in negligence cases can, in my judgment, only serve to confuse'. In *X (minors) v Bedfordshire County Council* [1995] 3 WLR 152, 170, in a slightly different context, Lord Browne-Wilkinson commented that: 'I do not believe that it is either helpful or necessary to introduce public law concepts as to the validity of a decision into the question of liability at common law for negligence.'   [41] [1997] 4 All ER 771.

The doctor who failed to attend said that had she attended the plaintiff she would not have intubated, and therefore the cardiac arrest and subsequent brain damage would have occurred in any event. There was evidence from one expert for the defendants, which the trial judge and the Court of Appeal chose to characterise as a responsible body of professional opinion, that he would not have intubated in the circumstances, although five medical experts for the plaintiff said that the child should have been intubated, and it was agreed that this was the only course of action that would have prevented the damage in this case. In the House of Lords the plaintiff submitted that the judge had been wrong in law to treat the *Bolam* test as requiring him to accept the views of one truthful body of expert professional advice, even though he was unpersuaded of its logical force, and that ultimately it was for the court, not for medical opinion, to decide what was the standard of care required of a professional in the circumstances of each particular case.

6.13 Delivering the judgment of the House, Lord Browne-Wilkinson agreed that the court was not bound to conclude that a doctor can escape liability for negligent treatment or diagnosis just because he leads evidence from a number of medical experts who are genuinely of opinion that the defendant's treatment or diagnosis accorded with sound medical practice. The court had to be satisfied that the opinion had a logical basis, which would involve the weighing of risks against benefits, in order to reach a defensible conclusion. His Lordship referred to the judgment of Sachs LJ in *Hucks v Cole* and the decision of the Privy Council in *Edward Wong Finance Co Ltd v Johnson Stokes & Master*[42] and commented:

> These decisions demonstrate that in cases of diagnosis and treatment there are cases where, despite a body of professional opinion sanctioning the defendant's conduct, the defendant can properly be held liable for negligence (I am not here considering questions of disclosure of risk). In my judgment that is because, in some cases, it cannot be demonstrated to the judge's satisfaction that the body of opinion relied upon is reasonable or responsible. In the vast majority of cases the fact that distinguished experts in the field are of a particular opinion will demonstrate the reasonableness of that opinion. In particular, where there are questions of assessment of the relative risks and benefits of adopting a particular medical practice, a reasonable view necessarily presupposes that the relative risks and benefits have been weighed by the experts in forming their opinions. But if, in a rare case, it can be demonstrated that the professional opinion is not capable of withstanding logical analysis, the judge is entitled to hold that the body of opinion is not reasonable or responsible.[43]

6.14 It is rare for the courts to condemn a commonly accepted practice as negligent. Normally, it will only be where the risk was, or should have been, obvious to the defendant so that it would be folly to disregard it, that the courts will take this step.[44] The point was stressed by Lord Browne-Wilkinson in *Bolitho v City and Hackney Health Authority*.[45] It would very seldom be right, said his Lordship, for a judge to reach the conclusion that views genuinely held by a competent medical expert were unreasonable. It would be wrong to allow the assessment of medical risks and benefits, which was a matter of clinical judgment, to deteriorate into seeking to persuade the judge to prefer one of two views both of which are capable of being logically supported: 'It is only where a judge can be satisfied that the body of expert opinion cannot be logically supported at all that such opinion will not provide the bench mark by reference to which the defendant's conduct falls to be assessed.' Where the case does not involve difficult or uncertain questions of medical or surgical treatment, or highly technical scientific issues, but is concerned with whether obvious and simple precautions could have been taken, it will be easier for the court to form its own judgment and the practice of experts, though not irrelevant, may be more readily discounted.[46] Where, however, there are difficult, uncertain, highly technical scientific questions requiring information not ordinarily expected of a practitioner, and where the state of medical knowledge was highly variable between scientists, public health authorities, and different medical communities, it is not appropriate for the court to find that a practice which conformed to what other similarly situated practitioners were following was negligent.[47] In these circumstances the court should confine itself to the prevailing standards of practice.

6.15 Before any question of complying with accepted practice can arise the court must be satisfied on the evidence presented to it that there is a responsible body of professional opinion which supports the practice. It is always open to the court to reject expert evidence applying the ordinary principles of credibility that would be applied in any courtroom.[48] In *Hills v Potter*, Hirst J denied that the *Bolam* test allows the medical profession to set the standard of care:

---

[44] *Paris v Stepney Borough Council* [1951] AC 367, 382, *per* Lord Normand: 'obvious folly'; *General Cleaning Contractors* (n 21 above), 193, *per* Lord Reid: 'obvious danger'; *Morris* (n 20 above), 579, *per* Lord Cohen: 'obvious risk'; *Stokes* (n 31 above), 1783; see also *O'Donovan* (n 35 above), 193, *per* Walsh J; *Gent v Wilson* (1956) 2 DLR (2d) 160, 165 *per* Schroeder JA (Ont CA).   [45] [1997] 4 All ER 771, 779.
[46] *Anderson v Chasney* [1949] 4 DLR 71, 86–87 *per* Coyne JA (Man CA); aff'd [1950] 4 DLR 223 (SCC); *Chapman v Rix* (1959) 103 SJ 940 *per* Morris LJ, CA.
[47] *ter Neuzen v Korn* (1993) 103 DLR (4th) 473, 506 (BCCA); aff'd (1995) 127 DLR (4th) 577 (SCC).
[48] For example, an expert witness should be independent. Evidence which, say, descends into advocacy may well be treated as less credible. See, eg, *Murphy v Wirral Health Authority* [1996] 7 Med LR 99, 104; *El-Morssy v Bristol and District Health Authority* [1996] 7 Med LR 232, 240; *Wiszniewski* (n 39 above), 254, 262. For discussion of the duties of an independent expert, see *National Justice Compania Naviera SA v Prudential Assurance Company Ltd, 'The Ikarian Reefer'* [1993] 2 Lloyd's Rep 68, 81–2; *Sharpe v Southend Health Authority* [1997] 8 Med LR 299, 303.

In every case the court must be satisfied that the standard contended for . . . accords with that upheld by a substantial body[49] of medical opinion, and that this body of medical opinion is both respectable and responsible, and experienced in this particular field of medicine.[50]

Similarly, in *Bolitho v City and Hackney Health Authority*, Farquharson LJ pointed out that:

There is of course no inconsistency between the decisions in *Hucks* v. *Cole* and *Maynard's* case. It is not enough for a defendant to call a number of doctors to say what he had done or not done was in accord with accepted clinical practice. It is necessary for the judge to consider that evidence and decide whether that clinical practice puts the patient unnecessarily at risk.[51]

Following accepted practice, or one of several such practices, is strong evidence of the exercise of reasonable care, but ultimately it is for the court to determine what constitutes negligence.[52] It will be rare for the court to conclude that a common practice was negligent, but when this does happen it will be through a finding that the practice was not 'responsible'. Once the practice followed by the defendant is acknowledged to be a 'responsible' practice it is not open to the court to hold that it was negligent, even where another body of 'responsible' professional opinion is critical of the practice. The inherent danger in the *Bolam* test, however, is that if the courts defer too readily to expert evidence, medical standards may decline, since where there

---

[49] In *De Freitas v O'Brien* [1995] 6 Med LR 108, it was argued that this reference to a 'substantial body of medical opinion' meant that the defendant could not rely on a small number of experts in the field as supporting a particular practice. The Court of Appeal rejected this argument. The test is whether there is a 'responsible body' of opinion, which cannot be measured in purely quantitative terms. On the facts, a body of 11 doctors who specialised in spinal surgery, out of a total of well over 1,000 orthopaedic and neurosurgeons in the country, could represent a responsible body of opinion.

[50] [1983] 3 All ER 716, 728. See also *per* Lord Diplock in *Sidaway* (n 28 above), 659, stating that the court must be satisfied by the expert evidence that a body of opinion qualifies as a 'responsible' body of medical opinion; *Dowdie v Camberwell Health Authority* [1997] 8 Med LR 368, 375 *per* Kay J: 'The mere fact that two distinguished expert witnesses have testified that it was within the range of acceptable practice to proceed in that way does not oblige me to accept their evidence and, on this issue, I accept the evidence of the plaintiff's experts . . .'

[51] [1993] 4 Med LR 381, 386. In *Chapman v Rix* (1960), [1994] 5 Med LR 239, 247 Lord Goddard said that a doctor cannot avoid a finding of negligence merely by finding two doctors to say that they would have acted as he did, provided there was evidence the other way. In *Gascoine v Ian Sheridan & Co.* [1994] 5 Med LR 437, 444 Mitchell J commented that 'as a matter of common sense . . . simply because a number of doctors gave evidence to the same effect, that does not automatically constitute an established and alternative "school of thought" if, for example, the reasons given to substantiate the views expressed do not stand up to sensible analysis: see *Hucks* v. *Cole ante* (*per* Sachs L.J.).'

[52] See *Jackson & Powell on Professional Negligence* (1992), 3rd edn, para 1.69; Dugdale and Stanton, *Professional Negligence* (1989), 2nd edn, paras 15.22–15.23; Norrie [1985] JR 145.

are competing views within the medical profession the *Bolam* test supports the lowest common denominator.[53]

2. Departures from Common Practice

6.16 A departure from accepted practice may be evidence of negligence,[54] but it is not conclusive.[55] If deviation from a common professional practice was considered proof of negligence then no doctor could introduce a new technique or method of treatment without facing the risk of a negligence action if something went wrong.[56] The fundamental test remains whether the defendant acted with reasonable care in all the circumstances, and the significance of compliance with or deviation from common professional practice lies in its evidential value. Sometimes, a departure from accepted practice may provide overwhelming evidence of a breach of duty, particularly where the practice is followed as a precaution against a known risk and the defendant has no good reason for not following the normal procedure. If the risk should materialise the defendant will have great difficulty in avoiding a finding of negligence.[57]

6.17 Some instances of departure from accepted practice are quite clearly negligent. In *Chin Keow v Government of Malaysia*[58] a doctor gave a patient an injection of penicillin without making any enquiry about the patient's medical history. Had he done so he would have discovered that she was allergic to penicillin. The patient died due to an allergic reaction to the drug. The doctor was aware of the remote possibility of this risk materialising but he carried on with his routine practice of not enquiring because he had not had any mishaps before. He was held to have been negligent. All the medical evidence was to the effect that enquiries, which would have taken no more

---

[53] In *Fallows v Randle* [1997] 8 Med LR 160 an operation to sterilise the plaintiff failed to achieve sterility. There were competing theories as to how the operation could have failed, one of which involved negligence by the defendant whereas the other did not. The trial judge preferred the plaintiff's explanation. Stuart-Smith LJ said, at 165, that the *Bolam* principle 'has really no application where what the judge has to decide is, on balance, which of two explanations—for something which has undoubtedly occurred which shows that the operation has been unsuccessful—is to be preferred. That is a question of fact which the judge has to determine on the ordinary basis on a balance of probability. It is not a question of saying whether there was a respectable body of medical opinion here which says that this can happen by chance without any negligence, it is a question for the judge to weigh up the evidence on both sides, and he is, in my judgment, entitled in a situation like this, to prefer the evidence of one expert witness to that of the other.' [54] *Robinson v Post Office* [1974] 2 All ER 737, 745.

[55] *Holland v The Devitt & Moore Nautical College* (1960) *The Times*, 4 March, QBD, where a slight departure from the standard textbook treatment was held not negligent, since the doctor had to treat a particular patient, whereas the textbooks deal with a subject generally; *Dunne* (n 10 above), 109.

[56] *Hunter v Hanley* 1955 SC 200, 206, *per* Lord President Clyde.

[57] See *Clark v MacLennan* [1983] 1 All ER 416. [58] [1967] 1 WLR 813.

than five minutes, were necessary. Similarly, in *Landau v Werner*[59] a psychiatrist who engaged in social contact with a female patient who had developed a strong and obsessive emotional attachment to him was held to have been negligent. His conduct was a departure from recognised standards in the practice of psychiatry and led to a serious deterioration in the patient's mental health. Sellers LJ said that:

> . . . a doctor might not be negligent if he tried a new technique but if he did he must justify it before the court. If his novel or exceptional treatment had failed disastrously he could not complain if it was held that he went beyond the bounds of due care and skill as recognised generally. Success was the best justification for unusual and unestablished treatment.

One consequence of the *Bolam* test is that where there are two competing **6.18** responsible bodies of professional opinion and the defendant adheres to one view, but carelessly fails to follow his own normal practice with the result that he complies with the alternative approach, he will not be held negligent because he will have conformed to a practice accepted as proper by a responsible body of professional opinion. Thus, where the doctor fails to give a warning about the risks of treatment which he would usually give, but there is a responsible body of medical opinion which, as a matter of deliberate policy, would not warn the patient of the particular risks, the defendant will not be liable since, though he has departed from his own clinical practice, he has conformed to a practice accepted as proper by a responsible body of professional opinion, albeit by accident.[60] In *Gascoine v Ian Sheridan & Co*,[61] a case of alleged negligent overtreatment, Mitchell J commented that: 'If on some hit-and-miss basis [the defendants] treated correctly (or correctly in the opinion of a respected reasonably competent body of thinking in 1978) then liability in negligence could not be established.'

Codified standards of professional conduct, though not conclusive, may **6.19** constitute significant evidence of what constitutes reasonable care.[62] In the context of health care, the introduction of medical audit could lead to the development of treatment protocols and best practice guidelines, providing a consensus view of experts in the field as to the proper standards. It might then become increasingly difficult for a doctor to argue that the protocol was rejected in favour of some alternative method, even if there are some doctors

---

[59] (1961) 105 SJ 257 and 1008 (CA).
[60] *Moyes v Lothian Health Board* [1990] 1 Med LR 463, 470.
[61] [1994] 5 Med LR 437, 458. See also *Lachambre v Nair* [1989] 2 WWR 749 (Sask QB).
[62] *Lloyd Cheyham & Co Ltd v Littlejohn & Co* (1985) 2 PN 154. See Gwilliam (1986) 2 PN 175. See also *Bevan Investments Ltd v Blackhall and Struthers (No 2)* [1973] 2 NZLR 45, 66 on engineering codes of practice.

prepared to state that they disagree with the protocol produced by the experts.[63] There is already evidence that the courts are prepared to consider, and accept as highly persuasive, guidelines produced by the medical profession on appropriate standards of conduct.[64]

6.20 The fact that a practitioner who departs from the accepted methods of treatment will normally have to provide some justification for doing so could have an inhibiting effect on doctors who seek to employ novel or experimental methods in the interests of their patients where traditional techniques have failed. There is a public interest in allowing the medical profession to develop new, and more effective methods of health care, without the fear that they may be sued for negligence simply for trying something different from established practice.[65] On the other hand, patients should not be recklessly subjected to untried and potentially dangerous experimentation.[66] The law has to reach a balance between these competing considerations. One response has been to say that in such circumstances the courts should be careful not to make a finding of negligence simply because the patient has sustained injury.[67] There is likely to be a time-lag between the development of new methods and their acceptance by the profession. Where the new treatment is not yet supported by a responsible body of medical opinion a defendant will have to justify his decision simply by reference to the 'reasonable doctor'. This will depend on the relative risk of the treatment in comparison to the alternative treatments and the nature of the illness for which it was prescribed. Where the patient's condition is very serious and the standard treatment is ineffective, a doctor will be justified in taking greater risks in

---

[63] Harpwood (1994) 1 Med Law Int 241, 250, 251. Instructive here are the CEPOD Reports into perioperative deaths which have identified certain systematic errors which can occur during surgery: see Buck, Devlin, and Lunn, *Report of a Confidential Enquiry into Perioperative Deaths* (Nuffield Provincial Hospitals Trust and the King's Fund, 1987); Campling, Devlin, Hoile and Lunn, *Report of the National Confidential Enquiry into Perioperative Deaths* (National Confidential Enquiry into Perioperative Deaths, London, 1990).

[64] See *W v Egdell* [1990] 1 All ER 835 in the context of confidentiality; and *Airedale NHS Trust v Bland* [1993] 1 All ER 821 in the context of the treatment for patients in a persistent vegetative state. See also *Pierre v Marshall* [1994] 8 WWR 478 (Alta QB) where the defendant was held to have been negligent for failing to follow the recommendations of the Alberta Medical Association and the Society of Obstetricians and Gynaecologists of Canada that there should be universal screening of pregnant women for gestational diabetes, notwithstanding that there was still controversy about the cost-effectiveness of universal screening.

[65] *Sidaway v Bethlem Royal Hospital Governors* [1985] 1 All ER 643, 657 *per* Lord Diplock.

[66] In *Coughlin v Kuntz* (1987) 42 CCLT 142 (BCSC); aff'd [1990] 2 WWR 737 (BCCA) the defendant was held to have been negligent for adopting a method of performing an operation which was experimental, unsupported by clinical study, and favoured by no other orthopaedic surgeon. The procedure was under investigation by the College of Physicians and Surgeons, which had urged the defendant to undertake a moratorium on the procedure.

[67] *Wilsher v Essex Area Health Authority* [1986] 3 All ER 801, 812 *per* Mustill LJ.

an attempt to provide some effective treatment. In *Zimmer v Ringrose* Prowse JA said that:

> A physician is entitled to decide that the situation dictates the adoption of an innovative course of treatment. As long as he discharges his duty of disclosure, and is not otherwise in breach of his duties of skill and care, e g has not negligently adopted the procedure given the circumstances, the doctor will not be held liable for implementing such a course of treatment.[68]

The defendant's method of sterilisation was 'experimental and quite unsupported by clinical study as a method acceptable for human beings'.[69] He was held to have been negligent in failing to inform the plaintiff that the technique had not been approved by the medical profession.

6.21 It is clear that the patient should not be exposed to excessive risk and there should be some attempt to provide scientific validation for a new technique. In *Hepworth v Kerr*[70] the defendant anaesthetist adopted a new hypotensive anaesthetic technique which he knew had never been attempted routinely before, in order to provide a blood-free field for the operating surgeon. He knew that he was experimenting, but did not embark upon any proper scientific validation of his technique in some 1,500 patients by the time of the plaintiff's operation. It was not a minor adjustment to well-established techniques, but a step completely outside conventional wisdom which was right at the margins of safety and effectively took patients 'to the very edge of existence'. McKinnon J held the defendant liable for the condition of anterior spinal artery syndrome (spinal stroke) which the plaintiff was subsequently found to have developed, despite the fact that this amounted to a condemnation of the defendant's 'life-time work'.

6.22 A degree of care is expected which is commensurate with the risk involved, and innovative treatment would be regarded as inherently 'risky' until it has become tried and tested. In *Independent Broadcasting Authority v EMI Electronics Ltd and BICC Construction Ltd*,[71] the House of Lords held that a defendant employed to design an experimental television mast had to demonstrate that he had exercised a high degree of care both in assessing the risks of the venture and the possible alternatives. He could not justify his actions simply by saying 'we were taking a step into the unknown and so the risks were unforeseeable'. There was an obligation to think things

[68] (1981) 124 DLR (3d) 215, 223–4 (Alta CA). See also *Waters v West Sussex Health Authority* [1995] 6 Med LR 362.
[69] (1978) 89 DLR (3d) 646, 652, *per* MacDonald J. See also *Cryderman v Ringrose* [1977] 3 WWR 109; aff'd [1978] 3 WWR 481 (Alta SC Appellate Division).
[70] [1995] 6 Med LR 139.   [71] (1980) 14 BLR 1.

through and to assess the dimensions of the 'venture into the unknown'.[72] This would apply to claims arising out of a systematic research project, whether therapeutic or non-therapeutic. An allegation of negligence in conducting research would involve proving that the design, the performance, or the follow-up of the experimental procedure was negligent, or that the disclosure of information concerning risks was inadequate. A researcher has a duty to investigate fully the possible consequences of the research using existing published literature and animal experiments where appropriate, prior to conducting research on human subjects.[73] Medical research must seek to minimise the risks to the research subjects, for example by providing for termination of the project if a serious risk of harm became apparent, by provision for emergencies, and by careful periodic observation of the subjects.[74]

3. Keeping Up To Date

6.23 Professional practice tends to change over time so that what was once accepted as the correct procedure may no longer be considered to be responsible. Doctors have an obligation to keep up to date with new developments in their particular field, although it can be difficult to determine precisely when a new development will render adherence to the old method negligent; there is a tension between the obligation to keep up to date and the obligation not to subject patients to untried methods of treatment unless the traditional approach has proved ineffective and the anticipated benefits are justified by the risks. Once the risks associated with the old procedure become generally known, so that an ordinary and reasonably competent practitioner can be expected to have altered his practice accordingly, it would be negligent to continue using that procedure. The problem is to identify precisely when it can be said that a risk has become generally known. For example, there may be a difference of knowledge and understanding between research scientists

---

[72] ibid, 31, *per* Lord Edmund-Davies.

[73] *Vacwell Engineering Co Ltd v BDH Chemicals* [1971] 1 QB 88, where the defendant was negligent in failing to check all relevant publications dealing with a little known chemical prior to marketing it.

[74] *Zimmer v Ringrose* (1978) 89 DLR (3d) 646, 656. It is also arguable that a research project which failed to comply with national or international ethical codes on medical experimentation could be found to have been conducted negligently, on the basis that the codes constitute evidence of what is reasonable care, by reference to the accepted practice of the profession: see Dugdale and Stanton, *Professional Negligence* (1989), 2nd edn, para 16.11. Both therapeutic and non-therapeutic medical research are governed by the guidelines of the *Declaration of Helsinki*. See further, the Royal College of Physicians, *Guidelines on the Practice of Ethics Committees in Medical Research Involving Human Subjects* (1990), 2nd edn, and Royal College of Physicians, *Research Involving Patients* (1990). See generally, Giesen (1995) 3 Med L Rev 22.

and clinicians, since research scientists are usually better informed about new discoveries in discrete areas of their discipline than practitioners, who have to rely on researchers and professional publications to keep them informed.[75]

The obligation is to make a reasonable effort to keep up to date. A doctor cannot realistically be expected to read every article in every learned medical journal,[76] but where a particular risk has been highlighted on a number of occasions the practitioner will ignore it at his peril.[77] The practices adopted or state of knowledge in other countries are not necessarily evidence of the appropriate standard in the United Kingdom.[78]   **6.24**

In *Crawford v Charing Cross Hospital*,[79] the plaintiff developed brachial palsy   **6.25**
in an arm following a blood transfusion. At first instance the defendants were held liable on the basis that the anaesthetist had failed to read an article published in *The Lancet* six months earlier, concerning the best position of the arm when using a drip. The Court of Appeal reversed this decision, taking the view that it would be too great a burden to require a doctor to read every article appearing in the current medical press.[80] It was wrong to suggest that a practitioner was negligent simply because he did not immediately put into operation the suggestions made by a contributor to a medical journal, although the time might come when a recommendation was so well proved and so well accepted that it should be adopted. In *Gascoine v Ian Sheridan & Co*[81] Mitchell J commented that a 'shop floor gynaecologist' had a responsibility to keep himself generally informed on mainstream changes in diagnosis, treatment, and practice through the mainstream literature, such as the leading textbooks and the *Journal of Obstetrics and Gynaecology*. However, it was unreasonable to suppose that he had had an opportunity to acquaint himself with the content of more obscure journals.

---

[75] *ter Neuzen* (n 47 above), 497–8. Moreover, there may be a lack of effective communication between public health officials and practitioners, again producing a 'time lag' in the knowledge of the profession.
[76] Although it is acknowledged that 'where there is developing knowledge, [the defendant] must keep reasonably abreast of it and not be too slow to apply it': *Stokes* (n 31 above), 1783, *per* Swanwick J; on the other hand, where the defendant's omission involves an absence of initiative in seeking out knowledge of facts which are not in themselves obvious 'the court must be slow to blame him for not ploughing a lone furrow': *Thompson v Smith Shiprepairers (North Shields) Ltd* [1984] 1 All ER 881, 894, *per* Mustill J.
[77] See e g, *Roe v Minister of Health* [1954] 2 QB 66; *McLean v Weir* [1977] 5 WWR 609; aff'd [1980] 4 WWR 330; *McCormick v Marcotte* (1971) 20 DLR (3d) 345 (SCC).
[78] *Whiteford* (n 24 above); *ter Neuzen* (n 47 above), where it was held that it was not open to a jury to find the common practice of Canadian practitioners to be negligent on the basis of knowledge available in Australia.   [79] (1953) *The Times*, 8 December.
[80] See also *Dwan v Farquhar* [1988] 1 Qd R 234, where an article in a journal concerning the risks of contracting the AIDS virus from blood transfusions was published in March 1983, and a patient contracted HIV from a blood transfusion performed in May 1983. It was held that there was no negligence.   [81] [1994] 5 Med LR 437, 447.

4. Assessing Degrees of Risk

6.26 In applying general principles to the assessment of whether a defendant has exercised reasonable care, the courts take into account a number of factors, including the foreseeability of the damage, the magnitude of the risk, the purpose of the defendant's conduct, and the cost or practicability of taking precautions. These issues are just as relevant to an action for medical negligence as any other type of negligence action, despite the heavy reliance which is often placed on expert medical evidence in the former. The decision of the House of Lords in *Bolitho v City and Hackney Health Authority*[82] now makes it clear that medical experts will have to be able to demonstrate that they have addressed the question of assessing the relative risks and benefits of adopting a particular medical practice, and that their opinion stands up to logical analysis.

Foreseeability of Risk

6.27 If a particular danger could not reasonably have been anticipated because it was unforeseeable, the defendant did not act negligently, because the reasonable man is not expected to take precautions against unforeseeable consequences. Whether a consequence was foreseeable is not determined by using hindsight but by reference to knowledge at the date of the alleged negligence. Thus, in *Roe v Minister of Health*[83] heard in 1954, the defendants were found not to have been liable for the injuries inflicted when contaminated anaesthetic was administered to the plaintiff in 1947, because the anaesthetic had become contaminated in a way which was unforeseeable at the time. The court 'must not look at the 1947 accident with 1954 spectacles', even though it would have been negligent to adopt the same practice in 1954 when the risk was more widely known.[84]

Magnitude of Risk

6.28 A defendant is not negligent simply because the damage was foreseeable.[85] In some circumstances it may be reasonable to ignore a small risk, because the chance of it materialising is remote and the cost of precautions high. By

---

[82] [1997] 4 All ER 771, 779.   [83] [1954] 2 QB 66.
[84] ibid, 86; *McLean* (n 77 above). There is some doubt as to whether the contamination of the anaesthetic in *Roe* was in fact caused by the manner in which it was stored: see Hutter (1990) 45 *Anaesthesia* 859.   [85] *Bolton v Stone* [1951] AC 850, 863, *per* Lord Oaksey.

contrast, where the cost of avoiding a risk is minimal it may be negligent to ignore even a remote risk.[86]

A degree of care commensurate with the risk created by the defendant's conduct is required, so that the greater the risk of harm the greater the precautions that must be taken.[87] This principle applies just as much to professional liability as it does to any other category of negligence: **6.29**

> . . . there is a clear relationship between the magnitude of the risk and the duty of care, in particular the standard of care. The greater the risks involved in any proposed course of treatment, the more carefully and anxiously must the medical practitioner weigh and consider the possible alternatives before deciding to resort to the proposed treatment.[88]

Thus, when an anaesthetist was handling a highly inflammable substance and knew of the hazard arising from electrostatic sparks in an operating theatre, the degree of care required was correspondingly high and he was bound to take special precautions to prevent injury to his patient.[89]

The magnitude of the risk involves two elements. First, the likelihood that the harm will occur. The more remote the chance that any damage to the plaintiff will arise, the more reasonable it will be to take fewer, or even no, precautions against the eventuality. Secondly, the degree of risk also takes into account the severity of the potential consequences. If the harm is likely to be serious, should it occur, then greater precautions must be taken. Thus, a risk that a patient may be accidentally infected with HIV from a contaminated blood transfusion will impose a high standard of care upon the supplier of the blood, given the seriousness of the consequences.[90] Where a doctor has **6.30**

---

[86] *Overseas Tankship (UK) Ltd v Miller Steamship Co Pty Ltd, The Wagon Mound (No 2)* [1967] 1 AC 617, 642.

[87] *Read v J Lyons & Co Ltd* [1947] AC 156, 173, *per* Lord Macmillan.

[88] *Battersby v Tottman* (1985) 37 SASR 524, 542 *per* Jacobs J; *Glasgow Corporation v Muir* [1943] AC 448, 456, *per* Lord Macmillan: 'Those who engage in operations inherently dangerous must take precautions which are not required of persons engaged in the ordinary routine of daily life'; *McAllister v Lewisham and North Southwark Health Authority* [1994] 5 Med LR 343, 347, QBD, where Rougier J commented that: 'The decision whether or not to operate is the product of a tripartite equation: 1. The risks of operating. 2. The benefits of operating. 3. The risks of not operating'; see also *O'Donovan* (n 35 above), 190, *per* Walsh J; *Buchan v Ortho Pharmaceuticals (Canada) Ltd* (1986) 25 DLR (4th) 658, 678–9, *per* Robins JA (Ont CA).

[89] *Crits* (n 9 above), 511 (Ont CA); *Darley v Shale* [1993] 4 Med LR 161, 168 (NSWSC).

[90] *E v Australian Red Cross Society* (1991) 105 ALR 53, 77 (Aus Fed CA) *per* Sheppard J. Despite the high duty, the defendants were found not to have been negligent in this case because of the very limited options for reasonable precautions against infection with HIV at the time (October 1984). A test specifically for HIV did not become available until March 1985. See also *Pittman Estate v Bain* (1994) 112 DLR (4th) 257, 319 *per* Lang J (Ont Ct, Gen Div). Note, however, that the importance of the blood supply in saving lives may justify the taking of greater risk than would otherwise be acceptable.

formed an opinion as to the appropriate diagnosis of a patient's condition, he should take into account the possibility that an alternative diagnosis would explain the symptoms, especially where the consequences of the alternative diagnosis, if correct, would be very serious.[91] The defendant must also take account of the known characteristics of the particular plaintiff where those characteristics make the likelihood of harm occurring greater than would be the case with a normal individual,[92] or where the damage is likely to be more severe.[93] In these circumstances greater precautions will be required than for the average individual.

6.31 The purpose of the defendant's conduct will also be taken into account in assessing what is reasonable. If sufficiently important, it may justify the assumption of abnormal risk.[94] Unsurprisingly, the saving of life and limb is likely to justify taking considerable risk[95] but this does not mean that this purpose can justify taking *any* risk. It is a matter of balancing the risk against the consequences of not taking the risk. If, for example, the patient's condition is such that he will almost certainly die without some form of medical intervention, then treatment with a high degree of risk will be justified, unless, of course, there is an equally effective alternative treatment that carries less risk.

Cost of Precautions

6.32 A further matter to be considered in assessing whether the taking of a foreseeable risk was justified is the practicability (or cost) of taking precautions. The practicability of taking precautions should be measured on an objective basis: the defendant's impecuniosity is not a defence if objectively a precaution was reasonably required.[96] If the risk can be avoided at small

---

[91] *Lankenau v Dutton* (1986) 37 CCLT 213, 232 (BCSC); aff'd (1991) 79 DLR (4th) 707 (BCCA); *Bergen v Sturgeon General Hospital* (1984) 28 CCLT 155 (Alta QB); *Law Estate v Simice* (1994) 21 CCLT (2d) 228, 236 (BCSC).

[92] A 'measure of care appropriate to the inability or disability of those who are immature or feeble in mind or body is due from others, who know of or ought to anticipate the presence of such persons within the scope and hazard of their own operations': *Glasgow Corporation v Taylor* [1922] 1 AC 44, 67, *per* Lord Sumner, approved by Lord Reid in *Haley v London Electricity Board* [1965] AC 778, 793.   [93] *Paris v Stepney Borough Council* [1951] AC 367.

[94] *Daborn v Bath Tramways Motor Co Ltd* [1946] 2 All ER 333, 336, *per* Asquith LJ.

[95] *Watt v Hertfordshire County Council* [1954] 1 WLR 835. See also the comments of Lang J in *Pittman Estate v Bain* (1994) 112 DLR (4th) 257, 313 (Ont Ct, Gen Div): 'In the case of blood, the societal need for the component produces different considerations. This is not a product that should be removed from the market if inherently dangerous. Blood is an essential source of life to many. Although a biologic, and, therefore, dangerous, the need for the product outweighs the risk.'

[96] In *PQ v Australian Red Cross Society* [1992] 1 VR 19, 33 (Vict SC) McGarvie J held that the actual resources of the defendants was not an issue relevant to the practicability of

cost or with a trivial expenditure of time and effort, it will be unreasonable to run the risk. Conversely, some risks can only be eliminated or reduced at great expense. A reasonable man would only neglect a risk if he had a valid reason for doing so, for example, if 'it would involve considerable expense to eliminate the risk . . . [h]e would weigh the risk against the difficulty of eliminating it'. However, a reasonable man would not ignore even a small risk 'if action to eliminate it presented no difficulty, involved no disadvantage and required no expense'.[97] In *Hucks v Cole*[98] Sachs LJ said that when risks of great danger are knowingly taken as a matter of professional practice then, however small the risks, the court must carefully examine the practice, particularly where the risks can be easily and inexpensively avoided. In *Coles v Reading and District Management Committee*[99] it was held to be negligent not to have given the patient an anti-tetanus injection, since it was a simple precaution, and the consequences of the infection are serious.

Some risks will be unavoidable. In this situation the risks of proceeding **6.33** have to be weighed against the disadvantages of not proceeding, taking into account the expected benefits to the patient's health. Where the consequences of not treating the patient are potentially very serious, then the doctor will normally be justified in taking greater risks.[100] Conversely, where the treatment is for a minor ailment even small risks should not be disregarded;[101] *a fortiori*, where a diagnostic test which carries a real risk of an adverse reaction is conducted when there are no clinical indications for performing such a test.[102] This balancing exercise must take account of the individual patient. In *Battersby v Tottman*[103] a doctor prescribed a very high

---

the precautions required to protect the plaintiff from HIV infection from a transfusion of blood products; cf *Pittman Estate* (n 95 above) where Lang J held that the conduct of a blood bank should be measured against that of other blood banks, not by reference to commercial organisations, on the basis that it was a 'professional service' not a commercial service. If other 'responsible' blood banks were unable or unwilling through lack of resources to take such precautions, the defendant would probably not be liable for failing to take the same precautions.

[97] *Overseas Tankship (UK) Ltd* (n 86 above), 642; and in the medical context see *Chin Keow v Government of Malaysia* [1967] 1 WLR 813, PC; *Leonard v Knott* [1978] 5 WWR 511, 516 (BCSC).   [98] (1968), [1993] 4 Med LR 393, 397.

[99] (1963) 107 SJ 115.

[100] *Davidson v Connaught Laboratories* (1980) 14 CCLT 251, 270, where the patient suffered an allergic reaction to a rabies vaccine, having come into contact with a rabid animal. Rabies is almost invariably fatal.

[101] The obvious example would be cosmetic surgery, although there may well be room for disagreement as to the importance to the individual patient of removing certain cosmetic defects. In *La Fleur v Cornelis* (1979) 28 NBR (2d) 569, 573 (NBSC) Barry J commented that cosmetic surgeons do not treat illnesses in the ordinary sense, and accordingly a 'doctor who undertakes to operate on the nose of a healthy person for cosmetic purposes has a very high duty indeed'.   [102] *Leonard* (n 97 above).

dose of a drug to a patient suffering from mental illness. He took the view that the benefits of the drug outweighed the risk of it causing serious and permanent eye damage, since without treatment the patient was 'dangerously suicidal', and other methods of treatment had failed. It was held that in these circumstances the decision to prescribe a dosage that was far in excess of the recommended dosages was not negligent.[104]

5. Specialists and the Inexperienced

6.34 A specialist is required to achieve the standard of care of a reasonably competent specialist in his field, exercising 'the ordinary skill of his specialty.[105] Thus, while a general practitioner must be judged by the standards of general practitioners and not specialists,[106] if a general practitioner were to undertake a specialist task, he would be judged by the standards of that specialty. If he is unable to meet those standards, he will be held negligent for undertaking work beyond his competence.

6.35 The standard of care within a specialist field is that of the ordinary competent specialist, not the most experienced or most highly qualified within the specialty.[107] However, where the defendant has knowledge of some *fact* that makes harm to the plaintiff more likely than would otherwise be the case, he must take account of that fact as a reasonable man (i e a greater than average knowledge of the risks entails more than the average or standard precautions).[108] This appears to require that a specialist must take greater precautions than an average doctor when undertaking the same task, if the specialist's actual knowledge and experience gives him a greater knowledge

---

[103] (1985) 37 SASR 524; see also Scott LJ in *Mahon v Osborne* [1939] 2 KB 14, 31 on the surgeon's problem of balancing competing risks and objectives when performing an operation.
[104] See also *Vernon v Bloomsbury Health Authority* (1986), [1995] 6 Med LR 297.
[105] *Maynard v West Midlands Regional Health Authority* [1984] 1 WLR 634, 638, *per* Lord Scarman; *Sidaway* (n 65 above), 660, *per* Lord Bridge; *Whitehouse* (n 7 above), 280 *per* Lord Fraser. See also *McCaffrey v Hague* [1949] 4 DLR 291; *Crits* (n 9 above); *Wilson v Swanson* (1956) 5 DLR (2d) 113, 119, *per* Rand J (SCC).
[106] *Langley v Campbell* (1975) *The Times*, 5 November; *Sa'd v Robinson* [1989] 1 Med LR 41; *Thornton v Nicol* [1992] 3 Med LR 41; *Gordon v Wilson* [1992] 3 Med LR 401 (Court of Session); *Stockdale v Nicholls* [1993] 4 Med LR 190; *Durrant v Burke* [1993] 4 Med LR 258; *Stacey v Chiddy* [1993] 4 Med LR 216 (NSWSC); aff'd [1993] 4 Med LR 345 (NSWCA).
[107] *O'Donovan* (n 35 above), 190, *per* Walsh J (Supreme Court of Ireland); *Giurelli v Girgis* (1980) 24 SASR 264, 277, *per* White J; *F v R* (1983) 33 SASR 189, 205, *per* Bollen J.
[108] *Stokes* (n 31 above), 1783, *per* Swanwick J; *Wilson v Brett* (1843) 11 M & W 113, 115, *per* Rolfe B: 'If a person more skilled knows that to be dangerous which another not so skilled as he does not, surely that makes a difference in the liability.'

of the risks that ought to be guarded against;[109] a clinician's conduct should not be judged by reference to lesser knowledge than in fact he had. On the other hand, he is not expected to use a higher degree of skill than comparable specialists.[110]

There may come a point where a sub-discipline develops within a specialty **6.36** such that it can be said that a practitioner undertaking that type of work must achieve the standards of the new 'specialty'.[111] Conversely, where it can be said that a new specialty has developed, the question of whether the defendant has conformed to the practice of a responsible body of professional opinion will be judged by reference to the standards of that specialty rather than the standards of doctors engaged in a more generalised practice. This may make it reasonable, for example, for a specialist surgeon to undertake intricate exploratory surgery, on the basis that this conforms to a practice accepted as proper by a responsible body of surgeons in the specialty, in circumstances where surgeons in other fields might consider the procedure to be too risky.[112]

The defendant who is inexperienced or who is just learning a particular task **6.37** or skill must come up to the standards of the reasonably competent and experienced person. His 'incompetent best' is not good enough.[113] This is a consequence of the rule that the standard of care expected of the reasonable man is objective, not subjective. It takes no account of the particular idiosyncrasies or weaknesses of the defendant.[114] This principle applies with as much force to an inexperienced doctor as it does to, say, an inexperienced motorist. In *Jones v Manchester Corporation*[115] a patient died from an excessive dose of anaesthetic administered by an anaesthetist who had only been qualified for five months. In an action which was concerned with the respective responsibilities of the junior doctor and the hospital authority, the Court of Appeal made it clear that it was no defence to an action by a patient to say

---

[109] A point accepted as correct by Webster J in *Wimpey Construction UK Ltd v Poole* [1984] 2 Lloyd's Rep 499, 506–7.

[110] In *Duchess of Argyll v Beuselinck* [1972] 2 Lloyd's Rep 172, 183 Megarry J suggested that a solicitor's client might be able to purchase a higher standard of care in contract, the obligation stemming from a contractual term that the solicitor would use the care and skill that he actually possessed rather than the care and skill of the average solicitor specialising in that field of law. Megarry J distinguished contractual duties from the tort of negligence, where 'the unusually careful and highly skilled are not held liable for falling below their own high standards if they nevertheless do all that a reasonable man would have done'; cf *Wimpey Construction UK Ltd (n 109* above), 506 *per* Webster J.

[111] See eg, *Poole v Morgan* [1987] 3 WWR 217.

[112] *De Freitas v O'Brien* [1995] 6 Med LR 108.

[113] *Nettleship v Weston* [1971] 2 QB 691, 698, 710.

[114] *Glasgow Corporation v Muir* [1943] AC 448, 457, *per* Lord Macmillan.

[115] [1952] 2 All ER 125.

that the anaesthetist did not have sufficient experience to undertake the task, or to say that the surgeon in charge was also to blame.

6.38 The issue arose in *Wilsher v Essex Area Health Authority*[116] in which a premature baby in a special care baby unit received excess oxygen due to an error in monitoring its supply of oxygen. An inexperienced doctor had inserted a catheter (by which the blood oxygen pressure was to be measured) into a vein rather than an artery. This in itself was not a negligent error. However, on checking the position of the catheter by means of an X-ray, the doctor had failed to spot that the catheter was mispositioned. He did ask a senior registrar in the unit to check the X-ray but the registrar also failed to notice the mistake. The baby was subsequently discovered to be suffering from retrolental fibroplasia which causes blindness, possibly as a result of the exposure to excess oxygen.[117] There was a marked difference of opinion on the question of the appropriate standard of care to be applied to the junior doctor. Sir Nicolas Browne-Wilkinson V-C, dissenting, said that it was unfair to apply an objective standard to a junior doctor in the first year after qualifying, or to someone who has just started in a specialist field in order to gain the necessary skill in that field. The doctor could not be said to be at fault if he lacked the very skills which he was seeking to acquire. His Lordship would only hold such a doctor liable for acts or omissions which a careful doctor with his qualifications and experience would not have done or omitted.

6.39 However, Mustill LJ said that the notion of a duty tailored to the actor, rather than to the act which he elects to perform, had no place in the law of tort. The effect of applying a subjective test would be that the standard of care that a patient would be entitled to expect would depend upon the level of experience of the particular doctor who happened to treat him. A professional person who assumed to perform a task must bring to it the appropriate care and skill, although his Lordship did add that the standard of care should be related, not to the individual, but to the post which he occupies, distinguishing 'post' from 'rank' or 'status'. It followed that the standard was not just that of the averagely competent and well-informed junior houseman (or whatever the position of the doctor) but of a person who holds such a post in a unit offering a highly specialised service, while recognising that different posts made different demands. The very structure of hospital medicine envisaged that the lower ranks would be occupied by those of whom it would be wrong to expect too much.

---

[116] [1986] 3 All ER 801.
[117] The decision of the Court of Appeal on the causation issue was reversed by the House of Lords: [1988] 1 All ER 871. There was no appeal on the question of the standard of care.

With respect, these comments appear to introduce an inconsistency since, **6.40** having rejected a subjective test of negligence, his Lordship seems to reintroduce variable standards of care by reference to the 'posts' occupied by different doctors.[118] Glidewell LJ simply applied the *Bolam* test, commenting that this was the standard by which to weigh the conduct of all the doctors in *Wilsher*:

> In my view, the law requires the trainee or learner to be judged by the same standard as his more experienced colleagues. If it did not, inexperience would frequently be urged as a defence to an action for professional negligence.[119]

It is submitted that this is the correct and long-established approach. A single standard of care for patients can only be achieved by relating the reasonableness of the defendant's conduct to the task that is undertaken, and what is objectively reasonable does not change with the experience of the defendant, or, for that matter, the post he holds.[120] This is at its most obvious if a doctor in a specialist 'post' undertakes some procedure which is completely outside the sphere of that specialty. He would be required to achieve the standard of the reasonably competent doctor in performing the procedure, and if it were a specialised procedure he would have to achieve the standards of the relevant specialty. This has nothing to do with his post. The duty arises by virtue of the fact that he has undertaken to perform the act, and by doing so professes that he has the competence to perform it with skill and care, just as an unqualified person would be held to the standard of a reasonably competent surgeon if he undertook surgery.[121] Thus, undertaking work which is beyond

---

[118] In *Djemal v Bexley Health Authority* [1995] 6 Med LR 269 Sir Haydn Tudor Evans held that the standard of care required of a senior houseman in an Accident and Emergency department was that of a reasonably competent senior houseman acting as a casualty officer, though without any reference to length of experience, applying the view of Mustill LJ.

[119] [1986] 3 All ER 801, 831; *Dale v Munthali* (1977) 78 DLR (3d) 588, 594; aff'd (1978) 90 DLR (3d) 763; *Wills v Saunders* [1989] 2 WWR 715 (Alta QB).

[120] See Dugdale and Stanton, *Professional Negligence*, 2nd edn, (1989), para 15.16; and para 15.20 making the same point in relation to the standard to be applied to specialists. The objective nature of the standard of care applies to other factors as well as inexperience. If the defendant is unable to measure up to the objectively required standard for any reason, be it stress, overwork, tiredness, or ill-health he will none the less be found negligent. Thus, old age or infirmity is not a defence for a negligent driver of a motor vehicle: *Roberts v Ramsbottom* [1980] 1 All ER 7, 15. In *Nickolls v Ministry of Health* (1955) *The Times*, 4 February, the surgeon who operated on the plaintiff was suffering from cancer. The question was whether he was in a fit condition to have undertaken the operation. It was held that, on the facts, he was and therefore he was not negligent. Clearly, if the conclusion had been that he was unfit, it would have been negligent to operate. In *Barnett v Chelsea and Kensington Hospital Management Committee* [1968] 1 All ER 1068, 1073 Nield J held that the doctor's failure to see and examine the deceased was negligent, commenting that: 'It is unfortunate that Dr Banerjee was himself at the time a tired and unwell doctor, but there was no-one else to do that which it was his duty to do.'

[121] *R v Bateman* (1925) 94 LJKB 791, 794, *per* Lord Hewart CJ; *Freeman v Marshall & Co* (1966) 200 EG 777.

one's competence constitutes negligence. As a matter of practice the inexperienced doctor will normally undertake less complex tasks than his experienced colleagues, but if he does perform tasks beyond the level of his competence, the fault lies not so much in not having the skills, which by definition he does not possess, but in him undertaking the task at all.[122] This principle is not limited to actions against newly qualified doctors. It can apply at any stage where a doctor 'gets in above his head'. The doctor who holds himself out as a specialist will be held to the standards of a reasonably competent specialist, 'even if he is a novice specialist',[123] and even where he is performing the procedure for the first time.[124] A doctor must recognise his limitations and where necessary seek the advice or supervision of more experienced colleagues, or refer the patient to a specialist.[125] The inexperienced doctor will discharge his duty of care by seeking the assistance of his superiors to check his work, even though he may himself have made a mistake.[126]

6. Emergencies

6.41　In an emergency it may well be reasonable for a practitioner inexperienced in a particular treatment to intervene, or indeed for someone lacking medical qualifications to undertake some forms of treatment. For example, a bystander who renders assistance at a road accident does not necessarily hold himself out as qualified to do so. He would be expected to achieve only the standard that could reasonably be expected in the circumstances, which would probably be

---

[122] In any event, it is possible that a health authority would be in breach of a primary duty of care to the patient for allowing inexperienced staff to practise without adequate supervision: *Jones* (n 115 above); *Wilsher* (n 116 above), 833 *per* Sir Nicolas Browne-Wilkinson V-C.

[123] *Poole v Morgan* [1987] 3 WWR 217, 254 (Alta QB). The defendant ophthalmologist was held to be inadequately qualified to use laser treatment, a procedure normally performed by a retina vitreous specialist, even though ophthalmologists were permitted to use laser treatment by their governing body.

[124] *McKeachie v Alvarez* (1970) 17 DLR (3d) 87 (BCSC).

[125] *Wilsher* (n 116 above), 833; *Fraser v Vancouver General Hospital* (1951) 3 WWR 337 (BCCA); aff'd [1952] 3 DLR 785 (SCC); *Payne v St Helier Group Hospital Management Committee* (1952) *The Times*, 12 July; *Dillon v Le Roux* [1994] 6 WWR 280 (BCCA).

[126] It was on this basis that the junior doctor was found not to have been negligent in *Wilsher v Essex Area Health Authority*, although the registrar was held negligent. See also *Junor v McNicol* (1959) *The Times*, 26 March, where the House of Lords held that a house surgeon who had acted on the instructions of a consultant orthopaedic surgeon was not liable; *Tanswell v Nelson* (1959) *The Times*, 11 February, where McNair J said that a dentist was entitled to rely on a doctor's opinion about a patient's response to antibiotics, unless that opinion was clearly inconsistent with the observed facts; *Leonard v Knott* [1978] 5 WWR 511 (BCSC), where it was held that a radiologist is entitled to rely on the judgment of the referring physician as to whether a radiological investigation is required, unless there is some obvious problem; cf *Davy-Chiesman v Davy-Chiesman* [1984] 1 All ER 321, 332, 335, stating that solicitors should not rely blindly on the advice of counsel, although in this case the solicitor had failed to detect an 'obvious error'.

very low.[127] This approach is clearly born of the emergency since, if there was no urgency, the unqualified person who undertook treatment beyond his competence would be held to the standard of a reasonably competent and experienced practitioner. For example, a person who holds himself out as trained in first-aid must conform to the standards of 'the ordinary skilled first-aider exercising and professing to have that special skill of a first-aider'.[128]

7. Defensive Medicine

The increase in medical malpractice litigation over the last 10 or 15 years has been accompanied by claims that, in response to the threat of litigation, doctors now practise defensively. This involves undertaking procedures which are not medically justified but are designed to protect the doctor from a claim for negligence. The most commonly cited examples are unnecessary diagnostic tests, such as X-rays, and unnecessary Caesarian section deliveries. However, applying the *Bolam* test, a reasonable doctor would not undertake an *unnecessary* procedure and so a doctor could not avoid a finding of negligence by performing one. In fact, to the extent that the procedure carries some inherent risk, a practitioner acting in this way may increase his chances of being sued.[129] Moreover, there is little clear understanding within the medical profession of what the term 'defensive medicine' means. 'Defensive' may mean simply treating patients conservatively or even 'more carefully', and this begs the question whether that treatment option is medically justified in the patient's interests. None the less, the courts have apparently acknowledged the existence of the phenomenon of defensive medicine, despite the fact that there is virtually no empirical, as opposed to anecdotal, evidence of such practices in this country.[130]

6.42

In non-medical cases the courts have occasionally relied on the prospect of unduly defensive practices developing in response to a potential liability in

6.43

---

[127] See eg, *Ali v Furness Withy* [1988] 2 Lloyd's Rep 379, where the question was the standard applicable to a ship's master diagnosing insanity in a crewman.
[128] *Cattley v St John's Ambulance Brigade* (1988) (unreported), QBD
[129] If a diagnostic test or procedure is unnecessary by reference to the standards of the medical profession, i e according to the standards of the reasonably competent doctor exercising and professing to have that skill, it will be negligence to perform it, and it will be actionable if the patient suffers injury as a consequence. See eg, *Leonard* (n 126 above).
[130] *Wilsher* (n 116 above), 810 *per* Mustill LJ; *Sidaway* (n 65 above), 653 *per* Lord Scarman. Lord Denning was particularly concerned about the risks of defensive medicine: *Roe* (n 83 above), 86–7; *Lim v Camden and Islington Area Health Authority* [1979] 1 QB 196, 217; *Whitehouse v Jordan* [1980] 1 All ER 650, 658; *Hyde v Tameside Area Health Authority* (1981) reported at (1986) 2 PN 26; *Hatcher v Black* (1954) *The Times*, 2 July. See also *per* Lawton LJ in *Whitehouse* (above), 659; *Sidaway* (n 28 above), 1031, 1035, *per* Dunne and Browne-Wilkinson LJJ.

order to deny the existence of a duty of care.[131] This option is not available in most cases of medical negligence, since the doctor undoubtedly owes a duty of care to his patient. In *Barker v Nugent*,[132] counsel for the defendant doctor argued that, as a matter of public policy, the courts should be slower to impute negligence to the medical profession than to others, in order to avoid an escalation of defensive medicine. Rougier J rejected the argument, with the comment that:

> I can think of only one thing more disastrous than the escalation of defensive medicine and that is the engendering of a belief in the medical profession that certain acts or omissions which would otherwise be classed as negligence can, in a sense, be exonerated.

Similarly, in *Wilsher v Essex Area Health Authority* Mustill LJ responded to his own acknowledgement of the risks of defensive practice with the comment that 'the proper response cannot be to temper the wind to the professional man. If he assumes to perform a task, he must bring to it the appropriate care and skill.' Nonetheless, the judicial perception of the risk of defensive practices developing may be reflected in the standard of proof that plaintiffs have to achieve in practice, although the formal standard of proof remains the same.

6.44   In *M (a minor) v Newham London Borough Council*[133] the question of defensive practice arose in circumstances where, unusually, it was open to the court to conclude that a duty of care should be held not to exist. A majority of the Court of Appeal held that a psychiatrist and a social worker did not owe a duty of care to a child or its parents when advising a social services authority whether the child had been physically or sexually abused, and as to the identity of the abuser. The child had been needlessly removed from its home into local authority care, and both the child and her mother claimed that they had suffered psychiatric harm as a result. The defendants argued that imposing a duty of care in these circumstances would have serious adverse consequences, particularly in terms of: (a) the financial implications for local authorities; and (b) the reaction of social workers and doctors working in the field of child protection to the risk of liability. Peter Gibson and Staughton LJJ accepted that it would not be desirable if actions in such circumstances resulted in a major diversion of resources to defending legal actions. Sir Thomas Bingham MR, dissenting, also accepted that, to a greater

---

[131] *Saif Ali v Sydney Mitchell & Co* [1980] AC 198; *Yuen Kun-yeu v A-G of Hong Kong* [1987] 2 All ER 705, 715–6; *Hill v Chief Constable of West Yorkshire* [1988] 2 All ER 238; *Rowling v Takaro Properties Ltd* [1988] 1 All ER 163, 173; *Elguzouli-Daf v Commissioner of Police of the Metropolis* [1995] 1 All ER 833; *Marc Rich & Co v Bishop Rock Marine Co Ltd* [1995] 3 All ER 307.   [132] (1987) (unreported), QBD.
[133] [1994] 2 WLR 554.

or lesser extent, the overstretched resources of local authorities would be diverted from the function of looking after children and wasted on litigation but said:

> . . . this is an argument frequently (and not implausibly) advanced on behalf of doctors: it has not prevailed. Other professions resist liability on the ground that it will in the end increase the cost to the paying customer; that resistance has not on the whole been effective either. Save in clear cases, it is not for the courts to decide how public money is best spent nor to balance the risk that money will be wasted on litigation against the hope that the possibility of suit may contribute towards the maintenance of higher standards.[134]

The defendants also argued that imposing a duty of care would lead to **6.45** defensive practices by social workers and doctors engaged in child protection work. Essentially the question was whether imposing liability in negligence would contribute to a deterioration in standards of conduct or lead to their improvement. It was said that the decisions that have to be taken in the context of child protection are difficult and delicate and involve an exercise of professional judgment. Imposing liability could lead to such decisions being taken in a 'detrimentally defensive frame of mind'. Staughton LJ very much doubted whether the imposition of a duty of care encouraged people not to be negligent, though it might encourage defensive practices. This appears to be inconsistent, for as Sir Thomas Bingham observed: 'The common belief that the imposition of such a duty may lead to overkill is not easily reconciled with the suggestion that it has no effect.'[135] His Lordship did not accept, as a general proposition, that the imposition of a duty of care makes no contribution to the maintenance of high standards. The task may be difficult, delicate, and judgmental in nature, but this simply means that it is difficult for a plaintiff to prove negligence. There was no reason, in a case such as *M (a minor) v Newham London Borough Council*, why a doctor's performance of his duty to form the best judgment and give the soundest advice that he could, would be inhibited by the knowledge that he might be held liable to the child:

> He might no doubt be anxious to be as sure as possible before expressing any opinion, and would be careful to express no opinion stronger than the facts in his judgment warranted, but both these results are to be encouraged. I do not think he would be deterred from prompt action where the facts appeared to warrant it, since he would be as vulnerable to criticism for failing to advise urgent action when the facts appeared to call for it as for acting precipitately when the facts did not. The doctor's only certain protec-

---

[134] [1994] 2 WLR 576.
[135] ibid, 572. Staughton LJ's view assumes that people on the one hand do not respond to liability rules by acting more carefully, while on the other it assumes that they do respond to liability rules by being over-careful.

tion would be sound performance of his professional duty, and that is how it should be.[136]

6.46   In the House of Lords, however, it was accepted that there was a risk of defensive practices developing and that local authorities would adopt a more cautious approach to their duties.[137] In circumstances where a speedy decision to remove a child may be vital there would be a substantial temptation to postpone making the decision until further inquiries had been made in the hope of getting more concrete facts. This was a factor in the conclusion that a duty of care should not be imposed for reasons of policy.

C. Common Types of Error

6.47   It is possible for any diagnosis or treatment to be performed in a careless fashion, or for some essential step to be negligently omitted. What follows is a consideration of some of the most common situations in which an action may arise, although these examples should always be measured against the general test for negligence embodied in *Bolam*.

1. Failure to Attend or Treat

6.48   A doctor who fails to attend his patient or who is dilatory in attending may be guilty of negligence if a reasonable doctor would have appreciated that his attendance was necessary in the patient's interests. This will depend upon the precise circumstances of the case: how serious was the patient's condition; what was the doctor told; what commitments to other patients did he have at the time?[138]

---

[136] ibid, 571–2. It might be added that the 'frame of mind' with which any professional person approaches the tasks to be carried out is so subjective to the individual as to be almost meaningless. What is 'defensive' for one may well be regarded as good practice by another. What counts is whether *objectively* the professional is exercising reasonable standards of professional conduct; and, moreover, questions of immunity aside, this is the only way in which the professional can be sure of being found not liable.

[137] sub nom. *X (minors) v Bedfordshire County Council* [1995] 3 WLR 152, 184, *per* Lord Browne-Wilkinson.

[138] *Smith v Rae* (1919) 51 DLR 323, 325–6 (Ont SC Appellate Div); see also *Cavan v Wilcox* (1973) 44 DLR (3d) 42, 53 (NBCA), where the information the doctor received over the telephone was not sufficiently serious to alert him to the emergency; *Barnes v Crabtree* (1955) *The Times*, 1 and 2 November, discussed in Nathan, *Medical Negligence* (1957), 37; on a general practitioner's 'duty to visit' see also *Kavanagh v Abrahamson* (1964) 108 SJ 320; *Stockdale v Nicholls* [1993] 4 Med LR 190; *Durrant v Burke* [1993] 4 Med LR 258; *Morrison v Forsyth* [1995] 6 Med LR 6, Court of Session, where the seriousness of the patient's condition was not made clear to the general practitioner.

The duty to attend also extends to post-operative treatment. Thus, in *Corder v* **6.49**
Banks,[139] a plastic surgeon who allowed the plaintiff to go home after an
operation on the plaintiff's eye-lids, but failed to make any arrangements for
the plaintiff to contact him if bleeding occurred during the first 48 hours after
the operation, was found to have been negligent. The duty to provide post-
operative attendance does not require the doctor to supervise routine procedures carried out by nursing staff.[140] In some circumstances the duty to
examine and/or treat the patient may arise independently of any request by
or on behalf of the patient. For example, in *Stokes v Guest, Keen and Nettlefold
(Bolts and Nuts) Ltd*,[141] it was held that a factory medical officer should have
instituted six-monthly medical examinations, given his knowledge of the risk
to employees of contracting cancer from their working conditions and the fact
that early diagnosis gave a significantly better chance of successful treatment.
The employers were held vicariously liable for the medical officer's negligence
in failing to implement a system of screening employees for the disease.

2. Diagnostic Errors

Diagnostic errors can arise from an inadequate medical history, errors in exam- **6.50**
ining the patient, errors in interpreting the patient's symptoms, a failure to
conduct tests or refer the patient for specialist consultation, or a failure to
monitor treatment and revise the diagnosis where a treatment is proving ineffective. Diagnosis should be preceded by the taking of a full history from the patient.

(a) Duty to Take Medical History

In *Chin Keow v Government of Malaysia*[142] a doctor was held liable in **6.51**
respect of a patient's allergic reaction to penicillin, having administered the
injection without first inquiring into the patient's medical history. In
Leonard v Knott,[143] the defendant physician conducted annual 'executive
health examinations' for client corporations. He referred the deceased for a
radiological examination of the kidneys and urinary tract by means of an
intravenous pyelogram. This was part of the 'package' included in the
annual check-up, and at that stage the defendant had never even met the
deceased, let alone examined him, taken a medical history, done any routine

---

[139] (1960) *The Times*, 9 April; see also *Videto v Kennedy* (1980) 107 DLR (3d) 612, 616–17;
rev'd on other grounds (1981) 125 DLR (3d) 127 (Ont CA), where the arrangements made by
the defendant doctor for post-operative care in the event of complications were 'just about non-
existent'; *Cherewayko v Grafton* [1993] 3 WWR 604, 626 (Man QB) on the failure to provide
for 'follow-up'.   [140] *Morris v Winsbury-White* [1937] 4 All ER 494.
[141] [1968] 1 WLR 1776.   [142] [1967] 1 WLR 813.
[143] [1978] 5 WWR 511 (BCSC).

tests, such as urine analysis, or sought any information from the family doctor. The patient died from an allergic reaction to the contrast medium used in the procedure, a risk which was known and foreseeable to the medical profession. The defendant was held liable for exposing the deceased to such a risk without taking a history, examining him, or consulting the family doctor, given that virtually all of the problems could have been thus determined and the deceased had never had any signs or symptoms relating to the kidneys or urinary tract.

6.52 The patient's medical history may include not only the signs and symptoms of the illness or injury for which the patient is seeking treatment, but also details of any previous treatment either for the same condition or, in appropriate circumstances, a previous injury or disease. In *Coles v Reading and District Hospital Management Committee*[144] a patient was given first aid treatment for a crushing injury to his finger at a cottage hospital but he was not given an anti-tetanus injection. He did not go to another hospital for further treatment, as advised, but saw his own doctor, who did not inquire as to what had happened at the cottage hospital but simply redressed the wound. The patient subsequently died of toxaemia due to tetanus infection. Both the cottage hospital and the general practitioner were held liable for omitting to take the elementary precaution of giving the deceased an anti-tetanus vaccination. The general practitioner was negligent in failing to make inquiries of the hospital or the deceased.[145]

6.53 The duty to take a full history requires the doctor to *listen* to what the patient is saying. Sometimes, particularly if the patient is considered to be 'difficult', a doctor may disregard or discount what the patient says and this can colour the diagnosis. A failure to listen to a patient who is describing symptoms which would affect diagnosis and treatment will amount to negligence, where harm results.[146] Of course, the patient also bears some responsibility to provide appropriate information when questioned by a doctor. If the information is misleading the doctor will not be held liable for acting upon it, at

---

[144] (1963) 107 SJ 115.
[145] In *Meyer v Gordon* (1981) 17 CCLT 1, hospital staff failed to take details of the patient's obstetric history, which would have revealed that her previous labour had been a rapid one and put the staff on notice that the labour must be closely monitored; *Schanczi v Singh* [1988] 2 WWR 465 (Alta QB).
[146] *Giurelli* (n 107 above). See also *Cassidy v Ministry of Health* [1951] 2 KB 343, 349 on the question of medical staff ignoring the plaintiff's complaints of intense and excessive pain; *Rietze v Bruser (No 2)* [1979] 1 WWR 31, where it was held that a doctor should not attribute the plaintiff's complaints of pain to 'anxiety' until all the possible causes of the symptoms have been explored; *Rhodes v Spokes and Farbridge* [1996] 7 Med LR 135, 145 on the duty to 'keep an open mind' when taking a history.

least where it is reasonable to rely upon the information.[147] There is a tendency on the part of patients to 'rationalise' their problem, that is, to tend to ascribe the problem to something which they themselves can identify; it may be dangerous for a doctor to be too ready to put symptoms down to the cause suggested by a patient.[148]

(b) Alternative Diagnoses

Whether an error of diagnosis is negligent depends to a large extent upon the **6.54** difficulty of making the diagnosis given the symptoms presented, the diagnostic techniques available, and the dangers associated with the alternative diagnoses. Where there are two possible diagnoses, one of which is potentially life-threatening but the less likely of the two alternatives, it will not be negligent to undertake diagnostic procedures intended to rule out or confirm that diagnosis before the results of tests for the other possible diagnosis are available.[149] The seriousness of the consequences of the condition proving to be life-threatening would justify the risks associated with the procedure. The difficulty of making a diagnosis will often excuse a defendant.[150] The diagnosis must be judged in the light of the facts at the time and a doctor cannot be expected to possess the vision and wisdom of hindsight.[151] Thus, the failure to diagnose cancer is not necessarily negligent[152], nor is to diagnose cancer mistakenly.[153]

---

[147] See eg *Venner v North East Essex Area Health Authority* (1987) *The Times*, 21 February, where the plaintiff assured the defendant gynaecologist immediately before a sterilisation operation that she could not be pregnant. The defendant did not perform a dilatation and curettage (D and C) which probably would have terminated any pregnancy. The plaintiff was in fact pregnant at the time of the sterilisation operation, and subsequently gave birth to a healthy child. Tucker J held that the defendant was not negligent in not performing a D and C as a matter of course. [148] *Bova v Spring* [1994] 5 Med LR 120, 127; *Djemal* (n 118 above).
[149] *Maynard v West Midlands Regional Health Authority* [1984] 1 WLR 634. See also *Dillon* (n 125 above).
[150] *Pudney v Union-Castle Mail SS Ltd* [1953] 1 Lloyd's Rep 73; *Crivon v Barnet Group Hospital Management Committee* (1958) *The Times*, 18 November, CA; *Walker v Semple* (1993) (unreported), CA; *Pilon v Bouaziz* [1994] 1 WWR 700 (BCCA).
[151] *Holmes v Board of Hospital Trustees of the City of London* (1977) 81 DLR (3d) 67, 91 (Ont HC); *Wilkinson Estate (Rogin) v Shannon* (1986) 37 CCLT 181 (Ont HC); *Roe* (n 83 above), 83, *per* Denning LJ.
[152] *Hulse v Wilson* (1953) 2 BMJ 890; *Phillips v Grampian Health Board* [1991] 3 Med LR 16; *Judge v Huntingdon Health Authority* [1995] 6 Med LR 223 (though the defendants were held liable on the facts); cf *Sutton v Population Services Family Planning Programme Ltd* (1981) *The Times*, 7 November, on the diagnosis of cancer; *Stacey* (n 106 above). Where a doctor suspects cancer he should refer the patient to a specialist or arrange for an immediate biopsy: *Wilson v Vancouver Hockey Club* (1983) 5 DLR (4th) 282, 288; aff'd (1985) 22 DLR (4th) 516 (BCCA). In *Taylor v West Kent Health Authority* [1997] 8 Med LR 251 there was a negligent failure to interpret a cytology report correctly. The doctors should have sought clarification of the report, and should have been alerted to the need for further investigations.
[153] *Whiteford* (n 24 above); *Crivon* (n 150 above); *Graham v Persyko* (1986) 27 DLR (4th) 699, 703–4, where a doctor who mistakenly diagnosed Crohn's disease was held not to have

6.55 Even where a particular condition cannot be diagnosed, the symptoms may indicate that the plaintiff is suffering from something serious which needs further investigation. The very difficulty of making a diagnosis may in itself suggest that the doctor should take additional precautions such as admitting the patient to hospital for observation, conducting further tests, or referring the patient to a specialist who was capable of making the diagnosis.[154] For example, in *Bova v Spring*[155] a general practitioner diagnosed a muscle strain in the chest of a patient who died two days later from pneumonia. The defendant was held to have been negligent for 'failing to recognise the uncertainties attending his diagnosis'. In *Langley v Campbell*[156] the patient presented with symptoms of fever, headache, and alternate sweating and shivering. His general practitioner diagnosed influenza, but the patient subsequently died from malaria, having recently returned from Uganda. Although general practitioners did not normally come across malaria, the deteriorating condition of a patient without the recognised complications of influenza should have been the cause of special concern. The defendant might not have been capable of diagnosing malaria, but should have been alerted to the possibility that the patient's illness might not be indigenous.

(c) Diagnostic Aids

6.56 Where diagnostic aids would assist a doctor in reaching an accurate diagnosis it may well be negligent to fail to use them, if available,[157] although this is not

been negligent. On missed fractures see: *McCormack v Redpath Brown & Co Ltd* (1961) *The Times*, 24 March; *Wood v Thurston* (1951) *The Times*, 5 May; *Newton v Newton's Model Laundry* (1959) *The Times*, 3 November; *Saumarez v Medway and Gravesend Hospital Management Committee* (1953) 2 *BMJ* 1109; *Fraser v Vancouver General Hospital* (1951) 3 WWR 337 (BCCA); aff'd [1952] 3 DLR 785 (SCC); *Walker v Huntingdon Health Authority* [1994] 5 Med LR 356.

[154] *Barnett* (n 120 above), 1073; *Seyfert v Burnaby Hospital Society* (1986) 27 DLR (4th) 96. In *Dale v Munthali* (1976) 78 DLR (3d) 588; aff'd (1978) 90 DLR (3d) 763 (Ont CA) the defendant diagnosed the patient as suffering from influenza, when in fact he had meningitis. There was no negligence in failing to diagnose meningitis, but the patient was so extremely ill that the defendant should have realised that it was more than gastro-intestinal influenza.

[155] [1994] 5 Med LR 120, QBD See also *Riddett v D'Arcy* (1960) 2 BMJ 1607 where a general practitioner who failed to examine a baby closely enough was held liable for failing to diagnose the early stages of pneumonia. On the failure to diagnose appendicitis, see *Edler v Greenwich (1953) The Times*, 7 March; *Bergen* (n 91 above).

[156] (1975) *The Times*, 5 November; see also *Sa'd* (n 106 above); cf *Stockdale* (n 106 above). On a general practitioner's 'duty to visit', see *Durrant* (n 106 above).

[157] *Bergen* (n 91 above); *Lankenau* (n 91 above); *Smith v Salford Health Authority* [1994] 5 Med LR 321, QBD, where it was held that the defendant should have undertaken a CT scan prior to performing a spinal fusion operation, because this would have been a far more sophisticated and informative piece of radiology than the X-rays upon which he relied in assessing the need for the operation and the technique that would be required. The simplest diagnostic tool may be a physical examination of the patient. See *Stacey* (n 106 above), 224–5.

necessarily the case.[158] Where a gynaecologist was aware that his patient could be pregnant, he should have conducted tests before subjecting her uterus to X-rays.[159] Doctors who ordered X-rays to be carried out but then delayed for five days before examining them were held negligent for failing to inform themselves of the factual data which they had themselves identified as pertinent and necessary to the plaintiff's diagnosis, and which they knew or ought to have known was available.[160] In *Pierre v Marshall*[161] a general practitioner who failed to screen a pregnant woman for gestational diabetes, contrary to the recommendations of the Alberta Medical Association and the Society of Obstetricians and Gynaecologists of Canada, was held to have been negligent. The defendant also had failed to do an ultrasound scan to confirm the expected size of the baby, despite his suspicion that the foetus was slightly larger than it should have been at 36 weeks. In *X and Y v Pal*,[162] it was accepted that an obstetrician who failed to test a patient for syphilis during her pregnancy was negligent.[163]

(d) Diagnostic Review

The diagnosis should also be kept under review as the treatment progresses. **6.57** There is a danger in acquiring 'tunnel vision' about the patient's condition.[164] This is even more important where the consequences of the alternative diagnosis, if it turns out to be correct, are likely to be serious.[165] In *Lankenau*

---

[158] *Whiteford v Hunter* [1950] WN 553.

[159] *Zimmer v Ringrose* (1981) 125 DLR (3d) 215, (Alta CA); aff'g (1978) 89 DLR 646, 656–7; *Gardiner v Mounfield* [1990] 1 Med LR 205, where the defendant dismissed the possibility that the plaintiff, who was overweight and had a history of amenorrhoea, was pregnant.

[160] *Holmes v Board of Hospital Trustees of the City of London* (1977) 81 DLR (3d) 67 (Ont HC).

[161] [1994] 8 WWR 478 (Alta QB). See also *Tucker v Tees Health Authority* [1995] 6 Med LR 54, where the defendant was held negligent for performing a laparotomy to remove a presumed ovarian cyst without first conducting an ultrasound scan to check whether the plaintiff was pregnant. On the other hand, a doctor should not be criticised for a refusal to offer a CT scan or any other diagnostic procedure which he considered inappropriate just because the patient was willing to pay and wanted reassurance: *Rhodes* (n 146 above), 146.

[162] (1991) 23 NSWLR 26; [1992] 3 Med LR 195 (NSWCA).

[163] There may also be negligence in failing to interpret test results properly: see e g *Fraser* (n 153 above), and *Roy v Croydon Health Authority* [1997] PIQR P444, on the negligent interpretation of X-rays; *Rance v Mid-Downs Health Authority* [1991] 1 All ER 801, an allegedly negligent failure to interpret an ultrasound scan of a foetus. A failure to read a report will be negligent: *Fredette v Wiebe* [1986] 5 WWR 222 (BCSC). On the other hand, a misleading pathology report may result in a finding that a surgeon was not negligent in embarking on radical surgery in a case of suspected cancer: *Abbas v Kenney* [1996] 7 Med LR 47.

[164] *Layden v Cope* (1984) 28 CCLT 140 (Alta QB); *Rietze* (n 146 above), 47 *per* Hewak J.

[165] *Bova v Spring* [1994] 5 Med LR 120, 129, QBD.

v Dutton[166] the medical evidence was that a surgeon confronted with a patient with paralysis after major surgery should not only attempt to diagnose the cause but also 'should make a differential diagnosis, that is to say that he should consider other likely causes of her condition and test them against her symptoms and be ready with an alternative theory to direct her treatment if his first diagnosis and treatment should fail to produce an improvement in her condition.'[167] The defendant had diagnosed an aortic dissection occurring during surgery, which was a reasonable initial diagnosis. As the patient's symptoms progressed, however, he failed to reassess the diagnosis, which resulted in the paralysis becoming permanent. The surgeon was held to have been negligent for clinging to the original diagnosis even though the symptoms should have made him question it, for failing to test his theory by X-ray, and for failing to seek the assistance of neurological experts quickly enough.[168]

(e) Obligation to Refer

6.58   The obligation to refer a patient to a specialist or to seek further advice will arise whenever a doctor is unable to diagnose or treat the patient.[169] Even a consultant in a specialist field may come across a problem that he has never previously encountered and accordingly may have a responsibility to seek advice.[170] In *Poole v Morgan*,[171] the defendant ophthalmologist was inadequately trained in the use of a laser, although he had often used it in his practice. The treatment that he gave to the plaintiff was usually performed by a retina vitreous specialist. Since the defendant was unable to come up to the standard of that specialty, he had a duty to refer the plaintiff to such a specialist.

---

[166] (1986) 37 CCLT 213 (BCSC); aff'd (1991) 79 DLR (4th) 707 (BCCA).

[167] ibid, 231, *per* Spencer J.

[168] In *Bergen v Sturgeon General Hospital* (1984) 28 CCLT 155 (Alta QB) a female patient, who was admitted to hospital complaining of pains in her abdomen, died from a ruptured appendix, having been provisionally diagnosed as suffering from acute gastroenteritis, with appendicitis to be checked out. A further diagnosis of pelvic inflammatory disease had been made, but no steps were taken to rule out appendicitis, despite the fact that it explained all the symptoms, that the patient's condition was not responding to treatment, and that appendicitis is life-threatening. The defendants were held negligent, not for the initial mistaken diagnosis but for failing to keep the diagnosis under review when the patient's condition did not improve. In *Law Estate* (n 91 above), 236, Spencer J observed that: 'Where a potentially life-threatening condition is included in a differential diagnosis, there is a duty on the physician to take prompt steps to confirm it or rule it out with reasonable dispatch.'

[169] *MacDonald v York County Hospital* (1973) 41 DLR (3d) 321, 349–50, *per* Dubin JA (Ont CA); aff'd sub nom *Vail v MacDonald* (1976) 66 DLR (3d) 530 (SCC).

[170] *Gascoine v Ian Sheridan & Co* [1994] 5 Med LR 437, 447, *per* Mitchell J.

[171] [1987] 3 WWR 217; *Layden v Cope* (1984) 28 CCLT 140, 148; *Lankenau* (n 166 above).

3. Failures of Communication

(a) Between Doctor and Patient

Failures of communication can arise between doctor and patient or between **6.59** the various health care professionals involved in a patient's treatment, but in either case the consequences for the patient can be serious. The doctor has an obligation to provide information to a patient about the nature, purpose, and consequences of proposed procedures, but in addition to the duty to warn patients in advance of the risks associated with the treatment, it is possible that in some circumstances the practitioner will be under a duty to inform the patient that something has gone wrong with the treatment.[172] In *Stamos v Davies*,[173] the defendant punctured the plaintiff's spleen while performing a lung biopsy, but did not tell the plaintiff, who was then discharged from hospital. The plaintiff was readmitted as an emergency three days later, due to bleeding into his abdominal cavity. The spleen was removed surgically and the plaintiff recovered uneventfully. Krever J held that the defendant was in breach of a duty to inform the plaintiff that the spleen had been punctured. The difficulty with any case of this nature, however, is proving that the breach of duty caused the plaintiff damage. The plaintiff's ignorance that something untoward has occurred will rarely contribute to any further loss, and since the damage has already occurred, the failure to be candid is not a cause of the harm.[174]

In some cases the failure to inform may cause further injury as if, for **6.60** example, the patient takes a risk that he would otherwise have avoided, or if

---

[172] See the comments of Sir John Donaldson MR in *Lee v South West Thames Regional Health Authority* [1985] 2 All ER 385, and *Naylor v Preston Area Health Authority* [1987] 2 All ER 353, 360. In *Gerber v Pines* (1934) 79 SJ 13 Du Parcq J said that as a general rule a patient was entitled to be told at once if the doctor had left some foreign object in his body; cf *Daniels v Heskin* [1954] IR 73, 87, *per* Kingsmill Moore J. But on *Daniels* see now *Walsh v Family Planning Services Ltd* [1992] IR 496, 520 (Supreme Court of Ireland). It has been suggested that there is an obligation to break distressing, though truthful, news to patients in a manner which reduces the risk of patients developing psychiatric illness in response to the news: *AB v Tameside & Glossop Health Authority* [1997] 8 Med LR 91, though the defendants were held not to have been negligent in choosing to inform patients that there was a small risk that they might have contracted HIV from a doctor by letter rather than face to face. See Dziobon and Tettenborn, 'When the truth hurts: the incompetent transmission of distressing news' (1997) 13 PN 70. *A fortiori* if, as a result of the defendants' negligence, the distressing information was *inaccurate* and the plaintiff suffered psychiatric harm from this distressing 'news', even where the incorrect information was imparted in a sensitive and appropriate manner: *Allin v City [1996]* 7 Med LR 167; Jones, 'Negligently inflicted psychiatric harm: is the word mightier than the deed?' (1997) 13 PN 111.
[173] (1986) 21 DLR (4th) 507 (Ont HC); Robertson (1987) 25 Alberta L Rev 215.
[174] *Daniels v Heskin* [1954] IR 73, 81, 88.

the patient's ignorance leads to delay in diagnosis (resulting in additional harm) or an emergency subsequently arises as a result of the injury of which he is unaware. In *Kiley-Nikkel v Danais*[175] the plaintiff's breast was removed following a mistaken diagnosis of cancer. She was not informed of the error, with the result that she sought follow-up treatment for cancer in another locality and lived with the belief that she had cancer for a considerable time. Part of the award of damages was for the psychiatric harm resulting from non-disclosure of the error in diagnosis, since the consequences of this would have been much less serious had she known immediately that she was not suffering from cancer. In *Pittman Estate v Bain*[176] a patient received a blood transfusion during the course of heart surgery. It was subsequently discovered that the blood he had received was contaminated with HIV. The defendants were found to have been negligent in failing to inform him that there was a risk, which in fact materialised, that the transfusion had infected him with HIV. Although there was no negligence in the administration of the transfusion, the failure to inform the patient meant that he did not have an opportunity to take measures which could have extended his life expectancy and, moreover, his wife also contracted the infection from unprotected sexual intercourse with her husband. The defendants were held liable for both of these consequences.

6.61 A doctor will often need the patient's co-operation, for example, in performing an examination or administering treatment. This may be as simple as requiring the patient to keep still or instructing the patient about taking medication. It may also be necessary to give the patient a warning about any danger signs to look out for, with instructions as to what should be done if they occur, such as stopping the medication or seeking medical assistance immediately.[177] Sometimes this will be absolutely vital. In these circumstances the doctor will be under a duty to take special care in giving the patient instructions, to make sure that the patient understands both the instructions and the importance of strictly adhering to them.[178] In *Joyce v Wandsworth Health Authority*[179] the plaintiff underwent an operative procedure which resulted in a partially occluded artery, leading three months later

---

[175] (1992) 16 CCLT (2d) 290 (Qué SC).
[176] (1994) 112 DLR (4th) 257 (Ont Ct, Gen Div).
[177] See eg, *Crossman v Stewart* (1977) 82 DLR (3d) 677 where the defendant doctor was held negligent for failing to identify the indications of side-effects.
[178] *Clarke v Adams* (1950) 94 SJ 599; *Stamos v Davies* (1986) 21 DLR (4th) 507. In *Sheridan v Boots Co Ltd* (1980) (unreported), QBD, a doctor who prescribed a potent anti-inflammatory drug but failed to give the patient a warning that if he experienced any stomach trouble he should stop taking the drug and consult a doctor immediately, was said to have been negligent, although the action failed on causation. [179] [1996] 7 Med LR 1.

to an upper brain-stem infarction causing almost total paralysis. The Court of Appeal held that the immediate follow-up care that the plaintiff had received was negligent because the patient was discharged from hospital without proper instructions and advice. In some instances the risk associated with the treatment may be so great that it will be negligent for a doctor to rely on a patient accurately reporting his symptoms, the obligation being to conduct regular tests.[180] There is also a responsibility to bring home to a patient the importance of obtaining further treatment, if necessary, and the dangers involved in failing to do so.[181] Similarly, where it is unwise for a patient to engage in certain types of activity following treatment, he should be warned of this danger.[182]

(b) Between Health Professionals

A breakdown in communication between health care professionals with responsibility for a patient can have dangerous consequences for the patient. These errors may be the result of isolated acts of carelessness (for example, failing to read the nursing notes)[183] or they may be the product of some organisational failure (for example, relying too heavily on casual exchanges).[184] The system of communication may be so poor that mistakes are almost inevitable, or the methods adopted may fail to take into account the risks of human error by providing some mechanism for checking. Thus, a hospital must have an adequate system for summoning specialist assistance when needed.[185] If a patient is injured by reason of a negligent breakdown in the systems for communicating material information to the clinicians responsible for her care, she is not to be denied redress merely because no identifiable person or persons are to blame for deficiencies in setting up and monitoring the effectiveness of the relevant communication systems.[186]

6.62

---

[180] *Marshall v Rogers* [1943] 4 DLR 68, 77 (BCCA); cf *Battersby v Tottman* (1985) 37 SASR 524 where, in the circumstances, a failure to monitor the known and serious side-effects of a drug was held not negligent.

[181] *Coles v Reading and District Hospital Management Committee* (1963) 107 SJ 115.

[182] *Brushett v Cowan* (1987) 40 DLR (4th) 488; aff'd (1990) 69 DLR (4th) 743 (Newfd CA), where the plaintiff was given crutches to use following a biopsy on her leg, but she was not warned that she should not bear weight on the leg. While engaging in ordinary activity without the crutches the leg broke at the site of the biopsy. The doctor was held negligent.

[183] *Holmes v Board of Hospital Trustees of the City of London* (1977) 81 DLR (3d) 67, 94 (Ont HC). [184] *Bergen* (n 168 above), 175.

[185] *Bull* (n 14 above), Of course, even the best systems may not be foolproof. In *Bolitho v City and Hackney Health Authority* [1997] 4 All ER 771 one doctor failed to attend an emergency call from a nurse because the battery in her bleeper was flat.

[186] *Robertson v Nottingham Health Authority* [1997] 8 Med LR 1, 13 *per* Brooke LJ This may give rise to a 'non-delegable duty' on the part of the hospital to 'set up a safe system of operation in relation to what are essentially management as opposed to clinical matters', ibid.

Thus, there must be a system for dealing with a surgeon's patients when the surgeon goes away for a weekend.[187] It is also to be expected that there will be a system for communication between hospitals, or between a hospital and general practitioners, about the treatment that a patient has received.[188]

6.63   Communication errors can occur from simply mishearing or misreading an instruction. This may be the result of a single lapse of concentration, but the further question will then arise as to whether there was any system for checking for such errors given that it is known that mistakes do sometimes happen. In *Collins v Hertfordshire County Council*,[189] a patient died after being injected with cocaine instead of procaine as a local anaesthetic. The surgeon had told a junior, unqualified medical officer over the telephone his requirements for the operation, and the word 'procaine' was misheard for 'cocaine'. The pharmacist dispensing the drug at the hospital pharmacy did not question the order for an 'unheard-of dosage' of a dangerous drug, and the surgeon did not check prior to injecting the solution that he was in fact injecting what he had ordered. It was held that both the surgeon and the medical officer were liable, as was the hospital authority for having an unsafe dispensing system.

6.64   A pathologist who has been given specimens for testing or analysis owes a duty to the patient not only to conduct the tests in a proper manner but also to take reasonable steps to communicate the results to the referring doctor, and it is irrelevant that the doctor also has a corresponding duty to find out the results.[190] A doctor who prepares a report or medical notes which he is aware may be relied upon by others for the treatment of the patient has a duty to exercise reasonable care in writing the report.[191] This also applies to the writing of a prescription, which should be reasonably legible.[192]

---

[187] *Cassidy v Ministry of Health* [1951] 2 KB 343, 359, *per* Singleton LJ; *Crichton v Hastings* (1972) 29 DLR (3d) 692, 700 (Ont CA).

[188] *Coles* (n 181 above); see also *Schanczi* (n 145 above) on a specialist's failure to obtain adequate information about a patient from the referring doctor before proceeding to surgery; cf *Chapman v Rix* (1960), [1994] 5 Med LR 239, HL.

[189] [1947] 1 KB 598; see also *Strangeways-Lesmere v Clayton* [1936] 2 KB 11, where a nurse who misread her instructions and gave an excess dose was held to be negligent.

[190] *Thomsen v Davison* [1975] Qd R. 93; see also *McKay v Essex Area Health Authority* [1982] QB 1166 on an alleged omission to communicate test results; *Gregory v Pembrokeshire Health Authority* [1989] 1 Med LR 81 CA; *Fredette* (n 163 above).

[191] *Everett v Griffiths* [1920] 3 KB 163, 213; *Price v Milawski* (1977) 82 DLR (3d) 130 (Ont CA).

[192] *Prendergast v Sam and Dee Ltd* [1989] 1 Med LR 36, CA. For similar cases of negligence by a pharmacist failing to spot prescription errors see *Collins v Hertfordshire County Council* [1947] 1 KB 598 and *Dwyer v Roderick* (1983) 127 SJ 806; McKevitt (1988) 4 PN 185; Crawford (1995) 2 J Law and Med 293.

4. Treatment Errors

Errors in treatment can take a multitude of forms. The mere fact that a doctor **6.65** has departed from the standard treatment will not necessarily indicate negligence, bearing in mind that doctors have to treat the individual patient and not the 'standard' patient found in textbooks; a slight departure from the textbook therefore will not necessarily be a mistake, let alone negligent.[193] On the other hand, a substantial departure from standard practice will place a heavy onus on the defendant to justify this decision.[194] If a doctor has made a considered decision about treatment, it may be more difficult to conclude that there has been negligence[195] than if he has made an unintentional or inadvertent 'error', since in the latter case there has been no balancing of risks and benefits.[196]

(a) Operations

The courts have long recognised that the mere fact that something has gone **6.66** wrong during the course of an operation is not per se indicative of negligence,[197] although knocking out four of the patient's teeth during a tonsillectomy was held to be negligent.[198] Where a patient sustains burns in an operating theatre, this is usually the result of negligence.[199] Perforation of the uterus during the course of performing a Dilatation and Curettage is relatively common, and not in itself negligent, but damage to the small bowel during the operation is so rare as to be outside the range of normal practice and does indicate a lack of reasonable care.[200]

In *Hendy v Milton Keynes Health Authority (No 2)*[201] the evidence showed **6.67** that it was possible for ureteric damage to occur during an abdominal

---

[193] *Holland* (n 55 above).   [194] *Clark v MacLennan* [1983] 1 All ER 416.
[195] See e g *Darley v Shale* [1993] 4 Med LR 161 (NSWSC).
[196] *Goode v Nash* (1979) 21 SASR 419, 423 (SC of South Australia).
[197] *White v Westminster Hospital Board of Governors* (1961) *The Times*, 26 October; *Ashcroft v Merseyside Regional Health Authority* [1983] 2 All ER 245; aff'd [1985] 2 All ER 96; see also *Chubey v Ahsan* (1977) 71 DLR (3d) 550 (Man CA); *Kapur v Marshall* (1978) 85 DLR (3d) 567, 573, *per* Robins J (Ont HC).   [198] *Munro v United Oxford Hospitals* (1958) 1 *BMJ* 167.
[199] *Crits* (n 9 above); *Paton v Parker* (1942) 65 CLR 187; *Crysler v Pearse* [1943] 4 DLR 738; *Clarke v Warboys* (1952) *The Times*, 18 March. Burns to the buttocks following surgery are, apparently, a common type of claim: Medical Defence Union, *Annual Report 1990*, 45; (1993) 9 *J of the MDU* 95. The Department of Health has issued specific warning to hospitals about the danger of inflammable liquids igniting during surgery: HC (Hansard) (90) 25.
[200] *Bovenzi v Kettering Health Authority* [1991] 2 Med LR 293, QBD.
[201] [1992] 3 Med LR 119, QBD. In *Ratty v Haringey Health Authority* [1994] 5 Med LR 413 the Court of Appeal upheld a finding of negligence where there was damage to the plaintiff's ureter during the course of colo-rectal surgery. The negligence consisted, not in the initial damage to the ureter, which could occur even with the exercise of reasonable care, but in failing to discover and correct the damage before the end of the operation. See also *Bouchta v Swindon Health Authority* [1996] 7 Med LR 62.

hysterectomy despite the use of a competent surgical technique, but these rare instances of non-culpable ureteric damage were attributable to anatomical variations outside the normal range. Most cases of ureteric damage where the anatomy was normal were due to poor technique, and therefore the most likely explanation of damage to the plaintiff's ureter, in the absence of any evidence of abnormal anatomy, was that there had been negligence.

6.68   Obstetric errors are frequently the subject of litigation, partly because the consequences for the child can be extremely serious, and partly because the parents' expectation is to have a normal, healthy child. In *Whitehouse v Jordan*,[202] an allegation that the defendant had pulled too long and too hard in the course of a forceps delivery, and thus was negligent in failing to proceed to a Caesarian section delivery, was ultimately rejected on the facts. In *Parry v North West Surrey Health Authority*[203] on the other hand, the defendant was held liable for attempting to deliver a child by forceps when it was too high in the mother's pelvis, and thus for failing to undertake a Caesarian section delivery. Human error is frequently implicated in obstetric accidents, many of which are avoidable,[204] although establishing the causal link between any negligence and the child's injuries can be extremely difficult.

6.69   A doctor may be liable for proceeding to surgery too quickly without first considering conservative treatment.[205] Conversely, a delay in recommending

---

[202] [1981] 1 All ER 267. See also *Hinfey v Salford Health Authority* [1993] 4 Med LR 143, where an allegation that the failure to undertake a Caesarian section delivery constituted negligence was rejected on the evidence; *James v Camberwell Health Authority* [1994] 5 Med LR 253, where a delay in proceeding to a Caesarian section was held not negligent on the facts; *Goguen v Crowe* (1987) 40 CCLT 212 (Nova Scotia SC); *Knight v West Kent Health Authority* [1998] Lloyd's Rep Med 18, CA.

[203] [1994] 5 Med LR 259. See also *Dowdie v Camberwell Health Authority* [1997] 8 Med LR 368 where the defendant was held to have been negligent in failing to proceed to a Caesarian section in a case of shoulder dystocia; *Wiszniewski* (n 39 above); *Hill v West Lancashire Health Authority* [1997] 8 Med LR 196; *Bowers v Harrow Health Authority* [1995] 6 Med LR 16. See also *De Martell v Merton and Sutton Health Authority* [1995] 6 Med LR 234 and *Robertson v Nottingham Health Authority* [1997] 8 Med LR 1 where the actions failed on causation.

[204] Ennis and Vincent (1990) 300 *BMJ* 1365. This reflects a number of general problems, including inadequate training and supervision of junior and middle ranking staff in the labour ward: ibid. See further the Department of Health's *Report on confidential enquiries into maternal deaths in England and Wales*, (HMSO, 1989).

[205] *Schanczi* (n 145 above), 472; see also *Coughlin* (m 66 above), 744; *Haughian v Paine* (1987) 37 DLR (4th) 625, 629–35 (Sask CA); *Mann v Judgeo* [1993] 4 WWR 760 (Sask QB), on the performance of aggressive surgery when 'first treatment surgery' was appropriate; *Cherewayko v Grafton* [1993] 3 WWR 604, 619 (Man QB), on an 'unnecessary' operation; *Doughty v North Staffordshire Health Authority* [1992] 3 Med LR 81, QBD; cf *De Freitas v O'Brien* [1995] 6 Med LR 108, where the defendant's decision to resort to spinal surgery, despite the absence of definite clinical and radiological evidence of nerve compression, was held not to have been negligent.

surgery may also be negligent. In *Powell v Guttman*[206] the plaintiff developed a condition of avascular necrosis following an operation on her leg performed by the defendant orthopaedic surgeon. The defendant failed to advise the plaintiff to undergo an arthoplasty operation to correct this. A year after the first operation another surgeon performed this operation, and during it the plaintiff sustained a rotary fracture of the femur. Due to the delay, the condition of the bone had deteriorated as a result of osteoporosis, and this was a 'significant cause' of the fracture that occurred. The defendant was held liable on the basis that the delay in the second operation was attributable to his negligence, and this had caused an increase in the osteoporosis rendering the femur more susceptible to the fracture.

(b) Team Negligence

Under modern conditions, most medical treatment is undertaken by a team **6.70** of health care professionals, and this is invariably true of surgical procedures. In *Wilsher v Essex Area Health Authority*[207] the Court of Appeal rejected the concept of 'team negligence' whereby each of the persons who formed the staff of the unit held themselves out as capable of undertaking the specialised procedures which the unit set out to perform. It would not be right, said Mustill LJ, to attribute to each individual member of the team a duty to live up to the standards demanded of the unit as a whole, because that would expose a student nurse to an action in negligence for a failure to possess the skill and experience of a consultant. Each member of the team will be responsible for his or her own contribution to the joint undertaking. For example, a doctor will not normally be responsible for the negligence of others, such as nurses, in carrying out instructions that have been given with regard to the patient's treatment,[208] and, conversely, nursing staff will not be considered to have acted negligently when faithfully carrying out the instructions of a doctor.[209] Acting under the instructions of a doctor, however, does not excuse a nurse from making any professional judgment. There may be circumstances where a nurse could be negligent when following a doctor's instructions; for example, if a doctor ordered an obviously incorrect and dangerous dosage of a drug and the nurse administered it without obtaining confirmation from the doctor or higher authority.[210] Similarly, a pharmacist

---

[206] (1978) 89 DLR (3d) 180 (Man CA).   [207] [1986] 3 All ER 801, 812–13.
[208] *Perionowsky v Freeman* (1866) 4 F & F 977; *Morris v Winsbury-White* [1937] 4 All ER 494, 498.   [209] *Gold v Essex County Council* [1942] 2 KB 293, 299, *per* Lord Greene MR.
[210] ibid, 313, *per* Goddard LJ, although his Lordship added that: 'In the stress of an operation, however, I should suppose that the first thing required of a nurse would be an unhesitating obedience to the orders of the surgeon.' See also the analogous case of *Davy-Chiesman v Davy-Chiesman* [1984] 1 All ER 321, 332, 335, stating that solicitors should not rely blindly on the advice of counsel.

has been held to be negligent for failing to check a request for an 'unheard-of dosage' of cocaine.[211] A doctor may be negligent if he knows or ought reasonably to have known that another person in the team, whether it be the anaesthetist or a nurse, has done something which puts the patient at risk but fails to take any steps to remedy the error.[212] Moreover, it is negligent for a doctor to rely on information provided by a nurse whom he knows or ought to know is overconfident in her own abilities and not qualified to make the clinical judgment in question.[213]

(c) 'Swab' Cases

6.71   The danger of swabs or surgical instruments being left inside a patient at the end of an operation is clearly something which must be guarded against. But even in this type of case a surgeon is not necessarily liable; he only has to exercise reasonable care to see that it does not happen.[214] However, the consequences can be very serious and accordingly the degree of care required in order to satisfy the requirement of reasonableness will be correspondingly high. It is not negligent for a surgeon to delegate the task of counting swabs to a nurse, but a surgeon will not necessarily avoid liability by relying on that count.[215] In *Urry v Bierer*[216] a surgeon conducting a Caesarian section relied almost exclusively on the count by the nurse. He was held to have been negligent in failing to take any additional precautions, such as using swabs with tapes, although it was said that different considerations might apply in an emergency. There was no reason why the surgeon should not have made some mental effort to remember where he had placed the swabs, particularly since he had chosen not to use tapes. In practice swab cases are usually settled as indefensible, and most of the cases that are litigated end in a finding of negligence.[217] Even if, on the facts, the

---

[211] *Collins v Hertfordshire County Council* [1947] 1 KB 598.
[212] *Perionowsky* (n 208 above), 982; *Wilsher* (n 207 above), where the registrar was held to have been negligent in failing to spot the senior house officer's error. In *Jones v Manchester Corporation* [1952] 2 All ER 125 the Court of Appeal took the view that the inexperienced doctor who administered the fatal injection was not as culpable as the experienced doctor who supervised her. See also *Collins* (n 211 above), on the question of responsibility for injections.
[213] *Wiszniewski v Central Manchester Health Authority* [1996] 7 Med LR 248, 256.
[214] *Mahon v Osborne* [1939] 2 KB 14, 31–2 *per* Scott LJ. Note, however, that Scott LJ dissented on the question of whether *res ipsa loquitur* applied to a swab case.
[215] ibid, 47, *per* Goddard LJ.   [216] (1955) *The Times*, 15 July, CA.
[217] See e g *James v Dunlop* (1931) 1 *BMJ* 730 which is considered in *Mahon* (n 214 above), *Dryden v Surrey County Council* [1936] 2 All ER 535; *Holt v Nesbitt* [1951] 4 DLR 478; *Garner v Morrell* (1953) *The Times*, 31 October; *Urry* (n 216 above); *Fox v Glasgow South Western Hospitals* 1955 SLT 337; *Cooper v Nevill* (1961) *The Times*, 10 March (PC); *Anderson v Chasney* 1949] 4 DLR 71 (Man CA); aff'd sub nom *Chasney v Anderson* [1950] 4 DLR 223 (SCC). The position will usually be the same in the case of a surgical instrument inadvertently left inside the patient's body: *Hocking v Bell* [1948] WN 21 (PC); *Gloning v Miller* [1954] 1 DLR 372; cf *McDonald v Pottinger* [1953] NZLR 196.

---

conclusion is that the surgeon was not negligent in leaving the swab inside the patient, the result will almost invariably be that the nurse conducting the count was negligent.[218]

(d) Infection

In Hospital

About 10 per cent of patients pick up infections while they are in hospital, at a cost to the NHS of more than £170 million a year. These infections cause 5,000 deaths a year and contribute to a further 15,000 (more deaths a year in the UK than road deaths or suicides).[219] Some of these cases are unavoidable, but some are due to medical staff ignoring basic hygiene rules.[220] Cases may arise from cross-infection, where patients acquire a disease from another patient, or they may result from surgical intervention. In the case of post-operative infection, the infection itself cannot be treated as evidence of negligence, because no one can guarantee that post-operative infection will not occur.[221] However, specialists should be quick to recognise the development of infection following surgery.[222] In *Voller v Portsmouth Corporation*[223] the plaintiff developed meningitis after the administration of a spinal anaesthetic. It was admitted that the illness must have been caused either by contamination of the anaesthetic or by an infection occurring during its administration. It could not be said precisely how the accident occurred but the court concluded that there must have been some failure to follow the appropriate sterilisation procedure resulting in contamination from the equipment used.

6.72

Unnecessarily exposing a patient to the risk of contracting an infection will be negligent. Thus, bringing a patient into contact with other patients who have an infectious disease can constitute negligence,[224] as can discharging an

6.73

---

[218] In *Frandle v MacKenzie* (1990) 5 CCLT (2d) 113 (BCCA) liability for not keeping a proper count of the swabs was ascribed 80 per cent to the surgeon and 20 per cent to the nurses.

[219] *Hospital Acquired Infections* (Office of Health Economics, 1997), reported in *The Independent*, 16 Sept 1997.

[220] (1990) *The Times*, 4 Sept (news report). It has been estimated that up to a third of hospital acquired infections could be prevented: *Hospital Acquired Infections* (Office of Health Economics, 1997). See also Cooke (1989) 5 *J of the MDU* 62.

[221] *Hajgato v London Health Association* (1982) 36 OR (2d) 669, 681 (Ont HC).

[222] ibid, 682; *Rietze v Bruser (No 2)* [1979] 1 WWR 31, 49–50, (Man QB); see also *Hucks v Cole* (1968), [1993] 4 Med LR 393, CA. [223] (1947) 203 LTJ 264.

[224] *Lindsey County Council v Marshall* [1937] AC 97, where the plaintiff was admitted to the defendants' maternity home notwithstanding an outbreak of puerperal fever in the home a week earlier. See also *Heafield v Crane* (1937) *The Times*, 31 July, where, after the birth of her child, the plaintiff was moved from the maternity ward to a general ward where a patient was suffering from puerperal fever, and the plaintiff caught the infection.

infectious patient from hospital prematurely, with the result that others who come into contact with him contract the disease.[225] It is not necessarily negligent, however, for a hospital to adopt a system for managing infectious smallpox patients by sterilisation rather than isolation, where the defendants conform to a practice accepted as proper by a responsible body of professional opinion.[226]

By Donor Organs or Bodily Fluid

6.74 Some cases of infection arise from the transplantation of human organs or the transfusion of bodily fluids from a donor who carried the infection.[227] Before a test for HIV was developed in 1985, there were a number of cases in Commonwealth jurisdictions concerning the liability of blood banks and hospitals for the infection of patients with HIV from blood transfusions.[228] When the risk of infection was unknown or unforeseeable, it could not be negligent to fail to take precautions against the risk.[229] Therefore actions involving allegations that defendants failed to adopt adequate screening of donors from groups known to be at high risk of being infected with HIV, or failed to adopt 'surrogate testing',[230] were not particularly successful. Surrogate testing, for example, namely testing blood for Hepatitis B core antibodies (the anti-HBc test) on the basis that there was an association between those who tested positive and those in high risk groups

---

[225] *Evans v Liverpool Corporation* [1906] 1 KB 160.

[226] *Vancouver General Hospital v McDaniel* (1934) 152 LT 56.

[227] See Norrie (1985) 34 ICLQ 442 for discussion of both the principles of liability in negligence and the question of consent. See further Giesen (1994) 10 PN 2. In *Morgan v Gwent Health Authority* (1987) *The Independent*, 14 December, CA, a young unmarried woman was negligently given a transfusion of Rhesus positive blood instead of Rhesus negative blood, which raised the level of antibodies in her blood and put at risk any future pregnancy. She was awarded £20,000 in damages.

[228] The one English case which raised this issue was settled before trial of the substantive matters. See *Re HIV Haemophiliac Litigation* (1990), [1996] PIQR P220, in which haemophiliacs treated with imported HIV-infected blood products commenced proceedings against the Department of Health, the Blood Products Laboratory, and the National Blood Transfusion Service, alleging *inter alia* negligence in screening donors, failing to treat the blood products to minimise the risk of infection, failing to warn donors of the risk, and failing to achieve a self-sufficiency in blood products within the NHS. The action raised novel points on the potential liability of the Department of Health and certain government agencies. Without determining the issues, the Court of Appeal accepted that the plaintiffs had made out at least an arguable case of negligence. For a comparable Canadian case see *Brown v Alberta* [1994] 2 WWR 283 (Alta QB).

[229] Thus, in *H v Royal Alexandra Hospital for Children* [1990] 1 Med LR 297 it was not negligent to fail to give a warning of the risk to doctors or patients in 1982, though by 1983 the situation had changed.

[230] ibid; *E v Australian Red Cross Society* (1991) 105 ALR 53 (Aus Fed CA); aff'g (1991) 99 ALR 601; [1991] 2 Med LR 303; *PQ v Australian Red Cross Society* [1992] 1 VR 19 (Vict SC); *Pittman Estate* (n 176 above). On infection with Hepatitis from blood products, see *Kitchen v McMullen* (1989) 62 DLR (4th) 481 (NBCA).

for AIDS, was highly controversial. It was also not a particularly effective test as there was a risk that introducing surrogate testing could lead to a reduction of the blood supply as a whole, as well as to an increase in the number of undetected donations of HIV-infected blood.[231] In addition, it was alleged that a blood bank or the hospital where a transfusion took place failed to warn doctors and/or patients of the risk of contracting HIV from blood transfusions.[232]

Between 1982 and 1984 the state of knowledge was in constant flux as scientists and health authorities sought to discover the causes of the newly identified condition of AIDS.[233] However, since the risk of transmission of HIV through blood products has become recognised, the question of negligence turns on whether reasonably practicable steps could have been taken to eliminate or reduce the risk although the standard of care to be expected of a blood bank reflects the fact that it is neither a commercial organisation operating for a profit nor a public health organisation, with a duty to monitor, investigate, and control the spread of disease.[234] **6.75**

Similar issues have arisen from the possibility of transmitting infection through the donor insemination of semen. In *ter Neuzen v Korn*[235] the plaintiff contracted HIV from artificial insemination in January 1985. In Australia it was known that HIV could be transmitted through blood transfusion by late 1994, and because the Elisa test for HIV being developed in the United States was soon to be available for clinical use, a decision had been taken to impose a moratorium on all bodily fluid and tissue transfers. However, the defendant and North American experts did not learn of the Australian moratorium until after September 1985 and the risk of infection from artificial insemination was not widely known in North America until mid-1985. It was held that this was not a case in which the jury, acting **6.76**

---

[231] This was because of the possibility of a 'magnet effect' whereby those who were at high risk of having contracted the 'AIDS virus' donated blood for the specific purpose of having the surrogate test performed on them. Given that a positive surrogate test had, at best, a 50 per cent coincidence with HIV infection, the numbers of donations screened out by the surrogate test might be more than offset by the additional donations from high risk donors.
[232] *H v Royal Alexandra Hospital for Children* (n 229 above); *PQ v Australian Red Cross Society* (n 230 above).
[233] See e g, the comments of Sheppard J in *E v Australian Red Cross Society* (n 230 above), 82.
[234] *Pittman Estate* (n 176 above), 313, 318–19. Lang J commented that the social need for a continued supply of blood created different considerations. It was not a product that could simply be removed from the market if inherently dangerous because it is an essential source of life to many. The need for the product outweighs the risk.
[235] (1993) 103 DLR (4th) 473 (BCCA); aff'd (1995) 127 DLR (4th) 577 (SCC). For discussion of the risks of sexually transmitted disease and HIV infection associated with donor insemination see Barratt and Cooke (1989) 299 *BMJ* 1178, and 1531.

judicially, could find the common practice of competent Canadian doctors to be negligent. The proper test was whether the defendant had conducted himself as a reasonable doctor, and this required the jury to confine itself to prevailing standards of practice in North America.

6.77 Surgeons who are infected with HIV or Hepatitis B and who knowingly continue to practise surgery, expose their patients to an unacceptable risk of infection, given the seriousness of the consequences, notwithstanding that the risk of passing on the infection is comparatively small. This would almost certainly be deemed to be negligent if a patient were infected in this way.[236]

(e) Miscalculating Drug Reactions

6.78 Doctors must take account of manufacturers' instructions and known side-effects when prescribing drugs, although they should not rely on the manufacturers' information unthinkingly.[237] Where a doctor ignores the manufacturer's instructions and warnings, it is the doctor who is responsible for any adverse reactions, though a decision to exceed the manufacturers' guidelines or dosages indicated in MIMMS in prescribing a drug is not necessarily negligent.[238] The manufacturer will not be liable since a warning addressed to the doctor will normally discharge the manufacturer's duty of care to the patient in the case of prescription drugs.[239]

6.79 Ignorance of known side-effects is negligent if the defendant ought reasonably to have been aware of them. Some mistakes may be isolated errors,[240] but in other cases the doctor is aware of the risk from side-effects, and yet calculates that it is a reasonable risk to run in the circumstances, given the condition for which the drug is prescribed. If the calculation is correct by reference to the standards of the profession he is not negligent, but if the risk was unreasonable in the circumstances he will be liable. For example,

---

[236] The General Medical Council Statement, *HIV Infection and AIDS: The Ethical Considerations*, June 1993, paras 8–10, advises doctors who are HIV positive to seek specialist advice on the extent to which they should limit their practice in order to protect their patients. Doctors should not continue in clinical practice 'merely on the basis of their own assessment of the risk to patients'. See further Mulholland (1993) 9 PN 79. One surgeon, a Hepatitis B carrier who had infected 19 patients and put hundreds of others at risk, was convicted of the offence of public nuisance and jailed: (1994) *The Times*, 30 Sept (news report). See also *R v Thornton* (1991) 1 OR (3d) 480 (Ont CA); aff'd (1993) 13 OR (3d) 744 (SCC).

[237] See e g, *Buchan v Ortho Pharmaceuticals (Canada) Ltd* (1986) 25 DLR (4th) 658 (Ont CA).

[238] *Vernon v Bloomsbury Health Authority* (1986), [1995] 6 Med LR 297.

[239] *Holmes v Ashford* [1950] 2 All ER 76; *Kubach v Hollands* [1937] 3 All ER 907; *Buchan* (n 237 above),669; *Davidson v Connaught Laboratories* (1980) 14 CCLT 251, 276 (Ont HC); Ferguson (1992) 12 OJLS 59; Peppin (1991) 70 Can Bar Rev 473.

[240] See e g, *Dwyer v Roderick* (1983) 127 SJ 806; *McCaffrey v Hague* [1949] 4 DLR 291.

in *Battersby v Tottman*[241] a doctor prescribed a very high dose of melleril to a patient who was suffering from a mental illness. He took the view that the benefits of the drug outweighed the risk that the drug would cause serious and permanent eye damage, since without treatment the patient was suicidal, and other methods of treatment had failed. The patient did sustain permanent eye damage. It was held that the decision to prescribe a dosage far in excess of the recommended dosage was not negligent as it was justified by the potential consequences of not using the drug. By way of contrast, in *Graham v Persyko*[242] the defendant gastro-enterologist wrongly, but not negligently, diagnosed that the plaintiff had Crohn's disease, for which there is no cure, and prescribed prednisone, a very potent drug with a multitude of serious adverse effects, and a low safety margin. This caused avascular necrosis of the patient's femoral heads, a rare but known complication. The decision to prescribe the drug was held to be negligent, because the risk from the side-effects was disproportionate to the anticipated benefit to the patient who was asymptomatic at the time.

It is also possible for the correct dosage of a drug to be undercalculated. A **6.80** number of cases have arisen in which patients undergoing surgery have been awake and conscious of pain but unable to communicate with medical staff due to being paralysed by muscle relaxant drugs. This may or may not be due to fault in the administration of the anaesthetic.[243]

(f) Injections

Injections may be given in the wrong place, the hypodermic may contain **6.81** the wrong substance or an excessive dose, or the needle may break.[244] Not

---

[241] (1985) 37 SASR 524 (SC of S Aus).
[242] (1986) 27 DLR (4th) 699 (Ont CA); (1986) 34 DLR (4th) 160 (SCC) leave to appeal refused.
[243] See *Ludlow v Swindon Health Authority* [1989] 1 Med LR 104; *Taylor v Worcester and District Health Authority* [1991] 2 Med LR 215; *Ackers v Wigan Health Authority* [1991] 2 Med LR 232; *Phelan v East Cumbria Health Authority* [1991] 2 Med LR 419; *Early v Newham Health Authority* [1994] 5 Med LR 214; *Jacobs v Great Yarmouth and Waveney Health Authority* [1995] 6 Med LR 192. For discussion see (1995) 1 *Clinical Risk*, (No 4).
[244] A broken needle is not necessarily an indication of negligence, since it may be due to a latent defect in the needle: *Brazier v Ministry of Defence* [1965] 1 Lloyd's Rep 26. See also *Gerber v Pines* (1935) 79 SJ.13; *Galloway v Hanley* (1956) 1 *BMJ* 580; *Daniels v Heskin* [1954] IR 73, 79; cf *Cardin v City of Montreal* (1961) 29 DLR (2d) 492 (SCC) where a doctor who administered a vaccine by hypodermic needle to a child who was struggling against his mother's efforts to keep him still was held to have been negligent in not postponing the injection until the child was in a less agitated state. Note that the fact that an instrument, such as a needle, has broken may indicate that the instrument itself was defective in which case there may be an action against the manufacturer either in negligence or under the Consumer

all errors, however, will give rise to a claim for negligence. An injection into the patient's surrounding tissues instead of a vein is not necessarily negligent if the vein is difficult to find.[245] On the other hand, a doctor must take responsibility for what he injects into a patient, and administering an excessive dose of a drug having misread the instructions is clearly negligent,[246] as is an excessive dose of anaesthetic given through misjudgment attributable to inexperience.[247] Even when allowing for the fact that the person who provides the hypodermic is skilled in such matters and the solution is made up in the hospital pharmacy, there remains an obligation upon a surgeon carrying out the injection to take reasonable steps to check that he is getting what he ordered.[248] In *Ritchie v Chichester Health Authority*[249] the treatment protocol for the administration of an epidural anaesthetic to a woman in the course of labour required both the midwife and the anaesthetist to check that the correct drug had been selected for injection by reading the name on the ampoule. The defendants were held liable on the basis that the anaesthetist must have injected a neurotoxic substance into the plaintiff when administering the epidural anaesthetic, despite the fact that there would have to have been a series of errors on the part of the medical staff involved. In *Caldeira v Gray*,[250] damage to the sciatic nerve following an injection in the buttocks was found to have been caused by negligence, but in *Wilcox v Cavan*,[251] the Supreme Court of Canada held that where gangrene had developed in the plaintiff's arm following an intra-muscular injection, the nurse who administered the

---

Protection Act 1987: see e g, *G v Fry Surgical International Ltd* (1992) 3 AVMA Medical & Legal *Journal* (No 4), 12, where the blade of a pair of arthroscopy scissors fractured during the course of an operation and a fragment was lost in the plaintiff's knee. An action under the Consumer Protection Act 1987 against the importers of the scissors, on the basis that the scissors were defective, was settled.

[245] *Williams v North Liverpool Hospital Management Committee* (1959) *The Times*, 17 January; *Prout v Crowley* (1956) 1 *BMJ* 580; *Gent v Wilson* (1956) 2 DLR (2d) 160.

[246] *Strangeways-Lesmere v Clayton* [1936] 2 KB 11; *Smith v Brighton and Lewes Hospital Management Committee* (1958) *The Times*, 2 May; *Sellers v Cooke* [1990] 2 Med LR 16, 19.

[247] *Jones v Manchester Corporation* [1952] 2 All ER 125.

[248] *Collins v Hertfordshire County Council* [1947] 1 KB 598, 607.

[249] [1994] 5 Med LR 187, QBD; cf *Muzio v North West Herts Health Authority* [1995] 6 Med LR 184, where an anaesthetist was found not negligent when, in the course of inserting a needle for a spinal anaesthetic, she penetrated the dura, leading the plaintiff to develop severe spinal headaches. See also Dr J Lunn, 'The Role of the Anaesthetist', in Action for the Victims of Medical Accidents, *Risk Areas in Medical Practice* (1993), 128–36; and Dr Hannington-Kiff, 'Overview of Obstetric Lumbar Epidural Blocks' (1993) 4 AVMA Medical & Legal Journal (No 1), 2.   [250] [1936] 1 All ER 540.

[251] (1974) 50 DLR (3d) 687 (SCC); *Fischer v Waller* [1994] 1 WWR 83 (Alta QB), where it was held that perforation of the globe of the eye during the course of administering a local anaesthetic prior to cataract surgery was a rare but recognised risk of the procedure which could occur in the absence of negligence.

injection was not liable under the principle of *res ipsa loquitur*. Although there was no explanation as to how the injection had found its way into the plaintiff's circumflex artery, the defendant's version of events was consistent with the absence of negligence.

(g) Failure to Monitor Treatment

A doctor has a duty to monitor treatment given to a patient, particularly **6.82** where the treatment carries a high risk of an adverse reaction.[252] This duty extends to post-operative conditions which the patient may develop.[253] A patient recovering from a general anaesthetic will require careful monitoring. In *Coyne v Wigan Health Authority*[254] the plaintiff sustained brain damage caused by hypoxia for a period of four to five minutes when she was in the recovery ward following an operation under general anaesthetic. The defendants accepted that the principle of *res ipsa loquitur* applied, seeking to explain the incident on the basis that the hypoxia was the result of silent regurgitation of gastric content. It was held that the evidence did not support the defendants' explanation, which was implausible because there was no recorded instance of silent aspiration leading to brain damage and only one such case was referred to in evidence. Accordingly, the appropriate inference was that there had been negligence in monitoring the patient.

D. Psychiatric Patients

The *Bolam* test[255] applies to the relationship between a psychiatrist and a **6.83** psychiatric patient just as it applies to any other doctor–patient relationship. Thus, it was negligent for a psychiatrist to engage in social contact with a female patient who had developed a strong and obsessive emotional attachment to him, leading to a serious deterioration in the patient's mental health, given that this was a departure from recognised standards of practice which no body of professional opinion supported.[256] In some cases the nature of the mental illness makes the patient dangerous, either to himself or to others, and

---

[252] *Marshall v Rogers* [1943] 4 DLR 68; *Male v Hopmans* (1967) 64 DLR (2d) 105, 113–15 (Ont CA); *Wilsher v Essex Area Health Authority* [1986] 3 All ER 801.
[253] *Bayliss v Blagg* (1954) 1 *BMJ* 709; *Ares v Venner* (1970) 14 DLR (3d) 4 (SCC) and *Harrington v Essex Area Health Authority* (1984) *The Times*, 14 November, QBD, on plaster casts; *Poole v Morgan* [1987] 3 WWR 217; *Cavanagh v Bristol and Weston Health Authority* [1992] 3 Med LR 49, QBD   [254] [1991] 2 Med LR 301, QBD.
[255] The plaintiff in *Bolam v Friern Hospital Management Committee* [1957] 2 All ER 118 was a psychiatric patient who sustained serious physical injuries in the course of electro-convulsive therapy administered to treat depression.
[256] *Landau v Werner* (1961) 105 SJ 257, and 1008, CA.

claims can arise out of an alleged failure to exercise control over the patient. A doctor undoubtedly has a duty to take reasonable steps to protect a psychiatric patient from harming himself, and in an institutional setting a hospital authority may be responsible for injuries inflicted on a patient by himself,[257] or by a fellow patient, where the injuries are the result of a failure to provide adequate control and supervision.[258]

1. Self-harm

6.84 This duty can include an obligation to make reasonable efforts to prevent suicide attempts.[259] In *Thorne v Northern Group Hospital Management Committee*,[260] the nursing staff on a medical ward of a general hospital were aware that a patient, who was a suspected depressive, had threatened suicide. The patient walked out of the hospital, went home and committed suicide while mentally ill but not legally insane. It was held that there had been no negligence, because, on the facts, constant supervision was not appropriate. In *Selfe v Ilford and District Hospital Management Committee*[261] on the other hand, it was accepted that reasonable care required continuous observation of a patient who was known to be a serious suicide risk. He was put in a ground floor ward with twenty-seven patients, four of whom were also suicide risks, and there were insufficient nurses available to cope with all the circumstances that could be expected to arise. The plaintiff climbed out of a window and jumped off a roof, sustaining serious injuries. Hinchcliffe J held the defendants liable. The degree of care required was proportionate to the degree of risk, and in this case there had been a breakdown in proper nursing supervision. However, the degree of care must also take into account the level of restraint or supervision appropriate in the light of the patient's mental condition. In some cases, imposing restraint on a patient may exacerbate the patient's condition, or at least inhibit effective treatment. If it is against the patient's wishes, it might undermine the trust between doctor and patient.

---

[257] *Jinks v Cardwell* (1987) 39 CCLT 168 (Ont HC); *Kelly v Board of Governors of St Laurence's Hospital* [1988] IR 402 (Supreme Court of Ireland).

[258] *Wellesley Hospital v Lawson* (1977) 76 DLR (3d) 688 where the Supreme Court of Canada assumed that such a common law duty existed. In *Ellis v Home Office* [1953] 2 All ER 149, prison authorities were held to owe a duty of care to a prisoner assaulted by another prisoner.   [259] Jones (1990) 6 PN 107.

[260] (1964) 108 SJ 484.

[261] (1970) 114 SJ 935. See also *Hay v Grampian Health Board* [1995] 6 Med LR 128, Court of Session, where the regime for supervising a known suicide risk broke down; *Mahmood v Siggins* [1996] 7 Med LR 76, where a general practitioner was held liable for failing to refer a known manic depressive to a community mental health team for assessment, treatment, and supervision; *Villemure v L'Hôpital Notre Dame* (1972) 31 DLR (3d) 454 (SCC). Where, on the other hand, the suicide attempt is unforeseeable there will be no liability: *Lepine v University Hospital Board* (1966) 57 DLR (2d) 701 (SCC); *Stadel v Albertson* [1954] 2 DLR 328 (Sask CA).

This judgment has to balance competing risks to the patient's health, including the risk of self-harm resulting in death.[262]

If a non-psychiatric patient makes a suicide attempt the question will be **6.85** whether non-specialist (ie non-psychiatric) staff ought to have realised that there was a genuine risk of a suicide attempt. This will not be judged by reference to whether a psychiatrist could have made this diagnosis but whether in the defendant's position a reasonable doctor or nurse would have identified the risk. In *Hyde v Tameside Area Health Authority*[263] the plaintiff was admitted to hospital with a painful shoulder. Twelve days later he jumped from a third floor window, having convinced himself, erroneously, that he had cancer. He suffered catastrophic injuries. It was alleged that the medical staff had negligently failed to identify the plaintiff's mental distress, and had failed to realize the patient needed psychiatric treatment. The Court of Appeal held that on the particular facts there was no negligence, merely a 'forgivable failure to achieve a standard approaching perfection'. The court will make allowance for the fact that a decision to introduce psychiatric treatment for patients who are not being treated for a psychiatric illness or disorder is one that involves competing considerations. Watkins LJ pointed out that many patients in hospital suffer from anxiety and worry about their medical condition. They may need reassurance and sometimes need drugs to ease pain or stress, but to tell a patient who requires surgery that he also needs psychiatric help may be counter-productive.[264]

It has been argued that, quite apart from the question of breach of duty, **6.86** claims for negligence based on suicide or attempted suicide should not be permitted, on the grounds of causation, *volenti non fit injuria*, *ex turpi causa non oritur actio*, or simply for policy reasons.[265] The causation argument states that the defendant's negligence merely provided the opportunity for the deceased's act of suicide, which amounted to a *novus actus interveniens*. In *Kirkham v Chief Constable of Greater Manchester Police*,[266] Tudor Evans J rejected this contention on the basis that the suicide was the very thing that the defendants had a duty to take precautions against,[267] and concluded that

---

[262] *Haines v Bellissimo* (1977) 82 DLR (3d) 215 (Ont HC).
[263] (1981), reported at (1986) 2 PN 26.   [264] ibid, 30.
[265] For consideration of the *volenti non fit injuria* and *ex turpi causa* defences see paras 7.42–7.45.   [266] [1989] 3 All ER 882; aff'd [1990] 2 WLR 987.
[267] Where the intervening conduct is the very thing that the defendant was under a duty to guard against, he cannot avoid liability by arguing that the conduct constituted an intervening act: *Haynes v Harwood* [1935] 1 KB 146, 156; *Perl (Exporters) Ltd v Camden London Borough Council* [1984] QB 342, 353. See also *per* Farquharson LJ in *Kirkham v Chief Constable of Greater Manchester Police* [1990] 2 WLR 987, 997 in relation to the defence of *volenti non fit injuria*.

on the evidence the patient's suicide would probably have been prevented.[268] It would appear that the deceased's state of mind is relevant to the question of causation, since his Lordship commented that although the act of suicide was a conscious and deliberate act 'the deceased's mental balance was . . . affected at the time'.[269]

2. Harm to Third Parties

6.87 It is uncertain whether, in this country, a psychiatrist would be held responsible for foreseeable harm inflicted by a patient on a third party.[270] Even if it were possible to identify reasonably practicable steps that a doctor could have taken (such as seeking compulsory admission for assessment or treatment under the Mental Health Act 1983), it is not clear that a duty of care would be held to exist. Where the patient is compulsorily detained, however, the greater degree of control exercised over the patient may be sufficient to tip the balance in favour of a duty of care being imposed.[271] In *Clunis v Camden & Islington Health Authority*[272] the Court of Appeal rejected a claim in negligence by a patient who had killed an innocent bystander. He alleged that had he received proper psychiatric treatment he would not have committed the offence and therefore he would not have been convicted of a criminal offence and sent to prison. The claim was struck out as contrary to public policy, because his plea of manslaughter by reason of diminished responsibility still required some degree of personal responsibility, even though it was accepted that his mental responsibility was substantially impaired. The Court of Appeal did, however, contemplate that there could be liability in negligence in such a case if it could be proved that the plaintiff did not know the nature and quality of his act or that what he had done was wrong.

---

[268] In *Hyde v Tameside Area Health Authority* (1986) 2 PN 26 O'Connor LJ said that he did not think that 'the fact that a patient commits suicide or attempts suicide will necessarily break the chain of causation if breach of duty is established against the hospital. It all depends on the circumstances of an individual case.' See also *Funk Estate v Clapp* (1986), reported at 68 DLR (4th) 229, and (1988) 54 DLR (4th) 512 (BCCA), where it was held that *novus actus interveniens* was not a defence to a claim following the suicide of a prisoner.

[269] [1989] 3 All ER 882, 889. In *Wright Estate v Davidson* (1992) 88 DLR (4th) 698 (BCCA) the deceased's suicide was held to constitute a *novus actus interveniens* where there was no evidence of disabling mental illness; cf *Costello v Blakeson* [1993] 2 WWR 562 (BCSC).

[270] See *Tarasoff v Regents of the University of California* 551 P 2d 334 (1976); *Thompson v County of Alameda*, 614 P 2d 728 (1980); *Brady v Hopper*, 751 F 2d 329 (1984); cf *Jablonski v US*, 712 F 2d 391 (1983).

[271] *Holgate v Lancashire Mental Hospitals Board* [1937] 4 All ER 19.

[272] *The Times*, 10 Dec, 1997. This case is not concerned with a claim *by* a third party against the health authority, though it is clear that had the patient's action against the health authority succeeded the deceased's spouse would have had better prospects of obtaining redress from the plaintiff.

3. Negligent Certification

A doctor who provides a written recommendation supporting the compulsory **6.88** admission of a patient into hospital under Part II of the Mental Health Act 1983 must exercise reasonable care.[273] This necessarily requires that the doctor examine the patient,[274] and make such further enquiries as are necessary.[275] On the one hand, the court must make due allowance for the difficulty in making an accurate diagnosis in some cases of mental illness, and on the other hand, they should require 'very considerable care' to be taken where a person is being deprived of his liberty.[276]

4. Procedural Bars

Section 139(1) of the Mental Health Act 1983 provides that no person shall **6.89** be liable to any civil or criminal proceedings in respect of any act purporting to be done under the mental health legislation unless the act was done in bad faith or without reasonable care. In addition, civil proceedings may not be instituted in respect of such an act without leave of the High Court.[277] Proceedings issued without leave are a nullity,[278] although the requirement for leave applies only to patients who are formally detained under the Act; voluntary patients do not need leave to bring an action.[279]

In *Winch v Jones*,[280] the Court of Appeal held that it was not necessary for the **6.90** plaintiff to establish a prima facie case of negligence against the defendant in order to obtain leave, because this would lead to a full dress-rehearsal of the action, and at the stage of seeking leave an applicant who has a reasonable suspicion that there has been negligence may be quite unable to put forward a prima facie case before discovery has taken place. The test is whether on the materials immediately available to the court 'the applicant's complaint appears to be such that it deserves the fuller investigation which will be

---

[273] *Hall v Semple* (1862) 3 F & F 337; *De Freville v Dill* (1927) 96 LJKB 1056; *Everett v Griffiths* [1921] 1 AC 631; *Harnett v Fisher* [1927] AC 573; *Buxton v Jayne* [1960] 1 WLR 783; [1962] CLY 1167.   [274] Mental Health Act 1983, s 12(1).
[275] *Hall v Semple* (1862) 3 F & F 337, 354, *per* Crompton J.   [276] ibid, 355–6.
[277] Mental Health Act 1983, s 139(2). See RSC Ord 32, r 9. This requirement does not apply to actions against the Secretary of State or a health authority: s 139(4). Accordingly, it does not apply to the Mental Health Act Commission, which is a special health authority: *X v A, B and C and the Mental Health Act Commission* (1991) 9 BMLR 91, 97, QBD. The fact that an application for leave under s 139(2) has been successful does not preclude a judge from subsequently concluding, following further investigation, that the action should be struck out under RSC Ord 18, r 19(1) as disclosing no reasonable cause of action: ibid.
[278] *Pountney v Griffiths* [1976] AC 314.   [279] *R v Runighian* (1977) Crim LR 361.
[280] [1985] 3 All ER 97.

possible if the intended applicant is allowed to proceed'.[281] Parker LJ said that the purpose of the section was to prevent harassment by clearly hopeless actions, not to see that only those actions which would be likely to succeed should go ahead.

6.91 In *James v London Borough of Havering*,[282] however, Farquharson LJ suggested that the court did have to decide whether the applicant had a prima facie case. He distinguished *Winch v Jones* and refused the applicant leave under section 139(2) saying that, because it was 'virtually unarguable' that the doctor and the social worker concerned in an emergency compulsory admission for assessment could have acted without reasonable care, an action by the applicant would be bound to fail. Farquharson LJ disagreed with the approach of Sir John Donaldson MR, on the ground that the object of section 139 was to protect a defendant from the consequences of a wrong decision made in purported compliance with the Mental Health Act, particularly in circumstances where decisions have to be made quickly for the safety of the patient or others. Section 139 was not only protection against frivolous claims; it was also a protection from error in the circumstances set out in the subsection.[283] It is arguable, however, that requiring a plaintiff to establish a prima facie case before discovery, and in circumstances where facts are in dispute, sets the procedural hurdle for plaintiffs too high, a point that had been accepted in *Winch v Jones*.

E. Evidence and Proof

1. Proof of Negligence

6.92 The burden of proving, on the balance of probabilities, that the defendant has been negligent and that the negligence caused damage to the plaintiff lies with the plaintiff. If there are two equally possible explanations for an accident, one of which indicates that the accident occurred without negligence by the defendant, the plaintiff's action will fail,[284] although it will only be in an exceptional case that the issue should be decided on the basis of the burden of proof.[285] The plaintiff does not have to provide direct evidence that the

---

[281] ibid, 102, *per* Sir John Donaldson MR.　　[282] (1992) 15 BMLR 1.
[283] ibid, 4.
[284] *Jones v Great Western Railway Co* (1930) 47 TLR 39, 45, *per* Lord Macmillan; *The Kite* [1933] P 154; *Harrington v Essex Area Health Authority* (1984) *The Times*, 14 November, QBD, where Beldam J felt unable to select either one of two possible explanations for the plaintiff's necrosis of the skin, and the plaintiff's action failed on the burden of proof.
[285] *Morris v London Iron & Steel Co Ltd* [1987] IRLR 182, CA; *The Popi M* [1985] 2 Lloyd's Rep 1, 6, HL.

defendant has fallen below the requisite standard of care. He may rely upon any legitimate inferences that can be drawn from the proved facts, and in the absence of evidence to the contrary, the inference may well be that the defendant has been negligent.

2. *Res Ipsa Loquitur*

The principle of *res ipsa loquitur* is an evidential principle which enables a **6.93** plaintiff who has no knowledge, or insufficient knowledge, of how a medical accident occurred to rely on the accident itself and its surrounding circumstances as evidence of negligence on the part of the defendant. There is no magic in the phrase; it is simply a submission that the facts establish a prima facie case against the defendant which would be sufficient to impose liability in the absence of evidence in rebuttal.[286] Of course, it does not follow that simply because the plaintiff is in a position to invoke *res ipsa loquitur*, that his action will necessarily succeed. The inference of negligence may be rebutted by evidence adduced by the defendant which explains how the accident occurred without negligence on his part[287] but the maxim prevents a defendant who does know what happened from avoiding responsibility simply by choosing not to give any evidence.[288]

In some cases it has been suggested that the principle has the effect of **6.94** reversing the burden of proof, requiring the defendant to show that the harm was not the product of his carelessness.[289] The better view would seem to be that this is incorrect. The burden of proof remains with the plaintiff, but *res ipsa loquitur* requires the defendant to offer some reasonable explanation as to how the accident could have occurred without negligence by him.[290] On this basis, *res ipsa loquitur* 'is no more than the use of a Latin maxim to describe the state of the evidence from which it

---

[286] *Roe v Minister of Health* [1954] 2 QB 66, 87–8, *per* Morris LJ; *Ballard v North British Railway Co* 1923 SC 43, 56, *per* Lord Shaw: 'If that phrase had not been in Latin, nobody would have called it a principle.'

[287] See e g, *Roe* (n 286 above); *Brazier v Minister of Defence* [1965] 1 Lloyd's Rep 26; *Moore v Worthing District Health Authority* [1992] 3 Med LR 431, QBD; *Lindsay v Mid-Western Health Board* [1993] 2 IR 147 (Supreme Court of Ireland); *Wilcox v Cavan* (1974) 50 DLR (3d) 687 (SCC); *Hajgato v London Health Association* (1982) 36 OR (2d) 669; aff'd (1983) 44 OR (2d) 264 (Ont CA).

[288] For example, patients under a general anaesthetic are not aware of what is going on about them, and the facts are peculiarly within the knowledge of the anaesthetist and others attending them: *Crits v Sylvester* (1956) 1 DLR (2d) 502, 510, *per* Schroeder JA (Ont CA); see also *Mahon v Osborne* [1939] 2 KB 14, 50, *per* Goddard LJ.

[289] *Henderson v Henry E Jenkins & Sons* [1970] AC 282; *Ward v Tesco Stores Ltd* [1976] 1 WLR 810; *Moore v R Fox & Sons* [1956] 1 QB 596; *Mahon* (n 288 above), 50 *per* Goddard LJ.

[290] *Ng Chun Pui v Lee Chuen Tat* [1988] RTR 298, PC.

is proper to draw an inference of negligence'.[291] Where an inference of negligence does arise, a general denial by way of defence will not be sufficient to rebut it.[292] If the defendant adduces no evidence, the plaintiff will have proved his case. If the defendant does adduce evidence that is consistent with an absence of negligence on his part, then the inference of negligence is rebutted. The plaintiff then has to produce positive evidence that the defendant has acted without reasonable care[293] although, in practice, it is unlikely that the plaintiff will be able to do this, since he would not have relied on *res ipsa loquitur* in the first place if he had such evidence. Where the explanation given by the defendant relates to a remote or unusual eventuality,[294] however, this will not necessarily rebut the presumption of negligence. The plaintiff does not have to disprove every theoretical explanation, however unlikely, that might be devised to explain what happened in a way which absolves the defendant.[295] Just as the plaintiff is not entitled to rely on conjecture or speculation to establish his case on the balance of probabilities, so the defendant cannot resort to this when he is called upon for an explanation of events, although on occasions the courts are tempted to accept an explanation of events which relies on the occurrence of extremely remote risks.[296]

6.95 *Res ipsa loquitur* may apply where the defendant, or someone for whom he is responsible, has 'control' of the thing or circumstances that caused the damage,[297] and the accident is such as 'in the ordinary course of things' is

---

[291] ibid, 300, *per* Lord Griffiths. In *Lloyde v West Midlands Gas Board* [1971] 1 WLR 749, 755, Megaw LJ regarded *res ipsa loquitur* as 'no more than an exotic, although convenient, phrase to describe what is in essence no more than a common sense approach, not limited by technical rules, to the assessment of the effect of the evidence'. See also *Lindsay* (n 287 above), 183–4 *Crits* (n 288 above), 510.

[292] *Bergin v David Wickes Television* [1994] PIQR P167, 168, CA.

[293] *Ballard v North British Railway Co* 1923 SC 43, 54, *per* Lord Dunedin.

[294] *Holmes v Board of Hospital Trustees of the City of London* (1977) 81 DLR (3d) 67, 82; *Glass v Cambridge Health Authority* [1995] 6 Med LR 91, where the defendant's explanation for the plaintiff's cardiac arrest under general anaesthetic was rejected as 'at best a highly unlikely possibility'.

[295] *Bull v Devon Area Health Authority* (1989), [1993] 4 Med LR 117, 138, CA, *per* Dillon LJ; *Ballard* (n 293 above), 54, *per* Lord Dunedin; cf *Lindsay* (n 287 above), 185 (Supreme Court of Ireland) where it was said that 'it was legitimate . . . for the defendant to adduce evidence of possibilities, remote though they might be, as an explanation; in contradistinction to saying that it could not offer *any* explanation of any description whatsoever' (original emphasis).

[296] See e g, *Howard v Wessex Regional Health Authority* [1994] 5 Med LR 57, QBD.

[297] Where the defendant is vicariously liable for all the staff who played some role in the plaintiff's treatment, this is sufficient control: *Cassidy v Ministry of Health* [1951] 2 KB 343; cf *Morris v Winsbury-White* [1937] 4 All ER 494, 499 where the patient's post-operative treatment was under the control of several people (nurses, and resident medical officers) as well as the defendant surgeon, and it was held that *res ipsa loquitur* did not apply.

one which does not happen in the absence of negligence.[298] However, if all the facts about the cause of the accident are known, the maxim does not apply. The question in such a case is whether, on the known facts, negligence by the defendant can be inferred.[299]

Despite the occasional suggestion that, since much of medical practice is out-side the common experience of life, *res ipsa loquitur* should not be invoked in the context of a medical negligence action,[300] the principle may be relied upon in an appropriate case, although the court will be cautious about drawing an inference of negligence simply because something has gone wrong with the treatment.[301] The occurrence of injury is not itself necessarily evidence of a lack of reasonable care, since medical treatment carries inherent risks.[302] None-theless, even within medicine, there are some circumstances where the maxim *res ipsa loquitur* will apply.[303] For example, leaving swabs or surgical instru-ments inside a patient after an operation will normally speak of negligence.[304]

6.96

---

[298] *Scott v London & St Katherine Docks Co* (1865) 3 H & C 596, 601; *Cassidy* (n 297 above) 353–4 *per* Singleton LJ.
[299] *Barkway v South Wales Transport Co Ltd* [1950] 1 All ER 392; *Johnston v Wellesley Hospital* (1970) 17 DLR (3d) 139, 146 (Ont HC).
[300] See e g, Scott LJ in *Mahon v Osborne* [1939] 2 KB 14, 23. In *Delaney v Southmead Health Authority* [1995] 6 Med LR 355, 359, Stuart-Smith LJ doubted whether the maxim was of much assistance 'in a case of medical negligence, at any rate when all the evidence in the case has been adduced'. In *Ritchie v Chichester Health Authority* [1994] 5 Med LR 187, 205, QBD, HH Judge Thompson QC did not understand Stuart-Smith LJ to be saying that *res ipsa loquitur* could not apply in cases of medical negligence, or that medical negligence was in a special category which put it outside the ordinary English law of negligence. Rather, the maxim may not be of much help where there has been a lot of medical evidence. See also *Nesbitt v Holt* [1953] 1 DLR 671 (SCC).
[301] *Hucks v Cole* (1968), [1993] 4 Med LR 393, 396 *per* Lord Denning MR.
[302] *Roe v Minister of Health* [1954] 2 QB 66, 80; *O'Malley-Williams v Board of Governors of the National Hospital for Nervous Diseases* (1975) 1 BMJ 635; *Delaney* (n 300 above), 360, *per* Dillon LJ; *Holmes* (n 294 above), 78; *Girard v Royal Columbian Hospital* (1976) 66 DLR (3d) 676, 691 (BCSC).
[303] *Clarke v Warboys* (1952) *The Times*, 18 March, CA, where a patient sustained a burn from a high frequency electrical current used for 'electric coagulation' of the blood; *Bull* (n 295 above), 131, CA, *per* Slade LJ, where there was a delay of 50 minutes in obtaining expert obstetric assistance at the birth of twins when the medical evidence was that at the most no more than 20 minutes should elapse between the birth of the first and the second twin; *Coyne v Wigan Health Authority* [1991] 2 Med LR 301, QBD, where, following an operation under general anaesthetic, a patient in the recovery ward sustained brain damage caused by hypoxia for a period of four to five minutes; *Roe* (n 302 above), where a spinal anaesthetic became contaminated with disinfectant as a result of the manner in which it was stored, causing paralysis to the patient; *Brazier* (n 287 above), 30, when a needle broke in the patient's buttock while he was being given an injection; *Crits* (n 288 above); *Cavan v Wilcox* (1973) 44 DLR (3d) 42 (NBCA); rev'd on the facts (1974) 50 DLR (3d) 687 (SCC); *Eady v Tenderenda* (1974) 51 DLR (3d) 79 (SCC); *Rietze* (n 222 above).
[304] *Mahon* (n 288 above), 50 *per* Goddard LJ; *Cassidy v Ministry of Health* [1951] 2 KB 343, 365–6 *per* Denning LJ; *Garner v Morrell* (1953) *The Times*, 31 October, CA; *Nesbitt v Holt* [1953] 1 DLR 671 (SCC).

Where a patient went into hospital for treatment of two stiff fingers but came out of hospital with four stiff fingers, he was entitled to call on the defendants for an explanation of how the injury could have occurred without negligence.[305] Similarly, the heart of a fit child does not arrest under anaesthesia if proper care is taken in the anaesthetic and surgical processes.[306]

Inherent Risks of Treatment

6.97   As a general rule, *res ipsa loquitur* will not apply where the injury sustained by the plaintiff is of a kind recognised as an inherent risk of the treatment, since such accidents obviously can occur without negligence.[307] However, if the risk is known but does not normally occur in the absence of negligence, the maxim will apply.[308] As Robins J said in *Kapur v Marshall*,[309] *res ipsa loquitur* only comes into play when common experience or the evidence in the case indicates that the happening of the injury itself may be considered as evidence that reasonable care had not been used; this will not be the case where the complication is a recognised, even if rare, risk inherent in the operation.[310]

---

[305] *Cassidy* (n 304 above); see also *Fraser v Vancouver General Hospital* (1951) 3 WWR 337, 343, *per* O'Halloran JA (BCCA). In *Moore v Worthing District Health Authority* [1992] 3 Med LR 431, 434, QBD, it was said that where a plaintiff goes into hospital with no impediment to the use of his upper limbs and no obvious risk to them, but comes out crippled, this creates a prima facie case of negligence; though on the facts the injury was found to be attributable to the plaintiff's abnormal susceptibility.

[306] *Saunders v Leeds Western Health Authority* (1984), [1993] 4 Med LR 355; *Lindsay* (n 287 above), 181 (Supreme Court of Ireland) *per* O'Flaherty J: '. . . it seems to me that if a person goes in for a routine medical procedure, is subject to an anaesthetic without any special features, and there is a failure to return the patient to consciousness, to say that that does not call for an explanation from defendants would be in defiance of reason and justice.' See also *Glass v Cambridge Health Authority* [1995] 6 Med LR 91, where it was held that *res ipsa loquitur* applied to a case where the heart of a healthy man went into cardiac arrest while under general anaesthesia.

[307] *O'Malley-Williams v Board of Governors of the National Hospital for Nervous Diseases* (1975) 1 *BMJ* 635; *Guertin v Kester* (1981) 20 CCLT 225; *Considine v Camp Hill Hospital* (1982) 133 DLR (3d) 11 (Nova Scotia SC); *Videto v Kennedy* (1980) 107 DLR (3d) 612, 618; rev'd on other grounds (1981) 125 DLR (3d) 127.

[308] *Holmes v Board of Hospital Trustees of the City of London* (1977) 81 DLR (3d) 67 (Ont HC).   [309] (1978) 85 DLR (3d) 566, 574 (Ont HC).

[310] *Fish v Kapur* [1948] 2 All ER 176, dentist broke the plaintiff's jaw during an extraction; cf *Lock v Scantlebury* (1963) *The Times*, 25 July; *Fletcher v Bench* (1973) 4 *BMJ* 17 CA; *Keuper v McMullin* (1987) 30 DLR (4th) 408, part of a dental drill was left embedded in the jaw; *Considine v Camp Hill Hospital* (1982) 133 DLR (3d) 11 (Nova Scotia SC), plaintiff became incontinent following a prostate operation; *Girard v Royal Columbian Hospital* (1976) 66 DLR (3d) 676, 691 (BCSC), patient suffered permanent partial paralysis of the legs following anaesthesia; *Kapur v Marshall* (1978) 85 DLR (3d) 566 (Ont HC), patient died from haemorrhage during the course of spinal disc surgery when the surgeon pierced an artery with a surgical instrument; *Rocha v Harris* (1987) 36 DLR 410 (BCCA), paralysis occurred following a cervical laminectomy; *Ferguson v Hamilton Civic Hospitals* (1983) 144 DLR (3d)

Standard of Proof

The standard of proof in cases of medical negligence is the same as for any   **6.98**
other case of negligence, namely 'on the balance of probabilities', but in
practice the cogency of the evidence that the courts require in order to
satisfy the test can vary with the issues at stake.[311] It has been suggested that
cases of professional negligence create particular problems, and this may
result in what is effectively a higher standard of proof than for 'ordinary'
cases of negligence.[312] This is particularly true of the medical profession.[313]
This may reflect the concern that has been expressed about the effect that
findings of negligence can have on the reputation of individual doctors, and
the more general consequences of medical malpractice litigation for the
practice of medicine. Thus, in *Hucks v Cole*, Lord Denning commented
that:

> A charge of negligence against a medical man, a solicitor or any other
> professional man, stands on a very different footing from a charge of
> negligence against a motorist or employer. The reason is because the con-
> sequences for the professional man are far more grave. A finding of negli-
> gence affects his standing and reputation. It impairs the confidence which his
> clients have in him. The burden of proof is correspondingly greater. The
> principle applies that: 'In proportion as the charge is grave, so ought the
> proof to be clear': see *Hornal v Neuberger Products Ltd* [1957] 1 QB 247 . . .
> A doctor is not to be held negligent simply because something goes wrong
> . . . He is not liable for mischance, or misadventure. Nor is he liable for an
> error of judgment . . . He is only liable if he falls below the standard of a
> reasonably competent practitioner in his field—so much so that his conduct

---

214 paralysis occurred following arteriography; *Whitehouse v Jordan* [1980] 1 All ER 650, 658,
661; *Goguen v Crowe* (1987) 40 CCLT 212 (Nova Scotia SC), a baby suffered cerebral palsy
following a forceps delivery; *Grey v Webster* (1984) 14 DLR (4th) 706, sterilisation operation
failed to render the plaintiff sterile; *Hobson v Munkley* (1976) 74 DLR (3d) 408 patient's ureter
damaged in the course of a tubal ligation operation.

[311] See Pattenden (1988) 7 CJQ 220. It is more difficult, for example, to establish that the
defendant has behaved fraudulently than to prove that he was negligent: *Hornal v Neuberger
Products Ltd* [1957] 1 QB 247.

[312] In *Dwyer v Roderick* (1983) 127 SJ 806 May LJ said that it was: 'to shut one's eyes to the
obvious if one denies that the burden of achieving something more than that mere balance of
probabilities is greater when one is investigating the complicated and sophisticated actions of a
qualified and experienced lawyer, doctor, accountant, builder or motor engineer than when one is
enquiring into the momentary inattention of the driver of a motor car in a simple running-down
action.'

[313] *Jackson & Powell on Professional Negligence*, 3rd edn, (1992), para 6.26. See also Robertson (1981) 44 MLR 457, 459 commenting on the 'strong pro-defendant policy' evident in
many medical negligence cases; Giesen (1993) 1 Med L Internl 3, 5.

may fairly be held to be—I will not say deserving of censure, but, at any rate, inexcusable.[314]

More rarely, perhaps, the courts also recognise that doctors are only human, and that even a conclusion that a defendant doctor has made a negligent mistake is not to be taken as a statement that the doctor is incompetent to practise medicine. This approach makes it easier for the court to make a finding of negligence without undermining the doctor's professional reputation.[315]

---

[314] (1968), [1993] 4 Med LR 393, 396. See also the comments of Lord Denning in *Roe v Minister of Health* [1954] 2 QB 66, 86–7; *Hatcher v Black* (1954) *The Times*, 2 July; *Whitehouse* (n 310 above), 658; *Hyde v Tameside Area Health Authority* (1981) reported at (1986) 2 PN 26. Similarly, in *Whitehouse* (n 310 above), 659, Lawton LJ commented that: 'The more serious the allegation the higher the degree of probability that is required. In my opinion allegations of negligence against medical practitioners should be considered as serious.'

[315] In *Whitehouse v Jordan* [1980] 1 All ER 650, 666 Donaldson LJ pointed out that very few professionals can claim never to have been negligent, and that often the only difference between those who are sued and their colleagues is that the error happens to have caused harm to the plaintiff; see also *Clark v MacLennan* [1983] 1 All ER 416, 433; *Thake v Maurice* [1984] 2 All ER 513, 523.

7

CAUSATION AND DEFENCES

A. Causation

1. Introduction

It is trite law that merely to show that a defendant was in breach of a duty owed to the plaintiff and that the plaintiff suffered damage does not suffice to ground an action in negligence. The defendant's breach must have caused the plaintiff's damage and, additionally, the damage must be such that the law regards it proper to hold the defendant responsible for it. These two requirements jointly constitute Causation; separately they are *Causation in Fact and Law* and *Legal Causation* or *Remoteness*. **7.01**

The concern here is whether there are considerations specific to medical law which call for a treatment of causation beyond that which can be found in standard works on the law of torts.[1] The answer is that there are. While the **7.02**

---

[1] See Fleming, J, *The Law of Torts*, 9th edn, LBC Information Services, 1998; and, particularly on Medical Negligence, Jones, M, *Medical Negligence* (Sweet and Maxwell, 1996), ch 5.

principles of causation may ordinarily be relatively straightforward, it is fair
to say that causation in the context of medical law is fraught with difficulty.[2]
This is due both to the complexity of the factual circumstances themselves
and to the (perhaps unnecessarily) complex nature of the law, when the
principles come to be applied to the facts. As for the former, the complicated
and, to some extent, indeterminate nature of medical science means that the
causal nexus between X and Y, while suspected, may be hard to demonstrate.
Indeed, it could be said that the more medicine is portrayed as a scientific
endeavour, rather than as an art or a combination of both art and science, the
more difficult it becomes on occasion to demonstrate to the satisfaction of the
law a causative link between breach and damage. As for the latter, the law
becomes ever more complex as it seeks to serve the twin aims of justice:
fairness to the patient and to the doctor. As Leggatt LJ put it in *Tahir v
Haringey HA*,[3] 'when a doctor has been at fault no court wishes to send his
patient away empty handed'. This, of course, is the crux. A breach of duty is
proved, or even admitted, and yet the doctor or hospital is found not liable
and the patient recovers nothing. The patient is left bemused. But, equally, if
whatever happened to the patient was not the result of the doctor's conduct, it
is hard to see why the doctor should be held liable. Only a system which
compensated damaged patients on the basis of need rather than proof of
someone else's misconduct could square this particular circle.

2. Causation in Fact and Law

(i) *Burden of Proof: Who bears it?*

7.03 In any examination of causation, the first question to ask is who bears the
burden of proving the causative link between breach of duty and damage. The
answer is unequivocally that in this, as in all other aspects of civil litigation, it
is the plaintiff who must prove causation. Proof must be on the balance of
probabilities. There was a brief period of time in which it was thought that, in
certain particular circumstances, medical law provided an exception to this
principle by reversing the burden and placing it on the defendant. As will be
discussed more fully below, it was Lord Wilberforce's speech in *McGhee v
National Coal Board*[4] that gave rise to this strain of reasoning. The plaintiff
had established a breach of duty, the failure to provide showers so as to be
able to wash off the brick dust which pervaded the work-place. The presence

---

[2] It was Lord Bridge in *Hotson v East Berkshire AHA* [1987] 2 All ER 909 who remarked,
'In some cases, perhaps particularly medical negligence cases, causation may be so shrouded in
mystery that the courts can only measure statistical chances.'
[3] Unreported (Jan 1995). For a Commentary, see [1996] 4 Med L Rev 92 (A Grubb).
[4] [1973] 1 WLR 1.

of the dust in the work-place was not itself a breach of duty. The result was that the brick dust continued to adhere to his skin while he cycled home. He contracted dermatitis. What he could not definitively demonstrate was that the extra time spent cycling home was causative of his dermatitis. Lord Wilberforce's speech was taken to mean that, in such a case, the burden of proof shifted to the defendant to show that his breach of duty did not cause the dermatitis. Certainly Pain J in *Clark v McLennan*[5] interpreted the speech in this way. In *Wilsher v Essex AHA*,[6] however, the House of Lords categorically reasserted that the burden of proof always remains with the plaintiff. *McGhee* was distinguished on its facts and Lord Wilberforce's speech was relegated by Lord Bridge to the status of a dissent. That marked the end of that brief period of heresy.

Of course, what *McGhee* and *Wilsher* drew attention to was the well-recognised fact of litigation in medical law, that proof of causation is often an extremely difficult hurdle for the plaintiff. The law appears to contemplate some kind of linear connection between X and Y, whereas in reality what is involved in medicine is often a series of interdependent and interacting events from which it is at best difficult to pluck one (the defendant's breach) and point to it as 'the cause'. The plaintiff's increased ill health may, for example, be as much the consequence of the natural progression of the disease as the defendant's breach. The defendant's breach may be only one of several independent or interacting causal agents, as was the case in *Wilsher*.[7] Or further, the state of medical science may be such that experts may properly disagree as to the exact aetiology of the plaintiff's condition, as in *Loveday v Renton*.[8] Obvious examples of this in common knowledge are the effects of passive smoking or radiation.   **7.04**

(ii) *Burden of Proof: What is it?*

(a) 'But For' Test

The standard approach to causation in the law of torts is represented by the   **7.05** 'but for' test: that the damage suffered by the plaintiff would not have been suffered but for the defendant's breach of duty. The assumption of the law is that it is possible to show (and, therefore, that the law should demand demonstration) that X would not have happened but for Y. The corollary

---

[5] [1983] 1 All ER 416.   [6] [1986] 3 All ER 801.
[7] The House of Lords found that there were at least 5 possible causes of the retrolental fibroplasia suffered by the plaintiff; see para 7.12.
[8] [1990] 1 Med LR 117, where the issue at stake was the relationship (if any) between the pertussis vaccine and brain damage. See also, *Kay v Ayrshire and Arran Health Board* [1987] 2 All ER 417.

is that if this cannot be demonstrated, causation is not proved and the defendant, regardless of any breach of duty, is not liable. While represented as a principle concerned with fact it is, of course, self-evident that what is involved is a matter of policy. A limit is placed on the potential liability of the defendant by demanding that a particular form of nexus be shown. And, as has been said, there are numerous circumstances, particularly in medical law, when this policy defeats the claim of the plaintiff. The clearest example is when the defendant's breach may have been part of the background leading to the plaintiff's damage. If the defendant can show that the damage would have occurred in any event, regardless of any breach of duty, then the plaintiff's action will fail. *Barnett v Kensington and Chelsea HMC*[9] was just such a case. The court found that the plaintiff would have died in any event, regardless of the defendant doctor's failure to provide proper medical care, because, by the time arsenic poisoning would have been diagnosed, it would have been too late to take any action to save him.

7.06 The difficulties associated with the 'but for' test in medical law are at their starkest when there are several causal factors contributing to the plaintiff's damage, or there are successive causes each of which is sufficient. The intrinsic complexity of medical evidence means, therefore, that if the law fails to mitigate the strict application of the 'but for' test, injustice may be done. One obvious mitigating device would be to *reverse the burden of proof*, providing certain conditions were met. As has been seen, tentative steps in this direction were firmly retraced by the House of Lords in *Wilsher*.[10] By contrast, a second mitigating device is an established part of the ordinary tort rules on causation. It may be relevant in medical law. It consists in the plaintiff being able to succeed if it can be shown that the defendant's breach was a *principal* or *substantial cause* of the damage suffered, if not the only cause (*Bonnington Castings v Wardlaw*).[11]

(b) Material Contribution

7.07 *Bonnington Castings* also made it clear that the defendant could be liable if the breach of duty, while not the sole or even a substantial cause, contributed in a material way to the damage suffered by the plaintiff. This is of some significance to the mitigation of the 'but for' test in medical law. In that case, there were two sources of the silica dust which the plaintiff inhaled, and because of which he contracted pneumoconiosis. The plaintiff could not point to the source of dust which was dubbed 'guilty', that is, arising from a breach of duty, as being the sole or even the more important source. But the plaintiff was allowed to succeed

---

[9] [1968] 1 All ER 1068.   [10] N 7 above.   [11] [1956] AC 613.

in his action by persuading the court to make an inference from the facts that the 'guilty' dust had made a material contribution to his illness.

The key factor was the court's preparedness, in the absence of any way of **7.08** knowing, with any degree of certainty, what actually caused the plaintiff's illness, to draw an inference of fact favourable to the plaintiff from all the available evidence. This is clearly, at bottom, a nice issue of judgment for any court. On one level, it can be represented as a matter of extremely technical legal analysis in which certain complex verbal formulae must be applied to the facts and, once applied, the solution to causation will emerge. More realistically, the court is ultimately in the business of seeking to honour what have been suggested as the two conflicting policy objectives, namely controlling liability while being fair to plaintiffs. Such a (more realistic or cynical) view would suggest that the verbal formulae are precisely that and little else. What the plaintiff and defendant must do is pile up as many factual arguments as they can muster in favour of their view of the case. The more facts, the more a court can find something to infer, or to deny that any inference can be drawn. Of course, once the decision is made, it will be expressed in the appropriate formulaic manner. But, while participating in this process, the parties to the litigation would be unwise to be so mesmerised by the complex taxonomy of causation that they overlook what is really going on.

The material contribution made by the defendant's breach may be to the **7.09** damage suffered by the plaintiff or to the risk of damage to which the plaintiff was exposed. This is the effect of the much discussed case of *McGhee*. Here, as in *Bonnington Castings*, the court was prepared to make an inference of fact, namely that the failure to provide showers materially contributed to the risk of contracting dermatitis from the brick dust. The reason for doing so was the lack of available evidence, such that the plaintiff could not meet the 'but for' test. Given the breach of duty by the defendant coupled with damage of the type which the duty was designed to avoid, the court was prompted to draw an inference of fact that the defendant had materially contributed to the risk of damage.

In their subsequent deconstruction of *McGhee*, the House of Lords in *Wilsher* **7.10** were anxious, as has been said, to reassert the basic principle that the burden of proof always remains with the plaintiff, who must show either that the damage would not have occurred but for the defendant's breach, or that the breach made a material contribution to it. For Lord Bridge in *Wilsher*, *McGhee* was merely a 'robust and pragmatic approach' to the undisputed primary facts. Thus, all that the court did in *McGhee* was to make a common sense inference of fact that increased exposure to the dust must have materially contributed to the plaintiff's dermatitis.

7.11   Of course, it is all very well to describe *McGhee* as common sense but it places the defendant in a well-nigh impossible situation. If the court is moved to draw an inference of fact because of the inherent uncertainty of the facts, the defendant cannot, *ex hypothesi*, disprove the inference (given the uncertainty!). Furthermore, to claim that an increase in the risk constitutes a material contribution is not only to make one step in the dark, but two. This is because it must also be assumed that the risk which was increased in fact materialised, since merely to increase a risk is not logically to cause anything. The underlying triumph of policy over logic is again laid bare.

7.12   The difficult question for the medical lawyer, however, is when will a court draw an inference of fact based on pragmatism or common sense. Unfortunately, there are a few pointers in the cases which can serve as reliable guides in the uncertain world which is the reality of medical science. One plausible guide is the distinction which may be drawn between uncertainty created by the existence of a range of contributing factors, any or all of which may be judged cumulatively to have made a material contribution, and uncertainty created by the existence of a number of possible contributing factors each of which is separate and distinct. Where the factors are cumulative, the court, following *Bonnington Castings*, has the option to find the defendant liable. If the factors taken together led to the plaintiff's damage, then the defendant's breach, as a contributing factor, may be held to have made a contribution which can be described as material, if it is not *de minimis*. By contrast, where the damage could have been caused by any one of a number of distinct factors, the material contribution principle will not work in the plaintiff's favour. This is illustrated by *Wilsher*. In *Wilsher*, the baby's RLF (retrolental fibroplasia) could have arisen from at least five separate and distinct factors. The defendant's breach was responsible for only one of these. It was impossible to assert that the breach was the sole or principal cause of the RLF. It was equally untenable to argue that the breach materially contributed to it. It may have had no effect whatsoever. What the House of Lords was deciding in *Wilsher* was that the sort of inference of fact made in *McGhee* was not available unless an existing risk, in this case of RFL, was enhanced. Excessive oxygen in *Wilsher* could only logically be said to have enhanced or increased the risk of RFL if it, in fact, caused RFL, since there were five distinct, quite separate, possible causes, which did not interact with each other. And, of course, if it could have been shown that excessive oxygen caused RFL, the plaintiff's case would have been much simpler. *Bonnington Castings* would have brought the case home, if not the straightforward application of the 'but for' test. It follows that the reasoning in *McGhee* based on material contribution to the risk of damage only applies where the risks are cumulative and interact, and not when they are discrete and separate. And, of course, as has been seen, it only applies then so as to give the court the option of finding the inference proved, rather than compelling such a conclusion.

Beyond that particular guideline, the territory of material contribution **7.13** becomes virtually impossible to chart. Where there is a breach of duty, and uncertainty as to what may have led to what, the court has the choice of favouring the plaintiff or the defendant. If the court chooses the latter, it can merely decide that the 'but for' test is not satisfied and the case is over. If, on the other hand, it is thought proper to assist the plaintiff in pursuit of a remedy, once a defendant is judged to have breached his duty, the Court in effect has two principal policy options. The most effective option, of course, is to reverse the burden of proof. But this has been rejected. The alternative is for the Court to use the principle of material contribution to draw appropriate inferences of fact.[12] The drawback for the plaintiff is the need to show that the contributing factors were cumulative rather than discrete and that an inference favourable to the plaintiff should be drawn. The drawback for both parties is the lack of certainty such an obviously policy-led approach represents.[13] These difficulties were rehearsed in the judgment of the Canadian Supreme Court in *Snell v Farrell*.[14] In *Snell*, Sopinka J revisited *McGhee* in the light of the House of Lords' decision in *Wilsher*. Beginning from the point that '[p]roof of causation in medical malpractice cases is often difficult for the patient', Sopinka J took the view that Lord Bridge's endorsement of a 'robust and pragmatic approach to the . . . facts' was a reminder to the courts not to adopt what he described as a 'too rigid application' of the traditional approach to causation. He cited with approval Lord Salmon's view in *Alphacell Ltd v Woodward*[15] that causation is 'essentially a practical question of fact which can best be answered by ordinary common sense rather than abstract metaphysical theory'. Relying on the crucial notion of drawing inferences, Sopinka J went on to state that '[i]n many medical malpractice cases, the facts

---

[12] It was Nourse LJ in *Fitzgerald v Lane* [1987] QB 781 who described *Wilsher*'s robust and pragmatic approach as the 'benevolent principle [which] smiles on . . . factual uncertainties and melts them all away'. See further *Lybert v Warrington* (1995), The Times, 17 May, CA.

[13] For a very helpful summary of propositions relating to causation, see Grubb, Commentary on *Tahir v Haringey Health Authority*, 4 Med L Rev 92. Grubb suggests that in cases of medical negligence, where 'causation is often difficult to establish', 'the plaintiff must establish one of the following: 1. that 'but for' the negligence he would not have suffered *any* injury (plaitiff recovers for all his injuries); or 2. that 'but for the negligence he would not have suffered *an identifiable part* (X) or *particular aggravation* (Y) of the injuries (plaintiff recovers for X and Y respectively); or 3. that the negligence *materially contributed* to the whole injury (Z) or an identifiable part (X) or particular aggravation (Y) of the injuries (plaintiff recovers for Z, X and Y respectively)' (emphasis in original). [14] (1990) 72 DLR (4th) 289.

[15] [1972] 2 All ER 475.

lie particularly within the knowledge of the defendant. In these circumstances, very little affirmative evidence on the part of the plaintiff will justify the drawing of an inference of causation in the absence of evidence to the contrary.' This was not, he emphasised, a matter of shifting the burden of proof or even the burden of adducing evidence. 'The legal or ultimate burden remains with the plaintiff, but in the absence of evidence to the contrary adduced by the defendant, an inference of causation may be drawn, although positive or scientific proof of causation has not been adduced. If some evidence to the contrary is adduced by the defendant, the trial judge is entitled to take account of Lord Mansfield's famous precept [referred to earlier, that] "[i]t is certainly a maxim that all evidence is to be weighed according to the proof which it was in the power of one side to have produced, and in the power of the other to have contradicted it".[16] It could be said that English law could greatly benefit if the courts were more ready to adopt Sopinka J's approach to causation in this most troubling area of litigation.

3. The Place of *Bolam*[17] in Causation

7.14 *Bolam* has traditionally been seen as the *locus classicus* of the test for the quantum of care required of a doctor by the law, so as to comply with his duty of care.[18] The question arose in the case of *Bolitho v City and Hackney HA*[19] as to whether *Bolam* also had a role to play in determining issues of causation. In *Bolitho*, the responsible doctor failed to attend a child patient, despite two separate requests from the senior nurse. The child suffered total respiratory collapse and a cardiac arrest and subsequently died. It was accepted during the course of the trial that had the child been intubated, the respiratory failure, had it occurred, would not have led to cardiac arest, and that such intubation would have had to be carried out before the final catastrophic event. The doctor's failure to attend (either in person or through a deputy) was conceded to be a breach of duty. The question then arose whether this breach caused the child's death.

7.15 It will be noticed that the breach of duty relied on by the plaintiff was the doctor's failure to attend the child, rather than a failure to intubate. This had significant consequences for the approach to causation adopted by the courts at all levels. The evidence given by the doctor was that, even if she had attended, she would not have intubated the child. Intubation of a two-year old child was, she said, a major intervention not free from risks. The symptoms of the child did not warrant it. On a straightforward application of the 'but for'

---

[16] *Blatch v Archer* (1774) 1 Cowp 63.
[17] *Bolam v Friern Hospital Management Committee* [1957] 2 All ER 118.
[18] But see *Bolitho v City and Hackney HA* [1997] 4 All ER 771.   [19] N 14 above.

test, the plaintiff fails at that point, provided, of course, that the defendant's evidence is believed, which it was. There is, however, an obvious reservation to be entered. As a precedent, does not such an approach lend itself to self-serving, *ex post facto* justification? Is it not particularly undesirable to base causation on this approach, when there may be evidence to suggest that the failure to carry out a procedure (on the basis that the defendant states that he would not have carried it out), itself constitutes a further breach of duty? It appears counter-intuitive to allow a defendant to avoid liability by pleading in aid the fact that he would have compounded the original breach of duty with a further breach.

Faced with this apparent difficulty, both the Court of Appeal (with Simon **7.16** Brown LJ dissenting) and the House of Lords (with Lord Browne-Wilkinson speaking for the House), decided that something had to be done. What they decided to do was, having asked the first question—would the doctor have attended the child?—and received a negative response, to ask a second question—*should* the doctor have attended the child? If the evidence was that she should have, then, their Lordships held, causation would be established. As it happens, the evidence was sufficiently equivocal to absolve the defendant.

Lord Browne-Wilkinson referred with approval to the judgment of Hobhouse **7.17** LJ in *Joyce v Merton, Sutton and Wandsworth HA.*[20] In that case, Hobhouse LJ, commenting on the Court of Appeal's judgment in *Bolitho*, said, '[the situation which arose in *Bolitho*] involves the factual situation that the original fault did not itself cause the injury but that this was because there would have been some further fault on the part of the defendants'. The response to this line of reasoning must first be that the 'original fault', if relied upon as the breach of duty on which the plaintiff's case is based, is the relevant fault for the law of causation. Secondly, the 'further fault' does not exist save as a hypothesis and is unrelated to the conduct of the particular defendant. While it is understandable that the Court would not want to be seen to allow a defendant to 'get away with it', it is at least doubtful whether the law of causation is the appropriate mechanism to achieve this. What the doctor *should* have done may be evidence of what the doctor *would* have done, but it is no more than that. As Grubb puts it, commenting on the Court of Appeal's decision, '[I]t is relevant to know what *should* have been done in deciding what a particular doctor *would* have done, but it cannot be conclusive . . . The fact that some doctors would have intubated the plaintiff while others would not cannot determine what *this doctor* would have done.'[21]

---

[20] [1996] 7 Med LR 1.
[21] Commentary (1993) Med L Rev 241. For a sustained assault on Hobhouse LJ's judgment in *Joyce*, see Grubb, Commentary (1996) Med L Rev 86.

7.18 The House of Lords' approach, therefore, is at best odd. What the doctor should or should not have done relates to her duty of care to the patient. It has nothing to do with establishing a causative link between breach (non-attendance in this particular case) and the child's injury and death. Causation purports to be a matter of fact, or, in cases of omission such as *Bolitho*, a matter of plausible hypothesis based on evidence of the past practice *of the defendant*. What others would have done cannot be conclusive.

7.19 It may seem that this is a somewhat churlish response to *Bolitho*, given that it sought to mitigate the difficulties encountered by the plaintiff in dealing with an entirely hypothetical situation: did the non-attendance cause the child's injury? The response must be that the route taken by way of mitigation is incoherent even by the standards of the law of causation. It is no answer that it allowed the House of Lords to endorse the move away from *Bolam* as the basis for establishing a breach of duty, which had been signalled by the Court of Appeal. Although this is particularly welcome, it is irrelevant for current purposes. What is relevant is that, in cases in which the breach of duty alleged is an omission to act, the legal enquiry into causation, which is represented as factual, will be converted into a normative investigation as to what the defendant should have done. Admittedly, it is clear from what has gone before, that the supposedly factual enquiry as to causation is not free from an accretion of policy issues. None the less, it has always ultimately resolved itself into a factual issue, even if the Courts have sometimes decided to infer one set of facts rather than another. *Bolitho* represents a significant departure from this approach. By introducing a normative element into causation in this way, it has added to the complexity (and, some would say, incoherence) of the law. It only remains to say that the alternative approach for the plaintiff in *Bolitho* was to have focused on the failure to intubate as the relevant breach of duty. There was little doubt that factual causation could link *this* breach to the child's subsequent injury and death. Had the case been approached in this way, the law of causation may have avoided the strange flirtation with *Bolam*, even at a time when *Bolam's* death-knell is being rung.

4. Causation and Breach of the Duty to Inform

7.20 Where a doctor has breached his duty to obtain a properly informed consent, the patient, if he is to succeed in an action in negligence, must still show that the breach caused the damage complained of. The damage, of course, is the fact that a procedure was carried out without consent. It is immaterial that it may have been carried out with all due skill. The proposition that the breach must cause the damage translates here into the assertion by the plaintiff that, if he had been properly informed, he would not have gone ahead with the procedure.

Obviously, it is open to the plaintiff, with the benefit of 'twenty-twenty vision' to assert that he would not have consented. Provided he is believable, this would clinch the case. Causation would be established on the basis his of say-so. Such a subjective approach to causation, however, may appear to tip the scales too heavily in favour of the plaintiff. One option is to insist on an objective test: what would the reasonable person in the plaintiff's position have done? The difficulty with this alternative is obvious. It rests the test of causation on a fiction, the decision of the reasonable person, rather than on the evidence of the particular patient. A further option is to cleave to the subjective approach, but require that the evidence adduced by the plaintiff be judged against some test of reasonableness, so as to inject some sort of check on the resort to hindsight. This last, hybrid position most closely reflects the current position in English law,[22] as is discussed more fully in Chapter 3, paras 3.140–3.142.

Loss of Chance

The argument here is that as a consequence of the defendant's breach of duty, the plaintiff did not receive any, or any proper, treatment and thereby suffered damage. In ordinary circumstances, there is no reason why the plaintiff should not be compensated for any such damage, even if it takes the form of not having his condition improved or having it become worse, rather than some discrete, identifiable additional damage. If the plaintiff can show that this change for the worse in his condition was, on the balance of probabilities, the consequence of the defendant's breach, the 'but for' rule will apply and recovery will follow. **7.21**

The problems arise when the evidence demonstrates that, even if the defendant had complied with his duty of care, it was more likely than not that the plaintiff's condition would *not* have improved. The plaintiff's alleged damage, then, is the loss of a *chance* of improvement, but a chance which was less than a 50 per cent chance. Clearly the 'but for' test cannot be satisfied in that the plaintiff cannot show that, on the balance of probabilities, but for the defendant's breach he would have recovered or his condition would have improved. **7.22**

In *Hotson v East Berkshire AHA*,[23] it was alleged by the plaintiff that the delay of five days in diagnosing the fracture of his left femoral epiphysis when he fell from a tree caused him to lose a chance of complete recovery. The chance was put at 25 per cent. The plaintiff argued that although there was always a 75 per cent chance of permanent injury, the defendant's breach made that a 100 per cent certainty. The defendant's response was straightforward. The **7.23**

---

[22] See *Smith v Barking, Havering and Brentwood HA* [1994] 5 Med LR 285 and *Smith v Tunbridge Wells HA* [1994] 5 Med LR 334.   [23] [1987] AC 750.

plaintiff's case must be established on a balance of probabilities, that is, that it was at least 51 per cent certain that the defendant's breach caused the damage. The evidence, the defendant argued, failed to meet that criterion. It was the fall from the tree that must have been more likely than not the cause of the plaintiff's damage. The law treats past facts, established on a balance of probabilities, as certain.[24] Hence, it was certain that the cause of the plaintiff's damage was not the delay in treatment. Simon Brown J, at first instance, preferred the plaintiff's argument. He held that the issue before him was not one of causation but of quantification; the proper quantum of damages, given the defendant's breach of duty. Assessing the damages arising from the avascular necrosis caused by the fracture at £46,000, he then awarded the plaintiff 25 per cent of this amount (£11,500) to compensate for the 25 per cent chance of avoiding permanent injury which had been lost.

7.24 On appeal, the Court of Appeal affirmed the High Court's decision. In the House of Lords, however, their Lordships saw the facts as raising an issue of causation. As Lord Bridge put it, 'on a balance of probabilities the injury caused by the plaintiff's fall left insufficient blood vessels intact to keep the epiphysis alive. This amounts to a finding of fact that the fall was the sole cause of the vascular necrosis.' Thus, the House of Lords held that the appeal must be allowed 'on the narrow ground that the plaintiff had failed to establish a cause of action'.

7.25 Standing back from the particular details of the case, it is clear that *Hotson* gave the House of Lords at least two opportunities to develop the law in a way more favourable to the plaintiff. It will be recalled that the position which the law puts the plaintiff in is to insist that, even though the defendant has been shown to be in breach of duty, the plaintiff must prove *on the facts* that the breach caused the damage suffered. By the very nature of things, in the sort of cases under discussion, this is precisely what the plaintiff cannot do. Thus, one opportunity open to the House of Lords was to develop the law by allowing 'loss of a chance' as a separate head of damage. Alternatively, their Lordships could have applied the reasoning in *McGhee*, even after its interpretation in *Wilsher*, and held that it was permissible in such cases to draw an inference of fact based on 'robust and pragmatic common sense'. Curiously, the unusual facts of *Hotson* prevented the House of Lords from adopting this latter course. Simon Brown J had held, as a fact, that the prospect of recovery was no more than 25 per cent. This somewhat precise quantification of the chance prevented any subsequent inference. If, instead, Simon Brown J had

---

[24] See *Judge v Huntingdon HA* [1995] 6 Med LR 223, citing Lord Diplock in *Mallet v McMonagle* [1970] 116, 'Anything that is more probable than not is certain'.

merely held that there had been a chance of a full recovery, that it was significant, and that it had been lost, it could have been open to the court to categorise this as having materially contributed to the plaintiff's damage and thus to have satisfied that test of causation. Admittedly, *Wilsher* makes it clear that merely to increase the risk of injury does not make the defendant necessarily liable. It has, however, an evidential quality allowing the court to infer that the defendant's breach made *the* difference as regards the plaintiff's damage. The same reasoning could apply to loss of a chance. To contribute materially to the plaintiff's prospects of permanent injury, denying him the chance of treatment, is just another way of materially increasing the risk of damage. Following *Wilsher*, therefore, the House of Lords could have said that, as a matter of principle, whatever the facts in the particular case may have been, a court may infer, where the facts allow, that the defendant's breach materially contributed to the plaintiff's damage in circumstances where what the plaintiff lost was the chance of treatment which would have been beneficial. After all, it could be said that the only difference between *McGhee* (even after *Wilsher*) and *Hotson* is that in *McGhee* it was impossible to estimate the extent of the increased risk, thereby allowing the court a free hand to draw inferences. By contrast, in *Hotson* the plaintiff had sought to put some estimate on the risk and thereby lost the case by pre-empting the court's ability to draw any inference. It is a strange policy if the law prefers the unknown to the estimation, in circumstances where nothing can be known for sure.

A further supporting argument in favour of allowing the plaintiff to recover is **7.26** that based on analogous cases from the law of contract. The most obvious case is *Kitchen v Royal Air Force Association*[25] in which the loss of a chance was clearly held to be recoverable. The solicitor's breach of duty in *Kitchen* had prevented the plaintiff from pursuing a civil action. The plaintiff recovered damages based on an estimation of his likely chance of success. Lord Bridge in *Hotson* dismissed the analogy somewhat airily, referring to (without specifying) 'formidable difficulties in the way of accepting the analogy'. It would be odd law, however, if a patient treated privately could maintain an action in contract against his doctor and recover damages for the loss of a chance of recovery or improvement, while a patient treated in the public sector and, therefore, restricted to an action in tort could not.

Perhaps a final point could be made in favour of allowing the plaintiff to **7.27** recover. It can be argued that, while the plaintiff is entitled to more than a fair share of sympathy, his position is no different from lots of other situations in which the defendant's breach is egregious but the plaintiff cannot establish causation and, therefore, loses. *Barnett*[26] is one such well known example.

---

[25] [1958] 1 WLR 563.   [26] N 9 above.

The answer may be, of course, that the fact that the plaintiff cannot establish causation is what is under discussion. And, given the policy 'tweaks' which the courts in *Bonnington Castings* and *McGhee* were prepared to contemplate, why should they not go a 'tweak' further?

7.28   Of course, to allow the plaintiff to recover in situations such as *Hotson* would not put an end to the legal problems which arise. The issue of fairness raises its head again. Simon Brown J's approach, it will be recalled, was to award the plaintiff a proportion of the total damages which would have been recoverable if the defendant had been wholly to blame. If, however, the court were to adopt an approach based on causation through an inference of fact (with no evidence of percentages before it), the plaintiff would be held to have made his case and the defendant would be completely (not proportionately) liable. This may seem unfair and may again, as in *Hotson* itself, be a triumph of logic over common sense. One answer could be to discount the plaintiff's damages (as in *Kitchen*) by an appropriate factor. The difficulty with this, however, is obvious. The court has no evidence before it as to what discount is appropriate. Indeed, the moment such evidence were submitted, the court would be bound by *Hotson*, either to deny the plaintiff any damages (if the discount was 50 per cent or more) or award the plaintiff the full claim, (if the discount was less than 50 per cent). The solution to these problems is not immediately obvious. Certainly, it is unlikely that this particular form of development in the law will endear itself to the courts.

7.29   An alternative opportunity to develop the law is at the same time more radical and yet more obvious. It is simply to recognise loss of a chance as being a head of damage recoverable in its own right. The premise again, it will be recalled, is that justice requires that a way be found to compensate a plaintiff when the defendant is in breach of duty and the plaintiff has suffered damage, in this case, the chance of treatment which could, perhaps, have been beneficial.

7.30   Their Lordships in *Hotson*, and particularly Lord MacKay, did not rule out the possibility of recovery by the plaintiff, although it appears that Lord MacKay was considering loss of a chance within the existing law of causation, rather than as a separate head of damage. It remains, therefore, a matter for further argument whether a plaintiff may bring an action based clearly and unequivocally on a claim that a chance of recovery or improvement was lost through the defendant's breach of duty. Using the facts of *Hotson*, the plaintiff would be able to point to the evidence of the lost chance, and to quantify it. The court would be able to respond to this factual evidence and indeed encourage it, rather then see the law continue to favour doubt over some sort of certainty. The damages to be awarded to the plaintiff would not be the 100 per cent recovery of all that flowed from the damage suffered, but merely 100 per cent of the lost chance, that is the proportion of the total damage attributable to the lost chance.

5. Causation in Law: Intervening Acts

There is little for causation in medical law in such issues as the impact of **7.31** intervening acts on the defendant's possible liability. The ordinary rules of tort law apply. The question for the court, where it is alleged that the intervening act of a third party has broken the chain of causation, is clearly a mixed question of law and fact. If the evidence demonstrates that there was some act of a third party which intervened between the defendant's breach of duty and the plaintiff's damage, the court must decide what degree of responsibility should still reside with the defendant. The word 'responsibility' is used to seek to demonstrate that the court, as ever, has a choice and that, essentially, the choice is a matter of policy. The policy at issue is, of course, that a defendant should only be held liable if his conduct is sufficiently blameworthy. This translates, in any particular case involving allegations of third-party intervention, into whether the defendant's breach of duty is sufficiently blameworthy that he should continue to attract condemnation through an award of damages.

Although there is little in the cases in medical law which can add to these **7.32** general propositions, there are a number of matters which warrant comment. The first is the case of *Knightley v Johns*,[27] in which it was made clear that a subsequent breach of duty by a third party may not break the chain of causation, and thereby absolve the defendant of his breach of duty, if the later breach was reasonably foreseeable. In *Knightley*, Stephenson LJ sought to prescribe some kind of hierarchy of third-party interventions, each of which might have a different effect on the defendant's liability: '[n]egligent conduct is more likely to break the chain of causation than conduct which is not; positive acts will more easily constitute new causes than inactions'. The difficulty with this type of 'analysis by list' is that it omits to identify and analyse the underlying criteria which might give rise to these various conclusions. Given that the criterion is ultimately accepted by Stephenson LJ as being 'common sense rather than logic on the facts and circumstances of each case', it may be wiser to avoid the formulaic approach and concentrate on the complex array of factors which persuade a court to shift responsibility away from a doctor in breach of his duty onto someone else.

A further matter warranting consideration is what is the status of an inter- **7.33** vention by a third party which takes the form of a failure to act—that is, there

---

[27] [1982] 1 WLR 349.

is no *actus interveniens*. There is some authority in the general law of torts for the proposition that an omission to act by a third party cannot intervene to break the chain of causation. This was the view expressed by Goff LJ in *Muirhead v Industrial Tank Specialities*.[28] In medical law, in the context of a doctor–patient relationship, it is difficult to sustain this approach. Arguably, it gives too much force to a literal interpretation of *actus*, rather than see it as conduct, a more neutral term embracing both commission and omission. Furthermore, given that doctors are liable for omissions once a doctor-patient relationship can be shown to exist, a failure to act, in breach of duty, which causes damage, should be eligible to be regarded as a cause, and in appropriate circumstances, an intervening cause.

7.34 A third issue relates to the plaintiff's conduct. It will be recalled that what is under discussion here is conduct of another which may break the chain of causation between the defendant's breach of duty and the plaintiff's damage. So, here, it must be assumed that the doctor is in breach of his duty. It is submitted that, in appropriate circumstances, the unreasonable behaviour of the plaintiff could be judged to be contributory negligence (as set out in para 738). Equally, in appropriate circumstances, there seems no reason in principle why it should not be regarded as an intervening cause, absolving the defendant. In such a case, the plaintiff would become the author of his own misfortune. That said, it is further submitted that, before a plaintiff would be held in medical law to have brought his own damage on himself, the court would probably demand a high degree of knowledge by the plaintiff of what he was doing, its implications and that it was not appropriate and would expose him to a risk of harm, and that he acted voluntarily and not under any duress or other factor reducing the capacity to choose.

7.35 A final issue, in the context of intervening cause, is the situation in which the plaintiff refuses further treatment. Again, the beginning point of analysis is a breach of duty by the defendant doctor. Can the plaintiff's refusal constitute an intervening cause? Arguing from first principles, it would appear that it should not be so regarded. A patient who is competent is entitled in law to refuse treatment. It is hard to see, therefore, how a refusal to undergo further treatment, so as to rectify a previous breach of duty by the doctor, can be judged adversely. The law may, however, be less simple. The proposition that a competent patient has the right to refuse is, of course, relevant to circumstances in which the patient's personal integrity and inviolability is at stake. Here, it could be argued that the law is concerned with something slightly different. The plaintiff has had treatment. All that is asked is that the doctor

---

[28] [1985] 3 All ER 705.

(or another) have the opportunity to take remedial action (for example, intervene surgically to ensure that an operation on the knee which was not done properly does not leave the patient with a permanent limp. Any difference, however, is at best superficial. The integrity of the patient is as much at stake here as in other situations. It would follow that the patient's refusal of further treatment, even if unreasonable or irrational, should not and does not serve as an intervening cause to break the chain of causation. An extreme example in support of this proposition can be found in the case of *Emeh v Chelsea and Kensington AHA*.[29] A doctor was found to be in breach of duty in not performing properly an operation to sterilise the plaintiff. She became pregnant and brought an action to recover, *inter alia*, the increased costs associated with the pregnancy and birth of a further child. The trial judge found that her failure subsequently to obtain an abortion was unreasonable and thereby broke the chain of causation. The Court of Appeal in three strongly worded judgments rejected this view. The Court went out of its way to make it plain that a woman's choice not to undergo an abortion should not be regarded as a reason for absolving the defendant doctor, whose breach of duty had confronted her with the very dilemma she sought to avoid.

6. Legal Causation and Remoteness

7.36 Again, the question here is whether there are any issues of remoteness of damage or legal causation which are peculiar to medical law. The answer is that the general rules of remoteness in the law of torts apply and that there is nothing of significance for the medical lawyer. That said, it may be worth adding that, in so far as the rules on remoteness embody conclusions of social and economic policy, they are applied and must be understood in the light of the application of those conclusions of policy to the practice of medicine. Thus, what is reasonably foreseeable, that is to say, what the defendant will pay for, must be analysed and understood against the values and economic circumstances according to which medicine is practised in the UK.

B. Defences

7.37 There are several potential defences available to a defendant in a medical negligence action but, in practice, with the exception of limitation, they are rarely relevant, given the nature of the relationship between doctor and patient. The defences that will be considered here are contributory negligence, *volenti non fit injuria*, *ex turpi causa non oritur actio*, and limitation of action.

---

[29] [1984] 3 All ER 1044.

1. Contributory Negligence

7.38 A doctor frequently needs the patient's co-operation, for example, to make an accurate diagnosis or for the purpose of administering treatment. Sometimes this will be absolutely vital. The doctor requires accurate information regarding the patient's symptoms and medical history. Similarly, the co-operation of the patient may be essential in implementing a treatment regime, for example, with regard to taking medication correctly, or returning for further treatment or tests. If the patient fails to follow proper instructions and this is a cause of his injuries, then it will be possible to argue that the patient has been contributorily negligent, or in an extreme case that his conduct is the sole cause of the damage.[30] Alternatively, where a patient has failed to communicate the nature of the symptoms from which she is suffering, the conclusion may simply be that the doctor was not negligent in failing to make a correct diagnosis on the basis of the available information.[31]

Law Reform (Contributory Negligence) Act 1945

7.39 Section 1 of the Law Reform (Contributory Negligence) Act 1945 provides that where damage is attributable partly to the fault of the defendant and partly to the fault of the plaintiff, then the award of damages may be reduced by reason of the plaintiff's contributory negligence.[32] The reduction will be to such extent as the court thinks just and equitable having regard to the plaintiff's share in responsibility for the damage. The Act applies to actions in contract where the defendant's negligent breach of contract would have given rise to liability in the tort of negligence independently of the existence of the contract.[33] Accordingly, the defence will be available in virtually all actions arising out of private medical treatment, since the obligations imposed by the contract are normally the same as the duty to exercise reasonable care in the tort of negligence. On the other hand, where:

---

[30] *Venner v North East Essex Area Health Authority* (1987) *The Times*, 21 February; *Murrin v Janes* [1949] 4 DLR 403, 406 (Newfd SC).

[31] *Morrison v Forsyth* [1995] 6 Med LR 6, Court of Session, where a general practitioner was found not liable for failing to visit a patient because the seriousness of the patient's condition was not made clear in the course of a telephone conversation; *Gordon v Wilson* [1992] 3 Med LR 401, Court of Session (Outer House); *Friedsam v Ng* [1994] 3 WWR 294 (BCCA).

[32] Section 4 provides that fault means 'negligence, breach of statutory duty or other act or omission which gives rise to a liability in tort or would, apart from this Act, give rise to the defence of contributory negligence'. The Act probably applies to actions in trespass to the person: *Barnes v Nayer* (1986) *The Times*, 19 December, CA; *Wasson v Chief Constable of the Royal Ulster Constabulary* [1987] 8 NIJB 34; *Murphy v Culhane* [1977] QB 94; cf *Lane v Holloway* [1968] 1 QB 379.

[33] *Forsikringsaktieselskapet Vesta v Butcher* [1988] 2 All ER 43, CA, approving the analysis of Hobhouse J at [1986] 2 All ER 488, 508.

(a) liability does not depend on negligence but arises from breach of a strict contractual duty; or

(b) liability arises from breach of a contractual obligation which is expressed in terms of exercising reasonable care, but does not correspond to a common law duty of care which would exist independently of the contract, apportionment under the legislation is not available.[34]

Thus, in the rare circumstances where a patient was able to establish that the doctor had given a contractual warranty to achieve a specific result, this would fall into category (a) and the damages could not be apportioned for contributory negligence. It is unlikely that there are circumstances where category (b) could be relevant to the doctor–patient relationship.

Although, in theory, there is no reason why contributory negligence should not **7.40** apply in a claim for medical negligence, in practice the defence is rarely invoked successfully, and this is reflected in a comparative dearth of cases.[35] It may be that the plea is considered to be inappropriate, given the inequality between the respective positions of doctor and patient. Patients do not generally question the advice or conduct of their doctors, even when they are aware that their condition is deteriorating or not improving. If the patient has ignored the doctor's advice (for example, by discharging himself from hospital or failing to return for further treatment) it may be easier to establish the defence. It would have to be shown that a reasonable person would have been aware of the significance of the advice, which will depend upon the nature of the advice and whether it was clear to the patient. Moreover, in some circumstances there may well be a responsibility upon the doctor to adopt a system for following up patients who do not comply with advice to re-attend for further treatment or tests. In fact, by raising a plea of contributory negligence, a defendant may highlight the extent of the doctor's duty to take special care in giving the patient instructions, and making sure that the patient understands both the instructions and the importance of strictly adhering to them. In *Marshall v Rogers*,[36] for example, the defendant alleged that the plaintiff's injury was caused by his own negligence in failing to follow the instructions that he had been given and to report his symptoms. It was held, however, that where a dangerous remedy was being attempted, the doctor was negligent in delegating his own professional duty to decide the true meaning of the patient's progressive symptoms to the patient himself, especially given that the patient was only able to make a subjective assessment. The defendant should have conducted daily tests.

---

[34] ibid; *Barclays Bank plc v Fairclough Building Ltd* [1994] 3 WLR 1057, CA.

[35] There would appear to be no reported case in this country in which the court has had to make a finding of contributory negligence against a patient. See Giesen, D, *International Medical Malpractice Law (1988)*, para 236; Picard, E, *Legal Liability of Doctors and Hospitals in Canada*, (2nd edn 1984), 243–7.   [36] [1943] 4 DLR 68, 77.

7.41 Some Canadian courts have made findings of contributory negligence against careless patients. In *Brushett v Cowan*,[37] the plaintiff was contributorily negligent in engaging in ordinary activities without crutches following a bone biopsy on her leg, because she had failed to ask for clear instructions regarding the use of the crutches. A failure to have a post-operative check-up, as suggested by the doctor, has been held to be negligent,[38] and in *Crossman v Stewart*,[39] a patient who obtained prescription drugs from an unorthodox source, and continued to use the drugs on a prolonged basis without obtaining prescription renewals or consulting the 'prescribing' physician, was described as 'foolhardy in the extreme'. She was held to be responsible for two-thirds of the damage to her eyesight caused by the side-effects of the drug.

2. *Volenti Non Fit Injuria*

7.42 *Volenti non fit injuria* consists of a voluntary agreement by the plaintiff to absolve the defendant from the legal consequences of an unreasonable risk of harm created by the defendant, where the plaintiff has full knowledge of both the nature and extent of the risk. This should not be confused with *consent* to medical treatment which provides a defence to what would otherwise be the tort of battery. The patient who consents to medical treatment does not thereby consent to run the risk of negligence by the doctor.[40]

7.43 The one situation where the *volenti* defence could plausibly apply to a medical negligence action is in the case of suicide by a patient in circumstances where the doctor was under a duty to take reasonable precautions to prevent a suicide attempt. In *Kirkham v Chief Constable of Greater Manchester Police*,[41] the Court of Appeal accepted that *volenti* could apply to a claim brought on behalf of the estate of a suicide or by a person who suffered injuries in an unsuccessful attempt, but said that the defence would only arise where the person was 'of sound mind'. Although the deceased in *Kirkham* was legally sane and his suicide was a deliberate and conscious act, none the less he 'was suffering from clinical depression. His judgment was impaired . . . [H]e was not truly *volens*.[42] Thus although insanity is not essential in order to defeat the

---

[37] (1987) 40 DLR (4th) 488; aff'd (1990) 69 DLR (4th) 743 (Newfd CA).
[38] *Fredette v Wiebe* [1986] 5 WWR 222 (BCSC).
[39] (1977) 82 DLR (3d) 677, 686 (BCSC). It is also possible that unreasonable behaviour by a patient after the defendant's negligent conduct could be characterised as a failure to mitigate his loss. In *Brain v Mador* (1985) 32 CCLT 157 (Ont CA) a patient who failed to take steps to seek further medical advice following a vasectomy which had developed complications was held to have acted unreasonably, and his damages were reduced by 50 per cent for failing to mitigate the loss.
[40] See *Freeman v Home Office* [1984] 1 All ER 1036, 1044, *per* Sir John Donaldson MR.
[41] [1990] 2 WLR 987.
[42] ibid, 992–3, *per* Lloyd LJ. See also *per* Farquharson LJ at 997.

volenti defence as some impairment of judgment will suffice, [43] it may be that suicides who cannot be categorised as suffering from some form of mental illness which impairs judgment will be met with this defence.

3. *Ex Turpi Causa Non Oritur Actio* and Other Policy Factors

(a) *Ex Turpi Causa*

The defendant in *Kirkham v Chief Constable of Greater Manchester Police* also argued that the principle *ex turpi causa non oritur actio* applied. The Court of Appeal accepted that the *ex turpi causa* defence is not confined to criminal conduct, but would apply to illegal or immoral conduct by the plaintiff 'if in all the circumstances it would be an affront to the public conscience to grant the plaintiff the relief which he seeks.[44] Awarding damages following a suicide would not 'affront the public conscience', at least where there was medical evidence that the suicide was 'not in full possession of his mind'.[45] Farquharson LJ said that an action could hardly be said to be grounded in immorality where 'grave mental instability' on the part of the victim has been proved, although 'the position may well be different where the victim is wholly sane'.[46] In the context of a claim following a suicide attempt it would appear that there is considerable overlap between the *ex turpi causa* defence and the *volenti* defence.[47]

7.44

The defence of *ex turpi causa* rests upon a principle of public policy that, in some cases, it would be inappropriate and bring the legal system into disrepute to permit a plaintiff to base an action for damages on circumstances which are tainted with illegality (or, after *Kirkham*, immorality). For example, in *Clunis v Camden & Islington Health Authority*[48] the plaintiff was convicted of manslaughter on the basis of diminished responsibility. He sued the health authority in negligence for failing to treat his mental condition and thereby

7.45

---

[43] cf *Robson v Ashworth* (1987) 40 CCLT 164, (Ont CA), where the fact that the deceased took his life 'knowingly and deliberately while he was sane' barred the action by his widow.

[44] [1990] 2 WLR 987, 993, *per* Lloyd LJ *Euro-Diam Ltd v Bathurst* [1988] 2 All ER 23, 28–9, *per* Kerr LJ, cited by Lloyd LJ in *Kirkham*; see also *Thackwell v Barclays Bank* [1986] 1 All ER 676; and *Saunders v Edwards* [1987] 2 All ER 651.

[45] [1990] 2 WLR 987, 944, *per* Lloyd LJ; see also *Funk Estate v Clapp* (1986), reported at 68 DLR (4th) 229, and (1988) 54 DLR (4th) 512.

[46] The meaning of the phrases 'grave mental instability' and 'wholly sane' is a matter of some conjecture, Query whether a person who is not insane, but whose judgment is impaired by an emotional, as opposed to a psychological, disturbance falls into the category of 'not wholly sane'.

[47] In *Hyde v Tameside Area Health Authority* (1981), reported at (1986) 2 PN 26, 29–30, Lord Denning MR was opposed to allowing actions based on suicide or attempted suicide, a view that was claerly based on considerations of policy, and in particular his Lordship's belief that '"medical malpractice" cases should not get out of hand here as they have done in the United States of America'. In *Kirkham v Chief Constable of Greater Manchester Police* [1990] 2 WLR 987, 995 Lloyd LJ did not share this view. [48] *The Times*, 10 Dec 1997.

failing to prevent him from committing the offence. The Court of Appeal struck out the claim as contrary to public policy, on the basis that the court would not lend its aid to a litigant who relied on his own criminal or immoral act. A plea of diminished responsibility accepted that the accused's mental responsibility was substantially impaired, but it did not remove liability for his criminal act. There could be no liability in negligence unless it could be shown that he did not know the nature and quality of his act or that what he had done was wrong. Similarly, where a mother had negligently been denied the opportunity to have an abortion, an action for negligence was denied on policy grounds in circumstances where the abortion would not have been lawful under the Abortion Act 1967, since the plaintiff could not have put the lost opportunity to benefit without breaking the law.[49] Accordingly, where potential claims arise out of the negligent performance of procedures which are unlawful, the likelihood is that they will be barred on the grounds of policy, whether or not this is referred to as *ex turpi causa*.[50]

(b) Other Policy Factors

7.46 Policy factors may also play a role, though rarely, at other points in a medical negligence action, usually in the form of denying the existence of a duty of care. For example, 'wrongful life' claims on the part of a child whose congenital disabilities the defendant negligently failed to diagnose are not actionable.[51] In *M (a minor) v Newham London Borough Council*,[52] a majority of the Court of Appeal held that neither a psychiatrist nor a social worker owed a duty of care in negligence to a child and her mother in respect of the manner in which they conducted an interview with the child for the purpose of identifying whether, and if so by whom, the child had been sexually abused. This was partly on the basis that the child was not the psychiatrist's patient, and therefore the

---

[49] *Rance v Mid-Downs Health Authority* [1991] 1 All ER 801, where the period of gestation was such that a termination of the pregnancy would probably have been unlawful. Following amendement of the Abortion Act 1967 by the Human Fertilisation and Embryology Act 1990, s 37, there is no time limit where the termination is necessary to prevent grave permanent injury to the health of the woman, where the pregnancy involves risk to her life, or where there is a substantial risk that the foetus would be seriously handicapped. Where any of these grounds applied the causation issue in *Rance* would be irrelevant. The time limit under s 1(1)(a), the Abortion Act, 1967 is 24 weeks.

[50] Possible examples would be an unlawful organ transplant operation contrary to the Human Organ Transplants Act 1989, or a procedure connected with surrogate motherhood in breach of the Surrogacy Arrangements Act 1985. In *Norberg v Wynrib* (1992) 92 DLR (4th) 449 the Supreme Court of Canada held that *ex turpi causa* did not apply to an action where the defendant doctor had supplied drugs to a patient who was addicted to pain-killers and tranquillisers in exchange for sexual contact. The patient had also been obtaining drugs from other doctors, and was convicted of the offence of 'double-doctoring'. The illegality was not causally linked to the harm suffered by the plaintiff.

[51] *McKay v Essex Area Health Authority* [1982] QB 1166; Congenital Disabilities (Civil Liability) Act 1976, s 1(1),(2).   [52] [1994] 2 WLR 554.

requisite degree of proximity was not established, and partly on the policy grounds first, that such a duty would lead to 'defensive' practices by the professionals involved in child protection and secondly, that actions against local authorities would have an adverse impact on the resources available for the purpose of child protection. This was accepted to be a proper basis for rejecting a duty of care in such circumstances by the House of Lords.[53]

Another ground of immunity stems from the fact that a witness in legal proceedings has immunity from suit with respect to evidence given in those proceedings,[54] and this immunity applies to a proof or report prepared for trial by a witness.[55] This is based on public policy in protecting the proper administration of justice so that witnesses are able to be frank when giving evidence free from the threat of civil proceedings, and to avoid a multiplicity of actions in which the truth of their evidence would be tried over again.[56] In the case of an expert witness, the immunity extends only to what can fairly be said to be preliminary to giving evidence in court. Thus, the production of a report for disclosure to the other side in litigation is immune, but work done for the principal purpose of advising the client (as to the merits of the claim, for example) is not.[57] In *Landall v Dennis Faulkner & Alsop*,[58] the plaintiff was suing, *inter alia*, a medical expert who had provided a number of reports on the condition and prognosis of his back for the purpose of a claim being brought by him against a negligent motorist. He alleged that the expert's report and/or advice was negligent in that his opinion relating to the prospects of further successful treatment for the plaintiff's back condition was unduly optimistic, with the result that the plaintiff settled his action against the motorist for much less than it was worth. The plaintiff argued that the reports provided by the expert were not simply for the purposes of the litigation, but also constituted advice to the plaintiff as to the potential benefits of a spinal fusion operation. This argument was rejected, however. The report constituted:

7.47

> pre-trial work . . . so intimately connected with the conduct of the case in court that it could fairly be said to be a preliminary decision affecting the way that the case was to be conducted when it came to a hearing.[59]

---

[53] sub nom *X (minors) v Bedfordshire County Council* [1995] 3 WLR 152, 184.
[54] *Rondel v Worsley* [1969] 1 AC 191, 268; *Saif Ali v Sydney Mitchell & Co* [1980] AC 198.
[55] *Evans v London Hospital Medical College* [1981] 1 WLR 184.
[56] *Watson v M'Ewan* [1905] AC 480; *Saif Ali v Sydney Mitchell &; Co* [1980] AC 198; *Evans v London Hospital Medical College (University of London)* [1981] 1 WLR 184.
[57] *Palmer v Durnford Ford* [1992] 1 QB 483, 488.   [58] [1994] 5 Med LR 268, QBD.
[59] *per* Holland J, applying *Saif Ali* (n 56 above) and *Palmer* (n 57 above).

Accordingly, the claim was struck out as disclosing no reasonable cause of action.[60]

4. Limitation Act 1980

7.48 Where an action is commenced outside the statutory limitation period the defendant can rely on the defence of limitation.[61] An action in tort cannot normally be brought more than six years from the date on which the cause of action accrued,[62] which in the case of an action for negligence is when damage occurs, but in torts actionable per se, such as trespass to the person, the cause of action accrues at the date of the defendant's wrong. In contract the limitation period is also six years from the accrual of the action.[63] These rules are modified, however in cases of personal injuries and death and plaintiffs under a disability. Medical negligence actions are usually, though not exclusively, concerned with claims for personal injuries or death, which are governed, as a general rule,[64] by the provisions of the Limitation Act 1980, sections 11–14 and 33. The scheme provides for a three year limitation period running from either (a) the date on which the cause of action accrued, or (b) if later, the plaintiff's date of knowledge of certain facts about the cause of action.[65] Additionally, even if this fixed period has expired, the court has a wide discretion to override the time limit and permit the action to proceed.[66]

---

[60] In *X (minors) v Bedfordshire County Council* [1995] 3 WLR 152, 188 the House of Lords held that a psychiatrist who, in the course of interviewing a child, was negligent in ascertaining the identity of the person who had sexually abused the child was protected by witness immunity (reversing the decision of the Court of Appeal in *M (a minor) v Newham London Borough Council* [1994] 2 WLR 554). The policy considerations which applied to witnesses in criminal proceedings were equally applicable to a local authority's investigation, in the performance of a public duty, of whether or not there is evidence on which to bring proceedings for the protection of children from child abuse. The psychiatrist knew that if abuse was discovered, proeedings for the protection of the child would ensure and that her findings would be the evidence on which those proceedings would be based. The investigations had an immediate link with possible proceedings in pursuance of a statutory duty, and therefore could not be made the basis of a subsequent action in negligence.

[61] For a more detailed discussion see Jones, M A, *Limitation Periods in Personal Injury Actions* (Blackstone Press, 1995). [62] Limitation Act 1980, s 2.

[63] ibid, s 5. The action in contract will accrue at the date of the breach of contract.

[64] The Limitation Act 1980 does not apply where a period of limitation is prescribed by other legislation: s 39.

[65] Limitation Act 1980, s 11(3) and (4). New claims which are outside a relevant limitation period cannot be brought by addition to or amendment of existing proceedings since this would have the effect of depriving a defendant of an otherwise valid limitation defence. The Limitation Act 1980, s 35, in combination with RSC Ord 15, r 6 and Ord 20, r 5, allows for limited exceptions to this rule.

[66] ibid, s 33. Similar rules apply to claims brought under the Consumer Protection Act 1987 in respect of defective products, except that there is an overall longstop which expires 10 years after the product was put into circulation by the defendant. The longstop is an absolute bar, and the court has no discretion to override this limit in personal injuries cases. See Limitation Act 1980, ss 11A, 14(1A), 28(7), 32(4A) and 33(1A).

(i) *Limitation Periods*

Section 11(1) provides that the three year period applies to 'any action for **7.49**
damages for negligence, nuisance or breach of duty' where the damages claimed
by the plaintiff consist of or include damages in respect of personal injuries. This
expressly includes breach of a contractual duty. In *Letang v Cooper*,[67] the Court of
Appeal held that the wording also applied to an action for trespass to the person,
but in *Stubbings v Webb*,[68] the House of Lords concluded that section 11(1) was
limited to personal injury resulting from accidents caused by negligence, nuisance, or breach of a duty of care.[69] The consequence of this is that actions for
trespass against the person against a doctor, for example, in respect of a failure to
obtain a valid consent to treatment, are not governed by section 11, but by section
2 of the Limitation Act 1980. This means the plaintiff must bring the action
within six years, without any possibility of the court's discretion under section 33
being available.[70] The omission to obtain the patient's consent may be the
product of carelessness, but none the less the cause of action is in battery because,
although battery is an intentional tort, the doctor has the relevant intention (the
direct application of force to the patient's body) and is simply careless as to
whether he has the *defence* of consent. On the other hand, a psychiatrist/psychol-
ogist who enters into an improper relationship with a patient commits a breach of
duty of care in negligence, not 'wilful conduct calculated to cause the plaintiff
injury', and therefore the three year limitation period specified by section 11
applies, not the six year period created by section 2 (which would be the case
following *Stubbings v Webb* if the conduct was intentional).[71]

'Personal injuries' includes any disease and any impairment of a person's **7.50**
physical or mental condition.[72] Where the breach of duty does not itself
cause the personal injuries, but deprives the plaintiff of a chance of receiving
compensation for the injuries, the three year period does not apply.[73] So
where a patient suffers purely financial loss due to a doctor's negligence (for
example, as a result of giving up work following a negligent misdiagnosis),[74]

---

[67] [1965] 1 QB 232; *Long v Hepworth* [1968] 1 WLR 1299.
[68] [1993] AC 498; [1993] 1 All ER 322.
[69] On the other hand, a daughter's allegation that her mother had been negligent in failing
to protect her from sexual abuse by her father during her minority falls within s 11 rather than
2: *Seymour v Williams* [1995] PIQR P470, CA.
[70] See *Dobbie v Medway Health Authority* [1994] 4 All ER 450, 458–9, CA. This would not
be the case, however, where the patient died and an action was brought by the dependants
under the Fatal Accidents Act 1976, since this action is governed by s 12 of the Limitation Act
1980, not s 11. On the other hand, a claim under the Law Reform (Miscellaneous Provisions)
Act 1934 is governed by s 11(5) of the Limitation Act, with the results that *Stubbings v Webb*
applies s 2, and the limitation period will be six years from the date of the battery.
[71] *Bowler v Walker* [1996] PIQR P22, CA.   [72] Limitation Act 1980, s 38(1).
[73] *Ackbar v Green & Co Ltd* [1975] 1 QB 582.
[74] See *Hedley Byrne & Co Ltd v Heller & Partners Ltd* [1964] AC 465, 517, *per* Lord Devlin.

the six year, rather than three year, period will apply. In *Walkin v South Manchester Health Authority*[75] the Court of Appeal held that a claim for the economic loss attributable to the birth of a child following a failed sterilisation operation fell within section 11, as a claim for 'damages in respect of personal injuries'. The unwanted conception was a personal injury because the physical change to the plaintiff's body was an unwanted condition which she had sought to avoid by being sterilised.[76]

7.51 Once the limitation period prescribed by section 2 of the Limitation Act 1980 expires there is no discretion to permit the action to proceed, though the commencement of the limitation period may be postponed in the case of deliberate concealment[77] or latent damage.[78]

(ii) *The Running of the Limitation Period*

7.52 Time begins to run from either the date on which the cause of action accrued or the date of the plaintiff's knowledge, if later.[79] Once the period has started to run it cannot be suspended; only the issue of the writ stops time running.

---

[75] [1996] 7 Med LR 211.

[76] cf *Pattison v Hobbs* (1985) *The Times*, 11 November, where the Court of Appeal had held that such an action was subject to s 2, as a claim in respect of financial loss. In *Walkin* Auld LJ said that *Pattison v Hobbs* was a decision of a two-judge Court of Appeal which turned on a point of pleading, whereas the question whether an action was for damages in respect of personal injuries was a matter of substance, not pleading.

[77] Where any fact relevant to the plaintiff's right of action has been deliberately concealed from him by the defendant, the limitation period does not begin to run until the plaintiff has discovered the concealment or could with reasonable diligence have discovered it: Limitation Act 1980, s 32(1). In *Sheldon v RHM Outhwaite Underwriting Agencies Ltd* [1995] 2 All ER 562, the House of Lords held that s 32(1)(b) operated to postpone the running of the limitation period in every case where there is deliberate concealment by the defendant of facts relevant to the plaintiff's cause of action, regardless of whether the concealment was contemporaneous with or subsequent to the accrual of the cause of action. Thus, subsequent concealment has the effect of bringing s 32 into play, thereby excluding ss 2 and 5, and the plaintiff has a full six years from the date of discovery of the concealment in which to bring the action.

[78] In cases of latent damage (other than personal injuries) the plaintiff has three years from the date on which he discovered or ought reasonably to have discovered significant damage, subject to an overall longstop which bars all claims brought more than 15 years from the date of the defendant's negligence: Limitation Act 1980, ss 14A and 14B. Section 14A is expressed in very similar terms to s 14 (see para 7.65 below) and the courts' approach to s 14A will closely mirror that taken to s 14: see *Spencer-Ward v Humberts* [1995] 06 EG 148, CA; *Hallam-Eames v Merrett Syndicates Ltd* [1996] 7 Med LR 122, CA. The latent damage provisions do not apply to claims in contract: *Iron Trade Mutual Insurance Co Ltd v JK Buckenham Ltd* [1990] 1 All ER 808; *Société Commerciale de Réassurance v ERAS (International) Ltd (Note)* [1992] 2 All ER 82. Where, however, the defendant owes concurrent duties in contract and tort the plaintiff is entitled to pursue the action which will give him a practical advantage on the question of limitation: *Henderson v Merrett Syndicates Ltd* [1994] 3 All ER 506, 525 *per* Lord Goff.

[79] For consideration of who has the burden of proof in respect of the limitation defence see *Fowell v Naional Coal Board* (1986) *The Times*, 28 May, CA; *Nash v Eli Lilly & Co* [1993] 1 WLR 782, 796, CA; *Driscoll-Varley v Parkside Health Authority* [1991] 2 Med LR 346, 357.

The parties may agree, expressly or impliedly, to extend the time, but the mere fact that negotiations towards a settlement were in progress when the three year period expired will not constitute such an agreement, unless the defendant's conduct is such that he is estopped from relying on the defence.[80]

In negligence the action accrues when damage occurs, whether or not the **7.53** damage is discoverable.[81] In the case of minor or trivial harm it will be a question of fact whether the plaintiff has sustained 'damage' sufficient for the cause of action to accrue. Damage will only be ignored if it falls within the principle *de minimis non curat lex*.[82] In an action for personal injuries, even if more than three years have elapsed since the action accrued, the primary limitation period will not have expired if the writ is issued within three years of the plaintiff's 'knowledge'. By section 14(1), references to a person's date of knowledge are references to the date on which he first had knowledge of the following facts:

(a) that the injury in question was significant; and
(b) that the injury was attributable in whole or in part to the act or omission which is alleged to constitute negligence, nuisance or breach of duty; and
(c) the identity of the defendant; and
(d) if it is alleged that the act or omission was that of a person other than the defendant, the identity of that person and the additional facts supporting the bringing of an action against the defendant . . .

The word 'knowledge' does not mean 'know for certain and beyond possibility of contradiction'.[83] Suspicion, particularly if it is vague and unsupported, will not be enough, but reasonable belief will normally suffice.[84] The court must assess the intelligence of the plaintiff, consider his assertions as to how he regarded the information that he had, and determine whether he had knowledge of the facts by reason of his understanding of the information.[85]

(a) Significant Injury

An injury is significant if the person whose date of knowledge is in question **7.54** would reasonably have considered it sufficiently serious to justify his instituting proceedings for damages against a defendant who did not dispute liability

---

[80] *Deerness v John Keeble & Son Ltd* [1983] 2 Lloyd's Rep 260; *K Lokumal & Sons (London) Ltd v Lotte Shipping Co Pte Ltd* [1985] 2 Lloyd's Rep 28.
[81] *Cartledge v Jopling & Sons Ltd* [1963] AC 758.   [82] ibid.
[83] *Halford v Brookes* [1991] 3 All ER 559, 573–4 *per* Lord Donaldson MR.
[84] For consideration of the degree of 'certainty' required to constitute knowledge see *Nash v Eli Lilly & Co* [1993] 1 WLR 782, 792, CA; *Skitt v Khan and Wakefield Health Authority* [1997] 8 Med LR 105; cf *Wilkinson v Ancliff (BLT) Ltd* [1986] 3 All ER 427, 238, and *Stephen v Riverside Health Authority* [1990] 1 Med LR 261, where it was said that reasonable belief is not sufficient to constitute knowledge.   [85] *Nash* (n 84 above), 792.

and was able to satisfy a judgment.[86] This is a combined subjective/objective test.[87] It is a question of what a reasonable man of the plaintiff's age, with his background, intelligence, and disabilities would reasonably have known.[88] Other personal reasons that the plaintiff may have had for not commencing proceedings are irrelevant, even if they are objectively reasonable.[89] 'Significant injury' refers to the gravity of the damage and its monetary value, not to the plaintiff's evaluation of its cause, nature, or usualness.[90] Section 14(2) makes most injuries significant in monetary terms, since it will not take much to justify instituting proceedings against a solvent defendant who admits liability.

7.55 Where the injury, though minor, is sufficiently serious to institute proceedings, and the plaintiff subsequently discovers a far more serious injury caused by the same accident, time will run from the date of the first injury.[91] In *Nash v Eli Lilly & Co*,[92] the plaintiffs alleged that they had suffered side-effects from the use of the prescription drug Opren. The Court of Appeal accepted that there was a valid distinction between an expected, or accepted, side-effect, which would not constitute significant injury, and an injurious or unacceptable consequence. Time would not begin to run until the plaintiffs had knowledge that the side effects were injurious or unacceptable.

(b) Causation

7.56 The plaintiff must have knowledge that the injury was attributable in whole or in part to the 'act or omission which is alleged to constitute negligence'. This refers to the plaintiff's knowledge of factual causation.[93] Ignorance of causation in law is irrelevant. Once the plaintiff has the broad knowledge that his injuries are attributable to the defendant's acts or omissions, he has sufficient knowledge for the purpose of section 14(1)(b), even if he does not know the specific acts or omissions and is not in a position to draft a fully particularised statement of claim.[94] Moreover, a plaintiff will be taken to

---

[86] Limitation Act 1980, s 14(2).
[87] *McCafferty v Metropolitan Police District Receiver* [1977] 1 WLR 1073, 1081, *per* Geoffrey Lane LJ; *Denman v Essex Area Health Authority* (1984) 134 New LJ 264.
[88] *Davis v City and Hackney Health Authority* [1991] 2 Med LR 366.
[89] *Miller v London Electrical Manufacturing Co Ltd* [1976] 2 Lloyd's Rep 284; *Buck v English Electric Co Ltd* [1997] 1 WLR 806; *McCafferty (n 87 above)*.
[90] *Dobbie v Medway Health Authority* [1994] 4 All ER 450, 457, *per* Sir Thomas Bingham MR, though his Lordship added that time does not run if the plaintiff would reasonably have accepted it as a fact of life or not worth bothering about.
[91] *Bristow v Grout* (1986) *The Times*, 3 November. The plaintiff's appreciation of the seriousness of an injury may depend upon the medical advice he receives: *Harding v Peoples' Dispensary for Sick Animals* [1994] PIQR P270, CA.   [92] [1993] 1 WLR 782, CA.
[93] *Dobbie (n 90 above)*, 462, *per* Steyn LJ. See e g, *Marston v British Railways Board* [1976] ICR 124.   [94] *Wilkinson v Ancliff (BLT) Ltd* [1986] 3 All ER 427, 438, CA.

know that his injury was 'attributable' to the defendant's act or omission if he knew that it was 'capable of being so attributed'.[95]

Where the plaintiff has a firm belief that his injuries are due to the acts or **7.57** omissions of the defendant, but on making inquiries is informed by expert opinion that he is mistaken, the quesiton of whether he had sufficient knowledge to start the limitation period running will be one of degree. If the plaintiff realised that his belief required further confirmation, then he will not acquire knowledge until he receives that confirmation.[96] On the other hand, if the plaintiff is convinced in her own mind that there is a causal link, even though objectively that belief is not reasonable in the absence of confirmation from an expert, she none the less has the requisite knowledge and it is not open to argue that her knowledge runs from the date of confirmation of that belief by an expert.[97] Moreover, if the plaintiff has acquired 'knowledge' sufficient to start the limitation period running, he cannot subsequently lose it simply because he receives expert advice which tends to undermine the belief.[98] Everything turns upon the degree of conviction with which the plaintiff holds his belief, and whether he realised that expert confirmation was required. The Court of Appeal has suggested that where a claimant has sought advice and taken proceedings there would be some difficulty in saying that he did not then have the relevant knowledge.[99] This would mean that where a protective writ had been issued the plaintiff would be deemed to have knowledge even where he then received negative expert advice leading him to discontinue the action.[100] In *Nash v Eli Lilly & Co*[101] the Court even went so far as to state that a person who embarks upon the preliminaries to the making of a claim for compensation by taking legal or other advice may be

---

[95] ibid. 'To "attribute" means 'to reckon as a consequence of': *Halford v Brookes* [1991] 3 All ER 559, 573, *per* Lord Donaldson MR.

[96] See *Davis v Ministry of Defence* (1985) *The Times*, 7 August; *O'Driscoll v Dudley Health Authority* [1996] 7 Med LR 408.

[97] *Spargo v North Essex District Health Authority* [1997] 8 Med LR 125, CA. Brooke LJ said, at 131: 'The test is a subjective one: what did the plaintiff herself know? It is not an objective one: what would have been the reasonable layman's state of mind in the absence of expert confirmation?' [98] *Nash v Eli Lilly & Co* [1993] 1 WLR 782, 795, CA.

[99] ibid.

[100] This occurred in *Stephen v Riverside Health Authority* [1990] 1 Med LR 261 and *Davis* (n 96 above), but it was held that the plaintiffs did not acquire knowledge until they received further expert advice confirming their original belief that there was a causal connection.

[101] [1993] 1 WLR 782, 792. In *Spargo* (n 97 above), 129, Brooke LJ said that 'attributable in this context means "capable of being attributed to" in the sense of being a real possibility'. A plaintiff would have the 'requisite knowledge when she knows enough to make it reasonable for her to begin to investigate whether or not she has a case against the defendant. Another way of putting this is to say that she will have such knowledge if she so firmly believes that her condition is capable of being attributed to an act or omission which she can identify (in broad terms) that she goes to a solicitor to seek advice about making a claim for compensation' (ibid at 130).

deemed to satisfy the level of 'certainty' required for acquiring 'knowledge' under section 14. It is arguable, however, that even issuing a writ should not be treated as *conclusive* evidence that the plaintiff had the relevant knowledge. In *Whitfield v North Durham Health Authority*[102] the Court of Appeal held that it was wrong to treat the issue of a protective writ as determinative, by itself, of the question of knowledge. The plaintiff may have a firm belief, even a conviction, that his injuries were caused in a particular way, but it subsequently turns out that he was mistaken and his injuries were caused by other acts or omissions of the defendant. In these circumstances he was 'barking up the wrong tree'[103] and on the wording of section 14(1)(b) he does not have the required knowledge until he discovers his mistake, notwithstanding the possibility that a writ has already been issued.

7.58 A particular problem which has arisen in the context of medical negligence actions is the degree of 'specificity' of knowledge required about the causal connection between treatment and the injury. Can it be said that a plaintiff's knowledge that the injury was attributable to an act or omission which is alleged to constitute negligence, where the plaintiff cannot identify the relevant acts or omissions? The difficulty arises because unlike, say, the typical road traffic accident or work accident, the plaintiff cannot regard the occurrence of injury itself as indicating that there must be a causal connection between the injury and 'act or omission which is alleged to constitute negligence'. Injury following an operation may arise without negligence or without even an error, as an unavoidable complication of the procedure. Alternatively, the operation may simply have been unsuccessful in preventing the plaintiff's medical condition from deteriorating as a consequence of the original disease or injury which was being treated.[104] Moreover, most people would not regard *successful* medical treatment as constituting an *injury*, so that if a patient is informed that surgery was successful, she would not even consider that she had been injured, let alone address her mind to the question of which acts or omissions had caused the 'injury'.

7.59 In order to distinguish those injuries which were unavoidable consequences of the procedure and those which are attributable to an 'act or omission which is alleged to constitute negligence', it is strongly arguable that the minimum knowledge a plaintiff would require is knowledge that 'something has gone

---

[102] [1995] 6 Med LR 32, 37.   [103] See the cases cited at n 108 below.
[104] See eg, *Harrington v Essex Area Health Authority* (1984) *The Times*, 14 November, where it was held that knowledge by the plaintiff that he had contracted an infection in the operating theatre, was not knowledge that the infection was attributable to an act or omission constituting negligence, since an infection can be contracted without negligence on the part of anyone.

wrong' with the treatment. This has been the approach taken in a number of cases.[105] Conversely, section 14(1) makes it clear that the plaintiff's ignorance that the defendant's acts or omissions would give rise to a cause of action in law is irrelevant to the running of the limitation period, and it might be argued that requiring knowledge that 'something has gone wrong' would import an element of knowledge about the defendant's negligence.

In *Broadley v Guy Clapham & Co*,[106] the plaintiff underwent an operation to **7.60** remove a foreign body from her knee and for at least seven months after the operation she needed two sticks in order to walk. It was held that by this time she had constructive knowledge of a potential cause of action because a reasonable person in her position would have sought further medical assistance or made further enquiries of the doctor. The plaintiff argued that she did not have knowledge until she knew of:

> some act or omission which could adversely affect the safety of the operation or proper recovery from the operation, such as unreasonable interference with the nerve or failure reasonably to safeguard it from damage, or failure properly to investigate and/or repair the nerve lesion in time.

Leggatt LJ said the use of the words 'unreasonable', 'reasonably', and 'properly' could not be justified because section 14(1) provided that 'knowledge that any acts or omissions did or did not, as a matter of law, involve negligence' was irrelevant. The words 'which is alleged to constitute negligence' simply pointed to the relevant act or omission to which the injury was attributable.[107] The situation would be different, said Hoffman LJ, if the plaintiff was 'barking up the wrong tree', that is, where the plaintiff thought that the complications from which she suffered had been caused in one way (for example, during the operation) but she later discovered that the real cause was not the operation but the subsequent premature removal of her leg from

---

[105] *Bentley v Bristol and Western Health Authority* [1991] 2 Med LR 359, 364, *per* Hirst J: '. . . the performance of a surgical operation . . . is not the act or omission which is itself alleged to constitute negligence. The act or omission which *is* alleged to constitute negligence in operation cases is some conduct or failure which can affect the safety of the operation' (original empasis); *Nash v Eli Lilly & Co* [1991] 2 Med LR 169, where Hidden J said that there must be a degree of specificity about the act or omission which is alleged to constitute negligence, which in *Nash* consisted of exposing the plaintiffs to a drug which was unsafe in that it was capable of causing persistent photosensitivity and/or in failing to take reasonable steps to protect the plaintiffs from such a condition. The Court of Appeal accepted that this was the appropriate degree of specificity: *Nash v Eli Lilly & Co* [1993] 1 WLR 782, 799, CA.; see also *Driscoll-Varley v Parkside Health Authority* [1991] 2 Med LR 346.

[106] [1994] 4 All ER 439, CA.

[107] ibid, 447. See also *per* Hoffmann LJ at 448. It followed that the decision in *Bentley* (n 105 above) was wrong, since it required knowledge on the plaintiff's part of all matters necessary to establish negligence or breach of duty, and this was too high a test.

traction.[108] In these circumstances the issue is the identification of the act which caused the injury and not the appreciation of whether the act was capable of being attributable to negligence or fault. Balcombe LJ said that detailed knowledge (ie sufficient knowledge to enable the plaintiff's advisers to draft a statement of claim) or qualitative knowledge (ie knowledge that the operation had been performed in such a way as unreasonably to cause injury to a nerve) were not required for the purpose of section 14(1). On the other hand, his Lordship accepted that 'broad knowledge' was required, which consisted of knowledge that the operation had been carried out in such a way that something went wrong.[109]

7.61 In *Dobbie v Medway Health Authority*[110] the plaintiff issued a writ in 1989 in respect of the removal of her breast during the course of a breast biopsy operation performed in 1973. Although the surgeon believed a lump to be malignant, subsequent pathological examination revealed that it was benign. The plaintiff was told by medical staff that the breast had been removed to be safe rather than sorry; that the hospital did not have facilities for testing breast lumps while the patient was under anaesthetic; and that she should be grateful that she did not have cancer. She subsequently suffered psychological problems attributable to the loss of her breast. It was argued that since the plaintiff had been told at the time that she had received the appropriate treatment, she did not know that she should not have had her breast removed until either she received an expert's report to this effect in 1990, or at the earliest in 1988 when she heard about a successful claim in a similar case. The Court of Appeal held that the plaintiff had sufficient knowledge to start the limitation period running in 1973. Sir Thomas Bingham MP said that knowledge that the breast had been 'unnecessarily' removed, or that something had gone wrong was irrelevant under section 14, because this would conflict with the closing words of subsection 14(1) that 'knowledge that any acts or omissions did or did not, as a matter of law, involve negligence, nuisance or breach of duty is irrelevant'. Though it was customary in discussing tortious liability to refer to acts and omissions, his Lordship did not believe that the meaning of section 14(1)(b) would be any different had the reference been to 'conduct'.[111]

---

[108] See eg, *Driscoll-Varley* (n 105 above) and the comments of Hoffmann LJ on this case in *Broadley v Guy Clapham & Co* [1994] 4 All ER 439, 449; *Khan v Ainslie* [1993] 4 Med LR 319; *Spargo v North Essex District Health Authority* [1997] 8 Med LR 125, 130 *per* Brooke LJ. In *Baig v City & Hackney Health Authority* [1994] 5 Med LR 221, 224, Rougier J commented that: 'It seems to me to be a travesty of language to hold that somebody who approaches his case in a wholly erroneous belief—however strong—as to the cause of his injury could ever have the requisite knowledge. On the contrary, he has the reverse.'
[109] [1994] 4 All ER 439, 446–7.
[110] [1994] 4 All ER 450, CA. Leave to appeal refused: [1994] 1 WLR 1553.
[111] [1994] 4 All ER 450, 456.

The plaintiff argued that the word 'injury' should be interpreted in a way **7.62** which distinguished between the normal or expected consequences of success-ful medical treatment and the consequences of faulty treatment. The man in the street would not regard himself as 'injured' by a successful operation. He would only regard himself as injured if he suffered consequences other than those normally attributed to the treatment. Beldam LJ rejected this argument because the definition of personal injuries in section 38(1), though not exhaustive, indicated that 'injury' could not be qualified by the addition of words implying its source or aetiology. Nor was there any need to import the perception of the reasonable patient.[112] However, the implication of refusing to draw a distinction between successful and unsuccessful surgery appears to be that any patient who undergoes a surgical operation is, by definition, 'injured' and knows that she has suffered injury immediately. The fact that she does not know that the surgery has gone wrong would be irrelevant to the running of the limitation period.

This conclusion is open to question. Consider, for example, a patient who has **7.63** an appendix removed. She would not consider, and reasonably so, that she had suffered any injury at the hands of the doctor. Appendectomy is a potentially life-saving procedure. The pain and suffering involved in the surgery, and the resultant scar, though clearly 'caused' by the surgeon's knife would not normally be thought of as an 'injury' when the operation is undertaken on reasonable grounds. If, however, the operation was totally unnecessary on the clinical signs, then a patient would reasonably consider that she had been damaged by having to undergo a needless operation. If the fact that the operation was unnecessary only became apparent much later, the patient only acquired knowledge that she had suffered an *injury* at that time. It is the decision to undertake the operation itself, rather than the perfor-mance of the operation (which may have been technically perfect) that is the gist or the 'essence' of her complaint.[113] However, the decision to perform the operation can only be characterised as an 'injury' if the decision was mistaken, and therefore the plaintiff can only acquire knowledge that she has suffered an injury when she learns that the decision was mistaken. She need not know that it was a careless or negligent mistake, but she has to know that there *was* a mistake, that is, that there was an error or that 'something had gone wrong', before she can have knowledge that she has even suffered an injury.

---

[112] ibid, 461. The Limitation Act 1980, s 38(1) provides that '"personal injuries" includes any disease and any impairment of a person's physical or mental condition, and 'injury' and cognate expressions shall be constructed accordingly'.

[113] See eg, *Gascoine v Jan Sheridan & Co* [1994] 5 Med LR 437, 422, where Mitchell J considered that the validity of the decision to treat was an 'act' quite independent from the 'act' constituting the conduct of the treatment.

7.64 While it is correct to say that ignorance of the law does not affect the running of the limitation period, the question of whether the plaintiff knew that the facts would give her a cause of action in law should not be confused with the question of the plaintiff being able to identify the relevant act or omission of the defendant as a cause of her injuries. Knowledge that the defendant's acts or omissions have or have not caused the plaintiff's injuries is knowledge about a fact, not about a law. The question is *which facts* must the plaintiff have knowledge of, given that section 14(1)(b) clearly does *not* state that it is sufficient to know that the injury was attributable merely to the defendant's *conduct*? The subsection directs attention to the specific conduct of the defendant which it is subsequently alleged by the plaintiff constitutes negligence, nuisance or breach of duty. The plaintiff need not be aware that this conduct would in law give rise to an action for damages, but she must have *some* knowledge of the relevant acts or omissions.[114] In a medical negligence action the plaintiff needs more than simply knowledge that the 'injury' was attributable to the treatment or operation.

7.65 This point has been made clear by the Court of Appeal in *Hallam-Eames v Merrett*,[115] which was concerned with the interpretation of the analogous provision in section 14A of the Limitation Act 1980 in respect of claims for economic loss. Hoffmann LJ said that:

> If all that was necessary was that a plaintiff should have known that the damage was attributable to an act or omission of the defendant, the statute would have said so. Instead, it speaks of the damage being attributable to 'the act or omission which is alleged to constitute negligence'. In other words, the act or omission of which the plaintiff must have knowledge must be that which is causally relevant for the purposes of an allegation of negligence.

The words 'which is alleged to constitute negligence' served to identify the facts of which the plaintiff must have knowledge. It was not sufficient for the plaintiff to know merely that the relevant damage had been caused by *an* act or omission of the defendant. Commenting on *Dobbie*, Hoffmann LJ said that Mrs Dobbie had to know more than that her breast had been removed. She had to know that a healthy breast had been removed. That was the essence of what she was complaining about. Nor did this require knowledge of fault or negligence:

---

[114] See eg, *Baig v City and Hackney Health Authority* [1994] 5 Med LR 221, 224, where Rougier J commented that the words of s 14(1)(b) admitted of no interpretation other than that the knowledge required is 'knowledge, at any rate in general outline, of just what it was that the defendant had either done or failed to do which had caused the damage'.

[115] [1996] 7 Med LR 122, 125.

The plaintiff does not have to know that he has a cause of action or that the defendant's acts can be characterised in law as negligent or as falling short of some standard of professional or other behaviour . . . He must have known the facts which can fairly be described as constituting the negligence of which he complains. It may be that knowledge of such facts will also serve to bring home to him the fact that the defendant has been negligent or at fault. But that in itself is not a reason for saying that he need not have known them.[116]

Many of the cases, including several Court of Appeal decisions, refer to a requirement of knowledge of some error relating to safety by the defendant before section 14(1)(b) is satisfied.[117] In *Nash v Eli Lilly & Co*,[118] the Court of Appeal accepted that the relevant acts or omissions of the defendants consisted of exposing the plaintiffs to a drug which was *unsafe*. Knowledge that their symptoms were simply attributable to taking a drug could not constitute knowledge by the plaintiffs of any relevant act or omission on the part of the defendant manufacturers. The reference to 'safety' clearly requires that the plaintiff know more than simply that the defendant's *conduct* caused the injury. It is submitted that she must either know, or have constructive knowledge, that 'something has gone wrong' sufficiently to consider investigating the circumstances.[119] **7.66**

In any event, where the plaintiff is informed at the time by the medical staff involved that nothing has gone wrong, and that her treatment was consistent with good medical practice, she does not know that she has suffered an injury because there is no basis for challenging either the performance of the treatment itself or the decision to proceed with the treatment. When Mrs Dobbie was informed that she was lucky to be alive, she was not simply being advised that the surgery to remove her breast had been technically competent, she was being advised that the decision to remove **7.67**

---

[116] ibid, 126. See also *Ostick v Wandsworth Health Authority* [1995] 6 Med LR 338, where it was held that it was not sufficient that the plaintiff knew she had received an injury that had not healed. It was necessary to know that there was a causal link between the treatment or lack of treatment and the subsequent physical disability, i e the fact that the injury had not healed. Similarly, in *O'Driscoll v Dudley Health Authority* [1996] 7 Med LR 408 it was held that knowledge that the plaintiff's injury could be attributed to hypoxia was not knowledge that the injury was attributable to the act or omission alleged to constitute negligence, because hypoxia was not itself that act or omission.

[117] *Davis v Ministry of Defence* (1985) *The Times*, 7 August, CA; *Wilkinson v Ancliff (BLT) Ltd* [1986] 3 All ER 427, 438, CA; *Farmer v National Coal Board* (1985) *The Times*, 27 April, CA.

[118] [1993] 1 WLR 782, 799.

[119] In *Broadley v Guy Clapham & Co* [1994] 4 All ER 439, 446, for example, Balcombe LJ accepted that 'broad knowledge' was required, and that this involved knowledge 'that something went wrong'.

her breast was not an error or a mistake. On that information, she did know that she had suffered an injury.[120]

7.68 Where the alleged negligence consists of an omission to treat, the plaintiff must know more than the mere fact that he has not been treated. In *Smith v West Lancashire Health Authority*[121] the plaintiff had been told that the initial treatment had not worked and that there was nothing further that could be done. He presumed that he had received proper treatment, but in fact the operation had been performed too late to achieve full recovery. Russell LJ said that the alleged negligence consisted of the omission to operate promptly, together with the failure properly to diagnose his condition. The reality was that the plaintiff did not know that there had been an omission to operate at all until he received advice to that effect from his own expert witness:

> True, he knew that he had not had an operation on or about November 12, 1981, but that knowledge cannot, in my judgment, be knowledge of an omission 'which is alleged to constitute negligence'. One cannot know of an omission without knowing what it is that is omitted. In this case, that was an operation to reduce the fracture dislocations, as opposed to conservative treatment. Simply to tell the plaintiff that the first course of treatment had not worked, is not the same as imbuing the plaintiff with the knowledge of an omission to operate.[122]

7.69 It is also clear that in cases where the plaintiff mistakenly believed that her injuries were attributable to a particular aspect of her treatment but she subsequently discovered that the injuries were caused by a different aspect of treatment, the plaintiff does not have knowledge as long as she is 'barking up the wrong tree'.[123] These cases indicate that knowledge that an injury was attributable simply to 'the treatment' or 'the defendant's conduct' is not sufficient.

(c) Defendant's identity

7.70 Identifying the defendant is not normally a problem in actions for medical negligence, although the plaintiff may not know which individual in a team caused the injury. However, where the plaintiff knows that the injuries were

---

[120] cf *Scuriaga v Powell* (1979) 123 SJ 406; aff'd 1980 (unreported), CA, where following an unsuccessful abortion on the plaintiff, the defendant lied to the plaintiff, telling her that the operation had failed because she had a physical defect. Time did not begin to run until the plaintiff discovered that the failure was due to the doctor's conduct of the operation. It is apparent that in many of these cases plaintiffs have been given reassurances ranging from statements that nothing further could have been done, implying that the plaintiff's problem is attributable to the underlying medical condition rather than anything done or omitted by the medical staff, to outright lies. It is unfortunate that plaintiffs should then be caught by the limitation period, having placed reliance on the professional advice of the very defendants that thay are now seeking to sue.   [121] [1995] PIQR 514.
[122] ibid, 517. See also *Parry v Clwyd Health Authority* [1997] 8 Med LR 243; *Hind v York Health Authority* [1997] 8 Med LR 377.   [123] See the cases cited in n 108 above.

caused by one or other of two defendants, but not both, and does not know which defendant is responsible, the plaintiff would be expected to sue both in the alternative.[124] This will only be relevant in cases of private medical treatment or in actions against general practitioners, since in cases of hospital treatment in the NHS, the plaintiff will sue the NHS Trust or the health authority which will be vicariously liable for the conduct of all of its staff.

(d) Vicarious liability

Section 14(1)(d) refers to the circumstances required to establish an employer's vicarious liability for the torts of employees committed in the course of employment, though the wording is wide enough to cover liability for the conduct of independent contractors where the defendant is under a relevant 'non-delegable' duty. The precise identity of the employee is irrelevant if the plaintiff is aware that the damage was caused by one or more of the defendant's employees acting in the course of employment.[125] The plaintiff's ignorance that on the facts the defendant would be held vicariously liable in law is irrelevant. **7.71**

(iii) *Constructive knowledge*

A person's knowledge includes constructive knowledge, which by virtue of section 14(3) means: **7.72**

> knowledge which he might reasonably have been expected to acquire—
> (a) from facts observable or ascertainable by him; or
> (b) from facts ascertainable by him with the help of medical or other appropriate expert advice which it is reasonable for him to seek;
>
> but a person shall not be fixed under this subsection with knowledge of a fact ascertainable only with the help of expert advice so long as he has taken all reasonable steps to obtain (and, where appropriate, to act on) that advice.

This is a combined subjective/objective test. The plaintiff is fixed with knowledge which *he* might reasonably have been expected to acquire from facts observable or ascertainable by *him*.[126] A failure to seek legal advice will give rise to constructive knowledge of the facts which would have been

---

[124] *Halford v Brookes* [1991] 3 All ER 559, 574, *per* Lord Donaldson MR.

[125] Where the defendant is responsible in law for all the staff who played some role in the plaintiff's treatment, it is unnecessary for the plaintiff to identify the particular employee who was at fault: *Cassidy v Ministry of Health* [1951] 2 KB 343.

[126] *Nash v Eli Lilly & Co* [1993] 1 WLR 782, 799, CA; *Colegrove v Smyth* [1994] 5 Med LR 111, 114; cf *Forbes v Wandsworth Health Authority* [1996] 4 All ER 881 where the Court of Appeal had some difficulty in seeing how the individual character and intelligence of the plaintiff in a personal injury case can be relevant to the question of constructive knowledge (doubting the view expressed by Purchas LJ in *Nash v Eli Lilly & Co*). See also *Slevin v Southampton and South West Hampshire Health Authority* [1997] 8 Med LR 175, following *Forbes*.

discovered after the data at which it would have been reasonable to seek such advice;[127] but where the question is whether it was reasonable for the plaintiff to seek expert advice, his personal circumstances should be taken into account. Thus, it may well be reasonable for a plaintiff who is seriously ill or dying not to seek legal advice.[128] Similarly, it may be reasonable for a plaintiff to delay seeking legal advice where she was still receiving treatment and did not wish to sour relations with the doctors who were treating her.[129] Some account will be taken of the limited resources available to the plaintiff by way of advice, where, for example, his solicitors could only seek expert advice to the extent that they were authorised to do so by the Legal Aid Board.[130] Constructive knowledge does not include the knowledge of a child's parents during the child's minority.[131] Moreover, an ordinary person of average intelligence and average understanding of medical matters is not expected to infer from the fact that a child is born with cerebral palsy that there was a real possibility that an act or omission of the medical staff was the cause of the injury.[132]

7.73 The proviso to section 14(3) prevents a plaintiff from being fixed with constructive knowledge where an expert has failed to discover or disclose a relevant fact that ought to have been revealed,[133] but it applies only to facts which are 'ascertainable only with the help of expert advice'. Where the plaintiff himself could have discovered the information, then he is fixed with any knowledge that the expert acting on his behalf ought to have acquired.[134]

---

[127] *Hills v Potter* [1983] 3 All ER 716, 728.

[128] *Newton v Cammell Laird & Co (Shipbuilders and Engineers) Ltd* [1969] 1 All ER 708; *Davis v City and Hackney Health Authority* [1991] 2 Med LR 366; *Driscoll-Varley v Parkside Health Authority* [1991] 2 Med LR 346, 357. This is a question of degree. In *Forbes* (n 126 above) the plaintiff underwent a bypass operation on his leg which was unsuccessful, and there was a second opertion carried out the next day, which was also unsuccessful. His leg was amputated to prevent gangrene. Almost nine years later the plaintiff consulted a solicitor, and was advised by an avascular surgeon that delay in treating him after the first operation had caused the damage that resulted in the amputation. The Court of Appeal held that, although the plaintiff had no actual knowledge he did have constructive knowledge. He expected the operation to be successful and it was not, and a reasonable man would have sought advice reasonably promptly. He should have sought expert medical advice some 12 to 18 months after he came out of hospital, by which time he would have had time to overcome his shock at losing his leg and take stock of his disability and its consequences.

[129] *Ostick v Wandsworth Health Authority* [1995] 6 Med LR 338.

[130] *Khan v Ainslie* [1993] 4 Med LR 319. On the other hand, in *Skitt v Khan and Wakefield Health Authority* [1997] 8 Med LR 105 the Court of Appeal held that though lack of funds to obtain an expert's report could be a factor, that has to be weighed against the seriousness of the injury and its consequences for the plaintiff in deciding whether objectively it was reasonable to seek expert medical advice. On the facts it was understandable that the plaintiff did not seek such advice, but it was not reasonable.

[131] *Parry v Clwyd Health Authority* [1997] 8 Med LR 243. [132] ibid.

[133] See eg, *Marston v British Railways Board* [1976] ICR 124; *Stephen v Riverside Health Authority* [1990] 1 Med LR 261; *Davis v Ministry of Defence* (1985) *The Times*, 7 August, CA.

[134] *Leadbitter v Hodge Finance Ltd* [1982] 2 All ER 167, 174–5; *Halford v Brookes* [1991] 3 All ER 559, 565.

Erroneous advice about the law is irrelevant and does not prevent time **7.74**
running.[135] Where the legal advice consists of a failure to discover relevant
facts, or a failure to suggest a line of enquiry that would have revealed the
facts, then in theory the proviso to section 14(3) applies, although in
Leadbitter v Hodge Finance Ltd,[136] a very narrow view was taken of the
facts which are ascertainable only with the help of expert advice. It is also
possible that section 14(3)(b) does not apply to *any* form of legal advice,
since it has been doubted whether a party's solicitor is an 'expert' within
the meaning of the subsection, which is directed to experts in the sense of
expert witnesses.[137] This would mean that a plaintiff is not constructively
fixed with the knowledge of his solicitor *by virtue of section 14(3)*, but
under the general law of agency it may be that a plaintiff is fixed with the
actual, and even the constructive, knowledge of his solicitor.[138] Of course,
it must be reasonable to attribute knowledge to the solicitor. In *Hepworth v
Kerr*[139] the plaintiff suffered paraplegia following an operation under general anaesthetic and, despite a suggestion in the medical notes that his
condition might have been attributable to the operation, he was assured on
several occasions by the neurosurgeon who subsequently treated him for
the paralysis that the operation had not caused his condition. A report by
the neurosurgeon to the plaintiff's solicitors came to the same conclusion.
The defendants argued that the plaintiff had constructive knowledge
because a competent solicitor should have realised that the neurosurgeon
was the wrong expert and that he had not indicated that he had read the

---

[135] Limitation Act 1980, s 14(1); *Farmer v National Coal Board* (1985) *The Times* 27 April,
CA. See also *Jones v Liverpool Health Authority* [1996] PIQR 251, 266 where Glidewell LJ said
that: 'if a person has been advised by one consultant, who considers on the informtion put
before him that the plaintiff probably does not have a cause of action, and years later the
plaintiff is advised by another consultant that, upon precisely the same facts, he has a possible
cause of action, he cannot thereafter claim that he did not gain knowledge for the purposes of
sections 11 and 14 . . . until he received the later opinion.' With respect, this rather assumes
that it is the function of medical experts to advise about the law, which, clearly, it is not. If the
first expert advised that in his opinion there was no causal connection between the relevant acts
or omissions and the plaintiff's injury, then the advice concerns a fact, notwithstanding that
the conclusion would also be that no claim in law would be sustainable because the injury
could not be attributed to the defendant's acts or omissions. If this was the only information
that the plaintiff had then he would only acquire the relevant knowledge when informed by the
second expert that there was a causal connection.   [136] [1982] 2 All ER 167, 174–5.
[137] *Fowell v National Coal Board* (1986) *The Times*, 28 May, CA; *Khan v Ainslie* [1993] 4
Med LR 319, 325.
[138] *Simpson v Norwest Holst Southern Ltd* [1980] 2 All ER 471, 476. See *Fowell* (n 137
above), where Parker LJ specifically left this point open. See further the discussion by Hidden J
in *Nash v Eli Lilly & Co* [1991] 2 Med LR 169; *Colegrove v Smyth* [1994] 5 Med LR 111; *Khan
v Ainslie* [1993] 4 Med LR 319, 325. The Court of Appeal in *Nash v Eli Lilly & Co* [1993] 1
WLR 782, 800 could see no reason to depart from Hidden J's general approach to this issue.
[139] [1995] 6 Med LR 135.

hospital medical notes. This argument was rejected by Latham J. To require the plaintiff or his solicitor to question whether the expert had obtained sufficient information from the medical notes or to question whether or not he was the appropriate expert was 'asking for a startling degree of scepticism'. Some solicitors might have been sceptical, but that did not mean that it was something that any reasonably competent solicitor would have done.

(iv) *Section 33 discretion*

7.75 Where the primary three year limitation period has expired, the plaintiff may seek to persuade the court to exercise its discretion under section 33.[140] The court's discretion is unfettered,[141] except that a plaintiff who issued a writ within the primary limitation period but did not proceed with the action and then issues a second writ outside the limitation period, cannot rely on this section. In *Walkley v Precision Forgings Ltd*[142] the House of Lords held that section 33(1) directs the court to have regard to the degree to which the operation of the primary limitation period has prejudiced the plaintiff, but where the plaintiff has issued a writ in time and then for some reason the action has not been pursued, he has not been prejudiced by the effect of sections 11 or 12 but by his own dilatoriness. This rule applies whatever the reason for the plaintiff not proceeding with the first action: whether it is because he or his solicitors failed to serve the writ in time; or because the action was dismissed for want of prosecution; or, for good or bad reasons, the action was discontinued by the plaintiff.[143] On the other hand, *Walkley* will not apply where the plaintiff has been induced to discontinue the action by a misrepresentation or other improper conduct by the defendant. The defendant is then estopped from relying on sections 11 or 12. This exception will be construed narrowly, however, and does not arise merely from an admission of liability and the making of an interim payment by the defendant.[144]

7.76 Where the first writ, although issued in time, is technically invalid, a second writ issued outside the three year period is not caught by *Walkley* and the plaintiff can invoke the court's discretion.[145] Finally, if it can be said that the plaintiff did not have sufficient knowledge to start the limitation period under section 14, even though an earlier protective writ has been issued,

---

[140] The burden of proving that it is equitable to allow the action to proceed is the plaintiff's: *Thompson v Brown Construction (Ebbw Vale) Ltd* [1981] 2 All ER 296, 303.

[141] *Firman v Ellis* [1978] QB 886; *Thompson* (n 140 above); *Donovan v Gwentoys Ltd* [1990] 1 All ER 1018, 1023, *per* Lord Griffiths. [142] [1979] 1 WLR 606.

[143] *Chappell v Cooper* [1980] 2 All ER 463; *Forward v Hendricks* [1997] 2 All ER 397.

[144] *Deerness v John Keeble & Son Ltd* [1983] 2 Lloyd's Rep 260; *Forward* (n 143 above).

[145] *White v Glass* (1989) *The Times*, 18 February, CA; *Wilson v Banner Scaffolding Ltd* (1982) *The Times*, 22 June; *Re Workvale Ltd (No 2)* [1992] 2 All ER 627, CA.

then *Walkley* is irrelevant, since the 'second' writ will be within the *primary* limitation period.[146]

Under section 33(1) the court may direct that the primary limitation period **7.77** shall not apply if it would be equitable to allow the action to proceed, having regard to the degree to which (a) sections 11, 11A, or 12 prejudice the plaintiff, and (b) the decision to allow the action to proceed would prejudice the defendant. The court has to balance the degree of prejudice to the plaintiff caused by the operation of the primary limitation period against the prejudice to the defendant if the action were to be allowed to proceed. The stronger the plaintiff's case is on the merits, the greater the prejudice to him; and conversely, the weaker his case, the less he is prejudiced.[147] On the other hand, if the defendant has a good case on the merits, there is probably less prejudice to him in allowing the action to proceed, although in *Thompson v Brown Construction (Ebbw Vale) Ltd*[148] Lord Diplock said that it was still highly prejudicial to a defendant to allow the action to proceed even where he has a good defence on the merits. The loss of the limitation defence *as such* is not the prejudice to the defendant that has to be taken into account, but rather the effect of the delay on the defendant's ability to defend.[149] This must be balanced against the prejudice to the plaintiff of being barred from pursuing the action.[150]

When considering the degree of prejudice to the parties the court is required by **7.78** section 33(3) to have regard to all the circumstances of the case, and in particular to:

(a) the length of and reasons for the delay on the part of the plaintiff;
(b) the extent to which, having regard to the delay, the evidence . . . is likely to be less cogent . . .
(c) the conduct of the defendant after the cause of action arose, including the extent (if any) to which he responded to requests reasonably made by the

---

[146] This occurred in both *Davis v Ministry of Defence* (1985) *The Times*, 7 August, and *Stephen v Riverside Health Authority* [1990] 1 Med LR 261. In *Nash v Eli Lilly & Co* [1993] 1 WLR 782, 795–6, however, the Court of Appeal queried whether it could be said that a plaintiff who has previously taken proceedings did not have relevant knowledge.

[147] *Dale v British Coal Corporation* [1992] PIQR 373, 380, *per* Stuart-Smith LJ, CA; *Forbes v Wandsworth Health Authority* [1996] 4 All ER 881, 894–5.

[148] [1981] 2 All ER 296, 301.

[149] *Hartley v Birmingham City District Council* [1992] 2 All ER 213, 224 *per* Parker LJ; *Ward v Foss* (1993) *The Times*, 29 November, CA, *per* Hobhouse LJ. It cannot always be said that where the ability of a defendant to defend on the merits has not been affected by the delay the defendant suffers no prejudice in having to defend a weak case, since disapplying the primary limitation period will put the defendant to the expense of defending the action. Allowing the action to proceed may simply enable a dilatory plaintiff to claim from the defendants a sum in settlement which reflects the risk in costs to the defendants rather than the fair value of the claim: *Nash v Eli Lilly & Co* [1993] 1 WLR 782, 804, 808, CA.

[150] *Ward v Foss* (1993) *The Times*, 29 November, CA, *per* Hobhouse LJ.

plaintiff for information or inspection for the purpose of ascertaining facts which were or might be relevant to the plaintiff's cause of action against the defendant;

    (d) the duration of any disability of the plaintiff arising after the date of the accrual of the cause of action;

    (e) the extent to which the plaintiff acted promptly and reasonably once he knew whether or not the act or omission of the defendant, to which the injury was attributable, might be capable at that time of giving rise to an action for damages;

    (f) the steps, if any, taken by the plaintiff to obtain medical, legal or other expert advice and the nature of any such advice he may have received.

The court should consider all the circumstances of the case, not simply the issues identified by section 33(3).[151] Provided this has been done, the Court of Appeal will be reluctant to interfere with the trial judge's exercise of discretion.[152]

(a) Length of and Reasons for Delay

7.79 'Delay' in subsection 33(3)(a) and (b) refers to the period between the expiry of the primary limitation period and the issue of the writ, not the period between the accrual of the action or the plaintiff's 'knowledge' and the issue of the writ.[153] However, in weighing the degree of prejudice to the defendant, the court is entitled to take into account the whole period of delay, including that within the primary limitation period, as part of all the circumstances of the case.[154] In these circumstances it is the delay between the commencement of the limitation period and notification to the defendant of the claim, rather than the issue of the writ, that is significant, the object being to bar 'thoroughly stale claims'. Therefore, there is a distinction between cases where the defendant was notified of the claim fairly promptly, and so had an opportunity to give it full consideration, but the limitation period has expired through an oversight by the plaintiff's solicitors,[155] and cases where the defendant first heard of the claim some years after the accident.[156]

7.80 A short delay probably causes little prejudice to the defendant,[157] indeed, a very short delay causes no prejudice at all, particularly where the defendant

---

[151] *Taylor v Taylor* (1984) *The Times*, 14 April, CA; *Donovan v Gwentoys Ltd* [1990] 1 All ER 1018, HL.

[152] *Conry v Simpson* [1983] 3 All ER 369; *Bradley v Hanseatic Shipping Co Ltd* [1986] 2 Lloyd's Rep 34, 38. The prejudice to each side may be 'obvious' and not have to be expressly considered: *Yates v Thakeham Tiles Ltd* [1995] PIQR 135, 139, *per* Nourse LJ, CA.

[153] *Thompson v Brown Construction (Ebbw Vale) Ltd* [1981] 2 All ER 296, 301; *Eastman v London Country Bus Services Ltd* (1985) *The Times*, 23 November, CA.

[154] *Donovan v Gwentoys Ltd* [1990] 1 All ER 1018, 1024.

[155] *Thompson* (n 153 above); see also *Simpson v Norwest Holst Southern Ltd* [1980] 2 All ER 471, 478.

[156] *Donovan* (n 154 above), 1024, *per* Lord Griffiths; *Dale* (n 147 above), 385, CA.

[157] *Firman v Ellis* [1978] QB 886; *Simpson* (n 155 above), 478.

was notified about the claim at an early stage,[158] whereas a delay of five or six years raises a rebuttable presumption of prejudice.[159] The length of the delay is probably of less significance than the reasons for the delay and the effect of the delay on the evidence. Reasons for the delay will vary considerably, and the plaintiff's subjective beliefs are taken into account.[160] The plaintiff may have been unaware of his legal rights,[161] or the injury may not have appeared so serious at first,[162] or he may have felt that he was 'sponging' if he sued and may have wanted to maintain good relations with the defendant,[163] or the plaintiff may have been in a debilitated physical and mental state throughout the relevant period.[164] Generally, where the plaintiff's conduct has not been personally blameworthy, this will carry considerable weight in persuading the court to exercise the discretion in his favour.[165]

(b) Cogency of the Evidence

The effect of the delay on the cogency of the evidence will be very significant. If documents have been destroyed or witnesses have disappeared, this is a different situation from cases where there is little real dispute about the facts, since the defendant's ability to defend the case has clearly been prejudiced.[166] Cases which are based on allegations about failures in systems of work are likely to be better documented than one-off accidents.[167] Cases of medical negligence should, in theory, be reasonably well documented in the medical records,[168] although this is not always the case.[169]

7.81

---

[158] *Hartley v Birmingham City District Council* [1992] 2 All ER 213; *Hendy v Milton Keynes Health Authority* [1992] 3 Med LR 114.

[159] *Buck v English Electric Co Ltd* [1977] 1 WLR 806; *Pilmore v Northern Trawlers Ltd* [1986] 1 Lloyd's Rep 552.

[160] *Buck* (n 159 above); *McCafferty v Metropolitan Police District Receiver* [1977] 1 WLR 1073; *Coad v Cornwall & Isles of Scilly Health Authority* [1997] 8 Med LR 154.

[161] *Brooks v Coates (UK) Ltd* [1984] 1 All ER 702, 713; *Coad* (n 160 above).

[162] *McCafferty* (n 160 above).

[163] *Buck* (n 159 above); *McCafferty* (n 160 above). A patient's natural reluctance to upset the doctor/patient relationship by engaging in litigation is relevant here.

[164] *Mills v Dyer-Fare* (1987) (unreported), QBD; *Birnie v Oxfordshire Health Authority* (1982) 2 *The Lancet* 281, QBD; *Pearse v Barnet Health Authority* [1998] PIQR P39.

[165] *Brooks* (n 161 above).

[166] *Dale v British Coal Corporation* [1992] PIQR 373, 385, CA; *Hattam v National Coal Board* (1978) 122 SJ 777; cf *Brooks* (n 161 above), 713—14.

[167] *Cotton v General Electric Co Ltd* (1979) 129 New LJ 73; *Pilmore v Northern Trawlers Ltd* [1986] 1 Lloyd's Rep 552; *Buck* (n 159 above).

[168] *Bentley v Bristol and Western Health Authority* [1991] 2 Med LR 359. In *Pearse v Barnet Health Authority* [1998] PIQR 39 it was held that there was no prejudice to the defendants from a delay between 1991 and 1994, in dealing with a case based on events in 1970 which would inevitably turn on the medical records (which were virtually complete). Where the defendants have had to investigate and prepare to meet another case on liability arising out of the same facts the cogency of the evidence may not be affected by the delay: *Bowers v Harrow Health Authority* [1995] 6 Med LR 16.

[169] In *Forbes v Wandsworth Health Authority* [1996] 4 All ER 881 the Court of Appeal

(c) Conduct of the Defendant

7.82 Section 33(3)(c) refers to the extent to which the defendant responded to reasonable requests for information or inspection for the purpose of ascertaining facts which were or might be relevant to the plaintiff's cause of action. A potential defendant does not have a duty to volunteer information but he should not obstruct the plaintiff in obtaining information.[170] This includes the conduct of the defendant's solicitors and his insurers. The defendant's conduct is relevant even where he has made an honest mistake in giving misleading information.[171]

(d) Duration of the Disability

7.83 If the plaintiff is under a disability at the date at which the cause of action accrued, the commencement of the limitation period is postponed until he ceases to be under a disability,[172] but supervening disability does not stop time running. It will be taken into account, however, in the exercise of the discretion. Since minority can never supervene, section 33(3)(d) applies to supervening mental incapacity. The plaintiff's physical disabilities can be considered under section 33(3)(a), as part of the reasons for the delay, or as part of 'all the circumstances of the case'.[173]

(e) Extent to which Plaintiff Acted Promptly

7.84 If the plaintiff has acted promptly and reasonably once he became aware of the cause of action, it is not to be counted against him that his lawyers have been dilatory and allowed the primary limitation period to expire.[174] In *Yates v Thakeham Tiles Ltd*,[175] the plaintiff consulted solicitors after the expiry of the primary limitation period, and the solicitors did not notify the defendants of a potential claim until a year later. The Court of Appeal held that this was

---

declined to exercise the discretion under s 33 in the plaintiff's favour having regard to the prejudice to the defendants after a long delay, caused by an inability now to locate medical records and witnesses, fading memories, the difficulty that experts would have in dealing with the appropriate standards of practice of 14 years earlier, and the fact that the plaintiff's case was supported by scanty evidence and had only modest prospects of success.

[170] *Thompson v Brown Construction (Ebbw Vale) Ltd* [1981] 2 All ER 296, 302. A serious delay in providing the plaintiff's medical records may be a relevant consideration: *Mills v Dyer-Fare* (1987) (unreported), QBD; *Atkinson v Oxfordshire Health Authority* [1993] 4 Med LR 18, QBD, where a failure to tell the plaintiff or his mother what had happened during the course of an operation meant that to a large extent the delay was of the defendants' own making.
[171] *Marston v British Railways Board* [1976] ICR 124.
[172] Limitation Act 1980, s 28. The word 'disability' in s 33 has the same meaning as in s 28, ie as defined in s 38 (see para 7.89, below). It does not incluse physical disability: *Yates v Thakeham Tiles Ltd* [1995] PIQR 135, CA; *Thomas v Plaistow* [1997] PIQR 540, CA.
[173] *Yates* (n 172 above); *Pearse v Barnet Health Authority* [1998] PIQR 39.
[174] *Thompson* (n 170 above), 303.   [175] [1995] PIQR 135, CA.

proper where the solicitors were obtaining all the relevant informtion to support the claim, such as advice from counsel, and obtaining legal aid.

(f) Steps Taken to Obtain Expert Advice

This includes legal advice and whether it was favourable or unfavourable.[176] **7.85**
Thus, while erroneous legal advice will not prevent time running under the three year limitation period, it is relevant under section 33.

(g) Other Factors

The availability of an alternative remedy (for example, against the plaintiff's **7.86**
negligent solicitors) is a 'highly relevant consideration', but it is not conclusive. Even where the plaintiff would have a cast-iron case against his solicitors, he will suffer some prejudice in having to find and instruct new solicitors, additional delay, and a possible personal liability for costs up to the date of the court's refusal of the application.[177] Where there is any real dispute about the solicitors' liability in negligence, then the chances of the plaintiff having an alternative remedy should be largely disregarded.[178] It is legitimate to take into account the insurance position of both defendant and plaintiff, as part of all the circumstances of the case,[179] but the court will not apply different principles to multi-party litigation from the principles applied to ordinary, single plaintiff actions when exercising the discretion. The merits of each case must be considered individually.[180] The fact that a medical negligence action is a claim for professional negligence may be a factor in the defendant's favour, because such actions have more serious consequences for defendants and should be prosecuted without delay.[181] This can only be

---

[176] *Jones v GD Searle & Co Ltd* [1978] 3 All ER 654.

[177] *Thompson* (n 170 above), 301–2.

[178] *Firman v Ellis* [1978] QB 886, 916, *per* Geoffrey Lane LJ. See further *Conry v Simpson* [1983] 3 All ER 369; *Ramsden v Lee* [1992] 2 All ER 204; *Donovan v Gwentoys Ltd* [1990] 1 All ER 1018.

[179] *Firman* (n 178 above) 916; *Liff v Peasley* [1980] 1 WLR 781, 789; *Hartley v Birmingham City District Council* [1992] 2 All ER 213, 224, CA. In *Kelly v Bastible* [1997] 8 Med LR 15 the Court of Appeal held that the fact that the defendant is insured was one of the factors that could be placed in the scales when weighing prejudice to the parties under section 33, but, if, treating the defendant and insurer as a composite unit, the delay had seriously prejudiced their ability to defend the action, and if the court would not have allowed the action to proceed had the defendant not been insured, the weight to be given to the mere fact that the defendant was insured should be nil.

[180] *Nash v Eli Lilly & Co* [1991] 2 Med LR 169; aff'd [1993] 1 WLR 782, 810, CA.

[181] *Jackson & Powell on Professional Negligence*, 3rd edn, (1992), para 1.131. In the analogous context of an application to strike out an action for want of prosecution, prejudice in the form of the worry that professional staff would suffer with the action hanging over them like the 'sword of Damocles', can be taken into account: *Biss v Lambeth Health Authority* [1978] 1 WLR 382, CA. It is exceptional, however, to treat the 'mere sword of Damocles, hanging for an unnecessary period' as a sufficient reason in itself to strike out: *Department of Transport v Chris*

relevant, however, where the defendant has had a claim intimated, but there has been a long delay in issuing the writ.[182]

(v) *Death*

(a) Fatal Accidents Act 1976

7.87   In an action for loss of dependency under the Fatal Accidents Act 1976, if the death occurred before the expiry of the deceased's three year limitation period, then a new three year period commences in favour of the dependants. This period runs from the date of death or the date of the dependants' 'knowledge', whichever is later.[183] If the action is not commenced within three years of the death or the date of knowledge of the dependants, the action is barred,[184] although the court may disapply the primary limitation period under section 33. If the deceased's three year limitation period had expired before he died, then in theory he could not have maintained an action at the date of his death and the dependants' action is barred. The court can exercise its discretion under section 33, however, having regard to the length of and reasons for the delay on the part of the deceased.[185] The court may disapply section 12 only where the reason why the deceased could no longer maintain an action was because of the time limit in section 11.[186] If he could no longer maintain an action for any other reason, there is no discretion to allow the dependants' action to proceed.

(b) Law Reform (Miscellaneous Provisions) Act 1934

7.88   The position in the case of an action on behalf of the estate of a deceased person under the Law Reform (Miscellaneous Provisions) Act 1934 is similar to that which applies to Fatal Accident Act claims. If the deceased died before the expiry of his three year limitation period, a new three year period commences which runs from either the date of death or the date of the personal representative's knowledge, whichever is later.[187] If this period

---

Smaller (Transport) Ltd [1989] 1 All ER 897, 905, *per* Lord Griffiths. See further *Slevin v Southampton and South West Hampshire Health Authority* [1997] 8 Med LR 175, 181 on the question of distress to the defendant as a factor in the exercise of the discretion under s 33 in medical negligence cases; and *Sims v Dartford and Gravesham Health Authority* [1996] 7 Med LR 381.

[182] *Dobbie v Medway Health Authority* [1994] 4 All ER 451, 462, *per* Beldam LJ. See *Birnie v Oxfordshire Area Health Authority* (1982) 2 *The Lancet* 281, QBD, Glidewell J.

[183] Limitation Act 1980, s 12. 'Knowledge' is defined in s 14. If dependants have different dates of knowledge, time runs separately against each of them: s 13(1).   [184] ibid, s 12(2).

[185] Limitation Act 1980, s 33(4).   [186] ibid, s 33(2).

[187] ibid, s 11(5). If there is more than one personal representative and their dates of knowledge are different, time runs from the earliest date: s 11(7).

expires the personal representative may request the court to exercise its discretion under section 33. Where the deceased died after the expiry of his three year limitation period, an action by the personal representative is barred by section 11(3), but again the court can exercise its discretion under section 33, having regard to the length of and the reasons for the delay by the deceased.

(vi) *Persons under a Disability*

A person is under a disability while he is an infant or of unsound mind.[188] An **7.89** infant is a person under the age of 18,[189] and a person is of unsound mind if, by reason of mental disorder within the meaning of the Mental Health Act 1983, he is incapable of managing and administering his property and affairs.[190] If a person to whom a right of action accrues is under a disability at the date when the action accrued, time does not run until he ceases to be under a disability or dies, whichever occurs first.[191] Thus, an infant has an indefeasible right to bring an action for personal injuries at any time before the age of 21,[192] and a person of unsound mind has three years from the date he ceases to be of unsound mind. If the accident itself caused immediate unsoundness of mind time will not begin to run.[193] The fact that a defendant may suffer prejudice from a long delay is immaterial.[194] If the plaintiff was not under a disability when the action accrued, supervening unsoundness of mind will not prevent time running,[195] though the discretion under section 33 is available.

---

[188] ibid, s 38(2).

[189] Family Law Reform Act 1969, s 1.

[190] Limitation Act 1980, s 38(3). Under the Mental Health Act 1983, s 1(2) mental disorder is defined as 'mental illness, arrested or incomplete development of the mind, psychopathic disorder, and any other disorder or disability of mind'. See also Limitation Act 1980, s 38(4) which identifies circumstances in which for the purposes of s 38(2) a person shall be conclusively presumed to be of unsound mind.

[191] Limitation Act 1980, s 28(1) and (6). If the person under a disability dies the primary limitation period starts to run, and there can be no further extension under s 28: s 28(3).

[192] *Tolley v Morris* [1979] 2 All ER 561.

[193] *Kirby v Leather* [1965] 2 QB 367, CA. This applies if the unsoundness of mind arises at any time before the end of the day on which the accident occurred; *Boot v Boot* (1991) (unreported), CA; *Turner v WH Malcolm Ltd* (1992) 15 BMLR 40, CA.

[194] *Headford v Bristol and District Health Authority* [1995] 6 Med LR 1, 4, CA, *per* Rose LJ.

[195] *Purnell v Roche* [1927] 2 Ch 142.

8

INSTITUTIONAL LIABILITY

8.01 Doctors and other health professionals working within the NHS function within an institutional framework.[1] Hospital doctors and nurses perform their professional duties for an institution which is usually an NHS Trust[2] or, though increasingly rarely, for a Health Authority in a so-called 'managed unit'. General practitioners provide general medical services in a relationship[3]

---

[1] Discussed in Ch 1.
[2] Constituted under the National Health Service and Community Care Act 1990.
[3] Under the National Health Service (General Medical Services) Regulations 1992, SI 1992/635 (as amended), the legal nature of the relationship remains unclear: see *Roy v Kensington*

with a Health Authority (formerly known as a Family Health Services Authority).[4] They may also provide 'personal medical services' under a 'pilot scheme' by virtue of the National Health Service (Primary Care) Act 1997.[4a] Nurses and others may work for the GP practice in which they are based. In addition to the personal liability of an individual for negligence,[5] the law also imposes liability in some circumstances upon the institution. First, the institution will be vicariously liable for the negligence of its employees committed in the course of their employment.[6] Secondly, the institution may owe a primary or direct duty owed to the patient which is breached by the failure to provide a safe 'health environment'[7] or, more controversially, by an act of negligence by any individual working within, and as part of, the institution.[8] The same questions arise in respect of the liability of a clinic or doctor in the context of private medical services.

The importance of liability being imposed upon the institution is that **8.02** practically (and legally) it shifts financial responsibility to the organisation providing the medical service. While, in the case of vicarious liability, the employee will in theory remain legally liable to the patient and the employer will have an indemnity[9] claim against the employee,[10] in practice it is the institution who is sued and who pays the damages award.[11] Indeed, as will be seen later in this chapter,[12] since 1 January 1990 within the NHS this practical position has been enshrined in the litigation arrangements following the introduction of the NHS Indemnity Scheme[13] and, since 1 March 1996, the Clinical Negligence Scheme for Trusts.[14] The only contexts in which a

---

and Chelsea and Westminster FPC [1992] 1 AC 624 (HL). However, even if there is a contractual element, the relationship is not one of employment. See Kennedy, I and Grubb A, *Medical Law*, 2nd edn, (Butterworths, 1994), 38–43.

[4] The change was brought about by the unification of health authorities under the Health Authorities Act 1995. Prior to the National Health Service and Community Care Act 1990, FHSAs had been known as Family Practitioner Committees.

[4a] See ch1, above. The first 'pilot schemes' came into existence on 1 April 1998.

[5] Discussed in Chs 5–7.   [6] See below, paras 8.03 *et seq.*

[7] See below, paras 8.15 *et seq.*   [8] See below, paras 8.20 *et seq.*

[9] Or for contribution if the employer is also in breach of an independent duty of care owed to the patient: *Jones v Manchester Corporation* [1952] 2 QB 852 (CA).

[10] *Lister v Romford Ice and Cold Storage Co Ltd* [1957] AC 555 (HL).

[11] Until 1 January 1990, an agreement dating back to 1954 between the medical protection organisations and the Department of Health meant that contribution or indemnity claims were settled privately and not in court: HM (54)32.   [12] See below, paras 8.74–8.88.

[13] HC (89)34, and now updated as HSG (96)48. Discussed by Brazier, M (1990) 6 *Professional Negligence* 88.

[14] See The National Health Service (Clinical Negligence Scheme) Regulations 1996, SI 1996/251, as amended by SI 1997/527, made pursuant to the National Health Service and Community Care Act 1990, s 21.

doctor remains personally liable in practice is where he is a GP[15] or in private practice. Even in these situations, the doctor will almost certainly have what is, in effect, insurance cover for his liability from one of the medical defence organisations.[16] As a consequence, he will be liable for his negligence but, in practice, any award of damages will be paid by the defence organisation.

A. Vicarious Liability[17]

8.03 Under the common law an employer is vicariously liable for the torts of his employees committed in the course of their employment.[18] The general statement applies within the NHS and private health care facilities.[19] The three relevant issues in determining the institution's liability are: (1) has the individual committed a tort?; (2) is he an employee of the defendant?; and (3) did he commit the tort in the course of his employment? The first question does not call for any further comment here.[20] As regards the third, if the negligence occurs on the premises of the institution, it is most unlikely that any question will arise of whether the employee is acting 'in the course of his employment'. He will be so acting, for example, where an employee (such as a doctor) injures a patient in the course of diagnosis or treatment, or an employee (such as a porter) drops the patient whilst lifting them onto a trolley. A doctor will be 'acting in the course of his employment' even if he commits a battery (or false imprisonment) when treating a patient, for example, where force[21] or restraint[22] is used upon an incompetent patient in their best interests but it is excessive and unreasonable. Only the most

---

[15] The NHS schemes do not apply to negligence actions against GPs arising out of the provision of general or personal medical services and, as will be seen, the relationship with a Health Authority is not one of employment giving rise to vicarious liability.

[16] The Medical Defence Union, Medical and Dental Defence Union of Scotland, and the Medical Protection Society.

[17] For a definitive account of the modern law, see Atiyah, P, *Vicarious Liability in Tort*, (Butterworths, 1967).

[18] The modern doctrine dates back to the seventeenth century and, perhaps, to the case of *Tuberville v Stamp* (1697) 1 Ld Raym 264. See generally Williams, G, 'Vicarious Liability and the Master's Indemnity' (1957) 20 MLR 220. For a general discussion, see eg, *Clerk & Lindsell on Torts*, 17th edn, (1997), ch 3.

[19] For discussion of the 'hospital' cases see Atiyah P, *Vicarious Liability in Tort* (n 17 above), 87–9; *Salmond and Heuston on the Law of Torts*, 21st edn, (eds R F V Heuston and R A Buckley, 1996), 437–8; *Winfield and Jolowicz on Tort*, 14th edn, (ed W V H Rogers, 1994) 597–8; *Street on Torts*, 9th edn, (ed M Brazier, 1993) 487–8 and Jones M, *Medical Negligence*, 2nd edn, (1996), 392–9.

[20] Vicarious liability extends not only to the tort of negligence but also to other torts such as battery committed in the course of employment.

[21] *Re MB (Medical Treatment)* [1997] 2 FLR 426 (CA).

[22] *Re C (Detention: Medical Treatment)* [1997] 2 FLR 180 (Wall J).

outrageous displays of individualistic behaviour by the employee, such as a porter who punches a patient, could isolate the institution from liability.[23] The second question is the crucial one: is the negligent person an employee of the hospital?[24]

1. Staff in NHS Trusts and Health Authorities

(i) Hillyer: *Vicarious Liability Excluded*

At one time, English law held to the view that hospitals could not be liable for **8.04** the negligence of their staff exercising their professional skills. In 1909 in *Hillyer v Governors of St Bartholomews Hospital*,[25] the Court of Appeal held that liability could only arise for 'purely ministerial or administrative duties' which, in essence, meant failures that did not involve judgment or the exercise of professional or clinical discretion. The decision was based on a view, now no longer tenable, that a person could not be an employee (for whom an institution could be vicariously liable) unless the institution has 'control' over the performance of the individual's duties.[26] The reasoning in the case is, and indeed was, flawed.[27] First, 'control' is not a satisfactory indicator of who is an employee.[28] It reflects a bygone era when workers carried out the tasks of their employer who was himself skilled in that work.[29] Today, as indeed in 1909, employees in many work-contexts possess skills far beyond their employer's abilities and work not for 'X' but for an institution in a management structure where those above occupy that position because they possess their own skills rather than of those they manage. Secondly, it is difficult to understand the reasoning in *Hillyer*. How could a particular individual have been an employee when carrying out some functions ('purely ministerial or administrative') but not when performing others ('professional skills')? Perhaps, as regards doctors, their functions were thought always to fall into the latter category: a very big assumption. But even if they did, other staff such as nurses carry out functions falling under both classifications. In principle, however, they either were, or were not, employees of the institution. As a result, until the 1950s, hospitals were not liable for medical negligence of their staff. Apart from the preserved

---

[23] eg, *Keppel Bus Co v Ahmad* [1974] 1 WLR 1082. Contrast situations of authorised force (nn 21 and 22 above) and see generally, Rose, F, (1977) 40 MLR 420.

[24] For the remainder of this chapter the term 'hospital' will be used to encompass all institutions within the NHS unless the context otherwise requires.

[25] [1909] 2 KB 820. See also, *Evans v Liverpool Corp* [1906] 1 KB 160.

[26] The modern 'composite' approach is set out in the Privy Council decision of *Lee Ting Sang v Chung Chi-Keung* [1990] 2 AC 374.

[27] See a criticism as far back as 1936 in *Lindsey CC v Marshall* [1936] 2 All ER 1076, 1094 *per* Lord Wright.   [28] See Atiyah, *Vicarious Liability in Tort* (n 17 above), ch 5.

[29] See Kahn-Freund, O, 'Servants and Independent Contractors' (1951) 14 MLR 504.

category of functions in *Hillyer*, their liability depended upon a breach of a primary or direct duty owed to the patient.

(ii) Cassidy *and* Roe: *Vicarious Liability Introduced*

8.05 The untenable basis of the *Hillyer* decision led to its eventual rejection in other countries such as Canada,[30] Australia[31] and Ireland.[32] English law gradually moved away from the 'control test'.[33] But, in the particular context of hospitals, it survived for over 30 years[34] until the Court of Appeal's decision in *Gold v Essex CC*.[35] In that case, a majority of the Court of Appeal[36] rejected *Hillyer* and held that a hospital was vicariously liable for the negligence of a radiographer. Whilst the case law developed cautiously, the judges came to accept that both permanent and temporary full-time members of a hospital's staff worked under contracts of service (as employees) rather than under contracts for services (as independent contractors).[37] The position of visiting staff remained unclear.[38] In the 1950s the Court of Appeal in *Cassidy v Ministry of Health*[39] and *Roe v Minister of Health*[40] effectively consigned *Hillyer* to the historical dustbin.[41] In *Cassidy*, Denning LJ remarked that the *Hillyer* rule was motivated by a desire 'to relieve the charitable hospitals from liabilities which they could not afford'.[42] The structure of health provision had markedly changed making this rationale no longer applicable and, of course, in particular the introduction of the National Health Service in 1948.[43] Thus, the

---

[30] *Sisters of St Joseph of the Diocese of London v Fleming* [1938] SCR 172 (Can Sup Ct). See Picard, E and Robertson, G, *Legal Liability of Doctors and Hospitals in Canada*, 3rd edn, (1996), 381–97. [31] *Henson v Perth Hospital* (1939) 41 WALR 15.

[32] *O'Donovan v Cork CC* [1967] IR 173.

[34] It survived in America until 1957 and the New York case of *Bing v Thunig* (1957) 143 NE 2d 3. The exclusion of liability was based upon an immunity for the charitable status of hospitals. This is now rejected by the majority of jurisdictions in America: see Furrow, B, Greaney, T, Johnson, S, Jost, T and Schwartz, R, *Health Law*, Vol 1 (1995), ch 7.

[35] [1942] 2 KB 293.

[36] MacKinnon and Goddard LJ, ibid, at 308–9 and 312–13 respectively. Lord Greene MR decided the case on the basis of the hospital's non-delegable duty to the patient, ibid at 301–2. Reliance was placed upon Goodhart, A, (1938) 54 LQR 553.

[37] eg, *Collins v Hertfordshire CC* [1947] 1 KB 598 (junior house surgeon employed on a temporary but full-time basis).

[38] ibid at 619 *per* Hilbery J. See also *Gold* (n 35 above), 310 *per* Goddard LJ and *Cassidy* (n 39 below), 351 *per* Somervell LJ (no vicarious liability).

[39] [1951] 2 KB 343 (vicariously liable for all permanent staff, including assistant medical officer).

[40] [1954] 2 QB 66 (vicariously liable for part-time staff, including anaesthetist).

[41] The Scottish courts followed suit in *MacDonald v Glasgow Western Hospitals* 1954 SC 453 (CS(IH)). [42] N 39 above, 361.

[43] The potential for charitable and non-profit bodies to be liable in has been clear in England since 1866: *Mersey Docks and Harbour Board Trustees v Gibbs* (1866) LR 1 HL 93.

negligence of all those who form part of the 'organisation'[44] such as doctors, nurses, porters and other staff are, in practice, caught by the doctrine of vicarious liability.[45] It has never been expressly decided that a consultant—the highest employment grade within the NHS—is an employee of a hospital[46] although in one case, Denning LJ asserted it.[47] There is no doubt today, however, that consultants within the NHS are properly seen as employees of NHS Trusts. Their higher employment status than 'junior doctors' is irrelevant for this purpose. They are as much employees of the institution as anyone else, albeit that their appointment is governed by statutory instrument.[48]

The correct question in determining whether a hospital is vicariously liable **8.06** for an individual is whether *in the particular case* that member of staff is, or is not, working under a contract of service as an employee. The issue is a factual one turning on the nature of the contractual relationship between the parties having regard to all the circumstances.[49] The court will look for 'indicia' of the employer–employee relationship without regarding any one factor as necessarily conclusive.[50] In practice, however, a hospital will be liable for the negligence of all its full-time and part-time staff,[51] whether permanently or temporarily engaged, on the basis that they are employees of the hospital.[52]

---

[44] *Roe* (n 40 above), *per* Morris LJ at 91.

[45] The view expressed in *Hillyer* (n 25 above) 826 *per* Farwell LJ, that nurses in an operating theatre are employees of the surgeon and not the hospital should no longer be relied upon: see, *Cassidy* (n 39 above), *per* Denning LJ at 361–2. See also *Morris v Winsbury-White* [1937] 4 All ER 494 (rejecting vicarious liability of surgeon for nurse in operating theatre) and *Gold v Essex CC* (n 35 above), 312–3 *per* Goddard LJ.

[46] The position of a consultant was distinguished by the judges in *Cassidy* (n 39 above), *per* Somervell LJ at 351 and Singleton LJ at 358. See also *Roe* (n 40 above), *per* Denning LJ at 82 ('consultants or anaesthetists selected and employed by the patient himself'); *Collins* (n 37 above), *per* Hilbery J at 619–20.

[47] *Razzel v Snowball* [1954] 1 WLR 1382, 1386.

[48] See National Health Service (Appointment of Consultants) Regulations 1996, SI 1996/701 and National Health Service (Appointment of Consultants) (Wales) Regulations 1996, SI 1996/1313. See also *Good Practice Guidance* (NHS Executive), March 1996.

[49] *Ready Mixed Concrete (South East) Ltd v Minister of Pensions* [1968] 2 QB 497 and *Lee Ting Sang v Chung Chi-Keung* [1990] 2 AC 374.

[50] See Atiyah, *Vicarious Liability in Tort* (n 17 above), chs 3–6.

[51] Including occupational physicians: see *Stokes v Guest, Keen and Nettlefold (Bolts and Nuts) Ltd* [1968] 1 WLR 1776.

[52] For a masterly survey of the law in common law and civilian jurisdictions see Giesen, D, *International Medical Malpractice Law*, (1988), 38–59.

(iii) *Paying Patients within the NHS*

8.07   Health Authorities[53] and NHS Trusts[54] have statutory powers to provide accommodation and services on a private basis to patients: so-called powers of 'income generation'.[55] What is the position of a patient treated privately within an NHS hospital in a so-called 'pay-bed'? Will the hospital be vicariously liable for the negligence of the doctors or nurses? The staff, both nurses and doctors, will usually be employees of the hospital in which the patient is being treated. The crucial legal issue, therefore, in determining the vicarious liability of the hospital will be whether the staff were acting 'in the course of their employment' or in a purely private capacity when treating the patient. The patient may be entitled to assume that he is an 'NHS patient', given the circumstances, and the hospital may, apart from payment and the level of services, deal with the patient as an NHS patient albeit a 'paying guest'. It may well be that the staff carry out their care of the patient on 'NHS time'.[56] It is possible, therefore, that this combination of factors will lead a court to distinguish this patient from one treated in a wholly private context,[57] and impose vicarious liability on the hospital.[58]

(iv) *'Borrowed' Doctors and Other Staff*

8.08   While it will generally be beyond doubt that, as a matter of fact, a member of the hospital staff is an employee, there are a few situations that call for comment: 'borrowed' or 'visiting' staff and agency staff. A doctor who is loaned by his employer, Trust 'X', to work in a hospital operated by Trust 'Y' probably, in law, remains an employee of Trust 'X'.[59] However, the

---

[53] National Health Service Act 1977, s 65.

[54] National Health Service and Community Care Act 1990, Sch 2, paras 14, 15.

[55] Discussed in Newdick, C, *Who Should We Treat?* (OUP, 1995), 73–5.

[56] The Clinical Negligence Scheme for Trusts applies: The National Health Service (Clinical Negligence Scheme) Regulations 1996 SI 1996/251 as amended by the National Health Service (Clinical Negligence Scheme) (Amendment) Regulations 1997 SI 1997/527, reg 2 substituting definition of 'relevant function' in reg 1(2) of 1996 Regulations.

[57] On which see below, para 8.13.

[58] This should be distinguished from situations where the patient is treated in a private clinic or hospital pursuant to an agreement with the health authority or GP fund-holder. While such patients remain 'NHS patients', the only possible liability of an NHS body would be for breach of a direct or primary duty; the doctors and nurses will not be employed within the NHS but by the private provider.

[59] *Mersey Docks and Harbour Board v Coggins and Griffith (Liverpool) Ltd* [1947] AC 1. There is a heavy burden on the permanent employer to shift his prima facie responsibility to

usual practice in this situation is for the doctor to enter into a temporary contract of service with Trust 'Y'. There is, in effect, a temporary transfer of his duties to another employer. In which case, it is Trust 'Y' who will be vicariously liable for his negligence; an outcome which more accurately places the responsibility on the appropriate party. To the outside world, and particular to patients of Trust 'Y', he will be seen as working for his 'new' employer, Trust 'Y'. It would simply be incongruous if, whilst being paid by and performing the functions of Trust 'Y', Trust 'X' remained liable for his negligence. It will be Trust 'Y' that possesses all the trappings of his *current* employer. It would be otherwise, of course, if a doctor working for Trust 'X' were on a visit to a doctor-friend at Trust 'Y' who asked him to examine a patient in the course of which he negligently injured them. Here, neither Trust will be liable for him. While he is an employee of Trust 'X', he will not in these circumstances be acting 'in the course of his employment' with Trust 'X'. As regards Trust 'Y', he is simply not an employee. The doctor would, of course, be personally liable but Trust 'Y's liability, if at all, would depend upon a breach of a primary or direct duty owed to the patient.[60]

(v) *Agency Staff*

In the case of agency staff such as nurses, a hospital is unlikely to be **8.09** vicariously liable for their negligence as they will remain employees of the agency (or independent contractors) unless a contract of service is entered into with the hospital.[61] Again, the hospital's liability, if any, will be for breach of a primary or direct duty owed to the patient.[62]

2. General Practitioners

(i) *Liability of Health Authorities*

General practitioners provide primary care to their patients on behalf of **8.10** Health Authorities who have a statutory duty to make provision for 'personal

---

the temporary employer, for example, by showing that the entire and absolute control over the employee has been transferred: see, *Bhoomidas v Port of Singapore Authority* [1978] 1 All ER 956 (PC)—no transfer on facts. It is not, therefore, beyond doubt in the hospital context.

[60] See below, para 8.14 *et seq*.

[61] Quaere whether the Clinical Negligence Scheme for Trusts applies as it covers, *inter alia*, a breach of duty by a person 'employed or *engaged*' by a Trust member (see The National Health Service (Clinical Negligence Scheme) Regulations 1996 (n 56 above), reg 4 (emphasis added)?

[62] See below.

medical services' to those for whom they are responsible.[63] In doing so, GPs are not employees of the Health Authorities (formerly Family Health Services Authorities).[64] As such, they are in an entirely different position to their hospital counterparts.[65] It is doubtful whether the relationship created under the Terms of Service in Schedule 2 of the National Health Service (General Medical Services) Regulations 1992[66] even amounts to a contractual relationship.[67] However, it is clear that general practitioners are independent contractors and, consequently, a Health Authority is not vicariously liable for the negligence of a GP.[68]

(ii) *Liability of a GP's Partners*[69]

8.11 General practitioners ordinarily work in partnerships with other GPs. By virtue of the Partnership Act 1890, the partnership will itself be liable for the negligence of a GP in treating a patient.[70] Equally, each of the GP partners will be jointly and severally liable for the negligence of the other partners.[71]

(iii) *Liability of GP for Practice Staff*

8.12 A general practitioner (and the partnership) will be vicariously liable for the negligence of his own professional or office staff such as practice nurses or receptionists[72] working within his surgery under contracts of service.[73] He

---

[63] National Health Service Act 1977, s 29. But note, the National Health Service (Primary Care) Act 1997, s 9(2).

[64] See the National Health Service Act 1977, s 8, as substituted by the Health Authorities Act 1995, s 1(1).

[65] The position would be otherwise if the GP is employed by an NHS Trust or other body under a 'pilot scheme' constituted under the National Health Service (Primary Care) Act 1997, Part I. See above, Ch 1.   [66] SI 1992/635 (as amended).

[67] See the differing views expressed in the Court of Appeal and House of Lords in *Roy v Kensington and Chelsea FPC* [1992] 1 AC 624 (HL) and [1990] 1 Med LR 328 (CA).

[68] This does not mean that a Health Authority could not in any circumstance be liable to an injured patient. It is conceivable that the courts would hold that a Health Authority owed a primary or direct duty to patients to exercise reasonable care in selecting and placing practitioners on the Medical List such that liability might flow for selecting (negligently) an incompetent GP. This would not assist a patient who was injured by a competent GP but whose negligence caused the injury. For primary liability see below, para 8.14 *et seq.*

[69] See Atiyah, *Vicarious Liability in Tort* (n 17 above), ch 11.   [70] S 10.

[71] S 12.

[72] *Lobley (A Minor) v Nunn* (1985) December 9 (CA)—no breach of duty by receptionist on facts.

[73] For a useful discussion in the Canadian context, see Picard, E and Robertson, G (n 30 above), 356–64.

will not, however, be vicariously liable for the negligence of his deputy or locum.[74] The latter is an independent contractor.[75] The GP's liability will, again, stand or fall on the basis of whether the GP himself owes a primary or direct duty of care to his patient which is breached. Providing the selection of the deputy was not negligent,[76] it follows that the GP's liability would only arise if he were as a matter of law under a non-delegable duty to ensure that his patient is treated carefully.[77] Notwithstanding the phrasing of the Terms of Service which limit the GP's obligations where the deputy is himself a doctor on the Medical List of a Health Authority,[78] it is arguable that such a duty could exist.[79]

3. Doctors in Private Practice

A doctor in private practice will usually be a sole practitioner. He will not be employed by anyone and hence no question of vicarious liability will arise for his negligence. Even in situations where the doctor treats a patient in a private clinic or hospital, it is unlikely that the relationship between the doctor and the clinic or hospital will be one of employment. More likely, there will be a contractual arrangement whereby the doctor has 'admission privileges', the private clinic providing the facilities and, perhaps, nursing staff for the patient's treatment. The doctor's position is likely to be somewhat analogous to the position in other countries where the doctors often are not employees, but are in private practice, and have 'admissions privileges' at the hospital under an agreement with that hospital.[80] The legal position is illustrated by one case where an Australian court[81] held that a doctor with 'admission privileges' was not an employee of the hospital. Whilst he was subject to some regulation under the hospitals rules, he was essentially in private practice 'borrowing' hospital space.[82] The clinic will, of course, be liable

8.13

---

[74] Acting on the GP's behalf under the National Health Service (General Medical Services) Regulations 1992, SI 1992/635, Sch 2, para 19(2).

[75] See *Rothwell v Raes* (1988) 54 DLR (4th) 193 (Ont H Ct). Discussed in Picard, E and Robertson, G (n 30 above), 361.

[76] On obligation imposed upon a GP by his 'Terms of Service', see National Health Service (General Medical Services) Regulations 1992, SI 1992/635, Sch 2, para 28.

[77] On which, see below, para 8.21 *et seq* and above, paras 5.28–5.29.

[78] National Health Service (General Medical Services) Regulations 1992 (n 74 above), Sch 2, para 20(2) (as amended by SI 1994/633, reg 8(5)).   [79] See above, para 5.28.

[80] Of course, the doctor may be employed by the clinic. Whether or not he is will, in each case, be a question of fact. Even if there is no employment relationship, the clinic may be liable for breach of a direct or primary duty owed to the patient.

[81] *Ellis v Wallsend District Hospital* (1989) 17 NSWLR 553; [1990] 2 Med LR 103 (NSW CA).

[82] See similarly, *Yepremian v Scarborough General Hospital* (1980) 110 DLR (3d) 513 (Ont CA).

for the negligence of any of its staff such as the nurses. There may also be a claim for breach of contract, depending upon whether there is a contract between the patient and the clinic and what are its terms, for example, if there is fault by the clinic in providing adequate staff or facilities.[83] Otherwise, its liability in tort will depend upon a breach of a primary or direct duty owed to the patient. This may be co-extensive with its contractual terms or, it might be argued, the clinic owes a non-delegable duty to care for the patient and hence it can even be liable for the negligence by the (non-employee) doctor. It is to these possibilities which we now turn.

B. Primary or Direct Liability

1. Within the National Health Service

8.14 In addition to being vicarious liable for the negligence of its employees, an NHS hospital[84] may be liable for a breach of a duty owed directly to the patient.[85] The duty of care will arise when the patient is admitted to the hospital[86] or presents himself at the casualty department seeking medical attention.[87] It is doubtful whether a duty will arise prior to this, for example, merely on receipt of a referral letter by a consultant from a GP or on the making of an appointment at the hospital.[88] There is, in these situations, no assumption of responsibility as yet for the health of the patient.[89] It is, perhaps, ironic that this form of liability which was largely all that was left in the post-*Hillyer* era, was all but

---

[83] To the extent that 'goods' or 'services' are provided by the clinic under contract, there may be liability under the Sale of Goods Act 1979 or, more likely, the Supply of Goods and Services Act 1982. There may also be liability in tort for injury caused by a 'defective product', either under common law or the Consumer Protection Act 1987, Part I. See Ch 14 below.

[84] Or, indeed, a private clinic.

[85] As with all negligence action 'breach', 'causation' and 'damage' must be proved: on these, see Chs 6 and 7 and below, paras 8.47–8.72.

[86] *Jones v Manchester Corp* [1952] QB 852, 867 *per* Denning LJ and *Cassidy v Ministry of Health* [1951] 2 KB 343, 360 *per* Denning LJ.

[87] *Barnett v Chelsea and Kensington HMC* [1969] 1 QB 428; [1968] 1 All ER 1068. Nield J distinguished the situation where the person presents themself and the A & E department is closed when no duty would arise; ibid, at 1072. See also, *Capital and Counties plc v Hampshire CC* [1997] 2 All ER 865 (CA), especially *per* Stuart-Smith LJ at 883. It is arguable that a hospital does owe a duty of care in these circumstances as it will have held itself out as being 'willing and able' to receive emergency patients and, thus, must give reasonable notice (or provide reasonable alternative facilities) to the public before closing: see Picard, E and Robertson, G, *Legal Liability of Doctors and Hospitals in Canada* (n 30 above), 10 and 371 citing *Baynham v Robertson* (1993) 18 CCLT (2d) 15 (Ont Gen Div).

[88] *Clunis v Camden and Islington HA* (CA) (1997) 40 BMLR 181 (no duty of care owed to mentally disordered patient referred to hospital and for whom an appointment had been made).

[89] See above, paras 5.23 *et seq* for a discussion in the context of a doctor's duty.

forgotten by the courts until the 1980s. There were probably two reasons for this. First, after the courts applied the doctrine of vicarious liability to hospital staff in the 1950s for all intents and purposes it became unnecessary in practice for injured patients to rely upon a breach of a duty of care owed by a hospital directly to the patient. Secondly, the agreement reached in 1954[90] between the Government and the medical defence organisations on how to apportion damages between the doctors' 'insurers' and the institution, served to obscure the fact that there might, in a particular case, be joint liability based upon different breaches of duty.[91] Hence, the fact that the patient's injuries might be attributable to a combination of a doctor's negligence and a hospital's breach of duty to provide, for example, sufficient staff or adequate facilities was hardly ever litigated.[92] Not, that is, until 1986 when it was referred to by the Court of Appeal in *Wilsher v Essex AHA*.[93] Indeed, Mustill LJ commented that counsel for the defendant had asserted that no health authority had, or could, ever be liable on the basis of breach of a primary duty.[94] Both assertions are incorrect. The former simply ignores the pre-1950s law.[95] As regards the latter, there are a number of subsequent Court of Appeal decisions in which the direct duty of an institution has been acknowledged.[96] Consequently, there is no doubt that an NHS institution such as an NHS Trust or Health Authority owes a direct duty to its patients: the real question is what is the nature of that duty.

(i) *The Duty to Provide a Safe 'Health Care Environment'*

What then is the scope of the hospital's direct or primary duty? In essence, the hospital's duty could be summed up as one 'to provide . . . a reasonable regime of care at its hospital'.[97] An analogy might be drawn with the employment context and the House of Lords' decision in *Wilsons & Clyde Coal Co Ltd v English*.[98] The duty owed to an employee is to provide a reasonably safe work place, including, equipment, facilities, fellow workers, systems of work, and the like.[99] In the health care context, the hospital's duty

8.15

---

[90] Circular HM (54)32.
[91] *Robertson v Nottingham HA* [1997] 8 Med LR 1, 13 *per* Brooke LJ.
[92] For a rare instance, see *Jones v Manchester Corp* [1952] 2 QB 852.
[93] [1987] QB 730; [1986] 3 All ER 801.   [94] ibid. 817.
[95] eg, *Vancouver General Hospital v McDaniel* (1934) 152 LT 56 (PC); *Lindsey CC v Marshall* [1937] AC 820 (HL); and, of course, *Hillyer* (n 25 above).
[96] eg, *Bull v Devon AHA* [1993] 4 Med LR 117 (CA); *Blyth v Bloomsbury HA* [1993] 4 Med LR 151 (CA) and *Robertson v Nottingham HA* (n 91 above).
[97] *Per* Brooke LJ in *Robertson* (n 91 above), 13 citing *Gold v Essex CC* (n 35 above), *per* Lord Greene MR at 302 and 304; *per* Goddard LJ at 309 and *Roe v Ministry of Health* (n 40 above), *per* Denning LJ at 72.   [98] [1938] AC 57.
[99] See Fleming, J, *The Law of Torts* 7th edn, (1987), ch 24, especially at 481–6.

includes providing sufficient and competent staff. In *Wilsher v Essex AHA*,[100] Browne-Wilkinson V-C stated that a hospital had a duty 'to provide doctors of sufficient skill and experience to give the treatment offered at the hospital'.[101] This, however, could not have been intended to be a complete description of the institution's duty, and it is not. The duty is broader and extends to providing adequate facilities, including equipment, and safe systems of care, including adequate supervision of junior doctors and others by experienced staff.[102]

8.16   The duty is concerned with the *fault of the organisation* rather than the negligence of an individual member of staff. It is important to bear in mind that the duty is one of *reasonableness* and not an absolute one. The hospital will not be in breach of its duty simply because a doctor or nurse is negligent. A breach of its primary duty will only occur if that doctor or nurse is incompetent (in general or to carry out the particular task) and the hospital has been negligent in employing him or allowing him to carry out that task. Hence, an inexperienced doctor who is not up to a particular task will be negligent[103] when he carries it out and the institution will be vicariously liable for his tort.[104] However, the hospital will also be liable for its own failure if it either should not have put him in the position of performing a task beyond his abilities[105] or it has allowed him to carry out the task without adequate supervision by a more experienced practitioner.[106]

8.17   Organisational or systems failures are at the heart of the institution's direct liability to a patient. In *Robertson v Nottingham HA*[107] Brooke LJ emphasised the distinction between the institution's liability based upon vicarious liability and breach of its primary duty. The alleged failure concerned a breakdown in communications between the medical and nursing staff during the confinement of a pregnant woman as a result of which, it was alleged, the plaintiff was born with severe physical and mental disabilities. Brooke LJ stated:[108]

> If effective systems had been in place at this hospital for ensuring that so far as reasonably practicable communications breakdowns did not occur in connection

---

[100] [1986] 3 All ER 803 (CA).   [101] ibid, 833. See also *per* Glidewell LJ at 831.
[102] For a useful discussion of the factual situations in the Canadian context see Picard and Robertson, *Legal Liability of Hospitals and Doctors in Canada* (n 30 above), 367–80.
[103] Inexperience is not relevant in setting the standard of care: *Wilsher* (n 100 above). See for discussion, Chapter 6 above.
[104] As would have been the case in *Wilsher* (n 100 above), except for the fact that the inexperienced doctor sought the advice of a more experienced doctor and thereby acted reasonably: see *per* Glidewell LJ at 831.
[105] See eg, *Hinfey v Salford HA* [1993] 4 Med LR 143 (no breach on facts).
[106] *Hinfey*, ibid, and *Wilsher* (n 100 above).   [107] [1997] 8 Med LR 1, 13.
[108] ibid.

with such a significant area of a patient's treatment then the health authority would be vicariously liable for any negligence of those of its servants or agents who did not take proper care to ensure, so far as was reasonably practicable, that the communications systems worked efficiently. If, on the other hand, no effective systems were in place at all . . . then the authority would be directly liable in negligence for this lacuna.

This basis of liability is of increasing importance within the NHS as working **8.18** and clinical protocols[109] become more common.[110] Failure to introduce a protocol or failure in setting the content of the protocol may give rise to a breach of the hospital's primary duty to the patient. But, a failure to follow or implement such a protocol in a particular instance will, if anything, be a question of breach of duty by a member of staff and vicarious liability for that breach of duty.[111] Of course, this is not to say that the hospital might not be liable itself if it negligently allowed, for example, a culture of non-compliance with a protocol by 'turning a blind eye' to its non-implementation.

The operation of an institution's primary duty can be seen in the case of *Bull* **8.19** *v Devon AHA*.[112] The plaintiff was born with severe brain damage. He was the second of twins to be born and, it was alleged, the delay in delivering him had caused his injuries. The hospital was based on two sites. Unfortunately, a suitably qualified doctor was not available on the site where the plaintiff's mother was in labour. Although attempts were made to summon a doctor from the other site, one did not arrive for some time. The Court of Appeal held that the defendant was liable for breach of its primary duty to the plaintiff.

Slade LJ held that the defendant had a duty to provide adequate staff, **8.20** facilities, and equipment for the provision of maternity services.[113] On the evidence he held there had not been a breach of this duty.[114] Looking at the issue on the basis of professional evidence, at the time the staffing arrangements were not inadequate, let alone, negligently inadequate. It was not necessary, in order for the hospital to comply with its duty, to have a doctor

---

[109] Though there may be differences, these may variously be termed protocols, clinical guidelines, guidance, or advice.
[110] See Newdick, C *Who Shall We Treat?* (n 55 above), 174–8. See also the proposal for a National Institute of Clinical Excellence in *The New NHS* (Cm 3807, 1997), para 7.11– 7.12.
[111] See eg, *Thomson v James* (1996) 31 BMLR 1 (no liability for failure to follow DoH guidelines). See also *AB v Tameside and Glossop HA* [1997] 8 Med LR 91 (CA). Though it may reflect on fault by the hospital: *Blyth v Bloomsbury HA* [1993] 4 Med LR 151 (hospital not liable for failing to apply warning system to plaintiff); discussed, Montgomery, J, (1990) 140 NLJ 1349.
[112] [1993] 4 Med LR 117 (CA) (decided 1989). See Kennedy (1993) 1 Med L Rev 384 (Commentary).   [113] ibid, 130.
[114] On the issue of institutional breach of duty, see below, paras 8.47 *et seq*.

immediately available.[115] However, Slade LJ determined that the defendant also had a duty to provide an adequate system for summoning an appropriate doctor to deal with maternity emergencies. On the facts, he concluded that the system for summoning the doctor must either have broken down or a member of staff must have negligently operated it.[116] Consequently, the defendant was liable either for breach of its primary duty[117] or on the basis of vicarious liability. Dillon LJ agreed that the defendant had a duty to provide adequate staff for its maternity services and the system in place was only acceptable if it worked 'with supreme efficiency'[118] which, on the facts, he held it had not: it had been operated negligently.[119] Mustill LJ agreed that the defendant was in breach of its primary duty because the system for summoning a doctor had broken down in its operation.[120] However, he went further and concluded that the system itself was inadequate: the defendant's duty was to provide immediately a doctor who could have delivered the plaintiff. Alternatively, the system was too sensitive to hitches.[121] In either case, the defendant was negligent and in breach of its primary duty to the patient.

(ii) *Non-Delegable Duty*

8.21 More controversially, it has been suggested that a hospital within the NHS owes a non-delegable duty to *ensure* that reasonable care (or skill) is taken of its patients.[122] The legal duty is that of the hospital which is performed on its behalf by its staff or, possibly, independent contractors within the hospital. Where reasonable care (or skill) is not taken of a patient, the institution is, through the breach of the staff member or independent contractor, in breach of its own non-delegable duty.[123] Significantly, if such a non-delegable duty did exist, the hospital would be liable for the negligence[124] not only of its employee but also of independent contractors acting on its behalf.[125]

---

[115] N 112 above, 131.   [116] ibid, 132.

[117] Applying the maxim *res ipsa loquitur*.   [118] N 112 above, 137.

[119] ibid, 137 and 138.

[120] ibid, 142. He declined to apply the maxim *res ipsa loquitur*.   [121] ibid, 141–2.

[122] See Jones, M, *Medical Negligence*, 2nd edn, (1996), 405–9.

[123] See *McDermid v Nash Dredging and Reclamation Co Ltd* [1987] AC 906 (HL).

[124] Providing it was not 'co-lateral', i e unrelated to the delegated task. See Atiyah, *Vicarious Liability in Tort* (n 17 above), ch 33, especially 376–8.

[125] ibid. See generally, McKendrick, E, 'Vicarious Liability and Independent Contractors— A Re-examination' (1990) 53 MLR 770.

(a) The English Cases

In the hospital context, the duty was first proposed in *Gold v Essex CC*[126] by **8.22**
Lord Greene MR to impose liability on a hospital for the negligence of a
radiographer.[127] MacKinnon and Goddard LJJ relied on vicarious liability.[128]
Lord Greene MR stated that the correct question in determining the defendant's duty to patients was to ask what obligation had it 'assumed' or 'undertaken'?[129] He concluded that the hospital assumed an obligation to treat the
patient rather than merely provide staff and facilities for his treatment. The
hospital was in breach of its duty to treat the patient when he was treated
negligently.[130] In the subsequent cases of *Cassidy v Ministry of Health*[131] and
Roe v Minister of Health,[132] Denning LJ (as he then was) applied a hospital's
non-delegable duty to fix it with liability for the negligence of all hospital
staff. In *Cassidy* Denning LJ stated:[133]

> . . . the hospital authorities accepted the plaintiff as a patient for treatment, and
> it was their duty to treat him with reasonable care. They selected, employed, and
> paid all the surgeons and nurses who looked after him. He had no say in their
> selection at all. If those surgeons and nurses did not treat him with proper care
> and skill, then the hospital authorities must answer for it, for it means that they
> themselves did not perform their duty to him.

The other judges in *Cassidy* and *Roe* rested the defendants' liability on vicarious **8.23**
liability.[134] No subsequent English case has directly faced up to whether a
hospital is under this more onerous duty. Curiously, in *X (minors) v Bedfordshire
CC*,[135] Lord Browne-Wilkinson, relying upon the earlier 'hospital' cases, stated:[136]

> even where there is no allegation of a separate duty of care owed by a servant of
> the [local social services and health authority] to the plaintiff, the negligent acts
> of that servant are capable of constituting a breach of the duty of care (if any)
> owed directly by the authority to the plaintiff.

What is to be made of this statement is unclear.[137] On the face of it, Lord **8.24**
Browne-Wilkinson is accepting the non-delegable duty in the hospital cases:
there is no other plausible explanation of what he said. He is only correct if
the non-delegable duty does exist; and, he does, after all, cite the judgments
of Lord Greene MR in *Gold* and of Denning LJ in *Cassidy* and *Roe*. His

---

[126] [1942] 2 KB 293.   [127] ibid, 301.
[128] ibid, 308–9 and 312–13 respectively; but notice Goddard LJ at 309 See above, para
8.05.   [129] ibid, 301–2.
[130] ibid, 304.   [131] [1951] 2 KB 343.   [132] [1954] 2 QB 66.
[133] N 131 above, 365.   [134] See above, para 8.05.
[135] [1995] 2 AC 633; [1995] 3 All ER 353 (HL).   [136] ibid, 372.
[137] See Cane, P, 'Suing Public Authorities in Tort' (1996) 112 LQR 13, 20–1.

reservation—'the duty of care (if any)'—is not a reservation about the hospital cases but rather about the duty owed in the child abuse context which he is considering in the *Bedfordshire* case and which the House of Lords went on to decide did not exist. Yet, a few sentences earlier he specifically said that he expressed 'no view on the extent of [the hospital's] duty'![138] Finally, in *Robertson v Nottingham HA*, Brooke LJ declined to address the question of whether a hospital owed a non-delegable duty to ensure care is taken of a patient.[139] Thus, the issue remains open in the modern case law.

(b) *Yepremian* and *Ellis*

8.25 By contrast, two Commonwealth decisions have considered in depth whether an institution has a non-delegable duty of care to its patients. In *Yepremian v Scarborough General Hospital*[140] the plaintiff attended the emergency department of the defendant's hospital. He was hyperventilating and had been vomiting, and also had an increased frequency of urinating and drinking. He was seen by the doctor on duty. The doctor failed to diagnose that the patient was suffering from diabetes and although he was subsequently admitted to the hospital he suffered a cardiac arrest and resultant brain damage. He sued the defendant for the negligence of the doctor. The doctor was not an employee of the hospital but had admission privileges. By a majority[141] the Ontario Court of Appeal held that the defendant was not liable since it did not owe the plaintiff a non-delegable duty to exercise reasonable care.[142] The court concluded that the only duty owed was to exercise reasonable care in picking its staff and there was no suggesting that this had been negligent or that the doctor was unqualified or incompetent.[143] The court distinguished the English cases of *Gold*, *Cassidy*, and *Roe* as simply reflecting the statutory framework of the NHS, namely the existence of a statutory duty to provide services and staff, which did not exist in Ontario. For good measure, the judges also concluded that any change in the status quo should come from the legislature and not the courts. The dissenting judges[144] held that a hospital could owe a non-delegable duty to patients: whether it did depended upon 'whether and to what extent a hospital assumes

---

[138] Notice his later reference to *Gold* (n 135 above, 392–3) as authority for the hospital being 'under a duty to those whom it admits to exercise reasonable care in the way it runs it'. This is a statement of the accepted, and less onerous, primary duty of a hospital.
[139] N 107 above, 13.   [140] (1980) 110 DLR (3d) 513 (Ont CA).
[141] McKinnon ACJO, Arrup and Morden JJA.
[142] A subsequent appeal to the Canadian Supreme Court was settled. See Picard, E and Robertson, G (n 30 above), 390.   [143] See eg, at 532 *per* Arrup JA n 140 above).
[144] Blair and Houlden JJA.

a direct duty' which 'depends upon the circumstances of the particular case'.[145] The other dissenting judge, Houlden JA, distinguished between two situations in applying this approach:[146]

> First, a general hospital may function as a place where medical care facilities are provided for the use of the physician and his patient. The patient comes to the hospital because his physician has decided that the hospital's facilities are needed for the proper care and treatment of the patient . . . . Where a hospital functions as merely the provider of medical care facilities then . . . a hospital is not responsible for the negligence of the physician . . . . Second, a general hospital may function as a place where a person in need of treatment goes to obtain treatment. Here the role of the hospital is that of an institution where medical treatment is made available to those who require it. . . . Does a hospital in these circumstances have a duty to provide proper medical care to a patient? In my judgment, it does.

8.26 On the facts, the minority concluded that the case fell into the second category. The approach of the minority is attractive. It reflects the general approach of English law of asking what duty has the defendant 'assumed' or 'undertaken', expressly or impliedly? Not only the approach, but also the conclusion of the minority in *Yepremian*, seems preferable.[147]

8.27 In the other Commonwealth decision of *Ellis v Wallsend District Hospital*,[148] the New South Wales Court of Appeal essentially applied the approach of the minority in *Yepremian*, although the judges differed in its application. The plaintiff suffered from severe neck pain. She consulted a neuro-surgeon. He advised her that she should undergo surgery and arranged for her to be admitted at the defendant's hospital where he had admission privileges. The doctor informed her that there was a slight risk of numbness but he did not tell her that there was a risk of paralysis or that the operation might not relieve her pain. Following the operation, the plaintiff developed quadriplegia. She sued the doctor and hospital alleging, *inter alia*, that it had been negligent not to warn her of the risk of paralysis and of failure. Had she known, she would not have agreed to the procedure. Her action against the hospital was based upon vicarious liability for the negligence of the doctor and for breach of its non-delegable duty of care to her. A majority of the Court of Appeal[149] held that the doctor was not an employee of the

---

[145] N 140 above, 579 *per* Blair JA. [146] ibid, 581.
[147] In Picard, E and Robertson, G (n 30 above), 391, it is stated that the subsequent case law in Canada has followed the majority's approach with the exception of *Lachambre v Nair* [1989] 2 WWR 749 where a Saskatchewan court stated that a hospital had a non-delegable duty to ensure that the patient had given an informed consent. For a different approach in England, see *Blyth v Bloomsbury HA* [1993] 4 Med LR 151 (CA).
[148] (1989) 17 NSWLR 553; [1990] 2 Med LR 103 (NSW CA).
[149] Samuels and Meagher JJA. Kirby P dissenting.

hospital. He was an 'honorary medical officer' with admission privileges, but was in private practice. Hence the hospital could not be vicariously liable.

8.28 As regard the hospital's direct duty to the patient, all the judges accepted that a hospital did owe such a duty. However, the extent of the duty was dependant upon the particular circumstances of each case. Samuels JA[150] stated that it was 'a question of what medical services the hospital has undertaken to supply'.[151] Samuels JA concluded, that in the circumstances of the case, the hospital was not under a non-delegable duty to ensure that care was taken of the plaintiff. Adopting an approach reminiscent of the minority in *Yepremian*, Samuels JA distinguished between the situation where the patient approached the hospital for treatment and where the patient approached a doctor who arranged for the patient to be admitted to hospital.[152] In the first situation, which was not that in *Ellis*, Samuels JA stated that the hospital by accepting the patient 'remains responsible to ensure that whatever treatment or advice [is given] is given with proper care; its duty cannot be divested by delegation'.[153] By contrast, in the second situation, which was *Ellis*, the patient looks to the doctor rather than the hospital for medical care. The hospital is merely the place where the medical treatment is performed. The hospital's duty is limited to the services it provides, such as nurses and possibly any other medical treatment following the operation. Kirby P dissented, holding that the doctor was an integral part of the hospital, and for reasons of policy and practice it was appropriate to impose a non-delegable duty upon the hospital; it was not a 'mere custodial institution designed to provide a place where medical personnel could meet and treat persons lodged there'.[154] The patient looked to the hospital to provide care and compensation when something went wrong.

(c) England Again?

8.29 What duty is owed by an NHS institution such as a Trust to a patient? As was noted earlier, the underlying approach of the minority in *Yepremian* and of the New South Wales Court of Appeal in *Ellis*, reflects English law.[155] The

---

[150] With whom Meagher JA agreed.   [151] N 148 above, 130.

[152] See also *Gold* (n 126 above), *per* Lord Greene MR at 302.

[153] N 148 above, 130.

[154] ibid, 112 quoting Reynolds JA in *Albrighton v Royal Prince Alfred Hospital* [1980] 2 NSWLR 542 (NSW CA) at 562.

[155] The essence of the issue is 'undertaking' and what responsibility has the hospital 'assumed', or is deemed to have assumed, to the patient: see *Kondis v State Transport Authority* (1984) 154 CLR 672 (Aust HCt), 687 *per* Mason J.

difficulty, as *Ellis* well illustrates, is applying the approach.[156] Certainly when a patient is seen at an accident and emergency department (A & E), it is likely that the law imposes a non-delegable duty on the institution to take care of the patient. In *Barnett v Chelsea and Kensington HMC*[157] Nield J, in part, placed the 'duty' in that case upon the defendant directly. It was a duty to ensure that care was taken which was breached by the negligence of the doctor in failing to examine the patient in the A & E department. However, this certainty in the legal position goes no further than situations *within* the A & E department. Once the patient is admitted, then that patient will be in a somewhat similar position to other patients who have been referred to the hospital by their general practitioner. What is their position? Of course, this is the very situation contemplated by Denning LJ in *Cassidy* and *Roe* as giving rise to the non-delegable duty. Is he correct?

The usual situation within the NHS is quite different from that in *Ellis*. A **8.30** doctor does not 'borrow' the hospital bed for his patient through an arrangement between himself and the hospital. The doctor will usually be an integral part of the hospital. The referral by the patient's general practitioner is altogether different and irrelevant. Certainly, the patient would not look to the GP for his care *whilst in hospital*. He will, of course, look to his doctor—the consultant under whose care he is admitted to the hospital—and, to that extent, it might be doubted whether the patient looks to the hospital rather than the doctor for care. But, it would normally be reasonable to say that notwithstanding this, an NHS patient looks to the hospital rather than the particular doctor. That, after all, is part of the ethos of the NHS. The patient is most unlikely to have chosen the doctor. His Health Authority or GP-Fundholder will have chosen the NHS Trust through the 'contracting' process, but no one will usually select the *particular* doctor. Consequently, it is suggested that Denning LJ may have been correct and that, within the NHS, a hospital does owe a non-delegable duty to its patients to ensure that reasonable care is taken of them during their time in hospital.[158] Even where a particular specialist doctor has been chosen by the patient's GP, *the patient* will still look to the hospital for his overall care.

In practical terms what, if any, is the effect of recognising this non-delegable **8.31** duty? The answer is almost none. A hospital will be liable for the negligence of any one acting on its behalf whether employee or independent

[156] See McKendrick (n 125 above), 774–6. See also, *Rogers v Night Riders* [1983] RTR 324 (CA) where it was held that a minicab service owed a non-delegable duty of care to a passenger who was injured by the negligence of an independent contractor-driver.
[157] [1969] 1 QB 428; [1968] 1 All ER 1068.
[158] For a more cautious account see, Kennedy and Grubb, *Medical Law* (n 3 above), 414.

contractor.[159] Rarely, however, will the negligent individual not be an employee for whom the hospital would be liable in any event on the basis of vicarious liability. In that rare case, perhaps of a visiting doctor or agency nurse who is not employed by the hospital but who negligently injures the patient, the non-delegable duty will impose liability where otherwise there would be none. Otherwise, however, in the NHS context this more onerous duty, novel in modern times, adds little. It may, however, have important consequences in cases of treatment in a private hospital or clinic.

2. In Private Practice

8.32 To what extent will a private clinic or hospital be liable for injuries caused to patients? The answer must principally depend upon the contract, if any, between the clinic and the patient. An action for breach of contract may lie against the clinic either for breach of an express or an implied term. In tort, it is likely the law will impose a direct duty upon the clinic. Depending upon the contractual arrangement, the duty is likely to encompass the exercise of reasonable care in the provision of the services and staff supplied under the contract with the patient.[160] What, however, of the negligence of a doctor? In some (perhaps unusual) situations the doctor will be an employee of the clinic; in which case the clinic will be vicariously liable for his negligence. Where he is not an employee, however, the clinic's liability will turn upon whether it has assumed a non-delegable duty to the patient. This must ultimately be a factual matter depending upon the particular situation. In principle, the legal approach must be the same as that discussed earlier in relation to NHS institutions. A patient who receives treatment in a clinic where the doctor only has admission privileges will not be owed a non-delegable duty of care by the clinic.[161] The patient must look solely to the doctor for compensation for his negligence. In the private context, however, reliance on a particular doctor or particular hospital's reputation is more likely, for instance in the context of infertility treatment. In the former case, the clinic probably does not undertake a non-delegable duty to the patient. It will be the doctor alone who will be liable for his negligence. In the latter case, it will be otherwise.

3. In the 'Internal Market'

8.33 Within the 'internal market' of the NHS the services which a 'provider' institution, such as an NHS Trust, must provide are set out in 'NHS

---

[159] For contracted-out services, see the Deregulation and Contracting Out Act 1994, s 72(2).
[160] If not an express term, it will certainly be implied.
[161] See *Ellis* (n 81 above) and *Cassidy* (n 131 above), *per* Denning LJ at 362 (referring to 'the patient [who] himself selects and employs the doctor').

contracts' made under the National Health Service and Community Care Act 1990.[162] Civil actions based upon the negligent *non-provision* of care through an 'NHS contract' or as a result of a refusal to make an extra-contractual referral are most unlikely to succeed.[163] The courts will leave the patient to what remedies, if any, that may lie in public law.[164] Could a patient sue a Health Authority or GP-Fundholder who had purchased inadequate care which resulted in injury to the patient? Would the Health Authority or GP-Fundholder owe a duty to exercise reasonable care in placing and providing for care under 'NHS Contracts'? Further, could an action lie if negligent care was provided and the Health Authority had failed properly to monitor the provider in the performance of the 'NHS contract'? To the extent that such actions involve the direct exercise of statutory powers by the Health Authority and raise questions of policy, it is most unlikely that the law would entertain any private, as opposed to public, law remedies against the Health Authority.[165] However, if the failure stems from a clinical judgment about the proper 'care package' needed, or from oversights or mistakes in monitoring, then in principle, a direct duty to exercise reasonable care would be owed to an injured patient even if there will be obvious difficulties of proving causation and, in the case of clinical judgments, of establishing a breach of duty.

4. The Secretary of State

The National Health Service Act 1977 places a duty upon the Secretary of State to provide a 'comprehensive health service' in England and Wales.[166] The Act further imposes a duty upon the Secretary of State to provide certain services such as hospital accommodation and medical, dental, nursing, and ambulance services.[167] The duty is not an absolute one but rather the more limited one to provide them 'to such extent as he considers necessary to meet all reasonable requirements'.[168] In practice, the vast majority of the Secretary of State's functions are delegated by statutory instrument to health authorities,[169]

8.34

---

[162] S 4.

[163] For a discussion of tort liability within the 'internal market', see Barker, K, 'NHS Contracting: Shadows in the Law of Tort?' (1995) 3 Med L Rev 161.

[164] See Jacob, J, 'Lawyers Go To Hospital' [1991] PL 255 and Longley, D, 'Diagnostic Dilemmas: Accountability in the National Health Service' [1990] PL 527.

[165] See below, paras 8.39–8.45.   [166] S 1.   [167] S 3(1).

[168] ibid. See also, *R v Secretary of State for Social Services, ex p Hincks* (1980) 1 BMLR 93 (CA).

[169] The power is in s 13 and the delegation is effected by National Health Service (Functions of Health Authorities and Administrative Arrangements) Regulations 1996, SI 1996/708.

although some functions are retained centrally.[170] It may be, as a matter of theory, that the duties under the 1977 Act are non-delegable in the sense that the Secretary of State remains responsible for failures to comply with the Act. However, the 1977 Act states that the Health Authority (or other) to whom the power or function has been delegated should be sued and not the Secretary of State.[171] Hence, a claim against the Secretary of State directly could only lie where the action arises out of (a) the exercise (or non-exercise) of a retained function; or (b) an ancillary function of the Secretary of State, such as providing advice to doctors or Health Authorities which is alleged to be negligent.

8.35 Could a civil action for damages be brought by a patient who suffered injury as a result of an alleged breach of the statutory duties contained in the 1977 Act? Almost certainly not; because there will be immense difficulties, first in establishing a breach of the duty[172] and, secondly in fixing the Secretary of State with liability in private, rather than public, law.

8.36 Crucially, however, will be the difficulty faced by a litigant in showing that any civil claim for damages can be established. The two possibilities are (a) civil liability for breach of statutory duty; and (b) negligence.

(i) *Breach of Statutory Duty*

8.37 A private cause of action for damages will arise for breach of a statutory duty only in exceptional circumstances. Usually, the only remedy for such breach will lie in public law. If, as a matter of construction, it can be shown that the statutory duty was imposed for the protection of a limited class of the public and that Parliament intended to confer on members of that class a private right of action, then a damages action can be brought.[173] What of the 1977 Act? It is almost inconceivable that the courts will construe the duties under the 1977 Act as giving rise to an action for damages. In *X (Minors) v Bedfordshire CC*, Lord Browne-Wilkinson observed that no case had been cited to the court where such an action had been recognised for

---

[170] The statutory duty to provide general medical, dental, ophthalmic and pharmaceutical services is statutorily placed on Health Authorities; see National Health Service Act 1977, ss 29, 35, 38, and 41.   [171] National Health Service Act 1977, Sch 5, para 15(1).
[172] See below, paras 8.47–8.72 and see for the difficulties of establishing a breach at the public law level: *R v Secretary of State for Social Services, ex p Hincks* (1980) 1 BMLR 93 (CA); *R v Central Birmingham HA, ex p Walker* (1987) 3 BMLR 32 (CA); and *R v Central Birmingham HA, ex p Collier* (1988) Jan 6 (CA).
[173] *X (Minors) v Bedfordshire CC* [1995] 3 All ER 353 (HL) *per* Lord Browne-Wilkinson at 364.

breach of 'statutory provisions establishing a regulatory system or scheme of social welfare for the benefit of the public at large'.[174] He concluded that:[175]

> Although regulatory welfare legislation affecting a particular area of activity does in fact provide protection to those individuals particularly affected by that activity, the legislation is not to be treated as being passed for the benefit of those individuals but for the benefit of society in general.

This account wholly covers the national health service legislation. Lord **8.38** Browne-Wilkinson may even have had the NHS in mind since it is the most obvious, and expansive, example of such a welfare scheme as he describes. In *Re HIV Litigation*,[176] the Court of Appeal held that sections 1 and 3(1) of the 1977 Act did not give rise to an action for breach of statutory duty. Referring to the nature of the duties imposed by the 1977 Act, Ralph Gibson LJ said that '[they] do not clearly demonstrate the intention of Parliament to impose a duty which is to be enforced by individual civil action'.[177] It is most unlikely that breach of any duty relating to the health service will be construed as giving rise to a claim for damages.[178]

(ii) *Negligence*

No less problematic will be a claim by a patient framed in negligence against **8.39** the Secretary of State (or his delegate) arising out of the exercise (or non-exercise) of the statutory powers under the 1977 Act. The reluctance of the courts to spell out a cause of action in negligence when the defendant is exercising statutory powers is well recognised.[179] The courts will require that the duty requirements applicable against a private defendant are satisfied, namely foreseeability, proximity, and public policy which may be difficult enough in this context for an injured patient.[180] Also, the courts will require that the patient establish that the defendant acted outside his statutory powers under public law principles, namely illegality and irrationality. As a consequence, a decision made under the 1977 Act which is discretionary must be shown to be ultra vires. Importantly, the courts will be unable to do this where the exercise (or non-exercise) of the discretion involved policy

---

[174] ibid, 364. [175] ibid. [176] [1996] PNLR 290 (CA). [177] ibid, 310.
[178] See *Danns v Department of Health* (1995) 25 BMLR 121 (Wright J) and *Ross v Secretary of State for Scotland* 1990 SLT 13 (Lord Milligan).
[179] eg, *X (Minors) v Bedfordshire CC* [1995] 3 All ER 353 (HL).
[180] eg, *Danns* (n 179 above). See, *X (Minors) v Bedfordshire CC*, ibid, *per* Lord Browne-Wilkinson at 371.

considerations which the court is unable to adjudicate upon on the basis that they are non-justiciable.[181] A negligence action which is based upon such a decision will, as a consequence, fail.

8.40 In some cases, the distinction is drawn between 'policy' decisions (non-justiciable) and 'operational' decisions (which may be justiciable). It is illustrated by the case of *Department of Health and Social Security v Kinnear*.[182] The plaintiff suffered injury allegedly caused by the pertussis or whooping cough vaccine. He sued the Department of Health on the basis first, that it had been negligent to promote immunization with the vaccine and secondly, that its advice to doctors on the circumstances when it should or should not be administered was negligent. The defendant sought to struck out the action. As regards the Department's policy on immunization, Stuart-Smith J struck out the claim on the basis that it was a policy within the powers of the Secretary of State. By contrast, he allowed that part of the action relying on the negligent advice to proceed because it fell within the 'operational' area of the statutory power and it was arguable that this could be the basis for a duty of care in negligence.

8.41 It is arguable that Stuart-Smith J misunderstood the 'policy'/'operational' distinction as it would be perceived today after the decisions of the House of Lords in *X (Minors) v Bedfordshire CC*[183] and *Stovin v Wise*.[184] It is not at all clear why the DoH policy was non-justiciable when it was argued that its basis was *factually* flawed due to negligence in the process leading up to the formulation of the policy.

8.42 Two subsequent Scottish cases have, however, taken a similar view in respect of government policies to promote the triple vaccine for whooping cough, diphtheria, and tetanus[185] and the vaccine for smallpox.[186] Indeed, in these cases it was also held that allegations of negligence in the promotional information and guidance sent to the medical profession could not found actions. In *Ross*, Lord Milligan stated that the pursuer's action in negligence related to 'decisions as to what information was to be issued to whom and how it was to be issued'.[187] As such, he concluded these were matters of 'policy and discretion'.[188] Even here, where Stuart-Smith J, in *Kinnear*, regarded the decision as justiciable because it was within the 'operational' area of the discretion, the courts will not impose a duty of care if the

---

[181] *X (Minors) v Bedfordshire CC* (n 179 above) and *Stovin v Wise (Norfolk CC, third party)* [1996] AC 923 (HL). [182] (1984) 134 NLJ 886.
[183] N 179 above. [184] N 181 above.
[185] *Bonthrone v Secretary of State for Scotland* 1987 SLT 34 (Lord Grieve).
[186] *Ross v Secretary of State for Scotland* 1990 SLT 13 (Lord Milligan).
[187] ibid, 17. [188] ibid.

discretion is exercised *bona fide*. In *Bonthrone*, Lord Grieve would have imposed a duty of care if the negligence did not relate to the *decision* of what information to disseminate or to whom it was to be given, but rather to the *actual act of dissemination* by, for example, negligently sending the information out so that not all doctors received it.[189]

Thus, the scope for imposing a duty of care when the Secretary of State (or his delegate) is engaged in the direct exercise of his statutory powers is extremely limited. Operational activities of the sort contemplated in *Kinnear* and *Bonthrone* will, by and large, be restricted to the actual provision of care by the delegate or on his behalf by a Trust within the NHS. Decisions about local or national policy of what care to provide, and to whom, within the NHS will not give rise to private law actions. A patient's remedy will lie, if at all, in public law.[190]   **8.43**

In *Re HIV Haemophiliac Litigation*,[191] the Court of Appeal went a little   **8.44**
further than this would suggest the law to be. The plaintiffs were haemophiliacs and their families who had been infected with HIV as a result of using the contaminated blood clotting agent, Factor VIII, imported from the USA. The plaintiffs sued, *inter alia*, the Secretary of State, alleging he had negligently failed to make the United Kingdom self-sufficient in blood products and thereby remove the greater risk of infection posed by blood products derived from the USA. As a preliminary matter the plaintiffs sought discovery of documents which was resisted on the basis that the plaintiffs did not have a cause of action against the Secretary of State. The Court of Appeal held that it was arguable that a duty of care was owed. While recognising the rarity of such a duty in this context, the Court of Appeal held that merely because the attack on the government's policy involved questions of resource allocation did not, ipso facto, prevent a duty arising. The judges identified the difficulties facing the plaintiffs in making good their case but they were not prepared to rule out the claim in negligence as unarguable.

Too much should not be made of this case.[192] First, it was an interlocutory   **8.45**
appeal relating to discovery of documents. The Court of Appeal only concluded that a negligence action *might* exist on the facts if established. Bingham LJ, in particular, was circumspect about the plaintiffs' prospects for success at trial.[193] The nature of the decisions that were being taken by the

---

[189] N 185 above, 41.
[190] eg, *R v Cambridge HA, ex p B* [1995] 1 WLR 898 (CA); cf *R v North Derbyshire HA, ex p Fisher* [1997] 8 Med LR 327 (Dyson J).   [191] [1996] PNLR 290 (CA).
[192] For a discussion of the action, see Grubb, A and Pearl, D, *Blood Testing, AIDS and DNA Profiling* (1990), 103–7.   [193] N 191 above, 323 and 324.

government about the provision of health care for haemophiliacs was a stereotypical one of discretion, laced with more than a tinge of policy and resource allocation which is outside the court's competence to enquire into. Had their actions come to court, they would surely have lost.[194] Secondly, even if the plaintiffs overcame these obstacles, like all other plaintiffs suing the Secretary of State, they would have had insuperable difficulties in establishing 'proximity'. It was, so it would seem from Bingham LJ's judgment, conceded in *Re HIV Haemophiliac Litigation* that such a relationship existed.[195] Why is not clear. There arguably was not a sufficiently close relationship between the parties to found a duty of care.[196]

8.46 The issue is similar to the one which arose more recently in *Danns v Department of Health*.[197] The husband of a couple underwent a vasectomy. Later his wife became pregnant and gave birth to a healthy child. At no time was the husband told the risk of natural reversal by a process known as 'late recanalisation' although the risk was known. They sued the Department of Health in negligence[198] alleging that in breach of the duty under section 2 of the Ministry of Health Act 1919, the Secretary of State had negligently failed to disseminate information concerning the risks to the public through 'Dear Doctor' letters. Section 2 provides that the Secretary of State must take all such steps as are desirable, *inter alia*, to publish and disseminate information relating to the prevention and cure of diseases and the treatment of physical and mental defects. Wright J dismissed the plaintiffs' actions. Having decided that no duty arose because the defendant was exercising a statutory discretion which entailed a policy decision, he applied the private law framework of 'foreseeability', 'proximity', and 'fair, just, and reasonableness' derived from *Caparo*. For good measure, Wright J also added that he thought that it would be contrary to public policy to impose a duty of care on the department.[199] He concluded:[200]

> By no stretch of the imagination . . . can the various civil servants in and the various advisers to the department be regarded as being sufficiently proximate to the various members of the public who might have an interest in the topic of male sterilisation by vasectomy. If it needs to be repeated again, questions of proximity are not to be judged merely on the basis of foreseeability.

The approach of Wright J in *Danns* is, it is suggested, correct and likely to be followed in analogous cases.

---

[194] See Grubb, A and Pearl, D (n 192 above), 105.   [195] N 191 above, 324.
[196] See Grubb, A and Pearl, D (n 192 above); 106–7.
[197] (1995) 25 BMLR 121. See Kennedy, (1996) 4 Med L Rev 324 (Commentary).
[198] And for breach of statutory duty: on which, see above, paras 8.37–8.38.
[199] N 197 above, 133.   [200] ibid.

C. Breach of Duty by Institution

The question asked here is what quantum of care is expected of an institu- **8.47** tional defendant, that is, a Health Authority *qua* hospital or an NHS Trust (any differences in the law when the defendant is a privately funded institution will be noted as they arise). Two different duties have been identified as being owed by an institution: a non-delegable duty and the duty to maintain a safe system of working. As regards the former, the issues of duty and breach are considered above. It is the latter which will be examined here.

Clearly, whether an institution is in breach of its duty to provide a safe system **8.48** of working is ultimately always a question of fact. But, while this is true, it leaves open certain issues of legal analysis. These are: the *quantum of care* which the law may properly expect of an institution; the *process of establishing breach*, most particularly the relevance, if any, of the *Bolam case*;[201] and the vexed question of the *relevance of resources*. These will be considered in turn.

1. Degrees of Care

Is the quantum of care the same for all institutions, or does it vary as between, **8.49** for example, a general hospital and a centre of excellence? Resort to first principles would suggest two propositions. One proposition is that there must be an irreducible minimum of care which is demanded of any and all institutions. This is reflected in the general law of torts in the well-known case of *Nettleship v Weston*.[202] The case did not involve institutional liability but, *mutatis mutandis*, would appear to apply with equal force here. Indeed, all of the judgments of the Court of Appeal in *Wilsher v Essex AHA*[203] seem to suggest, while not deciding the point, that an institution may be liable *primarily* if its services do not measure up to that which may properly be expected. As Browne-Wilkinson LJ put it in *Wilsher*, the Health Authority may be directly liable if it 'so conducts its hospital that it fails to provide doctors of sufficient skill and experience *to give the treatment offered* at the hospital' (emphasis added). The reference to 'the treatment offered' is crucial. It means that the Health Authority will be judged on what it represented as being available by way of treatment services. But, it also means that whatever treatment is offered must measure up to some basic level of care. This proposition is well illustrated by the decision of the Court of Appeal in

---

[201] *Bolam v Friern Hospital Management Committee* [1957] 2 All ER 118, and see now *Bolitho v City and Hackney HA* [1997] 4 All ER 771.   [202] N 93 above.
[203] [1987] QB 730.

Bull v Devon AHA.[204] In that case, the court found unanimously that the system for providing obstetric care was deficient. As Brooke LJ put it, in discussing *Bull* in the later case of *Robertson v Nottingham HA*,[205] the defendant did not operate 'a system whereby, except in unforeseen contingencies, a responsible doctor would have attended reasonably quickly in relation to such an emergency [as arose]'. The circumstances which a court is entitled to take account of in deciding what level of care can be expected of an institution are explored more fully at para 8.56 below.

8.50   Browne-Wilkinson LJ's reference to 'the treatment offered' also provides the second general principle by reference to which an institution's duty can be judged. While every institution must meet a minimum standard of care, if an institution offers more than the minimum, it will be held to whatever is judged to be the proper level of service for what it offers. (As was said earlier, it is a separate question, discussed at para 8.52 below, how the criteria of the appropriate level of care are determined). Thus, an institution which claims to have a specialist unit in, for example, child care will be expected to have available an appropriate range of skilled staff and equipment to meet the needs of such a unit. This proposition is no more than an application of the principle that a defendant will be held to the standard of care which he professes to offer (*R v Bateman*).[206] This is confirmed by Mustill LJ's comment in *Wilsher* that, had the case been argued on the basis of *primary* rather than vicarious liability, the plaintiff would have asserted that 'the defendants owed a duty to ensure that the special baby care unit functioned according to the standard reasonably to be expected of such a unit'. Thus, in conclusion, while a general hospital is held to a standard of care commensurate with the services it offers, a centre of excellence breaches its duty when it fails to meet appropriate levels of excellence.

2. Level of Care

8.51   As has been noted, to assert that an institution must meet the quantum of care expected of it or claimed by it, is not to determine how that level of care is arrived at, or, put another way, how breach of duty is established. To go to the heart of the question, what weight does the law assign to expert evidence and, even more critically, what role, if any, is played by *Bolam*? Browne-Wilkinson LJ observed in *Wilsher* that to hold an institution primarily liable would 'raise awkward questions'. He expressed the first of these awkward questions as follows. '[t]o what extent should the [health] authority by held

---

[204] N 112 above.   [205] N 107 above.
[206] (1925) 94 LJKB 791 (CCA).

liable if . . . it is only adopting a practice hallowed by tradition'? Although Browne-Wilkinson LJ merged this question into a further enquiry about resources (which will be discussed below at para 8.54), it is a question which must be addressed in its own right. Can an institution claim that it has complied with its duty because it has done that which other institutions of a like nature have done? It is important to state the question in this way to make it clear that what is under discussion is not any alleged breach of duty by the doctors or other staff, for which the hospital would be vicariously liable, but the quantum of care expected of an institution itself in meeting its obligation to patients.

What evidence is relevant in determining this quantum of care? A starting **8.52** point may be compliance with relevant Guidelines and Codes of Practice issued by the NHS Executive and laying down 'best practice'. A court will ordinarily regard failure to observe these as evidence of breach of duty, unless non-compliance can be justified on the facts, (see eg, *R v North Derbyshire HA, ex p Fisher*).[207] Thereafter, expert evidence of those involved in the management and operation of institutions would appear to be the most relevant. Such a view, of course, would suggest that the expert views of doctors and other health care professionals, unless they were managers rather than, or as well as, providing care for patients, would not be particularly relevant. But this must be right if it is institutional liability, the liability of those managing the institution, which is under discussion. The views of doctors and others will, of course, be a critical element in establishing and monitoring any system of medical care. However, there may be other factors which managers must also take account of. Leaving aside the issue of allocating scarce resources (which is discussed below at para 8.54), the extent to which the manager may depart from the considered opinion of medical and other staff may still depend on the facts. Clearly, if there is a divergence of opinion among the health care professionals as to which of the various systems of care should prevail, the manager is entitled, indeed obliged, to make his own decision which will ordinarily involve opting for one of the systems proposed. He will not be judged to be in breach of duty if some harm later ensues, if he can show that the choice he made was reasonable and justified based on all the available evidence. This is not an application of *Bolam*. Instead, it is an application of the more general principle of tort law that the defendant's conduct is to be measured against what a reasonable person in the defendant's position and circumstances would have done. It also follows from this conclusion that it is more likely that the expert evidence of

---

[207] [1997] 8 Med LR 327.

other managers of institutions, whether Health Authorities or hospitals, may be of greater relevance here than that of health care professionals. Of course, by contrast, where medical evidence all points in the same way as to the requirements for any particular system of care, and the manager has chosen to ignore it, a court will find it hard to avoid the conclusion that the institution is in breach of duty, whatever other managers may claim concerning the common practice of institutions.

8.53 What this proposed analysis makes abundantly clear is that, in the case of an alleged breach of duty by an institution, it must be for the *court*, as in the mainstream of tort law, to determine whether *on all the facts*, the defendant is in breach. *Bolam* can be seen to be only tangentially relevant, and even then, must be understood in the light of Lord Browne-Wilkinson's speech in *Bolitho v City and Hackney HA*.[208] As is too well-known, *Bolam* came to be regarded as authority for the proposition that in cases of medical negligence, the evidence of medical professionals that the defendant complied with a practice regarded as reasonable by a responsible body of medical opinion was enough to absolve him of liability. *Bolitho* represents an attempt (perhaps less than whole-hearted) to drag medical negligence back into the mainstream of negligence (and into line with other common law jurisdictions), by reserving to the court the final say on breach of duty. *Bolitho* does so by drawing on cases both within and outside medical negligence. *A fortiori* since institutional liability is not a form of medical negligence (although it involves the practice of medicine), after *Bolitho*, it is the cases outside medical negligence which will guide the court.

3. Relevance of Resources

8.54 One factor which a manager will inevitably have taken account of in establishing the system of working in any particular institution is the resources, both human and material, available. If, notwithstanding discussions about resources, the manager is none the less able to provide and maintain a system which complies with what the law may properly expect of the institution, no further questions arise. But circumstances may be, and usually are, otherwise. This is where Browne-Wilkinson LJ's second 'awkward question' in *Wilsher* comes in. 'Should the authority', he asks (sadly, rhetorically), 'be liable if it demonstrates that due to the financial stringency under which it operates, it cannot afford to fill the posts with those possessing the necessary experience' (or, fill them at all, it could be added).

---

[208] N 201 above

It is helpful in answering the 'awkward question' about resources to separate **8.55** out two strands of enquiry. The first relates to the factual circumstances: what response has the institution made to the fact that it has insufficient resources to provide all the services that it would otherwise wish to provide? The second relates to the legal basis of any liability: is any legal remedy founded in public law, through judicial review, or private law through the tort of negligence? In what follows, these two strands will be interwoven, but their importance should not be overlooked. Equally, a further, larger question should not be overlooked and will be discussed as part of the analysis. The question is to what extent, if at all, should matters of resource allocation be adjudicated upon by the courts when the distribution of scarce public resources is ordinarily perceived of as being a matter first for politicians and then for managers. The issue is one of justiciability, which itself is an issue ultimately of the perception by the courts of the proper reach of their authority and the limits of their competence.

(i) *Non-provision of Service*

The first response of an institution to scarce resources which calls for analysis **8.56** is when the institution simply decides not to provide a particular service or range of services. An example would be a decision not to offer accident and emergency services or a comprehensive orthopaedic service. This latter circumstance arose in the well-known case of *R v Secretary of State for Social Services, ex p Hincks*[209] (the defendant was the Secretary of State but would now almost always be the Health Authority). The Court of Appeal was in no doubt that the four plaintiffs, two elderly women, an elderly man, and a girl, who had been waiting for orthopaedic services for a number of years, had no case. The Secretary of State had, in the event, decided not to fund the proposed scheme to establish such services, preferring instead to allocate resources elsewhere. This non-provision of services did not, the Court held, give rise to a cause of action. Referring to the Secretary of State's duty, Lord Denning MR expressed himself in his usual pithy way as follows: 'It cannot be that the Secretary of State has a duty to provide everything that is asked for . . . [including] the numerous pills that people take nowadays: it cannot be said that he has to provide all these free for everybody.' Citing with approval Wien J's decision at first instance, that the Secretary of State was not under any absolute duty, but had a discretion as to how to allocate resources, he continued, '[t]he Secretary of State says that he is doing the best he can within

---

[209] (1980) 1 BMLR 93.

the financial resources available to him: and I do not think he can be faulted in the matter'. Bridge LJ, in a concurring judgment, explained that if there are not unlimited resources, the Secretary of State 'must plan to provide a service within the ambit of some limitation upon the resources which are going to be available . . . If there is to be some limitation . . . the limitation must be determined *in the light of current government economic policy*' (emphasis added).

8.57   The action in *Hincks* was an action in public law for judicial review. The Court of Appeal held that the Secretary of State was not acting unreasonably. Put into the context of the current analysis, the Court of Appeal was in reality deciding that the exercise of discretion about resources was a matter for government, not for the courts. The rationale for this judicial self-denial is not hard to find. Most important, government is elected by and answerable to the public as regards the raising and distribution of public funds. Courts are not. In addition, as Lord Denning MR made clear in *Hincks*, financial decisions about particular services are not made in isolation. They are made in the context of the totality of the services offered. An expenditure here is a saving (or cut) there, where the financial cake to be cut is of a constant (or diminishing) size. Courts lack the relevant information, the expertise and the experience to make such decisions. Indeed, the moment they were to presume to enter the field of resource allocation to remedy some particular non-provision of services, they would in effect be taking over the management and running of the Health Service. This is clearly not to be contemplated as long as the Health Service is organised in its current form, with politicians ultimately answerable for its operation.

R v Cambridge Health Authority, ex p B (A Minor)

8.58   Two further cases in which an action for judicial review was brought against Health Authorities challenging the lawfulness of their non-provision of service warrant mention here. The first is *R v Cambridge Health Authority, ex p B (A Minor)*.[210] This case achieved a certain notoriety because of the poignant nature of the facts. B, aged ten, having been diagnosed as suffering from common acute lymphoblastic leukaemia, received two courses of chemotherapy and then a bone marrow transplant. Sadly, less than a year later, she fell ill with acute myeloid leukaemia. On the basis of expert advice, the Health Authority declined to authorise payment for B to be treated outside the Health Authority (an extra-contractual referral, in the language of the then purchaser–provider split). The case became something of a *cause célèbre*, with

---

[210] [1995] 6 Med LR 250.

B's father claiming that his daughter had been denied treatment because of resources, while the Health Authority responded by saying that it was the pointlessness of the proposed further therapeutic interventions, in terms of effecting any cure, together with the discomfort which would accompany them, which formed the basis of their decision. They also pointed to the experimental and unproven nature of the therapy proposed. Interestingly, however, while the letter to B's father from the Health Authority's responsible officer sought to make it clear that the non-provision of treatment was *not* based on financial grounds, when it came time to put in an affidavit, this same officer was moved to assert that, 'I also had to consider whether it [the proposed treatment of B] would be an effective use of the [Authority's] limited resources, bearing in mind the present and future needs of other patients'. Thus, the case must be regarded as one raising, *inter alia*, the issue of the amenability to judicial review of resource allocation discussions.

At first instance, Laws J made a cautious but significant foray into the role of **8.59** the court on the resources issue. While accepting that judges should not make orders about resource allocation which would inevitably have implications for the wider health services when they are ignorant of the consequences for others, Laws J stated that, '[w]here the question is whether the life of a 10 year old might be saved by however slim a chance, the responsible Authority . . . must do more than toll the bell of tight resources . . . they must explain the priorities that have led them to decline to fund the treatment'. Laws J was, therefore, making two separate points. The first is that the court will not seek to interfere with any particular funding decision on its merits. This repeats the conventional approach. The second point is equally important, however. Judicial review is a remedy in public law which, while not addressing the merits of any particular decision by a public authority, is most anxious to ensure that the *process* by which the decision was reached was lawful, that is, that it took account of relevant factors and did not take account of irrelevant factors. This is what Laws J was seeking to establish in *B*. He was anxious to state that it was within the jurisdiction of the court, indeed it was the court's obligation, to insist that any Health Authority should demonstrate that it has asked itself the appropriate questions prior to its deciding not to fund a range of services or a particular treatment for a particular patient. For this reason, Laws J was concerned that the Health Authority explain its priorities. It could be objected that in calling on the Health Authority to do so, Laws J was crossing the line into an examination of the merits: the exercise by the Authority of its discretion. This objection can, however, be rebutted. What Laws J was in fact asserting was that English law recognises certain fundamental rights (as being part of the common law and by virtue of the European

Convention on Human Rights). This being so, any exercise of discretion must be made in the light of a prior process, whereby the relative values to be ascribed to the various rights at play are determined. Given the very high priority attached to the right to life, which, for Laws J, was at stake in the case, Laws J insisted that the Health Authority demonstrate the process by which this very important right had been made subservient to others.

8.60 This is a legitimate public law approach, concerned with the process of decision making. Its implications are, however, far reaching, in that they would, in effect, have meant that Health Authorities do something which they (and central government) have been scrupulous in avoiding. It would have required the Health Authority to make *explicit* the principles by reference to which resource allocation (or rationing) was determined. This would have been an enormously significant development. While avoiding involvement in the details of health service management, the courts would have found for themselves a crucial role. By insisting, in good public law tradition, on the transparency of decisions about resources, they would have become the agent for a development many consider long overdue, a proper, political discussion about rationing.

8.61 It will come as no surprise, therefore, that the Court of Appeal, in the form of Sir Thomas Bingham MR, took one look at what Laws J had decided, realised its implications and quickly rejected it. In Laws J's telling phrase, they tolled the bell of resources. 'Difficult and agonising judgements have to be made', Sir Thomas Bingham MR held, 'as to how a limited budget is best allocated to the maximum advantage of the maximum number of patients. This is not a judgement which the court can make.' Thus, at a philosophical level, British utilitarianism triumphed over any European notion of rights. At a legal level, the law was dragged back into its non interventionist mode. Non-allocation of resources was once again non-justiciable in public law.

R v North Derbyshire HA, ex p Fisher

8.62 The second case warranting attention here is *R v North Derbyshire HA, ex p Fisher*.[211] This again was a case in public law seeking judicial review of the decision by the Health Authority not to allocate resources for the prescription of beta-interferon for a patient suffering from relapsing remitting multiple sclerosis. Superficially *Fisher* could be regarded as a departure from the traditional approach of the courts to the non-provision of services. Dyson J declared the Health Authority's decision not to provide the drug to be

---

[211] [1997] 8 Med LR 327.

unlawful and ordered it to 'formulate and implement a policy which took full and proper account of national policy', which was that the drug should be introduced in a carefully managed way. Is this not an example of a court taking to itself a resource allocation decision? The simple answer is, that it is not. On proper examination, *Fisher* is entirely in accordance with the approach taken by all the previous courts. In *Fisher*, there was a national policy, set out in a Circular, that beta-interferon be introduced. The Health Authority refused to do so, and thereby denied Fisher his treatment. The reason was not entirely clear, but Dyson J concluded that it was basically because the Authority did not approve of the policy set out in the Circular. In taking this view, without good reason, Dyson J held that the Authority behaved unlawfully.[212] But, as will be recalled, he did not order the Authority to see to it that the drug was prescribed. He only ordered that it should introduce a policy which took 'full and proper account of national policy'. This is crucial. This is as far as the Court was prepared to go. Indeed, Dyson J accepted 'unreservedly' the proposition advanced by counsel for the Health Authority that 'clinical decisions must always be taken with due regard to the resources available', relying on *R v Cambridge Health Authority.* Moreover, at the conclusion of his judgment Dyson J repeated his view that the applicant should receive treatment, 'subject to clinical judgement *and the availability of resources*' (emphasis added). Thus *Fisher* does not break new ground. It affirms the existing view of the role of the courts in public law in matters of non-provision of resources: that such matters are non-justiciable and, thus, that it has no role.

For the sake of completeness it may be mentioned that the avenue of complaint in law for non-provision of services is through the public law remedy of judicial review. No private law remedy would appear to exist.[213] **8.63**

(ii) *Curtailed Provision of Service*

If the Courts regard the non-provision of services as non-justiciable, is this also true when services are provided but in a curtailed manner? An example would be when accident and emergency services are announced to be available only during the week and not on Saturdays and Sundays. Does a person seeking such services have any remedy because of the curtailed nature of their provision? Any remedy again would be in public law, through judicial review. **8.64**

---

[212] See, for a similar analysis, *R v NW Thames RHA, ex p Daniels* [1993] 4 Med LR 364.
[213] See *Re HIV Haemophiliac Litigation* (n 191 above) and Kennedy and Grubb, *Medical Law* (n 3 above), 414–19.

No private law remedy would appear to be available. What a court is being asked is to declare unlawful the decision of the Health Authority to allocate resources in this way. Expressed as such, it will be clear that if the courts will not get involved in non-provision, they are equally unlikely to get involved where only a curtailed provision is made. The reason is that the same element of discretion, which the court recognises as properly belonging to the Authority, is involved. The approach of the Courts is exemplified in two cases. In *R v Central Birmingham HA ex p Walker*,[214] MacPherson J had to consider the decision of the Health Authority. It chose not to expand the existing intensive care unit, because of a shortage of resources to hire specialist nurses. This meant that it could not extend its services to treat a baby needing surgery, given the existing immediately urgent calls on the unit. To this extent, the Authority chose to curtail, or put limits on, the service offered. MacPherson J held that 'this decision of the health authority is not justiciable, that is to say that it is not a matter in which the court should intervene'. Sir John Donaldson MR affirmed the lower court's decision, declaring, in a sentence which could serve as the *vade mecum* for this area of law, '[i]t is not for this court, or indeed any court, to substitute its own judgement for the judgement of those who are responsible for the allocation of resources'.

8.65 In a second case, *R v Central Birmingham HA, ex p Collier*,[215] Stephen Brown LJ delivered himself of a similar judgment. The complaint was that not all the beds in a hospital were being used and that this was unlawful, as posing, *inter alia*, an immediate threat to health. 'This court', Stephen Brown LJ held, 'is in no position to judge the allocation of resources by this particular Health Authority.' Citing and relying on *Walker*, Stephen Brown LJ went on to remark that the 'courts of this country cannot arrange the lists in the hospital'.

8.66 The cases on non-provision and curtailed provision of services suggest that no remedy lies in public law, by way of judicial review, to challenge the exercise of discretion by a Health Authority as to how resources should be used. A remedy will still lie, of course, if the decision is *Wednesbury* unreasonable.[216] But what the cases make clear is that it is not, of itself, *Wednesbury* unreasonable to make decisions about resources which lead to curtailed, or the non-provision of, services. That said, the cases leave open the question what a court would do if the non-provision of services was so profound as to throw into doubt whether the Health Authority was actually complying with the statutory duty, imposed on the Secretary of State and delegated to the Health Authorities, to 'provide a *comprehensive* health service' (emphasis added),

---

[214] [1987] 3 BMLR 32.   [215] 6 Jan 1988, unreported.
[216] *Associated Provincial Picture Houses Limited v Wednesbury Corpn* [1947] 2 All ER 680.

pursuant to section 1(1) of the National Health Service Act 1977. An example could be the failure of a Health Authority covering a large and populous urban area to provide any obstetrical and maternity care services. A court could well hold, in such an admittedly unlikely situation, that this exercise of discretion went beyond a mere decision not to provide certain services, and became a decision to fail to provide a health service.

It would, of course, be different if, rather than offering a curtailed service or no service at all, a Health Authority decided to spread its resources as widely as possible, offering some level of service but a level below that which, by common agreement and indeed by their own admission, was appropriate. This is what must now be considered.   **8.67**

(iii) *Inadequate Provision of Service*

The complaint here is that the services(s) provided by the Health Authority are inadequate. By contrast with what has gone before, any action will be in private law. The action will be in negligence, alleging harm caused through failure to provide an adequate or proper service. An example could be a hospital ward without sufficient nursing staff or staff of a sufficient level of skill and training, such that a patient suffers harm. In such an action, the first step will be for the plaintiff to prove a breach of duty by the Health Authority. This will be done through the use of relevant evidence, as was discussed earlier in paragraph 8.52. If it is found that the Health Authority has failed to meet what the evidence indicates is a proper level of service, then the Authority will *prima facie* be in breach of its duty. All things being equal, liability will follow. However, it is at this point that the issue of resources may be raised. The Health Authority may say that while admittedly their service did not measure up to the standard required, they have done their best *in the light of available resources*. In other words, the Authority is asking that lack of resources either be regarded as a defence, or that the quantum of care demanded by the law should be relaxed to the point at which it takes account of scarce resources.   **8.68**

The claim that lack of resources should be used as an excusing circumstance places the courts in great difficulties. To accept the argument would be to go against the grain of the general law of torts. As a matter of first principles, if a defendant cannot afford to do something properly, that is, to a standard regarded as reasonable, the law's answer is that he should not do it, rather than that he should be excused for doing it badly. It could, of course, be said that a publicly funded institution, such as an NHS Hospital, should be regarded differently. But the logic of the law of torts and the thrust of good   **8.69** public policy would suggest that it is not open to a defendant to concede that the law requires a certain level of care, to admit that this level has not been met, and then to ask none the less not to be judged to have been in breach of duty. However, as in all things, there is a counter-argument, which the courts are equally well aware of. To ignore the reference to resources, and to find that a Health Authority is liable in negligence, inevitably means that the court is drawn into decisions about resource allocation. It will be recalled that Stephen Brown LJ said in *Collier* that 'courts . . . cannot arrange the lists in the hospital'. Equally, the courts have been anxious not to challenge the exercise of discretion by Health Authorities as to how they allocate limited resources. A court may point to the inadequacy of a particular service, but a Health Authority may reply that, from its position, the provision of some, albeit substandard, service is a better option than no service at all, that, in other words, the logic of the law must give way to the realities of an imperfect world. Furthermore, the Authority could well go on to point out that the effect of holding it liable in negligence for inadequate service would be that they would simply take the advice of their risk manager and withdraw the service. It would be a matter of fine judgment, and one that courts are singularly ill-equipped to make, unaware as they are of most of the relevant facts that condition the judgment to be made and insulated as they are from political pressure.

8.70 Clearly, the arguments are finely balanced. In the cases in which the courts have expressed a view, the complexity of the situation has been well recognised. In *Wilsher*, Browne-Wilkinson LJ adverted to the issue, only to take refuge in the view that issues of resource allocation are 'social questions' which are for Parliament, not the courts. While this is, of course, true as far as it goes, does it go far enough? Once Parliament has set the broad parameters, Health Authorities have to set their budgets. Resource allocation at this level can also be described as a 'social question'. But does this description adequately fit a decision to provide inadequate care, whereby a patient is harmed? Perhaps it does in so far as the patient injured is a member of a larger group of actual or potential patients whose interests must also be weighed by the Health Authority.

8.71 In *Bull v Devon AHA*,[217] Mustill LJ was less prepared to regard this particular aspect of resource allocation as non-justiciable. While concluding that it did not need to be resolved in the particular case, he warned that issues were raised 'which the courts may one day have to address'. He adverted first to the issue of legal logic. 'Is there not a contradiction', he asked, 'in asserting at the same time that the system put the foetus at risk and that it was good enough?'

---

[217] N 112 above

As for the argument that as a public service, the Health Authority was doing its best on limited resources, Mustill LJ remarked that while hospital medicine was a public service,

> there are other public services in respect of which it is not necessarily an answer to allegations of unsafety that there were insufficient resources to enable the administrators to do everything which they would like to do. I do not for a moment suggest that public medicine is precisely analogous to other public services, but there is perhaps a danger in assuming that it is completely *sui generis*, and that it is necessarily a complete answer to say that even if the system in any hospital was unsatisfactory, it was no more unsatisfactory than those in force elsewhere [or was the best that could be done].

In *Knight v Home Office*,[218] Pill J repeated Mustill LJ's warning, although he found for the defendant (effectively Brixton Prison) on the facts. 'It is not a complete defence', he stated, 'for a Government department any more than it would be for a private individual or organisation to say that no funds are available for additional [but deemed necessary] safety measures.' Taking up the point made by Mustill LJ, Pill J went on to state that

> [i]n a different context [from the provision of medical services by a public body] lack of funds would not excuse a public body which operated its vehicles on the public roads without any system of maintenance for the vehicle [or, it may be added, an inadequate system of maintenance] if an accident occurred because of lack of maintenance. The law would require a higher standard of care towards other road users.

8.72 It can be said that both Mustill LJ and later Pill J were firing a shot across the bows of the NHS. Without having to find the Authority liable on the grounds of allocating resources in such a way as to lead to inadequate provision of services, the courts were warning that the day may come when liability will be imposed. But will it? It may be that the court's threat, as represented by these two cases, is somewhat empty. The courts know, as Browne-Wilkinson LJ saw, that resource allocation, even where it produces inadequate service, is an area they enter at their peril, for the reasons already advanced. They cannot know all the facts and are not charged with, nor answerable for, the wide range of services which make up the Health Service. In fact, what the cases may indicate more than anything else is an impasse. The Courts threaten, but find a way to avoid taking action: the Health Authorities cut the cake dangerously thin, but know that this is what they are there for and will be judged by. The occasional judicial skirmish may serve to remind those who need reminding that resource allocation involves hard choices. It is doubtful that it will lead to judicial intervention. Browne-Wilkinson LJ's counsel in

---

[218] [1990] 3 All ER 237.

Wilsher that resource allocation was for Parliament will be seen for the pragmatic recognition of reality which it is.

D. Paying Awards of Damages

8.73 The mechanisms for securing payment of awards of damages have undergone considerable changes in recent years. The National Health Service was unusual as an employer, in that prior to 1990 it required doctors employed in NHS hospitals to subscribe to a medical defence organisation as part of the term of the contract of employment.[219] In the event of a malpractice claim arising out of a doctor's professional duties, the defence organisation would meet the cost of the claim. Where there had been negligence on the part of other staff for whom the hospital was vicariously liable, such as nurses, or an organisational error in respect of which hospital was under a primary duty, the relevant district health authority would be responsible for meeting the claim. If there had been negligence by both nurses and doctor(s), then, in theory, liability could be apportioned amongst the defendants relying on the contribution legalisation,[220] but Health Circular HM (54)32 reduced the importance of this legalisation in the context of actions against NHS hospital doctors. The Circular established a private arrangement between the defence organisations and the Department of Health by which payment to the plaintiff is apportioned between the defendants by agreement amongst themselves in each case, or in the absence of agreement in equal shares. The purpose of the Circular was to provide a formal, though not legally binding, mechanism which would reduce defendants' costs and at the same time present a united front to the plaintiff in the conduct of the litigation.

1. NHS Indemnity

(i) *NHS Patients*

8.74 The arrangement was replaced from 1 January 1990 with the introduction of 'NHS indemnity' under which health authorities assumed responsibility for new and existing claims of medical negligence and no longer require their medical and dental staff to subscribe to a defence organisation.[221] The new

---

[219] The principal defence organisations are the Medical Defence Union, the Medical Protection Society, and the Medical and Dental Defence Union of Scotland

[220] Civil Liability (Contribution) Act 1978. See eg, *Jones v Manchester Corporation* [1952] 2 All ER 125; *Collins v Hertfordshire County Council* [1947] 1 KB 598, 623–5

[221] See *Claims of Medical Negligence Against NHS Hospital and Community Doctors and Dentists*, HC(89)34, HC(89)(FP) 22; Brazier (1990) 6 PN 88. The scheme contained

scheme was introduced as a result of substantial increases in the subscription rates of the medical defence orgainsations in the 1980s, and the growing pressure to relate subscription rates to the doctor's speciality, with high risk specialities paying a higher rate. It was considered that this could lead to distortion in pay and recruitment to the medical profession. NHS indemnity covers only health authority responsibilities, namely their vicarious liability for the negligence of staff acting in the course of their employment, and there is no attempt to seek contribution from the employee. This includes consultants and staff provided by external agencies, irrespective of the precise legal relationship between these individuals and the hospital (that is, whether or not they are in law employees of independent contractors).

Strictly speaking, Health Circular (89)34 did not determine the question **8.75** whether a health authority was in law vicariously liable for the negligence of, say, agency staff, but simply specified how health authorities were to deal with this in practice. If, for example, an NHS Trust hospital were to take a vicarious liability point in a particular case involving agency staff, the Circular could not change the position in *law*. Health authorities did not, in any event, take this point for agency staff and consultants before 1990. The Circular did not help on this point, since it merely stated that NHS Trusts would be responsible for claims against their medical and dental staff. If visiting consultants and agency staff are not in law employees of the NHS Trust, the Circular could not deem them to be employees. HSG(96)48 and the accompanying documentation[222] updated the guidance given in HC(89)34 and takes the view that in addition to staff acting in the course of their NHS employment, NHS indemnity also covers locums, medical academic staff with honorary contracts, students, researchers conducting clinical trials, charitable volunteers, and people undergoing professional education, training and examinations, 'whenever an NHS body owes a duty of care to the person harmed'.

Although there were no NHS Trusts constituted when NHS indemnity was **8.76** introduced, the intention of Health Circular (89)34 was that NHS Trusts

---

transitional provisions to deal with existing claims. The Department of Health was given a share of defence organisation reserves, which was made available to assist health authorities meet the cost of large claims. This was intended to meet claims usually, though not necessarily, arising from incidents before 1 January 1990. The Department of Health will meet 80 per cent of the costs, including legal costs, of a settlement over a threshold of £300,000, until these funds are exhausted: HC(89)34, para 11. Since there is a substantial delay in claims coming to light (see Hickey, J, (1995) 1(1) *Clinical Risk 43*) these transitional provisions will continue to be of significance for some time.

[222] *NHS Indemnity—Arrangements for Clinical Negligence Claims in the NHS* (NHS Executive, 1996). See also EL(96)11 (NHS Executive, 1 April 1996), setting out guidelines for NHS Trusts in handling clinical negligence and personal injury claims.

should be responsible for claims for negligence against their own medical and dental staff.[223] This was consistent with the objective of giving NHS Trusts financial autonomy and it is the basis upon which the scheme has operated since its inception. From 1 April 1991 NHS Trusts have had to bear their own losses arising out of claims for clinical negligence.

8.77 NHS indemnity does not apply to general practitioners except where the general practitioner has a contract of employment (for example, as a clinical assistant at a hospital or as a public health doctor) with a health authority or NHS Trust and the treatment is being given under that contract. If the health authority or Trust is essentially providing only hotel services and the patient remains in the general practitioner's care, the hospital authority will not be responsible, and the claim will be dealt with by the general practitioner's defence organisation. Where a case involves a claim against both a health authority or NHS Trust and a general practitioner the possibility of a contribution claim exists, but the Circular requests defendants' representatives to seek to reach agreement out of court as to the proportion of their respective liabilities, and to co-operate fully in the formulation of the defence.

(ii) *Private Patients*

8.78 NHS indemnity does not apply to private hospitals or private work performed by a consultant in an NHS hospital. It is accepted, however, that where junior medical staff are involved in the care of private patients in NHS hospitals, they would normally be doing so as part of their NHS contract. To the extent that NHS employees participate in the treatment, the hospital will be vicariously liable for their negligence. Work which is outside the scope of a junior doctor's employment (for example, reports for insurance companies or locum work for a general practitioner) is not covered by the scheme, and the doctor will have to rely on a defence organisation for indemnity. Similarly, a 'Good Samaritan' act of assisting at an accident is not covered, but negligence by a locum doctor, whether 'internal' or provided by an external agency is within the scheme.

---

[223] The Department of Health (relying on para 12) took the view that NHS Trusts did fall within the scheme, although para 12 simply stated that 'NHS Trusts will be responsible for claims for negligence against their medical and dental staff'. This was trite, since NHS Trusts are undoubtedly vicariously liable in *law* for the negligence of their staff. The question was whether the Trusts would no longer seek indemnity from their medical staff and therefore no longer require them to be members of a defence organisation as a part of their contract of employment. In practice, it is now clear that this is the case, and NHS Trust hospitals handle and bear the cost of claims against their clinical staff.

2. Funding Claims for Clinical Negligence

The NHS Litigation Authority is a special health authority established in **8.79**
November 1995 with the responsibility for administering schemes set up
under section 21 of the NHS and Community Care Act 1990 permitting
NHS bodies to pool the costs of injury, loss or damage to property, and
liabilities to third parties arising out of their NHS activities.[224] Its role is to
approve or not approve proposals to it by NHS bodies in the conduct of
medical negligence claims. The NHS Litigation Authority also has a duty to
advise the Department of Health about: novel or contentious claims or
claims with major repercussions; claims where the total value, including
costs, is more than £1 million; and developments in law and legal practice.
It is also responsible for devising and implementing risk management
strategies for the NHS. The NHS Litigation Authority administers two
principal[225] schemes:

(1) the Clinical Negligence Scheme for Trusts (CNST), covering liabilities
for clinical negligence where the adverse event occurred on or after 1
April 1995;[226] and

(2) the Existing Liabilities Scheme (ELS) covering incidents of clinical negligence which occurred before that date.[227]

CNST is funded by contributions from the NHS Trusts who are members of **8.80**
the scheme.[228] It is not an insurance fund, but a 'pay as you go' scheme which
only collects enough money each year in contributions to cover the actual

---

[224] *NHS Litigation Authority Framework Document* (NHS Executive, 1996).
[225] The NHS Litigation Authority also has responsibility for miscellaneous residual clinical
negligence laibilities of certain special health authorities and the Regional Health Authorities
(which were abolished from 1 April 1996).
[226] See the NHS (Clinical Negligence Scheme) Regulations 1996, SI 1996/251; which
came into force on 1 March 1996; NHS (Clinical Negligence Scheme) (Amendment) Regulations 1997, SI 1997/527. See further Hickey, J, 'The Clinical Negligence Scheme for Trusts',
(1995) 1(1) *Clinical Risk 43*.
[227] See the NHS (Existing Liabilities Scheme) Regulations 1996, SI 1996/686; NHS
(Existing Liabilities Scheme) (Amendment) Regulations 1997, SI 1997/526. Clinical negligence liability is defined as: 'any liability in tort owed by a member to a third party in respect of
or consequent upon personal injury or loss arising out of or in connection with the diagnosis of
any illness, or the care or treatment of any patient, in consequence of any act or omission to act
on the part of a person employed or engaged by a member in connection with any relevant
function of that member': NHS (Clinical Negligence Scheme) Regulations 1996, SI 1996/251,
reg 4. Similar wording, with appropriate amendments, applied to the Existing Liabilities
Scheme, which covers a health authority, a special health authority, an NHS Trust and the
Public Health Laboratory Service Board: NHS (Existing Liabilities Scheme) Regulations 1996,
SI 1996/686, regs 4 and 3.
[228] Membership is voluntary, but in 1995–6, 365 out of 433 NHS Trusts were members of
CNST.

costs which fall into that year, plus a small margin to form a contingency reserve and cover administrative expenses. The object is to permit NHS Trusts to spread the cost of the larger claims, while at the same time leaving the individual Trust responsible for a proportion of the claim. As a result of the significant time gap between an adverse event and settlement of the claim, the expectation is that contributions will be small in the early years, building up in future years. There are discounts of up to a maximum of 5 per cent of the Trust's contribution for putting into place appropriate risk management standards.

8.81 Under the *CNST Membership Rules*, September 1996, there are 'excess' levels which range from £10,000 to £500,000, which are also linked to an 'ultimate threshold' ranging from £100,000 to £1,000,000. For settlements, including costs, which are below the excess there is no financial benefit to the NHS Trust. Where the settlement is above the excess, but below the amount of the ultimate threshold, the Trust must pay the amount of the excess plus 20 per cent of the balance of the settlement. Where the settlement is above the ultimate threshold the Trust pays the amount of the excess plus 20 per cent of the amount between the excess and the ultimate threshold, the remaining amount being paid by the CNST.

8.82 CNST operates on a 'claims paid' basis, which means that it will cover an NHS Trust if the Trust is a member of the scheme continuously at the date of the adverse event which subsequently gives rise to the claim and the date of settlement. There are requirements for Trusts to report claims to CNST, in particular in relation to claims likely to settle for more than £1 million (including costs), claims which have 'significant implications' and claims which may set a precedent or constitute a test case of a 'serial claim'. Although the majority of claims are handled by the Trust's own legal advisers (who are selected and instructed by the Trust), the NHS Litigation Authority has the power to take over the conduct of any claim.

8.83 The Existing Liabilities Scheme (ELS) is funded by the Secretary of State, through the Litigation Authority. Under ELS the health authority or NHS Trust has to bear the first £10,000 of the total cost (damages and costs) of a settlement, 20 per cent of the amount between £10,000 and £500,000, with the remaining cost being met from the existing claims pool administered by the NHS Litigation Authority.[229]

---

[229] FDL(95)56. The NHS Executive estimates that outstanding liabilities against the NHS for incidents prior to April 1995 are likely to be greater than £1 billion: *NHS (England) Summarised Accounts 1995–96*, para 50.

3. Structured Settlements

The possibility that awards of damages in medical negligence actions can be **8.84** dealt with in the form of a structured settlement creates certain options for health authorities and NHS Trusts. A structured settlement normally takes the form of a private arrangement between the plaintiff and the defendant's liability insurer under which the usual lump sum damages award can be varied or 'structured' over a period of time.[230] The settlement may include a lump sum element, plus periodic payments intended to meet the plaintiff's future losses. The payments can be for a fixed period or until the plaintiff's death, and they can be index-linked. The payments are normally financed by the purchase of an annuity by the liability insurer with the money, or part of it, that would have been paid to the plaintiff as a lump sum. The annuity is held by the insurer on behalf of the plaintiff and, as a result of a concession by the Inland Revenue, the payment is not taxable as income in the plaintiff's hands. The insurer is not liable to tax on the annuity either. The result is that for large awards, where the tax liability on the income generated by investment of the lump sum damages would be high, the value of the arrangement to both plaintiff and insurer is substantially greater than the traditional lump sum award.[231] This has potential advantages for both plaintiffs and defendants.

There are significant differences in structured settlements in the context of **8.85** NHS medical negligence claims, however, because there is no liability insurer involved, and it is possible to structure a settlement without purchasing an annuity from a life insurer.[232] The previous practice was generally for health authorites to pay the Department of Health a lump sum to provide the reserves for the future liabilities arising under the structured settlement. Under the *CNST Membership Rules* NHS Trusts are required to consider the overall value for money to the public sector of proposing a structured settlement and for reporting to the Department of Health and the Treasury on their administration.

---

[230] See Allen (1988) 104 LOR 448; Lewis (1988) 15 J of Law and Soc 392; Lewis (1991) 10 CJQ 212; Allen (1993) 12 CJQ 8; Law Commission Report, *Structured Settlements and Interim and Provisional Damages*, Cm 224 (HMSO, 1994). For a detailed analysis of this subject see Lewis, R, *Structured Settlements: The Law and Practice* (Sweet & Maxwell, 1993).

[231] The sum awarded under a structured settlement should be smaller than for a lump sum payment, since there are tax savings which result in the same benefits accruing to the plaintiff: *Kelly v Dawes*, *The Times*, 27 Sept 1990. The discount tends to range between 8 and 15 per cent, though it can be higher or lower than this: see Lewis (1993) 143 New LJ 772.

[232] See Lewis (1993) 56 MLR 844; and Lewis, R, *Structured Settlements: The Law and Practice* (Sweet & Maxwell, 1993), ch 16. There are disincentives to the medical defence organisations structuring settlements: ibid, 251.

IV

SPECIFIC ISSUES

9

CONFIDENTIALITY AND MEDICAL RECORDS

Introduction

9.01 In the course of any consultation with a patient, a doctor collects information personal to the patient. That information will form the basis of the doctor's diagnosis and treatment plan, and it is essential that the patient makes full and frank disclosure to the doctor in order to ensure that the doctor is able to make recommendations taking into account all relevant matters. The situation inevitably arises that the doctor is privy to much that the plaintiff would regard as personal, and has come upon that information in circumstances in which it is appropriate that the doctor is under an obligation of confidence to the patient. This chapter considers first the manner in which the law regulates the use which the doctor may make of confidential information disclosed by the patient, and the circumstances in which the doctor is lawfully entitled to disclose that information to anyone other than the patient.

9.02 A second issue concerns the extent to which a doctor can control information which he collects and records in the course of his relationship with the patient. A patient's medical record will almost always include information over and above that which the patient himself has disclosed to the doctor. Much of this information is sensitive and the doctor or doctors who have contributed to the medical record over the years may be unwilling to disclose the contents of the record to the patient or his advisers. Although there is little dispute that the medical record is regarded at law as the property of the hospital or other health care institution, it is generally believed that patients ought to be entitled to require that they are given access to their medical records, other than when this might in fact be prejudicial to their interests.

9.03 This chapter therefore investigates two separate questions:

(i) When does the law allow a doctor to disclose information which is personal to the patient? and
(ii) When does the law require a doctor to disclose information which has been recorded in the course of the patient's medical treatment?

A. The Obligation of Confidence

1. Common Law

(i) *Legal Basis*

There is some uncertainty as to the jurisdictional basis for the obligation of **9.04** confidence, as the courts have tended to apply different principles in different cases. In *Morrison v Moat*[1] Turner VC said:

> Different grounds have indeed been assigned for the exercise of that jurisdiction . . . but, upon whatever grounds the jurisdiction is founded, the authorities leave no doubt as to the exercise of it.

It is generally thought that the action for breach of confidence is now a sui **9.05** generis action, finding its roots in principles of equity, contract, property and tort.

The action for breach of confidence enables one party who imparts informa- **9.06** tion in confidence to another to obtain relief against the recipient of that information if the latter, without permission, discloses that information directly or indirectly to a third party. In *Hunter v Mann* Boreham J con- sidered the question of whether a doctor owed an obligation of confidence to his patients and concluded that:

> [I]n common with other professional men, . . . the doctor is under a duty not to disclose [voluntarily], without the consent of his patient, information which he, the doctor, has gained in his professional capacity.[2]

The cases of *X v Y*[3] and *W v Egdell*[4] affirmed this position and there can now **9.07** be no question but that an obligation of confidence might arise out of the doctor–patient relationship, notwithstanding that the patient may have no contractual or proprietary rights over the information.

Where the parties are in a contractual relationship, the terms of the contract **9.08** may modify the nature and scope of the obligation of confidence which might otherwise have been owed. A contract which is silent on the matter of con- fidence is, however, no bar to the recognition of an obligation of confidence.

---

[1] (1851) 9 Hare 241, 255, 68 ER 492, 498.
[2] [1974] QB 767, 772. Noted by Boyle, C (1975) 38 MLR 69.
[3] [1988] 2 All ER 648.
[4] [1990] 1 All ER 835. First Instance decision noted by McHale, J (1988) 52 MLR 715.

(ii) *Scope*

(a) General

9.09 English courts have retained great flexibility in interpreting the scope of the doctor's obligation of confidence. First, the obligation is one which is focused upon 'confidential information'. Only where the subject of the disclosure is confidential will the law restrain a doctor from disclosing information.

9.10 Secondly, in *W v Egdell*, a case which arose out of the proposed disclosure to the Home Office of a report about the mental condition of a psychiatric patient in a secure hospital, the Court of Appeal accepted that the obligation of confidence was not absolute. Bingham LJ described the cases as establishing:

(1) that the law recognises an important public interest in maintaining professional duties of confidence; but
(2) that the law treats such duties not as absolute but as liable to be overridden where there is held to be a stronger public interest in disclosure.[5]

(b) Confidential Information

9.11 There is no precise definition of confidential information but English courts include within its scope all information which has 'the necessary quality of confidence about it, namely, it must not be something which is public property and public knowledge'.[6]

9.12 There are, however, no fixed rules to determine what suffices to confer confidentiality on any particular item of information. Rather, the courts approach the question in a pragmatic way, asking whether disclosure in the circumstances would be 'within the mischief which the law as its policy seeks to avoid . . .'.[7] This would clearly cover information which the doctor receives from the patient in the course of a professional relationship. Both information which is directly communicated by the patient, and information to which the doctor is privy by reason of his position, for example diagnostic test results, would be regarded as confidential. Similarly, information which is communicated to the doctor by a third party who is aware of the doctor's professional relationship with the patient might be subject to an obligation of confidence.

---

[5] *W v Egdell* [1990] 1 All ER 835, 848.
[6] *Saltman Engineering Co v Campbell Engineering Co Ltd* (1948) 65 RPC 203, 215.
[7] *Argyll v Argyll* [1967] 1 Ch 312, 330 *per* Ungoed-Thomas J. See also Gurry, F, *Breach of Confidence*, 70.

The position is less clear where the doctor receives information other than in **9.13** connection with a professional relationship. This situation could arise either where the patient discusses matters with the doctor for purely social purposes, or where a third party discusses the patient with the doctor but is unaware of the professional relationship between the doctor and that patient. The difficulty here is in determining whether or not the information has the 'necessary quality of confidence', although there is a strong argument that any information about a patient which the doctor receives should be subject to an obligation of confidence in order to maintain the essential relationship of trust upon which the effective provision of medical treatment depends.

Once information is in the public domain it will usually cease to be con- **9.14** fidential. This would only pertain to information communicated in the doctor–patient relationship where any possible disclosure by the doctor would not add anything to that which was already in the public domain. Thus, for example, the fact that the patient had known about her condition for a particular length of time might be confidential notwithstanding that she has disclosed to the public at large that she has the condition. Moreover, it will always be a question of degree whether the information is sufficiently broadly disseminated that it can be said to have lost its confidential character.

Further, it is possible that a court might recognise a continuing obligation of **9.15** confidence in respect of information in the public domain where it would be unconscionable to allow the party to make use of the information in the circumstances. For example, if English courts were to accept that a doctor owed a fiduciary obligation to his patient, it might be held on analogy with the Californian case of *Moore v Regents of the University of California*[8] to be a breach of that obligation to allow the doctor to use information which was disclosed in circumstances of confidence for his own financial gain.

(c) Circumstances of Confidence

English law clearly provides that information is only subject to an obligation **9.16** of confidence when it is communicated in circumstances of confidence.[9] In the context of the doctor patient relationship this will almost always be assumed to be the case since, according to Megarry J in *Coco v AN Clark* (a case not concerned with doctors) the test should be whether or not a

> reasonable man in the shoes of the recipient of the information would have realised that upon reasonable grounds the information was being given to him in confidence . . .[10]

---

[8] (1990) 793 P 2d 479.
[9] *Coco v AN Clark (Engineering) Ltd* [1969] RPC 41, 47–8 *per* Megarry J. [10] ibid.

9.17 One remaining question is whether or not the description of information as confidential depends upon some expectation of secrecy in the mind of the person communicating the information. Two views are possible here. First, information could objectively be described as confidential where it possesses the basic attribute of inaccessibility to others,[11] and where the reasonable man in the shoes of the confidant knew or ought to have known that the information has been disclosed for a limited purpose only. Gurry, in his seminal work on breach of confidence, would appear to support this view when he states that the relevant circumstances to be taken into account in determining whether or not an obligation of confidence arises include both

> the confider's own attitude to the preservation of the confidentiality of the information . . . [and circumstances] apparent from custom—such as the custom, 'which was believed to be universal' that actors do not disclose the details of the plot of a play before its first performance.[12]

9.18 Alternatively, it is possible to argue that information can only be described as confidential where there is an expectation, actual or inferred, of confidence on the part of the person communicating the information.[13] If that person were not capable of forming such an expectation, therefore, the information could not be said to be confidential. Those cases in which it has been held that the deliberate seeking of publicity operated to destroy the confidence of personal information could be argued to support this position.[14] These cases can, however, also be explained on the basis that the information in question was in fact already in the public domain.[15]

(d) Anonymised Information

9.19 There is clearly no obligation of confidence owed with respect to information in a form which is not capable of identifying the patient, or any other person to whom an obligation of confidence might also be owed. Whether or not information is or is not sufficiently anonymised to excuse the doctor from any obligation of confidence is a question for the court, to be determined upon all of the evidence. If an initial disclosure presents a risk of identification, for example where it would lead to further media investigation and ultimately to tracing of the identity of the patient, then this may be sufficient

---

[11] Gurry (n 7 above) discusses the characteristics of confidentiality at 70–85. The only case providing direct authority on this question is *Franklin v Giddins* [1978] Qd R 72 (noted at (1979) 95 LQR 323) where the defendant stole samples of the plaintiff's special fruit trees and the court held that the thief owed an obligation of confidence because this was clearly a 'trade secret'.
[12] Gurry (n 7 above), 120 (footnotes omitted).   [13] Footnote omitted.
[14] See for example *Woodward v Hutchins* [1977] 1 WLR 760 (CA) and *Lennon v News Group Newspapers Ltd* [1978] FSR 573 (CA).   [15] See Gurry (n 7 above), 101.

to justify imposing an obligation of confidence.[16] Similarly, where information is capable of identifying a particular patient because, for example, the patient's symptoms are very rare or the patient is one of a very small community then an obligation of confidence would be owed in respect of that information.

Where information has been obtained in breach of confidence, publication of **9.20** that information may be restrained by injunction even where it is sought to publish the information in a form which would not be capable of identifying the plaintiffs. According to Rose J in *X v Y*:[17]

> The risk of identification is only one factor in assessing whether to permit the use of confidential information. In my judgment to allow publication in the recently suggested restricted form, would be to enable both defendants to procure breaches of confidence and then to make their own selection for publication. This would make a mockery of the law's protection of confidentiality when no justifying public interest has been shown.

(e) Disclosure with the Patient's Consent

Consent provides a lawful justification for disclosure provided that the patient **9.21** is competent to give a valid consent and understands the nature of the disclosure proposed. English courts are most likely to agree with the view of the General Medical Council (GMC) that doctors may 'release confidential information in strict accordance with the patient's consent, or the consent of a person properly authorised to act on the patient's behalf'.[18]

This general principle is subject to the requirement that, at the time of giving **9.22** consent, patients are able to understand what will be disclosed, the reasons for disclosure and the likely consequences.[19]

Consent need not be express but might be inferred from conduct. It could be **9.23** argued, for example, that a patient implicitly consents to information about her medical condition being shared with members of a health care team responsible for her care. For example, according to the General Medical Council:

> Where the disclosure of relevant information between health care professionals is clearly required for treatment to which a patient has agreed, the patient's explicit consent may not be required.[20]

In this regard, however, the GMC advises that the doctor **9.24**

---

[16] The question was considered but not resolved by Rose J in *X v Y* [1988] 2 All ER 648, 657.
[17] [1988] 2 All ER 648, 661.
[18] *Guidance from the General Medical Council on Confidentiality*, 4.   [19] ibid, 2.
[20] ibid, 4.

must make sure that patients are informed whenever information about them is likely to be disclosed to others involved in their health care, and that they have the opportunity to withhold permission.[21]

9.25 Where a patient has explicitly refused consent for information to be shared amongst team members the doctors involved are advised to respect those wishes.

9.26 Where doctors undertake to assess patients on behalf of third parties such as employers, insurance companies, or local authorities the GMC advises that the assessment should not take place unless the patient understands the nature of the doctor's obligations to the third party and has consented to the disclosure of personal information in accordance with those obligations.[22]

(f) Disclosure Required by Law

9.27 It is clear that the doctor's duty of confidence may be overridden in circumstances where the doctor is required by law to disclose information which would otherwise be subject to an obligation of confidence. In 1974 in *Hunter v Mann*,[23] Boreham J considered whether or not a statutory obligation to provide information to the police investigating an allegation of dangerous driving could apply to doctors.[24] Having considered both the clear and unambiguous language of the statute and the nature of the doctor's obligation of confidence to his patients, Boreham J concluded that the doctor could be under no obligation of confidence to his patients in relation to information which he was compelled by law to disclose. Rather, the doctors obligation is one not 'voluntarily' to disclose, without the consent of his patient, information which he has gained in his professional capacity.

(g) Disclosure in the Public Interest

9.28 The sui generis obligation of confidence is largely based upon recognition of important public interests favouring confidentiality where personal information is communicated in circumstances in which it is clear that the recipient is expected to respect the privacy of that information. It follows from this that the obligation of confidence may be modified where countervailing public interests favouring disclosure are overriding.

---

[21] ibid, 2.   [22] ibid, 5.   [23] [1974] 1 QB 767.
[24] The relevant provision was the Road Traffic Act 1972, s 168(2), which provided that 'Where the driver of a vehicle is alleged to be guilty of an offence to which this section applies . . . any other person shall if required as aforesaid give any information which it is in his power to give and may lead to the identification of the driver . . .' The doctor in that case had been charged with the offence of failing to provide the relevant information to the police.

There is no judicial guidance upon the precise circumstances in which the doctor's obligation of confidence can be overridden in the public interest. In both *W v Egdell* and the earlier case of *X v Y* the courts paid great heed to the advice provided by the General Medical Council contained in what is now known as 'The Duties of a Doctor', but the question remains one for the courts and not for professional bodies.   **9.29**

The courts balance the public interests favouring confidentiality against those favouring disclosure in the particular circumstances of each case. The balance of the public interest in the context of an action to restrain what was alleged to be a potential breach of medical confidentiality was first considered by English courts in 1987 in the case of *X v Y*.[25] The defendants in that case intended to publish an article identifying two doctors with AIDS who were carrying on general practice in England after having sought and received appropriate medical advice and counselling. The health authority where the doctors' medical records were held sought to restrain publication. The question for the court was whether or not the defendants were justified in the public interest in publishing and using the information about the two doctors.   **9.30**

Rose J emphasised that the concern of the courts was with public and not private interests. Thus it was not necessary to show any detriment to the individual plaintiffs. It would be unlawful to disclose the information provided the public interests in maintaining confidence, in this case those in loyalty and confidentiality both generally and particularly in relation to the hospital records of patients with AIDS, outweighed the public interests in disclosure, here having a free press and an informed public debate.[26]   **9.31**

Subsequently the scope of medical confidentiality was considered by the Court of Appeal in *W v Egdell*.[27] W had been convicted of manslaughter on the grounds of diminished responsibility after having shot and killed five people in an indiscriminate display of violence. At the time of the action for breach of confidence, he was compulsorily detained in a secure hospital but had taken steps to apply to a mental health tribunal for a conditional discharge. To that end his solicitors instructed Dr Egdell to report on W's mental state. His report conflicted substantially with that of W's own medical advisers and he recommended further investigation of this conflict in opinion. Further he recommended that attention should be given to other information, including W's confession that he had a continuing and long standing interest in explosives, which apparently had not been noted in other reports. W subsequently withdrew his application for conditional discharge   **9.32**

---

[25] [1988] 2 All ER 648.   [26] [1988] 2 All ER 648, 661.
[27] [1990] 2 WLR 471.

and his solicitors refused to forward Dr Egdell's report to those responsible for his care and for any future recommendations as to his discharge. Dr Egdell nonetheless sent a copy of his report to the hospital and also pressed for a copy to be sent to the Home Office to be considered by those responsible for reviewing W's case.

9.33 W's solicitors commenced an action for breach of confidence against Dr Egdell, claiming damages and injunctive relief. The Court of Appeal emphasised that in determining whether or not there had been a breach of confidence the court should balance the public interests implicated, and should not focus on the private interests of the doctor or the patient. Bingham LJ quoted with approval from the speech of Lord Goff of Chieveley in *Attorney-General v Guardian Newspapers Ltd (No 2)*:[28]

> [A]lthough the basis of the law's protection of confidence is that there is a public interest that confidences should be preserved and protected by the law, nevertheless that public interest may be outweighed by some other countervailing public interest which favours disclosure. . . . It is this limiting principle which may require a court to carry out a balancing operation, weighing the public interest in maintaining confidence against a countervailing public interest favouring disclosure.[29]

9.34 The court must reach its own decision on the balance. However, in doing so it is legitimate for the court to give 'such weight to the considered judgment of a professional man as seems in all the circumstances to be appropriate'.[30] On the facts that balance:

> clearly lay in the restricted disclosure of vital information to the director of the hospital and to the Secretary of State who had the onerous duty of safeguarding public safety.

9.35 The disclosure in *W v Egdell* was justified by reference to the public interest in ensuring that a properly informed decision was made by those responsible for considering W's release in order to avert a 'real risk of consequent danger to the public'.[31] This raises the question of what risks of harm might be sufficient to justify disclosure of confidential information in the public interest. It has been suggested that, in order to justify disclosure, the risk of harm must be real and not fanciful, and it must be a risk involving the danger of *physical* harm.[32]

9.36 Even if these qualifications are accepted, it is necessary to decide whether or not a doctor will be justified in disclosing information whenever he reason-

---

[28] [1988] 3 WLR 776, 807.   [29] Quoted at [1990] 2 WLR 471, 489.
[30] [1990] 2 WLR 471, 490–1.   [31] ibid 493 *per* Bingham LJ.
[32] See Kennedy, I and Grubb, A, *Medical Law: text with materials*, 2nd edn (Butterworths, 1994), 657; Brazier, M, *Medicine, Patients and the Law*, 2nd edn (Penguin, 1992), 56.

ably believes that such a risk has arisen, or whether he must prove objectively that a real risk of physical harm does in fact exist. This point was not resolved in *W v Egdell*, since it is possible to read the judgments as saying that either might be in the public interest. The earlier decision of the New Zealand High Court in *Duncan v Medical Practitioners' Disciplinary Committee*[33] similarly left the question open:

> The doctor must then exercise his professional judgment based upon the circumstances, and if he fairly and reasonably believes such a danger exists then he must act unhesitatingly to prevent injury or loss of life even if there is to be a breach of confidentiality. If his actions are later to be scrutinised as to their correctness, he can be confident any official inquiry will be by people sympathetic about the predicament he faced.

(iii) *Guidance from the General Medical Council*

In 'The Duties of Doctor' the GMC provides detailed guidance for doctors **9.37** on the scope of their obligation of confidence. According to the GMC, the obligation of confidence is founded upon both a patient's right to expect confidentiality from a doctor, and the danger that otherwise patients may be reluctant to give doctors information which they need in order to provide good care.[34] Although the GMC adopts the general principle that confidential information should only be disclosed with the patient's consent, it has recognised that circumstances may arise in which a doctor may be justified in disclosing such information notwithstanding that the patient has not consented to the disclosure. It should be remembered, however, that the courts are not bound to follow the guidance from the GMC in determining the scope of the legal, as opposed to the professional, obligation of confidence.

(a) Caring for the Patient

The GMC recognises four circumstances in which concern for a patient's **9.38** welfare might necessitate the disclosure of confidential information without consent. First, where the patient is mentally incapable of giving a valid consent to disclosure by reason of immaturity, illness or mental incapacity. In such circumstances the GMC suggests that disclosure may be justified if it is 'essential in the patient's medical interests'.[35]

Secondly, where a patient is unable to give or withhold consent by reason of **9.39**

---

[33] [1986] 1 NZLR 513, 521.
[34] *Guidance from the General Medical Council on Confidentiality*, 3.
[35] ibid, 5–6.

either neglect or physical or sexual abuse the GMC recommends that disclosure to the appropriate responsible person or statutory agency would be justified if it is both in the patient's best medical interests and essential to prevent further harm to the patient. The distinction between this and the first category is not altogether clear. The GMC appears to take the view that patients might be either incapable of giving a valid consent to treatment, in which case they would fall into the first category, or may otherwise be 'unable' to give consent, for example, because they are under undue influence or otherwise precluded from making an appropriate medical treatment decision, in which case they would fall into the latter category. It may be that, from the legal point of view, the second category is better viewed as encompassing those cases where the patient *is capable of giving a valid consent* to disclosure but the circumstances are such that disclosure without the patient's consent is *justified in the public interest.*

9.40 The third situation in which the GMC accepts that disclosure of confidential information may be justified, albeit rarely, in the patient's own interests, is where disclosure serves the patient's medical interests but the seeking of consent to disclosure may itself be damaging to the patient.[36]

9.41 Finally, where necessary to prevent a risk of death or serious harm to the patient the GMC takes the view that disclosure to an appropriate person or authority would be justified.[37]

(b) Teaching, Research and Audit

9.42 For the purposes of teaching, research and audit it is advised that, wherever possible, information should be effectively anonymised in order to protect the confidentiality of the patient. In relation to audit and teaching, the GMC takes the view that patients' consent must otherwise be obtained in order to justify disclosure. In relation to research, however, the position is slightly different. First, the GMC suggests that every reasonable effort must be made to inform patients that they may withhold consent to the disclosure of personal information for research purposes. The implication here is that consent might then be inferred if a patient does not at this stage register any objection to his medical information being used for research purposes.

9.43 Secondly, where consent cannot be obtained, this should be disclosed to a research ethics committee which must then decide whether or not the public interest in the research being carried out outweighs the patients' right to confidentiality. This assumes that a research ethics committee will always be

---

[36] ibid, 6.   [37] ibid, 8.

involved prior to the disclosure of confidential information. The reality is, however, that research ethics committees are not routinely involved in much which may be published or discussed as clinical research, for example procedures carried out on a named patient basis, observations of unusual patient symptoms or responses, or trials of new surgical methods. In such circumstances it may well be the case that information is shared for research purposes without first obtaining the consent either of the patient or of a research ethics committee. This would appear to fall outside of the exception to the obligation of confidence recognised by the GMC and may, indeed, be regarded as professionally improper since according to the GMC: 'Disclosures to a researcher may otherwise be improper, even if the researcher is a registered medical practitioner.'[38]

(c) Preventing Harm to Others

Where necessary to prevent the risk of death or serious harm to the patient **9.44** or others, disclosure to an appropriate person or authority will not be regarded as professional impropriety. The situations chosen to illustrate this exception are disclosure to the Driver and Vehicle Licensing Authority where a patient continues to drive when unfit to do so, disclosure of the fact that a colleague is placing patients at risk as a result of illness or another medical condition, and disclosure necessary for the prevention or detection of a serious crime.[39]

(d) HIV and AIDS

Where a patient is diagnosed as being HIV positive or having AIDS, parti-   **9.45** cular problems might arise from the apparent conflict between the obligation of confidence owed to the patient and the doctor's obligation to safeguard the welfare of other doctors or health care professionals caring for the patient or of the patient's sexual partner. In relation to the former, the GMC advises that the patient should be counselled about the need for disclosure and the difficulties which a refusal of consent to disclosure may cause for the team providing his medical care. If, however, he does refuse consent to disclosure, his wishes ought to be respected unless 'the failure to disclose would put the health of any of the health care team at serious risk'.[40]

The GMC clearly regards this as an exceptional situation. Accordingly, it   **9.46** must be necessary to show some particularly significant risk of exposure to the

---

[38] *Guidance from the General Medical Council on Confidentiality,* 7.   [39] ibid, 8.
[40] *Guidance from the General Medical Council on HIV and AIDS: the ethical considerations,* 8.

virus, for example, where careful barrier precautions would be unlikely to succeed in guarding against infection.

9.47 Disclosure to a sexual partner of the patient would, in the view of the GMC, be justified only where the patient has been appropriately counselled and nonetheless refuses to inform his partner of the infection, and 'there is a serious and identifiable risk to a specific individual who, if not so informed, would be exposed to infection'.[41] In such circumstances, the GMC advises that a doctor is in fact *under a professional duty* to ensure that any sexual partner is informed in order to safeguard such persons from infection.

(iv) *Special Cases*

(a) **Children**

9.48 No English case has dealt with the question of the doctor's obligation of confidence to a child. Whereas the common law has developed in relation to the question of a child's ability to consent or refuse consent to medical treatment itself, there is still some doubt about the correct analysis of the doctor's obligation to maintain the confidentiality of information which he obtains in the course of his professional relationship with a child.[42]

9.49 There are two possible positions which could be taken here. The first would be to suggest that there is nothing unique about the doctor–child patient relationship. According to this view, the obligation of confidence depends not upon the patient's expectation that information will be kept confidential, but upon that information itself 'having the necessary character of confidence about it'.[43] More particularly, that information may be described as confidential where the law would impose an obligation of confidence and not merely where it could be said that the person communicating the information thought of it as confidential to him.

9.50 If information disclosed within the doctor–child patient relationship could be so described as confidential, in every case a balance would have to be struck between the public interests favouring confidentiality in the circumstances and the public interests favouring disclosure. Where a child is very young and

---

[41] ibid, 9.

[42] The recent Disclosure and Use of Personal Health Information Bill introduced into the House of Lords (HL Bill 37), clause 5(1) contains a proposed statutory obligation of confidence in relation to minors.

[43] *Per* Lord Greene MR in *Saltman Engineering Co Ltd v Campbell Engineering Co Ltd* (1948) 65 RPC 203, 215.

the lawfulness of medical treatment depends upon a parent's consent being given, then there will clearly be a public interest served by disclosure of information about the child's medical condition to the parent. Of course that is not to say that the information should be disclosed to anyone else. As the child grows in maturity and intelligence, the public interest in the disclosure of medical information to his parents will correspondingly decrease since in many cases treatment will lawfully be provided without the need for consent to be given by his parents or anyone else.[44]

The alternative is to regard the doctor's obligation of confidence as being dependent upon the child being competent to form a relationship of confidence with the doctor. The description of information as confidential is, according to this view, dependent upon some expectation on the part of the person communicating it that it will be kept secret. Thus, no obligation of confidence could be owed to a child unless the child was able to understand what secrecy entails, and to make a decision whether or not to restrict disclosure of medical information. Just as a child cannot consent to treatment unless competent, a child could not be owed an obligation of confidence unless capable of understanding what that entails. It would follow that a doctor owes no obligation of confidence at all unless a child patient is competent. If necessary, however, an order specifically restricting the disclosure of information which relates to child patients could be sought from a court exercising its *parens patriae* jurisdiction, or exercising powers specifically conferred under the Children Act 1989.

(b) Incompetent Adults

The analysis described above applies equally to incompetent adults.[45] Thus, according to one view an obligation of confidence is owed by the doctor because information disclosed in the relationship could objectively be described as confidential, although this obligation is liable to be overridden where disclosure can be justified in the public interest. The alternative position is that no obligation of confidence can be owed unless the patient is competent at the time of disclosure. The patient who was once competent but ceases to be so may be owed an obligation of confidence in respect of information communicated at a time when he was competent. But a patient

---

[44] Note however that in exceptional circumstances it may be prudent for doctors to involve the parents in the treatment decision even where the child is competent. See for example *Re W (a minor)(medical treatment)* [1992] 4 All ER 627.
[45] See also clause 5(2) of the Disclosure and Use of Personal Health Information Bill (HL), HL Bill 37.

who has never been competent, or who is incompetent at the time of disclosure, is owed no obligation of confidence whatsoever.

9.53 Since English courts have no *parens patriae* power in respect of adults the consequence of the latter view is that there is no legal basis upon which a doctor could be restrained from disclosing information relating to adult incompetent patients. The only relevant legal action which could be brought would be to sue in the tort of negligence where disclosure caused actual harm to the patient and was judged to be unreasonable in the circumstances.

(c) Deceased Patients

9.54 There is no settled law determining whether or not an obligation of confidence survives the death of the patient.[46] Since it is a personal obligation owed to the deceased, absent any statutory provision to the contrary, English courts are most likely to find that the obligation of confidence does not survive death.[47] In this regard the analogy with the policy underlying the law of defamation is persuasive, that is that where the deceased's reputation and feelings are at stake the interest should not survive for the benefit of the estate. The position is much the same as that of third parties whose interests might be affected by disclosure of information communicated within the doctor–patient relationship, but to whom the doctor owes no obligation of confidence.

(d) Express Prohibition

9.55 Difficulties arise where a patient forbids a doctor to disclose information which he has gained in his professional relationship. Although there is no case law, it is probably correct to say that disclosure contrary to an express prohibition would generally be a breach of confidence since there must be a strong public interest favouring confidentiality in such circumstances. This would probably apply even to information which is not in a form capable of identifying the patient although in that case there is some argument that no confidence of the patient has been infringed.

9.56 Since, however, the lawfulness of disclosure even where the patient has expressly forbidden disclosure must depend upon whether or not disclosure could be justified in the public interest, there may be exceptional circumstances in which even an express prohibition on disclosure could be over-

---

[46] cf the recommendation of the General Medical Council that a doctor's obligation to keep information confidential survives the patient's death. See *Guidance from the General Medical Council on Confidentiality*, 6–7.

[47] The Access to Health Records Act 1990 allows the personal representatives of a deceased patient to seek access to his medical records.

ridden. Clearly where disclosure is required by law there would be no breach of confidence. Probably also where disclosure is necessary in order to prevent an imminent risk of serious harm it would also be lawful. A doctor would not, however, be justified in disclosing the confidential information for the patient's own benefit, for example, by informing the patient's general practitioner or other health professionals caring for the patient. Similarly, disclosure contrary to an express prohibition for the purposes of teaching or research would probably not be lawful.

2. Disclosure for the Purpose of Litigation

(i) *Actions against a Health Authority, Trust, or Doctor*

9.57 Where litigation relating to personal injuries or death is actual or in contemplation an individual who is 'likely to be a party to subsequent proceedings' can apply to the High Court to compel a doctor or hospital to make such disclosures as may be relevant to an issue arising or likely to arise out of a claim for personal injuries provided that the doctor or hospital is also likely to be a party to the proceedings.[48] The court must be satisfied that disclosure is necessary either to dispose of the case fairly or to save costs.[49] It is not, however, necessary for the patient to show that he is likely to succeed on the merits of his claim, or that he has sufficient evidence to base a claim at the time of making the application for disclosure.

9.58 In the leading case of *Dunning v Board of Governors of the United Liverpool Hospitals*[50] the Court of Appeal held that to hold otherwise would be to frustrate the purpose of the legislation which is to enable potential litigants to discover whether there is sufficient evidence to bring a claim for compensation before incurring the expense of commencing proceedings. According to Lord Denning MR, the court

> should construe 'likely to be made' as meaning 'may' or 'may well be made' dependent upon the outcome of discovery.[51]

9.59 Conversely, it is clear that an application for pre-action discovery can not be

---

[48] Supreme Court Act 1981, s 33, and RSC Ord 24. See also the County Courts Act 1984, s 52. Pre-action discovery under these statutes is not limited to the applicant or claimant's own medical records but may include notes of other patients or accident reports.

[49] See RSC Order 24 r 8, and CCR Order 13, r 7.

[50] [1973] 2 All ER 454, decided under the Administration of Justice Act 1970, s 31, the wording of which is identical to the Supreme Court Act 1981, s 33(2).

[51] [1973] 2 All ER 454, 475.

used as a 'fishing expedition' and the plaintiff must show that there is a reasonable prospect of him making a claim in the circumstances.[52]

9.60 Courts considering these applications must balance the public interest in favour of disclosure against the public interest in maintaining the confidentiality of the information, and the relevant legislation empowering the High Court to make such orders prohibits the making of an order for discovery where 'compliance with the order, if made, would be likely to be injurious to the public interest'.[53]

9.61 The burden is on the party seeking to maintain the confidence of the information to establish that the court should refuse to order disclosure, since it is generally the case that the public interest in the administration of justice will be overriding. It is clear that the mere fact of information having been communicated confidentially within the confines of the doctor–patient relationship will not of itself be sufficient to justify the court exercising its discretion. Some further consideration would be required before a court would exercise its discretion to refuse to require medical information to be disclosed in the context of litigation.[54]

(ii) *After proceedings have been commenced*

9.62 Once litigation has commenced the High Court has the power to order disclosure between the parties to the litigation of any documents which are relevant to an issue arising out of the claim.[55] It also has the power under section 34 of the Supreme Court Act 1981 to order that a person who is not himself a party to the proceedings must disclose whether or not he possesses certain documents, and if so, to disclose them to the plaintiff or defendant or his advisers.[56] These powers are, once again, dependant upon a finding that it

---

[52] See in particular James LJ in *Dunning* [1973] 2 All ER 454, 460 and *Harris v Newcastle upon Tyne Health Authority* [1989] 1 WLR 96. See also the discussion in Cowley, R, *Access to Medical Records and Reports* (NAHAT, Radcliffe Medical Press, Oxford, 1994), 43.

[53] Gurry, F, *Breach of Confidence* (Clarendon Press, 1984), at 326 notes that the public interest here represents a higher interest which overcomes the interest in confidentiality for certain purposes. See also *Campbell v Tameside Metropolitan Borough Council* [1982] 1 QB 1065 (CA).

[54] For a discussion of the court's discretion in relation to medical information see *Re C* (16 Jan, 1991) on Lexis. Where the claimant is legally aided the court may see it as particularly important that information should be provided at an early stage in order to ascertain the likelihood of the action succeeding; see *Shaw v Vauxhall Motors* [1974] 1 WLR 1935, 1040 *per* Buckley LJ.

[55] The High Court has an inherent power to order disclosure between the parties to proceedings which have been commenced.

[56] See also the County Courts Act 1984, s 53.

is not against the public interest to order disclosure,[57] and that disclosure is necessary either to dispose of the case fairly or to save costs.[58]

Even as between parties to the litigation English courts have in the past shown **9.63** their willingness to exercise their discretion to refuse to order disclosure of information where there is an important public interest in maintaining the confidentiality of the information in the circumstances. Thus, for example, in *D v NSPCC*[59] (an action for breach of duty and negligence against the NSPCC), the House of Lords held that documents disclosing the source of a complaint to the NSPCC should be immune from inspection on discovery since otherwise the society's capacity to perform its public functions may be put at risk.[60] It may be that in particular cases information which would otherwise be confidential, for example information disclosed for purposes of maintaining public health or containing the spread of infectious diseases, may similarly be immune from disclosure in legal proceedings on the basis that disclosure might jeopardise an important public interest.

(iii) *In the Courtroom.*

It will often be the case that a doctor or other health professional is requested **9.64** to supply information as evidence orally or in a written statement either as a witness or in order to defend the claim. In such cases, the doctor is entitled to include confidential information in his evidence provided that it can be shown that it is in the public interest that such information is before the court.[61] As discussed above, the presumption in favour of disclosure rests upon the weight of the public interest in the administration of justice. In order to justify non-disclosure therefore, a doctor must be able to establish that the public interest in confidentiality in the circumstances outweighs the public interest in disclosure. If the doctor is not able successfully to justify non-disclosure he may be liable for contempt of court if he refuses to give evidence in court regardless of the fact that the information is confidential to his patient.[62] This position has been subject to some criticism, as one commentator has noted.

---

[57] Supreme Court Act 1981, s 35(1). See also *Science Research Council v Nassé* [1979] 3 All ER 673 (HL). [58] RSC Order 24, r 8.
[59] [1977] 1 All ER 589. [60] See the discussion in Gurry (n 53 above) at 347–8.
[61] For a recent consideration of the Crown Court's power to set aside a witness summons which would have required the witness to produce records relating to lawful abortions see *Morrow v DPP* (1993) 14 BMLR 54, noted by Kennedy, I, [1994] 2 Med L Rev 99.
[62] See *Duchess of Kingston's Case* (1776) 20 State Trials 355; *Nuttall v Nuttall and Twynan* (1964) 108 Sol J 605. For a discussion of the balancing process see *D v NSPCC* [1977] 1 All ER 589, 597.

The patient can stop his doctor from disclosing details of his confidential information in virtually all situations save in the courtroom.[63]

3. Confidentiality, Warning and Negligence Liability

(i) *Negligent Disclosure*

9.65 In New Zealand in the case of *Furniss v Fitchett*[64] it was held that liability in negligence might arise from a disclosure of information in breach of confidence. Barrowclough CJ clearly felt that the obligation to take reasonable care to respect confidences might be owed in any situation in which it was reasonably foreseeable that disclosure might injure the plaintiff's mental health.

> I have not forgotten that the certificate was true and accurate, but I see no reason for limiting the duty to one of care in seeing that it is accurate. The duty must extend also to the exercise of care in deciding whether it should be put in circulation in such a way that it is likely to cause harm to another.

9.66 No English court has followed this authority and there must be some doubt as to whether an action in negligence could arise out of a breach of confidence. There is, however, a strong argument that in any case in which it could be shown that a doctor had breached the obligation of confidence which he owed to his patient in circumstances where it was foreseeable that this could harm the patient, he must also have breached the duty of care which he owed to that patient. Even if other doctors might similarly have disclosed the information, it could hardly be described as 'responsible' medical practice to act unlawfully in breach of a patient's confidence.[65] This is particularly so given that the finding of a breach of confidence itself is predicated upon there being no overriding public interest in disclosure in the circumstances.

9.67 In most cases, however, a plaintiff will not have suffered damage compensable in the tort of negligence. In order to succeed in a negligence action a plaintiff would have to show some personal injury, or possibly economic loss.[66] Even if

---

[63] McHale, J, *Medical Confidentiality and Legal Privilege* (Routledge, London, 1993), 12. Pursuant to the Coroners Act 1988 s 2(1) a doctor may be required to provide information to the court. See also the rules relating to investigations by the GMC contained in *Guidance from the General Medical Council on Confidentiality*, 9.

[64] [1958] NZLR 396. Noted by Davis, AG, (1958) 21 MLR 438.

[65] See eg the modern interpretation of *Bolam* [1957] 2 All ER 118 in *Smith v Tunbridge Wells HA* [1994] 5 Med LR 334 (Morland J).

[66] The recovery of economic loss in actions for medical negligence based upon a breach of confidence would involve a substantial expansion in the law governing the recovery of economic loss which is unlikely given the present 'incremental' approach favoured by English courts in this area; see for example *Murphy v Brentwood District Council* [1990] 2 All ER 908.

the doctor's disclosure caused the patient to suffer from psychiatric injury of a type going beyond mere grief and distress there is some doubt as to whether the plaintiff could recover damages unless his symptoms could be said to have been induced by shock.[67]

(ii) *Negligent Failure to Disclose*

In certain circumstances a doctor might be justified in disclosing confidential **9.68** information in the public interest. Does this mean that a doctor might also have a duty to disclose confidential information in order to avert a risk of harm either from his patient or from some other source? No English cases have considered this question, and case law from the United States suggests a variety of different possible responses. Distinctions may have to be made between:

(a) an imminent and real risk of physical harm to an identified third party, as for example where a patient threatens immediate physical violence against another;

(b) a real but not immediate risk of physical harm to an identified third party, as for example where a patient carries a transmissible disease where transmission is possible but not inevitable; and

(c) a risk of physical harm to unidentified third parties, or to the public at large.

The most well known United States authority dealing with the doctor's duty **9.69** to warn of a risk of harm from his patient is *Tarasoff v Regents of the University of California*[68] where it was held that a psychologist could be held liable in negligence for failing to warn of his patient's intention to kill a named victim. The court accepted that:

> the therapist's obligations to his patient require that he not disclose a confidence unless such disclosure is necessary to avert danger to others.[69]

Where, however, there was a real risk of physical harm to a named person: **9.70**

> If the exercise of reasonable care to protect the threatened victim requires the

---

[67] In *Walker v Northumberland CC* [1995] 1 All ER 737 an employee successfully sued his employer for negligently caused psychiatric injury caused by stress at work. The Law Commission in its Consultation Paper on *Liability for Psychiatric Injury* (No 137) at 35, described the *Walker* case as supporting the view that in 'a primary victim case like this . . . it is not a prerequisite for liability that the psychiatric illness has been shock induced', then went on to suggest that '[o]ther miscellaneous situations in which a primary victim *probably* can recover for a negligently inflicted psychiatric illness . . . include: where a patient suffers a psychiatric illness because of negligent treatment by his psychiatrist . . .' (at 35).
[68] (1976) 131 Cal Rptr 14 (Cal Sup Ct).   [69] ibid, 27.

therapist to warn the endangered party or those who can reasonably be expected to notify him, we see no sufficient societal interest that would protect and justify concealment. The containment of such risks lies in the public interest.[70]

9.71 It is likely that English courts, which have traditionally been slow to recognise a duty to act, as opposed to a duty to avoid causing harm, would take a more conservative approach but would nonetheless find a duty to warn in limited circumstances. In determining whether or not non-disclosure was negligent the court would take account of the likelihood and seriousness of harm, the ease with which it could be prevented, and the strong public interest in maintaining patient confidentiality to encourage dangerous individuals to seek medical care in an open and trusting environment. In this context risks of physical aggression towards identified individuals and risks of transmitting serious infection to identified individuals might be viewed as sufficiently great to merit disclosure provided it was the only available precaution against that harm.[71]

4. Remedies

(i) *Injunction*

9.72 A patient may apply to the court for an injunction to restrain publication of confidential information, either absolutely or in part. An injunction is available at the discretion of the court and may be granted upon whatever terms the court thinks appropriate. At the interlocutory stage, when most of these issues come to be tried, the availability of an injunction depends upon showing that there is a serious issue to be tried.[72] An interlocutory injunction will be of considerable practical significance for a plaintiff in a breach of confidence action since, unless publication is restrained, it will usually be pointless for him to continue with his action.[73]

---

[70] ibid, 27–8.

[71] *Gamill v US* (1984) 727 F 2d 950 (duty to warn family and other foreseeably at risk of transmission of hepatitis). See also *Bradshaw v Daniel* (1993) 854 SW 2d 865 (SC Tennessee) where the risk was not of direct transmission of infection but of an infection indirectly being transmitted to other family members (known as a clustering of infection). See also the *Guidance from the General Medical Council on HIV and AIDS* discussed above at paras 9.45–9.47.

[72] Applying the principles laid down in *American Cyanamid Co v Ethicon* [1975] 1 All ER 504. [73] See Cowley, R, *Access to Medical Records and Reports*, (n 52 above), 80.

(ii) *Declaration*

In some circumstances a plaintiff may be satisfied with a declaration from the   **9.73**
court that a breach of confidence took place, or that a particular disclosure
which is reasonably anticipated by the parties would amount to a breach of
confidence.

(iii) *Damages*

If a doctor's breach of confidence caused financial harm to a patient, as for   **9.74**
example if it had adverse implications for his employment or business
opportunities, this loss could be compensated in an action for breach of
confidence. Where, however, the breach of confidence causes mere mental
distress and anxiety, the law governing the recovery of damages is less
certain.[74] If the patient were able to frame his claim as one in negligence,
then damages could be recovered for any personal injury caused by the
disclosure and possibly also for psychiatric injury so caused.[75] Of course, as
noted below, English courts may award damages under section 23 of the Data
Protection Act 1984 for any damage caused by unauthorised disclosure of
personal data falling within the provisions of the Act.

In an action for breach of a contractual obligation of confidence it is   **9.75**
possible,[76] but unlikely,[77] that damages could be claimed for mental distress
and anxiety. If the court were to take the view that one purpose underlying
the contractual relationship between the doctor and the patient was to
provide peace of mind and freedom from distress, it might be possible for
damages to be awarded for a breach which compromised that very object.

(iv) *Restitutionary Damages*

If a doctor were to profit financially from a breach of patient confidentiality it   **9.76**
is possible that he might be liable to account for those profits to the patient.

---

[74] The *Law Commission Report on Breach of Confidence* (Law Commission No 110) at para
4.81 recommended against the recovery of damages for embarrassment or distress caused by a
non-contractual breach of confidence.

[75] Depending upon the interpretation of *Walker v Northumberland* and *Page v Smith*. Note
that the Law Commission in *Consultation Paper* envisages that damages might be recoverable
for psychiatric injury in an action by a patient against, for example, a psychiatrist.

[76] See *Jarvis v Swan Tours Ltd* [1973] QB 233

[77] See Scott J at first instance in *W v Egdell* [1989] 1 All ER 1089.

The situation could arise, for example, where a doctor sells a patient's story to the press, or makes use of confidential information derived from the patient for his own financial gain from scientific research or development.

5. Statutory Modifications to the Obligation of Confidence

9.77 There are three different ways in which statute may modify a doctor's obligation of confidence. First, it might reinforce the common law obligation of confidence by providing specific penalties for unjustified disclosure, or extend its application to cover circumstances in which the doctor might have been justified in disclosing information at common law. Secondly, it might empower the doctor to disclose information in certain limited circumstances, although not in fact requiring him to do so. Thirdly, a statute might positively require disclosure provided specified conditions are satisfied, leaving the doctor no discretion whether or not to disclose.

(i) *The Data Protection Act 1984*

9.78 The Data Protection Act 1984 provides a legal framework for controlling the use of personal data stored in an electronic form. The Act covers all personal data defined as:

> data consisting of information which relates to a living individual who can be identified from that information (or from information in the possession of the data user), including any expression of opinion about the individual but not any indication of the intentions of the data user in respect of that individual.[78]

9.79 The Act provides a registration system (operated by the Data Protection Registrar)[79] for data users, defined as persons who hold, process, or control data in an electronic form.[80] Generally, the data user will be an organisation such as a health authority or NHS Trust but it is possible that an individual doctor may qualify as the data user in a particular case. Difficult questions may arise as to whether the purchaser of health care services or the provider of those services is the data user in respect of the patient's personal data. The *Guidelines* suggest that various factors will be considered in deciding who is the data user and therefore required to comply with the registration requirements in the 1984 Act. Generally, it is recommended that the parties involved should clarify the situation between themselves, and one party should take on the responsibilities of the data user under the 1984 Act. Otherwise, the factors which appear to be relevant are who has authority to decide the extent

---

[78] Data Protection Act 1984, s 1(3).   [79] S 3.   [80] S 1(3).

to which records should be kept, what sort of information should be collected, whether the information should be updated, added to, amended or deleted; whether and when the information should be available to the other party or third parties; and who keeps the information after the relationship between the parties has ended.[81] Moreover, the fact that, for example, a provider of health care services may be supplied personal information for the limited purpose of providing one particular treatment service would not preclude it being designated as the data user provided it is responsible for using its skill and judgment in compiling the data record.[82]

The Act makes it an offence to be a data user unless registered with the Data **9.80** Protection Registrar, and also to use personal data for an unregistered purpose or disclose or transfer it otherwise than in accordance with the details in the register.[83] The Registrar also has discretionary powers of enforcement should he find that there is a breach of one of the data protection principles set out in Schedule 1 of the Act. These include requirements that personal data is kept confidential, in particular that it shall be obtained and processed fairly and lawfully,[84] that it shall not be used or disclosed in any manner incompatible with the purposes noted on the register, and that appropriate security measures shall be taken against unauthorised access to personal data.

Provided that the registration requirements and the Data Protection Princi- **9.81** ples are complied with an individual has no right under the Act to object to disclosure of information held by the data user provided that:

(a) the person to whom the disclosure is made is described in the disclosures section of the data user's register entry; or

(b) the disclosure is covered by one of the non-disclosure exemptions set out in the Act. Disclosure falling within one of these exemptions will not be regarded as breaking any of the Data Protection Principles and the Registrar cannot take any action in respect of the disclosure.[85] They are as follows:

   (i) disclosure where the person making it has reasonable grounds for believing that it is to or with the consent of the data subject;

   (ii) disclosure where the person making it has reasonable grounds for

---

[81] *The Guidelines, Third Series, November 1994*, Office of the Data Protection Registrar, 24–7.

[82] See for example *The Data Protection Registrar v Francis Joseph Griffin* (High Court, Feb 1993, unreported). [83] S 5.

[84] The *Guidelines* emphasise that this includes an obligation to take care to ensure that in disclosing information data users do not breach any duty of confidence: *The Guidelines, Third Series, November 1994*, Office of the Data Protection Registrar, 9.

[85] *The Guidelines, Third Series, November 1994*, Office of the Data Protection Registrar, 97.

believing that it is to or with the consent of someone acting on the data subject's behalf;[86]

(iii) disclosure by a data user to its employees or agents in order to enable them to perform their duties as employees or agents;

(iv) disclosure in order to avoid a substantial chance of prejudicing the prevention or detection of crime, the apprehension or prosecution of offenders, or the assessment or collection of any tax or duty;[87]

(v) disclosure made to safeguard national security;[88]

(vi) disclosure where required by statute, made for the purposes of the data user taking legal advice, or made for the purpose of, or in the course of, legal proceedings in which the person making the disclosure is a party or a witness;[89] and

(vii) disclosure urgently required for preventing injury or other damage to anyone's health.[90]

9.82 Section 23 of the 1984 Act gives an individual the right to compensation for damage *and any distress* which he suffers by reason of the disclosure of data, or access having been obtained to the data, without 'such authority as aforesaid'. This does not apply to any disclosure by a registered data user to a person described as a potential recipient of data in the register. There is some ambiguity surrounding this section, in particular the meaning of the phrase 'without such authority as aforesaid'. Guidelines issued by the Office of the Data Protection Registrar make it clear, however, that: 'Unauthorised' means without the authority of the data user or the computer bureau concerned'.[91]

9.83 Accordingly, compensation can only be awarded where personal data held by a registered data user are disclosed without the data user's authority and outside the terms of the data user's register entry, or where personal data are in the possession of a computer bureau and access to it is obtained without the data user's authority. Further, although the Act makes no mention of these the *Guidelines* provide that no compensation should be payable if the data user or computer bureau can prove that all reasonable care was taken to prevent the disclosure or access, and that damage should include financial loss or physical injury but not mere distress suffered by the individual data subject. Damages for distress should only be awarded in conjunction with a claim for personal injury or financial loss.[92]

---

[86] Curiously the *Guidelines* appear to contemplate someone acting to protect the data subject as falling within this category notwithstanding that they may not be specifically authorised to do so by the data subject: *The Guidelines, Third Series, November 1994*, Office of the Data Protection Registrar, 98. [87] ibid, 99.
[88] ibid, 100.   [89] ibid, 100.   [90] ibid, 101.   [91] ibid, 8.
[92] ibid, 81–2.

The fact that a particular disclosure falls within one of the non-disclosure **9.84** exemptions discussed above does not inhibit a court's power to award compensation for damage suffered because of an unauthorised disclosure.

(ii) *Abortion*

Pursuant to the Abortion Regulations 1991[93] any registered medical practi- **9.85** tioner who terminates a pregnancy in England or Wales is required to provide the Chief Medical Officer with notice of the termination together with any other information specified in the prescribed form of notification.[94] The regulations also prohibit disclosure of the notice or other information provided to the Chief Medical Officer other than for the purposes set out in the regulations themselves.[95]

(iii) *Infectious Diseases*

The National Health Service (Venereal Diseases) Regulations 1974[96] prohibit **9.86** the disclosure by a Health Authority of identifying information which was obtained:

> with respect to persons examined or treated for any sexually transmitted disease . . . except—
> (a) for the purpose of communicating that information to a medical practitioner, or to a person employed under the direction of a medical practitioner in connection with the treatment of persons suffering from such disease or the prevention of the spread thereof, and
> (b) for the purpose of such treatment and prevention.[97]

There is no specific requirement that the patient consent to disclosure under **9.87** the regulations, but clearly disclosure would only be lawful 'for the purpose of treatment' where the recipient of the information was in fact treating the patient for the sexually transmitted disease itself. Disclosure for the purpose of preventing the spread of disease, however, could be lawful even in the face of the patient's objection if, for example, it was felt necessary to inform a doctor responsible for the medical treatment of the individual's partner in order to prevent transmission. A further limitation on the scope of the

---

[93] SI 1991/499. Wilful contravention or wilful failure to comply with these requirements is an offence under s 2(3). See *R v Senior* [1981] 1 QB 283 at 290 *per* Lord Russell for a discussion of what amounts to 'wilful' in these circumstances.   [94] Para 4(1).
[95] See para 5.   [96] SI 1974/29.
[97] Para 2. See also NHS Trust (Venereal Disease) Directions 1991.

regulations is that the disease must have been transmitted to the individual sexually, hence they could not authorise disclosure where, for example, HIV had been transmitted other than by sexual intercourse.[98]

9.88 The Public Health (Control of Disease) Act 1984 (supplemented by the Public Health (Infectious Diseases) Regulations 1988)[99] requires a doctor to notify 'the proper officer of the local authority for that district' of identifying particulars and other relevant information set out in the section if he

> becomes aware, or suspects, that a patient whom he is attending within the district of a local authority is suffering from a notifiable disease or from food poisoning . . . unless he believes, and has reasonable grounds for believing, that some other registered medical practitioner has complied with this subsection with respect to the patient . . .[100]

9.89 Notifiable disease means any of the following: acute encephalitis, acute meningitis, acute poliomyelitis, anthrax, cholera, diphtheria, dysentery, food poisoning, leprosy, leptospirosis, malaria, measles, meningococcal septicaemia, mumps, opthalmia, neonatorum, paratyphoid fever, plague, rabies, relapsing fever, rubella, scarlet fever, small pox, tetanus, tuberculosis, typhoid fever, typhus, viral haemorrhagic fever, viral hepatitis, whooping cough, and yellow fever.[101]

(iv) *Drug Misuse*

9.90 Pursuant to the Misuse of Drugs (Notification of Supply to Addicts) Regulations 1973 doctors are required to notify the Chief Medical Officer at the Home Office of identifying particulars about any person who

> he considers, or has reasonable grounds to suspect, is addicted to any notifiable drug . . .[102]

9.91 This does not, however, apply where the doctor

> is of the opinion, formed in good faith, that the continued administration of the drug or drugs concerned is required for the purpose of treating organic disease

or, where the particulars have already been supplied to the Chief Medical Officer (although not necessarily by the doctor) during the period of twelve months ending with the date of the doctor's attendance of the patient.[103]

---

[98] See the discussion in Kennedy, I and Grubb, A, *Medical Law: text with materials* (Butterworths, 1994), 646.   [99] SI 1988/1546.
[100] S 11(1).
[101] S 10, as added to by the Public Health (Infectious Diseases) Regulations 1988, SI 1988/1546.   [102] Reg 3(1).
[103] Reg 3(2).

(v) *Births*

Any person in attendance on the mother is obliged to notify the district **9.92**
medical officer of the birth of any child born dead or alive after the twenty-
eighth week of pregnancy.[104] This obligation may be discharged by instructing another person to notify the birth.

(vi) *Fertility Treatment*

As discussed in Chapter 10 there are specific provisions in the Human **9.93**
Fertilisation and Embryology Act 1990 as modified by the Human Fertilisation and Embryology (Disclosure of Information) Act 1992 which regulate
confidentiality.

(vii) *In Connection with the Investigation and Prevention of Crime*

Under the Police and Criminal Evidence Act 1984, certain material is **9.94**
excluded from the ordinary provisions enabling courts to make special procedure orders for the production of documents required for criminal investigations.[105] This material is described as 'excluded material' and covers both
personal records created or acquired for professional purposes and held in
confidence, and human tissue or tissue fluid taken for the purposes of
diagnosis or medical treatment and held in confidence.[106] Personal records
are in turn defined in section 12 to include records from which an individual
can be identified and which relate to his physical or mental health.

Recently in *R v Central Criminal Court, ex p Kellam*[107] it was held that **9.95**
hospital records detailing which of a psychiatric hospital's patients were
absent from the hospital on a particular day fell within the definition of
'personal records' because they enabled patients to be identified by reference
to their state of mental health. The fact that the document was created for the
purpose of calculating National Insurance payments was not relevant to this

---

[104] The National Health Service Act 1977, s 124(4); and the National Health Service
(Notification of Births and Deaths) Regulations 1982, SI 1982/286.
[105] Police and Criminal Evidence Act 1984, s 9(1).
[106] If, for example, blood was taken to determine an individual's blood-alcohol level it
would not be 'excluded material'. Bullets are not excluded material.
[107] (1993) 16 BMLR 76 (Evans LJ and Morland J). Noted by Grubb, A, (1994) 2 Med L
Rev 370.

enquiry since the critical question is whether or not the information in the record relates to the physical or mental health of the individual who may be identified therefrom. In the context the phrase 'relating to physical or mental health' is to be construed broadly.

9.96 Police may seize excluded material without a court order if they come upon material whilst lawfully on premises for another purpose, provided they have reasonable grounds for believing that it is relevant evidence in relation to an offence and that it is necessary to seize it to prevent it from being destroyed.[108] A court order to produce excluded material will only be given if there are (a) reasonable grounds to believe that there is material which includes excluded or special procedure material on the premises; (b) a search warrant for that material might otherwise, ie before PACE, have been given; and (c) the issue of a warrant would, in the circumstances, have been appropriate. The person who is subject to the order must be given notice and cannot then lawfully destroy material.[109]

9.97 The only situation in which police can compel the disclosure of medical records is in connection with offences of terrorism under the Prevention of Terrorism (Temporary Provisions) Act 1989 with either an inspection or search warrant, or, in cases of extreme urgency, a written order by an officer of not less than the rank of superintendent. In addition, section 18 of the Prevention of Terrorism (Temporary Provisions) Act 1989 requires the disclosure of information to police where the information might be of assistance:

> in preventing the commission . . . of an act of terrorism connected with the affairs of Northern Ireland; or in securing the apprehension, prosecution or conviction of any other person for an offence involving the commission, preparation or instigation of such an act.[110]

9.98 Section 172(b) of the Road Traffic Act 1988 provides that, where the driver of a vehicle, or rider of a bicycle, is alleged to be guilty of a road traffic offence:

> any other person shall if required . . . give such information which it is in his power to give and may lead to identification of the driver.[111]

9.99 *Hunter v Mann* confirmed that this section applied to doctors who received the information in confidence from a patient, and that doctors have the power to disclose such information if so required by statute, even where

---

[108] Police and Criminal Evidence Act 1984, s 19.   [109] ibid, Sch 1.

[110] S 18(2) makes it an offence 'without reasonable excuse' to fail to provide information in accordance with s 18.

[111] S 172(4) makes it an offence to fail to give information in accordance with such a request.

they might not be entitled otherwise voluntarily to disclose such information without the patient's consent.[112]

6. Europe

(i) *The European Convention on Human Rights*

English courts have accepted that article 8(1) of the European Convention on Human Rights may protect an individual against the disclosure of information which is subject to an obligation of professional confidence. Article 8(2), however, provides that disclosure might be justified in circumstances where interference with the right to privacy is justified in accordance with law and where necessary in a democratic society in the interests of public safety or the prevention of crime.[113]

9.100

(ii) *The European Directive*[114]

The European Parliament on 25 July 1995 adopted a Directive on the Protection of Individuals with regard to the processing of personal data and on the free movement of such data. The Directive covers all personal data, defined as:

9.101

> any information relating to an individual or identifiable natural person ('data subject'); an identifiable person is one who can be identified, directly or indirectly, in particular by reference to an identification number or to one or more factors specific to his physical, physiological, mental, economic, cultural or social identity.[115]

The Directive applies both to the 'processing of personal data wholly or partly by automatic means' and to processing 'otherwise than by automatic means of personal data which form part of a filing system or are intended to form part of a filing system'.[116] This could clearly cover most, if not all, manually stored hospital or medical records since filing system is defined as:

9.102

> any structured set of personal data which are accessible according to specific criteria, whether centralized, decentralized or dispersed on a functional or geographical basis.

---

[112] *Hunter v Mann* [1974] 1 QB 767.
[113] See the discussion in *W v Egdell* [1990] 2 WLR 471, 493.
[114] [1995] OJ L281. Adopted by the European Parliament on 25 July 1995 and by the European Council on 24 October 1995. Thus, the English Parliament has until 25 July 1998 to comply with the Directive.   [115] Art 2.
[116] Art 3.

9.103 The Directive operates to buttress patient confidentiality in a similar manner to the Data Protection Act 1984. Article 6 imports various principles relating to data quality (much like the Data Protection Principles discussed above) which require, *inter alia*, that member states must provide that all personal data is processed fairly and lawfully, collected for specific purposes and not further processed in a way incompatible with those purposes, and kept in a form which permits identification of data subjects for no longer than is necessary for the purposes for which the data were collected or for which they are further processed. For those concerned with the health care context it is significant that the Directive stipulates that:

> further processing of data for historical, statistical or scientific purposes shall not be considered as incompatible provided that Member States provide appropriate safeguards.

9.104 Accordingly, it appears that hospitals and health authorities may use information which it holds about patients for further research irrespective of whether or not the information was originally collected with those purposes in mind. It is the responsibility of each Member State to lay down specific safeguards, however, to ensure the security of information which is further processed for research purposes.[117]

9.105 The second mechanism by which the Directive effectively reinforces the common law obligations of confidence (in respect of which no analogy can be found in the Data Protection Act 1984) is by laying down specific principles which govern the lawfulness of the processing of personal information.[118] Information concerning health or sex life is designated as a 'special category of data' requiring separate attention.[119] The processing of such data must be prohibited by member states but this requirement is subject to a number of exceptions of broad application in the health care context. Most importantly in the health care context, the prohibition does not apply where:

> the processing of data is required for the purposes of preventative medicine, medical diagnosis, the provision of care or treatment or the management of health care services, and where those data are processed by a health professional subject under national law or rules established by national competent bodies to the obligation of professional secrecy or by another person also subject to an equivalent obligation of secrecy.[120]

This will cover most if not all cases of disclosure of information in the health care context.

---

[117] Art 6(e).
[118] Art 7. This is described as a 'striking feature of the Directive' by Bainbridge, D and Pearce, G, 'Controls and Constraints on processing of personal data' (1995) NLJ 1579, 1579.
[119] Art 8.   [120] Art 8(3).

The final means by which the Directive imposes additional obligations of confidence upon those who 'process' personal information is by requiring that data controllers (ie 'the natural or legal person, public authority, agency or any other body which alone or jointly with others determines the purposes and means of the processing of personal data'[121]) and processors guarantee security in relation to the processing of personal information. The Directive prohibits any person under the authority of the controller or the processor from processing personal information except on instructions from the controller.[122] Moreover, the controller is obliged to take appropriate technical and organizational measures to protect personal data against unauthorized disclosure or access, in particular where the 'processing involves the transmission of data over a network'.[123]

9.106

The Directive stipulates that a judicial remedy must be available for any breach of the rights guaranteed therein[124] and that any person who suffers damage as a result of any processing which is either prohibited by provisions adopted pursuant to the Directive or is inconsistent with such provisions must be entitled to receive compensation from the controller.[125] Only if the controller can establish that he is not responsible for the event giving rise to the damage can he escape the obligation to pay compensation.[126]

9.107

B. Rights of Access to Medical Records

1. General

It is generally accepted that good clinical care requires that doctors

9.108

> keep clear, accurate, and contemporaneous patient records which report the relevant clinical findings, the decisions made, information given to patients and any drugs or other treatment prescribed . . .[127]

In order to provide a comprehensive picture of a patient's history and medical prognosis these records will frequently include details of all aspects of patients' past and present medical care, including medical and other opinions about the patient's physical and mental condition, together with other information which may be relevant to any doctor treating the patient. That good

9.109

---

[121] Art 2(d).
[122] Art 16. This is subject to an exception where such processing is required by law.
[123] Art 17(1).   [124] Art 22.   [125] Art 23(1).   [126] Art 23(2).
[127] *Good Medical Practice: Guidance from the General Medical Council on Good Medical Practice* (London, 1995) 2. See also NHS Management Executive EL(95)60 *Code of Practice on Openness in the NHS—Guidance on Implementation*, 13.

medical practice will usually require that access be provided voluntarily is recognised by Guidance issued by the NHS:[128]

> The Department of Health policy has long been that as a matter of principle patients should be allowed to see what has been written about them . . .[129]

9.110 This section investigates the circumstances in which a patient may be entitled to claim access to medical records as of right. Two distinctions are important here. First, we are not concerned with situations in which it might be alleged to be negligent for the doctor or hospital to refuse access to the plaintiff's medical records, or not to have disclosed certain information therein to the patient.[130] In such cases the patient's claim is that the doctor has a duty to avoid causing harm, including harm which is caused by withholding medical information from him or his advisers. The claim is not, however, that the patient has a right of access to his medical records *per se*. In the words of Kirby P (dissenting) in the New South Wales Court of Appeal in *Breen v Williams*:

> there is a quantum leap from the entitlement of a proper explanation by a medical practitioner about the dangers of medical procedures as incidental to treatment to an affirmative obligation to give access to information in records by a medical practitioner who has not been sued and who has never been said to have failed in his duty of explanation to his patient.[131]

9.111 Secondly, we must distinguish claims for access to medical records as part of pre-action disclosure under section 33 or 34 of the Supreme Court Act 1981 and RSC Order 24 r 7A[132] where litigation is actual or in contemplation. Again where a patient claims that he has a right of access to his medical records in such circumstances his claim is founded upon the potential usefulness of those records in anticipated litigation, it is not a claim that he has a right of access to the records as such.

---

[128] Health Service Guidance (91)6. See also the Patient's Charter which states that 'every citizen has the "right" to have access to your health records'; EL(93)44.

[129] The argument that these gave rise to a legitimate expectation on the part of patients that they would voluntarily be given access to their medical records was rejected by Popplewell J at first instance in *Martin*.

[130] See *Sidaway v Governors of Bethlem Royal Hospital* [1985] 1 All ER 643, [1985] 2 WLR 480 (HL); *Lee v South West Thames Regional Health Authority* [1985] 2 All ER 385 (CA); *Naylor v Preston Area Health Authority* [1987] 2 All ER 353, [1987] 1 WLR 958 (CA).

[131] *Breen v Williams* [1995] 6 Med LR 385, 418. The judgments of the High Court of Australia in *Breen v Williams* are considered below.

[132] See also *C v C* (1946) 1 All ER 562 where a court ordered that access to medical records should be given for the purpose of litigation.

2. Statutory Rights of Access

(i) *In the Course of Litigation*

As discussed above, patients may have to seek a court order for access to their **9.112**
medical records where they have already commenced, or are contemplating
commencing, legal proceedings.[133] Prior to the commencement of proceedings
a patient is only entitled to court ordered access of documents held by a person
who is likely to be a party to any proceedings which may be instituted.[134] If,
however, litigation has already been commenced, a patient may seek a court order
against a person who is not a party to proceedings on a matter which is relevant to
the proceedings in hand.[135] Accordingly, reliance upon court ordered disclosure is
effectively conditional upon a patient already having sufficient information to
identify a potential defendant against whom she may bring a claim.

It is possible that access to medical records might be provided even without a **9.113**
court order. In this regard the Department of Health has issued guidance to
health authorities that:

> In considering requests from patients or their authorised representatives for
> disclosure of case notes or information from them in connection with actual or
> possible litigation, . . . [i]t would not be appropriate for health authorities to
> adopt a more stringent test than would be likely to be applied by the court when
> considering an application under section 33(2) or 34(2) of [the Supreme Court
> Act 1981] since this could have the effect of forcing the applicant to resort to
> court action when there was no real doubt as to the outcome.[136]

In the view of the Department of Health, hospitals would not be well advised **9.114**
to insist on their strict legal rights in considering requests for access to
medical records for the purpose of anticipated legal proceedings,

> except for some good reason bearing on the defence to the particular claim or on
> the ground that the request is made without substantial justification.[137]

In general the Department of Health advises that each request for disclosure of **9.115**
medical records in connection with litigation must be examined on its own
merits, and in all cases which involve medical matters (as opposed for example
to merely administrative matters) any member of staff directly concerned in the
outcome of the claim or involved in the patient's treatment should be con-

---

[133] Supreme Court Act 1981, County Courts Act 1984, and the court's inherent power to
order disclosure for the purpose of legal proceedings which have already been commenced:
discussed above at paras 9.62–9.63.   [134] Supreme Court Act 1981, s 33.
[135] Supreme Court Act 1981, s 34.   [136] HC(82)16, para 5.
[137] HC(82)16, Annex A, para 3.

sulted. This is to ensure that any extracts which are given are not misleading, and that disclosure would not in any way be harmful to the applicant.

(ii) *Data Protection Act 1984*

9.116 The Data Protection Act 1984,[138] which applies to medical records stored in an electronic form,[139] requires that individuals shall be entitled, at regular intervals and without undue delay or expense, to be informed by any data user whether personal data are held by them, to have access to any such data, and, if appropriate, to have such data corrected or erased. More particularly, section 21(1) entitles a data subject to be supplied with a copy of the information constituting this personal data, together with any explanation necessary to make the record intelligible. Failure to comply with such a request is not a criminal offence, but may entitle an individual either to complain to a court who may order the data user to comply with the request unless it seems unreasonable to do so,[140] or to the Data Protection Registrar who may serve an enforcement or de-registration notice, failure to comply with which would be a criminal offence.

9.117 The right of access applies provided three criteria are satisfied. First, that the request is made in writing.[141] A separate application must be made for each entry in the register where, for example, information is being held for more than one different purpose.[142] Secondly, the applicant is obliged to provide sufficient information to enable him to be identified and to locate the information sought.[143] Thirdly the applicant must pay the statutory fee for access.[144]

9.118 There are several exceptions to this statutory right of access.[145] Moreover, according to *The Guidelines* issued by the Data Protection Registrar, where information is entitled to be withheld under one of the exceptions discussed

---

[138] The Act came into force in 1987 but applies to records compiled prior to this date provided they fall within the statutory definitions.

[139] Data are defined in sub-s 1(2) of the Act as 'information recorded in a form in which it can be processed by equipment operating automatically in response to instructions given for that purpose. For a detailed discussion of the meaning of 'personal data' see Cowley, R, *Access to Medical Records and Reports* (NAHAT, Radcliffe Medical Press, 1994), 4.

[140] *The Guidelines, Third Series, November 1994*, Office of the Data Protection Registrar, 74.   [141] S 21(2).

[142] S 21(3).   [143] S 21(4)(a).

[144] S 21(2). Delay in payment of the fee does not justify delay in processing the application since the 40 day period within which the application must be processed runs from the date on which the other two criteria are satisfied and does not take the date of payment into account (see HC(87)26).

[145] See also Chapter 10 which discusses the exemption in the Data Protection Act 1984, s 35(A), introduced by the Human Fertilisation and Embryology Act 1990.

below, the data user is not obliged to inform the patient of this fact. Thus it would be perfectly legitimate for a health authority to respond to a request for information which it is entitled to withhold by denying that it has in its possession any information which it was required to disclose.[146] In such circumstances the patient is effectively disentitled from challenging the decision to refuse access, since he may not even be aware that such a decision has been made.[147]

First, the data user is not obliged to comply with a request for access where the data would identify another person unless he satisfies himself that that other person has consented to the disclosure of information to the applicant.[148] This is expressly said to cover the situation where the record identifies another person as the source of information about the patient, for example, if the record indicated that a patient's husband had discussed her physical or mental problems with their doctor.[149] A doctor is nonetheless obliged to give the patient: 9.119

> so much of the information sought by the request as can be supplied without disclosing the identity of the other individual concerned, whether by omission of names or other identifying particulars or otherwise.[150]

Secondly, section 34 provides that the Secretary of State may by order exempt personal data from subject access provisions where disclosure is prohibited or restricted by any enactment. However, before making an order, the Secretary of State must carry out a balancing exercise, deciding whether the prohibition or restriction ought to prevail over the interests of the data subject of others.[151] 9.120

Thirdly, the Act appears to assume generally that it is only the data subject (or his duly authorised agent)[152] who is entitled to access to his computerised records. Although the Act does not make this explicit, that the request should come from the data subject himself is implicit in the scheme of section 21 which is based around an individual's entitlement to be informed about data held about him *should he so choose*. This of course begs the question whether patients who are not capable themselves of satisfying the formal requirements of access of making a request in writing and paying a prescribed fee are 9.121

---

[146] *The Guidelines, Third Series, November 1994*, Office of the Data Protection Registrar, Guideline 6, 101–2.   [147] Para C.1.2, Guideline 6, issued by Data Protection Registrar.
[148] See also the Data Protection (Subject Access Modification) (Health) Order 1987, discussed below.   [149] S 21(4).
[150] S 21(5).
[151] Information about human embryos is specifically exempt from the subject access provisions pursuant to section 35A.
[152] See Guidance from the Data Protection Registrar, para 2.32, Guideline 5, discussed in Cowley, R, *Access to Medical Records and Reports* (n 139 above), 5.

excluded from the subject access provisions altogether. Further, it is unclear whether or not there is some threshold of capacity which must be satisfied in order to be entitled to access to data under the Act, or whether it is sufficient that the request satisfy the formal requirements in the Act.

9.122 In relation to adults, section 21(9) enables the Secretary of State by order to provide for a request to be made *on behalf of* any individual who is incapable by reason of mental disorder of managing his own affairs.[153] This clearly enables an application for access to be made by such a person, but does not preclude an individual who is mentally disordered from exercising his rights under the Act provided he is capable of satisfying the formal requirements. Thus it is entirely consistent with an interpretation of the Act which holds that the only 'capacity' relevant to an application under the Act is that to make a request in writing and to pay the prescribed fee.

9.123 The Act does not specifically deal with the question of whether or not children should be able to apply for access to their computerised records. It might be possible to argue that, since the Act does not expressly require that the request in writing comes from the data subject him or herself a child should be entitled to apply for access through his parents, or some other person who is able to supply a request in writing and payment to the data user.[154] Alternatively a competent child might appoint his parents as his agent for these purposes and thereby entitle his parents to apply for access to medical records on his behalf.[155]

9.124 *The Guidelines* suggest that the subject access provisions only entitle a competent child, meaning a child who is capable of understanding the nature of the request which he has made, to seek access, in which case the data user should reply to the child himself. Moreover, if the child is competent *The Guidelines* state that personal data should only be supplied to the parents if the data user is satisfied that the child has authorised the request. In relation to incompetent children, *The Guidelines* state that a parent or guardian is entitled to make a request on behalf of the child and to receive a reply, but that such requests should only be made in the child's and not the parents' interests.[156]

---

[153] See *Re K* [1988] Ch 310, [1988] 1 All ER 358 (considering the Enduring Powers of Attorney Act 1985).

[154] Kennedy and Grubb suggest that a competent child might appoint his parent as his agent and might thereby be entitled to access under the subject access provisions: See Kennedy, I and Grubb, A, *Medical Law, Text with Materials*, 2nd edn (Butterworths, 1994), 628.

[155] The non-disclosure provisions preserving patient confidentiality (ie s 34(6)) assume that both patients and their agents might be entitled to apply for access under the Act.

[156] *The Guidelines, Third Series, November 1994*, Office of the Data Protection Registrar, 79.

Guidance issued by the Department of Health[157] also suggests that a parent's **9.125** power to claim a right of access under the 1984 Act is subject to the proviso that:

> the parent or legal guardian considers it necessary to have access to the data for the purpose of carrying out the duty to take care of the child.[158]

The guidance states that such requests should only be made in the interests of **9.126** the child, presumably suggesting that information should only be provided if the data user is satisfied that it would be in the child's interests to do so.[159] Subsequently the Department of Health has advised that:

> Health authorities should assume, unless there are grounds to suggest the contrary, that a parent or legal guardian making a request on behalf of a dependent child who lacks capacity is acting in that child's best interests and access should be allowed.[160]

Fourthly, personal data held only for the purpose of preparing statistics or **9.127** carrying out research are exempt from the subject access provisions in section 21. It is a condition of this exemption, however, that that data is only used for the specified purpose and that the results of the research are not made available in a form which identifies the data subjects or any one of them.[161]

Fifthly, the Act does not require a data user to supply information where to **9.128** do so 'would expose him to proceedings for any offence other than an offence under this Act'.[162]

Finally, the Data Protection (Subject Access Modification) (Health) Order **9.129** 1987[163] partially exempts from the subject access provisions data relating to the physical or mental health of the data subject where the data are held by a health professional or were first recorded by or on behalf of a health professional. The provisions apply only where informing the patient or supplying the data:

(a) would be likely to cause serious harm to the physical or mental health of the data subject; or

[157] See 'Data Protection Act 1984: Modified Access to Personal Health Information' HC(87)26 as amended by HC(89)29.
[158] See Health Circular (89)29 'Data Protection Act 1984: Modified Access to Personal Health Information', para 6.
[159] Specific guidance about evidence of capacity etc is contained in 'Data Protection Act 1984: Modified Access to Personal Health Information' HC(87)26 as amended by HC(89)29.
[160] See Health Circular (89)29 'Data Protection Act 1984: Modified Access to Personal Health Information', para 6. [161] S 33.
[162] S 34(9).
[163] SI 1987/1903, promulgated by the Secretary of State pursuant to the power established in s 29(1) of the Act.

(b) would be likely to disclose to the data subject the identity of another individual (who has not consented to the disclosure of the information) either as a person to whom the information or part of it relates or as the source of the information or enable that identity to be deduced by the data subject either from the information itself or from a combination of that information and other information which the data subject has or is likely to have.[164]

9.130 This does not cover the situation where the only other person identified is the health professional and 'the information relates to him or he supplied the information in his capacity as a health professional'. Nor does it exempt a data user from the obligation to disclose so much of the information as can be supplied without causing serious harm or enabling the identity of another to be deduced.[165] Moreover, a data user other than a health professional must consult the appropriate health professional[166] prior to making a decision whether or not to provide or refuse access to data to which the Data Protection (Subject Access Modification) (Health) Order 1987 applies.

9.131 The precise scope of this last exemption is unfortunately unclear. Although the Order does place a duty upon the data user who is not a health professional to consult the 'appropriate' health professional before either supplying or withholding health data covered by the Order, unlike the Access to Health Records Act 1990 which contains a similar provision exempting certain records from the entitlement to access, the exemption appears on a literal reading of the Order to depend upon showing that access would in fact be likely to cause serious harm to the physical or mental health of the data subject. Accordingly it would not be sufficient merely for a doctor to be *of the opinion that* access might have such an effect, if he cannot objectively satisfy the court that this opinion was correct. *The Guidelines* state merely that:

> The decision as to whether serious harm is likely to be caused, or the identity of a third party is likely to be deduced, is to be based on the judgement of a health professional.[167]

(iii) *Access to Health Records Act 1990*

9.132 The Access to Health Records Act 1990 applies to records created after 1 November 1991, and to records created before that date if 'in the opinion of the record holder the giving of access is necessary in order to make intelli-

---

[164] Para 4(2).
[165] Note the partial overlap of para 4(2)(b) and s 21(4)(b) of the Data Protection Act 1984 discussed above.   [166] Defined in para 4(6).
[167] *The Guidelines*, 106–7.

gible' records created after 1 November 1991. Health records are defined as records which:

> consist of information relating to the physical or mental health of an individual who can be identified from that information, or from that and other information in the possession of the holder of the record.[168]

The Act applies to all records made: **9.133**

> by or on behalf of a health professional[169] in connection with the care[170] of the individual.[171]

The possibility of overlap between the 1990 Act and the earlier Data Protec- **9.134** tion Act 1984 is precluded by section 1 which provides that the definition of health record does not include any information to which an individual might be entitled under the Data Protection Act 1984.

The scheme of the Act is to allow applications for access to health records to **9.135** be made to the holder of the record[172] and to oblige that person to provide access unless excused from doing so under one of a number of specific exceptions. Unlike the Data Protection Act 1984, the 1990 Act sets out precisely who may apply for access to their health records. An application may be made by:

(a) the patient;
(b) a person authorised in writing to make the application on the patient's behalf;
(c) where the record is held in England and Wales and the patient is a child, a person having parental responsibility for the patient;
(d) where the record is held in Scotland and the patient is a pupil, a parent or guardian of the patient;
(e) where the patient is incapable of managing his own affairs, any person appointed by a court to manage those affairs; and
(f) where the patient has died, the patient's personal representative and any person who may have a claim arising out of the patient's death.[173]

The application must be made in writing[174] and contain sufficient informa- **9.136**

---

[168] S 1(1)(a).   [169] Defined in s 2.
[170] Defined in s 11 to include 'examination, investigation, diagnosis and treatment'.
[171] S 1(1)(b).
[172] The holder of the record is defined in s 1(2) and s 11 to include, where relevant, general practitioners on whose list the patient is included, the FHSA on whose list the patient's most recent general practitioner was included, the health services body (i e health authority or trust) on whose behalf the record is held or the health professional by or on whose behalf the record is held.
[173] S 3(1). S 5(4) provides that access shall not be given under s 3(1)(f) to any part of the record which, in the opinion of the holder of the record, would disclose information which is not relevant to any claim which might arise out of the patient's death.   [174] S 11.

tion to identify the patient. If it is made by someone other than the patient it must include information sufficient to establish that he or she is entitled to make the application.[175] A fee may be charged where access is given to information none of which was recorded during the forty days immediately preceding the application,[176] or where the applicant is supplied with a copy of the record.[177]

9.137 Depending upon the time frame to which the application relates, the holder of the record has either twenty-one (if it relates even in part to a record made within forty days preceding the application) or forty days to respond to the request either by giving access to the record or part of the record. The applicant must be allowed to inspect the record (or so much of the record as is not excluded) or part of the record to which the application relates, or be supplied with a copy of the record or extract.[178]

9.138 A child under the age of sixteen[179] is entitled to request access under the Act provided that the holder of the record 'is satisfied that the patient is capable of understanding the nature of the application'.[180]

9.139 If so, the only means by which a parent can apply for access to the child's medical records under the Act is if he or she is 'authorised in writing to make the application on the patient's behalf'.[181] Presumably where a patient is between the ages of sixteen and eighteen, hence not within the definition of child in the Act, his or her application would be treated as being identical with that of any other adult patient.[182]

9.140 Where a child patient under the age of sixteen 'is incapable of understanding the nature of the application and the giving of access would be in his best interests', a person with parental responsibility for the child may apply for access under the Act provided always that the child has consented to the making of the application.[183]

9.141 Unfortunately the Act does not specifically deal with the question of whether or not a mentally incapacitated adult is entitled himself to apply for access to his health records where he is capable of making a request in

---

[175] S 3(6).

[176] The fee may not exceed the maximum chargeable under s 21 of the Data Protection Act 1984 (s 3(4)(a)).

[177] The fee may not exceed the cost of making the copy and, where relevant, the cost of postage (s 3(4)(b)). [178] S 3(2).

[179] Child is defined in s 11 as someone under the age of 16. [180] S 4(1)

[181] S 3(1)(b).

[182] See the discussion in Kennedy, I and Grubb, A, *Medical Law: text with materials*, 2nd edn (Butterworths, 1994), 630. [183] S 4(2).

writing and paying the appropriate fee. Unlike with respect to children, there is no minimum standard for competence when an application is made by an adult.

There are two exceptions in the Act which are of particular importance here.   **9.142**
First, the Act provides that access shall not be given to any part of the record which:

(a) in the opinion of the holder of the record, would disclose—
    (i) information likely to cause serious harm to the physical or mental health of the patient or any other individual.[184]

Secondly, access should also be excluded in respect of any part of the record   **9.143**
which:

(a) in the opinion of the holder of the record, would disclose— . . .
    (ii) information relating to or provided by an individual, other than the patient, who could be identified from that information,[185]

unless the individual concerned has consented to the application, or is a health professional who has been involved in the care of the patient.[186]

Where access under the Act is excluded, the record holder is under no   **9.144**
obligation to inform the applicant that information exists and has been excluded. All that is required is that the record holder inform the patient that he does not hold any information which he is required by law to disclose.

(iv) *Access to Medical Reports Act 1988*

The Access to Medical Reports Act 1988, which came into force on 1   **9.145**
January 1989, gives patients the right to see certain medical reports prepared about them for employment or insurance purposes.[187] The right of access conferred by the Act is a right to inspect or be supplied with a copy of the report.[188]

An important limitation on the scope of the Act comes from the fact that   **9.146**
'medical report' is defined to mean:

a report relating to the physical or mental health of the individual prepared by a

---

[184] S (5)(1)(a)(i).   [185] S (5)(1)(a)(ii).   [186] S 5(2).
[187] S 1, defined in s 2(1).
[188] S 4(4). See also s 5(2) conferring upon the individual the right to request corrections to the report.

medical practitioner who is or has been responsible for the clinical care of the individual.[189]

9.147 Care is in turn defined in the Act to include 'examination, investigation or diagnosis for the purposes of, or in connection with, any form of medical treatment'.[190] Accordingly, reports prepared by an independent medical practitioner who is not, and has not been, involved in a therapeutic doctor–patient relationship with the individual concerned are not covered by the Act.[191] Difficult questions arise in relation to the position of an occupational health doctor who is employed to advise employers and employees about issues involving health and safety at work. Whether or not reports prepared by such a doctor will fall within the scope of the Access to Medical Reports Act 1988 will most likely depend upon the degree of involvement with the employees and, in particular, whether the physician has, or has had, any direct responsibility in relation to the mental or physical well-being of the individual concerned.[192]

9.148 The Act provides that the employer or insurance company must obtain the individual's consent when it seeks the report, and that the individual may at that time make his consent conditional upon being given access to the report prior to the supply to the employer or insurance company.[193] Even if he does not so stipulate at the time of giving his consent, he may nonetheless, by notice to the doctor supplying the report, request access prior to the report being given to the employer or insurance company[194] or, again by notice to the doctor, within six months of the report being so supplied.[195]

9.149 The individual's right of access to medical reports under the Act is not absolute. There are three situations in which doctors are justified in refusing to provide access. First, where disclosure would:

> in the opinion of the practitioner be likely to cause serious harm to the physical or mental health of the individual or others . . .[196]

9.150 Secondly, where disclosure would 'indicate the intentions of the practitioner in respect of the individual'.[197]

9.151 Thirdly, where disclosure would:

> be likely to reveal information about another person, or to reveal the identity of another person who has supplied information to the practitioner about the individual unless—
> (a) that person has consented; or
> (b) that person is a health professional who has been involved in the care of the

---

[189] S 2(1).   [190] ibid.
[191] They may, however, be covered by the Access to Health Records Act 1990.
[192] See the discussion in Cowley, R, *Access to Medical Records and Reports* n 139 above, 27.
[193] S 3(1).   [194] S 4(3).   [195] S 6.   [196] S 7(1).   [197] ibid.

individual and the information relates to or has been provided by the professional in that capacity.[198]

Contrary to the position under the Access to Health Records Act 1990, the doctor is obliged to inform the individual that his request for access has been denied under one of the exceptions.[199] The individual is entitled to apply to the county court for an order that the doctor must provide him access under the Act.[200]   **9.152**

(v) *European Directive on the Protection of Individuals with Regard to the Processing of Personal Data and on the Free Movement of such Data*

As discussed above, the Directive applies both to information which has been processed automatically and to information which is manually processed but which is accessible according to specific criteria. The Directive guarantees a right of access both physically to such records themselves, and also to information relating to the existence of the records, by whom they are held or processed, and to whom information is disclosed.[201] In addition, the Directive requires that data subjects are informed of the existence of their right of access to data where this is necessary to guarantee fair processing in respect of the data subject.   **9.153**

The Directive also requires that member states guarantee a right of access to personal information which is processed 'in an intelligible form' together with information about the purposes for which the data was processed and the recipients or categories of recipients to whom the data has been disclosed.[202]   **9.154**

The Directive enables members states to derogate from these provisions in a number of circumstances. In the health care context the most important of these is likely to be where it is necessary to restrict access in order to protect the data subject or to protect the rights or freedoms of others.[203] A second exception of significance to those conducting scientific research enables Member States to enact legislation to restrict an individual's right of access to personal information: **9.155**

> when data are processed solely for the purposes of scientific research or are kept in personal form for a period which does not exceed the period necessary for the sole purpose of creating statistics.

Unlike the former exception, however, the Directive allows such derogation only where it is 'subject to adequate safeguards, in particular that the data are not used for taking measures or decisions regarding any particular individual'.[204]   **9.156**

---

[198] S 7(2).   [199] S 7(3).   [200] S 8.   [201] Art 10.   [202] Art 12.
[203] Art 13(1)(g).   [204] Art 13(2).

3. The Common Law

(i) *Basis for a Right of Access*

9.157 There are essentially four possible legal bases for asserting a common law right of access to medical records. First, the court could recognise an innominate common law right which is general but which may be made subject to exceptions. Since there is no historical precedent for such a right, any such analysis must depend upon judicial assertion and upon the demands of practical justice. Secondly, the common law could recognise such a right in furtherance of the protection of basic human rights recognised in such documents as the European Convention of Human Rights. Since the Convention does not form part of English domestic law, this must depend upon judicial interpretation of the current common law position as ambiguous hence justifying reference to the European Convention. Since *R v Mid Glamorgan Family Health Services Authority, ex p Martin*, it would appear that any such argument is unlikely to find success in an English court.[205] Thirdly, a common law right of access could have been based upon a patient having a proprietary interest in his or her medical records.[206] There can, however, no longer be any doubt that patients have no proprietary interests in their medical records. Rather these are regarded as the property of the relevant health authority or trust in the public sector, whilst in the private sector ownership may depend upon the precise contractual relationship between the parties. Fourthly, a duty of disclosure and a corresponding right of access may be found to arise as part of a series of fiduciary obligations which could be held to arise in the context of the doctor–patient relationship.

(ii) *Judicial Development of a Right of Access*

9.158 The first English decision to deal with the question of a common law right of access to medical records was *R v Mid Glamorgan Family Health Services Authority, ex p Martin*.[207] Prior to *Martin*, however, the Supreme Court of

---

[205] See in particular the judgment of Evans LJ in *Martin* [1995] 1 All ER 356, 365.
[206] This position is reluctantly accepted by the BMA: see *Medical Ethics Today: Its Practice and Philosophy* (BMA, 1993), 44. Acceptance of this position is also clear in the judgments in the Court of Appeal in *Martin*. See also *McInerney v MacDonald* (1992) 93 DLR (4th) 415, 421; *Breen v Williams* (1996) 70 ALJR 772. See also The National Health Service (General Medical Services) Regulations 1992 SI 1992/635, Sch 2, para 36.
[207] [1995] 1 All ER 356 (CA), noted by Grubb, A (1994) 2 Med L Rev 353 and Feenan, D (1996) 59 MLR 101.

Canada in *McInerney v MacDonald* had considered the question and determined that a common law right of action could be found from the general fiduciary nature of the doctor patient relationship.[208] The case arose when a patient sought access to the whole of her prior medical records after discovering that she did not in fact need the thyroid pills which she had been prescribed for a number of years. Her current doctor, Dr McInerney gave the plaintiff copies of all notes, memoranda, and reports which she had prepared herself, but refused to produce copies of reports and records she had received from other physicians on the grounds that, in her view, it would be unethical for her to release them. The Canadian Supreme Court found on these facts that the patient had a common law right of access to her medical records, including those compiled by doctors other than Dr McInerney.

LaForest J, delivering the judgment of the Canadian Supreme Court, **9.159** accepted that the medical records were the property of the physician, institution, or clinic which compiled them.[209] Nonetheless, in his view, the critical factor was that the relationship between physician and patient, within which medical records are compiled, is one in which trust and confidence must be placed in the physician. Thus he characterised the relationship as fiduciary and confidential then went on to analyse the precise character of the relationship in this context, since in his view the shape and content of a fiduciary relationship depends upon the demands of the situation.[210] In the case of the doctor–patient relationship LaForest J found that the fiducial qualities of the relationship created a duty upon the physician to grant access to the information the doctor uses in administering treatment,[211] and that this duty extends to requiring the disclosure of information which has been conveyed to the current holder by another doctor.[212]

In England the Court of Appeal in *R v Mid Glamorgan Family Health Services* **9.160** *Authority, ex p Martin* reached a broadly similar conclusion that a patient might have a limited common law right of access to medical records, but this was based on reasoning far removed in substance from that of the Canadian Supreme Court.[213] The plaintiff sought judicial review of the decision of two health authorities to deny him access to medical records relating to two

---

[208] (1992) 93 DLR (4th) 415 (Canadian Supreme Court). See also *R v Dyment* (1988) 55 DLR (4th) 503 and *Halls v Mitchell* [1928] 2 DLR 97.
[209] 93 DLR (4th) 415, 421. Noted by Kennedy, I (1993) 1 Med L Rev 378. Cf *Re Mitchell and St Michael's Hospital* (1980) 112 DLR 3d 360. [210] ibid, 423.
[211] ibid, 424. See *Emmett v Eastern Dispensary and Casualty Hospital* 396 F 2d 931 (DC Cir 1967) and *Cannell v Medical and Surgical Clinic* 315NE 2d 278 (Ill App Ct 1974).
[212] (1992) 93 DLR (4th) 415, 425.
[213] For argument in favour of the view that the doctor–patient relationship is fiduciary see Grubb, A, 'The Doctor as Fiduciary' [1994] CLP 311.

specific incidents in his past, both of which involved his psychiatric treatment, which he sought in order that he might better come to terms with his own personal development. His repeated requests for access had been refused, on grounds ranging from possible detriment to his overall best interests to a perceived duty to 'protect retired colleagues'. At one stage access was offered provided that the patient would give an assurance that 'the Authority and/or any of its staff are not implicated in any potential litigation being contemplated by Mr Martin in respect of his South Glamorganshire treatment'. Finally in 1993, after the patient had instituted proceedings for judicial review of the decision not to give him access to his medical records, the respondents agreed to disclose the patient's medical records to his medical advisers, but not to the patient himself.

9.161 At first instance Popplewell J, in the course of a judgment which denied the existence of a common law right of access to medical records, rejected the fiducial approach in *McInerney* on the basis that Lord Scarman in the House of Lords (and Browne Wilkinson LJ in the Court of Appeal) in *Sidaway*[214] had rejected this characterisation of the doctor–patient relationship.[215] Accordingly his judgment contains little examination of whether or not English courts should recognise fiducial qualities in the doctor–patient relationship, and the point was not discussed when the case reached the Court of Appeal.

9.162 The Court of Appeal declined to consider whether or not a patient has an unconditional right of access at common law to his medical records, preferring to limit consideration to the question whether or not

> a doctor or a health authority, as the owner of a patient's medical records, [is] entitled to deny him access to them on the ground that their disclosure would be detrimental to him?[216]

9.163 In this regard, the Court of Appeal considered that the fact that the holder of the records was a public body was irrelevant to the legal principles which should be applied.[217] Nourse LJ, with whom Evans LJ and Sir Roger Parker agreed, held that access to medical records could be denied where it was in the best interests of the patient to do so, for example where disclosure would be

---

[214] '[T]here is no comparison to be made between the relationship of doctor and patient with that of solicitor and client, trustee and *cestui qui trust* or the other relationships treated in equity as of a fiduciary character', 884.

[215] Moreover, Popplewell J criticised the judgment in *McInerney* for failing to distinguish between information in the medical records which had been collected from the patient, and conclusions which a doctor reaches based on that information but which should remain wholly the property of the doctor.

[216] [1995] 1 All ER 356, 359 *per* Nourse LJ, 365 *per* Evans LJ.

[217] ibid, 363 *per* Nourse LJ.

detrimental to the patient's health. Given that the health authorities had offered to disclose the patient's medical records to his medical advisers, there was clearly no ground for granting the patient the relief sought in his action for judicial review of the health authorities' decisions. Unfortunately, the narrow basis of this question considered by the Court of Appeal precluded any helpful guidance being issued on questions such as who has the onus of proving that disclosure would be harmful to the patient, and upon what other grounds might access lawfully be denied.

Of greater interest is the Court of Appeal's analysis of the possible bases upon which a patient could claim a common law right of access to his medical records. Each of the judges found that a health authority has no absolute right to deal with medical records in any way that it chooses.[218] According to Nourse LJ, this right is limited by a doctor or health authority's general duty to act at all times in the best interests of the patient, a duty which he identifies as resting upon the speech of Lord Templeman in *Sidaway v Bethlem Royal Hospital Governors*.[219] By contrast, Evans LJ based the duty to disclose upon the need not to frustrate the very purposes for which medical records are created in the first place. In his view those purposes were to enable a patient's doctor and his successors best to treat the patient, and to provide a record of diagnosis and treatment in the case of future inquiry or dispute.[220] Sir Roger Parker preferred not to set out the scope of the doctor's duty of disclosure because 'the circumstances in which a patient or former patient is entitled to demand access to his medical history as set out in the records will be infinitely various'.[221] He gave the example of a patient requiring access in order to facilitate his medical treatment if he is about to emigrate and his condition is such that he might need treatment before he can nominate a successor doctor. **9.164**

The difficulty with the judgments of the Court of Appeal are that they rest more on assertion of the need to qualify a doctor or health authority's right to deny access to medical records than upon any analysis of the possible basis in the common law for a right of access to medical records. **9.165**

The lack of any principled foundation for the right of access to medical records, identified by the Court of Appeal in *Martin*, was recognised by the High Court of Australia in *Breen v Williams*.[222] The case arose after a woman was denied access to her medical records which had been compiled by her doctor after treatment he had provided in the private medical sector in connection with complications from a breast augmentation operation which **9.166**

---

[218] ibid, 363 *per* Nourse LJ, 365 *per* Evans LJ, 366 *per* Sir Roger Parker.
[219] [1985] 1 All ER 632, 665–6, [1985] AC 871, 904.   [220] [1995] 1 All ER 356, 365.
[221] ibid, 366.   [222] (1996) 70 ALJR 772.

had been performed by another doctor. She sought access to her medical records in order to participate in settlement of breast implant litigation in the United States, but access was refused by her doctor unless she agreed to release him from any possible claim which might arise in relation to his treatment of her. Unlike in *McInerney* and *Martin*, in *Breen* there was no suggestion that disclosure of the information in the records could have any adverse effect on the plaintiff's physical or mental health.

9.167   In *Breen* it was held that, unless a patient had a contractual right of access to her records, or disclosure of the information in the records was in her best interests such that it would be negligent to withhold the information, there was no common law obligation on a doctor or hospital to provide access. Moreover, there was no basis for implying such a term into the contractual relationship between the doctor and the patient. Rejecting the authority of *Martin*, the High Court found that the relationship between a doctor and patient is not such that a patient has a *right* to see her medical records.[223] Also of interest was the High Court's rejection of the argument that the fiduciary qualities of the doctor–patient relationship were such that a doctor would be under a fiduciary obligation to provide a patient with access to her medical records. Whilst accepting that a doctor was a fiduciary in some respects, the High Court held that the fiduciary duty as understood in Australia did not provide any foundation for an obligation to provide access to a patient's medical records, or more generally to act in the patient's best interests.[224]

(iii)   *The Scope of the Common Law Right of Access*

9.168   In England, the most that can be said with any certainty is that the courts implicitly accept that the owner of medical records does not have an unfettered discretion to deal with them as he or she chooses. The legal basis for qualifying these ownership rights could be based upon one of three possible grounds. First, that patients have a general 'innominate' right of access to medical records subject to certain exceptions. Secondly, that in certain defined circumstances doctors are obliged to disclose information in the medical records or hand over the records themselves to patients. These circumstances include where it is necessary to do so to avoid liability in negligence and where so required by the rules governing disclosure for the purposes of litigation. Thirdly, it is still possible that either the Court of Appeal or the House of Lords should adopt the reasoning of the Canadian

---

[223]   (1996) 7 ALJR 772, at 784, 789–90, 804.
[224]   (1996) 70 ALJR 772, at 776–7, 781–2, 793, 800–801.

Supreme Court in *McInerney* and of Kirby P in dissent in *Breen v Williams*, and hold that the fiducial qualities of the doctor–patient relationship impose an obligation upon doctors to provide patients with access to their medical records.

10

MEDICALLY ASSISTED REPRODUCTION

A. Introduction

10.01   This Chapter examines infertility and the ways in which the law in England and Wales responds to the practices developed by the medical profession to alleviate the problem.

10.02   Infertility has been defined as 'the involuntary, significant reduction of reproductive capacity'.[1] At the time of the Warnock Inquiry, 'a commonly quoted

---

[1] *per* Canadian Law Reform Commission, *Medically Assisted Procreation* (Working Paper 65, 1992).

figure [was] that one couple in ten [was] childless'.[2] However, the Inquiry conceded that accurate statistics were not available and noted that the proportion of this figure relating to couples who chose not to have children was not known. Higher estimates have been suggested elsewhere,[3] and it is likely that infertility is anyway on the increase so that ten per cent can be considered a gross underestimate today.

There are a large number of techniques which have been developed for treating the infertile, ranging from artificial insemination using donated sperm through various in vitro fertilisation methods to surrogacy. Not all assisted reproductive techniques require medical intervention but even those that do not are often carried out under medical supervision.   **10.03**

Donor insemination (AID as it was once called) has existed for the best part of a century[4] and surrogacy is an age-old institution, some would say with biblical roots.[5] However, it is with the development of IVF procedures in the 1970s[6] that medically assisted reproduction has come to concern policymakers throughout the world.[7] There were inquiries into donor insemination (DI) shortly after the Second World War (the Fisher report[8] recommended that it be criminalised)[9] and in the late 1950s the Feversham Committee, which reported in 1960, concluded that AID was an undesirable practice to be discouraged. A more positive response was made in the Peel report in 1973[10]—AID should be available at accredited NHS centres for those for whom it was appropriate—but this led to nothing, and no system of accreditation was established. Modern thinking begins with the Warnock report.[11]   **10.04**

---

[2] See Report of the Committee of Inquiry into Human Fertilisation and Embryology (Cmnd 9314) (HMSO, 1984), para 2.1.

[3] In Canada the estimate is 15%: in the US it was estimated as 13.9% in 1982.

[4] There is a claim that the first human donor insemination was in the United States in 1884. See Snowden, R and Mitchell, GD, *The Artificial Family* (Unwin, 1983), 13.

[5] See Singer, P and Wells, D, *New Ways of Making Babies: The Reproduction Revolution* (Oxford University Press, 1984), 107–8, citing Genesis 16 (the story of Abram and Sarai).

[6] Louise Brown, the first 'test-tube' baby was born in 1978.

[7] See McLean, SAM, *Law Reform and Human Reproduction* (Dartmouth, 1992). Bonnicksen, AL, *In Vitro Fertilization: Building Policy from Laboratories to Legislatures* (Columbia University Press, 1989).

[8] Artificial Human Insemination: the report of a Committee appointed by his Grace the Archbishop of Canterbury (SPCK, 1948).

[9] Home Office and Scottish Home Department, Departmental Committee on Human Artificial Insemination, (Cmnd 1105) (HMSO, 1960).

[10] British Medical Association, Annual Report of the Council, Appendix V: Report of the Panel on Human Artificial Insemination, British Medical Journal Supplement, 7 Apr 1973 vol II, 3–5.

[11] Subsequently reprinted with an introduction by the chairwoman as *A Question of Life* (Basil Blackwell, 1985).

1. The Warnock Report

10.05 The Warnock Inquiry was established in 1982 'to consider recent and potential developments in medicine and science related to human fertilisation and embryology; to consider what policies and safeguards should be applied, including consideration of the social, ethical and legal implications of these developments; and to make recommendations'.[12] The committee reported in 1984. It took the view that 'actions taken with the intention of overcoming infertility can, as a rule, be regarded as acceptable substitutes for natural fertilisation'.[13] Infertility was not to be seen as 'something mysterious, nor a cause of shame, nor necessarily something that has to be endured without attempted cure'.[14] It is, the Inquiry concluded, 'a condition meriting treatment'[15] and in the light of its analysis, it recommended statutory regulation of medically assisted reproduction.

2. History of Regulation

10.06 The Medical Research Council and the Royal College of Obstetricians and Gynaecologists responded by establishing the Voluntary Licensing Authority in 1985. This was subsequently called the Interim Licensing Authority. This body instituted a self-regulatory mechanism for licensing infertility treatment and research on human embryos and gametes. The V(I)LA operated for six years, approving IVF centres and licensing research projects. It established voluntary guidelines for such research work, including provisions for donor consent and prior ethical committee approval of the work.[16] It ceased to exist on 1 August 1991 when the Human Fertilisation and Embryology Act 1990 came into force. This established the Human Fertilisation and Embryology Authority.

10.07 The Human Fertilisation and Embryology Act 1990 (hereafter the 1990 Act) regulates infertility treatments that involve the use of donated genetic material, whether sperm, eggs or embryos, or those that involve the creation of an embryo outside the human body. In addition, the 1990 Act regulates the storage of all genetic material. The 1990 Act is not directly concerned with the practice of surrogacy; only insofar as a surrogate birth is effectuated through the use, in part or whole, of donated genetic material or using IVF techniques is the framework or the 1990 Act applicable. The moral panic[17] fanned by the

---

[12] N 2 above.   [13] ibid, para 2.4.   [14] ibid.   [15] ibid.

[16] On its work see Gunning, J and English, V, *Human In Vitro Fertilization*, (Dartmouth, 1993).

[17] See Dyer, C, 'Baby Cotton and the Birth of a Moral Panic', *The Guardian*, 15 Jan 1985 and Hutchinson, A and Morgan, D, 'A Bill Born from Panic', *The Guardian*, 12 July 1985.

birth of 'Baby Cotton' in January 1985[18] resulted in an attempt to regulate the practice of surrogacy in legislation passed in 1985 (the Surrogacy Arrangements Act 1985[19]). Surrogacy is thus best considered separately later in this chapter.[20]

B. The Human Fertilisation and Embryology Authority

1. Establishment of the Authority

The 1990 Act established the Human Fertilisation and Embryology Author-   **10.08**
ity (hereafter HFEA).[21] This is a body corporate and consists of a chairman and deputy chairman and such number of other members as the Secretary of State appoints.[22] In making appointments the Secretary of State is to have regard to the desirability of ensuring that the proceedings of the authority, and the discharge of its functions, are informed by the views of both men and women.[23] S/he must also ensure that there is a majority of members who are neither doctors nor research scientists.[24] Neither the chairman nor deputy chairman may come from either of these professional groups. The first two chairs have both been academic lawyers/university heads (Sir Colin Campbell, the Vice-Chancellor of the University of Nottingham and Ruth Deech, the Principal of St Anne's College, Oxford).

Appointments to HFEA are for renewable periods of three years.[25] An   **10.09**
appointed member who is absent from meetings without HFEA permission for six consecutive months, who becomes bankrupt or makes an arrangement with creditors, or who is unable or unfit to discharge the functions of a member of the Authority may be removed.[26] A member of the House of Commons is not eligible to become a member of HFEA;[27] there is no similar restriction on members of the House of Lords.

2. Functions of HFEA

The principal functions of HFEA are: **10.10**

(i)   to license treatment services, the storage of gametes and embryos, and research on embryos;[28]

---

[18] Reported as *Re C* (1985) FLR 846. A more personal account is *Baby Cotton: For Love or Money* (Dorling Kindersley, 1985).
[19] On which see Freeman, MDA, 'After *Warnock*: Whither The Law?' (1986) 39 CLP 33, 37–48.   [20] Paras 10.128–10.158.
[21] S 5.   [22] S 5(2).   [23] Sch 1, para 4(2).   [24] Sch 1, para 4(4).
[25] Sch 1, para 5(2).   [26] Sch 1, para 5(5).   [27] Sch 1, para 6.   [28] S 11.

(ii) to monitor and inspect premises and activities carried out under statutory licence;[29]

(iii) to submit an annual report to the Secretary of Sate on its activities;[30]

(iv) to maintain a code of practice as guidance for the proper conduct of activities carried out under a licence. (Two editions have been published: a third will be published in 1997).[31]

In addition it has the following 'general functions':[32]

(i) to keep under review information about embryos and any subsequent development of embryos, and about the provision of treatment services and activities governed by the 1990 Act, and advise the Secretary of State, if s/he asks it to do so, about those matters;

(ii) to publicise the services it provides or which are provided in pursuance of licences it grants;

(iii) to provide advice and information for persons to whom licences apply or who are receiving treatment services, or providing gametes or embryos for use for the purposes of activities governed by the 1990 Act, or may wish to do so;

(iv) to perform such other functions as may be specified in regulations.

C. Licensing

1. Types of Licence

10.11 The 1990 Act provides that HFEA may grant any one of three types of licence authorising:

(i) activities in the course of providing treatment services;[33]

(ii) the storage of gametes and embryos;[34]

(iii) activities for the purpose of a project of research;[35]

10.12 In the course of providing treatment services a licence may authorise any of the following:[36]

(i) bringing about the creation of embryos in vitro;

(ii) keeping embryos;

(iii) using gametes;

(iv) practices designed to secure that embryos are in a suitable condition to be placed in a woman or to determine whether embryos are suitable for that purpose;

---

[29] S 9.   [30] S 7.   [31] S 25.   [32] S 8.
[33] S 11(1)(a) and Sch 2, para 1.   [34] S 11(1)(b) and Sch 2, para 2.
[35] S 11(1)(c) and Sch 2, para 3.   [36] Sch 2, para 1(1).

(v) placing any embryo in a woman;

(vi) mixing sperm with the egg of a hamster, or other animal specified in directions, for the purpose of testing the fertility or normality of the sperm, but only where anything which forms is destroyed when the test is complete and, in any event, not later than the two cell stage; and

(vii) such other practices as may be specified in, or determined in accordance with, regulations.

A licence for the purposes of research may authorise the bringing about of the creation of embryos in vitro and the keeping or using of embryos[37] but it cannot authorise any activity unless it appears to the Authority 'to be necessary or desirable'[38] for the purpose of: **10.13**

(i) promoting advances in the treatment of infertility;

(ii) increasing knowledge about the causes of congenital disease;

(iii) increasing knowledge about the causes of miscarriages;

(iv) developing more effective techniques of contraception; or

(v) developing methods for detecting the presence of gene or chromosome abnormalities in embryos before implantation; or for such other purposes as may be specified by regulations, but these are limited to projects which 'increase knowledge about the creation and development of embryos, or about disease, or enable such knowledge to be applied'.[39]

A research licence cannot authorise altering the genetic structure of any cell while it forms part of an embryo, except in such circumstances, if any, as may be specified in or determined in pursuance of regulations.[40] **10.14**

A licence can only authorise activities to be carried on in premises specified in the licence and under the supervision of an individual designated in the licence.[41] No licence can authorise more than one research project; each proposed project requires a separate licence.[42] No licence can authorise more than one individual who is to be responsible for the licensed activities,[43] nor apply to premises in different places.[44] A licence which authorises treatment services, or a licence which authorises research, can also permit the storage of embryos or gametes, but a treatment licence cannot authorise research, nor a research licence authorise treatment: each activity must be considered in a separate licence application.[45] **10.15**

Licences are granted to an individual, described in the 1990 Act as the 'person responsible'.[46] Treatment licences authorise particular classes of treatment to **10.18**

---

[37] So long as they have not developed a primitive streak (s 3(3)(a), (4)).
[38] Sch 2, para 3(2).   [39] Sch 2, para 3(3).   [40] Sch 2, para 3(4).
[41] S 12(a).   [42] Sch 2, para 4(2)(b).   [43] Sch 2, para 4(2)(c).
[44] Sch 2, para 4(2)(d).   [45] Sch 2, para 4(2)(a).   [46] S 17.

be carried out under the control of the 'person responsible' at the designated premises. Licences for research are granted for a specific project of research for one or more of the purposes set out in Schedule 3, paragraph 2 (and see para 10.13 above).

10.19 Licences are subject to a maximum time-limit. This is five years in the case of licences for treatment[47] or for storage[48] and three years in the case of licences for research.[49] Twelve months is the standard duration.[50]

2. Licence Conditions

10.20 Licences may be granted subject to conditions.[51] The 1990 Act lays down both general conditions[52] and conditions for licences for each of treatment,[53] storage,[54] and research.[55]

(i) *General Conditions*

10.21 The general conditions are:

(i)   licensed activities can only be carried on in the premises to which the licence relates and under the supervision of the 'person responsible';[56]

(ii)   proper records must be maintained in the form specified by HFEA.[57] Copies of extracts from those records or any other specified information is to be provided to HFEA when and how it specifies.[58]

(iii) the requirements as to written consent (see para 10.84 below) must be complied with;[59]

(iv)   no money or other benefit is to be given or received in the supply of gametes or embryos other than in accordance with authorisation given by HFEA in directions.[60]

It has been suggested[61] that the waiving of charges for private treatment in consideration of the donation of eggs would be waiving a payment for advantage and not a 'payment in money or money's worth', and therefore would have fallen outside the precursor of this provision. 'Money's worth' is not an identical concept to 'other benefit'. It is submitted that the latter is wider and that the example used should fall within the prohibition of section

---

[47] Sch 2, para 1(5).   [48] Sch 2, para 2(3).   [49] Sch 2, para 3(9).
[50] See HFEA, Second Annual Report 1993, para 1,2.   [51] See generally Sch 2.
[52] S 12.   [53] S 13.   [54] S 14.   [55] S 15.
[56] S 16, 17, and Sch 2, para 4(1).   [57] S 12(d).   [58] S 12(g).
[59] S 12(c) and Sch 3.   [60] S 12(e).
[61] By Morgan, D and Lee, R, *Blackstone's Guide To The Human Fertilisation and Embryology Act 1990* (Blackstone Press, 1991), 99.

12(e). Expenses, however, may be reimbursed, though it is not entirely clear how far this extends.[62] It is suggested that compensation for loss of earnings should be acceptable but more dubious is recompense for inconvenience and discomfort. Morgan and Lee express the view that 'there is a good case for allowing financial benefit to be greater where more invasive procedures are used. However, the medical profession has generally disdained payments calibrated according to use. This would seem to militate against large sums of money being offered for the supply of healthy eggs'.[63] In 1996 HFEA, which originally allowed donors to be paid up to £15 per donation plus reasonable expenses, concluded that a donation should be 'a gift, freely and voluntarily given.' However, it accepts that donors should not be out of pocket as a result of becoming donors so that 'reasonable direct expenses', such as for travel and child care, can be reimbursed. A Working Party is currently examining the implementation of this policy in detail.[64] It should be added that a person to whom a licence applies and who gives or receives any money or any benefit, other than in accordance with HFEA directions, commits an offence.[65] Further general conditions are:

(v) where gametes or embryos are supplied by one licence holder to another, the supplier is to give to the recipient such information as HFEA may specify in directions;[66]

(vi) any member or employee of HFEA is to be permitted to enter and inspect premises as well as equipment and records. Such persons may also observe any activity. Inspections are to be carried out at reasonable times. If required to do so the member or employee must produce identification.[67]

10.22 HFEA may also attach further conditions.[68] It reports that 'Licence conditions have been used, when appropriate, as a means of applying pressure on centres to conform quickly in areas where there have been observed deficiencies in their practice'.[69] Many of the conditions imposed have related to counselling, confidentiality and security, the welfare of the child, and information for patients. As HFEA notes, these are 'all new statutory obligations which some centres are considering for the first time'. HFEA's view is that 'it

---

[62] It is reported that a loophole in the Act is being exploited and that a treatment centre is using an agency in order to pay women to donate eggs. This has been condemned by Baroness Warnock (and see *The Guardian*, 2 Nov 1995). [63] N 61 above, 99.
[64] HFEA, Fifth Annual Report, July 1996, 23–4.
[65] Under s 41(8) of the 1990 Act. The maximum punishment is six months' imprisonment or a fine not exceeding level 5 on the standard scale. [66] S 12(f).
[67] S 12(b). See also the enforcement powers in s 39, which include retaining embryos or gametes (s 39(3)).
[68] The conditions listed in ss 12–15 are those which must be imposed: others may (and are). [69] See HFEA, Second Annual Report.

is reasonable for the Authority to recognise that in some centres it may take a little time to develop adequate procedures'.[70]

(ii) *Treatment Licence Conditions*

10.23 The 1990 Act prescribes conditions of licences for treatment. These relate to record-keeping. Such information is to be recorded as HFEA may specify in directions which relate to the persons for whom the services are provided in pursuance of the licence; the services provided; the persons whose gametes are kept or used for the purposes of services provided in pursuance of the licence or whose gametes have been used in bringing about the creation of embryos so kept or used; any child appearing to the person responsible to have been born as a result of treatment in pursuance of the licence; any mixing of egg and sperm and any taking of an embryo from a woman or other acquisition of an embryo; and other matters specified by HFEA in directions.[71] Records are also to record consents required under Schedule 3[72] of the 1990 Act.[73] No information may be removed from any records maintained in pursuance of the licence before the expiry of such period as may be specified in directions for records of the class in question.[74] Where a treatment licence holder does not know whether a child has been born following the provision of treatment services, the information held shall be maintained for a period of not less than fifty years from when it was first recorded.[75]

10.24 Two other conditions of licences for treatment, dealing with counselling[76] and the prospective welfare of any child born as a result of treatment[77] are considered below (see paras 10.78 and 10.55–10.62).

(iii) *Storage Licence Conditions*

10.25 The 1990 Act prescribes conditions of storage licences.[78] Every licence must require that 'gametes of a person or an embryo taken from a woman shall be placed in storage only if received from that person or woman or acquired from a person to whom a licence applies', and that 'an embryo the creation of which has been brought about *in vitro* otherwise than in pursuance of that licence shall be placed in storage only if acquired from a person to whom a licence applies'.[79] An embryo may not be placed in storage if it has

---

[70] ibid.   [71] S 13(2).   [72] As to which see para 10.75 below.   [73] S 13(3).
[74] S 13(4).   [75] S 24(1).   [76] S 13(6).   [77] S 13(5).
[78] S 14.   [79] S 14(1)(a).

been created in vitro by an unlicensed person. The words 'a person to whom a licence applies' are ambiguous. Literally interpreted it would include persons not licensed to bring about the creation of embryos (persons, indeed, who may have committed an offence in so doing). The better interpretation must be that it envisages persons licensed to bring about the creation of embryos.

10.26 In addition it is a condition of every licence authorising the storage of gametes or embryos that gametes or embryos which are or have been stored shall not be supplied to a person otherwise than in the course of providing treatment services unless that person is a person to whom a licence applies.[80]

10.27 The statutory storage period for gametes may not exceed ten years:[81] for embryos the period must not exceed five years.[82] If still stored at the end of these respective periods they must be allowed to perish.[83] An embryo created from stored gametes may itself be frozen and stored for five years. Accordingly, an embryo could be used for treatment services or for the purposes of research for up to fifteen years after the egg or sperm from which it derives was donated. Regulations may, however, provide for a shorter maximum period of storage[84] and, in circumstances as may be specified, a longer period.[85]

10.28 The Human Fertilisation and Embryology (Statutory Storage Period) Regulations 1991 have extended the storage period for gametes where:

the gametes were provided by a person:
(a) whose fertility since providing them has or is likely to become, in the written opinion of a registered medical practitioner, significantly impaired,
(b) who was aged under 45 on the date on which the gametes were provided, and
(c) who does not consent to the gametes being used for the purpose of providing treatment services to persons other than that person, or that person and another together, and has never so consented while the gametes were ones to which this regulation applied.[86]

Thus the storage period for a 25 year-old, about to undergo radiotherapy for cancer, would be thirty years, that is the normal ten years maximum for storage of gametes plus twenty further years.

---

[80] S 14(1)(b). [81] S 14(3). [82] S 14(4). [83] S 14(1)(c).
[84] S 14(5)(a). [85] S 14(5)(b). [86] SI 1991/1540, reg 2(2).

(iv) *Research Licence Conditions*

10.29 The conditions of research licences are that the records maintained in pursuance of the licence shall include such information as the Authority may specify,[87] that no information shall be removed from any records maintained in pursuance of the licence before the expiry of such period as may be specified in directions for records of the class in question,[88] and that no embryo appropriated for the purposes of any project of research shall be kept or used otherwise than for the purposes of such a project.[89]

3. Prohibited Activities

10.30 Sections 3 (as amended, see below para 10.40) and 4 of the 1990 Act prohibit certain activities in connection with embryos (s 3) and gametes (s 4).

10.31 No person may bring about the creation of an embryo or keep or use an embryo except in pursuance of a licence.[90] 'Embryo' is defined as a 'live human embryo where fertilisation is complete',[91] but it also puzzlingly includes 'an egg in the process of fertilisation',[92] though, for this purpose, 'fertilisation is not complete until the appearance of a two cell zygote'.[93] The embryo is thus both complete in the process of fertilisation and not complete until that process is over. The intention of Parliament is to require a licence for any activity which results in the creation of an embryo ex utero: the language it uses is confusing and clumsy.

10.32 The placing in a woman of a live embryo other than a human embryo or any live gametes other than human gametes is prohibited.[94]

10.33 Research on embryos is permitted provided HFEA has licensed the research project.[95] However, a licence cannot authorise using an embryo after the appearance of the primitive streak,[96] and the primitive streak is to be taken to have appeared in an embryo not later than the end of the period of fourteen days beginning with the day when the gametes are mixed, not counting any time during which the embryo is stored.[97]

10.34 A licence cannot authorise the placing of an embryo in any animal.[98] There is no similar prohibition on the placing of human sperm and an egg in an

---

[87] S 15(2). [88] S 15(3). [89] S 15(4). [90] S 3(1). [91] S 1(1)(a).
[92] S 1(1)(b). [93] ibid. [94] S 3(2). [95] Sch 2, para 3(1)(b).
[96] S 3(3)(a).
[97] S 3(4). This endorses the opinion of the majority of the Warnock Committee (n 2 above, para 11.30). [98] S 3(3)(b).

animal. The mixing of gametes with the live gametes of an animal is prohibited (except in pursuance of a licence[99]), but what is envisaged here is different. The placing of human sperm and eggs in an animal would probably require a licence: it would if the gametes were then 'stored' in the animal's uterus.[100] Although this seems a far-fetched argument, it would have the merit of bringing any such experiment within the framework of licensing and presumably, therefore, stopping it.[101]

A licence cannot authorise the keeping or using an embryo in any circumstances in which regulations prohibit its keeping or use.[102]   **10.35**

A licence cannot authorise replacing a nucleus of a cell of an embryo with a nucleus taken from the cell of any person, embryo or subsequent development of an embryo.[103] Thus nucleus substitution and cloning (if they are different[104]) are prohibited.   **10.36**

The storing of gametes, and thus their freezing, requires a licence.[105] So does the mixing of gametes with the live gametes of any animal.[106]   **10.37**

A licence cannot authorise storing or using gametes in any circumstances in which regulations prohibit their storage or use.[107]   **10.38**

No person is to place sperm and eggs in a woman in any circumstances specified in regulations except in pursuance of a licence.[108] Regulations could bring gamete intra-fallopian transfer (GIFT), which currently falls outside the 1990 Act, into the regulatory framework of the Act, but this has not been done. Further, no person, in the course of providing treatment services for any woman, is to use the sperm of any man, unless the services are being provided for the woman and man together. Nor can the eggs of any other woman be used.[109] It is clear from the wording of section 4(1)(b) that the Act does not apply where the sperm of a male partner is being used.   **10.39**

Also now prohibited is the use of 'female germ cells taken or derived from an embryo or a foetus' or the use of 'embryos created by using such cells' where this is done 'for the purpose of providing fertility services for any woman'.[110]   **10.40**

---

[99] S 4(1)(c).   [100] S 4(1)(a). On the meaning of 'stored' see also s 2(2).
[101] Carl Wood and Anne Westmore (see *Test-Tube Conception*, Allen and Unwin, 1984) apparently did try, unsuccessfully, to introduce human eggs and sperm into the fallopian tube of a sheep. They were 'relieved' when it failed since 'it may have been difficult to convince the community that the sheep was an appropriate place for human fertilisation and early human development'.   [102] S 3(3)(c).
[103] S 3(3)(d).
[104] The Warnock Report treats them as separate (n 2 above, paras 12.11 and 12.14).
[105] S 4(1)(a) and s 2(2).   [106] S 4(1)(c).   [107] S 4(2).   [108] S 4(3).
[109] S 4(1)(b).
[110] S 3A, inserted by the Criminal Justice and Public Order Act 1994, s 164.

The proposer of this amendment, Dame Jill Knight, wanted 'to send a message out to scientists that there is no point in spending any more time on research [on aborted foetuses], or in messing about with aborted mouse eggs, rat eggs, or anything similar. The end product from using aborted human eggs for fertilisation purposes will simply not be allowed to be used'.[111] But the new provision does not go as far as this; it prohibits only the use of cells from an aborted foetus to create an embryo 'for the purpose of assisting women to carry children'. As a result, cells or eggs from an aborted foetus may still be used to create an embryo for the purpose of research (provided it complies with the limits on this imposed by the 1990 Act, in which see para 10.13 above). It is also still possible to do research on the cells themselves.

10.41 Although not its primary purpose, the new provision also clarifies the law on the use of foetal eggs for treatment. As the HFEA Report on Donated Ovarian Tissue in Embryo Research and Assisted Conception points out, the 1990 Act, as originally formulated, controls only the use of mature eggs or 'gametes'.[112] Foetal eggs, however, are not gametes. Thus, for example, under the 1990 Act a licence is required and the donor's consent must be obtained only for the storage or use of gametes (and see para 10.84 below); the storage and use of foetal eggs were not controlled by the original Act at all. The new section 3A makes it clear that the statutory prohibition extends to the use of foetal germ cells or eggs for treatment.

10.42 As indicated above (para 10.40), the use of foetal eggs for research is not banned or controlled by either the 1990 Act or its 1994 amendment. The Polkinghorne report[113] recommended that the use of foetal material for research purposes should be allowed subject (i) to the consent of the mother[114] (though not the father[115]); (ii) that consent should be general rather than specific;[116] (iii) that there should be no inducements.[117] The

---

[111] *Hansard*, HC vol 241, col 158.

[112] *Report on Donated Ovarian Tissue in Embryo Research and Assisted Conception*; HFEA, July 1994, para 20.

[113] *Review of The Evidence on the Research Use of Fetuses and Fetal Material*, Cmnd 762 (HMSO, 1989).   [114] ibid, paras 3.10 and 6.3.

[115] ibid, para 6.7. His relationship to the foetus was said to be less intimate. The Council of Europe would require the freely-given written consent of the donor parents. The HFEA report (n 112 above) endorses the Polkinghorne recommendation that the mother's consent should be obtained (see paras 5 and 17).

[116] It thought it was undesirable to allow the woman to specify possible uses of foetal tissue since this might influence the timing and techniques used in the abortion procedure. In the United States it is a criminal offence for any person to use foetal tissue pursuant to a promise that the tissue will be transplanted into a recipient specified by the donor or into a relative of the donor (Federal Register Vol 58, No 166 at 45496).

[117] HFEA Report (n 112 above), para 7.

Polkinghorne committee rejected the need for legislation, favouring instead regulation through research ethics committees. The European Parliament, however, has said that 'it is not enough to regulate the problems by means of guidelines within the medical profession'.[118] The European Convention on Bioethics[119] is likely to require legislation (there will need to be sanctions for infringments of principles in the Convention). The 1994 amendment, hastily drafted and barely debated, has obstructed proper Parliamentary consideration of these issues, and further legislation can be expected.[120]

4. The Licensing Procedure

The licensing procedure is set out in the 1990 Act in sections 9, 10 and 16–22. HFEA published an explanatory *Manual for Centres* in June 1991, since updated. **10.43**

HFEA is to maintain one or more committees to discharge its functions relating to the grant, variation, suspension, and revocation of licences.[121] Such committees are known as 'licence committees'. Licence committees consist of five members of the Authority with a quorum of three. Licence committees must be guided by the Act and the Code of Practice. Where new or major issues arise (home insemination was one such), licence committees have taken policy advice from the Authority. Guidance has then been given as an addition to the Code of Practice which, following consultation, has been revised accordingly.[122] **10.44**

When an application is received, there is a site visit by a team of inspectors, consideration of the application and inspection report by a licence committee and notification of the outcome to the applicant. If the applicant is not content with the decision, representations may be made to the committee before the decision takes effect. This may be followed by an appeal to the full **10.45**

---

[118] European Parliament, Committee on Legal Affairs and Citizens' Rights, *Ethical and Legal Problems of Genetic Engineering and Human Artificial Insemination*, Luxembourg, 1990, Resolution 31.

[119] See Art 21 of the *Draft Convention for the Protection of Human Rights and Dignity of the Human Being with regard to the application of Biology and Medicine: Bioethics Convention and Explanatory Report*, Strasbourg 1994, Dir/JUR (94) 2.

[120] See, further, Plomer, A and Martin-Clement, N, 'The Limits of Beneficence: Egg Donation under the Human Fertilisation and Embryology Act 1990', (1995) 15 Legal Studies 434.

[121] S 9(1). The then Health Minister, Virginia Bottomley, described these as committees at the 'cutting edge of the Authority'. They were its 'central force'. See HC *Official Report*, Standing Committee B, 15 May 1990, cols 113–14.

[122] See HFEA, *Second Annual Report, 1993*.

Authority and, finally, on a point of law, an applicant may appeal to the High Court.

10.46 There have been few refusals. Where treatment licences have been refused, the reasons for the refusal have been given to the applicants. According to HFEA:

> Generally these have been cases where the centres failed in significant ways to meet the standards required by the Act and Code of Practice, and where it appeared to the licence committee that the centre would be unable to meet the required standard within a reasonable period of time.[123]

10.47 As HFEA acknowledged in its Second Annual Report, 'while much of the licensing procedure is set out in statute [the 1990 Act], the corresponding administrative arrangements are entirely at the discretion of the authority'. It is, therefore, aware that 'it is important to ensure that the right information is available to centres, to inspectors and to licence committees'. It has accordingly standardised licence conditions 'to maintain consistency'[124] and to show how they relate to particular parts of the Code of Practice.

10.48 It is provided that an applicant for any licence must file in an approved form an application accompanied by an initial fee.[125] Before a licence committee can grant a licence it must be satisfied that certain requirements are met. The application must name an individual who is to be responsible for supervising the activities.[126] The licence committee must be satisfied that the applicant is a suitable person to hold a licence.[127] The premises must also be suitable.[128] The committee must also be satisfied that all other requirements of the Act have been complied with.[129]

5. Challenging Decisions

10.49 If a condition is imposed which the applicant does not like s/he may apply for variation of that condition.[130] Applications may be made by the person responsible or the nominal licensee. However the licence can only be varied so far as it relates to the activities authorised by the licence by changing the manner in which the licensed activities are conducted or the conditions of the licence.[131] To the extent that the licence authorises the conduct of activities on licensed premises, the licence can be varied only as to extend or restrict the premises to which the licence relates.[132] So an application to vary a licence cannot add new premises which were previously unlicensed, nor can it add new services, nor can it authorise the conduct of an activity, not previously

---

[123] *Second Annual Report, 1993*, 7. [124] ibid. [125] S 16(2)(b)(ii), (c).
[126] S 16(2)(d). [127] S 16(2)(e). [128] S 18(2)(c). [129] S 17(1)(d).
[130] S 18(4). [131] S 18(6)(a). [132] S 18(6)(b).

authorised, which will need a separate application for a new licence. However, it may, on an application by the nominal licensee, vary the licence so as to designate another individual in place of the person responsible if the committee is satisfied that the character, qualifications and experience of the other individual are such as are required for the supervision of the activities authorised by the licence and that the individual will discharge the duties stipulated in section 17 of the 1990 Act.[133]

The other avenue open to an aggrieved applicant is recourse to ordinary public law remedies. Thus the conditions imposed by HFEA must be *Wednesbury* reasonable.[134] As formulated by Lord Greene MR, 'a person entrusted with a discretion must . . . direct himself properly in law. He must call his own attention to the matters which he is bound to consider. He must exclude from his consideration matters which are irrelevant to what he has to consider'.[135] In *Secretary of State for Education and Science v Tameside Metropolitan Borough Council*, Lord Diplock said that 'the very concept of administrative discretion involves a right to choose between more than one possible course of action upon which there is room for reasonable people to hold differing opinions as to which is to be preferred'.[136] Thus, for example, to impose upon a treatment centre a condition as to the frequency with which services may be offered would be reasonable; to insist that it employed only nurses with blonde hair would not. **10.50**

HFEA must not fetter its discretion. This does not mean that it may not exercise its discretion by means of a policy or rule. But it must 'be prepared to make an exception to that rule or policy in a deserving case'.[137] Thus, if, for example, a decision was taken that a certain category of research within Schedule 2, para 3(2)(a)–(e) could never be pursued, the courts might be prepared to conclude that this offended against legality by fettering discretion. Interested parties (treatment clinics) must be allowed the opportunity to persuade the licensing authority to amend or deviate from the rule or policy, but the rule against fettering does not extend to the point of requiring any particular form of hearing or any particular technique of making or receiving representations.[138] **10.51**

Decisions may also be challenged for procedural ultra vires. This can take two forms: failure to follow the directions of the Act, and failure to observe the **10.52**

---

[133] S 18(5)(a). The other individual's consent is also required (see s 18(5)(b)).
[134] See *Associated Provincial Picture Houses v Wednesbury Corporation* [1948] 1 KB 223.
[135] ibid, 229.   [136] [1977] AC 1014, 1064.
[137] De Smith, Woolf and Jowell, *Judicial Review of Administrative Action* (Sweet and Maxwell, 1995), 505.
[138] See *R v Secretary of State for the Environment, ex p Brent LBC* [1982] QB 593.

principles of natural justice. As regards directions under the Act, there are both mandatory prescriptions (where disobedience will normally render invalid what has been done) and directory ones, in which case disobedience may be treated as an irregularity not affecting the validity of what has been done.[139] It is not always easy to distinguish the two requirements but it may be said that where statutory words require things to be done as a condition of making a decision, especially when the form of words requires that something *shall* be done, an inference is raised that the requirement is mandatory, so that failure to do the required act renders the decision unlawful.[140] Examples in this Act are a determination by a licence committee which is improperly constituted in breach of the regulations determining the composition of such committees,[141] and the failure by a licence committee to give notice of a determination of a licence application contrary to the requirement in section 19(5). Where the procedures are merely directory,[142] the courts will not normally find committees bound, with the result that failure to meet the procedural requirements will not generally be fatal to the validity of the decision taken. It is important to grasp that all statutory requirements are prima facie mandatory.[143] In order to decide whether a presumption that a provision is mandatory is in fact rebutted, the whole scope and purpose of the Act must be considered: one must assess 'the importance of the provision that has been disregarded, and the relation of that provision to the general object intended to be secured by the Act'.[144]

10.53 A key element of procedural propriety is the duty to observe the principles of natural justice. The Act itself embodies these,[145] but recourse must still be had to common law principles. It has been said that rules of natural justice 'mean no more than the duty to act fairly'.[146] The courts have offered some guidance as to which interests should be protected by fair procedures. In *McInnes v Onslow Fane*,[147] three situations were distinguished: 'forfeiture' or 'deprivation' cases where there is a decision which

---

[139] See n 137 above, 265 *et seq*. See also *Cullimore v Lyme Regis Corporation* [1962] 1 QB 715.

[140] But the decision is presumed valid until set aside or otherwise held to be invalid by a court of competent jurisdiction (*Smith v East Elloe RDC* [1956] AC 736).

[141] S 9(5).

[142] An example is where a licence committee may by notice suspend a licence (s 22(1)).

[143] See n 136 above, 267.

[144] *Howard v Bodington* (1877) 2 PD 203, 211. See also *R v Tower Hamlets Health Authority, ex p Tower Combined Traders Association* [1994] COD 325.

[145] See the 'right to be heard' in the Act and Regulations and protections against bias (eg Sch 1 para 10(1)).

[146] *per* Lord Diplock in *O'Reilly v Mackman* [1983] 2 AC 237, 275.

[147] [1978] 1 WLR 1520.

takes away some existing right or position (in our context the operation of an existing licensed treatment clinic), 'application' cases (for example, to run a treatment clinic), and an intermediate category of 'expectation' cases, where there is a reasonable expectation of a continuation of an existing benefit (the renewal of a licence, for example) which falls short of a right. A fair hearing, the court suggested, should be granted in cases involving 'forfeiture' and, normally, 'expectation', but not in those involving a mere 'application'. A strict application of this reasoning could result in injustice, with one clinic securing a licence and another not, so the courts have held that deciding bodies are under a duty to give an applicant an opportunity to make representations and to be apprised of all information on which the decision may be founded.[148] It has been argued that 'wherever a public function is being performed there is an inference, in the absence of an express requirement to the contrary, that the function is required to be performed fairly'.[149] This inference is all the more compelling where a decision may adversely affect a person's rights or interests or when a person has a legitimate expectation of being fairly treated, as is clearly the case with applications for licences under the Act. 'The court is the arbiter of what is fair';[150] whether fairness is required and what is involved to achieve fairness is a decision for the courts as a matter of law.

D. Access to Treatment

1. Introduction

The Warnock committee was 'not prepared to recommend that access to **10.54** treatment should be based exclusively on the legal status of marriage'.[151] It did, however, express its view that 'as a general rule it is better for children to be born into a two-parent family, with both father and mother'.[152] It concluded that 'eligibility' raised difficult questions and that 'hard and fast rules' were not applicable to its solution.[153] Instead the Warnock committee recom-

---

[148] See *R v Huntingdon DC, ex p Cowan* [1984] 1 WLR 501. The obligation may be qualified by a right to refrain from disclosing the source and precise content of highly confidential information: *R v Gaming Board for Great Britain, ex p Benaim and Khaida* [1970] 2 QB 417, 431.   [149] N 137 above, 405.

[150] *per* Wolff and Lloyd LJJ in *R v Panel on Takeovers and Merger, ex p Guinness* [1990] QB 146. The test is not whether no reasonable body would have thought it proper to dispense with a fair hearing.

[151] Report of the Committee of Inquiry into Human Fertilisation and Embryology (n 2 above), para 2.5.   [152] ibid, para 2.11.

[153] ibid, para 2.13.

mended that where consultants declined to provide treatment 'they should always give the patient a full explanation of the reasons'.[154] In fact, during the passage of the 1990 Act through Parliament, an attempt was made to restrict access to infertility treatment to married couples or, at least, to heterosexual couples in a stable relationship but it failed.[155]

2. The Welfare of the Child

10.55 The Act only addresses the question of access to treatment in one provision and then obliquely rather than directly. Section 13(5) provides: 'A woman shall not be provided with treatment services unless account has been taken of the welfare of any child who may be born as a result of the treatment (including the need of that child for a father), and of any other child who may be affected by the birth'.

10.56 Kennedy and Grubb point to the significance of this provision and its novelty:

> Parliament has required that the clinical judgment of the doctor must be exercised having regard to others and not just in the 'best interests' of his patient. In this respect, the 1990 Act departs from what would be the normal understanding of a doctor's duty to his patient.[156]

10.57 The provision is incoherent. It refers to the welfare of children as yet unconceived ('who are only a twinkle in the doctor's eye'[157]). It asks us to compare the utilities of not being born with being born to a single mother; surely a nonsense for existence will nearly always be preferable to non-existence.[158] Equally nonsensical at face value is to emphasise 'the need of that child for a father'. All children have fathers; what the provision requires is a *social* father.

10.58 The provision only requires 'account' to be 'taken of the welfare of any child who may be born as a result of the treatment' and 'of any other child who may be affected by the birth'. There is no indication as to the weight, if any, to be attached to the welfare of either set of children. An amendment which would have made the welfare of the child paramount did not pass.[159] But

---

[154] ibid.

[155] An amendment moved in the House of Lords to make it an offence to provide treatment services for an unmarried couple was defeated by a single vote (see HL Hansard vol 515, col 787 (6 Feb 1990)).

[156] Kennedy, I and Grubb, A, *Medical Law: Text with Materials* (Butterworths, 1994), 781.

[157] See Douglas, G, *Law, Fertility and Reproduction* (Sweet and Maxwell, 1991), 121.

[158] And see Parfit, D, *Reasons and Persons* (Oxford University Press, 1984); Harris, J, *Wonderwoman and Superman* (Oxford University Press, 1992).

[159] See n 157 above, 122.

what is meant by 'account'? On whom exactly does the duty fall?[160] What has to be shown to demonstrate that it has been discharged? Who can challenge a decision taken allegedly in breach of the duty? The 1990 Act is silent on locus standi.[161] Nor does the Act define 'welfare', though conventionally this is given a broad definition.[162] It clearly includes material welfare so that presumably the poverty of the prospective mother should be taken into account. The fact that an existing child would stand to inherit less as a result of the birth of a new medically-assisted sibling would detrimentally affect that child's welfare.

10.59 These thoughts did not enter the minds of those responsible for section 13(5). This was introduced and passed expressly to prevent the creation of one-parent families through assisted reproduction, and, implicitly, to prevent lesbian women from receiving treatment services. The provision, say Morgan and Lee, 'has all the hallmarks of a profamilist ideology. Assisted conception is to be, for the most part, for the married, mortgaged middle-classes'.[163]

10.60 The width of the provision should also be noted. It extends to any treatment service, defined in the Act to mean 'medical, surgical or obstetric services provided to the public or a section of the public for the purpose of assisting women to carry children'.[164] In theory, antenatal services could be denied to a lesbian woman on the ground that it would be better for the child if she miscarried. No one, it is assumed, would put this construction on s 13(5), but extraordinarily it is capable of bearing this meaning.

10.61 The provision also clearly applies to surrogacy (on which see para 10.128 below). This means that treatment services to a surrogate must take account of both the abilities of the commissioning parents (or parent where the surrogate's egg is being used) to advance the child's welfare (clearly very relevant in terms of Parliament's intention where the commissioning parent

---

[160] Nor is it clear what are to be the consequences if services are provided in breach of the statutory obligation.

[161] See the discussion by Morgan and Lee (n 61 above), 145–6.

[162] On the meaning of 'welfare' Lord Mackay referred to a well-known discussion in a New Zealand decision (*Walker v Harrison* [1981] 257 New Zealand Recent Law), where 'welfare' was described as an 'all-encompassing word. It includes material welfare . . . More important are the stability and the security, the loving and understanding care and guidance, the warm and compassionate relationships, that are essential for the full development of the child's own character, personality and talents' (see Hansard HL col 1097 (6 Mar 1990)). Despite this 'smokescreen', it is suggested that the focus is not on the welfare of children at all, but rather on the suitability of prospective parents.

[163] *Blackstone's Guide To The Human Fertilisation and Embryology Act 1990* (Blackstone, 1991), 146. See also Haimes, E, 'Recreating the Family? Policy Considerations Relating To The "New" Reproductive Technologies' in McNeil, M, Varcoe, I and Yearley, S (eds) *The New Reproductive Technologies* (Macmillan, 1990), 154. [164] S 2(1).

is a homosexual man), and the psychological effect that a woman giving birth and then giving the child away will have on her other children.[165]

10.62   HFEA's *Code of Practice* (1995) accepts 'the right of people who are or may be infertile to the proper consideration of their request for treatment'.[166] It goes on to list the 'factors' to be considered by those offering treatment services. The Code states:

> 3.15   Centres should take all reasonable steps to ascertain who would be legally responsible for any child born as a result of the procedure and who it is intended will be bringing up the child. When clients come from abroad, centres should not assume that the law of that country relating to the parentage of a child born as a result of donated gametes is the same as that of the United Kingdom.
>
> 3.16   People seeking treatment are entitled to a fair and unprejudiced assessment of their situation and needs, which should be conducted with the skill and sensitivity appropriate to the delicacy of the case and the wishes and feelings of those involved.
>
> 3.17   Where people seek licensed treatment, centres should bear in mind the following factors:
> a.   their commitment to having and bringing up a child or children;
> b.   their ability to provide a stable and supportive environment for any child produced as a result of treatment;
> c.   their medical histories and the medical histories of their families;
> d.   their ages and likely future ability to look after or provide for a child's needs;
> e.   their ability to meet the needs of any child or children who may be born as a result of treatment, including the implications of any possible multiple births;
> f.   any risk of harm to the child or children who may be born, including the risk of inherited disorders, problems during pregnancy and of neglect or abuse; and
> g.   the effect of a new baby or babies upon any existing child of the family.
>
> 3.18   Where people seek treatment using donated gametes, centres should take the following factors into account:
> a.   a child's potential need to know about their origins and whether or not the prospective parents are prepared for the questions which may arise while the child is growing up;
> b.   the possible attitudes of other members of the family towards the child, and towards their status in the family;

---

[165] Krimmel, H, 'The Case Against Surrogate Parenting', *Hastings Center Report*, Oct 1983, 35 quotes a 9-year old girl who, when told that the child her mother was carrying would be given away to another family, responded: 'All right . . . but if it's a girl, let's keep it and give Jeffrey (her 2-year old brother) away'.   [166] HFEA, *Code of Practice* (1995), 1.

    c. the implications for the welfare of the child if the donor is personally
       known within the child's family and social circle; and

    d. any possibility known to the centre of a dispute about the legal
       fatherhood of the child . . .

3.19   Further factors will require consideration in the following cases:
    a. where the child will have no legal father. Centres are required to have
       regard for the child's need for a father and should pay particular
       attention to the prospective mother's ability to meet the child's needs
       throughout their childhood. Where appropriate, centres should con-
       sider particularly whether there is anyone else within the prospective
       mother's family and social circle willing and able to share the respon-
       sibility for meeting those needs, and for bringing up, maintaining and
       caring for the child . . .

The *Code of Practice* goes on to list the enquiries to be made. It states: **10.63**

3.23   Centres should take a medical and social history from each prospective
    parent. They should be seen together and separately. This should include
    all information relevant to paragraphs 3.15 to 3.19 above [and see para
    10.63].

3.24   Centres should seek to satisfy themselves that the GP of each prospective
    parent knows of no reason why either of them might not be suitable for
    the treatment to be offered. This would include anything which might
    adversely affect the welfare of any resulting child.

3.25   Centres should obtain the client's consent before approaching the GP.
    However, failure to give consent should be taken into account in con-
    sidering whether or not to offer treatment.

3.26   If any of these particulars or inquiries give cause for concern, eg,
    evidence that prospective parents have had children removed from their
    care, or evidence of a previous relevant conviction, the centre should
    make further inquiries of any relevant individual, authority or agency as
    it can.

3.27   Centres should obtain the client's consent before approaching any indi-
    vidual, authority or agency for information. However, failure to give
    consent should be taken into account in deciding whether or not to offer
    treatment.

The *Code of Practice* also emphasises multi-disciplinary assessment. On this it   **10.64**
states:

3.28   The views of all those of the centre who have been involved with the
    prospective parents should be taken into account when deciding whether
    or not to offer treatment. Prospective parents should be given a fair
    opportunity to state their views before any decision is made and to meet
    any objections raised to providing them with treatment.

3.29   If a member of the team has a cause for concern as a result of information
    given to them in confidence, they should obtain the consent of the
    person concerned before discussing it with the rest of the team. If a
    member of the team receives information which is of such gravity that

confidentiality *cannot* be maintained, they should use their own discretion, based on good professional practice, in deciding in what circumstances it should be discussed with the rest of the team.

3.30 The decision to provide treatment should be taken in the light of all the available information. Treatment may be refused on clinical grounds. Treatment should also be refused if the centre believes that it would not be in the interests of any resulting child, or any child already existing, to provide treatment, or is unable to obtain sufficient information or advice to reach a proper conclusion.

3.31 If treatment is refused for any reason, the centre should explain to the woman and, where appropriate, her husband or partner, the reasons for this and the factors, if any, which might persuade the centre to reverse its decision. It should also explain the options which remain open and tell clients where they can obtain counselling.

3.32 Centres should record in detail the information which has been taken into account when considering the welfare of the child or children. The record should reflect the views of all those who were consulted in reaching the decision, including those of potential parents.

10.65 The *Code of Practice* does not exclude any category of persons as such from access to services for assisted reproduction. But, as can be seen above, it does emphasise 'the child's need for a father' and stresses that treatment should be refused if the centre believes that 'it would not be in the interests of any resulting child, or any child already existing'. It leaves decisions to rest with individual centres' assessments of an applicant's suitability. It also emphasises the importance of giving reasons for decisions. Where these prove inadequate, the possibility is opened up of challenge by judicial review.

10.66 There is only one reported example of a challenge in this way and the case antedates both the legislation and the Code. In *R v Ethical Committee of St Mary's Hospital (Manchester), ex p H*,[167] the applicant, who had been turned down as a suitable foster or adoptive parent because she had a criminal record involving prostitution offences and a 'poor understanding' of fostering, was removed from the IVF waiting list after the hospital became aware of her background. At St Mary's Hospital the criteria for offering treatment were that couples 'must, in the ordinary course of events, satisfy the general criteria established by adoption societies in assessing suitability for adoption[168] . . . (and there) must be no medical, psychiatric or psychosexual problems which would indicate an increased probability of a couple not being able to provide satisfactory parenting to the offspring or endanger the mother's life or health if she became pregnant'.

---

[167] [1988] 1 FLR 512.
[168] See, generally, Campion, M J, *Who's Fit To Be A Parent?* (Routledge, 1995). On adoption see ch 2, on assisted reproduction ch 4.

The applicant sought judicial review of the decision to refuse to treat her. She **10.67** failed because she had been given an opportunity to make representations against the refusal. There was, accordingly, no procedural unfairness (as to which see paras 10.52–10.53 above). Schiemann J was prepared to accept obiter that a blanket policy to refuse treatment to 'anyone who was a Jew or coloured' might be illegal. The hospital's criteria, however, were acceptable, and not *Wednesbury* unreasonable (as to which see para 10.50 above). Why Schiemann J had any doubt as to the propriety of a policy which denied treatment on grounds of race or colour is surprising; under the Race Relations Act 1968 such policies would clearly be unlawful. Discrimination on grounds of religion is not, however, unlawful under any legislation in operation in England.

It was reported in June 1991 that St Mary's Hospital in London rejected a **10.68** couple where both were HIV positive; rejection was based on the risk of transmitting the infection to the child and of the likelihood that the child would be orphaned at some (early) stage in his/her childhood. This seems convincing but it is the case that HIV-infected pregnant women are given the choice of continuing their pregnancy rather than terminating it. In 1996 the decision of Hammersmith Hospital to give infertility treatment to a woman who was HIV positive proved controversial: so did the decision to assist a woman in Solihull whose partner seemed less than supportive (the more so in this case when it was revealed she was expecting eight children).

The 1990 Act deals with treatment services only within the United Kingdom. **10.69** However, section 24(4) of the Act does invest the Authority with a discretion to permit a licence-holder to export sperm. Accordingly, the possibility of using treatment services abroad, most especially within the European Union, and the legal implications of so doing, has arisen in two cases. In *R v Human Fertilisation and Embryology Authority, ex p Blood*,[169] when Mrs Blood was denied permission to take her dead husband's semen to Belgium with a view to treatment services being performed in a Brussels clinic, she invoked provisions of the Treaty of Rome.[170] The Court of Appeal held that the prohibition on exporting gametes, imposed by the Human Fertilisation and Embryology Authority, was tantamount to a denial of the right of access to medical treatment abroad and could only by justified if, in the public interest, it were absolutely necessary. The court would interfere with the Authority's decision only if it wrongly evaluated criteria to an extent which went beyond the margin of appreciation allowed by European law. The court was unim-

---

[169] [1997] 2 WLR 806.   [170] Arts 59 and 60.

pressed by the floodgates of argument.[171] It said that, since this case would make it clear that sperm could not be lawfully stored without written consent, there should be no further cases. In *U v W (Attorney-General Intervening)*[172] Wilson J considered that section 28(3) of the 1990 Act (on which see para 10.122 below) represented a restriction on the freedom to provide services under Article 59. But he held the restriction to be justified on the grounds that an unmarried man joining with a woman in seeking treatment with donor sperm had to be aware of all the consequences and given an opportunity to make an informed choice; a short, clear answer should be available to any question whether treatment had been provided for a woman and a man together; and the issue of paternity could arise long after the birth of a child, when the licence-holder's records would be the best source of evidence as to the identity of the alleged father. Further, on making a provision relating to non-genetic paternity, a Member State had been given considerable discretion under Community law to determine which restriction was proportionate to its legitimate objectives, and thus the licensing system with its code of practice was a restriction which was not out of proportion to the reasons which justified the restriction. Therefore, the requirement of treatment under licence in the 1990 Act is not an infringement of Article 59 of the Treaty of Rome.

E. Conscientious Objection

10.70 The 1990 Act contains a conscientious objection provision designed to permit individuals to opt out of participating in any of the activities covered by the Act. It provides in section 38(1): 'No person who has a conscientious objection to participating in any activity governed by this Act shall be under a duty, however arising, to do so'. But 'in any legal proceedings the burden of conscientious objection' rests 'on the person claiming to rely on it'.[173]

10.71 The provision is modeled on section 4 of the Abortion Act 1967 (as to which see Chapter 11) but there is an important difference. The 1990 Act does not contain an exception to the right to object where action is necessary to save a patient's life or prevent grave permanent injury.[174] However, it will be noted that section 38 refers to 'any activity governed by this Act' and abortion is, of course, in part governed by the 1990 Act.[175] There is thus a conflict between section 4 of the Abortion Act 1967 and section 38 of the

---

[171] But cf Delany, L and Doyle, K, 'Fathers—Who Needs Them—*HFEA v Blood*', (1997) 27 Fam Law 261, 262.   [172] [1997] 2 FLR 282.
[173] S 38(2).   [174] As the Abortion Act 1967 does.   [175] S 37.

1990 Act, one which was, it is submitted, created unintentionally, perhaps thoughtlessly, but one which nevertheless has to be resolved. The better view must be that the exception does not apply to activities covered by the 1990 Act except abortion. However two points may be noted. First, life-threatening conditions are not likely to arise in the context of infertility treatment. Secondly, if they do, there is a common law duty on doctors to intervene to arrest conditions which are life-threatening or are causing grave physical injury.[176] The omission and the conflict are therefore not of great significance.

10.72 The objection must be 'conscientious'. 'Conscience' is widely interpreted and will include not only religious beliefs but also other principled reasons which impel a person to believe that an activity is inherently wrong.

10.73 The provision states 'no person' with a conscientious objection is under a duty to participate in any of the Act's activities. This clearly extends to doctors and nurses,[177] but, in the light of the House of Lords' decision in *Janaway v Salford Area Health Authority*,[178] whether it extends any further will depend on how 'participate' is interpreted. There can be no doubt that a research scientist or laboratory technician may invoke the conscience clause. Whether a secretary, instructed to type letters or forms in connection with, for example, embryo research to which she takes moral objection, would be similarly protected is generally thought unlikely after *Janaway*.[179] But the language of the abortion provision, interpreted in *Janaway*, and section 38 are not identical. Section 4 of the Abortion Act refers to participation in *any treatment* authorised by the Act and section 38 is couched more widely in terms of *any activity* governed by the Act. A secretary does not, so it has been held, participate in treatment, but it is not stretching language too far to hold that she does participate in an activity governed by the 1990 Act. In support of this it may be noted that Lord Keith in *Janaway* argued that: 'If Parliament had intended the result contended for by the applicant (i.e. that typing a letter amounted to participating in treatment), it could have procured it very clearly and easily by referring to participation "in anything authorised by this Act" instead of "in any treatment [so] authorised"'.[180] In effect this is what Parliament has done in the 1990 Act. It is thus arguable that even activities remote from treatment are covered by the conscience clause in section 38.

---

[176] See *F v Berkshire Health Authority* [1990] 2 AC 1. And see Ch. 11 above.
[177] See *Royal College of Nursing of the United Kingdom v Department of Health and Social Security* [1981] AC 800. [178] [1989] AC 537.
[179] That a secretary was not participating in abortion when she typed a letter referring a patient on to a second doctor for a second opinion.
[180] [1989] AC 537, 570.

Whether section 38 in addition reverses the ruling in *Janaway* (note the argument in para 10.71 above that abortion is an activity covered by the 1990 Act) must at least be arguable, although there can be no doubt that Parliament had no such intention.

10.74 The conscience clause permits an individual to object to *any* activity governed by the 1990 Act. S/he may thus, for example, object on conscientious grounds to embryo research without also objecting to assisted reproduction. However, two difficult questions arise in relation to this. Can an individual who accepts assisted reproduction conscientiously object to the use of IVF in the case, for example, of a single woman or a lesbian? Does acceptance of an activity entail acceptance of all instances of that activity? It has been argued[181] that the conscientious objection provision could be successfully invoked by those who do not wish to treat lesbians. This is not very convincing for two reasons: first, such an objection would be based more on prejudice than it would on conscience[182] (a definitive understanding of 'conscience' awaits clarification by the courts); and, secondly, it does not seem that the person invoking conscientious objection is objecting to the activity at such, but rather to the sexual orientation and lifestyle of the person who is the potential beneficiary of the activity.[183] It would be straining language to hold that the objection is to the activity of creating unconventional families. This is not the natural meaning of the language used, nor was it Parliament's intention.

F. Consent to Use of Genetic Material

10.75 A donor of genetic material (for example, eggs) or a patient undergoing infertility treatment must consent to the medical interventions involved. This principle is firmly entrenched in the common law[184] and needs no further exposition in this context (and see Chapters 3 and 4). In the case of medically assisted reproduction the common law is supplemented by the 1990 Act, and by the *Code of Practice* (revised in 1995).

The *Blood* litigation in 1996–7[185] re-emphasised the necessity of consent. Sperm was removed from Mr Blood, who was in a coma dying from menin-

---

[181] See Douglas, G (n 157, above), 122.
[182] And see Dworkin, R, *Taking Rights Seriously* (Duckworth, 1977), ch 10.
[183] See for agreement Kennedy and Grubb, *Medical Law* (n 156 above), 788.
[184] See *Sidaway v Governors of Royal Bethlem Hospital* [1985] AC 871; *Re F* [1990] 2 AC 1; and *Airedale NHS Trust v Bland* [1993] AC 789.
[185] *R v Human Fertilisation and Embryology Authority, ex p Blood* [1997] 2 WLR 806.

gitis, on the instructions of his wife. According to Lord Woolf MR, 'humanity dictated that the sperm was taken and preserved first and the legal argument followed'.[186] There was argument that Mr Blood's consent could be implied from conversations that he and his wife had had about starting a family. The Court of Appeal agreed with the Human Fertilisation and Embryology Authority that consent had to be express and written, as stipulated in the 1990 Act,[187] and could not be constructed in this way. It also agreed with the Authority that the storage of Mr Blood's sperm was 'technically' a criminal offence: it was contrary to section 41(2)(b) of the Act. Although the Court of Appeal did not address the issue, it is also clear that Mrs Blood had no capacity to consent on behalf of her husband. Such capacity would need to be grounded on the need 'to save life or to ensure improvement or prevent deterioration in physical or mental health',[188] and none of these criteria could possibly have applied. Further, if treating Mr Blood in this way was not in his best interests, it is difficult to see how he could have an interest in treatment which was designed to produce offspring after his death.

G. Provision of Counselling and Information

The 1990 Act provides in section 13(6) that: **10.76**

> A woman shall not be provided with any treatment services involving—
>   (a) the use of any gametes of any person, if that person's consent is required under paragraph 5 of Schedule 3 to this Act for the use in question,
>   (b) the use of any embryo the creation of which was brought about *in vivo*, or
>   (c) the use of any embryo taken from a woman if the consent of the woman from whom it was taken is required under paragraph 7 of that Schedule for the use in question, unless the woman being treated and, where she is being treated together with a man, the man, have been given a suitable opportunity to receive proper counselling about the implications of taking the proposed step, and have been provided with such relevant information as is proper.

This confirms and reinforces the common law and supplements it by requir-   **10.77**
ing an opportunity for counselling and the provision of relevant information. The need for counselling was recognised in the Warnock report.[189] It envisaged 'non-directional' counselling aimed at 'helping individuals to understand their situation and to make their own decisions about what steps should

---

[186] ibid, 814.   [187] Sch 3, para 8.
[188] *per* Lord Brandon of Oakbrook in *Re F* [1990] 2 AC 1, 55.
[189] N 151 above, paras 3.3–3.4.

be taken next'.[190] The Act does not state what counselling is to consist of, nor when it is to be made available, nor whether a centre can direct or merely encourage the use of counselling services. However the *Code of Practice* is very specific on the content of counselling (see para 6 of the *Code*, below) and on the question of time, it is clear that it should take place 'before' any consent is given (see para 6.1 of the *Code* below). However the 1990 Act is expressed in the present continuous tense ('being treated'); this raises the question, not addressed in the *Code*, as to whether proper counselling must also be offered each time the patient or patients return for treatment. Given resource constraints the better interpretation may be to limit the obligation to before initial treatment is offered. On the question as to whether counselling may be directed or merely offered, the *Code* is clear that what is required is the making available of counselling (see para 4 of the *Code* below).

1. Provision of Counselling

10.78   As regards the provision of counselling, the *Code of Practice* (1995) provides:

General

6.1   People seeking licensed treatment (i.e. *in vitro* fertilisation or treatment using donated gametes) or consenting to the use of storage of embryos, or to the donation or storage of gametes, *must* be given a suitable opportunity to receive proper counselling about the implications of taking the proposed steps, before they consent.

6.2   Counselling should be clearly distinguished from:
   a. the information which is to be given to everyone, in accordance with the guidance in Part 4 [see below];
   b. the normal relationship between the clinician and the person offering donation or seeking storage or treatment, which includes giving professional advice; and
   c. the process of assessing people in order to decide whether to accept them as a client or donor, or to accept their gametes and embryos for storage, in accordance with the guidance given in Part 3.

6.3   No-one is obliged to accept counselling. However, it is generally recognised as beneficial.

6.4   Three distinct types of counselling should be made available in appropriate cases:
   a. *implications counselling*: this aims to enable the person concerned to understand the implications of the proposed course of action for themselves, for their family, and for any children born as a result;
   b. *support counselling*: this aims to give emotional support at times of particular stress, eg when there is a failure to achieve a pregnancy;

---

[190] ibid, para 3.4.

c. *therapeutic counselling*: this aims to help people to cope with the consequences of infertility and treatment, and to help them to resolve the problems which these may cause. It includes helping people to adjust their expectations and to accept their situation.

Centres *must* make implications counselling available to everyone. They should also provide support or therapeutic counselling in appropriate cases or refer people to sources of more specialist counselling outside the centre.

6.5 Centres should present the offer of counselling as part of normal routine, without implying either that the person concerned is in any way deficient or abnormal, or that there is any pressure to accept. Centres should allow them sufficient time to consider the offer.

6.6 Centres should allow sufficient time for counselling to be conducted sensitively, in an atmosphere which is conducive to discussion. The length and content of counselling, and the pace at which it is conducted, should be determined by the needs of the individual concerned.

6.7 Centres should offer people the opportunity to be counselled by someone other than the clinician responsible for their treatment, donation or storage. Such counselling should be independent of the clinical decision-making process.

6.8 Centres should offer people the opportunity to be counselled individually and with their partner if they have one. Group counselling sessions may also be offered, but it is not acceptable for a centre to offer only group sessions.

6.9 People should be able to seek counselling at any stage of their investigation or treatment. However, counselling should normally be made available after the person seeking treatment or providing the gametes or embryos has received the oral and written explanations described in paragraph 4.4 and 4.5 [see below]. Discussion may then focus on the meaning and consequences of the decision, rather than on its practical aspects.

Implications Counselling

6.10 Counsellors should invite potential clients or providers of gametes and embryos to consider the following issues:

a. the social responsibilities which centres and providers of genetic material bear to ensure the best possible outcome for all concerned, including the child;

b. the implications of the procedure for themselves, their family and social circle, and for any resulting children;

c. their feelings about the use and possible disposal of any embryos derived from their gametes;

d. the possibility that these implications and feelings may change over time, as personal circumstances change;

e. the advantages and disadvantages of openness about the procedures envisaged, and how they might be explained to relatives and friends.

6.11 Counsellors should invite *clients* to consider in particular:

a. the client's attitude to their own, or partner's infertility;

b. the possibility that treatment will fail.

6.12 Where treatment using donated gametes or embryos is contemplated, clients should also be invited to consider:

a. their feelings about not being the genetic parents of the child;

b. their perceptions of the needs of the child throughout his or her childhood and adolescence.

6.13 If a woman is already undergoing infertility treatment when the question of treatment with donated gametes or embryos derived from them arises, counselling about the implications of receiving donated material should be offered separately from counselling about the other implications of treatment. Treatment with donated material should not proceed unless the woman and, where appropriate, her partner have been given a suitable opportunity to receive counselling about it.

6.14 If a woman is undergoing infertility treatment and the possibility of her or her partner becoming a donor also arises, counselling about the implications of donation should be undertaken separately from counselling about the implications of treatment in the first instance. If the possibility of donation arises at a later stage in the treatment, donation should not proceed unless the woman and, where appropriate, her partner have been given a suitable opportunity to receive counselling about it.

6.15 Counselling about the implications of donation may be combined with counselling about the other implications of treatment at a later stage, if this is advisable in the light of the initial counselling sessions and the client's or potential donor's wishes.

6.16 Counsellors should invite potential *donors* of gametes and embryos to consider in particular:

a. their reasons for wanting to become a donor;

b. their attitudes to any resulting children, and their willingness to forego knowledge of and responsibility for such children in the future;

c. the possibility of their own childlessness;

d. their perception of the needs of any children born as a result of their donation;

e. their attitudes to the prospective legal parents of their genetic off-spring;

f. their attitudes to allowing embryos which have been produced from their gametes to be used for research.

6.17 If a person seeking to donate or store genetic material is married or has a long-term partner, the centre should counsel them together if they so wish. If a partner wishes to be counselled separately about the implications of donation or storage, centres should take all practicable steps to offer counselling at the centre, or to assist them in contacting an external counselling organisation.

Later Counselling

6.18   Centres should take all practicable steps to provide further opportunities for counselling about the implications of treatment, donation or storage after consent has been given, and throughout the period in which the person is providing gametes, or receiving treatment, if this is requested. If someone who has previously been a donor or client returns to the centre asking for further counselling, the centre should take all practicable steps to help them obtain it.

Support Counselling

6.19   Centres should also take all practicable steps to offer support to people who are not suitable for treatment, whose treatment has failed, prospective donors who are found to be unsuitable and people who have previously unsuspected defects, to help them come to terms with their situation.

6.20   These steps should include, wherever practicable, reasonable assistance in contacting or establishing a support group.

6.21   Centres should ensure that, as part of their training, all staff are prepared to offer appropriate emotional support at all stages of their investigation, counselling and treatment to clients who are suffering distress.

Therapeutic Counselling

6.22   Procedures should be in place to identify people who suffer particular distress and to offer them, as far as is practicable, therapeutic counselling, with the aim of helping them to come to terms with their situation.

6.23   If a client experiences mental ill-health or a severe psychological problem which may or may not be related to infertility, for which it would be more appropriate to seek help and advice outside the centre, the centre should take all practicable steps to help him or her to obtain it.

Records

6.24   A record should be kept of all counselling offered and whether or not the offer is accepted.

6.25   All information obtained in the course of counselling should be kept confidential, subject to paragraph 3.29, above.

2. Provision of Information

As regards the duty to give information, the *Code of Practice* lays down the   **10.79** following:

General Obligation

4.1   Before anyone is given licensed treatment (ie, in vitro fertilisation or treatment using donated gametes) or consents to the use of storage of embryos, or to the donation or storage of gametes, they *must* be given 'such relevant information as is proper'. This should be distinguished from the requirement to offer counselling, which clients and donors need not accept.

4.2   Clients and donors should be given oral explanations supported by relevant written material. They should be encouraged to ask for further information and their questions should be answered in a straightforward, comprehensive and open way.

4.3   Centres should devise a system to ensure that:

a. the right information is given;

b. the person who is to give the information is clearly identified, and has been given sufficient training and guidance to enable them to do so; and

c. a record is kept of the information given.

Information to be Given to Clients

4.4   Information should be given to people seeking treatment on the following points:

a. the limitations and possible outcomes of the treatment proposed, and variations of effectiveness over time. This should include the centre's own live birth rate per treatment cycle and the national live birth rate per treatment cycle;

b. the possible side effects and risks of the treatment to the woman and any resulting child, including (where relevant) the risks associated with ovarian hyperstimulation syndrome (OHSS) and with multiple pregnancy;

c. the possible disruption of the client's domestic life which treatment will cause, and the length of time he or she will have to wait for treatment;

d. the techniques involved, including (where relevant) the possible deterioration of gametes or embryos associated with storage, and the possible pain and discomfort;

e. the availability of embryo freezing facilities, including the likelihood of success of embryo freezing, thawing, transfer and implications of storage;

f. any other infertility treatments which are available, including those for which a licence is not necessary;

g. that counselling is available;

h. the cost to the client of the treatment proposed and of any alternative treatments;

i. the importance of telling the treatment centre about any resulting birth;

j. who will be the child's parent or parents under the Act. Clients who are nationals or residents of other countries, or who have been treated with gametes obtained from a foreign donor should understand that the law in other countries may be different from that of the United Kingdom . . . ;

k. the child's right to seek information about their origins on reaching 18 or on contemplating earlier marriage;

l. the information which centres must collect and register with the Authority and the extent to which that information may be disclosed to people born as a result of the donation;

m. a child's potential need to know about their origins;

n. the centre's statutory duty to take account of the welfare of any resulting or affected child; and

o. (where relevant) the advantages and disadvantages of continued treatment after a certain number of attempts.

Information to be Given to People Providing Gametes and Embryos

4.5 Information should be given to people consenting to the use or storage of embryos, or to the donation or storage of gametes, on the following points:

a. the procedure involved in collecting gametes, the degree of pain and discomfort and any risks to that person, eg, from the use of super-ovulatory drugs;

b. the screening which will be carried out, and the practical implications of having an HIV antibody test, even if it proves negative;

c. the purposes for which their gametes might be used;

d. whether or not they will be regarded under the Act as the parents of any child born as a result;

e. that the Act generally permits donors to preserve their anonymity;

f. the information which centres must collect and register with the Authority and the extent to which that information may be disclosed to people born as a result of the donation;

g. that they are free to withdraw or vary the terms of their consent at any time, unless the gametes or embryos have already been used;

h. the possibility that a child born disabled as a result of a donor's failure to disclose defects, about which he or she knew or ought reasonably to have known, may be able to sue the donor for damages;

i. in the case of egg donation, that the woman will not incur any financial or other penalty if she withdraws her consent after preparation for egg recovery has begun;

j. that donated gametes and embryos created from them will not normally be used for treatment once the number of children believed to have been born from them has reached 10, or any lower figure specified by the donor; and

k. that counselling is available.

As will be seen, the level of detail required by the *Code of Practice* far exceeds **10.80** the requirements of the common law. The question therefore arises as to the liability of a doctor who fails to comply with the *Code of Practice*. Section 25(6) states that: 'A failure on the part of any person to observe any provision of the code shall not of itself render the person liable to any proceedings . . . '. On its face this suggests that failure to observe a provision of the *Code of Practice* will not, without more, be sufficient to render a doctor liable to civil or criminal proceedings. However, a case may be made that the *Code of Practice* establishes what is to be regarded as good medical practice and thus what a reasonable doctor would do (that is the test established in *Bolam v Friern Hospital Management Committee*,[191] on which see Chapter 4 above),

---

[191] [1957] 1 WLR 582.

with the consequence that failure to comply with it would constitute breach of duty and expose the doctor concerned to a civil action for negligence. The latter is the better view and, in the absence of a legal ruling to the contrary, should be followed.[192]

10.81 It should additionally be noted that a licence committee, in considering whether or not to vary or revoke a licence, may take into account any observance or failure to observe the provisions of the *Code of Practice*.[193]

H. Control of Gametes and Embryos

10.82 The 1990 Act in Schedule 3 sets out an elaborate framework, the purpose of which is to vest control of gametes and embryos in those who provide this genetic material.

10.83 It is a requirement of the 'licence condition' that the consent provisions in Schedule 3 are complied with.[194] Failure to observe the provisions will breach the duty upon the 'person responsible' for the licensed activities to ensure that the conditions of the licence are complied with.[195] A breach of such duty, for example proceeding without an effective consent, is a ground for the revocation of the licence.[196]

10.84 The Schedule requires that a gamete provider must, at the time the gametes are procured, indicate in a written consent to what use or uses the gametes may be put.[197] The gametes, and any resulting embryos, may only be used in accordance with the consents (including in accordance with those consents as varied).[198]

10.85 A gamete provider must specify the purposes to which the gametes may be put. They may not be used for treatment services unless there is an 'effective consent'[199] by that person to their being so used and they are used in accordance with the terms of the consent.[200] Nor may they be kept in storage unless there is an effective consent by that person to their storage and they are stored in accordance with the consent.[201] Nor may they be used to bring about the creation of an embryo in vitro unless there is effective consent by

---

[192] A small number of specialists, such as exists within the field of assisted procreation, is sufficient to constitute a responsible body of medical opinion. See *De Freitas v O'Brien and Connolly* [1995] 6 Med LR 108, 115 *per* Otton LJ.   [193] S 25(6)(b).
[194] S 12(c).   [195] S 17(1)(e).   [196] Under s 18(1)(c).
[197] Sch 3, para 2(1). Conditions may be specified: for example, the gametes may only be used for the consent given or only for treatment services.   [198] Sch 3, para 4.
[199] 'Effective consent' means consent which has not been withdrawn. See Sch 3, para 1.
[200] Sch 3, para 5.   [201] Sch 3, para 8(1).

that person to such a creation.[202] In this case the gamete provider must both consent to the future use and/or storage of the embryos.[203]

10.86 A consent to the use of any embryo may specify conditions subject to which the embryo may be so used.[204] Similarly, a consent to storage of gametes or embryos may specify conditions subject to which they may remain in storage.[205] But may the provider specify any conditions? Would a condition which stipulated that the gametes not be used for the treatment of individuals from a particular ethnic or religious group be valid or invalid? There can be little doubt that such a condition would be regarded as invalid[206] and a treatment centre should not accept gametes or embryos subject to such conditions. Whether such a condition would invalidate the 'effective consent' is a more contentious question. The better view is, I believe, that the invalid condition could be severed.[207] However, Kennedy and Grubb have expressed the view, using the testamentary analogy, that 'the consent would only be valid if what remained once the condition was excised still gave effect to the gametes provider's underlying intention'.[208] They say this would 'probably' be followed by a court. I would hope that the public interest in making gametes available would prevail over the selfish prejudice of the provider.

10.87 A consent to the storage of any gametes or embryos must specify the maximum period of storage, if less than the statutory storage period[209] (on which see paras 10.27–10.28 above) and state what is to done with the gametes or embryo if the person who gave the consent dies or is unable because of incapacity to vary the terms of the consent or to revoke it.[210] The 1990 Act does not state what should happen, only that the provider of gametes and embryos should address the issue.

10.88 Before a person gives consent under Schedule 3 s/he must be given a suitable opportunity to receive proper counselling about the implications of taking the proposed steps and must be provided with such relevant information as is proper.[211] Before a person gives consent s/he also must be informed of its effect.[212]

---

[202] Sch 3, para 6(1). [203] Sch 3, para 6(3). [204] Sch 3, para 2(1).
[205] Sch 3, para 2(2).
[206] See *Re Dominion Students' Hall Trust* [1947] Ch 183; *Re Lysaght* [1966] Ch 191.
[207] As happens with charitable trusts. Certainly, this should happen if, once the invalid condition is removed, the public interest in having gametes and embryos preserved could be upheld. [208] *Medical Law* (n 156 above), 796.
[209] Sch 3, para 2(2)(a). [210] Sch 3, para 2(2)(b). [211] Sch 3, para 3(1).
[212] Sch 3, para 3(2). This includes the knowledge that terms are not variable and consents cannot be withdrawn once the embryo has been used in providing treatment services or for the purposes of any project of research (see Sch 3, para 4(2)).

10.89 Consent can be varied and withdrawn[213] by notice. By implication notice must be in writing[214] though this is not specifically stated in the legislation. Nor does the Act say what notice must be given; the assumption must be that any notice will suffice. The terms of any consent to the use of any embryo cannot be varied, and the consent cannot be withdrawn once the embryo has been used in providing treatment services or for the purpose of any project of research.[215]

10.90 An embryo taken from a woman[216] must not be used for any purpose unless there is an effective consent by her to the use of the embryo for that purpose and it is used in accordance with the consent,[217] or it is used for the purpose of providing that woman with treatment services.[218] Nor must it be kept in storage unless there is an effective consent by her to this.[219]

10.91 A person's gametes must not be kept in storage unless there is an effective consent by that person to their storage and they are stored in accordance with the consent.[220] An embryo, the creation of which was brought about in vitro, must not be kept in storage unless there is effective consent by each person whose gametes were used to bring about the creation of the embryo to the storage, and the embryo is stored in accordance with those consents.[221] It follows that upon the valid withdrawal of consent by at least one gamete provider, any gametes or embryos may no longer be lawfully stored. They must then either be used in accordance with any remaining consents to their use or, if no such consent exists, must presumably be 'allowed to perish'.[222] I say, 'presumably' because the 1990 Act does not actually say what should happen in these circumstances but no other consequence is possible in terms of the general scheme of the Act.

10.92 A centre which fails to comply with these provisions would be in breach of a condition of its licence, and this could be reviewed by HFEA, and revoked. The 1990 Act is silent on whether gamete or embryo providers have any remedy in law. There would appear to be four possibilities.[223]

---

[213] Sch 3, para 4(1).
[214] The definition of 'notice' in s 46 does not require notice to be in writing but the language of s 46(2) ('delivering', 'leaving', 'sending by post') strongly suggests this.
[215] Sch 3, para 4(2). This provision seeks to overcome the problems which arise where there are disputes over frozen embryos (for example, over their 'custody', as happened in *Davis v Davis* (1992) 842 SW 2d 588). [216] By lavage.
[217] Sch 3, para 7(1), (2). [218] Sch 3, para 7(3). [219] Sch 3, para 8(3).
[220] Sch 3, para 8(1). [221] Sch 3, para 8(2).
[222] The *Code of Practice* (1995), paras 7.24–7.26 requires the procedure for disposal to be 'sensitively devised', given the special status of the human embryo.
[223] And see Kennedy and Grubb (n 156 above), 797–9.

One possible avenue of redress is by way of an application for judicial review **10.93** (and then to seek a declaration or mandamus). For this to succeed it would be necessary to show that the licence-holder was exercising a public function.[224] Although Kennedy and Grubb characterise it as a private activity[225] and, therefore, not subject to judicial review, there is a strong argument for saying that even a private clinic would be carrying out a public function. It is, after all, licensed by an institution established by the state, HFEA, and is highly regulated.

A remedy in contract is a second resource. In default of express terms, **10.94** Kennedy and Grubb argue, rightly I believe, that Schedule 3 'could be said to be implied into the contract such that a claim for breach of contract could be brought against the licence-holder'.[226] Remedies would include injunction, or specific performance as well as damages.[227] It may be more difficult to argue in contract where treatment or storage is provided under the aegis of the National Health Service; but, even here, when there is payment, it should be possible to proceed in contract.

Although section 25(6) (and see para 10.80 above) states that breach of the **10.95** *Code of Practice* does not render the person concerned liable to any proceedings, it is arguable that a breach of statutory duty, for example, the duty to allow embryos to perish, could give rise to a private right of action. The 1990 Act is silent on whether civil liability can exist for breach of the Act. Kennedy and Grubb, however, argue that the Act is so emphatic in its commitment to the wishes of gamete providers that a court might well take the view that a private right of action should arise. The provisions of Schedule 3 clearly contemplate gamete providers as the beneficiaries of the obligations imposed upon licence-holders.[228] They add that this argument 'gains force'[229] from the absence of any other remedy. However it is argued that remedies may well exist in judicial review and in contract.

Whether or not there is a property claim has not been aired in any English **10.96** case. The Tennessee decision of *Davis v Davis*[230] is no support for the gamete providers' claim to exercise a property right over their embryos where the licence-holder fails to comply with the 1990 Act.[231]

---

[224] See *R v Panel on Take-Overs and Mergers, ex p Datafin plc* [1987] QB 815.
[225] N 156 above, 798.   [226] ibid.
[227] Perhaps including for distress, given the personal nature of the contract: see eg *Hayes and Another v Dodd* [1990] 2 All ER 815.
[228] N 156 above, 799.   [229] ibid.   [230] (1992) 842 SW 2d 588 (Tenn Sup Ct).
[231] It may be otherwise with sperm or eggs (though not in the view of *Hecht v Superior Court* (1993) 20 Cal Rptr 2d 275 (California). The case of *Moore v Regents of the University of California* (1990) 793 P 2d 479 (Cal Sup Ct) may assist, but it rejected a property right in cells.

I. Access to Information

10.97 Section 31 of the 1990 Act imposes upon HFEA a statutory obligation to keep a register of information relating to:

(a) the provision of treatment services for any identifiable individual, or

(b) the keeping or use of the gametes of any identifiable individual or of an embryo taken from any identifiable woman,

or if it shows that any identifiable individual was, or may have been, born in consequence of treatment services.[232] The 1990 Act requires licence-holders to collect this information and provide it to HFEA.[233]

10.98 Who has access to the statutory information held by HFEA? Section 31(3) gives applicants over the age of 18 access to specified and limited information, or will do when regulations are made. The only information which will be vouchsafed is that which HFEA will be required by regulations to give.[234] The Warnock report recommended that the child (on reaching the age of eighteen) should have access to only 'basic information about the donor's ethnic origin and genetic health'.[235] It is unlikely that regulations when made will go further than this, though the European Court of Human Rights has held that article 8 of the European Convention on Human Rights requires that 'everyone should be able to establish details of their identity as individual human beings'.[236] By way of a striking contrast, adopted children have the legal right to discover their genetic parents.[237]

10.99 Regulations will not be able to require HFEA to give any information as to the identity of a person whose gametes have been used, or from whom an embryo has been taken, if a person to whom a licence applied was provided with the information at a time when the Authority could not have been required to give information of the kind in question.[238] A donor of gametes (or embryos) will thus always know exactly what information may be given to a resulting child eighteen years after that child is born. This means that even if, as is likely, regulations subsequently expand the amount of information made available to assisted procreation children, only children who are the products of post-regulation donations will benefit.

10.100 The *Code of Practice* requires that treatment centres should take into account,

---

[232] S 31(2).   [233] S 12(g).   [234] S 31(5).

[235] Report of the Committee of Inquiry into Human Fertilisation and Embryology (n 2 above), para 4.21.   [236] *Gaskin v United Kingdom* [1990] 1 FLR 167.

[237] Adoption Act 1976 s 51 (though it is not an absolute right: see *R v Registrar General, ex p Smith* [1991] 2 QB 393).   [238] S 31(5).

among other factors, 'a child's potential need to know about their origins'.[239] A 'potential need' is not, of course a 'right', and the epithet 'potential' in itself suggests that the need to know is only a remote contingency and not one of overwhelming importance. The way the *Code of Practice* deals with the counselling of adults who wish to become recipients of gamete donation (and see also para 6.1 above at para 10.78) also shows thin understanding of rights issues. Thus, clients are to be invited to consider 'the advantages and disadvantages of openness about the procedures'[240] and 'their perceptions of the needs of the child throughout their childhood or adolescence'.[241] There must be doubt as to whether in this respect the *Code of Practice* complies with the United Nations Convention on the Rights of the Child.[242] This provides for the recognition of the right to identity,[243] which is stipulated for the first time in any international human rights document. It also stipulates a right to know parents, though this is hedged with the qualification 'as far as possible'.[244]

10.101 The 1990 Act additionally provides that information may be made available to someone between the ages of sixteen[245] and eighteen where that person is concerned that someone whom he or she proposes to marry may be genetically related.[246] It is provided that the minor must be given a suitable opportunity to receive proper counselling about the implications of compliance with the request.[247] This provision is actually defective because only on the application of both intending marriage partners would HFEA be able to disclose whether this is a genetic relationship.[248] It is, however, worthy of note that an application by a child is only permitted before marriage, and therefore to protect against the very remote possibility of in-breeding.

10.102 The Registrar General may request information from HFEA in fulfilling his statutory functions. The Authority is bound to comply with any request made by the Registrar General by notice (presumably in writing, though the 1990 Act does not so stipulate) to disclose whether any information on the register (which the Authority is obliged by section 31 to keep) tends to show that a particular man may be the father of the child[249] and, if it does, disclose that

---

[239] Para 3.18.   [240] Para 6.10.e.   [241] Para 6.12.b. See also Para 4.4.m.
[242] See Stewart, G, 'Interpreting the Child's Right To Legal Identity in the UN Convention on the Rights of the Child', (1992) 26 Family Law Quarterly 221.   [243] Art 8.
[244] Art 9.
[245] But not to someone under 16 who may be able to marry according to his/her personal law (for an example see *Mohamed v Knott* [1969] 1 QB 1).   [246] S 31(6).
[247] S 31(6)(b).
[248] To like effect see also Morgan and Lee, *Blackstone's Guide To The Human Fertilisation and Embryology Act 1990* (n 61 above), 166.
[249] By virtue of s 28 of the 1990 Act, discussed below at paras 10.120–10.127.

information.[250] This provision applies where a claim is made before the Registrar General that a man is or is not the father of a child and it is 'necessary or desirable' for the purpose of any function of the Registrar General to determine whether the claim is or may be well-founded.[251]

10.103   A court may require HFEA to disclose information (excluding that relating to any donor)[252] where in any proceedings the question of whether a person is or is not the parent of a child by virtue of the status provisions of the 1990 Act (on which see paras 10.118–10.127 below) falls to be determined. The court cannot do this of its own motion; it requires an application by any party to the proceedings.[253] The court must not comply unless it is satisfied that the interests of justice require it to do so, taking into account any representation by any individual who may be affected by the disclosure and the welfare of the child if a minor and of any other minor who may be affected by the disclosure.[254] If the proceedings are civil proceedings, the court may direct that they (or part of them) be held in camera[255] and applications for an in camera direction must themselves be heard in camera.[256]

10.104   A court may require HFEA to disclose the identity of a donor when a child wishes to bring a claim for injury caused before birth under section 1 of the Congenital Disabilities (Civil Liability) Act 1976[257] (see further Chapter 12). The 1976 Act provides for civil liability in the case of children born disabled in consequence of the intentional act, negligence or breach of statutory duty of some person prior to the birth of the child. The Act covers children who live for at least forty-eight hours after birth. The defendant is answerable to the child if s/he was liable to one or both parents in respect of matters which gave rise to the disability at birth. Such matters could arise either before conception, during pregnancy or in the process of childbirth. The 1990 Act contemplates the situation where it is necessary to identify a person who is the genetic (but because of the Act not the legal) parent of the child. The provisions of subsections (2) to (4) of section 34 (see para 10.103 above) apply to these applications as well. The provision becomes a resource of importance where a child wishes to sue a donor for *his* or *her* negligence.[258]

10.105   The 1990 Act (in section 33(8)) inserts into the Data Protection Act 1984 a new provision[259] which exempts from the subject access provisions of the 1984 Act personal data consisting of information showing that an identifiable

---

[250] S 32(2).   [251] S 32(1).   [252] S 34(1) and s 31(2)(b).   [253] S 34(1).
[254] S 34(2).   [255] S 34(3).   [256] S 34(4).   [257] S 35(1).
[258] But note this includes s 29 which provides that donors are not to be treated as either the mother or father of the child in question.
[259] S 33(8), inserting a new s 35A into the Data Protection Act 1984.

individual was, or may have been, born in consequence of treatment services, except in so far as their disclosure is made in accordance with the provisions of section 31 of the 1990 Act (on which see paras 10.97, 10.98, 10.101 above).

10.106 The data protection access provisions apply to personal data relating to gamete donors.[260] A donor, whose gametes are stored, or used in providing treatment services, or used in creating an embryo which is stored or used, may require HFEA to furnish a copy of the information which it has directed a treatment centre to keep.[261] Also within the subject access provisions of the 1984 Act is the personal information held by virtue of the provision (in section 14(1)(d)), which requires any clinic holding a licence enabling it to store frozen gametes or embryos to hold, in respect of any person whose consent is necessary under the Act (see Schedule 3, para 10.84 above) for continued storage of those gametes or embryos, such information as HFEA may specify in directions.

10.107 It should also be noted that where records are manually stored, the 1984 Act does not apply,[262] and the provisions of the Access to Health Records Act 1990 will also not apply to HFEA because HFEA is not a 'holder' within the meaning of section 1(2) from whom information may be sought.

10.108 However, treatment centres will have to comply with the Access to Health Records Act 1990[263] (as to which see Chapter 9), though this is now[264] subject to the Access to Health Records (Control of Access) Regulations 1993[265] which, in Regulation 2 provides:

> Access shall not be given under section 3(2) of the [Access to Health Records] Act to any part of a health record which would disclose information showing that an identifiable individual was, or may have been, born in consequence of treatment services within the meaning of the Human Fertilisation and Embryology Act 1990.

10.109 The 1990 Act imposes a strict secrecy requirement for statutory information held by HFEA and by licence-holders. As regards HFEA it is provided:

(1) No person who is or has been a member or employee of the Authority shall disclose any information mentioned in subsection (2) below which he holds or has held as such a member or employee.

(2) The information referred to in subsection (1) above is—

---

[260] S 13(2)(c).   [261] By virtue of s 13(2), 22 and 23.
[262] See the Data Protection Act 1984, s 21(1).
[263] If the licence-holder is a health professional.
[264] The Data Protection Act 1984 had limitations on it as regards children born as a consequence of infertility treatment that were overlooked by the Access to Health Records Act 1990.   [265] SI 1993/746.

(a) Any information contained or required to be contained in the register kept in pursuance of section 31 of this Act, and

(b) any other information obtained by any member or employee of the Authority on terms or in circumstances requiring it to be held in confidence'.

10.110 As regards a licence-holder, section 33(5) of the 1990 Act provides:

> No person who is or has been a person to whom a licence applies and no person to whom directions have been given shall disclose any information falling within section 31(2) [as to which see para 10.97 above] of this Act which he holds or has held as such a person.

The requirements of the 1990 Act have been relaxed by amending legislation: namely, the Human Fertilisation and Embryology (Disclosure of Information) Act 1992. This permits a greater degree of disclosure by licence-holders than did the 1990 Act. The law on disclosure by HFEA remains as set out in the 1990 Act.

10.111 As regards disclosure by HFEA of *statutory information*, the following is permitted:

(a) Disclosure to a person who is a member or employee of HFEA;[266]

(b) Disclosure to a person to whom a licence applies for the purposes of his/her functions as such;[267]

(c) Disclosure of such information so that no individual to whom the information relates can be identified;[268]

(d) Disclosure in pursuance of a court order[269] or to the Registrar General in pursuance of a statutory request;[270]

(e) Disclosure in accordance with section 31[271] [on which see paras 10.98 and 10.101 above];

(f) Disclosure to patients or donors which relates exclusively to themselves;[272] where an individual is treated together with another, disclosure is permitted to both of them.[273]

10.112 As regards confidential information held by HFEA which is not 'statutory information', the 1990 Act imposes a statutory obligation of confidence.[274] But this does not apply to disclosure of information made to members or employees of HFEA acting in that capacity[275] or where disclosure is made with the consent of the person or persons whose confidence would otherwise be protected[276] or which has been lawfully made available to the public before the disclosure is made.[277]

---

[266] S 33(3)(a).   [267] S 33(3)(b).   [268] S 33(3)(c).   [269] S 33(3)(d).
[270] S 33(3)(e).   [271] S 33(3)(f).   [272] S 33(7).   [273] S 33(7)(b).
[274] S 33(2)(b).   [275] S 33(4)(a).   [276] S 33(4)(b).   [277] S 33(4)(c).

Licence-holders' duties as regards confidence are governed both by the **10.113** common law[278] and by statute (the 1990 Act section 33(6), as amended by the 1992 Act). The common law duty of confidentiality, though never in much doubt, was only authoritatively stated recently. It is discussed fully in Chapter 9.

The 1990 Act goes further than the common law in limiting disclosure. In **10.114** addition a licence-holder or nominal licensee who gives or receives any money or other benefit, not authorised by directions, in respect of the supply of gametes or embryos, is guilty of a criminal offence.[279]

Disclosure of statutory information is permitted only in circumstances listed **10.115** in section 33(6), (6A), (6B), (6C), (6D), (6E), (6F), (6G), (7), and (9). Disclosure is permitted:

(a) to a person as a member or employee of the Authority;
(b) to a person to whom a licence applies for the purposes of his functions as such;
(c) so far as it identifies a person who, but for the Act [as to which see paras h–k below] would or might be a parent of person who instituted proceedings under section 1A of the Congenital Disabilities (Civil Liability) Act 1976, but only for the purpose of defending such proceedings, or instituting connected proceedings for compensation against that parent;
(d) so that no individual to whom the information relates can be identified;
(e) in pursuance of directions given by virtue of section 24(5) or (6) of the 1990 Act;[280]
(f) 'necessarily' for any purpose preliminary to proceedings or for the purposes of, or in connection with, any proceedings.

The word 'necessarily' imports objectivity into what is otherwise a wide provision. It is insufficient that the doctor thinks it is necessary to disclose information or that s/he is acting in good faith. 'Any proceedings' is defined[281] to include 'any formal procedure for dealing with a complaint', but not any further.[282] The width of (f) is such that the preliminary proceedings do not, it seems, need to be proceedings in which doctors are involved. But disclosure which identifies a donor is not permitted, at any rate where a child was, or may have been born, as a consequence.[283] However, as Kennedy and Grubb point out, 'the latter information may be important where the

---

[278] See *X v Y* [1988] 2 All ER 648 and *W v Egdell* [1990] 1 All ER 835. [279] S 41(8).
[280] S 33(6)(e). [281] S 33(9).
[282] Though they would include any proceedings brought against a licensed doctor; a complaint against a GP (licensed to provide DI) under the National Health Service (Service Committee and Tribunal) Regulations 1992, SI 1992/664; and a complaint against an NHS hospital doctor under the complaints procedure (HC(88)37). [283] S 33(6A)(a).

medical negligence claim is based on inadequate screening of the donor(s) or testing of the donated material. Here what passed between the doctor and the donor may well be important to the doctor's defence and yet he cannot disclose any identifying information to his legal advisers.'[284] A court has the power to order disclosure of information which identifies a donor (see discussion of section 35 in para 10.104 above) but this is only for the purpose of instituting proceedings against the donor.

(g) for the purpose of establishing for the purposes of a parental rights order in a surrogacy case[285] (as to which see para 10.151 below) whether the conditions as to parentage for such an order are met;

(h) under section 3 of the Access to Health Records Act 1990[286] (and see Chapter 9);

(i) with the consent of the patient.[287]

Where a man and a woman are treated together, disclosure may be made with the consent of both,[288] or if disclosure is made for the purpose of disclosing information about the provision of treatment services for one of them, to disclosure with the consent of that individual.[289] It is provided[290] that consent to disclosure must be to a specific person, except where it is to a person who needs to know in connection with the provision of treatment services, or any other description of medical, surgical or obstetric services, for the individual giving the consent, or in connection with the carrying out of an audit of clinical practice or in connection with the auditing of accounts.[291] A patient's consent is not valid[292] unless reasonable steps have been taken to explain to the patient the implications of the disclosure.[293]

(j) in an emergency by a doctor who is 'satisfied that it is necessary to make the disclosure to avert an imminent danger to the health' of a patient and 'it is not reasonably practicable to obtain that patient's consent'.[294] If it is 'reasonably practicable' the patient's consent must be obtained. The doctor must be satisfied that disclosure is necessary (cf (f) above); there is more leeway for subjective judgment here. But danger to health must be 'imminent' and not, for example, likely at some time in the future.

---

[284] *Medical Law* (n 156 above), 814.   [285] S 33(6)(g).   [286] S 33(6)(h).
[287] S 33(6B)–(6D).   [288] S 33(6B)(b)(i).   [289] S 33(6B)(b)(ii).
[290] S 33(6C).
[291] This avoids the circuitous procedure which HFEA formerly advised, whereby a patient was to be given a sealed envelope to deliver to his/her GP; and see further, *Code of Practice* (1995), para 3.7.   [292] S 33(6D).
[293] Implications must be interpreted broadly in terms of what the person concerned would understand.   [294] S 33(6E)(a), (b).

Disclosure which is 'necessarily incidental' to disclosure under this provision is also permitted.[295]

(k) in such circumstance as may be specified in Regulations promulgated by the Secretary of State.[296]

J. The Status of Children

Until statutory intervention in 1987[297] parentage was tied by the common law to genetics; a sperm donor was the father, although in practice a combination of a common law presumption (the husband of a mother was presumed to be the father of her child) and pious perjury[298] (the child was often registered as the husband's child) meant that social fatherhood often prevailed. There was little discussion of egg or embryo donation[299] before the advent of surrogacy in the mid-1980s; in theory the genetic should have prevailed here too, though in practice it is thought the gestational mother was regarded as the mother.[300]   **10.116**

In 1987 the Family Law Reform Act[301] tackled the situation of the married couple who had a child through donor insemination. It reversed the common law rule and made the husband of a woman who was artificially inseminated the father of the child unless it was proved that he did not consent to the procedure. However this legislation did not deal with egg or embryo donation or other techniques such as GIFT. This provision has now been repealed and replaced by a more comprehensive set of provisions in the 1990 Act.   **10.117**

1. Statutory Motherhood

The 1990 Act provides[302] that a woman who is carrying or has carried a child as a result of the placing in her of an embryo or of sperm and eggs, and no other woman, is to be treated as the mother of the child. The gestational woman is thus in law the mother of any child born as a result of IVF procedures or GIFT or zygote intra-fallopian transfer (ZIFT). Where egg donation does not involve IVF, GIFT or ZIFT, that is where the egg is directly implanted in the woman for natural fertilisation, the Act does not apply and who is the mother is a question that would fall to be determined by the   **10.118**

---

[295] S 33(6F).   [296] S 33(6G).   [297] The Family Law Reform Act 1987 s 27.
[298] Pious or not, it was an offence under the Perjury Act 1911.
[299] See Freeman, MDA, 'The Unscrambling of Egg Donation', in McLean, SAM (ed) *Law Reform and Human Reproduction* (Dartmouth, 1992), 273.
[300] As in California: see *Johnson v Calvert* (1993) 851 P 2d 776 (Cal Sup Ct).
[301] In s 27.   [302] S 27(1).

common law, which, as indicated (see para 10.116) can offer no conclusive answer.

10.119 Where the mother is a surrogate, the legislation does not achieve the objective of tying legal to social motherhood[303] and the gestational mother becomes the legal mother even though she is not intended by the parties involved to be the social mother. The social mother is denied the status of parent, even in the situation where her egg, fertilised by the sperm of her husband or partner, is used. She can, if married, seek a section 30 parental order (as to which see para 10.151 below).

2. Statutory Fatherhood

(i) *The Married Mother*

10.120 The 1990 Act also provides[304] that if a married woman becomes pregnant following embryo transfer, GIFT, ZIFT, or DI, her husband is to be treated as the father of any child who results from such treatment. It has been said to be contrary to Parliament's express wish to treat such a man differently from the father of any other child when considering an application for contact.[305] The court held it would go against the principles of justice to deny rights to a man who had consented to, and participated fully with the mother in, fertility treatment merely because of an absence of a biological link between him and the child. If he can show that he did not consent to the treatment service, he is not to be treated as the father under section 28(2), although he will remain the presumed father by virtue of section 28(5), which preserves the common law presumption of paternity. In normal circumstances this would be a rebuttable presumption but it is difficult to see what scope, if any, there is for rebuttal beyond showing that he did not consent to the treatment service. Although it is not clear, it may be supposed that a husband who consented to the treatment service, but changed his mind in the nine months between treatment and birth will also be the presumed father, if he is not treated as the father under section 28(5).

10.121 It is not a requirement of treatment that a married woman should get her husband's consent; however, the *Code of Practice* does advise that this be sought as a matter of good practice,[306] and research shows that clinics are sensibly reluctant to treat without it.[307]

---

[303] Hence the need for the parental order established by s 30 and discussed in para 14.24.
[304] S 28(1) and (2). [305] *Re CH* [1996] 1 FLR 768. [306] See para 5.7.
[307] See Douglas, G, *Access To Assisted Reproduction—Legal and Other Criteria for Eligibility* (Cardiff Law School, 1992).

(ii) *The Unmarried Mother*

The 1990 Act also provides[308] that, if no man is treated as the father of the   **10.122**
child by virtue of section 28(2) (in effect because the woman is unmarried),
and an embryo is placed in the woman 'in the course of treatment services
provided for her and a man together by a person to whom a licence applies,
and the creation of the embryo carried by her was not brought about with the
sperm of that man, then . . . that man shall be treated as the father of the
child'. This is subject to the presumption in section 28(5) (discussed in para
10.120 above). There is, it has been said, 'a conundrum about what the
unmarried man must have said and/or intended and/or done before it can be
concluded that treatment services not involving the use of his own sperm
were provided for the woman and him together'.[309] This conundrum concerned Johnson J in *Re Q (Parental Order)*.[310] He needed to look at section
28(3) only in passing for it was patently applicable to the case he was
considering. But he remarked 'it seems plain to me that the subsection
envisages a situation in which the man involved himself received medical
treatment, although as presently advised I am not sure what treatment is
envisaged since the subsection refers to a man whose sperm was not used in
the procedure'.[311] The notion of the provision or receipt of treatment services
for or by a woman and a man together is found elsewhere in the 1990 Act (see
section 4(i)(b) and Schedule 3, para 5(3)), both of which Bracewell J
addressed in *Re B (Parentage)*.[312] In that case the woman's boyfriend had
under medical supervision donated sperm with which, five months later, after
the breakdown of their relationship, she was inseminated. The judge concluded that the man's gametes had been used (that is presumably at the time
of insemination for the purpose of their receiving treatment services
together). In *R v Human Fertilisation and Embryology Authority, ex p Blood*,[313]
the Court of Appeal approved the analysis of *Re B (Parentage)* by the
President of the Family Division, Sir Stephen Brown in the Family Division,
namely that the man '. . . was a willing, consenting party to the treatment
which they had commenced together when the sperm sample had been
removed and that he had not subsequently withdrawn his deemed consent.'[314]
In the *Blood* case (see para 10.75a above) the man had died and posthumous
use of sperm taken from him while in a coma was inevitably held not to be

---

[308] S 28(3).
[309] *per* Wilson J in *U v W (Attorney-General Intervening)* [1997] 2 FLR 282, 293.
[310] [1996] 1 FLR 369.   [311] ibid, 371.   [312] [1996] 2 FLR 15.
[313] [1997] 2 WLR 806.   [314] ibid, 816.

capable of constituting 'treatment . . . together'. It has been said that there is a 'mental element inherent in the notion of 'treatment' . . . together'.[315] This is not:

> whether the man consented either to be deemed in law to be the father of the prospective child or to become legally responsible for him: it is whether the relevant treatment services were provided for the woman and him together. It stretches the requisite mental element in the man too far to require either form of such consent . . . [W]hat has to be demonstrated is that, in the provision of treatment services with donor sperm, the doctor was responding to a request for that form of treatment made by the woman and the man as a couple, notwithstanding the absence in the man of any physical role in such treatment.[316]

In this case (*U v W (Attorney-General Intervening)*) it was held that treatment services had been provided for the parties together since they had attended the clinic together, received information together, and both had signed a form permitting the use of donor sperm. However, in the particular case, since the treatment services had been given at a clinic in Rome, and were therefore not licensed treatment, the implications of the sub-section did not apply, and the court was unable to give a declaration that he was the father, with the result that the woman was unable to obtain a maintenance assessment under the Child Support Act 1991.

10.123   Where a man is, by virtue of section 28(2) or (3) treated as the child's father, section 28(4) provides that no other man is to be so regarded. Also there is a provision in the 1990 Act[317] ensuring that the provisions dealing with the meaning of 'father' apply whether the woman was in the United Kingdom or elsewhere at the time of the placing within her of the embryo or the sperm and eggs or her artificial insemination.

(iii)   *The Legally Fatherless Child*

10.124   Section 28(6) is intended to protect a donor whose sperm is used with his consent to establish a pregnancy in a married woman whose husband has not consented. It also protects the donor of sperm when this is given to an unmarried woman. It provides that the donor is not to be treated as the father of the resulting child. The sperm donor accordingly is not at risk of being exposed to the responsibilities of a father. But if neither the mother's husband nor the donor is the father, who is? The answer is, it seems, no one; in law the child has no father. If the sperm is used without the donor's

---

[315]   *per* Wilson J in *U v W (Attorney-General Intervening)* [1997] 2 FLR 282, 294.
[316]   ibid, 295.   [317]   S 27(3).

consent, the donor may not be protected by section 28(6)(a), and may, as a result, be treated as the child's father without his consent. Although it is unlikely that this could happen, the possibility may arise where a man has, for example, agreed to donate sperm for research purposes, but not for treatment services, and it is accidentally used in infertility treatment.

The 1990 Act creates a further category of the legally fatherless by the way it **10.125** regulates posthumous births. Section 28(6)(b) provides that where the sperm of a man, or an embryo the creation of which was brought about with his sperm, is used after his death, he is not to be treated as the father of the child. The result of this is that a child, produced using frozen sperm left in storage by a soldier, who falls in battle after expressly consenting to his wife using it after his death, does not have a legal father, and is also illegitimate, since the marriage ended upon the soldier's death.[318] However, if the widow remarried before the child's birth, her new husband would be treated as the child's father under section 28(2) (see para 10.120 above).

(iv) *Unlicensed Services*

If an infertile couple do not use licensed treatment services (for example, if **10.126** they use DIY insemination), then, if they are married, section 28(2) applies and the husband will be deemed to be the father of the child unless it can be shown that he did not consent, which may be more difficult in a non-regulated environment. The presumption of legitimacy also applies. If, on the other hand, they are not married, the 1990 Act does not apply; section 28(3) is restricted to situations where the woman 'together' with a man *receives treatment services* under the Act. Parentage will be decided according to the common law, and the donor will be legally the father of any child born as a result of the insemination.

(v) *Post-Mortem Inseminations*

The 1990 Act does not address paternity or legitimacy in the context of post- **10.127** mortem inseminations. No presumption of legitimacy can apply because the marriage ended on death. It has been argued by Morgan and Lee[319] that a statutory provision[320] dealing with void marriages may by analogy be used as

---

[318] Even though her pregnancy is in accordance with his express consent given under Sch 3, para 2(2)(b). [319] *Blackstone's Guide* (n 61 above), 158.
[320] Legitimacy Act 1976, s 1(1) as amended by the Family Law Reform Act 1987, s 28(1).

an interpretational device. A child of a void marriage is legitimate if at the time of insemination resulting in his or her birth, or at the time of the child's conception, or at the time of the celebration of the marriage if later, both or either of the parties reasonably believed that the marriage was valid (the so-called 'putative marriage'). If, for the purposes of conception in vitro, conception takes place when the egg is fertilised, and not when the resulting embryo or zygote is replaced in the uterus, then if either of the parties believed the marriage was valid, a child born years later from a frozen embryo, even after the man's death, would be legitimate. But whether this argument can be successfully invoked is dubious; it would seem to place such a child in a better position than one whose parents were married. The courts, it may be supposed, might wish to resist such a conclusion.

K. Surrogacy

10.128   Surrogacy, as defined in the Warnock report, is 'the practice whereby one woman carries a child for another with the intention that the child should be handed over after birth'.[321] It can take a number of forms: the commissioning mother may be the genetic mother, in that she provides the egg, or she may make no contribution to the establishment of the pregnancy. She may simply lease her womb. The genetic father may be the husband of the commissioning mother, or of the gestational mother, or he may be a donor. Surrogacy may involve payment and this may vary from reimbursement of expenses to a substantial fee. There is also so-called altruistic surrogacy, as, for example, where one sister carries the pregnancy for another.

10.129   The practice of surrogacy has proved very controversial.[322] Warnock even went so far as to describe surrogacy, for convenience—a most uncommon practice anyway but the one nevertheless the committee chose initially to focus on—as 'totally ethically unacceptable'.[323] Even where there were 'compelling medical circumstances', the report castigates the practice of surrogacy using Kantian language: 'That people should treat others as a means to their own ends, however desirable the consequences, must always be liable to moral objection'.[324] Although the committee was more concerned with the commercial exploitation of surrogacy, it recommended the criminalisation of

---

[321] N 2 above, para 8.1.
[322] See Freeman, M, 'Is Surrogacy Exploitative?' in McLean, SAM (ed) *Legal Issues In Human Reproduction* (Gower, 1989), 164. More generally see Field, MA, *Surrogate Motherhood* (Harvard University Press, 1988).   [323] N 2 above, para 8.17.
[324] ibid.

surrogacy agencies, both profit-making, and non-profit making organisa-tions.[325] It also recommended that it be provided by statute that all surrogacy agreements are illegal contracts and unenforceable in the courts.[326] Legisla-tion was passed within a year of the Warnock inquiry's report but this speed of response is attributable to the first major surrogacy case in the United Kingdom, the so-called 'Baby Cotton' case.[327] The Surrogacy Arrangement Act 1985 (hereafter the 1985 Act) did not go as far as Warnock recom-mended; it distinguished the practice of commercial agencies from those which are non-profit making, and it said nothing about the status of the surrogacy contract. The latter issue was picked up, after the 1987 White Paper had addressed the issue,[328] in the 1990 Act.

1. Surrogacy Agreements

The status of surrogacy agreements can be examined from the perspectives of both the criminal law and the civil law. **10.130**

(i) *The Criminal Law*

As far as the criminal law is concerned, there are a number of ways in which surrogacy may be thought to be sanctioned. Most obviously, an offence may be committed under section 57 of the Adoption Act 1976 if the commission-ing couple intend to adopt the child once born. This provides that: **10.131**

> it shall not be lawful to make or give to any person any payment or reward for or in consideration of (a) the adoption by that person of a child; (b) the grant by that person of any agreement or consent required in connection with the adoption of a child; (c) the handing over of a child by that person with a view to the adoption of the child; or (d) the making by that person of any arrangements for the adoption of a child.

However, in *Re An Adoption Application (Payment for Adoption)*,[329] Latey J put a somewhat liberal construction on this statutory provision. He held that whether there is 'any payment or reward' 'for adoption' is a 'question of fact to be decided on the evidence'.[330] He could see 'nothing commercial in what happened',[331] although the couples admitted sums of £10,000 and £5,000 had changed hands. In his view, it 'was only after the payments had been

---

[325] ibid, para 8.18.   [326] N 2 above, para 8.19.
[327] *Re C (A Minor)* [1985] FLR 846.
[328] *Human Fertilisation and Embryology: A Framework for Legislation* (Cd 259, 1987), paras 66–75.   [329] [1987] Fam 81.
[330] ibid, 86.   [331] ibid, 84.

made and the baby was born that any of them began to turn their minds in any real sense to adoption and the legalities'.[332] 'Legalities' may be a Freudian slip on his Lordship's part; he clearly meant 'illegalities'. He seems to have been influenced by the absence of a written contract and the fact that lawyers were not consulted until after the baby was born. The arrangement was one of 'trust which was fully honoured on both sides'.[333]

10.132 Even if there is a payment or reward, section 57(3) of the Adoption Act 1976 provides: 'This section does not apply . . . to any payment or reward authorised by the court to which an application for an adoption order in respect of a child is made'. And in *Re An Adoption Application (Payment for Adoption)*, Latey J held that 'authorised by the court' covered not only authorization in advance of making a payment but could also cover retrospective authorization. Otherwise, he held, it would mean, that:

> any payment, however modest and however innocently made, would bar an adoption and do so however much the welfare of the child cried aloud for adoption . . . and that, be it said, within the framework of legislation whose first concern is promoting the welfare of the children concerned.[334]

He did not believe Parliament intended to produce such a result; it 'produced a balance by setting its face against trafficking in children . . . but recognising that there may be transactions which are venial and should not prohibit adoption'.[335] Accordingly an adoption order was made. Whether Latey J was right to construe 'authorization' to include subsequent ratification by a court may be doubted.[336]

10.133 It is not unlawful under the Adoption Act 1976 for a surrogate mother to receive a payment for handing over her child to another nor is there a crime of 'baby selling'.

10.134 The criminal law might also be invoked if the agreement were thought to constitute a conspiracy to corrupt public morals or outrage public decency.[337] Although a body of opinion would support this,[338] it seems unlikely that such a prosecution would be brought. No English case has addressed this question and there has been ample opportunity for the Director of Public Prosecutions to initiate a prosecution should s/he have wished to do so.

---

[332] ibid, 86.   [333] ibid, 84.   [334] ibid, 87.   [335] ibid.   [336] ibid.
[337] On which see *Shaw v Director of Public Prosecutions* [1962] AC 220, and *Knuller v Director of Public Prosecutions* [1973] AC 435.
[338] Best represented by Lord Devlin, though he did not write on surrogacy as such. See *The Enforcement of Morals* (Clarendon Press, 1965).

(ii) *The Civil Law*

From the perspective of the civil law it is now clear that a surrogacy arrange- **10.135** ment is unenforceable. The 1990 Act inserted a new section 1A into the 1985 Act: 'No surrogacy arrangement is enforceable by or against any of the persons making it'.

(iii) *Public Policy*

Is the agreement also void on grounds of public policy? In *Re P (Minors)* **10.136** *(Wardship: Surrogacy)*, Sir John Arnold P said obiter that there was a view that an element of the surrogacy agreement was 'repellent to proper ideas about the procreation of children, so as to make any such agreement one which should be rejected by law as being contrary to public policy'.[339] In *A v C*, Comyn J held that an agreement made between a prostitute and a man that she would bear his child and hand it over to him was contrary to public policy as 'a purported contract for the sale and purchase of a child'.[340] In the Court of Appeal, in the same case, Ormrod LJ described the arrangement as 'most extraordinary and irresponsible, bizarre and unnatural' and as a 'sordid commercial bargain';[341] Cumming-Bruce LJ characterised the arrangement as 'a kind of baby-farming operation of a wholly distasteful and lamentable kind'.[342] Thus there can be little doubt that the courts regard surrogacy arrangements as contrary to public policy.

This question remains of importance despite the insertion of the new provi- **10.137** sion in the 1985 Act (see para 10.135 above). The new provision applies to 'surrogacy arrangements' as defined in the 1985 Act.[343] These do not include agreements reached after the child is conceived and which are intended to result in the child being handed over by the surrogate mother. Such arrange- ments would remain governed by the common law and, on the basis of the case law considered in paragraph 10.136, would be held to be both contrary to public policy and unenforceable.[344]

---

[339] [1987] 2 FLR 421, 425.   [340] [1985] FLR 445, 449 (decided in 1978).
[341] ibid, 455, 457.   [342] ibid, 459.   [343] S 1(2)(a) of the 1985 Act.
[344] See n 313–16.

(iv) *Activities Connected with Surrogacy*

10.138 English law does not prohibit surrogacy arrangements although the 1985 Act prohibits a number of activities in connection with surrogacy. Where IVF or DI techniques are used to achieve pregnancy (and the latter does not employ DIY), the activities will be licensed activities under the 1990 Act[345] and, as such, HFEA may regulate the use of the techniques to achieve a surrogate pregnancy. Its *Code of Practice* (1995) provides:

> The application of assisted conception techniques to initiate a surrogate pregnancy should only be considered where it is physically impossible or highly undesirable for medical reasons for the commissioning mother to carry the child.[346]

Clearly, to assist a surrogacy for convenience (see para 10.129 above) would be contrary to the Code. A licence-holder may have his/her licence withdrawn or varied if s/he assists a surrogate pregnancy for other than compelling medical reasons.[347]

10.139 Attention should also be drawn to the British Medical Association's *Changing Conceptions of Motherhood* (1996) which contains guidelines for practitioners. The attitude taken to surrogacy is more relaxed than in its previous report of 1990. No longer are doctors to exercise 'extreme caution' before helping to achieve a surrogate pregnancy but it is still stressed that they should do so only as 'a last resort'. Surrogacy is now described as 'an acceptable option of last resort in cases where it is impossible or highly undesirable for medical reasons for the intended mother to carry a child herself'.[348] The report stresses that the interests of the potential child must be paramount, and the risks to the surrogate mother must be kept to a minimum.

2. Surrogacy Agencies

(i) *Statutory Provisions*

10.140 The 1985 Act, as amended by the 1990 Act,[349] seeks to outlaw commercial surrogacy agencies. It provides[350] that:

---

[345] S 2(1) of the 1990 Act. [346] Para 3.20.
[347] This follows from the *Code of Practice* [1995], para 3.20. See, for agreement, Kennedy and Grubb (n 156 above), 846.
[348] *The Changing Conceptions of Motherhood—The Practice of Surrogacy in Britain* (BMA, 1996), 59. [349] S 36(2).
[350] S 2(1).

No person shall on a commercial basis do any of the following acts in the United Kingdom, that is—
  (a) initiate or take part in any negotiations with a view to the making of a surrogacy arrangement,
  (b) offer or agree to negotiate the making of a surrogacy arrangement, or
  (c) compile any information with a view to its use in making, or negotiating the making of, surrogacy arrangements,

and no person shall in the United Kingdom knowingly cause another to do any of those acts on a commercial basis.

An act is done on a 'commercial basis' if 'any payment is at any time received by himself or another in respect of it' or 'he does it with a view to any payment being received by himself or another in respect of making, or negotiating or facilitating the making of, any surrogacy arrangement'.[351] Contravention of these prohibitions is a criminal offence.[352] However, a person is not to be treated as doing an act on a commercial basis by reason of having received a payment if it is proved that he did not do the act knowing or having reasonable cause to suspect that any payment had been received in respect of the act or, where payment was received after he did the act, that he did not do the act with a view to payment being received.[353]

(ii) *Statutory Definitions*

10.141 For this purpose 'payment' does not include payment 'to or for the benefit of a surrogate mother or prospective surrogate mother',[354] and both she and the commissioning couple are specifically excluded from the provisions of the legislation under section 2(2).

10.142 It has been seen (para 10.140 above) that the provision outlawing the negotiation etc of surrogacy arrangements is broadly defined. But there have been no reported prosecutions and there was reluctance, it seems, on the part of the Director of Public Prosecutions to get involved in a case where the payment was for the writing of a pregnancy diary.[355]

10.143 'Surrogate mother' and 'surrogate arrangement' are also broadly defined.[356] 'Surrogate mother' means 'a woman who carries a child in pursuance of an arrangement made before she began to carry the child' with a view to the child being handed over and parental responsibility being met by another person or persons; it therefore does not cover an arrangement reached after

---

[351] S 2(3).   [352] S 2(2).   [353] S 2(4).   [354] S 2(3).
[355] As reported in the *Daily Telegraph*, 15 May 1986.
[356] S 1(2) and s 1(3)–(6) respectively.

'conception'. The 1990 Act[357] has extended the meaning of this (and therefore of a surrogacy arrangement) to include not just insemination and embryo transfer but also 'the placing in [the woman] . . . of an egg in the process of fertilisation or of sperm and eggs . . . that results in her carrying the child'.

10.144 In determining whether an arrangement is made with a view to the child being handed over to, and parental responsibility being met by, another person or persons:

> regard may be had to the circumstances as a whole (and, in particular, where there is a promise or understanding that any payment will or may be made to the woman or for her benefit in respect of the carrying of any child in pursuance of the arrangement, to that promise or understanding).[358]

An arrangement may be regarded as made with such a view although there are conditions relating to the handing over of the child.[359] 'Payment' is defined to include 'money's worth'.[360]

(iii) *Advertising*

10.145 It is a criminal offence to publish an advertisement seeking a surrogate mother or offering to act as a surrogate mother in a newspaper or periodical.[361] The offence is committed by the proprietor, editor or publisher.[362] An offence is also committed by a person who conveys an advertisement through radio or television[363] or through the internet or otherwise (for example, a shopkeeper who places a notice in his or her window would commit an offence).[364] Whether the potential surrogate mother and the commissioning couple also commit offences is far from clear. It could be argued that they 'cause' an advertisement to be 'conveyed' or 'published' or 'distributed' by placing the advertisement with the publisher.[365]

3. Parenthood

10.146 Where a child is born as a result of a surrogacy arrangement, who are his/her parents? Legally the child's mother will always be the surrogate; the woman of the commissioning couple is not the mother even if her eggs were used.[366]

---

[357] By substituting in s 1(6) for 'or, as the case may be, embryo insertion', 'or of the placing in her of an embryo, of an egg in the process of fertilisation or of sperm and eggs, as the case may be' (see 1990 Act, s 36(2)).   [358] S 1(4).
[359] S 1(5).   [360] S 1(8).   [361] S 3(4).   [362] S 3(2).   [363] S 3(3).
[364] S 3(5).   [365] S 3(4) (and see Kennedy and Grubb (n 156 above), 849).
[366] S 27(1), discussed at para 10.118, above.

Where the surrogate is married, her husband is the father unless he can prove that he did not consent to the procedure and the man of the commissioning couple is not the father even if his sperm is used for DI or IVF.[367] Where the surrogate is unmarried, the commissioning man will be the father if his sperm is used in DIY insemination or the child is conceived as a result of sexual intercourse. This is the common law position and it is not affected by the 1990 Act. If there is medical intervention, section 28 of the 1990 Act (on which see para 10.120 above) will alter the position if the surrogate and the commissioning man are being treated 'together'.[368] Everything hinges on what 'together' means. Interpreted literally it will not be difficult to find that 'togetherness' is satisfied. But if 'together' is construed more purposefully and contextually, doubts arise. The purpose of fertility treatment is to produce families; 'together' suggests that the man and woman being treated together will bring up the child produced as a result of the treatment as a couple. Nor can the history and context of the 1990 Act be ignored; these suggest that the legislature envisages treatment services for conventional two-parent families. Section 13(5) (discussed in para 10.55 above) should not be overlooked in interpreting the meaning of 'together'. The better view is that the surrogate and the commissioning man are not being treated 'together'. The consequence of this is that the provision of treatment must be licensed because the commissioning man's gametes will constitute donated material. As a donor his consent to the use of his sperm is then required[369] and when it is used with his consent 'he is not to be treated as the father of the child'.[370] The resulting child will have no legal father.[371]

4. Parental Orders

In most cases after the birth of the child, s/he will be handed over by the surrogate mother to the commissioning couple. A number of legal avenues are then open to them.[372]   **10.147**

(i) *Adoption*

For full details in relation to this standard books on child law should be consulted. In short, much depends on whether or not the surrogate is   **10.148**

---

[367] S 28(2), (3) and (4).   [368] S 4(1)(b).   [369] Sch 3, para 5.
[370] S 28(6)(a).   [371] See para 10.124, above.
[372] To cement the relationship. Only adoption will imitate nature and confer total parental status. A s 30 order, however, comes sufficiently close to this to make little difference. With wardship only care and control is conferred.

married, whether or not assisted procreation was used and, if she is married, whether or not her husband consented to her becoming a surrogate.

10.149 Where the surrogate is unmarried, or the pregnancy was achieved after sexual intercourse or by DIY, or she is married and her husband did not consent to the assisted procreation procedure, the commissioning father is the 'putative father' and as such a 'relative'.[373] An adoption order can be made, provided the child is at least nineteen weeks old and has at all times during the preceding thirteen weeks lived with the commissioning parents. A single applicant can adopt,[374] so that a single commissioning father is not barred from applying, though whether an adoption order would be made is more doubtful.[375] A joint adoption order can only be made in favour of a married couple; a cohabiting couple cannot adopt together.[376] It follows that two homosexual men who commission a child through a surrogate cannot both become the legal parents of any child that results. It is possible to make an adoption order in favour of one person together with a joint residence order in favour of two unmarried persons[377] but again it is unlikely that a court would countenance this.

10.150 Where the surrogate is married and the child results from assisted procreation procedures *with* the husband's consent, the surrogate's husband rather than the commissioning father would be the legal father. As a result, before an adoption order will be made, the child will have to have lived with the commissioning parents for at least twelve months.[378] Unless the child has been placed by an adoption agency (and it is difficult to envisage circumstances where this could have occurred), an offence is committed; independent placements for adoption, other than by relatives, are not allowed,[379] unless sanctioned by an order of the High Court (although this can be done retrospectively).[380] The commissioning parents will have to notify the local authority which will report to the court on their suitability as parents. It will

---

[373] See the Adoption Act 1976, s 72(1).

[374] See the Adoption Act 1976, s 15. And see *Re W (Adoption: Homosexual Adopter)* [1997] 2 FLR 406: s 15 should not be construed narrowly.

[375] No proposals for change are made by the *Review of Adoption Law: Report To Ministers of an Inter-Departmental Working Group* (1992). See paras 26.13 and 26.14.

[376] See the Adoption Act 1976, ss 14, 15. The possibility exists of an adoption order in favour of one and a joint residence order: see *Re AB (Adoption: Joint Residence)* [1996] 1 FLR 27. An adoption order may be made in favour of a separated couple jointly: see *Re WM (Adoption: Non-Patrial)* [1997] 1 FLR 132.

[377] See *Re AB (Adoption: Joint Residence)* [1996] 1 FLR 27.

[378] See the Adoption Act 1976, s 13(1) and (2).   [379] See the Adoption Act 1976, s 11(1).

[380] See *Re Adoption Application (Non-Patrial: Breach of Procedures)* [1993] 1 FLR 947, 955 *per* Douglas Brown J. Followed by the Court of Appeal in *Re G (Adoption: Illegal Placement)* [1995] 1 FLR 403.

also have to tell the court that the ban on private placements has been broken. A reporting officer will be appointed to ensure that the necessary agreements have been given (for example, the surrogate's husband's agreement is required[381]). In adoption cases generally, a guardian ad litem must also be appointed to safeguard the child's interests,[382] where the child's welfare is thought to require this. Where surrogacy is involved it is thought that a guardian ad litem will almost certainly be appointed.

(ii) *The Section 30 Parental Order*

The 1990 Act introduced an alternative to adoption. The commissioning **10.151** parents may seek a parental order.[383] Before a court may make this order (which provides for the child to be treated in law as the child of the commissioning parents)[384] a number of conditions must be satisfied:

(i) the child must have been born to a surrogate as a result of assisted procreative techniques;[385]

(The s 30 procedure is not applicable where DIY has been used or the commissioning father has had sexual intercourse with the surrogate)

(ii) the gametes of the husband or the wife, or both, were used to bring about the creation of the embryo;[386]

(iii) the applicants must be husband and wife;[387]

(the Act is silent on polygamy but it would be consonant with current trends[388] to regard them as husband and wife even if the marriage was polygamous or potentially so)

(iv) the applicants must apply within six months of the birth of the child;[389]

(v) the child must have his or her home with the applicants both at the time of the application and at the time of the order;[390]

(vi) at least one of the applicants must be domiciled in a part of the United Kingdom or in the Channel Islands or the Isle of Man;[391]

(vii) both husband and wife must be at least eighteen years old;[392]

(viii) the court must be satisfied that the child's father, where he is not the husband, and the surrogate mother freely agree to the making of the order. When an unmarried woman, acting as a surrogate for a married couple, carried and gave birth to a child created from the egg of the

---

[381] If, as is likely, he is the legal father.   [382] See the Adoption Act 1976, s 65.
[383] Under s 30.   [384] S 30(1).   [385] S 30(1)(a).   [386] S 30(1)(b).
[387] S 30(1).
[388] See Poulter, S, *English Law and Ethnic Minority Customs* (Butterworths, 1986), ch 3.
[389] S 30(2).   [390] S 30(3)(a).   [391] S 30(3)(b).   [392] S 30(4).

wife fertilised by sperm donated at a clinic under a licenced arrangement rather than the sperm of the husband, it seems that there is no man who is to be treated as the father and whose consent is therefore required to the making of the parental order.[393] The agreement must be unconditional and with full understanding of what is involved.[394] No agreement is required of a person who cannot be found or is incapable of giving agreement.[395] The surrogate is not allowed to agree until six weeks have elapsed since the child's birth;[396]

(ix) the court must be satisfied that no money or other benefit (other than for expenses reasonably incurred) has been given or received by the husband or the wife for or in consideration of the making of the parental order, any agreement required, the handing over of the child to the applicants or the making of any arrangements with a view to the making of the order. The court can, however, authorise payments.[397]

10.152 This new procedure will be helpful where all the parties are agreed. Where they are not, the requirement that the child's home must be with the applicants at the time of the application may be difficult to fulfil. The requirement that the applicants must be a couple and married to each other may also prove a stumbling block to some commissioning parents. A single applicant can adopt but not obtain a section 30 order. The requirement that there must be a genetic link (at least one of the commissioning parents must be a genetic parent of the child) means that it is not possible for a couple to commission another couple to produce an embryo for them and have a surrogate carry this to term, and then use the section 30 procedure.

10.153 An application for a parental order is not governed by the paramountcy principle.[398] Nor is the child's welfare even a 'first consideration', as it is in adoption legislation.[399] Further, the court is not constrained to desist from making orders unless doing so would be better for the child.[400] The welfare checklist in the Children Act 1989 is also irrelevant.[401]

10.154 The Parental Orders (Human Fertilisation and Embryology) Regulations 1994[402] apply many of the provisions of the Adoption Act 1976 to section 30 applications and orders. Thus, applications are heard in private,[403] a

[393] *Re Q (Parental Order)* [1996] 1 FLR 369.   [394] S 30(5).   [395] S 30(6).
[396] S 30(6).   [397] S 30(7).   [398] In the Children Act 1989, s 1(1).
[399] See the Adoption Act 1976, s 6.
[400] See the minimal intervention principle in the Children Act 1989, s 1(5).
[401] Children Act 1989, s 1(3).   [402] SI 1994/2767.
[403] Reg 2, Sch 1, applying the Adoption Act 1976, s 64(b), to applications for parental orders.

guardian ad litem is appointed for the child[404] and the court has a duty to safeguard and promote the welfare of the child.[405]

Children cannot be parties to these proceedings. One result of this is that **10.155** guardians ad litem are not able to instruct solicitors for the children whose interests they represent.[406]

(iii) *Children Act 1989*

Proceedings under section 30 are 'family proceedings' within the meaning of **10.156** the Children Act 1989.[407] This means that the powers available under that Act are also available on an application for a parental order, including the power to make section 8 orders.[408] The court could grant the applicants a residence order instead of a parental order; the former would confer parental responsibility on them,[409] whilst not removing it from the parents (in most cases the surrogate and her husband); under the latter, the child would be treated in law as the child of the applicants (from their viewpoint clearly the more desirable option). The court could also make a contact order[410] in favour of the surrogate in addition to the section 30 order, and could attempt to regulate disputes by making a specific issue order[411] (perhaps relating to the religion in which the child is to be brought up) or a prohibited steps order[412] (for example, relating to the removal of the child from this country).

(iv) *Wardship*[413]

In effect this is the only way in which a dispute between the surrogate and the **10.157** commissioning parents as to who should bring up the child can be resolved. If the surrogate mother refuses to hand over the child, the commissioning parent or parents may invoke the inherent jurisdiction of the High Court

---

[404] See the Family Proceedings (Children Act 1989) (Amendment Rules) 1994, SI 1994/2166 and Family Proceedings (Amendment) (No 2) Rules 1994, SI 1994/2165. See generally Timms, J E, *Children's Representation: A Practitioner's Guide* (Sweet and Maxwell, 1995), ch 8, particularly 295–304.

[405] Reg 2, Sch 1, applying the Adoption Act 1976, s 6, to applications for parental orders.

[406] 'The Guardian is, therefore, acting without the benefit of legal advice for the child, in an extraordinarily complicated and sensitive area', Timms, *Children's Representation*, n 387 above, 305. [407] Children Act 1989, s 8(3), (4).

[408] That is to make residence orders, contact orders, specific issue orders and prohibited steps orders. [409] Children Act 1989, s 12(2).

[410] Children Act 1989, s 8. [411] ibid. [412] ibid.

[413] As to which see Lowe, N and White, R, *Wards of Court*, 2nd edn (Barry Rose, 1986).

as *parens patriae* to decide matters relating to the child's welfare. In *Re P (minors) (wardship: surrogacy)*, Sir John Arnold P said:

> The court's duty is to decide the case, taking into account as the first and paramount consideration [now the paramount consideration], the welfare of the child or children concerned and if that consideration leads the court to override any agreement that there may be in the matter, then that court is fully entitled to do.[414]

In this case 'preserving the link with the [surrogate] mother to whom they [there were twins in this case] are bonded and who has . . . exercised over them a satisfactory level of maternal care'[415] tipped the balance in favour of the surrogate and against the commissioning parents.

10.158 It would be possible for a court to grant commissioning parents contact with the child whilst leaving him/her with the surrogate mother. In the notorious *Baby M* case[416] in New Jersey, the commissioning parents were awarded custody but the Supreme Court of New Jersey decided that the surrogate mother should have 'visitation'.[417] The issue has only been considered in one English case (*A v C*), where the Court of Appeal firmly rejected it. To Ormrod LJ it would lead to 'the whole of this sordid story . . . be[ing] revived weekly or monthly . . . The mother's position will be handicapped, and the handicapping of her position handicaps the child'.[418] Although the facts were different from most surrogacy cases (the 'contract' resulted from a casual encounter with a prostitute), courts are unlikely today to make a 'contact order' in favour of commissioning parents if they decide that the child should continue to reside with the surrogate mother. Nor are they likely to follow the precedent of *Baby M* and award contact to a surrogate mother.

---

[414] [1987] 2 FLR 421, 425.   [415] ibid, 427.
[416] (1988) 537 A 2d 1227 (NJ Sup Ct).   [417] 'Contact' in English terminology.
[418] [1985] FLR 445, 458.

11

ABORTION

A. Abortion and the General Law

Abortion is the termination of a pregnancy by surgical or medical means **11.01** intended to result in the death of a foetus.[1] As with other medical procedures the general requirements of medical law apply, in particular, the law of consent and negligence.[2] Consequently, either the patient[3] or another must validly consent to the abortion or, in the case of an incompetent adult, it must be lawful to carry out the termination notwithstanding the fact that the patient is

---

[1] It is arguable that Parliament also intended 'late terminations of pregnancy' to be dealt with as 'abortions', where only the pregnancy, but not the child, is unwanted. Hence some intended live births are brought within the Act: see Kennedy, I and Grubb, A, *Medical Law*, 2nd edn (Butterworths, 1994), 923–4 and Scowen, E and Grubb, A, 'Is Induction of Labour Unlawful?' (1991) 1(3) Dispatches 4.

[2] See Chapter 4 (consent), Chapters 5–7 (negligence) and Chapter 11 (pre-natal actions).

[3] For the requirements of consent, see Ch 3.

unable to consent.[4] Consequently, a competent patient, whether child[5] or adult, must consent to the procedure.[6] In the case of an incompetent child the consent of the parents[7] or the court[8] must be obtained acting in the child's best interests.[9] And, if the patient is an incompetent adult, an abortion may only be performed if the principle of necessity permits it in the best interests of the patient.[10] Except in the case of a child who is already a ward of court,[11] there is no requirement to seek the court's consent or a declaration of the procedure's legality.[12]

B. Statutory Regulation of Abortion

1. The Abortion Act 1967

11.02 In addition to the general law, however, the Abortion Act 1967 regulates the availability and delivery of terminations of pregnancy in England, Scotland, and Wales.[13] Unusually, the availability of abortion, unlike other medical procedures, is not left to agreement between the doctor and patient.[14] An abortion or termination of pregnancy must, to be lawful, be covered by the provisions of the 1967 Act. The Abortion Act 1967 operates by creating a defence to what would otherwise amount to the criminal offence of 'procuring a miscarriage' under section 58 of the Offences Against the Person Act ('OAPA') 1861[15] or, if

---

[4] *Re F (A Mental Patient: Sterilisation)* [1990] 2 AC 1.
[5] Under the Family Law Reform Act 1969, s 8 (aged 16–18) or the common law if *Gillick*-competent (under 16). See discussion, Ch 4, paras 4.51 *et seq*.
[6] It appears that the court may, in some circumstances, consent even if a competent child *refuses* to consent: *Re W (A Minor) (Medical Treatment)* [1992] 4 All ER 627 (CA); but probably the parents cannot override the refusal; ibid *per* Nolan LJ at 648–9. For discussion, see ch 4, above.
[7] A parent or other with 'parental responsibility' under the Children Act 1989. It is impossible to imagine circumstances where the 'carer' provision in the Children Act 1989, s 3(5), could be applied to abortion.
[8] Under its inherent jurisdiction (requiring leave under the Children Act 1989, s 100), under the Children Act 1989, s 8, or, unusually under the wardship jurisdiction if the child is already a ward of court.
[9] See e g, *Re P (A Minor)* [1986] 1 FLR 272; *Re B (Wardship: Abortion)* [1991] 2 FLR 426. See discussion, paras 4.75 *et seq*.
[10] eg, *Re SG (Adult Mental Patient: Abortion)* [1991] 2 FLR 329 and *Re AMHN* (1994) 2 Med L Rev 374. [11] *Re G-U (A Minor) (Wardship)* [1984] FLR 811.
[12] *Re SG (Adult Mental Patient: Abortion)* [1991] 2 FLR 329.
[13] The Act does not apply to Northern Ireland where the common law still applies: see *Northern Health & Social Services Board v F and G* [1993] NI 268 (Sheil J) and Grubb, (1994) 2 Med L Rev 371 (Commentary); *Re AMNH* (1994) 2 Med L Rev 374 (MacDermott LJ); *Re SJB (A Minor)* (Pringle J) 28 Sept 1995, and *Re CH (A Minor)* (Sheil J) 18 Oct 1995.
[14] Another important instance of Parliamentary intervention is in the area of assisted reproduction through the Human Fertilisation and Embryology Act 1990. See Ch 10.
[15] In Scotland, it is a common law crime. For the position in Scotland, see Norrie, K, 'Abortion in Great Britain: One Act, Two Laws' [1985] Crim LR 475, especially 481–6.

the foetus is 'capable of being born alive', of the offence of 'child destruction' contrary to the Infant Life (Preservation) Act 1929.[16]

11.03 The Abortion Act 1967 regulates the availability of abortion in a number of ways. First, it sets out four grounds, one of which must exist, for an abortion to be lawful.[17] Secondly, the Act lays down the time-limits within which an abortion may be carried out.[18] Thirdly, it stipulates who may carry out abortions[19] and where they may be performed, providing in the latter case for a system of licensing for private clinics.[20] Finally, it provides for regulatory matters such as reporting, certification, and confidentiality.[21]

2. Background to the 1967 Act

(i) *Section 58 OAPA 1861 and* Bourne

11.04 The present legislation dates back to 1967 and began life as a Private Member's Bill sponsored by David Steel MP. It came into force on 27 October 1967. It replaced the common law as stated in *Bourne*.[22] In *R v Bourne*[22a] it was held that an abortion would not be 'unlawful' under section 58 of the OAPA 1861 if it was 'done in good faith for the purpose only of preserving the [life of the mother]'. Macnaghten J adopted an expansive interpretation of this phrase to include cases where the probable consequence of the continuance of the pregnancy would be to make the woman a physical wreck. Subsequent case law made it quite clear that a doctor could perform an abortion to preserve the mental or physical health as well as the life of the mother.[23]

(ii) *The Infant Life (Preservation) Act 1929*

11.05 However, until 1991, the Abortion Act 1967 had to be read subject to the effect of the Infant Life (Preservation) Act 1929. Compliance with the 1967 Act did not provide a defence to the crime of 'child destruction' created by the

---

[16] Abortion ('procuring a miscarriage') has been a statutory offence since 1803. Whether there was a crime of abortion at common law is uncertain, though the better view is that there probably was. For discussions of the common law and the legislation between 1803 and 1861, see Keown, J, *Abortion, Doctors and the Law* (1988) and Grubb, A, 'Abortion Law in England: The Medicalisation of a Crime' (1990) 18 Law, Medicine and Health Care 146.   [17] S 1(1).
[18] Ss 1(1)(a) and 5(1).   [19] S 1(1): only 'registered medical practitioners'.
[20] S 1(3) and (3A). Notice the emergency exception in s 1(4).
[21] S 2 and The Abortion Regulations 1991, SI 1991/499.   [22] S 6.
[22a] [1939] 1 KB 687.
[23] *R v Bergmann* [1948] 1 BMJ 1008 (Morris J) and *R v Newton and Stungo* [1958] Crim LR 469 (Ashworth J). For a recent discussion in an Australian context, see *CES v Superclinics (Australia) Pty Ltd* (1995) 38 NSWLR 47 (NSW CA) and Grubb, A (1996) 4 Med L Rev 102, 107–9 (Commentary).   [24] S 5(1) as originally enacted.

1929 Act.[24] In fact, the Infant Life (Preservation) Act 1929 was enacted to close a loophole in the law where a child was killed in the course of being born; which was neither an offence under section 58—it could not be said to be procuring a 'miscarriage'—nor murder or manslaughter because the child would not yet have 'an existence independent of its mother'. However, section 1(1) of the 1929 Act is broader in its scope. It provides that 'any person who, with intent to destroy the life of a child capable of being born alive, by any wilful act causes a child to die before it has an existence independent of its mother' shall be guilty of an offence. Aborting a foetus 'capable of being born alive' could amount to the offence under the 1929 Act.

11.06 As a result, the 1929 Act had the practical effect until 1991 of setting the upper time-limit for an abortion when the foetus was 'capable of being born alive'. The meaning of this statutory phrase is not, however, clear and unambiguous.[25] The Act itself gives one indicator: section 1(2) creates a presumption that a 28-week old foetus is 'capable of being born alive'. That, however, is no more than a presumption and the courts have interpreted the Act as applying to less mature foetuses. In *C v S*[26] the Court of Appeal rejected the argument that the 1929 Act prevented the destruction of any foetus which showed 'recognisable signs of life'. The court concluded that the 1929 Act required that the foetus should have the capacity to survive and, hence, did not apply to a foetus of 18- to 21-weeks gestation which could not because its lungs were insufficiently developed.

11.07 In *Rance v Mid-Downs HA*[26a] Brooke J held that a 26-week old foetus was 'capable of being born alive' within the terms of the 1929 Act because ' . . . after birth, it exists as a live child, that is to say breathing and living by reason of its breathing through its own lungs alone, without deriving any of its living or power of living by or through any connection with its mother'. Brooke J rejected an argument that the foetus must have the capacity to survive for a reasonable period when it is born.

11.08 Thus, prior to 1991,[27] the time limit for a legal abortion was, because of the impact of the 1929 Act, somewhere between 22 and 24 weeks depending

---

[25] *Per* Heilbron J in *C v S*, and see Keown, J, 'The Scope of the Offence of Child Destruction' (1988) 104 LQR 120.

[26] [1987] 1 All ER 1230 (Heilbron J and CA). Discussed, Grubb, A, and Pearl, D, (1987) 103 LQR 340.   [26a] [1991] 1 All ER 801, 817.

[27] When the Abortion Act 1967, s 5(1) was amended so as also to create a defence to the crime of 'child destruction' under the 1929 Act.

upon the development of the particular foetus.[28] Hence, the 1929 Act continued to dictate the upper time limit for lawful abortion where the foetus was 'capable of being born alive'.[29]

3. Section 37 of the Human Fertilisation and Embryology Act 1990

Despite numerous back-bench attempts to change its terms, in particular, to **11.09** lower the upper time-limit for abortions and to restrict the grounds upon which an abortion could be carried out, the substance of the 1967 Act remained unaltered until 1991. During the passage of the Human Fertilisation and Embryology Act 1990 through Parliament the Government allocated time in order to allow a full debate upon what should be the law. In the result, section 37 of the Human Fertilisation and Embryology Act 1990, which came into force on 1 April 1991,[30] amended the 1967 Act principally in *four* ways:[31]

(1) it substituted (and enlarged) the grounds for abortion contained in s 1(1) of the 1967 Act;[32]

(2) it disengaged the 1967 Act from the Infant Life (Preservation) Act 1929 and the time-limit it imposed so that compliance with the 1967 Act created a defence both to the 1861 and 1929 Acts;[33]

(3) it set an upper time-limit of 24 weeks for the most common ground for an abortion under the new s 1(1)(a) of the 1967 Act and removed any time-limit for the other grounds;[34]

(4) it sought to clarify the law, and make legal, the procedures of selective reduction and foeticide.[35]

4. Abortion and Post-Coital Contraception[36]

It is important to determine the scope of the regulation of abortion given the **11.10** criminal prohibition contained in section 58 of the Offences Against the Person Act 1861. The most important situation, in practice, concerns certain birth control practices which may not be purely contraceptive in their effects.

---

[28] This will remain important where the legality (or availability) of an abortion prior to 1 April 1991 is still relevant, for example, in a 'wrongful birth' claim arising before that date: see *Rance v Mid-Downs HA* [1991] 1 All ER 801. See discussion below, Ch 12.

[29] Unless the abortion was carried out 'in good faith for the purpose only of preserving the life of the mother': s 1(1). The burden of proof lies on the prosecution.

[30] The Human Fertilisation and Embryology Act 1990 (Commencement No 2 and Transitional Provision) Order 1991, SI 1991/480.

[31] For discussions of s 37, see Grubb, A, [1991] Crim LR 659; Montgomery, J, (1991) 45 MLR 524, 531–3; Murphy, J, [1991] JSWFL 375.   [32] See s 1(1)(a)–(d).

[33] See s 5(1).   [34] Combined effect of ss 1(1)(a) and 5(1).   [35] See s 5(2).

[36] See Norrie, K, *Family Planning Practice and the Law* (1991), Ch 2.

A contraceptive is a medicinal substance or device which prevents fertilisation of the egg by the male sperm. Obvious examples of this are the so-called 'pill' or barrier methods such as condoms. These prevent by chemical or physical means fertilisation. Other methods may not prevent fertilisation but act in such a way that the fertilised egg, if any, does not implant in the woman's uterus. Examples of these are post-coital methods like the so-called 'morning after pill' or intra-uterine devices (IUDs) whether fitted post-coitally or not. In these situations it is better to term the methods as contragestive rather than contraceptive since they act *only* to prevent gestation. Further complications may arise, and will be returned to later, in that the agents may act not to prevent gestation but to end it. In other words, after the developing embryo has implanted they effect its expulsion from the woman's uterus. Are any of these properly subject to the legal regulatory regime for terminations or abortion? The answer depends principally upon one issue: do they effect a 'miscarriage' so as to fall within the criminal prohibition in the 1861 Act?

11.11 It is clear that a purely contraceptive agent does not produce a 'miscarriage'. A failure to fertilise cannot properly be considered a 'miscarriage'. By contrast it is widely accepted that if the effect is to cause an implanted embryo to be expelled from the mother's uterus that is a 'miscarriage' and the effect is abortifacient rather than contraceptive. The Abortion Act 1967 must be complied with for this to be done legally. What, however, of the contragestive method? Is a failure to implant also a 'miscarriage'? In one sense, the woman has ceased to 'carry' and, hence has 'miscarried'. What was previously within her body will be expelled. However, this does not tally within the ordinary notion of 'miscarriage' which would entail a lost 'pregnancy' (ie which had become established to the woman's knowledge). This, of course, only occurs once a period is missed which itself can only follow the implantation of the developing embryo. Also, a broad notion of 'miscarriage' is not consistent with modern medical usage. While legislation has to be interpreted in the sense intended at the time of its enactment (originally 1803), attempts to show that the broader meaning was intended merely illustrate the ambiguity in the language used or the relative ignorance of the time about the reproductive process.[37] In short, little of any value can be gleaned about the meaning of 'miscarriage' by reliance on early or late nineteenth century medical or legal dicta.

11.12 What then amounts to a 'miscarriage'? The weight of legal writing supports the view that 'carriage' requires the developing embryo to have implanted.[38] This comports most easily with accepted notions of what it is to be pregnant

---

[37] Keown, J, 'Miscarriage': A Medico-Legal Analysis' [1984] Crim LR 604.
[38] Kennedy, I, *Treat Me Right* (1988) ch 3; Williams, G, *Textbook of Criminal Law* (2nd edn, 1983), 294–5 and Kennedy and Grubb, *Medical Law* (n 1 above) 692–4. Contrast Keown, J, ibid; and Tunkel, V, [1974] Crim LR 461.

and for it to end by means of an abortion. Further, there is no convincing public policy argument which would bring contragestive measures within the mischief or desirable scope of the law regulating abortions.

In addition, there is strong support for the need for implantation from the **11.13** (then) Attorney General in a written answer in the House of Commons in 1983[39] and Parliament has, in effect, accepted that the concept of 'carriage' requires implantation in the Human Fertilisation and Embryology Act 1990. Section 2(3) provides, for the purposes of the 1990 Act,[40] that 'a woman is not to be treated as carrying a child until the embryo has become implanted'. Other jurisdictions have made this interpretation explicit in their legislation based upon the 1861 Act.[41]

As a result, purely contragestive methods of birth control are not regulated by the **11.14** 1967 Act. However, where the method may work pre- or post-implantation, the position may be otherwise. This may occur with an IUD. The legal issue is whether the doctor acts 'with intent' to procure a miscarriage. Certainly, if he believes the woman is pregnant, in the sense of 'carrying' a foetus in utero, what he is doing falls within the 1861 Act and he must comply with the requirements of the Abortion Act. Hence, where a doctor fitted an IUD to a woman whom the doctor believed to be about 14 weeks pregnant, the Court of Appeal upheld his conviction under section 58.[42] In that case, of course, there could be no doubt as to his intention given his knowledge.

Where, however, an IUD (or whatever) is fitted much sooner after sexual inter- **11.15** course has taken place the doctor's knowledge will inevitably be much less. It is not necessary for the offence under section 58 to be committed that the woman be pregnant or, as the section quaintly puts it, 'be with child'.[43] But does a doctor who carries out a procedure trying to prevent implantation if that has not yet occurred (not a 'miscarriage') or, if it has, to dislodge the implanted embryo (a 'miscarriage') have the 'intent to procure a miscarriage'? If the doctor undertakes the procedure prepared if necessary to bring about a 'miscarriage', his conditional state of mind ('Do "X" if necessary') is an intent to procure a miscarriage. If 'miscarriage' is entailed as an acceptable outcome of what he is doing, then he has the requisite mens rea. If his state of mind is otherwise, he will only be reckless as

---

[39] 42 Parl Deb HC 238, 239.
[40] Thus, it is not directly applicable to the Offences Against the Person Act 1861, ss 58 and 59. [41] Crimes Act 1961 (NZ), s 182A.
[42] See eg, *R v Price* [1969] 1 QB 541 (CA).
[43] Contrast the news report of *R v Dhingra, Daily Telegraph*, 25 Jan 1991. On the basis of expert evidence that the woman could not have been pregnant (ie, implantation had not occurred) after 11 days, when the IUD was fitted, Wright J withdrew the case from the jury. It is only explicable on the basis that the defendant must have known this, therefore, he could not possibly have intended to procure a 'miscarriage'.

to procuring a miscarriage which is insufficient for a conviction under section 58. In such circumstances there may be considerable difficulty in establishing beyond a reasonable doubt that the doctor intended to procure a miscarriage.

C. The Abortion Act 1967 (as amended)[44]

11.16   Section 1(1) of the 1967 Act states that:

> Subject to the provisions of this section, a person shall not be guilty of an offence under the law relating to abortion when a pregnancy is terminated by a registered medical practitioner if two registered medical practitioners are of the opinion, formed in good faith—
>> (a) that the pregnancy has not exceeded twenty-four weeks and that the continuance of the pregnancy would involve risk, greater than if the pregnancy were terminated, of injury to the physical or mental health of the pregnant woman or any existing children of her family; or
>> (b) that the termination is necessary to prevent grave permanent injury to the physical or mental health of the pregnant woman; or
>> (c) that the continuance of the pregnancy would involve risk to the life of the pregnant woman, greater than if the pregnancy were terminated; or
>> (d) that there is a substantial risk that if the child were born it would suffer from such physical or mental abnormalities as to be seriously handicapped.

1. The Scope of the Act

11.17   The Abortion Act 1967 creates a defence to the offences of 'procuring a miscarriage' under sections 58 and 59 of the OAPA[45] and of 'child destruction' under the Infant Life (Preservation) Act 1929.[46] The Act contemplates a number of prerequisites to a lawful abortion.[47]

(i) '. . . a pregnancy is terminated . . .'

11.18   The wording of section 1(1) of the 1967 Act states that the woman's 'pregnancy' must be 'terminated'.[48] This is a curious formulation since it seems to presuppose that the crime—to which the 1967 Act provides a defence—is

---

[44] By the Human Fertilisation and Embryology Act 1990, s 37, with effect from 1 April 1991.

[45] S 6 defines 'the law relating to abortion' as meaning the Offences Against the Person Act 1861, ss 58 and 59, and, rather mysteriously, 'any rule of law relating to the procurement of abortion'. It is not clear what this latter phrase relates to.   [46] S 5(1).

[47] For a discussion of other procedural requirements under the 1967 Act and Abortion Regulations 1991, see below, para 11.53 *et seq*.

[48] For difficulties in respect of 'selective reduction', see below, paras 11.78 *et seq*.

couched in similar terms. Of course, the 1861 Act is not. It makes no reference to a 'pregnancy' but to a 'miscarriage'[49] and, more importantly, it does not require that a miscarriage actually should occur. Section 58 creates an offence where the person does one of the specified acts[50] 'with intent to procure the miscarriage' of a woman. The crime is committed even if the person is unsuccessful providing that was his intention and, in the case of anyone except the woman herself,[51] even if she is, in fact, not 'carrying' or pregnant. On the face of it, however, the 1967 Act does not apply where the pregnancy is not terminated in these circumstances. This would be a most bizarre outcome. A person would have a defence if the abortion was successful but not where it failed or where the woman was wrongly believed to be pregnant; even though both amount to offences under section 58. In practical terms, the situation could arise where a doctor undertook 'speculative' action in case the woman should be pregnant.[52] It is not clear that the 1967 Act applies to him.[53] His conditional intent to procure a miscarriage if the woman was pregnant would suffice for an offence to be committed under section 58.

When the issue was raised in the case of *Royal College of Nursing v DHSS*,[54] the **11.19** Law Lords, who discussed it, expressed differing views. Lord Diplock considered that the 1967 Act should be interpreted to cover 'the whole treatment undertaken' and not merely, should it occur, the miscarriage.[55] Lord Wilberforce (dissenting) took the opposite view. For him, the 1967 Act did not apply: '[t]ermination is one thing; attempted and unsuccessful termination wholly another'.[56] Lord Edmund-Davies (also dissenting) agreed with Lord Diplock on the effect of the 1967 Act, in these circumstances, but for a different reason. For him, a doctor would not be acting unlawfully because he was attempting to do that which was lawful, namely 'terminate' the woman's pregnancy.[57] Whether he was successful did not, therefore, matter. Even though the issue cannot be said to be free from doubt, it is suggested that the approaches of Lord Diplock and Lord Edmund-Davies represent a commonsense interpretation of a Private Member's Bill which would be adopted by a court.

---

[49] For a discussion of the meaning of 'miscarriage', see above, paras 11.10–11.15.
[50] The 'act' means administer a poison or other noxious thing or use any instrument or other means to procure the miscarriage.
[51] If the woman is charged she must be 'with child'. She may, however, commit an attempt if she believed she was pregnant, or be charged an accessory to another's crime or with conspiracy: *R v Sockett* (1908) 24 TLR 893 and *R v Whitchurch* (1890) 24 QBD 420.
[52] See Tunkel, V, 'Abortion: How Early, How Late, How Legal?' (1979) BMJ 253 discussing the procedure known as 'menstrual extraction'.
[53] See Lane Committee (Committee on the Working of the Abortion Act, Cmnd 5579, 1974) which recommended an amendment to the Act to make the law clear.
[54] [1981] AC 800; [1981] 1 All ER 545 (HL).   [55] ibid, 828.
[56] ibid, 823.   [57] ibid, 832–3.

(ii) '. . . *by a registered medical practitioner* . . . .'

11.20 The 1967 Act also requires that the pregnancy is terminated by a registered medical practitioner, that is, a doctor registered with the General Medical Council. To the extent that an abortion is effected by a surgical procedure, there is no difficulty. Later abortions, however, where labour in induced using prostaglandin, involve a team of health care professionals, including both doctors and nurses who carry out composite parts of the woman's treatment. Indeed, it may be more directly the actions of the nurses which bring about the termination. In the *Royal College of Nursing* case, the House of Lords was asked whether the nurses' involvement in such abortions meant that the 1967 Act did not apply as the pregnancy was not being terminated by a doctor. By a majority (3–2), the House of Lords held that the Act did apply. The majority (Lords Diplock, Roskill, and Keith) adopted a broad interpretation of section 1(1) so as to take account of modern medical practice and of the notion of the health care 'team'. The termination was within the Act if the treatment was prescribed or determined by a doctor, carried out in accordance with his directions and he remained in charge throughout. Lord Diplock stated that which acts were performed by a doctor personally and which by others, such as a nurse, did not affect the application of the Act providing what was done was 'in accordance with accepted medical practice'.[58] The case effectively settles the law in respect of the procedures currently, and indeed foreseeably, used to effect an abortion.[59]

11.21 Where a pregnancy is terminated by a doctor, any person who might otherwise be guilty of an offence under section 58 has a defence.[60] This would include nurses carrying out parts of the procedure as contemplated in the *Royal College of Nursing* case. However, if a late abortion is being carried out (ie one where the foetus is 24 weeks or more), it is not clear whether a nurse has a defence to the crime of child destruction under the Infant Life (Preservation) Act 1929. Section 5(1) of the 1967 Act states that the offence will not be committed by 'a registered medical practitioner who terminates a pregnancy' in accordance with the 1967 Act. Clearly, therefore, the doctor has a defence but the nurse would not where her involvement amounts to a wilful act causing the death of a child capable of being born.[61] Parliament

---

[58] [1981] AC 800; [1981] 1 All ER 545 (HL), 828–9.
[59] For a discussion of the use of RU-486 ('Myfigene' or 'Mifepristone') where the woman herself administers the drug, see Kennedy and Grubb, *Medical Law* (n 1 above), 916–17.
[60] S 1(1).
[61] S 1(1) of the 1929 Act, unless done 'for the purpose only of preserving the life of the mother' which is unlikely.

plainly overlooked this possibility and has, as a result, left an unfortunate gap in the law.

(iii) '. . . *two registered medical practitioners are of the opinion, formed in good faith . . .*'

Section 1(1) of the 1967 Act requires that two doctors certify that one or more of the grounds for abortion set out in the Act applies. The 'certificate of opinion' must be in the form specified in the Abortion Regulations 1991.[62] The certificate is known as the 'blue form' because of its colour.[63] Except in emergencies, the certificate must be completed prior to commencement of the treatment.[64] In the case of emergencies, it may be signed[65] if it is not practicable to do so before commencing treatment within 24 hours of the termination.[66] The certificate must be retained by the doctor who terminates the pregnancy for at least three years following the termination.[67] **11.22**

It may well be that the two doctors who sign the certificate will be the woman's GP and the consultant gynaecologist who carries out the abortion. However, the Act does not require that any particular doctor should sign the form. Indeed, there is no legal requirement that either doctor should have seen, let alone examined, the woman,[68] and the Act would be complied with even, for example, if the doctor carrying out the abortion had not signed the certificate. It also seems consistent with the wording of section 1(1) that the doctor performing the abortion need not himself be one of the certifying doctors. Though in practice this would be unusual, it would be lawful. Section 1(1) only requires that the pregnancy is terminated by a doctor and two doctors certify that a statutory ground exists. Thereafter, a 'person', who may be a completely different doctor or another such as a nurse involved in the procedure, has a defence under the 1967 Act. **11.23**

The 1967 Act does not require that one of the statutory grounds actually exists. Instead, it merely states that two doctors must form the opinion 'in good faith' that the particular ground exists. Both certifying doctors must form an opinion that a ground under the Act is satisfied. It does not appear from the wording of the Act that the doctors need agree on which ground is **11.24**

---

[62] SI 1991/499, reg 3(1). See Sch 1: Certificate A (usual case), Certificate B (emergencies).
[63] Previously, under the Abortion Regulations 1968, SI 1968/390 it was green and known as the 'green form'. [64] Abortion Regulations 1991, SI 1991/499, reg 3(2).
[65] In this instance it need only be signed by one doctor: s 1(4) and Sch 1 (Certificate B).
[66] ibid, reg 3(3). [67] ibid, reg 3(4).
[68] Notice that the certificate asks the signing doctor to strike out as appropriate 'Have/have not seen/and examined' the woman.

satisfied; they may take a joint or several view of the basis for the abortion. Also, an abortion will be lawful even if the doctors are mistaken about the woman's condition providing they honestly believe the ground to exist.[69] Even an unreasonable belief will, in law, be sufficient although, of course, the unreasonableness of the doctor's belief will be relevant in determining whether the belief was actually held.

11.25 The upshot of the wording of the 1967 Act is that it will be very difficult to establish that an abortion does not fall within the Act if two doctors conscientiously conclude that a ground, usually under section 1(1)(a), is fulfilled providing always that the required procedures under the 1967 Act and Abortion Regulations 1991 are followed.[70] Remembering also, that in a criminal case, the prosecution has the burden of proving beyond reasonable doubt that the 1967 Act was not complied with. The 1967 Act in effect places a 'great social responsibility' firmly 'on the shoulders of the medical profession.'[71] In *Paton v BPAS*,[72] a case in which a husband sought an injunction to prevent his wife having an abortion, Sir George Baker P stated that it would not only

> be a bold and brave judge . . . who would seek to interfere with the discretion of doctors acting under the 1967 Act, but I think he would really be a foolish judge who would try to do such a thing, unless possibly, there is clear bad faith and an obvious attempt to perpetrate a criminal offence.

11.26 In extreme circumstances, the conduct of the doctor may call into question the bona fides of his opinion. In the only reported case of a successful prosecution,[73] the doctor concerned carried out a limited examination of the pregnant woman, did not obtain a medical history, but agreed to carry out the procedure a week later for cash. No further investigations or enquiries were carried out and a second opinion was not sought until given by the anaesthetist on her admission. The doctor's conviction under section 58 was upheld by the Court of Appeal. On the facts, the Court of Appeal concluded that the jury had been entitled to take the view that the doctor had not formed his opinion in 'good faith'.

---

[69] *R v Smith* [1974] 1 All ER 376 (CA).   [70] *Paton v BPAS* [1978] 2 All ER 987, 992.
[71] *R v Smith* [1974] 1 All ER 376, 378 *per* Scarman LJ.
[72] [1978] 2 All ER 987, 992. See also *C v S* [1988] QB 135; [1987] 1 All ER 1230, 1243 *per* Sir John Donaldson MR.
[73] *R v Smith* (n 69 above). For two unreported prosecutions both ending in acquittals, see *R v Dhingra* (n 43 above) and *R v Dixon*, *The Times*, 22 Dec 1995 (news report).

2. The Grounds For Abortion

The amended section 1(1) of the 1967 Act does not extend or narrow the **11.27** substance of the grounds for abortion which previously existed. There are four grounds of abortion based upon

(i) risk to maternal physical and mental health;[74]

(ii) where necessary to prevent grave permanent physical or mental injury;[75]

(iii) risk to maternal life;[76] and

(iv) where there is a substantial risk that the child will suffer from physical or mental abnormalities so as to be seriously handicapped.[77]

Prior to 1991, grounds (i) and (iii) were combined in the old section 1(1)(a) of the Act and ground (iv) merely reproduces exactly what was previously in section 1(1)(b). Ground (ii) did not explicitly exist, except as a basis for carrying out emergency abortions not in an NHS hospital or approved clinic.[78] The amended section tidies up the grounds and, importantly, was necessary because only the ground in the new section 1(1)(a)—where there is risk to the mother's physical or mental health—is subject to a time-limit.

(i) 'Risk of Physical or Mental Injury'—s 1(1)(a)

Section 1(1)(a) is, in practice, the most commonly relied upon ground for **11.28** abortions. It is also, as we shall see below, limited to cases where the woman's pregnancy has not exceeded its twenty-fourth week. There are, in fact, two distinct grounds contained within section 1(1)(a) relating first, to a risk to the *mother's* health and secondly, to that of the *existing children of her family*.[79]

(a) The Comparative Exercise

This ground for abortion[80] requires that the certifying doctors engage in a **11.29** comparative exercise and decide whether there is a greater risk to the mother's (or existing children's) physical or mental health if the pregnancy continues than if it were terminated. It is not sufficient merely that the pregnancy creates a risk to the mother's (or existing children's) physical or mental health.

---

[74] S 1(1)(a).   [75] S 1(1)(b).   [76] S 1(1)(c).   [77] S 1(1)(d).

[78] S 1(4).

[79] The Abortion Regulations 1991, S1 1991/499, Sch 1, distinguish between these two bases for relying on s 1(1)(a): see Certificate A indication 'C' and 'D' respectively.

[80] As does s 1(1)(c) relating to risk to the mother's life.

(b) 'Risk to Woman's Mental Health'

11.30   As regards the risk to the pregnant woman, the ground is very broad in its scope. It covers any risk of any physical or mental injury providing the comparative exercise is satisfactorily performed. Many of the terminations carried out under it involve what have become known as 'social abortions' performed because the pregnancy is unwanted and an inconvenience to the mother and her family. In truth, of course, the doctors must always be satisfied of the effect on her health. However, distress and pressure generated by the unwanted child are readily seen as creating a risk to the 'mental health' of a pregnant woman. Two doctors are easily able to certify that there is a greater risk to a pregnant woman's mental health if she is forced to have an unwanted child than if an abortion is performed, certainly early on in the pregnancy where the risks inherent in the abortion procedures are very low. The Act is concerned with the 'risk' to the woman's mental health and not the certainty or even probability of its occurring and the notion of 'mental health' under the Act is itself very broad indeed. Mental health is not to be equated with recognised psychiatric injury. It is much broader and less well defined. It means, in effect, 'mental well-being' encompassing all deleterious effects upon a woman's emotional life.

(c) The Statistical Argument

11.31   A further reason why abortions under section 1(1)(a) have come to be seen as being carried out 'on demand' is because of the so-called 'statistical argument'. This is that early in a pregnancy—usually in the first twelve weeks—the risks to a 'normal' mother of continuing the pregnancy are always greater than the risks involved in the techniques used to terminate pregnancy. Therefore, the comparative exercise always falls out in favour of the pregnant woman's decision to seek an abortion. Ultimately, of course, the two doctors must form an opinion that the ground applies to this *individual* and not solely on the basis of abstract statistics though, as we have seen, there is no legal requirement that they examine her. Thus, the argument is logically inescapable, providing there is nothing in the individual woman's circumstances to upset the 'statistical argument'. The only doubt that remains, since the amendments in 1991, is the extent to which it can be based solely on the risk of morbidity rather than mortality. A risk to the 'health' of the woman is all that is left under section 1(1)(b) since the separation out of 'risk to life' is now contained in section 1(1)(c) of the Act. However, it is likely that the statistical argument would, in practice, stand up to expert evidential scrutiny under either ground if tested. Jointly or severally the risks to the woman's health or life are greater by remaining pregnant in the early stages of the pregnancy.

(d) 'Foreseeable Environment'

In applying section 1(1)(a) and assessing the effect on the pregnant woman[81] **11.32**
of continuing the pregnancy, section 1(2) states that 'account may be taken of
the pregnant woman's actual or reasonably foreseeable environment'. Consequently, the comparative exercise mandated under the Act cannot be
restricted to the risks (of continuing or terminating) fixed in time at the
point at which the decision whether or not to abort is made. Parliament has
clearly indicated that the risks to the woman's health of the 'continuance of
the pregnancy' extend beyond the pregnancy itself. As a result, the social and
family circumstances of, for example, having another child may be taken into
account to the extent that this would impact upon her physical or mental
health. Thus, potential deleterious consequences of having a child too young
and not able to cope, of having too large a family to deal with socially or
economically or the effect on a woman's career prospects and potential, could
all be bases for forming a 'good faith' view of injury to the woman's mental
health. It is even possible that an abortion sought on the basis that a child of a
particular sex was undesired—so-called 'sex selection'—could fall within the
Act if the birth of a child on such circumstances would adversely affect the
mother's mental health.[82] All will, in the end, depend upon the medical
evidence. Of course, the obverse is also true. A privileged background or
highly supportive family environment will also be relevant and may be taken
into account when engaging in the statutory comparative exercise.

(e) 'Risk to Existing Children of her Family'

We have already noted how section 1(1)(a) contemplates an abortion because **11.33**
of the risk to the physical or mental health of the woman's existing children
having, of course, engaged in the comparative exercise required. The former
possibility, of the risk of physical injury to an existing child, is perhaps
difficult to imagine though not impossible. For example, it could occur
were it known that the unborn child would be a physical danger or health
risk to others. More likely, of course, is the impact that another child will
have on the mental health of existing children. It is unlikely, however, to
entail a risk to them *during the pregnancy*, although the circumstances might
create this situation. The doctors may, as we have already seen, have regard to
the 'reasonably foreseeable environment' after the pregnancy comes to term.

---

[81] Or of 'existing children of her family'.
[82] See Morgan, D, 'Legal and Ethical Dilemmas of Fetal Identification and Gender Selection'
in Templeton, A and Cuisine, D (eds), *Reproductive Medicine and the Law* (1990) 53, 71–3.

For instance, this might arise where the already greatly impoverished family circumstances will be even more stretched by having an 'extra mouth to feed'. The effect on the children of the adversely changed social circumstances may, in the doctors' opinion, have the requisite impact on their mental (or physical) health to satisfy section 1(1)(a).

11.34 The risk must be to 'existing children of [the pregnant woman's] family'. Who does this entail? The Act offers no definition but there is no reason to adopt a restrictive interpretation. The statutory phrase expresses a sociological concept rather than a purely legal one whereby Parliament intended to include all those who would be cared for by the pregnant woman and who would be affected if her pregnancy continued.[83] Hence, it would cover *any* child whose mother is legally the pregnant woman or whom the woman has taken in as part of her family, for instance, a child of her current or former partner or husband. Also, it is suggested that the word 'child' should not be narrowly construed and given its legal meaning of a person under 18. Given the aim of Parliament, it should also include older 'children' who remain within the woman's care and are dependent upon her because, for example, they are disabled and live with her.

(f) 'Pregnancy not Exceeded its 24th Week'[84]

11.35 As we saw earlier, the 1991 amendment of the 1967 Act resulted in a time-limit being introduced into the Act for the first time. Only section 1(1)(a) is subject to a time-limit: the pregnancy must not have exceeded its 24th week. There are no time-limits in the other grounds under section 1(1). However, section 1(1)(a) does not specify the point in time which starts the clock running in calculating the 24 weeks. There are four possibilities:

(A) the first day of the woman's last period;
(B) the date of conception (up to 14 days later);
(C) the date of implantation (up to 10 days later); and
(D) the first day of the woman's first missed period (about 4 weeks after (A)).

11.36 In England the medical profession calculates the length of gestation of a baby on the basis of (A) because it is the most certain date of any of these alternatives. Options (B) and (C), namely the date of conception and the date the fertilised egg implants into the woman, by contrast, cannot be

---

[83] See Hoggett, AJ, 'The Abortion Act 1967' [1968] Crim LR 247.
[84] This section is based upon Grubb, A [1991] Crim LR 659, 665–6.

known for certain. There are difficulties with option (D) even though the first day of the woman's first missed period is certain.[85]

An interpretation of section 1(1)(a) consistent with the medical profession's **11.37** approach in (A) would achieve certainty. More importantly, however, it was the basis upon which Parliament introduced the 24-week time limit in section 1(1)(a). The 24-week limit represents Parliament's view of the stage of development when a foetus is capable of surviving. At this point the legislative intent was that the foetus should not be aborted except under the further grounds set out in the remainder of section 1(1). If any of the other options for starting time to run were accepted, this premise would be nullified.

By contrast, there are arguments favouring options (B) or (C). First, it is wrong **11.38** to adopt an interpretation which leads to the absurd conclusion that a woman is pregnant in the 14 days (approximately) between the first day of her last period and the time of conception when this is patently not the case. Secondly, the medical profession's approach exemplified in option (A) could act to the detriment of a defendant since it results in the shortest possible time for the 24-week period to run. A pregnancy calculated on the basis of (A) at 25 weeks is likely, in fact, to be a case where conception and implantation will have occurred less than 24 weeks before the abortion. Ambiguities in criminal statutes should be construed in a defendant's favour and not against him, particularly when interpreting a section providing a defence to a criminal offence.

On balance, however, it is suggested that (C) is legally the most justifiable.[86] **11.39** As a matter of common sense, the Abortion Act should be interpreted so that the defence to the crime in section 58 operates from the point in time when that crime could first be committed. That offence only applies after an embryo has implanted.[87]

(ii) 'Necessary to prevent Grave Permanent Injury to Physical or Mental Health'—s 1(1)(b)

Section 1(1)(b) introduces a new substantive ground for abortion. Prior to **11.40** 1991 it had merely justified not carrying out an abortion at an NHS hospital

---

[85] It would be quite misleading to indicate the length of pregnancy where, for example, following conception during the last week of a cycle the woman does not miss the next period but only the one that follows. The date calculated on the basis of (D) could be about 5 weeks after conception has actually occurred.

[86] There is even indirect Parliamentary support for this interpretation in s 2(3) of HUFEA 1990 which states that '[f]or the purposes of [HUFEA], a woman is not to be treated as *carrying* a child until the embryo has become implanted' (emphasis added).

[87] See above, paras 11.10–11.15.

or approved clinic.[88] There is no time-limit in section 1(1)(b). As with the remaining grounds under the Act, Parliament did not wish to impose a time-limit on abortions where serious dangers to the woman's health existed. Though section 1(1)(b) is still concerned with the pregnant woman's health, it requires injury of a different order to that under section 1(1)(a). Parliament clearly intended manifest proof of the more serious danger specified. The examples given by Lord Mackay LC, in the House of Lords' debates on the provision of when 'grave permanent injury' might arise, were where a woman suffered from severe hypertension and continuation of the pregnancy might result in permanent kidney, brain, or heart damage.[89]

11.41 Where does section 1(1)(b) apply? Unlike section 1(1)(a), the comparative exercise is, on the face of it, abandoned. It requires the certifying doctors to decide that the termination is 'necessary to prevent grave permanent injury to the physical or mental health' of the woman. The termination must be 'necessary' to avoid all or some injury of this kind. On the other hand, a *risk* of 'grave permanent injury', however great, will not fall within section 1(1)(b). Section 1(i)(b) only contemplates preventing what will actually, or is reasonably certain to, occur. In any other case, the doctors would have to rely upon sections 1(1)(a), bearing in mind that there is a 24-week time-limit for any abortion. Equally, a termination will only be necessary if there is no other alternative course available to avoid the effect on the woman's health. Section 1(1)(b) not only lays down a very stringent requirement of harm—'grave permanent injury'—it also only applies where termination is effectively a last resort.

(iii) *'Risk to Woman's Life'—s 1(1)(c)*

11.42 Prior to 1991, the ground in section 1(1)(c) was lumped in together with what is now section 1(1)(a). Both require the two certifying doctors to engage in the comparative exercise of whether the risk to the pregnant woman—here to her 'life'—is greater if the pregnancy is continued than if it is terminated. The risk must be to *her*; there is no equivalent in this ground to that which we saw earlier of risk to her existing children. The ground only requires that the termination *reduces* the risk to her life. It does not require that the termination eliminate the risk altogether. There may exist a continuing, though lesser, risk to her life but the termination will fall within section 1(1)(c) nevertheless if she stands a better chance of surviving there having been a termination. As we shall see later, this may be important in respect of

---

[88] S 1(4).   [89] *Hansard*, HL Vol 522 Col 1039.

selective reduction procedures where one or more foetuses are killed in utero when the woman has a multiple pregnancy.[90]

As we saw in respect of section 1(1)(a), an abortion under this ground may **11.43** also be justified on the basis of the 'statistical argument' in early pregnancy (ie approximately the first 12 weeks).[91] Beyond this time, however, the risk to the woman increases by undergoing the abortion, and consequently to satisfy section 1(1)(c) there would have to be a greater countervailing risk to her life by remaining pregnant.

The ground looks to the risk to the woman's *life*. In *R v Bourne*[92] and **11.44** subsequent cases,[93] the courts took a broad view at common law of what was meant by a risk to a pregnant woman's life so as to include risks to her health.[94] This broad interpretation cannot be applied to section 1(1)(c) since it would be inconsistent with the other grounds in the Act, in particular section 1(1)(a) where Parliament intended to restrict to 24 weeks abortions performed solely because of the risk to the woman's health.

(iv) 'Substantial Risk (so as to be) Seriously Handicapped'—s 1(1)(d)

The final ground for abortion is in section 1(1)(d) which states that a **11.45** pregnancy may be terminated if two doctors are of the opinion that there is 'a substantial risk' that if the child is born it will be 'seriously handicapped' due to 'physical or mental abnormalities'. The interpretation of this ground is not without difficulty. Since 1991, there has been no time-limit applicable to this ground. In theory at least an abortion on the basis of foetal abnormality could be obtained up to full-term. However, in practice very few abortions are performed after the foetus is 24 weeks old. Although there are a few cases where foetal abnormality is not detected before 24 weeks gestation, more generally the trend is towards earlier rather than later abortions with ever earlier detection of abnormalities. Also, many gynaecologists will not be prepared to perform an abortion late in pregnancy on the ground that the foetus is seriously handicapped unless the handicap is unusually severe as, for example, in the case of anencephaly where most, if not all, of the foetus's higher brain will be missing.

---

[90] See below, paras 11.85 *et seq.*   [91] See above, para 11.31.
[92] [1939] 1 KB 687.
[93] *R v Newton and Stungo* [1958] Crim LR 469 and *R v Bergmann* [1948] 1 BMJ 1008.
[94] See above, para 11.04.

(a) Substantial Risk

11.46 It is unclear what is meant by a 'substantial risk' of physical or mental abnormalities so as to be seriously handicapped. What degree of risk is contemplated? Proof of certainty is clearly not essential. No doubt, a substantial risk exists if there is more than 50 per cent chance that the child will have the disability. But, will a one in four chance of disability suffice? It is simply not clear from the Act. It has been suggested that whether a risk is 'substantial' cannot be viewed in isolation from the nature of the disability.[95] Hence, a relatively low risk of a very serious disability may be 'substantial' whereas a rather higher risk of a less serious disability would be required. However, there is no justification for conflating the magnitude of the risk with the nature of the disability. The Act treats them as distinct and separate. The interpretative difficulty will be exacerbated in 'double risk' cases where there is a risk that the child will inherit a genetic condition but it is not certain, if he does, what effect that will have upon him. There will, however, be an increased risk of him developing a particular disability. There may be a 'substantial' risk of inheriting but this must necessarily be seen in the context of the risk of developing the disability. The latter will statistically dilute the former and it is the overall risk (the risk of suffering physical or mental abnormalities so as to be seriously handicapped) which must be 'substantial'.

11.47 When is a risk 'substantial'? Answering this question may increase in importance as medical science develops better and more sophisticated methods of detecting pre-natal and genetic abnormalities. On the other hand, the answer may decrease in significance as these tests achieve a greater certainty in the diagnosis of foetal abnormalities. The answer cannot be found by recourse to the 'safe haven' of medical evidence and the two doctors' 'good faith' opinions. Of course the courts will look to medical evidence to determine what are the risks in a particular instance, but whether they are 'substantial' requires an interpretation of the statute and, as such, it is a legal issue. Equally, two doctors may, in good faith, conclude that a particular risk is substantial but that will not be conclusive that section 1(1)(d) has been complied with. If their mistake is factual, for example, if they thought the risk was 50 per cent when it was only 25 per cent, their honest beliefs ('good faith') will protect them under the Act. However, if their mistake is not factual but rather whether 25 per cent is a 'substantial' risk, their 'good faith' will not protect them under the Act if a court takes the view that that is a misinterpretation of the Act. They will, simply, have misdirected themselves in law. No doubt,

---

[95] Williams, G, *Textbook of Criminal Law* (2nd edn, 1983), 298.

however, the courts will give doctors considerable leeway and perhaps consider any risk which a reasonable parent would consider significant in making
an abortion decision to be one which is 'substantial'.

(b) Seriously Handicapped

A further problem of interpretation arises in relation to the meaning of the **11.48**
phrases 'physical or mental abnormalities' so as to leave a child 'seriously
handicapped' under section 1(1)(d). The former phrase will largely be a matter
of medical evidence and rarely be problematic. The latter phrase, however,
seems to be incapable of precise definition. What counts as a 'serious handicap'? Again, like the meaning of the phrase 'substantial risk', this is a question
of law for the court. The courts will be guided by medical evidence of the
nature of the condition. Certainly, the child does not have to have a life-
threatening condition for it to be 'seriously handicapped'. Nor is the phrase
restricted to children who would be 'grossly abnormal and unable to lead any
meaningful life'.[96] There is no basis for taking such a narrow view of the scope
of section 1(1)(d) which, though phrased in terms of the foetus's condition, is
really concerned with the parents' ability to cope with a 'seriously' disabled
child.[97] Further, the woman's interests implicated in carrying and bringing up
the child means that it is inappropriate (and unnecessary) to interpret its scope
consistently with the limited situations where a severely handicapped newborn
child may be allowed to die solely *in its own best interests*.[98]

In practice, and quite properly, much less serious conditions form the basis **11.49**
for abortions under section 1(1)(d). Providing the condition is not trivial,
easily correctable (such as harelip), or will merely lead to the child being
disadvantaged, the law will allow doctors scope for determining the seriousness of a condition.[99] At a minimum, it is suggested, a 'serious handicap'
would require the child to have physical or mental disability which would
cause significant suffering or long-term impairment of their ability to function in society. The most serious genetic or other conditions which manifest
themselves at birth or almost immediately thereafter are, by and large, likely
to fall within the scope of section 1(1)(d).

When must the serious handicap exist? Must it exist at birth or immediately **11.50**
thereafter, or could it be a latent condition which develops later in the child's

---

[96] Report of the Select Committee on the Infant Life (Preservation) Bill (HL Paper (1987–
88) No 50), 18.   [97] See Williams, G, *Textbook of Criminal Law* (n 95 above), 297.
[98] Contrast Morgan, D, 'Abortion: The Unexamined Ground' [1990] Crim LR 687.
[99] The Abortion Regulations 1991 require the doctor carrying out the termination to notify
the Chief Medical Officer of the suspected condition in the foetus and the method by which it
was detected.

life. Section 1(1)(d) is concerned with the life of the 'child' 'if born'. Consequently, the condition must exist after birth at some point. However, to require the condition, and its manifestation, to exist at the point of birth or immediately thereafter is too narrow a reading of the Act. The Act is concerned with 'the child'. A reasonable interpretation would allow the doctors to project forward during the child's life, if born, and assess what its condition would be and whether it would suffer 'serious handicap'. An example of such a condition is Tay-Sach's disease. Of course, there must be a 'physical or mental abnormality' during this time. This would not be broad enough to catch a carrier of a defective gene which did not manifest itself in the child, for example, a recessive condition such as sickle-cell anaemia or cystic fibrosis. There is no basis for including physical abnormalities (if that's what these are) of this kind within the Act. In any event, the carrier child would not be 'seriously handicapped'. His only impairment in life would be to make wise reproductive choices in the future in case his partner were also a carrier of the recessive gene.

11.51   Some conditions might, however, fall within the Act even though there is no manifestation at birth. Will, for example, an abortion be justified if a baby is diagnosed as HIV-positive in its mother's womb? It would have to be established that the HIV-antibodies which are detected are the baby's own and not its mother's for it to be established that there be 'a substantial risk' of the child being infected. Even so, would the HIV-positive baby suffer from 'physical abnormalities' given that it would almost certainly be asymptomatic at birth? Pathologically, the baby will suffer from a physical abnormality (the infection) even if there are no symptoms; but is the baby 'seriously handicapped'? On one view the baby is not even handicapped because it is asymptomatic and so suffers no appreciable medical detriment. However, this is a very narrow meaning of 'handicap' and, given the social conditions, including the prejudice and discrimination, that the baby will exist in, it is quite plausible to say that the baby will be 'seriously handicapped' because of its infection.

11.52   Some conditions do not, however, manifest themselves and so lead to 'serious handicap' until much later in the child's life after birth, for example, Huntingdon's Disease.[100] Are these within section 1(1)(d)? On one view they are not. The Act speaks of the 'child' if born suffering from 'physical or mental abnormalities as to be seriously handicapped'. Huntingdon's Disease does not usually manifest itself until a person is in his forties. Only a broad construction of "child" could encompass this situation. And, although it is difficult on the wording of section 1(1)(d) to include adulthood conditions, once it is

---

[100] Even if HIV infection is not seen in itself as a serious handicap, AIDS-Related-Complex and AIDS which will develop later are undoubtedly serious handicaps.

accepted that the handicap need not manifest itself at birth, it would seem to undermine the purpose of the ground to restrict it narrowly to childhood.

3. Operation of the Abortion Act

The 1967 Act together with the Abortion Regulations 1991[101] provide a   **11.53** statutory regulatory framework for abortion. Any person who wilfully contravenes or wilfully fails to comply with the requirements of the 1991 regulations commits a summary offence.[102] In particular, they provide for (1) the places where terminations may be performed; (2) the certification of the grounds for the abortion; (3) notification to the Chief Medical Officer of information about the abortion performed; and (4) the restriction on disclosure of information.

(i) *Places*

Section 1(3) of the Abortion Act 1967 provides that an abortion ('termina-   **11.54** tion of pregnancy') may only be carried out in an NHS hospital, an NHS Trust, or a place approved by the Secretary of State. An exception is provided for in cases of emergencies. Section 1(4) states that a termination need not be carried out in such a place where the doctor:

> . . . is of the opinion, formed in good faith, that the termination is *immediately necessary to save the life or to prevent grave permanent injury to the physical or mental health of the pregnant woman.*

(a) The Private Sector

Private clinics require the approval of the Secretary of State to carry out   **11.55** abortions. In effect, though not name, a licensing procedure exists for the approval of private sector places under section 1(3) of the Act.[103] The system entails an application process, monitoring, and inspection by the Department of Health. Approval is conditional upon an applicant agreeing in writing to a number of conditions (technically 'assurances') relating to the conduct of the clinic or hospital. Approval is also conditional upon registration as a 'nursing home' under the Registered Homes Act 1984 by the appropriate health authority. The details are contained in the Department of Health's *Compendium of Guidance*.[104] One matter of interest concerns the performing of 'late abortions'. Specific approval is required from the Secretary of State for

---

[101] SI 1991/499 (made pursuant to s 2).
[102] Abortion Act 1967, s 2(3). Liable to a fine not exceeding level 5 on the standard scale.
[103] See *Abortion Act 1967: Compendium of Guidance* (DoH, July 1994).   [104] ibid.

abortions after the 20th week of gestation, and abortions after the 24th week of gestation are prohibited.[105] Also, approved places are required to comply within NHS guidelines, for example on the disposal of foetuses and foetal tissue,[106] determining gestational age and counselling patients.[107] In addition, approved places are required to keep and maintain records and registers on the patients and procedures performed which must be available for inspection by the Department of Health.

(b) Medicinal Abortions[108]

11.56 The Human Fertilisation and Embryology Act 1990[109] introduced a new section 1(3A) into the 1967 Act. It provides:

> The power under subsection (3) of this section to approve a place includes power, in relation to treatment consisting primarily in the use of such medicines as may be specified in the approval and carried out in such manner as may be specified, to approve a class of places.

11.57 The provision is intended to allow for the use of *medicinal agents* as an abortifacient. In particular, it is intended to allow the use of the drug 'Mifepristone' or RU-486[110] which is widely used, and was developed in, France. Mifepristone is an anti-progesterone which prevents the implantation of a fertilised egg in a woman's uterus and as such it operates as a contragestive and not as an abortifacient. However, the drug also can dislodge any fertilised eggs which have implanted at the time of treatment and so it can also function as an abortifacient. It is the latter use which necessitated amendment to the 1967 Act. In 1991 Mifepristone was licensed under the Medicines Act 1968 for use as an abortifacient.[111]

11.58 The use of Mifepristone does not require the initial hospitalisation of the patient. The drug has been proven to be safe with few side-effects.[112] All that is required is that the woman should be prescribed the drug; that she should take a course of the drug for three days followed by a prostaglandin vaginal pessary which ensures that the termination is successful and that no products of conception remain in the uterus. While it is essential that the woman

---

[105] Since 1 February 1986: see 'Estimation of Gestational Age of Cases at 20–23 Weeks of Pregnancy', Letter from Department of Health dated 22 May 1986.

[106] HSG(91)19, EL(91)144 and Polkinghorne Committee Report on the *Review of the Guidance on the Research Use of Fetuses and Fetal Material* (Cm 762 1989)

[107] HC (77)26.

[108] This section is based upon Grubb, A, [1991] Crim LR 659.   [109] S 37(3).

[110] Product name 'Myfigene'.   [111] *The Times*, 4 July 1991.

[112] Couzinet *et al*, 'Termination of Early Pregnancy by Antiprogesterone RU486 (Mifepristone)' (1986) 315 *New Eng J Med 1565* and Cherfas, J and Palca, J, 'The Pill of Choice?' (1989) 245 *Science 1319.*

should remain under the care of a doctor, apart perhaps from the adminis-tration of the prostaglandin pessary, the remainder may be carried out at a General Practitioner's surgery or in a hospital clinic as an outpatient. For the rest of the time the woman can go home and carry on her normal life.

Section 1(3) would require the Secretary of State to approve each place (such as an individual GP's surgery) separately. Section 1(3A) permits him to approve such places as a *class*. It is not clear whether the Secretary of State has yet approved a class of places under his new power in section 1(3A). In any event, section 1(3A) may fail to achieve its desired goal. It assumes that the 'treatment for the termination of pregnancy' in the 1967 Act is restricted to the prescrip-tion of the drug and, perhaps, the administration of the prostaglandin pessary. However, a much broader interpretation of the statutory phrase is possible. Arguably, the 'treatment' begins with the prescription of the drug and con-tinues until the pregnancy is terminated. In *Royal College of Nursing of United Kingdom v DHSS*[113] the House of Lords adopted a wide interpretation of 'treatment' under the Abortion Act to include all the activities undertaken by the 'hospital team' designed to bring about the termination of a woman's pregnancy. 'Treatment for the termination of pregnancy' is, in the case of Mifepristone, a process spanning a number of days. A woman will only be at one or more of the classes of places contemplated as falling for approval under section 1(3A) for part of the time that the 'treatment' is taking place. Only if the Secretary of State approves all the places a patient might visit between the prescription of Mifepristone and the eventual abortion will the Act be com-plied with. It is doubtful whether section 1(3A) allows the approval of places for terminations outside the medical environment. Even if it did permit approval of such places as patients' homes, public transport etc, this is an absurd possibility to contemplate. If this is correct, section 1(3A) requires further amendment to achieve its desired aim.

11.59

(ii) *Certification*

The two doctors' opinions given in 'good faith'[114] and required under section 1(1) of the 1967 Act must be given in the prescribed form of the 'certificate of opinion' set out in Schedule 1, Part 1[115] to the Abortion Regulations 1991.[116] No other form of certification is permissible.[117] The certificate

11.60

---

[113] [1981] AC 800. See discussion above, para 11.20.
[114] See also paras 11.22–11.26 above. [115] Certificate A.
[116] SI 1991/499. Colloquially known as the 'blue form' because of its colour. Under the previous Abortion Regulations 1968, (SI 1968/390) the certificate was known as a 'green form' for a similar reason. [117] ibid, reg 3(1).

must be completed 'before the commencement of the treatment for termination of the pregnancy'.[118] Where the termination is to be carried out in an emergency under section 1(4),[119] then a single doctor's opinion will suffice and that opinion must be given in accordance with the certificate set out in Schedule 1, Part II[120] to the 1991 Regulations. Unlike the usual case, in this situation the certificate must be completed before the commencement of treatment or, if that is not reasonably practicable, not more than 24 hours after the termination.

11.61 The certificate must be retained by the practitioner who terminates the pregnancy for not less than three years beginning with the date of the termination[121] and, thereafter, if it is no longer to be preserved it must be destroyed by the person having custody of it.[122] Wilful failure to comply with the Regulations is a criminal offence.[123]

(iii) *Notification*

11.62 The Abortion Regulations 1991 provide that a doctor terminating a pregnancy must within seven days of the termination provide the appropriate Chief Medical Officer[124] (and only that person[125]) with notice of the termination and information relating to it as required by Schedule 2 to the Regulations. The notification form is extensive in the information it requires the doctor to supply. The information relates to the personal and medical history of the woman, to the circumstances of the termination, its statutory basis, and details of the foetus's gestational age and, if over 24 weeks, a 'full statement' of the medical condition of the woman and the foetus.

(iv) *Disclosure of Information*

(a) **The Restriction**

11.63 As in other situations of medical treatment, the common law protects the confidentiality of the information provided by, or relating to, the pregnant woman.[126] However, the 1991 Abortion Regulations go further and give stat-

---

[118] ibid, reg 3(2).
[119] ie, where the doctor is of the opinion that it is 'immediately necessary to save the life or to prevent grave permanent injury to the physical or mental health of the pregnant woman'. See above, para 11.40 *et seq*. [120] Certificate B.
[121] SI 1991/499 reg 3(4).   [122] ibid, reg 3(5).
[123] Abortion Act 1967, s 2(3) and above, para 11.53.   [124] Of England or Wales.
[125] Abortion Act 1967, s 2(2).   [126] See Ch 9.

utory protection to this information. Regulation 5 imposes a duty not to disclose a 'notice given or any information' supplied to the Chief Medical Officer in pursuance of the Regulations except[127] as provided in the Regulation. The Regulations are widely drawn. They do not merely prohibit disclosure of the notice under Schedule 2 of the Act but also 'any information' contained in it. However, the Regulations do not specify upon whom the 'duty' is imposed. They merely state that the notice or information 'shall not be disclosed'. There can be little doubt that the Regulation applies to everyone.[128] Of course, the criminal offence created by the 1967 Act if a breach occurs is only committed if the discloser acts 'wilfully'.[129] Also, the Regulations do not, in themselves, create a civil cause of action enforceable by a patient. However, given the specificity of their scope and the obvious person whose confidences they are designed to protect, the courts are likely to construe the Regulations as creating a civil cause of action in the pregnant woman's favour.[130] She alone[131] could seek an injunction, and perhaps damages, to prevent disclosure in breach of the Regulations.

(b) The Exceptions

There are *eight* circumstances specified in Regulation 5 in which disclosure of the 'notice' or 'information' supplied to the Chief Medical Officer is permitted:[132] **11.64**

(1) to an authorised officer of the Department of Health or Welsh Office or to the Registrar General (or an authorised member of staff) for the purpose of carrying out their duties;

(2) to the DPP (or an authorised member of staff) for the purposes of carrying out his duties in relation to offences under the Abortion Act 1967 or the law relating to abortion;[133]

(3) to a police officer not below the rank of Superintendent (or a person authorised by him) for the purposes of investigating whether an offence has been committed under the Abortion Act 1967 or the law relating to abortion;[134]

---

[127] See below, para 11.64.   [128] Including the Chief Medical Officer himself.
[129] Abortion Act 1967, s 2(3).
[130] Alternatively, on the basis of *Gouriet v UPOW* [1978] AC 435, as the person suffering 'special damage'.
[131] Leaving aside the Attorney-General who could do so as the guardian of the public interest.   [132] Reg 5(a) to (h).
[133] Namely, the Offences Against the Person Act 1861, ss 58, 59. Notice that this does not include an offence under the Infant Life (Preservation) Act 1929 which might well have been significant prior to the 1991 amendment of the Abortion Act 1967.   [134] See ibid.

(4) pursuant to a court order for the purposes of proceedings[135] which have begun;

(5) for the purposes of bona fide scientific research;

(6) to the medical practitioner who terminated the pregnancy;

(7) to a medical practitioner,[136] with the consent in writing of the woman whose pregnancy was terminated;

(8) to the President of the GMC (or an authorised member of staff) when requested by him for the purpose of investigating whether there has been serious professional misconduct by a[137] medical practitioner.

(v) *Conscientious Objection*[138]

11.65 The Abortion Act 1967 does not require a doctor to perform an abortion even if the particular circumstances of the pregnant woman fall within one or more grounds in the Act. To this extent, however, the doctor is in no better position and the pregnant woman no worse position than in any other medical consultation. English law will not require a doctor to treat a patient if he considers it inappropriate in his clinical judgment.[139] The doctor–patient relationship is perceived by the law to be one of partnership requiring joint agreement for treatment to go ahead.[140] The objection will, however, usually be a matter of clinical judgment rather than personal preference or predilection. In the context of abortion, a doctor (or other) may have a conscientious objection to be involved in the procedure as a result of their moral or religious beliefs. The Abortion Act 1967 provides specifically for this situation.

11.66 Section 4(1) of the Abortion Act 1967 provides that:

> no person shall be under any duty, whether by contract or by any statutory or other legal requirement, to participate in any treatment authorised by this Act to which he has a conscientious objection.

11.67 The 'conscientious objection' cannot be relied upon in emergencies. Section 4(2) provides that

---

[135] Not limited to *court* proceedings providing always that a court has ordered disclosure, for example, in disciplinary proceedings on the basis of 'fairness' or natural justice.

[136] But not anyone else, even with the woman's consent.

[137] But not necessarily *the* doctor who terminated the pregnancy so, for example, the investigation could relate to another certifying doctor.

[138] For a general discussion, see Braithwaite, C, *Conscientious Objection To Compulsions Under the Law* (1995).

[139] See *Re J (A Minor) (Wardship: Medical Treatment)* [1992] 4 All ER 615 (CA).

[140] ibid, and *Re R (A Minor) (Wardship: Medical Treatment)* [1991] 4 All ER 177, 184 *per* Lord Donaldson MR.

[n]othing in subsection (1) . . . shall affect any duty to participate in treatment which is necessary to save the life or to prevent grave permanent injury to the physical or mental health of the pregnant woman.[141]

Subject to the exception, section 4(1) allows a doctor or nurse not to **11.68** participate in an abortion which they otherwise would be required to by virtue of their legal duty to their employer or to the patient. The burden of proving the conscientious objection lies upon the individual.[142] There are two essential elements to the 'conscientious objection': first, that the person's objection is *conscientious*; and secondly, that they would otherwise be asked to *participate* in an abortion.

(a) Matters of Conscience

Rarely will this be a problem in practice.[143] 'Conscience' is not used here in **11.69** the sense of a mere thought or state of mind of an individual but rather as a conviction or belief based upon a moral assessment. The *Oxford English Dictionary* refers to

> [t]he internal acknowledgment or recognition of the moral quality of one's motives and actions; the sense of right and wrong as regards things for which one is responsible; the faculty or principle which pronounces upon the moral quality of one's actions or motives, approving the right and condemning the wrong.

A matter of 'conscience' is widely understood to cover, for example, religious, **11.70** moral, or other principled beliefs which lead the individual to conclude that the activity is wrong. Thus, objections based upon prejudice rather than principle would not be covered. However, a doctor who took a particular view of the sanctity of human life—including foetal life—would have a conscientious objection whether his belief was religious or secular.

It seems also that the Act permits a doctor (or other) to have a conscientious **11.71** objection to some but not all abortions. Section 4(1) speaks of the person having a conscientious objection to '*any* treatment' covered by the Act. Although it is not free from doubt, this provision would seem to allow a doctor to object to, say, late abortions only, or to terminations on the basis of foetal disability while not objecting to others. Providing the limited nature of his objection is 'conscientiously' based, rather than misguided or 'borne of prejudice', he need not participate in the termination.

---

[141] ie, falling within s 1(1)(b) and in extreme cases under s 1(1)(c).
[142] For proof in Scotland, see s 4(3).
[143] The position may be otherwise under s 38 of the Human Fertilisation and Embryology Act 1990: see Kennedy and Grubb (n 1 above), 787–8.

(b) Who is Covered?

11.72 Section 4(1) applies to any 'person', and not just the doctor carrying out the termination, providing that they would be 'participat[ing]' in the 'treatment authorised' under the Act. Undoubtedly, nurses and others who perform acts as part of the 'team' under the direction of the responsible doctor[144] will be covered by section 4(1). But what of others less directly involved?

11.73 The issue arose in *Janaway v Salford Health Authority*.[145] The plaintiff was a receptionist/secretary at a health centre. She was asked by a doctor working there to type a letter referring a patient for an appointment with a consultant with a view to him forming an opinion as to whether the patient's pregnancy should be terminated under the Abortion Act. She refused and was dismissed. She brought judicial review proceedings seeking to quash the decision on the basis that she was entitled to rely on the 'conscientious objection' provision in section 4(1) of the 1967 Act. Nolan J (at first instance) refused her application and her appeal was subsequently dismissed by the Court of Appeal[146] and House of Lords.[147] The House of Lords rejected the approach of a majority of the Court of Appeal[148] that section 4(1) should be interpreted as covering any activity which would be a criminal offence either as a principal or as an accessory under the Offences Against the Person Act 1861.[149] Instead, the Law Lords held that the word 'participate' had to be given its ordinary and natural meaning. The plaintiff was entitled to rely on section 4(1) because she was not

> actually taking part in treatment administered in a hospital or other approved place . . . for the purpose of terminating a pregnancy.[150]

11.74 The interpretation of section 4(1) adopted by the House of Lords is a narrow one and would exclude from its ambit all health care professionals and other staff who are not directly taking part at the hospital or clinic in the patient's treatment under the 1967 Act (ie the termination). Also, incidental or unrelated activities carried on within a hospital would not fall under the

---

[144] See *Royal College of Nursing v DHSS* [1981] AC 800 discussed above, paras 11.20–11.21.
[145] [1989] AC 537 and [1988] 3 All ER 1079 (HL).
[146] ibid, noted Grubb, A, [1988] CLJ 162.   [147] Noted Grubb, A [1989] CLJ 17.
[148] N 145 above *per* Slade and Stocker LJJ.
[149] The majority of the Court of Appeal held that the plaintiff lacked the mens rea of an accessory since her intention was 'merely to carry out the obligations of her employment' (*per* Slade LJ at 452). This narrow view is problematic on the facts (see Grubb, A [1988] CLJ, 163) and in the House of Lords, Lords Keith and Lowry probably disagreed (n 145 above, 1083 and 1083–4 respectively).   [150] N 145 above, 570 per Lord Keith.

umbrella of section 4(1). It is doubtful whether nurses involved in the general care of the woman or ancillary staff looking after her, for example, by changing the bed sheets or delivering her meals, could rely on section 4(1) since they are not involved in the 'treatment' authorised by the Act.

One situation which remains problematic concerns the doctor, usually a **11.75** general practitioner, who refuses to act as one of the statutory 'opinions' and sign the certificate for conscientious reasons. Is he entitled to rely on section 4(1)? In *Janaway* Lord Keith left the point open. However, this much is clear: on the basis of the House of Lord's interpretation of 'participate' such a doctor could not be said to be participating in the treatment authorised under the Act. Indeed, as Lord Keith acknowledged, the certificate must come into existence 'before the commencement of the treatment'.[151] It is logically impossible to construe signing the certificate as 'participation' in the treatment and at the same time it occur prior to the treatment. Consequently, such a doctor would not be able to rely upon section 4(1) to relieve him of any duty he would otherwise have to sign the certificate or refer the pregnant woman. The crucial question, therefore, is whether he has such a duty under the law assuming that the abortion is medically justified, ie, it falls within the Act.

In the Court of Appeal in *Janaway*, Stocker LJ took the view that a doctor had **11.76** a legal duty to sign the certificate.[152] Whether this view is correct turns upon the GP's obligations under the Terms of Service.[153] Paragraph 12 of the Terms of Service provide:

(1) . . . a doctor shall render to his patients all necessary and appropriate personal medical services of the type usually provided by general practitioners.
(2) The services which a doctor is required by sub-paragraph (1) to render shall include the following . . .
(d) arranging for referral of patients, as appropriate, for the provision of any other services under the Act . . .

There is no doubt that a termination of pregnancy amounts to 'other services' **11.77** provided under the National Health Service Act 1977. Consequently, at the very least the GP has the legal duty under his Terms of Service[154] to refer the patient to another doctor in respect of her pregnancy. It could be argued that it suffices if he refers her to another GP who may act as the first statutory 'opinion' by signing the certificate.[155] However, it is plausible to argue that, in this context, 'referral' within paragraph 12(2)(d) also contemplates referral to a consultant, having himself signed the form, for the purpose of obtaining

---

[151] ibid, 572. See Abortion Regulations 1991, SI 1991/499, reg 3(2) and above, para 11.60.
[152] N 145 above, 556.
[153] National Health Service (General Medical Services) Regulations 1992, SI 1992/635, Sch 2.
[154] Which will reflect his duty to the patient.   [155] Grubb, A [1989] CLJ 17, 18.

the second 'opinion' and if so the termination—as occurred in *Janaway* itself.[156]

(vi) *Selective Reduction*[157]

(a) The Techniques

11.78 Modern technology has developed techniques whereby a multiple pregnancy may be reduced by killing one or more foetuses in utero. This has become particularly important in cases where infertility treatment has led to a multiple pregnancy. The greater the number of foetuses carried by a woman the greater is the risk to her health during pregnancy and at delivery. Equally, in these circumstances there is the risk of foetal mortality and of foetal handicap, including cerebral palsy, blindness, and mental retardation. Consequently, it is often desirable out of the interests of the mother and/or the foetuses that the pregnancy should be reduced in number.[158] This is usually done in the first 14 weeks of the pregnancy by either injecting potassium chloride into the amniotic sac or into the heart of the foetus or by aspiration. The foetus(es) will die and may be spontaneously expelled or, more likely, will remain in the mother, wither, and what remains will be expelled at the time the remaining healthy foetuses are delivered. This procedure is known as 'selective reduction'.

11.79 In addition, a similar procedure may be used later in pregnancy when one of a number of foetuses (usually twins) is discovered to be seriously handicapped. Because of the slightly differing circumstances when it is used, it is sometimes distinguished from selective reduction and is sometimes known as selective foeticide.[159]

(b) Legal Position Before 1991

Miscarriage

11.80 It was not clear under the law prior to 1 April 1991 whether selective reduction and selective foeticide were covered by the abortion legislation. It could be argued that, in cases where the 'reduced' foetus(es) is (are) not expelled, no 'miscarriage' occurs within the terms of section 58 of the

---

[156] Kennedy and Grubb (n 1 above), 896.
[157] This section is based upon Grubb, A [1991] Crim LR 659, 667–9.
[158] See Howie, P W, 'Selective Reduction—Medical Aspects' in Templeton, A and Cuisine, D (eds), *Reproductive Medicine and the Law* (Churchill Livingstone, 1990), 25.
[159] The procedures are discussed in Berkowitz *et al*, 'Selective Reduction of Multifetal Pregnancies in the First Trimester' (1988) 318 *N Engl J Med 1043* and Howie, P W, 'Selective Reduction in Multiple Pregnancy' (1988) 297 *BMJ 664*.

Offences Against the Person Act 1861.[160] The better view is, however, that the term 'miscarriage' does not require expulsion of the contents of the womb but merely that some or all of the contents cease to be carried alive within it. This would bring both procedures within section 58 of the 1861 Act. In any event, the argument overlooks the fact that, ultimately, the withered and dead products of the foetus will be expelled at the time the remaining foetuses are delivered.

Termination of Pregnancy

A further complication was raised as to whether selective reduction was a 'termination of pregnancy' within the Abortion Act 1967 because the woman is still pregnant in the sense that one or more of the healthy foetuses remains after the procedure. If there was no termination of pregnancy, then the procedure could never be lawful because what was being done would not fall within the wording of the Abortion Act.[161] There would then be a potential crime but no possible defence. It is most likely that a court would have taken the view that the destruction of one or more foetus was a termination of a pregnancy. Hence, providing a doctor complied with the terms of the Abortion Act, he would have acted lawfully in performing a selective reduction. The matter is now entirely academic since Parliament has intervened. **11.81**

(c) Legal Position After 1991

In an attempt to put the matter beyond doubt, section 5(2) of the 1967 Act was amended by the Human Fertilisation and Embryology Act 1990[162] to include the following: **11.82**

> . . . in the case of a woman carrying more than one foetus, anything done with intent to procure her miscarriage of any foetus is authorised by [section 1] if—
> (a) the ground for termination of the pregnancy specified in subsection (1)(d) of that section applies in relation to any foetus and the thing is done for the purpose of procuring the miscarriage of that foetus, or
> (b) any of the other grounds for termination of pregnancy specified in that section applies.

The effect of the amended section 5(2) is to bring the two procedures of selective reduction and selective foeticide within the Abortion Act and to require compliance with its terms if a doctor is to act lawfully. Interestingly, section 5(2) assumes that the procedures do result in a 'miscarriage' for the purposes of the 1861 Act. The first of the difficulties mentioned is now put **11.83**

---

[160] The argument is put and rejected by Keown, J, 'Selective Reduction of Multiple Pregnancy' (1987) 137 NLJ 1165.

[161] Price, D P T, 'Selective Reduction and Feticide: The Parameters of Abortion' [1988] Crim LR 199. [162] S 37(4).

beyond doubt because a court is very unlikely to reach a contrary conclusion given this assumption by Parliament.

Selective Foeticide

11.84 Section 5(2)(a) covers the procedure of selective foeticide where the particular foetus is identified by pre-natal screening (using, for example, amniocentesis or chorion villus sampling techniques) as suffering from a physical or mental abnormality which would lead to the child being 'seriously handicapped' within section 1(1)(d) of the Act when it is born. As a result of section 5(2)(a), providing the foetus could be aborted on the foetal abnormality ground had it been a singleton (ie the whole pregnancy would be terminated), it alone may be aborted as part of a multiple pregnancy.

Selective Reduction

11.85 Section 5(2)(b) covers the procedure of selective reduction. If a doctor would be justified in terminating the whole pregnancy under section 1(1) of the Act because of the risk to the mother's health or life or because of the serious injury she will suffer if the pregnancy continues, he may reduce the number of foetuses in the multiple pregnancy in order to remove (or reduce) the risk of danger to her.

11.86 Unlike section 5(2)(a), which requires the doctor to kill only the handicapped foetus which specifically falls within the ground under the Act, section 5(2)(b) permits the doctor randomly to select which foetus(es) to kill. He may selectively reduce any foetus(es) where a multiple pregnancy creates a risk to the mother's health within one of the grounds in section 1(1). This difference between the two provisions is inevitable because no one foetus can be singled out as a threat to the mother; rather it is the cumulative effect of the presence which creates the risk to her.

11.87 One final point to notice. Selective reduction may be desirable because a multiple pregnancy can risk damage to the foetuses themselves. Section 5(2) does not permit selective reduction in this situation because a risk of injury to a foetus is not a ground for abortion under section 1(1).[163] Only a risk to the mother would satisfy the Act but this will probably exist in the case of quadruplets, quintuplets or sextuplets and even in the case of triplets.

---

[163] But note the comment by Lord Mackay of Clashfern LC, *Hansard*, HL Vol 522, cols 1041–2.

D. Injunctions to Prevent Abortions

In what, if any, circumstances, will a court grant an injunction to prevent a woman undergoing an abortion? Courts throughout the world have rejected claims by the father of an unborn child for such an injunction: Australia,[164] Canada,[165] Scotland,[166] and England.[167] In America it has been held unconstitutional for a state to require that a husband's consent be sought prior to an abortion[168] or even that he be consulted.[169] English law regards the decision whether or not to terminate a pregnancy as exclusively one for the patient and her doctor subject to the regulatory requirements. Third parties, such as fathers or others, have no legal role to play in that process although, of course, a father might well be involved in practice with the consent of the pregnant woman.

11.88

There are a number of grounds upon which a father has claimed an injunction: (1) as a representative of the foetus in order to prevent a wrong being committed against it; (2) on his own behalf to enforce his right to agree or be consulted as the foetus's father; and (3) as a public spirited citizen on the basis that in the particular circumstances the abortion will be a crime.

11.89

1. As Next Friend of the Foetus

In order for a father (or other) to act on behalf of the foetus, the law would have to regard the foetus as a legal person possessing rights which could be enforced by a 'next friend'. In England, as elsewhere,[170] the courts have conclusively rejected the view that an unborn child has legal personality. Hence, for example, an unborn child cannot be made a ward of court,[171] bring an action for pre-natal injury until it is born,[172] and is not protected by the criminal law of murder or manslaughter if killed in utero.[173] In the

11.90

---

[164] *A-G of Queensland (ex rel Kerr) v T* (1983) 46 ALR 275 (Aust HCt).
[165] *Tremblay v Daiglé* (1989) 62 DLR (4th) 634 (Can Sup Ct).
[166] *Kelly v Kelly* 1997 SLT 896 (CS (IH)).
[167] *Paton v Trustees of BPAS* [1978] 2 All ER 987 (Baker P) and *C v S* [1987] 1 All ER 1230 (Heilbron J and CA).
[168] *Planned Parenthood of Central Missouri v Danforth* (1976) 428 US 52 (US Sup Ct).
[169] *Planned Parenthood of SE Pennsylvania v Casey* (1992) 112 S Ct 2791 (US Sup Ct).
[170] Recently by the Canadian Supreme Court in *Winnipeg Child and Family Services (Northwest Area) v DFG* (1997) 152 DLR (4th) 193. See also *Tremblay v Daiglé* (1989) 62 DLR (4th) 634 (Can Sup Ct).   [171] *Re F (In Utero)* [1988] 2 All ER 193 (CA).
[172] *Burton v Islington HA* [1992] 2 All ER 833 (CA) and Congenital Disabilities (Civil Liability) Act 1976, s 4(2)(a).
[173] *Attorney-General's Reference (No 3 of 1994)* [1997] 3 All ER 936 (HL). See also, *R v Tait* [1989] 3 All ER 682 (CA): foetus not 'a third party' so that a threat to kill the foetus amounts to a crime of threatening to kill 'a third party' under s 16, Offences Against the Person Act 1861.

context of paternal injunctions, in *Paton v BPAS*[174] and in *C v S*,[175] courts denied injunctions based upon an unborn child's right. In the latter case, Heilbron J (at first instance) stated:[176] ' . . . there is no basis for the claim that the foetus can be a party, whether or not there is any foundation for the contention with regard to the alleged threatened crime . . . '

11.91 Most recently in the Scottish case of *Kelly v Kelly*[177] a father claimed an interim interdict—the Scottish equivalent of an interlocutory injunction—to prevent his estranged wife from undergoing an abortion. The Inner House of the Court of Session approached his claim by asking whether the foetus had any legal rights at all which could be enforced on its behalf by the father. The court concluded that it did not since it was not a legal (or juridical) person until birth. The court referred to, and adopted, the English, Commonwealth, and American jurisprudence that denies an unborn child legal status. The court accepted in *Kelly* that, therefore, the father had no claim on behalf of the foetus because the foetus could have no legal claim of any kind until it was born alive.

11.92 While current English law is clear, it is not certain what impact the European Convention on Human Rights will have when enacted into domestic law.[178] There will essentially be two questions: Is an 'unborn child' a person within Article 2 of the Convention protecting 'everyone's right to life'? And, if it is, how will that right be accommodated with the pregnant woman's right to life under Article 2 or her right to her 'private life' including autonomy in decision-making and respect for her bodily integrity under Article 8? The case law under the Convention is undeveloped on these questions. Whether an 'unborn child' had a right under Article 2 was left open by the Commission in *Paton v United Kingdom*.[179] The Commission preferred to determine that Article 2—assuming it applied—did not create an absolute right and could be 'trumped' if the woman's own life or health was at risk. The fundamental question about the application of Article 2 may yet arise in the European Court of Human Rights.[180] It is most unlikely, however, that (whatever view is taken of Article 2) it would not be interpreted to accommodate the pregnant woman's rights to life and privacy at least to the extent that her health was affected by continuing the pregnancy.

---

[174] [1978] 2 All ER 987 (Baker P).   [175] [1987] 1 All ER 1230.
[176] ibid, 1235. The Court of Appeal decided the case on the basis that no crime would be committed under the Infant Life (Preservation) Act 1929. However, the judges did not doubt the approach of Heilbron J or that in *Paton*: see, especially, *per* Sir John Donaldson MR at 1243.
[177] 1997 SLT 896. Grubb, (1997) 5 Med L Rev 329 (Commentary).
[178] See discussion in Kennedy and Grubb (n 1 above), 902–5.
[179] (1980) 3 EHRR 408.
[180] See e g, *Open Door Counselling Ltd and Dublin Well Woman Centre Ltd v Ireland* (1992) 18 BMLR 1 (ECtHR).

2. As a Father

Does a father have any right himself to prevent an abortion? The English **11.93**
courts have dismissed the idea that a husband or partner of a pregnant woman
has any right, common law or otherwise, in his unborn child, or which is
implicated by her decision to have an abortion. Not least, the courts have
reached this conclusion because such involvement would run counter to the
structure of the Abortion Act 1967 which contemplates a private decision
reached between doctor and patient.[181] For these reasons, English law does
not confer upon a husband (or partner) a right which entails the need for his
consent or that he be consulted.

3. As Guardian of the Public Interest

The final basis upon which to claim an injunction might be the criminal nature of **11.94**
the proposed abortion. An 'interested' individual might argue that an injunction
should be granted to prevent the commission of an offence under section 58 of
the Offences Against the Person Act 1861 (or the Infant Life (Preservation) Act
1929) if the Abortion Act 1967 has not been complied with. Leaving aside the
difficulty of substantiating such an allegation where two doctors have conscientiously concluded that the Abortion Act 1967 applies, would an individual have
locus standi? Common law jurisdictions throughout the world have rejected a
father's locus standi to enforce the criminal law through the civil courts following
the House of Lords' decision in *Gouriet v UPOW*.[182] Absent a private wrong, a
citizen will only in *the most* exceptional circumstances, if ever, be allowed by the
courts to claim a civil remedy to prevent a criminal offence.

In practice, only an application by the Attorney General will be entertained **11.95**
by the courts, and then rarely.[183] The English cases have not yet applied the
Gouriet reasoning in a paternal injunction case either because there was no
suggestion that the abortion was illegal[184] or because the court chose, for
whatever reason, to ignore the procedural issue and dismiss the claim on its
merits.[185] There can be no doubt, however, that *Gouriet* would be fatal to the
standing of a father in this sort of case even if the abortion was outside the
terms of the Abortion Act.[186] The matter would be for the Crown Prosecution

---

[181] *Paton* (n 174 above). See also *C v S* (n 175 above), 1235 *per* Heilbron J and *Tremblay v Daiglé* (n 165 above), 665.
[182] [1978] AC 435. See also *League for Life in Manitoba v Morgentaler* [1985] 4 WWR 633 (Man QB). [183] See eg, *Attorney General v Able* [1984] 1 All ER 795 (Woolf J).
[184] *Paton* (n 174 above). [185] *C v S* (n 175 above).
[186] See *C v S* (n 175 above), *per* Sir John Donaldson MR at 1243.

Service to determine whether a criminal trial was in the public interest after the abortion had been performed. For this reason, a judge's decision in 1996 (reported in the newspapers) to grant an ex parte injunction, albeit temporarily, to a pro-life group to prevent a woman undergoing an abortion on the basis that it did not fall within the Act must seriously be called into question.[187]

E. Abortion and Homicide[188]

1. Killing In Utero

11.96 It is neither murder nor manslaughter to kill a foetus in utero. Homicide requires the death of 'a person in being' (or *in rerum naturae*), namely that the child is fully extruded from the mother's body and is 'breathing and living by reason of its breathing through its own lungs alone, without deriving any of its living or power of living by or through any connection with its mother'.[189] The rule was recently re-affirmed by the House of Lords in *Attorney-General's Reference (No 3 of 1994)*.[190] The common law rule is widely recognised throughout the world[191] but not universally.[192] Consequently, an abortion which results in the death of the foetus in utero will not amount to homicide.

2. Killing Ex Utero

11.97 What, however, would be the position if the abortion procedure results in the foetus being born and dying *ex utero*? Could this be murder or manslaughter? It is helpful to consider two situations: first, where the doctor terminates the pregnancy intending to kill the unborn child in utero but for whatever reason the child dies after birth; and secondly, where the intention is to produce a live birth and let the child die. Clearly, in both situations it would have to be proved that the doctor's action in terminating the pregnancy caused or substantially contributed to the child's death after birth. This will be a factual matter turning upon expert evidence. More problematic legally are the questions of whether the doctor has the requisite mens rea for murder or man-

---

[187] See 'Selective Abortions Hit the Headlines' (1996) 313 *BMJ 380*.

[188] See Skegg, P D G, *Law, Ethics and Medicine* (1994), 19–26.

[189] *Rance v Mid-Downs HA* [1991] 1 All ER 801, 817 *per* Brooke J. For a discussion of the historical precedents, see Atkinson, S, 'Life, Birth and Live-Birth' (1904) 20 LQR 134.

[190] [1997] 3 All ER 936, 948 *per* Lord Mustill.

[191] See e g, *Keeler v Superior Court* (1970) 470 P 2d 617 (Cal Sup Ct): not murder under California Penal Code to kill an unborn child; cf now s 187 amended in 1970 to include killing of a foetus in definition of murder.

[192] *Commonwealth v Lawrence* (1989) 404 Mass 378 (Mass Sup Jud Ct): killing of viable foetus in utero is murder.

slaughter and, if he does, whether he has any defence on the basis that what he did was lawful under the Abortion Act 1967.

(i) *Death In Utero Intended*

(a) Murder and Manslaughter

Where a doctor intends to terminate the pregnancy by killing the unborn child in utero, he will lack the mens rea of murder, namely an intention to kill or cause serious injury to a legal person since, prior to birth, the unborn child has no legal personality. However, could the doctrine of 'transferred intention' apply?[193] Thus, the intention to kill the foetus is transferred to the child once born.[194] In *Attorney-General's Reference (No 3 of 1994)*[195] the House of Lords decided that for murder the doctrine of 'transferred intention' could not be applied where the only intention was directed against the pregnant woman, because that would require a 'double transfer': first, from the mother to the foetus, and secondly, from the foetus to the child subsequently born. This was a fiction too-far for the House of Lords. However, where the intention is directed against the foetus—as it will be in the situation of an abortion—the House of Lords' decision leaves open the possibility of transferring the intention from the foetus to the child subsequently born: a single transfer and 'fiction'. The better view is, however, that the doctor's intention cannot be transferred because he does not intend to kill a 'legal person'. First, as a matter of principle, the House of Lords held that the foetus was not 'the mother' but a 'distinct organism . . . living symbiotically'.[196] Secondly, the foetus itself is not a legal person. These reasons also prevent the doctor's conduct amounting to manslaughter by an 'unlawful act' even though the House of Lords held that a 'double transfer' of intention was, by contrast to murder, possible. In the situation of abortion, unlike that of a violent attack on the pregnant woman, there will not for the reasons given above be any intention to injure a 'legal person', only the discrete organism that is the foetus.

11.98

One possibility of an offence does, however, exist where the doctor in the course of a termination inadvertently brings about a live birth and the child dies.[197]

11.99

---

[193] For a discussion of the doctrine in this context see Tempkin, J, 'Pre-Natal Injury, Homicide and the Draft Criminal Code' [1986] CLJ 414.

[194] As was held in *R v West* (1848) 2 Cox CC 500 (murder) and *Kwok Chak Ming v R* [1963] HKLR 349 (manslaughter).

[195] [1997] 3 All ER 936 (HL), overruling the Court of Appeal, [1996] 2 All ER 10.

[196] ibid, 943 *per* Lord Mustill. See also Lord Hope at 954. See discussion in Grubb, 'Unborn Child (Pre-Natal Injury): Homicide and Abortion' (1995) 4 Med L Rev 302, 306–8 (Commentary).

[197] *R v Senior* (1832) 1 Mood CC 346 (gross negligence by midwife leading to death ex utero).

The doctor could commit the offence of manslaughter by gross negligence if his negligence in bringing about the live birth and subsequent death was characterised as sufficiently serious by a jury.[198]

(b) A Lawful Justification

11.100 In any event, the law would, in all probability recognise that the doctor would have a defence to a charge of murder or manslaughter if the child died after birth as the result of a lawful abortion. In *Attorney-General's Reference (No 3 of 1994)*,[199] the Court of Appeal stated that a doctor's action in terminating the pregnancy, unlike that of the violent assailant, would not be unlawful if the terms of the 1967 Act were complied with, and hence he would have a defence to a charge of murder or manslaughter. However, the basis for the defence is not clear.[200] Such a defence is analytically problematic. First, the Abortion Act 1967 does not expressly or impliedly create a defence to a charge of murder or homicide. The legislative intention behind the 1967 Act is clear from its provisions which remove criminal liability for an offence under 'the law relating to abortion' which means under the 1861 Act.[201] Parliament was only concerned with offences prohibiting in utero deaths.[202] Secondly, murder does not require an unlawful act. What murder requires is that *the death be caused unlawfully*: but by this the law means merely not in circumstances where the defendant has a defence, for example, self-defence, provocation, diminished responsibility, etc. Murder may be committed by a wholly lawful act. The same is true for manslaughter committed by 'gross negligence' but not, of course, for 'unlawful act' manslaughter.

11.101 It is suggested that the answer to the doctor's criminal liability really lies in the mother's ability in law to consent to the harm to herself—which a 'miscarriage' undoubtedly is—and to the foetus which the Abortion Act 1967, as matter of public policy in England, permits a woman to do if the termination falls within the grounds set out in section 1 of the 1967 Act. If the mother's consent is sufficient to exempt the doctor from liability under sections 20 or 18 of the Offences Against the Person Act 1861 (for serious harm caused to her) and under section 58 (for the miscarriage of the foetus), the legality of the abortion procedure is established and there is no good reason why the unintended fact that the child is born should affect that.

---

[198] See *R v Adomako* [1994] 3 All ER 79 (HL).
[199] [1996] 2 All ER 10 (CA). The issue was not addressed by the House of Lords.
[200] See Grubb, 'Unborn Child (Pre-Natal Injury): Homicide and Abortion' (1995) 4 Med L Rev 302, 308–10 (Commentary).
[201] Ss 1(1) and 6(1) and, since 1990, under the Infant Life (Preservation) Act 1929: s 5(1).
[202] See Skegg, P D G, *Law, Ethics and Medicine* (Clarendon Press, 1984), 23–6.

(ii) *Death Ex Utero Intended*

In the unlikely situation that a doctor carried out an abortion intending the **11.102** foetus to die after birth, he would commit murder if the child were 'born alive'. More likely in practice would be the situation were the doctor inadvertently brought about a live birth and the child then dies. Here, the doctor would commit the offence of manslaughter by gross negligence if his negligence in bringing about the live birth and subsequent death was characterised as sufficiently serious by a jury.[203] In these situations, it is arguable that the doctor would not have a defence or lawful justification. Certainly, as regards murder, if the true basis of his defence is the woman's consent, she could not lawfully consent to the death of her child once born.

In addition, the law imposes a duty upon a doctor to act reasonably in trying **11.103** to save the child's life once born. Of course, this is not an absolute duty. The courts have already recognised that a doctor will not necessarily breach his duty by allowing a severely disabled premature newborn to die.[204] The fact that the child was born following a termination would in itself, however, be irrelevant. The doctor would have to take reasonable steps given the gestational age, the physical and mental condition, and prognosis of the child to save its life. Once born it would be entitled to the same care from the doctor and protection from the law as any premature baby in its circumstances. Undoubtedly the surest way to avoid a charge of murder or manslaughter is to prevent the situation arising altogether by adopting a method of termination which will certainly kill the foetus in utero.

---

[203] *R v Senior* (n 197 above) and para 11.99 above.
[204] See eg, *Re J (A Minor) (Wardship: Medical Treatment)* [1990] 3 All ER 930 (CA) and Ch 4, paras 4.28–4.35 above.

12

ACTIONS ARISING FROM BIRTH

A. Introduction

12.01 The scope of this Chapter[1] is the investigation of the nature of events occurring before birth, whether or not preceding conception, which give a

---

[1] For academic discussion generally, see: Cane, P F, 'Injuries to Unborn Children' (1977) 51 ALJ 74; Eekelaar, J M and Dingwall, R W J, 'Some legal issues in Obstetric Practice, (1984) JSWL 258; Fortin, J E S, 'Is the "Wrongful life" Action Really Dead?, (1987) JSWL 306; 'Legal Protection for the Unborn Child' (1988) 51 MLR 54; Kennedy, I and Grubb, A, *Medical Law: Text and Materials*, second edition (1994) Butterworths, ch 13; Lovell, P H and Griffith Jones, R H, 'The Sins of the Fathers—Tort Liability for Pre-Natal Injuries' (1974) 90 LQR 531; Mullis, A, 'Wrongful Conception Unravelled' (1993) 1 Med L Rev 320; Pace, P J, 'Civil Liability for Pre-Natal Injuries' (1977) 40 MLR 141; Rogers, W V H, 'Wrongful Life and Wrongful Birth: Medical Malpractice in Genetic Counselling and Testing' (1982) 33 SCL Rev 713; 'Legal Implications of Ineffective Sterilization's (1985) LS 296; Sarno, G G, 'Tort Liability for wrongfully causing one to be born' (1978) 83 ALR 3d 15; Symons, C R, 'Policy Factors in Actions for Wrongful Birth', (1987) 50 MLR 269; Tedeschi, I, 'On Tort Liability for "Wrongful Life" 4 Israel Law Rev 513; Teff, H, 'The Action for "Wrongful Life", in England and the United States' (1985) 34 ICLR 423; Whitfield, A, 'Common Law Duties to Unborn Children' (1993) 1 Med L Rev 28.

right of action to the child who is eventually born or to a member of his family. It will be seen that claims can only be made by or on behalf of children who are born alive or by parents, and not by other relations.

Most claims by children in England and Wales will now be brought under the **12.02** Congenital Disabilities (Civil Liability) Act 1976, which by section 4(5) replaces the common law in respect of all births after its passing on 22 July 1976. However, it is necessary also to discuss the common law rights of children, partly because of their relevance to other jurisdictions and partly because, under the Limitation Act 1980,[2] some children born before the Act came into effect may have claims which are not and may never become statute barred. Furthermore, all claims by a parent will be brought under the common law.

The general assumption is that, whether at common law or under statute, children **12.03** can only claim for disabilities which they have suffered as a result of some prenatal event, and not for the mere fact of being born or for so-called 'wrongful life'. A parent, on the other hand, may have a claim for the so called 'wrongful conception' or 'wrongful birth' of a child who is born alive but who would not have been born alive but for negligence. The parent may also have, in addition to a right of action in respect of personal injuries resulting from the circumstances of birth, a strictly limited claim in the case of a miscarriage or stillbirth.

However, it is unfortunately not possible to keep the categories of claims **12.04** completely separate, and problems can overlap. For example, where one event is responsible both for the conception of, and for a disability in, a child eventually born, does that child's claim succeed as a prenatal injury claim? Does it fail as a 'wrongful life' claim? How would it dovetail with any claim by a parent arising out of the same event? These, and other problems, await final analysis.

B. Claims by Living Children for Injuries Caused Before Birth

1. Claims for Injuries at Common Law

(i) *The Status of the Foetus*[3]

An unborn child has no 'legal personality'. In *Paton v British Pregnancy* **12.05** *Advisory Service Trustees*[4] Sir George Baker P considered an application by

---

[2] The Limitation Act 1980 appears to apply to all causes of action which have not accrued before 4 June 1954; see *Arnold v Central Electricity Generating Board* [1988] 1 AC 228 and *Keenan v Miller Insulation and Engineering Ltd* (1988) PMILL Vol 4, No 3, 11.

[3] The form 'fetus' is preferred by many purists to 'foetus', though, for consistency, the latter spelling is used throughout this volume. Etymologically the word is connected with the obscure Latin verb 'feo', meaning 'bear' or 'produce', as are the words 'fecundus' (fruitful), 'felix' (fortunate) and 'femina' (woman).

[4] [1979] QB 276. The husband later took the case to the European Commission of Human

a husband to restrain his wife and the British Pregnancy Advisory Service from causing or permitting an abortion, for which she had obtained a certificate under the Abortion Act 1967, from being carried out upon her. The case thus raised the question of the rights of the unborn child. He concluded: 'in England and Wales the unborn child has no right, no right at all, until birth.'[5]

12.06 In *C v S and Another*,[6] where a putative father of a foetus also failed in an application for an injunction to restrain an abortion, Heilbron J said:

> The authorities, it seems to me, show that a child, after it has been born, and only then in certain circumstances, based on his or her having a legal right, may be a party to an action brought with regard to such matters as the right to take on a will or intestacy, or for damages for injuries suffered before birth. In other words, the claim crystallises upon the birth, at which date, but not before, the child attains the status of a legal persona, and thereupon can exercise that legal right.[7]

These views were endorsed by the Court of Appeal in *Re F (in utero)*[8] when deciding the somewhat different issue of whether it had jurisdiction to ward an unborn child. The answer, that it had not, was primarily based on the fact that the unborn child has no existence independent of the mother.

12.07 In this respect, the law of Scotland appears identical; in *Hamilton v Fife Health Board*[9] Lord McCluskey said:[10]

> An unborn person, a foetus, is not a person in the eyes of the law—at least in relation to the law of civil remedies—and there can be no liability to pay damages to a foetus, even although the foetus sustained injuries resulting from a negligent act or omission constituting a breach of duty owed.

However, it is important to understand the limits of these propositions. While a foetus has no legal personality, and therefore cannot sue or recover damages, it does not follow that there is no duty to exercise reasonable care not to injure a foetus. It may lack legal capacity when unborn, but it does not follow that it is unprotected by the common law.

Rights, which rejected his complaint under Articles 2 and 8: *Paton v United Kingdom* [1980] EHLR 408.

[5] ibid, 279.   [6] [1988] QB 135.   [7] ibid, 140.   [8] [1988] Fam 122.
[9] [1993] SC 369, [1993] SLT 624 and [1993] 4 Med LR 201. Generally, the common law world does not confer rights upon children as legal persons. See *Attorney-General (Qld) ex re Kerr v T* [1983] 46 ALR 275 (Aus H Ct); *Trembley v Daigle* [1989] 62 DLR (4th) 634 (Can Sup Ct); *R v Sullivan* [1989] 1 SCR 489 (Can Sup Ct); *Roe v Wade* [1973] 410 US 113 (US Sup Ct). But cf *In the matter of Baby P (an unborn child)* [1995] NZFLR 255, and [1997] Med L Rev 143.   [10] ibid, at 382, 629 and 206.

(ii) *The Civil Law*

By contrast, the civil law very clearly protects the rights of an unborn child. **12.08**
There is a well-established rule of civil law that an unborn child shall be
deemed to be born whenever its interests require it.[11] The application of that
maxim is typically in the field of succession. For example, a gift to a class of
children living on a particular date is held to benefit a child *en ventre sa mère*
at that date but later born alive within that class. The rule appears in certain
Latin versions, one of which is '*nasciturus pro iam nato habetur quotiens de eius
commodo agitur*' ('one about to be born will be held already to have been born
whenever that is to his advantage'). It is to be noted that it was under the
influence of that principle that Sir Robert Phillimore held in the Admiralty
Court in *The George and Richard*[12] that a child born after the death of its
father—in that case a ship's carpenter, drowned in a shipwreck—counted as a
'dependent' for the purposes of bringing an action under Lord Campbell's
Act, the Fatal Accidents Act 1846. As will be seen, the influence of the civil
law upon developments in this branch of the common law has been
considerable.

(iii) *The Criminal Law*

The criminal law provides sanctions against some, but not all, conduct **12.09**
directed against a foetus. Its destruction by abortion is made unlawful by
section 58 of the Offences Against the Person Act 1861, save in the circumstances set out in the Abortion Act 1967 as amended by section 37 of the
Human Fertilisation and Embryology Act 1990. The Act of 1861 did not
criminalise the taking of a child's life while it was being born and before it was
fully born, but that loophole was blocked by the Infant Life (Preservation)
Act 1929. However, section 5(1) of the 1967 Act as amended provides that no
offence is committed under the Act of 1929 if termination is in accordance
with the Act of 1967. It is to be noted that three grounds for termination
under the 1967 Act as amended, namely those under Section 1(1) (b), (c) and
(d), are not subject to any time limit and so termination on any such ground
can lawfully be carried out at any stage of the pregnancy. Once the child has

---

[11] See *Villar v Gilbey* [1907] AC 139, where the rule is fully discussed.
[12] [1871] LR 3 A and E, 466. See also *Williams v Ocean Coal Ltd* [1907] 2 KB 422, in
which reliance was placed on the principle to establish the dependency of a posthumous child
under the Workmen's Compensation Act 1897, and *Burton v Islington HA* and *de Martell v
Merton and Sutton HA* [1933] QB 204 *per* Dillon LJ at 227.

'an existence independent of its mother'[13] its life is protected by the law of homicide.[14]

12.10 In *R v Tait*[15] the Court of Appeal decided that the threat 'I am going to kill your baby' addressed to a pregnant woman, if meant as a threat to kill the foetus *in utero*, was not a threat to kill 'a third person' within the meaning of section 16 of the Offences against the Person Act 1861. The reason was that the foetus *in utero* was not, in the ordinary sense, 'another person' distinct from its mother.

12.11 However, if a child is injured *in utero* but is later born alive and dies of that injury, then assuming the necessary *mens rea* the person who inflicted it is guilty of manslaughter or murder. Thus in *R v Senior*[16] an incompetent male midwife broke a child's skull with a knife as he became visible during birth. The child died immediately after he was born: a conviction for manslaughter was upheld. The justification for that result is the 'born alive' rule, namely that the child, having been born alive, then becomes 'a person' independent of the mother and thus is so at the time of death.

12.12 A more complex set of facts was considered in *Attorney General's Reference (No. 3 of 1994)*[17] The respondent stabbed his girlfriend, whom he knew was pregnant, in the abdomen, penetrating the foetus. Two weeks later she gave birth at twenty-six weeks' gestation, but the child died from the complications of prematurity. He was charged with murder, but acquitted on the judge's direction that the facts adduced by the prosecution could not result in a conviction for murder or manslaughter. The Court of Appeal, on a reference under section 36 of the Criminal Justice Act 1972, did not consider the question of causation but only whether, assuming proof of a causal link between the wound and the death, the facts could justify such a conviction. It held that they could. The reasoning was as follows. In law a foetus was to be treated as an integral part of the mother, so an injury to the foetus was thus as unlawful as an injury to any other part of her, and where, having subsequently been born alive, the child died of that injury, the *actus reus* of homicide would be proved. As to *mens rea* the Court invoked the doctrine of transferred

---

[13] Infant Life (Preservation) Act 1929 s 1(1). For a full discussion see *Rance v Mid-Downs HA* [1991] 1 QB 587, 620 *per* Brooke J. See also Russell, EJ, 'Abortion Law in Scotland and the Kelly Foetus', 1997, SLT Issue No 24, 187.
[14] Note the Infanticide Act 1938 in relation to the killing by a mother of her child under the age of twelve months.   [15] [1990] 1 QB 290.
[16] [1832] 1 Mood CC 346. For summaries of the case-law identifying the moment of birth see *Rance v Mid-Downs HA* (n 13 above) and Archbold, *Criminal Pleading, Evidence and Practice*, (1998 edn), 19–17.   [17] [1996] QB 581, [1996] 2 All ER 10.

malice[18] (whereby if A intends to kill B but instead kills C he is as guilty as if he had intended to kill C). It held that it was irrelevant that the foetus had no separate existence at the time of the act, and that the respondent's intention in relation to the mother could be transferred to the child after its birth.

This line of reasoning did not commend itself to the House of Lords.[19] In the **12.13** event it decided that the doctrine of transferred malice simply could not be stretched far enough to justify a conviction for murder, but that as manslaughter was a crime of 'basic intention' an unlawful and dangerous act directed at a woman who later gave birth to living child which died could give rise to a conviction for manslaughter. However, it roundly rejected the identification of the foetus with the mother, principally on obvious physiological grounds.[20] One can go further. The proposition that an unborn child has no legal status does not imply that it has no interest of any kind. Were that so, the problems which have arisen when a mother declines caesarean section required in the interests of her unborn child would simply not exist.[21] Indeed, the Abortion Act 1967 and the Human Fertilisation and Embryology Act 1990 clearly recognise that a foetus is a separate organism whose interests must be considered. What is more, the whole issue as to whether and how a civil claim can be brought for damages for injury to a child inflicted prenatally would never arise if there was identity of mother and child for all purposes. It is therefore unsurprising that in *R v Tait*[22] Mustill LJ referred to the 'confused and unsatisfactory state of the law' and to:

> the complex legal issues not yet fully worked out which concern the status of the unborn child in the community and the obligation of the community and its members towards the unborn child.

(iv) *The Development of the Common Law*

No English decision dealt with the question of the common law duty of care **12.14** to an unborn child before *Burton v Islington Health Authority* and *De Martell v Merton & Sutton Health Authority*.[23] The common law, however, had

---

[18] See eg *R v Mitchell* [1983] QB 741. 76 Cr App R 293, CA. A struck B, who fell against C causing C to fracture her femur; death resulted; and the conviction for manslaughter was upheld. See *R v Latimer* [1886] 17 QBD 359: A aimed a blow at B but hit C; the conviction of unlawful and malicious wounding was upheld. See also Archbold, *Criminal Pleading, Evidence and Practice*, (1998 edn), 19–219.   [19] [1997] 3 WLR 421: [1997] 3 All ER 936.
[20] *Per* Lord Mustill at 428–429, 943 and Lord Hope at 440, 954.
[21] See *Re MB* [1997] 8 Med LR 217.
[22] [1990] QB 290, 299, 300. See also the discussion in (1995) 3 Med L Rev 302.
[23] [1993] QB 204.

developed in other jurisdictions, gradually moving from denial of claims by those injured *in utero* to their general acceptance.

12.15 Early objections are illustrated by two American decisions. In *Dietrich v Inhabitants of Northampton*[24] Mr Justice Holmes considered a case where, as a result of a fall by the mother, a child was born at four or five months' gestation and survived its premature birth only by ten or fifteen minutes. He declined to follow the criminal and civil law analogies, and rejected a claim based on the infant's loss of life on the grounds that it was not a 'person' recognised by law at the time of its injury. He went on to rule that

> as the unborn child was a part of the mother at the time of the injury, any damage to it which was not too remote to be recovered for at all was recoverable by her.[25]

12.16 Objections to claims at common law were put more succinctly in *Drobner v Peters*.[26] The plaintiff was an infant allegedly injured when, eleven days before his birth, his mother fell down a coal-hole left uncovered in the sidewalk. Numerous arguments were raised by the defendant.

> The reasons given to defeat recovery in such a case are: lack of authority; practical inconvenience and possible injustice; no separate entity apart from the mother and, therefore, no duty of care; no person or human being *in esse* at the time of the accident.[27]

In the event the claim was rejected on the ground that the injuries were to the mother, and the defendant owed a duty of care to her alone.

12.17 A further obstacle to the development of such claims was the Irish case of *Walker v Great Northern Railway Company of Ireland*.[28] In that case a mother claimed for injuries allegedly sustained by her unborn child in a railway accident. On a demurrer, a court of the Queen's Bench Division decided that the Statement of Claim disclosed no cause of action. On any analysis, the decision is unsatisfactory. The majority view was based principally on the failure to plead a contract of carriage with the unborn child, an approach based on the fallacy that privity of contract is a prerequisite to a duty in tort. The court also drew support from the plaintiff's failure to plead that the carrier knew of the pregnancy and, further, from the absence of any case law on the matter. However *Donoghue v Stevenson*[29] exploded the 'privity of contract' fallacy and, based as it was upon the technical issue of the pleadings, *Walker* has become irrelevant.

---

[24] [1994] 138 Mass 14 (Mass Sup Jud Ct).   [25] ibid, 17.
[26] [1921] 25 NY 220 (NYCA).   [27] [1921] 25 NY 220, 222. (NYCA)
[28] [1891] 28 LR Ir 69   [29] [1932] AC 562.

A turning point was the influential decision of the Supreme Court of Canada   **12.18**
in *Montreal Tramways v Leveille*,[30] a decision under the Civil Code of
Quebec, Article 1053 of which provided:

> every person capable of discerning right from wrong is responsible for the
> damage caused by his fault to another, whether by positive act, imprudence,
> neglect or want of skill.

Recognising that judicial opinion in common law courts tended to deny the
right of a child when born to maintain an action for prenatal injury, the
majority of the court held that the civil law fiction should apply and that 'a
child will . . . be deemed to have been born at the time of the accident of the
mother'.[31] However, of greater interest to the common lawyer is the judgment
of Cannon J. It was delivered in French: the ratio appears in translation in the
Australian case of *Watt v Rama*[32] in these terms:

> [T]he cause of action arose when the damage was suffered and not when the
> wrongful act was committed. The plaintiff's right to compensation came into
> existence only when she was born with the bodily disability with which she
> suffered. It was only after birth that she suffered the injury, and it was then that
> her rights were encroached upon and she commenced to have rights.[33]

This judgment, as will be seen, contains the genesis of the modern analysis of
the problem.

Eventually, the right of a child when born alive to sue for injuries caused by a   **12.19**
prenatal event became recognised not only in Canada, in the United States of
America (where every jurisdiction now permits such a claim)[34] but also in
Australia,[35] South Africa,[36] Scotland,[37] Ireland (by statute),[38] and in
England and Wales by virtue of the Court of Appeal decision in *Burton
and De Martell*.[39]

---

[30] [1933] 4 DLR 337.   [31] ibid, 346.   [32] [1972] VR 353 (Sup Ct of Victoria).
[33] ibid, 357 to n 27. For further Canadian decisions see *Duval v Sequin* (1972) 26 DLR
(3d) 318 and *Cherry v Borsman* (1991) 75 DLR (4th) 668 (British Columbia Sup Ct), [1991]
2 Med LR 396.
[34] Prosser, WL and Keeton, P, *Torts* (5th edn) (West Publishing, 2984) 368: see Second
Restatement of the Law of Torts, 1977 para 869.
[35] *Watt v Rama* (n 32 above); *X and Y v Pal and another* [1991] 23 NSWLR 26, [1992] 3
Med LR 195 (NSWCA): *Lynch v Lynch and Another* [1992] 3 Med LR 62 (NSWCA).
[36] *Pinchin and another v Santam Insurance Co Ltd* [1963] 2 SA 254.
[37] *Hamilton v Fife Health Board* (n 9 above); for a commentary see (1993) 1 Med L Rev
392.   [38] Civil Liability Act 1961, s 58.
[39] N 23 above.

(v) *The Legal Basis of the Right*

12.20 A large number of Commonwealth cases depend as much upon assertion as analysis. For at least fifty years it has been generally accepted that denials of claims for prenatal injury are unjust. However, in various ways the courts have been oppressed by the argument that because at the time of the insult the foetus, the child-later-to-be-born, has no legal personality, therefore no duty can be owed to it. In *Burton*, it was further argued at first instance[40] that, because all the physical injury occurred to an entity without legal personality, it must follow that any damage sustained by the 'legal person' which first came into being upon birth was purely economic and as such irrecoverable by reason of the House of Lords decisions in *Caparo Industries plc v Dickman*[41] and *Murphy v Brentwood District Council*.[42]

12.21 The closest analysis of the law appears in the decision of the Supreme Court of Victoria in *Watt v Rama*.[43] The claim was brought by the plaintiff allegedly injured *in utero* by the negligent driving of the defendant, and the defendant took the preliminary point that the allegations disclosed no cause of action on the grounds that at the time of the collision the defendant owed no duty of care to the infant plaintiff who was then unborn; that he owed the infant plaintiff no duty not to injure her mother; and that the damages sought to be recovered by the infant plaintiff were in law too remote. The majority (Winneke CJ and Pape J) defined the issue as:

> not whether an action lies in respect of pre-natal injuries but whether a plaintiff born with injuries caused by the pre-natal neglect of the defendant has a cause of action in negligence against him in respect of such injuries.[44]

The solution was to define the relationship of the defendant to the plaintiff *in utero* as 'contingent or potential' which would 'crystallise' or 'ripen into a relationship imposing a duty' when the plaintiff's identity as a legal person became defined by birth. At that stage the act of neglect could be treated as a breach of duty, and the inter-uterine damage as 'merely an evidential fact relevant to the issue of causation and damage': the damage consisted of 'injuries as a living person'.[45] Thus, duty, breach, and damage remained potential until at and after birth, at which point they became actual. This line of reasoning was adopted by Potts J at first instance in *Burton*.[46]

---

[40] [1991] 1 QB 638, 651.   [41] [1990] 2 AC 605.   [42] [1991] 1 AC 398.
[43] [1972] VR 353 (Sup Ct of Victoria).
[44] [1972] VR 353, 358. (Sup Ct of Victoria)   [45] ibid, 360–1 and 366.
[46] [1991] 1 QB 638.

In contrast with the majority, the approach of Gillard J in *Watt v Rama* was **12.22** less metaphysical. He derived from *Donoghue v Stevenson*[47] and *Grant v Australia Knitting Mills Limited*[48] the proposition that:

> it would be immaterial whether at the time of fault the victim was in existence or not, so long as the victim was a member of a class which might reasonably and probably be affected by the act of carelessness.[49]

He noted that the pleaded and relevant '*damnum*' or damage was 'physical disabilities at and after her birth'. From this he inferred that the only difference made to a plaintiff by the passage of time was that by birth she acquired capacity to sue. He then went on to provide two linked answers to the contention that prior to birth no duty could be owed to an unborn child because it was not a legal person:

> The first depends on the views I have already expressed. The cause of action for negligence only comes into existence when the damage is suffered. The infant plaintiff at that period . . . is, I repeat, a *persona juridica*, with capacity to institute proceedings and to whom a duty might be owed. The injury while *en ventre sa mère* was but an evidentiary incident in the causation of damage suffered at birth by the fault of the defendant . . . As a second answer there is probably at the time of the defendant's fault also *damnum* contemporaneous with the *injuria* to a subject which is sufficiently protected by the rules of the common law, so that when it reaches the capacity of a person in being by subsequent birth to institute legal proceedings, it is entitled to bring those proceedings for its own benefit in relation to the damage suffered.[50]

(vi) Burton *and* de Martell

It was the first answer of Gillard J which attracted Phillips J at first instance in **12.23** *de Martell*:[51]

> To say that the plaintiff suffered his injuries the moment after his birth rather than in the period leading up to his birth involves a legal fiction. But the fiction is that which denies the living creature which became the plaintiff a *persona* in the period prior to birth. It is that legal fiction which the health authority relies upon in denying liability to the plaintiff. It is not open to the health authority to deny liability on the ground that the organism that they injured was not in law the plaintiff and yet to deny responsibility for the defects with which the plaintiff was born on the ground that they inflicted them before birth. In law

---

[47] [1932] AC 562.   [48] [1936] AC 85.
[49] N 43 above, 373. See also Lovell and Griffith-Jones, *The Sins of the Fathers* (n 1 above), 534, for the argument that unborn children, as a class, are foreseeable in their own right.
[50] N 43 above, 374–5.   [51] [1993] QB 204, 219.

and in logic no damage can have been caused to the plaintiff before the plaintiff existed. The damage was suffered by the plaintiff at the moment that, in law, the plaintiff achieved personality and inherited the damaged body for which the health authority (on the assumed facts) was responsible. The events prior to birth were mere links in the chain of causation between the health authority's assumed lack of skill and care and the consequential damage to the plaintiff.

The second answer given by Gillard J effectively identifies a complete cause of action at the time of the initial trauma, with the reservation only that it cannot be enforced until after a live birth. This, it is submitted, raises without resolving the problem of how a being with no legal identity can possess a 'chose in action', and is the less preferable analysis.

12.24 The Court of Appeal heard the defendants' appeals in *Burton* and *De Martell*[52] together and dismissed them without calling on the appellants. The majority followed *Watt v Rama*[53] without analysing its different approaches or expressing preference for either of the two first instance decisions. In a short concurring judgment, however, Leggatt LJ appears to express a preference for the first formulation of Gillard J, stating the issue as follows:

> [T]he plaintiffs claim that each was injured when at birth he or she became a legal person damaged by the prior act of the respective defendants, and that when each such act was done it was reasonably foreseeable that it might result in the plaintiff being born damaged.[54]

(vii) *The Common Law Right Defined*

12.25 The common law of England and Wales, thus analysed, now seems to be clear.

(a) There is a duty not by lack of reasonable care to cause damage to a person;

(b) an act or omission which is in breach of that duty is actionable at the suit of the injured party once the injury occurs;

(c) a human being injured as a result of a prenatal event first sustains injury for the purposes of the law and acquires a right to sue when, at birth, he or she first becomes a person recognised as such by the general law.

---

[52] ibid; for a commentary see (1993) 1 Med LRev 103.
[53] [1972] VR 353 (Sup Ct of Victoria).   [54] ibid.

(viii) *Pre-conception Occurrences*

From the premise that a claim can be made by a living child for the effects of **12.26** an occurrence which preceded its birth, it is but a short step to conclude that a living child can also make a claim for the consequences of an incident which preceded its conception. However, it is probably too simplistic to approach 'pre-conception occurrences' as if they formed one category susceptible of one answer in law. Distinctions may have to be made between:

(a) bringing about an injury to a child not yet conceived at the time of the act complained of but who would have been conceived whatever the defendant did;

(b) bringing about the conception of a child who, having been conceived, is doomed to disability for reasons unconnected with the act of the defendant, and

(c) bringing about both the conception of and the injury to the child.

This section considers only the first of these categories: the other two are discussed later.[55]

The problem was considered in *X and Y v Pal and Others*.[56] In that case the **12.27** New South Wales Court of Appeal considered the claim of an infant plaintiff, born with congenital syphilis, that her disabilities were caused by the negligence of her mother's gynaecologists in failing to screen and treat the mother for syphilis before she became pregnant. The defendants argued that the doctors owed no duty to the infant plaintiff: the argument failed. Clarke JA said:[57]

> [I]n principle . . . it should be accepted that a person may be subjected to a duty of care to a child who was neither born nor conceived at the time of his careless act or omission such that he may be found liable in damages to that child. Whether or not that duty will arise depends upon whether there is a relevant relationship between the careless person and the class of persons of whom the child is one.

A number of pre-conception occurrences may give rise to injuries to a child **12.28** subsequently conceived. For example, a doctor may perform an operation which negligently weakens the uterus so that some years later it ruptures at the end of pregnancy and injures the child. A further example would be that of pre-conception exposure to chemicals or radiation which caused gene mutation and consequent disability to children later conceived. It may also

---

[55] See below, paras 12.58–12.67 and 12.70–12.73.
[56] [1991] 23 NSWLR 26, [1992] 3 Med L Rev 195.   [57] ibid, 41 and 205.

be the case that some trauma to the mother leads to disability in a child not yet conceived when it occurs. *Burton* and *de Martell*[58] have removed the objection to such claims that the child was not alive at the time of the trauma. The extent to which such claims are likely to succeed, however, requires some discussion. There will in many cases be difficulties of proof in showing that, 'but for' the occurrence complained of, the child would have been born and born without the relevant disability. Leaving questions of evidence aside, however, there is also difficulty in predicting which categories of incident are most likely to give rise to successful claims.

12.29 Since *Caparo Industries plc v Dickman*[59] it has become clear that in a novel situation, such as that of a child claiming for injuries resulting from an incident which preceded his conception, a plaintiff must demonstrate that the damage was not only foreseeable but that a relationship of 'proximity' or 'neighbourhood' existed between him and the defendant. He must also show that it would be fair, just and reasonable for the law to impose a duty in the novel situation, and in general the courts only do so incrementally and by analogy with established categories of duty situations.

12.30 In America there has been reluctance to permit such claims to be brought against negligent motorists, on the ground that there is no 'special relationship' between the careless driver and the future child or the woman he injures.[60] However, where the child's disabilities are caused by the conduct of a doctor or pharmaceutical manufacturer, a 'special relationship' has been said to exist and such claims have been permitted.[61] Without the 'special relationship', injury to the future (as yet unconceived) child is as a matter of law treated as unforeseeable, and hence no duty of care is owed to the child.[62] It remains to be seen whether English courts would be so reluctant to find the existence of a duty of care. Such common law claims are unlikely to arise in

---

[58] [1993] QB 204.

[59] [1990] 2 AC 398; see in particular 617G–618E *per* Lord Bridge and 633F–635F *per* Lord Oliver.

[60] *Hegyes v Unjian Enterprises Inc* (1991) 286 Cal Rptr 85 (Cal App 2 Dist) (driver of motor vehicle not liable to child subsequently conceived and suffering disability in utero as a result of mother's injuries sustained in the accident). A majority of the Court of Appeal held that a 'special relationship' only existed between a doctor and a female patient and between a manufacturer of pharmaceuticals and their users. See also *McAuley v Wills* 303 SE 2d 258 (1983) (Ga Sup Ct).

[61] See eg *Bergstresser v Mitchell* 577 F 2d (1978) (8th Cir) (negligent caesarean section leading to weakened uterus); *Renslow v Mennonite Hospital* 367 NE 2d 1250 (1977) (Ill Sup Ct) (negligent blood transfusion leading to injury due to its incompatible Rhesus factor); and see cases cited in *Hegyes* (n 60 above).

[62] See *Hegyes* (n 60 above), 93 and 103 *per* Woods JA (Lillie PJ concurring). Contrast Johnson JA (dissenting) at 108. See also *Yeager v Bloomington Obstetrics and Gynaecology Inc* (1992) 585 NE 2d 696 (Ct App Indiana) and the commentary at (1993) 1 Med L Rev 247.

England now, and answers will be theoretical. Child plaintiffs injured *in utero* by vehicle accidents were successful in *Watt v Rama*[63] and also in *Lynch v Lynch and another.*[64] While it could be argued that a woman injured prior to conception is less likely to have an injured child than one injured during pregnancy, it cannot really be argued that injury caused to a child by a pre-conception event is 'unforeseeable'. It is suggested that as the Congenital Disabilities (Civil Liability) Act 1976[65] allows a claim for injuries to a child resulting from an incident which occurred before its conception, it would not be unfair if the common law did the same. However, the extension of a defendant's duty to such a situation would indeed be great, and the English courts might well find that the 'proximity' test was satisfied and a duty imposed on a defendant only where that defendant, as might a doctor or drug manu-facturer, knowingly acted in a way which might affect a parent's health.

(ix) *The Liability of Parents*

A parent can be liable to a child injured by his or her negligent driving of a car. It is not difficult to imagine other contexts in which parental liability might arise, for example where there is persistent refusal by a parent to take a child to hospital despite specific medical advice in obvious circumstances. This view is reinforced by the dictum of Lord Donaldson MR in *Re J (Wardship: Medical Treatment)* where he stated plainly:[66]

12.31

> [T]he parents owe the child a duty to give or withhold consent [to medical treatment] in the best interests of the child and without regard to their own interests.

Furthermore, analysis of the law set out in *Burton* and *de Martell*[67] implies that a parent may owe a duty at common law not to damage the health of a child as yet unborn.

The Law Commission,[68] however, was much troubled by the idea of a child having an unfettered right to sue his or her mother in respect of injuries arising from some antenatal event. It felt that such a right of action could further stress the already difficult relationship between mother and disabled child, or become a weapon between parents in a matrimonial conflict to its further detriment. It was impressed by the difficulty and unseemliness of possible allegations against mothers, such as those of excessive drinking and smoking, and pointed to the fact that in any event a mother, even if liable,

12.32

---

[65] S 1(2)(a).   [66] [1991] Fam 33, 41.   [67] [1993] QB 204.
[68] Law Commission Report No 60: *Report on Injuries to Unborn Children* 1974, Cmnd 5709, paras 54–63.

would probably be unsupported by funds. In the end it recommended that a woman should only be liable for causing antenatal injury to her child if she was negligent in driving when she knew or ought reasonably to know herself to be pregnant. However, the Law Commission did not recommend any such special exemption for a father.[69]

12.33 These considerations of policy would be likely to affect any court considering a common law claim by a child against a parent for an antenatal occurrence. There may be further difficulties. For example, the interests of the foetus and the parents do not always coincide. Thus a pregnant mother may exercise her individual right to refuse caesarean section and thereby, perhaps knowingly, injure a viable foetus.[70] By parity of reasoning it is not easy to envisage a court actually finding a mother negligent in refusing or delaying other treatment to herself which might benefit her unborn child. Furthermore, if the standard of care to be expected to the mother cannot be identified, then it cannot be imposed upon her, and no claim will succeed.[71] For example, it will be extremely difficult to identify the point at which drinking or smoking in pregnancy became negligent.

12.34 It would, however, be going too far to say that no child could ever sue a parent at common law for injuries resulting from some antenatal occurrence. Thus, in *Lynch v Lynch*[72] a mother was successfully sued by a child injured in utero in a driving accident. Equally, if a mother failed to follow explicit prenatal advice which involved no assault upon her (eg to stop water skiing or the consumption of damaging drugs)[73] there would be no particular difficulty in judging her conduct. It could be assessed by the same standards as those which would apply, for example, to a teacher who disregarded a school doctor's instructions on how to react to a pupil's sudden illness, or to one who knowingly gave a child damaging substances. It is therefore suggested that where, as in motoring cases, a parent's conduct can be assessed by the same tests as those which can be applied to non-parents, then in the absence of a very good reason it is strongly arguable that lack of care by parents which damages a foetus may be actionable by the child, if and when born alive.[74]

---

[69] ibid, para 61.   [70] See *Re MB* (n 21 above).
[71] See *Jackson v Harrison* [1978] CR 438 (H Ct of Australia), 455—6 *per* Mason J: *Pitts v Hunt* [1991] 1 QB 24, 50–1 *per* Balcombe LJ, where the principle is discussed in the context of illegal joint enterprises (joy-riding). See also *Gala v Preston* [1991] ALJR 366.
[72] N 64 above.   [73] ibid, 71 *per* Clarke JA.
[74] See *Surtees v Royal Borough of Kingston* [1992] 1 PIQR 101, 121: 'the development of duties owed by a parent to his child has tended to result from claims by third parties either for damages or for contribution': *per* Beldam LJ, dissenting in the result. There are dicta in all three judgments on the need for care in imposing duties on a parent in the home context: *per* Stocker LJ at 111–2, Beldam LJ at 121, Browne-Wilkinson V-C at 123–4.

(x) *Transgenerational Claims*

It is possible to envisage something happening to a person as a result of which **12.35** not (or not only) his or her child but that child's child and indeed succeeding generations may be injured. The establishment of a causal link between the occurrence and the subsequent harm to later generations may be difficult to establish, but at least in logic the claim of successive generations might be thought to be entitled to succeed under the *Burton*[75] principle. It is, however, likely that such claims will be rejected on straightforward policy grounds. The Law Commission[76] was of the view that no duty should be owed to any but the immediate children of the parent affected by the occurrence. The same conclusion has been reached in the litigation of the American DES daughters. Diethylstilbestrol (DES) was a drug which, between 1947 and its banning in 1971, was given to millions of pregnant women to prevent miscarriages. It was alleged that *in utero* exposure to DES resulted in genital tract abnormalities to daughters later born, who in turn and as a result suffered obstetric problems including premature births. In *Enright v Eli Lilly & Co*,[77] the granddaughter of a woman who had ingested the drug during pregnancy alleged that in consequence her mother had given birth prematurely, as a result of which she suffered from cerebral palsy, and sued the manufacturers of the drug. The New York Court of Appeals rejected the claim, strongly influenced by policy considerations including the unquantifiable extent of the potential liability of drug companies to future generations. It is suggested that English courts would be extremely reluctant to reach a different conclusion.

(xi) *Exclusion and Restriction of Liability*

An unborn child is not a 'person' in law,[78] and it is difficult to envisage how **12.36** any contract term or notice given by a defendant while it is *in utero* can exclude or restrict a defendant's liability for injuries with which the child is born. Certainly, in strict law the mother can hardly be described as an agent, fixing the foetus as a legally non-existent principal with notice or with the terms of a contract to which she was a party.

This conclusion, however, did not attract the Law Commission,[79] which **12.37** concluded on social grounds that it would be unfair on a defendant if he could not limit liability to a child as yet unborn to the same extent as he could limit liability to the mother. In the context of prenatally inflicted injuries,

---

[75] See para 12.25 above.   [76] N 68 above, paras 79–80.
[77] (1991) 570 NE 2d 198 (NYCA).   [78] See para 12.05 above.
[79] N 68 above, paras 67–71.

however, the debate has now become of limited practical importance since the Unfair Contract Terms Act 1977.[80] Section 2(1) of the Act provides:

> a person cannot by reference to any contract term or to a notice given to persons generally or to particular persons exclude or restrict his liability for death or personal injury resulting from negligence.

This language is sufficiently broad to refer to injury arising from a prenatal event.

12.38 The protection provided by section 2(1) is however not completely all-embracing. 'Negligence' is defined[81] so as to include 'contractual' as well as common law negligence, and also an occupier's common duty of care, but it does not include 'any stricter duty' than common law negligence (such as an obligation under *Rylands v Fletcher*)[82] nor breaches of any statutory duty other than those of an occupier. Nevertheless, for the reasons given above[83] it is thought that, even in the absence of the protection conferred by the Act of 1977, a defendant cannot restrict his liability for injuries inflicted before birth.

(xii)   *Volenti Non Fit Injuria*

12.39 Should a parent's voluntary assumption of a risk to his or her as yet unborn child negative a defendant's liabilities, as a result of his conduct, to the child if later born injured? On strict legal analysis, a parent's assumption of a risk would only absolve a defendant of a duty not to injure an unborn child if he or she was treated as having authority to consent on behalf of the child, which is highly artificial. The Law Commission[84] thought it unfair that a defendant should be liable to the child born of a *volens* mother, and proposed that legislation should counter this injustice. Nevertheless, the problem remains at common law. One practical solution, it is suggested, is that although the doctrine of *volenti non fit injuria* might not exempt a defendant from his duty to a child as yet unborn, yet the fact of the mother's consent might prevent the defendant's conduct from amounting to a breach of that duty. Theoretically, that might not always be so. If, for example a pregnant woman insisted on a bizarre birth plan that might absolve her medical attendants of liability to her. However, if her child was later born injured as a result he might well

---

[80] S 31(2) of the 1977 Act provides: 'nothing in this Act applies to contracts made before [1 February 1978]; but subject to this it applies to liability for loss or damage which is suffered on or after that date'.
[81] Unfair Contract Terms Act 1977, s 1(1).
[82] [1868] LR 3 HL 330 [1861–73] All ER Repl HL.   [83] See para 12.36 above.
[84] N 68 above, paras 67–9.

wish to argue that it was their duty to him (as opposed to his mother) forcefully to try and persuade her to follow an alternative course which avoided the risk of inter-uterine damage, and that if proper persuasion had been employed it would have changed the mother's mind and avoided the injury. Thus, in highly unusual circumstances it might be arguable that a mother's consent would not protect the defendant against a claim by the child. In practice, however, it is not easy to see such an argument succeeding.

2. Claims for Injuries under the Congenital Disabilities (Civil Liability) Act 1976

(i) *The Purpose of the Act*

The 1976 Act has its origins in the Law Commission Report on Injuries to Unborn Children.[85] The proposed legislation was justified on five grounds,[86] namely: **12.40**

(a) because in the absence of English authority there was doubt whether a child had a cause of action at all for injuries caused before birth;

(b) because the basis upon which the cause of action existed in other common law jurisdictions varied;

(c) to avoid the cost of law reform falling upon one individual;

(d) because the first factual situation litigated would almost certainly leave a number of ancillary questions unanswered, and

(e) because it recommended departures on social grounds from the probable results of strict application of legal principles, eg to claims by a child against the mother.[87]

(ii) *The Availability of the Act*

The Act applies to a child who is 'born disabled' after 22 July 1976, and in respect of such births it replaces the common law. By 'born'[88] is meant being 'born alive (the moment of a child's birth being when it first has a life separate from its mother)'.[89] To take advantage of the Act however, the child need not be 'disabled' in the ordinary sense of the word because disability denotes: 'any deformity, disease or abnormality, including pre-disposition (whether or not   **12.41**

---

[85] N 68 above.   [86] ibid, para 110.

[87] In retrospect it must be asked whether this difficult Act, a reaction to the thalidomide cases (see *S v Distillers Co* [1970] 1 WLR 114), was really necessary, and whether it is an improvement on the common law as now established.

[88] S 1(1), s 4(5).   [89] S 4(2)(a).

susceptible of immediate prognosis) to physical or mental defect in the future'.[90] In other words, any child born alive with any personal injury has a claim in appropriate circumstances. Social disadvantage, however, does not found a claim under the Act.

(iii) *The Scope of the Act*

12.42 To succeed, the child must prove that the disability resulted from an occurrence within the meaning of section 1(2) of the Act, namely:

one which—

(a) affected either parent of the child in his or her ability to have a normal, healthy child; or

(b) affected the mother during her pregnancy, or affected her or the child in the course of its birth, so that the child is born with disabilities which would not otherwise have been present.

Section 1(2) requires two comments. First, although its sub-sections were intended to deal with pre-conception occurrences and post-conception occurrences respectively,[91] they are not mutually exclusive. For example, a badly performed caesarean section may affect the mother's subsequent ability to have a normal healthy child, but also affect her during a later pregnancy. Second, the language of the statute does not make it absolutely clear that section 1(2)(b) covers all post-conception occurrences which might damage the foetus. For example, it might be the case that X-rays and inter-uterine investigations affected the foetus without 'affecting' the mother, at least in the sense of injuring her. However, despite that lack of clarity it is most unlikely that a court would adopt so narrow a construction and thereby deprive the child of a statutory right of action. This is particularly so because a child has a right of action even though the mother has not been injured.[92] It is therefore likely that a court would construe 'affected' as meaning not 'injured' but rather as merely meaning 'involved'.[93]

(iv) *Infertility Treatments*

12.43 Section 1 of the Act has been extended to a child's disabilities which result from certain infertility treatments, namely:

---

[90] S 4(1).
[91] See note 5 to Clause 1 of the Draft Bill, Appendix 1 to the Report, n 68 above.
[92] See s 1(3).
[93] Note 5 (n 91 above) uses the verb 'involve' as equivalent to 'affect'.

an act or omission in the course of selection, or the keeping or use outside the body, of the embryo . . . or of the gametes used to bring about the creation of the embryo.[94]

(v) *The Mother as a Defendant*

12.44 With one exception, a child born disabled has no claim against its mother.[95] The exceptional case is that of claims arising from the negligent driving of a motor vehicle by a woman when she knows (or ought reasonably to know) herself to be pregnant. In such circumstances the mother owes a direct 'duty to take care for the safety of the unborn child', who may sue her if later born with disabilities. It is to be noted that this right of action extends only to the driving of motor vehicles and not, for example, to the riding of a bicycle or horse. In other words, it extends to claims covered either by insurers or by the Motor Insurance Bureau. In these circumstances the policy arguments for disallowing claims against a mother are much diminished.

(vi) *The Father as a Defendant*

12.45 It is to be noted that a father does not enjoy the same immunity from action as does the mother. This apparent anomaly was justified by the Law Commission's views that, *inter alia*, there would be less ways in which congenital disabilities could be caused by a father than by a mother: that a father's responsibility for a child's injuries would be less likely to raise family disputes than a mother's: and that a child born disabled as a result of an assault by a man on the mother (even a rape which caused the conception) should have a cause of action against the man.[96]

(vii) *The Derivative Nature of the Claim*

12.46 The basis of liability under the Act is unique, because, save in claims against a mother for motoring injuries,[97] a defendant is liable to the child only if the defendant has committed a breach of duty to a parent. He:

---

[94] S 1A, inserted by the Human Fertilisation and Embryology Act 1990, s 44(1).
[95] The general rule appears in s 1(1), the exception in s 2 of the Act.
[96] N 68 above, paras 92–3. See Cane, P F, 'Injuries to Unborn Children' (n 1 above), 154–5 for criticism of this 'inequality of treatment of parents' liabilities'.
[97] See above, para 12.44.   [98] S 1(3).

is answerable to the child if he was liable in tort to the parent or would, if sued in due time, have been so: and it is no answer that there could not have been such liability because the parent suffered no actionable injury, if there was a breach of legal duty which, accompanied by injury, would have given rise to the liability.[98]

In other words, a child's claim is derivative from a breach of duty to the parent which gives rise to, or would if accompanied by damage give rise to, liability in tort. This includes not only tortious liability at common law but also cases where such liability is created by statute when the wrong, though commonly called 'breach of statutory duty' is a proper analysis the infringement of a private law right created by statute.[99] However the Act does not apply where the injury to the parent is a breach of a term in a contract, whether express or implied. Thus, a child born injured as a result of breach of a term implied by the Sale of Goods Act 1989 as amended as to the quality of goods bought by her would have no remedy under the 1976 Act.

12.47 It may be thought that this approach seems unnecessarily tortuous. However, it avoids a number of anomalies. For example, an occupier's duty may require a different level of care to be exercised towards lawful visitors from that which is owed to trespassers;[100] to impose an unrestricted duty of care to unborn children upon an occupier could mean that he owed a higher duty to the unborn child than to its trespassing mother. Thus, by making the child's action derivative on a breach of duty to a parent, the Act avoids the problem which would arise if a defendant owed two levels of duty in respect of one incident. More importantly, this approach enables the child to sue the maker of a negligent misstatement to the mother. This would not otherwise have been possible. For if the only duty upon which an action could be based was one owed directly to a child as yet unborn, it is not easy to see how liability could be imposed for negligent advice given to the mother before the birth.

12.48 Nevertheless, this approach is not entirely without disadvantage to the child. First, if the parents' actions would have given rise, had they sued, to a defence, then the child is without remedy; this might arise if the mother perversely refused appropriate treatment such as a caesarean section in appropriate circumstances, or refused to go into hospital despite a warning that the labour was high risk. Here the child will be without remedy either against the medical attendant or against the mother (because she is immune from action save in motoring claims). Furthermore, undue solicitude for the

---

[99] See *X (Minors) v Bedfordshire CC* [1995] 2 AC 633, 731C–732B *per* Lord Browne-Wilkinson.
[100] See *Herrington v British Railways Board* [1972] AC 877: Occupiers' Liability Act 1984: s 1(3).

mother, even at risk to the child, might not be a breach of any duty to her, and the child injured by such excess of care would be without remedy.[101] Cane gives an example of another anomaly.[102] A manufacturer of a drug known to create a risk to both mother and foetus warns the mother of the risk to herself but negligently states that the drug is safe for the foetus. The mother consumes the drug: only the foetus is injured. Because the child's claim is derivative only on an assumed breach of duty to the mother, he has no claim against the drug manufacturer. This is clearly unjust. As yet, these problems remain unlitigated.

(viii) *Product Liability*

Section 6(3) of the Consumer Protection Act 1987 provides that: **12.49**

> Section 1 of the Congenital Disabilities (Civil Liability) Act 1976 shall have effect the purposes of this Part as if—
>
> (a) a person were answerable to a child in respect of an occurrence caused wholly or partly by a defect in a product if he is or has been liable under section 2 above in respect of any effect of the occurrence on a parent of the child, or would be so liable if the occurrence caused a parent of the child to suffer damage;
>
> (b) the provisions of this Part relating to liability under section 2 above applied in relation to liability by virtue of paragraph (a) above under the said section 1; and
>
> (c) subsection (6) of the said section 1 (exclusion of liability) were omitted.

In brief, it extends the protection of product liability legislation to the unborn child, while adopting the general scheme of the Act of 1967 in making liability to the child derivative on liability to a parent under the Act of 1987.

(ix) *The Statutory Standard of Care*

The special position of the professional attendant is recognised by section **12.50** 1(5) of the Act which provides

> the defendant is not answerable to the child, for anything he did or omitted to do when responsible in a professional capacity for treating or advising the parent, if he took reasonable care having due regard to then received professional opinion applicable to the particular class of case; but this does not mean that he is answerable only because he departed from received opinion.

---

[101] See Eekelaar J M and Dingwall, R W J, 'Some legal issues in Obstetric Practice' (n 1 above).   [102] See Cane, P F, 'Injuries to Unborn Children' (n 1 above), 707–8, n 42.

This is an attempted codification of the common law, of which the Law Commission said:

> [I]t demands of a professional man that he should exercise such care as accords with the standards of reasonably competent medical men at the time unless he has in fact greater than average knowledge of any risks in which case his duty will be that much greater.[103]

Emphasis is correctly placed by the subsection both on the standards of the day and on the principle that departure from approved practice is not necessarily a breach of duty.[104] No reference is made to responsibility for diagnosis (as opposed to treatment or advice) but this distinction is unlikely to commend itself to a Court: no distinction was made between 'diagnosis' and 'treatment' in *Hunter v Hanley*.[105] Finally, the language, it is suggested, gives some comfort to those who seek to argue on policy grounds that the *Bolam*[106] test is unduly favourable to medical defendants. While accepting the relevance of medical opinion to the question of negligence it stops short of making it determinative of the issue.

(x) *Transgenerational Claims*

12.51 It will be recalled[107] that difficult questions arise at common law in considering whether a child should have a claim for injuries caused by a pre-conception occurrence which affects not the parent but a grand-parent or more remote ancestor. The Act, in somewhat obscure language, excludes such a claim. Section 1(3) makes a child's claim dependent upon his establishing that a defendant is 'liable in tort' to the parent or would, if sued in time, have been so. However section 4(5) of the Act provides that:

> [I]n section 1(3) of this Act the expression 'liable in tort' does not include any reference to liability by virtue of this Act or to liability by virtue of [any law in force before its passing whereby a person could be liable to a child in respect of disabilities with which it might be born.]

This means that the liability in tort to a parent from which a plaintiff's rights

---

[103] *Report on Injuries to Unborn Children* (n 68 above), para 94. In this connection see *Newell v Newell and Goldenberg* [1995] 6 Med LR 371, 374 *per* Mantell J: 'The *Bolam* principle provides a defence for those who lag behind the times. It cannot serve those who know better'.
[104] See Kennedy, I and Grubb, A, *Medical Law, Text and Materials* (n 1 above), 463–5.
[105] [1955] SLT 213.
[106] *Bolam v Friern HMC* [1957] 1 WLR 582. See also *Maynard v West Midlands RHA* [1984] 1 WLR 634; *Sidaway v Board of Governors of the Bethlem Royal Hospital* [1985] AC 871; and *Bolitho v City and Hackney HA* [1997] 3 WLR 1151, [1997] 4 All ER 771.
[107] See para 12.35 above.

under the Act derive must arise from an event taking place after the parent's birth. Therefore, a defendant would not be under any liability for an occurrence which affects the second or subsequent generation from the victim of the original occurrence.

(xi) *Exclusion and Restriction of Liability*

The question of the exclusion or restriction of liability to children to whom the Act does not apply has been discussed above.[108] Those to whom it does apply are equally protected, because section 1(6) of the Act provides: **12.52**

> [L]iability to the child under this section may be treated as having been excluded or limited by contract made with the parent affected, to the same extent and subject to the same restrictions as liability in the parent's own case; and a contract term which could have been set up by the defendant in an action by the parent, so as to exclude or limit his liability to him or her, operates in the defendant's favour to the same, but no greater, extent in an action under this section by the child.

This confers on a child born disabled the same extensive protection against exclusion clauses in contracts with the parents as they, if injured, would enjoy by virtue of section 2(1) of the Unfair Contract Terms Act 1977. In product liability claims the same effect is achieved even more directly because, although section 6(3)(c) of the Consumer Credit Act 1987 excludes the operation of section 1(6) of the 1967 Act, section 7 provides:

> [T]he liability of a person by virtue of [Part I of the 1987 Act] to a person who has suffered damage caused wholly or partly by a defect in a product, or to a dependant or relative of such a person, shall not be limited or excluded by any contract term, by any notice or by any other provision.

(xii) Volenti Non Fit Injuria *and Parental Knowledge of Risks*

If a claim by a parent arising out of the occurrence which injured the unborn child would have been defeated by the defence of *volenti non fit injuria*, then the child will be unable to succeed under the Act. This is because, as has been pointed out,[109] the child's claim is derivative, and presupposes that the defendant would have been liable to the parent. **12.53**

However, children born with a disability face another obstacle. Section 1(4) of the Act provides: **12.54**

---

[108] See, paras 12.36–12.38 above. [109] See para 12.46 above.

[I]n the case of an occurrence preceding the time of conception, the defendant is not answerable to the child if at that time either or both of the parents knew of the risk of their child being born disabled (that is to say, the particular risk created by the occurrence); but should it be the child's father who is the defendant, this subsection does not apply if he knew of the risk and the mother did not.

This subsection requires certain comments. First, it is probable that the Law Commission[110] intended this to be a statutory form of *volenti non fit injuria*. However, such a provision would be unnecessary,[111] and in any even knowledge without assumption of that risk does not make a plaintiff *volens*.[112] Perhaps unintentionally, a defence of *scienti non fit injuria* has been introduced. Second, section 1(4) does not apply to a risk attaching to post-conception occurrences, but only to those attaching to occurrences which precede conception. Nor, in cases where the child sues the father, can the father claim that his knowledge of the risk amounted to a defence unless that knowledge was shared by the mother. Were the law otherwise, a man who knew he had syphilis, of which a woman was unaware, and who in raping her infected a child thus conceived with that disease might be able to plead his own knowledge of it as a defence, which would be absurd. Third, a comparable but not identical provision applies to claims arising out of the infertility treatments referred to in section 1A(3)[113] of the Act, providing that

[T]he defendant is not under this section answerable to the child if at the time the embryo, or the sperm and eggs, are placed in the woman or at the time of her insemination (as the case may be) either or both of the parents knew the risk of their child being born disabled (that is to say, the particular risk created by the act or omission).

In the circumstances contemplated, as neither parent will be responsible for the infertility treatment, and thus neither will be a defendant, there is no reason why either's knowledge of the risk involved should not be a defence available to those who provided it.

(xiii) *Contributory Negligence by Parents*

12.55 Section 1(7) of the Act provides:

[I]f in the child's action . . . it is shown that the parent affected shared the responsibility for the child being born disabled, the damages are to be reduced

---

[110] N 103 above, paras 71 and 93, and note 10 to the Draft Bill, Appendix 1 to the Report, suggesting a defence 'if either or both of the parents knew of the risk of their child being born disabled *and accepted it'.* [111] See para 12.53 above.
[112] *Smith v Baker* [1891] AC 325, 355 *per* Lord Watson. [113] N 94 above.

to such extent as the court thinks just and equitable having regard to the extent of the parent's responsibility.

This in effect gives a partial or complete defence on grounds equivalent to the contributory negligence of a parent. In doing so, the Act recognises the injustice which would otherwise result to a wrongdoer who is made to pay damages in full when his fault was slight compared with that of the parent. By implication, it also recognises the responsibility of a parent for the well-being of a child as yet unborn. The disadvantage is that (save in motoring claims) a child may have his damages severely reduced by reason of the mother's responsibility, and yet because of her exemption from liability have no right to recover the balance of compensation from her.[114]

(xiv) *Radiation Injuries*

The Nuclear Installations Act 1965 as amended provides compensation provi- **12.56** sions for those injured by a nuclear incident, and the Act of 1967 extends them to children subsequently born disabled. Section 3(2) of that Act includes as an injury for the purposes of the compensation provisions of the Act of 1965:

anything which
(a) affects a man in his ability to have a normal, healthy child or
(b) affects a woman in that ability, or so affects her when she is pregnant that her child is born with disabilities which would not otherwise have been present.

Section 3(3) then provides that a child's disabilities resultant on such an injury caused by a breach of a duty under sections 7 to 11 of the 1965 Act are also compensatable. The child's compensation is however by section 3(4) subject to a reduction caused by the contributory fault of the parent within the limits of section 13(6) of the 1965 Act, namely by: 'any act . . . committed with the intention of causing harm to any person or property or with reckless disregard for the consequences of his act;. Finally, section 3(5) of the 1976 Act provides:

compensation is not payable in the child's case if the injury to the parent preceded the time of the child's conception and at that time either or both of the parents knew the risk of their child being born disabled (that is to say, the particular risk created by the injury).

Detailed discussion of the Act of 1965 is beyond the scope of this work.

---

[114] See Pace, PJ, 'Civil Liability for Pre-Natal Injuries' (n 1 above), 157 for arguments that this provision is unfair and inconsistent with the Law Commission's wish to avoid bitterness in the family.

(xv) The Nature of the Remedy

12.57 Finally, section 1(1) of the Act confers a remedy in these terms: 'the child's disabilities are to be regarded as damage resulting from the wrongful act . . . and actionable accordingly.' The scope of that remedy is defined by section 4(3): 'liability is to be regarded as liability for personal injuries sustained by the child immediately after its birth.' One purpose of this provision is to exclude a right to compensation for any prenatal suffering, and to provide for damages to be assessed as if the prenatal injury had been inflicted after birth without the disabilities due to the prenatal wrong.[115] Secondly, the intention was to limit the claim to damages for personal injuries. Whether this has been achieved will be discussed below.[116] When the Act was passed there was a right to damages for loss of expectation of life, and therefore (to avoid the apparent absurdity of a child which survives only for a few minutes having such a claim) section 4(4) the Act provided that no damages should be recoverable for loss of expectation of life unless the child lived for at least forty-eight hours. However, in respect of causes of action accruing after 31 December 1982 damages in respect of any loss of expectation of life were abolished save in respect of claims for damages in respect of loss of income.[117] In most actions under the Act such claims will be worthless, because claims for loss of income during the 'lost years' are not recoverable on behalf of a young child save to the extent that they may be reflected occasionally in 'some small adjustment to the multiplier'.[118] Occasionally, however, claims are made on behalf of those injured as a result of a prenatal occurrence but do not reach court until after the plaintiff's maturity. In those circumstances, there is no reason why a claim should not be made for loss of income during any 'lost years'.

C. Claims by Living Children for 'Wrongful Life'

1. 'Wrongful Life' Claims at Common Law

(i) The 'Wrongful Life' Claim

12.58 In *McKay v Essex AHA*,[119] the Court of Appeal considered claims arising from the birth of a child born disabled as a result of an infection of rubella suffered

---

[115] N 103 above, para 100. [116] See paras 12.74–12.77 above.
[117] Administration of Justice Act 1972, s 1.
[118] *Housecroft v Burnett* [1986] 1 All ER 332, 345. See also *Croke v Wiseman* [1982] 1 WLR 71, [1981] 3 All ER 853. [119] [1982] QB 1166.

by the mother during pregnancy. One claim brought by the child was that, but for the negligence of the defendants in managing the pregnancy, the mother would have had a lawful abortion and the child would not, as the Statement of Claim alleged, have 'suffered . . . entry into a life in which her injuries are highly debilitating, and distress and loss and damage'.[120] It was clear that the injuries resulted not from the negligence but from untreated rubella. The claim by the child was therefore analysed as one for negligently allowing her to be born alive in an injured condition: a claim now traditionally described as one for 'wrongful life'.

(ii) *Objections to a 'Wrongful Life' Claim*

That claim was struck out, essentially on three grounds: first, that it was **12.59** contrary to public policy as being inconsistent with the concept of the sanctity of human life; second, that despite the possible legality of an abortion a doctor was under no obligation to the child to give the mother an opportunity to terminate its life; and third, that as a court could not evaluate non-existence it could not award damages for life, ie for the denial of non-existence. These three arguments require separate discussion.

(iii) *Public Policy and the Sanctity of Life*

The argument that public policy should not permit a claim for 'wrongful **12.60** life' requires some care in its deployment. First, while such policy in general may support life actually in existence, it cannot apply in a case in which an abortion is lawful under the Abortion Act 1967, for in such a case the termination has in effect been approved by Parliament as being consistent with the public interest. Second, the argument cannot be applied to bar claims for 'wrongful life' arising out of preconception events such as negligently performed sterilization or vasectomy or negligently given contraceptive advice or indeed rape, as a result of which the child is in fact conceived. For public policy actively supports the provision of contraceptive services and advice, and condemns rape as a crime. Therefore, generalised appeals to 'the sanctity of life' are of doubtful weight in countering 'wrongful life' claims.

---

[120] ibid, 1174.

(iv) *The Nature of the Doctor's Duty*

12.61　The second objection to 'wrongful life' claims is more formidable. It is that there is an insuperable problem in establishing a duty to a child to bring about, or help to bring about, its non-existence. The legality of contraceptive services or abortion does not imply an obligation on a doctor to provide such services or perform an abortion: and it is difficult to impose on a doctor in this context a duty to do more than advise the parent or parents. On what basis could such a duty be owed to the child? No duty can be owed to the hypothetically non-existent, so any duty would have to be owed to the child in fact born in some way to facilitate his non-existence. But tort law is concerned with defendants who make plaintiffs worse, not with those who merely make plaintiffs exist. Unless existence is to be defined as an injury to the person who exists, or some other damage can be identified, nothing can be identified as the injury to be avoided by reasonable care.

(v) *Identifying Damage and Quantifying Damages*

12.62　In *McKay* the Court was unable to quantify damages, and therefore unable to identify compensatable damage. It was argued,[121] by analogy with cases in which damages were assessed for loss of expectation of life, that difficulties in computation should not bar the claim. The argument was rejected. Stephenson LJ[122] said:

> [I]n measuring the loss caused by shortened life the courts are dealing with a thing, human life, of which they have some experience; here the court is being asked to deal with the consequences of death for the dead, a thing of which it has none. To measure loss of expectation of death would require a value judgment where a crucial factor lies altogether outside the range of human knowledge.

To the same effect Ackner LJ[123] said:

> [H]ow can a court begin to evaluate non-existence, 'the undiscovered country from whose bourne no traveller returns?' No comparison is possible and there-fore no damage can be established which a court can recognise. This goes to the root of the whole cause of action.

The objection is, and will remain, formidable.

---

[121] [1982] QB 1166, 1170.　　[122] ibid, 1181–2.　　[123] ibid, 1189.

(vi) *American Authorities*

A number of American cases were considered in *McKay*, and some of the   **12.63**
thinking is illustrated by three of them. In *Gleitman v Cosgrove*[124] the
Supreme Court of New Jersey by a majority rejected a claim by a child
born disabled as a result of intra-uterine rubella on the grounds that the
action did not give rise to damages cognisable in law, in that a child could not
complain that it would have been better off not being born.

However, a different approach was taken in *Curlender v Bio-Science Labora-*   **12.64**
tories.[125] There the Californian Court of Appeal considered a case in which it
was alleged that, as a result of negligently conducted genetic tests, a child was
born suffering from Tay-Sachs disease, which was defined as 'amaurotic
familial idiocy'. The court, accepting that the real crux of the problem was
whether the breach of duty was the proximate cause of an injury cognisable at
law, was able to identify as such an injury not the physical defect (for which
the defendant was not responsible) nor the birth alone, but the composite
concept of 'the birth of the plaintiff with such defect'. It therefore ruled that
damages could be quantified for: 'the pain and suffering to be endured during
the limited lifespan available to such a child and any special pecuniary loss
resulting from the impaired condition.'[126]

This development was curtailed by the Supreme Court of California in   **12.65**
Turpin v Sortini.[127] There, the Court considered the claim by a child Joy
that clinicians had been negligent in failing to advise her parents that the
deafness of an elder sister Hope was hereditary. The claim was for 'general
damages for being deprived of the fundamental right of a child to be born as a
whole, functional human being without total deafness',[128] and special
damages were also claimed for expenses necessary to treat the hereditary
illness. Unlike the *Curlender* court, that in *Turpin* rejected the claim for
general damages. Taking into account the benefits of life itself as well as
the detriment of the affliction, it ruled:

> [B]ecause of the incalculable nature of both elements of this harm–benefit
> equation, we believe that a reasoned, non arbitrary award of general damage
> is simply not obtainable.[129]

Special damages were however allowed for the extraordinary expenses of
specialized teaching, training, and hearing equipment as there was no benefit

---

[124] 49 NJ 22, 227 A 2d 689 (1967).   [125] (1980) 165 Cal Rptr 477 (Cal CA).
[126] ibid, 489.   [127] (1982) 643 P 2d 954 (Sup Ct Cal).
[128] ibid, 956.   [129] ibid, 964.

or amenity enjoyed by the plaintiff which could fairly be set off against these requirements.

12.66 It has been persuasively argued[130] that English courts could follow *Turpin*, as has been done in two other American jurisdictions.[131] It can be said that quantifiable and foreseeable loss occurs as a function of a defect which becomes apparent on birth which itself was caused by negligence. The difficulty here is that, as the defect was not caused by the defendants, and as birth is not an injury to the one who is born,[132] the harm recognisable in law or 'damage' necessary to constitute the tort of negligence must be economic loss alone.

12.67 It remains to be decided whether the approach of the House of Lords to economic loss will be modified to permit such claims.[133] Such a change would be a prerequisite to adoption of the *Turpin* solution of awarding compensation for financial loss and expense alone in 'wrongful life' cases. There would be social justice in it, because the multiplier used to calculate such a claim would be based only on the child's expectation of life, rather than (as in the case of a parent's 'wrongful birth'[134] claim for caring for a disabled child) on the period for which a parent would be expected to survive and provide care. It is, however, to be expected that general 'policy' considerations such as led the Law Commission to recommend[135] the exclusion of 'wrongful life' claims from statutory remedy, however arguable, will prevail and with them the authority of *McKay*.

(vii) *Disadvantaged Life*

12.68 In *Zepeda v Zepeda*,[136] an illegitimate child sued his father for conferring on him the status of illegitimacy by fraudulently inducing his mother to have sexual relations with a promise of marriage when he was already married. In *Williams v State of New York*[137] a child, conceived as a result of the rape of the mother when she was a patient in a state mental hospital, asserted that the

---

[130] See Kennedy, I and Grubb, A, *Medical Law, Text and Materials* (n 1 above), 971–3.
[131] See *Harbeson v Parke-Davis Inc* (1983) 656 P 2d 483 (Wash Sup Ct); *Procanite v Cillo* (1984) 478 A 2d 755 (NJ Sup Ct).
[132] See *P's Curator Bonis v Criminal Injuries Compensation Board* [1997] SLT 1180, 1189 (OH) in which Lord Osborne said that congenital disabilities could not be regarded as injuries because there was no 'pre-injury state which is capable of assesment and comparison with the post-injury state'. But see paras 12.83–12.86 below: unwanted birth may be an injury to the parents. [133] For discussion of this problem see paras 12.87–12.88 below.
[134] See paras 12.108–12.109 below. [135] *Report* (n 68 above), para 89.
[136] (1963) 190 NE 2d 849 (Ill CA). [137] (1966) 223 NE 2d 343 (NYCA).

conception resulted from negligence in the hospital and that in consequence she was: 'deprived of property rights; deprived of a normal childhood and home life; deprived of proper parental care, support and rearing; caused to bear the status of illegitimacy.' In *Stills v Gratton*,[138] a child alleged that, as a result of a negligently performed abortion, he was born out of wedlock and 'various reasons' affected him to his detriment.

All these imaginative claims failed. The courts have refused to recognise the social incidents of existence itself, however depressing, as 'injury' for the purposes of the law of negligence. Moreover, not surprisingly there has been a strong policy element in their approach: **12.69**

> It is not the suits of illegitimates which give us concern, great in numbers as these may be. What does disturb us is the nature of the new action and the related suits which would be encouraged. Encouragement would extend to all others born into the world under conditions which they might regard as adverse. One might seek damages for being born of a certain colour, another because of race; one for being born with a hereditary disease, another for inheriting unfortunate family circumstances; one for being born into a large and destitute family, another because a parent has an unsavoury reputation.[139]

It can be said with confidence that no such claim will be allowed in England.

(viii) *Events which cause Injury and Birth*

So far we have considered cases at common law where prenatal occurrences cause injury (in which damages claims by children may lie) and where they cause birth (where *McKay* effectively prevents such claims). Situations may, however, arise, particularly in a preconception context, in which an occurrence can cause both the injury and the birth. The Law Commission[140] gave the examples of the negligent supply of damaged sperm for artificial insemination or of a contraceptive pill which might prove both ineffective and damaging to the child consequently born because of its ineffectiveness. More dramatically, under the heading 'wrongful life' it asks the following question: 'if a man suffering from syphilis has intercourse with a woman without telling her that he is infected, would the child resulting from the assault have a cause of action against him?' There is justice in the view that in such a case there **12.70**

---

[138] (1976) 127 Cal Rptr 652 (Cal CA).
[139] *Zepeda v Zepeda*, (n. 136 above), 858, *per* Dempsey PJ. See also *Cowe v Forum Group Inc* (1991) 575 NE 2d 630 (Sup Ct Indiana), a claim for 'wrongful life' base on rape of plaintiff's intellectually disabled mother and Commentary at (1993) 1 Med L Rev 261.
[140] *Report* (n 68 above), paras 7 and 88.

should be compensation, not for the fact of being born but for the disability itself.

12.71   This problem has however been considered, and the opposite conclusion arrived at, by the Supreme Judicial Court of Massachusetts in *Payton v Abbott Labs et al.*[141] The plaintiffs were women whose mothers had ingested during pregnancy the drug diethylstilbetrol (DES) which was manufactured by the defendants and designed to prevent them miscarrying, but which could cause abnormalities in their daughters. Thus, the one drug could be responsible both for giving life and for causing injury to the 'DES daughters'. The claims, however, were not for 'wrongful life' but only for injury. The allegation was that the defendants were negligent in marketing without adequate testing or warnings. One question was put:

> [I]f the trier of fact concludes that a plaintiff would probably not have been born except for the mother's ingestion of DES, is that plaintiff barred from recovery because of physical or emotional damage suffered as a result of the mother's ingestion of DES?[142]

The plaintiffs contended that, just as rescuers have a duty to exercise reasonable care in their efforts to save or protect the lives of others, so by analogy the defendants as manufacturers of a drug designed to preserve life were under a duty to exercise reasonable care in connection with their drug. It was however pointed out that the analogy was not exact, because whereas in a 'rescue' case the plaintiff might be better off if no attempt had been made to save her than if an attempt had been made negligently, in a DES case she would simply not have been born but for the drug, and just could not say that in those circumstances she would have been better off than if born, albeit injured, as a result of its use by the mother. In those circumstances the claims were rejected as if they had been claims for wrongful life, the court concluding:

> the provider of the probable means of the plaintiff's very existence should not be liable for unavoidable, collateral consequences of the use of that means.[143]

12.72   It is suggested that this conclusion is not wholly satisfactory, certainly as an authority for the proposition that a plaintiff can never sue for injury caused by an occurrence which gave him life. First, it is not in every case that the collateral injurious consequences are 'unavoidable': might it not be open to a drug manufacturer to eliminate the dangerous side-effects from some life-giving drugs? Second, and more generally, it hardly lies in the mouth of one who has caused a disability to say that it is non-compensatable because he has

---

[141] (1982) NE 2d 171 (Sup Ct Jud Mass).   [142] ibid, 181.   [143] ibid, 182.

also caused the life which bears the disability.[144] To allow such an argument would be to permit such a defendant to rely on the child's very existence to defeat a claim. It is suggested that since, as we have seen, the courts prevent a plaintiff from relying on that existence to raise a 'wrongful life' claim, they should also in fairness prevent a defendant from seeking to rely upon it to defeat a claim for injury.

To be distinguished from such occurrences, each of which may have the **12.73** double effect of causing both life and injury, is the case of a set of circumstances one of which causes injury and another of which causes life. Let us suppose that a gynaecologist negligently damages a foetus, and then goes on negligently to fail to warn the parents of what has happened with the result that they are deprived of the opportunity, which would have been accepted, of a lawful abortion: in the result the child is born disabled. It is suggested that in such a case the child would succeed in an action against the gynaecologist by arguing that the dominant event was the intra-uterine injury, and that the gynaecologist could not escape liability for the consequences of that act by relying on a further act of negligence, saying that if he had been more careful the plaintiff would never have been born, and that the action was really only one for 'wrongful life'.

2. 'Wrongful Life' Claims Under the Congenital Disabilities (Civil Liability) Act 1976

(i) *The Intention of the Statute*

The view of the Law Commission,[145] that no claim should lie by statute by **12.74** 'wrongful life', was influenced by such reasoning as the following:

> [S]uch a cause of action, if it existed, could place an almost intolerable burden on medical advisers in their socially and morally exacting role. The danger that doctors would be under subconscious pressures to advise abortions in doubtful cases through fear of an action for damages is, we think, a real one.

It was therefore the clear intention of the legislature that the Congenital Disabilities (Civil Liability) Act 1976 should allow no such cause of action. It attempted to achieve this result by section 1(2) which provides:

---

[144] See the remarks of Lord Osborne in *P's Curator Bonis v Criminal Injuries Compensation Board* (n 132 above), 1200. Considering a child born as a result of incestuous rape with disabilities due to consanguinity he said, obiter, 'I consider that (a jury) would accept that the birth of the child and its disabilities were both directly attributable to the same criminal act.' [145] *Report* (n 68 above), para 89.

[A]n occurrence to which this section applies is one which—
  (a) affected either parent of the child in his or her ability to have a normal, healthy child; or
  (b) affected the mother during her pregnancy, or affected her or the child in the course of its birth, so that the child is born with disabilities which would not otherwise have been present.'

In *McKay*[146] Stephenson LJ and Ackner LJ interpreted section 1(2)(b) as being worded so as:

to import the assumption that, but for the occurrence giving rise to a disabled birth, the child would have been born normal and healthy, not that it would not have been born at all.

They thus concluded that the Act excluded claims by children for 'wrongful life', and Griffiths LJ agreed.[147]

(ii) *Academic Support for 'Wrongful Life' Claims*

12.75 It is, however, to be noted that academic writers have raised three reasons for doubting this conclusion. First, it has been suggested by Jane Fortin[148] that the Act does not really abolish any common law right of action for 'wrongful life'. The argument is as follows. Section 4(5) of the Act provides:

[T]his Act applies in respect of births after (but not before) its passing, and in respect of any such birth it replaces any law in force before its passing, whereby a person could be liable to a child in respect of disabilities with which it might be born.

A 'wrongful life' action is not, so the argument runs, an action 'in respect of disabilities', but rather in respect of life itself: therefore, section 4(5) leaves intact any pre-existing common law right to sue for 'wrongful life'. It has, however, to be said that, even if the English courts could be persuaded that such actions could be brought at common law, which is doubtful, they would probably hesitate long before allowing such an interpretation and bypassing the intention of the statute so as to permit a 'wrongful life' claim by a disabled child. In any event the phrase 'in respect of' is extremely wide. Thus in *Paterson v Chadwick*[149] the phrase 'a claim in respect of personal injuries' was held to include a claim against a solicitor for permitting a medical negligence action to become statute-barred, on the ground that the nature and extent of the plaintiff's personal injuries formed an essential ingredient in the proof of the claim. It is true that *Paterson* was distinguished in *Ackbar v CF Green and*

---

[146] [1982] QB 1166, 1178 and 1186–7. [147] ibid, 1191.
[148] See Fortin, J E S (1987) (n 1 above). [149] [1974] 1 WLR 890.

Co Ltd[150] and its principle disapproved, obiter, in *Howe v David Brown Tractors (Retail) Ltd*[151] by Nicholls LJ who said that in such a claim:

> the damages claimed do not consist of or include damages in respect of personal injuries. The damages claimed comprise damages in respect of the solicitor's failure to issue a writ in time.[152]

However, in the *Howe* case the Court held that a firm's claim for financial loss arising from an injury to one of its partners was 'in respect of personal injuries', on the grounds that the same facts gave rise both to the firm's claim and to the partner's claim for personal injury. It is suggested that, by parity of reasoning, the Courts would probably proceed on the basis that, as both the child's life and 'the disabilities with which it might be born' came into existence simultaneously at the moment of birth, it would be artificial to separate the two concepts: that therefore a 'wrongful life' claim by a child born disabled was 'in respect of disabilities', and was therefore excluded by section 4(5).

Second, it has been pointed out by Kennedy and Grubb[153] that the *McKay* **12.76** dicta cited above referred to sub-section 1(2)(b), and not to sub-section 1(2)(a), of the 1976 Act. It is suggested that negligence in a pre-conception context, for example in the course of genetic counselling, could amount to an occurrence which affected the parents' opportunity to have a normal healthy child, and therefore his or her 'ability' so to do within the meaning of Section 1(2)(a). To give a concrete example: let us assume that a doctor has negligently advised a mother that conception after the age of forty-five created no greater risk of Down's Syndrome than conception after the age of thirty-five: that as a result the mother started her family ten years later than she would otherwise have done; that a child is born with Down's Syndrome, and that he or she is able to demonstrate that that syndrome was a function of the delayed conception. There is an argument of reasonable strength that the child was, to summarise section 1 of the Act: 'born disabled as the result of . . . an occurrence . . . which . . . affected [the mother] of the child in . . . her ability to have a normal healthy child.' Under Section 1(1): 'the child's disabilities are to be regarded as damage resulting from the wrongful act of that person and actionable accordingly at the suit of the child'. By this reasoning the statute would in fact give the child a remedy in such circumstances, whatever was its intended policy. And indeed there would be some justice in this conclusion, for damages could be computed by reference to the life of the child not (as in a 'wrongful birth' claim)[154] by reference to the, frequently shorter, life of the caring parent.

---

[150] [1975] QB 582.   [151] [1991] 4 All ER 30.   [152] ibid, 42.
[153] *Medical Law, Text and Materials* (n 1 above), 976–7.
[154] See paras 12.108–12.109 below.

12.77 Third, Kennedy and Grubb[155] also draw attention to Section 1A of the 1976 Act, which allows a child to claim for negligence in the course of infertility treatment. They point to the fact that the section covers negligence in the 'selection' of the embryo that becomes the child. From this they go on to reason that since (but for the negligence) some other embryo would have been selected and the child plaintiff himself would never have been born, therefore the claim can truly be classified as one for 'wrongful life'. It is, however, suggested that the courts may approach the section more cautiously. Section 1A provides:

> [I]n any case where—
>   (a) a child carried by a woman as the result of the placing in her of an embryo or of sperm and eggs or her artificial insemination is born disabled,
>   (b) the disability results from an act or omission in the course of the selection, or the keeping or use outside the body, of the embryo carried by her or of the gametes used to bring about the creation of the embryo, and
>   (c) a person is under this section answerable to the child in respect of the act or omission,
>
> the child's disabilities are to be disregarded as damage resulting from the wrongful act of that person and actionable accordingly at the suit of the child.

There is at least a risk that the courts would interpret the whole phrase 'in the course of the selection' so as to restrict claims to those based on acts or omissions during the selection process, rather than on the very act of choice. If they did not, they would have no alternative but to quantify the difference between the condition of the disabled plaintiff as it was in fact on the one hand and his non-existence on the other hand, a process from which they will continue to shrink. The alternative, to compare the plaintiff's disabled state with that of a healthy but hypothetical child who might otherwise have been born had the selection process been different, is an even less realistic exercise.

D. Claims by Parents of Children Born Alive

1. Claims by Parents for Wrongful Birth

(i) *Introduction*

12.78 Claims by the family of unwanted children born alive are, for reasons to be discussed, available only to the father or the mother and not to siblings or more remote relations. To distinguish them from 'wrongful

---

[155] N 152 above, 977.

'life' claims, that is those which (if permitted) would be brought by the children themselves, they are usually categorised as claims for 'wrongful birth'.

(ii) *Factual Contexts*

Such claims may arise in various factual contexts, all of which are medical in nature. Where the patient undergoes an operation designed to prevent conception, there may be negligence in pre-operative counselling (eg a failure to warn of the risk of recanalisation of the vas), in the operation itself (eg if the doctor ligates a ligament during an operation for female sterilization rather than a fallopian tube), in post-operative testing (eg a failure to carry out sperm tests properly after vasectomy), or in post-operative counselling (eg if there is a failure to warn of the need to use contraceptives until sperm tests after vasectomy have proved negative).[156] Claims may also be brought if a child is born after an attempt at an abortion has failed.[157] There may also be negligence quite outside the context of an operation, for example in failing to give appropriate contraceptive advice to a young person who needs or requires it.

12.79

(iii) *Terminology*

There is, however, some variation in the terminology. Some commentators[158] have used the term 'wrongful pregnancy' or 'wrongful conception' to denote claims by parents where a child subsequently born is healthy, confining the term 'wrongful birth' to cases where the child is not only unwanted but born with a disability. The distinction between these two categories of claim, however, is not based on any difference in the legal bases for the claims, but only on different factual bases for quantifying damages. An alternative approach would be, for example, to define 'wrongful conception' claims as those where the wrong consists in responsibility for an unwanted conception, and 'wrongful birth' claims as being those where the fault lies in permitting a pregnancy to continue to birth. This distinction may have significant consequences. However, in this Chapter it is proposed, for the sake of simplicity, to use only the generic term 'wrongful birth' to include all claims by parents

12.80

---

[156] See Mullis, A, 'Wrongful Conception Unravelled' (n 1 above).
[157] See *Scuriaga v Powell* [1979] 123 SJ 406, aff'd, [1980] CA Transcript 597.
[158] See Kennedy, I and Grubb, A (n 153 above), 977. See also Rogers, WVH, Teff, H and Sarno, GG, (n 1 above) for different terminologies.

arising out of an unplanned or unwanted birth, whether or not the child suffers from a disability.

(iv) *Problems in 'Wrongful Birth' Claims*

12.81 No appellate court in the United Kingdom has as yet fully analysed the legal nature of 'wrongful birth' claims.[159] The problems may be illustrated in this way. Where an operation is carried out, it may be conducted negligently in a way which causes injury to the patient other than the physiological conseqeunce which the operation was designed to procure. An example already given is of a ligament being damaged by mistake in the course of an ineffective sterilisation. If an unwanted child is born as a result, the true claim by the mother is not just for a damaged ligament (which is clearly a personal injury) but for an unwanted pregnancy, labour, and child and their financial consequences. The legal problem becomes more acute when the operation has produced no unwanted injury but only the desired result, for example a successful vasectomy, yet a child is born because the father was not warned to use contraceptives until sperm tests proved negative. Here, the doctor's patient was the father, whose body was given the treatment he required, no more no less, and whose only injury may be to his pocket. The only person who was physically affected was the mother, who was not the doctor's patient, who was not operated upon, who received no misleading advice, and whose only complaint may be that she has had a baby which she will doubtless come to love and which may result in no financial loss to her but only re-distribution of family income, all of which is provided by the father.

12.82 Thus 'wrongful birth' actions raise at least seven questions.

(a) are pregnancy and birth to be considered 'personal injuries'?

(b) to what extent, if at all, are 'wrongful birth' claims restricted by the current state of the law on 'economic loss'?

(c) how do the answers to those questions affect the application to the Limitation Act 1980?

(d) is a doctor liable not only to his patient but also to his patient's spouse or sexual partner?

(e) to what extent are such claims restricted by considerations of public policy?

(f) what is the effect of a mother's refusal to terminate an unwanted pregnancy?

(g) how are damages for 'wrongful birth' to be quantified?

---

[159] *Allen v Bloomsbury HA* [1993] 1 All ER, 651, 657 *per* Brooke J. See Commentary at (1993) 1 Med L Rev 238.

(a) Pregnancy and Birth as Personal Injury

Whether or not pregnancy and birth can be treated as 'personal injury' is a **12.83** question with double significance. First, damages can only be awarded for 'pain, suffering and loss of amenity' caused by pregnancy and birth if they can be so treated. Second, unless the 'wrongful birth' claim is one where the damages claimed for negligence, nuisance, or breach of duty consist of or include damages in respect of personal injuries to the plaintiff or any other person,[160] the limitation period will be six years and not the three year period appropriate[161] to personal injury cases.

The phrase 'personal injury' has been by section 38 of the Limitation Act **12.84** 1980 which provides: '"personal injuries" includes any disease and any impairment of a person's physical or mental condition, and "injury" and cognate expressions shall be construed accordingly'.[162] Pregnancy and birth, as elements in the natural process of reproduction, are not self-evidently injuries. However, in *Allen v Bloomsbury HA*[163] Brooke J considered a claim by a mother who was negligently deprived of the opportunity to have a pregnancy terminated:

> for the discomfort and pain associated with the continuation of her pregnancy and the delivery of her child [as] a claim for damages for personal injuries . . . comparable to, though different from, a claim for damages for personal injuries resulting from the infliction of a traumatic injury.[164]

The question was fully considered by the Court of Appeal in *Walkin v South Manchester Health Authority*,[165] where a mother who had given birth following a failed sterilisation tried to avoid the three year limitation period under Section 11 of the Limitation Act 1980 by bringing an action only in respect of financial loss. It was held that 'failure of the attempt to sterilise the plaintiff was not of itself a personal injury. It did her no harm; it left her as before'.[166] Equally, it was held that the birth itself was not the injury,[167] but in the event, the court decided that the conception was a personal injury because it was unwanted, and because the consequent physical change in the plaintiff's body was in effect an 'impairment' of her physical condition. There is academic support for this view.[168] The reasoning is that an unwanted

---

[160] Limitation Act 1980, s 11(1): see s 14 for 'date of knowledge'.
[161] Subject to extension under s 28 in the case of disability and discretionary exclusion under s 33.   [162] See also RSC Order 1, Rule 4 for a similar definition.
[163] N 159 above.   [164] ibid, 657–8.
[165] [1995] 1 WLR 1543, 4 All ER 132. For a full discussion see (1996) 4 Med L Rev 94.
[166] ibid, 1550, 139 *per* Auld LJ.   [167] ibid, 1554, 144 *per* Neill LJ.
[168] See Mullis, A (n 156 above), 324–5.

pregnancy can very readily be viewed as such an impairment because it 'involves an element of danger, certain discomfort and possibly severe disruption of the woman's employment and pattern of life'.[169]

12.85 Yet the *Walkin* case leaves certain problems unresolved. First, failure in itself of an attempt to sterilise (such as might result, as in that case, from the failure of diathermy to seal the fallopian tubes) may not of itself be an injury, yet it may be the case that sterilisation does not take place because the surgeon inflicts an injury instead, for example by operating not on the tube but on a ligament. If that occurred it would be for consideration whether, following *Walkin*, there would be two injuries, one consisting in the damage to the ligament and the other consisting of the unwanted conception, occurring at different times. Second, the identification of conception as an injury in any one case depends upon whether or not the mother wanted to conceive. This presents the conceptual difficulty of the plaintiff's right to damages being dependent not upon the defendant's acts but upon the plaintiff's attitude to the defendant's act. It also presents some practical problems. What should the just solution be if at the time of conception the woman would not wish it, but has changed her mind and wants to become pregnant by the time that she finds out? Roch LJ in *Walkin* identified a further problem:

> I have some difficulty in perceiving a normal conception, pregnancy and the birth of a healthy child as 'any disease or any impairment of a person's physical or mental condition' in cases where the only reasons for the pregnancy and subsequent birth being unwanted are financial.[170]

In such a circumstance it is not the pregnancy which is unwanted but the financial difficulties. The tendency to restrict 'wrongful birth' claims was further illustrated in *R v Croydon AHA*.[171] In that case the Court of Appeal considered a claim by a woman who wanted and indeed had a healthy child, but would not have done so had a radiologist, who misinterpreted an x-ray taken in the course of a pre-employment health check, picked up an abnormality which would have indicated that pregnancy and birth would place her own health at risk. A breach of duty had been conceded. However, the Court of Appeal held that:

> when the mother wants both the pregnancy and a healthy child there is simply no loss which can give rise to a claim in damages in respect of either of the normal expenses and of trauma of pregnancy or the cost of bringing up the child.

---

[169] See Rogers, WVH (1985) (n 1 above), 310.
[170] [1995] 1 WLR 1543, 1553; 4 All ER 132, 142.
[171] 25 Nov 1997, CA; *Independent*, 4 Dec 1997.

It further held that the plaintiff's family life fell outside the scope of the conceded duty and accordingly confined her claim to damages for injury to her own health.

Third, if the claim against a doctor was for failure to diagnose an unwanted   **12.86**
pregnancy in time for termination, then the *Walkin* definition of injury could hardly apply: if it did then the injury (unwanted pregnancy) would pre-date the breach of duty (failure to diagnose). In such a case the injury would have to be the unwanted continuation of pregnancy. Fourth, let us suppose that the pregnancy is wanted, but that there is a failure to diagnose a possible foetal abnormality in time for termination. Again, the *Walkin* definition of the injury could hardly apply, because the pregnancy was wanted. The injury would presumably be either the continuation of the pregnancy after the time when it should have been diagnosed and would have been terminated, or the birth itself. Fifth, if the criterion for conception amounting to an injury is that it is unwanted by the woman, then a woman who wants a child but has one by a man who does not but becomes a reluctant father only because his vasectomy has, through negligence, failed, would have no personal injury claim herself. Nor would the man, the failure would have left him as before.[172] His claim, if any, would be for economic loss.[173]

(b) Claims for Economic Loss

Is it then possible for the parent of an unwanted child to bring a claim for   **12.87**
such economic loss which was not the consequence of injury, however defined? The law here is still developing. In *Spartan Steel & Alloys Ltd v Martin & Co (Contractors) Ltd*,[174] the supply of power to the plaintiff's factory was interrupted by the defendant's negligence. It was held that while the plaintiff could recover damages for the physical damage to metal actually in its furnaces at the time of a power cut and for loss of profits on its sale, it could not recover loss of profits on further operations which they would have completed but for the power cut. The reason was that although the second category of loss resulted from the defendant's negligence, it was economic loss not immediately consequential on the physical damage to the plaintiff's property. Application of that principle to 'wrongful birth' claims presents problems. In a failed sterilisation case a mother would be able to claim for loss of earnings and expense resulting from the pregnancy and birth itself, but the costs of rearing the child (either direct, consisting of financial outlay, or

---

[172] *Naylor v Preston AHA* [1987] 1 WLR 938, 971, *per* Sir John Donaldson MR, cited in *Walkin* at 1550 *per* Auld LJ.   [173] *per* Roch LJ in *Walkin* (n 165 above), 1553, 142.
[174] [1973] 1 QB 27.

indirect, such as wages foregone while the mother brought the child up) would not be immediately consequential on the physical injury, which would end once the mother recovered from the birth, but only on the existence of the child itself. A claim for such costs would therefore be a claim for purely economic loss and thus, on a strict application of *Spartan Steel*, irrecoverable. More obviously, any claim by a father for rearing costs, whether the child was born as a result of negligence in advice, in the performance of a sterilisation, or in the performance of a vasectomy, would be pure economic loss[175] not consequent on any injury to him at all.

12.88 However, the fact that such losses are economic does not mean that they are necessarily irrecoverable. First, if the loss results from a negligent misstatement it will be actionable under *Hedley Byrne & Co Ltd v Heller & Partners Limited*.[176] Secondly, in *Lonhro plc v Tebbit* Browne-Wilkinson V-C, having pointed out that the law on the duty of care to protect from economic loss is in a state of flux, accepted that the right question to ask was: 'is the relationship between the plaintiff and the defendant sufficiently proximate to constitute the special relationship required to give rise to a duty of care to prevent economic loss?'[177] In practice, the degree of proximity will in part be affected by the amount of reliance which has been placed by the plaintiff upon the defendant. As Clarke JA said in *X & Y v Pal and Others*:

> the fundamental elements underlying [the doctor's] proximity relationship with his patient was assumption of responsibility and reliance. The doctor assumed the responsibility of exercising due care in the treatment of his patient and the patient relied on him to administer the treatment with due care.[178]

In the context under discussion it is plain that when a husband, wife, or indeed regular sexual partner agrees to undergo an operation designed to procure infertility, each partner will rely equally on the doctor's skill: both, indeed, will probably have been involved in the pre-operative counselling. In most cases where a woman undergoes a lawful abortion, her husband or partner will have been involved in the decision, or will at least have placed reliance on that skill. It is therefore likely that most plaintiffs, whether or not formally patients, will be able to establish sufficient foreseeability by a doctor of economic loss and proximity with the doctor to found a duty of care owed to them to avoid such loss, and that the courts will thus not consider it reasonable to discriminate between patient and non-patient so as to allow only a claim by the former. In short, it is anticipated that should the House of

---

[175] See Mullis, A (n 1 above); *Allen v Bloomsbury HA* [1993] 1 All ER 651, 657–8.
[176] [1964] AC 465.   [177] [1991] 4 All ER 973, 986.
[178] [1992] 3 Med L Rev 195 (NSWCA), 206.

Lords consider claims for the costs of rearing unwanted but healthy children, it will not disallow them on the ground that the loss is purely economic.

(c) Limitation Act Problems

Failed Sterilisation

Section 11(1) of the Limitation Act 1980 applies a three year limitation **12.89** period:

> to any action for damages for negligence, nuisance or breach of duty . . . where the damages claimed for the negligence, nuisance or breach of duty consist of or include damages in respect of personal injuries to the plaintiff or any other person.

In *Allen v Bloomsbury HA*[179] Brooke J touched on a problem. He expressed the view, obiter, that a claim by a mother in a 'wrongful birth' action which is not for damages for personal injuries but only for economic loss, such as lost wages or the cost of upkeep of an unwanted child, might well be subject to the different six year limitation period, since it is hard to see how section 11 of the Limitation Act 1980 would apply to a claim limited to the financial costs associated with the upbringing of an unwanted child. However, it is now clear that a plaintiff actually injured by a tort cannot escape from the three year limitation period merely by abandoning a claim for physical injuries and pursuing a claim for economic loss. The earliest authority was *Ackbar v C F Green & Co Ltd*,[180] in which Croom-Johnson J said that the proper test for deciding whether an action fell within the section was to ask 'what is the action all about?' That case was cited in the Court of Appeal in *Howe v David Brown Tractors (Retail) Limited*[181] in which Nicholls LJ expressed the view that a plaintiff injured by medical negligence could not escape the application of the three year limitation period by abandoning any claim for physical injury and claiming only damages in respect of loss of earnings.[182] The Court of Appeal reached a decision to the same effect in *Walkin v South Manchester HA*.[183] Although there was no claim for pain, suffering, or inconvenience as a result of the failed sterilisation operation, pregnancy, or birth, but only for financial loss, on a preliminary issue it was held that the claim was 'in respect of personal injuries', that time ran from the moment of conception and that the action was therefore statute-barred. Consistently with that approach, the suggestion of Brooke J in the *Allen* case, that different limitation periods might apply to physical injury and economic loss was disapproved.

---

[179] [1993] 1 All ER 651, 658.   [180] [1975] QB 582.
[181] [1991] 4 All ER 30.   [182] ibid, 40–41.   [183] N 165 above.

Failed Vasectomy

12.90   An apparently inconsistent conclusion had been reached by a two-judge Court of Appeal in *Pattison v Hobbs*.[184] In that case a vasectomy which had been performed by the defendant doctor failed, and in consequence the husband remained fertile and the wife conceived a child. Both sued, neither claiming damages for personal injury as such but only for financial loss. On an application to strike out for want of prosecution the question of limitation was raised, and the Court of Appeal held that the six year limitation period applied as the claim was not for 'damages in respect of personal injuries' within the meaning of Section 11 of the Limitation Act 1980. A distinction between the failed sterilisation and the failed vasectomy cases may certainly be made, in that in the former it is the mother who was the patient and who clearly sustained personal injury, whereas in a failed vasectomy case it is the father who was the patient yet sustained no physical injury, being able to complain only that a planned operation was ineffective, but only economic loss.

12.91   However, it does not follow that a male plaintiff in a failed vasectomy case can thus escape the three year limitation period. His loss may be purely financial, and for that reason Roch LJ in *Walkin*[185] reserved the question of a proper limitation period. Yet it is likely that if the pregnancy was unwanted by the woman the man's claim will be interpreted as 'in respect of personal injuries to . . . any other person' within the meaning of, and thus caught by, section 11 of the Limitation Act 1980.[186] If, on the other hand, the woman wanted a pregnancy which resulted only because, as a result of negligence, a vasectomy had failed, it might well be that, as there was no personal injury, the man would have the benefit of a six year limitation period.[187] One must comment that these paradoxes and anomalies suggest that the time is now right for reconsideration of the law of limitation in this context.

(d)   A Doctor's Duty: Contract

12.92   In *Eyre v Measday*[188] and *Thake v Morris*[189] the Court of Appeal considered cases of failed laparoscopic sterilization and vasectomy respectively. In each

---

[184]   *The Times*, 11 Nov 1985, CA Transcript 85/676. Technically *Pattison* should bind later Courts of Appeal even though only a two-judge court: *Langley v North West Water Authority* [1991] 3 All ER 610 (CA).

[185]   [1995] 1 WLR 1543, 1553, 4 All ER 132, 142.

[186]   ibid, *per* Auld LJ at 1552, 142.

[187]   ibid, *per* Neill LJ at 1555, 144.   [188]   [1986] 1 All ER 488, CA.

[189]   [1986] QB 644, [1986] 1 All ER 497 CA.

case claims were made in contract. In *Eyre* the mother alone was the plaintiff. In explaining the operation the doctor had emphasised that it was 'irreversible'. She thus argued that he had contracted to render her absolutely sterile, that the use of the word 'irreversible' amounted to an express guarantee that the operation would achieve its object of sterilising her, and that alternatively there was an implied warranty to that effect. All those arguments failed. The Court of Appeal held that the contract was only to carry out the particular type of operation and not to sterilise: that 'irreversible' meant only that the operation could not be reversed and not that it would achieve its object, and that in a contract to operate the Court will imply an obligation to exercise reasonable skill and care but would be:

> slow to imply against a medical man an unqualified warranty as to the results of an intended operation, for the very simple reason that, objectively speaking, it is most unlikely that a responsible medical man would intend to give a warranty of this nature.[190]

In *Thake* both parents sued. They too sued in contract but, (Kerr LJ dissenting) **12.93** this claim failed. The possibility of an enforceable warranty was firmly rejected by the majority. Neill LJ said:

> a reasonable man would have expected the defendant to exercise all the proper skill and care of a surgeon in that speciality: he would not have expected the defendant to give a guarantee of 100% success.[191]

More firmly still, Nourse LJ said:

> of all sciences medicine is one of the least exact. In my view, a doctor cannot be objectively regarded as guaranteeing the success of any operation or treatment unless he says as much in clear and unequivocal terms.[192]

A Doctor's Duty: Tort

It therefore follows that 'wrongful birth' claims by parents must in reality be **12.94** founded upon an alleged breach of a duty of care. Now a doctor, of course, owes such a duty to the patient whom he or she is treating or advising. But is such a duty owed to the patient's partner? In *Thake* both parents sued, and it was not submitted that the mother (upon whom no operation had been performed) had no right of action. It is probable that the court would have rejected so discriminatory a suggestion, particularly as both had been advised directly about the vasectomy and had signed forms consenting to it. Support

---

[190] N 188 above at 495 *per* Slade LJ.   [191] N 189 above at 685, 510.
[192] ibid, 688, 512.

for the proposition that a doctor may owe a duty to a person who is not a patient has been sought in cases where the courts have accepted that one person may owe a duty to another to prevent a third person causing him harm.[193] Thus, in *Carmarthenshire County Council v Lewis*[194] an education authority was held responsible to a driver who was killed in avoiding a child who was negligently allowed to wander out of a nursery school onto the road. The parallel, however, seems a little far fetched. It is suggested that the existence or otherwise of a duty owed by a doctor to the partner of a patient can more easily be assessed by reference to more recent formulations of principle than by such analogies.

12.95 As has been pointed out,[195] the criteria for deciding whether a duty is owed are foreseeability, proximity, and an assessment of whether it is fair, just, and reasonable to impose a duty to the plaintiff on the defendant. If this principle is applied, there should be no difficulty in finding that a doctor may owe a duty of care, at least in the abstract, to the known sexual partner of the patient. However, it does not follow that the doctor would owe a duty to every sexual partner of the patient, for example to every woman impregnated by a man whose vasectomy he had negligently performed.

12.96 This problem was addressed by the Court of Appeal in *Goodwill v British Pregnancy Advisory Service*.[196] The plaintiff was a woman who, at about the time of her divorce, had commenced a sexual relationship with a married man who had had a vasectomy and negative semen tests arranged by the defendants about three years earlier. She became pregnant because the vasectomy had undergone spontaneous reversal and brought an action claiming not for personal injury but only for financial loss. The allegations of negligence were of failure to warn the man of the possibility of late spontaneous reversal of the vasectomy and its consequences. Curiously, *Walkin v South Manchester Health Authority*[197] was not cited, and the decision turned on whether the plaintiff's claim fell within the principles either of *Hedley Byrne v Heller and Partners Ltd*[198] as explained in *Caparo Industries PLC v Dickman*[199] and *James*

---

[193] See the discussion by Mullis, A, 'Wrongful Conception Unravelled' (n 1 above), 326.
[194] [1955] AC 549.
[195] See para 12.29 above. For a general discussion of duties to non-patients, see Giesen, D, *International Medical Malpractice Law* (JCB Mohr, Paul Siebeck, 1988), 157–61. See also *Tarasoff v Regents of the University of California* (1976) 551 p 2d 334 (Sup Ct Cal) (psychiatrist's duty to inform third party of threats made against her by his patient): cf *Webb v Jarvis* (1991) 575 NE 2nd 992 (Sup Ct of Indiana) (plaintiff shot by patient: defendant physician not in breach of duty to avoid harm to plaintiff in his prescribing of medicine to patient). See Commentary at (1993) 1 Med L Rev 265.
[196] [1996] 2 All ER 161. [197] N 164 above. [198] N 176 above.
[199] [1990] 2 AC 398.

McNaughton Papers Group Ltd v Hicks Anderson & Co[200] or of *White v Jones*.[201] The claim was struck out, principally on the basis that it could not be shown that, at the time it was given, the defendant knew that its advice was likely to be acted upon by the plaintiff without independent enquiry, or that it had in fact been so acted upon by the plaintiff to her detriment. But dealing with the question of a doctor's duty to a non-patient Peter Gibson LJ said:[202]

> the doctor is concerned only with the man, his patient, and possibly that man's wife or partner if the doctor intends her to receive and she receives advice from the doctor in relation to the vasectomy and the subsequent tests. Whether the avoidance of pregnancy is a benefit or a disadvantage to a sexual partner of the man will depend on her circumstances. If the existence of that partner is known to the doctor and the doctor is aware that she wishes not to become pregnant by the man and the vasectomy is carried out to meet her wish as well as the man's wish, it may be said that the doctor is employed to confer that benefit on her.

More succinctly Thorpe LJ said:[203]

> the doctor in the circumstances regards himself as advising the patient and, if a married man, the patient's wife. It cannot be said that he knows or ought to know that he also advises any future sexual partners of his patient who chance to receive his advice at second-hand. Presented with such a set of facts a doctor is entitled to scorn the suggestion that he owes a duty of care to such a band so uncertain in nature and extent and over such an indefinite future span.

In short, it would seem that the scope of duty extends only to a patient's spouse or known sexual partner at the time of the advice who is likely to be affected by it.[204]

(e) 'Wrongful Birth' and Public Policy

In the United States of America there is a body of judicial opinion[205] which opposes the recovery by a parent of the costs of rearing a healthy (as opposed to disabled) child on policy grounds. This view briefly prevailed in the law of England. In *Udale v Bloomsbury AHA*,[206] Jupp J considered the case of a claim by a mother for a child born as a result of an unsuccessful sterilisation operation, and decided that it was contrary to public policy to allow damages

12.97

---

[200] [1991] 2 QB 113.   [201] [1995] 2 AC 207, 1 All ER 691.
[202] N 196 above at 167.   [203] ibid, 170.
[204] See *Miller v Rivard* (1992) 585 NYS 2d 523 (Sup Ct NY, App Div) on the distinction between known and casual sexual partners. See also Rogers, WVH (1985), n 1 above.
[205] For reviews of authorities see *Burke v Rivo* (1990) 551 NE 2d 1 (Mass Sup Jud Ct) and *Lovelace Medical Center v Mendez* (1991) 805 P 2d 603 (NM Sup Ct). For commentary see (1993) 1 Med L Rev 249.   [206] [1983] 1 WLR 1098, 2 All ER 522

for the cost of carrying out necessary extensions to the home and bringing up a child. He gave four reasons:

(a) it was highly undesirable that a child should learn that a court had declared that his life and birth was a mistake and that he was unwanted or rejected:

(b) before making such an award the court would have to set off against the inconvenience and financial disadvantages which accompany parenthood the mother's love and joy at the birth of the child, with the result that maternal instincts would be penalised:

(c) medical men would be under subconscious pressure to encourage abortions in order to avoid claims for medical negligence which will arise if a child was born:

(d) the birth of a child is 'a blessing and an occasion for rejoicing'.

12.98 By contrast, in *Thake v Morris*,[207] Peter Pain J critically considered the reasons of Jupp J in *Udale* one by one. He reasoned that:

(a) damages would not lead to the rejection of the child because, even if it did learn that the conception was unwanted, what mattered to a child was how it was received when it entered life:

(b) the joy of having a healthy child should not be set off against the costs of rearing, for that joy was largely of the parents' own making in welcoming the child into the family, and they should not be penalised for doing so:

(c) there was little force in the argument that such claims might influence doctors towards an abortion in view of the divisions within the medical profession, and anyway the decision whether or not to abort would usually rest with an obstetrician who might well be quite independent of the defendant:

(d) finally, social policy, which permitted abortion and vasectomy, implied that it was generally recognised that the birth of a healthy child was not always a blessing.

12.99 Subject to the views of the House of Lords, the debate has been resolved by the preference of the Court of Appeal in *Emeh v Kensington & Chelsea & Westminster HA*[208] for the views of Peter Pain J in *Thake*. The present state of English law is that public policy does not prevent a claim for the costs of rearing an unwanted child. However, from time to time judicial unease surfaces. Thus, in *Jones v Berkshire AHA*[209] Ognall J said:

---

[207] [1986] QB 644; [1984] 2 All ER 513.
[208] [1985] QB 1012, [1984] 3 All ER 1044.   [209] 2 July 1986, Unreported.

I pause to observe that, speaking purely personally, it remains a matter of surprise to me that the law acknowledges an entitlement in a mother to claim damages for the blessing of a healthy child. Certain it is that those who are afflicted with a handicapped child or who long desperately to have a child at all and are denied that good fortune would regard an award for this sort of contingency with astonishment. But there it is: that is the law.

As Lloyd LJ said in *Gold v Haringey HA*, 'many would no doubt agree with the observation.'[210]

(f) Refusal by a Mother to Terminate an Unwanted Pregnancy

In *Emeh v Kensington & Chelsea & Westminster HA*,[211] where a sterilisation operation had failed, it was argued, and the judge at first instance accepted, that the mother had behaved unreasonably in failing to have an abortion, and that her refusal was so unreasonable as to amount to a *novus actus interveniens*, or failure to mitigate damage which eclipsed the negligence for which the Health Authority was responsible. The Court of Appeal reversed the first instance decision on the ground that the Health Authority had, by its negligent failure to effect a sterilisation, created the very dilemma which the plaintiff had sought to avoid, and thus had no right to expect that she would undergo an abortion with its attendant risks, pain, and discomfort. The child in was in fact born with a disability. There was no evidence that this was or could have been known before the birth, and so there was no discussion of the question of whether the mother would have been held unreasonable had she known of the disability but nevertheless declined the offer of a lawful abortion on the grounds 'that there [was] a substantial risk that if the child were born it would suffer from such physical or mental abnormalities as to be seriously handicapped'.[212] Nevertheless, it is possible that there may be cases in which a mother's refusal to terminate the pregnancy may defeat her claim. In *Emeh* Slade LJ[213] said:

12.100

> save in the most exceptional circumstances, I cannot think it right that the court should ever declare it unreasonable for a mother to decline to have an abortion, in a case in which there is no evidence that there were any medical or psychiatric grounds for terminating this particular pregnancy,

and Purchas LJ[214] said:

---

[210] [1988] QB 481, 484. See however *Allan v Greater Glasgow Health Board* (1993) 17 BMLR 135 (CS) where arguments that public policy bars claims in a failed sterilisation case for general and special damages and rearing costs were rejected. See also *McCallion or Anderson v Forth Valley Health Board*, 14 Nov 1997 (unreported) and *McFarlane v Tayside Health Board* (I.H.) 9 Jan 1998 (unreported) allowing the reclaiming motion from [1997] SLT 211.
[211] N 208 above.   [212] Abortion Act 1967 s 1(i)(b).
[213] N 208 above, at 1024, 1053.   [214] ibid, 1027, 1055.

if the sole motivation of a plaintiff [for continuing a pregnancy] was in order to promote an action, [that] would be at least a factor to be taken into account in deciding whether, on an objective test of unreasonableness, there had been a break in the chain of causation.

12.101   The question was discussed somewhat elliptically in the wrongful birth case of *Goodwill v British Pregnancy Advisory Service*.[215] The facts are not completely clear from the judgments, but it appears that the plaintiff originally thought that her symptoms meant that she had an ovarian cyst, and was pleased later to discover that she was pregnant. Nevertheless, she was worried because the father was still married and living with his family, and feared the prospect of single parenthood. She:

> spent a couple of weeks in a great state of turmoil and anxiety before deciding to go ahead with the pregnancy. Although it might have been still possible to terminate the pregnancy, the implications were much more serious because the foetus was so well developed and because of her belief that life was sacred. She also knew in her heart of hearts that she could not abort the life that she had previously thought was an omen of death.[216]

Yet despite this emotional ambivalence, in circumstances which can hardly be described as exceptional, the plaintiff's decision to continue with the pregnancy influenced the Court in its view that a claim should be struck out as frivolous, vexatious, and an abuse of process.[217]

12.102   It would appear impossible to reconcile the dicta in *Emeh* with the approach in *Goodwill*. This anomaly may have arisen because the earlier case was not drawn to the attention of the *Goodwill* Court. Alternatively, one may simply be witnessing a change in judicial attitude. Thorpe LJ commented in *Goodwill*:[218]

> in reality a woman exploring the development of a sexual relationship with a new partner takes much on trust before experience corroborates or exposes his assurances. Her responsibility is to protect herself against unwanted conception and to take independent advice on whatever facts he presents.

This is a far cry from the language, twelve years earlier, in *Emeh*. The courts' assessment of 'the reasonable woman' may be changing.

12.103   In summary, it is of course the case that a woman cannot be criticised for failure to agree to termination of a pregnancy unless an abortion would be lawful.[219] Correlatively, the mere existence of grounds for a lawful abortion does not mean that a woman is unreasonable in refusing to have one. Yet, if

---

[215] [1996] 2 All ER 161.   [216] ibid, 165 *per* Peter Gibson LJ.
[217] ibid, 169 *per* Peter Gibson LJ, 170 *per* Thorpe LJ.   [218] ibid, 170.
[219] See *Rance v Mid-Downs HA* [1991] 1 QB 587.

the reasons for a termination are such that a court concludes that no reasonable woman in the plaintiff's position would decline one, then, a defendant's argument that her conduct amounts to a novus actus interveniens or failure to mitigate her claim becomes strong. In particular, if the claim is based not on a defendant's responsibility for an unwanted conception but on his failure to take steps which, if properly performed, would have led to termination of an existing pregnancy (such as antenatal screening for congenital defects or an attempted abortion) it is difficult to see how a mother's refusal of the offer of a lawful termination, made soon after such a failure, could be seen as anything but unreasonable. In those circumstances her claim should be limited to pain and suffering and to financial loss, if any, up to the time when she would have started earning after the lawful termination which she rejected.[220] But where the court will draw the line is currently hard to predict.

(g) Quantification of Damages in an Action for 'Wrongful Birth'

General Damages

The mother will have a claim for the discomfort and suffering of pregnancy and childbirth, but in calculating damages there should be taken into account any suffering she may have been spared. For example if (but for the negligence) a pregnancy would have been terminated, the unpleasantness of that avoided procedure must be set against what the plaintiff in fact suffered. **12.104**

The next question is whether a claim can be made for the value of family care provided to the child, for a 'wrongful birth' claim is a claim by the parent for the injury suffered by him or her. It is therefore unlikely that such a claim can be made in respect of care provided to the child by anyone but the parent. Moreover, a distinction must be made between cases where the child is born healthy and cases where the child is born disabled. In relation to the former type of case, Brooke J summarised the law in *Allen v Bloomsbury Health Authority*[221] summarised the law in the following words: **12.105**

> [A]lthough the law recognises that it is foreseeable that if an unwanted child is born following a doctor's negligence a mother may suffer wear and tear and tiredness in bringing up a healthy child, the claim for general damages she might otherwise have had on this account is generally set off against and extinguished by the benefit of bringing a healthy child into the world and seeing one's child grow up to maturity.

This 'set-off' approach is known in America as the 'benefits rule'.[222]

---

[220] For American law on failure to mitigate damage by aborting a foetus, see 2 ALR 5th 301 at 321–3 and *Lovelace Medical Center v Mendez*, n 20s above, which rejected the argument that the plaintiff should have had an abortion or placed the child for adoption as a matter of law.   [221] [1993] 1 All ER 651, 657.
[222] See 'Wrongful Pregnancy Damages', 89 ALR 4th at 632.

12.106 Where, however, the child is born handicapped, the position is different. In *Allen* Brooke J continued:[223]

> [H]owever, the law is willing to recognise a claim for general damages in respect of the foreseeable additional anxiety, stress and burden involved in bringing up a handicapped child, which is not treated as being extinguished by any counter-vailing benefit, although this head of damages is different in kind from the typical claim for anxiety and stress associated with and flowing from an injured plaintiff's own personal injuries.

He referred to a 'claim for damages for the loss of amenity associated with bringing up a handicapped child', and stated:

> [I]n a case where the future child is foreseeably born handicapped, for example because the effects of rubella have not been explained to its pregnant mother by a negligent defendant, I can see reasons why a court is willing to award the mother an extraordinary item of general damages for the burden of bringing up a handicapped child.

So the law allows an award to the parent, classified as general damages, for caring for a child who is foreseeably handicapped. The question of foreseeability will be construed very broadly. It is not necessary that the defendant should have foreseen the precise disability of the unwanted child or even that such a child, more probably than not, would have been born disabled. That this is so emerges from *Emeh v Kensington AHA*, a case of failed sterilisation following which an unwanted child was born with congenital abnormalities requiring constant medical and parental supervision. Waller LJ[224] said:

> [I]n my view it is trite to say that if a woman becomes pregnant, it is certainly foreseeable that she will have a baby, but in my judgment, having regard to the fact that in a proportion of all births—between 1 in 200 and 1 in 400 were the figures given at trial—congenital abnormalities might arise, makes the risk clearly one that is foreseeable, as the law of negligence understands it. There are many cases where even more remote risks have been taken to be 'foreseeable' . . . [T]his child would need to be under constant supervision, both medically and by her mother, and her abnormalities would have to be carefully watched . . . [T]hose conditions which arose by reason of birth were, in my judgment, not too remote to be taken into account when considering what damages should be awarded for the admitted negligence of the defendant's doctors in this case.

---

[223] N 221 above 657–8, 662. See also *Emeh v Kensington AHA*, n 208 above, where the award of general damages included compensation for the 'extra care' of a disabled child, and *Thake v Maurice*, n 189 above.   [224] N 208 above, 1019–20, 1049–50.

Claims for the Financial Consequences of 'Wrongful Birth'

In *Allen* Brooke J divided a mother's claim for the economic consequences of 'wrongful birth' into two heads:[225]   **12.107**

(a) the financial loss she suffers because when the unwanted baby is born she has a growing child to feed, clothe, house, educate and care for until the child becomes an adult;

(b) the financial loss she suffers because she has lost or may lose earnings or incur other expense because of her obligations towards her child which she would have sought to avoid.

It will be noted that Brooke J's language suggests that the costs of upkeep can be claimed 'until the child becomes an adult'. The question arises, however, as to whether a claim can be made for upkeep costs after the child becomes eighteen, when a parent's legal responsibility for the child ceases.[226] There are several American authorities[227] on the point. the gist of whose arguments seems to be that if under the relevant State law the parents remain liable for the support of a disabled child after majority, then they can recover for such expenditure by them attributable to such disabilities (see the New Hampshire case of *Smith v Cote*[228] and the Massachusetts case of *Viccaro v Milunsky*).[229] If, on the other hand, there is no legal obligation on parents to support a disabled child after majority, then they cannot recover the cost of extraordinary expenses for continued support and special care of a disabled child even though they have a moral obligation to provide it; see the New York case of *Bani-Esraili v Lerman*.[230]   **12.108**

In the absence of any statutory obligation upon a parent to provide upkeep, even for a disabled child, after majority in this country, the American distinction would obviously favour defendants here. They could argue that as the parent has no legal obligation to provide for the child after s/he is eighteen, there is no legal obligation on the defendants to compensate for any such provision. This argument was however rejected by Swinton Thomas J in *Fish v Wilcox*.[231] The claim was for wrongful birth of a child who had spina   **12.109**

---

[225] N 159 above, at 657.
[226] cf Social Security Administration Act 1992, s 78(6) and s 105 as amended (parental liability to maintain children under the age of 19).
[227] See Louisell, D W and Williams, M, *Medical Malpractice*, Vol 1, para 18.09.
[228] **513** A 2d 341 (1986) (Sup Ct NH).
[229] **551** NE 2d 8 (1990) (Sup Ct Jud Mass).
[230] **505** NE 2d 947 (1987) (NYCA).
[231] Unreported, 9 Apr 1992. The point was not pursued on appeal: [1994] 5 Med LR 230, 231.

bifida but was likely to survive into adult life. The Judge accepted as a matter of general principle the plaintiff's argument that: 'the measure of damages must be a sum of money which will put the party who has been injured in the same position as she would have been in if she had not sustained the wrong', and clearly would have awarded damages for maternal services after the age of eighteen had he not found as a fact that the child would not require them. It is likely that this approach will be followed, and damages awarded for the cost of upkeep, if reasonably incurred, into adult life. One may point to the parallel that under the Fatal Accidents Act 1976 the question of the 'dependency' of children is a question of fact, and it may well continue beyond the age of eighteen years when many are still being educated. It is, however, not possible to see how a parent's claim for loss can be projected beyond the anticipated date of that parent's death.

12.110 The next question which arises is how the cost of upkeep should be quantified. In *Emeh v Kensington & Chelsea & Westminster AHA*,[232] Purchas LJ adopted the following approach which was outlined in *Sherlock v Stillwater Clinic*:[233]

> [W]e hold that in cases such as this an action for 'wrongful conception' may be maintained, and that compensatory damages may be recovered by the parents of the unplanned child. These damages may include all prenatal and postnatal medical expenses, the mother's pain and suffering during pregnancy and delivery, and loss of consortium. Additionally, the parents may recover the reasonable costs of rearing the unplanned child subject to off-setting the value of the child's aid, comfort and society during the parents' life expectancy.

12.111 The question of what costs of upkeep are 'reasonable' was discussed in *Allen v Bloomsbury HA*[234] in which Brooke J summarised and reviewed a number of earlier authorities. He noted that in two earlier cases[235] judges had referred to defendants as being expected to do no more than provide 'necessaries', and that it was likely that they had in mind a definition of 'necessaries' in section 3 of the Sale of Goods Act 1979 as 'goods suitable to the condition in light of the minor and to his actual requirements at the time of sale and delivery'. On that basis, consistently with the decision in *Bennar v Kettering HA*,[236] he concluded that if the unplanned child was born into a family which educated their children privately, then the defendant would have to pay the cost of private education as being appropriate to that childs condition in life. On the

---

[232] N 208 above, 1028, 1056. [233] (1977) 260 NW 2d 169 (Sup Ct of Minn)
[234] [1993] 1 All ER 651.
[235] *Thake v Maurice*, (n. 207 above) *per* Peter Pain J: *Bennar v Kettering HA* [1988] 138 NLJ 179 *per* Hodgson J. [236] N 235 above.

facts of that case, however, he accepted that the claim was reasonably based on the average National Foster Care Association figures.[237]

It is not easy to predict how the courts will approach the concept of offsetting **12.112**
the value of the child's aid, comfort and society against rearing costs as was suggested in *Sherlock v Stillwater Clinic*.[238] In adopting that suggestion in *Emeh v Kensington & Chelsea & Westminster HA*[239] Purchas LJ merely said:

> where the arrival of the child has mitigating features, such as those referred to in the judgement to which I have just referred, then, in the ordinary assessment of damages, there will be an appropriate diminution in the damages awarded.

In fact, *Sherlock* and other American cases contemplate a setting off against the economic costs of child rearing the dollar value of the emotional gains of having a normal healthy child.[240] However, those emotional gains are best set off against the stress of child-rearing,[241] and should not be set off again against the economic costs of caring. In reality, the only benefit likely to be set off against a claim for such costs would be some economic advantage to the parents derived from the birth.[242] Dependency on the child's future income is likely to be so speculative and heavily discounted for accelerated receipt as to be valueless, it is conceivable that some form of inheritance might possibly go to reduce a claim.

Avoided Loss

In calculating a claim for the extra costs of care, the rule against the recovery **12.113**
of avoided loss will be strictly applied. In *Salih v Enfield HA*[243] the parents of two children then had a third, a boy who suffered from congenital rubella syndrome. They successfully sued a Health Authority for negligent failure to diagnose and warn of the danger, as a result of which the mother had been unable to have the pregnancy terminated. The family had in fact planned to have four children in all, but the strain of bringing up their handicapped son was such that they decided not to have any more children after him. The Court of Appeal held that the consequential saving of likely future expenditure on children was a factor to be taken into account in assessing damages, and that as on the evidence the parents would, but for the

---

[237] Contrast *Robinson v Salford HA* [1992] 3 Med LR 270 *per* Morland J.
[238] N 233 above.   [239] N 208 above, 1028, 1056.
[240] See the sources in n 205 above.
[241] See para 12.105 above: *pace* Swinton Thomas J in *Fish v Wilcox*, n 231 above.
[242] See Kennedy, I and Grubb, A, *Medical Law* (n 1 above), 1001.
[243] [1991] 3 All ER 400.

negligence, probably have had not just the two elder children and the handicapped son but four healthy children in all, they could not recover the basic costs of rearing that son. The cost of his special needs, however, remained recoverable.

Claims by Siblings

12.114 The question which finally arises is whether the siblings of children born in consequence of negligence can claim damages on the basis that the 'wrongful birth' has prejudiced them, socially, emotionally, or economically. Such claims have been described as 'wholly without merit'.[244] Three points may be made. First, in a normal case it will be difficult to persuade a court that any financial loss was foreseeable, because if the parents have a 'wrongful birth' claim (as ex hypothesi they will) then damages recovered should prevent existing siblings from suffering financial loss, save possibly on inheritance. Second, it is unlikely that a court would find sufficient proximity between a sibling and the parents' doctors to found any duty of care. Third, if a court is reluctant to permit a claim by a child born into a disadvantaged family, as is undoubtedly the case,[245] by parity of reasoning it will hardly find it fair, just or reasonable to allow an action by a sibling claiming to be disadvantaged by an unplanned new arrival in the family.[246]

2. Claims by Parents for Physical and Psychiatric Injuries and Disruption of the Family

(i) *Physical Injury*

12.115 Circumstances which lead to neonatal injury or death may also injure the mother. The leading English case is *Kralj v McGrath*.[247] In that case the mother was admitted to hospital for the birth of twins. After attempted internal cephalic version of the second twin without any anaesthetic, a procedure described as horrific and completely unacceptable, he was delivered by caesarean section, but died eight weeks later. The mother claimed, *inter alia*, for aggravated damages and damages for grief arising out of the loss of a

---

[244] *Sala v Tomlinson* 422 NYS 2d 506 (1979) (Sup Ct App Div): cf *Bowman v Davies* 48 Ohio St 2d 41 (1976). In *Fish v Wilcox*, (n 231 above), Swinton Thomas J considered, obiter, the possibility of the father and brothers of a damaged child being joined in a wrongful birth action brought by the mother so that they might recover damages for the services they had provided to the child. It is doubtful that this is correct.
[245] See paras 12.68–12.69 above.   [246] As to these criteria, see para 12.29 above.
[247] [1986] 1 All ER 54.

child. Woolf J held that the concept of aggravated damages should not be introduced into personal injury actions, although to the extent that the mother's experience of her baby's injuries and death made it more difficult for her to overcome the consequences of her own injuries, the award would correspondingly be increased. He further ruled that while damages cannot be awarded for grief in isolation at common law, the mother could be compensated for the shock she had sustained as a result of being told what had happened and of seeing her son, and, to the extent that grief had made her injuries have a more drastic effect on her, that could be taken into account in calculating the personal injury award.

A further, and not unimportant, factor in computing damages was identified by Rose J in *Grieve v Salford HA*[248] The facts of that case were that, following a negligent obstetric procedure, a psychiatrically vulnerable unmarried woman had a stillborn child. The stillbirth was held to be particularly damaging because she had been given a variety of inconsistent explanations as to what had been the cause of death. In two cases Sir John Donaldson MR[249] has expressed the view, obiter, that a doctor's general duty of care requires him to tell a patient what has gone wrong. One of the difficulties facing plaintiffs who allege that they have suffered from such a breach of duty must be in establishing that they have suffered damage in consequence. The approach of Rose J sidesteps that difficulty by treating a failure to inform a patient of what has gone wrong not as a separate tort but as a factor increasing an award for the original wrong.[250] **12.116**

(ii) *Psychiatric Injury*

The law relating to damages for psychiatric injury is in a state of evolution, and following the Law Commission consultation paper 'Liability for Psychiatric Injury' further developments can be expected.[251] At the time writing the following propositions seems to be accepted. **12.117**

(a) A person physically injured by negligence can recover for the psychiatric concomitants of that physical injury.

(b) A person who sustains a psychiatric illness as a result of an incident in

---

[248] [1991] 2 Med LR 295 at 296.
[249] *Lee v South West Thames RHA* [1985] 1 WLR 845, 850–1: *Naylor v Preston AHA* (n 172 above), 967.
[250] See the discussion in Kennedy, I and Grubb, A, *Medical Law* (n 1 above), 230–2.
[251] Law Commission Consultation Paper No 127. See, for a wide ranging and critical discussion, Mullany, NJ and Handford, PR, 'Tort Liability for Psychiatric Damage', (The Law Book Company, Sweet and Maxwell, 1993).

which he or she was directly involved as a participant may be described as a 'primary victim' and will be able to recover damages for that illness if the defendant could reasonably foresee that his conduct would expose the primary victim to the risk of some injury, either physical or psychiatric. It is no answer that the primary victim was predisposed to psychiatric injury.[252]

(c) Where a person sustains a recognised psychiatric injury as a result of the shock of seeing or hearing an event, or the immediate aftermath of such event, which injures one with whom he or she has a close tie of affection he or she may have a claim as a 'secondary victim' of that event.[253]

12.118 The application of these principles to medical negligence claims is still being worked out. For present purposes the relevant question is whether a parent can claim for psychiatric injury consequent on perinatal injury to a child. In the important decision of *Jaensch v Coffey*[254] the High Court of Australia, in considering a claim for 'nervous shock' by the wife of a victim of a road traffic accident whom she visited in hospital, gave important general guidance which, *inter alia*, emphasises the requirement that in a claim by a secondary victim the illness must be caused by 'shock'. Of particular relevance is the passage in a judgment of Brennan J in which he said:[255]

> [T]he spouse who has been worn down by caring for a tortiously injured husband or wife and who suffers psychiatric illness as a result goes without compensation; a parent made distraught by the wayward conduct of a brain-damaged child and who suffers psychiatric illness as a result has no claim against the tortfeasor liable to the child.

12.119 In *Taylor v Somerset HA*,[256] a widow, whose husband's death resulted from medical negligence, unsuccessfully claimed damages for psychiatric shock allegedly resulting from seeing his body in the hospital mortuary. It was successfully submitted to Auld J that, in order to succeed, a plaintiff had to demonstrate that the defendant's breach of duty did not just cause injury or death to the plaintiff's relation, but had actually resulted in 'some external, traumatic event in the nature of an accident or violent happening'. That submission was repeated to the Court of Appeal in *Sion v Hampstead HA*,[257] a case in which a father unsuccessfully claimed for psychiatric shock allegedly caused by witnessing his son's gradual death in hospital as a result of mis-diagnosis. However, Peter Gibson LJ said:[258]

---

[252] See *Page v Smith* [1996] 1 AC 155; [1995] 2 All ER 736.
[253] See *McLoughlin v O'Brian* [1983] 1 AC 410; *Alcock v Chief Constable of South Yorkshire Police* [1992] 1 AC 310; *McFarlane v EE Caledonia Ltd* [1994] 2 All ER 1.
[254] [1984] 155 CLR 549.   [255] ibid, 565.   [256] [1993] 4 Med LR 34, 37.
[257] [1994] 5 Med LR 170 CA.   [258] ibid, 176.

[I]t is the sudden awareness, violently agitating the mind, of what is occurring or has occurred that is the crucial ingredient of shock. I see no reason in logic why a breach of duty causing an incident involving no violence or suddenness, such as where the wrong medicine is negligently given to a hospital patient, could not lead to a claim for damages for nervous shock, for example where the negligence has fatal results and a visiting close relative, wholly unprepared for what has occurred, finds the body and thereby sustains a sudden and unexpected shock to the nervous system.

The application of these principles appears in the decision of *Tredget v Bexley HA*.[259] In that case, as a result of admitted negligence in failing to deliver by caesarean section, a child was born severely asphyxiated, and died two days later. The father was present at the birth. The judge found that:[260] **12.120**

the actual birth with its 'chaos' or 'pandemonium', the difficulties that the mother had of delivery, the sense in the room that something was wrong, and the arrival of the child in a distressed condition requiring immediate resuscitation was, for those immediately and directly involved as each of the parents was, frightening and horrifying.

He found that the period from onset of labour until the child's death was effectively one event, that there was no need to invoke the 'aftermath' doctrine, and that the parents were victims of an experience sufficient to establish liability even though a full appreciation of the gravity of that child's condition only developed in the forty-eight hours between birth and death. As that composite event was a powerful factor in contributing to the pathological grief thereafter suffered by the parents, each was entitled to damages for psychiatric injury.

Thus far, claims by parents who have sustained psychiatric injury as a result of perinatal injury to their child have been presented and evaluated on the assumption that the parents are 'secondary victims'. On that basis the requirement that a secondary victim, to recover, must prove that he sustained the injury as a result of the shock caused by witnessing the horrifying event or its immediate aftermath leaves uncompensated the parent whose psychiatric illness develops only as a result of learning of and experiencing the injury to the child (devastating cerebral palsy, for example), a long time after the birth. The question, however, may be asked: if such a mother is, as she must be, the patient of the obstetrician,[261] can she present her claim as if she was a primary victim? If so, would it be possible for her to claim that her psychiatric illness was a foreseeable consequence of the long-term stress caused to her by the **12.121**

---

[259] [1994] 5 Med LR 178.   [260] ibid, 183.
[261] To whom the duty is owed: see s 1(3) of the Congenital Disabilities (Civil Liability) Act 1976: see also para 12.46 above.

negligence of her obstetrician? In *Walker v Northumberland CC*[262] an employee succeeded in a claim against his employer for a severe nervous breakdown caused by stress at work, and in *Johnstone v Bloomsbury HA*,[263] the Court of Appeal refused to strike out a claim by a hospital doctor caused by stress and depression caused by long working hours. Although it may be clear that psychiatric injury caused by stress should be compensatable in an action by a primary victim,[264] the problem is that while a mother traumatized by the circumstances of birth is clearly a primary victim, one injured by developing stress suffers not because of the circumstances of birth but because she later witnesses her child's developing disability. It is questionable whether there refinements result in justice.

(iii) *Stillbirths and 'Dashed Hopes'*

12.122 It has been held that a stillbirth in itself may give rise to a claim for damages. In *Bagley v North Herts HA*,[265] the negligent failure to carry out a blood analysis in pregnancy deprived the plaintiff of her opportunity of successful delivery by caesarean section, and the child was stillborn. Simon Brown J considered that the mother was entitled to compensation for 'dashed hopes', that is to say the loss of the satisfaction of bringing her pregnancy, confinement and labour to a successful, indeed joyous conclusion. In similar circumstances in *Grieve v Salford HA*,[266] Rose J came to the same conclusion. However, in *Kerby v Redbridge HA*,[267] Ognall J disagreed. He was considering the case not of a stillbirth but of a neonatal death resulting from negligence. He rejected a 'dashed hopes' formulation of the claim partly on the basis that it would duplicate statutory damages for bereavement[268] (which are of course not available in the event of a stillbirth) but also because it amounted to no more than awarding damages for 'the normal emotions by way of grief, sorrow or distress attendant on the loss of a loved one'[269] which are not compensatable in law. It is suggested that he was probably correct in identifying a difficulty in treating 'dashed hopes' as the subject matter of a separate head of damages, rather than as a factor in quantifying a personal injury claim.

---

[262] [1995] 1 All ER 737. [263] [1992] QB 333 (Leggatt LJ dissenting).
[264] See the dissenting judgment of Sir Thomas Bingham MR in *X v Bedfordshire CC* [1995] 2 AC 633, 663–4. [265] [1986] NLJ 1014.
[266] N 248 above. [267] [1993] 4 Med LR 178. [268] See para 12.123 below.
[269] N 267 above, 179, quoting *McLoughlin v O'Brian*, (n 253 above), 431 *per* Lord Bridge.

(iv) *Claims by Parents: Bereavement Awards*

Where a child has died after 31 December 1982 the parents (if it was **12.123** legitimate) or the mother (if it was illegitimate) are entitled to a statutory award of damages for bereavement.[270] The award is conventional. In relation to death before 1 April 1991 it is £3,500, and in relation to subsequent death it is £7,500.[271] Where both parents have an entitlement, the award is to be divided equally between them.

(v) *'Shattered Family Plans'*

In *Kralj v McGrath*[272] the parents had always intended to have three children. **12.124** They already had one when the mother gave birth to twins. One twin died as a result of the defendant's negligence, and the claim included damages for the consequences, including financial loss, of having another child to replace the one who had died. On the evidence the probability that the mother would become pregnant again was only sixty-six per cent. However, Woolf J awarded £18,000 under this head to take account of the financial loss which would arise if a pregnancy occurred and the loss of satisfaction of achieving the planned family if it did not. Similarly, in *Bagley v North Herts HA*,[273] following the stillbirth, the parents decided not to attempt another pregnancy, because that would have carried a fifty per cent risk of mortality. Simon Brown J. made it plain that he was not able to award damages for loss of the society of the stillborn child, but that he was able to compensate for loss of the pleasure of bringing up an ordinary healthy child who would now not be born. Such an entitlement was, however, like the 'dashed hopes' claim, doubted by Ognall LJ in *Kerby v Redbridge HA*,[274] His views were *obiter*, because the plaintiff planned to get pregnant again and indeed was awarded £1,500 for the prospect of 'the rigours of a further pregnancy'. However, the judge took the view that the plaintiff, in making a claim for damages for 'shattered family plans', was doing no more than advancing 'the normal facet of a mother or a mother's emotions when bereaved of a child'. In support of his view it can be pointed out that in *Kralj v McGrath*[275] no statutory bereavement award was available, as the child's death pre-dated 1 January

---

[270] Fatal Accidents Act 1976, s 1A, inserted by Administration of Justice Act 1982, s 3: for commencement see s 73(1).
[271] Damages for Bereavement (Variation of Sum) (England and Wales) Order 1990, SI 1990/2775. [272] [1986] 1 All ER 54.
[273] N 265 above. [274] N 267 above. [275] N 272 above.

1983, nor was one available in *Bagley v North Herts HA*[276] because the child was stillborn. However, it is suggested that the statutory bereavement award does not in fact replace a claim for 'shattered family plans' of the type contemplated in those two cases, which are based not on grief but on interference with the ordered planning of life and the economic and other consequences of such interference.

E. Stillbirths and Neonatal Deaths: Claims on Behalf of the Estate

1. Stillbirths

12.125 In *Burton v Islington HA*[277] and *de Martell v Merton & Sutton HA* Dillon LJ said, obiter,:

> I doubt very much whether there are any claims now outstanding which are not statute barred, in respect of children stillborn before 22 July 1976 or any children born before that date, who are locked in litigation with their mothers over whether the mother tasted alcohol or followed a diet other than that recommended by the current phase of medical opinion during pregnancy.

This dictum appears to imply that a claim can be brought on behalf of a stillborn child. If so, it is surprising. At common law, there can be no actionable breach of duty to those born dead: before they are born they are not 'persons',[278] and after they are born, because they never lived, they have no legal rights. Nor is the position different under statute. In a number of American states, recovery by a child who has died *in utero* as a result of the defendant's negligent conduct has been admitted under Wrongful Death Acts. The Second Re-statement of the Law of Torts, however, states that 'if the child is not born alive, there is no liability unless the applicable wrongful death statute so provides'.[279]

12.126 The English position is that where a child is stillborn there is no liability under statute to anyone, for the following reasons. First, it is a precondition for recovery under the Congenital Disabilities (Civil Liability) Act 1976 that the child is born alive. Secondly, no right either of bereavement or dependency can arise out of the Fatal Accidents Act 1976, because death is a precondition of such rights. A court will inevitably conclude that one who,

---

[276] N 265 above.   [277] [1993] QB 204, 232.
[278] See para 12.05 above. For the definition of a still-birth, see Still-Birth (Definition) Act 1992.   [279] Para 369(2).

in the eyes of the law, has never become a 'person',[280] cannot be said to have obtained life, and therefore cannot be said to have suffered death. Third, for the same reason there will be no claim under the Law Report (Miscellaneous Provisions) Act 1934 which applies only simply 'on the death of any person'.[281]

2. Neonatal Deaths

Three types of claim are possible on behalf of the estate of a child dying as a result of a birth injury. First, there may be a claim for reasonable funeral expenses.[282] Second, in respect of deaths before 1 January 1983 a claim could be made for loss of expectation of life; in *Kralj v McGrath*[283] the award was £1,650, less than the conventional £1,750, as the child survived for only eight weeks. (Such claims, however, will almost inevitably be statute barred by now). Finally, a claim for the pain, suffering and loss of amenity of the child before death will survive for the benefit of the estate but will be modest. In *Kralj v McGrath*[284] the award was £2,500;: in *Kerby v Redbridge HA*,[285] where the child survived only for 3 days, the award was £750.

12.127

---

[280] See para 12.05 above. [281] S 1(1).
[282] Law Reform (Miscellaneous Provisions) Act 1934, s 1(2)(c). [283] N 247 above.
[284] ibid. [285] N 267 above.

13

RESEARCH AND EXPERIMENTATION

A. Introduction

13.01 This Chapter is concerned with biomedical research on human subjects.[1] Research here principally refers to any intervention by touching or more, whereby the law as it relates to the inviolability of the person is engaged. This approach highlights the perspective of human rights which has been the central focus of discussion and analysis, particularly since the end of the Second World War. It also offers a way of understanding the underlying principles which inform and condition the law. To qualify as research, an intervention must form part of a programme of enquiry based on a scientifically plausible hypothesis, must follow a scientifically valid methodology, and be intended to produce data of a generalisable nature. The principal focus in this Chapter is on the doctor as medical researcher.[2] Research which

---

[1] For discussion of research on embryos and foetuses, see Chapters 10 and 15.
[2] Thus, this Chapter will not be concerned with such matters as the regulatory systems under which medicinal products or devices are licensed, once tested satisfactorily.

does not involve touching, for example, observational or epidemiological research, will also be briefly discussed. In such research, the legal interests engaged are those of privacy and confidentiality.

Research on human subjects is most commonly associated with the develop- **13.02** ment and testing of pharmaceutical products. Of course, research is conducted in all areas of medicine, but it should be noted that the case of surgery is somewhat exceptional. Developments in surgery are often described and reported as 'innovative therapy'.[3] This may not reflect any desire to avoid or finesse the regulatory mechanisms surrounding research. It may merely mean that surgeons oftentimes do not see themselves as engaged in research when they test out new procedures or techniques. The response of the law is that any innovation which departs from standard practice(s) will be regarded as research if it can be shown that the ordinary principles defining research (see para 13.01) apply. In such a case, the researcher will be expected to have observed the regulatory procedures, (see para 13.65). If the innovation does not qualify as research, the ordinary rules of the common law apply.

The focus in this Chapter is on the law. Much has been and, increasingly, is **13.03** being written on the ethics of research.[4] There also exist a growing number of Codes of Ethics relating to research, both nationally—emanating from the medical profession, through, for example, the Royal Colleges and their Faculties, from industry, and from public bodies—and internationally from international agencies.[5] Clearly, the law takes account of and seeks to reflect what is thought to be ethically appropriate. Codes of Research Ethics may indeed set the standards which the law will seek to adopt.[6] Despite the very considerable growth in the number of Codes and the range of activities they address, however, the law, by contrast or maybe because of the increased availability of Codes, remains singularly underdeveloped. Remarkably, perhaps, there is no specific regime of law regulating research on humans. This is in contrast to the comprehensive legislative framework regulating the conduct of research on non-human animals.[7] Furthermore, there are no cases in English law directly related to the conduct of research, (and few in the

---

[3] See Kennedy and Grubb, *Medical Law: Text with Materials* (2nd edn, Butterworths, 1994), 1073 *et seq.*

[4] See eg, *Manual For Research Ethics Committees* (4th edn, Centre of Medical Law and Ethics, King's College London, 1996).

[5] ibid. And see Council of Europe's Convention on Human Rights and Biomedicine, 1997, Arts 16 and 17 and the Explanatory Report thereto from the Directorate of Legal Affairs, DIR/JUR(97)1. A detailed Protocol on Research is under consideration by the Council of Europe.

[6] See, for example, the detailed ethical requirements relating to consent set out in the European Guidelines on Good Clinical Practice, *Manual* (n 4 above).

[7] Consolidated currently in the Animals (Scientific Procedures) Act 1986.

Commonwealth), on which to draw. Thus, the exposition of the law which follows is fundamentally a matter of applying the relevant common law principles—particularly the law relating to consent and to the torts of battery and negligence—and the relevant European law.[8]

13.04 At the most general level, there are two major areas which need to be examined:

(a) the lawfulness of any proposed research procedure; and

(b) the relevant regulatory/supervisory mechanisms.

B. Lawfulness

13.05 It will be recalled that the principal concern here is with research which involves touching the research subject. For the purposes of analysis, the common classification of research as being either **therapeutic** or **non-therapeutic** will be adopted. These two types of research are distinguished from each other by reference to the intention of the researcher. In the case of therapeutic research, there is a dual intention, both to seek to benefit the patient who is the research subject *and* to gather data of a generalisable nature. In non-therapeutic research, there is only a *single* intention: to gather data. Whether any proposed intervention qualifies as research (see para 13.01) is measured, prima facie, by reference to the views of peers. This means that, as regards any claim for damages brought by someone harmed as a consequence of alleged research, the complainant must show that the procedure should not have been carried out because it had no scientific plausibility or the methodology was flawed. The cause of action would be in negligence. The court would largely rely on expert evidence such that *Bolam*[9] would apply, as modified by *Bolitho*.[10]

13.06 There are certain general legal themes which are common to the considera-tion of all forms of research. The most important is the theme of **consent**. As regards medical *treatment*, the general law provides that consent is required before a patient may lawfully be touched, (save in the special circumstances of

---

[8] See further, Kennedy and Grubb (n 3 above), ch 14. Curiously, one of the very, very few examples of legislation concerned with research on human subjects can be found in the rather obscure statutory instrument, SI 1992/3146, Sch 3 implementing 90/385/EEC, The Active Implantable Medical Devices Regulations 1992. By Sch 3, clinical investigations must be carried out in accordance with the Declaration of Helsinki, as amended (on which, see *Manual*, n 4 above).

[9] *Bolam v Friern Hospital Management Committee* [1957] 1 WLR 582.

[10] *Bolitho v City and Hackney Health Authority* [1997] 4 All ER 771, and see discussion in Chapter 7.

an emergency). The consent must come from the patient, if competent, or, in the case of an incompetent child, from someone with parental responsibility. Failure to obtain consent will result in liability for battery or negligence. The current law contemplates circumstances in which a doctor would not be liable in negligence for failing, in the process of obtaining consent to treatment, to pass on certain information to a patient, if, in the opinion of fellow professionals, it would not be in the patient's interests to do so. This approach, (not without its critics[11]), will be examined later as to its application to research, (see paras. 13.23–13.25). However, the law allows no exception to the requirement that, at the very least, that degree of consent necessary to defeat a claim in battery must be obtained from a patient prior to treatment. By the same token, the law is clear that a patient who refuses consent may not thereafter be treated.[12] *A fortiori*, therefore, the general law applies in the case of therapeutic *research*. *Consent*, at least sufficient to counter any claim in battery, *is required*.

Participation in research entails an act of altruism. Thus, the law's concern for the need to obtain legally valid and effective consent to any proposed research comes as no surprise. As will be seen later, however, this concern for consent is not free of difficulties. In particular, it creates problems for those who wish to conduct certain forms of research, for example on young children and on incompetent adults. **13.07**

The examination of consent which follows will concentrate on the various, interrelated legal issues which arise from the law's concern for consent. The first is concerned with **competence** to consent to research. The second relates to **who** may consent: whether the law recognises the authority to consent of anyone other than the research subject. The third issue is how the **validity** of any apparent consent is established. The fourth issue is what may be consented to: the **limits** of consent. **13.08**

As a matter of everyday practice, the various legal issues considered here, in so far as they are also matters of ethics, are scrutinised by Research Ethics Committees (RECs)[13] to which research proposals are ordinarily submitted. The role and status of these Committees will be considered later (see para 13.70 *et seq*). Suffice it to say here that they have developed working practices which require researchers to give their minds to, and set out their responses to, the legal issues arising from the conduct of research. **13.09**

---

[11] See eg Kennedy, I, *Treat Me Right* (Clarendon Press, 1992), ch 9; and Chalmers and Schwartz, '*Rogers v Whitaker* and Informed Consent in Australia' (1993) 1 Med L Rev 139.   [12] *Re MB* [1997] 8 Med LR 217.
[13] On which see *Manual* (n 4 above).

C. Therapeutic Research

Research Subjects

13.10 For the purposes of analysing the legal issues referred to (para 13.08 above), it is helpful to consider research on **children** (ie persons under 18 years of age) and on **adults** (ie persons over 18 years of age) separately.

1. Children

(i) *Consent: Competence*

13.11 If it is the word '*therapeutic*', in the term therapeutic research, which is dominant, then the ordinary common law should apply. This would mean that a child over sixteen years of age would appear, by virtue of section 8(1) of the Family Law Reform Act, 1969,[14] to have the capacity to consent to therapeutic research. As regards a child under sixteen, the law as laid down in *Gillick v West Norfolk and Wisbech AHA*[15] would apply, namely that such a child's consent would be valid in law if the child had sufficient maturity and understanding. Of course, since something more than treatment alone is involved, the degree of understanding required would be commensurately high. On this view, however, there would be no general rule that therapeutic research on children under the age of sixteen may not be carried out solely on the basis of the child's consent, despite the child's apparent competence. The decision would rest on the facts of each case. Alternatively, and this is the more cautious view adopted by a number of bodies concerned with the ethics of research, it may be that the law would take a paternalistic position and decide that as regards any procedure other than the very simple and risk-free, there would be the strongest presumption against competence.[16] By contrast, should a competent child refuse permission rather than consent to take part in a therapeutic research project, current law could have it that the child's refusal may be ignored if the parents give consent. This is the case as regards medical treatment *simpliciter*.[17] The criticism to which this view has been

---

[14] See Kennedy and Grubb (n 3 above), 108–9.

[15] [1986] AC 112, and see Kennedy and Grubb (n 3 above), 109 *et seq*.

[16] See eg, *Research Involving Patients* (Royal College of Physicians, 1990), para 7.32. The Department of Health's guidance goes further and states that 'it would . . . be unacceptable not to have the consent of the parent or guardian where the child is under 16', Local Research Ethics Committees, HSG (91) 5 para 4.2.

[17] *Re W (A Minor) (Medical Treatment)* [1992] 4 All ER 627, but cf the view taken in HSG (91) 15, written before the decision in *Re W*.

subjected,[18] however, would suggest that it would be unwise to ignore the refusal of a competent child. Certainly, the prevailing view in medical ethics is that the refusal of a competent child, or even the dissent of a child not deemed competent, should be honoured.

If the word 'research' is dominant, then section 8(1) may not apply. Lord **13.12** Donaldson MR and Nolan LJ in *Re W (A Minor) (Medical Treatment)*[19] made it clear that the wording of the section was limited to 'surgical, medical or dental *treatment*' (emphasis added), and did not apply to non-therapeutic research. It could well be that this reasoning could be extended to therapeutic research. In this case, the common law would govern until the child reached adulthood. The question then becomes whether the different emphasis, whereby the word research is stressed, would lead to a different view of the common law from that just stated (para 13.11). The probable answer is that it would reinforce the more cautious view of the law. Thus, save in those cases involving the most trivial intervention, carrying minimal risk or inconvenience, a child would be deemed—by virtue of being a child and thus presumed to be lacking maturity and the ability to weigh risks against benefits—as a matter of law to be incompetent to consent to therapeutic research.

Where a child is judged incompetent to give a valid consent, a researcher **13.13** must seek consent elsewhere. Although not strictly required in law, it is deemed proper to seek the assent of the child before proceeding. Equally, while, in principle, the refusal of an incompetent child to participate lacks any legal effect, it is deemed good ethical practice at the very least to take seriously any refusal or expression of dissent by the child.[20]

(ii) *Consent: Who*

Where a child is competent and the proposed intervention is deemed to be **13.14** one to which the child can consent, the child's consent will be valid. In this regard, the child is in no different a position in law than the competent adult, such that references hereafter to a competent child can be read as referring equally to a competent adult. Where the child is not competent, consent must be obtained from a parent, or person with parental responsibility, (including, where relevant, the court).

---

[18] See eg, Kennedy and Grubb (n 3 above), 392–6.   [19] N 17 above.
[20] *Research Involving Patients* (n 16 above), para 7.34.

(iii) *Consent: Validity*

13.15 Does the law stipulate the *form* in which consent to participate in therapeutic research must be expressed? The general common law rule relating to medical treatment is, of course, that there are no requirements as to form. This is so despite the elevation of the 'consent form' to the status of an icon in medical practice (at least in hospitals though, oddly, not in general practice). It is trite law that the consent form may be evidence of consent, but the law's real concern is with real consent, as established by all the evidence and not just a consent form. The law relating to therapeutic research may not be different, even though superficially it may appear to be. It is standard practice for RECs to require that they be informed about the procedures to be adopted by the researcher in order to obtain consent. This will normally involve the submission of a draft consent form to the REC for approval. It does not follow that any failure to use the approved form would render legally invalid any consent obtained which is otherwise valid. It may well be that the researcher would be guilty of unethical conduct, but, provided the law was satisfied that real consent was, in fact obtained, the precise form would be of no concern.

13.16 Consent, to be valid, must be both *voluntary*, that is freely given, and properly *informed*. The ordinary principles of the common law apply, but given that research is involved, observance of them is subject to particular scrutiny. Both of the requirements pose problems in the case of children.

13.17 As regards *voluntariness*, in the, perhaps rare, case in which a child may be judged prima facie competent, the law's concern is to be vigilant to ensure that no pressure or persuasion has been brought to bear which could have overborne the child's capacity to refuse participation. Clearly, there is an interaction here with the law on competence, since in both cases a high level of maturity would be insisted upon. Where a child is incompetent to consent, it may be thought that the problem of voluntariness would be less serious, since the parents would be involved and have to consent. However, parents caring both for and about sick children are vulnerable to pressure. The law would again be vigilant to ensure that they have freely agreed that their child should participate in the proposed research. In other words, there must be no indication of pressure, however subtle, by, for example, being told that their child must be part of the research project as a condition of receiving any treatment, (save in the rare case where this is so). In practice, the relevant REC will have explored this issue, if it is doing its job properly. As has been said, it is standard practice for RECs to require consent forms to be submitted by researchers as part of the research proposal. These must then be approved, as must any accompanying information sheet. In the relatively rare case where research is conducted without prior submission to an REC, the law would probably treat evidence of what RECs regard as reasonable practice as its guide.

As regards *information*, again, in the case of a child who is prima facie   **13.18**
competent, there is an obvious interaction between competence and being properly informed. The relative complexity of the information which it is intended to pass on to the child and the child's ability both to comprehend it and deal with it emotionally will necessarily condition any view as to the child's competence. That said, there is clearly a duty properly to inform the competent child. The general law on the doctor's duty to inform a patient about proposed treatment is currently that laid down in *Sidaway v Governors of Bethlem Hospital*.[21] In the context of research, however, there must be added to the somewhat minimalist approach of *Sidaway*, the law's proper recognition of the fact that the patient is acting in the public interest. Consequently, any discretion not to disclose information which may be enjoyed by doctors under the general law is limited, in the context of research, by the law's desire to ensure that the patient's interests are appropriately secured. Thus, at the very least, the doctor is under a duty to inform the competent child of the fact that the treatment being proposed is part of a research project, and also of the implications and consequences of this fact. The former means that the patient is entitled to be told how involvement in research will affect the proposed therapeutic procedure and future health status. It also involves being told, for example, if the proposed research is, as is usual in the case of pharmaceutical research, a Randomised Controlled Trial (RCT) and what this means.[22] The latter involves such questions as whether there will be more than the usual number of interventions (for example, more blood samples taken), or more visits to the hospital or doctor than would be normal, or whether a lengthier than usual stay in hospital will be required, or more follow-up examinations called for. It also requires that the patient must be told of such matters as the foreseeable risks (both present and longer term), what provision exists for after care in the event that matters do not proceed as intended, and what alternatives exist to the therapeutic research being proposed. It may also involve, if the circumstances warrant it, informing the patient of any arrangements for compensation should things go wrong. Critically, patients must be told that they can withdraw from the research at any time without incurring any disadvantage in treatment, or

---

[21] [1985] AC 871.
[22] For an explanation and discussion of RCTs, see *Research Involving Patients* (n 16 above), para 7.93 *et seq*.

generally (save in the unusual circumstances in which treatment is only available under a research protocol).[23]

13.19 The REC, in carrying out its responsibility to approve the proposed consent form and information sheet, is concerned to insist on what is judged to be ethically appropriate. It is unlikely that the ethical and the legal will diverge. To the extent that they do, the requirements of the law must be observed, if otherwise that which is judged ethically appropriate detracts in any significant way from that required by law. To the extent that the REC requires more of the researcher than the current law demands, the point may arrive at which such requirements themselves become incorporated into the law. Such a view is a consequence of the reasoning in the *Bolam/Sidaway* approach, namely that the views of the REC reflect a responsible body of informed and expert opinion, including that of doctors. In this way, the law will develop a framework of regulation which meets proper ethical standards, drawing *inter alia* on such principles as those laid down in the various International Conventions post-Nuremberg, as well as more recent European developments.[24]

13.20 It is important here to notice a development in Europe, the precise legal effect of which remains unclear. The Committee for Proprietary Medicinal Products (CPMP) of the European Community in 1991 issued its *Guidelines on Good Clinical Practice for Trials on Medicinal Products in the European Community*.[25] As the name indicates, the *Guidelines on GCP* do not themselves have the force of law although they were intended to be, and have since become, the basis for the conduct of the relevant research. The *Guidelines on GCP* have extensive provisions relating to 'informed consent' which could be thought to go beyond the requirements of the common law, in detailing the extent of the researcher's duty to disclose.[26] Subsequently, as part of the process of the harmonisation of European law relating to the testing and licensing of medicinal products, Directive 91/507/EEC was issued. This was incorporated into English law by the Medicines (Applications for Grant of Product Licences—Products for Human Use) Regulations 1993.[27] The

---

[23] The matters referred to are among the many addressed in such guides as *Research Involving Patients* (n 16 above) and form part of the legal duty to inform to the extent that, in the circumstances, the patient reasonably needs to know them so as to make a considered decision.

[24] For instance, the European Convention on Human Rights and Biomedicine.

[25] See *Manual* (n 4 above). These *Guidelines* have been superseded by International Guidelines, ICH Good Clinical Practice, Step 4 Consolidated Guideline i.5.96 (CPMP/ICH/135/95) but there is no reference to them in any law which could justify the argument that *they* have been incorporated by reference into European and hence English law.

[26] See the text and dicussion in Kennedy and Grubb (n 3 above), 1047–8.

[27] SI 1993/2538.

Directive, (and thus the Regulations), provides that, '[a]ll phases of clinical investigation . . . shall be designed, implemented and reported in accordance with *good clinical practice*' (emphasis added).[28] On one view, this reference to 'good clinical practice' incorporates by reference the 1991 *Guidelines on GCP* into English law, at least as regards research leading to an application for a product licence for a medicinal product. Thus, the consent requirements generally, and specifically those relating to the researcher's duty to inform, must be read in the light of the *Guidelines on GCP*. Alternatively, and perhaps this is the better view with regard to the researcher's *legal* duty, the *Guidelines on GCP* were not incorporated into English law by the Regulations. Thus, their legal significance lies not in the fact that they are embodied in delegated legislation, but rather that they represent what a reasonable REC should require and take account of. As such, of course, they begin to mark out the boundaries of the researcher's legal duty.

The fact that the child, though competent, is, by definition, ill (in that the concern here is with therapeutic research), may appear to serve as a ground for arguing that, notwithstanding the general principles discussed above (para 13.18), *Sidaway* (discredited as it may be) allows the doctor engaged in the research a wide discretion as to what to tell the child. The response is that the law would not permit a researcher to use the fact of illness as a ground for not properly informing the patient. It has been argued, for example, that a patient suffering from cancer should not be told that she is involved in a research project, since that would inevitably involve telling her that she had cancer, something which the attending doctors had decided not to do. However, this is to turn on its head the respect for the person which underlies the law. It is to suggest that if consent to participate in research may be difficult to obtain, it should be dispensed with. The law's response is that if informing a competent patient of the fact that she is participating in a research project would not be in the patient's interests, the patient should not participate. To argue that it is in the interests of the patient, who is otherwise competent, to be protected from information, is either to say that the patient (here a child), in fact is not competent, or that the pursuit of research has a greater priority under the law than the protection of a patient's rights, a proposition which the law would emphatically reject. **13.21**

Where a child is incompetent to give a valid consent, it is the person with parental authority who must be informed. Here there is no room at all for arguments in favour of allowing doctors a discretion as to what parents (or others) should be told. The duty placed on them by the law to act in the **13.22**

---

[28] Para 1.1, Part 4B, Annex to Directive 91/507/1991.

child's best interests[29] means that as regards treatment *simpliciter*, a doctor has a duty to inform the parents as fully as possible. Only thus will a parent be able to fulfil the role which the law imposes. Consequently, a doctor has no discretion to withhold any information necessary for making a considered decision about treatment. *A fortiori*, no such discretion exists when there is the added dimension that the parent is being asked to involve a child in research, at least in part for the common good. It follows that parents must be given all that information which will allow them properly to weigh the risks and benefits and thus determine the interests of the child.

(iv) *Consent: Limits*

13.23 As was discussed above, the competent child can, theoretically at least, consent to anything which is otherwise permissable under the general law. In practice, however, the better view is that the law will be slow to find a child competent, save in those cases in which the proposed intervention is trivial. Thus, to the question, to what may a competent child consent, the answer is, not very much: only that which is readily comprehensible and does not pose any but the remotest risk, in the form of short or long-term physical or psychological harm.

13.24 As regards the incompetent child, the law is obviously keen to set limits to what the child may be volunteered for by the parent or other. As will be seen, these limits differ depending on whether the proposed research is therapeutic or non-therapeutic. As regards therapeutic research, given the therapeutic element, the relevant legal criterion as regards the limits of consent is the same as that which the law uses in the case of treatment *simpliciter*, namely, the best interests of the child. The parent must weigh up the risks and benefits to the child of participating in the research project. Clearly, the more ill the child, the more potentially beneficial the consequences if the child is exposed to what is proposed, and the more dire the consequences if the child is not, the greater the risks to which the parent may expose the child. This is no more than an application of the more general proportionality test, which must be satisfied so as to honour the law's commitment to the paramountcy of the child's welfare.[30]

13.25 The European *Guidelines on Good Clinical Practice*, referred to above (para 13.20) specifically address the issue of research on those unable to consent. As

---

[29] See, Kennedy and Grubb (n 3 above), 255 *et seq.*   [30] ibid.
[31] Para 1.13, Guidelines on GCP, *Manual* (n 4 above).

regards therapeutic research on children, they contemplate that this is both ethical and lawful, provided there is approval from the REC and from those with parental authority, on the basis that the research will promote the interests and welfare of the child.[31]

2. Adults

(i) *Consent: Competence*

The criteria of competence to consent to participate in therapeutic research mirror those laid down by Thorpe J in *Re C*[32] as regards consent to treatment; namely, that the patient first, comprehends and retains treatment information, secondly, believes it and thirdly weighs it in the balance to arrive at a choice.[33] The only question which arises is whether the fact that the patient is consenting to something in addition to treatment means that the criteria for consent are more demanding. The answer must be that the comprehension referred to in *Re C* must extend to participation in the research project. Thus, the criteria are not different, they must merely be applied to the facts of involvement in research. **13.26**

(ii) *Consent: Who*

Obviously, in the case of the *competent* adult, it is the adult and no one else whose consent must be sought and given. **13.27**

As regards the *incompetent* adult, the picture is less clear. It is settled law that, unlike a child, no one can consent to treatment on behalf of an adult in English law.[34] This cannot mean, however, as the House of Lords in *Re F* made clear, that the inability to consent makes it always unlawful to treat an incompetent adult. Such a result would be grotesque. Rather, the law is that consent, in the case of the incompetent adult, is no longer the relevant legal consideration. Instead, the doctor stands as a proxy and is entitled in law to treat if such treatment is in the patient's best interests. Where what is contemplated is therapeutic research, the therapeutic element would suggest that the same rule applies. By this reasoning, the doctor may involve the incompetent adult in therapeutic research if what is to be undertaken is in the **13.28**

---

[32] *Re C (Refusal of Medical Treatment)* [1994] 1 FLR 31 as explained in *Re MB* (n 12 above).
[33] ibid, 36. See also the similar approach adopted by the Law Commission in *Mental Incapacity*, Law Com No 231 (1995).
[34] *Re F (A Mental Patient: Sterilisation)* [1990] 2 AC 1.

patient's best interests. Clearly, if the treatment holds out a prospect of benefit and is not available other than in a research project, or if the prospects of benefit outweigh both any risks that may be involved and the consequences of not being exposed to the procedure, the involvement of the incompetent adult would seem to be prima facie lawful.[35]

13.29   Much depends, however, on what is chosen as the appropriate legal basis for determining best interests. One approach is that *Bolam* governs;[36] that a patient's best interests are determined by reference to what an informed body of medical opinion would decide. This approach, however, could weight the scales in favour of a view that being involved in research is, ipso facto, in a patient's best interests, not least because most doctors are persuaded of the benefits of carrying out therapeutic research and can rationalise their decision by referring, for example, to the heightened quality of care often associated with involvement in research. An alternative, and arguably more defensible position, is that *Bolam* is not relevant and that any determination of best interests must be made by reference to more explicit and objective criteria. The question remains where the onus should be. If research, even therapeutic research, is seen as raising human rights issues, (which are, of course, always lurking in medical law), then the onus ought to be on those proposing the research to justify it and to do so by means of evidence which addresses specific questions, rather than allowing research to go through on the nod of interested parties, for example, doctors. This would entail the development of a conceptual shortlist of the sort of matters relating to best interests which are raised by research.

(iii) *Consent: Validity*

13.30   As regards the *form* which consent must take, the law relating to research on the competent adult is *mutatis mutandis* the same as that set out above (para 13.15). In the case of the incompetent adult, as has been made clear, consent, strictly speaking, has no place. Rather, the doctor must make a judgment of the patient's best interests. The intention to involve incompetent adults in a research project will have been made clear to the REC, which will have insisted on being satisfied that the proposed research was, in fact, in the patient's best interests. The recording of the REC's approval and the doctor's judgment in the patient's notes will, if the involvement of the patient is thereafter challenged, serve as evidence that consideration was given by the

---

[35] See further, the discussion in Kennedy and Grubb (n 3 above), 1052–4.
[36] See *Re F* (n 34 above), *per* Lord Goff, and discussion in Kennedy and Grubb (n 3 above), 321 *et seq*.

doctor to the relevant issues. It would, of course, only be evidence of form. It would still be open to a court to conclude that the research was not, in fact, in the patient's best interests.

What was said previously (paras 13.16–13.20) concerning the need for **13.31** consent to be both *voluntary* and *informed* applies *mutatis mutandis* to therapeutic research on the competent adult. These requirements cannot, of course, apply in the case of the adult who is incapable of giving consent. That said, the law will regard it as part of the doctor's obligation, in reaching the conclusion that involvement in a research project is in the patient's best interests, to have taken account of and weighed appropriately all relevant information before reaching this conclusion.

(iv) *Consent: Limits*

As noted above (para 13.23) the law limits the extent to which a competent **13.32** child may consent to therapeutic research by the device of adopting a demanding set of criteria for establishing competence. The law's concern to protect the vulnerable is less pronounced in the case of such research on competent adults. The assumption, intrinsic to the notion of competence, applies that people should be left to make their own decisions. Thus, the law places no limit on what the competent adult may consent to by way of therapeutic research, subject to any overarching prohibitions contained in the general law.[37] The prior scrutiny of an REC will, of course, serve to ensure that the patient is not invited to consent to that which it would be unethical to carry out.

When the adult patient is incompetent, the limits to what therapeutic **13.33** research may be carried out are contained within the concept of best interests. This being so, it is clearly desirable, as was suggested above (para 13.29), that, from the point of view of safeguarding the patient, some flesh, by way of explicit criteria, should be put on the bones of the otherwise unsatisfactorily vague concept of best interests. The Law Commission made some efforts in this direction in its Report on Mental Incapacity.[38] These do not have the force of law but they do suggest and, it is argued, reflect the kind of factors a

---

[37] See eg, *R v Brown* [1993] 2 All ER 65.

[38] N 33 above, Part III, para 3.26 *et seq*. A 'checklist of factors' is proposed in para 3.28. In its Consultation Paper, 'Who Decides?' (Cm 3803) (1997), which reviews the Law Commission's Report, the Government 'endorses the need for guidance as to the criteria that must be taken into account when a decision-maker is considering what is in a person without capacity's best interests' but seeks views on whether the proposed checklist 'would prove workable, and useful, in practice', at 14.

court should take into account. Thus, they and other similar considerations are what should guide the REC, in its prior evaluation of a research proposal, and the doctor, in deciding whether to involve an incompetent adult patient. Above all, in therapeutic research, where there is an intention to benefit the particular patient as well as to produce generalisable data, the principle of proportionality applies. If the patient is severely ill, greater risks may be taken if the possibility of benefit is medically plausible and the alternative is otherwise bleak. Clearly, if the research involves extra interventions, or greater inconvenience or pain, the justification, that it is in the patient's best interests, must be that much stronger. As has been said, these would be matters that the REC would be expected to examine.

13.34 The question then arises whether, if the researcher has complied with the criteria of best interests stipulated by the REC, this would serve as a defence to any action subsequently brought by a patient or his representative, alleging that the research project was not in his best interests? The answer must be that compliance would be good evidence of the reasonableness of the doctor's judgment as to the patient's best interests, such that an action, whether in battery or negligence, would be unlikely to succeed.

D. Non-Therapeutic Research

Introduction

13.35 Non-therapeutic research, it will be recalled, is research carried out to produce generalisable scientific data but with no intention to benefit the research subject. It is ordinarily conducted on healthy volunteers, although it may, rarely, be carried out also on patients if it is concerned with matters other than the patient's specific illness and does not expose the patient to any additional risk of harm. Clearly, because of the altruism of the volunteer and of the fact that no benefit is intended, since no procedure can be free of risk, the law is, arguably, particularly vigilant to ensure that the volunteer is protected from harm or exploitation. This is, however, an assertion of general principle, since, as was pointed out at the outset, there is, surprisingly, no specific regime of law governing medical research, not even non-therapeutic research.

13.36 In the paragraphs which follow, the issues considered earlier in the context of therapeutic research will again be analysed as they affect non-therapeutic research. As before, the principal focus of the law is on **consent**. The same distinctions will be drawn between the child under eighteen years of age and the adult, and between the competent and the incompetent.

1. Consent: Competence

The criteria governing competence to consent are the same for non-thera-   **13.37**
peutic as for therapeutic research. While the application of these criteria is
relatively unproblematic in the case of *adult* volunteers, the legal position
regarding a *child* volunteer is not without difficulty. The law's concern to
protect the vulnerable even from themselves could, on one view, suggest that a
child should always be regarded, as a matter of law, as incompetent to
consent. Such a view is hard to support. It would involve the adoption of a
status approach to competence, (that competence depends on the fact of
minority), rejected by the House of Lords in *Gillick*[39] in favour of an
approach based on comprehension. As a matter of law, therefore, there is
no room for a blanket assumption of incompetence. Furthermore, as a matter
of logic, it is perfectly plausible to contend that, in certain circumstances, a
particular child may be competent to consent to a particular non-therapeutic
research procedure. Such a view, of course, reflects the pragmatism of the
common law and its commitment to the supremacy of the particular facts. It
is, however, a view which causes concern lest it go too far.[40] The best view,
therefore, may be as follows. A sweeping prohibition on all non-therapeutic
research on children relying solely on the child's consent, on the basis of an
irrebuttable presumption of incompetence to consent, cannot be justified. A
strong presumption exists, however, against the use of a child volunteer,
without the involvement of parents, such that very clear evidence of competence to consent will be required before non-therapeutic research may legitimately be carried out on the child.

2. Consent: Who

In the case of a competent adult, it is the adult whose consent must be sought   **13.38**
and given. In those, albeit very limited, circumstances in which a child is
deemed competent, it is the child who must consent.

In the case of an incompetent child, the general law provides that it is the   **13.39**
person with parental responsibility who may consent on behalf of the child.
The criterion governing this power to consent is, as before, the best interests
of the child. Here a difficulty arises. It can be argued that non-therapeutic
research, because it is not intended to benefit the child and is never entirely
free of risk when some form of intervention is to be carried out, can never, as

---

[39] N 15 above.
[40] See eg, the view taken in the Department of Health's guidance (n 16 above), para 4.3.

a consequence, be said to be in the child's *best* interests. On the other hand, it can be objected that some non-therapeutic research on incompetetent children ought to be permissable. It is clear that children suffer from children's diseases. Thus, data on healthy children are essential, for example, so as to identify what deviations from a norm are pathological. Data generated from research on adults may not be relevant. In such circumstances, it would be at least unfortunate, the argument goes, if such data could not be collected because of an overall ban on non-therapeutic research on incompetent children.

13.40 A compromise which is probably acceptable to the law is as follows. The criterion for consent to non-therapeutic research by those with parental responsibility should be the more relaxed test of whether the proposed research is *not against* the child's interests, rather than the need to show it is in the child's best interests.[41] The law should only follow this approach, however, subject to two crucial provisos. The first is that the research be approved independently by an REC. The second is that there should be strict limits to that for which the parent may volunteer the child. These all important limits are considered below (paras 13.55–13.56). Translated into legal analysis, therefore, the law would be that it would serve as an answer to an action, whether in battery or negligence, for the researcher to point to the fact that the child's interests had been carefully considered and a decision had been taken that what was proposed was not against the child's interests, viewed objectively and provided the proper limits were observed.

13.41 It is important to note that this view appears to be at odds with that expressed in the European *Guidelines on GCP*. By paragraph 1.15, '[c]onsent must always be given by the signature of the subject in a non-therapeutic study,[42] ie when there is no direct clinical benefit to the subject'.[43] If a subject is incompetent to consent, *ex hypothesi* no valid signature can be given. Thus, non-therapeutic research on such a subject is prohibited. A parent, consequently, may not authorise non-therapeutic research on a child. As has been seen, there is some doubt as to whether the *Guidelines on GCP* form part of English law even in that area to which they are addressed, namely research leading to an application for a product licence for a medicinal product. If they do, the view taken above (para 13.40) on the conduct of non-therapeutic research on incompetent children may to that extent need to be revised. Such

---

[41] For discussion of this test, see Kennedy and Grubb (n 3 above), 256–8, 1061–5 and *S v S, W v Official Solicitor* (or *W*) [1972] AC 24, *per* Lord Reid.

[42] It should be noted that the ICH Guidelines (n 25 above) appear to be somewhat less restrictive as regards research on the incompetent (para 4.8.14), but the wording is by no means unequivocal. [43] See *Manual* (n 4 above).

a consequence, however, may well be regarded as unfortunate, and would provide an argument for a court's holding that the Regulations translating European Directive 91/507/EEC into English law do not, in fact, incorporate the *Guidelines on GCP.*

Non-therapeutic research on an incompetent *adult* poses even greater pro-   **13.42**
blems. As has been seen, no one has authority to consent on behalf of an adult. Moreover, a proxy decision-maker must act in the best interests of the adult. Given the nature of non-therapeutic research (that it confers no benefit but carries some risk), it would appear to follow that a proxy decision-maker, who unlike the person with parental responsibility is not consenting on behalf of the adult, has no authority to volunteer an incompetent adult for involvement in such research. From this would follow the inevitable conclusion that non-therapeutic research on an incompetent adult is unlawful.

Furthermore, the interaction of the European *Guidelines on GCP,* Directive   **13.43**
91/507/EEC, and the 1993 Regulations, which was examined above (paras 13.20 and 13.41), adds further force to this view. The apparent prohibition on non-therapeutic research on the incompetent, at least in the context of research leading to an application for a product licence for a medicinal product, would clearly apply to the incompetent adult. It is no surprise, therefore, that the Law Commission in its Report on Mental Incapacity also concluded that non-therapeutic research on adults incompetent to consent for themselves is currently unlawful.[44]

It is important, therefore, to identify what, if any, legal counter-arguments   **13.44**
may exist to justify some, albeit very limited, research on the incompetent adult. First, the same sort of arguments set out in para 13.39 above can be advanced here. Research into certain diseases which result in incompetence may be impeded if, for example, tests on the incompetent themselves, so as to discover possible variations from the norm, were outlawed. On the other hand, concern to protect the vulnerable from exploitation is particularly keen in this context. The law cannot be seen to condone circumstances in which the incompetent are converted into guinea pigs for the benefit of the more fortunate. The central question is as follows. The law may, as was suggested above (para 13.40), accept a less demanding test of when non-therapeutic research may be carried out on incompetent children, namely that the proposed research is not against the child's interests, provided certain safeguards are observed. Even if this is the law as regards children, does it apply to incompetent adults, (whether generally, or, in the event that they are part of

---

[44] N 33 above, paras 6.28 *et seq.*

English law, where the *Guidelines on GCP* do not apply)? Clearly, there is no definitive answer to this question. Equally clearly, any view expressed by the Law Commission, that non-therapeutic research on incompetent adults is currently unlawful, would not lightly be disregarded by a court. Nonetheless, the view taken here is that such non-therapeutic research on incompetent adults may be lawful, subject to the strictest safeguards, as set out below (paras 13.55–13.56). The basis of its lawfulness rests on the reasoning and the test advanced above (paras 13.39–13.40), that the research is *not against* the interests of the incompetent person and is subject to strict limits, supervised by the REC.[45] The position of the Law Commission can, perhaps be explained by its desire to expose the uncertainties of current law with a view, then, to proposing a comprehensive legislative solution. This case is better made if the current law is viewed abstractly in the least favourable light rather than pragmatically as being the only law there currently is.

13.45 Indeed, the Law Commission recommended that non-therapeutic research *should* be lawful if, besides involving no more than minimal risk and invasiveness, the research was into the condition which the patient suffered from and provided that certain procedures were satisfied. (The recommended procedures are in Clause 11(i) of the Draft Bill). The insistence that the research be limited to the condition which a patient has seems difficult to justify. Apart from the hope that the patient may one day benefit, which, by definition is not the intended reason for doing the research, the patient's incompetence presumably relates as much to his own condition as to others. It seems, therefore, that what is being offered is an apparent ethical life-line to those seeking to justify the otherwise unjustifiable, in particular so as to allow research on such conditions as Alzheimer's Disease to be conducted on those suffering from it. The Government's response in its Consultation Paper is suitably cautious about contemplating even this limited degree of non-therapeutic research on the incompetent. Baldly it asks, 'Should procedures not intended to benefit the patient be allowed?'[46]

3. Consent: Validity

13.46 *Competent* volunteers, as a matter of law, may consent to non-therapeutic research without observing any particular *form*, providing they have in fact given consent. Ordinarily, of course, the relevant REC will have insisted on written consent, in an approved form, as a requirement of the ethical accept-

---

[45] Support for this approach, from an ethical point of view, can be found, for example, in guidance from the Medical Research Council, *The Ethical Conduct of Research on the Mentally Incapacitated*, 1991.   [46] See 'Who Decides?' (n 38 above), 41.

ability of the research proposal. To the extent that the *Guidelines on GCP* are part of English law, (as discussed in para 13.20 above), they stipulate, in Para 1.14, that consent must 'always be given by the signature of the subject', that is to say, in writing.

As regards non-therapeutic research on an *incompetent child*, to the extent, **13.47** argued above, that such research can be lawful, the law does not specify any particular form which consent must take. If consent may be given, it must be given by the person with parental responsibility, and, as a matter of proper caution, it would be wise for it to be set down in writing. Ordinarily, of course, the REC, in deciding whether to approve the research proposal, will have insisted on written consent.

In the case of research involving the *incompetent adult*, strictly speaking, the **13.48** form of consent does not arise, since consent does not. However, if the view expressed above (para 13.44) represents the law and non-therapeutic research, generally or subject to the application of the *Guidelines on GCP*, may lawfully be carried out within limits, some formal recording of the process leading to the decision would appear to be at least desirable. The decision-maker would wish to record the factors taken into account in reaching the view that the proposed non-therapeutic research was not against the adult's interests, and the fact that the relevant REC had been consulted and given its approval. This record, although not formally required as a prerequisite for undertaking the research, would serve as evidence that the researcher's mind was directed to the factors deemed relevant by the law, (assuming that the view of the law being advanced is valid), should the involvement of the adult be challenged.

As has been seen earlier, consent to be valid must be given voluntarily and **13.49** must be properly informed. The requirement of *voluntariness*, which, of course, only applies to the competent volunteer, is of particular importance in the case of non-therapeutic research. More generally, the fact that no benefit is intended to accrue to the volunteer causes the law to be vigilant to ensure that participation results from genuine agreement rather than from duress or coercion. Mention of duress is not intended to suggest that strong-arm tactics might be employed by medical researchers. Rather, it is to draw attention to the many pressures, subtle and otherwise, which may operate on the mind of the person asked to volunteer.

Two particular areas of difficulty warrant mention here. The first relates to **13.50** *payment*. There are those who argue that the payment of research subjects puts at risk the voluntariness of their participation. Certainly, concern has been expressed, for example, at the recruitment of participants for drug trials in areas of high unemployment, where involvement in such research could take on the quality of alternative employment. The argument is that financial exigencies cause people to expose themselves to risks they would otherwise choose to avoid. This is a complex subject, not free from an element of paternalism. Suffice it to say that it has caused considerable concern to RECs and has resulted in an uneasy compromise in which payment (in addition to reasonable expenses) is tolerated, provided it is not inappropriate or dispro-portionately large.[47] The law's position would tend to be rather more robust. Payment is unlikely to be regarded as vitiating consent unless, applying the principle of proportionality, it is so obviously out of proportion to that which was asked of the volunteer, that the ability of a reasonable person, in the volunteer's shoes, to refuse would have been overborne.

13.51 The second area of difficulty relates to those who, by virtue of their status or *relationship* with the researcher, may find it difficult to refuse consent, though they might wish to do so. What these groups have in common is their vulnerability to exploitation. Examples include: students asked to participate by teachers who also are responsible for grading their examinations; armed forces personnel asked by their superiors in rank; employees recruited by employers, explicitly on terms that no reward, by way of promotion or preferment will follow, but where the employee believes some reward will in fact follow; prisoners, again in circumstances where they hope for advan-tage despite explicit disclaimers; and mentally disordered persons, who, by virtue of their condition may be particularly vulnerable. One ethical response is that such relationships are so affected by the inevitable imbalance of power that research involving these and similar categories of persons should not be permitted. An alternative approach is that prohibition is too extreme and unnecessary. Instead, wherever the consent of someone in such a relationship is involved, extra vigilance is called for to ensure that the apparent consent is in fact real. Whatever view is taken on the ethics, the law probably reflects this latter position. Perhaps before moving on, it is worthwhile noticing here another group as regards whom extra vigilance is urged before they be involved in non-therapeutic research. The group is women. The argument advanced is that all women of child-bearing age should, on the precautionary principle, be regarded as potentially pregnant (subject to obvious exceptions). This being so, the research could put at risk the life of the embryo/foetus and, thus, cannot be justified. This approach, not suprisingly, has been strongly criticised as discriminating against women by distorting the data generated by

---

[47] The Department of Health's guidance (n 16 above), states, for example, in para 3.16 that '[p]ayment in cash or kind . . . should only be for expense, time and inconvenience reasonably incurred. It should not be at the level of an inducement which would encourage people to take part in studies against their better judgement.'

research. Data become, in fact, data on men not on people. Given the differences between men and women, this distortion can only act to the detriment of women.[48] Whatever the merits of the arguments, it will be obvious that the origin of the exclusionary principle lies with lawyers. It is an eminently sensible piece of preventive lawyering to counsel against the recruitment of women in circumstances where liability might flow if the woman were pregnant and damage were done to the unborn child. It is a matter for speculation whether an explicit waiver of responsibility, excusing the researcher of any liability, by the woman on her own and any unborn child's behalf would be legally valid or ethically acceptable.

The issue of voluntariness obviously does not arise in the case of those **13.52** incompetent to consent. This does not mean that factors such as money or other possible inducements—which might cause the decision-maker to decide in favour of volunteering someone for non-therapeutic research—cease to be important. They remain relevant and, to the extent that the law allows, form part of the assessment of whether a particular procedure is or is not against the interests of the person involved.

As regards the *information* which must be supplied to the volunteer, the **13.53** starting point for the law is that, since no therapeutic benefit is intended, there can be no case for withholding any information necessary to allow the volunteer to make a reasoned decision. The researcher's duty, as has been said, is not confined to what was set out by the House of Lords in *Sidaway*.[49] Rather, it is a much more extensive duty, namely, to bring to the attention of the volunteer all that information which, from what the volunteer has said and the researcher knows and reasonably ought to know, the volunteer would wish to know. What is known to the researcher about such matters as risks, inconvenience, or side-effects of the proposed procedure must be passed on to the volunteer in a manner and form which is comprehensible. Furthermore, the comprehensibility should be tested and checked to ensure, to the extent that is reasonably possible, that in the particular case the volunteer has, in fact, understood. As has been said before, the REC will ordinarily have called for and seen both an information sheet and a consent form, thereby providing a mechanism for translating the legal duty into practice.

In those circumstances, if any, in which the law permits non-therapeutic **13.54** research on those incompetent to consent, the issue of information translates, if the legal analysis offered above is valid, into the duty of the decision-maker not to act against the incompetent person's interests. Thus, not only is it the

---

[48] See eg, Institute of Medicine, *Women and Health Research* (National Academic Press, 1994). [49] N 21 above.

duty of the researcher to impart all relevant (as defined in para 13.53 above) information, but it is also the duty of the decision-maker, (whether parent or otherwise) to seek out this information, weigh it and reach a view on how it affects the incompetent person's interests. Again, the REC's involvement will tend to ensure that these duties are complied with.

4. Consent: Limits

13.55 The law's concern here is to set proper limits to that which volunteers may be exposed to, so as to protect the more eager from themselves and the more vulnerable from others. The question of limits, therefore, is of the greatest importance. The focus of attention clearly must be on the level or degree of *risk* involved in any particular procedure. The prevailing ethical standpoint is that volunteers in non-therapeutic research should never be exposed to a risk greater than that which can be described as *minimal*.[50] This limit also reflects the position in law. Thus, to expose a healthy volunteer or, in those circumstances in which it may be permissable, an incompetent child or adult, to risks other than those which objectively can be categorised as minimal (and, clearly, the test must be objective), is to behave unlawfully. The consent, real or apparent, of the research subject would be no defence to possible criminal liability.[51] Equally, it would probably not be admissable as a defence of consent or voluntary assumption of risk in any civil suit, whether in battery or negligence, for reasons of public policy.

13.56 In addition to setting the limit to non-therapeutic research at minimal risk, two further limits are recognised as ethically appropriate in the case of research on those incompetent to consent, where such research is permissable. The first is that the case for carrying out the research on the incompetent should be compelling. It is not enough merely to wish to know. What is required is strong evidence that the information which is sought will be gained and that, once gained, it is likely to have significant practical consequences. The second additional limitation is that the researcher must clearly demonstrate that the research must be carried out on the incompetent, or, put another way, no other group of research subjects would be suitable to generate

---

[50] See eg, Department of Health's guidance (n 16 above) para 4.3 and see the definition offered in *Research on Healthy Volunteers*, Royal College of Physicians 1986, *Manual* (n 4 above): 'We . . . use the term "minimal risk" to cover two types of situation. The first is where there is a small chance of a recognised reaction which is itself trivial, eg a headache or feeling of lethargy. The second is where there is a very remote chance of a serious disability or death. We regard this second risk to the healthy volunteer as comparable, for example, to that of flying as a passenger in a scheduled aircraft.' For further discussion, see Kennedy and Grubb (n 3 above), 1060.   [51] See eg, *R v Brown* (n 37 above).

the desired data. There is no doubt that these two ethical concerns would be recognised as a legally relevant part of the process of determining whether the proposed research is or is not against the interests of the incompetent child or adult.

5. Research not Involving Intervention

Not all medical research involves intervention by way of touching so as to **13.57** bring into play the law of battery and negligence. Psychologists and psychiatrists, for example, may conduct research through observation and recording of patients and volunteers.[52] Epidemiologists carry out research which usually will not even bring them into contact with the research subject. Their concern is with aggregates of patients or healthy volunteers, rather than individuals. Such research attracts its own ethical guidance.[53] The task here is to identify areas of legal concern. The approach adopted will be to identify possible harm or grounds for complaint which might flow from these forms of research and analyse the law's response.

The first area of concern is that *psychiatric or psychological research* could **13.58** expose the research subject to *psychological damage* actionable in negligence.[54] Such damage may occur as a consequence of therapeutic research on a patient or non-therapeutic research on a volunteer. The law's response is that the researcher in either set of circumstances is under a duty of care owed to the subject, which must not be breached. A breach may occur because the research was ill-conceived or improperly conducted, or because the subject was not properly informed as to what might transpire. How will the law define the standard of care? The situation in which it is alleged that the research was ill-conceived, in that it lacked scientific plausibility, is different from the others. The court would rely there on expert evidence. In the other cases, the standard of care to which the researcher will be held will not be determined simply by reference to *Bolam*.[55] The views and practice of other researchers (*per Bolam*) would be regarded by the court as relevant but by no means determinative of the degree of care required by law. The fact that research was involved and, thus, that someone was acting altruistically, would persuade the court to impose its own standard. In the context of *therapeutic* research, if the complaint was as to the conduct of the research, the court would weigh the risks against the alleged benefits, in the light of

---

[52] See Guidelines issued by the Royal College of Psychiatrists and the British Psychological Society in *Manual* (n 4 above).
[53] See eg, British Sociological Association, Statement of Ethical Practice, in *Manual* (n 4 above).   [54] On which see *Alcock v Chief Constable of South Yorkshire* [1992] 1 AC 310.
[55] N 9 above.

the circumstances, not least the subject's mental state. If the complaint rested on breach of the duty to inform, it is equally unlikely that *Sidaway*[56] *simpliciter*, derived as it is from *Bolam*, would be relied on. Instead, the court in all probability would opt for a test based on the reasonable patient in the particular patient's position.[57] In the context of *non-therapeutic* research, the fact that no benefit is intended to accrue to the subject would, *a fortiori*, result in the court going beyond *Bolam*. Researchers would be held to a standard of care which, though it took account of, was not determined by evidence of professional standards or practice.

13.59 The second area of concern relates to *privacy* and *confidentiality*. There are a number of circumstances in which a research subject might complain of an invasion of privacy or a breach of confidence.

13.60 The first relates to research involving *observation* of the subject. By its nature this would ordinarily be non-therapeutic research. Obviously, if the subject has given effective consent beforehand, no problems arise. This is what an REC would insist on. But, what of the situation in which, whatever the REC may have stipulated, the research is conducted surreptitiously, without consent? The question arises whether the subject, once aware of what has taken place, can bring any legal action if upset thereby. There is no doubt that, as a matter of ethics, the subject has been wronged. Recourse to the relevant Professional Codes of Conduct[58] would, therefore, be an option open to the subject. It is doubtful, however, that any legal redress would be available. The English law of privacy is extremely undeveloped.[59]

13.61 The following question then arises: what if it were proposed to carry out such research on someone incompetent to consent? The limitations on carrying out non-therapeutic research on the incompetent have been set out in detail above. It could be argued, however, that these limitations do not apply here. It could be said that they apply only to those circumstances in which the incompetent person is touched and thereby put at risk. Whatever the validity of this view, it is likely that, from an ethical perspective, in the case of research on an incompetent child, the consent of the person with parental responsibility will be required. Furthermore, the parent will be constrained in what may be consented to, whether by reference to the child's best interests or that the research is not against the child's interests. It is most likely, moreover, that

---

[56] N 21 above.
[57] Following, eg, the reasoning in *Reibl v Hughes* (1980) 114 DLR (3rd) 1.
[58] See eg, nn 52 and 53 above.
[59] See eg, Salmond and Heuston, *Law of Torts*, 21st edn (Sweet and Maxwell, 1996), 32–4. It is a separate question whether an action would be sustainable under Article VIII of the European Convention on Human Rights, once all domestic remedies were exhausted.

this also represents the legal position, bearing in mind the law's paramount concern for the welfare of the child. Thus, any research carried out without the parent's consent or which, despite consent, violates the child's interests, will be unlawful.[60] In the case of an incompetent adult, it may similarly be argued that the limits or prohibitions on non-therapeutic research discussed above (para 13.44) do not, or should not, apply to research which does not involve touching. The answer would be that the primary ethical concern would be to safeguard the interests of the incompetent adult, at the very least so as to ensure that nothing is done which is against those interests. Whether the incompetent adult would have any legal redress if those interests were violated is by no means clear. As has been said, the law of privacy is wholly undeveloped. Clearly, if some harm were suffered as a consequence of negligence, an action would lie. Equally, a remedy may exist if harm were caused intentionally. Beyond these, the subject's protection lies with those who police the relevant Ethical Codes.

The second situation which could give rise to legal complaint is where *access to personal medical details* relating to a current or former patient is granted to a researcher, ordinarily in the context of non-therapeutic research. Again, no complaint can be made if the patient has given effective consent, whether at the time of treatment or subsequently. If the patient is an incompetent child, arguably the person with parental authority could authorise access. It may well be, however, that the test against which any decision would be judged would be the traditional test of the child's best interests. There does not seem to be a strong argument in favour of the more relaxed test of 'not against the child's interests' in this context, bearing in mind the possible damaging effect to a child of the release of personal medical details. What if the patient is an adult, incompetent to give, or have given, consent? As has been seen, the general law makes it clear that no one else has authority to consent *to treatment* on behalf of an adult. Does this prohibition apply equally where what is at issue is not treatment but access to personal medical details, usually in the form of records? It could be said that those who have the responsibility of managing the affairs of the incompetent person could give consent, all other things being equal, namely that the adult's interests are not violated. This may not be the law, however, since medical records are not the property of the patient.[61] Thus, if the authority to manage affairs is limited to property, it would not extend to authorising access to medical details. If

13.62

---

[60] It is a separate question, and one not easy to resolve, whether the conduct described as unlawful would give rise to a civil cause of action at the suit of the child. Negligence suggests itself as one candidate, if the child suffered harm. Clearly, family law remedies would also be available to seek to protect the child for the future.
[61] See Kennedy and Grubb (n 3 above), 610 *et seq.*

the authority goes further—and Ungoed-Thomas J's judgment in *Re W* (*EEM*)[62] is somewhat equivocal, since it draws the line at treatment decisions and what is being considered here is somewhere in-between—access could be granted. Perhaps the better view is that the authority does not, in fact, extend this far. Thus, prima facie, access is impermissable. If such a conclusion were judged to be too restrictive in circumstances where very good reasons could be advanced for access, the law could adopt a more permissive position. This could be that access is lawful, provided that it is not against the interests of the incompetent adult and is deemed acceptable by a reasonable body of informed people, by being approved, after proper deliberation, by an REC.

13.63 In the absence of lawful authority, the person granting access, usually the doctor, has committed a breach of confidence. This would be actionable at the suit of the patient.[63] The legal position in the case of those incompetent to consent, however, is less clear. While any release of personal medical details to persons other than those who need them for the purposes of rendering medical care would provoke ethical disapproval and, perhaps, sanction, it is by no means clear that any legal action would lie in the case of an incompetent child or adult.[64] If such an action were to lie, the only possible defence would be to argue that the public interest in pursuing the particular research outweighed the public interest in maintaining the law's commitment to confidentiality. It is difficult to envisage circumstances in which such a defence would succeed.

13.64 The third situation warranting attention here is where *information is published* as part of a research project which allows a research subject, usually a patient, to be identified. The publication can take such diverse forms as personal details in a learned paper, a photograph in an article or book illustrating a particular condition, or a video shown at a research conference. Once again, if effective consent has been given, no problem arises. By contrast, it would be hard to justify publication in any other case, whether of those who are incompetent to consent or those whose consent has not been sought. The reasons are twofold. First, it would appear to be a significant intrusion into

---

[62] [1971] Ch 123.

[63] It should be noticed that the NHS executive in HSG (96) 48, *The Protection and Use of Patient Information*, takes a different view. Broadly speaking, it contemplates that NHS records are available to any NHS employee for NHS purposes. This somewhat self-serving view, by which a number of managerial tasks can be more readily accomplished, flies in the face of long-standing medical tradition and the law. In the context of research and access to personal medical details, it advises that NHS staff may have access to patients' notes for the purpose of research without the consent of the patients. With all due respect, this is not the law and the NHS Executive does itself no favours by taking the position that by saying something frequently enough it will become true. [64] Kennedy and Grubb (n 3 above), 640 *et seq.*

the privacy of the research subject. Secondly, publication of identifying details is rarely, if ever, necessary. Data can be anonymised. Photographs and other pictorial representations can be so disguised as to prevent identification. Professional bodies regard the anonymisation of data, wherever possible, and consent, if feasible, when anonymisation is not possible, as required from an ethical perspective.[65] The legal position, however, is less clear. Once again, what is being complained of is, in essence, an invasion of privacy. As was said above in (para 13.60) the existence of any legal remedy is, at best, problematical.

E. Regulatory/Supervisory Mechanism

1. Introduction

As was said at the outset, there is no overarching statutory framework **13.65** regulating the conduct of biomedical research on humans. With the limited exception of the Regulations referred to above (para 13.20), those conducting research must, therefore, look to the common law for guidance. As the foregoing exposition has made clear, it is no easy task to state the law with any degree of certainty. This is because, until very recently, medical research has been conducted out of the public limelight, in an atmosphere of trust (or at least tolerance) and responsibility, and, apparently, with very few cases of harm ensuing. For these among many reasons, remarkably, no cases involving research have been brought to the English courts from which guidance could be obtained.

2. HSG *(91) 5—Department of Health Guidelines*

In the absence of any specific regulatory system, various institutional bodies, in **13.66** particular the Royal College of Physicians and the Association of the British Pharmaceutical Industry, began to develop frameworks for guidance during the early 1980s.[66] Eventually, the Department of Health, having taken advice, issued Guidelines in 1991 through the NHS Management Executive (HSG (91) 5). Perhaps the principal factor which persuaded government to act, albeit in a non-statutory manner, was a concern at the lack of legal protection available to research subjects. The Guidelines which emerged, entitled *Local Research Ethics Committees*, are the closest the United Kingdom government has come to regulating the conduct of research on human subjects.

---

[65] See eg, *Duties of a Doctor: Confidentiality* (General Medical Council, 1995), paras 15 and 16.   [66] See, *Manual* (n 4 above).

13.67 The Guidelines lay certain duties on various bodies within the NHS under the auspices of which research is conducted. Ultimately, the duties fall upon the relevant District Health Authority (DHA). Principal among these duties is the creation of a local REC and consultation of it in matters relating to the ethics of any proposed research project. These duties form part of the contractual obligations of the manager of the DHA. In turn, through its contractual relationship with NHS employees, management then ensures that the procedures and safeguards set out in the Circular are observed. In this way, the provisions of the Guidelines, at least as they affect those employed within the NHS, operate as if they had the force of law.

13.68 The Guidelines only apply, of course, to activities undertaken within the ambit of the NHS. To that extent, those who conduct research outside the NHS are under no duty to comply with them. Given the status of the Guidelines, in practice if not in law, as some form of quasi-legislation, this limitation on their reach might seem to represent a significant hiatus. In practice, however, this limitation may be more apparent than real. First, the Circular extends to any research involving the use of NHS patients or premises. To the extent that non-NHS researchers, (that is, researchers who are not employed within the NHS), might wish to conduct research, it is difficult to do so without using NHS patients or premises. Secondly, companies sponsoring research will ordinarily wish to ensure that the Guidelines are followed, both because they represent considered public policy but also because it is clearly in their commercial interests to be seen to behave responsibly. Thirdly, the Guidelines' most significant regulatory mechanism, the REC, is now a standard feature of biomedical research, whether conducted within or outside the NHS. Indeed, bodies which provide financial support for research and editors of journals which publish research results both tend to insist on evidence that research has received approval from an REC.

13.69 Nonetheless, whatever the situation may be in practice, it remains odd, and some would say unfortunate, that there is no formal law regulating research. It means, among other things, that, as a matter of law, there is no requirement that a research proposal even be submitted to, let alone be approved by, an REC. Thus, in principle at least, the safeguards referred to earlier whereby, for example, RECs will have had to be satisfied as to the scientific plausibility of a research proposal and have called for and approved consent forms or information sheets, may not always apply. To this extent, the law's protection of the interests and welfare of research subjects is less than satisfactory. Of course, the common law remains. However, the extent and prevalence of biomedical research suggest that something better than relying on the common law is called for, not least something which is prescriptive, setting out in a pro-active manner what ought to be done, rather than a system which only provides for complaint after the event, when damage may already have been done.

As will have become clear, the REC is seen as the single most important and, **13.70** *ex hypothesi*, most effective mechanism to ensure that research proceeds in a way which meets the twin public policy objectives widely recognised as justifying biomedical research: that it should proceed without unnecessary impediment; and that the welfare and safety of research subjects should at all times be the primary consideration in deciding whether to proceed. Therefore, given the significance of the REC, it is important, first, to notice the membership. The Guidelines make certain recommendations but, in practice, the size and composition vary considerably.[67] It is equally important to determine its precise legal status. The short answer is that the REC, in law, is no more than a group of individuals. It has no separate legal personality, distinct from its members.[68] Thus, any action complaining of an REC's conduct must be brought either against the individual members or the Health Authority, as the appointing body and, as regards some at least of the members, the employer. That said, in the case of *R v Ethical Committee of St Mary's Hospital* (*Manchester*), *ex p H*,[69] the court, by admitting the suit, appeared to accept that RECs are amenable to judicial review in the exercise of their functions. This must be right since they are a quasi-public body, chosen by government to perform an important public role.

Although there is no legal requirement that RECs should exist, and although, **13.71** once established, they have no legal personality, the members, once appointed, take on a number of legal duties. As has been seen, the REC is amenable to judicial review in the exercise of these duties and members are also individually responsible. Principal among these duties is the duty of each member to act with due care. The role of each member is to review proposals for research and make recommendations as to the ethical propriety, or otherwise, of them. In carying out this role, members must take account of the twin aims, referred to above (para 13.70), of fostering research while safeguarding the welfare of research subjects. Members must, therefore, seek to understand, so as to take an ethical view about, complex issues of, *inter alia*, biomedical science, statistics and moral philosophy. The members' duty, expressed in this way, may seem somewhat daunting. The standard of care demanded by the law, however, is that of reasonableness. The REC member

---

[67] See eg, Neuberger, *Ethics and Healthcare: The Role of Research Ethics Committees in the UK*, King's Fund Research Report No 13, 1992.
[68] See Brazier, 'Liability of Ethics Committees and Their Members', (1990) PN 186.
[69] [1988] 1 FLR 512.

must behave as a reasonable REC member. While this does not mean that the quantum of care demanded of a member may be intentionally kept at a low point through the expedient of appointing members whose experience and expertise is limited, it does mean that the law recognises that it will be a rare member who is at home in all areas of concern to the REC. The upshot is that the member will not be held to too high a standard, but at the same time will be expected to recognise the limits of his own expertise. Where such limits exist, the law would expect that the member would not take a view until information and reassurance had been sought from others. A member, and the Health Authority, would also be expected to take advantage of whatever training opportunities may exist. Equally, a member has a duty to ensure that the decision-making process which the REC operates is one which, for example, ensures that expertise is drawn upon and shared, that decisions are only taken after proper consultation and that the REC follows appropriate standing procedures.[70]

13.72 It is fair to say that not all RECs function in as appropriate a manner as the law would expect.[71] Standing operating procedures may not exist or may not be observed. The expertise available within the REC may be too limited. The REC may be dominated by one section of the local community, whether medical, nursing or anti-medical. These deficiencies are unfortunate when it is recalled that RECs are the bodies with which the pharmaceutical industry, with its huge investment in research, must deal. Arguably, the industry should be entitled to a rather more professional and, it would follow, better resourced system than the somewhat amateurish and overworked RECs which currently exist in some parts of the country. Moreover, it will be clear from what has been said that the industry, among others, is limited as regards any redress it may have in the face of adverse decisions by the REC. An action in theory exists against any member who has failed to behave reasonably, for example, by reaching a perverse decision or simply failing to read the papers before making a decision. Not only would it be difficult to prove breach but it would also be extremely difficult to demonstrate any actionable harm or a causal link between the conduct complained of and the harm suffered. Furthermore, only those members of the REC who were employees of the Health Authority would have any insurance cover to meet any claim, such that the existence of a cause of action against members is more theoretical than real. That said, the threat exists that a test case, whether by judicial review or common law action, may be brought by researchers

---

[70] See eg, Bendall, 'Standard Operating Procedures for Local RECs', *Manual* (n 4 above).
[71] See Neuberger (n 67 above).

frustrated by the conduct of an REC which has very considerable power and very little accountability.

The alternative to ensuring greater professionalism and accountability of RECs through litigation is though political action. The development of a new system for dealing with *multi-centre trials* illustrates this latter approach. Multi-centre trials, as their name makes clear, are trials, usually of a medicinal product, conducted simultaneously at a number of places, often in a number of countries. Conflict has arisen over the years because RECs at different research centres, in considering a proposal for multi-centre research, have reached different decisions as to the acceptability of the research or have imposed different terms as the condition for acceptability. Those in charge of multi-centre trials have complained about the variability of approach, its unpredictability and, hence, its cost. RECs have responded that they exist to make independent judgments. Local circumstances may well affect the ethical acceptability of a proposal, such as, for instance, the ethnic composition of a particular area. Furthermore, they have urged that on issues of ethical acceptability, it should not be assumed, nor may it be desirable for every REC to take the same view. In the event, after considerable consultation between industry, RECs and the Department of Health, a compromise position was agreed. HSG (97) 23 was issued. It is concerned with the ethical review of multi-centre research. Eleven new MRECs, (multi-centre RECs) were established, one each in Scotland, Northern Ireland, and Wales and the remainder in England. They will consider all multi-centre research proposals involving the use of human subjects. RECs at local level will still be involved in review but their powers have been limited. They may insist on changes to the patient information sheet, but only if local reasons justify them. They are not, however, permitted to change the scientific basis of the research proposal.[72]

13.73

The final matter which warrants mention is *compensation* for research subjects who may be injured as a result of their participation in research. Of course, it is open to any research subject to pursue an action at common law. The difficulties of doing so and the uncertainty of success, coupled with the argument that, as public-spirited volunteers, research subjects deserved some special treatment, led to the emergence of proposals that compensation be available without the need for litigation. The Association of the British Pharmaceutical Industry (ABPI) proposed a scheme whereby compensation based on no-fault would be paid to the subject.[73] The subject still had to

13.74

---

[72] See, for the full text, HSG (97) 23.
[73] For a discussion of this and other schemes, see Hodges, 'Harmonisation of European Controls over Research: Ethics Committees, Consent, Compensation and Indemnity', in Goldberg, (ed) *Pharmaceutical Medicine and the Law* (1991). and Kennedy and Grubb (n 3 above), 1067–73.

prove that it was the research which caused the harm complained of. The Royal College of Physicians, in its 1986 guidance, made a number of proposals designed to ensure that a research subject who was harmed through taking part in research would obtain compensation with a minimum of legal obstacles and delay.[74] The Department of Health's Guidelines, however, are somewhat guarded on the issue, not least because of the Treasury convention that open-ended financial commitments are not made by government. It cannot be said, therefore, that arrangements for compensation outside the framework of litigation, regarded by most as eminently desirable, are currently satisfactory.

---

[74] *Research on Healthy Volunteers* (n 50 above).

14

PRODUCTS LIABILITY

A. Introduction

'Products liability' may be broadly defined as the liability of manufacturers **14.01**
and other suppliers of products for injury or loss caused by their defective
condition.[1] Liability for medicinal products is thus a particular instance of

---

[1] cf the 'civil liability of manufacturers and others where damage or loss is caused by
products which fail to meet the standards claimed expressly or impliedly for them or which are
defective or otherwise dangerous'. Miller, C and Lovell, P, *Product Liability* (London, 1977) 1.
'The term 'products liability' is an American invention. It does not describe a distinct category
of law in the United Kingdom'. Royal Commission on Civil Liability and Compensation for
Personal Injury (the 'Pearson Commission') (London, 1978) Cmnd 7054 Vol 1, para 1216.

liability for products which cause injury because of the way in which they have been designed, manufactured, or marketed. In the 1960s an elaborate regulatory structure was established for medicines, in the wake of the thalidomide tragedy.[2] The protracted litigation over thalidomide proved to be a catalyst for proposals during the 1970s, both in the UK[3] and in Europe,[4] to introduce strict liability regimes for injuries caused by defective products. The culmination of this activity was the European Community Directive on Products Liability (1985),[5] as implemented in England by Part I of the Consumer Protection Act 1987 (hereafter the CPA).[6]

14.02 Products liability may arise by virtue of contract, tort, or statute. In contract, reflecting the development of implied warranties in the nineteenth century, the main focus has been on merchantability—the condition or *quality* of the product in the light of presumed consumer expectations. Tort law, on the other hand, has stressed the defendant's *conduct* and society's interest in product *safety*. The distinction is somewhat superficial, since 'almost all defects in goods can at some level be more accurately described as attributable to human agency'.[7] Most importantly now, in the guise of strict liability, a new statutory framework for the protection of consumers has emerged in the CPA. The CPA appears to blur the tort/contract divide by defining product *safety* in terms of consumer expectations. Defectiveness under the Act depends on proof that 'the safety of the product is not such as persons generally are entitled to expect . . .'.[8] However, it would seem that the CPA's conception of 'defectiveness' is rooted in product safety, rather than merchantability.[9]

14.03 The different sources of civil liability do not blend into a single, coherent body of legal doctrine. Leaving to one side the questionable logic of differentiating

---

[2] Medicines Act 1968.

[3] The Law Commission and the Scottish Law Commission, *Liability for Defective Products* (1977) Cmnd 6831; Royal Commission on Civil Liability and Compensation for Personal Injury (n 1 above), ch 22.

[4] EEC Draft Directive on products liability, OJ No C 241, 14.10.76 (first draft), OJ No C 271, 26.10.79 (second draft); *Strasbourg Convention on Products Liability in Regard to Personal Injury and Death*, 27.1.77 (1977).

[5] EEC Directive on the approximation of the laws, regulations and administrative provisions of the Member States concerning liability for defective products: 85/374/EEC, OJ No L 210/29, 7.8.85.

[6] The CPA does not apply to damage caused by defects in products supplied before 1 March 1988: CPA, s 50(7); CPA (Commencement No 1) Order 1987, SI 1987/1680.

[7] Stapleton, J, *Product Liability* (London, 1994) 329.   [8] S 1(3).

[9] Department of Trade and Industry, 'Implementation of the EC Directive on Product Liability. An Explanatory and Consultative Note' (London, 1985), para 55. Cf EEC Draft Directive (first draft) (n 4 above), Explanatory Memorandum, Art 4.

between the provision of products and services,[10] the CPA provides only an alternative or additional basis for a cause of action in damages.[11] Actions in tort and contract remain available for situations either not covered or less adequately covered by the 1987 Act. In addition to providing these civil actions, the law endeavours to enhance consumer protection by means of regulatory measures which contain criminal penalties for failure to comply with specified standards.[12] In recent years, such provision has become more elaborate following a series of EEC initiatives.[13]

Effective medicines are seldom risk-free. Determining whether or not they **14.04** have caused harm can present difficulties which, in the case of other products, either do not arise or are typically less pronounced. Problems include the unpredictable long-term or delayed effects of certain drugs,[14] idiosyncratic or allergic reactions, the synergistic effects of some drug interactions with other drugs or foods, and the difficulty of distinguishing the effects of medication from the natural progression of illness.[15] A causal complication of a different kind may arise when vaccines and, increasingly, drugs are generically prescribed, with the result that their source of origin is not readily identifiable.[16]

---

[10] See generally, Stapleton, J 'Three Problems with the New Product Liability', in Cane, P and Stapleton, J (eds), *Essays for Patrick Atiyah* (Oxford, 1991), ch 11.

[11] CPA, s 2(6). See *AB v South West Water Services Ltd* [1993] QB 507, CA, where, as well as claiming under the CPA, s 2(1), the plaintiffs pleaded breach of statutory duty; *Rylands v Fletcher*, breach of contract, nuisance, and negligence.

[12] eg under the Medicines Act 1968. The provisions of this Act may not be construed as conferring a civil right of action in respect of contraventions of the Act or of any regulations or order made under it: s 133(2). By contrast, safety regulations made under the Consumer Protection Act 1961 and the Consumer Safety Act 1978 did entitle a person injured by certain goods, which included cosmetics and asbestos products, to bring an action for breach of statutory duty against any seller in the chain of supply. These two Acts (and the Consumer Safety (Amendment) Act 1986) were repealed by the CPA, which has extended the regulation-making powers and which does permit an individual injured by infringement of a safety regulation to bring an action for breach of statutory duty: CPA, s 41. See eg the Active Implantable Medical Devices Regulations 1992, SI 1992/3146, as amended by SI 1995/1671. However, 'licensed medicinal products' and tobacco are not subject to regulatory control under the CPA: CPA, s 10(7)(e) and s 10(7)(f), respectively. See also, Miller, C, 'Consumer Protection' in Guest *et al* (eds) *Benjamin's Sale of Goods* (London, 1992, 4th edn), ch 14.

[13] ibid, para 14–001. See esp Product Safety Directive: 92/59/EEC, OJ L.228/24, 11.8.92, as implemented by the General Product Safety Regulations 1994, SI 1994/2328.

[14] See eg *Sindell v Abbott Laboratories* (1980) 26 Cal 3d 588 (DES).

[15] DHSS, *Product Liability: Special Features of the Medical Sector*, Medicines Division Consultation Paper (London, 1979); Newdick, C, 'Defective Medicines: Unavoidable Danger or Unacceptable Risk?' (1990) 1 *Intl J of Risk and Safety in Medicine*, 195.

[16] As in *Loveday v Renton and Wellcome Foundation Ltd* [1990] 1 Med LR 117 (pertussis). On generics, see *Mann and Close v Wellcome Foundation Ltd* (unreported) (1989) QBD; *Sindell v Abbott Laboratories* (n 14 above).

14.05 The scope of products liability in the medical sphere may also be affected by the way in which a particular substance is legally defined. For example, though the common law has resisted classifying human bodies as 'goods',[17] there are unresolved doubts over whether human organs can be so regarded, or whether supplying bodily fluids could connote a sale of goods rather than a supply of services. It thus remains unclear whether or not transplants and blood transfusions constitute a supply of 'goods' within the Supply of Goods and Services Act 1982[18] and whether they involve the transfer of 'products' under the CPA.[19] Similarly, the applicable legal principles will vary according to a product's statutory classification and the manner in which it has been supplied. It may have been sold as a 'medicinal product'[20] on the General Sale List (GSL) or as a pharmacy medicine (P). Alternatively, it may have been a Prescription Only Medicine (POM)[21] made available either under the legal regime for drug prescription under the National Health Service or on private prescription.[22] In some circumstances, it would have been directly administered by way of injection.

14.06 The term 'product(s) liability' is primarily associated with claims against manufacturers or producers. However, in attributing or apportioning responsibility for harm it may be necessary to consider other suppliers in the chain of distribution, including the retailer. In the case of medicinal products, liability may attach to retail or hospital pharmacists and to doctors. In principle, it would seem that an action could also be brought against a

---

[17] See further para 14.20 below.
[18] Bell, AP, 'The Doctor and the Supply of Goods and Services Act 1982' (1984) 4 *LS*, 175, 178. See further para 14.21 below.   [19] See para 14.56 below.
[20] Under the Medicines Act 1968, a 'medicinal product' is 'any substance or article (not being an instrument, apparatus or appliance) . . . for use wholly or mainly' for a 'medicinal purpose', that is, to treat, prevent, or diagnose disease; to ascertain the existence, degree, or extent of a physiological condition; for contraception; to induce anaesthesia, or otherwise prevent or interfere with the normal operation of a physiological function: s 130(1), (2). Some biological, surgical, dental, and ophthalmic materials which were medicinal products within the Act or its subordinate legislation are now controlled under the CPA. They include IUDs and contact lens fluids. See Council Dir 93/42/EEC and the Medical Devices Regulations 1994, SI 1994/3017. Cosmetics with remedial or curative functions are also subject to licensing provisions. On judicial review of classification, see *R v Medicines Control Agency, ex p Pharma Nord Ltd, The Times*, 29 July 1997.
[21] See Medicines Act 1968, s 51 (General Sale list), and s 58 (Prescription Only medicinal products). See also the Medicines (Prescription Only, Pharmacy and General Sale) Amendment Order, SI 1989/1852, and the Medicines Act 1968, s 58A, inserted by the Medicines Act 1968 (Amendment)(No 2) Regulations 1992, SI 1992/3271, reg 2 (implementing Council Dir 92/26/EEC, L 113/5). See generally Medicines Control Agency, *Towards Safe Medicines* (London, revised edn, 1997).
[22] In the UK, approximately 80% of drugs are POMs supplied under the NHS. See Hancher, L, *Regulating for Competition: Government, Law, and the Pharmaceutical Industry in the United Kingdom and France* (Oxford, 1990), 72.   [23] See n 12 above.

regulatory agency with a licensing function, such as the Licensing Authority and its advisory bodies established under the Medicines Act 1968. Although such an action could not be for breach of statutory duty,[23] it might lie in negligence, a possibility contemplated by the Court of Appeal in respect of haemophiliacs injured by blood products contaminated with HIV.[24]

Though numerous claims of drug-induced injury have been settled, no **14.07** United Kingdom court has yet held a pharmaceutical company liable in negligence for injuries caused by a medicinal product. There is scant judicial analysis of what constitutes an absence of 'reasonable care' by pharmaceutical manufacturers and, at the time of writing, there has been only one reported case of any description involving Part I of the CPA.[25] As well as the lack of English authority on substantive aspects of medical products liability, a number of recent drug injury claims have highlighted the procedural complexity and funding difficulties commonly associated with group actions.[26]

B. Contractual Liability

Historically, the boundaries of liability for injurious products largely derive **14.08** from the law on sales warranties. Since, under the doctrine of privity, the

---

[24] *Re HIV Haemophiliac Litigation* (1990) 140 NLJ 1349, where the Committee on Safety of Medicines, the Licensing Authority and the Department of Health were joined as defendants. See also *Brown v Alberta* [1994] 2 WWR 283 (Alta. QB); cf *H v Royal Alexandra Hospital for Children* [1990] 1 Med LR 297 (SC of NSW). Arguably, however, the only duty (of care) is to the public at large: Barton, A, 'The Basis of Liability of the Licensing Authority and its Advisers under the Medicines Act 1968 to an Individual' in Goldberg, A and Dodds-Smith, I (eds) *Pharmaceutical Medicine and the Law*, (London, 1991). See further para 14.46 below.

[25] *AB v South West Water Services Ltd* [1993] QB 507, CA. For the European Court of Justice ruling on the UK formulation of the 'development risks' defence in the CPA, s 4(1)(e), see paras 14.65–14.68. below. See also Mildred, M, 'The Impact of the Directive in the United Kingdom', in Goyens, M, *Directive 85/374/EEC on product liability: ten years after* (Louvain-la-Neuve, 1996) 37–57.

[26] See *Nash v Eli Lilly & Co*. [1991] 2 Med LR 169 (Opren); Oliphant, K, 'Innovations in Procedure and Practice in Multi-Party Medical Cases' in Grubb, A (ed) *Choices and Decisions in Health Care* (Chichester, 1993); cf the benzodiazepine litigation: see the Supreme Court Procedure Committee, *Guide for Use in Group Actions* (London, 1991); Legal Aid Board, *Issues Arising for the Legal Aid Board and the Lord Chancellor's Department from Multi-Party Actions* (London, 1994). See further para 14.71 below.

[27] *Dunlop Pneumatic Tyre Co v Selfridge & Co Ltd* [1915] AC 847; *Daniels and Daniels v R White & Sons Ltd and Tarbard* [1938] 4 All ER 258; *Woodar Investment Development Ltd v Wimpey Construction UK Ltd* [1980] 1 WLR 277, HL. Contrast the relaxation of the privity rule in the United States Uniform Commercial Code s 2–318, extending the seller's liability for breach of warranty to other members of the purchaser's household (including guests); cf *Henningsen v Bloomfield Motors Inc 161* A 2d 69 (1960), and most importantly, *Greenman v Yuba Power Products Inc 377* P 2d 897 (1963), where 'strict' liability in tort heralded the widely adopted rule in Section 402A of the Restatement (Second) of Torts (1965), making

seller of a defective product is contractually liable only to the buyer,[27] in practice contract has limited relevance to claims for harm caused by medicinal products. Pharmaceutical companies very rarely have a contractual relationship with consumers for the supply of goods, unless they are private patients buying medical equipment direct from the manufacturer. Patients injured by the more potent drugs will usually have obtained them through NHS prescription. In such circumstances there is no contract with the prescribing doctor, or with the pharmacist, who is statutorily obliged to dispense drugs on presentation of a prescription and payment of any fixed charge.[28] A pharmacist could however be liable in contract for injury caused by privately prescribed drugs or by non-prescription medicines sold over-the-counter. Equally, a doctor or hospital supplying drugs or other medical materials privately could be contractually liable.[29]

1. General Principles of Liability

14.09 Sales of medicinal products, being subject to the common law and statutory principles generally applicable to consumer sales, can give rise to liability for innocent misrepresentation[30] or breach of contract. In addition to grounding a claim for the breach of any express or implied terms at common law, such transactions are subject to the implied terms of the Sale of Goods Act 1979 (hereafter the SGA 1979), which in essence consolidates the Sale of Goods Act 1893. Thus the seller can be held liable if the goods sold do not correspond with their description,[31] or do not meet the 'quality conditions', either because they are not of 'satisfactory quality'[32] or not fit for their particular purpose.[33] Liability for breach of the implied terms is 'strict', there being no need to prove fault or negligence on the part of the vendor.[34] There

---

commercial sellers strictly liable to the ultimate user or consumer for physical harm caused by 'unreasonably dangerous' products.

[28] *Pfizer Corp v Ministry of Health* [1965] AC 512, 535–6, *per* Lord Reid; *Appleby v Sleep* [1968] 1 WLR 948, 954–5.

[29] In such cases, liability can in principle move back up the chain of supply via third-party proceedings and successive indemnities. See para 14.16 below.

[30] Misrepresentation Act 1967, s 2(1).

[31] S 13(1). 'Description' is construed broadly to include the purpose and use to which goods are put; cf *Holmes v Ashford* [1950] 2 All ER 76, CA; *Kubach v Hollands* [1937] 3 All ER 907.

[32] Sale and Supply of Goods Act 1994, s 1. The term 'satisfactory quality' has replaced the long-established expression 'merchantable quality' (SGA 1979, s 14(2)), which had been criticised as outmoded and inappropriate for consumer transactions: Law Commission, *Sale and Supply of Goods* (London, 1987) paras 2.9 and 2.10.   [33] SGA 1979, s 14(3).

[34] *Frost v Aylesbury Dairy Co Ltd* [1905] 1 KB 608, CA. See also *Kendall (Henry) and Sons (a firm) v William Lillico and Sons Ltd* [1969] 2 AC 31, 84, *per* Lord Reid; *Vacwell Engineering Co Ltd v BDH Chemicals Ltd* [1971] 1 QB 88.

are comparable provisions regarding contracts for services in the course of which goods are 'supplied', in the Supply of Goods and Services Act 1982 (hereafter the SGSA).[35]

Where a medicinal product is defective because of a manufacturing fault there may be a breach of the implied condition of satisfactory quality, namely, that the goods 'meet the standard that a reasonable person would regard as satisfactory'.[36] For such liability to arise, there is no need for the buyer to have relied on the seller's skill or judgment. In principle this provision could also ground liability for unforeseen side effects resulting from defective design. However, it might be deemed unreasonable to expect drugs not to present any such dangers, and it would often be difficult to demonstrate that unavoidable risks of a powerful drug are incompatible with 'satisfactory quality'.   **14.10**

As regards fitness for purpose, inability of the seller to detect an unforeseen side effect is not in principle a defence.[37] However, 'where the circumstances show that the buyer does not rely, or that it is unreasonable for him to rely, on the skill or judgment of the seller . . .', the implied condition is inapplicable.[38] The onus is on the seller to show that there was no such reliance. Thus a dispensing pharmacist might be able to show that the implied condition was negated by a private patient's reliance on the judgment of the prescribing doctor. In addition, no liability arises in respect of the buyer's unexpected sensitivity unless it has been expressly or impliedly made known to the seller.[39] A pharmacist would therefore not normally be liable if unaware of a customer's abnormal condition or allergy.[40]   **14.11**

Since both of the 'quality conditions' refer to 'the goods supplied under the contract', liability can arise in respect of packaging, containers, and instructions which render goods of unsatisfactory quality and/or unfit for their particular purpose(s).[41] However, the mere fact that a drug is potentially harmful will not ground liability if it is safe when taken according to the instructions.   **14.12**

---

[35] See paras 14.18 and 14.19 below
[36] SGA 1979, s 14(2A) and (2B), as amended by the Sale and Supply of Goods Act 1994, s 1.
[37] *Aswan Engineering Establishment Co v Lupdine Ltd* [1987] 1 WLR 1, CA; *Hill (Christopher) Ltd v Ashington Piggeries Ltd* [1972] AC 441, 498; *Frost v Aylesbury Dairy Co. Ltd* [1905] 1 KB 608, CA; *Kendall (Henry) and Sons (a firm) v William Lillico and Sons Ltd* [1969] 2 AC 31; cf 'it is well settled that the implied condition as to fitness extends to latent defects': *Young and Marten v McManus Childs Ltd* [1969] 1 AC 454, 479, *per* Lord Wilberforce.
[38] SGA 1979, s 14(3).
[39] *Griffiths v Conway (Peter) Ltd* [1939] 1 All ER 685, CA (sale); cf *Ingham v Eves* [1955] 2 QB 366, CA (work and materials).
[40] For constructive knowledge, see Atiyah, P, *Sale of Goods* (9th edn Adams, J) (London, 1995), 168.
[41] *Vacwell Engineering Co Ltd v BDH Chemicals Ltd* [1971] 1 QB 88; *Wormell v RHM Agricultural (East)* [1987] 1 WLR 1091, CA.

14.13 Unlike the condition as to description, the quality conditions apply only to goods sold 'in the course of a business'.[42] This expression would appear to cover transactions undertaken by a private hospital. The position with regard to NHS hospitals is less clear. A statutory provision making records relating to a 'business' admissible in criminal proceedings has been held not to apply to the medical records of an NHS hospital,[43] on the ground that its commercial functions were ancillary to its main purpose. However, under legislation concerned to promote consumer protection, which defines a 'business' to include a 'profession' and the activities of a 'public authority',[44] there is a strong case for regarding the commercial transactions of NHS hospitals (*a fortiori* if they are Trusts), as taking place 'in the course of a business'.[45]

2. Exclusion of Liability

14.14 The right of the parties to a contract to exclude or restrict the implied conditions of description, satisfactory quality and fitness for purpose in the SGA 1979 is subject to the provisions of the Unfair Contract Terms Act 1977 (hereafter the UCTA).[46] Consequently, as regards sales 'in the course of a business',[47] any such exclusion or restriction is unenforceable against a party who 'deals as a consumer',[48] and enforceable only if 'reasonable' in other transactions.[49] More generally, a party cannot by reference to a term of the contract exclude or restrict liability for death or bodily injury caused by negligence.[50]

3. Privity and Collateral Contracts

14.15 By virtue of the doctrine of privity,[51] the consumer-purchaser of a medicinal product will not normally have a contractual right of action against the manufacturer unless there is a collateral contract between them. Only rarely have the courts so construed agreements arising from manufacturers' representations about their products.[52] Although in *Carlill v Carbolic Smoke Ball Co*,[53] the

---

[42] SGA, ss 14(2), (3)
[43] Criminal Evidence Act 1965, s 1(1)(4); *R v Crayden* [1978] 1 WLR 604, 609, CA.
[44] SGA, s 61(1).
[45] See *Davies v Sumner* [1984] 1 WLR 1301, HL; *Benjamin's Sale of Goods* (n 12 above), 11–030; cf *E v Australian Red Cross Society* (1991) 105 ALR 53 (FC) (blood contaminated with HIV): public hospital marginally engaged in business activities a 'trading corporation' within the Commonwealth Trade Practices Act 1974. Cf CPA s 45(1) (n 223 below).
[46] SGA 1979, s 55(1).   [47] UCTA, s 1(3)(a).   [48] UCTA, s 6(2) and s 12.
[49] UCTA, s 6(3).   [50] UCTA, s 2(1).   [51] See para 14.08 above.
[52] eg *Wells (Merstham) Ltd v Buckland Sand and Silica Co Ltd* [1965] 2 QB 170: specific and personal assurance to buyer by manufacturer; cf *Shanklin Pier Ltd v Detel Products Ltd* [1951] 2 KB 854.   [53] [1893] 1 QB 256, CA.

defendants were held liable on the basis of a very specific collateral warranty in their advertisement, even factual representations contained in promotional material are seldom construed as intended to have contractual effect.[54] *A fortiori*, English law has not followed those United States decisions in which collateral contracts based on implied warranties of quality and fitness have been derived from the mere presence of goods on the market.[55]

However, the consumer-purchaser may in effect be compensated by the manufacturer via third-party proceedings and successive indemnities. Thus, harm caused by non-prescription products sold by retail pharmacists can result in contractual claims that move back up the chain of supply. Intermediaries may, of course, prove to be insolvent, uninsured, or unidentifiable. Suing them could also prove to be impracticable if they trade exclusively outside the jurisdiction.[56] In sales between non-consumers, the chain of liability may be broken by a 'reasonable' exemption clause.[57]   **14.16**

Though the seller of a defective product is liable in contract only to the purchaser, very occasionally purchasers have been treated as contracting agents for some other individual who has suffered injury.[58] In such situations, they may recover for their own resultant losses[59] or, arguably, as contracting expressly for the benefit of another.[60]   **14.17**

4. Contracts Involving the Supply of Products: Supply or Services?

Where a contract for private medical treatment is exclusively for the provision of services, at common law a doctor who has not been negligent will not normally be liable for injury.[61] Similarly, under the SGSA, there is an implied term that the supplier need do no more than carry out such services with 'reasonable care and skill'.[62] If, for example, an operation on a private patient   **14.18**

---

[54] *Lambert v Lewis* [1980] 2 WLR 299, CA. Contrast the position in some United States and Commonwealth jurisdictions: eg *Baxter v Ford Motor Co 35* P 2d 1090 (1934); *Henningsen v Bloomfield Motors Inc 161* A 2d 69 (1960); Rest. 2d para 402A (1965); *Murray v Sperry Rand Corp* (1979) 96 DLR (3d) 113; *Leitz v Saskatoon Drug & Stationery Co Ltd* (1981) 112 DLR (3d) 106. And see Australia's Federal Trade Practices Act 1974 (Cth), s 76G. See also, Atiyah, *Sale of Goods* (n 40 above) 227–8.

[55] As in *Henningsen* (n 54 above); cf Miller and Lovell *Product Liability* (n 1 above), 65 and Atiyah, *Sale of Goods* (n 40 above), 227–8. See also CPA, s 3(2)(a), para 14.57 and n 239 below.

[56] Though 'extended' jurisdiction over foreign manufacturers is provided for under RSC O 11: *Distillers Co (Biochemicals) Ltd v Thompson* [1971] AC 458.

[57] UCTA, ss 6(2) and 6(3). See *Lambert v Lewis* [1980] (n 54 above).

[58] See eg *Lockett v A & M Charles Ltd* [1938] 4 All ER 170.

[59] *Preist v Last* [1903] 2 KB 148, CA.

[60] *Jackson v Horizon Holidays Ltd* [1975] 1 WLR 1468, CA. See also *Woodar Investment Ltd v Wimpey UK Ltd* [1980] 1 All ER 571, 576–7, *per* Lord Wilberforce.

[61] Nathan, Lord, *Medical Negligence* (London, 1957), 10–11.   [62] SGSA, s 13.

for sterilisation has been unsuccessful, in the absence of negligence there will be no breach of contract unless the doctor has guaranteed a successful outcome.[63] When, however, a doctor supplies or administers drugs or other medical materials to a private patient, as when giving an injection or anaesthetic, or applying an ointment, it may not be clear whether the contract is primarily for the provision of services or for the supply of medicines. The same problem can arise when a private doctor (or hospital) supplies medical equipment, such as a prosthesis or other medical device. Even when such products are supplied, the doctor's professional role in diagnosis, advice and/ or treatment will commonly be regarded as the dominant feature of the transaction, so that it is not viewed as comparable to a contract of sale.[64]

14.19 However, at common law, a contract which in substance is for the supply of work and materials may contain implied terms analogous to those applicable to sales.[65] More importantly, when goods are supplied (or administered) 'in the course of a business',[66] either by way of transfer, as in the case of drugs, prosthetics, dentures, and injections, or hire, as in the temporary use of splints or crutches, the contract would now be subject to the strict liability provisions of the SGSA. Essentially, as regards the quality and fitness for purpose of any such 'goods', these provisions replicate the SGA s 14(2) and s 14(3) in respect of goods 'transferred'[67] or 'hired'[68] to the patient. In practice, most medical contracts for work and materials involve transfer, as the patient becomes the owner of the materials used. In some instances of temporary use, however, the contract will be one of hire.[69]

5. Medical Products as 'Goods'

14.20 Most of the materials used in medicine are undoubtedly 'goods' which can be the subject of commerce, but the position regarding human body products is

---

[63] *Eyre v Measday* [1986] 1 All ER 488, CA; *Thake v Maurice* [1986] QB 644, CA; cf *Grey v Webster* (1985) 14 DLR (4th) 706 (NBCQB).

[64] *Benjamin's Sale of Goods* (n 12 above), para 1–046. And see Nathan *Medical Negligence* (n 61 above), 19. cf case 353/85 *Commission v United Kingdom* [1988] STC 251. But note *Commissioners of Customs and Excise v Wellington Private Hospital Ltd* [1997] STC 445 (CA) (supply of drugs and prostheses to private hospital in-patients constitutes a separate supply of goods for the purposes of VAT).

[65] *Samuels v Davis* [1943] KB 526, CA; *Dodd v Wilson* [1946] 2 All ER 691. The more like sale the transaction, the stricter the implied obligations: *Young & Marten Ltd v McManus Childs Ltd* [1969] 1 AC 454, 476, *per* Lord Wilberforce. In many American jurisdictions, pharmacists, unlike other retailers, have been characterised as professionals providing a service and not subject to strict liability: e g *Murphy v ER Squibb and Sons Inc 710* P 2d 247, 251–3 (1985).

[66] SGSA, ss 4, 9 and 18(1); cf para 14.13 above.   [67] SGSA, s 4.   [68] SGSA, s 9.

[69] See further Bell, A, 'The Doctor and the Supply of Goods and Services Act 1982' (n 18 above).

not free from difficulty. Judicial abhorrence at the idea of defining human beings, alive or dead, as 'goods or materials'[70] has raised doubts about the legal status of transactions involving human organs and bodily fluids such as blood and semen.[71]

It is possible, for example, that organ transplantation, artificial insemination **14.21** and the transfusion of whole blood and blood-products involve a supply of goods capable of giving rise to strict liability under the SGSA. The argument is most cogent where commercial supply of the substance in question is both long-established and socially accepted, as in the case of blood transfusion.[72] In the United States there has been widespread resistance to a strict liability approach, partly in recognition of the need for available and affordable transfusion. Nearly all American jurisdictions have followed *Perlmutter v Beth David Hospital*[73] in defining blood transfusion as a service which does not involve sale.[74] When *Perlmutter* was rejected in *Cunningham v MacNeal Memorial Hospital*,[75] many states enacted 'blood shield statutes' to the effect that supplying blood or blood products constituted a service 'for all purposes', so that neither the manufacturer nor anyone else in the supply chain would be subject to an implied warranty of merchantable quality.[76] Recent case law has made it clear that the blood shield statutes apply to blood infected with HIV.[77]

---

[70] *Bourne (Inspector of Taxes) v Norwich Crematorium Ltd* [1967] 1 WLR 691, 695; cf *Williams v Williams* (1882) 20 Ch D 659, 662–3 and *Dobson v North Tyneside Health Authority* [1997] 1 WLR 596, CA. It is not certain that property rights could not exist in such materials at common law: *Benjamin's Sale of Goods* (n 12 above), 1-087; Skegg, P, 'Human Corpses, Medical Specimens and the Law of Property' (1976) 4 *Anglo-Am LR 412*; *Doodeward v Spence* (1908) 6 CLR 406 (Aust).
[71] See Bell, AP, 'The Doctor and the Supply of Goods and Services Act' (n 18 above) p 178; Atiyah, P, *Sale of Goods* (n 40 above), 22–3; Meyers, D, *The Human Body and the Law* (Edinburgh, 1990, 2nd edn), ch 7.
[72] Trading in human organs is prohibited by the Human Organ Transplants Act 1989, s 1. See further Kennedy, I and Grubb, A, *Medical Law* (London, 1994, 2nd edn) ch 15.
[73] *Perlmutter v Beth David Hospital 123* NE 2d 792 (1954).
[74] See eg *Coffee v Cutter Biological 809* F 2d 191 (USCA) (1987).
[75] *Cunningham v MacNeal Memorial Hospital 266* NE 2d 897 (SC of Ill) (1970).
[76] See eg *Miles Laboratories v Doe 556* A 2d 1167 (Md CA) (1989). In *Belle Bonfils Memorial Blood Bank v Hansen 579* P 2d 1158 (Colo Sup Ct) (1978), supply by a blood bank—as distinct from a hospital—was construed as a sale of goods permitting an action for strict liability and breach of warranty. However, in a subsequent hearing, blood and blood products were held to fall within Comment k of the Restatement (Second) of Torts, section 402A, which excludes the application of strict liability to 'unavoidably unsafe' products: *Belle Bonfils Memorial Blood Bank v Hansen 665* P 2d 118 (Colo Sup Ct) (1983).
[77] *Hyland Therapeutics v Superior Court 175* Cal App 3d 509, 220 Cal Rptr 590 (1985). See further Giesen, D, 'Liability for the transfusion of HIV-infected blood in comparative perspective' (1994) 10 *PN 2*. See also *E v Australian Red Cross Society* (1991) 105 ALR 53 (FC): blood transfused by hospital not an act 'in trade and commerce' where the defendants had not been paid for the blood as such. Cf *Pittman Estate v Bain* (1994) 112 DLR (4th) 257 (Ont Ct Gen Div); *ter Neuzen v Korn* (1995) 127 DLR (4th) 577 (SCC): no implied warranty of

C. Tort: Negligence

1. The Duty of Care

14.22   The expression 'products liability' has most commonly been used to describe the liability in negligence of those who supply products in the course of a business. In practice, the primary target has been the manufacturer who by act or omission has failed to take reasonable care to avoid injury to the ultimate consumer. The classic formulation of the manufacturer's duty is the 'narrow rule' in *Donoghue v Stevenson*:

> A manufacturer of products which he sells in such a form as to show that he intends them to reach the ultimate consumer in the form in which they left him, with no reasonable possibility of intermediate examination, and with the knowledge that the absence of reasonable care in the preparation or putting up of the products will result in injury to the consumer's life or property, owes a duty to the consumer to take that reasonable care.[78]

(i) *Who Owes The Duty?*

14.23   The duty owed by manufacturers has been extended to cover anyone in the chain of distribution and supply.[79] Thus, in respect of drugs it could apply to the product licence holder, a subsequent distributor, the prescribing doctor or the dispensing pharmacist. Pharmacists, for example, may incur liability if they cause injury by negligently dispensing the wrong drug, or the wrong strength of drug.[80] Likewise, a doctor may be liable in negligence for injury attributable to a carelessly written prescription,[81] or which results from prescribing a drug without having taken reasonable steps to explore the risks of side effects, reactions with other drugs or contra-indications. In principle, it might also be possible to impose liability for negligence on the Licensing Authority and its expert committees.[82]

---

quality by doctor in contract to administer artificial insemination which included the supply of (infected) semen. And see Grubb, A and Pearl, D, *Blood Testing, AIDS and DNA Profiling* (Bristol, 1990) ch 5.

[78] [1932] AC 562, 599, *per* Lord Atkin.

[79] e g *Watson v Buckley, Osborne, Garrett & Co* [1940] 1 All ER 174; *Fisher v Harrods Ltd* [1966] 1 Lloyd's Rep 500.

[80] e g *Prendergast v Sam & Dee Ltd* [1989] 1 Med LR 36, CA (doctor held 25% liable; pharmacist 75%). And see McKevitt, T, 'Doctors, Pharmacists and Prescriptions: The Standard of Care Owed to the Patient' (1988) 4 *PN 185*. See also Civil Liability (Contribution) Act 1978.

[81] ibid; cf *Dwyer v Roderick* (1983) 127 SJ 806, CA.   [82] See paras 14.42–14.47 below.

(ii) *Products Sold*

The 'narrow rule' in *Donoghue v Stevenson* represents no more than a parti-   **14.24**
cular instance of liability for negligence. There being no separate category of
'products liability' as such at common law, no need arises in cases based on
negligence to define 'product'. Though Lord Atkin's dictum refers to 'products', the general principles of negligence liability have been interpreted as
covering the whole range of production-related negligent acts.[83] Similarly,
there is no reason to confine liability to goods 'sold', as distinct, for example,
from free samples distributed by a manufacturer.[84]

2. The Standard of Care

In general terms, manufacturers are under an obligation to exercise such care as is   **14.25**
reasonable in all aspects of the production process under their control. Liability
may arise from inadequate care in matters as diverse as research and design,
manufacture, presentation, and instructions for use, including warnings about
risks.[85] Determining the requisite standard has sometimes been described as an
exercise in cost–benefit analysis,[86] centring on such well-established negligence
criteria as magnitude of risk,[87] probability of harm,[88] the burden of taking
adequate precautions,[89] and the social utility of the defendant's conduct.[90]

The attempt, in essence, to establish where the balance of social interest lies   **14.26**
can be unusually difficult in the case of medicinal products, the full risks and
benefits of which may not become apparent for many years, if at all. The
anticipated utility of any given drug, and the advantages of its early availability, may or may not be outweighed by its potential for harm. The benefits

---

[83] eg *Herschtal v Stewart and Arden Ltd* [1940] 1 KB 155; *Malfroot v Noxal Ltd* (1935) 51
TLR 551; *Howard v Furness Houlder Argentine Lines Ltd and A and R Brown Ltd* [1936] 2 All
ER 781.
[84] *Hawkins v Coulsdon and Purley UDC* [1954] 1 QB 319, 333, *per* Denning LJ; cf *Griffiths
v Arch Engineering Co Ltd* [1968] 3 All ER 217, 220. And see Miller and Lovell, *Product
Liability* (n 1 above), 308–9.
[85] *Cartwright v GKN Sankey Ltd* [1972] 2 Lloyd's Rep 242, 259, CA; *Devilez v Boots Pure
Drug Co Ltd* (1962) 106 SJ 552.
[86] As notably articulated in American case law and literature. See *US v Carroll Towing 159
F 2d* 169, 173 (1947), *per* Judge Learned Hand. See further Posner, R, 'A Theory of
Negligence' (1972) 1 *J Leg Studies 29*, 33. And see Stapleton, *Product Liability* (n 7 above),
chs 5 and 6.
[87] *Paris v Stepney Borough Council* [1951] AC 367; *Wright v Dunlop Rubber Co* (1972) 13
KIR 255.   [88] *Bolton v Stone* [1951] AC 850.
[89] *Latimer v AEC Ltd* [1953] AC 643. And see *PQ v Australian Red Cross Society* [1992] 1
VR 19.
[90] *Buchan v Ortho Pharmaceuticals (Canada) Ltd* (1986) 25 DLR (4th) 658, 668 (Ont CA).

of elaborate safety precautions may or may not outweigh the inhibiting effects on innovation of cost and delay.[91] A marginally more effective new drug may be inherently less safe than available alternatives.[92] Many otherwise valuable drugs present a significant risk to a minority of the public, and it has been suggested that a product which is safe for most people should be considered dangerous 'if it might affect other users who had a higher degree of sensitivity than normal, so long as they were not altogether exceptional'.[93]

(i) *Common Practice*

14.27 Whether or not the defendant's conduct is deemed negligent is judged by reference to the prevailing state of scientific and technical knowledge.[94] Conformity with industry standards or custom, though prima facie evidence of reasonable prudence on the part of a manufacturer,[95] is not dispositive.[96] A general indication of what constitutes appropriate pre-marketing research for pharmaceutical products is contained in the guidelines produced by the regulatory authorities (the Licensing Authority and its advisory bodies) and the industry (the Code of Practice for the Pharmaceutical Industry). However, compliance with recommended testing procedures, for example, is not ipso facto a defence in any given case. Non-compliance with accepted practice would be strong, though not conclusive, evidence of negligence.[97] Similarly, the views of expert official committees are relevant but not determinative.[98]

---

[91] Newdick, C, 'The Impact of Licensing Authority Approval on Pharmaceutical Product Liability: A Survey of American and UK Law' (1992) 47 *F & DLJ 41*; Teff, H, 'Regulation under the Medicines Act 1968: A Continuing Prescription for Health' (1984) 47 MLR 303, 309–318.

[92] See *Nicholson v John Deere Ltd* (1986) 34 DLR (4th) 542, 549 (Ont HC).

[93] *Board v Thomas Hedley* [1951] 2 All ER 431, 432, CA, *per* Denning, LJ. See also *Griffiths v Conway (Peter) Ltd* [1939] 1 All ER 685; Miller and Lovell, *Product Liability* (n 1 above), 324–6. For the duty to warn, see paras 14.32 and 14.33 below.

[94] *Vacwell Engineering Co v BDH Chemicals* [1971] 1 QB 88; *Stokes v Guest, Keen and Nettlefold (Bolts & Nuts) Ltd* [1968] 1 WLR 1776, 1783; cf *Fuller v Baxenden Chemical Co Ltd* QBD (1985) (unreported): failure to update company literature in line with changed knowledge and practice of others; *Ogden v Airedale Health Authority* [1996] 7 Med LR 153.

[95] cf *R v British Pharmaceutical Industry Association Code of Practice Committee, The Independent*, 1 Nov 1990.

[96] *Morris v West Hartlepool Navigation Co* [1956] AC 552; *Cavanagh v Ulster Weaving Co Ltd* [1960] AC 145. Miller and Lovell, *Product Liability* (n 1 above), 264 *et seq*.

[97] *Chin Keow v Government of Malaysia* [1967] 1 WLR 813, PC.

[98] *Thompson v Johnson and Johnson Pty Ltd* [1992] 3 Med LR 148, 171–2 (SC of Victoria, App Div).

(ii) *Compliance With Statutory Provisions*

Even full compliance with statutory requirements does not conclusively pre- **14.28** clude liability for negligence at common law.[99] Hence the issue of a product licence does not automatically constitute a defence to a claim.[100] However, the courts would be loath to impose a standard of care that effectively penalised compliance with specific, statutorily prescribed, standards,[101] and they would be reluctant to hold negligent a manufacturer who had been granted a product licence for a drug after having disclosed to the Licensing Authority all the information deemed relevant to its safety.[102]

(iii) *Manufacturing Defects*

Defects arising from error in the manufacturing process are relatively rare in **14.29** the pharmaceutical industry. Examples would include a failure to combine ingredients in the correct proportions, excessive potency and toxicity,[103] the presence of some impurity or foreign body,[104] and deterioration of the product from contamination or faulty packaging.[105] Though the full burden of proof is formally on the plaintiff,[106] once it has been proved that there is a defect in the product[107] which probably did not occur after it had left the manufacturer's control,[108] there is an 'inference of negligence' akin to *res ipsa*

---

[99] *Bux v Slough Metals Ltd* [1973] 1 WLR 1358, CA; *Dickson v Flack* [1953] 2 QB 464; *Best v Wellcome Foundation Ltd* [1994] 5 Med LR 81 (Irish Sup Ct). As licence holders, pharmaceutical companies are subject to regulation under the Medicines Act 1968 and its subordinate legislation. See further Newdick, C, 'The Impact of Licensing Authority Approval on Pharmaceutical Product Liability: A Survey of American and UK Law' (n 91 above), 52.

[100] cf 65/65/EEC OJ 22, 9 Feb 1965, 369.

[101] *Budden v BP Oil and Shell Oil* (1980) 124 SJ 376, CA; cf the defence under the CPA, s 4(1)(a) (paras 14.59 and 14.60 below).

[102] cf *R v Licensing Authority Established under Medicines Act 1968, ex p Smith, Kline & French Laboratories Ltd* [1989] 1 All ER 578, 590, *per* Lord Templeman.

[103] *Best v Wellcome Foundation Ltd* [1994] 5 Med LR 81 (Irish Sup Ct) (pertussis component in DTP vaccine).

[104] cf *Donoghue v Stevenson* [1932] AC 562; *Daniels and Daniels v R White & Sons Ltd and Tarbard* [1938] 4 All ER 258.

[105] eg *Fisher v Harrods Ltd* [1966] 1 Lloyd's Rep 500; *Adelaide Chemical & Fertilizer Co Ltd v Carlyle* (1940) 64 CLR 514; *Hill v James Crowe (Cases) Ltd* [1978] 1 All ER 812.

[106] E g *Mason v Williams and Williams Ltd* [1955] 1 All ER 808, relying on *Donoghue v Stevenson* [1932] AC 562, 622, *per* Lord MacMillan.

[107] *Grant v Australian Knitting Mills Ltd* [1936] AC 85; cf *Hill v James Crowe (Cases) Ltd* [1978] 1 All ER 812; *Shandloff v City Dairy Ltd* [1936] 4 DLR 712, 719 (Ont CA).

[108] *Mason v Williams and Williams Ltd* [1955] 1 All ER 808, *Evans v Triplex Glass* [1936] 1 All ER 283.

loquitur, if not tantamount to automatic liability.[109] In fact, the stronger the evidence that the defendant has a careful quality control system, the more likely is it that a particular defect will be attributed to negligence in the production process.[110] In principle, if manufacturers have an appropriate system for ordering raw materials and components and adequate testing and inspection procedures, they will not incur liability for the negligence of an independent contractor,[111] though occasionally the manufacturer's duty has been treated as non-delegable.[112]

(iv) *Design Defects*

14.30 Manufacturers are liable for harm caused by their failure to take reasonable care to ensure that a product has been safely designed.[113] Though they cannot, by definition, be liable in negligence for not knowing about undiscoverable defects, some cases have suggested that a high standard of care is expected, especially in the research that goes into the design of intrinsically dangerous and novel products.[114] However, though the manufacturer is under a duty to keep abreast of medical and scientific discoveries,[115] proof that design defects are attributable to negligence is often elusive, and seldom more so than in the case of medical products.[116]

14.31 A major obstacle to proof of negligence in medical products litigation is that what counts as 'knowledge' can be both intrinsically problematic and complicated by the fact that scientists and medical researchers may legitimately

---

[109] *Lockhart v Barr* (1943) SC (HL) 1.

[110] *Grant v Australian Knitting Mills Ltd* [1936] AC 85, 101; *Hill v James Crowe (Cases) Ltd* [1978] 1 All ER 812, 816.   [111] *Taylor v Rover Co* [1966] 1 WLR 1491.

[112] *Winward v TVR Engineering Ltd* [1986] BTLC 366, CA; *Cynat Products Ltd v Landbuild (Investment and Property) Ltd* [1984] 3 All ER 513.

[113] *Hindustan Steam Shipping Co Ltd v Siemens Bros & Co* [1955] 1 Lloyd's Rep 167.

[114] eg *Vacwell Engineering Co Ltd v BDH Chemicals Ltd* [1971] QB 88, 109: liability imposed for failure 'to provide and maintain a system for carrying out adequate research into scientific literature to ascertain known hazards' and for failure to conduct such research. The defendants had based their research on several modern texts (including the standard work on the industrial hazards of chemicals) which did not mention the explosive hazard documented in earlier literature. Cf *Independent Broadcasting Authority v EMI Electronics Ltd and BICC Construction Ltd* [1981] 14 Build LR 1, HL. And See Howells, G, *Comparative Product Liability* (Aldershot, 1993) 74–5; Newdick, C. 'The Future of Negligence in Product Liability' (1987) 103 *LQR 288*, 293–4.

[115] *Stokes v Guest, Keen & Nettlefold (Bolts & Nuts) Ltd* [1968] 1 WLR 1776, 1783; *Cartwright v GKN Sankey Ltd* [1972] 2 Lloyd's Rep 242, 259.   [116] See para 14.04 above.

hold conflicting views.[117] There will often be a grey area between speculation, hypothesis, or information, on the one hand, and 'hard' knowledge on the other,[118] and the courts are mindful of the need to guard against hindsight.[119] Also, though 'the law requires even pioneers to be prudent',[120] it also reflects the importance attached to innovation. In determining the level of acceptable risk for new drugs, allowance will be made for the fact that they need to be potent to be useful and that there are practical limits on discovering risks at the stage of pre-market testing on relatively small populations in animal studies and clinical trials. By contrast with the approach of the courts towards manufacturing defects, a previous good design safety record is of distinct evidential value to the defendant.

(v) *Marketing Defects*

(a) Warnings and Instructions

An important aspect of due care in the supply of products is the provision of **14.32** adequate instructions for their use and, where necessary, of warnings about risks of which the defendant has actual or constructive knowledge. 'Failure-to-warn claims are now the most common form of litigated product case in the US.'[121] Since the manufacturer is required to make available such information as will enable products to be used safely,[122] any warnings must be readily intelligible and commensurate with risks,[123] bearing in mind that informing the medical profession normally suffices in respect of prescription medicines. Risks, in turn, must not be minimised by promotional material.[124] The

---

[117] See Lee, R, 'Vaccine Damage: Adjudicating Scientific Dispute' in Howells, G (ed) *Product Liability Insurance and the Pharmaceutical Industry: An Anglo-American Comparison* (Manchester, 1991); Newdick, C, 'The Development Risk Defence of the Consumer Protection Act 1987' (1988) 47 CLJ 455, 462.   [118] See para 14.68 below.
[119] *Roe v Minister of Health* [1954] 2 QB 66, 86, CA, *per* Denning LJ; cf *Thompson v Smiths Shiprepairers (North Shields) Ltd* [1984] 1 All ER 881, 894, *per* Mustill J; *Mann and Close v Wellcome Foundation Ltd* (1989) QBD (unreported).
[120] *Independent Broadcasting Authority v EMI Electronics Ltd and BICC Construction Ltd* (n. 114 above), 28, *per* Lord Edmund-Davies.
[121] Stapleton *Product Liability* (n 7 above), 252.
[122] *Kubach v Hollands* [1937] 3 All ER 907; *Holmes v Ashford* [1950] 2 All ER 76, CA; *Devilez v Boots Pure Drug Co* (1962) 106 SJ 552.
[123] *Vacwell Engineering Ltd v BDH Chemicals Ltd* [1971] 1 QB 111, CA (varying [1971] 1 QB 88); cf *Ward v Hopkins* [1959] 3 All ER 225, 239, CA.
[124] *Watson v Buckley, Osborne, Garrett & Co Ltd* [1940] 1 All ER 174; cf *Vacwell Engineering Ltd* (n 123 above); *Buchan v Ortho Pharmaceuticals (Canada) Ltd* (1986) 25 DLR (4th) 658, 678–9 (Ont CA); *Rothwell v Raes* (1989) 54 DLR (4th) 193, 341–2 (Ont CA); *R v Roussel Laboratories; R v Good* (1989) 88 Cr App R 140. By virtue of an EC Directive on labels and

manufacturer would normally be expected to warn of a drug's inherent and irreducible risks, though there is no duty to warn of a danger which is either patent or a matter of common knowledge.[125] There can, however, be liability for injury resulting from reasonably foreseeable misuse which has not been warned against.[126] A warning or instructions may also be needed where the danger is known to the user, but not the means of avoiding the risk. At the same time, the manufacturer may have regard to such factors as the remoteness of any danger and the possibility of causing needless alarm.[127] Where there has been a total failure to warn there is little scope for defences such as contributory negligence[128] or volenti, since the user will normally have been unaware of any danger. In principle, there is some scope for them where an inadequate warning has been given.[129]

(b) Allergic Reactions

14.33 Particular difficulties surround the issue of allergic reactions. If a manufacturer knows or ought to know of the danger, in appropriate circumstances a

---

leaflets, the provision of package leaflets for human medicinal products is now obligatory, unless all the required information is on the pack or label: Council Dir 92/27/EEC, OJ 30.4.92, L 113/8, as implemented by the Medicines (Labelling) Amendment Regulations 1992, SI 1992/3273, amends SI 1976/1726; and the Medicines (Leaflets) Amendment Regulations 1992, SI 1992/3274, amends SI 1977/1055; the Medicines (Labelling and Leaflets) Amendment Regulations 1994, SI 1994/104, further amends SI 1976/1726 and SI 1977/1055, by implementing in part Council Dir 92/73/EEC, OJ 13.10.92, L 297/8.

An EC Directive on advertising medicinal products for human use provides a common framework for advertising and promotion within the Community. It prohibits misleading advertising and the advertisement to the public of prescription only medicines. It also requires all advertising to conform with the terms of market authorisation: Council Dir 92/28/EEC, OJ 30.4.92, L 113/13, as implemented by the Medicines (Advertising) Regulations 1994, SI 1994/1932 and by the Medicines (Monitoring of Advertising) Regulations 1994, SI 1994/1933. See generally, Bogaert, P, *EC Pharmaceutical Law* (London, 1992); Medicines Control Agency *Towards Safe Medicines* (n 21 above).

[125] *Farr v Butters Bros & Co* [1932] 2 KB 606, CA; *Devilez v Boots Pure Drug Co* (1962) 106 SJ 552; cf *Deshane v Deere & Co* (1993) 106 DLR (4th) 385 (Ont CA). See also Miller and Lovell, *Product Liability* (n 1 above), 239. In the United States there is some support for the view that manufacturers should provide a warning for any users whom they know or should reasonably expect to be less informed than themselves about the dangers associated with the product. See eg *Micallef v Miehle Co 39* NY 2d 376 (1976).

[126] *Hill v James Crowe (Cases) Ltd* [1978] 1 All ER 812.

[127] *Thompson v Johnson & Johnson Pty Ltd* [1992] 3 Med LR 148 (SC of Victoria, App Div) (tampons and toxic shock syndrome).

[128] But see *Devilez v Boots Pure Drug Co* (1962) 106 SJ 552.

[129] See Miller and Lovell, *Product Liability* (n 1 above), 293–6. See also *Cippolone v Liggett Group Inc 112* S Ct 2608 (1992) (tobacco).

warning would be required for the benefit of a vulnerable minority.[130] In the United States, courts have often relied on the 'narrow formulaic requirement that a certain percentage of persons must suffer an allergic reaction from the product before the manufacturer will be held liable'.[131] However, in any given case, whether or not failure to warn is reasonable could involve consideration of such factors as the severity of the consequences, the social value of the product, the availability of substitutes, and the plaintiff's access to information about allergy.[132]

(c) Causation

Inadequate warning or failure to warn is normally easier to establish than defective design, and plainly is more easily rectified. It will not, of course, result in liability without proof of causation. The court must be satisfied that the plaintiff would not have used the product had a proper warning been given.[133]

14.34

(vi) *Continuing Duty Of Care*

If, after its potential for harm had become apparent, a marketed product caused injury, there could be liability in negligence for not having modified it or made its availability subject to a suitable warning,[134] for not having removed it from the market and, it would seem, for not having warned previous purchasers.[135] As regards prescription drugs, it would be negligent not to take reasonable steps to warn prescribing doctors[136] and presumably in certain instances not to issue

14.35

---

[130] *Ingham v Emes* [1955] 2 QB 366, CA; *Parker v Oxolo Ltd and Senior* [1937] 3 All ER 524; *Chin Keow v Government of Malaysia* [1967] 1 WLR 813 (PC). See Newdick, C, 'Strict Liability for Defective Drugs in the Pharmaceutical Industry' (1985) 101 *LQR 405*, 412.
[131] Rogerson, C and Trebilcock, M, 'Products Liability and the Allergic Consumer: A Study in the Problems of Framing an Efficient Liability Regime' (1986) 36 UTLJ 52, 57. Typically an 'appreciable number': *Crotty v Shartenberg's New Haven Inc 162* A 2d 513 (Conn, 1960).   [132] See Miller and Lovell, *Product Liability* (n 1 above), 324–6.
[133] *Buchan v Ortho Pharmaceuticals (Canada) Ltd* (1986) 25 DLR (4th) 658 (Ont CA); *H v Royal Alexandra Hospital for Children* [1990] 1 Med LR 297 (SC of NSW); *Davidson v Connaught Laboratories* (1980) 14 CCLT 251 (Ont HC). In *Buchan*, as in English law, the test of causation was subjective. See also *Hollis v Dow Corning Corp* (1996) 129 DLR (4th) 609 (SCC). Presumably, where causation depends on what the prescribing doctor would have done if adequately warned, the test would be subjective to that doctor: Jones, M, *Medical Negligence* (London, 2nd edn, 1996), 434–5, paras 8-038 and 8-039.
[134] *Wright v Dunlop Rubber Co Ltd* (1972) 13 KIR 255, 272, CA.
[135] *Walton v British Leyland UK Ltd* (1978) QBD (unreported); *Hobbs (E) (Farms) Ltd v Baxenden Chemical Co Ltd* [1992] 1 Lloyds Rep 54, 65; Carroll v Dunlop Ltd (1996) *Product Liability Intl*, Apr 1996, 58–9. Cf *Rivtow Marine Ltd v Washington Iron Works* [1973] 40 DLR (3d) 530, 536 (SCC).
[136] *Hollis v Dow Corning Corp* (1996) 129 DLR (4th) 609 (SCC).

public warnings.[137] To this end, manufacturers need proper procedures for monitoring adverse reactions and product recall.[138]

(vii) *Intermediate Examination*

14.36 Lord Atkin described the manufacturer's liability for a defective product as contingent on there being 'no reasonable possibility of intermediate examination' before it reaches the ultimate consumer.[139] In effect this requirement is simply an aspect of reasonable foreseeability, there being no liability[140] unless the manufacturer could reasonably have anticipated that the examination conducted by the intermediary would be of such a type as to reveal the defect.[141] It is now clear that there must be a reasonable 'probability' of such examination if the manufacturer is to avoid liability.[142]

14.37 Plainly patients cannot normally be expected to have conducted the kind of inspection of medicinal products that would reveal their potential for harm, but the position of doctors and pharmacists is less clear.[143] The manufacturer will normally be absolved from liability where the pharmacist has failed to observe manifest defects connected with the production or distribution process, such as deterioration or lack of sterility of products that have not been properly packaged or stored. In addition, the manufacturer may be able to invoke the 'learned intermediary' rule against either the doctor or the pharmacist.[144]

(viii) *The 'Learned Intermediary' Rule*

14.38 An important aspect of the pharmaceutical manufacturer's duty of care is to see that the ultimate user is adequately warned about risks.[145] However, it is

---

[137] *Buchan v Ortho Pharmaceuticals (Canada) Ltd* (n 133 above), 667, 678.

[138] *McCain Foods Ltd v Grand Falls Industries Ltd* (1991) 80 DLR (4th) 252 (NBCA). For pharmaceuticals, the existence of such procedures is a prerequisite for the grant of a product licence: Medicines (Standard Provisions for Licences and Certificates) Regulations 1971, SI 1971/972, Sch 1, para 6, as amended. On the 'yellow card' scheme for reporting adverse reactions to the CSM see Teff, H, 'Regulation under the Medicines Act 1968: A Continuing Prescription for Health' (n 91 above). [139] *Donoghue v Stevenson* [1932] AC 562, 599. See para 14.22 above.

[140] Subject to any possibility of apportionment under the Civil Liability (Contribution) Act 1978, or of contributory negligence by the consumer.

[141] *Herschtal v Stewart & Ardern Ltd* [1940] 1 KB 155; *Griffiths v Arch Engineering Co (Newport) Ltd* [1968] 3 All ER 217; *Aswan Engineering Establishment Co v Lupdine Ltd* [1987] 1 All ER 135, 153, CA, *per* Lloyd LJ.

[142] eg *Paine v Colne Valley Electricity Supply Co Ltd* [1938] 4 All ER 803, 808–9; *Griffiths v Arch Engineering Co Ltd* (n 141 above).

[143] As is that of certain regulatory bodies in regard to design defects. See paras 14.42–14.47 below.

[144] See Ferguson, P, 'Liability for Pharmaceutical Products: a Critique of the "Learned Intermediary" Rule' (1992) 12 OJLS 59.

[145] See paras 14.32 and 14.33 above; cf *Thompson v Johnson and Johnson Pty Ltd* [1992] 3 Med LR 148 (SC of Victoria, App Div).

not usually necessary for the relevant information to be communicated directly to the consumer when a product is to be used under expert supervision; adequate warning to a responsible intermediary normally suffices.[146] As regards prescription drugs, in many jurisdictions it has been held sufficient for the manufacturer to warn the doctor as 'learned intermediary'.[147] There is no express authority on the rule in England, but its spirit is reflected in the applicable regulatory regime. Though the 'standard labelling particulars' on directions for use and precautions required for OTC products[148] do not apply to 'dispensed medicinal products', a drug may not be promoted to doctors unless, within the preceding fifteen months, they have received a copy of the manufacturer's data sheet specifying any necessary warnings or contra-indications.[149] A drug manufacturer cannot assume that doctors will have read all the relevant scientific literature: 'They rely on the drug companies to supply them with the necessary data.'[150]

Nevertheless, in any given case, doctors are still required to use their independent judgment in prescribing, based on their knowledge of the individual patient and the drug. However, under English law, they have considerable leeway as to what information they need to disclose. By virtue of the '*Bolam* principle' they can normally discharge their duty in this respect by acting in accordance with any standard of practice recognised as proper by a responsible body of medical opinion.[151] It therefore follows that, in England, adherence to the 'learned intermediary' rule could in practice mean that patients have less effective legal protection against failure to warn in respect

14.39

---

[146] cf *Holmes v Ashford* [1950] 2 All ER 76, CA.

[147] A term first used in *Sterling Drug, Inc v Cornish 370* F 2d 82 (8th Cir) (1966). See e g *Reyes v Wyeth Laboratories 498* F 2d 1264, 1276 (5th Cir) (1974); *Buchan v Ortho Pharmaceuticals (Canada) Ltd* (1986) 25 DLR (4th) 658, 680–1 (Ont CA) *per* Robins JA. Cf *H v Royal Alexandra Hospital for Children* [1990] 1 Med LR 297 (SC of NSW); *McKee v Moore 648* P 2d 21 (Okla) (1982). See Ferguson, 'Liability for Pharmaceutical Products: a Critique of the "Learned Intermediary" Rule' (n 144 above), 61.

[148] Medicines Act 1968, s 85(1) and the Medicines (Labelling) Regulations 1976, SI 1976/1726, as amended (see n 124 above).

[149] Medicines Act 1968, s 96 and the Medicines (Data Sheet) Regulations 1972, SI 1972/2076, as amended (see n 124 above).

[150] *Davidson v Connaught Laboratories* (1980) 14 CCLT 251, 276 *per* Linden J (Ont HC). Awareness that a report of an official advisory committee has been circulated to medical practitioners does not absolve the manufacturer from a common law duty to inform them: *Buchan v Ortho Pharmaceuticals (Canada) Ltd* (n 147 above), 680–1 *per* Robins JA. See also *Hollis v Dow Corning Corp* (1996) 129 DLR (4th) 600 (SCC), (1993) 103 DLR (4th) 520 (BCCA), and Stapleton, *Product Liability* (n 7 above), 252–5.

[151] *Bolam v Friern Hospital Management Committee* [1957] 1 WLR 582; *Sidaway v Board of Governors of the Bethlem Royal Hospital and the Maudsley Hospital* [1985] AC 871.

of prescription drugs than in the case of the typically less powerful over-the-counter products.[152]

14.40 Considerations of policy may argue against applying the 'learned intermediary' rule to certain medical procedures. For example, in the United States it has not always been applied to mass immunisation.[153] Some courts have stressed that voluntary participants in a procedure which benefits society at large should not be deprived of a remedy against the manufacturer; that the injections are not necessarily administered by someone who is indisputably a 'learned intermediary', and that, even when they are, there may be no 'individualized assessment' of risks and benefits.[154] Nor does the rule invariably hold for the prescription of oral contraceptives, when the case for insisting on communication to the user is underlined by the typically 'heightened participation' of patients in the decision; the danger of doctors giving inadequate information about risks and allowing unmonitored long-term and repeat prescriptions, and the elective, non-therapeutic nature of the treatment.[155] American courts have, however, generally retained the 'learned intermediary' rule for contraceptive devices.[156]

3. Proving Causation

14.41 In determining whether or not a medicinal product is responsible for harm, the problems of extrapolating from biochemical findings, animal studies and relatively small-scale tests on humans are frequently compounded by competing scientific views on evidence and the 'mismatch of legal and scientific notions of causation'.[157] As a result, proof that on the balance of probabilities a given product caused or materially contributed to the plaintiff's injuries[158] is often

---

[152] See Ferguson (n 144 above), 72.
[153] *Davis v Wyeth Laboratories Inc 399* F 2d 121 (9th Cir) (1968); *Reyes v Wyeth Laboratories 498* F 2d 1264 (5th Cir) (1974).[154] *Givens v Lederle 566* F 2d 1341 (5th Cir) (1974).
[155] eg *Seley v GD Searle & Co 423* NE 2d 831 (1981); *Lukaszewicz v Ortho Pharmaceutical Corp 510* F Supp 961 (Wis) (1981); *Stephens v GD Searle & Co 602* F Supp 379 (Mich) (1985); *MacDonald v Ortho Pharmaceutical Corp 475* NE 2d 65 (Mass) (1985); *Odgers v Ortho Pharmaceutical Corp 609* F Supp 867 (DC Mich) (1985). Cf *Buchan v Ortho Pharmaceuticals (Canada) Ltd* (1986) 25 DLR (4th) 658, 670, 688–9 (Ont CA).
[156] *McKee v Moore 648* P 2d 21 (Okla) (1982); contra *Hill v Searle Laboratories 884* F 2d 1064 (8th Cir) (1989).
[157] Lee, R, 'Vaccine Damage: Adjudicating Scientific Dispute'. See n 117 and para 14.31 above; cf *Brock v Merrell Dow Pharmaceuticals Inc 874* F 2d 307 (5th Cir) (1989). See also, Goldberg, R, 'Scientific Evidence, Causation and the Law—Lessons of Bendectin (Debendox) Litigation' (1996) 4 Med L Rev 32.
[158] *Bonnington Castings Ltd v Wardlaw* [1956] AC 613.

elusive.[159] Any suggestion that, following the decision in *McGhee v National Coal Board*,[160] negligent conduct which materially increased the risk of injury would suffice to ground liability unless the defendant could show that it was not the cause has been rejected by the House of Lords. The burden is on the plaintiff to prove that such negligence was more likely than not to have caused or materially contributed to the injury.[161] The limitations of orthodox causation theory are also apparent in cases where injury is attributable to generic drugs but the plaintiff is unable to identify the manufacturer in question.[162]

4. Claims Against Regulatory Authorities

Legal responsibility for harm caused by products is not necessarily limited to those directly engaged in their production and distribution. It is convenient at this point to outline the statutory framework for the control of safety, quality and efficacy of medicines, with a view to considering whether any actions might lie against the relevant regulatory bodies. **14.42**

Under the Medicines Act 1968,[163] the manufacture and distribution of medicines is regulated by a Licensing Authority (LA), comprising the UK Ministers of Health and Agriculture.[164] Its executive responsibilities in respect of the pharmaceutical sector are now discharged by the Medicines Control Agency (MCA). Under the 1968 Act, the right to grant a product licence or market authorisation is vested in the LA,[165] which receives advice from the Medicines Commission and various specialist committees.[166] These include the Committee on the Safety of Medicines (CSM), whose **14.43**

---

[159] See eg *Kay v Ayrshire and Arran Health Board* [1987] 2 All ER 417, HL (penicillin and deafness). On pertussis, see eg *Loveday v Renton* [1990] 1 Med LR 117; *Rothwell v Raes* (1988) 54 DLR (4th) 193, aff'd (1990) 76 DLR (4th) 280 (Ont CA). But see also *Best v Wellcome Foundation Ltd* [1994] 5 Med LR 81 (Irish Sup Ct). And see Jones, *Medical Negligence* (n 133 above), 243–54; Newdick, C, 'Strict Liability for Defective Drugs in the Pharmaceutical Industry' (1985) 101 LQR 405, 420–30.
[160] *McGhee v National Coal Board* [1973] 1 WLR 1, HL.
[161] *Wilsher v Essex Area Health Authority* [1988] AC 1074; cf *Snell v Farrell* (1990) 72 DLR (4th) 289 (Can SC). And see cases cited at n 159 above.
[162] See eg *Mann v Wellcome Foundation Ltd* (1989) QBD (unreported). For a radical and controversial solution based on defendant companies being held liable in proportion to their share of the national market, see *Sindell v Abbott Laboratories 607* P 2d 924 (1980). Cf *Hymowitz v Eli Lilly & Co 73* NY 2d 487 (1989); *Doe v Cutter Biological Inc 971* F 2d 375 (1992): applied to HIV-infected Factor VIII, despite the fact that the manufactured product is not uniformly dangerous.
[163] In force from 1 Sept 1971. And see the Medicines for Human Use (Marketing Authorisations etc) Regulations 1994, SI 1994/3144.
[164] Medicines Act 1968, ss 1 and 6(1).   [165] ibid, s 6(1).
[166] ibid, s 2 and s 4, respectively. See further Medicines Control Agency, *Towards Safe Medicines* (n 21 above).

advice the LA may seek on questions of safety, quality, and efficacy of new medicines for human use.[167] If the CSM provisionally advises against granting a licence, the applicant has a right to a hearing before it and, thereafter, a right of appeal to the Medicines Commission. Products to be marketed only in the UK continue to be validated by this national procedure. In addition, there have been a series of EC initiatives aimed at achieving a single European market in pharmaceuticals.[168] In 1995, following the establishment of the European Medicines Evaluation Agency (EMEA), a new dual EC licensing system was introduced. There is a centralised procedure, mandatory for most biotechnological medicines and optional for other high-technology medicines and those which contain a new active substance.[169] Applications are submitted to the EMEA and marketing authorisation is valid for all Member States. There is also a mutual recognition (decentralised) procedure for all other human medicines, compulsory since 1 January 1998, where it is sought to have an existing marketing authorisation recognised by one or more other Member States.[170]

14.44 Where injury is attributable to the defective design of medicinal products, it is unclear whether or not an action lies against the LA, which authorises their sale or supply, and against the other statutory bodies which advise on their safety, quality and efficacy, or where appropriate, against the Department of Health. No such right is conferred under the Medicines Act 1968, but neither does the Act purport to derogate from any pre-existing rights of claimants.[171] Bodies which license or advise on products do not attract liability under the CPA, as they are providers of services, not suppliers of products. Though the licensing authority and the CSM have occasionally been joined as defendants in negligence actions,[172] there has been no definitive ruling. The issue turns primarily on how far regulatory bodies enjoy immunity from suit in discharging their statutory duties. In accordance with the distinction adopted by Lord Wilberforce in *Anns v Merton*, discretionary policy decisions have been

---

[167] ibid, ss 19–20. In respect of the safety, quality, and efficacy of products on the market before the Medicines Act 1968 took effect, the LA was advised by the Committee on the Review of Medicines. The Committee was disbanded in 1992.
[168] See Council Dir 65/65/EEC. OJ No L 22, 9.2, as amended.
[169] See Council Reg (EEC) 2309/93.
[170] Council Dir 65/65/EEC as amended, and Medicines for Human Use (Marketing Authorisations etc) Regulations 1994, SI 1994/3144.
[171] Medicines Act 1968, s 133(2).
[172] See *Davies v Eli Lilly & Co* [1987] 3 All ER 94, CA (Opren), and *Re HIV Haemophiliac Litigation* (1990) 140 NLJ 1349 (contaminated blood), where the Court of Appeal considered that the plaintiffs had 'made out at least a good arguable claim in law based upon common law negligence' against, *inter alia*, the LA, the CSM and the Department of Health. See also *Brown v Alberta* [1994] 2 WWR 283 (Alta QB).

deemed non-justiciable and operational ones subject to a common law duty of care,[173] though the dividing line can be elusive. Promoting childhood vaccination has been treated as a non-justiciable exercise of statutory discretion, whereas claims that the DHSS had provided inadequate advice on contra-indications have been allowed to proceed, as have claims against the DoH in respect of Creutzfeldt-Jakob disease contracted following growth hormone treatment.[174]

It is uncertain, however, whether, or to what extent, the policy/operational   **14.45** distinction still obtains, given the criticism to which Lord Wilberforce's speech in *Anns v Merton* has been subjected and the tendency in later appellate decisions to favour extensive immunity for regulatory bodies in the performance of their statutory functions.[175] Dicta to the effect that, in the context of consumer protection, it is perhaps 'best left to the legislature' to state the extent and limits of any such liability[176] may be seen as symptomatic of a general retreat from the expansion of liability for negligence, and if the distinction does remain, courts are likely to take a broad view of 'policy'. Regulatory agencies are only indirectly involved in the 'supply' of products, and the courts take a relatively strict approach to causation. In the context of prescribed drugs, they may be slow to find negligence against bodies which, in practice, exert only limited control over other potential defendants with more direct causal responsibility; though this argument seems less cogent when

---

[173] See *Anns v Merton London Borough Council* [1978] AC 728, 754, *per* Lord Wilberforce; *Rowling v Takaro Properties* [1988] AC 473 (PC); *Home Office v Dorset Yacht Co Ltd* [1970] AC 1004, 1067–8, *per* Lord Diplock; *Sutherland Shire Council v Heyman* (1985) 157 CLR 424, 469, *per* Mason J. cf on drug licensing: *R v Licensing Authority Established under Medicines Act 1968, ex p Smith, Kline & French* [1989] 1 All ER 578, 590, HL; *Gray v United States and Eli Lilly & Co* 445 F Supp 337 (DC Tex) (1978).

[174] *Department of Health and Social Security v Kinnear* (1984) 134 N LJ 886 (the point was not ultimately pursued to judgment). cf *Rothwell v Raes* (1989) 54 DLR (4th) 193, 346 (Ont HC). But see *Bonthrone v Secretary of State for Scotland* [1987] SLT 34, where the nature and extent of such warnings was deemed a discretionary matter. Cf *Ross v Secretary of State for Scotland* [1990] 1 Med LR 235. Under the Vaccine Damage Payments Act 1979, anyone suffering at least 80% disablement, who can establish that it was caused by vaccination against certain specified diseases, is entitled to no-fault compensation, up to a maximum of £30,000: Vaccine Damage Payments Act 1979 Statutory Sum Order 1991, SI 1991/939. S 6(4) of the Act provides for the deduction of such payment from any award based on negligence. For growth hormone treatment, see *N v United Kingdom Research Council: sub nom Creutzfeldt-Jakob Disease Litigation* [1996] 7 Med LR 309.

[175] eg *Yuen Kun-yeu v A-G of Hong Kong* [1988] AC 175; *Murphy v Brentwood District Council* [1991] 1 AC 398. cf *Hill v Chief Constable of West Yorkshire* [1989] AC 53; *X (Minors) v Bedfordshire County Council* [1995] 2 AC 633, and *Stovin v Wise, Norfolk County Council (Third Party)* [1996] AC 923.

[176] eg *Murphy v Brentwood District Council* [1991] 1 AC 398, 472, *per* Lord Keith; cf 491, *per* Lord Oliver, and *D and F Estates Ltd v Church Commissioners for England* [1989] AC 177, 193 and 210, *per* Lord Bridge.

applied to those therapeutic categories for which NHS prescription is confined to drugs on the 'selected list'.[177]

14.46 Each case must now be considered in its context. There may be more scope for impugning the operational decisions of public bodies in respect of personal injury than for pure economic loss, the primary focus of judicial retrenchment. The courts have of late laid much stress on 'statutory purpose' in determining whether or not a private right of action exists.[178] Traditionally, the role of statutory bodies has been to protect the general public interest rather than to confer rights on individuals,[179] though a duty to individuals is now more readily acknowledged where an agency has been established specifically to protect the public from dangerous practices.[180] Granted judicial disinclination to impugn discretionary decisions on the 'distribution of risks',[181] the public interest in early availability of valuable drugs must be set against the risks of allowing dangerous products onto the market, bearing in mind that protection of the public is the primary objective of the statutory bodies entrusted with the safety and licensing of medicinal products.[182] It has been suggested that 'a duty of care, by this test, would appear to be owed to the class of patients as a whole rather than individually.'[183] Equally, there may be 'cogent reasons of social policy'[184] for maintaining that such a 'statutory purpose' supports the case for granting a remedy to individual citizens.[185]

14.47 Assuming the existence of such a remedy, on whom would the duty lie and what standard of care would it entail? Though the LA is formally the ultimate

---

[177] National Health Service (General Medical and Pharmaceutical Services) Amendment Regulations 1985, SI 1985/290, and ibid, Amendment No 2 Regulations 1985, SI 1985/540.

[178] See eg *Governors of the Peabody Donation Fund v Sir Lindsay Parkinson & Co Ltd* [1985] AC 210.

[179] *Atkinson v The Newcastle and Gateshead Waterworks Company* (1877) 2 Ex D 441, CA.

[180] See *Swanson v The Queen in Right of Canada* (1991) 80 DLR (4th) 741 (Fed CA) *per* Linden J (commercial airlines).

[181] *Rowling v Takaro Properties Ltd* [1988] AC 473, 501, PC, *per* Lord Keith. And see Craig, P, *Administrative Law* (London, 3rd edn, 1994) 618–27.

[182] eg 'The principal task of the licensing authority is to protect the public . . . its duty [is] to safeguard the health of the nation . . . ' (*R v Licensing Authority Established under Medicines Act 1968, ex p Smith Kline & French Laboratories* [1990] 1 AC 64, 103, *per* Lord Templeman. cf Council of EC Directive: '. . . the primary purpose of any rules concerning the production and distribution of proprietary medicinal products must be to safeguard public health . . .' (65/65/EEC, as amended).

[183] Barton, A, 'The Basis of Liability of the Licensing Authority and its Advisers under the Medicines Act 1968 to an Individual' in Goldberg and Dodds-Smith (eds), *Pharmaceutical Medicine and the Law* (n 24 above), 99.

[184] *Murphy v Brentwood District Council* [1991] AC 398, 482, *per* Lord Bridge. cf *Re HIV Haemophiliac Litigation* (1990) 140 NLJ 1349.

[185] See Jones, *Medical Negligence* (n 133 above), 424, para 8-019.

decision-making body under the Medicines Act,[186] delegation of its advisory role to the CSM, as statutorily provided for,[187] should normally afford it protection against liability for negligence. It has also been argued that the CSM is, by the very nature of its composition, a 'responsible body of medical opinion' against which a finding of negligence is effectively precluded under the *Bolam* test.[188] It is not however self-evident that the *Bolam* principle extends beyond the spheres of professional clinical practice and advice in the context of such practice.

D. Liability under the Consumer Protection Act 1987

1. The European Directive on Product Liability

The lengthy process of reassessing products liability law which began in the **14.48** 1970s culminated in the European Directive on Product Liability of 1985,[189] on which Part I of the Consumer Protection Act 1987 is substantially based.[190] The preamble to the Directive expressed concern that divergences between the laws of Member States could distort competition and result in differential protection of consumers. It also asserted that the imposition of liability without fault on producers was the fairest method of apportioning risk.[191] Accordingly, with a view to harmonising national laws, the Directive required all members of the European Community to introduce a strict liability regime for defective products.

Though Part I of the CPA implements the EC Directive, there are some **14.49** significant differences of wording, most notably on the 'development risks' defence.[192] English law subscribes to the doctrine of 'indirect effect', whereby

---

[186] Medicines Act 1968, s 6.   [187] ibid, s 4.
[188] *Bolam v Friern Hospital Management Committee* [1957] 1 WLR 582. See Barton, A (n 183 above), 101.
[189] 85/374/EEC. See generally Goyens, M (ed) *Directive 85/374/EEC on product liability: ten years after* (n 25 above).
[190] See Stapleton, *Product Liability* (n 7 above), ch 3. The Act's provisions extend to the whole of the United Kingdom. See Consumer Protection (Northern Ireland) Order 1987, SI 1987/2409. No liability arises under the Act in respect of goods put into circulation by the producer prior to 1 Mar 1988: CPA, s 50(7); SI 1987/1680.
[191] '. . . liability without fault on the part of the producer is the sole means of adequately solving the problem peculiar to our age of increasing technicality, of a fair apportionment of the risks inherent in modern technological production . . .'
[192] See paras 14.65–14.68 below. The term 'development risks' is normally used to refer to undiscoverable defects which come to light only after a product has been in use. It may be distinguished from 'state of the art', an expression which commonly signifies the most up-to-date technology and standards in a given industry. In both the Directive and the CPA, the defence actually refers to discoverability of the *defect*, not of a *risk*; Art 7(e) and s 4(1)(e), respectively.

any ambiguity in the domestic legislation which implements directives is, as far as possible, construed so as to conform with Community law obligations.[193] In fact, the CPA itself states that Part I of the Act 'shall have effect for the purpose of making such provision as is necessary in order to comply with the product liability Directive and shall be construed accordingly.'[194] This novel form of stipulation seemingly invites English courts to apply the Directive whenever the terms of the CPA appear to be incompatible with it. At the same time, assistance in construing ambiguous or obscure statutory wording may now be derived from clear Parliamentary statements of a Minister or other promoter of a Bill.[195] On the 'development risks' defence, in particular, several such statements suggest that the UK Government intended the Act to have a different meaning from that generally attributed to the Directive. The European Commission brought an action against the UK, under Article 169 of the EC Treaty, seeking a declaration of non-compliance. However, the European Court of Justice ruled that the UK formulation of the defence did not clearly conflict with the Directive.[196]

14.50 The European Court of Justice has held that non-discretionary provisions in a directive which are unconditional and sufficiently precise may be relied on directly by an individual against the state, if the state has failed to implement the directive correctly.[197] In addition, in certain circumstances, the state might be liable in damages.[198] In practice, the potential application of the doctrine of direct effect to products liability is severely limited. It could not apply to the 'development risks' defence, as the Directive permits derogation from it.[199] More generally, directives have direct effect only insofar as a state body is the defendant.[200] However, the doctrine could in principle apply to a health authority,[201] in the capacity, for example, of producer or supplier of pharmaceuticals, aids, appliances and blood products, or where equipment or products have been substantially modified by health authority employees.

---

[193] *Von Colson and Kamann v Land Nordrhein-Westfalen* [1986] CMLR 240; *Garland v British Railway Engineering Ltd* [1983] 2 AC 751, 771, *per* Lord Diplock; *Pickstone v Freeman plc* [1989] AC 66; *Litster v Forth Dry Dock & Engineering Co Ltd* [1990] 1 AC 456. And see Steiner, J, 'Coming to Terms with EEC Directives' (1990) 106 LQR 144.
[194] CPA, s 1(1).   [195] *Pepper (Inspector of Taxes) v Hart* [1993] AC 593.
[196] *European Commission v United Kingdom* (case c-300/95) [1997] All ER (EC) 481. See further paras 14.65–14.68 below.
[197] Case 103/88 *Fratelli Costanzo SpA v Commune di Milano and Others* [1990] 3 CMLR 23a, para 29; *Becker v Finanzamt Munster-Innenstadt* Case 8/81, [1982] ECR 53. European Communities Act 1972, ss 2(1), (4).   [198] *Francovich v Italy 1* ECR 5357, [1993] 2 CMLR 66.
[199] Art 15(1)(b). And see para 14.65 below.
[200] *Marshall v Southampton and South-West Hampshire Area Health Authority* Case 152/84, [1986] 1 CMLR 688.   [201] ibid.

2. The Act

(i) *The 'Strict Liability' Regime Under the CPA*

A general principle of strict civil liability is contained in section 2(1) of the   **14.51**
Act:

> Where any damage is caused wholly or partly by a defect in a product, every person to whom [s 2(2)] applies shall be liable for the damage.

The above wording points to the Act's stated focus on the condition of the product rather than on the conduct or state of mind of its producer. Once the plaintiff has proved that there is a 'defect' in the product and that the relevant damage was wholly or partly caused by it, the onus shifts to the defendant(s), for whom several specific defences are available under the Act.[202] Liability under Part I of the Act may not be limited or excluded by any contract term, notice or other provision.[203]

(ii) *Causation*

Many of the more intractable problems associated with proving causation in   **14.52**
drug-related claims based on negligence[204] remain under the Act. Moreover, its silence on causation and remoteness leaves a number of issues unresolved. For example, though, unlike negligence, the Act does not confine recovery to damage of a foreseeable kind,[205] the courts might still be disposed to treat 'cause' as importing foreseeability of consequences.[206] Medicinal products which cause injury through unforeseeable misuse would presumably not be deemed 'defective'. It should be noted that whereas, in negligence, inter-mediate examination is seen as breaking the chain of causation as regards defects existing when the manufacturer put a product into circulation, under the Act the manufacturer would be jointly and severally liable with any culpable intermediary.[207] Where damage is caused partly by a defect in the product and partly through the plaintiff's fault, contributory negligence may be invoked as a partial defence.[208] Any consequent reduction in the plaintiff's

---

[202] S 4. See paras 14.59–14.68, below.
[203] S 7.   [204] See paras 14.04 and 14.41 above.
[205] *Overseas Tankship (UK) Ltd v Morts Dock & Engineering Co Ltd, The Wagon Mound (No 1)* [1961] AC 388.
[206] See Whittaker, S, 'The EEC Directive on Product Liability' (1985) 5 *Yearbook of European Law 233*, 253–4.   [207] S 2(5); and see n 218 below.
[208] Law Reform (Contributory Negligence) Act 1945, s 6(4).

damages might be less than in negligence, given that, under the Act, the defendant's liability is not contingent on negligence.

(iii) *Who May Sue?*

14.53 The Act confers a right of action on any person[209] who suffers damage from a defective product. 'Damage' is defined so as to cover death, personal injury and loss of or damage to property.[210] 'Personal injury', which includes 'any disease and any other impairment of a person's physical or mental condition'[211] would seem broad enough to cover claims for psychiatric damage.[212] No remedy is provided for loss of or damage to the product itself,[213] or for pure economic loss.

(iv) *Who May Be Strictly Liable?*

14.54 Primary liability is imposed on the 'producer',[214] 'own brander',[215] and any person who has imported a product into the EC in order to supply it to another in the course of a business.[216] In addition, any persons in the chain of supply can be held strictly liable if they have failed, on request, to identify within a reasonable time either the 'producer' or their own supplier, where identification is not reasonably practicable for the person who has suffered the damage.[217] Typically it is the manufacturer of the finished product who would incur liability, as 'producer'; but the manufacturer of a defective component part (or the producer of some raw materials) responsible for the damage caused by the finished product is also liable as a 'producer',[218] as is a person who has 'abstracted' a 'substance which has not been manufactured.'[219] So, too, is the processor where the 'essential characteristics' of a product are attributable to an industrial or other process.[220] Depending on

---

[209] Including persons who have suffered ante-natal injury: CPA, s 6(3).
[210] S 5(1). Actionable damage to property is limited to property of a kind ordinarily intended for private use, occupation or consumption and mainly so intended by the plaintiff, where the amount to be awarded exceeds £275: s 5(3)(4).   [211] S 45(1).
[212] *Alcock v Chief Constable of the South Yorkshire Police* [1992] 1 AC 310; *Page v Smith* [1996] AC 155.
[213] CPA, s 5(2).   [214] ibid, s 1(2).   [215] ibid, s 2(2)(b).
[216] ibid, s 2(2)(c).   [217] ibid, s 2(3).
[218] ibid, s 1(2). Where two or more persons are liable for the same damage their liability is joint and several: s 2(5), subject to any rights of contribution or indemnity. See s 2(6) and the Civil Liability (Contribution) Act 1978.   [219] S 1(2)(b).
[220] S 1(2)(c).

the circumstances, the assembly of products might fall within the definition, though presumably not mere packaging.[221]

It is thus apparent that the application of the Act to the production and supply of medicinal products is, in principle, far-ranging. In addition to pharmaceutical companies, hospital and individual pharmacists manufacturing their own finished products, doctors, dentists, and any other health care staff who mix drugs for a prescription or an injection, or modify a piece of equipment, may be deemed producers.[222] The pharmacist, doctor or dentist dispensing drugs, and other health care personnel supplying medical equipment, could be held liable as suppliers if they were unable to identify the 'producer' or their own supplier.[223] There are, then, potentially draconian consequences for innocent intermediaries as a result of this legislative attempt to assist consumers in tracing producers and importers. All suppliers are now well advised to keep adequate records of their source of supply, and producers are similarly advised to label otherwise 'anonymous' products. Identification of source can pose acute problems in the distribution of pharmaceuticals, especially as, increasingly, generic drugs and blood products supplied in bulk originate from a variety of companies, and some forty per cent of NHS prescriptions are for generics.[224] In practice, suppliers would need to keep records for eleven years to avoid liability.[225]

14.55

---

[221] Except as regards defects in the packaging itself, ie *qua* product. See Dodds-Smith, I, 'The Implications of Strict Liability for Medicinal Products under the Consumer Protection Act, 1987' in Mann, R (ed) *Risk and Consent to Risk in Medicine* (Carnforth, 1989).

[222] Under the Medicines (Labelling) Regulations 1976, the containers of all medicines prepared or dispensed must be labelled with the name and address of the supplying chemist. It seems unlikely that this of itself would amount to a holding out so as to make the chemist an 'own-brander', and hence a producer within the meaning of the CPA, s 2(2)(b). *Aliter* where the chemist's own brand name is attached to a product without indicating that it was manufactured by others. See also Directive 92/27/EEC OJ 30 Apr 1992, L.113/10.

[223] 'Supplying goods' is, *inter alia*, defined as providing them 'in or in connection with the performance of any statutory function': s 46(1)(e). In the case of NHS employees, the effective 'producer' or 'supplier' will be the health authority. Part I of the CPA binds the Crown: s 9. The activities of a 'public authority' are included within the definition of 'business' for the purpose of producer or supplier liability: s 45(1).

[224] Ferguson, P, 'Pharmaceutical Products Liability: 30 Years of Law Reform?' (1992) JR 226, 236.

[225] ie the limitation period of 10 years after the product was put into circulation by the defendant: CPA, Sch 1; Limitation Act 1980, s 11A(3), plus a year for service of the writ.

(v) *The Meaning of 'Product'*

14.56 'Product' is broadly defined under the Act, as 'any goods or electricity', including 'a product which is comprised in another product'.[226] Moreover 'goods' include 'substances', defined as 'any natural or artificial substance'.[227] However, the still broader definition in the Directive—'electricity' and 'all movables'[228]—might be invoked in respect of problematic substances.[229] Though criticism of the refusal to exempt pharmaceutical products from the statutory regime was defused by the inclusion of the 'development risks' defence,[230] there remains, as in the law of sale, uncertainty over the classification of borderline articles such as human blood, plasma, human tissue and organs.[231] The inclusion of the term 'substances' strengthens the case for regarding them as 'products' within the Act, more especially when they have been abstracted,[232] for example by a surgeon. Equally, the processor of such products might be deemed a producer.[233] But, depending on the facts, any of these transactions might be more appropriately characterised as a provision of services. According to the Department of Trade and Industry, 'medicinal materials used in trials before marketing' would 'generally be exempt', not having been put into circulation in the normal course of business.[234] In fact, use for research purposes would seem to fall within the statutory definition of 'supply',[235] though, in any event, a product which is still being researched would rarely be deemed 'defective'.[236]

(vi) *The Meaning Of 'Defect'*

14.57 Proof by the plaintiff that a product has a 'defect' is essential to liability under the Act. A product is deemed defective if 'its safety is not such as persons

---

[226] S 1(2).   [227] S 45(1).

[228] Art 2. 'Movables' have elsewhere been defined by the ECJ as anything capable of money valuation and of being an object of commercial transactions: 7/68 *EC Commission v Italy* [1968] ECR 423.   [229] ie under CPA, s 1(1). See para 14.49 above.

[230] See para 14.65 below.

[231] See 14.20 and 14.21 above. See further Grubb and Pearl (n 77 above), ch 5; Grubb, A (1993) 1 Med L Rev 259, and Stern, K, 'Strict Liability and the Supply of Donated Gametes' (1994) 2 Med L Rev 261.

[232] S 1(2)(b). See also the Pearson Commission (n 1 above), para 1276.   [233] S 1(2)(c).

[234] Department of Trade and Industry, *Implementation of EC Directive on Product Liability—An Explanatory and Consultative Note* (London, 1985) 14, para 56(a).

[235] S 46(1).

[236] See ss 3(1),(2), paras 14.57 and 14.58 below. See also s 4(1)(e) ('development risks' defence), paras 14.65–14.68 below.

generally are entitled to expect . . .'.[237] In determining the issue, 'all the circumstances shall be taken into account . . .'.[238] These include 'the manner in which, and purposes for which, the product has been marketed, its get-up, . . .' and any instructions or warnings concerning its use;[239] 'what might reasonably be expected to be done with or in relation to the product',[240] and 'the time when the product was supplied by its producer to another . . .'.[241] The choice of the date of supply as a factor in the evaluation of defectiveness means that, under the Act, no less than in negligence, the plaintiff has the burden of establishing what safety standards were acceptable at some time in the past, perhaps many years previously in the case of drugs. The Act does not 'require' an inference of defectiveness to be drawn from the fact 'alone' that a product marketed at a later date is more safe,[242] though, where appropriate, liability could be imposed on the producer of the original product for its continued supply.

(vii) *The 'Consumer Expectation' Test*

Interpreted in the spirit of the Directive's Preamble,[243] the 'consumer expectation' test would make it easier for plaintiffs to establish liability than is currently the case in negligence. However, it is not clear precisely how this objectively framed test will be applied, particularly as regards design defects and failure to warn. As the 'learned intermediary' principle implies, with many medicinal products there is a certain artificiality in trying to determine what 'persons generally are entitled to expect'.[244] The equivalent American criterion of a product in a 'defective condition unreasonably dangerous'[245] is now commonly subjected to elaborate risk-utility analysis.[246] It remains to be seen whether the English courts will move in this direction and away from their traditionally more intuitive approach. Under an avowedly strict liability regime, the courts may be inclined to require higher standards both as regards the condition of products and the information, warnings and promotional material which accompany them. But the reference to 'all the circumstances' in section 3(2), as well as its explicit focus on how and why a product has been marketed and on the nature of any instructions or warnings, have a familiar ring. The likelihood is that determinations on defectiveness of design

14.58

---

[237] S 3(1).   [238] S 3(2).   [239] S 3(2)(a).
[240] S 3(2)(b). This subsection would permit liability for foreseeable misuse.
[241] S 3(2)(c).   [242] S 3(2).   [243] See n 191 above.
[244] cf Atiyah, *The Sale of Goods* (n 40 above), 236–7.
[245] Section 402A of the Restatement (Second) of Torts.
[246] See especially *Barker v Lull Engineering Co* 573 P 2d 443 (1978).

and adequacy of warning will continue to revolve around issues of relative safety, reasonable care, and foreseeability,[247] thereby perpetuating the kind of balancing act characteristic of negligence and of American 'strict' products liability regimes alike.[248]

(viii) *Defences*

14.59 If the plaintiff can prove that damage has been caused by a 'defective product' (as defined above) for which the defendant is responsible under the Act, the burden shifts to the defence to establish any of six specific defences listed in section 4.

(a) **Section 4(1)(a)**

14.60 That the defect 'is attributable to compliance with any requirement imposed by or under any enactment or with any Community obligation'.[249]

Compliance with such a requirement is not in itself a defence. The defendant must show that the defect was caused by the compliance. Thus mere compliance with licensing regulations under the Medicines Act 1968 is not a defence, though it will often be strong evidence that the 'consumer expectation' test of safety has been met, and some indication that the producer has demonstrated the degree of scientific and technical knowledge needed to satisfy the 'development risks' defence.[250] The requirement relied upon must be mandatory.[251]

(b) **Section 4(1)(b) and Section 46**

14.61 That the defendant 'did not at any time supply the product to another'.[252]

This defence derives from Article 7(a) of the Directive, under which a producer can avoid liability by proving that 'he did not put the product into circulation'. It could be relied on where, for example, damage has arisen

---

[247] Perhaps also considerations of cost in regard to design defects
[248] cf '. . . even where strict liability is ostensibly the chosen regime, doctrine is likely to reflect the long and enduring reach of negligence principles': Rogerson, C and Trebilcock, M, 'Products Liability and the Allergic Consumer: A Study in the Problems of Framing an Efficient Liability Regime' (n 131 above), 52. cf Whittaker, S, 'The EEC Directive on Product Liability' (1985) (n 205 above), 233; Stapleton, J, 'Products Liability Reform—Real or Illusory?' (1986) 6 OJLS 392; Newdick, C, 'The Future of Negligence in Product Liability' (n 113 above); Stoppa, A, 'The Concept of Defectiveness in the Consumer Protection Act 1987: a Critical Analysis' (1992) 12 LS 210; Atiyah, *The Sale of Goods* (n 40 above), 235–9.   [249] S 4(1)(a).
[250] See paras 14.65–14.68 below.
[251] cf 'mandatory regulations issued by the public authorities': European Directive (n 189 above), Art 7(d).   [252] SS 4(1)(b) and 46.

from the theft of drugs or from the use of defective products, provided that they were not yet in the distribution chain.[253]

(c) Section 4(1)(c)

That the defendant did not supply the goods 'in the course of a business' and, in the case of the producer, 'own-brander' or importer (ie a section 2(2) defendant), with a view to profit.[254]   **14.62**

(d) Section 4(1)(d) and Section 4(2)

That the defect 'did not exist in the product at the relevant time'.[255]   **14.63**

It is a defence for section 2(2) defendants to prove that the defect was not present when they supplied the product. A supplier[256] can succeed under the defence by showing that the defect did not exist when the product was last supplied by the producer, 'own-brander' or importer. The supplier is thus apparently not liable, under the Act, for introducing the defect into the product. The defence would be available to a pharmaceutical manufacturer where, for example, a product had deteriorated because of inadequate storage or poor handling by a wholesaler or pharmacist, or where injury was shown to have resulted from a pharmacist having removed a patient leaflet. It could also cover situations where a supplier had altered the original specifications of a product, as well as instances of criminal tampering.

(e) Section 4(1)(f)

That the defect in a component is wholly attributable to the design of the finished product in which it was comprised or to compliance with the instructions of that product's producer.[257]   **14.64**

Components manufacturers (and producers of raw materials) are not liable, under the Act, if their product is defective only as a consequence of the design of the finished product or of compliance with instructions given by its producer. In the European Directive, unlike the CPA, the defence that the defect was attributable to instructions is not confined to instructions given to the component manufacturer, and could cover instructions for use.[258]

---

[253] As regards products still under research, see para 14.56 above.
[254] S 4(1)(c). 'Business' includes NHS provision: see para 14.55, n 223 above. The defence would not be available for promotional free samples.   [255] S 4(1)(d), (2).
[256] S 2(3).   [257] S 4(1)(f).   [258] Art 7(f).

(f) Section 4(1)(e): The 'Development Risks' Defence[259]

14.65 That: . . . the state of scientific and technical knowledge at the relevant time
was not such that a producer of products of the same description as the
product in question might be expected to have discovered the defect if it had
existed in his products while they were under his control . . . .

This provision is the most contentious feature of the legislation. The pharmaceutical industry had been very prominent in the intensive lobbying to
have a 'development risks' defence, emphasising concern about innovation
and insurability. The availability of such a defence in the European Directive[260] was a key factor in obtaining the agreement of all Member States,
especially the UK, to the introduction of a strict liability regime.[261] At the
same time, there has been much criticism that it signifies a reversion to
negligence, is conceptually incompatible with strict liability and threatens
to undermine the social and economic objectives of products liability
reform.[262] These concerns were reflected in the Directive's requirement
that, after ten years,[263] the European Commission would have to report on
how 'consumer protection and the functioning of the common market' had
been affected by court rulings of Member States based on the defence, to
determine whether or not Article 7(e) should be repealed.[264]

(g) Section 4(1)(e) and Article 7(e)

14.66 The controversy has been exacerbated by the difference in terminology
between section 4(1)(e) and Article 7(e).[265] Under the Act, manufacturers
need only show that the state of knowledge when they supplied the product
was not such that 'a producer of products of the same description . . . might

---

[259] S 4(1)(e). See Newdick, C, 'The Development Risk Defence of the Consumer Protection
Act 1987' (n 117 above), 455; Newdick, C, 'Risk, Uncertainty and "Knowledge" in the
Development Risk Defence' (1991) Anglo-Amer LR 127; Stapleton, 'Products Liability
Reform—Real or Illusory?' (n 248 above), 392; Stapleton, *Product Liability* (n. 7 above),
236–42; Whittaker, S, 'The EEC Directive on Product Liability' (n 206, above), 233; Stoppa,
A, (1992) 'The Concept of Defectiveness in the Consumer Protection Act 1987: A Critical
Analysis' (n 248 above), 218–21. [260] Art 7(e).
[261] Under Article 15(1)(b), Member States were given the option of adopting or derogating
from the defence. [262] See references at n 248 above.
[263] ie in 1995.
[264] Art 15(3). In its first report on the application of the Directive, the Commission did not
propose any amendments to it. *First Report on the application of Council Directive on the
approximation of laws, regulations and administrative provisions of the Member States concerning
liability for defective products* (85/374/EEC): COM (95) 617 final, 13 Dec 1995, 2.
[265] See references at n 259 above.

be expected' to have discovered the defect.[266] The Directive requires the defendant to prove that the state of knowledge 'was not such as to *enable* the existence of the defect to be discovered.'[267] The Directive is concerned with what is objectively discoverable; the CPA only with what might be expected of producers of a particular category of products.

Clearly this is a distinction which could have major implications for the **14.67** pharmaceutical industry in cases of defective design.[268] The imprecise wording of the CPA defence appeared to permit exactly the kind of balancing act which is familiar in negligence analysis. It seemed to leave the court free to consider what are appropriate standards within the industry, having regard to such factors as the resources of the producer and the feasibility of discovering a particular defect at the pre-marketing stage, in the light of the various financial and scientific constraints on investigative procedures. It has often been asserted that, by virtue of section 4(1)(e), the thalidomide victims might not have recovered damages under an Act which was in part prompted by their struggle. Certainly it is possible that Distillers could have shown that pharmaceutical manufacturers of comparable products might not have been expected to conduct the kind of tests that would have revealed the defect.[269] On the other hand, the reverse onus of proof and the expectations engendered by a strict liability regime would have made their task harder. In fact, according to two experienced practitioners in the field:

> There is widespread expectation that any court would feel obliged to construe the defence in accordance with the Directive and thus in effect to override the literal words of the Act. Indeed, insurance is widely believed to be on this basis.[270]

---

[266] It is not entirely clear what is meant by 'a producer of products of the same description as the product in question'. In the pharmaceutical context, it could refer to drug manufacturers in general or might be limited to producers of drugs of the same therapeutic class, always assuming that they exist.

[267] Emphasis added. Art 7(e) reads in full, 'that the state of scientific and technical knowledge at the time when he put the product into circulation was not such as to enable the existence of the defect to be discovered'.

[268] The section would seem to have little, if any, relevance for manufacturing defects, which already effectively attract strict liability at common law, and may not be within the scope of s 4(1)(e), which is concerned with the individually defective product. See Miller, C, *Product Liability and Safety Encyclopaedia* (London, 1979) Division III, 178. See also, Newdick, 'The Development Risk Defence of the Consumer Protection Act 1987' (n 117 above), 469–73. The comparable German provision under the *Produkthaftungsgesetz* (Product Liability Act 1990) has no application to unavoidable manufacturing defects: Bundesgerichtshof (VI ZR 158/94, May 9, 1995) [1995] 1504.

[269] See generally Teff, H and Munro, C, *Thalidomide: The Legal Aftermath* (Farnborough, 1976).

[270] Mildred, M and Pannone, R, 'Liability in Tort: Class Actions' in Miller, *Product Liability and Safety Encyclopaedia* (n 268 above), Division IIIA, para 94 (1996).

In 1997, in response to infringement proceedings brought by the European Commission, the European Court of Justice ruled that the test of scientific and technical knowledge under Article 7(e) is an objective one. It includes the most advanced level of such knowledge at the time when the product was put into circulation, provided that knowledge was accessible at that time. The Court found that section 4(1)(e) did not impose any restriction on the state of scientific and technical knowledge to be taken into account and, more particularly, did not suggest that the availability of the defence depended on the subjective knowledge of a producer taking reasonable care in the light of standard precautions in the industrial sector in question. The Court further noted that section 1(1) of the Act expressly provided that relevant provisions be construed in conformity with the Directive. It therefore concluded that section 4(1)(e) did not clearly conflict with Article 7(e).[271]

14.68 Yet the wording of the Directive is not free from ambiguity and there are practical difficulties in trying to apply it in a literal fashion. What does it mean to say that the state of scientific and technical knowledge enables the existence of a defect to be discovered? First, there is a fundamental problem of definition. How reliable and beyond challenge must findings be, what level of recognition must they have achieved within the scientific community, before they can be said to constitute 'knowledge' at all, let alone 'the most advanced level of such knowledge'?[272] Does 'knowledge' exist within the meaning of the section when the failure to discover a defect results from not having drawn appropriate conclusions, or from not having made the relevant connections, from data which already exist? Secondly, it has been forcefully argued that 'scientific and technical knowledge' cannot be said to exist merely because of what someone, somewhere knows, or may have published in an obscure journal.[273] A court assessing the relevant state of scientific and technical knowledge would hardly 'require the defendant to prove . . . a worldwide absence of knowledge of the defect'.[274] The ruling by the European Court of Justice that the knowledge in question must have been 'accessible' indicates that, even under the Directive, only reasonably discoverable knowledge is in issue.[275]

---

[271] *European Commission v United Kingdom* (Case C-300/95) [1997] All ER (EC) 481.
[272] Newdick, 'Risk, Uncertainty and "Knowledge" in the Development Risk Defence' (n 259 above). Cf para 14.31 above.
[273] Newdick, 'The Development Risk Defence of the Consumer Protection Act 1987' (n 117 above), 461–7. Cf Atiyah, *Sale of Goods* (n 4o above), 239–40; Stapleton, *Product Liability* (n 7 above), 236–42.　　　　　　　　　　　　　　　　[274] Newdick (n 117 above), 459.
[275] In the United States a number of jurisdictions permit a development risks defence along the lines of the European Directive. Since the mid-1980s, the American courts have largely retreated from strict liability in cases based on defective design and failure to warn. Contrast *Beshada v Johns-Manville Products Corp* 447 A 2d 539, 546 (1982) (Sup Ct of New Jersey)

(ix) *Limitation Of Actions*

The normal principles of limitation of actions apply under the Act, except in **14.69** two respects.[276] First, the limitation period for damage to property is the same as for personal injury, namely three years from the date that the plaintiff became aware or should reasonably have become aware of the material facts relating to the damage.[277] Secondly, in no circumstances may an action be brought under the Act after ten years from when the defendant supplied the actual defective product which caused the damage.[278] This cut-off point is of particular significance in respect of drugs, since the latency period for adverse effects can be considerable,[279] but it does not preclude the possibility of a subsequent action in negligence (or breach of contract).

(x) *Jurisdiction*

For the purposes of jurisdiction, liability under Part I of the Act is treated as **14.70** liability in tort,[280] and the normal rules as to conflict of laws apply.[281] Generally speaking, and despite the scope for derogation under the Directive, there has not been such a degree of divergence in its implementation by Member States as to encourage widespread forum shopping. Nonetheless, apart from any extrinsic considerations as to choice of forum, several points merit attention. First, because the Directive applies only to products put into circulation once the domestic implementing law has come into force, liability for products supplied prior to that date is based on the applicable national law at the relevant time. Secondly, though nearly all Member States have implemented a 'development risks' defence, the UK's version is the one most open to a broad interpretation. However, specifically in respect of pharmaceutical

---

with the same court's holding in *Feldman v Lederle Laboratories 479* A 2d 374, 387 (1984). In *Brown v Superior Court (Abbott Laboratories) 751* P 2d 470, 480–2 (1988), the California Supreme Court held that the exemption from strict liability for 'unavoidably unsafe' products in Comment k to section 402A of the Restatement (Second) of Torts covered all prescription drugs in respect of failure to warn. Contrast *Shanks v Upjohn Co 835* P 2d 1189 (Alaska 1992). See also Stapleton, *Product Liability* (n 7 above), ch 2.

[276] See s 6(6) and Sch 1, amending the Limitation Act 1980.
[277] Limitation Act 1980, ss 11A(4) and 14(1A).
[278] Limitation Act 1980, s 11A(3).
[279] See e g *Sindell v Abbott Laboratories 607* P 2d 924 (Cal 1980).   [280] S 6(7).
[281] See Attree, R, 'Jurisdiction, Enforcement of Judgments and Conflicts of Laws' in Kelly, P and Attree, R (eds) *European Product Liability Law* (London, 2nd edn, 1997), ch XVIII.

products, Germany has a statutory scheme under which manufacturers are subject to strict liability.[282]

E. Multi-Plaintiff Actions

14.71 Our substantive law, the Rules of the Supreme Court and the legal aid system were all essentially designed to deal with individual claims. Because defective medical products and devices may cause injury on a large scale, they are liable to generate multi-plaintiff actions which raise comparable, but often not identical, issues of liability[283] and which pose intractable problems of procedure and case management.[284] In a legal system which does not provide for 'class actions',[285] and where it remains uncertain whether a representative action[286] can be maintained when damages are claimed for individuals,[287] there is a pressing need for a more coherent approach to litigation of this kind.[288]

---

[282] Drug Administration Act (*Arzneimittelgesetz*) 1976 BGBI, 1S 2445, amended 20 July 1988 BGBI, IS 1050.

[283] 'In the case of pharmaceutical products . . . patients of differing susceptibilities will have taken different quantities of the drug over differing periods of time and during different stages of the advancement of scientific knowledge, so that the issue of negligence or "defective product" will vary. Equally, patients taking the same drug may complain of different ill-effects, and so the issue of causation may vary.': Supreme Court Procedure Committee, *Guide for Use in Group Actions* (n 26 above), 6.

[284] *Nash v Eli Lilly & Co* [1991] 2 Med LR 169 (Opren); *AB v John Wyeth & Brother Ltd* [1994] 5 Med LR 149, CA (benzodiazepine). And see Oliphant, K, 'Innovation in Procedure and Practice in Multi-Party Medical Cases' (n 26 above); Legal Aid Board, *Issues arising for the Legal Aid Board and the Lord Chancellor's Department from Multi-Party Actions* (n 26 above).

[285] See eg *Davies v Eli Lilly & Co* [1987] 1 WLR 1136, 1139, CA, *per* Lord Donaldson MR. Contrast the position in the United States and certain Commonwealth jurisdictions which provide for numerous plaintiffs with related claims against the same defendant to have them disposed of in a single action. See further Mildred and Pannone, 'Liability in Tort: Class Actions' (n 268 above), Division IIIA.   [286] RSC Ord 15, r 12.

[287] Contrast *Markt & Co Ltd v Knight Steamship Co Ltd* [1910] 2 KB 1021, 1040, CA: 'absolutely inapplicable', *per* Fletcher Moulton LJ, with *Prudential Assurance Co Ltd v Newman Industries Ltd* [1979] 3 All ER 507 and *Irish Shipping Ltd v Commercial Union Assurance Co Plc* [1991] 2 QB 206, CA.

[288] See eg *Chrzanowska v Glaxo Laboratories Ltd* [1990] 1 Med LR 385, 386 (Myodil); Supreme Court Procedure Committee, *Guide for Use in Group Actions* (n 26 above); Legal Aid Board, *Issues arising for the Legal Aid Board and the Lord Chancellor's Department from Multi-Party Actions* (n 26 above); Woolf, Lord, *Access to Justice* (Final Report) (London, 1996), ch 17 and *Access to Justice: Multi-Party Situations: Proposed New Procedure. A Consultation Paper* (London, 1997).

15

DONATION AND TRANSPLANTATION OF ORGANS AND TISSUES

A. Introduction

1. The Scope of this Chapter

The list of materials in the human body that can be removed and transplanted **15.01** into another person's body for therapeutic, cosmetic, reproductive or other purposes is growing.[1] Further, human cells outside the body can be cultured

---

[1] See Nuffield Council on Bioethics, *Human Tissue: Ethical and Legal Issues* (London, 1995)

787

by biotechnological processes and otherwise developed into commercially valuable products,[2] and surplus materials of human origin, such as placentas and umbilical cord blood that result from childbirth, can be of considerable therapeutic and industrial use.[3] Dead bodies, living persons and such products of human conception as foetal tissues can be sources of materials for transplantation, scientific research, industrial development, and medical and related education.

15.02 The focus of this Chapter is donation of human organs and tissues for transplantation into patients. Donations for purposes other than therapeutic transplantation, such as development of commercial products and therapeutic agents, are not the present concern. Transfers of materials including sperm, ova and pre-embryos for reproductive purposes are addressed directly in Chapter 10 and indirectly in Chapter 12, and research uses of human bodily materials used in treatments such as gene therapy and storing of materials in tissue or genetic data banks are addressed in Chapter 14. Further, plans are being elaborated to narrow the gap between the demand for human organs for transplantation and their supply, by employment of transgenically-prepared animal organs and tissues, such as from pigs and baboons.[4] Concerns with legal aspects of xenotransplantation, however, such as breeding of and care for selected animals and the legal status of their separated organs pending implantation, are touched on only from the narrow perspective of the intended human recipients. Despite the expanding range of transplantable human materials, this Chapter will standardize its approach by citing primarily kidney transplantation as representative of organ transplantation, and bone marrow as representative of transplantable tissues, except when specific tissue raises special concerns, such as reproductive tissue.

2. Organs and Tissues

15.03 The historical common law was more concerned with lost limbs and digits than organs and tissues. Obtaining organs or tissues from living persons would usually require that they be cut, but, particularly before the develop-

---

Appendix 3, 144. For a somewhat critical extended review of the report, see Matthews, P, 'The Man of Property' (1995) 3 Med L Rev 251–74.

[2] See *Moore v Regents of the University of California* (1990), 793 P 2d 479 (Cal Sup Ct), cert denied (1991), 111 S Ct 1388 (US Sup Ct), concerning a cell line with a potential market worth over three billion dollars by 1990.

[3] See Royal Commission on New Reproductive Technologies, Final Report, *Proceed with Care* (Ottawa, 1993) ch 31, 981–5.

[4] See Nuffield Council on Bioethics *Animal-to-Human Transplants: The Ethics of Xenotransplantation* (London, 1996).

ment of sterile practice in surgery, the law recognized that any breaking of the outer surface of the skin endangered life itself, and was a wound that might constitute an unlawful maim (or mayhem). The law also recognized the distinction between natural and induced separation of bodily materials from the person, such as in the contrast between release of waste products and the shedding of blood. However, the modern legal distinction between organs and tissues is based on legislation. In Britain, the Human Tissue Act 1961,[5] dealing with cadaveric removal of materials, deals with them in an undifferentiated way, but the Human Organ Transplants Act 1989,[6] addressing donations from living persons, provides that the Act deals only with 'organs'. Section 7(2) of the Act provides that:

> 'organ' means any part of a human body consisting of a structured arrangement of tissues which, if wholly removed, cannot be replicated by the body.

Although unreplicable structured tissues are organs, 'tissue' remains the generic description of bodily materials, so that the Human Tissue Act 1961 is appropriately titled in not distinguishing organs from unstructured tissues. Under the 1989 Act, the whole liver for instance is an organ, but a liver segment is not since, following surgical removal of the segment, the liver remaining in the donor's body spontaneously regenerates itself. The major purpose of the Act, as stated in its long title, is 'to prohibit commercial dealings in human organs intended for transplanting', but its narrow definition of 'organ' leaves some objectionable commerce in human tissues beyond its reach.

The legislation of each jurisdiction warrants particular attention, since statutory language and definitions do not conform to any coherent pattern, although underlying purposes may be similar. In Ontario, for instance,[7] the legislation covering both inter vivos gifts for transplantation and post mortem gifts is The Human Tissue Gift Act.[8] Section 1(c) provides that: **15.04**

> 'tissue' includes an organ, but does not include any skin, bone, blood, blood constituent, or other tissue that is replaceable by natural processes of repair.

Accordingly, 'tissue' under this Act appears comparable to 'organ' under the British 1989 Act.[9] Blood is a tissue according to the 1989 Act, but not the Ontario Act. The former addresses only organs as defined, but leaves uncertainty regarding its application to important transplantable materials such as

---

[5] 9 & 10 Eliz 2 ch 54, as amended. [6] Human Organ Transplants Act 1989.
[7] Principal contrasts in this Chapter will be between the laws in England and Ontario.
[8] Human Tissue Gift Act, RSO 1990, c H-20.
[9] On uncertainties in the statutory language, see Kennedy, I and Grubb, A, *Medical Law: Text with Materials* (London, 2nd edn, 1994), 1087–9.

bone marrow. It is a matter of biology whether this is 'a structured arrangement of tissues', but if it is so considered it may be an 'organ' under the 1989 Act since it may not be replicated if 'wholly removed', although it regenerates in time if removed in limited and safe amounts. Since bone marrow is usually not considered to be structured tissue, however, it falls outside the 1989 Act and the prohibition, for instance, of commercial exchange.[10] In contrast, the prohibition of commerce in the Ontario Act applies to 'any tissue . . . or any body or part or parts thereof other than blood or a blood constituent',[11] which includes bone marrow.[12]

B. Issues Common to Living and Post Mortem Donation

1. Introduction

15.05 A functional distinction between tissues and organs is that the former tend to be donated primarily by live donors, whereas experience and policy favour the acquisition of organs primarily from cadaveric sources. This is largely self-evident where donations of vital organs such as hearts are concerned, but kidneys and organ segments from, for example, the liver and pancreas (which segments may be legally classified as tissues rather than organs[13]) may be donated by persons while living. Nevertheless, strong international endorsement supports the recovery of organs for transplantation from cadavers rather than from live donors, where local cultures, influenced by religious beliefs, are sympathetic to the practice.[14] The World Health Assembly has endorsed certain Guiding Principles for human organ transplantation proposed by the World Health Organization that include the principle that:

> Organs for transplantation should be removed preferably from the bodies of deceased persons.[15]

The Commentary on Guiding Principle 3 states that this provision:

> is intended to emphasize the importance of developing cadaveric donation programmes . . . and to discourage donations from living, genetically unrelated

---

[10] N 6 above, s 1(1)(a).   [11] N 8 above, s 10.

[12] On practical problems from the prohibition of commerce, and more generally, see Law Reform Commission of Canada, *Procurement and Transfer of Human Tissues and Organs* (Ottawa, 1992, Working Paper 66), 29 *et seq.*   [13] See para 15.03 above.

[14] For comparative international legislation and international institutional activity, see World Health Organization *Legislative Responses to Organ Transplantation* (Dordrecht, Boston, London, 1994).

[15] World Health Organization *Human Organ Transplantation: A Report on Developments under the Auspices of WHO (1987*–1991) (Geneva, 1991), 8, Guiding Principle 3.

donors, except for transplantation of bone marrow and of other acceptable regenerative tissues.[16]

The purpose is both to serve the humanitarian goal of sparing living persons from the physical and emotional burdens of organ donation, and to reduce the incidence of donations that are inspired by material reward and the related commercialization of inter vivos organ donation.

Cadaveric recovery of organs for transplantation depends in law[17] on appro- **15.06** priate consents (see below at paras 15.28 *et seq*) and application of the legal criteria of death.[18] Persons in a persistent vegetative state, including those it is legally permissible to let die by withdrawal of artificial means of life support or of nutrition and hydration, are not dead because vital signs remain, notably spontaneous brain-stem activity.[19] However, following death, respiration and cardiac action may be artificially undertaken in order to preserve the tissue quality of organs for purposes of transplantation. Since both patients receiving intensive care and the bodies of deceased persons may be attached to medical devices that maintain heartbeat and oxygenation of tissues, the process of distinguishing the former from the latter is of legal significance.

The Human Tissue Act 1961 provides that death is determined when a **15.07** registered medical practitioner is satisfied by personal examination of a body that life is extinct.[20] In contrast, the legislation for instance in Ontario[21] provides in section 7 that:

(1) For the purposes of a *post mortem* transplant, the fact of death shall be determined by at least two physicians in accordance with accepted medical practice.

(2) No physician who has had any association with the proposed recipient that might influence the physician's judgment shall take any part in the determination of the fact of death of the donor.

(3) No physician who took any part in the determination of the fact of death of the donor shall participate in any way in the transplant procedures.

This provision recognizes both that while the criteria of death are governed by law, the law may defer to 'accepted medical practice', which is provable in judicial proceedings by expert evidence, and that the legally set criteria of

---

[16] ibid, 10.
[17] The issue is not just legal, however; see Hazony, O, 'Increasing the Supply of Cadaver Organs for Transplantation: Recognizing that the Real Problem is Psychological not Legal', (1993) *Health Matrix*, 3 219–57. [18] See Chapter 17.
[19] *Airedale National Health Service Trust v Bland* [1993] 1 AC 789 (HL).
[20] N 5 above, ss 1(4), 1(4A). [21] The Human Tissue Gift Act (n 8 above).

death are applied by physicians as a matter of judgment. This judgment determines the fact of death.

15.08 The Ontario legislation makes explicit what the Human Tissue Act 1961 leaves implicit, namely that a physician who determines death of a person must avoid any conflict of interest arising from any professional or personal association with the proposed recipient of that person's organ.[22] Management of such conflict is a matter both of law and of professional ethics. Physicians capable of determining death may be engaged in transplantation procedures in general. However, they are barred from making a determination when a potential donor may be the source of an organ of which one of their patients may be a recipient. The British Medical Association's ethical advice to the profession observes that:

> Awareness of a potential conflict of interest between donors and recipients has influenced the development of organ transplantation. The medical response to this in the conventional adult donor situation is to have two quite separate health care teams: one responsible for the care of the donor, the other responsible for the care of the recipient.[23]

Regarding dying patients who are potential donors, the advice is that '[n]o patient can be considered as a potential donor until all treatments for the benefit of that patient have been exhausted.'[24] As a patient, the dying potential donor may be expected to receive care from a health care team separate from that attending a potential recipient of that patient's posthumously donated organs. Departure from this principle may be excusable on grounds of unexpected emergency and necessity, but physicians would have to demonstrate that the welfare of the dying patient was not compromised and that they acted in good faith without advance knowledge of the likelihood of the recipient being a patient for whose care they become responsible.

15.09 Physicians and other health care professionals are legally accountable to their licensing or other disciplinary authorities, such as the General Medical Council, for unethical behaviour, such as failing satisfactorily to resolve conflicts of interest. Their duty to conduct themselves in accordance with professional ethics may be an implied term of contracts they enter, such as contracts for professional services. While Canadian courts are developing legal incidents of the fiduciary duties that physicians owe their patients,[25]

---

[22] Shaw, BW Jr, 'Conflict of Interest in the Procurement of Organs from Cadavers Following Withdrawal of Life Support', (1993) 3 *Kennedy Institute of Ethics J*, 179–87.
[23] British Medical Association, *Medical Ethics Today: Its Practice and Philosophy* (London, 1993), 26. [24] ibid, 28.
[25] *Norberg v Wynrib* (1992), 92 DLR (4th) 449 (Sup Ct Can); *McInerney v MacDonald* (1992), 93 DLR (4th) 415 (Sup Ct Can).

this approach has been rejected in England and other common law jurisdictions. However, whether as an incidence of a fiduciary duty or the common law duty of care, the duty to determine death competently, avoiding any conflict of interest, such as professional or personal commitments to potential recipients of organs that may be donated by or from patients whose deaths such physicians may be called on to determine, may be legally enforceable.

2. Anencephalic Neonates and Donors

Children born with the congenital absence of the cerebral cortex and of major **15.10** portions of the skull and scalp, described as anencephaly, may never achieve consciousness but nevertheless have a functioning brain stem, and so are not stillborn but born alive.[26] The condition is ordinarily incompatible with continuation of life beyond a few days, but measurement of the lifespan of anencephalic newborn children is compromised by the inability to apply brain death criteria to infants within the first few days after birth.[27] Claims that such infants are stillborn, however, or that they may be characterized if not as brain stem dead then as 'brain absent',[28] have no legal foundation. Because such children, born alive but dying, do not necessarily suffer genetic defects, their organs may be deemed appropriate for transplantation after death. Natural death, however, usually results in organ deterioration due to hypoxia and ischemia, so mechanical means may sometimes be used to maintain the quality of organs for posthumous transplantation. The acute shortage in the availability of infant-sized organs makes anencephalic sources particularly valuable to preserve the lives of newborn children suffering from organ failure. However, the Royal Medical colleges take the view that:

> organs for transplantation can be removed from anencephalic infants when two doctors who are not members of the transplant team agree that spontaneous respiration has ceased.[29]

Any removal may be legally authorized by a parent of the deceased infant[30] but it is doubtful whether a parent has legal power to consent to the use of mechanical means before death to preserve organs for posthumous recovery.[31]

---

[26] See *In the Matter of Baby K* (1993), 832 F Supp. 1022 (ED Va), affirmed (1994), 16 F 3d 590 (4th Cir), certiorari denied (1994), 115 S Ct 95 (US Sup Ct); and Chapter 17.

[27] See criteria for the diagnosis of brain stem death, (1995) 29 *J Royal College of Physicians*, 381, para (e), and Furrow, B R, Johnson, S H, Jost, T S and Schwartz, R L *Health Law: Cases, Materials and Problems* (St Paul, Minn, 2nd edn, 1991), 1049.

[28] McCullagh, P, *Brain Dead, Brain Absent, Brain Donors: Human Subjects or Human Objects?* (Chichester, 1993).

[29] Report of the Working Party of the Conference of Royal Medical Colleges and their Faculties in the United Kingdom on Organ Transplantation in Neonates, 1988.

[30] See para 15.33 below.   [31] See Chapter 17.

3. Foetal Tissue Donation

15.11   Foetal tissues include not only organs and cells from foetuses aborted spontaneously and electively, but also placentas and umbilical cord blood[32] available following childbirth. They have a variety of uses in research and increasingly in therapy, such as the employment of placental tissues in the manufacture of therapeutic pharmaceutical products and the treatment of burn victims, and the transplantation of foetal cells into patients suffering for instance from diabetes and such neurological disorders as Parkinson's disease.[33] Foetal tissue possesses four qualities that make it valuable for transplantation to overcome a range of medical problems. It can proliferate when implanted, undergo cell and tissue differentiation, produce growth factors, and, in contrast to adult tissue, not always provoke a significant immune response from the host tissue.[34] Products of spontaneous abortion may be valuable in types of research,[35] but their utility for therapeutically intended transplantation will remain very limited due to the high incidence of genetic abnormalities in foetuses that are spontaneously aborted. If miscarriage occurs late in pregnancy due to a traumatic event or comparable misfortune, however, foetal organs may become available and be suitable for transplantation into infants suffering organ failure. For purposes of gathering vital statistics, abortions may be distinguished from stillbirths, the latter being marked by such criteria as delivery of a dead foetus after twenty weeks of pregnancy or of foetal weight of 500 grams or more.[36] However, the terms 'abortion' and 'miscarriage', whether spontaneous or induced, may be regarded as synonymous.[37]

---

[32] Marshall, E, 'Clinical Promise, Ethical Quandry' (1996) 271 *Science*, 586–8 (transplanting umbilical cord blood as an alternative to bone marrow to treat a variety of life-threatening diseases).

[33] Because it is still novel and unproven, foetal neural cell transplantation into patients with Parkinson's disease tends to be classified as experimental, although it is therapeutic research, designed to benefit the patients, rather than pure research, designed to achieve generalizable knowledge for its own sake: see Goddard, J E, 'The NIH Revitalization Act of 1993 Washed Away Many Legal Problems with Fetal Tissue Transplantation Research But a Stain Remains', (1996) 49 Southern Methodist Univ L Rev, 375–99, 378, and Gelfand, G and Levin, T R, 'Fetal Tissue Research: Legal Regulation of Human Fetal Tissue Transplantation', (1993) 50 Washington and Lee L Rev, 647–94.

[34] Morgan, B, 'The Regulation of Fetal Tissue Transplantation' (1991) 14 Univ of New South Wales L J, 283–301, 284.

[35] The United Kingdom's Medical Research Council has maintained a centralized foetal tissue bank in London since 1957, which distributes between four and five thousand tissue samples each year, derived from some 800 foetal specimens: see Royal Commission (n 3 above), 983.   [36] See eg The [Ontario] Vital Statistics Act, RSO 1990, ch V-4 s 1.

[37] See Keown, I J, 'Miscarriage: a Medico-Legal Analysis' (1984) Criminal L Rev, 604–14.

Most contentious in foetal tissue transplantation, although minor in current **15.12** practice, is recovery of such tissues as foetal neural cells that can stimulate dopamine production when transplanted into patients suffering from Parkinson's disease,[38] and recovery of foetal islet cells from the pancreas for treatment of diabetes.[39] Recovery of such foetal tissues is controversial because it depends on elective abortions scheduled, for instance, before nine weeks of gestation in the case of treatment of Parkinson's disease, and during the fourteenth week for treatment of diabetes.[40] Further, the type of abortion procedure employed will affect the quality of the tissue and its utility for transplantation. A hysterotomy, similar to a caesarian section delivery, provides superior tissue because the foetus is damaged least, so that tissues can more easily be differentiated and recovered, but it presents the greatest risk of an adverse outcome to the health and future childbearing of the pregnant patient. In contrast, when appropriate to the stage of gestation, dilation and curettage procedures affect the patient the least, but are most destructive to foetal tissues.[41]

Recovery of foetal tissues for purposes of transplantation or research raises **15.13** central issues of patients' informed consent to abortion itself, its timing, and its method, since decisions on these matters affect the utility of resulting tissues for these purposes. Use for transplantation is closely analogous to use in research, and before transplantation becomes a therapeutic treatment of choice its procedures constitute clinical research. The Committee to Review the Guidance on the Research Use of Foetuses and Fetal Material (The Polkinghorne Committee) recommended that 'great care should be taken to separate the decisions relating to abortion and to the subsequent use of fetal material. The prior decision to carry out an abortion should be reached without consideration of the benefits of subsequent use.'[42] The Code of Practice the Committee recommended includes the provisions, among others, that:

> The decision to carry out an abortion must be reached without consideration of the benefit of subsequent use.[43]

---

[38] See Gelfand and Levin (n 33 above), 652.   [39] ibid.   [40] ibid.
[41] ibid.
[42] Review of the Guidance on the Research Use of Fetuses and Fetal Material, 1989, HMSO Cm 762, 9 para 4.1; see also Royal Commission (note 3 above); Recommendation 281 (b) at 998, and Recommendation 283, at 999, on separation of decisions on timing and methods of abortion from subsequent use of tissues. For a critique of the Royal Commission's approach, see Dickens, BM, 'The Ethics of Fetal-Tissue Donation: Consensus and Contradiction' (editorial) (1994) 151 *Canadian Med Assoc J*, 285–9.
[43] Review (n 42 above), 22 Code of Practice, para 3.1.

> The written consent of the mother must be obtained before any research or therapy involving the fetus or fetal tissue takes place.[44]

> Consent to the termination of pregnancy must be reached before consent is sought to the use of fetal tissue, and without reference to the possibility of that use. Provided the question of use is not introduced until consent to the termination of pregnancy has been obtained, it is permissible to deal with the two issues on the same occasion.[45]

The Committee required that the question of subsequent use of the foetus not be raised with a patient by counsellors until she had made the decision to terminate pregnancy, but recognized that it is impossible to prevent her putting questions about the method and timing of abortion in relation to subsequent use. The Committee considered, however, that 'since it will not be permissible to give any indication of the use to which any particular fetus might be put, or even if it will be used at all, it will not be possible to give advice of this kind.'[46]

15.14   General concerns regarding the legality of elective abortion[47] frame the legal issue of control of foetal tissues that could become available thereby for transplantation. Assuming that the pregnant woman will survive the procedure, which, under medical management, is now almost invariably the case,[48] the issue is whether:

(i)   she may give consent as a living donor of her own tissues;

(ii) she and/or the biological father or husband may give consent as for tissues of a deceased infant; or

(iii) she is precluded from participation in the consent process on the analogy that a person who kills another is usually unable to donate the victim's tissues.

The Code of Practice recommended by the Polkinghorne Committee requires the mother's consent, and observes that:

> It may be desirable to consult the father since, for example, tests on fetal tissue may reveal a finding of potential significance to him, and because he may have knowledge of a transmissible or hereditary disease, but his consent shall not be a requirement nor should he have the power to forbid research or therapy making use of fetal tissue.[49]

---

[44] ibid, 23, Code of Practice, para 4.1.   [45] ibid, para 4.2.
[46] Review (n 42 above) 14, para 6.6.   [47] See Chapter 11.
[48] Between 1984 and 1988, six women died from abortion in the United Kingdom, while 1,044,099 abortions were performed, including on women from outside the UK. The death rate of under one in 100,000 procedures makes abortion about 20 times as safe as pregnancy and childbirth; Lloyd, L 'Abortion and Health Care Ethics III' in Gillon, R and Lloyd, A (eds) *Principles of Health Care Ethics*, (Chichester, 1994), 559–576 at 566–7.
[49] Review (n 42 above), 23, para 4.3.

In the United States, the Uniform Anatomical Gift Act, adopted by all states, **15.15** generally with some modification, defines a 'decedent' as a 'deceased individual and includes a stillborn infant or foetus'.[50] This leaves some ambivalence regarding donation of foetal tissues, since either parent may consent to donation of tissues from a deceased infant. The Uniform Anatomical Gift Act permits the 'parents' of a decedent to donate the body or its parts,[51] but does not define 'parent'. This failure leaves open the issues of whether 'parent' includes a biological unmarried father, and whether paternity presumptions apply to the husbands of married women. The distinction has been proposed that:

> once the fetus is removed from the woman's body, it is no longer accurate to call it 'her' tissue in the same way that her liver or spleen would be called her tissue. The fetus is genetically distinct from her. It is a whole entity, not a functional part of an entity as is a woman's spleen, liver or kidney.[52]

This is not persuasive of a father's rights of disposition, however, since an intact dead foetus falls within the definition of an 'organ', which is controlled by the living source, under the Human Organ Transplants Act 1989,[53] and, like the foetus, the placenta is also genetically distinct from the mother, but it has never been suggested that it is at the biological father's disposal.[54]

Legal approaches to foetuses and foetal tissues are also conditioned by **15.16** judicial assertions that foetuses are not to be equated to persons. In *R v Tait*,[55] the Court of Appeal (Criminal Division) quashed the conviction of a man who threatened to kill a foetus in utero. He had been convicted of the offence against section 16 of the Offences against the Person Act 1861, as amended,[56] of making a threat to kill another 'or a third person'. The trial judge had directed the jury that 'Parliament . . . has not put any restriction on the definition of a third party,'[57] and left members of the jury to decide whether the unborn baby was such a person. The Criminal Division held this to be a misdirection, since 'the foetus in utero was not, in the ordinary sense, "another person", distinct from its mother.'[58] Similarly, the Supreme Court of Canada considered itself to be expressing the long-standing

---

[50] Uniform Anatomical Gift Act §1(2), 8A Uniform Laws Annotated (ULA) 9 (1987).
[51] ibid, §§3, 8A ULA 17.
[52] Bell, NMC, 'Regulating Transfer and Use of Fetal Tissue in Transplantation Procedures: The Ethical Dimensions', (1994) 20 Amer J Law and Medicine, 277–94, 287.
[53] See text at n 6 above.
[54] See the Royal Commission (n 3 above), Recommendation 276 at 983: 'Hospitals obtain consent from women, by means of written consent forms, regarding the disposal of placentas.'
[55] [1989] 3 WLR 891 (CA).
[56] 24 & 25 Vict ch 100 s 16, as substituted by the Criminal Law Act 1977, s 65, Sch 12.
[57] N 55 above, 895.   [58] ibid, 899.

common law in *R v Sullivan*[59] in observing that the expressions 'human being' and 'person' are synonymous, and that a foetus in the birth canal is not a person, so that negligence resulting in the pregnant woman suffering stillbirth is not convictable as manslaughter or criminal negligence causing death.[60]

15.17 Recipients of tissues from elective abortions, and of products developed from such tissues, who oppose such procedures in principle and consider any participants in or beneficiaries of their use to be complicit in immoral behaviour[61] may claim a legal right to know if any medical procedures or products proposed for them are tainted by this association.[62] The claim may be based on battery, alleging that consent to conduct of the transplant was vitiated by omission of information material to the patient's choice, or negligence in giving information, although in the latter, damage may be difficult to establish. Physicians proposing foetal neural cell transplants will usually inform patients, perhaps in naming the procedure. However, products developed from use of foetal tissues, such as vaccines against polio, measles, rubella, and other diseases and diagnostic tests for viral diseases including hepatitis, influenza and human immunodeficiency virus (HIV), tend not to disclose their development from foetal tissues, including from elective abortions, in information to the public. Patients with strong sensitivities may ask about the origins of products proposed for their use, of course, and must be honestly answered[63] with specific regard to their concerns. Fee-paying patients may so claim under contractual law on misrepresentation. Others' claims for negligent non-disclosure are buttressed where no 'therapeutic privilege' of non-disclosure is recognized,[64] but they still have to establish damage. Patients are entitled to decline use of products for their own purposes to which they have moral objections but, on analogy to Jehovah's Witness parents and blood transfusions, are not legally entitled to violate the legal duties they owe their children to supply them with medically indicated health care, including preventive health services.[65]

---

[59] (1991), 63 CCC (3d) 97 (Sup Ct Can).   [60] ibid, 106.
[61] See para 15.69 below.
[62] Finnis, J, 'Abortion and Health Care Ethics II' in Gillon and Lloyd, *Principles of Health Care Ethics* (n 48 above), 547–557, 554.
[63] See Lord Bridge, obiter in *Sidaway v Board of Governors of the Bethlem Royal Hospital* [1985] AC 871 (HL), 898.
[64] English law does not recognize 'therapeutic privilege'; see Kennedy and Grubb (n 8 above), 211–15.
[65] See *In re B (A Minor) (Wardship; Sterilisation)*, [1988] 1 AC 199 (HL) and para 15.21 below.

4. The Legal Status of Tissues Outside the Body

Dead bodies have long been governed by the 'no property' rule of the **15.18** common law, despite its insecure historical foundations,[66] and, since the abolition of slavery, living persons have not been considered the subject of property.[67] This raises the issue of the legal status of tissues that have come from persons while they are living[68] or following death.[69] A highly visible modern case in the Supreme Court of California, *Moore v Regents of the University of California*,[70] concerned a man from whose tissues (acquired without his understanding the purpose for which they were requested), a valuable cell-line was developed and patented for commercial exploitation. He sued on thirteen causes of action, but was finally allowed to proceed only on his claims for lack of his informed consent to non-therapeutic tissue donation, which in essence was a claim in negligence,[71] and for breach of fiduciary duty.[72] His claim for violation of alleged property rights in his tissue, based on the tort of conversion, was rejected.[73] The Court found that, because Moore had voluntarily surrendered his tissues to his physicians, he clearly did not expect to retain possession of them, and no precedents supported his claim of ownership, either directly or indirectly.[74] The narrower ground on which the property claim was rejected was California's Health and Safety Code, which required human tissues, following conclusion of scientific use, to be disposed of by interment, incineration, or any other specified method to protect public health and safety.[75] The Court concluded that:

> the statute's practical effect is to limit, drastically, a patient's control over excised cells . . . the statute eliminates so many of the rights ordinarily attached to

---

[66] Matthews, P, 'Whose Body? People as Property', (1983) 36 Current Legal Problems, 193–239.

[67] For a pre-abolition case of property in slaves, see *Gregson v Gilbert* (1783) 3 Dougl 232, 99 ER 629 (KB).

[68] For background, see Dickens, B M, 'The Control of Living Body Materials', (1977) 27 Univ Toronto Law J, 142–98.

[69] For a modern analysis, see Dworkin, G and Kennedy, I, 'Human Tissue: Rights in the Body and Its Parts', (1993) 1 Med L Rev, 291–319. [70] N 2 above.

[71] *Cobbs v Grant* (1972) 501 P 2d 1 (Cal Sup Ct); in Canada, compare *Reibl v Hughes (1980)*, 114 DLR (3d) 1 (Sup Ct Can). [72] N 2 above, 485.

[73] ibid, 493–7.

[74] In *R v Stillman* (1997) 113 CCC (3d) 321, 348, the Supreme Court of Canada indicated that when a person voluntarily surrenders or abandons bodily tissues, others may acquire and use them without the person's consent. For an argument in favour of a person's inchoate right of ownership in tissues involuntarily severed from the person's body, see Dickens, B M (n 68 above), 180–3. [75] California Health and Safety Code §7054.4 (West Supp 1992).

property that one cannot simply assume that what is left amounts to 'property' or 'ownership' for purposes of conversion law.[76]

The broader ground on which the Court refused to extend the tort of conversion to protect Moore's interest in the tissues which were removed, was the chilling effect this would have on biotechnological development, since conversion of property is a tort of strict liability[77] that would create legal liability in even innocent and bona fide holders of the property. The Court observed that:

> Research on human cells plays a critical role in medical research. This is so because researchers are increasingly able to isolate naturally occurring, medically useful biological substances and to produce useful quantities of such substances through genetic engineering . . . Products developed through biotechnology . . . include treatments and tests for leukaemia, cancer, diabetes, dwarfism, hepatitis-B, kidney transplant rejection, emphysema, osteoporosis, ulcers, anaemia, infertility and gynaecological tumours to name but a few.

> The extension of conversion law into this area will hinder research by restricting access to the necessary raw materials.[78]

In expressing the pragmatic basis of its conclusion, however, the Court left open the issue of principle. It declared that:

> We do not purport to hold that excised cells can never be property for any purpose whatsoever . . .[79] and emphasized that its concern was the protection of:

> innocent parties who are engaged in socially useful activities, such as researchers who have no reason to believe that their use of a particular cell sample is, or may be, against a donor's wishes.[80]

15.19 Accordingly, a living source of tissue outside the body who made clear that he or she had no intention of abandoning or donating it in general, or in an unrestricted way, could in principle assert a property interest in it.[81] This might be particularly so if he or she, like those the Supreme Court of California was concerned to protect, was 'engaged in socially useful activities', such as being an altruistic tissue donor to a designated recipient like a family member affected by organ failure.[82] The pragmatism that protects a medical

---

[76] N 2 above, 492.
[77] See eg *Byer v Canadian Bank of Commerce* (1937) 65 P 2d 67 (Cal Sup Ct).
[78] N 2 above, 494 (citations omitted).   [79] ibid, 493.
[80] N 2 above, 494 (citations omitted).
[81] See the differing views of Weisman, J, 'Organs as Assets', (1994) 27 Israel L Rev, 610–23; Tedeschi, G, 'Ownership of Organs Taken from a Living Person', ibid, 624–51, and Weisman, J, '"Ownership", "Assets" and "Transferability of Property Rights"' ibid, 652–60.
[82] Where A donates an organ for the benefit of B, but the organ is transferred to C, claims of A and B against the transferor and C would be governed by principles of property law on transfer between A and B, but the transferor and perhaps C might be convicted on prosecution for theft or conspiracy if they acted knowingly.

or scientific researcher's property interest in abandoned human cells over that of the source's would also operate to protect the source's property interest in tissue that the source intended for a comparably valuable social interest such as organ donation, for instance to a family member.[83]

A reason to resist recognition of human tissues as property, whether from living or deceased sources,[84] is the way recognition might open to objectionable commerce.[85] However, legislation and judicial policy, for instance on contracts held to be void as being contrary to public policy, may offer adequate safeguards against commercialization of human organs and other tissues.[86] Indeed, the legislative prohibition of commercial traffic in human tissue[87] may confirm its legal status as property.[88]   **15.20**

Tissue banking is increasingly common, including eye banks, blood banks, breast milk banks and, for instance, cord blood stem cell banks. Operators of banks require legal security in their control of the materials they gather and preserve. Particularly sensitive are reproductive tissues and pre-embryos.[89] Beyond objections to treating a pre-embryo as property based on concepts of ensoulment are Kantian objections to treating people as objects, or only as means to ends, and to treating potential people as objects. Nevertheless, in *York v Jones*,[90] the US District Court for the Eastern District of Virginia found a bailor–bailee relationship to arise from the contract between a couple whose pre-embryo was preserved in the freezing facility of an infertility clinic, and the clinic,[91] thereby creating the implication that the pre-embryo was property. In 1992, the Tennessee Supreme Court rejected the implication that frozen pre-embryos are subject to property rights, however, and held them to   **15.21**

---

[83] See Dickens, BM, 'Living Tissue and Organ Donors and Property Law: More on *Moore*', (1992) 8 J Contemp Health Law and Policy, 73–93.

[84] On non-proprietary remedies for improper removal of cadaveric material, see Skegg, PDG, 'Liability for the Unauthorised Removal of Cadaveric Transplant Material' (1974) 14 Medicine, Science and Law, 53–7; Kennedy, I, 'Further Thoughts on Liability for Non-observance of the Provisions of the Human Tissue Act 1961' (1976) 16 Medicine, Science and Law, 49–55; Skegg, PDG, 'Liability for the Unauthorized Removal of Cadaveric Transplant Material: Some Further Thoughts', (1977) 17 Medicine, Science and Law 123–6.

[85] See Wagner, DM, 'Property Rights in the Human Body: The Commercialization of Organ Transplantation and Biotechnology', (1995) 33 *Duquesne Law Rev*, 931–59.

[86] See discussion of the Human Organ Transplants Act 1989, para 15.36 below.

[87] Influenced by the *Moore* case (n 2 above), for instance, the California State Legislature enacted a law that prohibits donors from receiving any 'valuable consideration' for donation. Cal Health and Safety Code §7155(a) (West Supp 1992).

[88] The Nuffield Council (n 1 above) made further recommendations for elimination of commerce, including the use of non-commercial agencies and payments for expenses only: see ch 6, 49–53.

[89] Meaning embryos prior to implantation in utero; see McCormick, RA, 'Who or What is the Preembryo?', (1991) 1 *Kennedy Institute of Ethics J*, 1–15.

[90] (1989), 717 F Supp 421 (EDVa).   [91] ibid, 425.

be neither property nor living beings, but sui generis.[92] The Court observed that:

> pre-embryos are not strictly speaking either 'persons' or 'property', but occupy an interim category that entitles them to special respect because of their potential for human life.[93]

Nevertheless the Court, while stating that the formerly married couple did not have a 'true property interest' in the pre-embryos, held that:

> they do have an interest in the nature of ownership to the extent that they have decision-making authority concerning disposition of the pre-embryos, within the scope of policy set by law.[94]

Despite declaring the pre-embryos' entitlement to special respect because of their potential for life as human persons, the Court permitted the ex-husband's right not to procreate to outweigh his ex-wife's interest in donating them to a childless couple, while suggesting obiter that only the ex-wife's interest in using the pre-embryos herself could outweigh the ex-husband's right, and then only if she could not become pregnant with her own genetic child by any other means.[95]

15.22 In *Hecht v Superior Court*,[96] the California Court of Appeals, reversing the trial court, held that a man who died, by suicide, could bequeath to his girlfriend an interest in sperm he had previously deposited in a sperm bank, just as he could bequeath an interest in stock. However, under Schedule 3 of the Human Fertilisation and Embryology Act 1990,[97] section 2(2)(b) requires that a consent to the storage of any gametes or any embryo must 'state what is to be done with the gametes or embryo if the person who gave the consent dies'. In *R v Human Fertilisation and Embryology Authority, ex p Blood*,[98] sperm samples were taken from a comatose man at his wife's request shortly before his death. He gave no consent or directions as to their posthumous use. The Court of Appeal upheld a ruling that storage of the sperm did not comply with legal requirements under the Act, and that the HFEA was entitled to refuse to allow the wife exceptional use of the sperm without the donor's written consent. However, the Court also held that, since the donor's wife was entitled to receive medical treatment in the European Community under articles 59 and 60 of the European Community Treaty,[99] and the HFEA is entitled under section 24(4) of the 1990 Act to authorise the sending of gametes outside the United Kingdom, where limits of the 1990

---

[92] *Davis v Davis* (1992), 842 SW 2d 588 (Tenn Sup Ct).   [93] ibid, 597.
[94] ibid.   [95] ibid, 604.   [96] (1993), 20 Cal Rptr 2d 275 (Cal Ct App).
[97] 1990 ch 37.   [98] [1997] 2 WLR 806 (CA).
[99] OJ 1992 No C224, p 6.

Act do not apply, the Authority's refusal to allow the sperm to be sent abroad would be set aside and the Authority be invited to reconsider whether to authorise release of the stored sperm in another member state.[100] This is consistent with the European Court of Human Rights limiting state restriction of individuals' intimate consensual conduct.[101]

The operation of sperm, ova and embryo storage facilities in the United **15.23** Kingdom must comply with the terms of licences granted by the Human Fertilisation and Embryology Authority under the 1990 Act.[102] At the private level, sperm banks properly treat sperm as property of the donors,[103] and third party holders of ova and pre-embryos might be advised to act on the same basis. Nevertheless, in order not to violate legal prohibitions on sales of human tissues and to avoid breach of warranty provisions, sperm donation is usually treated as a service[104] rather than a commodity transaction,[105] and ova and pre-embryo donation may be approached similarly. A service can include an incidental transfer of property, maintaining the status of gametes and pre-embryos as legal property. Interests in preserving availability of such materials for scientific research and education may be protected in terms of the agreements under which possession of them may lawfully be transferred and managed. Donors' property rights protect their interests against uses they do not authorize. However, compensation for property loss or damage alone is usually set at its fair market value, but in the case of gametes and embryos legislation or judicial policy may preclude a market evaluation.[106]

---

[100] See Chapter 10.

[101] See for instance, *Dudgeon v United Kingdom* (1981), 45 Eur Ct HR (ser A) (Eur Ct HR). [102] See n 97 above, and Chapter 10.

[103] See Collins, J L, '*Hecht v Superior Court*: Recognizing a Property Right in Reproductive Material' (1994–95) 33 J Family Law, 661–84, 669, 675.

[104] By directions made in Britain by the Human Fertilisation and Embryology Authority (HFEA Directions, as amended Feb 1996; see HFEA Fifth Annual Report, July 1996, 18) individual donors of gametes may be paid a maximum of £15 for each donation plus reasonable expenses incurred. The Authority intends eventually to phase out payment (HFEA *Second Annual Report*, 1993, 29).

[105] See Dickens, B M, 'Reproduction Law and Medical Consent', (1985) 35 *Univ Toronto L J*, 255–86, 284, and Hodgson, A M, 'Note: The Warranty of Sperm: A Modest Proposal to Increase the Accountability of Sperm Banks and Physicians in the Performance of Artificial Insemination Procedures' (1993) 26 Indiana L Rev, 357–86, 367.

[106] For an alternative basis of assessment of loss see Collins (n 103 above), 682–3.

C. Post Mortem Use

1. Introduction

15.24   Recovery of transplantable organs from cadavers raises fewer legal issues than their donation by living persons, but issues that arise are nevertheless profound and at time complex. Development of the concept of brain-stem death or neurological death permits recovery of materials for transplantation from bodies of persons who are diagnosed to be dead, even though their hearts continue to beat through the artificial means that have been used for their care, and their organs thereby remain transfused and viable for transplantation.[107] Where a distinction is drawn between organs and tissues, turning on the potential for spontaneous regeneration,[108] it remains relevant notwithstanding the death of the source, since the distinction is generic to the materials themselves and not specific to the individual human source.

15.25   The historical management of bodies of dead persons under provisions of ecclesiastical law, the common law's so-called 'no property' rule which affected testamentary gifts and intestate succession,[109] and the emergence of medical transplantation only in the last few decades, denied the common law system opportunities to develop long standing principles on removal of materials for therapeutic purposes. Modern laws on post mortem recovery of organs and tissues for transplantation rest on legislation, historically founded on removal of corneas.[110] Legislation may govern post mortem availability of the whole body for educational, research or therapeutic purposes, and therapy would involve transplantation of particular organs or tissues.

15.26   The terms of the consent would govern the availability of individual organs or tissues for transplantation, and the range of users and recipients. Most donations are in general terms, but a consent may be limited to recipients in specified disease categories, or for instance to users in a particular institution such as a named hospital or university medical centre, perhaps as a response to an institutional drive to increase donations or a publicized case. Individuals making donations in anticipation of their death, and persons in lawful possession of bodies after death who are permitted under the terms of legislation to authorize acquisition of materials for transplantation, may specify the extent of the donation or authorization they are willing to approve. In principle this is a private discretion, although circumstances

---

[107]   See Chapter 17, paras 17.04–17.09 on Development of Criteria of Brain Stem Death.
[108]   See para 15.03 above.   [109]   See Chapter 17, para 17.38.
[110]   See the Corneal Grafting Act 1952.

may arise in which the person lawfully in possession of a body is a public or quasi-public officer, such as when a person dies in a public facility like a prison, public shelter, or hospital and no family member claims the body for burial or cremation. A concern for potential recipient institutions is whether they may lawfully accept a donation or authorization that draws an invidious distinction, for instance among members of racial groups for whose thera-peutic care materials may be used. A positive selection, such as to favour residents of a specified area, a hospital with an affinity with a religious denomination, or recipients in given age categories may be more acceptable than a negative selection, such as to deny transplantation to members of a given race or religion, but each form of expression must be critically assessed to determine whether the purpose is to exclude identified persons as recipients on an offensive ground. Acceptance of donations made on discriminatory terms may violate international and national human rights principles enforce-able by law, and, more immediately, an institution's own by-laws.

2. Legislation on Post Mortem Use for Transplantation

In Britain, the Human Tissue Act 1961[111] provides in section 1 that: **15.27**

(1)   If any person, either in writing at any time or orally in the presence of two or more witnesses during his last illness, has expressed a request that his body or any specified part of his body be used after his death for therapeutic purposes or for purposes of medical education or research, the person lawfully in possession of his body after his death may, unless he has reason to believe that the request was subsequently withdrawn, authorise the removal from the body of any part or, as the case may be, the specified part, for use in accordance with the request.

(2)   Without prejudice to the foregoing subsection, the person lawfully in possession of the body of a deceased person may authorise the removal of any part from the body for use for the said purposes if, having made such reasonable enquiry as may be practicable, he has not reason to believe

   (a)   that the deceased had expressed an objection to his body being so dealt with after his death, and had not withdrawn it; or

   (b)   that the surviving spouse or any surviving relative of the deceased objects to the body being so dealt with.

(3)   Subject to subsections (4) and (5) of this section, the removal and use of any part of a body in accordance with an authority given in pursuance of this section shall be lawful.

---

[111] N 5 above.

(4) No such removal shall be effected except by a fully registered medical practitioner, who must have satisfied himself by personal examination of the body that life is extinct.

(4A) No such removal of an eye or part of an eye shall be effected except by

    (a) a registered medical practitioner who must have satisfied himself by personal examination of the body that life is extinct; or

    (b) a person in the employment of a health authority or NHS trust acting on the instructions of a registered medical practitioner who must, before giving those instructions, be satisfied that the person in question is sufficiently qualified and trained to perform the removal competently and must also either

        (i) have satisfied himself by personal examination of the body that life is extinct, or

        (ii) be satisfied that life is extinct on the basis of a statement to that effect by a registered medical practitioner who has satisfied himself by personal examination of the body that life is extinct.[112]

(5) Where a person has reason to believe that an inquest may be required to be held on any body or that a post-mortem examination of any body may be required by the coroner, he shall not, except with the consent of the coroner,

    (a) give an authority under this section in respect of the body; or

    (b) act on such authority given by any other person.

(6) No authority shall be given under this section in respect of any body by a person entrusted with the body for the purpose only of its interment or cremation.

(7) In the case of a body lying in a hospital, nursing home or other institution, any authority under this section may be given on behalf of the person having the control and management thereof by any officer or person designated for that purpose by the first-mentioned person.

(8) Nothing in this section shall be construed as rendering unlawful any dealing with, or with any part of, the body of a deceased person which is lawful apart from the Act.

(9) In the application of this section to Scotland, for subsection (5) there shall be substituted the following subsection

    (5) Nothing in this section shall authorise the removal of any part

---

[112] Section 4A was added, with related adjustments, by the Corneal Tissue Act 1986, s 1.

from a body in any case where the procurator fiscal has objected to such removal.

(i) *Consent: The Deceased Donor*

A person who wishes to express a request that the person lawfully in posses- **15.28** sion of his or her body or parts of it authorise use of tissues following death for transplantation may do so in one of two forms. The more usual is in writing. No specified form has been established for this purpose by legislation or regulation, and the form attached for instance to a motor vehicle driving licence has no special legal status. Donation post mortem in writing need not be witnessed and no confirmation of capacity is required. If the purported donor lacks relevant capacity,[113] or if capacity is questionable, the person lawfully in possession of the body may nevertheless authorize removal of any part from the body for transplantation under section 1(2), unless there is reason to believe that the deceased had expressed an objection and not withdrawn it.[114] If doubt exists about a donor's competence to give the consent that was expressed, the person in possession of the body may under-write that consent through that person's authority under section 1(2). How-ever, if there is doubt about the capacity of a person who expressed an objection to donation, the person in possession might be advised not to consent in his or her own capacity. Incapacity on the part of the deceased may be a separate ground for caution in use of material for transplantation, of course, if the condition has a genetic origin or may be due, for instance, to AIDS-related dementia.

The alternative to written consent is oral consent expressed in the presence of **15.29** two or more witnesses during the donor's last illness. What constitutes a last illness is a matter of medical evidence of the cause of death and of the natural pathology of the disorder. An oral statement by a sick person who shortly afterwards suffers death from a cause unrelated to the illness, such as a road traffic accident, might not be considered adequate for purposes of section 1(1) of the Act, although evidence of the statement may reinforce consent given by the person lawfully in possession of the body under section 1(2). However, the donor's suicide in the course of that illness may be considered to be pathologically related to it, although a coroner's jury's verdict of suicide while the balance of the mind was disturbed may cast doubt on contempora-neous capacity. In the case of testamentary documents, witnesses attest only to the freedom of the testator's signature, not that the testator competently

---

[113] See generally Chapter 4.   [114] See s 1(2)(a).

intends the consequences of the will. Under the 1961 Act, however, witnesses have to recognize the nature of the donor's oral expression, and be satisfied that the donor intends to make the request and any limitations or conditions that accompany it. Further, unlike witnesses to a will, they are apparently not precluded from subsequently becoming beneficiaries under the donation. The Act contains no requirement that witnesses be adults, but the younger a witness is, or the less capacity a witness possesses for a reason unrelated to age, the less reliable the oral statement may appear.

15.30 The Act similarly sets no minimum age to request donation. Section 8(1) of the Family Law Reform Act 1969[115] provides that the consent to medical treatment of a minor of sixteen or above 'shall be as effective as it would be if he were of full age'. Although a request for donation is not 'treatment',[116] this may be applied by analogy to posthumous donation. However, the oral expression of a person younger than sixteen may serve only as reinforcement of consent given under section 1(2). Equally problematic is whether the written donation request of a minor would be effective under section 1(1). Posthumous donation is not the type of medical procedure to which section 8(1) of the 1969 Act applies, but the Act may embody the common law mature minor rule in this regard despite the Act's general purpose to reform the law. Again, if a donor younger than eighteen, or sixteen, cannot make an effective written posthumous donation request, willingness to donate may be the basis of a section 1(2) consent given by the person in possession of the young person's body.

15.31 It must be noted, however, that the donation of even an adult of unquestioned capacity in anticipation of death does not compel the person in subsequent possession of the donor's body to make it available for recovery of transplantable materials. Section 1(1) of the Human Tissue Act 1961 describes a donation only as 'a request', and provides that the person lawfully in possession of the body after death 'may . . . authorise the removal from the body of any part or, as the case may be, the specified part, for use in accordance with the request.' The request is not simply for medical assessment of the body's suitability for recovery of transplantable materials, but for favourable exercise of discretion by the person in lawful possession. The request may be frustrated not simply because, at death, the body is unsuitable for use of its materials, for example due to organ damage, genetic defect, or infection of tissue, but also because the person in lawful possession of the body declines to respect the request, for whatever reason. It is doubtful that a

---

[115] 1969, ch 46.
[116] *Re W (A Minor) (Medical Treatment)* [1992] 4 All ER 627, *per* Nolan LJ at 647.

potential recipient person or institution has standing to compel that person's exercise of discretion in favour of compliance with the deceased person's request,[117] or that a request for posthumous donation constitutes an enforceable trust binding the person subsequently in possession of the body. If the 'person' lawfully in possession of the body is a public body such as a hospital trust, its exercise of discretion might be amenable to judicial review to determine whether it had been lawfully exercised but, unless its decision is patently unreasonable, courts will be slow to interfere.[118]

By section 1(2), the person in possession of a body may not authorise recovery of materials for transplantation if, 'having made such reasonable enquiry as may be practicable', which the person is obliged to make, he or she has reason to believe that the deceased objected to such dealing with the body, or 'that the surviving spouse or any surviving relative of the deceased objects to the body being so dealt with.'[119] The Act sets no limits on proximity of relatives who are empowered to veto the deceased person's request, or on the relative's age or capacity.[120] Accordingly, remote relatives who are identified after the reasonable enquiry that it is practicable for the person in lawful possession of the body to make, may veto the deceased person's request, and apparently the concurring request of that person's spouse and of a more proximate relative. A remote relative who takes an initiative to notify the person in lawful possession of the body of his or her objection will not depend on the person's reasonable enquiry[121] for the veto to have effect. The Act seems to afford the person in possession of the body no power to follow a near relative's consent to removal of materials over a more distance relative's objection. The veto may be open to legal challenge, however, if, for instance, the deceased had failed to express a request in conformity with section 1(1) but could be shown to have wished for posthumous donation to assist survival of a more proximate relative than the objector, such as a child, brother or sister of the deceased. By contrast to the Human Tissue Act, legislation may explicitly favour the deceased person's preference of donation

15.32

---

[117] Difficulties in potential recipients' enforcement are recognized in Jardine, DG, 'Liability Issues Arising Out of Hospitals' and Organ Procurement Organizations' Rejection of Valid Anatomical Gifts', (1990) Wisconsin L Rev, 1655–94, 1680–6.

[118] See *R v HFEA, ex p Blood* (n 98 above), 821, and *R v Sheffield Health Authority, ex p Seale* [1996] 3 Med L Rev 326 and accompanying Commentary.

[119] Section 1(2)(b) (n 5 above).

[120] Skegg, PDG argues that 'relative' is limited to genetic or blood relatives, as opposed to a relative by marriage, since the Act contrasts the spouse with 'any surviving relative'; see 'Human Tissue Act 1961', (1976) 16 *Medicine, Science and Law* 193–9, 197.

[121] On 'reasonable enquiry', see Skegg, PDG, ibid, and Dworkin, G, 'The Law Relating to Organ Transplantation in England' (1970) 33 MLR, 353–77, 364–5. Kennedy and Grubb (n 9 above) at 1155 favour the latter's interpretation.

over the interest of an objecting relative, including a spouse. For instance, Ontario's Human Tissue Gift Act[122] permits the donor's consent to posthumous use of body materials to prevail over family members' opposition. Section 4(3) provides that:

> Upon the death of a person who has given a consent under this section, the consent is binding and is full authority for the use of the body or the removal and use of the specified part of parts for the purpose specified, except that no person shall act upon a consent . . . if the person has reason to believe that it was subsequently withdrawn.

(ii) Consent: The Person in Lawful Possession of the Body

15.33 It has been held that executors of a deceased person's estate have a right to lawful possession of the body.[123] Burial or cremation expenses are a charge on the deceased's assets, and those responsible for their administration possess legal power to direct disposition of the deceased's mortal remains. Since recovery of materials for transplantation may affect plans for disposition, the 1961 Act gives those in possession of the body power to authorize removal of such materials. However, without affecting the financial responsibility for disposal of remains, subsection 7 of section 1 of the 1961 Act provides that when a body is lying in such an institution as a hospital or nursing home, power to authorize removal of any part of the body for purposes of the Act may be given by the institution through someone designated by the person having control and management of the institution.

15.34 This is a matter on which details of legislation vary. For instance, in contrast to the 1961 Act, Ontario's Human Tissue Gift Act[124] establishes a hierarchy of persons entitled to consent to removal of transplantable material from the body of a person who, when living, neither expressed consent nor demonstrated objection. The spouse, child, parent, brother or sister and other next of kin are ranked in that order, one higher in rank who is readily available displacing all lower in rank. A peer in rank who objects might negate another's consent, since:

> no person shall act on a consent given under this section if the person has actual knowledge of an objection thereto by the person in respect of whom the consent was given or by a person of the same or closer relationship to the person in respect of whom the consent was given than the person who gave the consent.[125]

---

[122] N 8 above.   [123] *Williams v Williams* (1882), 20 ChD 659.
[124] N 8 above.   [125] ibid, s 5(4).

In the absence of a ranked family member and of other next of kin, consent may be given by 'the person lawfully in possession of the body other than, where the person died in hospital, the administrative head of the hospital.'[126] The 'person lawfully in possession of the body' further excludes the Chief Coroner and a coroner in possession of the body under provincial legislation governing coroners, the Public Guardian and Trustee in possession for purposes of burial or cremation, an embalmer or funeral director and the superintendent of a crematorium.[127] Canadian case law[128] recognizes a general right to possession of the body of a deceased person in the surviving spouse or next of kin. It is not clear that a similar right is recognized under the British 1961 Act, or that that Act excludes coroners as such, since section 1(8) provides that nothing in section 1 renders unlawful any dealing with a body or part of a body that is lawful apart from the Act. A coroner's consent is necessary for removal of material from a body where an inquest or post mortem examination may be required, in addition to that of any other person,[129] and in Scotland no removal is authorized where the procurator fiscal has objected.[130] Further, in no case shall authority be given to remove materials from any body 'by a person entrusted with the body for the purpose only of its interment or cremation.'[131]

An addition to the Ontario legislation, designed to enhance the utility of **15.35** recovered materials, is that, in advance of the imminent death of a person incapable of giving consent to posthumous donation, a family member may approve such donation. Section 5(2) provides that:

> Where a person who has not given or cannot give a consent . . . dies, or in the opinion of a physician is incapable of giving a consent by reason of injury or disease and the person's death is imminent,
>
> (a) the person's spouse; or
> (b) if none or if the spouse is not readily available, any of the person's children
> . . .
>
> may consent,
>
> (g) in a writing signed by the spouse, relative or other person; or
> (h) orally by the spouse, relative or other person in the presence of at least two witnesses; or
> (i) by a telegraphic, recorded telephonic, or other recorded message of the spouse, relative or other person,
>
> to the body or the part of parts thereof specified in the consent being used after death for therapeutic purposes, medical education or scientific research.

---

[126] ibid, s 5(2)(f).   [127] ibid, s 5(5).
[128] *Edmonds v Armstrong Funeral Home Ltd* [1931] 1 DLR 676 (Alta SC).
[129] N 5 above, s 1(5).   [130] ibid, s 1(9).   [131] ibid, s 1(6).

The section repeats the hierarchy of relatives and others empowered to consent, and is subject to the condition that no person may give consent who has reason to believe that the person whose death is imminent would have objected. The provision anticipates, for instance, a sudden trauma such as a road traffic injury, and a relative rushing to a hospital emergency department or being reached by telephone. Further, although a coroner normally has jurisdiction only over dead bodies, section 6 of the Act provides that where, in the opinion of the physician, the death of a person is imminent by reason of injury or disease and the physician has reason to believe an inquest or post mortem examination will be held but that consent has been given to posthumous donation, the physician may obtain the coroner's directions in advance of death to remove relevant materials after death. This places the coroner on notice of intended donation, and permits the coroner to give such directions as will optimize recovery of materials after death for transplantation.

(iii) *Payment: Legislation*

15.36 The Human Organ Transplants Act 1989[132] provides in section 1 that:

> (1) A person is guilty of an offence if in Great Britain he
>
> > (a) makes or receives any payment for the supply of, or for an offer to supply, an organ which has been or is to be removed from a dead or living person and is intended to be transplanted into another person whether in Great Britain or elsewhere;
> >
> > (b) seeks to find a person willing to supply for payment such an organ . . . or offers to supply such an organ for payment;
> >
> > (c) initiates or negotiates any arrangement involving the making of any payment for the supply of, or for an offer to supply, such an organ; or
> >
> > (d) takes part in the management or control of a body of persons corporate or unincorporate whose activities consist of or include the initiation or negotiation of such arrangements.
>
> (2) Without prejudice to paragraph (b) of subsection (1) above, a person is guilty of an offence if he causes to be published or distributed, or knowingly publishes or distributes, in Great Britain an advertisement
>
> > (a) inviting persons to supply for payment any such organs as are mentioned in paragraph (a) of that subsection or offering to supply any such organs for payment; or
> >
> > (b) indicating that the advertiser is willing to initiate or negotiate any such arrangement as is mentioned in paragraph (c) of that subsection.

---

[132] N 6 above.

(3) In this section 'payment' means payment in money or money's worth but does not include any payment for defraying or reimbursing

   (a) the cost of removing, transporting or preserving the organ to be supplied; or

   (b) any expenses or loss of earnings incurred by a person so far as reasonably and directly attributable to his supplying an organ from his body.

(4) In this section 'advertisement' includes any form of advertising whether to the public generally, to any section of the public or individually to selected persons.

Section 4 of the Act provides that:

(1) Where an offence under this Act committed by a body corporate is proved to have been committed with the consent or connivance of, or to be attributable to any neglect on the part of, any director, manager, secretary or other similar officer of the body corporate or any person who was purporting to act in any such capacity, he as well as the body corporate is guilty of the offence and is liable to be proceeded against and punished accordingly.

(2) Where the affairs of a body corporate are managed by its members, subsection (1) above shall apply to the acts and defaults of a member in connection with his functions of management as if he were a director of the body corporate.

(iv) *Payment: Commodities and Services*

The distinction between organs and tissues is significant to the prohibitions **15.37** and punishments of the Human Organ Transplants Act 1989, since they apply only to organs. Section 7(2) provides that:

> In this Act, 'organ' means any part of a human body consisting of a structured arrangement of tissues which, if wholly removed, cannot be replicated by the body.

Accordingly, payments for naturally replicable materials such as blood and bone marrow would not violate the Act.[133] In contrast, the Ontario Human Tissue Gift Act,[134] for instance, provides in section 10 that:

> No person shall buy, sell or otherwise deal in, directly or indirectly, for a valuable consideration, any tissue for a transplant, or any body or part or parts thereof other than blood or a blood constituent, for therapeutic purposes, medical education or scientific research, and any such dealing is invalid as being contrary to public policy.

---

[133] But see the following section on contracts that are void as contrary to public policy.
[134] N 8 above.

The extension of the prohibition to a body and its parts is significant, since the Act defines 'tissue' much as the British 1989 Act defines 'organ', and it 'does not include . . . tissue that is replaceable by natural processes of repair.'[135] It has been seen that sperm donors receive payment not for the sperm themselves but for the time and inconvenience, including for instance repeated HIV testing, of making them available.[136] Payment for service is consistent with section 1(3) of the 1989 Act, which permits payment for costs and expenses involved in organ donation. Clause (b) of the section, permitting recovery of expenses which a person incurs that are attributable 'to his supplying an organ from his body', clearly relates only to donations made by living persons, but clause (a) allows reimbursement of 'the cost of removing, transporting or preserving the organ to be supplied', which would allow repayment of costs to executors and others responsible for deceased persons' assets when organ recovery increases costs of management of the body. Where physicians who remove materials for transplantation are paid on a fee-for-service basis, for instance, the estate may be charged, since costs may not be directly transferable to a recipient patient or institution, particularly when organs are transferable to distant locations and countries. Accordingly, donors' estates may pay these costs directly, and be entitled to appropriate reimbursement.

15.38 The legislation in Ontario that renders commercial dealings 'invalid as contrary to public policy' may reflect the position at common law that results from the criminalization of commercial dealings achieved by the 1989 Act. Common law provisions on entitlement to money or other consideration actually exchanged under an illegal agreement will apply, as will provisions on recovery of money and its equivalent, and the illegal agreement will not be enforceable by any court. It must be asked, however, how common law principles apply to commerce in tissues, the exchange of which for reward is not prohibited under the terms of the 1989 Act. Courts may apply the spirit of the Ontario legislation, and conclude that these agreements are void as being contrary to public policy. Recipients of money, and of tissues, under such void agreements may nevertheless be recognized to have obtained legal title to them. Lawyers who draft agreements that are merely unenforceable face no professional disciplinary charges. Many agreements for personal services, such as in the conduct of the entertainment and sports industries, are valid though not enforceable by order of a court. However, where agreements not criminal in themselves are unenforceable and invalid as contrary to

---

[135] ibid, s 1.
[136] See the payment limits set by the Human Fertilisation and Embryology Authority (n 104 above), and the Nuffield Council review of principles of payment (n 1 above at 130).

public policy, lawyers who draft them and physicians and other health care professionals who give effect to their terms may become liable to professional disciplinary sanctions for offending the public interest.

The effect of public policy considerations is relevant to proposals[137] that **15.39** people may be induced to request posthumous use of their organs and tissues by the prospect of payments going to others they name at the time of donation if, after death, the person's organs or tissues are available for transplantation. The 1989 Act makes it an offence to offer, make or receive any payment,[138] and payment to a person other than a donor appears to be covered by the scope of the Act. The Act intends that donation be altruistic, and directing an intended payment to a person other than the donor, whether at the time the request for donation is made or later, appears to violate that intention no less than giving money directly to the donor. However, the definition of 'payment' excludes the cost of removing an organ,[139] and a donor's agreement that such costs be paid to the estate on removal of an organ would not violate the Act.

More speculatively, an agreement made at donation that, on posthumous **15.40** recovery of an organ, a specified payment be made to a charity designated by the donor or, for instance, by a family member, might not violate the purpose of the 1989 Act to bar commercial dealings.[140] An arrangement of this nature would not seem to offend public policy, and would preserve the altruism the Act is designed to protect. Instead of the donor's altruism being directed to an unknown recipient, however, it would be directed to a charitable cause which the donor would identify, or to one approved for instance by a family member. The strategy to promote donation and recovery of transplantable organs post mortem by agreeing to make payments to charities on organs being recoverable might accordingly not be invalid as against public policy, nor offend the terms of the Act, and lawyers', physicians' and others' involvement in such agreements might not be offences or causes of disciplinary sanctions. Payments offered by prospective private recipients, whether individuals or institutions, might indicate the self-interest characteristic of

---

[137] Explored, for instance, by the US National Kidney Foundation and United Network for Organ Sharing; see Dejong, W, Drachman, J, Gortmaker, S L, *et al*, 'Options for Increasing Organ Donation: The Potential Role of Financial Incentives, Standardized Hospital Procedures, and Public Education to Promote Family Discussion' (1995) 73 *Milbank Quarterly* 463–79.
[138] N 6 above, s 1(1).   [139] ibid, s 1(3).
[140] This is different from creating organ 'futures', by which a person receives payment for promising that, following death, organs will be made available; see Spurr, S J, 'The Shortage of Transplantable Organs: An Analysis and a Proposal' (1993) 15 Law and Policy, 355–95, 373–4, and Cohen, L R, 'Increasing the Supply of Transplant Organs: The Virtues of a Futures Market' (1989) 58 George Washington Law Rev, 1–51.

commerce, but payments offered by public agencies might be compatible with the public interest and not legally or otherwise objectionable. A public health service authority intending to spare itself the expense, and patients the mounting health hazards, of dialysis might want to add an incentive to donation for posthumous recovery, and allocate organs in its customary way according to patients' needs, not recipients' means to pay. The unlinking of donating from receipt of a material reward might take the arrangement outside the purpose of the 1989 Act. Nevertheless, agreements of this nature appear contrary to the language of clauses 1(1)(a) and 1(1)(c) of the Act. Any progress towards such agreements might require action in court for a favourable declaratory judgment, or a favourable opinion of the Attorney-General, or perhaps of the Director of Public Prosecutions, without whose consent no proceedings for an offence under section 1 may be instituted.[141]

(v) *The Removal of Organs and Tissues*

15.41   The common law respects the integrity of corpses by apparently recognizing an offence of causing indignity to a dead body[142] and of violating public decency by improper handling.[143] The Human Tissue Act 1961[144] provides qualified relief in section 1(3), which states that 'Subject to subsection (4), (4A) and (5) of this section, the removal and use of any part of a body in accordance with an authority given in pursuance of this section shall be lawful.' The fact that the provision renders conduct in compliance with it lawful indicates that, in the absence of this provision, removing and using part of a body would be unlawful.[145] Although the provision refers only to 'any part of a body', section 1(1) allows donation of an entire body or any specified part or parts of it, so that subsection 1(3) may be read accordingly. Section 1(4) limits implementation of any authorization to obtain materials from a dead body by providing that: 'no such removal, except of eyes or parts of eyes, shall be effected except by a registered medical practitioner, who must have satisfied himself by personal examination of the body that life is extinct.'

---

[141] N 6 above, s 5.

[142] *Foster v Dodd* (1866) LR 1 QB 475 *per* Blackburn J at 485.

[143] See *R v Gibson* [1991] 1 All ER 439 (CA) and Skegg, PDG, 'Medical Uses of Corpses and the "No Property" Rule', (1992) 32 Medicine, Science, and Law, 311–18.

[144] N 5 above.

[145] By s1(8), see para 15.43 below, the section does not make unlawful actions that are lawful apart from the 1961 Act, indicating that the section makes lawful what is otherwise unlawful.

Organ removal requires the skills of a surgeon, who would have to be suitably **15.42** registered as a medical practitioner,[146] but various tissues may be recoverable by the skills of health care practitioners who are not so registered. It appears that a medical practitioner who is registered would usually have to be satisfied by personal examination of the body that life is extinct,[147] but may then authorize the removal of tissues by an unregistered person. This appears so from analogy with the law on abortion. Although only registered medical practitioners are authorized to perform abortions under the Abortion Act 1967,[148] it was held in *Royal College of Nursing of the UK v Department of Health and Social Security*[149] that, provided that a physician remains in charge of a procedure and bears responsibility throughout, particular acts may lawfully be undertaken by others acting along extended lines of authority. The purpose of the 1967 Act was to widen access to the procedures it governs, and the same expansive purpose appears applicable to the 1961 Act, which may be understood similarly.

Acquisition of materials intended for transplantation from a dead body other **15.43** than in accordance with the 1961 Act would risk prosecution for a common law or other offence,[150] although the Act itself contains no sanction for non-compliance.[151] Further, section 1 of the Act imposes no new legal liabilities, since section 1(8) provides that 'Nothing in this section shall be construed as rendering unlawful any dealing . . . which is lawful apart from this Act.' A registered physician whose only non-compliance with the Act was the removal of organs without the consent, prior to death, of the deceased or of the person lawfully in possession of the body might be guilty of offending public decency, but a charge of causing indignity to a dead body might not be made out if the procedure of removal was identical to that which would have been performed had due authorization been granted. Further, the defence of necessity might be invoked to excuse any failure to comply with the terms of the Act where materials were intended for a life-preserving transplantation.[152] The same defence might resist any charge, for non-conformity with section 1(5) of the 1961 Act, which requires a person who has reason to believe that

---

[146] See the Medical Act 1983, s 56, Sch 6, paras 11, 20.

[147] Personal examination by a registered medical practitioner might not be necessary where death is self-evident, such as in cases of decapitation or other conditions incompatible with life; for earlier law concerning survival and inheritance rather than transplantation, however, see *Gugel's Administrator v Orth's Executors* (1950), 236 SW 2d 460 (Kentucky CA) (a decapitated woman held to have survived her husband whose heart and respiration had ceased, because blood gushed from her severed neck, evidencing heartbeat). [148] S 1(1).

[149] [1981] 1 All ER 545, HL.

[150] See *R v Lennox-Wright* [1973] Crim L Rev 529 (Cent Crim Ct).

[151] See Kennedy and Grubb (n 9 above), Ch 15, 1156–9.

[152] See *R v Bourne*, [1939] 1 KB 687 (Cent Crim Ct).

an inquest or post mortem examination may be required to have consent of the relevant coroner before giving or acting on authority to remove materials from a body, and any charge of breach of statutory duty.[153]

15.44 Subsection 1(4A) was added to the 1961 Act by the Corneal Tissue Act 1986,[154] section 1. It provides that no removal of an eye or part of an eye shall be effected from a body except by a registered medical practitioner who by personal examination of the body is satisfied that life is extinct, or by a person in the employment of a health authority[155] acting on the instructions of a registered medical practitioner who, before giving such instructions, is satisfied that the person in question is sufficiently qualified and trained to perform the removal competently, and who is satisfied by his or her own examination of the body or by confirmation of another such medical practitioner who has so examined the body that life is extinct. In light of the judgment in the *Royal College of Nursing* case,[156] this addition may have added little of substance, but it avoids doubt and the need for the type of litigation resulting in that judgment that afforded non-physicians the confidence to act under a physician's instructions.

(vi) *The Duty to Supply Information*

15.45 By section 3(1) of the Human Organ Transplants Act 1989,[157] the Secretary of State for Health is empowered to make regulations requiring specified persons to supply particular information to a given authority 'with respect to transplants that have been or are proposed to be carried out in Great Britain using organs removed from dead or living persons.' The authority shall keep a record of such information.[158] Any person who without reasonable excuse fails to comply with the regulations is liable to summary conviction and fine, as is any person who, in purported compliance with the regulations, knowingly or recklessly supplies information that is false or misleading in a material respect.[159]

---

[153] See Kennedy and Grubb (n 9 above) at 1158, doubting that this common law offence applies to the 1961 Act.   [154] 1986 ch 18.
[155] The Act above added sub-s 1(10) to the 1961 Act, defining a 'health authority' in relation to England and Wales according to the meaning given by the National Health Service Act 1977, s 128(1).   [156] See n 149 above.
[157] N 6 above.   [158] ibid, s 3(2).
[159] ibid, s 3(3). S 4 further provides that any director, manager, secretary or other similar officer of a body corporate or any person purporting to act in such a capacity who consents to, connives in, or otherwise contributes to an offence by a body corporate is also liable to conviction and punishment, as are members of an offending body corporate who manage its affairs.

The Human Organ Transplants (Supply of Information) Regulations 1989[160] **15.46**
came into force on 1 April 1990. The Regulations define a 'relevant organ' to
which they apply as any kidney, heart, lung, pancreas or liver.[161]

D. Donation from Living Donors

1. Consent

The legal power of persons to donate materials from their bodies while they **15.47**
are alive, for transplantation into others, exists at common law, and is implicit
rather than explicit in legislation. The Human Organ Transplant Act 1989[162]
rests on the foundation that people may give organs from their bodies while
alive within the general framework of the law. The Act does not address
donation of non-organic materials such as blood and, probably, bone marrow,
which therefore fall outside the Act's prohibition of commercial dealings.[163]
Similarly, such legislation as the Human Fertilisation and Embryology Act
1990[164] regulates, but is not the origin of, the right to transfer human
reproductive materials including pre-embryos. The common law on 'maim'
places limits on what bodily invasions people can consent to for the purpose
of donation,[165] and they cannot give legally effective consent to have death
inflicted on them[166] by donation of vital organs such as the heart.[167] In many
circumstances, however, people have the legal power to risk inadvertent death
or injury, and civil liability for death or injury may be reduced or excluded by
the donor's assumption of risk, expressed in the doctrine *volenti non fit
injuria*. Within this general framework, people in principle may lawfully
consent to donate certain organs and other tissues while living, for transplantation into others.

Blood donation has almost invariably been undertaken anonymously for the **15.48**

---

[160] SI 1989/2108, as amended by SI 1991/1645.   [161] SI 1989/2108, reg 1(2).
[162] N 6 above.   [163] See para 15.03 above.   [164] 1990 ch 37.
[165] *R v Wright* (1603), Co Lit f 127 a-b (cutting off a beggar's hand with his approval to
increase sympathetic responses was held convictable); see also *State of North Carolina v Bass*
(1961), 120 SE 2d 580 (NC Sup Ct). In *R v Brown* [1994] 1 AC 212, on limits to sado-
masochistic practices, the House of Lords addressed the modern relevance of the historical law
of maim.
[166] The Criminal Code of Canada, RSC 1985, ch C-46, for instance, codifies the common
law in providng in s 14 that 'No person is entitled to consent to have death inflicted on him,
and such consent does not affect the criminal responsibility of any person by whom death may
be inflicted on the person by whom consent is given.'
[167] For an argument that respect for autonomy requires accepting a person's decision to die
in order to donate organs to others, see Rakowski, E, 'Taking and Saving Lives' (1993) 93
Columbia L Rev, 1063–1156, 1107–9.

benefit of strangers, and donation for instance of gametes, bone marrow,[168] and breast milk may be similar. Designated donation of blood has gained some attention due to awareness of risk of contamination of donated blood, particularly by the human immunodeficiency virus (HIV). However, organs as defined in the 1989 Act[169] are almost invariably donated only to specifically identified recipients.[170] Indeed, the intention to assist survival of the person identified, as opposed to anyone else, is the motivating factor in donation. This alone explains the donor's willingness to give consent.[171]

15.49 The legal requirement that consent to a proposed medical intervention be appropriately informed, express, and freely given applies to altruistic donation of body materials no less than to therapeutic procedures.[172] No laws compel individuals to render the resources of their bodies to sustain the lives of other human beings.[173] Parents have no legal duty to make, for instance, medically-indicated blood or bone marrow donations from their own bodies to sustain their children's lives, although it is arguable that a woman who declines to breastfeed her newborn child without medical reason when there is no accessible alternative source of nutrition for the infant might be convictable, for instance, for denying her child a necessity of life[174] or for a comparable offence of child neglect.[175] The legal basis of removing an organ or other tissue from a living person's body in order to transplant it into that of another person is freely given, express and appropriately informed consent.

15.50 Donors who are admitted to hospital for the purpose of donation, particu-

---

[168] See Anderson, M A, 'Encouraging Bone Marrow Transplants from Unrelated Donors: Some Proposed Solutions to a Pressing Social Problem' (1993) 54 Univ Pittsburgh L Rev, 477–530, and Hartman, R Q, 'The Privacy Implications of Professor Anderson's Proposed Mandatory Registry for Bone Marrow Donation: A Reply', ibid. 531–51.

[169] See para 15.03 above.

[170] Considerable controversy exists in the scholarly literature regarding the propriety of permitting, and of prohibiting, designation of recipients of foetal tissues from induced abortion. On the so-called 'designer fetus' concern, see Robertson, J A, *Children of Choice: Freedom and the New Reproductive Technologies* (Princeton, NJ, 1994), 207–19.

[171] See Jones, M A and Keywood, K, 'Assessing the Patient's Competence to Consent to Medical Treatment' (1996) 2 Medical Law International, 107–47.

[172] See *Sidaway* (n 63 above); contrast *Reibl v Hughes* (1980) 114 DLR (3d) 1 (Sup Ct Canada), and *Rogers v Whitaker* (1992), 67 ALJR 47 (High Ct Australia).

[173] See *McFall v Shimp* (1978), 10 Pa D&C 3d 90 (Allegheny Cnty Ct); see also Grey, T C, *The Legal Enforcement of Morality* (New York, 1983), 187–97.

[174] See *The Queen v Instan* [1893] 1 QB 450 (CCCR), citing *Rex v Friend*, R & R 20 on the indictable offence at common law of refusing or neglecting to provide sufficient food to an infant of tender years.

[175] In *R v Brooks* (1902) 5 CCC 372 (Sup Ct Brit Columbia), it was held that the duty of parents to provide 'necessaries of life', under s 215(1)(a) of the Criminal Code of Canada (n 166 above), includes the duty to provide medical aid, although breast-feeding may be considered the supply of nutrition and liquids rather than of medical treatment.

larly donation of an organ removed through surgery, are likely to be admitted and cared for under the description that they are 'patients'. Surgery will clearly require that they be prepared, operated on, and given after care in this capacity. They differ from other patients, however, in that they tend not to be sick or in need of medical treatment as the condition of admission to hospital. There is no concern for their therapeutic advantage that would justify or excuse physicians withholding counter-therapeutic information relevant to their management, and, for instance, they would not be acting contrary to medical advice if they decided to discharge themselves, were they to decide not to undertake the procedures for which they were admitted. They are entitled to be told all of the implications that donation would have for them, such as preparation by drugs or diet, hospital admission, and otherwise, including the risk of nosocomial infection, the actual process of organ or tissue removal, including anaesthesia, the risk of surgical error and accident,[176] including iatrogenic injury, the process of medical recovery from the procedure and of physical rehabilitation, and the level of restoration of their capacity to function which they could reasonably expect following removal of the organ or other tissue in question. Failure to offer them appropriate information would be liable to be pursued in law in an action for negligence, although actual surgery competently conducted within the scope that the patient authorized would probably not sustain a successful claim for battery.[177] Excessively graphic information given to a potential donor of the intended recipient's decline and process of death if transplantation is not undertaken may give rise to liability in negligence if it induces or pressures donation that results in injury to the donor, even if the injury itself, such as in surgery, is not caused by negligence.[178] Similarly, presenting too optimistic a prognosis of success of a transplant may leave a donor ill-prepared for the sense of loss and bereavement that follows its failure. In the United States, for example, a separate claim has been recognized for negligent infliction of emotional harm or distress,[179] such as regret that a donation was made, or remorse and guilt when a loved one died following donation refusal, or devastation when transplantation following donation fails.[180]

---

[176] See *Whitehouse v Jordan* [1981] 1 All ER 267 (HL).
[177] See *Hills v Potter* [1983] 3 All ER 716 (QBD) and *Reibl v Hughes* (n 172 above).
[178] See *Whitehouse v Jordan* (n 176 above).
[179] See Furrow *et al* (n 27 above), 164–71.
[180] For development of the law on recovery of damages for nervous shock, see *Page v Smith* [1995] 2 All ER 736 (HL).

(i) *Capacity of Adult Donor*[181]

15.51 Adults must be legally competent to give consent.[182] People of adult years enjoy the general presumption in law that they are competent to undertake the routine activities and risks of daily living, including acceptance of medical procedures, but the implications that are inherent in organ donation, and perhaps donation of other tissues such as bone marrow, take it beyond the nature of a routine activity. Competence in law is specific to particular functions;[183] for instance, a person proposing to execute a will must give satisfactory evidence of possessing testamentary capacity, and is liable to be questioned for establishment of such capacity, whereas a person may revoke a will in relatively informal ways, and without a prior need to show competence. Similarly in medical care, it has been observed that 'the common law test of competence to consent to medical treatment is functional and the threshold currently set for competence is low.'[184] The law seeks to minimize conditions and obstacles to a patient adhering to the conscientious advice offered by a disinterested physician discharging the duty to care for the patients' well-being.[185]

15.52 In contrast, organ and other tissue donation is not an indicated physical therapy for a donor, and may be a source of physical harm, however much the donor considers the risk of harm to be justified or overborne by benefit to the recipient and satisfaction to the donor. If the transplant fails, however, and the recipient succumbs to disease and death, the donor's grief may be aggravated by a sense that the donation was ill-advised or futile. Accordingly, since donation is not intended for the donor's advantage and may be a source of physical and emotional detriment, a higher level of competency may be required. An analogy may be drawn with participation in medical experimentation or research, which is entered altruistically with no intention of personal benefit. Not every person legally competent to consent to indicated medical therapy is competent to consent to participation in research,[186] and the same is true of organ and tissue donation. Capacity to consent is related

---

[181] 'Capacity' here refers primarily to mental or intellectual capacity. Legal capacity of live donors distinguishes between donors related and donors unrelated to intended recipients. The latter are considered at para 15.66 below.   [182] See Jones and Keywood (n 171 above).
[183] See Gunn, M, 'The Meaning of Incapacity' (1994) 2 Med L Rev, 8–29, 13.
[184] Brazier, M and Bridge, C, 'Coercion or caring; analysing adolescent autonomy', (1996) 16 LS 84–109, 90.
[185] See *Chatterton v Gerson* [1981] 1 QB 432 (QBD); *Re C (adult; refusal of medical treatment)* [1994] 1 All ER 819 (Fam D).   [186] See Chapter 13.

to the nature of the donation proposed, organ donation and bone marrow donation requiring greater capacity, for instance, than blood donation.

Capacity involves intellectual ability to appreciate the range of implications of the decision on donation, but also the ability to resist undue pressures, perhaps from close family members, and undue inducements. Pressures and inducements are inherent in the decision when donation is motivated by the urgent need of a close family member or friend. The pressure to act to relieve a loved one from the threat of organ-failure and disease is natural,[187] and inescapable. Undue pressure may be brought to bear, however, such as by family members' threats of ostracism, that compromises a potential donor's legal capacity to act voluntarily. The inducement of achieving a loved one's survival may appear irresistible and sufficient for acceptance of the known risks of donation. However, when the trusted informant significantly downplays chances of transplantation failure or factors likely to compromise the recipient's survival, the inducement to donate may become undue, and vitiate a potential donor's capacity to exercise choice voluntarily. Coercion negates consent, and non-consensual removal of tissues may constitute battery or criminal assault to which those who use pressure or deception are parties. **15.53**

Physicians and other health care professionals responsible for informing and counselling prospective donors must be alert not only to intellectual obstacles to choice but also to donors' vulnerability to forces that compromise their freedom of choice. Findings that prospective donors are unsuitable to donate organs or tissues may afford such people relief from improper persuasion to donate,[188] though perhaps at a cost to needful potential recipients' well-being or very survival. Physicians bear legal obligations to those on whom they propose to undertake medical procedures—particularly procedures that are major, irreversible and non-therapeutic—to be reasonably assured that they are competent to give, and do actually give, adequately understood and voluntary consent. Physicians addressing prospective donors bear no corresponding duty to protect the interests and well-being of potential recipients of materials that may be donated. They must satisfy themselves that potential donors are acting voluntarily by questioning them, by seeking opinions from other physicians, psychologists, social workers or chaplains, or by seeking legal advice. **15.54**

---

[187] *Urbanski v Patel* (1978) 84 DLR (3d) 650 (Manitoba QB) (father successfully sued doctor who negligently removed daughter's only kidney, causing father to donate a kidney). See also Spencer, J, 'Tissue Donors: Are They Rescuers, or Merely Volunteers?' (1979) CLJ 45–7.
[188] Fox, RC and Swazey, JP, *Spare Parts: Organ Replacement in American Society* (New York, 1992), 43–72.

15.55 The strongest safeguard in cases of doubt might be to seek a judicial declaration of the prospective donor's legal capacity to consent, but in many cases this would be impracticable, disruptive, or even destructive of relationships which the potential donor wants to preserve. Physicians may have to bear the burden, therefore, of acting with good sense and conscience to decide if they have received the quality of consent they require to give effect to a person's request to donate an organ or other tissue for transplantation. It may be of little comfort for physicians to know that Staughton LJ has observed that:

> I cannot find authority that the decision of a doctor as to the existence or refusal of consent is sufficient protection, if the law subsequently finds otherwise. So the medical profession . . . must bear the responsibility unless it is possible to obtain a decision from the courts.[189]

(ii) *Capacity of Adolescent Donors*

15.56 There is doubt that the power of minors aged sixteen and above to consent to medical treatment on their own behalf, under section 8(1) of the Family Law Reform Act 1969,[190] applies to organ donation,[191] although they may be able to give their own consent to blood and perhaps bone marrow donation that serves a special interest of theirs. There is therefore related doubt that the general law on adolescent therapy applies to donation. For instance the 'mature minor' rule recognized in the *Gillick* case[192] regarding adolescents aged under sixteen may be inapplicable. Although a court may find that, for instance, bone marrow donation from a person incapable of providing legally effective consent may be of emotional, psychological and social benefit and in that person's best interests,[193] it may be doubted that a person aged under sixteen may make the decision to donate independently of judicial or at least adult concurrence. The power of parents to consent to donation by their adolescent children over the children's objection may similarly not be governed by legal principles regarding parental power to consent to therapeutically indicated procedures.[194] In this case, the 'strong predilection to give effect to the child's wishes'[195] will prevail. Further, the likelihood that parents may influence dependent children to express wishes

---

[189] *Re T (Adult) (Refusal of Medical Treatment)* [1992] 4 All ER 649 (CA), 670.
[190] See n 115 above and related text.   [191] See *Re W* (n 116 above).
[192] *Gillick v West Norfolk and Wisbech Area Health Authority* [1986] AC 112 (HL).
[193] See *In re Y (Mental Patient: Bone Marrow Donation)* [1997] 2 WLR 556 (Fam Div); [1997] Fam 110 (Fam Div).
[194] See *Re W (A minor) (Medical Treatment)* [1992] 4 All ER 627 (CA) *per* Lord Donaldson, 635.   [195] ibid, *per* Balcombe, LJ at 643.

favourable to their own[196] may require that a parental proposal for organ donation and perhaps bone marrow donation from an adolescent child with the child's agreement receive judicial or other independent scrutiny,[197] Any proposed removal of an organ for transplantation to a genetically unrelated recipient would be subject to review by the Unrelated Live Transplant Regulatory Authority.[198]

(iii) *Capacity of Young Children as Donors*

The strict proposition that parents may use their legal powers to consent to medical treatment on their young, dependent children only for the therapeutic benefit of the children[199] may be interpreted more widely to allow their consent to non-beneficial treatments provided that they risk no more than the harms naturally arising in everyday life.[200] Both common law and legislation permit parents to submit young children to blood-testing for paternity claims,[201] for instance, and the use of reasonable constraints to compel compliance,[202] even though the benefit for the child is speculative, dependent in some measure on what the test result discloses.[203] It may be questioned whether kidney or similar organ donation can ever be legally authorized by a parent from the body of a young child,[204] and whether even bone marrow or blood donation is within the limits of permissible parental authority. An analogous case decided in Kentucky in 1969 demonstrates the vulnerability of dependent people to the judgment of their guardians on becoming sources of transplantable materials, and has been a basis of reaction. In *Strunk v Strunk*[205] the court approved kidney removal from an incompetent adult for transplantation to his twin brother, on the ground that, had his brother died, the loss would have caused him psychological and emotional injury. The incompetent adult had a mental age of six years.

15.57

---

[196] See *Re T* (n 189 above).   [197] See generally Chapter 4.

[198] See para 15.64 below.

[199] See Kennedy and Grubb (n 9 above) at 1061, citing Dworkin G.

[200] Brazier, M finds authority for parental consent for non-therapeutic procedures on children as long as they are not 'clearly against the interests' of the children; *Medicine, Patients and the Law* (London, 2nd edn, 1992), 423.   [201] *S v McC, W v W* [1972] AC 24 (HL).

[202] ibid.

[203] The Court reasoned (ibid) that paternity testing was of sufficient benefit to the child to be justifiable as legitimate pursuit of benefit; see also *In re H (A Minor) (Blood Tests: Parental Rights)* [1996] 4 All ER 28 (CA). On the legitimacy of venepuncture of a young child for non-beneficial medical research, see Chapter 13.

[204] See Skegg, P D G, *Law, Ethics and Medicine* (Oxford, 1984), 61; see also Mason, J K and McCall Smith, RA, *Law and Medical Ethics* (London, 4th edn, 1994), 295–8.

[205] (1969) 445 SW 2d 145 (Ky CA).

15.58 Similarly in *Hart v Brown*,[206] the court accepted that the psychological benefit to the child that a sibling would survive and be a continuing companion considerably outweighed the risks of donation and justified removal of an organ for transplantation. A more remarkable and no less controversial incident received public attention when a couple in the US planned and conceived a child, and continued the pregnancy only on receiving evidence from foetal diagnosis of tissue compatibility, in order that, following birth, the child would serve as a source of bone marrow for transplantation to a teenage daughter suffering from leukemia. The transplantation took place in June 1991 when the child so conceived, a girl, had reached the age of fourteen months.[207] Public and academic discussion centred on the ethics rather than on the legality of executing this plan.[208]

15.59 Several jurisdictions in the common law and civil law traditions have reacted to the prospect of parentally authorized acquisitions of organs from younger children by legislatively enacted prohibitions,[209] and similar controls on acquisition of tissues.[210] In jurisdictions where the defence of necessity is recognized, however, breach of prohibitive legislation may be excused on the ground that the urgency of the circumstances, the imminence of the recipient's death, and the relatively minor comparative risk to the child from whom materials were removed rendered the violation defensible by objective risk-to-benefit criteria.[211] Removal of bone marrow or other regenerative tissue might be more easily defensible on this basis than removal of a kidney or lung. Nevertheless, because conduct excused by necessity is not lawful, even though not punishable, lawyers risk liability for professional misconduct in positively advising that it be undertaken. They may only advise that it may be judicially excused.

15.60 The claim that parents can necessarily identify the best interests of a potential donor child has been questioned. It has been observed that:

> [I]t is increasingly suggested that the family may express interests which may not always adequately represent the best interests of the incompetent, especially with regard to non-therapeutic interventions. While family interests must be outweighed only by compelling interests, the proper forum for deciding must

---

[206] (1972) 289 A 2d 386 (Conn Sup Ct).
[207] 'Teen Gets Baby Sister's Marrow', *New York Times*, 5 June 1991, A-23.
[208] See Rachels, J, 'When Philosophers Shoot From the Hip' (1991) 5 *Bioethics*, 67–71.
[209] See Giesen, D, *International Medical Malpractice Law* (Tübingen, Dordrecht, Boston, London, 1988) 611 n 72. [210] ibid, 611–12, nn 63–9.
[211] On necessity, see *R v Bourne* (n 152 above), and the discussion in *Perka v The Queen* (1984) 14 CCC (3d) 385 (Sup Ct Can). See also Wilson, W and Smith, K J M, 'The Doctors' Dilemma: Necessity and the Legality of Medical Intervention' (1995) 1 Medical Law International, 387–410.

objectively weigh all considerations with predominant emphasis on the best interests of the incompetent individual.[212]

When it is intended to provide an organ or tissue such as bone marrow from a child incapable of understanding or of resistance for transplantation to another on the basis of parental consent, consideration will have to be given to a wide range of factors. These include the risks during surgical removal of the material, the risks of the child's immediate adverse reaction to removal, the child's longer-term prospects of physical and emotional dysfunction due to the loss, the child's prevailing and prospective emotional proximity to the intended recipient, the likelihood of the transplant succeeding in restoring or achieving the recipient's well-being, the effect on the child on learning of the donation on reaching an age of understanding, the effect on parent–child relations and attitudes if the child either serves, or does not serve, as a donor, the effect on the child if the intended recipient does, or does not, survive and, for instance, consequences for the child–parent relationship if the recipient survives or does not survive, with or without the transplantation procedure.[213]

Parents' natural anxieties concerning the child in need of the transplant, and their hopes for that child's well-being if the other provides an organ or tissue, present a classic conflict of interest in their management of the potential donor child's care. They may be liable to project their own fears, hopes and perception of benefit onto the potential donor child, and claim that its best interests, as well as their own, would be served by donation. The depth of detached consideration that needs to be given to parental assertions, the range of professional disciplines and expertise that would have to be applied to make the assessments called for, and the improbability of any generally agreed outcome being reached, persuade some analysts that prohibition, particularly of organ removals for transplantation, is the only appropriate legal policy. For instance, Professor Dieter Giesen wrote that: **15.61**

> It is submitted that in the case of mentally incompetent persons who do not understand what removal of organs or tissue may entail, such a procedure is never permissible. It is likewise submitted that the same line should generally be taken with regard to minors. No exception should be allowed with regard to *non*-regenerative tissue or organs in the case of minors who are not yet of an age at which they can properly understand what is at stake with regard to their own health . . .
>
> A less rigid approach has been recommended with reference to isotransplanta-tions, which, especially in the case of kidney transplantation between histo-

---

[212] Law Reform Commission of Canada, *Medical Treatment and the Criminal Law* (Ottawa, Working Paper 26, 1980), 69.
[213] See the factors weighed in the balance in *In re Y* (n 193 above).

compatible siblings, are said to have shown such exceptionally good results as to justify the procedure, provided that parents and minors have given their consent based on full and detailed information. We do not share this view. The vulnerability of minors to exploitation and manipulation is particularly problematic here, and exceptions to the general rule in this field will impose unacceptable pressures upon siblings or other relatives that are avoided only if the law prohibits the removal of non-regenerative organs in every case.[214]

Removals of regenerative tissues such as bone marrow from young children may be acceptable, however, subject to the objective and detached assessments indicated above. Because parents who are responsible for the protection of the well-being of adequately healthy prospective donor children are almost invariably also responsible for the well-being of the intended recipients whose health and very survival are in jeopardy, parents alone cannot necessarily be relied on to exercise the required objectivity of assessment. Before acting on parents' volunteering of their children as sources of transplantable materials, hospitals should receive favourable assessments of the children's interests from paediatricians, psychologists, social workers, or similar experts whose testimony courts would require to establish the children's psychological benefit and minor risk from donation. With this type of screening and assessment, young children may be accepted as donors of bone marrow and similar materials.

2. Relationships Between Donors and Recipients

15.62 In order to deter commerce in human organs and tissues that has arisen from impersonal, market-oriented dealings between suppliers and recipients, the Human Organ Transplants Act 1989[215] not only prohibits payments for organs, and advertising for and of organs,[216] but also regulates transplants between living persons not genetically related to each other. The purpose is to limit live persons' donations to strangers, while accommodating donations by relatives presumably moved to unrewarded altruism and self-sacrifice by sympathy for and affinity with their family members. The requirement of a genetic link both confirms the family relationship and increases the likelihood of transplantation success, although developments in immuno-therapy reduce recipients' dependency on the genetic compatibility of tissues. A limitation of this policy is that in itself it excludes transplants between spouses and members of unmarried unions. They may have the strongest incentives to be donors based on affection, but may also come under the greatest pressure due to such factors as economic and other dependency. A system that screens

---

[214] N 209 above, at 611, emphasis in original, footnotes omitted. [215] N 6 above.
[216] See para 15.36 above.

transplantations to ensure genetic links between donors and recipients must also accommodate exceptions for sympathetic cases of adequately voluntary donations where no genetic links to recipients exist.

Section 2 of the Human Organ Transplants Act 1989 provides that:

(1) Subject to subsection (3) below, a person is guilty of an offence if in Great Britain he—

  (a) removes from a living person an organ intended to be transplanted into another person; or

  (b) transplants an organ removed from a living person into another person, unless the person into whom the organ is to be or, as the case may be, is transplanted is genetically related to the person from whom the organ is removed.

(2) For the purposes of this section a person is genetically related to—

  (a) his natural parents and children;

  (b) his brothers and sisters of the whole or half blood;

  (c) the brothers and sisters of the whole or half blood of either of his natural parents; and

  (d) the natural children of his brothers and sisters of the whole or half blood or of the brothers and sisters of the whole or half blood of either of his natural parents; but persons shall not in any particular case be treated as related in any of those ways unless the fact of the relationship has been established by such means as are specified by regulations made by the Secretary of State.

(3) The Secretary of State may by regulations provide that the prohibition in subsection (1) above shall not apply in cases where—

  (a) such authority as is specified in or constituted by the regulations is satisfied -

    (i) that no payment has been or is to be made in contravention of Section 1 above;[217] and

    (ii) that such other conditions as are specified in the regulations are satisfied; and

  (b) such other requirements as may be specified in the regulations are complied with.

15.63 With effect from April 1990, the Human Organ Transplants (Establishment of Relationship) Regulations 1989[218] came into effect under authority of section 2(2) of the 1989 Act. The Regulations provide:

  1.—(1) These Regulations may be cited as the Human Organ Transplants (Establishment of Relationship) Regulations 1989 and shall come into force on 1st April 1990.

    (2) In these Regulations—

---

[217] ibid.   [218] SI 1989/2107.

'donor' means a living person from whom an organ is proposed to be removed which is intended to be transplanted;

'tester' means a person approved by the Secretary of State to carry out the tests described in regulation 2 of these Regulations.

The Establishment of the Genetic Relationship

2.—(1) The means by which the fact of a genetic relationship is to be established for the purposes of section 2 of the Human Organ Transplants Act 1989 are the carrying out by a tester of the appropriate tests described in paragraph (2) of this regulation.

(2) The tester shall carry out on the donor and the recipient and on such relatives of each as appear to the tester to be necessary—

(a) tests for the antigenic products of the Human Major Histocompatibility system HLA-A, HLA-B, HLA-DR, using conventional serological techniques, and

(b) tests to establish HLA-DR beta and HLA-DQ beta gene restriction fragment length polymorphisms, and

(c) where the tests in the preceding sub-paragraphs do not establish a genetic relationship between the donor and the recipient, tests to establish DNA polymorphisms, using at least 2 multi-locus gene probes, and

(d) where the tests in the preceding sub-paragraphs do not establish a genetic relationship between the donor and the recipient, further tests to establish DNA polymorphisms, using at least 5 single locus polymorphic probes.

15.64 The need to accommodate donations by persons not genetically related to intended recipients is met through creation of the Unrelated Live Transplant Regulatory Authority (ULTRA),[219] under section 2(3) of the 1989 Act. The Human Organ Transplants (Unrelated Persons) Regulations 1989[220] provide in regulation 3 that:

(1) The prohibition in section 2(1) of the [Human Organ Transplants] Act (restriction on transplants between persons not genetically related) shall not apply in cases where a registered medical practitioner has caused the matter to be referred to the [Unrelated Live Transplant Regulatory] Authority and where the Authority is satisfied:—

(a) that no payment has been, or is to be, made in contravention of section 1 of the Act;

(b) that the registered medical practitioner who has caused the matter to be referred to the Authority has clinical responsibility for the donor; and

(c) except in a case where the primary purpose of removal of an organ from a donor is the medical treatment of that donor, that the conditions specified in paragraph (2) of this regulation are satisfied.

(2) The conditions referred to in paragraph (1)(c) of this regulation are:—

---

[219] Established by the Human Organ Transplants (Unrelated Persons) Regulations 1989, SI 1989/2480, reg 2. [220] See Kennedy and Grubb (n 9 above) at 1091–2.

(a) that a registered medical practitioner has given the donor an explanation of the nature of the medical procedure for, and the risk involved in, the removal of the organ in question;

(b) that the donor understands the nature of the medical procedure and the risks, as explained by the registered medical practitioner, and consents to the removal of the organ in question;

(c) that the donor's consent to the removal of the organ in question was not obtained by coercion or the offer of an inducement;

(d) that the donor understands that he is entitled to withdraw his consent if he wishes, but has not done so;

(e) that the donor and the recipient have both been interviewed by a person who appears to the Authority to have been suitably qualified to conduct such interviews and who has reported to the Authority on the conditions contained in sub-paragraphs (a) to (d) above and has included in his report an account of any difficulties of communication with the donor or the recipient and an explanation of how those difficulties were overcome.

Although not expressed in the terms of regulations, it seems that in operation they are likely to bar organ donations by young children, and by adolescents vulnerable to coercion or undue inducement. It must be remembered, however, that the 1989 Act defines 'organ' as any part of a human body consisting of a structured arrangement of tissues which, if wholly removed, cannot be replicated by the body,[221] and therefore does not govern such replicable tissues as blood or probably, bone marrow.

3. Payment and the Supply of Information

Developments in organ transplantation techniques and immunosuppressive pharmacology fuelled early speculation that people might in time come to sell their organs. The speculation quickly proved true with revelation that markets in organs from living donors[222] had indeed emerged.[223] The reality was given an identifiable human face in 1989 when it was discovered that impoverished Turkish visitors had come to England in order to sell their kidneys to unrelated recipients.[224] A prompt legislative reaction was the enactment of the Human Organ Transplants Act 1989,[225] the primary purpose of which was to eliminate commerce in human organs and any asso-   **15.65**

---

[221] N 6 above, s 7(2).
[222] It has been observed that 'donors' are voluntary givers, not sellers, and that even for voluntary giving a better description should be explored; see Gerrand, N, 'The Notion of Gift-Giving and Organ Donation' (1994) 8 *Bioethics*, 126–50.
[223] Dorozynski, A, 'European Kidney Market', (1989) 299 *British Med J*, 1182; and Roscam Abbing, HDC, 'Transplantation of Organs: A European Perspective', (1993) 21 J Law, Medicine and Ethics, 54–8.   [224] Mason and McCall Smith (n 204 above), 299.
[225] N 6 above.

ciated advertisements and the involvement of health professionals. The Act requires that donation be gratuitous and altruistic, but permits commercial services to attend the recovery, preparation and transport of donated organs, and donors themselves to recover their reasonable expenses. In defining the prohibition of payment, section 1(3) of the Act provides that:

> 'payment means payment in money or money's worth but does not include any payment for defraying or reimbursing—
>
> (a) the cost of removing, transporting or preserving the organ to be supplied; or
>
> (b) any expenses or loss of earnings incurred by a person so far as reasonably and directly attributable to his supplying of an organ from his body.

15.66 The cost of removing and transporting an organ may reasonably be taken to extend to the cost of implanting it on a fee-for-service basis, unless, as is unlikely, the Act limits implantation surgery to physicians remunerated on a salaried basis by publicly maintained hospitals or clinics. Implantation fees may be considered 'expenses . . . incurred by a person . . . attributable to his supplying an organ,' even if the person is not expected to meet those expenses thereby incurred, or 'the cost of . . . preserving the organ.' Expenses attributable to supplying an organ include not just surgical fees, but preliminary testing of prospective donors to minimize the risk of organ donations transmitting genetic hazards or infections such as sexually transmitted diseases or HIV. Some materials from a human source may be stored so that donors tested immediately before donation can be recalled for instance six or more months later for re-testing. If the later test shows no infection, the tissue given earlier may be removed from storage and transplanted. Fresh tissue is better not used if its liability to transmit infection cannot be detected. In particular, the AIDS virus is undetectable during its incubation period, but transmissible. However, solid organs are currently not preservable for transplantation for any length of time, and, although donors will be tested before donation to reduce the risk that transplantation will transmit infection, the risk cannot be eliminated, and is part of the disclosure that must be made to prospective recipients.[226]

15.67 A cultural issue affected by the 1989 Act is gift-exchange. Cultures attuned primarily to dealings among strangers and to the identification of monetary exchanges with materialism and self-interest, including the mutual self-interest of bargained trade, consider a monetary payment in exchange for donation of an organ, whether immediate or following death, as commerce.[227]

---

[226] See para 15.73 below.

[227] The view that commerce is dysfunctional in the supply of tissues remains strongly influenced by Titmus, R, *The Gift Relationship: From Human Blood to Social Policy* (London, 1970).

Cultures based on mutuality or reciprocity might require, however, that a spontaneous act of altruism be reciprocated in some appropriate way, thereby ritualizing and personalizing gift-exchange that is culturally distinguishable from commerce. To the former, so-called 'rewarded gifting'[228] is a shallow euphemism for buying and selling. To the latter, however, failing appropriately to reciprocate organ donation would be an outrage to cultural values, discrediting the recipient of the gifted organ. Giving a reciprocal gift 'in money or money's worth'[229] would appear to be in breach of the 1989 Act. However, since the Act is also concerned with confining live donations to those between persons genetically related to each other, they are likely to have shared cultural values, so that a donor would be aware of the likelihood of the gift being appropriately reciprocated and the recipient would be similarly familiar with the expectation. One response may be that, in light of probable family links and the continuing association of donor and recipient, the reciprocal gesture might not be immediate, but made in due course. It might be so postponed as to escape scrutiny through the United Kingdom Transplant Support Service Authority,[230] which receives information, *inter alia*, of a kidney, lung, pancreas, or liver removed for transplantation from a living donor.[231] A commercial payment centres on negotiation and prearrangement, including of the times within which obligations must be discharged, whereas the operation of the culture of reciprocity is neither negotiated nor dependent on explicit arrangement and mutual performance at or by an agreed time. Accordingly, rewarded gifting may not amount to 'payment' as defined under the 1989 Act, nor, if it falls within the Act, be easily detected and proven beyond reasonable doubt.[232]

Special duties to supply information are created under the Human Organ **15.68** Transplants (Supply of Information) Regulations 1989.[233] The Schedule to the Regulations, containing details of information to be supplied to the Transplant Support Service Authority, includes an identically worded provision in Part I on organs removed and in Part II on organs that have been or are proposed to be transplanted. Section 5 of the former and section 6 of the latter require disclosure:

---

[228] Daar, AS, 'Rewarded Gifting', (1992) 24 *Transplantation Proceedings*, 2207–11.
[229] 1989 Act (n 6 above) s 1(3).   [230] See para 15.45 above.
[231] United Kingdom Transplant Support Service Authority Regulations, 1991 S1 1991/408. The requirement to supply information of removal and implantation of a 'liver' may not include the supply of information of liver segment removal. This is consistent with a liver segment constituting only tissue, as opposed to an organ as defined in the 1989 Act.
[232] The Nuffield Council (n 1 above) considered that rewarded gifting arrangements should be viewed as commercial transactions; at 52, para 6.36.   [233] N 160 above.

If the donor was living at the time of the removal of the organ—

(a) whether or not, for the purposes of section 2(2) of the [1989] Act, a genetic relationship to the recipient has been established by the means specified in the Human Organ Transplants (Establishment of Relationship) Regulations 1989,[234]

(b) if such a genetic relationship to the recipient has been established, the name of the person who carried out the test to establish that relationship,

(c) where no such genetic relationship to the recipient has been established, the reference number if any in respect of the proposed transplant allocated by the authority specified in or constituted by regulations made under section 2(3) of the Act.

The Unrelated Live Transplant Regulatory Authority (ULTRA)[235] may approve transplantation in a case referred to it as an exception to the restriction on unrelated donation if it is satisfied that no payment has been, or is to be, made in contravention of section 1 of the 1989 Act.[236] The regulations establishing the Authority may provide no appeal against its decisions, but they appear judicially reviewable by prerogative order.[237]

4. Transplant Recipients

(i) *Informed Choice*

15.69 Transplant recipients would appear to be the principal beneficiaries of the advances in surgical, pharmacological, and related techniques that have made transplantation the treatment of choice in routine cases—such as involve kidney and bone marrow transplantation and such a mundane matter as blood transfusion—and an option when more complicated treatments are indicated such as cardiac and multiple-organ transplantation. Recipients are patients in the same way as others, however, and have basic legal entitlements to receive material information and exercise voluntary choice.[238] Their choice may be implicit rather than explicit—for instance when a sudden life threatening crisis requires a life preserving initiative to treat a patient who is unconscious or otherwise incapacitated[239]—but prospective transplant recipients who have achieved mental capacity for choice are free outside unanticipated conditions of emergency, explicitly to decline the possibility of

---

[234] SI 1989/2107.   [235] See n 219 above.   [236] ibid, reg 3(1)(a).
[237] Principles of administrative law that authorities such as ULTRA must observe, and liability to judicial review, are helpfully summarized and explained, with regard to the Human Fertilisation and Embryology Authority but with application to comparable authorities, in Morgan, D and Lee, RG, *Blackstone's Guide to the Human Fertilisation & Embryology Act 1990* (London, 1991), 105–9.   [238] See Chapter 3.
[239] See the doctrine of necessity, *R v Bourne* and *Perka v The Queen* (n 211 above), and Chapter 4.

implantation, including refusing unwanted blood transfusion.[240] Patients are increasingly encouraged to complete advance medical directives[241] to express their preferences, and those declining indicated care tend to carry more weight than those requiring care that is not considered medically appropriate.[242]

The ordinary rules of the common law[243] require that prospective recipients **15.70** must be informed of such general matters as their health diagnosis and prognosis, options for their management including not seeking transplantation, preparation necessary for transplantation if that is to be pursued, their prospects of transplantation success, and their predictable capacity to function under the range of likely outcomes of the procedure. Current English law probably does not stipulate, however, that prospective transplant recipients must be informed of their likely advance to the top of any waiting list, alternative reasonably accessible waiting lists and means of entry to them, including any prioritisation criteria applied by list managers.[244] One reason may be that these factors are beyond the power of the treating doctor to control. Another is that a court still operating the *Bolam*[245] approach may not regard these matters as pertaining to the doctor–patient relationship.

Although recommendations for patient management may appear to be a **15.71** matter of professional judgment for which medical personnel bear legal responsibility,[246] patients may have an interest in knowing how medical options are prioritised, and in contributing to the decision-making process. For instance, some medical practitioners may consider transplantation to be the option of last resort, and will recommend the range of alternatives other than transplantation before addressing its possibility and prospects. On the other hand, others may consider transplantation to be an option competing equally with others to advance a patient's interests in restoration or maintenance of health or capacity. The different approaches have different implications for a patient. If transplantation is considered the last resort, its prospects of success may be compromised by delay in seeking an organ or other tissue necessary for transplantation, and by the physical effects of the alternative treatments used, such as the drugs that are taken before that

---

[240] See *Walker (Litigation Guardian of) v Region 2 Hospital Corporation* (1994) 116 DLR (4th) 477 (New Brunswick CA).
[241] See Stern, K, 'Advance Directives' (1994) 2 Med L Rev, 57–76, and *Re C (Adult: Refusal of Treatment)* [1994] 1 WLR 290 (Fam D).
[242] See Stern, K (n 241 above), 66.
[243] Reflected in legislation in some jurisdictions, such as in Ontario's Health Care Consent Act, Stats Ont, 1996, c 2, Sch A.   [244] See para 15.79 below.
[245] *Bolam v Friern Hospital Management Committee* [1957] 2 All ER 118 (QBD), applied in *Sidaway* (n 63 above).   [246] See *Whitehouse v Jordan* (n 176 above).

option is pursued. That is, earlier treatments may reduce the likelihood that transplantation will succeed. In contrast, turning to transplantation sooner rather than later in the patient's plan of management may preserve the patient's subsequent options for care should transplantation fail, but at the cost of exposing the patient to the risks of subjection to a major procedure and its complications when a less invasive and less drastic procedure might have been no less or even more effective to preserve the patient's life and capacity. Patients might want to be engaged in deciding how such competing options for care are exercised.

15.72 It was thought that one of the effects of the House of Lords' decision in *Sidaway* was that patients who ask questions about treatment strategies, or about alternatives to what their physicians or surgeons recommend, must be given the information they request.[247] The decision of the Court of Appeal in *Blyth v Bloomsbury HA*,[248] however, casts doubt on the existence of such a duty. Moreover, how forthcoming physicians must be at their own initiative is governed by the general law on patients' consent.[249] Physicians cannot be certain to meet the legal standard of disclosure by giving patients voluminous data, because that may be overwhelming to them or confusing, preventing patients' adequate understanding of choices.[250]

15.73 Care must be exercised in the selection of organs and tissues for transplantation.[251] In the case of cadaveric tissue, the cause of death must be reliably known, and even if it was traumatic rather than pathological, any reasonably detectable diseases affecting the deceased person including harmful genetic conditions should be diagnosed. Patients should be informed, however, that a risk remains that some diseases will be undiagnosable. When live donors offer organs or tissues, family histories should be taken, and genetic and other protective tests conducted before materials are removed. However, when cadaveric materials such as organs remain transplantable for only a short time, before full testing can be completed, transmission of infection remains an irreducible risk of their use. Further, some tissue tests bear an irreducible risk of producing a false negative result, which means that organs or tissues may become eligible to be transplanted when they actually bear the harmful infection for which they were tested. The test result is not due to negligence,[252] but disclosure that materials for transplantation from donors carry

---

[247] See n 63 above.   [248] *Blyth v Bloomsbury HA* [1993] Med LR 151 (CA).
[249] See n 63 above and Chapter 3.
[250] For discussion of negligence by excessive disclosure, see *Natanson v Kline* (1960) 350 P 2d 1093 (Kan SC).   [251] See Chapter 5 on negligence.
[252] See *Whitehouse v Jordan* (n 176 above).

some degree of risk of bearing adverse properties notwithstanding due testing reinforces physicians' positions in the event of suit.[253]

If it appears following transplantation or transfusion that the procedure had inadvertently, whether negligently or not, exposed the recipient to transmission of infection, it may be considered that the recipient is legally entitled to be informed.[254] The duty may be binding on tissue management agencies, hospitals, and attending and family physicians, depending on the source of detection of the infection risk and the extent of subsequent communication. Family physicians undertaking continuing care of patients have no legal duty to take independent measures to verify, for instance, the safety of transplanted organs or bone marrow, or that transfused blood was uncontaminated, but when they are given notice of a patient's past exposure they must ensure the patient's knowledge.[255] Information of exposure to even an apparently incurable condition such as HIV infection may allow the patient to limit the risk of spreading the infection, and to make social, business, and other plans, lifestyle adjustments and, for instance, relevant advance medical directives in light of that information. Where the transmitted risk is of susceptibility to harm rather than of harm itself, care may need to be taken to offer the patient appropriate counselling, in order to limit the patient's liability to overreact and take unnecessary protections or seek unnecessary and unproven remedies that could cause injury.

15.74

Informed patients for whom transplantation is proposed are free to reject the option. They may prefer not to take the risks of surgery or infection, not want relatives to take the risks of live donation, not want dead persons' materials in their bodies or, for instance, not want to receive transgenically prepared animals' organs. They may enquire (if they are not informed) whether organs they may receive come from members of races different from their own, from other countries, or from involuntary 'donors', and may be made aware of organ recovery, for instance, from executed prisoners.[256] Their decisions on whether or not to accept transplantation at all or from particular sources can give expression to their philosophical, social, religious, cultural, or other convictions. Those with parental responsibility are not necessarily free,

15.75

---

[253] On a possible product liability claim, see Chapter 14 and Kennedy and Grubb (n 9 above) at 1144–5.

[254] See *Pittman Estate v Bain* (1994) 112 DLR (4th) 257 (Ont Ct Gen Div). English law may be less clear, particularly since the decision of the Court of Appeal in *Powell*.

[255] *Pittman Estate v Bain* (n 254 above).

[256] See Owen, A K, 'Death Row Inmates or Organ Donors: China's Source of Body Organs for Medical Transplantation', (1995) 5 Indiana International & Comparative Law Rev, 495–517; and Patton, L- H M, 'A Call for Common Sense: Organ Donation and the Executed Prisoner' (1996) 3 Virginia Journal of Social Policy and Law, 387–434.

however, to make decisions on children's welfare on the same basis as they make decisions for themselves. It is trite law that while they may martyr themselves for their convictions, they cannot martyr their children who depend on them for protection and care.[257] Parents may balance such risks as transmission of infection against prospective benefits of transplantation for their children, and will not casually be contradicted by courts on procedures as invasive as organ transplantation.[258] However, courts are frequently willing to reverse refusals of blood transfusion for children incapable of making their own decisions that parents make on principles of the parents' religious faith.[259] The basis of the common law's intervention is the limited risk and overwhelming benefit when transfusion is medically indicated to sustain life.[260] Advances in organ and other tissue transplantation proposed for children may in time reach comparable levels of safety and efficacy. Courts may react similarly to parents' refusals of foetal tissues on the ground that their newborn children should not benefit from induced abortions.

(ii) *Selection Criteria*

15.76 The gap between the demand for organs for transplantation and the supply may be self-perpetuating, since the availability of organs provides an incentive for physicians to advise patients to consider the option, and to place them on waiting lists. Scarcity of organs, and of personnel and other resources for transplantation, compels selection among candidate recipients, and development of principles for this purpose.[261] Public agencies must ensure that the selection criteria they invoke in principle and apply in practice are lawful. Principles and practices must not be discriminatory, for instance, on the basis of race or sex, or perhaps of age, and unreasonable criteria will be amenable to judicial review.[262] Some centres equate reformed alcoholic patients with non-

---

[257] *Prince v Massachusetts* (1944) 321 US 158, 166 (US Sup Ct).

[258] See *In re T (A Minor) (Wardship: Medical Treatment)*, [1997] 1 All ER 906 (CA) and Moore, D A, 'Challenging Parental Decisions to Overtreat Children', (1995) 5 *Health Matrix* 311–23.

[259] See Mason and McCall Smith (n 204 above), 222–5 and Giesen (n 209 above), 468–75.

[260] See generally Chapter 4 on court-ordered blood transfusion for children and pregnant women, and Arch, R R, 'The Maternal-Fetal Rights Dilemma: Honoring a Woman's Choice of Medical Care During Pregnancy' (1996) 12 J Contemp Health Law and Policy 637–73, 661–7.

[261] See Dickens, B M, 'Ethics Committees, Organ Transplantation and Public Policy' (1992) 20 Law, Medicine and Health Care, 300–6.

[262] See *R v Sheffield Health Authority* (n 118 above).

alcoholic patients, but disfavour liver transplantation of unreformed alcoholic patients, for instance, on the ground that it would afford them only a brief respite from their affliction. However, if alcoholism is seen as a physical or mental health dysfunction rather than a moral failing, it may seem perverse to deny patients respite from suffering on the ground that they are sick.[263] Medical futility, if adequately defined,[264] is a legitimate basis to withhold non-indicated treatment,[265] and patients may be stratified into those whose conditions render forms of management appropriate, or inappropriate for them and of no potential benefit. However, to refuse organ transplantation to a patient on a medically unrelated ground such as low intelligence may expose the decision-maker to judicial review.

It is understandable that courts will be disinclined to contradict how health **15.77** authorities determine the allocation of resources to serve an individual patient's best interests and the authority's obligation reasonably to provide effective treatment for the population of patients for whose health care services it is responsible.[266] It has been observed that '[d]ifficult and agonizing judgments have to be made as to how a limited budget is best allocated to the maximum advantage of the maximum number of patients. That is not a judgment which the court can make.'[267] Considering a particular patient's circumstances and wishes and declining to accommodate them on grounds of economy may be distinguishable from declining to consider them on an impersonal ground of the patient's race, sex, age, intelligence or other status.

United States courts may consider whether denials of medical care offend **15.78** the Americans with Disabilities Act of 1990.[268] Canadian courts, by contrast, have not found clear means to regulate alleged discrimination in access to health services under federal constitutional or provincial human rights provisions,[269] which are themselves absent from United Kingdom legislation. Although more explicit on individuals' rights to require just treatment from public authorities, the European Convention on Human Rights does not express a right to health services, and covers

---

[263] Coehn, C and Benjamin, M, 'Alcoholics and Liver Transplantation' (1991) 265 *J Amer Med Assoc*, 1299–1301.

[264] See generally Symposium on Medical Futility, (1995) 25 Seton Hall Law Rev, 873–1073 and Smith, G P, 'Utility and the Principle of Medical Futility' (1995) 12 J Contemp Health Law and Policy, 1–39. [265] See also Stern, K (n 241 above).

[266] See *R v Cambridge Health Authority, ex p B* [1995] 2 All ER 129 (CA).

[267] ibid, *per* Sir Thomas Bingham, MR, 137.

[268] Public Law, 101–336, 104 Stat 327 (1990).

[269] See *Eldridge v British Columbia (Attorney-General)* (1997), 151 DLR (4th) 577 (Sup Ct Can) on the Canadian Charter of Rights and Freedoms.

discrimination in health care only by implication of Article 14, which provides that:

> The enjoyment of the rights and freedoms set forth in this Convention shall be secured without discrimination on any ground such as sex, race, colour . . . birth or other status.

The absence of explicit reference to such criteria as age or physical or mental disability is not conclusive that these are not so-called 'non-enumerated' grounds of prohibited discrimination, but places a heavy burden on those who argue that the Convention bars discrimination on these grounds in the allocation of health care services such as transplantation. Dissatisfied patients may have greater prospects of resisting apparently discriminatory policies and practices by referring to the codes of ethics of health professionals and institutions rather than broadly based international declarations of aspirations to equality for all.[270]

(iii) *The United Kingdom Transplant Support Service Authority*

15.79 In exercise of powers conferred by various sections and Schedule 5 of the National Health Service Act 1977[271] and section 3(1) of the Human Organ Transplants Act 1989,[272] the Authority was established by Regulations in 1991.[273] The Regulations empower the Authority to provide instruction and services (such as for diagnosis and treatment) relevant to transplantation, to conduct research into causes and prevention of illnesses that result in demands for transplantation, and to collaborate with others for these purposes. The Authority may also, within limits, make available supplies of human blood and other bodily materials, and supplies of other substances and preparations not otherwise readily obtainable, and make appropriate charges, in order to assist, facilitate, and promote services for organ transplantation. The Authority records information about donors and recipients of organs and of available organs, identifies potential recipients, notifies transplant centres accordingly, and may arrange transport of organs. Its concerns extend to practices in respect of storage, transport, and use of organs. An important function is provision of an organ matching and tissue-typing service. The Authority reports to the Secretary of State for Health as required and at least annually, and furnishes such informa-

---

[270] For a helpful bibliography, see McCarrick, PM, 'Organ Transplant Allocation' (1995) 5 *Kennedy Institute of Ethics J*, 365–83.
[271] 1977 ch 49 as amended; see SI 1991/408 note (a) for relevant amendments.
[272] See n 6 above.   [273] SI 1991/408, as amended by SI 1991/1645.

tion from time to time as the Secretary requires in connection with its functions.

E. Anonymity

Neither the Human Tissue Act 1961[274] nor the Human Organ Transplants **15.80** Act 1989[275] addresses anonymity between recipients and donors of transplanted materials. In contrast, Ontario's Human Tissue Gift Act[276] provides in section 11 that:

(1) Except where legally required, no person shall disclose or give to any other person any information or document whereby the identity of any person,

    (a) who has given or refused to give a consent;

    (b) with respect to whom a consent has been given; or

    (c) into whose body tissue has been, is being or may be transplanted, may become known publicly.

(2) Where the information or document disclosed or given pertains only to the person who disclosed or gave the information or document, subsection (1) does not apply.

Anonymity prevents a living donor and family member of a deceased person from whose body materials were recovered and transplanted from approaching the recipient to request payment or other recognition of indebtedness, and prevents a recipient from acknowledging an obligation in a personalized way. There may be no need for provisions concerning anonymity in Britain, since live donors are confined primarily to genetic relations of recipients, both of whom will probably know the other's identity, and the 1989 Act is intended to preclude and punish transactions of a commerical nature.[277] Blood donation is conventionally anonymous, but has been the subject of litigation in some jurisdictions. Recipients who have contracted HIV infection from contaminated blood transfusions have sought to discover donors' identities to establish negligent donor recruitment and testing by blood supply agencies.[278] Some courts have given priority to donors' anonymity on the ground that disclosure of identity would prejudice the public interest in donation[279] and risk publicizing a

---

[274] N 5 above.   [275] N 6 above.   [276] N 8 above.

[277] In practice, cadaveric donation is almost invariably anonymous: see Fox and Swazey (n 188 above), 37.

[278] See *PD v Australian Red Cross Society (NSW Division)* (1993), 30 NSWLR 376 (NSWCA), and US cases discussed in the case commentary by Grubb, A, 'Discovery: Identity of Blood Donor' (1994) 2 Med L Rev, 111–13.

[279] See *AB v Scottish Blood Transfusion Service*, [1990] SCLR 263 (Ct Session, Outer House).

donor suffering from AIDS, but courts that have granted disclosure have set limits confining plaintiffs' access to essential information, and precluding any wider release, for instance to news media. Courts attempt to balance public interest in donation against plaintiffs' interests in obtaining compensation for negligent infliction of devastating infections, and hope to reconcile the interests.[280]

---

[280] See Kennedy and Grubb (n 9 above), 1133–9.

16

ENDING LIFE

A. The Law and the Protection of Human Life

Human life is unquestionably the most important value which the law sets **16.01** out to protect. In the criminal law context, any action which is calculated to endanger, or which is reckless in relation to, human life may be the subject of criminal prosecution, and acts which are intended to destroy human life are particularly severely punished by the law of homicide. In this respect, the criminal law is doing no more than reflect the intense attachment of most ethical systems to the preservation of human life as the supreme moral value.[1] Moral consensus on death, however, has been considerably undermined by a fundamental questioning of the basic premise that death is to be avoided at all costs. The notion that there are certain persons for whom death is preferable, whether as a result of their own choice or of the paternalistically-motivated choice of others, now commands fairly wide acceptance: to describe death as a right might have seemed counter-intuitive in the past, but sounds less inappropriate in an era of right to die societies and right to die legislation. The sanctity of life doctrine, previously widely-accepted, is now routinely described by moral philosophers as unreflective and vague.[2] Defences of a

---

[1] For recent philosophical discussion of this fundamental moral question, see Kamm, F M, *Morality, Mortality*, Vol 1 (Oxford University Press, 1993).

[2] See, for example, Kuhse, H, *The Sanctity-of-Life Doctrine in Medicine*, (Clarendon Press, 1987).

strict doctrine of the sanctity of life are now the exception, and, when they are made, encounter the additional hurdle of objections based on moral pluralism.[3] This change in moral climate is profound, and has inevitably affected the nature of the legal discussion of death.

16.02   The protection of human life which the law has traditionally provided, is not absolute; there are recognised exceptions to the prohibition of killing. Certain forms of human life (such as the human embryo and the foetus) are protected only to a limited degree against destruction, and the law also recognises the legitimacy of the intentional taking of human life in circumstance of self defence and, in some jurisdictions, coercion.[4] The circumstances in which the deliberate killing of another will be legally permissible are, however, very limited; in English law, for example, although few would hold one who killed under threat of death to be morally culpable, the taking of life under duress has been explicitly disapproved of in a decision of the House of Lords[5] and courts have occasionally stressed that even the last few moments of life are of very considerable value for the individual and not be treated as disposable.[6]

16.03   Even if moral attitudes have changed, it is against a background of respect for the value of human life that the reaction of the law to the medical treatment of the dying must be considered. The basic legal value—that of the protection of human life—may be unambiguous, but the requirements of patients for whom prospects are poor have necessitated a delicate dialogue between the law and medicine, the aim of which has been to allow doctors to treat dying patients within the law but with room for the exercise of discretion. In English law this has been achieved without recourse to legislation, and indeed legislation on the central issue of euthanasia is not currently contemplated.[7]

1. Euthanasia: Active and Passive

16.04   Euthanasia is the process whereby human life is ended by another in order to avoid the distressing effects of an illness. It may be voluntary, in the sense that the person killed either requests death or agrees to it, or it may be involuntary, in that the person killed either objects or is incapable of expressing an opinion either way and has not given consent in the past. The term 'euthanasia' is not restricted to acts performed within a medical context; any taking of life for this reason is euthanasia.

---

[3] For a pluralistic vision of the ethics of euthanasia (and other issues) see Charlesworth, M, *Bioethics in a Liberal Society* (Cambridge University Press, 1993).

[4] See discussion in Devine, P E, *The Ethics of Homicide* (Ithaca, Cornell University Press, 1978).   [5] *R v Howe* [1987] AC 417.

[6] For example, Mars-Jones J in *R v Carr* (unreptd) *Sunday Times*, 30 Dec 1986, 1: 'However gravely ill a man may be . . . he is entitled in our law to every hour . . . '

[7] Government Response to the Report of the Select Committee on Medical Ethics, (London, HMSO, 1994) (Cmnd 2553).

The distinction between 'active' and 'passive' euthanasia is one which has bedevilled the discussion of this issue, at least from the point of view of the ethics of euthanasia. The distinction is of such significance—even if for many it is wholly misleading—that no analysis of the subject can avoid it, and indeed it continues to underpin the legal response to the issue. In spite of philosophical criticism, the law appears reluctant to abandon the notion that there is a significant difference between bringing about a desired result through active intervention and merely allowing that same result to occur through inaction.[8]

16.05

The term 'active euthanasia' is used in ethical discussion to refer to the process whereby death is brought about by a specific act directed towards the causing of death. The act must be accompanied by an intention on the part of the actor that death result, and this intention must be the predominant one rather than a secondary, or oblique intention. This means that if the principal intention of the actor is to relieve immediate pain, any act directed towards that end will not amount to the intentional ending of the patient's life if, as a consequence, the life of the patient is shortened. Passive euthanasia, by contrast, occurs where the doctor, or other person caring for the patient, refrains from performing a particular act, with the specific intention that the patient should die as a result. It would be an act of passive euthanasia, for example, to refrain from treating a simple infection in a terminally ill person in the hope that the infection will lead to the patient's death and thereby bring to an end current or future suffering.

16.06

Arguments over the moral distinction between active and passive euthanasia are generally indistinguishable from the broader argument as to the moral difference between acts and omissions. Many moral philosophers now discount any such difference, pointing out that omissions are as causally potent as actions and are therefore capable of bearing the same consequences for responsibility.[9] In this view, there is no moral distinction between the administration of a fatal injection to a patient and refraining from offering a treatment if, in each case, the intention is that the patient should die as a result. Indeed, it is sometimes argued that the course of ending suffering quickly—by positive intervention—is morally preferable to standing by while death occurs slowly.

16.07

Whether or not the distinction between active and passive euthanasia is of any moral weight, the criminal law nonetheless reflects a stark discrimination

16.08

---

[8] Discussed below, in the context of the omission/commission distinction.
[9] There is a considerable literature on this point. See, in particular, Steinbock, B, (ed) *Killing and Letting Die* (New Jersey, Prentice-Hall, 1980); Harris, J, *The Value of Life* (Routledge and Kegan Paul, 1985); Kuhse, H, *The Sanctity-of-Life Doctrine in Medicine* (Clarendon Press, 1987), 58–81.

between act and omission. As a general rule, the law is slow to impose liability for omissions, and will generally only do so where there is a close relationship between persons or where there has been previous conduct which gives rise to a duty to act. In view of this attitude to omissions, it is not surprising that the law on euthanasia should itself embody this distinction between acting and refraining to act. In general, active euthanasia attracts legal attention; passive euthanasia, being an omission, will attract legal attention only in very unusual circumstances.

2. The Prohibition of Euthanasia

16.09   In criminal law, the motive with which an act is committed is, in general, irrelevant to the question of criminal guilt. Thus an accused person's concern to end the victim's pain will have no effect on liability for an intentional act of homicide, even if it may incline the court to accept in an appropriate case a mitigating plea of diminished responsibility. Euthanasia, even if voluntary and resorted to for the highest motives, is therefore a legally hazardous undertaking. It may be charged as murder, on the grounds that the mens rea of murder is present. There is intention to kill and an act is committed which brings about death. Consequently, unless there are grounds for the reduction of the offence to manslaughter, the person who performs an act of euthanasia faces the mandatory sentence of life imprisonment.

16.10   In spite of the legal prohibition, doctors and others do resort to active euthanasia, both consensual and otherwise. Where this is done medically, it may well go undetected; where the act of euthanasia is committed by a relative or friend of the patient it is more likely to be brought to the attention of the authorities. The exercise of prosecutorial discretion—where this is possible—may result in a decision not to proceed with charges, not necessarily on the grounds of inadequate evidence but out of sympathy for the accused.[10] As research on the plea of diminished responsibility has disclosed, where a charge is brought in such cases it will more likely be one of manslaughter rather than murder,[11] although there are noted cases in which the charge has been that of murder. The bringing of the lesser charge may be justified legally on the grounds that the evidence does not support the inference of the mens rea of murder, or, more commonly, a plea of diminished responsibility is readily accepted by the prosecution. This requires medical evidence, but the readiness of doctors to diagnose a reactive depression in these circumstances is unlikely to be challenged by the court in a case

---

[10]   See Otlowski, M, 'Mercy killing cases in the Australian Criminal Justice System' (1993) Crim LJ 10, 16. In this study of 19 cases over a period of 30 years, the author identified a number of cases where sympathy on the part of state prosecutors resulted in the discontinuation of proceedings.

[11]   Dell, S, *Murder into Manslaughter* (Oxford University Press, 1984), 35–6.

which engages sympathies.[12] Even if a charge of manslaughter is brought, juries may be unwilling to convict out of sympathy for the accused, and, even if there is a conviction, the sentence is likely to be light. Mercy killing not uncommonly attracts a sentence of probation,[13] or even conditional discharge.[14] If a term of imprisonment is imposed, it is unlikely to be lengthy, and even where a mandatory life sentence is imposed on a conviction for murder, the actual time spent in prison may be short.[15]

Whatever the actual response of prosecutors, juries, and judges may be, in theory the taking of any step directly intended to bring to an end the life of a terminally-ill patient constitutes the crime of murder. (Omissions constitute a distinct problem, which is dealt with below.) There are relatively few reported English cases on the subject, although prosecutions of this sort, especially those involving a medically qualified accused, attract considerable attention. *R v Adams*,[16] a case in which the accused doctor was acquitted of the murder of a patient to whom he had given large doses of morphine, posed the question of the legitimacy of the administration of pain-killing drugs in such doses as to shorten the patient's life. In *R v Carr*[17] a doctor was charged with the attempted murder of a terminally ill patient into whom he had injected a very large dose of phenobarbitone; he too was acquitted. Other cases in which fatal injections were administered include *R v Lodwig*,[18] in which the prosecution was abandoned after the Crown offered no evidence in respect of the administration of a fatal dose of potassium chloride and lignocaine, and the Scottish case of *HM Advocate v Watson*.[19] In the latter case, the accused had administered ten times the normal dose of diamorphine to a patient suffering from intractable pain. He was unable to explain why he administered such a dose, but was none the less acquitted of culpable homicide.

16.11

In *R v Cox*,[20] by contrast, a conviction was achieved, in this case for attempted murder. Dr Cox, a rheumatologist, was charged with attempted murder after

16.12

---

[12] For example, *R v Johnson*, *The Times*, 2 July 1960: diminished responsibility accepted in the case of a father who killed his 3 month old Down's syndrome child having decided that it was not in the best interests of the child to survive, a decision which appears to have been based on a rational assessment of the child's prospects. See comment by Leng, R, 'Mercy killing and the CLRC' 1982 NLJ 76.

[13] *R v Taylor* [1980] CLY 510; 12 months' probation for the killing by a father of his 9 year old autistic son with a mental age of around 2 years.

[14] *R v Jones*, *The Guardian*, 4 Dec 1979.

[15] Otlowski (n 10 above) refers to the South Australian case of *Johnstone* (unreptd, 21 Jan 1987, S Ct of South Australia), in which the non-parole period of a life sentence imposed on a man convicted of the murder of his mentally ill wife (who had asked for his assistance in dying) was fixed by the court at 10 days.

[16] Unreptd, 1957. Palmer, H, 'Dr Adams' Trial for Murder' [1957] Crim LR 365. See the full treatment of the case by the presiding judge, Devlin, P, *Easing the Passing* (1985).

[17] (1993) 12 BMLR 1.   [18] (1990) *The Times*, 16 Mar, 3.

[19] (1991) *The Scotsman*, 11 June, 8; 12 June, 3.   [20] (1992) 12 BMLR 38.

he had injected a fatal dose of potassium chloride into a patient suffering from pain which was not otherwise relievable. Two aspects of the case are noteworthy: firstly, the drug employed was not one which has generally-recognised pain-killing properties and Dr Cox was therefore unable to establish that his action had been intended to have a therapeutic effect; secondly, the charge was one of attempted murder, rather than murder, although the patient had died. The first of these factors made it difficult for the prosecution authorities not to act, without implicitly accepting the legitimacy of active euthanasia; had Dr Cox been in a position to employ an accepted pain-killer, then prosecution may well have been unlikely. The second factor—that of the charge of attempted murder—is explicable by the Crown's doubts as to its ability to prove causation (the body had been cremated), although another explanation might be the unwillingness of the Crown to risk acquittal by a jury which would quite simply not be prepared to contemplate a life-sentence being imposed on a man with whose motives individual jurors might well be expected to be in some degree of sympathy. The sentence imposed was non-custodial, although Dr Cox was admonished by the General Medical Council and suffered some professional restriction in his employment.[21]

16.13 Cases of this sort are, from the legal point of view, relatively uncomplicated, even if juries may be unwilling to convict members of the medical profession accused of such a serious crime as murder or attempted murder. Where considerable difficulty may arise, however, is in those cases where the drug administered to the patient is one which has a recognised analgesic effect, as is the case with morphine or other pain-killing agents. Such drugs may be administered with a view to controlling pain, but may have the additional effect of precipitating death. Morphine, for example, administered in sufficient quantities will suppress respiration and lead to cardio-respiratory failure. The use of this drug therefore requires a balancing of the pain-killing effect with the possible consequence of the shortening of the patient's life.

16.14 A programme of treatment with a pain-killing drug, in the knowledge that the drug will shorten life, will not be criminal provided that the aim of the treatment is to control pain rather than to bring life to a premature end. As Devlin J said in his instructions to the jury in the trial of Dr Adams:

> If the first purpose of medicine, the restoration of health, can no longer be achieved, there is still much for a doctor to do, and he is entitled to do all that is proper and necessary to relieve pain and suffering, even if the measures he takes may incidentally shorten life.[22]

[21] Dyer, C, 'GMC tempers Justice with Mercy in Cox Case' (1992) 305 *BMJ 1311*.
[22] *Easing the Passing* (n 16 above), 171.

In *Airedale NHS Trust v Bland*[23] this principle is described by Lord Goff, in obiter remarks, as the 'established rule that a doctor may, when caring for a patient who is, for example, dying of cancer, lawfully administer painkilling drugs despite the fact that he knows that an effect of that application will be to abbreviate the patient's life.' Such a decision, he observes, may be made as part of the care of the living patient, in his best interests; and on this basis, the treatment will be lawful. This principle is based simply on the issue of intention; where the predominant intention is to relieve pain, the existence of an unavoidable side-effect will not necessarily make the act illegal. This is the doctrine of double-effect, which recognises that acts may have more than one effect. Where there is more than one effect, or consequence, the status of the act may be determined according to the nature of that consequence which is selected—according to objectively defensible moral (or legal) criteria—as being of adequate weight to justify the act. In a case in which a doctor realises that the control of pain will have the additional effect of the shortening of life, the control of pain may clearly be a consequence of such weight that it obscures, in moral terms, the additional consequence, namely, the shortening of life. Obviously this principle is subject to limitations; it would be unacceptable to use such extreme measures in a case where there is an effective, safe alternative to the drug in question, and it might not be appropriate where the illness is not terminal. The mere fact of intractable pain alone may not justify the use of a drug which will radically shorten life; it is questionable, for example, whether the use of a life-shortening drug would be legally permissible in a case where the patient, although in considerable pain, is not dying.

B. The Intentional Ending of Life

1. Defining the Boundaries

While the criminal law is unambiguous in its prohibition of any act intended **16.15** to end the life of another, considerable difficulties attend the issue of what constitutes such an act. We have already seen that acts intended to relieve pain may be permissible even if they have the effect of shortening life; in other cases attention may be focused on inaction or refraining from treatment, or the cessation of treatment which is already being provided. Legal discussion of this issue is intricately linked with the ethical debate. In essence the issue is one of the duty to act and of the circumstances in which the existence of this duty will make an omission criminal.

English criminal law in general is reluctant to impose liability in respect of **16.16** omissions; hence the absence in the common law of a general duty to rescue.

---

[23] [1993] 1 All ER 821.

Thus, at its most extreme, a doctor who fails to render assistance to a person in distress commits no criminal offence, provided that he has no contractual or other legally-relevant relationship with that person, and provided that past actings on his part do not lead to a duty to act. It is under these concepts of relationship and past actings that the courts have succeeded in imposing liability for omissions.

16.17 The distinction which the law has traditionally made between omissions and acts of commission has long bedevilled the discussion of the law relating to euthanasia. Much confusion stems from the rigidity with which this distinction has been advanced, with the suggestion that the fact that death is caused by an omission rather than a positive act is sufficient defence to any inference of responsibility for the death. This line of defence was advanced, for example, in the case of *R v Arthur*.[24] As a result of this lingering reluctance to convict on the basis of omissions, much effort has been devoted to the elucidation of the distinction, and to the classification of some forms of conduct as omissions rather than acts of commission. The distinction, however, can sometimes seem to be no more than semantic. For example, a failure to administer a particular form of treatment can be seen as an omission—the doctor omits to take steps to provide the treatment—or it can be seen as a positive act—the doctor makes a decision not to provide the treatment. Alternatively, it can be seen as a *particular form* of positive action—the treating of the patient in such a way as to exclude a particular form of treatment.

16.18 The making of an act/omission distinction depends to an extent on the isolation of events within a course of action. There are certainly circumstances in which there occurs what might be termed a 'pure omission'; as, for example, where a person sees a crime being committed and does not report the matter. This is an omission in the pure sense because the failure to act occurs in isolation from any factors such as relationship or past actings. By contrast, the non-provision of a particular form of treatment will occur in the context of previous care and, even more significantly, in the context of an existing duty to the patient. The non-provision of treatment is therefore more readily viewed as a potentially faulty form of conduct.

16.19 The act/omission distinction may therefore be viewed as confusing, and, in any event, is of controversial moral weight; yet it continues to play an important role in criminal jurisprudence and whether conduct is classified as an act or an omission may determine the question of criminal liability. In *Airedale NHS Trust v Bland*[25] the issue of the withdrawal of artificial nutrition and hydration was portrayed by the Official Solicitor as an act of

---

[24] (1993) 12 BMLR 1.   [25] [1993] 1 All ER 821.

commission which could amount to murder. This argument was rejected by Lord Goff, who took the view that 'the mere failure to continue to do what you have previously done is not, in any ordinary sense, to do anything positive; on the contrary it is by definition an omission to what you have previously done'.

Omissions may be criminal in the presence of some factor which makes them exceptional. This factor is readily identified as a duty to act; in the absence of such a duty the omission is legally irrelevant. The duty is inferred on the basis of the relationship between the parties, and the reasonable expectations that the patient may have of the doctor. If a patient is entitled to expect a particular course of action of the doctor, then the doctor's failure to do what is expected of him becomes legally relevant.   **16.20**

The difficult issue is not when the duty of care arises but setting its extent, and it is this issue which dominates the topic of selective non-treatment. The essential question is whether a duty to care for another, once it has come into existence, involves a duty to do everything possible to preserve life. If this is the case, any omission to act potentially constitutes a culpable failure. In so far as there is consensus on this issue, contemporary medical ethics recognises that limits should be placed on the provision of treatment and endorses the view that heroic efforts for the preservation of life at all costs are not only unnecessary, but may also be an affront to the dignity of the patient. The fact that modern medicine is capable of sustaining life well beyond what are widely seen as 'natural limits' has led to the rise in North America of the 'natural death' movement, which has sought to protect patients in the face of this medical onslaught at the end of life.[26] Continuing treatment is therefore potentially as bad as stopping it prematurely; what must be sought is a position where patients are protected against premature cessation of treatment (in the interests of convenience, or as a form of involuntary euthanasia), and where the patient's interests are taken into account in determining whether a course of treatment is futile and will only lead to an undue prolongation of life.   **16.21**

The actual formulation of such a policy has proved to be difficult. Various approaches have been suggested, many of which are mere linguistic reworkings of earlier formulae. The distinction between 'ordinary' and 'extraordinary' means played an important part in the earlier debate. Ordinary means were taken to be those treatments which were not scientifically novel, and which were part of the everyday range of treatments available to the doctor. Antibiotics and common operations fell into this category. Extraordinary means were those which involved an element of scientific novelty, entailed   **16.22**

---

[26] Berger, AS, *Dying and Death in the Law and Medicine* (Praeger, 1993). An argument for the need for restraint in the face of high technology medicine is made by Callahan, D, *Setting Limits* (Simon and Schuster, 1987).

a considerable degree of medical effort and expense, or which might lead to considerable discomfort to the patient. This distinction was evidently helpful, but it tended to focus on the status or classification of the medical procedure rather than on the situation of the individual patient.

16.23 An alternative approach is to ask whether the procedure in question was 'appropriate' or 'inappropriate' for the patient. This at least focuses on the circumstances of the individual, and appears to allow greater flexibility. Thus it might be considered inappropriate to embark on a course of antibiotic treatment of a respiratory infection in a ninety-year-old patient with a very poor quality of life and a very poor prognosis. Antibiotic treatment in itself is an ordinary treatment, but there may be little point in providing it in such a case. The terms 'appropriate' and 'inappropriate', however, do little to illuminate the real nature of the decision being taken, although they are useful in emphasising the subjective and consequentialist nature of such decisions. In an attempt to address this issue, reference might be made to the *interest* of the patient, which should draw attention to the issues of suffering, dignity, and autonomy which are crucial factors in this context.

2. The 'Switching Off' Issue[27]

16.24 The removal of artificial ventilation is perhaps the starkest of the forms of cessation of treatment in that it normally, although not always, involves the fairly rapid death of the patient. For this reason it tends to be seen as a significant intervention in which death follows upon an act of the doctor. If the cessation of artificial ventilation is to be treated as legitimate, it must be distinguished from acts such as the administration of a lethal injection, which amounts to homicide. In one view, what distinguishes the two situations is the fact that the removal of the ventilator merely allows death to follow on from an already existing cause (damage to the capacity to breathe spontaneously), whereas the act of administering a lethal injection is a more self-sufficient cause of death, for which the doctor bears responsibility as the *initiator* of what follows. In causal terms, it might be argued that the two acts are qualitatively different. Analyses of causation are notoriously contentious, and such an analysis as this is no exception. The causal significance attributed to a particular act depends on the perspective from which it is approached and on the moral weighting given to particular events in a sequence. The actual (or immediate) cause of death in the ventilator case is surely the withdrawal. Similarly, the lethal injection occurs in the context of other causes, namely the patient's underlying condition. Ultimately, causal arguments may stand as cyphers for more general moral decisions and it is

---

[27] For an extended discussion of treatment-limiting decisions in relation to competent patients, see Ch 3 above, and in relation to incompetent patients, see Ch 4 above.

therefore unprofitable to rely on causation to provide any real key solution to the moral dilemmas involved in such cases.

Once the patient has become reliant on the respirator, not every withdrawal **16.25** will be appropriate. The following possibilities should be considered here:

(i) Where the Patient's General Condition May Be Expected to Improve, and Where the Capacity For Spontaneous Respiration May Develop

In such a case the withdrawal of mechanical assistance might amount to a **16.26** wrongful act, actionable at civil law and possibly even attracting criminal liability for criminal negligence. A difficulty in such a case will be deciding the boundaries between this stage and those stages in which the prognosis is sufficiently poor to merit withdrawal. This is a matter which would require to be resolved by expert evidence.

(ii) Where the Patient's Ability to Breathe Spontaneously is Temporarily Compromised, but Where the Patient is Likely to be Severely Brain-Damaged Should He Survive Removal From the Respirator

Here the decision to remove the patient from ventilation may be prompted **16.27** in part by the desire to avoid the patient's survival in a badly damaged state. The conclusion might be reached that the quality of life which the patient would enjoy would be so poor that his survival is not in his own best interests. This decision is one which doctors may properly make, and is covered by the principle that treatment need not be given if its effect will be to prolong inappropriately a life which is marred to an unacceptable degree by factors such as pain, gross disability, or very limited awareness of self and surroundings.

(iii) Where the Patient has Suffered Such a Degree of Brain Damage as to be Incapable of Surviving Disconnection From the Respirator

Patients in this position might have suffered such damage to the brain-stem as **16.28** to be unlikley to survive for very long even if connected to the respirator. In other cases, the damage to the brain-stem may not be so great as to amount to brain-stem death, but assistance with breathing will still be necessary. Where there is brain-stem death, some commentators have argued that since such persons can be considered dead from a legal and moral point of view their disconnection from the respirator gives rise to no ethical or legal difficulty. In practice, however, the disconnection of patients in this category would be covered by the proposition in (ii) above in that it would amount to a proper treatment decision made in the light of the poor prognosis.

The courts have considered the question of the cessation of artificial ventila- **16.29** tion in a number of cases where it has arisen as a causation issue in homicide trials. One of the earlier cases was a Scottish one, *Finlayson v HM Advocate*[28] in which the appellant had caused the deceased to go into a coma after he injected him—consensually—with Temazepam. He was convicted of culpable homicide, and appealed on the grounds that the act of doctors in withdrawing the victim from the respirator actually constituted a *novus actus interveniens*. The Court of Criminal Appeals rejected this argument and treated the act of withdrawal, after proper medical consideration and consultation, as being a normal incident of the deceased's medical treatment. A similar conclusion was later reached by the Court of Appeal in England in *R v Malcherek, R v Steel*,[29] where cessation of artificial ventilation was held not to interrupt the causal link between the original assault and the death of the victim.

16.30 The decision in *Re A*[30] provides a clear statement as to the lawfulness of withdrawing respiratory support in cases where there is clear medical evidence that brain-stem death has occurred and where there is no medical purpose served in continuing to ventilate the patient. The parents of the patient opposed—for medico-legal reasons—the decision to discontinue ventilation, but the court ruled that the respirator could be withdrawn. In his judgment, the judge ruled that the child was in fact dead, and that 'it would be wholly contrary to the interests of the child, as they may now be, for his body to be subjected to what would seem to me to be the continuing indignity to which it is subject'. It was also, he said, 'quite unfair to the nursing and medical staff' that ventilation should continue in these circumstances. This is a significant decision, in that it amounts to an explicit judicial recognition of brain death criteria of death, although the actual circumstances—those of disagreement between doctors and parents as to continued ventilation—are unlikely to rise with any frequency.

16.31 In *Auckland Area Health Board v Attorney-General*[31] a declaratory judgment was successfully sought from the court to the effect that no criminal offence would be committed if a patient suffering from Guillian-Barré syndrome were to be removed from the respirator upon which he relied. Under New Zealand legislation, the court is technically empowered to make such a declaration as to the criminal law, and the court took the view that this was an appropriate case in which to exercise this power.[32] In his judgment Thomas J said:

---

[28] 1979 JC 33.   [29] [1981] 2 All ER 422.   [30] [1992] 3 Med LR 303.
[31] [1993] 4 Med LR 239.
[32] On the status of pronouncements by civil courts on criminal matters, see *Imperial Tobacco Ltd v Attorney-General* [1980] 1 All ER 866; cf *R v Sloan* [1990] 1 NZLR 474; *Sankey v Whitlam* (1978) 21 ALR 505.

I have come to accept that the doctors' request for guidance is wholly reasonable. I do not consider that the doctors should be required to pursue their 'healing vocation inhibited in making their independent medical judgments for the well-being of their dying patients' under the threat of a nightmarish criminal prosecution if they, or their advisers, prove to be in error in their evaluation of the law or the legal process. In such circumstances I consider that it is appropriate for the court to respond by clarifying the law.

16.32 The judgment turns on the wording of the relevant section of the New Zealand Crimes Act, which creates a duty—in specified circumstances—to provide the necessities of life to the vulnerable and provides for criminal conviction if this duty is not discharged and death is caused by such an omission. The questions for resolution by the court were therefore: (1) whether the patient's death could be regarded as being caused by the withdrawal of the respirator; and (2) whether the provision of ventilation was a necessity of life.

16.33 On the issue of causation, the court considered the argument that in circumstances of this sort the cause of death would not be the withdrawal of artificial ventilation in itself but the underlying disease. This issue, it was felt, could only be determined if the prior question of the lawfulness of the withdrawal was settled. An unlawful withdrawal of ventilation would be the *legal cause* of death; a lawful withdrawal—one made *with lawful excuse*—would not be the cause of death in these terms. The important issue, then, becomes that of whether artificial ventilation is a necessity of life which has to be provided by those caring for the patient. On this issue, Thomas J said:

> . . . the provision of artificial respiration may be regarded as a necessary of life where it is required to prevent, cure or alleviate a disease that endangers the health or life of the patient. If, however, the patient is only surviving by virtue of the mechanical means which induces heartbeat and breathing and is beyond recovery, I do not consider that the provision of a ventilator can properly be construed as a necessary of life. It is repugnant that a doctor who has in good faith and with complete medical propriety undertaken treatment which has failed should be held responsible to continue that treatment on the basis that it is, or continues to be, a necessary of life.

16.34 This approach still requires a medical decision as to whether the point has been reached at which treatment serves no further therapeutic purpose. The court held that this decision must be made in accordance with 'good medical practice', a standard which the court stipulated includes taking into the account the patient's best interests, the views of the recognised bodies concerned with medical ethics, and close consultation with the patient's family.

3. Assisted Suicide

16.35 Assisted suicide is a central issue in the debate on euthanasia because it provides a possible middle-ground between the apparently irreconcilable positions of the legalisation of euthanasia and the preservation of the existing criminal law prohibition. The proponents of euthanasia argue that if legislatures feel disinclined to legalise euthanasia outright, then allowing physician-assisted suicide would at least make the process of dying easier for those who wish to end their life in these circumstances. It is perhaps for this reason that opponents of the legalisation of euthanasia see such measures as a mere semantic device under which euthanasia itself will rapidly be subsumed. This difference requires the initial question to be addressed: is there any moral difference between helping another to kill himself and taking that life oneself? If there is no such morally-significant distinction, then any justification that the law might have for embodying that distinction is itself weakened.

(a) Defining Suicide

16.36 The moral assessment of suicide requires a satisfactory definition of the act itself. To commit suicide is to bring one's life to an end intentionally. Death must be wanted for itself, as opposed to accepted. For example, it is not suicide to engage in an heroic, and inevitably fatal endeavour. Captain Oates did not commit suicide when he stepped out into the wastes, even if he knew that his death was inevitable; nor does the altruistic self-experimenter who submits himself to an experimental procedure in the knowledge that there is a very high chance of his dying in the process. Suicide requires that death be sought not as a means to an end, but as an end in itself. The person who proposes to take a fatal dose of a drug in order to escape from insupportable pain or mental distress might argue that death is not wanted in itself; what is wanted is relief from pain, and this, in the particular circumstances, can only come about through death. His death, then, should be classified in the same way as the polar explorer's or the self-experimenter's deaths are classified—as acts intended to achieve a goal other than mere death.

16.37 This argument, however, has obvious flaws. Firstly, this interpretation deprives the concept of suicide of virtually all meaning, and possibly leaves it only with those acts in which death is sought for frivolous reasons or for no reasons at all. Secondly, it ignores the point that what the suicide actually desires is death, whatever the motive may be; those who engage in hazardous activities—even those which involve a certainty of death—do not desire their death; the achievement of death is not their dominant reason for acting.

(b) The Morality of Assisted Suicide

16.38 The moral status of suicide has in the past had an important bearing on its legal status, and, in an important sense, it is still a relevant matter in discussions of the legal response to the issue of assisting another to commit suicide. If suicide is considered to be a wrong, then there are grounds for criminalising attempts to commit suicide. Suicide is no longer widely considered to be a morally wrongful act, however, and the grounds for its criminalisation have consequently disappeared. There may still be respects in which suicide causes harm to others, of course, but such harm (distress or financial hardship, for example) is not considered to be sufficiently weighty to justify punishing the attempted suicide. Added to this, of course, is the general objection to punishing those whose acts speak to inner distress.

If suicide is not wrongful, then a person has the right to commit suicide. This **16.39** means that if a person chooses to kill himself, attempts to interfere with the exercise of this right are themselves wrong, unless they are made for the legitimate protection of others. Furthermore, if a person has the right not to be interfered with in the exercise of a right, then this prohibition of interference should extend to attempts to stop his being assisted in the exercise of his right. This leads to the proposition that if it is lawful to do *x*, then it should be lawful to assist a person to do *x*. Consequently, if suicide is not a crime, then it should not be a crime to assist another to commit suicide. The logic of this is recognised in both German and French criminal law where it is acknowledged that since suicide is not a criminal offence it cannot be an offence to help another to commit suicide. Many legal systems, however, including English law, reject this reasoning and continue to punish as a criminal offence any act which is intended to assist another to take his life. This continued penalisation requires justification, in the light of the substantial rights-based critique to which it has been subjected.

(c) Justifying the Illegality of Assisted Suicide

The justification of the continued prohibition of aiding and abetting suicide **16.40** may be based on pragmatic grounds or on principle. The consequentialist argument for the existing law is that to allow someone to assist another to commit suicide raises the possibility that the would-be suicide may be subjected to external pressure in the making of the decision. The ready provision of assistance may serve to encourage those who might otherwise be reluctant to act and brings others into the penumbra of a decision which should be uninfluenced by others. The issue of voluntariness gives rise to some concern.[33] A request for assistance in suicide may be made in response to a feeling of guilt over financial and physical dependence; it may also be associated with depression, possibly caused by the illness. To deny help in suicide in some cases may be to thwart a considered and long-held desire to die and may

---

[33] For discussion of the voluntariness issue, see Drickamer, MA, Lee, MA and Ganzini, L, 'Practical Issues in Physician-Assisted Suicide' 1995 (126) *Annals of Internal Medicine*, 146.

therefore involve a substantial restriction on individual autonomy, but it is also to prevent a situation where a person might wish to live, but feels that dying compliantly is expected of them. It may be difficult to resolve this conflict of values, which is essentially a moral rather than a legal issue.

16.41 The principled objection to allowing assisted suicide focuses on the proposition that competence to perform a particular act may properly be restricted to the actor himself. This is a privacy-related argument; suicide is a private matter in which no person other than the suicide has any *locus*. To assist another in suicide, then, is to intrude into the private sphere of another, and such intrusions may legitimately be prohibited by the criminal law. An obvious objection to this view is that it ignores the plight of those who are incapable, through physical disability, of performing the act in question. If they are denied assistance, then they may claim to be at a considerable disadvantage as compared with those who do have the ability to act within this private sphere. The issue then is whether society is to redress this disadvantage by allowing assistance in such cases, or whether the value of protecting the privacy of such acts precludes the making of any exceptions.

16.42 A further argument of principle holds that life is the supreme value endorsed by the law. The weakening of this endorsement, by any recognition of the legitimacy of taking life, threatens the value itself. If a life is seen as disposable, even if only at the instance of the holder of that life, then the moral awe with which life is viewed is compromised. The direct response to this view, of course, is that there is nothing valuable in life itself; what gives value to life is the capacity for enjoyment of and engagement in the world. If this is destroyed, then life itself becomes a burden which there should be no need to endure. The decision to commit suicide then becomes a legitimate exercise of the autonomous right vested in every person to shape and control his existence.

(d) Means of Assisting Suicide

16.43 The legal prohibition of direct acts of euthanasia may lead to a request to medical or nursing personnel to provide assistance to a patient who wishes to end his own life. The provision to such a patient of the means of committing suicide or advice as to an appropriate technique may amount to a criminal offence, although the patient's own act of suicide is not criminal. Suicide has not been a crime in English law since the Suicide Act 1961 decriminalised the act of attempted suicide. The offence of aiding and abetting a suicide was retained under section 2 of this Act. The mens rea of aiding and abetting suicide is probably an intention to assist another to take his own life. It is not clear whether the offence can be committed recklessly, but it is submitted that it would be an offence to furnish the means of suicide where one knows that they might be used to take the recipient's life. For example, it would be aiding and abetting suicide to give a bottle of potentially lethal pills to a person whom one knows to be depressed and who has talked of committing suicide. By analogy with the form of recklessness required for assault in *Spratt*[34] and *Parmenter*[35] the form of recklessness which would be required would probably be subjective recklessness of the *Cunningham* variety, rather than objective, *Caldwell* recklessness.[36]

The provision of advice as to means of ending life was considered in *Attorney-* **16.44** *General v Able*.[37] In this case the question arose as to whether the publication or circulation of a booklet setting out suicide techniques could amount to aiding and abetting suicide. The case was a civil one, the Attorney General seeking a declaration to this effect. The court declined to issue the declaration, but it also declined to say that the supply of the booklet was lawful. The judge did say, however, that a supplier of such advice could be guilty of the offence of aiding and abetting suicide if he intended to encourage the suicide of the recipient and if the recipient was, in fact, encouraged or assisted to commit suicide. This suggests that the link between the act of the accused and the deceased's act of suicide must be a close one. The *Able* case is unsatisfactory authority on the scope of criminal liability for aiding suicide, but it is significant that the supply of books detailing methods of suicide now appears to have been officially tolerated, with such books even being made available in book shops rather than to members of voluntary euthanasia societies.

(e) Homicide

As an alternative to the statutory offence, in an appropriate case it is possible **16.45** that a prosecution might be brought for homicide. Theoretically, the charge could be murder or manslaughter, depending on whether the intention necessary for murder could be established—it is certainly possible to envisage a situation where an accused has provided a drug to another with the full intention that the other person should use it. The only reason why this should not be homicide is that the act of the victim amounts to a *novus actus interveniens* breaking the chain of causation between the accused's act and the result (the death).

The English courts have not pronounced on this point, but similar questions **16.46** of causation have arisen in other contexts. The nearest analogy is provided by those cases in which there has been an initial unlawful act on the part of the

---

[34] [1991] 2 All ER 210.   [35] [1991] 2 All ER 225.
[36] For further discussion, see Smith, JC and Hogan, B, *Criminal Law* (8th edn, London, Butterworths, 1996), 392.   [37] [1984] 1 All ER 277.

accused, followed by a response by a self-harming response by the victim. The applicability of the analogy depends on whether the act of assistance is in itself unlawful. This would depend on whether it is considered an unlawful act to give to another the means of harming himself or herself, in the knowledge that the means might be used.

16.47 In a number of cases, a suicidal or self-endangering act of the victim has not been considered to be a *novus actus*. In a series of cases involving a self-injuring escape attempted in the face of a threat which the accused has made, the courts have held that the victim's act does not necessarily constitute a *novus actus*. This was so in *Williams*,[38] where the court stressed that the victim's act must be proportionate to the threat and not so unreasonable as to make it a voluntary act that breaks the chain of causation. Other escape cases reach a similar conclusion.[39] The test, then, would appear to be whether the act of the deceased was an unforseeable one, something that a reasonable person would not have expected to happen. As Brennan J says in the leading Australian case on this point, *Royall v R*:[40]

> The question whether an accused whose conduct has led to a death is criminally responsible for the death when the death has been caused by a final fatal step taken by the victim thus depends on the reasonableness (or proportionality) of the victim's attempt at self-preservation and the accused's foresight, or the reasonable foreseeabilty of the possibility that a fatal final step might be taken by the victim in response to the accused's conduct.[41]

16.48 *R v Dalby*[42] involved an appeal against a conviction of manslaughter in a case where the appellant had illegally supplied a drug of abuse to the victim, who had then injected it in excessive quantities and died as a result. The appellant's conviction of manslaughter was set aside by the Court of Appeal on the grounds that the act of supplying the drugs to the victim was not one 'directed against the victim'. It was held that manslaughter requires an act of this nature, and that the provision of drugs could not be so interpreted because it would 'itself have caused no harm unless the deceased had subsequently used the drugs in a form and quantity which was dangerous'. Waller LJ concluded:

> In the judgment of this court, where the charge of manslaughter is based on an unlawful and dangerous act, it must be an act directed at the victim and likely to cause immediate injury, however slight.[43]

16.49 This approach to the unlawful and dangerous act basis of manslaughter has led to confusion, which was clarified, to an extent, in *Goodfellow*[44] in which a

---

[38] [1992] 2 All ER 183.
[39] For example, *Roberts* (1971) 56 Crim App Rep 95; *DPP v Daley* [1980] AC 237.
[40] (1991) 65 ALJR 451. [41] ibid, 460. [42] [1982] 1 All ER 916.
[43] ibid, 919. [44] (1986) 83 Crim App Rep 23.

conviction of manslaughter was upheld where the accused, having set fire to a house, caused the death of two persons when the fire spread. Even if he had not directed his act against his victims, it was still an objectively dangerous act which caused death and therefore an unlawful and dangerous act. The decision in *Dalby*, it was said, was only intended to stress that there must not be a *novus actus interveniens* to break the causal link. *Dalby*, however, is capable of constituting a hurdle for any attempted manslaughter or murder prosecution in a case where a drug has been supplied to a prospective suicide. The difficulty may be overcome by distinguishing *Dalby* on its facts. It is one thing to give a drug to a drug abuser who might be expected to use it in normal quantities; it is another to pass on such a drug to one whom one knows is going to take a fatal dose. In the former case, it might be accepted that the act is not 'directed against' the victim, whereas in the latter, in view of the foreseen consequence (death), the act may clearly be described as being so directed.

4. Assisted Suicide in Other Jurisdictions

(a) United States

The paucity of English case law authority on this matter lends particular interest to the experience of other jurisdictions. In the United States, where in many states there is legislation prohibiting the aiding and abetting of suicide, challenges have been made to the constitutionality of such measures.[45] In *Vacco v Attorney General of New York*[46] the matter eventually came before the United States Supreme Court, which ruled in favour of the constitutionality of such provisions. In the case of New York the legislation in question was the New York Penal Law, section 12.15, which provides: 'A person is guilty of manslaughter in the second degree when . . . (3) he intentionally causes or aids another person to commit suicide.' Section 12.30 of the same legislation states: 'A person is guilty of promoting a suicide attempt when he intentionally causes or aids another person to attempt suicide.'

16.50

The appellants in *Vacco* argued that this law infringed the Fourteenth Amendment of the United States' Constitution in that it treated different classes of dying patients unequally. The Court of Appeals agreed, observing:

16.51

> New York law does not treat equally all competent persons who are in the final stages of fatal illness and who wish to hasten their deaths . . . [T]hose in the final stages of terminal illness who are on life support systems are allowed to hasten their deaths by directing the removal of such systems; but those who are

---

[45] Legal attitudes vary within the US: in Texas the courts have held that since there suicide is not a crime it cannot be a crime to assist another to take his own life: *Aven v State* 277 SW 1080 (1925).   [46] United States Supreme Court, 26 June 1997.

similarly situated, except for the previous attachment of life sustaining equipment, are not allowed to hasten death by self administering prescribed drugs.

The Supreme Court reversed this decision, holding that there was a distinction, widely recognised and endorsed in the medical profession, between suicide and withdrawing life sustaining treatment. This distinction, the court said, was a rational one; a person who commits suicide with the assistance of a doctor has a specific intention to end his own life, while one who refuses or discontinues treatment might not have such an intention. There were other grounds too; Chief Justice Rehnquist identified the State's motives in the following terms:

> New York's reasons for recognising and acting on this distinction—including prohibiting intentional killing and preserving life; preventing suicide; maintaining physicians' role as their patients' healers; protecting vulnerable people from indifference, prejudice, and psychological and financial pressure to end their lives; and avoiding a possible slide towards euthanasia . . . these valid and important public interests easily satisfy the constitutional requirement that a legislative classification bear a rational relation to some legitimate end.

(b) Scotland

16.52 In Scotland, where there is no counterpart of the Suicide Act 1961, and where suicide has not been a criminal offence in modern times,[47] diverging views have been expressed as to the legality of assisting a person to take his own life. In one view, it could be the common law offence of 'recklessly endangering life' to supply information on suicide to one who is likely to put it into effect; and, if death results, this could possibly amount to culpable homicide. The grounds of a culpable homicide prosecution would be that death resulted from the illegal act of the accused (that is, from the reckless endangerment). This is open, however, to the challenge that the act of the deceased in taking his life amounted to a *novus actus interveniens*, relieving the accused of responsibility for the death. It is not clear how a Scottish court would respond to this argument, although in *Ulaqh v HM Advocate*[48] a case involving the supply of solvents for purposes of ingestion, the court declined to regard the act of the recipients in using the solvents as amounting to a *novus actus*. Similarly, in *Lord Advocate's Reference (No 1 of 1994)*[49] the High Court ruled that a culpable homicide conviction was competent where the supplier of illicit recreational drugs gives drugs to another who then administers them himself, with fatal results.

---

[47] See discussion by Gordon, *Criminal Law* (Green, 2nd edn, 1978), 23.01.
[48] 1990 SCCR 593.   [49] 1995 SLT 248.

(c) Canada and New Zealand

Patients suffering from progressive and severe neurological conditions have **16.53** been involved in litigation in Canada and New Zealand in a series of cases which have attracted considerable attention. In *Nancy B v Hôtel-Dieu de Quebec*,[50] the plaintiff, who suffered from Guillain-Barré syndrome (which entails the development of the 'locked-in' syndrome, in which the mind becomes trapped in a totally immobile body), had lost almost all her capacity to move and was dependent on a respirator; her mental faculties, however, remained unaffected. She sought an injunction against the hospital in which she was a patient to the effect that she could lawfully be removed from the respirator even if this inevitably resulted in her death. This was granted on the grounds that artificial respiration constituted treatment and that every patient is entitled to reject treatment if he or she so desires.[51] The court cited with approval the opinion expressed in the United States case, *Re Conroy*,[52] in which it was pointed out that: ' . . . declining life-sustaining medical treatment may not properly be viewed as an attempt to commit suicide. Refusing medical treatment merely allows the disease to take its natural course; if death were eventually to occur, it would be the result, primarily, of the underlying disease, and not the result of a self-inflicted injury.' As far as possible criminal liability was concerned, the court also observed that in removing the respirator, the doctors would not be committing an offence under the law of homicide.[53]

In treating the issue as one of cessation of treatment, the court in *Nancy B* did **16.54** not need to pronounce on the question of assisted suicide, although the decision provides clear support for the right of the individual to determine the point at which his or her life comes to a 'natural end'. In *Rodriguez and Attorney General of British Columbia et al*[54] the Supreme Court of Canada was confronted with a direct challenge to the legality of the section in the Criminal Code which makes it an offence to aid or abet another to commit suicide. The plaintiff in this case was afflicted by a motor neurone disease from which she would not recover and which would, in time, deprive her of movement and therefore of any ability to take her own life. She sought a declaration to the effect that she was entitled to assistance in ending her life, a course of action which would otherwise result in criminal liablity under section 241 of the Criminal Code (which punishes the aiding and abetting

---

[50] 86 DLR 4th 385.
[51] A principle recognised in Canada in *Malette v Shulman* (1990) 67 DLR (4th) 321.
[52] 486 A 2d 1209, 1224.
[53] This was on two grounds: (1) s 45 of the Criminal Code states that surgical operations do not give rise to criminal liability if they are *reasonable*; and (2) such conduct would not manifest a wanton or reckless disregard for the life of another.   [54] 107 DLR (4th) 342.

of suicide). The Supreme Court determined, by a narrow majority, that the validity of section 241 should be upheld in face of the challenge that it infringed the provision of the Charter of Rights and Freedoms which recognises and protects the right of individual autonomy.[55] The majority judgment rejects at the outset the argument that a terminally ill person who takes his own life is merely determining the time and manner of death rather than actively 'choosing death'. Even so, it accepts that to prevent a person seeking assistance to commit suicide does, in fact, impinge upon the security of the person, and may cause distress and discomfort. This does not mean the principles of fundamental justice, protected by section 7 of the Charter are thereby compromised; the relationship between the state interest in the preservation of life and the individual's interest in autonomy has to be considered. This, the court said, involves a balancing process which, in the end results in a victory for the state interest. As Sopinka J pointed out:

> The issue here . . . can be characterised as being whether the blanket prohibition on assisted suicide is arbitrary or unfair in that it is unrelated to the state's interest in protecting the vulnerable, and that it lacks a foundation in the legal tradition and societal beliefs which are said to be represented by the prohibition.[56]

It is clear that in preferring the state interest the majority was swayed by the fact that the blanket prohibition of assistance in suicide was endorsed in the overwhelming majority of legal systems and that to adopt a contrary approach would be to invite abuse.[57] There is, thus, a strong policy flavour to this decision.

C. Euthanasia: Legislative Reform

16.55 Euthanasia, in the sense of a positive act intended to bring about death, remains universally a criminal offence, even if permissible in certain circumstances in the Netherlands. In the Common Law homicide liability is determined by intention, and there is therefore no distinct category of 'mercy killing'. Consequently it is only if a mitigating defence such as diminished responsibility is applied, or prosecutorial discretion is shown in charging with the lesser offence of manslaughter, that the courts are free to recognise the considerably lower level of moral guilt entailed in euthanasia. Other jurisdictions typically recognise more categories of gravity in homicide, with the result that the courts may have considerable sentencing discretion in relation to the punishment of acts of euthanasia. Swiss criminal law allow for the

---

[55] Section 7 of the Charter states: 'Everyone has the right to life, liberty and security of the person and the right not to be deprived thereof except in accordance with the principles of fundamental justice.'   [56] N 54 above, 396.
[57] See the majority judgment, ibid at 410 g–h.

reduction of punishment where a homicide is committed 'for honourable motives';[58] German law similarly recognises a broad concept of extenuating circumstances. In Norway, there is explicit recognition of mercy killing, with a lesser punishment being provided for in such cases.[59]

Punishing acts of euthanasia leniently does not meet many of the objections of those who favour a fundamental change in the criminal law. Pro-euthanasia campaigns claim widespread support for the principle of voluntary euthanasia, and to a great extent this is borne out by public attitude surveys.[60] There would also appear to be a measure of support in the medical profession for a change in the law, although many doctors are uneasy about the legalisation of euthanasia.[61] In spite of this evidence of considerable support for legal change, no attempt to introduce a parliamentary measure has ever succeeded in the United Kingdom and only two jurisdictions, the Netherlands and the Northern Territory in Australia, have taken substantial steps in the direction of legalising the practice of voluntary euthanasia. **16.56**

1. The Experience of the Netherlands

Euthanasia is widely and openly practised in the Netherlands. Estimates of the incidence of the practice differ, and a degree of caution should be exercised over the statistics, particularly in the light of concerns over under-notification. Most studies, however, reveal a rise in incidence since the practice became legally tolerated.[62] In theory, all homicide is illegal in the Netherlands: Article 293 of the Penal Code makes it an offence to cause another's death at his request, and this article remains in force.[63] However, in a series of decisions the Dutch courts have allowed a defence of necessity to **16.57**

---

[58] Penal Code, s 155.   [59] Penal Code, s 235.

[60] There are numerous surveys on this issue. For examples, see Wise, J, 'Public supports euthanasia for most desperate cases', 1996 (313) *BMJ 1423*, discussing a survey which revealed public support for the permissibility of euthanasia—in some circumstances—at 86 per cent. Emanuel, EJ, Fairclough, DL, Daniels, ER, and Clarridge, BR, 'Euthanasia and physician-assisted suicide: attitudes and experiences of oncology patients, oncologists, and the public' (1996) 347 *The Lancet*, 1805: two thirds of the patient group and the public expressed support for euthanasia and physician-assisted suicide for those afflicted with unremitting pain.

[61] Coulson, J, 'Doctors oppose legal mercy killing for dying', *BMA News Review*, Mar 1995, 15: revealing 57 per cent of the sample of doctors as being opposed to the legalisation of assisted suicide. See also: Bachman JG, *et al*, 'Attitudes of Michigan physicians and public toward legalizing physician-assisted suicide and voluntary euthanasia' 1996 (334) *NEJMed*, 303.

[62] For a general survey, see van der Maas, PJ, van Delden, JJM, and Pijnebourg, L, *Euthanasia and Other Medical Decisions Concerning the End of life* (New York, Elsevier, 1992); also, Hendin, H, *Seduced by Death* (Norton, 1997).

[63] The legal position in the Netherlands is discussed by Keown, J, 'The law and practice of euthanasia in the Netherlands' (1992) 108 LQR 51; Griffiths, J, 'The Regulation of Euthanasia and Related Medical Procedures that Shorten Life in the Netheralnds' (1994) 1 Med L Int, 137.

doctors who have taken the lives of patients in order to protect them from undue suffering. The effect of such decisions was to hold that where there is a conflict between the duty to preserve life and the duty to alleviate suffering, opting for the latter may be the right choice. The defence of necessity was therefore available to doctors reaching a decision to take life in such cases, but there was anxiety in the medical profession that it would still be possible to face prosecution. In 1990 an agreement was reached between the Ministry of Justice and the Royal Dutch Medical Association whereby a doctor would not face prosecution if he complied with the agreed notification procedure and this agreemnet was subsequently given formal legal status.

16.58 The working of the Netherlands provisions are of considerable interest in the light of pressure for change in other countries. It is a common warning that tolerance of euthanasia under limited conditions will lead to its application in an increasingly wide range of cases. To an extent, the Netherlands experience bears this out; certainly the courts have applied the necessity principle in cases which would not have met earlier criteria. In its decision in the *Chabot* case in 1994,[64] the Supreme Court held that the euthanasia of a patient suffering from psychological as opposed to physical distress was admissible as a case of necessity, even if in the case in question the doctor could not claim the defence because of his failure to seek an independent opinion. Other cases have involved the euthanasia of infants, which offends the voluntary principle.[65] There is also evidence that the procedural safeguards set out are not always observed, and this is taken as supporting the argument that it may be difficult to control the practice of euthanasia once it is admitted.

16.59 If proper procedures are followed, euthanasia in the Netherlands is available if there is a voluntarily-made request which is the result of proper reflection, and which emanates from a patient whose suffering is unacceptably severe. Before the request can be complied with, a doctor must have obtained the agreement of another doctor. He must subsequently notify the medical examiner, who reports in turn to the local state prosecutor. Critics point out that these procedures are not always followed and that there are now many cases, particularly involving vulnerable or confused patients, in which the voluntary principle has to all intents and purposes been abandoned.[66]

---

[64] This case is discussed at length by Hendin (n 62 above), 60.

[65] Sheldon, T, 'Dutch appeal court dismisses case against doctor' 1995 (311) *BMJ 1322*.

[66] See, for example, Keown, J, 'Euthanasia in the Netherlands: Sliding down the Slippery Slope?' in Keown J (ed) *Euthansia Examined: Ethical, Legal and Clinical Perspectives* (Cambridge University Press, 1995), 269.

2. Legalisation in Australia: The Northern Territory's Legislation

In 1995 The Northern Territory of Australia introduced the Rights of the **16.60** Terminally Ill Act which allowed for voluntary euthanasia in specified conditions. This Act provided that 'a patient who, in the course of a terminal illness, is experiencing pain, suffering and/or distress to an extent unacceptable to the patient, may request the patient's medical practitioner to assist the patient to terminate the patient's life'.[67] The Act set out a list of conditions which had to be satisfied for assistance to fall within its provisions. These included the obtaining of a second medical opinion confirming the prognosis of terminal status, and the obtaining of a psychiatric opinion as to the absence of depressive illness in relation to the condition and confirmation of the reality of consent and of due reflection by the patient.[68]

This legislation was subjected to challenge in the courts on the ground that it **16.61** was ultra vires of the Legislative Assembly of the Northern Territory to legislate on this matter. This challenge failed,[69] but a more successful attack was raised at a Commonwealth level with the passing of the Euthanasia Laws Act 1997. This Act provided that the powers conferred on the Legislative Assembly of the Northern territory by virtue of the Northern territory (Self-Government) Act 1978 did not include the power to make laws with respect to the intentional killing of a patient, nor did it include the power to repeal legal sanctions against attempted suicide.

---

[67] S 4.   [68] S 17.
[69] *Wake and Gondarra v Northern Territory of Australia and Administrator of the Northern Territory,* Northern Territory, Supreme Court, 24 July 1996.

17

DEATH

A. Introduction: The Historical Criteria of Death

17.01 The historic common law regarded death as an event rather than a process. The determination of death was addressed more as a matter of common observation than of medical science. The ecclesiastical courts dealt with many of the spiritual and social incidents of death, and the royal courts were interested in fines and forfeitures to the Crown when deaths were caused by crimes. The criminal law provided that if a victim's death occurred at a time later than a year and a day from an offence such as the infliction of a wound, the offence was not convictable as culpable homicide.[1] The common

---

[1] The Law Commission recommended abolition of this historic rule; see The Law Commission (Law Com No 230) *Legislating the Criminal Code: The Year and a Day Rule in Homicide* (London, 1995), and it was abolished by the Law Reform (Year and a Day Rule) Act 1996.

law evolved to address death as an indication for other events to occur, notably burial, distribution of estates and payments under life insurance policies. In contrast, increasingly sophisticated medical concepts evolved to regard death primarily as a process.[2] In 1979 the Conference of Royal Colleges and their Faculties (UK) published a report that observed that:

> Exceptionally, as a result of massive trauma, death occurs instantaneously or near-instantaneously. Far more commonly, death is not an event, it is a process, the various organs and systems supporting the continuation of life failing and eventually ceasing altogether to function, successively and at different times.[3]

Nevertheless, death is considered a matter of legal status, medicine serving to determine whether or not the legal criteria of death have been satisfied.[4]

The utility of organs and tissues from recently deceased persons for transplan-   **17.02** tation has created some modern urgency to determine whether or not deaths have occurred. Before this development, death was usually established only relatively to the time of death of another. In the absence of evidence of which of two or more persons died first, the common law presumption as to *commorientes* (people who die together) applies. The presumption reflects nature in deeming older persons to have died before younger persons. When spouses had made common wills, each leaving the bulk of the estate to the other in the event of surviving the testator, and they perished in a common disaster, the families of the two spouses might seek evidence of their family member's survival of the partner. In an Ontario case in 1936,[5] a husband was found to have survived his wife in a common drowning accident because the volume of water in his lungs was greater than the volume in hers, assessed proportionately to lung size. Respiration was taken as evidence of life, and the greater volume of water in his lungs indicated that he was breathing after his wife ceased to breathe. Similarly, in a macabre Kentucky case in 1950,[6] a couple died in a railway level-crossing tragedy. The wife was decapitated, and was found with blood surging from her trunk. The husband's body was observed at the same time motionless and not bleeding. The court concluded that, since the husband was neither breathing nor bleeding when his wife's body was gushing blood, she had survived him. Heart-beat or respiration were legal evidence of life, and her bleeding provided evidence that her heart was beating.

---

[2] See Kennedy, I and Grubb, A, *Medical Law with Materials* (2nd edn, 1994), ch 18, 1370–1406; and Morison, RS 'Death: Process or Event?', (1971) 173 *Science*, 694–8.
[3] 'Memorandum on the Diagnosis of Death', (1979) 1 *Brit Med J*, 332, para 2.
[4] For criticism of legal involvement in medical decision-making at the end of life, see Flick, MR, 'The Due Process of Dying', (1991) 79 California Law Rev, 1121–67.
[5] *Re Warwicker, McLeod et al v Toronto General Trust Co.* (1936) 3 DLR 368 (Ont SC).
[6] *Gugel's Administrator v Orth's Executors* (1950) 236 SW 2nd 460 (Kentucky CA).

B. Brain Stem Death

1. Introduction

17.03   The development of artificial means to preserve patients' vital functions, such as by mechanical ventilators to maintain patients' oxygen supply and heartbeat, affords patients an opportunity to survive when they are incapable of breathing spontaneously and maintaining heart function. In response to this development, the law preserved its focus on respiration and pulsation as evidence of life, but accepted the artificial source of energy sustaining vital functions as the equivalent of a person's spontaneous maintenance of such functions. A patient dependent for survival on artificial life support equipment is clearly alive. It became increasingly clear, however, that heartbeat and respiration alone are not necessarily sufficient to preserve human life. Although the heart retains its conventional status as the source of human sentiment, it has become progressively recognized that the seat of human personality and character is the brain, the location of human intellect. Accordingly, the neurological status and prognosis of a human being assumed increasing legal significance, eventually paving the way to concurrent legal recognition of death due to failure of heartbeat and respiration, and of so-called 'brain death', now medically described as brain stem death.[7]

2. Development of Criteria of Brain Stem Death

17.04   The first case in a common law jurisdiction to recognize the concept of basing death on neurological criteria appears to have been one decided in 1967 in Kansas.[8] A husband whose wife was suffering from terminal cancer fired five revolver shots into her head and then shot himself with the same weapon. Evidence showed that she had bled profusely, whereas he appeared not to have bled at all. By conventional tests of evidence of heart-beat, she would have been considered to have survived him,[9] if only for a brief time. The court accepted, however, not only that the severe brain damage suffered by the wife was incompatible with survival, but that it had caused an immediate and irreversible end to her vital functions, and that she had died before her husband killed himself. The court did not address refined explanations of brain structure and function nor the process of neocortical death, but applied a common sense, if crude, approach to the facts. Without addressing the

---

[7] 'Criteria for the diagnosis of brain stem death', (1995) 29 *J Royal College of Physicians*, 381–2.
[8] *United Trust Co v Pyke* (1967) 427 P 2d 67 (Sup Ct Kansas).
[9] See *Gugel's Administrator* (n 6 above).

decisive function of the brain stem, the court responded to an intuitive perception that the permanent loss of brain capacity would quickly lead to organ failure and satisfaction of physiological criteria of death.

Although the classical tests of death, amounting to the irreversible loss of **17.05** cardiopulmonary function, were widely accepted, due perhaps to their relatively easy application and the absence of an accessible, easily operable alternative, they were not fully satisfactory. The tests did not always produce true results, even advanced mechanical methods sometimes failing to detect faint pulse and shallow breathing associated for instance with the taking of drugs, and afforded continuing currency to popular superstitious fears of being buried alive.

The tests were also frustrated by the fact that mechanical means could appear **17.06** to satisfy them. Patients on mechanical life support systems appeared permanently incapable of resuming consciousness and yet continued to maintain a pulse and breathe. Use of mechanical means that were pioneered to maintain patients for the different purpose of preserving tissue quality in organs destined for transplantation[10] aggravated medical dissatisfaction with the legal criteria of death, and confounded legal decision-making on matters of public concern. Medical acceptance that the best way to preserve an organ until transplantation was in the body in which it had grown, transfused by its own blood, led to increasing employment of mechanical organ support in bodies of recently deceased persons. Because conventional legal criteria of death might record death in persons capable of medical revival, and life in persons treated medically as having died, pressures arose to develop more satisfactory criteria of death that the law could accept.

The first well accepted definition of death to include what then was described as **17.07** brain death was developed in 1968 by the Ad Hoc Committee of the Harvard Medical School to Examine the Definition of Brain Death.[11] The Ad Hoc Committee used the term 'irreversible coma' to define what is now generally called brain stem death, and described two reasons why a new definition of death was needed. The first was the need to provide a basis for withdrawal of resuscitative and supportive measures applied in the hope of saving desperately injured patients, when their comatose state could not be relieved although their hearts could be induced to continue beating. The second reason was that obsolete criteria for the definition of death can lead to controversy in obtaining organs for transplantation. The Ad Hoc Committee observed that no change in the law would be necessary to adopt its criteria, since 'the law treats this question

---

[10] See the discussion of *Potter* (n 68 below), at para 17.26.
[11] Report of the Ad Hoc Committee of the Harvard Medical School, 'A Definition of Irreversible Coma', (1968) 205 *J Amer Med Assoc*, 337–40.

[the establishment of death] essentially as one of fact to be determined by physicians'.[12] This observation was unduly optimistic in light both of legal caution in identifying what fact physicians are called on to determine, and of continuing controversy among physicians themselves.

17.08   The Ad Hoc Committee presented the first authoritative statement of medical criteria of death under modern conditions of medical care, but it proved to be far from the last word. The 1976 Report of the Conference of Medical Royal Colleges and their Faculties in the United Kingdom,[13] supplemented in 1979 to address brain death,[14] which now appears to be given legal effect in UK courts,[15] is one of several authoritative but slightly differing formulations developed by medical professional bodies in the English-speaking world.

17.09   The widely discussed case of Karen Quinlan,[16] decided by the New Jersey courts in the mid-1970s, alerted public attention in many countries to the medico-legal need to distinguish not just between the living and the dead but between those affected by cortical or higher-brain death, brain-stem death and whole brain death, and to issues in legal management of patients in a persistent vegetative state. It was primarily for neurologists and related medical specialists to distinguish patients whose higher-brain had suffered irreversible damage, such as Karen Quinlan, from others, such as those whose higher-brains were substantially intact but whose brain-stem functions were severely compromised,[17] and to distinguish both categories of patients from those whose brain-stem had irreversibly ceased to function, and who were therefore dead.[18] Issues were raised to which several jurisdictions proposed legislative responses.

3. Legislative Approaches to Criteria of Death[19]

17.10   Historically, the criteria and processes for the determination of death were governed by common law, but the pressures that led the Ad Hoc Committee at Harvard to propose criteria appropriate in modern circumstances of medical care also persuaded legislatures in North America and beyond to take action. Their incentives were partially to resolve legal uncertainties, but also partially to quell public disquiet at the appearance of a collection of

---

[12] ibid, 338.   [13] 'Diagnosis of Brain Death', (1976) 2 *Brit Med J*, 1187–8.
[14] 'Memorandum on the Diagnosis of Death', (1979) 1 *Brit Med J*, 332, para 2; now see also n 7 above.   [15] See *Re A (A Minor)* [1992] 3 Med L Rev 303 (Fam Div).
[16] *In re Quinlan* (1976) 355 A 2d 647, 664 (NJ Sup Ct).
[17] See Pearce, J M S 'The Locked In Syndrome' (1987) 294 *Brit Med J*, 1989; Allan, CMC, 'Conscious but Paralysed: Releasing the Locked-in' (1993) 17 *Lancet*, 130–2.
[18] See n 7 above.
[19] For valuable references to international legislation, see Giesen, D, *International Medical Malpractice Law* (Tübingen, Dordrecht, Boston, London, 1988), 612, n 73.

physicians settling among themselves the criteria according to which patients could be declared dead and their organs taken for medical transplantation.[20] The tendency of legislation was to incorporate medical criteria into a framework of legislative overview.

The first North American jurisdiction to enact a statute incorporating brain death was Kansas.[21] The Kansas legislation of 1970 addressed both cardio-pulmonary and brain death as equally available alternatives by providing that: **17.11**

> A person will be considered medically and legally dead if, in the opinion of a physician, based on ordinary standards of medical practice, there is the absence of spontaneous respiratory and cardiac function and . . . attempts at resuscitation are considered hopeless; and, in this event, death will have occurred at the time these functions ceased; or A person will be considered medically and legally dead if . . . there is the absence of spontaneous brain function; and if based on ordinary standards of medical practice, during reasonable attempts to either maintain or restore spontaneous circulatory or respiratory function in the absence of aforesaid brain function, it appears that further attempts at resuscitation or supportive maintenance will not succeed, death will have occurred at the time when these conditions first coincide.

The statute was quickly copied in several other states, but it was also subjected to criticism on a variety of grounds,[22] not least that its references to when a person was considered 'medically and legally dead' perpetuated the very notion of medical death and legal death being different in principle which the legislation was designed to end. To meet this criticism, some legislatures adopted brain death as the only legal criterion. For instance, Manitoba amended its Vital Statistics Act in 1975 to provide that:

> For all purposes within the legislative competence of the Legislature of Manitoba the death of a person takes place at the time at which irreversible cessation of all of that person's brain function occurs.[23]

This brought together legal and medical criteria of death, but for constitutional reasons had to leave open whether Canadian federal law, governing, for instance, criminal law, would take the same approach.[24] Other legislatures codified cardiopulmonary criteria of death, but added a brain death test for **17.12**

---

[20] Capron, AM and Kass, L, 'A Statutory Definition of the Standards for Determining Human Death', (1972) 121 Univ Pennsylvania Law Rev, 87–118.

[21] Kan Stat Ann ch 77–202.

[22] See Kennedy, I, 'The Kansas Statute on Death: An Appraisal', (1971) 285 *New Eng J Med*, 946–50, and Capron and Kass (n 20 above).

[23] See now R Stats Man 1987, ch V60, s 2.

[24] In the criminal case of *R v Kitching and Adams* (1976) 32 CCC (2d) 159 (Man CA) a brain stem death criterion was applied; organ removal, prior to death certification, was found not to have broken the chain of criminal causation between an injury and the victim's death: see para 17.26 *et seq* below.

application only when artificial life support precludes the use of such criteria, some requiring the opinion of a specialist in neurology, neurosurgery or electroencephalography as a condition of use of the brain death criterion.[25]

17.13 In many jurisdictions there is no legislation defining death for general purposes, but legislation on cadaveric organ donation for transplantation specifies how death is to be determined before organ recovery.[26] This necessarily covers brain death, since organ recovery frequently depends on artificial ventilation or other means being applied to a body at death to preserve the suitability of organs for transplantation. Such legislation usually contains no criteria of death, but requires that usual medical practice be observed. Typical is the Human Tissue Gift Act of Ontario[27] section 7(1) of which provides that:

> For the purposes of a post mortem transplant, the fact of death shall be determined by at least two physicians in accordance with accepted medical practice.

In the event of litigation or other need of clarification, expert medical opinion will be obtained to establish accepted medical practice, by reference to prevailing literature, codes of practice and their application. This approach may not resolve philosophical, spiritual or similar uncertainties, but it affords physicians the security of knowing that their demonstrable conformity to the practice of their profession will be respected by the courts.

4. Judicial Approaches to Brain Stem Death

17.14 In England, as in many other jurisdictions in the English-speaking world, no legislation establishes criteria of death. However, modern judgments now confirm that criteria of what may generically be called brain death[28] developed among leaders of the medical profession are incorporated into the law. A Family Division judgment confirming that a young child was dead (see below), and a House of Lords judgment finding that an adult in a persistent vegetative state was not (see below), showed that the English courts have subscribed to the brain stem criterion of brain death. This may be distinguished from the so-called 'whole brain death' test adopted, for instance, by the Manitoba legislature[29] and which may be favoured by

---

[25] In 1978 the US National Conference of Commissioners on Uniform State Laws adopted a Uniform Brain Death Act, which in 1980 was superseded by the Uniform Determination of Death Act. This provides alternative definitions of death, but presents death as a phenomenon that can be tested by alternative criteria: See Furrow, B R, Johnson, S H, Jost, T S and Schwartz, R L, *Health Law: Cases, Materials and Problems* (St Paul, Minn, 2nd edn, 1991), 1046.

[26] See Jones, D, 'Retrospective on the Future: Brain Death and Evolving Legal Regimes for Tissue Replacement Technology', (1993) 38 McGill Law J, 394–415.

[27] RSO 1990, ch H-20.

[28] But see the growing medical use of 'brain stem death' (n 7 above).   [29] N 23 above.

courts elsewhere.[30] Simply put, the brain stem controls reflexive functions of the body including breathing and heartbeat, while the higher-brain controls consciousness and interaction with surroundings, that is, sensation and cognition. Brain stem function is necessary to sustain higher-brain function, but a functioning brain stem will keep alive a person, such as Karen Quinlan (see para 17.09 above), whose higher-brain no longer allows recovery of consciousness.

(i) *Re A (A Minor)*

Re A (A Minor)[31] concerned a child aged under two years who was found to **17.15** have no heartbeat on admission to a hospital's accident and emergency department. Extensive resuscitation attempts were unsuccessful, and he was transferred into another hospital for intensive care and assessment, and placed on a ventilator. When briefly removed from the ventilator to test whether he could breathe independently, he made slight gasping noises, indicating to the consultant that he was not brain stem dead. The next day, however, when tests were conducted, the consultant was satisfied that A was brain stem dead. A consultant paediatric neurologist repeated the tests the following day, which confirmed the earlier finding. Both physicians made efforts to determine whether A's state could have been explained on other grounds before reaching the conclusion of brain stem death.

The boy was kept on ventilation and fed intravenously, and the proceedings **17.16** were brought to clarify the legality of the consultant's proposal to withdraw ventilation. The consultant explained to the judge that she was aware of recommendations on the definition of death made by the Royal College of Surgeons, the Royal College of Physicians, and a working party of the British Paediatric Association, and had applied the criteria laid down by her profession. The judge expressed no hesitation in holding that A had been dead, according to the medical procedures that had been followed to reach the conclusion of brain stem death, since the consultant made her initial determination. The judge also found, *inter alia*, that he had jurisdiction to declare that it would not be unlawful to disconnect A from the ventilator.[32]

---

[30] See Furrow *et al* (n 25 above).
[31] [1992] 3 Med L Rev 303 (Fam D).
[32] For a somewhat critical commentary on the judge's rulings on his finding of A's earlier death, see Kennedy, I, 'Commentary' (1993) 1 Med L Rev, 99–100.

(ii) *Airedale NHS Trust v Bland*

17.17 The criterion of brain stem death was incorporated into English law more explicitly by the House of Lords in *Airedale National Health Service Trust v Bland*.[33] A patient diagnosed as being in a persistent vegetative state was maintained in a hospital that proposed withdrawal of artificial nutrition and hydration, with the foreseeable consequence of his death through dehydration. He breathed unaided, but could not swallow, and was fed by a nasogastric tube.

17.18 In proceedings to determine the legality of this proposed course of conduct, an issue central to the courts' jurisdiction in the case was whether the patient was currently alive, since, if he were not, the approach to the courts and their jurisdiction would be quite different. Their Lordships were aware through judgments of the courts below of medical criteria relevant both to brain stem death and to the persistent vegetative state. They accepted the medical conclusion that, by this test, the patient was not dead, and accordingly accepted their jurisdiction in the case. Lord Keith observed that:

> [i]n the eyes of the medical world and of the law a person is not clinically dead so long as the brain stem retains its function.[34]

Lord Goff similarly stated that:

> as a result of developments in modern medical technology, doctors no longer associate death exclusively with breathing and heart beat, and it has come to be accepted that death occurs when the brain, and in particular the brain stem, has been destroyed . . . . The evidence is that Anthony's brain stem is still alive and functioning and it follows that, in the present state of medical science, he is still alive and should be so regarded as a matter of law.[35]

17.19 Lord Browne-Wilkinson went so far as to describe a ventilator-assisted being whose heart was beating 'even though the brain stem, and therefore in medical terms the patient, is dead', as 'the ventilated corpse',[36] but was careful to exclude the patient Anthony Bland from that category. Having located him among the living, however, their Lordships accepted the medical evidence that he was persistently vegetative and would never regain consciousness. Specifying the conditions under which courts could so act[37] their Lordships approved withdrawal of artificial nutrition and hydration. The court found that the resulting death would not leave those responsible for his medical care liable in law.

[33] [1993] 1 AC 789 (HL (E)).   [34] ibid, 856.   [35] ibid, 863.
[36] ibid, 878.
[37] See Practice Note [1994] 2 All ER 413.

(iii) *Jurisdictional Difficulties*

The problem that a judicial finding of death poses to a court's jurisdiction **17.20** warrants brief attention. In *Re TC (A Minor)*[38] the Family Division of the High Court of Justice in Northern Ireland accepted the diagnosis of brain stem death in a child on a ventilator who was a ward of court, but nevertheless granted declarations that the application for a declaration should have been brought before the court because a wardship was involved, and that the body could be removed from ventilation when the hospital's medical staff considered removal appropriate. It has reasonably been objected that, in view of the finding of the ward's death, the court had no further wardship jurisdiction to determine her legal status, nor to provide for subsequent ventilation of her dead body at the discretion of the hospital's medical staff except under very special conditions.[39] As against this, however, to deny the court its general supervisory jurisdiction because of the ward's death would paradoxically make answering the question whether the ward was alive or dead a precondition to asking it. Courts may have to be afforded some jurisdictional latitude to try cases from which a legal finding of death may result.

(iv) *The US Approach*

Homicide cases in the United States have occasionally been defended, although **17.21** never successfully,[40] on the ground that physicians' motives to acquire organs for transplantation caused them to terminate the lives of injured ventilated patients who otherwise could have survived, and that those responsible for their injuries were not responsible for their deaths. Rejection of the defence motivated two states to accept the brain death criterion for homicide cases only,[41] and others to recognize brain death for more general and perhaps civil purposes.[42] The particular form of brain death that these cases accept is whole brain rather than brain stem death, although it has been doubted that the distinction merits emphasis except in very unusual circumstances.[43]

---

[38] Reported and discussed in (1994) 2 Med L Rev, 376–7. [39] ibid.

[40] See Furrow *et al* (n 25 above), 1052.

[41] See *Commonwealth v Golston* (1977), 366 NE 2d 744 (Mass Sup Jud Ct); *State v Meints* (1982) 322 NW 2d 809 (Neb Sup Ct).

[42] See *People v Eulo* (1984) 472 NE 2d 286 (NYCA), *State v Matthews* (1986) 353 SE 2d 444 (SC Sup Ct) and *State v Velarde* (1986) 734 P 2d 449 (Utah Sup Ct).

[43] See Mason, K and McCall Smith, RA, *Law and Medical Ethics* (London, Dublin, Edinburgh, 4th edn, 1994), 284.

5. Persistent Vegetative State (PVS) and Anencephaly

(i) *Introduction*

17.22 In 1995, the Royal College of Physicians produced an updated review 'of the criteria used in the diagnosis of brain stem death (hitherto known as brain death)'[44] which was endorsed by the Conference of Medical Royal Colleges and their Faculties in the United Kingdom. This noted that:

> Problems relating to the diagnosis and management of the persistent vegetative state must not be confused with those relating to brain stem death.[45]

Similar confusion has concerned anencephalic newborn children, whom some want to consider dead or 'brain absent', although they have functioning brain stems.[46] By prevailing legal criteria, however, both PVS patients and anencephalic newborn children are alive.

(ii) *Persistent Vegetative State*

17.23 In *Airedale NHS Trust v Bland* the House of Lords, addressing the issue of letting die those patients diagnosed to be in a persistent vegetative state, specified measures to be adopted as a precondition to legality. These included attempting rehabilitation such as by coma arousal programmes,[47] and are now amplified in a Practice Note.[48] Although current methods of diagnosing PVS are not infallible,[49] their Lordships unanimously accepted, as did all judges below, that Anthony Bland's brain stem functioned, and that he was therefore not dead.[50]

(iii) *Anencephaly*

17.24 Anencephaly is a condition in which children suffer a congenital disorder resulting in the absence of major portions of the brain, skull

---

[44] See n 7 above at 381.   [45] ibid, para (f).
[46] See Kennedy and Grubb (n 2 above) at 1402, and Furrow *et al* (n 25 above) at 1049–51.
[47] N 33 above, *per* Lord Goff at 870–1.   [48] See n 37 above.
[49] ibid, para 2, referring to the Medical Ethics Committee of the British Medical Association guidelines on treatment decisions for PVS patients, of July 1993; for discussion of the diagnosis and of other conditions with which PVS is sometimes confused, see Appendix 4 and paras 156–162 and 251–258 of the *Report of the House of Lords Select Committee on Medical Ethics* (HL Paper (1993–94) 21–I), and text at n 45 above.
[50] See also *Frenchay Healthcare NHS Trust v S* [1994] 2 All ER 403 (CA), applying the Bland judgment (n 33 above).

and scalp.[51] Lacking the higher-brain, the cerebral cortex, they will never achieve consciousness, and it is highly doubtful that they feel sensations such as pain and discomfort. The large majority of anencephalic foetuses are stillborn or aborted when detected prenatally,[52] since the condition is incompatible with consciousness and survival. However, they have at least rudimentary brain stems, and some are born alive and survive for a few days, although rarely exceeding ten.[53] Because anencephalic children show some brain stem activity, they are neither brain stem dead, nor whole brain dead, but must be considered to have been born alive as human beings.[54] The 1995 review of criteria for brain stem death by the Royal College of Physicians suggested that, in children over the age of two months, brain stem death criteria should be the same as those in adults. It found, however, that '[t]here is insufficient information on children under the age of two months and on premature babies to define guidelines.'[55] In the normal course of events, anencephalic children born alive are given only comfort measures until death,[56] since aggressive care is futile. In the exceptional *Baby K* case in Virginia,[57] however, the US laws on emergency medical treatment and disability were held to compel a hospital to give ventilation and other care to such a child at its mother's request, made on religious grounds,[58] resulting in its survival for two and a half years.[59]

A medical incentive to ventilate and otherwise care for such children is to   **17.25** preserve their organs for transplantation on death. Anencephaly is not a genetic condition, and normal organs would be transplantable if tissue quality

---

[51] See Medical Task Force on Anencephaly, 'The Infant with Anencephaly', (1990) 322 *New England J Med*, 669–74.

[52] Medearis, DN and Holmes, LB, 'On the Use of Anencephalic Infants as Organ Donors', (1989) 321 *New England J Med*, 391–3.   [53] See Furrow *et al* (n 25 above) at 1049.

[54] *In re TACP* (1992) 609 So 2d 588 (Florida Sup Ct). In *Montreal Tramways v Léveillé* [1933] SCR 456, the Supreme Court of Canada held that the status of being a human being is dependent on being born alive and viable, but the viability condition has not been pursued in later jurisprudence: see *R v Sullivan* (1991) 63 CCC (3d) 97 (Sup Ct Canada).

[55] See n 7 above at 381, para (e).

[56] Death is determined on physiological indications, in the absence of brain stem death indications; see Furrow *et al* (n 25 above) at 1049.

[57] *In the Matter of Baby K* (1993) 832 F Supp 1022 (ED Va) affirmed (1994) 16 F 3d 590 (4th Cir), certiorari denied (1994) 115 S Ct 95 (US Sup Ct).

[58] The US legislation invoked included the Emergency Medical Treatment and Active Labor Act, 42 USC ch 1395 and the Americans with Disabilty Act, 42, USC ch 12112; See Flannery EJ 'One Advocate's Viewpoint: Conflicts and Tensions in the *Baby K* Case', (1995) 23 J Law, Medicine and Ethics, 7–12; Clayton, EW, 'Commentary: What is Really at Stake in Baby K? A Response to Eileen Flannery', ibid, 13–14; and Bonanno, MA, 'The Case of Baby K: Exploring the Concept of Medical Futility', (1995) 4 Annals of Health Law, 151–72.

[59] The cost of infant care, covered by a private insurance carrier, was reported to be $1464 each day; Knepper, K, 'Withholding Medical Treatment from Infants: When is it Child Neglect?' (1994–95) 33 Univ Louisville J Fam Law, 1–53.

can be preserved in vivo. Deterioration of organs would almost invariably occur in the course of the child's natural death, due to hypoxia and ischemia. Recovery of organs following natural death is unlikely to provide any suitable for transplantation. Invasive mechanical support for the organ systems of a living anencephalic child on the parents' consent could maintain tissue quality in organs, but raises legal and ethical concerns. Such treatments would not be intended for the child's benefit,[60] but for that of prospective transplant recipients. Usually, parents have at best restricted legal capacity to consent to non-therapeutic medical care for their children.[61] Mechanical support might be considered acceptable, however, since it would not be counter to the child's interests. Treatment administered with parental consent that postpones death may escape legal condemnation, for instance for constituting child abuse, because the child is incapable of experiencing distress, and it cannot be considered to have any interest in early as opposed to slightly later death.

17.26 According to the brain stem criteria approved in the *Bland* case,[62] anencephalic children are not dead, and describing them as 'brain absent' is a euphemism the law does not accommodate.[63] Similarly, arguments that they be registered at birth as stillborn cannot stand, for reasons both of the same law and of medical practice; some children living longer than expected have been shown on further examination to be microcephalic or otherwise to be misdiagnosed, and not anencephalic.[64] Nevertheless, the *Bland* preconditions to withdrawal and denial of care such as nutrition, hydration, and ventilation appear not to apply, since anencephalic newborn children do not have comparable interests in the exercise of due caution.[65] Taking a proposal for non-active treatment to court for approval is possible, but does not seem mandatory, since, unlike Anthony Bland, such children are in the process of natural death. Further, for physicians to meet the condition of twelve months of patient insentience[66] before they request a judicial declaration on the legality of withdrawing care seems not to serve any patient's interest, and to contradict good husbanding of scarce health care resources. Unless legislation is interpreted to require application of any

---

[60] The *Baby K* case (n 57 above), may offer a basis for an argument that active care is in the child's interests.
[61] See Giesen (n 19 above) at 440, and Dickens, BM, 'The Modern Function and Limits of Parental Rights', (1981) 97 LQR, 462–85.
[62] N 33 above.
[63] McCullagh, P, *Brain Dead, Brain Absent, Brain Donors: Human Subjects or Human Objects?* (Chichester, 1993).
[64] McDowell, D T, 'Death of An Idea: The Anencephalic as an Organ Donor', (1994) 72 Texas LR, 893–930, 929.
[65] See Steinbock, B, *Life Before Birth* (New York: Oxford, 1992), 35.
[66] Practice Note (n 37 above), para 2.

procedures, anencephalic newborn children may be given only basic comfort measures while they are allowed to die, although the use of mechanical supports until death is determined by physiological tests seems permissible.[67]

6. Termination of Mechanical Life Support Systems and Legal Liability

When human life can be sustained by use of an artificial life support system, a legal concern is whether withdrawal is in law a culpable cause of the death that follows. Recognition of different uses of life supports arose in consideration of the Director of Public Prosecution's advice to lay a charge only of common assault in the 1963 case of *R v Potter.*[68] The accused inflicted a severe head injury on the victim during a fight. The victim stopped spontaneous breathing fourteen hours after admission to hospital, and was then placed on an artificial ventilator for twenty-four hours. After this time, with the consent of his wife and a coroner, a kidney was removed for transplantation. The ventilator was then shut off and, lacking spontaneous respiration and circulation, the victim was pronounced dead. A coroner's inquest led to a decision to charge the accused for his offence that resulted in the death. By traditional criteria of death, the victim was alive when the kidney was removed, because he had both respiration and heartbeat, although by mechanical means. The accused claimed that the physicians' actions in removing the kidney and shutting off the ventilator broke the chain of causation between the assault and death, and that he accordingly could not be convicted of a crime based on causing death.

17.27

The Director of Public Prosecutions appears to have been responsive to this conventional interpretation of the law in advising a charge of assault rather than of manslaughter, which requires proof that the accused caused the death. Nevertheless, both the surgeon who removed the kidney on the wife's consent, and the coroner, whose jurisdiction is primarily over dead bodies, appear to have treated the victim as dead, and the ventilator as preserving the tissue quality of the organ to be removed for transplantation rather than the life of the victim. Inconsistently, however, death was not pronounced until the ventilator was shut off. Death might have been pronounced before initiation of ventilation on the basis of a neurological or 'brain death' criterion, had the law at that time clearly so permitted.

17.28

---

[67] See Chapter 15 on Donation and Transplantation of Organs and Tissue.
[68] *The Times, 26* July 1963; discussed in (1963) 4 Med Science and Law, 59–64: (1964) 31–37 *Medico-Legal J*, 195 and Myers, D, *The Human Body and the Law*, (Edinburgh, 2nd edn, 1990), 196.

17.29 In a civil case in Virginia in 1972,[69] a person suffered serious cranial injuries in a fall, and was placed on a ventilator in a hospital. When an electroencephalogram showed a total absence of neocortical activity, physicians stopped ventilation, pronounced him dead and immediately removed his heart for transplantation. His brother sued them, claiming that at the time of heart removal he was alive, since the traditional signs of life, heartbeat and respiration, were still present. The judge directed the jury members that they could establish the time of death by either the classical cardio-vascular tests or the new, neurological criteria which the defendant physicians explained they had applied. The jury found the defendants not liable.

17.30 Courts have been uniformly resistant to claims that physicians incur legal liability when, in the course of conscientious and competent management of patients, they terminate life support systems and patients' deaths follow.[70] *R v Malcherek, R v Steel*[71] involved victims of separate attacks who were placed on life support systems that were eventually withdrawn, whereupon they died. The defendants, who were convicted of causing their deaths, claimed that the physicians attending their victims failed, in different ways, to conform to the Code of Practice for the diagnosis of brain death established in 1976 in the Report of the Conference of Medical Royal Colleges and their Faculties.[72] The failures were alleged to have broken the chain of causation between the attacks and the deaths. In each case, the trial judge withdrew from the jury the question of whether the defendant's attack had caused the victim's death, since there was no evidence that might permit the jury any doubt that they had. Although juries determine facts, they must do so on evidence, and whether or not there is any evidence is a matter of law to be determined by the judge. In the Court of Appeal, Lord Lane CJ stated that:

> [t]he way in which the [defendants'] submissions are put . . . is as follows: the doctors, by switching off the ventilator and the life support machine, were the cause of death or, to put it more accurately, there was evidence which the jury should have been allowed to consider that the doctors, and not the assailant, in each case may have been the cause of death.[73]

---

[69] *Tucker v Lower*, May 1972, Richmond VA no 2831 (unreported); discussed in Converse, R, 'But When Did He Die?: *Tucker v Lower* and the Brain Death Concept', (1975) 12 *San Diego L Rev*, 424–35.

[70] See, for instance, *Finlayson v HM Advocate* (1978) SLT (Notes) 60 (Scotland); *R v Kitching and Adams* (n 24 above); *R v Kinash* [1982] Qld R 648 (Queensland CCA); *Nancy B v Hôtel-Dieu de Québec* (1992) 86 DLR (4th) 385 (Quebec Superior Ct). If care is not competent, however, physicians may be convictable: see *People v Eulo* (n 42 above) at 297, and *R v Prentice* [1993] 4 All ER 935 (CA).

[71] [1981] 2 All ER 422 (CA).   [72] See n 13 above, and the addendum, n 14 above.
[73] N 71 above, 427.

Lord Lane upheld the trial judge's direction that the defendants had caused their victims' deaths, and observed that:

> [w]here a medical practitioner adopting methods which are generally accepted comes bona fide and conscientiously to the conclusion that the patient is for practical purposes dead, and that such vital functions as exist (for example, circulation) are being maintained solely by mechanical means, and therefore discontinues treatment, that does not prevent the person who inflicted the initial injury from being responsible for the victim's death. Putting it in another way, the discontinuance of treatment in those circumstances does not break the chain of causation between the initial injury and the death.[74]

There can be more than a single cause of death,[75] but the physicians are not considered to have any part in such causation. Indeed, Lord Lane added, obiter, that:

17.31

> [w]hatever the strict logic of the matter may be, it is perhaps somewhat bizarre to suggest, as counsel have impliedly done, that where a doctor tries his conscientious best to save the life of a patient brought to hospital in extremis, skilfully using sophisticated methods, drugs and machinery to do so, but fails in his attempt and therefore discontinues treatment, he can be said to have caused the death of the patient.[76]

Nevertheless, where organs are proposed to be recovered for transplantation or other use is intended for the body,[77] prudence suggests that death should be pronounced and certified beforehand. Lord Lane's apparent endorsement of a physician's power to discontinue life support methods on reaching a conscientious assessment that a patient is 'for practical purposes dead'[78] begs a number of legal questions concerning more abstract or speculative purposes,[79] and falls short of legal acceptance of the concept of brain stem death reviewed, for instance, by the Royal College of Physicians and endorsed by the Conference of Medical Royal Colleges.[80] Lord Lane observed that '[i]t is no part of the task of this court to inquire whether the criteria, the Royal Medical College confirmatory tests, are a satisfactory code of practice',[81] but it is doubtful whether courts will permit physicians who establish death for removal of organs for transplantation to apply less rigorous criteria of brain stem death than their profession expects of them.

17.32

---

[74] ibid, 429.   [75] See *R v Kitching and Adams* (n 24 above), 175.
[76] N 71 above, 429.
[77] See eg Hayes G J, 'Issues of Consent: The Use of the Recently Deceased for Endotracheal Intubation Training', (1994) 5 *J Clinical Ethics*, 211–16. For discussion of a controversial incident in Germany, see Tuffs, A, 'Keeping a Brain-dead Pregnant Woman "Alive"', (1992) 340 *Lancet*, 1029–30.   [78] N 71 above, 429.
[79] See Hayes (n 77 above).   [80] N 7 above.   [81] See n 71 above, 427.

C. After Death

1. Coroners' Powers

(i) *Procedure*

17.33 The Coroners Act 1988[82] consolidates the English Coroners Acts 1887 to 1980, but regulations made under the repealed legislation continue in force unless legislation or regulations provide otherwise.[83] A doctor who has attended someone during the last illness must report the cause of death to the local registrar of births and deaths.[84] Although there is no statutory duty to report a death to the coroner, it is usual practice for a doctor to do so in the event of doubt or suspicion. Upon receipt of information that the body of a person is lying within the coroner's district, even though death may have occurred elsewhere,[85] and there is reasonable cause to suspect that the deceased (a) died a violent or unnatural death;[86] (b) died a sudden death of unknown cause; or (c) died in prison or in such a place or circumstances as to require an inquest under other legislation,[87] the coroner shall hold an inquest into the death as soon as practicable.[88]

17.34 Whether sitting with or without a jury,[89] the inquest shall consider how, when and where the deceased died. The evidence before the inquest is not limited to what is admissible at a criminal trial,[90] but is limited to evidence that establishes facts. The inquest is further limited to finding only proven particulars.[91] The inquest may identify a person found to have caused death by criminal means, except that a coroner's inquest cannot present a finding of murder, manslaughter or infanticide, and accordingly cannot charge a person on inquisition with any of these offences.[92] A verdict should be framed in a way that does not appear to determine any question of criminal or civil

---

[82] Stats 1988, ch 13.   [83] Interpretation Act 1978, s 17(2)(b).

[84] Births and Deaths Registration Act 1953, s 22(1), and Registration of Births and Deaths Regulations 1987, SI 1987/2088, reg 40(1)(a), Sch 2, Form 14.

[85] *R v West Yorkshire Coroner, ex p Smith* [1982] 3 All ER 1098 (CA).

[86] See *R v Poplar Coroner, ex p Thomas* [1993] QB 610 (CA).

[87] N 82 above, s 8(1).

[88] *In Re Hull* (1882) 9 QBD 689 it was held that an interval of five days between receipt of information and the holding of the inquest was too long.

[89] N 82 above, s 8. Procedures for summoning a jury prescribed by this Act and by the Coroners Rules 1984, SI 1984/552 are mandatory; *R v Merseyside Coroner, ex p Carr* [1993] 4 All ER 65 (QBD).   [90] See *The Times*, 18 Mar 1890, Will J in charge to a grand jury.
[91] *R v Huntbach, ex p Lockley* [1944] KB 606.   [92] N 82 above, s 11(6).

liability on the part of a named person.[93] A finding of a cause of death should be construed narrowly, to refer to the means of death rather than the broad circumstances that resulted in death.[94]

It is usual for a coroner's inquest to consider results of an examination of the body of the deceased person conducted by a physician or a forensic pathologist. Where a coroner has reason to believe that an inquest ought to be held but that, owing to the destruction of the body by fire or otherwise, or because the body is lying in a place from which it cannot be recovered, no examination of the body is possible, the coroner may report the facts to the Secretary of State for the Home Department.[95] The Home Secretary may then direct a coroner's inquest into the death if that is considered desirable, and the provisions of the Coroners Act and additional relevant law shall apply with any necessary modifications.[96]

17.35

(ii) *Post-Mortem Examinations*

When informed that a body is lying within the coroner's district and there is reasonable cause to suspect that the person died a sudden death of unknown cause, the coroner may, if of the opinion that a post-mortem examination may prove an inquest unnecessary, direct a legally qualified medical practitioner to conduct a post-mortem examination of the body and provide the coroner with a written report.[97] The coroner is not authorized to dispense with an inquest, however, when there is reasonable cause to suspect that the deceased died a violent or unnatural death, died in prison or in such other circumstances as require an inquest under other legislation.[98] A coroner may request that examination of a body be conducted by a person considered to possess special qualifications for conducting a special examination,[99] and if summoned as a witness at an inquest such person may give evidence of any matter arising out of the examination, and express an opinion as to how the deceased died.[100]

17.36

(iii) *Medical Witnesses*

At an inquest into death, the coroner may summon as a witness any medical practitioner who appears to have attended at the death or during the last

17.37

---

[93] Coroners Rules 1984, SI 1984/552, r 42; see *R v Surrey Coroner, ex p Campbell* [1982] QB 661.   [94] *R v North Humberside Coroner, ex p Jamieson* [1994] 3 All ER 972 (CA).
[95] N 82 above, s 15(1).   [96] ibid, s 15(2), (3).   [97] ibid, s 19(1).
[98] Coroners Act, 1988 s 19(4).   [99] ibid, s 20(1)(b).   [100] ibid, s 20(2).

illness of the deceased, or, where there appears to have been no such practitioner, any medical practitioner in actual practice in or near the place where the death occurred. Any medical witness summoned to appear may be asked to express an opinion as to how the deceased died.[101] In the summons for attendance of a medical witness, or at any time after its issue and before the end of the inquest, the coroner may also direct the medical witness to conduct a post-mortem examination of the body of the deceased.[102] This does not apply where a person has stated to the coroner on oath a belief that death was caused entirely or in part by the medical practitioner's improper or negligent treatment of the deceased.[103] A medical practitioner who fails to obey a coroner's summons to attend an inquest shall, unless able to show good and sufficient cause for such failure, be liable on summary conviction to a fine not exceeding £1,000.[104] Prosecution can be brought by the coroner or by any two members of the coroner's jury.[105] Scheduled fees are payable to medical witnesses and to those who conduct required post-mortem examinations.[106]

(iv) *Exhumation*

17.38 Under section 23 of the Coroners Act 1988, a coroner may by warrant order the exhumation of the body of a person buried within the coroner's district when this appears necessary for its examination for an inquest or for discharge of any other of the coroner's functions in relation to the body or the death. The same powers exist for the purposes of any criminal proceedings instituted or contemplated in respect of the death of the person whose body is to be exhumed for examination, or of some other person who died in circumstances connected with the death of that person.[107]

---

[101] ibid, s 21(1).

[102] ibid, s 21(2). An interested party, such as the deceased's spouse, may compel a coroner to order a post-mortem examination unless there are good grounds for refusal; see *R v Greater London Coroner, ex p Ridley* [1986] 1 All ER 37 (QBD).

[103] Criminal Justice Act 1991, s 17(3)(a), Sch 4 Pt 1.   [104] ibid, s 21(3), as amended.

[105] N 82 above, s 21(5).

[106] ibid, s 24; see Home Office Circulars detailing fees, which are circulated to all local authorities.   [107] ibid, s 23(1)(b).

2. Legal Status and Medical Uses of Corpses

(i) *Legal Status*

On a person's death, the corpse does not constitute part of the estate for **17.39** purposes of testate or intestate succession.[108] Questions therefore arise as to who may lawfully deal with the body. The executor of the estate is usually empowered to direct disposition of the body because the costs of burial, cremation or other lawful disposal are a charge on the estate. English legislation on organ and tissue recovery from cadavers for transplantation and other uses permits legally effective consent to be given for such recovery by 'the person lawfully in possession of the body' except when the deceased person when alive gave consent to posthumous recovery, or had expressed an objection.[109] A surviving spouse or any surviving relative of the deceased may also object to recovery,[110] preventing such use by those having charge of the body. It has been held that executors have a right to possession of a corpse, until its burial or other lawful disposition.[111] In 1931 a Canadian appeal court found that a right to possession of a body was held by the surviving spouse or next of kin,[112] whose rights of burial were described as a 'quasi-property' interest. Family members' interests have been extended to recovery of organs for transplantation by legislation such as exists, for instance, in a number of Canadian provinces. Consent to cadaveric organ and tissue recovery may be given by deceased persons' spouses, children, parents, brothers or sisters or, failing availability of any of these, a next of kin, unless the deceased when living had consented or objected to such recovery.[113]

(ii) *Medical and Other Uses*

The Human Tissue Act, 1961 and comparable legislation in other jurisdictions **17.40** addresses recovery of cadaveric materials for therapeutic purposes, meaning transplantation, and for research and medical education. Recovery for other purposes may find legal justification elsewhere. Cosmetic treatment may be

---

[108] See Skegg, P D G, 'Medical Uses of Corpses and the "No Property" Rule', (1992) 32 *Med Sci Law*, 311–18; Matthews, P, 'Whose Body? People as Property', (1983) 36 CLP 193–239.
[109] The Human Tissue Act 1961, s 1(2)(a).   [110] ibid, s 1(2)(b).
[111] *Williams v Williams* (1882) 20 Ch D 659; see generally Kennedy and Grubb (n 2 above), 1149–52.
[112] *Edmonds v Armstrong Funeral Home Ltd* [1931] 1 DLR 676 (Alberta CA); See also *Burney v Children's Hospital in Boston* (1897) 47 NE 401 (Sup Ct Mass).
[113] See Chapter 15 on transplantation.

therapeutic or non-therapeutic, depending for instance on the recipient's mental health needs, but where 'tissue' includes human hair, its acquisition for manufacture of wigs appears commercial rather than cosmetic or therapeutic. The legislative reference to 'research'[114] does not appear limited to medical or academic research, so that commercial research and development might be included, but use of human (including foetal) materials for purposes of routine manufacturing processes of pharmaceutical or other products would appear to fall outside the legislation. On the common law principle that whatever is not prohibited is permitted, and in the absence of generally recognized property rights in dead bodies,[115] recovery of materials appears lawful provided that it does not offend the law on public decency,[116] or against causing indignity to a dead body.[117] Medical removal of materials by routine surgical or other medical procedures that do not cause indignity when conducted with consent would appear not to cause indignity even when undertaken in the absence of consent.

17.41 The Anatomy Act 1984[118] provides for removal of cadaveric materials for examination, and for use of a body in 'the course of teaching or studying or researching'.[119] The Act provides a scheme for retention of body materials through licensing by the Secretary of State, licensees being entitled to use the body and its tissues for instruction, and to retain them. Licensees' interests in possession may be described as proprietary, although whether courts would, for instance, uphold the so-called 'no property' rule in dead bodies, deliberately reject or modify the rule, or deny that it ever possessed the influence attributed to it, remains unclear.[120] The matter may be resolved in a variety of contexts, including for instance in proceedings under the Theft Act 1968.[121] The Australian case of *Doodeward v Spence*[122] suggests that in special circumstances a corpse may become the subject of property. However, in *Dobson v North Tyneside Health Authority*[123] the Court of Appeal dismissed a claim by next of kin to a property interest in brain tissue of a deceased person left following an autopsy, which the next of kin wanted for development of forensic evidence in litigation. In the Californian *Moore* case,[124] involving

---

[114] N 109 above, s 1(1).

[115] See Skegg (n 108 above), and *Dobson v North Tyneside Health Authority* [1996] 4 All ER 474 (CA)

[116] In *R v Gibson* [1991] 1 All ER 439 (CA), the display of freeze-dried aborted foetuses as earrings was held convictable as outraging public decency.

[117] See *Foster v Dodd* (1866) LR 1 QB 475, *per* Blackburn, J at 485.

[118] Stats 1984, ch 14.   [119] ibid, s 3(3).

[120] See Skegg, and *Dobson v North Tyneside Health Authority* (nn 108 and 115 above).

[121] 16 & 17 Eliz 2, c 60.   [122] (1908) 6 CLR 406 (High Ct Aust).

[123] N 115 above.

[124] *Moore v Regents of the University of California* (1990) 793 P 2d 479 (Sup Ct Cal), certiorari denied (1991), 111 S Ct 1388 (US Sup Ct).

the status of tissue from a living person, the court rejected property-based claims on grounds both of history and of modern benefits of third parties being able to use such tissues for therapeutic and other purposes unrestrained by the need to obtain consent from the human source. This approach to tissues, from both living and cadaveric sources, may not preclude comparably instrumental reasoning leading to recognition of property interests.[125] The court specifically left open this possibility, observing that 'we do not purport to hold that excised cells can never be property for any purposes whatsoever.'[126]

Management of tissues from the dead is at an historic point of transition from the sacred to, if not the profane, at least the commercial. Proprietary claims in products from human tissues and tissues themselves are likely to grow under the impact of developments in biotechnology and the advancing understanding of human genetics. Control and protection of human tissue banks that not only preserve cadaveric tissues but 'immortalise' them will become a growing legal concern. Patented cell lines developed from human, including cadaveric, tissues have immense commercial potential. The value of the cell line in the *Moore* case was assessed to be three billion dollars in 1990. Legal regimes will influence the direction of commercial, and social, reactions to possibilities opened up by biotechnology and new knowledge of the human genome, and those possibilities and new realities will influence developments and proposals for development in the law.[127] **17.42**

---

[125] Dickens, BM, 'Living Tissue and Organ Donors and Property Law: More on *Moore*', (1992) 8 *J Contemp Health Law and Policy*, 73–93. [126] N 124 above, 493.
[127] See recommendations of the Nuffield Council on Bioethics, in *Human Tissue: Ethical and Legal Issues* (London, 1995), and Chapter 15 above.

INDEX

907

code of practice   10.138
contracts   10.130–10.139
criminal offences   10.130–10.134, 10.142,
   10.145
definitions   10.128, 10.143
enforcement   10.129, 10.135
mothers,
   gestational   10.119
parental orders   10.147–10.158
parenthood   10.119, 10.146–10.158
payment   10.128, 10.133, 10.140–10.145
public policy   10.136–10.137
wardship   10.157–10.158
Warnock Committee   10.129
welfare of child   10.62, 10.153
swabs   6.61

terrorism   9.97
third parties
   abortion   11.88
   best interests of the patient   4.153–4.157
   causation   7.31–7.36
   dangerous patients   5.48–5.68
   data protection   9.119
   duty of care   5.47–5.104
   medical reports   9.151
   omissions   5.61
   psychiatric patients   6.77
'Three Wise Men' procedure   2.63
time limits *see* limitation periods
tissue donations
   abortion   15.11–15.14, 15.17
   banking   15.21, 15.23
   best interests of the patient   4.186–4.188,
      4.190
   children   4.183–4.184
   codes of practice   15.13–15.14
   consent   15.14, 15.17, 17.34
   corpses   17.39, 17.41–17.42
   courts   4.185
   criminal offences   15.16
   European Union   15.22
   families   4.188–4.190
   fiduciary duties   15.18
   foetuses   15.11–15.17, 15.75
   hysterectomies   15.12
   incompetent patients   4.182–4.192
   legal status   15.18–15.27
   medically assisted reproduction
      15.22–15.23

mental disabilities   4.189
miscarriages   15.11
organs   15.03–15.05
parents   15.15
proprietary rights   15.20
removal   15.41–15.45
research   15.13
sperm   15.22–15.23
stillborns   15.15
total purchasing pilots   1.05, 1.23–1.27, 1.82
training *see* **education and training**
transplants *see* **organ donation**
transsexuals *see* **gender reassignment**
transparency
   codes of practice   1.78, 1.80
   Ombudsman   2.89
   standards   1.76, 1.78, 1.80–1.82

UK Central Council   2.28–2.32
   appeals   2.45
   composition   2.28
   disciplinary procedure   2.33, 2.36,
      2.42–2.43, 2.62
   education and training   2.29–2.30
   European Union   2.32
   midwives   2.31
   Preliminary Proceedings Committee   2.42
   professional conduct   2.33
   Professional Conduct Committee   2.42
   qualifications   2.32
   registration   2.01, 2.09, 2.29–2.31, 2.47
   Secretary of State   2.28
unborn children *see also* **abortion, congenital
   disabilities, wrongful births**
   best interests of the patients   4.33–4.34
      mothers   4.29, 4.33
   caesarians   4.33
   civil law   4.25–4.27, 12.08
   common law   12.14–12.19
   consent   4.28–4.35
refusal, of   4.35
   courts   4.27, 4.30–4.35
   criminal law   4.23–4.25, 12.09–12.13
   damages   4.27
   death   4.35
   exceptions   4.32–4.35
   homicide   12.11–12.13
   incompetent patients   4.23–4.35
   injunctions   4.27, 4.31, 4.33
   medical negligence   4.26